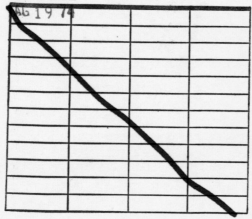

# HARLAN FISKE STONE:

## *Pillar of the Law*

CHIEF JUSTICE HARLAN FISKE STONE
(*Portrait by Charles Fox*)

# HARLAN FISKE STONE:

## *Pillar of the Law*

### BY ALPHEUS THOMAS MASON

"It doth appear you are a worthy judge;
You know the law, your exposition
Hath been most sound: I charge you by the law,
Whereof you are a well-deserving pillar . . . "
　　　　—Shylock in *The Merchant of Venice*, Act IV, Scene 1.

ARCHON BOOKS
1968

LIBRARY OF CONGRESS CATALOG CARD NUMBER: 68-21687
PRINTED IN THE UNITED STATES OF AMERICA

*To Christine*

# Contents

# *Illustrations*

*Following page 290:*

The Stone family in 1914

Fishing trip at Pyramid Lake, Nevada, 1933

Sons of the Vine in the Santa Cruz Mountains, California, 1941

The opening day of the trout season, Long Island Country Club, April 6, 1924

Attorney General Stone and Secretary of State Charles Evans Hughes, 1924

With Associate Justice Joseph McKenna, 1925

Summer cottage at Isle au Haut, Maine

Residence at 2340 Wyoming Avenue, Washington, D. C.

With Justices Holmes and Brandeis in 1930

The newly appointed Chief Justice with his grandsons

Being sworn as Chief Justice of the United States, July 3, 1941

Mural, "The Triumph of Justice," by Leon Kroll

Chief Justice Stone and his bench, 1941

Harlan Fiske Stone, 1941

# *Acknowledgments*

Work on this book began in the summer of 1950, when the late Chief Justice Stone's widow authorized its preparation and gave me unrestricted access to his personal correspondence, private and public papers. Included among these was a formidable mass of Supreme Court documents—slip opinions in various stages of preparation, memoranda to and from members of the Court, and Stone's own record of the manner in which certain crucial decisions were hammered into shape. These papers, on deposit at the Library of Congress, were sent to the Princeton University Library for my use. I am under further obligation to the Manuscript Division of the Library of Congress for assistance in the examination of the Hughes and Taft papers. Members of the Stone family and their friends made available their recollections, dating from Stone's idyllic boyhood in Mill Valley to his somewhat harassed Chief Justiceship.

For the formative period, my greatest debt is to the late Luther Ely Smith, Stone's Amherst classmate and lifelong friend, and Claude F. Walker, a contemporary and fellow townsman in Amherst, Massachusetts. Smith had a natural archival bent and indulged it to the limit in assembling memorabilia about his class, especially Stone. Walker, son of the Reverend Charles S. Walker, the chaplain with whom the future Chief Justice tangled in a chapel "rush" that may have changed for the better the course of his college and public career, had more than a normal incentive to be helpful. Whatever success I have achieved in reviving the Mill Valley spirit of the late nineteenth century and assessing its impact is due in considerable measure to him. Among those assisting in this effort were: Professor Emeritus Charles A. Peters, University of Massachusetts; Director William F. Merrill and Librarian Emeritus Charles R. Green, Jones Library of Amherst; Rena Mary Durkan, Curator, Edward Hitchcock Memorial Room, Amherst College; Marian G. Todd, Assistant Librarian, Newburyport (Mass.) Public Library, and Margaret Rose, City Library, Springfield, Mass.

To expedite exploration of Stone's work as teacher and dean, the Columbia Law School sent its entire files for 1910-1923 to the Princeton University Library. Young B. Smith, a participant on Stone's side in some of the wrangles that lent drama to the deanship, recreated in a single interview the passions animating those academic skirmishes. M. Halsey Thomas, Curator *Columbiana,* and Samuel F. Howard of Columbia University put within reach sources not easily available.

On Stone's law practice, I am under special obligation to Karl T. Frederick, a young lawyer in the firm of Wilmer, Canfield and Stone; to John Vance Hewitt, Stone's student at the Columbia Law School and later on his companion in piscatorial expeditions; and to Murray MacElhinny of Satterlee, Warfield and Stephens.

Assistance on the Attorney Generalship came from Stone's co-workers, Paul Shipman Andrews and Mabel Walker Wildebrandt, from Burton K. Wheeler, J. Edgar Hoover, and Louis B. Nichols, all of whom supplied detailed memoranda and answered specific inquiries. I also had the advantage of illuminating talks with Judge Alexander Holtzoff and John Lord O'Brian.

For insight into Stone's judicial contributions, the Justices them-selves cooperated: Hugo L. Black, William O. Douglas, Felix Frank-furter, the late Robert H. Jackson, Stanley Reed, and the late Owen J. Roberts. Learned Hand who, in 1924, was promoted on Attorney Gen-eral Stone's recommendation to the U.S. Circuit Court, 2nd District, responded to my requests. Noel T. Dowling, a close student of Stone's constitutional jurisprudence, was of assistance through his published writings and the detailed notes he made for me on various aspects of the Chief Justice's thought and methods. I am especially grateful to those who worked with Stone most intimately—his law clerks: Bennett Boskey, Alexis Coudert, Allison Dunham, Edward B. Friedman, Jr., Warner W. Gardiner, Walter F. Gellhorn, Harold Leventhal, Louis Lusky, Alfred McCormack, Eugene H. Nickerson, Herbert Prashker, Herbert Wechsler and Howard C. Westwood. Mrs. Gertrude Regis, the Chief Justice's secretary throughout most of his two decades on the bench, furnished much more than the usual amanuensis gleanings.

Because Stone understood and enjoyed life as well as work, I had perforce to enter fields normally beyond the ken of both the judge and the political scientist—the arts, wine, and food. His friends pleasantly introduced me to the joys of the Sons of the Vine. David E. Finley, Director of the National Gallery of Art, prepared a detailed memo-randum on another of the Justice's favorite hobbies. Mrs. Elizabeth B. Eustis gave me glimpses of the Stones on vacation at their beloved Maine retreat, Isle au Haut. The late Adolph Miller talked to me revealingly of how a European vacation nourished the Justice's soul. For a picture of the fun-loving Judge at Mrs. Stone's weekly teas, I am indebted to Mrs. Katherine McCook Knox.

In the actual work of assembling and sorting materials and getting the book into manuscript, I have had many helpers: Paul Tillett, Jr., was my research assistant during the early stages. Robert L. Tienken helped me in the summer of 1954. Mrs. Hazel Annis researched the Taft papers. Undergraduate assistant James H. Duffy checked the documentation against original sources, prepared the index, and performed numerous other tasks. At hand throughout was the mainstay of scholars and writers in the Princeton University Library, Miss Helen Fairbanks. Some of these services were made possible by financial awards. The Princeton University Research Fund thus furthered the project. A John Simon Guggenheim Fellowship released me from teaching duties at a critical time.

I am grateful also to various law journals for permission to use material printed in their pages: *Columbia Law Review, Harvard Law Review, University of Pennsylvania Law Review,* and *Yale Law Journal.*

It is often said that research and teaching are natural helpmates. Such was the case in the writing of this biography. Princeton seniors James M. Guiher, Jr., Robert P. Stranahan, Jr., and James S. Young, in doing their dissertations on different aspects of Stone's career, furthered their own education and substantially aided me.

In preparing the manuscript for the printer, Jerry Heringman Sper gave the book incisiveness by rigorous application of her editorial skill.

Since death struck the Chief Justice as he sat on the bench and in full vigor, his papers came to me as he left them. He had no chance, even if there had been inclination, to sort them out, make selections, impose restrictions, much less prepare notes for the guidance of his biographer. The freedom thus permitted has been balanced by a corresponding responsibility. Though my helpers gave me the advantage of friendly counsel and advice, the full weight of responsibility for final decisions as to both selection and interpretation of material was mine.

A. T. M.

*Princeton, N. J.*
*June 25, 1956*

MEMORIAL AT CHESTERFIELD, NEW HAMPSHIRE, ERECTED IN 1948

FREDERICK L. AND ANNE BUTLER STONE, PARENTS OF HARLAN FISKE STONE

HOUSE IN WHICH HARLAN FISKE STONE WAS BORN, OCTOBER 11, 1872

# HARLAN FISKE STONE:

## *Pillar of the Law*

# *Profile*

"A good many years ago," Chief Justice Stone commented a few months before his death, "I made up my mind that those who have a happy and useful life are those who resolve to do the job nearest to them with enough interest and enthusiasm so that it leaves them no opportunity to think much about what is beyond."[1]

Harlan Fiske Stone reached high position, not by definitely planning it, but "as the dog went to Dover, leg-by-leg."[2] Each step came naturally without that ugly vainglorious striving which mars so many public careers.

Thoroughly and faithfully, he did each day the particular task at hand. After thirteen years as Dean of the Columbia Law School he was appointed Attorney General of the United States, then an Associate Justice of the Supreme Court, and later Chief Justice—all "because someone who had authority to invite me to occupy the position asked me to do so." The secret of his steady advance lay in the reason President Coolidge appointed him Attorney General: "I think he had confidence in me, and that about tells the whole story."[3]

A sturdy son of the Yankee middle class, Stone held fast to the values that nurtured his youth—honesty, industry, thrift, self-reliance. Until the day he died he kept in a prominent place on his desk stark reminders of the four things that are supposed to have contributed to the advancement of New England—Eat it up; Wear it out; Make it do; Do without it. The New England crab-apple quality, however, disfigured neither his countenance nor his character. Though he valued thrift, he prized life more. The economic independence he sought was that of the freehold farmer who could look, as Jefferson said, "to the sun in heaven, the soil at his feet, and the labor of his own hands for his sustenance."[4] Economic security was not the main end, but an important means for achieving things more worth while.

Stone had dignity but not too much. He was a boy in many ways—his pockets always stuffed with a piece of string, a nut or two, scraps of paper, a button, an unusual stone—anything. Even as Chief Justice men and women in all walks of life remembered his dancing twinkle, his love of mischief, his delightful humor. An accomplished storyteller

3

himself, he collected Scotch yarns; friends and colleagues, notably Justice Sutherland, added to them. His special delight came from stories about himself. When his son Marshall demanded an independent search of title for the house he bought in Cambridge, the bank attorney said that a routine search would be quite enough. "Why do you want another?" "My father suggested it," young Stone replied. "Is your father a lawyer?" the bank official shot back.

The human streak of vanity was marked in him. "A man's got to live with himself," he would often say. But he cherished the discerning acclaim of others and loved admiration, attention, and praise. The flattery his classmates Luther Ely Smith and Sterling Carr showered on him for nearly half a century gave him genuine pleasure. But it rarely ever trapped him into a false estimate of his own powers or moved him to make a rash decision or take a false step. "Most of us," he remarked in 1928, "have a judgment of our own with respect to what we can do, and I think sometimes it is wisest to follow that and let recognition come when it will."[5]

In every relation of life he sought balance. He was calm and deliberate, stable and steady, famous as a liberal but utterly lacking in the qualities associated with the zealot and fanatic. Moving glacier-like, rather than skyrocketing into prominence, he advanced without exciting envy. Public recognition of his work won ready acceptance and approval. Senior Associate at the time of his appointment as Chief Justice, he became the only man in American history to occupy consecutively every seat on the Supreme Bench. Somehow he left each way-station with the good will of those who stayed behind.

In demeanor Stone was markedly modest and self-effacing. But whether one met him on campus, at lunch in the Columbia faculty club, or saw him at work as head of the Department of Justice, one was impressed with his commanding presence. Sheer force of character, extraordinary ability to inspire confidence in those whose lives he touched, tolerance and humaneness—these are the qualities that set him apart. His reputation at the New York bar was soon established, but professional adversaries remembered him especially for his eminent fairness. As Dean of Columbia Law School, where the Harlan Fiske Stone Chair of Constitutional Law honors his memory, he opened new vistas in legal education, but he is remembered more for his humanity than for his innovations.

Men generally saw Stone as one who exemplified "all that in human nature is most humane," as one who recognized the "sadness in being a man," but who also knew that "it was a proud thing, too."[6] Human beings could, he believed, develop ability to control themselves. The "sheer force" of man's "spiritual vitality" would "ultimately broaden

our social horizons and give us new social values."[7] Though his attachment to tested moorings was strong, he accepted change with calm
detachment.

The American political process itself calls for tolerance, the spirit of
give and take to ensure steady balance of opposing forces. The recurring interjection of such qualifiers as "I think," or "it seems to me,"
which characterize his formal and informal writings, stands for more
than scholarly prudence; these manifest an ingrained sense of man's
inherent limitations, distrust of extremes, the search for balance. His
favorite short story, "The Devil and Daniel Webster," suggests his attitude of mind. "One could admit all the wrong that had ever been done
and yet recognize that out of the wrong and the right, something new
had come. And everybody had played a part in it, even the traitors."[8]

Self-righteous extremes, whether right or left, gave him pause. A
hard and fast position stirred lurking doubt that it might not be firmly
grounded. "O what a brave thing it is," he might have exclaimed with
Rabelais, "in every case and circumstance of a matter to be thoroughly
well informed." Stone believed with Burke that government exists for
"the very purpose of opposing a sovereign reason to will and caprice,
in reformers and reformed, in the governors or in the governed, in
kings, in senators or in people." In public as in private affairs he felt
instinctively that "it is never wise to press a good situation too far."[9] A
maxim never far from the mind of Aristotle, Stone adopted as a rule of
life: "The right, or the good, or the beautiful, appears as something
which is neither too much nor too little. The limit suggested forms no
restraint; it rather acts as a guide, a principle imposed by reason to
conduct man along the proper path."[10] To some, Stone's distrust of
extremes made him appear lacking in courage and conviction, "as a
person who turned neither to partiality on the one hand, nor to impartiality on the other."[11] It seems more probable that such distrust
sprang from open-mindedness, tolerance, judicial temperament, suggesting the outlook of a man who, having pondered failures and successes in the "endless journey of mankind," fathomed the "inwardness
of it."[12]

The bulk of Stone's essential work does not lend itself to drama. No
essayist, as was Holmes, no social architect, as was Brandeis, Stone was
a judge's judge. His idiom was that of the law. The uncanny knack he
exhibited for narrowing down the issue in a case, deciding and writing
about that only, often enabled him to straighten out and clarify a mass
of apparently confusing precedents and doctrine, so that his opinion
could be used later on to resolve really tough issues, by saying no more
than "this has always been the law," or that "follows from the opinion
in 282 U.S." On occasion he could bring the Court right up to discard-

ing outmoded dogma without seeming to do so. Each case, even those of minor importance, was used "to blaze the path of the law a little further along its rough."[13]

It is difficult for the lay mind to grasp the fact that one may, and sometimes should, regard an act as constitutional even though it is bad legislation. That was precisely what Stone did in case after case. He strove against well-nigh insuperable odds to keep the judicial function within proper bounds. Judges disagree as to what those bounds are; some see them as narrow and confined; others as almost limitless. But, however interpreted, few judges would deny that the future of constitutional government in the United States depends on keeping the Court under some restraint. Stone had an abiding faith in this system; he believed profoundly that radical change is neither necessary nor generally desirable. Such change could be avoided "if fear of legislative action, which Courts distrust or think unwise, is not overemphasized in interpreting the document."[14] A free society needs continuity "not of rules but of aims and ideals which will enable government, in 'all the various crises of human affairs,' to continue to function and to perform its appointed task within the bounds of reasonableness."[15] This was the essence of his creed.

Stone had not always been so flexible. He did not emerge full grown; he lived and learned. In 1915 he shared the belief of conventionally minded lawyers that popular clamor for social justice and criticism of courts were "essentially lawless and subversive of all orderly judicial procedure."[16] Twenty years later the great changes wrought in the nation had convinced him of the necessity for more forceful political leadership, for strong government with the courage and will to prevent any group from dominating others.

A free society must reform in order to conserve; government must act constructively to preserve the essentials. "Today," he said in 1940, "it is more important, I believe, than at any time in my life, that we do not seek escape from our problems by leaving them to be solved by chance, or by those who have no more responsibility for their solution than ourselves. We should hold firmly to the belief that man by his very nature is bound to find the answers to his difficulties by intelligent, courageous, diligent intellectual effort. For that there is no substitute in the world in which we live."[17]

Temperamentally Stone was conservative, in the best sense of that much-abused label. For nostrums, panaceas, any and all world-rectifying schemes—and for their projectors—he had innate distrust. In human affairs there can be no perfect, no final solutions, but only adjustments or, to use his favorite expression, accommodations. Respect for facts, unremitting intellectual effort in the face of social perplexities, gave him an understanding that on occasion led to what observers identified as the liberal position. The accolade was unwanted and not wholly deserved. Gifted with an extraordinary sense of proportion, he kept his eye on the entire pattern of the law, and since he could not be "deceived by the false allure of a single case," he did not pass quickly from the conviction that legislation was bad to the conclusion that it was unconstitutional.[18] Thus, by tempering predilection with restraint and craftsmanship, he made the personal preference for social policy but one factor in his quest for judgment. In short, he became the statesman without ceasing to be the lawyer.

Stone had an abiding sense of duty. Judging preoccupied him almost completely. For him there was no more sacred duty than being a judge. "I have never found anything quite so absorbing as work on the Supreme Court. It just seems to exclude everything else."[19] The Chief Justiceship was onerous partly because "the business of running a court made it difficult to maintain decent standards of judicial writing."[20] In that aggregate of formal equals that is the Supreme Court, his contributions loom large. These must be weighed, however, not so much by the extent to which he kept his own notions out of law, but by the values he applied, their intrinsic merit, the influence he exerted on the course of events. If these endure, it is because he grasped social forces more profoundly than did other judges; divined more surely the course of their evolution, came closer to keeping his views in line with the "sober second thought of the community"—that "firm base on which all law must ultimately rest."[21]

PART ONE

# *Beginnings*

## CHAPTER ONE

# Heritage

*New England—a beauty which enters into the soul of the true New Englander and becomes a permanent part of his being.*

On the southeastern edge of the placid village of Chesterfield, New Hampshire, a dirt road, tortuous and rocky, wends its way through the woods to a clearing. All around lie pine- and birch-clad hills, hiding from vision greater heights—New Hampshire's bold Monadnock toward the east, and to the west lofty Haystack, Pisgah, and Stratton beyond the Connecticut River in Vermont. On a nearby slope stands a small story-and-a-half farmhouse, white frame with green trim. Its spindly chimney towers above the sturdy roof; a weathered porch surrounds it precariously on two sides; attached to the kitchen is a large shed that betokens rural New England architecture.

East of the house, and a little in front of it, stands a massive granite boulder bearing a tablet:

HARLAN FISKE STONE
Oct. 11, 1872–Apr. 22, 1946
Dean of Columbia Law School
Attorney General
of the United States
Associate Justice of
the United States Supreme Court
Chief Justice of the United States

This eight-room house was the birthplace of that country boy, son of a roughhewn New Hampshire farmer, who rose to the highest judicial office in the land. More than a marker for a homesite, this slab of granite, taken from one of the fields belonging to the farm, is an articulate glacial fragment of New Hampshire. The name it commemorates goes back through space and time to distant fields in England.

If Captain Peter Stone, Revolutionary soldier of 1777 and the first of the Stones to settle in Chesterfield, had inherited a nose for lineage, he might have exhumed an impressive line of American forebears. Blessed with Biblical names all, there were before him three Simons in succession, then Benjamin, then Peter. The first Simon broke ancestral ties to face the hardship of an ocean crossing from England.

For many generations the Stone family had been deeply rooted in the soil of the mother country. In and around the parishes of Little Bentley, Ardleigh, and Great Bromley in County Essex, England, bearers of the name Stone had long tilled as yeomen lands in leasehold from the lords of the manors. Simon Stone, the Chief Justice's English forebear, was born in Great Bromley, February 9, 1585.[1] In the spring of 1635 Simon, with his wife Joan and their five children, sixteen years to five weeks in age, joined a large Puritan emigration to America, which sailed from London, April 15, on the ship *Increase.*

Simon arrived on these shores innocent of the New England frontier, its discomforts and loneliness, its deadly peril. Settling in Watertown, an extended pioneer area west of Cambridge on the north bank of the Charles, he became grantee of eight lots, and to these added five more. It was his first investment in land, an expression of thrift that would motivate his posterity. On the south slope of Mount Auburn, well back from the Charles tidelands, Simon built his many-windowed, high-gabled frame dwelling, and soon became "one of the largest landowners in the town." Rising at once to the stature of freeman, this erstwhile yeoman immigrant served, before his death at eighty, as church deacon and Watertown selectman.

Simon, Jr., inherited a share of his father's landed estate and continued to occupy the family homestead in Watertown. Like his father, he planted his ground and held the offices of deacon and selectman, serving also as town clerk and deputy to the General Court of the Bay Colony. With an eye that looked ahead, he acquired extensive acres in Groton, a wild country twenty-five miles northwesterly from Watertown. A share of these lands he passed on to his son Simon, who became known as Deacon Simon.

This Simon had a more adventurous life. When King Philip's Indian uprising set New England aflame in 1675, he served in the militia and helped to defend garrison houses. In the spring of 1676 he marched with that doughty fighter, Captain Joseph Sill. Captain Sill's orders were to join Captain Henchman and seek out the enemy, whenever and wherever found. "Have your hearts lifted up to God in Jesus Christ, set the soldiers a good example in piety and virtue, have their heads covered in day of battle, get corn if found for plunder," the order said.[2] Whether Simon repelled murderous fire from a stockade, or sought the enemy along a blood-marked forest path, we know not, but we do know that posterity recognized and honored his intrepid courage and amazing vitality.

The first American edition of Reverend Cotton Mather's *Magnalia,* published in 1820, includes the fantastic account of one Simon Stone, soldier, who, though desperately wounded by Indians, fully recovered. The incident had occurred in 1690, early in King William's War, when Lieutenant Bancroft rescued the Exeter, New Hampshire, garrison from redskin attack. "At this time," Mather records, "there happened a remarkable thing . . . that one *Simon Stone* being here wounded with shot in *nine* several places, lay for *dead* (as it was time!) among the *dead*. The Indians coming to strip him, attempted with *two* several blows of an hatchet at his *neck* to cut off his *head*, which blows added . . . more enormous wounds unto those *port-holes* of *death*, at which the *life* of the poor man was already running out as fast as it could . . . and the English now coming to bury the dead, one of the soldiers perceived this poor man to fetch a gasp; whereupon an Irish fellow then present, advised 'em to give him another dab with an hatchet and so bury him with the rest. The English detesting this barbarous advice lifted up the wounded man and poured a little *fair water* into his mouth, at which he coughed; then they poured a little *strong water* after it, at which he opened his eyes. . . . *Simon Stone* was thoroughly cured, and is at *this* day a very lusty man; and as he was born with *two thumbs* on one hand, his neighbors have thought him to have at least as many *hearts* as *thumbs*."

"*Reader*," Mather moralized, "let the remembrance of such things cause thee to live, preparing for death continually. But . . . that nothing may be dispaired of, remember *Simon Stone*."[3]

No scion of the Watertown Stones could doubt that Mather's hero was their forebear, Deacon Simon Stone, who had fought King Philip, and then, after fourteen years of peaceful tilling of the soil and raising offspring, had picked up his musket and hurried to Exeter.

Deacon Simon Stone was to his last a "very lusty man." In his old age he received from the Province of Massachusetts a tangible reward for his military service. Of the long-promised "Narragansett" grants, he drew Lot 15, Township No. 6, in the untamed region some eighteen miles westerly from Groton. A part of this settlement Simon passed on to his son Benjamin.

True to Stone tradition, Benjamin, born in 1706, stuck to his patrimonial acres; he married Emme Parker, raised a family, and died in 1758. Benjamin's son Peter, born at Groton in 1741, was seventeen when his father left him a share of the "Narragansett" grant, Township No. 6, which in 1762 became Templeton, Massachusetts. The times were stirring. As the boy turned the home furrows, he heard this distant frontier calling.

In and around Boston the tide toward revolution was nearing flood. Many by the name of Stone were among the aroused patriots. On August 30 and 31, 1774, portentously close to hostilities, representatives of the Committee of Safety from every town and district of Middlesex County met in Concord "to consult upon measures proper to be taken at the present very important day." Among them were James Stone, Captain Jonas Stone, Captain Josiah Stone, and Ebenezer Stone—all Deacon Simon Stone's family stock. The Convention deliberated mainly upon the late acts of the British Parliament, entitled "an act for the better regulating of the government of the Province of Massachusetts Bay in New England." Following debate, a committee was appointed to take that measure in consideration and report to the Convention. Captain Josiah Stone of Framingham, brought in a series of resolutions for the committee, protesting overt conditions and proclaiming certain rights that Jefferson immortalized two years later:

Resolved, That no state can long exist free and happy where the course of justice is obstructed, and that, when trials by juries, which are the grand bulwarks of life and property, are destroyed or weakened, a people falls immediately under arbitrary power.

Resolved, That the late act which gives the governor of this province a power of appointing judges of the superior and inferior courts, commissioners of oyer and terminer, the attorney general, provosts, marshals, and justices of the peace, and to remove all of them, the judges of the superior court excepted, without consent of council, entirely subverts a free administration of justice; as the fatal experience of mankind, in all ages, has testified, that there is no greater species of corruption, than when judicial and executive officers depend for their existence and support, on a power independent of the people.

Resolved, That by ordaining jurors to be summoned by the sheriff only, which sheriff is to be appointed by the governor, without consent of council, that security which results from a trial by our peers is rendered altogether precarious, and there is not only an evident infraction upon our charter, but a subversion of our common rights as Englishmen.

Concluding the report are these words:

Our fathers left a fair inheritance to us, purchased by a waste of blood and treasure. This we are resolved to transmit equally fair to our children after us. No danger shall affright, no difficulties intimidate us; and if, in support of our rights, we are called to encounter even death, we are yet undaunted, sensible that he can never die too soon, who lays down his life in support of the laws and liberties of his country.[4]

Harlan Fiske Stone did not learn of Josiah Stone's forthright prerevolutionary action until 1941, shortly after his appointment as Chief Justice of the United States. Then his correspondent, enclosing a copy of the above excerpts, suggested that "your appointment was foreordained, in the neighborhood of Concord, Massachusetts, 167 years ago." The Chief Justice was "delighted." "What a wonderful story it is," he commented. "I wonder if there are any small communities in the United States today which could produce such a statesmanlike document."[5]

In rapid succession, after the Middlesex County resolutions, came Concord Bridge and Bunker Hill, the Declaration of Independence and, in 1777, the Bennington alarm. On August 21, 1777, Sergeant Peter Stone of Templeton marched in Colonel Sparhawk's regiment to Bennington; they arrived too late for the engagement, fought August 26, and marched home again.

Peter's ten days as a Continental opened his eyes. He had seen bare hills and lofty wooded mountains. He had crossed the Connecticut River, whose restless waters, freed from restraint of northern heights, meandered strong and wide past towns of bloody memory. On Templeton's northwestern horizon the Great Monadnock rose solitary above dark forests and sunny intervales in New Hampshire. Peter could see that noble landmark as he returned to the harvest on his farm. New ambition stirred him. Virgin fields awaited. In 1778 Peter Stone of Templeton, in the fifth generation of Deacon Simon of Watertown, bought partly cleared land in the town of Chesterfield, New Hampshire, and settled there with his family. He was the first in the Chief Justice's New Hampshire line.

Chesterfield, a rectangular tract of about forty square miles on the east bank of the Connecticut River, was named by provincial Governor Benning Wentworth in honor of the Earl of Chesterfield.[6] Settled in 1761, it was a post town in Cheshire County, ninety miles from Boston, with a population of about nine hundred when Peter Stone moved there. For the six miles adjacent to the water, wooded heights approached the river's side. North of the central village lay the beautiful, pure water of Spafford's Lake.[7] The primeval woods, bordering river and lake, were well stocked with deer, bear, and wild turkey.

Early Chesterfield inhabitants, stalwart pioneers, looked out first of all for themselves and turned every advantage of earth and water and sky to full account. While they cleared and planted their stubborn soil, they scanned the heavens for augury, kept track of seasons and weather, and even explored their granite ledges for hidden wealth. "We should be induced at every opportunity," admonished a writer of that day, "to examine our grounds and farms for other metals (than copper and iron), not however in a secret mysterious manner, with chimerical notions about the existence of precious ores, but with good and honest hearts, willing not only to benefit ourselves, but our state and country."[8]

Peter Stone, with no urge to engage in searches after plutonic treasure, attended to the practical business of earning a livelihood. He did not, however, confine himself to peaceful pursuits. The Revolu-

tionary fighting spared Chesterfield, but Peter remembered Bennington. Being able-bodied and free from religious scruples, he enrolled in
the militia and held the rank of captain in the local company. Like his
forebears, he was also active in civic affairs, serving as selectman in
1784 and 1795. But Peter's proudest achievement was his part in
founding Chesterfield Academy. The Preamble to the Act of January
12, 1799, incorporating the academy, says that "Peter Stone of Chesterfield, gentleman, and sundry other persons, have voluntarily contributed certain sums of money for the purpose of establishing and
supporting a public school or academy, in said Chesterfield." Opened
August 14, 1794, this institution soon attained pre-eminence. By 1808
it possessed a "Philesian Society" and a library of valuable books. For
a considerable time the Academy was Chesterfield's most illustrious
ornament, holding "a place among the academies of New Hampshire
second only to that of Phillips Academy at Exeter."[9]

For this impressive memorial to Captain Peter Stone's humanity and
foresight, the co-founder paid heavily. Toward the end of his life dire
financial straits obliged him to mortgage his farm, and eventually he
lost it. Though permitted to remain in his home because of age and
infirmity, he preferred to spend his closing days in the Academy he
helped to build.[10] He died there October 18, 1820, aged seventy-nine.

Peter's son, Amaziah, and grandson, Lauson, continued to live on
Chesterfield's granite uplands and follow the ancestral occupation of
farming. Lauson, the Supreme Court Justice's grandfather, was born
there, June 22, 1806. When he was only fourteen years old his father
died, and for the next ten years Lauson bore the responsibility of
helping his mother raise her six younger children. On April 26, 1832,
he married Hannah Fiske of Chesterfield, daughter of Joseph and
Polly Bingham Fiske, who bore him three children. One was Harlan's
father, Frederick Lauson, born September 12, 1836.

Harlan's grandfather was determined that nothing whatever should
interfere with the education of his children. Each snowy winter morning he would get the family up early, do the chores, pile firewood, and
plow the roads out to get the young ones off to school.[11] The boy
Frederick traveled a devious road to maturity, and finally achieved
moderate wealth. His mother died in 1841 when he was only five years
old. Two years later his father married Thankful Dodge of Dum-
merston, a Vermont river town across from Chesterfield.[12] One of
Chief Justice Stone's earliest recollections was visiting his grandfather
in his West Chesterfield home where he resided with his third wife,
whom he married in July 1876 at the age of seventy.[13]

Frederick's childhood was clouded by the loss of his mother and the
uncongenial home atmosphere created by his disagreeable stepmother.

Though he attended the public schools and the academy, he was not of a scholarly turn of mind, and preferred swapping jackknives or breaking steers to mastering a textbook. At fourteen he cut firewood at seventy-five cents a cord.

Frederick's continued unhappiness at home led him, at fifteen, to find refuge in Canada, where he joined a company of carpenters building stations on the Grand Trunk Railroad, along the north shore of Lake Ontario, from Cobourg to Toronto. After two and a half years he returned to New Hampshire, worked as a carpenter in Keene, and operated a butcher shop there. Ill fortune continued to dog him. He went back to Chesterfield, but the meat business he started failed because his partner kept the books and pocketed the profits. In these financial straits, October 26, 1861, Frederick married Ann Sophia Butler, a Chesterfield schoolteacher, daughter of Marshall Butler, farmer and lumberman. Five dollars was all the money the bridegroom had in the world. This he gave to the officiating minister, who, knowing of the young man's poverty, presented the greenback to the bride.[14]

Nor was Frederick Stone's wife Ann without hardening experience. Her father was killed when thrown from an oxcart, leaving his widow with four small children. To help support her family, thirteen-year-old Ann waited on table in a local hotel. Nevertheless her instinct toward learning led her to attend Chesterfield Academy. After her graduation she taught in the public schools. She had sympathy with children and understood their mental needs.

Ann Sophia Butler Stone's ancestors were of old New England stock. The Butlers, like the Stones, had lived in Chesterfield for three generations, working as farmers or innkeepers. Ann's grandfather was the son of Josiah Butler, tavernkeeper of Hinsdale, the New Hampshire town that separated Chesterfield from the Massachusetts line. Mrs. John Butler, Harlan's great-grandmother, practiced midwifery and traveled on horseback, carrying her equipment in saddlebags.

After their marriage Frederick went to work teaming, while his wife eked out their livelihood braiding palm-leaf hats. They soon saved $400, enough to make a $100 down payment on a $1550 farm and purchase stock, tools, and household furniture. Two and a half years later Stone sold out at a profit and bought a country hotel. Again fortune smiled. Two years later to a day he sold out with a net gain of $3000.

There was no nonsense about Fred Stone. Holding fast to old-fashioned ways of thought and action, he plowed his fields in fall and spring and snowbanks in winter. New methods of doing things had to await proof that they were more profitable as well as more practical. It took him a long time to quit churning his own cream and making his own cheese and send his milk to the cooperative creamery. To Fred Stone, one load of barnyard manure was more valuable than any highfalutin commercial fertilizer. To sell hay and fodder crops off the farm was much the same as selling the farm itself, bit by bit. He fed his crops to his cattle so he might feed the soil. Only when convinced by actual facts did he gradually adopt new ways and means. But he could change when the advantages in so doing were proved.

In his book, thrift required that his family live off the products of the farm. To live out of the butcher's cart and the grocery store and to heat his house with coal and light it with gas seemed to him an extravagance. His boys kept the woodshed filled with dry stovewood, and when winter came his wife had her pantry supplied with rye, Indian meal, and maple sugar. Only such things as could not be made or grown on the farm were bought at the store, and these were often to be paid for by bartering chickens, eggs, and butter. When winter storms or rain prevented outdoor work, there was plenty to do in the house or shop.[15]

True to family tradition, Frederick took a practical interest in civic affairs. He was chairman of the Chesterfield Republican Town Committee, and held office as selectman, assessor, and tax collector. Chastened but not dismayed by early misadventure, he prospered as farmer and trader.

For a decade Frederick's wife was engrossed in rearing and teaching their first son, Winthrop, born June 12, 1862. Not a robust boy, he was unfit to cope successfully with the rigors of farm life. His mother's discerning eye soon recognized the boy's latent intellectual gifts. Since the academy had failed, these talents could not be developed in Chesterfield; the only educational advantages offered were in the district school, and the practice of "going away to college" was unknown. Nevertheless, Frederick and Ann Stone, with their individual ideas as to the meaning and benefits of education, were determined that Winthrop should enjoy the best schooling that could be had.

A second son was born October 11, 1872, and christened Harlan Fiske.* The father thought he detected budding intellectual interest one day when the infant crawled across the floor and examined the name on the kitchen stove, tracing each shiny raised letter with his tiny finger.[16] This dubious evidence of promise hardened the Stones'

---

* Perhaps named for John Marshall Harlan (1833-1911), Jurist, Attorney General of Kentucky, conservative Republican leader after Civil War, defeated for governorship of Kentucky in 1872 and 1875, appointed Associate Justice of the Supreme Court in 1877.

Commenting on his first name, Stone said that he didn't know how his family happened to pick it, "but I have always supposed that it was the result of the prominence of Justice Harlan in public life, and they chose it because they liked it. At any rate, I have always been satisfied with their choice." (H. F. S. to Irving Brant, April 20, 1937.)

resolution to leave Chesterfield and resettle in a place where their children could enjoy greater educational opportunities.

In 1874 the Stones moved forty miles south of Chesterfield, to the Massachusetts college town of Amherst. Fred had bought a good farm there, on Fort River in Mill Valley, a sequestered locality a mile and a half south of the village green. Here they lived until 1897, well past the day when Harlan, school and college completed, left home to strike out for himself.

The decision to move had not been easy. For Ann the move meant separation from her mother as well as her brother Warren. There were also close friends like the Hermon C. Harveys. Young Mrs. Harvey and Ann frequently exchanged visits. When Agnes Harvey was born, Ann Stone hastened to be among the first to see the new arrival. She tussled with Harlan, then a year old, to slip on coat and hood, but he had other ideas, pulling off each garment as fast as his mother could put it on. Ann persisted. Mother and son arrived at the Harveys' in time to take a peek at the day-old baby. After little Agnes had been seen and duly admired, Ann turned to the task of dressing Harlan for the return trip. Again he rebelled against coat and hood, stoutly refusing to go home. This was the Chief Justice's first meeting with the future Mrs. Harlan Fiske Stone.*

Though Harlan's parents took him away from Chesterfield when he was less than two years old, he never doubted that the rugged qualities of the Yankee hill farmer were born and bred in him. His birthplace was in a corner of New Hampshire, near the point where three states meet, in the heart of New England's last frontier. "Just to prove that I am a New Englander," the Chief Justice proudly asserted, "I might mention that I am [in] the ninth generation of direct descendants of Simon Stone, who settled in Massachusetts Bay Colony in 1635. Five generations, of which I was the last, lived in the little town of Chester-field, New Hampshire, where I was born; and so far as I know, I am the first American member of the family to leave New England, and the first lawyer in the whole lot."[17]

Though New England was a cultural unit, common heritage and ethos did not preclude the existence of enmity among the several sovereign states. The ill feeling between New Hampshire and Vermont was of long standing. A boundary dispute flared up after the Duke of York was granted what is now New York and Vermont. The latter attempted to extend its jurisdiction over a section of New Hampshire which included the town of Chesterfield. One of Stone's ancestors on his grandmother's side, by name of Bingham, resisted legal processes

* "Harlan told President Coolidge this tale," Mrs. Harlan Stone recalled in July 1950. "It amused him greatly, and the first time I met the President, he wanted to know if it was a true story."

issuing from Vermont and was arrested and jailed for it. The dispute was once adjudicated previous to the Revolutionary War by the British Privy Council, but was not finally settled till over a hundred and fifty years later. When the Supreme Court resolved the conflict, the opinion was written by Associate Justice Harlan Fiske Stone.[18]

The case was decided on strictly legal grounds, but the final arbiter was at heart a loyal son of New Hampshire with strong sympathy for one's natural attachment to his native soil. "I never could see any good reason," Justice Stone wrote Louis Adamic, October 28, 1943, "why a former citizen of Yugoslavia or even of Germany should be expected not to cherish the folkways of his native land, any more than I, born in New Hampshire, should not continue to take delight in the traditions of that state which are unknown to most others. If you will read Stephen Benét's delightful story of New Hampshire, 'Daniel Webster and the Devil,' you will discover that a native-born American citizen may have a special place in his heart for New Hampshire from which all others are excluded, even Vermont."

Massachusetts commanded secondary loyalty. In later years it was his birthplace, rather than Amherst, the town of his upbringing, that he looked back to with deepest affection. His words always "came back at the end to New Hampshire ground, and the one spot of land that each man loves and clings to."[19] After his elder brother Winthrop met an untimely tragic death in July 1921, while mountain climbing near Banff, Canada, Harlan pictured the country of his birth in a paper prepared as a memorial.

"Chesterfield was, as it still is," he wrote, "like many another New England hill town, except that its natural beauty is rather more wild and rugged than that of the gentler slopes and quieter valleys which lie farther to the south. . . . In summer its pastured hillsides are dotted with grazing cattle. One hears along its wooded slopes the tinkling of cowbells mingled with the music of crystal brooks running swiftly to the valleys below. Remote from cities and from the turmoil of business and the great currents of commerce, its life is simple, natural and untroubled. . . . Its granite-bound hills are eternally clad in verdure. Even when wrapped in the snows of winter the tall pines, the verdant hemlocks and spruce, clothe its heights with a beauty which enters into the soul of the true New Englander and becomes a permanent part of his being."[20]

Harlan Fiske Stone's ancestors on both sides, like uncounted other frontier pioneers, through frugality, hard work, and self-denial, wrung a sufficient livelihood from the reluctant New Hampshire soil. He was a New England product. Early lineage instilled in him, as in Holmes, an abiding love of "granite rock and barberry bushes." Certain enduring qualities of mind and heart—independence, self-reliance, sound judgment, a sense of civic responsibility, love of freedom—all these were a solid inheritance from forebears who had lived and toiled on New Hampshire's unchanging hills.

## CHAPTER TWO

# Boyhood in Mill Valley

When the Stones arrived from New Hampshire, the town of Amherst retained much of the rural simplicity of earlier years. Neither the literary and scientific institutions dominating the central plateau, nor the straw hat shops beside the railroad on the eastern slope, nor even the minor industries scattered in the outskirts, could weaken the sturdy Amherst farmer's faith in his calling. Broad acres surrounded three outlying communities, each with church, school, and smithy. Alluvial plains at the base of the mountains and high wooded lots contributed to the well-being of their owners. The indefatigable energy and purpose of those who owned and tilled the land had made the most of these natural advantages. Fred Stone and his wife were determined to continue and improve tradition in a community far more elevated in tone than that to which they were accustomed.

Among the resources that blessed the Amherst domain was Fort River,* a rapid, sizable stream rising in Pelham on the northeast and in the foothills of the Holyoke range on the southern border. Uniting its waters in the South Amherst farmlands, the river flowed in rockbound pools and eddies through deep woods and across Hadley meadows to the Connecticut. Fort River got its name from a fortification against the Indians that once stood near the river's mouth. The water power, gristmill, and sawmill known as "Clark's Mills" antedated the town and gave this little community the name Mill Valley. Fred's acres of open fertile land, bought from his uncle Charles McMaster, fitted into a retired corner adjacent to the valley, a mile and a half from Amherst Center.

Ann Stone, in her thirties, found the simple appointments of the Mill Valley homestead, with its squat story-and-a-half farmhouse, adequate to her needs. Large of form and feature, "a little on the fleshy side," as the saying went, she was forceful and energetic. She fed and cared for her small family—including the hired man—and did

* Known colloquially as "Freshman" River.

her share in gathering and salvaging the products of dooryard and field. These chores performed, she kept a watchful eye on the slender, fast-growing schoolboy, Winthrop, and prepared roly-poly Harlan for school days to come. What Harlan wrote many years later about his mother's guidance of Winthrop applied to himself and to his brother Lauson, eleven years his junior; also to their sister Helen, born when Harlan was ready for high school. "Her devotion, rare good sense, and force of character, guided his [Winthrop's] intellectual discipline, until the time came to experience the rough-and-ready training of the Mill Valley district school."[1]

Fred Stone found his conveniently located acres well fitted to his design and purpose. His land responded with profit to his skillful touch. But Fred was not satisfied. He looked with inquiring interest upon the doings of his fellow landholders. Refusing to be seduced by ephemeral schemes of quick enrichment, he benefited others with no loss to himself. An expert trader, Fred liked to attend public auctions, where he would buy up a lot of things. Then, when he had a sufficient accumulation, he would have an auction of his own. Before long Fred had his fingers in so many pies that his son Harlan was at some pains, in later years, to tell an inquirer "just what my father's occupation was." "If you happened to have read *David Harum*," the Justice commented in 1933, "I could answer by saying that my father was the David of his community. He was a small businessman, distinctively the product of a small New England community. He owned and bought and sold farms, woodland, cattle, horses, and almost any kind of property that was dealt with in such communities. On one or two occasions I know he owned churches."[2]

Memory pictures the Stone farmhouse, for all its rural plainness, as an attractive and comfortable home. Around the yard ran a white picket fence with rambler roses and trailing vines; the gate served Harlan, and years later his brother Lauson and sister Helen, as a swing. In summer the apple trees and elms cast their shadows around the house, and the garden seemed alive with the hum of bees amid the flowers. Though outwardly small, this low-roofed dwelling was amazingly spacious—five bedrooms, a parlor, a dining room, and a good-sized kitchen that opened to a shed. The shiny kitchen stove, the sink with hand pump, and out in the summer kitchen an iron pot set over a brick furnace with Dutch oven—these were housekeeper Ann's stock tools in trade.

One red-letter day Fred replaced the pump on the kitchen sink with a faucet. Ann proudly showed this modern device to a visiting maiden aunt.

"Isn't it wonderful?" Ann asked excitedly.

Aunt Sophia, gaunt but energetic, looked skeptically at the sparkling

# ! AUCTION !

Hold on just a minute! I've something to tell,
I'm to have a BIG AUCTION, and all things to sell,
My home is in Amherst and I'm everywhere known,
As the man who looks out for the good of FRED STONE.

My home is situated one mile from town,
Prices that were once high have now come down,
Be assured a warm welcome awaits you,
If you attend my PUBLIC VANDUE.

All who attend will have time to consider,
As everything offered goes to the highest bidder,
Having disposed of my home and no place to stay,
I want my friends to come and take something away.

I have Horses and Wagons, and all kinds of rigs,
Cows, Heifers and Bulls, Brood Sows and their Pigs,
Hay Tedders, Horse Rakes, every sort of machine,
It's an Auction you've read of, but not yet seen.

Having rented my Farm I shall offer at Public Auction

# FRIDAY, APR. 16

## AT 9 O'CLOCK SHARP.

All of my personal property consisting of Horses, Cattle, Hogs, Wagons, Sleighs, Harness, Farm Implements, Furniture, &c. &c.    ☞  Terms made known at time and place of sale.

### F. L. STONE.

# GUY C. ALLEN, Auctioneer.

*April 1897*

trickle and retorted, "It must be pretty hard to stand still and wait for the kettle to fill!"[3]

More to the liking of Winthrop and Harlan than austere Aunt Sophia was genial Uncle Charles McMaster, whose occasional visits enlivened farm life. A fisherman at the Grand Banks, he had a fund of yarns to enthrall young as well as older folk.

Yet Harlan, swinging by himself on the front gate, must have been lonely. The boys saw and felt their father's presence, heard his insistent talk at table in the kitchen, but all day he was out of sight and hearing at the barn or on the farm. Each morning the mother would fill a lunch-box for Winthrop, send that tall slim youth on his long uphill walk to school at the Center, and then turn to her housework. In the workaday kitchen there must have been moments of fun and frolic for three-year-old Harlan, some juvenile tales told or picture books shown, to lighten the hours. However, Harlan spoke only of the "intellectual discipline" the children received from their mother. Winthrop, at fourteen, home from school in the afternoon, finished the day by help-ing his father with the chores. Saturdays and holidays, and dur-ing vacations, though none too sturdy, he performed his task in the fields.

In preschool days Harlan achieved a degree of freedom from parental confines and walked with Nature on the Hadley road. Wild flowers painted the countryside and the grassy slopes along the canal. No longer a solitary, he made this realm his own. Like Winthrop, this fledgling botanist collected and preserved flowers. The Valley teemed with life; he was part and parcel of it. Without understanding, the boy felt and accepted, in full measure, his environment. Born during these plastic years was his "passionate love of the mysterious workings of nature in growing things; his deep and abiding love of intimate contact with nature when she unveils her secrets and her beauty."[4]

One memorable day in the latter seventies, he climbed down from his swinging gate, wandered across the rutted road to the riverbank, then continued his adventurous way to the Mill. With eyes and mind alerted and imagination fired, he entered into a new world. High branches swayed in the wind and the river ran boisterously. He could see the water swirling among the smooth stones in its bed and forming silent pools in shaded nooks. The mystery of men carrying poles and lines now was solved. The boy stood wide-eyed on the bridge and looked up the boiling stream to the dam, where the water poured over in one glistening sheet. From the pond, on the north bank, a leaky pentstock led past the sawmill to Asahel Dwight's pump shop; on the south side a canal carried power to an overshot water wheel, in the depths of the gristmill. This lower region was a fearsome place. When Miller Holley, lantern in hand, opened the door to the stairway lead-ing down, few of the children playing on the mill floor dared follow him into that dank cavern.

John Holley's Mill, standing close to the highway, midway a group of homesteads, was heart and soul of Mill Valley. Two huge gambrel-roofed houses frowned upon each other from opposite banks of the river. On the north, the Clark mansion, west of the highway, proudly faced the Mill. It stood between modest twin houses—the McMaster farmhouse on Hadley road and the Dexter place on the highway. A few rods further north, across the street, stood the schoolhouse. On the south, the Gaylord mansion looked across the highway to the Linehan house and Miller Holley's cottage. These homesteads were hives of industry. Each owner was master of his farm, mill, or shop. Children came in endless succession. Boys and girls crowded the district school. Big boys labored on the farm or climbed up the long rise to school and college. When school was out, the Holley children and their friends played in the mill, their voices pitched high above the grinding.[5] The highway was busy too. South Amherst farmers drove their horses or oxen with grist to the mill, loitered for talk in the doorway, or continued over the rattly bridge to stores and bank, or town meeting, in the Center.

Harlan never forgot Holley's Mill. "I can remember well," he wrote years later, "when the loads of grain came from the Smith farm and were ground at the mill. Father did the same thing when I was a small lad. The grist was used for cattle feed. Both the Smith farm and Father kept very large numbers of cattle through the winter. Another thing that I remember was that we always selected corn and rye to have them ground on the old millstones, a supply enough to last us all through the winter. This was used in making the kind of bread that I have never seen anywhere else, except in Agnes's family. It was made of rye and corn, was deep brown in color with a brown crust, and was perfectly delicious."[6]

Throughout his life, in spite of wide acquaintance with other foods and styles of cooking, Harlan's relish for New England fare never diminished. He always liked to see on his table such dishes as corn on the cob, honeycomb tripe, pig's feet, summer sausage, Vermont cheese, and buttermilk. He never forgot the grist that came right off the millstones into his mother's kitchen. Rye and wheat were made into bread, corn meal into johnny cake, buckwheat into flapjacks. In the late 1930s, when a "For Sale" sign appeared on ancient Holley's Mill, this broken-down landmark of boyhood days awakened in Supreme Court Justice Stone memories more gastronomic than romantic.

Chubby and good-natured—a sort of "fat boy"—Harlan was, like his mother, large of frame and feature. His contemporaries remember him as "quite different from his brother Winthrop—had no style, you wouldn't look at him twice." A great reader, Sunday afternoons usually found him in a hammock, poring over a book.[7] When the Hermon Harveys, with their four young ones, drove down in their commodious carriage from Chesterfield to visit, Harlan proved himself a resourceful host. With Agnes and her three brothers, he had lively games of tag, made mud pies, and hung milkweed up to dry, pretending it was tobacco. He sometimes made overnight visits to his cousins, the Hubbards, in East Amherst. "I often think of our boyhood days," the Chief Justice wrote Dwight Hubbard in 1941, "and what a great experience it was for me to be permitted to go over to spend a day or two with you boys. How hard we did play and how many kinds of mischief we did get into!"[8]

Soon the schoolhouse called. Mill Valley District School No. 7 stood on open ground well back from the highway, its solid brick rectangle a monument to the wisdom of the fathers. Two worn-out millstones served as doorsteps and announced the locale to passersby. The weathered woodshed and privies hid shamefacedly behind it. No belfry dignified the structure; a schoolmistress in the doorway swinging her hand bell gave summons enough. The playground was ample and inviting. The dubious mixing in one room of infants and adolescents, of both sexes, aged five to twenty, for instruction ranging from primer to calculus, motivated by corporal punishment, had long been abandoned. The school was reorganized for primary teaching—reading, spelling, arithmetic, introductory geography. On this solid base, tough and talented pupils would be ready for intermediate instruction —reading and spelling continued, with writing, intellectual and practical arithmetic, modern geography, parts of speech and inflection. No formal music, beyond its spontaneous expression from the hearts of the children. No manual art, except self-imposed busywork by boys with jackknives and chalk. No social subjects. No gay cutouts in the windows to mark each joyous season. No textbooks furnished by the town. No flag on the building. The committee decreed a female teacher for Mill Valley, who ruled by ferule rather than rattan.[9]

Ann Stone, who herself had been a schoolteacher, insisted upon mental drill for Harlan before he was old enough for school. She bought his schoolbooks at school committeeman Nelson's store and carefully selected his home reading from the town library or from the Morgan Library at the College. Harlan took school in stride, and always found time to wrestle and play rough games and tease his girl schoolmates. Yet Flora King, the young mistress of the red schoolhouse, who taught Harlan from the age of seven through ten, probed beneath his prankishness and noted the boy's marked deliberateness. He never talked "merely to show off," as other boys often did, but always "thought a thing over before making a statement or asking a question." One day, the Reverend Warren H. Beaman,[10] the visiting school superintendent, explained to the scholars that they should be thankful for the advantages they enjoyed in the North. "Why, in the South," he said, "the children have to work all day and go to school at night!" Harlan scanned the schoolroom dubiously; nowhere did he see any lamps. "How could they see if they went to school at night?" he queried. The superintendent appeared stumped. Though he had often repeated that talk, no one had ever before questioned it.

Without being disquietingly precocious, Harlan continued to show unusual mental alertness. Miss King boarded at the home of a neighbor. On his way from school Harlan often dropped in to see her. Many a time, before the family and visitors, the teacher observed rotund Harlan engaged in timely debate, "talking like an old man" with persons many years his senior.

Miss King, young and resourceful, taught fractions by cutting up apples to demonstrate to her pupils that one-half is larger than one-third, even though the number in the denominator is smaller. At an "examination" at the end of the school year a member of the committee turned to chubby Harlan and asked, "Would you rather have half or a third of a pie?" Harlan looked at him gravely and politely answered, "Well, sir, if the pie was the kind of a pie I liked, I'd want a half. But if it wasn't a good pie, I'd take a third."[11] Everyone laughed. The teacher's method had not been unsuccessful, but she could not take all the credit. "Figure sense" ran in the Stone family. Fred Stone had uncanny ability to compute interest and make other mathematical calculations in his head—a talent that reached full flower in Harlan's son Marshall, who at an early age became a distinguished mathematician.

Though we are not informed that Harlan was a truant from school, we know that he ran away from home. When his mother tethered him with a long rope, Harlan accepted his punishment. Resignedly he walked to the end of the rope, lay down, and fell asleep. When Harlan was ready to leave Miss King for the daily trudge uphill to school at the Center, he was a big boy, overgrown, bright and amiable, self-conscious to a degree, and manifesting a tendency to be seen and heard by his fellows—a quality that often led him into mischief.

At twelve Harlan, whenever home from school, carried his share of the chores on the farm. His brother Lauson was then one year old. Winthrop was done with school and college. In two more years, on July 4, 1886, Ann Stone, at forty-four, would present her husband with a daughter, Helen.

As a small boy Harlan liked to play "Doctor." He had trundled his outgrown baby carriage to nearby houses, offering his own concocted remedies and announcing, "Doctor Stone calling!" To his admiring gaze the itinerant village doctor seemed a very big man. So Harlan, when questioned, would say, "I want to be a doctor!" From this came the nickname "Doc," which stuck to him throughout his life.

After Harlan was vaccinated, as required by town enactment, he begged his mother to let him perform the same operation on his little brother Lauson and baby Helen. Somewhat reluctantly Mrs. Stone gave her consent. Using a jackknife, Harlan scraped each patient's arm and placed "serum" on the raw spots. Lauson's vaccination "took," but nothing happened to Helen's.

Harlan's father had the gift of self-contrived surgery. One day, when coasting in the farmyard, Harlan's sled ran into a sleigh, and the boy's right forefinger was broken. His father, summoned by the child's screams, set the bone and pushed the flesh back into place. The resulting scar was Harlan's memento of his father's natural skill as a surgeon.

The routine of life in Mill Valley for the Stones was agreeably broken by occasional visits to Chesterfield, as business or family affairs required. Along with tilling the soil Fred Stone bought underfed cattle at low prices and after a period of fattening sold them in the fall at a substantial profit. During the summer months the cattle grazed on the lands he owned in Chesterfield. About Decoration Day, Fred, with a hired man and a boy or two to help, drove the lean cattle to Chesterfield, taking two days for the forty-mile trip. This was an exciting and eagerly awaited expedition. For days ahead the aroma of cakes, pies, and roasts came from the kitchen, where Ann Stone was preparing large quantities of food for the travelers. When Harlan was old enough to be useful he was taken along, and one of the Hubbard boys, glad to help his Uncle Fred and eager for a lark, might join the party. After much ado the outfit, including a shepherd dog and a pair of horses to draw the vehicle, was ready to set out. Each man and boy took his turn driving the cattle, and the dog did his part. One time the cattle got out of hand in North-field and overran the premises of Evangelist Dwight L. Moody. The irate preacher dashed out on his lawn, gesticulating wildly, and shouted orders to Stone to withdraw his animals. Fred surmised that the calm deliberateness with which he obeyed the orders may not have soothed Moody's ruffled feelings.

On these trips the Stones visited Harlan's grandmother or the Harveys for a day or two. Sometimes Ann Stone went along, and they all joined the Harveys for supper. In the evening there was likely to be a prolonged and lively discussion of current public affairs. As each adult member of the circle held definite and positive views, the meeting would grow heated. Ann Stone was often sharp-tongued, quite over-awing Agnes and the other children. A well-read person, she liked nothing better than a lively intellectual bout. But she was never so loquacious as was her husband, who, to the great annoyance of his wife, was always loath to tear himself away from a chance to talk, anytime, anywhere, even as dinner lay cooling on the table.

Ann Stone was inclined to be severe in disciplinary matters. Fred, too, had ideas of discipline. The Puritanism in his veins sanctioned corporal punishment, stern and inexorable. Far from sparing the rod, he added to its terror by delaying action until his temper had cooled. The horror of the punishment he administered was further enhanced by fear of Fred's tremendous strength. Though lithe and spare, he prided himself on being able to grasp a heavy sledge hammer by the extreme end of the handle, lift it, and hold it out horizontally, at arm's length, for several minutes. If the boy's offense was serious, the culprit was led off to the barn and punished with a horsewhip. To the psychologist of today such treatment of a child seems barbaric, and of no good effect. Not so to Harlan Stone. In later years he insisted that his father's harshness had been wholly salutary; it had made "a man" of him. The younger generation lacked courtesy, he said, because they were not "licked enough." "When I was a boy I received some mighty valuable whalings, especially when the Governor thought I was not sufficiently polite. That's one thing that makes me so humble nowadays."[12]

In matters of moral discipline, Fred Stone and his wife were staunch allies. Though not himself a churchgoer, Stone supported her policy of church and Sunday school attendance for their children. Winthrop or Harlan would spend Saturday evening learning the Bible lesson, and the next day walk more than two miles to attend the East Congregational Church and remain for Sunday school. Fred supplemented the moral and religious precepts inculcated in the church, and in the required teaching in the public schools, by citing ugly examples of the curse of alcohol. Harlan's sister remembered that her father always called attention to a drunken person, feeling that the spectacle of one in that forlorn condition was as good a lesson to his children as a long-faced preachment on the subject. Fred was in keeping with his times. In spite of its licensed liquor traffic, the town of Amherst, following the Total Abstinence movement, remained a crusading ground for Temperance Reform.

Though an exceptionally bright pupil, Harlan was no bookworm. Healthful outdoor sports, baseball, skating, and swimming, attracted him; as a fisherman he excelled. With Winthrop he would dig worms, properly bait his hook, and philosophically await the doomed trout. On the bank of the "boiler," as he called the river, he whiled away many a spare afternoon. Flat on his stomach, fish pole or spear in hand, he bided his time—and fisherman Stone reveled in it. Asked one day if the fishing was good, he solemnly replied, "There were so many in the brook that my rubber boots were filled to the top, and I just took them off and dumped the fish on the ground."

At a more veracious age Harlan would join his schoolmate Dick Fletcher[13] on a fishing expedition to Forge Pond, in Granby, beyond Amherst's southeasterly boundary. "These trips were," Stone recalled in 1943, "the ones that stand out in my memory. Forge Pond, in those days, was a famous place for fishing horned pouts or bullheads. The horned pout becomes interested in the lures of fishermen only after sundown and this meant that our expedition began in late afternoon and ended at some time in the wee small hours of the morning. It was usually possible for me to provide horse-driven transportation for the expedition. With plenty of tackle and bait, and a substantial luncheon, we usually arrived at Forge Pond a little before sundown, located our boat according to the proper bearings, and settled down to our fishing as long as the bullheads were responsive, which was usually sometime after midnight. Then we found our way back over the Holyoke range, sometimes barely escaping ditching ourselves on dark nights. It was great fun, and one of my youthful experiences I best like to recall."[14]

When the older boys went swimming Harlan went along. We do not know who helped him learn to swim. In those gladsome days the shy beginner who slowly took off his clothes, then let himself timorously down the bank into the shallow water, was frowned upon. Better for him to jump off the bank into the hole, flounder, and dog-paddle to safety. A boy as oversized as Harlan, bobbing like a cork, could take his time. It is recorded that Harlan Stone, "not being an accomplished swimmer, preferred a leisurely breast stroke." It is also known that one day at the swimming hole, in nature's garb, Harlan suffered considerable discomfiture when he inadvertently seated himself upon a hill of red ants.[15]

During these years in Mill Valley, Harlan's life, as he later recalled, was "like that of many another New England farm boy." He got up early to milk the cows; he grew husky plowing fields, and mowing, and pitching hay. His days were not always idyllic. In vain the robust country boy sometimes heard the playground and river calling; he longed for his hammock and book. "Harlan never enjoyed doing manual labor, but he did it just the same," Fred Stone recalled resignedly.[16] Years after, Attorney General Stone, like any other American father, stressed the disciplinary "advantage" of farm work, and expressed the usual regret that his own boys "could not have had a like experience."[17]

The practical benefit of farm life was exemplified on one occasion when Fred went off for several days. Winthrop, home from college on vacation, took over, and work proceeded about as usual. "Business is brisk," he wrote his father July 30, 1880. "I've had a chance to sell a horse, cow, pig, mowing machine, too. Sold a pig for $2.40 by working hard. Mr. Bolter of South Amherst wants a mowing machine. Byron Smith will want two *good* cows in a month or six weeks, so keep your eye out for them. We have got in three loads of oats this afternoon, in splendid condition. The rest will go in tomorrow if fair."

Farm life was not without its hazards. Harlan once risked serious body injury, and proved his courage, when, as he was on his way home after a game of baseball, one of his father's bulls became enraged and threatened a neighbor's little girl. Seeing her danger, Harlan ran into the pasture, stepped in front of the beast, and subdued the animal with his bat.[18]

In spite of its rural setting, Mill Valley was a center of high intelligence and moral purpose. Fred Stone's neighbors were among Amherst's stalwart citizens. As Fred had served Chesterfield with distinction, so in Amherst he achieved leadership in town affairs.

That the Amherst town meeting, in the seventies, could resolve its growing complex of problems was due largely to the integrity and homely sagacity of the moderator, Levi Stockbridge. Born dirt farmer in North Hadley, Stockbridge never went to college, but he became a professor at the Agricultural College and served for nearly two years as its president. In cooperation with the German scientist Dr. Goessmann, Stockbridge fed plants with chemicals and concocted newfangled manures that were both potent and pungent. Together they developed the idea that grew into an experiment station, which, in 1882, set the pace for enlightened farming in every progressive state in the post-Civil War nation.

Another fellow citizen who attracted Fred Stone's inquiring interest at town meetings was a well-built ministerial man, Julius Hawley Seelye. Seelye preached each Sunday to college boys in the church on the hill. In 1876, still retaining his professorship of moral philosophy and metaphysics, he was elected president of Amherst College. Never relaxing his vigilance, or stinting his good will among the rank and file of solid citizens, he watched Fred Stone's civic advancement with an appraising eye. Fred, an old-line Republican, was elected in 1884 to serve three years as selectman; he was re-elected in 1887 and again in 1890. In 1889 Stone became, under the new law, the first highway superintendent, taking full responsibility for the road machine and its crew. The day was not far distant when Seelye, in his completeness of years as President of Amherst College, would influence the life pattern of Fred's promising younger son.

It seems not unlikely that the upbringing of their children was among the most provocative topics discussed by Fred and Ann Stone at the family table. Fred's salty representation of Levi Stockbridge as professor may have evoked a tart yet complaisant rejoinder from the refined and book-conscious Ann. In 1874, Winthrop, at twelve, had entered high school, and we may only surmise his part in the decision that sent him to the Massachusetts Agricultural College, known colloquially as "M.A.C." or "Aggie." Here Winthrop absorbed the science and practice of agriculture from Stockbridge and made chemical experiments under Goessmann. In 1882 he became a Bachelor of Science, the first in Fred's line to receive a college degree. After a term as chemist at the experimental farm in Mountainville, New York, he was employed in the new State Experiment Station just getting under way at M.A.C.

One September morning in 1883 Harlan began his daily trudge up the long Pleasant Street hill to the four-turreted brick schoolhouse that for five years would be his grammar and high school home. Here there were intellectual stimulus and guidance for his inquisitive mind. Teaching was set at graded levels—arithmetic and algebra, United States history, English, physical geography. For three exacting years "examples" were done, dates and events memorized, maps and charts copied or drawn from memory, spelling lists learned, words and sentences parsed, compositions written, "pieces" learned and spoken. No part of a textbook might be skipped, nothing skimmed over lightly. Harlan's early subjection to his mother's mental drill stood him in good stead. At the end of his last grammar year he was one of four members of his class to be admitted to high school without examination.

The principal of the high school, Sidney A. Sherman, an Amherst College honor graduate, whose outward sternness disguised his innate friendliness, was respected for his erudition. To the book-hungry son of a Mill Valley farmer the classical library that graced the wall cabinet in the study room was of greatest worth. Whenever Harlan was missing from some rough-and-tumble melee in the gravelly yard in front of the schoolhouse, he could be found up in the schoolroom, reading a book. While proficiency in the classroom won the respect of teachers, his proclivity toward prankishness endeared him to schoolmates. No dullard, where there was horseplay Harlan was suspect. He played jokes of a non-malicious sort, calculated to get the teacher's or someone else's "goat."

One teacher's decided views on the deadly sin of card playing were well known. On a certain day, the story goes, Harlan sneezed with intention and slowly drew out his handkerchief, managing to scatter a pack of cards under the desk of the boy next to him. The upshot was a hair-raising sermon preached at the innocent victim, while Harlan buried himself in his geography lesson.* He may have been a "case" in the eyes of his more indulgent neighbors and friends, but he was not prodigal of his talents or his time. He never loafed in the streets, cared little for society of the formal sort, and when school was dismissed went straight home to do his bit on the farm.

* It is related that this highly respected teacher, a deeply religious person, had been known to interrupt a recitation to offer fervent prayer for the return to grace of a particularly refractory pupil.

During these years, Harlan picked up numerous "facts" with intimations of how to use them. He learned to study and make learning count. He sensed teacher-pupil-subject interrelations and became alert to human values in his zest for school life. Principal Sherman was the first college-bred man, other than Winthrop, to find a place in Harlan's expanding world. For two years Sherman supplemented, but did not supplant, Fred Stone's influence. Edith Field and Jessamine Dixon proved to be understanding teachers.

"I think of you," Miss Dixon wrote many years later, "as the growing and groping boy of about sixteen to whom I used to talk in the musty old classroom of the old high school: a rather obstinate and self-willed boy as I remember, but thoroughly likable and interesting and very ambitious. There were splendid boys in that class, but none quite as interesting to me, or as able as you. . . . I used to say, 'Harlan Stone will sit in the White House.' Instead, one of these days, you will probably be Chief Justice, which will, perhaps, suit you quite as well."[19]

Of equal weight with the "intellectual enlightenment" attributed to good teaching was Harlan's deepening knowledge of his fellows. For five pivotal years the farm-bred son of Selectman F. L. Stone mixed with boys, older and younger, who came from Amherst homes distinguished for culture and refinement. Some were sons of clergymen, returned from foreign lands; or children of doctors, merchants, artisans. There were faculty boys in goodly number—the "Amherst College gang," who enjoyed their distinction without being exclusive or snobbish.

Measured by today's standards, Harlan's educational opportunities were limited. But he never regarded them in that light. On the contrary, the community in which he was reared afforded peculiar advantages. For him, the benefit as well as the pleasure of intellectual effort depended primarily on one's self.

The fun he got out of his studies was the outward reward for power of mental application, instilled in him by his mother. Though he seldom sought help over hard places, his tried and forgiving teachers liked him for his scholarly traits that made him deserving of help. Years later, at the close of his teaching days, he paid a touching tribute to one of his former pupils, a university teacher who had won promotion. "I feel," he said, "that peculiar warmth of affection which the teacher must always have for his student who has the rare distinction of being both sound and brilliant."[20] Harlan too had that rare distinction. And many years afterward, warmth of affection and desire to be helpful were Chief Justice Stone's prominent traits. "I was trying to help you, Counsel," was his reassuring phrase to many a confused attorney at the bar. The words reflected the insight, kindliness of heart, and capacity for understanding which reconcile differences.[21]

In the spring of 1888, toward the end of his second year in high school, he announced to his parents that he intended to take the entrance examinations for M.A.C. and forego a classical education. Winthrop was at this time studying for his doctorate in Göttingen. Viewing the matter from an overseas prospective, and knowing Harlan well, he had misgivings. "Harlie writes me he proposes to take examinations at M.A.C.," the elder brother advised a former university teacher. "I suppose his brother's brilliant example inspires him to go and do likewise, but I shall sit on it at present. He is too young to get the most benefit from such a course, quite too young. But he is a good scholar. I believe there is none better among all his schoolmates. He has better natural qualities and aptitudes than I. I can see it plainly —steadiness, solidarity, perseverance, and physical qualities that will enable him to do a vast amount of work some day. I am proud of the boy, and wish I could stand by and help guide him along, as I can do in some respects from my standpoint better than the folks at home. He has a good deal of faith in me and generally listens to my advice."[22]

Harlan, following his own counsel, took and passed the examinations, and one September morning in 1888 found him in the Massachusetts Agricultural College Chapel with the freshmen of '92. At fifteen, he had "started out to be an agriculturalist."[23]

CHAPTER THREE

# Challenge and Defeat

## 1888-1890

Shortly before Harlan's admission to the Massachusetts Agricultural College the faculty had revised the course of study so as to provide a practical education along with study in basic cultural subjects. The sciences stood high; English, not considered utilitarian, occupied a minor place. It was felt that the student should study things in themselves rather than representations of things, that he should strive to achieve mastery of himself and his environment. The advantage of military drill and discipline was stressed. The "lecture method" was firmly rooted, and, except in chemistry, experimentation by students was slight. Physical training was unthought of. Manual of arms, bayonet and saber drill, and marching in formation gave exercise enough.[1]

The first year Harlan's course included English, mathematics, and Latin, which repeated or continued his high school studies, and botany, chemistry, physiology (one term), and agriculture. French followed Latin the second year, and drawing and military tactics found their places. There were no electives. A subject good enough for one was considered sufficient for all, and Harlan's entire class trooped from one building to another on a faculty-made schedule. His best subjects were mathematics and chemistry; his poorest Latin, French, and English, with deportment good to excellent.[2]

There were five "town boys" besides Harlan in the class of '92, and they were all held in high esteem in spite of their separation from many intimacies of college life. Harlan's neighbor and boon companion, Claude A. Magill, became class president, and Harlan himself was elected class historian. His immediate duty was to compose the freshman class "history" for *The Index*, the Junior annual, whose appearance was a highlight of the Christmas season. This illustrated paper-bound volume was the only printed chronicle of Aggie activities read by all the students. In addition to the year's happenings, it contained the usual good-natured digs at students and professors.[*] Harlan's freshman literary effort was so successful that he was re-elected historian for the sophomore year. When the class of '92 set up its own board of *Index* editors, Harlan Stone and Ned Holland, both "town boys," were elected.

Athletics were not neglected. For two seasons Harlan played quarterback on the football team. He did not join the Washington Irving Literary Society, which imposed its semblance of liberal culture upon the rustic campus, although his brother Winthrop had been an active supporter. Nor did Harlan follow his brother's example in joining a fraternity.

Everyone called him "Doc," and in any group where clear thinking and forceful action were in order he took the lead. "Harlan Stone," a classmate recalled, "was the most intellectual man I ever knew. He

* *The Index*, '91 (Vol. XXI, 1889), contains among its quips several citations of "Stone." From these we may infer that the Mill Valley youth was, in unconsidered campus opinion, susceptible to feminine comradeship and sociability; he was "fresh" and "green," inclined to talk and write about himself, and voluble in the classroom. His future prospect indicated "sheep driving." Harlan's own contribution, his first published writing, to *The Index* (Vol. XX, 1888) is in a more serious vein. After discussing athletics, he wrote: ". . . of greater importance than these minor affairs of college life is the fact that we now stand at the theshold of one of the most important epochs of our lives. May we be impressed with its value, and enter faithfully and energetically into the duties as well as the pleasures of college life." The next year, with equal gravity (XXI), he noted: "It is only the laggards that fall behind, while 'strong men and true' keep to the front. . . . May we estimate the remainder of our work here at its true worth . . . and accomplish it in a manner worthy of its value."

had the finest mind. He showed it in the classroom and on the campus
. . . everywhere."[3]

Brain more than brawn was to distinguish Harlan's college career.
Yet he rated the pleasures of campus life almost on a par with its
duties. Whenever his idea of pleasure expanded into downright fun,
his natural prankishness came into full play. When trouble with the
faculty ensued, he was in that too.

The fact that he lived several miles distant from the campus prevented full participation in after-dark freshman activities. His room
was never "stacked" by night-roving sophomores, nor was he dragged
out of bed, paraded in his nightshirt, and dumped into the fountain.

Of deeper import than freshman hazing were the physical collisions
between freshmen and sophomores, known as "rushes." Rushes had
been conspicuous in the college mores since the institution began.
These outbursts of excess energy took place when classes, following
an immutable schedule, met face to face en route between recitations.
They occurred in early fall, again at the approach of Freshman Night
in June, and erupted sporadically whenever interclass tension ran high.
While each class was led by its "captain"—a daring individual elected
to bear the brunt and lead the cheering—the fracas usually resolved
into lesser encounters, and when the rough-and-tumble scrap was over,
each group would surround its captain and give the class yell in token
of victory. These manifestations of animal spirits were ignored by the
understanding faculty, except when recitations suffered or property
was damaged.

Rushes were right in Harlan's line; he reveled in them. His baptism
of fire came early in his freshman term, when sophs were distributed
over the hall and walk one morning after chapel. This affray, at an
ill-chosen time and on dangerous ground, had blocked the doorway
to the chemistry lab, and Professor Wellington complained. Harlan,
like other full-blooded boys in his class, could be hot-headed and
quick-tempered, and when thoroughly aroused would go the limit.[4]
President Goodell, who saw where the blame lay, summoned Freshmen Stone and Boynton, both "town boys" well known to him. These
unrepentant malefactors were full of explanations. "Freshmen and
sophomores were all mixed up," they declared. "No one started anything. It just happened—spontaneous. How can any one person be
charged with starting such a fracas? How can one or two be picked
out and held responsible?"

"I understand," the adamant President said. "But these things have
got to stop! If one of them happens again, something will be done."[5]

One did happen again; it was a serious ruckus, and "something" was
done.

Stone's drama of misbehavior at M.A.C. unfolded slowly. Chastened by presidential caveat, the unruly sophomores abstained from rushing until examination week, June 1889, when '92 and '91 had another set-to. Freshman Night came on Friday the 14th. The chaplain's morning prayer—"May we do nothing in the dark that we would be ashamed to do at noonday"[6]—boded trouble. That night the freshmen impressed the college fire hose as a weapon of attack or defense. One length of hose was ruined, and '92 was assessed to replace it.[7]

President Goodell was much aroused, but in the few days before graduation could take no final action. The accused ringleaders spent that summer under a cloud. On September 4 the President reported to the faculty the names of Taylor, Stone, and two other members of the class as guilty of "disorderly conduct at the close of the last term." The outcome was that these four were held on probation until, at the President's dictation, they signed a pledge of good behavior. September 17 Goodell reported to the faculty that the culprits had fulfilled the conditions and had been allowed to "go on with their studies."[8] Harlan Stone was back in good standing, but not for long.

The new freshman class gave promise of becoming doughty antagonists, and the '92 leaders, though sobered by the sting of probation, were far from unwilling to join battle. Several attempts, however, proved abortive, and the faculty did what they could to keep order. When several collisions did finally occur, the punishment handed out seemed never to yield the count on either side. Animosity grew; tension mounted.

At morning prayers one March day in 1890, the hymn was announced by Dr. Walker, who in addition to dispensing rhetoric, political economy, and mental science in the classroom, performed as chaplain at the compulsory services. The four classes that filled the low-ceilinged chapel room, led by a reedy organ and a "choir," sang in good spirit if not complete reverence. The chaplain read the Scripture, then prayed for guidance: "May we love our enemies . . . never avenge ourselves . . . know that righteousness is better than malice. . . . May we cherish a forgiving spirit. . . ."[9] On this spring day it happened that President Goodell was not on the platform, nor was there a professor in the audience. At a signal the four classes, with some grating of settees and scuff of feet, arose en masse and made for the single exit. Seniors, then juniors, passed through the narrow door, pressed on by the restless sophs. Suddenly the freshmen, disregarding the order of seniority and violating a faculty rule, pushed ahead of the sophomores into the hall. With stairway jammed and banister swaying perilously, the rush was on in full force. Observing the physical danger to all concerned, and conscious of his responsibility, Dr. Walker barged in, and with one free hand (books and hat in the other) seized bulky Harlan Stone by the collar.

The embattled sophomore, feeling someone grab him from behind, turned about and repelled the attack, shouting in his excitement, "Take your damn hands off me!" Dr. Walker was an active man of medium stature and frame, with leonine reddish beard and eyeglasses on a cord, his garb a black frock coat. The onset upon the person of this highly respected member of the faculty, and the epithet hurled in the heat of conflict, aside from the breach of a faculty rule of conduct, transformed this rush into a very serious affair.* One week later the college closed for the Easter recess, and Harlan Stone failed to return for the spring term. It was commonly understood that he had been expelled for his part in the chapel brawl.

Stone's own account of his undoing was not recorded until 1944, when the Amherst College Trustees were holding a meeting in Washington, D.C. After the official business was finished the Trustees, including Stone, were chatting and recalling incidents of college days. Stone said something about the difficulty he had encountered in gaining admission to Amherst because of his inability to bring an honorable dismissal from the institution at the other end of the town. At this point Stone's classmate, Alfred Stearns, broke in: "Look here, Doc, here's the chance for you to tell us just what did actually happen to you at the Aggie. You know the story that went the rounds when you joined us was that you had gotten mad at one of your profs up there and had knocked him down. You're among friends now, the Aggie profs of your day are all in their graves, and it isn't likely that the truth could possibly mar your record as it stands today. Anyway, we'd like mightily to know whether you really did knock a prof down."

Stone waited a minute and then, as a broad grin spread over his genial face, replied, "No, I didn't knock him down—we were all in a rough-and-tumble scuffle when someone grabbed me by the shoulders. I turned and grabbed him and shook him until his teeth rattled. I continued shaking him till I suddenly discovered who he was!"[10]

Stone's recollections, more than fifty years after the event, omit certain important details. When President Goodell called the popular class leader and two lesser miscreants before the faculty to explain

---

* Dr. Walker's own statement of his part in the "chapel rush," long delayed, appeared in the *Boston Sunday Globe*, April 6, 1924. "The professor who led the chapel," wrote the reporter, "long ago retired from teaching and now one of Amherst's most respected sages, explained that he grabbed young Stone by the nape of the neck." Dr. Walker described Harlan as "a farmer's boy who in college was so full of youthful energy that he became a leader of the sophomores and ready to fight anywhere and at any odds for the glory of the class. His zeal, however, exceeded his discretion when he was rushing a freshman before he left the chapel door at morning prayers. But the young man soon learned to master himself and to concentrate his physical, mental, and moral powers upon ends better worth while than pounding a fellow student." (Adapted from Charles S. Walker's unpublished ms. in the Jones Library, Amherst, Mass.)

their actions, he reported that, prior to the climactic episode of March 19, Harlan, while on probation, had been guilty of "five different violations"* of college regulations. Harlan admitted these but made sundry statements with a view to commending himself to considerations of leniency. His statements were in vain. The faculty voted, March 25, 1890, to dismiss Harlan Stone from college. The other two, freshmen, were suspended for one year but were reinstated in April.

Harlan's class came promptly to his support, pleading with the faculty that he be reinstated. This petition was denied. Later a petition from the student body was presented by the president of the senior class. This too was of no avail. April 29 Harlan himself asked to be readmitted but again was refused.† His year and two terms of duty and pleasure at M.A.C. were ended.

* The precise nature of the violations is unknown. It seems not unlikely that they were trivial, routine infractions.

† The following excerpts from minutes of faculty meetings cover all mention of Harlan Stone, including the decision to dismiss him:

May 1, 1889 . . . The faculty met and listened to the speakers from the Freshman Class and by vote selected as the prize speakers: Stone, Magill, Davidson, and Clark.

May 4, 1889 . . . A petition from Stone was read asking to be excused from prayers. It was voted that his petition be not granted. . . .

Sept. 4, 1889 . . . The President reported his action in reference to the disorderly conduct of students at the close of last term.

It was voted that Baldus, Stone, Taylor, and Willard be placed upon probation and sign such a pledge as the President shall demand.

It was voted that tomorrow at prayers the President suspend Stone, Willard, and Taylor on the ground that they have not complied with the demands of the President. . . .

Sept. 17, 1889 . . . The President reported that the students, whose names had been reported to the faculty for disorderly conduct at the last meeting, had fulfilled the conditions required of them and had been allowed to go on with their studies. . . .

March 24, 1890 . . . The facts concerning the collision between the Freshman and Sophomore Class in the chapel were stated. It was voted that action concerning Stone, Gregory, and Woodbrey be deferred until they should have an opportunity to state their side of the case to the faculty. . . .

March 25, 1890 . . . Stone presented himself before the faculty. The President stated that while Stone was on probation he had been guilty of five different violations of college discipline. In reply Stone admitted the truth of the indictment, but made sundry statements with a view, while not attempting to excuse his conduct, to commend himself to the leniency of the faculty. . . .

. . . It was voted that Stone be dismissed from College. . . .

March 27, 1890 . . . The President stated that he had notified Stone, Woodbrey, and Gregory of the action of the faculty concerning them.

A petition was received from the class of '92 asking that Stone be reinstated.

It was voted that the President notify the petitioners that their petition had been received but that their petition cannot be granted.

It was voted that the letter, presented by the President, be sent to the father of Stone announcing the action of the faculty in his case.

A petition from the college, asking that the men expelled, in the opinion of the petitioners, unjustly, be reinstated.

It was voted that the petition be returned to the President of the Senior Class

Thus Harlan's intense class loyalty, his impulsive temper, had brought him unconscionably to grief. Selectman Stone was outraged. "Your school days are over. You're through! From now on it is the farm for you," he said to his son. Harlan was sober, very sober—and indignant. "I'll be in a position," he bragged to George Taylor, president of the class of '92, "to thumb my nose at them yet!" His words were accompanied by the appropriate gesture.[11] In the '92 *Index*, Taylor, editor-in-chief, sponsored a lengthy poem, "Paradise Lost," memorializing the chapel rush in dubious Miltonic phrase:

> Still, quiet did predominate,
> Until that well-remembered morn,
> When at the chapel door a mighty rush ensued.
> The Sophomore and the Fresh thought of naught else
> Save the stupendous onslaught.
> Ye who have ne'er beheld such human conflict
> Know nothing of its fury; e'en nature's wildest spasms
> Bear but a tame resemblance; volcanoes,
> Earthquakes, tidal waves and cyclones
> Dwindle to insignificance before the rush terrific.

> As key-*Stone* in the route, one was suspected—
> A ready writer and a scholar apt, of his ability perhaps too well aware,
> Yet he, the class historian, trembled among the guilty.[12]

This number of *The Index*, published in December 1890, and notable for enlarged format, red cloth binding, and attractive new features, made grateful acknowledgment to Harlan F. Stone, "ready writer and scholar apt," for assistance rendered before his untimely removal from the board of editors.

The days that followed were filled with baffling uncertainty. Harlan sought out his high school teachers, Jessamine Dixon and Edith Field. Both warmly assured him he was not "through," as his irate father had said. "I have been so sorry to hear of the unhappy circumstances in which you are placed," Miss Dixon wrote on April 4, 1890. "It may

---

with the endorsement that the faculty have considered it, but find no reason to grant the petition.

It was voted that a copy of a letter, read by the President, announcing the suspension of the Freshman and the reasons of it, be sent to the parents or guardian of each member of the Class of '93, or, in case the Freshman is of age, to the Freshman himself. . . .

April 29, 1890 . . . A petition from Mr. Harlan Stone was received asking for reinstatement in the Sophomore Class. After discussion it was voted that the President notify Mr. Stone that the faculty have considered the petition but cannot grant it. . . .

(All minutes signed: C. S. Walker, Secretary.)

These transcripts from the Minutes of the Faculty were obtained by Professor Emeritus Charles A. Peters, by permission of President (now Emeritus) Ralph A. Van Meter, University of Massachusetts (1951).

not be necessary, but I want to assure you of my sympathy and of the friendly interest I have always had in you. . . . I don't want this unfortunate affair to interfere with your plans for life. It will teach you something, and ought to make you stronger—not weaker. We all expect great things of you; don't disappoint us, or fail of your highest good. . . ."[13]

Harlan was apprehensive lest his beloved teacher, Edith Field, might not understand. "And did you really think that my friendship might not be equal to that?" she wrote him reassuringly July 5, 1890. "My dear boy, it is strong enough to bear a good deal harder strain than it has been put to yet. . . . Perhaps it will be just a little bit of comfort to you to know that I didn't believe you deserved it [dismissal]. . . . It is very hard to bear injustice even in little things; and when it touches one's honor, and defeats one's plans for a life, it is trouble indeed. But remember, Harlan, that if you *had* deserved the penalty, it would have been a great deal worse. . . . But you will not let this interfere very long with the making of the man you're going to be by and by. I hope you will be able to go to just the place where the best training for you is to be had—and that this dead stop, for which you are not to blame, will not prove a serious hindrance to your study and work."[14]

"Why not go to Amherst, and make good?" Miss Field suggested. "I'll help you make up the work." But it would be no easy task to meet Amherst's stiff entrance requirements. With only two years of high school it seemed well-nigh impossible. Worse still, Fred Stone, a "father of the old school," stood adamant.

In desperation Harlan turned to his cousin, Helene May Butler, begging her to come for a visit and reason with his father. Helene responded at once. During three weeks' stay she searched out all the facts and lost no time in championing Harlan's cause. So eloquent was her plea that Fred yielded. Harlan was overjoyed and deeply grateful. Later, while in Amherst College, he wrote his cousin: "Nellie, always remember, if I ever make anything of myself, I owe it all to you, because had you not spoken to Dad, I'd probably still be behind the plow."[15]

CHAPTER FOUR

# Proving His Mettle

## 1890-1894

Getting his father's permission to continue his education was only half the battle. How could an institution of Amherst's standing overlook the stigma of dismissal from M.A.C.? Harlan appealed directly to President Julius H. Seelye, who later talked with Fred Stone.

"Seelye sent for me, and I went up there," Fred recalled in talks with a fellow townsman. "Your son Harlan has applied for admission to Amherst College," the President began. "While it is not customary for this institution to accept candidates from another college where they are not in good standing, an exception may be made. Harlan has admitted doing what he ought not to have done; we may give him a chance. How do *you* feel about it, Mr. Stone?" "It is all right with me," Fred told the President.

Fred Stone, never a man of hurried action, returned home, but said nothing that night. The next morning he stood watching Harlan in the stable, cleaning out manure with a fork. Knowing his son's strong distaste for manual labor, the father was the more elated by the news he had to convey. "Harlan," he announced, "you will not have to do that kind of work any longer. Amherst College will accept you!" Harlan stopped—then hurled the fork clear across the stable.[1]

"I shall never forget my interview with President Seelye when I applied for admission to Amherst College with a record of dismissal from another college," Harlan wrote many years later. "The kindliness and friendliness of his treatment of me is one of my most vivid recollections. He refused to waste any time on the rather trivial matters which had brought me into disgrace with another institution. The only thing that really seemed to interest him was whether I was sincerely desirous of getting an education at Amherst College, and whether I was worth it. I, a very crude and callow youth, felt no embarrassment in his presence. I came away with the indelible opinion that I had been in contact with a 'big man,' with a feeling of self-confidence, inspired by the thought that he really understood me and had found something in me which Amherst College ought to encourage and develop."[2]

FROM "PRIEST FACTORY" TO LIBERAL EDUCATION

Justice Holmes once said that the education of a child begins two hundred and fifty years before birth. Institutions also may be the living consequence of well-nigh forgotten antecedents. So it was with Amherst College. Situated on a hilltop, in the Connecticut Valley of western Massachusetts, the college was founded to train indigent young men for the Congregational ministry. In its origins, Amherst was devout, conservative, independent, with students as poor as they were pious. Its charter was secured in 1825 from a reluctant legislature. Harvard, Williams, and Brown fought recognition of the new school. Newspapers hurled opprobrious epithets, calling it a "Priest Factory."[3] Though the struggling college could not be so neatly defined, many students entered with the intention of becoming ministers of the Gospel. It was not until the administration of President Seelye (1876-90) that the college was transformed into an institution of liberal education. Seelye introduced elective courses and nearly doubled the faculty. Picking teachers with judicious care, he allowed virtually complete freedom of thought and expression. Besides academic changes, he was responsible for the famed "Amherst System" of student self-government.

With Seelye's withdrawal from the presidency early in Stone's freshman year, it became apparent that nineteenth-century ideas and values, especially the conviction that the college must transfer to each generation a body of accepted truth, were living on borrowed time. The questioning attitude of Science had already begun to steal into the most conservative centers of learning as more and more scholars went to Germany for advanced degrees. There the prospective educator encountered the spirit of research, "scientific method," as the new pathway to knowledge. The German approach suggested that truth was, perhaps, not yet entire, that man might discern its nature and content without divine revelation or intuitive perception. In the wake of doubt and inquiry thus inspired, the sturdy bastions of orthodoxy began to crumble. Ironically enough, Seelye's own liberal educational policy, in spite of his dogged adherence to the faith, had helped in opening the doors to alien ideas.[4]

College life in Harlan's day seems, by present standards, austere and drab. Early morning chapel exercises were compulsory, but to "the best of his recollection," Stone commented many years later, "I always avoided attending whenever possible."[5] At these gatherings President Seelye gave sonorous recitals of his favorite aphorism: "Perfect freedom is perfect obedience to perfect law."[6] His successor, Merrill Edward Gates, reverted to an earlier version of the cramped, pietistic outlook. Every day the students were exhorted to become God-fearing Christians. Uprightness and service were the watchwords.

In keeping with the more liberal spirit, however, Amherst College had changed its admission requirements so as to accept Bachelor of Science candidates without preparation in Greek. It was this fortuitous circumstance that made it possible for the well-disposed Seelye to find a place for Harlan at Amherst in the "Scientific" course. Having contritely won admission under a probationary cloud, Harlan buckled down to serious study. Late into the night his student lamp burned in the room he shared with his brother Lauson. One time when Cousin Nellie was visiting the Stones, Harlan came down to breakfast about eight o'clock and said, "Nellie, what time do you think I went to bed? . . . The sun was shining in my window."[7]

During these first months Harlan kept in touch with his former high school teachers. Their letters consoled and encouraged him. "After all," Jessamine Dixon wrote, "your experience at the M.A.C., though hard, will work for your good in the end. You are stronger for it, and you are in a better place; I mean a place better fitted for you."[8]

In October of his freshman year Edith Field counseled and commended him:

> I was very glad to hear of your success in your examinations. I knew you would have no trouble with them. . . . I think the time will come when you will feel very thankful for the change in plans and colleges you were compelled to make, and even for the bitter experience and the injustice which made it necessary. . . . I do not care one whit about your carrying off the honors of your class. I do not think the one who gets the highest marks in recitation is always the one who does the most thorough work and goes to the foundation of things. . . . I think of the boys—little boys— I used to teach growing up into men, going through college, and way, way ahead of me in their pursuit of knowledge, where I can never go. Don't forget the teachers you will leave so far behind, Harlan.[9]

As one of the "Scientific" men in his class, his chief interests lay in chemistry, biology, and physics—subjects he had taken at M.A.C. "Our first sight of Doc Stone in 1890," one classmate remarked long afterward, "gave an impression of strong body and sturdy legs as he came lumbering up from the Freshman River. He carried the same sense of weight in his class. . . . Stone had a sense of power very early."[10]

In the fall term of his sophomore year Harlan was elected president of his class. The vote, however, was not unanimous. On the first informal ballot he was tied for fourth place. The second informal ballot put him ahead, but still without a majority. On the first formal ballot, Stone led by a substantial margin, and on September 30, 1891, was declared the new president of the class of '94, which numbered seventy-three members. Harlan succeeded Willis D. Wood, who left college to enter business. At the same meeting the class appropriated twenty-five dollars from the treasury for detective work concerning the class "goddess," Sabrina. Harlan was elected chief caretaker of Sabrina, and three '94 men were chosen to assist him. He continued as class president for three years, being re-elected in his junior and senior years by acclamation.[11]

At Amherst there was a strong tradition against hazing, and Harlan's class voted to abstain from this pastime. Rushing also was frowned on. Determined to abolish it altogether, the classes of '94 and '95, on June 18, 1892, jointly pledged that there should be no "rushing or class demonstrations of any kind during the remainder of the college year."[12] There were three signatories from each class, and the name "H. F. Stone," president of the class of '94, ranked the list. The claim voiced in later years that Harlan "abolished rushing at Amherst College" had more than a grain of truth.

Other issues cried for reform, the most urgent being compulsory chapel and church attendance. This college-wide revolt was no seasonal outburst of exuberant healthful spirits, but rather the demand of sentient youth for freedom, with deep moral implications. The fight was long and hard, and at times approached violence. In the spring of 1894 morning prayers were marked by disorder. Stone, who lived at home and so was exempt from required church attendance, had become the acknowledged leader of the student body. In 1892, the class of '94, except for one member, had "gone on record for non-compulsory church."[13] Two years later, in June 1894, the class, with Harlan presiding, again voted against compulsory church—a last defiant gesture against a college system outmoded and doomed.

### SABRINA—SHADOW AND SUBSTANCE

As "Guardian" of Sabrina, Harlan Stone carried a burden as exacting as it was unique. The Sabrina that Amherst College knew was the statue of a comely young woman, in easy sitting posture, with torso and limbs undraped, four and a half feet in height, cast in three hundred and fifty pounds of bronze. Made in replica of the Nymph of the "smooth Severn stream" in England, the statue had been donated in 1857 by a friendly art patron of dubious taste[14] and mounted upon a stone pedestal between North College dormitory and Hitchcock's Octagon. Chemistry Professor Clark, with a countryman's desire to brighten drab austerity, had superintended the planting on the site of a profusion of flowering plants. There, in her garden beside the "many-windowed colleges" Sabrina sat serene under the appraising eyes of sedate professors on their way to morning prayers.

About 1860 a predatory student invaded the backyard of the local Young Ladies' Institute and stole from the line a supply of the Victorian garments of the day in which he dressed the nearly naked maiden.[15] From that time on every student took notice of Sabrina. For many years, extending into President Seelye's regime, she was an object of abuse, the butt of ridicule. She was dressed in variegated garments, whitewashed, painted black or parti-color. Once she was plunged into a barrel of tar. Missed from her pedestal, she would appear on a bewildered professor's desk or on top of the Chapel Tower or the roof of the Octagon.

At last Sabrina was avowed a nuisance, and in 1884 President Seelye ordered a colored servitor known as "Professor Charley" to remove the statue from the college grounds and destroy it. This the faithful "Professor Charley" was presumed to have done. But in June 1887 a group of freshmen ('90) forcefully reclaimed the statue from the building where "Professor Charley" had kept it hidden. In June 1888 freshmen of '91 stole it from a wagon in which it was being drawn to the depot to be entrained for the sophomore ('90) banquet in New London. June 1889 Sabrina appeared at '91's sophomore celebration. That fall she was formally handed down by '91 to '93, and the sacred right of her possession by heritage or combat was established. In February 1890 the newly inherited "goddess" appeared at '93's freshman supper in Springfield. That the odd-numbered classes would continue the struggle for her possession seemed assured. It was equally certain that more serious crises were ahead.

Lifting, transporting, and lowering by hand a heavy bronze casting of troublesome dimensions and disturbing contour endangered property, life, and limb. Perilous, too, was the hauling of the statue by flimsy wagon many miles over rutted country roads in the dark. A gash cut in the statue's cheek by an excited student with an ax was but partly effaced. The broken leg of the man who jumped from a window in a '90 vs. '91 ruckus, in the Chapel Tower, was costly, as was the restoration of a stairway smashed on that occasion. The problem of hoisting the mass of metal out of the college well nearly stumped the authorities. The statue had been boxed and expressed or freighted to barns or warehouses in adjacent states. Such rail journeys were expensive, difficult to manage. A more ready refuge for the watery Nymph, in the Connecticut River bed, was abandoned as precarious.

In Harlan's freshman year Sabrina was the "subject of floating rumors and detached bits of alumni reminiscence." There were "Sabrina men" and "non-Sabrina men" in college, but no Sabrina partisans on the faculty to meliorate undergraduate sins committed in the heat of "even" or "odd" class loyalty.

As Sabrina's "Guardian," Stone faced a threefold challenge—the protectional custody of the bronze statue opportunely rescued from '93, its presentation to '94 at their sophomore banquet, and its final disposition to the expectant '96. Willis D. Wood, while '94 president, having discovered that '93 was banqueting in Boston, strongly suspected that Sabrina would be there. Ben Hyde, well financed by certain of his classmates, was sent to Boston to get her.[16]

With Sabrina in their secure possession, Stone and his helpers with great secrecy planned '94's sophomore banquet. Big and solid at eighteen, wise in the lore of countryfolk, he was a well-qualified "Guardian." Harlan's close associates in the hidden cause were Ben Hyde, son of a Boston lawyer; Walter Howe, Boston suburbanite and Andover man; Nathan Weeks, another near-Bostonian; and Harry Whitcomb, of Worcester.[17]

The river town of Brattleboro, Vermont, a mill and farming center, stood on the New Hampshire boundary, ten miles from the Massachusetts line and forty from Amherst. A malefactor in Brattleboro might quickly effect a switch of jurisdiction by crossing the state line. Here, in the palatial Brooks House, the Amherst sophomores of '94 held their memorable feast. Here, "Guardian" Stone presented the "fostering deity" to the even-numbered "Sabrina men"—a relationship that continued inviolate for twenty-nine years.

Late that evening the statue was removed, reboxed, and loaded into the wagon. Stone guided the horses ten miles across the Connecticut, along dark and tortuous roads, to the Harvey farm in Chesterfield. Faithful to the trust Harlan had placed upon him, Hermon Harvey had torn up his barn floor and dug a spacious hole beneath it. From her window Agnes Harvey watched the wagon drive up. Quick to anticipate Harlan's needs, she rushed from the house and held a lantern while the young men ruthlessly dragged forth the statue, lowered it into the space beneath the barn floor, and covered it with hay and chaff from the stalls. The victorious captors then hastened off lest someone discover the secret of Sabrina's whereabouts. Meanwhile they entrusted her to Agnes. The lantern she held for fun-loving Harlan that night was symbolic of the role she was destined to play in later years as he went on to a professional and public career.

Yet extreme vigilance was not to be relaxed. Nathan Weeks has recalled how fear gripped '94 men, when, at an athletic meet in Springfield, a stranger asserted that he could disclose Sabrina's hideaway. "I still remember," Weeks commented, "how calmly Doc received the information and how quickly he sized up the situation."

" 'It is just a stunt to scare '94,' Stone warned him, 'into attempting to move Sabrina, in the hope that '93 may thereby get a line on where she is hidden.' The fact that nothing happened proved Stone was right."[18]

January 12, 1894, in Nassau, New Hampshire, after nearly three years of guardianship, Harlan Stone formally delivered Sabrina to "Guardian" Charles J. Staples, class of '96. As president of Amherst College's senior class, near to graduation, Stone felt deeper loyalties than Sabrina might evoke, whether "in shadowy legend or in more tangible bronze."[19]

### THE GATES REBELLION

Events so mildly exciting could not suffice as an outlet for exuberant undergraduate energies even in the quiescent 1890s. Politely conducted rushes and sporadic hazing were seasonably confined to lower classes, and the Sabrina outbreaks were timed at wide intervals and subsided into periods of tolerated inactivity. Something more was needed—and that something came like a bolt from the blue.

"When we graduated from Amherst in 1894," Chief Justice Stone remarked, with a touch of facetiousness, at the fiftieth reunion of his class in 1944, "nothing could have been further beyond the reach of our imagination than the thought that we were destined to witness two of the most devastating wars in all history. In truth, we were so convinced of a peaceful future that we felt impelled to add a little variety to what would otherwise have seemed a humdrum life, by organizing our own little private war. It has now taken its place in history as 'the Gates Rebellion.' "[20]

Stone was a veteran of this local "war," a conflict significant for Amherst, and in the educational world generally, for it marked an important stage in the evolution of student self-government.

Before 1884 undergraduates at Amherst, as elsewhere, had been treated as non-voters, on the level of academy or high school boys. For President Seelye this *in loco parentis* college government, this denial of men of voting or near-voting age of the right to be self-governing, was both noxious and ridiculous. That is why Seelye carried the unique Amherst System to completion. The change effected was fundamental. With origins dating back to 1828, it meant a substitution of democracy for autocracy.[21]

Central to the functioning of the system was the so-called "contract." "A student," the 1892 college catalogue declares, "whose recommendations have been approved and whose examinations have shown him capable of admission to Amherst College, is received as a gentleman, and, as such, is trusted to conduct himself in truthfulness and uprightness, in kindness and respect, in diligence and sobriety, in obedience to law and maintenance of order, and regard for Christian institutions as becomes a member of a Christian college. The privileges of the college are granted only to those who enter into agreement to fulfill in all respects this trust."

Under this agreement, designed to appeal to "manly and generous instincts," the faculty ceased to be a governing body punishing under-graduates for infractions of "law." The faculty's responsibility became exclusively instructional; it reserved for itself the right to say whether the student complied with established scholastic requirements. All matters pertaining to moral conduct, all questions of order and deco-rum, were left to the undergraduates themselves. The "contract" was as valid as any other between man and man, the only difference (and it was an important one) being that, unlike a contract made at com-mon law, no penalty attached to its breach or forfeiture. If a student acted like a rowdy or was otherwise guilty of conduct at odds with "truthfulness and uprightness," he simply ceased to be a member of the college community.

Administration of the new system was placed in a student senate of ten members—four seniors, three juniors, two sophomores, one fresh-man, elected by their respective classes in the fall term of the college year. This body had the power to determine whether the "contract" had been broken and whether, if broken, it should be renewed. Its jurisdiction extended "over such procedures of any body of students, relating to order and decorum as affect the whole college." The Presi-dent of the college presided at all meetings, with power to introduce business, participate in discussion of all questions, and vote thereon.

Despite the bright auspices attending its beginnings, the Amherst System soon became a bone of contention. On October 27, 1890, Dr. Merrill Edward Gates succeeded Dr. Seelye. Gates was the first lay-man to head the college, and his election was hailed as a triumph of "efficiency and liberal ideas." One prominent Trustee confidently pre-dicted that the new President would bring Amherst "fresh inspiration through his own specialty, political ethics, and through practical lessons in good citizenship."[22] The omens, as seen by the "elder states-men," were very good indeed. But all such optimistic forecasts mis-judged the incoming President completely. Apparently the Trustees had measured Gates by his dignified presence and Chesterfieldian manner, accented by eyeglasses on a flowing black ribbon.[23] The undergraduates, on the other hand, with the mordant discernment of youth, soon penetrated the President's showy exterior. They noted his frequent references to the intimacies he enjoyed with the great; they heard rumors that his "extemporary" speeches and brilliant oratory, so highly prized in the Amherst of that day, were memorized and re-hearsed before a mirror for dramatic effect.

The new President naturally chose to teach his subject, political ethics, and the announcement of this was accompanied with fanfare and an impressive prospectus. Besides the two basic texts, Francis Lieber's *Political Ethics* and John W. Burgess's *Political Science and Constitutional Law,* Gates introduced the student to classics such as Hobbes' *Leviathan,* Locke's *Second Treatise on Civil Government,* Rousseau's *Social Contract.* Prospective students were told that, in addition to lectures by the President, they would hear questions of social and political reform discussed "by specialists from other institutions," by men "prominent for their practical knowledge."[24]

One day in the spring of 1892 the President strode into the classroom with more than his usual pomp and swagger. Placing his high silk hat carefully upon the table, the lecturer began: "When I was in Washington, I and the President . . ." Far from being impressed, the class greeted these histrionics with catcalls, shuffling of chairs, and stamping of feet. This so provoked Gates that he picked up his hat, strode down the aisle and out the door, not to return that year.

At the end of his senior year Stone soberly recorded his opinion of the President's course and the manner of its presentation. "The man who feels an interest in his fellow men as individuals, or in the prospects of the race, is drawn inevitably sooner or later to an interest in political science. For political science is the science of the origin of nations, the conduct of the state of society jurally organized. The conduct of the tutor of *Political Ethics* is the most outrageous imposition during my college course."[25]

President Gates's "practical lesson in good citizenship" failed as miserably as did his course in political ethics. Indeed, it seems not unlikely that the indignities accorded him in the classroom may have stimulated in him a grim determination to scuttle President Seelye's much publicized Amherst System. In any event, an abrupt reversal of the system's good fortune occurred January 4, 1894, when Gates, ignoring the senate, summarily dismissed a senior who had intercepted a letter from the secretary of the faculty to the student's father, telling of the son's unexcused absences from classes. The real issue was not whether the student broke his "contract," but who should sit in judgment on the case, the faculty or the student senate. The faculty had thus struck hard at the very foundation of the Amherst System, in effect, carrying the administration of discipline back to the discredited *in loco parentis* theory Seelye had so firmly abandoned nearly a decade earlier.[26]

At a meeting of the senate it was moved and seconded that the senate "request Mr. Harlan F. Stone to state what he knew of the Mr. C. E. Clutia case."[27] "Mr. Stone told what he knew," and after the meeting President Gates shouted at the undergraduate leader, "You have done the college a very serious injury." "I made no reply," Stone recalled many years later.[28]

The depth of undergraduate feeling became evident when the senior class appointed a committee of five to consider what action to take to preserve self-government. Stone was the committee chairman. It was on his insistence that the committee set out to marshal the facts. "The opinions of outstanding alumni, of faculty members whom we trusted, and even of prominent men outside the Amherst field were sought and carefully weighed. Fortified with the wide support given us, we, or better Stone, prepared our devastating reply. . . ."[29]

The report, written by Stone, was presented at a mass meeting in the chapel, on March 19, by Eugene W. Lyman, one of the class senators. "We call attention," the report began, "to the following points. . . . First, the faculty, by extending their business in dealing with a student so far beyond what is demanded by the contract relation . . . vitiate the contract relation, which is the foundation of the Amherst System. Second, the faculty find the justification for their action in regard to Mr. X not in the written constitution of the senate, but in an assumed unwritten constitution. We can discover nothing actual in the way of an unwritten constitution that is at all able to overbalance the express statements of the written constitution. Third, by the acts of closing the case of Mr. X and refusing to arbitrate, and in explicit statements as well, the faculty claims the right of deciding questions of jurisdiction and of interpreting the constitution of the senate. The power thus assumed makes it possible for the faculty to modify, or even to nullify, any portion of the constitution at will. Their decision in the case in question is a restriction of the constitution. But the constitution gives to the senate alone the right of making amendments. Hence to modify the constitution in any other way than through the senate is a revolution of the senate system.

"These acts of the faculty," Stone's report went on, "reduce the senate from the position of a governing body coordinate with the faculty, and acting in a sphere different in kind from that of the faculty, to a subordinate position having such a share in the government of the college as the faculty see fit to give. Such a subjection of the senate is inconsistent with its independent action. We believe in the Amherst System as it really is, but the subordination of the contract relation and of the senate has undermined that system. Responsibility for student conduct is lifted from the students themselves, where the Amherst System placed it, and assumed, in part at least, by the faculty, who stand once more *in loco parentis* to the students. . . .

"It remains, then," Stone concluded, "for the students to decide if they will acquiesce in the establishment of a new Amherst System and give it their support. Our unanimous opinion is that it would not be for the best interests of the college to do so. The senate is not an end in itself; it exists only as a means for securing good student government, and however much it may have contributed to Amherst's reputation in the past, it should be maintained only so long as it is useful for good student government. We believe that the senate system which would be established by this precedent would be of little usefulness as a governing body and would not secure the respect and cooperation of the students. The question is one which concerns the entire body of undergraduates and should be decided by them."[30]

After Lyman finished reading the report, Stone called for a discussion. General debate followed. To implement the report a resolution was offered, and strongly defended, recommending the withdrawal of the senators. A junior class senator spoke in favor of further conference with the faculty. But the weight of Stone's argument overcame conservatism, and on a final vote the resolution was adopted with only scattered dissents.

As soon as this assembly broke up, each of the four classes held separate meetings and requested the resignation of their senators. The resignations followed without delay, and student self-government at Amherst College was dead.

Besides the principle of self-government the rebellion had another purpose—to destroy "an egostistical and narrow-minded fundamentalist"—President Gates.[31] "The truth is," Stone commented in 1935, that "beneath President Gates' rather showy exterior were only a shallow intellect and shallow character. When this opinion became widespread, Gates was doomed." But, in 1939, when Amherst College historian Claude M. Fuess placed Stone in the role of head rebel, the Justice demurred. "I was not aware that I was so exclusively the moving spirit in starting the 'Senate Rebellion.' I had supposed it was more spontaneous."[32] But once the fight was on, Stone represented his constituency well and gave the movement a firmness of direction it might otherwise not have had.

"At the root of the trouble," Stone explained, "lay the fact that President Gates did not know how to deal with young men, and especially how to appeal to the manly and generous instinct of young men. It was inevitable that a clash would occur and . . . that the students having aptitude and some skill for conducting controversy should come to the front. I suppose that is how I happened to play a part in the controversy of that day. Perhaps my love for a righteous fight, or what I believed to be a righteous fight, helped it on."[33]

### RIGHT GUARD ON THE GRIDIRON

In October 1892, Harlan's junior year, Amherst College was all out to win its first football championship in the recently organized "triangular league," which included Amherst's hardened rivals, Williams and Dartmouth. To do this the coach and physical-education director had to muster all available resources. A canvass of prospects showed a dearth of material for the line, with special weakness at right guard. Harlan's five feet ten inches of height and 175 pounds of weight, hardened by years of pitching hay and plowing fields, made him a most likely prospect.[34] But when Captain George Pratt asked him to throw in his lot with the team, Harlan expressed doubt, mentioning the pressing necessity he was under to "make good" in the classroom. He would need a few days to think the matter over. Also his mother feared lest some permanent physical handicap result from the precarious game of that day. Even after Doc consented to go out for the team, his mother stood firm against any football for him.

"I remember," Harlan's sister Helen recalled, "old Dr. Hitchcock of the physical-education department, sitting on the slippery horsehair sofa in the parlor, trying to get Mother's consent. For a time he came every day (it seemed to me) to convince her that not everyone who played football was killed. . . . He would get more and more excited until his voice became high pitched, as it often was when he was offering prayer. Of course Mother finally capitulated."

Stone played his first game October 22, 1892, against Tufts. Though defeated, Amherst's hopes soared. The Tufts bout, in no sense decisive, was merely "the kind of practice needed for the championship games." So it proved to be. Three weeks later *The Amherst Student* triumphantly blazoned the news: *"The Football Pennant is Amherst's . . .* Amherst 60, Williams 0; Amherst 30, Dartmouth 2." For the first time in Amherst history she had won the championship of a New England Intercollegiate Football League.[35]

There was, however, no rejoicing in Mill Valley. Harlan had returned from the Dartmouth game with a broken nose, and his mother was adamant. He was the only member of the family, she insisted, who had a decent nose, and now it was ruined. The whiffs of liniment and other medicaments from the boy's room made the whole family look upon football as a barbarous calling. The impending crisis brought two or three distraught boys from the college to see Harlan and his parents, in order to get him to play again.

"They were down," his brother Lauson recalled, "just at the time of the evening chores, and Harlan took them with him into the cow stable while he did his milking. This made a great impression on me, because I was very sensitive about farm work. But this situation did not bother him a bit. It was a characteristic that always remained with him through life, even in his Washington days when I visited him. . . . At large social functions he was just as unconcerned and talked just as freely about these experiences as he acted then."[36]

Harlan did continue to play varsity football in senior year, but the pressure to get him into the game and keep him there was due to the paucity of material rather than to his superior power as a lineman. There is no foundation for the statement that Stone was "a whiz," "one of the nation's best football stars . . . back in '93 and '94."[37] Contemporary college papers indicate that Stone had neither great interest in, nor superior ability on, the gridiron.

Though something of a giant physically, Stone was not a natural athlete. He was more at home with a pitchfork or fishing rod, and made no claim to football greatness. "I have sometimes wondered," he wrote, November 4, 1937, "whether I carried my weight in the football team of those days, but I never had suspected before that I won any games alone and unaided. Some of the best fiction appears in our newspapers."[38]

### FRATERNITY MAN

Doc was a gregarious, popular man in college and made many lifelong friends and acquaintances, including Calvin Coolidge, a member of the class behind him. Stone, however, dispelled the notion, current in 1924 when President Coolidge appointed him Attorney General, that he and the Vermonter had been college chums:

> We were not of the same class and therefore were not intimates, although I doubt if many were intimate with him. His extreme reticence made that difficult. To those who knew him casually he no doubt seemed "odd" or "queer," but it only required slight acquaintance to appreciate his quiet dignity and self-respect, which commanded the respect of others. But most of us did not realize what was going on under that quiet exterior until years afterward. I gained a glimpse of it when I listened to his Grove oration a year after my own graduation, and was impressed by the humor, quiet dignity, and penetrating philosophy of his oration.[39]

By the time Harlan entered Amherst the Greek letter fraternities were well established. With the gradual relaxation of social strictures that came as a result of declining religious ardor in New England colleges, they had taken over, much to the chagrin of the faculty, many of the activities performed by literary groups. Tuesday night ("Goat Night") was set apart in the chapter houses for literary exercises, and each member was expected to make his contribution, in declamation, debate, essay, or talk upon some current topic. Fraternities provided a place where college boys could commune in an informal atmosphere and occasionally let off excess energy, long shackled by carking fear of hell fire and damnation. There were seasonal receptions and dancing parties, sobered by elaborate chaperonage and the inflexible rule against intoxicants.

Most freshmen hastened to join one of the nine Amherst fraternities.

Each chapter had an attractive house, with parlor, reading room, and living quarters for upperclassmen. Most of the greater faculty lights who influenced Stone belonged to one or another of the three oldest brotherhoods.[40]

Inter-fraternity rivalry was fierce. As a freshman, Harlan had received bids from three societies, including Alpha Delta Phi, all of which he promptly declined. On February 19, 1946, Chief Justice Stone told why he did not join a fraternity until halfway through college:

When I came to college I was a rather independent youngster with some rather original convictions. One was that it was foolish to do things just because the Joneses do. And another related idea was that the whole fraternity scheme was a rather artificial way of forming friendships. The result was that when I entered college I ignored the rushing approaches and did not turn up for interviews with the elder brethren of the fraternities. Nevertheless, three fraternities did give me invitations to join, which I politely declined.

During freshman and sophomore years I was thrown a good deal with the Alpha Delt groups in my class and so it ultimately came about in a natural way that I was invited to join that fraternity early in my junior year, and did so because it seemed to me that I had a real reason for doing it.[41]

Harlan's free spirit showed itself in other ways. He sold insurance and typewriters, not because of his father's inability or unwillingness to finance him, but because he "wanted to enjoy a certain amount of independence."[42]

## NATIONAL POLITICS IN COLLEGE AND TOWN

At Amherst, Harlan was an ardent Republican—as rock-ribbed as his father. In the spring of 1892 a mock convention in College Hall defined the campaign issues, and the son of Fred Stone was stirred to action. Through the summer he distributed leaflets to the voters, and in the hill town of Pelham he was speaker at the flag raising. When on October 1, W. C. Breed, president of the Amherst College Republican Club, resigned, Vice-President Harlan Stone was unanimously made president. In cooperation with the town he began at once to plan an anti-Cleveland rally.

On the evening of October 13 President Stone, introduced by Chairman Stratton of the Republican Town Committee, presided at a rally, following the flag raising and procession. One of the speakers presented by Harlan was John L. Dodge, Harvard graduate and president of the Harvard Republican Club. The main floor of the hall was well filled with voters from both colleges and from the village, while interested ladies looked down from the gallery.

These campaign activities had heated repercussions. The *Boston Journal,* October 17, 1892, published a pro-Cleveland appeal, signed by eighteen Amherst College professors—an unprecedented act that brought fiery denunciation from the Republican press, alumni and parents, and voters at large. Harlan and his cohorts warmly denied the implication that Amherst College was not overwhelmingly Republican. Posters were issued and distributed in protest. Of 145 student voters in college, only 20 were Democrats, it was confirmed. A spontaneous college parade on October 24 carried the placard: "*18 Profs can't fool us—Tammany Faculty—Christian College.*" A week later the Republican leaders of the town, deeply aroused, staged a mammoth demonstration, with uniformed marchers and bands from both colleges, fireworks, and speakers of power. A year later Harlan Stone, aged twenty-one, became chairman of the Amherst Republican Town Committee.[43]

The great majority of the Amherst student body was Republican, but the country swept Grover Cleveland back into office, producing in the GOP considerable alarm lest tariff rates be smashed. In the wholesome American spirit of a good loser, Harlan, writing to a victorious Democrat, on Republican Club stationery, said:

Dear George:

Your letter enclosing election returns is at hand. There was once a minister who being a very humble individual always began his prayers as follows: "O Lord, I am a mass of bruises, wounds, and putrefied sores." This is a story from which you can draw your own moral. However, I still live and shall not go into mourning until the Democrats take the tariff off of sackcloth and ashes. Gen. Grant used to say that "Give the Democrats rope enough and they would surely hang themselves." There is no doubt but what they have a sufficiency of rope, and four years will tell us whether they will reduce suicide to a fine art. I congratulate you on the biggest Democratic walkover which has occurred since the war.

Yours in haste,

H. F. S.

P.S. A three-dollar hat awaits you. Call at Blodgett's.[44]

Harlan was more prophetic than he guessed, for suicide aptly described the Democratic debacle of 1896.

## AN ABIDING INFLUENCE—PROFESSOR GARMAN

Among the moral forces that had a powerful impact upon Harlan Stone during his Amherst College years, none exceeded that of Charles Edward Garman.[45] Harlan's experience was not unique. An old saying has it that if you scratch an Amherst man who graduated just before or after the turn of the century, you will find the quickening spirit of Garman. This high tribute was bestowed upon a human being whose bodily circulation was so deficient that he had to wrap himself in a heavy overcoat in the middle of June. To prevent dangerous drafts from reaching his scarfed neck, his classroom windows all remained closed, and the temperature was kept abnormally high. Yet it was Garman's power of intellect, not his eccentricity, that Stone put into his description of 1933:

A tall, spare man, clean shaven; hair and eyes were coal black, the latter deep, cavernous, glowing. . . . His personality was impressive. Casual acquaintance with him gave the impression that he was a mystic. Fuller acquaintance with him revealed that he was a great teacher, and a man of great intellectual power. His influence was not limited to the classroom. He had close personal contacts with most of his students. . . . In the home no one could be more charming, or attractive, especially to young men. Everything he said or did stirred their higher aspirations and their desire for worthy accomplishment.[46]

Garman was an amazing synthesis of evangelical faith and scientific outlook, then rapidly gaining favor. While retaining Seelye's basic beliefs, he attacked philosophical and theological dogma in the relentless spirit of scientific inquiry. Over the supposedly unbridgeable gulf between science and religion, Garman wove a persuasive bond. His was a theistic philosophy, founded on implicit trust in God's goodness and omnipotence.

Garman's course in philosophy began with the assumption that his students believed, however vaguely, in a Supreme Being. He felt that man is an integral part of the Spirit that motivates and gives purpose to all of life.[47] To demonstrate that man is not a bundle of automatic reflexes responding to stimuli, Garman compared mental operations to a jury trial. Witnesses reveal the facts just as our brain records impressions. But the process does not rest there. The jury weighs and decides on the evidence presented just as the brain receives sensory impulses, considers them, and makes final judgment. This independent action of the brain is the basis of personality, which in turn is the agent of man's spirituality.

From this point, it was a natural step to Garman's stress on the individual's duty and responsibility to his fellow men. The concept of stewardship resolved the conflict between the individual and society. The individual should be selfless in his effort to administer to his neighbors, for they were all drops in the same ocean. It was, however, a reciprocal arrangement. Society and government (the less the better) were to exercise restraint with due regard for individual rights. The functioning basis of society was mutual cooperation between individuals, and between individuals and the community. The doctrine of stewardship, of service, thus became "the climax of Garman's course and the heart of his philosophy."[48]

Neither social Darwinism nor Spencer's doctrine of the survival of the fittest destroyed man's creative social usefulness:

It is no longer necessary to have the masses perish in order that the few fittest may survive, because the individual may be regenerated. If his likes and dislikes are wrong, he may resist them and restrain himself. Not selfishness, but service, becomes the process of the moral life. The law, " 'A' can determine himself only through 'B,' " brings the social order into a condition of peace and interdependence instead of war and independence. Utilitarianism is the order of Darwinian evolution; justice and mercy are the order of moral evolution. Brain paths are on the side of the former. Of course, it is not easy to change a point of view when the whole stress of physical heredity is against the spiritual life. But man is made in the image of God as truly as in the image of the animals, and he thus inherits the divine nature with all its possibilities. It is for him to decide which set of impulses shall control his career.[49]

This creed, translated into terms of social action, heralds worldly salvation. "In regenerating business and charity, in purging them of all that is selfish and merely traditional, and placing them squarely on the basis of service, we shall have a second coming of Christ, the realization of the Kingdom of God on earth."[50]

Garman's approach was skeptical and inductive. After months given to questioning prevalent dogmas and creeds, he would at the end set his own positive and constructive position in a personalized context.

There comes a time when the young man must assume responsibility for what he does; there must be self-possession and self-direction instead of dependence on authority, and this is a new experience to him, an experience which many shrink from even in very little things.

Those who decline to follow this unfolding of their nature, and there are many of them, begin to fossilize. If they are religious they soon become Pharisaical, get lost in particulars, are unable to discriminate the essential from the accidental, and take refuge in doing something, and their religious activity is often times such as exhibits zeal, but without knowledge. If they are not religious they become fastidious in imitating social customs and very soon develop a degree of indifference toward everything except mere form; they become heartless, selfish, many cynical. There is no hope for a young man at this time if he does not meet the obligations of life with the spirit of self-reliance, but to do this he must have some confidence in his own judgment and the standards by which he judges. This is the spirit of philosophy.[51]

Stone's motivating philosophy in mature years reflected Garman's teachings. The Justice's hope for mankind, like Garman's, rested on "individual apprehension of the moral duty of stewardship." Reform begins in the souls of men, in changing the leopard's spots, in taming the lion within man's nature. Since all mankind is the extension of

God's personality, "like the waves of the sea," the spirit of brother-hood, responsibility, and humanitarianism are necessarily the fountain-head of human behavior. Selfishness, individual and deliberate, is the root of all evil.

But it was Garman's method, perhaps more than the substance of his teachings, that impressed Stone. "His great contribution," the Justice wrote in 1933, "has seemed to me to be in his method by which he taught young men to stand on their own feet intellectually, and to encompass in their thinking spiritual as well as material values."[52]

Instead of lecturing or hearing recitations based on assigned text-book reading in philosophy, Garman handed out pamphlets—written by himself and printed at his own personal expense—dealing with specific problems. The students worked these over and came to class ready for a lively intellectual bout. While each student drew on his own limited metaphysics, the bundled-up professor sat motionless. Then, by careful, judicious questioning, the mentor would appraise and perhaps reduce the dialectic to its now glaring fallacies. "The student's critical faculties," Stone recalled, "were stimulated; he was required to weigh evidence, to draw his own conclusions and defend them. This method was, I think, the ultimate secret of Garman's pro-found influence with his students. For the first time in their daily lives they were made to realize that they possessed a thinking apparatus of their own. It was only by the use of it that they could become masters of their own moral and intellectual destiny."[53]

Stone often noted the similarity between Garman's method and that introduced earlier by Professor C. C. Langdell at the Harvard Law School. He wondered whether the two educators had ever exchanged ideas, or whether they had developed the same technique inde-pendently.[54] "What a lawyer Garman would make!" Stone was heard to remark one day after a session in philosophy. In the crossfire of abstract ideas that erupted under this teacher's flashing black eyes, the pupil envisioned a discipline worthy of lifelong dedication. In this man of wasted body but fiery spirit the future Chief Justice may have recognized the hero he would emulate in the law.

Professor Garman recognized Stone's superior talent and at the end of senior year commended his "marked success, great ability, and thoroughly scholarly methods." "The faculty all agree," Garman wrote, "in their high esteem of Mr. Stone as a Christian gentleman, a faithful student and able thinker, thorough and comprehensive and very clear in his power of expression. . . . In my judgment he has large business ability and will make an able and efficient organizer. His clear powers of presenting a subject make it impossible for students to fail to grasp his meaning. What he sees himself he can make others see." He will not "disappoint high expectations," Garman confidently concluded.[55]

Stone's acquaintance with Garman went beyond the formal class-room meetings. Eugene W. Lyman, a fellow student and later professor of the Philosophy of Religion at Union Theological Seminary, recalled the undergraduate practice of going to Professor Garman's house by twos and threes to discuss philosophy. Stone was often one of these. "Once when I was there and Stone was not," Lyman wrote, "Garman alluded to his abilities and added, 'I haven't yet begun to show you what is in that man.' "[56]

Besides Garman, the Amherst faculty included other remarkable teachers, especially in the science departments. Chemistry, Harlan's first love, was taught by Professor Elijah P. Harris, '55, known to generations of Amherst men as "Derwall." Professor Harris, one of the more colorful solons of the hill, had the habit of rapidly scribbling formulas on the blackboard without pause or explanation, lecturing and gesticulating at such a clip as to rouse critical comment. "Those who want to know chemistry will stop after class and get it," the professor told a complaining student. "I haven't time to fool with the fellows who don't want to learn."[57]

Harlan must have been one of those who stayed after class. A fellow student in the laboratory, looking back and recalling Doc's aptitude in chemistry, suggested that "Stone could have been as great a scientist as he was a lawyer, which is saying a very great deal. Besides his brain and executive ability, he had a beautiful disposition —good, kind, and simple in the best sense of the word."[58]

Though matriculating in science, Stone did not limit himself in either the depth or the compass of his learning.* His electives in social subjects, as in science, were taught by distinguished Amherst graduates, who ranged far beyond their own special disciplines—Anson D. Morse in history and John Bates Clark in political economy. Literature and the arts, however, were lacking in an otherwise well-rounded program.[59]

"After forty years of contact with all sorts of men both in and out of educational institutions," Justice Stone wrote a fellow alumnus, "Garman, Morse, and 'Old Ty' are still in my opinion great men, and I still look upon Olds, Harris, Emerson, Kimball, and others as men of distinguished quality of intellect and personality. Even Eph Wood, with his sarcasm . . . was master of his subject and highly proficient in the exposition of it."[60] Years later, the Chief Justice, now an Amherst trustee, wrote President Stanley King: "The real value of the training I received from Amherst College was contributed by three or four

---

* In junior year Harlan was one of nine elected on the first drawing to Phi Beta Kappa, with a general average of 87.87. He barely made it, however, for until the spring of that year B.S. candidates were ineligible.

teachers—Professors Garman, Morse, Harris, and Emerson. They, and they alone, are responsible for whatever education I succeeded in getting in college."[61] Long association with men in civic and professional life did not alter Stone's judgment that his Amherst teachers "had an understanding of education, and of the change it should work in the lives of men."

Stone's letter of 1925 to Nicholas Murray Butler hints at certain considerations which may have moved him to abandon science as a career: "I am wondering whether perhaps today the solution of our difficulties does not lie with the philosophers rather than the scientists. Huxley and Tyndall were great scientists, but they were also great philosophers, and they made their deep impression on the current of popular thought through the philosophy grounded as it was on scientific knowledge."[62] It was Garman's philosophy, not old Derwall's chemistry, that prevailed in Justice Stone's mind as he phrased his letter to the president of Columbia University.

## PUBLIC SPEAKING AND DEBATE

During Stone's undergraduate days a great deal of energy and time went into debates and declamation, some form of platform speaking being required all four years. These courses, conducted by Professor Henry Allyn Frink, went beyond the mechanized ritual of declamation. "The course," Frink declared, "has to do with the student as thinker and writer as well as speaker."[63]

In freshman and sophomore years every student was called upon to deliver three "speeches" before the assembled college class. The young orators coached one another. At the end of the year "Frinkie" picked fifteen freshmen and fifteen sophomores, who competed for the coveted Kellogg prizes. A panel of judges, usually alumni from surrounding towns, selected five from each fifteen. The so-called Kellogg Fives then competed at Commencement for "excellence in declamation"—$100 first prize, $50 second prize. Stone, who had won a first prize in oratory at M. A. C., made the Kellogg Fifteen his first year and the Kellogg Five his second, with an oration on "The Amnesty of Jefferson Davis."

In junior year Harlan won the Whiteman oration prize with "Patrick Henry and Kossuth." The award, given by Alonzo J. Whiteman of Duluth, Minnesota, to members of the class in public speaking who "excel in oratorical composition," carried with it a prize of forty dollars' worth of books. In senior year Stone made the Hyde Fifteen, in competition for a prize of one hundred dollars awarded to "that member of the senior class who may produce the best oration."

Stone's undergraduate addresses and papers exhibit a sparkle and buoyancy conspicuously absent from the mature and responsible utterances of his later years. In these early literary pieces one notes the effort to create mood and color. A passage from his junior oration, "The New Reconstruction," is typical:

Consider for a moment the condition of the South in 1865. The feverish vision of conquest and victory had fled. A great people was humiliated and impoverished, and over the South settled the gloom and agony of defeat. As the soldier turned away from the surrender at Appomattox his future was no longer bright with hope but dark with foreboding. Think of the pent-up bitterness that rushed over his very soul as he beheld the land of his childhood ravaged by the invader's armies, her cities in ashes, his home in ruins. Here for two centuries his ancestors had been building up a social system based on human slavery, a system more feudal than that of the middle ages and more exhausting in its results. At a single stroke that social system had been revolutionized. The Emancipation Proclamation that had struck the shackles from four millions of bondsmen left the master weaker than the slave and turned against each other two great and antagonistic races.

For a young man who had never been within two hundred miles of the Potomac River, such projected emotion indicates fertile imagination. Provincialism finally caught up with him, however, in a flourish that portrayed the South as a Yankee colony whose rejuvenation must await northern exploitation:

Into this land of rich promise, let northern capital, northern energy, and northern thrift make its invasion. . . . On to Richmond then with northern energy and industry. On to every city and village in the South with the civilizing power of modern business. This is the mission of the new reconstruction. Already the South is responding to northern influence. She cannot avert her future. Northern civilization will pour along her railways and river courses. . . .

Chosen by the faculty as one of eight senior commencement speakers, Stone took as his topic "Two Epochs of Socialism." The speaker began with a colorful description of the violent excesses of the French Revolution—the first "epoch" of socialism. Unable to assimilate the Revolution, France returned to the authoritarian forms she had tried to overthrow. The failure of republicanism was manifest in the rise of the "ignorant" and "vicious." Finding the "second Epoch" of socialism in America, the speaker cited the horrible spectacle of Coxey's Army, the "waves of Populism," and finally drew an analogy between the "unrestrained socialism" of the Terror and the "extremist" demands of inland American farmers. Could America withstand this "peasant onslaught?" the speaker inquired.

Genuine reason for alarm was seen in violent outbursts such as the Chicago Pullman strike, in the Populist demands for government con-

trol of the railroads, and in the frantic agitation for inflationary currency. But the speaker's inability to comprehend the catalytic value
of the melting pot or to understand the economic and social problems
of the vast areas outside New England marks his provincialism. The
oration concluded on a note quite extreme even for the late nineteenth
century: "As the earlier epoch of socialism failed, so will its American
prototype, not because of its own frenzied bloodshed and violence, but
because of an unsurmountable obstacle—patriotic Americanism."

Stone scored another oratorical triumph in the traditional senior
Hardy Prize debate, June 25, 1894, the second day of commencement.
The topic, "Resolved: That the State of New York should extend the
suffrage to women," was timely, as the New York constitutional convention was then in session at Albany drafting a new constitution, and
the question of suffrage for women was being promoted and discussed.
Stone, on the anti-feminist side, took second place and a prize of
thirty dollars.* Luther Ely Smith, chosen by the class as its "brightest"
member, won first prize. "There were no weaknesses in Doc's arguments," Smith commented many years later. "He made what seemed
to me a very convincing presentation, and I believed then, as now,
that he should have had the first prize."[64]

### PRIZES AND PROPHECY

During his last college year, 1893-94, Stone proved his executive
ability as business manager of *The Amherst Student*, the campus
weekly newspaper. In the fall of 1893 the editor-in-chief and the business manager, both newly elected, had resigned, and in the special
election the vote for editor-in-chief was tied; Harlan was elected business manager. In this unprecedented crisis the board prepared to
suspend publication, but Stone, conscious of obligations to advertisers, conducted the paper until the election of Luther Ely Smith to
the editorial vacancy.[65] In March 1894 all the '94 editors ended their
service, except Stone. He remained at his post until the Commencement issue, June 26, 1894. No editor-in-chief appeared on the mast-
head during the spring term.[66] Stone did not want the post but was
drafted, because "everyone admired and trusted him."[67] The trust was
well placed, for at the end of that fiscal year the *Student* had $1000
in unexpended funds.

Thus the four years at Amherst drew to a close. At the senior
banquet, the class of '94 had much to look back on. Though Harlan's
natural inclination had been to remain on the periphery of college

* In senior year Stone also won $125 as one of two winners of the Roswell
Dwight Hitchcock Memorial Fellowship, "offered by the Alpha Delta Phi fraternity
for excellence in history and the social and economic sciences."

activities rather than plunge in, and though his participation had been the accidental or direct result of fortuitous circumstance, he had pitched in for all he was worth once opportunity embraced him. Marked intellectuality, ability to inspire confidence, not qualities of aggressive leadership, won for him in college, as in later years, a preeminent place among his fellows.

An interested spectator at Harlan's Commencement was his childhood sweetheart, Agnes Harvey. During all his college years letters had been exchanged at least two or three times a week. The busy summers on the farm had often been relieved by visits to Chesterfield. Pleasures in those days were simple—picnics, walks, drives about the countryside. In Agnes, Harlan found a companion who shared his love of nature and the out-of-doors—an artistic girl who would one day express in water colors the beauty she saw around her. Together they roamed through wooded hillsides, rowed on Spofford Lake, and fished in crystal mountain brooks. A common taste for outdoor life formed a bond that endured. In later years it became an integral part of their lives, setting the pattern for their vacations.

Stone's graduation was an exciting event for the young guest from Chesterfield. "When Harlan graduated from Amherst," Mrs. Stone recalled in 1950, "I was invited to his house for Commencement. It was a great treat and very interesting to attend the many activities in which he participated. He never cared much for dancing, as most people did at that time, so we did not go to the fraternity parties except to look in for a few minutes."

Commencement lasted four days. Initiated by the Baccalaureate sermon on Sunday, June 24, the activities were solemn and proper. On Wednesday, June 27, the fifty-nine members of the class of '94 received the Bachelor's degree—fifty-two A.B. candidates followed by seven B.S. men. The name of Stone, distinguished leader of them all, closed the list.

In the class poll Harlan was second in the vote for "the most popular man" and ranked fourth among "the brightest." Two of his classmates answered the question, "What is the greatest benefit the college has got from the town?" by naming Doc Stone. On the traditional question "Who is most likely to succeed?" the class recorded: "Doc Stone will take warning and proceed to be the most famous man in '94."[68]

CHAPTER FIVE

# High School Teacher and Law Student

## 1894-1898

Prospects for employment were none too bright for Harlan the summer of 1894, and it was not until late in August that he found a suitable opening.

"I always thought his mind was turning to law," the Reverend Frederick D. Hayward later recalled, "but one morning, walking up College Hill, we talked of school teaching. Some days later a newspaper clipping came to me concerning a vacancy in the science department at the Newburyport (Mass.) High School. I handed the clipping to Doc. 'Go down and try for it,' I said. 'You are scientific. He went and got the job."[1]

"Do you remember," Stone wrote Hayward in 1941, "that you pointed me to my first job in Newburyport? I liked it so much that I came near never leaving it."[2]

In the fall of 1894 Harlan, nearing his twenty-second birthday, with $250 in prize money and the promise of a $1000 salary, struck out for himself.

Newburyport was a picturesque place to begin one's career. Wide streets skirted the waterfront, past relics of wharves and warehouses. Spacious dwellings, the product of skills that built and launched the clipper ships, lined High Street. The imposing brick high school stood on High Street, looking across the Mall. From there could be glimpsed the granite pile of the jail, its massive wall crowned with iron spikes. Diagonally across from the school, at the water's edge, stood the building that was to become the future Chief Justice's favorite haunt—the courthouse.

On September 1 the *Newburyport Daily Herald* announced the new teacher's arrival "ready for business." "He will make his home during the winter with Deputy Collector of Customs Arthur Huse," the paper said. School and community warmly welcomed him. Stone quickly oriented himself and began to dig in.

The teaching of science at Newburyport was already well established. Natural science, introduced by physics and chemistry, or botany and zoology, ran through three years. Frederick Tarr, Amherst '91, had impressed upon the high school laboratory the full tradition of "Old Derwall," and Stone continued their experimental routine. In his underground laboratory, hidden from adult invasion, save by Principal Enoch C. Adams on his rounds or Mr. Badger the fireman, Stone zealously applied the knowledge and methods he had gained at Amherst.

In later years he was remembered by his pupils as disciplinarian as well as teacher. One day, when he discovered two boys squirting streams of water at each other in the laboratory, he injected his big form into the fray and grabbed each culprit by the neck. "I ought to knock your heads together," he warned. Then, after a pause, he let the delinquents go.[3] In 1945 a former student, recalling a visit to Washington, D.C., commented: "There sat big Chief Justice Stone with his strong face that looked like New England. My mind instinctively reverted to the worry and care my classmates imposed upon the 'Good Old New Englander.' I could sympathize with him in those trying days. As soon as he undertook the uplifting of the class of '95, he recognized that he would need a stiff upper lip, and a sense of right and justice."[4]

The "Big Room" on the first floor, used for study, at times became the life center of the school. On Monday mornings the whole school gathered there to listen to devotional exercises. Principal Adams was usually on the platform. Mr. Stone, with round boyish face and big body, sat next to him. Other teachers were posted among the nearly three hundred boys and girls. One morning, when the principal was absent, Stone was called upon to conduct the service, which commenced with repeating the Lord's Prayer. He started all right, but had proceeded only a short way before he seemed to forget the text. He began to mumble, hoping the students would proceed without him, but without his leadership all sounds ceased. An embarrassing silence prevailed. Eventually he got under way, to the relief of all. Some students afterward said that instead of saying "daily bread" he substituted the word "biscuit."[5] When reminded of the incident in 1924, Stone commented ruefully that the incident only served to prove that he was "much better adapted to the legal profession than the ministerial."[6]

With teaching and slight administrative duties Stone combined the coaching of athletics. On the gridiron especially, his experience at Amherst made his coaching a heartening prospect for Newburyport High. Only two years before, the school had refused a challenge for lack of a line-up. Now, with the arrival of the right guard on Amherst's famous championship team, interest ran high. "Football is King of outdoor games," the *School Record* declared. But despite the progress made under Coach Stone's direction, the season was disappointing. The students were grateful nonetheless "for his earnest endeavors in their behalf."[7]

Harlan's interests ranged beyond formal school work and play. In January the Century Club listened to his "very interesting address" on "whether strikes are a benefit to the workman or not."[8] He frequented the YMCA and the public library. In leisure hours Harlan gained his first and lasting knowledge of the sea—its perpetual life and exalted beauty, and the fun it held. Beyond all these was Stone's chief extracurricular activity—attendance at the session of the court.

In September 1894 the Superior Court at Salem faced a full calendar of cases, criminal and civil. There had been murder, forgery, and robbery in rural towns north of the River, and manslaughter in Andover, while the seamy Haverhill "boodle cases" cried out for settlement. Out of more than five hundred pending cases, Chief Justice Mason assigned fifty-five to the September civil term in Newburyport. Arthur Bishop, the father of one of Stone's pupils, a deputy sheriff from Rowley, very often had to attend the Newburyport court. After school the boy would cross the street to the courthouse and wait for a ride home with his father. In 1954 Wilbert A. Bishop remembered that, "each day after school, Mr. Stone, when court was in session, would go to the courthouse to listen to the cases being tried. Sometimes he would sit with the lawyers behind the bar."[9] Here he became friendly with the district attorney, William H. Moody. Moody, recently returned from Europe, and widely esteemed for his knowledge of law and his relentless enforcement of it, was Stone's mentor and friend.* It was at his suggestion young Stone turned to the study of law.

In June 1895 it became known that Stone might not return to his post in the fall. "The school will meet a great loss if Mr. Stone leaves, as he is planning to do," the *School Record* announced. "He is not decided whether he will teach another year, or enter the law school at Cornell."[10] On June 25 the *Newburyport Daily News* reported that the school committee had "voted to increase the salary of Harlan F. Stone . . . from $1000 to $1200." The doubt, if any, in the teacher's mind was soon resolved. "We regret," Superintendent Lunt reported, "that Mr. Stone felt that his own interests called upon him to resign at the end of a single year. He is an able young man, of great energy and steadfastness of purpose, and does with his might what his hands find to do."[11]

---

* In 1895, after five intense years as district attorney (Essex County), Moody was sent to Congress. As a member of Theodore Roosevelt's Cabinet (1902-1909), and on the Supreme Court bench, he obtained high repute as administrator and judge. For Stone, Moody embodied the qualities of those early legal giants whose shades still haunted the courthouse on the Mall.

A half-century later twenty men and women of Newburyport High School, class of '95, planned a reunion, with Chief Justice Stone, their respected former "teacher and disciplinarian," as guest of honor. After lunch and a visit to the ruins of the old building, recently gutted by fire, the honored guest was tendered a reception at the new high school. At the Golden Reunion banquet that evening in the school library, speeches of remembrance were made, dubious poetry read, and mementos exchanged. Stone received two pieces of silverware of Newburyport craftsmanship. A small engraved plaque, recording the Chief Justice as "Teacher—N. H. S.—1895," was presented by the class to the school. Stone's gift was his photograph, inscribed in his bold script: "With regards to all students, former, prospective and present, of the Newburyport High School. Harlan F. Stone."[12] The plaque and the portrait are displayed today in the high school library.

"It was very kind of him to attend our reunion," Ernest Foss wrote Mrs. Stone after the Chief Justice's death less than a year later. "I had really built up the occasion on the possibility of his coming. When he came it was so easy for us to think of him and ourselves as of fifty years ago. I suspect some of our best-looking girls—we had precious few of them—again felt a heart flutter as they remembered the handsome, athletic, unmarried young man only a few years their senior. We tried hard to give the little affair that flavor, and I think he liked it."[13]

In early September 1895 Harlan left staid New England for New York City. He had decided to enter Columbia Law School, attracted perhaps by the number of Amherst men on its faculty. To finance the move he got a job as history teacher at Adelphi Academy in Brooklyn, against the "better judgment" of another famous son of Amherst, Charles S. Whitman (later on Governor of New York), who had gone directly from college to Adelphi, where he taught Latin and Greek while attending New York University Law School. When Stone's name came up, Whitman was asked for his opinion of Stone as a teacher. "I told them," he recalled, "that I didn't think Stone would do; he wasn't good enough." With a chuckle the Governor added, "Shows how poor my judgment is; he turned out to be much better than I was."[14]

Under Stone's instruction, history at Adelphi came alive. A former student sharply contrasted his predecessor, "a young blond-bearded Harvard graduate, almost dumb from fright," with the new history teacher. "Only a glance was needed for an electric change to come over the students," she wrote. "The quiet, pleasant, outgoing attractive young man—Harlan Fiske Stone—commanded instant interest. Ancient history became a favorite study overnight. Students lingered after recitations for any special assignment Mr. Stone suggested. Everyone came to class alert with interest. Instinctively, we did our best."[15]

Another Adelphi student recalled Stone as "the finest teacher I ever had. I shall always remember the definition of history he gave us—'the record of the progress of mankind.'" Still another former pupil remembered Stone's stress "on the effect of geography on history."[16]

Principal Charles H. Levermore and Stone were in complete rapport. The principal's stress on the inductive method betokened the scientific spirit. In the Newburyport laboratory, objective knowledge of science had reassured and guided Stone. History at Adelphi dealt with the stream of human events; it required imagination, reflection, exploration of the past to understand the present. In the study of law these two disciplines were not mutually exclusive or antagonistic, but complementary. At Amherst, Professor Garman had encouraged his students to look to a science of law as evidence of man's spiritual goal. "Statute law, a supplement to the common law," Garman pointed out, had "grown up through many generations, expressing precedents and traditions of previous ages."[17]

In later years Stone looked back on his year of teaching at Newburyport and his part-time work at Adelphi Academy with satisfaction. The necessity of earning enough money to go to law school was itself educational. It made him realize that "college and law school education did not grow on every bush for students in my position in life." It reinforced "the belief that diligence and loyalty to my immediate job would best serve to fit me for some useful achievement in the years to come."[18]

Stone's arrival at Columbia came shortly after the Trustees had placed the Law School on a full-time basis. It was a period of high expectations. In 1890 William A. Keener had been called from Harvard to introduce the case system of instruction. This inductive approach, this stress on original sources, fitted in with Stone's own experience both as a student and teacher. Yet this blatant heresy—the "case system" so-called—incubated at Harvard, started a stream of controversy that flooded the whole domain of the law. And when to this was added instruction by the political science faculty in constitutional history, comparative jurisprudence, and Roman law, "there was a roar of disapproval that shook the institution to its foundations."[19]

"There were many doubts and much shaking of heads over these innovations," Stone recalled. "Certain members of the bar were doubtful whether any law student could find enough to do in the mere study of law to occupy his whole time. They were quite clear that for a youth just out of college to attempt the study of law in any analytical and critical fashion would be a waste of time." One member of the bar warned Stone that if he went to Columbia he "would begin by studying law as it was at the time when the Scots came across the border to raid peaceful England," and he added, "of course, you would never win cases with such stuff."[20]

Many years later Stone, as a practicing lawyer, had the satisfaction of sending the giver of this advice the brief of a case he had argued before the United States Supreme Court. By historical research into English common law procedure, going back to the time the Scots "crossed the border," he succeeded in persuading the Justices that the foreign attachment laws of Delaware, founded upon the ancient Custom of London, were in accord with the due process clause of the Fourteenth Amendment.*

Stone and his classmates, in fact, found the law school on solid ground. "There is no uniform method of instruction in this school," Dean Keener wrote in 1893. "Each instructor is at liberty to pursue the method of instruction which, in his opinion, will be productive of the best results. At the present time three methods of instruction are used:

"First, the system of instruction by lectures with reference to and the incidental discussion of cases. This method prevails in the courses in Public Law.

"Second, the system of instruction based on the study and discussion of some standard treatise, and the consideration of cases by way of illustration. This method prevails in a few of the courses in Private Law.

"Third, the system of instruction based on the study and discussion of cases. This is the method generally used in the courses in Private Law. In the first year, however, the study of cases in Contracts, Pleading, Torts, and Real and Personal Property is preceded or accompanied by the study of a standard treatise."[21]

Introduction of the case system, only one aspect of the revolution, meant that accepted doctrines were subject to re-examination and analysis; it meant deepening as well as broadening legal education. More and more, the subject matter of courses was extended so as to include not only doctrines and techniques useful to the practitioner but also the study of legal principles relating to the organization and structure of society. For second- and third-year students the curriculum included Comparative Jurisprudence, Administrative and Comparative Constitutional Law, Institutes of Roman Law, and so on. These courses were taught by the political science faculty, which included a former Amherst man, Professor John W. Burgess, as dean, Monroe Smith, Frank J. Goodnow, and John Bassett Moore. Dean Burgess has spoken of the decade from 1890 to 1900 as "the period of bloom,"[22] the School of Political Science serving as a model for such faculties and schools throughout the country. These changes, along with many others, were reflected in the Board of Trustees' resolve of February 3, 1896, that Columbia College, "in its enlarged activities, might for convenience bear the name Columbia University."

* See pp. 185-87.

Professor George W. Kirchwey vividly pictured the emergence of the Law School—the library with its large well-lighted reading room, tables and chairs in the stacks, conference room on the one side, dean's office on the other; the floors above, with the rooms of the professors, and lecture rooms large and small. "The law student," Kirchwey wrote, "going to and from his lecture room, passes open doors of rooms filled with books, and of recitation rooms of professors of philosophy, history, and political science." There exists "a degree of comfort and studied ease; the 'still air of delightful studies' breathes through rooms that might otherwise gain too exclusively a professional atmosphere."[23]

"To my delight and satisfaction," Stone recalled in 1924, "I found at Columbia a group of men engaged in studying and teaching law as a science is studied and taught."[24]

The teacher of Jurisprudence and Equity was Dean Keener. A great hulk of a man with a full red beard, he made a sharp impression, not only because of his physical appearance, but also because of his mastery of Socratic dialogue. Adding to his repute was his pre-lecture habit of waving aloft a big red bandanna handkerchief and then violently blowing his nose.[25] He had a penchant for branding facts on students by use of biting sarcasm and merciless questioning.[26] Some were tempted to pull his whiskers, others merely referred to him profanely as "the red-bearded so and so."

Of an altogether different stamp was John Bassett Moore. A profound scholar and thinker, teacher of Criminal Law and Procedure, and a noted authority on international law, Moore was described by Stone as "the wise and kindly counselor of all those students who sought his guidance and instruction." Much like Moore in both friendliness and learning was rotund, fatherly George F. Canfield, professor of Agency and Evidence. A man of wisdom and scholarship, Canfield bore his burden of learning lightly. The "perfect exemplar," Stone commented, of the phrase "a gentleman and scholar."[27] Canfield's law partner spoke of "his gracious manners, his cheerful personality, and his consideration for the opinion of others. . . . He was patient and moderate in debate, and open-minded to suggestions. . . . Many a young lawyer who sat before him in the classroom or worked in his office has reason to be thankful for his teaching and influence."[28]

Remembered for his ready wit and literary ability was George Washington Kirchwey. When his class in real and personal property grew restless, he always had a "few more pearls to cast." Stone liked to tell of the encounter his classmate, Edward R. Finch, had with Professor Kirchwey. As the lecture hour drew to its close the discussion waxed warm. Finch (later judge of the New York Court of Appeals), not altogether satisfied with the professor's exposition, exclaimed, "But I want some test—some sign." Just then the bell rang, signaling the end of the hour. The professor gathered up his papers, gazed intently at his inquisitor, and said, "A wicked and adulterous generation seeketh a sign, but no sign shall be given." In recalling the incident, Stone said that to the best of his recollection no sign was ever given.[29]

These teachers did more than stimulate and discipline their students' intellectual processes. By breaking down the barriers of professionalism they created a sense of delight and satisfaction in the study of law and developed a love of it as an institution. Stone's acquaintance with Keener, Canfield, and Moore grew into warm and lasting friendships.

With the June 1896 Commencement at Adelphi, Stone ended his secondary teaching, bade Brooklyn farewell, and moved his personal belongings to Manhattan, to lodge with his Amherst college mate Clinton E. Bell at 17 East 46th Street. The next year they settled in Miss Katharine Kerr's boarding house at 417 West 117th Street, only a block from the new location of Columbia University on Morningside Heights. Living in the same house were two other Amherst graduates, Grosvenor H. Backus and Dwight Morrow. To these old friends Harlan added Jackson E. Reynolds, Edward R. Finch, Sterling Carr, and Walter Carter, Yale's famous baseball pitcher "Dutch Carter," son of the senior member of Carter, Dwight and Hughes. Bonds of enduring friendship developed among them. All soon recognized Stone's great ability as a leader. Almost unconsciously there arose the feeling that ultimately he would occupy high judicial office.*

There were about fifteen students living in the house and some others came in for lunch. Meal times were periods of great pleasure, particularly dinner, and Stone shone at these periods in all of his kindness, wit, and good humor. He and Walter Carter admired each other greatly. Carter was especially gifted in humor, and Stone had a faculty for inciting it and bringing it forth.[30]

Judge Edward R. Finch has written of the "friendliness and affectionate regard" that permeated the boarding-house group. City born and bred, Finch never ceased to admire Stone's "rugged physique." In that sturdy countryman he saw "how large a part the human will may play in constructing ability and personality." "These were days and nights of hard work," Finch recalled. He pictured "Stone buried in textbooks, clad in a well-known red sweater, a favorite garment, when all-night work was necessary. . . . As indicating his seriousness

* "While we were undergraduates," Philip Nelson wrote Stone, April 3, 1924, "our chief debate was, 'Why don't they make the Dean judge of the Court of Appeals or of the Supreme Court?' and the only answer then was, 'Columbia needs him too much.'" Stone's appointment to the Supreme Court in 1925 merely confirmed "the prediction made by us all at 417 West 117th Street during our law school days." (Sterling Carr to H.F.S., Jan. 11, 1925.)

of purpose, when a member of the class suggested that we have a class tea, to which young ladies should be invited, Stone in scorn inquired whether we were attending a law school or a young ladies' academy."[31]

But Stone's life was not all work and no play at law school—or ever. He often went to the vacant lot across from the boarding house where some of the group kicked a football around or watched Carter display his skill as a pitcher. He seldom took part himself, but encouraged those who did.[32]

Stone was a member of the legal fraternity, Phi Delta Phi, where he enjoyed the social amenities. "For so serious a chap," Jackson E. Reynolds observed, "he lent himself to that lighter side of life and contributed greatly to the enjoyment of our sessions."

Stone also came in close association with fellow students in Hamilton Moot Court, of which he was a member. "There," Reynolds recalled, "we argued 'close' cases of great interest pending in the courts. Two students argued for the plaintiff, two for the defendant, and four acted as judges. Stone was never outstanding as an advocate in Hamilton Court; but he was the best we had when sitting on the bench. Even in those early days his judicial attitude was a striking quality in his character. . . ."

"In classwork," Reynolds continued, "Stone was easily 'tops.' He was not particularly astute, or effective in his use of words in presenting his views, but he had a rugged self-confidence and a dogged tenacity that made every student look up to him. The professors, including hard-bitten old red-whiskered Keener, the dean, had a real respect for him and his views in his student days."[33]

Stone must have been acutely aware of his difficulty in achieving clarity of thought and expression. It was perhaps with a purpose of developing greater facility that he became the leader of two or three study groups, directing and reviewing the work of previous weeks. "It was my good fortune," Sterling Carr wrote, "to be a member of one group. He was remarkable for his capacity to bring forth from each member earnestness and understanding."[34] "My room," Judge Finch writes, "was only a few feet from that occupied by Harlan Stone. One of the things that impressed me was the way in which he clarified his thought." Coming into Stone's room one day, Finch found him "trying to express out loud the legal principles he had just learned."[35]

In three crowded days, beginning Sunday, June 5, 1898, Columbia University held its first Commencement on Morningside. The Reverend Doctor Henry Van Dyke preached to the candidates on Sunday. Monday was class day for the college. Wednesday's graduation reflected pomp and ceremony. The procession of more than seven hundred marchers started at the library, crossed South Court, moved through 116th, the Boulevard and 120th, to the gymnasium, where exercises were held. Dean Keener presented the eighty-five candidates for the LL.B. degree.[36] The Law School then seemed on the threshold of a remarkable push forward. At the first anniversary meeting of Columbia alumni, Professor Nicholas Murray Butler, speaking on behalf of the graduates in Philosophy, Law, Political Science, and Pure Science, noted that "great advance has placed the study of law upon a true university basis." "It is the testimony of the bench and bar and students alike," he said, "that we are now performing a great educational service in that branch of the University."[37]

The December 1898 issue of the *Columbia University Quarterly* carried the terse announcement that Herbert Noble, lecturer on bailments and insurance, had resigned and that Harlan Fiske Stone, B.S., LL.B., would take his place. Stone was now twenty-six. "His career in the Columbia Law School," the magazine noted, "was of the most distinguished character, and being admitted to the bar, soon after graduation, he at once entered upon the active work of his profession in the office of Sullivan and Cromwell."

Harlan's years at the Columbia Law School had generated "faith in a great profession, and hope for its future." Later the world became somewhat cynical about law and lawyers—and not without reason. "We were not cynical then," Stone recalled in 1937. "Now is the time," he went on, "to renew our faith, and take a fresh resolve to make it worthy of the faith and loyalty which we pledged to it thirty-five years ago."[38]

PART TWO

# *Toward the Goal*

———

## CHAPTER SIX

# Lawyer, Teacher, and Dean

## 1898-1923

Through the years Harlan never forgot Agnes Harvey. They corresponded regularly. Part of his vacation was always spent in her home town of Chesterfield. Gradually affection for his childhood playmate matured and deepened. As a token of his love (they could never fix precisely on the engagement date), he gave her a ring with nine small diamonds set around a pearl, perhaps symbolizing the nine years since 1890 during which they were pledged to each other. The marriage was at the bride's home on September 7, 1899—a simple ceremony performed by the Reverend Mark Tisdale before some twenty relatives and friends. The bride and groom themselves gathered the evergreens and asters to decorate the parlor. After a wedding breakfast they drove to Brattleboro, Vermont, to board the train for New London. They spent a few days at Block Island and then left for New York.

During the first year of their marriage the Stones rented the second floor in a boarding house at 912 West End Avenue. It was a comfortable apartment with bedroom, bath, and large living room facing the avenue. The house lodged several students, including an architect and four Columbia Law School men. Relative freedom from housekeeping gave the bride opportunity to adjust to New York, look for an apartment, and buy furniture.

The year following graduation from Columbia, Harlan was a clerk in the Wall Street legal firm of Sullivan and Cromwell. In October 1899 he became connected with Wilmer and Canfield at 49 Wall Street. Until 1905 this association meant simply that he had a desk there and used the office facilities. The same connection was maintained for one or two other men of the law faculty who were friends of Mr. Canfield and needed downtown offices.

With law practice Harlan combined part-time teaching at the Columbia Law School. The salary was pitifully small—only $2000. In December 1900 President Low proposed to increase it to $2250. At first Harlan did not feel justified in accepting it in view of the other opportunities now open to him which "promised much greater remuneration." "I have my family to support and my own future to provide for," he told the President.[1] The young lawyer was convinced, moreover, that at his age "some further experience in the practice of my profession would be of great advantage both to the Law School and to myself."[2] For a while he doubted whether it was feasible to continue dividing his time between teaching and practice. With the increased pay went a heavier teaching load and a new course in code practice and equity pleading. The demands seemed too heavy.

"It has always been my practice," he wrote Dean Keener, "never to go before a class, however familiar I might be with the subject, without first having carefully gone over the work and mapped out a fresh plan of presenting the subject to the class. . . . It is my opinion that law will never be successfully taught by the case system in any other manner. . . ."[3] Stone finally accepted the salary on a reduced schedule and with the understanding that he would be allowed to engage regularly in the practice of his profession either in an office of his own or as a partner in a firm. But he added, "I may say that I should not enter into this arrangement were it not my desire to remain in the service of the Law School on some permanent basis."[4]

In 1903 Stone was promoted to adjunct professor, with a seat in the Faculty of Law, at a salary of $2750. Though his pay was raised to $3000 the next year, he felt generally unhappy. By this time Nicholas Murray Butler had become president of the University, and differences immediately ensued over matters of policy. In March 1905 Stone resigned and joined the law firm of Wilmer and Canfield. For the moment he had decided to devote all his time to private practice. "For this action," he wrote Professor Kirchwey, "I have a number of reasons. . . . My principal reason, however, is that the demands of practice are becoming daily more exacting, and I do not feel that I can continue to do justice to the work downtown and to the work at Columbia."[5]

His resignation had repercussions that could hardly have been anticipated in the case of a faculty member who, like Stone, had never given his full time to the University. On April 6, 1905, the senior class addressed to him an ardent plea to reconsider:

. . . The members of the class have learned of your intention to leave the School with great regret. Could they by any act or expression persuade you to a different view, they would go far to see that result accomplished. They feel that the School is losing in you a most efficient and capable force in its teaching staff, one whose courses have been instructive, interesting, and stimulating—urging the student to constant, careful, and discriminating thought. The case method of teaching, which is followed in the Law School, is by no means a simple method, and the members of the graduating class, having at heart the interests of the School, and the maintenance of its present high standard, appreciate what it means for it to be deprived of one who has so well mastered his work. The teacher from whom one gathers power as well as knowledge is not so often seen as to go unnoticed.

We want, also, to assure you, speaking for all members of the class, that in addition to their respect for your ability, they have a warm admiration for you personally. The patience, geniality, and broad spirit with which you have met them at all times, give an added force to their regret at your departure. They wish you every possible success in your future career, and count it a privilege to have had the benefit of your instruction, and the charming influence of your personality.

Stone stuck to his decision. Among the reasons for doing so were his growing family responsibilities. He was now the father of two sons, Marshall, born April 8, 1903, and Lauson, born on November 28, 1904. Largely for the sake of their children, the Stones in 1906 bought a house in Englewood, New Jersey. A large roomy place, painted cocoa brown with white trim, it was dubbed by their friends the chocolate and whipped-cream house. While excellent for the children, the move meant a long and arduous day for "Father." He had to leave early and returned late, prompting him to remark that "on the way home he expected to see himself coming back." But there were compensations. He fished and hiked along the Palisades near his home and frequently took advantage of his membership in the Long Island Country Club. In the winter the Stones enjoyed the theater, opera, and local meetings of the Shakespeare Society. He found time for a flower and vegetable garden and prided himself on having the first flowers of the season. Gardening absorbed him on Sundays, hours that might have been spent in church. One day a caller inquired for Mr. Stone, and, learning that he was not in, asked when he might find him at home. Mrs. Stone, not realizing that this was the new Congregational minister, replied, "You can always find Mr. Stone in the garden on Sunday mornings."

Less than two years after Stone severed connections with Columbia, discussions were under way with President Butler, looking toward the possibility of his returning to the Law School as professor and dean. Butler offered him the post in December 1906.[6] The lawyer expressed his willingness to accept it on condition that he would have "reasonable freedom" in making faculty appointments. The President agreed, but soon thereafter appointed Harry Alonzo Cushing without consulting his new dean. Stone's letter of January 2, 1907, withdrawing his name, was perhaps his sharpest run-in with the authoritarian educator, but not the last:

I have decided to withdraw my name from further consideration for the position of Dean of the Law School, and I desire to state to you briefly my reasons for so doing. Before advising you of my willingness to accept the position, and, in fact, before giving it serious consideration, I stated to you in substance, among other things, that I regarded a reasonable freedom in the choice of new men who from time to time might be called to professorships in the Law School as essential to carrying out my plans for its development, and that unless as a preliminary matter I could feel assured of such freedom, I would not give any further consideration to the suggestion that I undertake the work. I then understood you to acquiesce cordially in my views, and it was on this basis that I a few days later advised you of my willingness to accept the position when it should be formally tendered. My views on this subject were again stated in my letter to you of the 14th ultimo.

Some four or five weeks after this interview, I was apprised by you that arrangements had been perfected whereby several important changes were to be made in the personnel of the corps of instruction and that a new professor had been selected to devote his entire time to the Law School, and that the fact of his selection had already been communicated to him. This arrangement was made entirely without my knowledge. Whether it was before or after my interview with you to which I refer seems not very material, since if before, and I had then been informed of it and advised that the terms which I then proposed could not be satisfied, I should not have proceeded further with the matter.

While it does not affect the principle involved, I did not and do not approve of the selection as made. It was both inherently objectionable for reasons which I have already stated to you, and judged upon a comparative basis, it was not acceptable because I had other plans, which I think all interested in the Law School would agree to be preferable, because those plans assure to us an immediate and unqualified success which the selection actually made does not and cannot do. It has now become apparent from your letter of the 26th ultimo that this arrangement cannot be modified in any substantial manner and that the University cannot comply with an essential condition of my acceptance of the position. I am, therefore, compelled with great regret to withdraw my name from further consideration. . . .

In this first encounter Butler acted vindictively. He not only kept Cushing on as professor, but in February 1907 made him acting dean. Subsequent events proved what Stone had foreseen—that Cushing's appointment was not in the best interests of the School. From the beginning, student horseplay made Cushing's life miserable. One day early in November 1909, without notice to anyone, not even his wife, this imposing-looking gentleman, six feet tall, with a heavy black beard, walked off the campus never to return. A maid in his flat told reporters that Professor Cushing had been dividing his time between the University and his law office. But newsmen tried in vain to elicit information about him at either location.

"If there is any explaining to be done it had better be done by Professor Cushing himself," an anonymous University official said. "This is the first time in my knowledge that a Columbia professor has skipped his classes in such a manner. . . . It is altogether a very unusual proceeding, but further than that I cannot go."[7]

Reporters were more successful in their interviews with students. Cushing was not, they said, "altogether popular with his classes." He had recently been "intensely nervous," "laboring under severe strain," and "several times had apologized to his class." At the beginning of the fall term the students had drafted a petition for submission to the Trustees requesting that when it came time to appoint a permanent dean, Professor Cushing's name not be considered. The petition "was suppressed before it reached the hands of the Trustees."[8]

The first official attempt to clarify these strange doings appeared on November 14, in a laconic notice signed by President Butler and posted in a students' coatroom: "Professor Cushing, acting dean of the Faculty of Law, having tendered his resignation as Professor of Law and withdrawn from the services of the University, the President has designated Professor Kirchwey to serve as acting dean pending action by the Trustees."

The thought of returning to Columbia had never been out of Stone's mind since the abortive discussions of 1906. Meanwhile, former students, faculty, and members of the Board of Trustees had continued pressing him to abandon his practice, at least in part, and return to teaching. Even before the Cushing fiasco, he had about made up his mind. There were lurking doubts, not least among them being profound distrust of President Butler's authoritarian ways. Butler's centralized theory of university organization, his belief that every department and school was directly under his supervision, clashed with Stone's federalistic views. Butler saw nothing wrong in his appointment of Cushing. It was entirely in keeping with his theory of presidential sovereignty.

Stone's request for advice from his old friend William S. Booth elicited a full reply. "I am interested in what you say about Columbia University," Booth wrote, November 5, 1909. "They seem to want you, don't they? It is very temptatious to have a steady job like that at which you can do things that you like. Without strings too. *If that be so*, and you can be sure of it, and sure that there is no trickery lurking behind it, I should be inclined to think it over well before turning it down. . . . You might keep up your practice to some extent at the same time."

Booth, mindful of Butler's tendency to welsh on his promises, expressed concern lest Stone find himself tied to Butler's plans "whether you will or not." But Stone could not, in any event, Booth suggested, "help becoming a factor and an important one too." He especially liked the professorship as "affording a chance to do work of a constructive kind. . . . You are working too closely at money making, and are not getting rest enough for your mind or for your body," Booth admonished.

At a meeting of the Board of Trustees' Committee on Education,

December 16, Stone was unanimously nominated Professor of Law and Dean of the Law Faculty, to take office July 1, 1910, at an annual salary of $7500. On January 3 President Butler notified him of this action and suggested that he confer, at an early date, with Acting Dean Kirchwey and other members of the faculty.

Announcement of the appointment brought forth a flood of congratulations and good wishes from former classmates, law teachers, and practicing lawyers. It was, they all said, "a well-merited honor." Even before the negotiations for Stone's return had been consummated, Professor Charles K. Burdick looked forward confidently to "a new and happier dispensation."[9] F. P. Keppel told of one man who for "the past few years had unwillingly been compelled to advise men to go to Harvard if they came East to study law." Keppel reported that this gentleman "saw no reason for doing so in the future."[10]

Though most of the letters were suffused with praise, a few were outspoken in their criticism of the way things had been going at Columbia. Feeling that this dissatisfaction was a fact to be reckoned with, Stone selected from forty or more letters a few that seemed fairly typical and sent them to President Butler. "I believe," he told him, "that the dissatisfaction is due principally to the feeling that some serious mistakes have been made in the selection of teachers in the past and that sufficient effort has not been made to perpetuate the kind of teaching and the standards of scholarship which distinguished the school at the time when Professor Keener was at its head."[11]

From Professor Anson D. Morse of Amherst came a suggestion that Stone was to take to heart. Stone had, Morse wrote, made the right decision, for "the country has greater need of the excellent work you will do as head of the Columbia Law School than the excellent work you would have continued to do as an active practitioner. . . . It seems to me," Morse continued, "that of the more important reforms that we wait for, few are needed so urgently as those which would modernize and rationalize the law itself, and both expedite and deepen its processes. And who can do more, or perhaps as much, to make justice sure and speedy and not a source of bankruptcy to those whose purses are not long, than the Dean of the Columbia Law School? He can kindle in the young the desire for better things. I know it will be uphill work; but that will not discourage you."[12]

Stone was already taking steps in this direction. On January 15 he sent a five-page letter to President Butler, outlining his plans for the coming year. Among the persons recommended for teaching assignments were two of Stone's law school classmates, Jackson E. Reynolds and Goldthwaite Dorr; both were robust personalities, both had been conspicuously successful in law school. If these additions to the faculty, along with certain other suggested changes, could be readily approved, Dean Stone assured the President that an attractive circular would be ready for the printer within a few weeks.[13] Two days later it appeared that the course in trusts was without an instructor. Though Stone had not contemplated doing any teaching until fall, he agreed to undertake it rather than allow the course to "go begging" for an instructor. This extra work necessitated employing additional assistance in his own office. "I hope that the compensation may be as liberal as the circumstances permit," he wrote Butler, "so that at least I shall not be out of pocket as a result of taking on extra work."[14] One thousand dollars was appropriated for the course.

The new dean had no complete blueprint, no brand-new ideas to present to the Trustees, but he did have standards.[15] The high requirements he set for himself, he was prepared to demand of others.

It was a fitting coincidence that in Stone's first year Kent Hall was dedicated. Though the Law School had to share these quarters with the Department of Political Science, the new building provided much-needed space for the growing school. Later he was plagued by its inadequacies, but for the time being it served as a symbol for his inauguration of the "era of legal scholarship."

For the first few years Stone was occupied with seemingly small matters. New elective courses were opened to second- and third-year men. Courses were added in English Legal History, Admiralty, Federal Jurisdiction, Patent Law, Law of Mining and Irrigation, Trial Evidence, Readings in the Digest of Justinian, Modern Civil Law, and History of European Law. These additions enriched the curriculum and gave students a better balanced selection of courses. The new course in Mining and Irrigation Law was calculated to attract students from the Far West. "It is important," he said, "both for the cause of legal education and for the school itself, that it should never be exclusively local in its character and influence."[16] The dean also recommended that the summer session be increased from six to eleven weeks, thus making it practically equivalent to corresponding courses in the regular session. Later he urged that summer session students receive the same recognition as night school students, which they did not under the rules relating to admission to the New York bar.[17]

In 1916 Stone crystallized the major objectives he had been working toward since his induction: "(1) More productive scholarship. (2) More *esprit de corps* on the part of the faculty, such as results from having a larger number of teachers here whose main interest in life is the promotion of the interests of the school and legal scholarship. (3) The organization of the school upon a more permanent basis so that there is less shifting about of courses and assignments of work."[18] Systematic efforts to achieve these goals marked the period 1910-16.

Scholarship came first; it was the core of Stone's theory of legal education. During the preceding century the common law had grown in mass and confusion to the point where, if it were to continue its historic function, it would have to be subjected to thorough analysis and clarification. The law schools had the talent, the library facilities, and the opportunity to do this. Besides, every law student, even if he never went near Blackstone again, ought to come into contact while in school with the deeper significance of the common law and should thus be instilled with the urge for creative scholarship. Stone was much opposed to establishing law schools merely to prepare for the bar examinations. The student should gain a knowledge of the historical roots of the law and understand the relationship between law and society, and see law, not as a conglomeration of confusing precedents, but as embodying fundamental principles established after long years of evolution.

Columbia had been among the first to provide a fourth year of study leading to the Master of Laws degree. In operation since 1895, it had been a failure. Even in 1910 it amounted to little more than taking left-over courses unnecessary for practice and not adaptable to work leading to a higher degree. Though Stone recommended the graduate degree of Juris Doctor as early as 1911, nothing was accomplished. In 1916 his recommendation was emphatic. "The great task of legal scholarship in this and the coming generation" was, he said, "the study of our law both historical and analytical, in comparison with other systems, for scientific purposes. This is pre-eminently the task of the University." Postgraduate courses should be offered beyond the three years required for the LL.B., and the degree of Juris Doctor authorized.* The research classes would not be large, but the influence on professional training would be highly beneficial. The effect would be to elevate preparation for the law above that of the trade school, to make law a profession rather than a guild. "The result which may be reasonably foreseen," he prophesied, "is a broadening and deepening of legal scholarship in the United States with the ultimate improvement of our law, both in its content and its administration."[19]

Though the Faculty of Law, the Faculty of Political Science, and the University Council jointly recommended the degree of Juris Doctor, the Trustees refused to endorse it. The next year war intervened and the proposal had to be shelved.

---

* In 1923, years after Stone first proposed establishment of the doctorate in law, the Trustees finally authorized it.

Stone believed that a by-product of the postgraduate program would be the stimulation of productive scholarship among members of the faculty. Four of them were actively engaged in outside practice; all were lecturing seven or eight hours a week, spending a tremendous amount of time grading examination papers, and under constant necessity of shifting courses to meet exceptional conditions. Stone himself was teaching six or seven hours a week in addition to his administrative duties. But he managed to publish some notable articles and addresses in his "spare" time, thus setting an example for his colleagues.

"In younger and more innocent days, with no premonition of the future," Justice Stone remarked jovially to the American Bar Association in 1928, "I took the time from busy days at the bar to write occasional articles in the law journals of scientific and technical interest, only to experience, in a repentant old age, the unhappy fate of hearing them, on occasion, cited to me in court in support of both sides of the same question."[20] Even before he went on the bench, lawyers and judges alike found authoritative support for their conclusions in his essays written exclusively for the *Columbia Law Review*. At various times his analyses were cited by the United States Supreme Court, several lower federal courts, and the appeals courts of at least eight states.[21] Bone-dry, humorless, and technical, these articles were so well received by law students, teachers, practitioners, and judges that eight of them were collected in 1922 and published under the title *Articles by Harlan Fiske Stone*.

The standards of scholarship he established were hard to meet. After six years of effort he was far from satisfied. "It is a fact," he reported, "that this school has not given the evidence of productive scholarship which a great school of law should give, and its performance in this respect falls short of the standards set by other schools."[22] But the publication record he built up for himself set no inflexible standard for others. Each teacher must use his own judgment in deciding whether to publish or not. "The printed page," he wrote, "is not the only measure of creative scholarship. To reckon the university's influence in terms of published volumes is as narrow and mechanized as to measure its success in terms of buildings and equipment or the number of its students."[23]

## THEORY VERSUS PRACTICE

The *esprit de corps* of the faculty could be improved, Stone thought, by maintaining a balance between the practical and the theoretical, between teaching abstract elements of law and the utilitarian aspects of procedure, legal forms, handling clients, and so on.

The scales might be tipped toward theory, since "the entire history of legal education teaches us that the law school is peculiarly the place for the student to become master of the principles of law from the scholarly and theoretical point of view." Scientific study of law would result both in better lawyers and greater concern for law reform. Though actual experience could come later, its importance must not be overlooked in the making of a teacher. In 1912 Stone delivered an address at the American Bar Association meeting on "The Importance of Actual Experience at the Bar as a Preparation for Law Teaching." "The man who would become a law teacher and who possesses the talent for stimulating intellectual activity in others will, as a teacher, possess greater power, exert a wider influence, and render a more useful service to his students and to his profession, if he has had experience in practice." If the young law graduate starts teaching immediately upon graduation without first-hand experience in actual practice, "there is always the danger that... he will lack the intellectual balance which should come from a practical knowledge of his profession, and he will inevitably be a stranger to its sentiments and traditions."[24]

Though law teachers should have experience at the bar, they should begin both a writing and teaching career early. In middle age mental habits tend to be fixed and inflexible. "I have often observed," he commented many years later, "that law teachers who fail to write early in their teaching experience seldom do worth-while writing."[25] Nor is success at the bar a "guaranty of success in the professor's chair, not because the incumbent has been in practice, but because he does not possess the gift. . . . The fact is," Stone explained, "that competent teachers of law are born, not made exclusively by training or environment. Of the thousands who prove themselves competent students or practitioners of the law only a few can be depended upon to become successful teachers of law."[26]

Stone liked to see young lawyers take up part-time instructing and then, if they were successful and liked it, move more and more into full-time teaching. The effect would be to discharge "the main business of the law school: sound theoretical training by competent instructors of practical experience." Ultimately the faculty would be staffed mostly with men giving "their whole time to the work of law teaching and to promoting the interests of the law school as an educational institution."[27]

Stone himself set the example. From 1910 to 1923 he taught the second-year course in Trusts and the third-year course in Mortgages. In 1911 he began giving the third-year course in Equity, making it peculiarly his own. From time to time he also taught Wills and Administration, Criminal Law, and Personal Property I. Yet throughout his years of teaching he maintained at least a nominal law practice. His informal professional relationship with Wilmer and Canfield proved to be both happy and profitable. Stone had become well acquainted with Canfield during his student days at Columbia. The two men became even better friends when they were associated in law practice and in teaching. A man of scholarly instincts, Canfield continued to teach and maintain an active practice until his death in 1931.

Wilmer, a Southerner, was for Stone "one of the most kindly and generous-hearted men I have known and, without qualification, the truest Christian." Though he was engaged in law practice most of his life and took an active part in all the controversies which arose in the profession, his first thought always seemed to be, "What course of conduct does the Christian faith require me to take?" Having settled that point, he pursued it to the end. Stone especially recalled Wilmer's devotion to younger people. "Young married people who were not getting on well together, others who had gotten into trouble through failure to observe the law or sound principles of conduct, were his special concern."[28]

Stone and his wife maintained friendly social relations with both Canfield and Wilmer, especially with the latter. Until his death in 1907, Wilmer often stopped in for dinner or spent an evening with the young couple.

In 1907, two years after Stone temporarily dropped teaching, the firm became Wilmer, Canfield and Stone. In the early days, indeed throughout, it was never predominantly a litigating firm. The greater part of its practice was that of solicitors—or what is sometimes called "practice in chambers." This was in line with Stone's conception of the lawyer's function. The chief value of legal counsel to the client, and to the economy, was, he believed, in guiding and aiding the client to conduct his affairs in such a way as to avoid possible pitfalls. Lawyers should not be merely a salvage crew to rescue as much as possible after a crash. The lawyer's job was rather to prevent litigation by helping the client to do his job properly. This meant dealing with the relatively unspectacular matters of banking, with the affairs of importing and exporting houses, with problems relating to letters of credit and other arrangements for lending and security, with technical and unique questions arising from the use of "trust receipts," with the ordinary run of "corporation law," with the preparation of wills and trusts and the settlement of estates. He was retained from time to time as counsel by other lawyers, sometimes for trial work or for advice regarding briefs or the argument of appeals, but more often for his opinions on difficult legal problems.

Stone's characteristically scholarly approach was demonstrated in his work on the law of "trust receipts." Frequently used by banks in connection with importations of merchandise, a trust receipt permitted the delivery of the merchandise to, and its use by, the importer without the recording of the lien or security title. In spite of general use in a somewhat narrow field, its place in the legal system and the principles of law governing it were not well understood. Stone's analysis led to a decision in his favor.[29] Opposing counsel, later an eminent and highly respected professor of law at the University of Virginia, was so interested in the legal theories involved and so completely convinced that the decision was wrong that he wrote a book in support of his theories. In 1922 one of Stone's younger partners, Karl T. Frederick, published an article that settled the law on this subject and upheld the position Stone had taken.[30]

In the early summer of 1909 Stone was asked by his friend Raynal Bolling, then general counsel for the United States Steel Corporation (and for whom Bolling Field near Washington was later named), to handle several cases for a subsidiary of the corporation. These involved the recovery of the purchase price for fabricated steel furnished for the building of a large part of the Queensboro Bridge in New York City. The amounts at stake were substantial, the defense resourceful, and the litigation protracted. Conscious that polish and maturity of approach were sometimes lacking in his trial work, Stone tried to give his argument and brief before the appellate courts a persuasive finish. The judges' compliments on his craftsmanship were gratifying. "No one can do a worse job than I when I am not well prepared," he commented, "but I believe I can do as good a job as anyone when I am thoroughly prepared."[31]

When Herbert L. Satterlee joined the firm at the beginning of 1913, it was thought that he would bring in lucrative J. P. Morgan and Company business. A son-in-law of the elder J. P. Morgan, Satterlee had great personal charm and enjoyed a wide circle of friends. But the idea that Satterlee, Canfield and Stone was about to become an important Wall Street firm, dealing largely with great financial affairs, did not materialize. Though Satterlee had been in practice for some years as a member of the small and respected firm of Ward, Hayden and Satterlee, he had never handled any substantial amount of business for J. P. Morgan and Company, nor was a small firm such as Satterlee, Canfield and Stone equipped to carry on the sort of financial practice which the popular mind associated with "Wall Street." Despite the hullabaloo raised over his Wall Street connections in 1925, Stone appeared in only one important case bearing the Morgan name. It was this litigation, however, that afforded him the only opportunity he had, before going to Washington as Attorney General, to argue a case before the Supreme Court of the

United States.* Stone, in later years, proudly referred to this triumph
as demonstrating the practical value of studying the roots of legal
doctrine.

Another appellate case that gave him special satisfaction was
*Alexander* v *Equitable Life Assurance Society*.[32] In 1888 James W.
Alexander and his wife, the plaintiff, entered into a written contract
with the Equitable (of which Alexander was then vice-president and
director, and later president) by which the defendant agreed to pay
to Mrs. Alexander an annuity during her life and after his death of
$18,000 a year. The consideration for this arrangement was stated to
be his past and future services rendered the corporation. Alexander
resigned all connection with the defendant company in 1905 and died
in 1915. There was no evidence of any such "past and future services." As counsel for the Equitable, Stone succeeded in convincing
the Court of Appeals that a sealed contract by an insurance company
to pay an annuity to a widow of an officer of the company in consideration of past and future services to be performed by such officer
was *ultra vires* and without consideration. The important effect was
to discourage the loose and unsound methods, formerly in common
use, for milking the treasuries of wealthy corporations.

In his methods of work as a lawyer, Stone was highly individualistic
and apparently rather disorganized. He possessed an unusually
active and retentive memory and relied on it heavily. His large desk
was always deeply covered with letters, legal papers, memoranda, and
similar material. No one else ventured to look for anything there, but
he was always able to recall instantly the appearance, whereabouts,
and contents of any desired document. Lack of organization in his
work was, however, much more apparent than real. He was quick
physically; his clear and perceptive mind was even quicker. He did
not flounder or indulge in reconsideration or amendment. His ideas
were clear before he began to put them on paper. He dictated to his
secretaries with clarity and with great speed—indeed, they were often
put to it to keep up with him. He was thus able, after teaching became
his chief activity, to keep up with the demands of a moderately active
practice. He would usually appear at his office in the middle of the
afternoon, and in an hour dictate enough to secretaries, working in
relays, to amount to a respectable day's work.

Stone's career as a practicing lawyer, free of other serious and
steady commitments, was comparatively brief. His private practice
was secondary and a considerable part of it quite unspectacular. As
a law clerk it covered about one year (1898-99); as a full-fledged
lawyer it extended over five years (1905-10), and another brief
period of about six months (1923-24). From 1898 to 1924 approxi-

* See Chapter XII, the Ownbey case.

mately nineteen and a half years were devoted to teaching. It is not surprising, therefore, that before he became a Supreme Court Justice his measure should derive mainly from his work as a teacher.

## TEACHER

Stone's absorbing interest in education reflected the high value he placed on the beneficial influence of the teaching profession. He took no stock in Bernard Shaw's much-quoted aphorism, "Those who can, do; those who can't, teach." Shaw overlooked the fact that "teachers are the big doers because they influence the whole course of human thought and action."[33] Christ and Socrates, Stone pointed out, were teachers.[34] "I am quite sure," he wrote several years after becoming a Supreme Court Justice, "that my work as a teacher* will be far more influential and lasting than anything I ever do as a judge."[35]

Stone's love of teaching had been heightened by Dean Keener's "powerful dialectic mind." In Stone's opinion, Keener was "one of the greatest of legal teachers."†[36] Both were dedicated to the Socratic method. Through a series of questions and answers Stone would indicate the direction of his thinking and let the student find the path for himself. Never satisfied until he had gone to the very heart of a legal problem, he would continue his questioning, kindly but firmly, until the student was made to see for himself the point the teacher was trying to bring out. Students who liked canned knowledge were never quite happy in his classes.[37] Stone's objective was to enlighten the mind, not to stuff it. "The end sought by the case method of instruction," he explained, "is not practice in dialectics or public speaking, but the leading of the entire class, step by step, through the intellectual processes by which the cases are analyzed and compared and their true legal significance developed. This is accomplished not by having every member, or indeed any large number of members, of the class participate orally in the discussion, but by insuring that every member of the class is a sharer in it

* This was not mere talk; it was considered judgment, repeated throughout the years. "The most interesting part of my life, and perhaps the most useful, was in my teaching days, when I was in daily association with young men working their way into the legal profession," he wrote O. R. Angelielo, April 2, 1937. And on Nov. 20, 1937, he wrote Thurman Arnold: "A little time spent in the governmental atmosphere goes a long way, and sometimes I recall my teaching days with nostalgic longing."

† Stone was not always so handsome in his praise of Dean Keener as a teacher: "His reliance on logic and complete acceptance of the conclusions which logic brought him made him intolerant of the views of others, and this intolerance showed itself in a rather lofty disdain of those views which, in the classroom, he carried almost to the point of brutality." (H. F. S. to Underhill Moore, Feb. 11, 1928.)

intellectually. This problem presents no difficulty to the competent instructor. With him every member of the class knows that he may be called on at any moment, at any stage of the discussion, to participate in it, to present his own views as critic or coadjutor of those who have already contributed to the discussion, and who may be called upon to resume it."[38]

Stone's conviction that education is merely an aid to intellectual self-help* ruled out the formal lecture. "As a leading method of imparting knowledge or stimulating thought," the lecture should "have become obsolete with the invention of the printing press."[39] In his classroom the give and take of discussion had three main objectives: (1) to ascertain the exact point decided by any given case; (2) to direct attention to the underlying reason on which the rule of law is based; (3) to determine whether the rule is what it ought to be.†

Many students, some now in high places, bear witness to his greatness as a teacher. "Those of us who were privileged to be students of Harlan Fiske Stone," Associate Justice William O. Douglas commented soon after his death, "will without exception, I believe, consider him as one of the very best, if not the best, law teachers we ever had." He was the conscientious students' teacher, concentrating on stimulating thought and discussion rather than on entertainment. "Wit and humor were not a part of his teaching techniques," Douglas wrote, "but his classes were never tedious or boring. His razorlike mind,

* Some years after he became a Supreme Court Justice, Stone took the trouble to spell this out to an Amherst undergraduate debater who sought his views on the constitutionality of government ownership and control of public utilities.

"I take this opportunity to express to you the disappointment I feel that any student in my old college, capable of participating in a college debate, should think that such casual information as could be given in a brief letter would be of any particular value in the conduct of such a debate. You must appreciate from your work as a student, that any information gathered in that manner would only be of the most superficial character, and that a debate based upon it would be equally superficial and worthless. Any debate, to command respect, must be grounded on intimate and diligent study of the question to be debated. Until such study is carried to the point where you have ideas of your own, of which you feel sure because you have studied and reflected upon them, you can have no confidence in what you say, and it will not command the confidence of others. You have in the college library a considerable volume of literature dealing with the whole problem of government ownership. Your librarian will aid you in gaining access to studies of the problem which give you data upon which it will be possible for you to form a judgment of your own. An idea which is really your own, because it is based upon study and reflection, will be more interesting and convincing than anything I could say which you would retail to your listeners merely because I have said it."

† A former student, John Vance Hewitt, has written: Perhaps at times a student left his classes with a degree of uncertainty and troubled by a desire for an exact and unchangeable answer to the legal problem. But this too was part of the method. It was rather in after life that the student fully appreciated the value of such training. (John Vance Hewitt to A.T.M., Sept. 19, 1955.)

his quick reply, his penetrating questions, were energizing influences."
Douglas sketched a clear picture of the teacher in action:

He always stood behind the desk and against the blackboard, twirling
his tortoise-shell glasses in his hand, his casebook usually closed and on the
desk before him. He did not often lecture. He used the Socratic method,
which he had developed to a high degree of perfection. His questions
seldom referred to cases, but to problems raised or suggested by them. It was
not easy to be prepared, for his questions in one session would sometimes
cover large areas of the course; and at times many hours would be spent
around one case, tracing its roots into early law and pursuing its modern
ramifications.

His technique of teaching was apt to be disconcerting to beginners.
He seldom stated what the law was or which of two competing principles
he favored. The positive statements would usually come from the students
whom he would ply with questions and whom he would pit one against
the other. Yet one soon learned from the inflections in his voice when the
scent was fresh, in what direction the answer was to be found, and when
the quest was over. But on occasion he would stop to summarize a segment
of the course. No analysis or exposition was ever more lucid; a jumble of
odds and ends would at his touch become a mosaic.

His emphasis in teaching was not primarily on the functioning of law
in modern society. His effort was to acquaint students with the techniques
of using legal tools, with the art of painstaking analysis, with the significance
of a rule's beginning to its present purpose, with the adaptability of law
in its evolution. The end product of a course was a synthesis of his own
creation—a putting together of relevant and at times seemingly irrelevant
currents of thought into a symmetrical and living system of law.

He instilled skepticism of absolutes, inquisitiveness as to the origins of
principles, respect for precision and intolerance for the lack of it, disrespect
of dogma, habits of close analysis, and belief in the sturdiness and vitality
and adaptability of law.[40]

It was, however, his capacity for friendliness quite as much as,
if not more than, his method and grasp of subject matter that was
the secret of his influence. A line from the Spanish novelist and
playwright Pérez Galdós gave one of Stone's most brilliant students
a clue to his power. "There is no possible teaching without blessed
friendship, which is the best conductor of ideas between man and
man."[41] At a time when he was doing three full-sized jobs—lawyer,
professor, and dean—he always had time for his students.* "No
personal problem was too small to discuss with him. He was never
too hurried to give a clue to the solution of some baffling problem

* In later years his law clerks also stressed the personal side: "From the standpoint of Stone's law clerks, the personal side of him is more memorable than the
judicial. He delighted in his contact with young men fresh from the Law School;
and they were the beneficiaries of his irrepressible desire to teach." (Alfred
McCormack, "Recollections of a Law Clerk," *Columbia Law Review*, Sept., 1946.)

of the law. He was never too harried to talk out a problem—to explore it to the edge and back, if necessary, to dispel doubt and confusion."[42]

Scores of grateful students wrote him through the years: to thank him for "the hours you were kind enough to spend with me and other members of the review";[43] to express "eternal gratitude" for his "magnanimous action when I did not know there was a time limit to examinations";[44] for "words of courage that strengthened the belief that what I was trying to do was wholly within the range of possibility," and for Mrs. Stone's magazine subscriptions that enabled "me to earn some of the money needed to keep me at the law school."[45] Sometimes gratification went beyond mere words. Frank W. De Friece, a self-styled hillbilly and son of a sharecropper, sent to the Secretary of the Columbia Alumni Fund a $500 Federal Coupon Bond as a mark of his appreciation of Stone's "friendly interest and generous act" in making it "possible for me to finish my law course in Columbia University."[46] On occasion Stone lent needy students money. Once, after having refused a request for a tuition loan of $180, he recalled the student and said: "I have discovered a dormant scholarship fund and I am going to let you have the $180 that you requested." Afterward, the student, now Justice Henry Clay Greenberg, learned that the dean had paid this money out of his own pocket. "I have no doubt," Justice Greenberg declared, "that my case was not unique."[47]

Another quality that endeared Stone to his students was his unfailing humor. One day in 1916 a group of law students, their last exam over, gathered outside Kent Hall. One of them, in a particularly carefree mood, exclaimed, "The last exam is finished, and now for noise and naked women." Exuberance was momentarily subdued when he felt a hand on his shoulder, and, turning around, saw it was the dean, who said, "Young man, with that motto, I predict you will go a long way in the law."[48] He has.

Stone considered this aspect of the teacher's task a greater contribution to the school than any other. Then, as later, his views ran counter to the dominant faculty opinion. He deplored the tendency on the part of some instructors to minimize the importance of "looking after students," and along with it the notion that one teacher was about as good as another, that a law school's duty was "performed if it has found someone to give the course." The unending debate among instructors on scholarship *versus* teaching was, in his mind, pointless. There was "not the slightest inconsistency between scholarship and thorough performance of the daily work of the law school. They actually go hand in hand." Yet, he told Butler, "in the present-day law school world . . . the opinion exists that thorough classroom work and a sense of personal obligation to students is a little beneath the dignity of a scholar." "There is nothing in it," Stone commented emphatically.[49]

Stone strongly believed that the teacher, especially the law teacher, could contribute toward easing the social tension of his time. He placed responsibility for the deterioration of the business conscience of the country squarely on the legal profession. Formerly bar associations had taken a lively interest in bar requirements and in legal education. Now their attention centered on the needs of business:

> I do not think it can be denied that there has been in the last twenty years a distinct and much to be regretted loss of the old-fashioned professional spirit which characterized the profession a generation ago. I sometimes wonder whether this may not be in some measure due to changes in the methods of legal education. When the young lawyer received his training in the office, he "grew into" the profession and acquired its sentiments and traditions by contact with older members of the bar, who were his teachers, guides, and mentors. Now he receives his professional training in a law school, a training which on the intellectual side is unquestionably superior to that of the law office, but it does not necessarily imbue him with the traditions and sentiments of the profession. I am confident that the law schools of the country are capable of dealing adequately with this situation, but it is a question in my mind whether they have done so up to the present time.[50]

The bar associations having failed in their responsibility for legal education, the Association of American Law Schools (of which Stone was president in 1919) was organized because, as he said, "the representatives of the leading law schools found it impossible to secure through the [American Bar Association] any adequate expression of their legitimate aspirations." The existence of two levels of legal education raised the old and difficult dilemma of higher standards *versus* democracy. If the bar was to be kept accessible to the rank and file, standards, it was said, could not be raised appreciably. Stone thought that such reasoning misinterpreted the true meaning of democracy. Though this country was founded upon the principle that all men are created equal, the American government is a republic. Special power is delegated to chosen representatives. These possess great power but at the same time carry great responsibility. This was Stone's ideal for the legal profession. If lawyers were to regain their position as community leaders, they must meet a rigorous test.[51]

"My own observation," he commented, "is that there is far greater danger to our profession and to this Republic by the reverence we do to the cult of incompetency masquerading in the guise of democracy than there will ever be by our adherence to the principle that even a democracy is entitled to have its functions performed by the competent and the well trained." There was something disingenuous in the thought that "the bar in the United States or elsewhere will become an undemocratic institution because of reasonably increased educational standards. . . ."[52] Democracy cannot survive without the guidance of a creative minority.

"True democracy," he maintained, "does not insist on the performance of every public function by every one of its members. Democracy is compatible with the division of labor based on fitness for the function to be performed, provided only that each function shall remain open to those who are fitted to perform it regardless of their social or economic status. . . . The remedy is to be found not in the abject surrender to the forces that are degrading the bar, but in a genuine effort to provide such educational facilities, both liberal and professional, as will keep the path open to the bar for the competent poor boy as well as the rich, and impose such educational requirements as will close it to the incompetent rich as well as the poor."[53]

"The profession of law," he warned, "because of its public and political character, must not be allowed to become the monopoly of any social or economic class." Stone, himself only once removed from the soil, believed that "our bar has traditionally been recruited" from youth of "slender financial resources."[54] Through the use of scholarships, it had become almost "a truism to those interested in liberal education that the man of good health, who is worth educating, can today give himself a college and professional education."[55]

Beginning in his first year as dean, Stone had urged the American Bar Association to bring pressure to raise the bar examination standards, to classify the law schools and to exercise "visitorial powers" over them. He often cited the success of the medical profession, after classifying medical schools, in raising from 6 per cent to 80 per cent the number of students attending high-grade professional schools. The experience in law, on the other hand, had been just the opposite. In the preceding fifteen years the number of students in low-grade schools had increased four times as much as those in high-grade schools. Entrance to the bar, he said, was "actually easier than it was a generation ago." There was, in his opinion, a direct relation between this fact and the declining influence of the bar. "Unless bar associations take a real interest in this movement," he admonished, "I do not see any solution of a problem which to me is a very real one and the most important one which the bar has to solve."[56]

When the Root Committee of the American Bar Association finally recommended the minimum of two years of college training and three years of law school, Stone was encouraged but not satisfied. For by this time the dean of Kent Hall had discovered that even a college degree is only "presumptive evidence" of a student's fitness for law school work. His annual report of 1922 noted that the colleges

fall far short of fitting one to do the intensive intellectual work necessary for the mastery of the intricacies of the law and for gaining some insight into its relations to our social structure. Too often the college graduate begins law study with mind undisciplined, with the critical faculty undeveloped, without the habit of logical thought, and with little or none of those powers of discrimination and analysis which should be the first fruits of a liberal education. Far too much time during the first year of law school is devoted to supplying these deficiencies.

How a subject was taught was more important than what was taught. Almost any liberal arts college offered an adequate program for training the educated man, if the material was studied under guidance and methods which excited intellectual curiosity and developed self-reliance. "Some of my colleagues," he observed as early as 1911, "think that courses in English history and in economics are essential. They are of course desirable, as they give to the student a good background for his law studies. My own feeling, however, is that those courses should be preferred which induce the student to do his own thinking. This you will understand is of course quite as much a matter of instructors as it is the subject matter of instruction."[57]

The lawyer's primary tool was his mind. It must be honed and sharpened by law school training. But if the lawyer was to discharge his responsibility to society more than brains was necessary. Stone called on the law schools to instill in the student a sense of responsibility to the profession and to society.* Rather than modify the law to fit changing conditions, he wanted enlightened lawyers to use the traditional principles of the common law to meet the new

* His views remained virtually unchanged after more than a decade on the Supreme Court. In answer to a request from Earl W. Crecraft for his opinion as to the most suitable program of study for pre-law students, he wrote, Oct. 20, 1938:

"Beginning law students need intellectual discipline and mathematics is one of the disciplines which often helps to satisfy this need. Of course, there are many other subjects which will fulfill, in varying measure, the same need. Often it is quite as much a matter of skill of the teacher as of subject matter. In my own college days I had the benefit of intellectual discipline of great value, largely because certain of my courses were given by skillful teachers who saw the importance of making the student think. In the hands of other teachers the same courses might have been much less effective.

"Then too, in addition to mere mental discipline, it is desirable that the man who is to study law should gain some understanding of the structure of the society in which we live, of the functions of courts and legislatures, and the methods which they use in order to resolve the clashing interests of the various elements in a complex society."

problems of the community. He summed up his theory of legal education thus:

To teach law as a science rather than as an instrumentality of a money-making trade; to teach it from its theoretical side by teachers experienced in practice; to encourage legal research and the production of legal literature and finally, to stimulate in the student knowledge of, and respect for, the professional obligations of the lawyer, are at once the high privilege and duty of the law schools of this country.[58]

He consistently reaffirmed the importance of this broader aspect of legal education. In 1930 John Bassett Moore wrote of a lecture he proposed to give on raising educational requirements for admission to the bar as a remedy for the evil practices so much in evidence. He proposed to say that those who discuss this subject are "too much disposed to leave out of account the capacity of persons with inadequate moral standards to acquire technical information and put it to improper uses; that we need to broaden the basis of our legal education, to incorporate in it more of legal philosophy and of legal history, to give more attention to foreign law and ancient law (especially Roman law) and legal ethics."[59]

Stone replied: "I thoroughly agree with you in what you say of legal education. I am taking the liberty of enclosing one or two excerpts from reports or addresses dealing with that aspect of the matter. What I said on this subject, both formally and informally, fell on deaf ears. My associates were then too much occupied in the search for some new educational discovery which would take the world by storm, to be interested in such old-fashioned notions."[60]

The lawyer, not the law itself, was the primary instrument for bringing about social justice. To achieve this was an uphill struggle. The bar, instead of becoming the conscience of business, had become more and more the mouthpiece of Mammon.* What was the remedy for a situation in which the bar had become virtually an adjunct of business? Must the law be transformed from an effective technical science into an elastic social science?

* This theme, discussed by Stone in "Bar Associations and the Development of Our Legal Institutions" (delivered before the New Jersey State Bar Association, Feb. 26, 1921), was not new. Two years earlier he had written: "As was perhaps inevitable the march of economic events has substituted for the leadership of the advocate and the legal scholar the leadership of the business lawyer and specialist. At his best he is the skillful, resourceful solicitor, and at his worst a mere hired man of corporations. Such leadership undoubtedly requires a training and intellectual power of the first order and at its best it is no less honorable than that of the great jurist or the barrister, but it has tended to give to the practice of law more and more the characteristics of business rather than of a learned profession and has contributed not a little to the decline of professional standards and the corporate spirit and activity of the bar which began some two generations ago." ("The Lawyer and His Neighbors," *Cornell Law Quarterly*, June 1919, p. 182.)

In his annual report of 1921 Stone wrote that "too long have we studied and taught law as though its problems were like the problems involving mathematical formulae." But instead of broadening study to include economics and sociology, he urged that more should be done "to humanize law study, to stimulate interest in a more intimate knowledge of its relation to the great events in history, of its great personalities, the part they have played in its development, and of the human figures who as lawyers and judges and teachers and writers have influenced its progress and reform. . . . We will do well to remember," he cautioned, "that our law schools cannot become schools of economics and sociology and maintain their present position; that excessive nicety in terminology tends to degenerate into logomachy, and that the over-refinement of law itself tends to defeat its end as an agency of social order by the very restrictions it sets on its generality and certainty. To make the work of our school progressive and enlightened without loss of a due sense of proportion and at the same time to preserve unimpaired our sense of the practical aim of law as an agency for administering justice and securing social order, must in this as in every case be the guiding principle in determining all questions of Law School policy."[61]

Blind adherence to the *status quo*, not conservatism, was the evil to be overcome. It was not surprising "that teachers of law, as well as practicing lawyers . . . should have become so absorbed in the study and exposition of its technique as to have lost sight of its social function, and to regard it as a body of learning quite distinct from those social forces which created it, much as the scientist regards the body of natural law which he investigates as something distinct and apart from social organization and development."[62] Balance should be struck between veneration for the old and agitation for the new:

The lawyer's habit of caution which so often protects his client from the consequences of rash action is a real conservative force in the community which should not be lightly valued. But the conservative mind is subject to two great dangers—the danger of intolerance and the danger of its becoming a "closed mind." I would not be understood as regarding intolerance as exclusively a vice of conservative minds. It is a fault of the radical as well, and I find almost as much intolerance among those who pride themselves on their liberal opinion as among the conservatives who are impatient and distrustful of the innovator. . . . I would not have lawyers any less conservative in their judgments; I would not have them hold any less reverence for the past or any less confidence in the capacity of the common law to adjust itself to new conditions. But I would have them approach these new problems with open and inquiring minds.[63]

Stone conceded the necessity of bringing "to bear on the actual exposition and judicial declaration of technical legal doctrine a well-grounded knowledge of the social and economic phenomena of our times." He was not sure, however, at what point the knowledge of social sciences might best be injected into legal training.[64] Of one thing Stone had no doubt—knowledge of the social sciences would be of little or no value unless students left the law schools with trained minds and great souls. The goal of social improvement must be reached through better men. The law was a negative or at best a neutral force in social advance. It could not take the place of "social morality." The failure of prohibition graphically illustrated that abstinence could not be legislated; it could only come about if the people honestly wanted it. Laws lacking the sanction of public morality were not only a nuisance, they blocked the road to improvement.*

The year 1923 marked the one hundredth anniversary of Chancellor James Kent's appointment as Professor of Law at Columbia.[65] Secretary of State Charles Evans Hughes, among others, delivered a "notable oration" on Chancellor Kent.[66] Stone used the occasion to reiterate his own objectives. On the "era of legal scholarship," he commented:

In carrying out this purpose, it has looked beyond mere preparation for bar examinations. It has had in mind the kind of lawyers its students are to be long after their bar examinations have been passed and they are well on in their professional careers. Its aim has been to make its graduates distinguished as men of intellectual breadth and depth as well as for their technical knowledge of law, and it has had faith that the way to accomplish this is to teach and study law as a science, applying to the process all the resources of scholarship. . . .

If I were to attempt to describe the school in a single sentence I would speak of it as a place where a limited number of selected students may receive the intellectual and moral inspiration and training which come from intimate contact of students with a group of gifted teachers and scholars, engaged in the common enterprise of study and investigation of our system of law.[67]

A gap yawned between the sort of society Stone ardently desired and the contemporary community in which men were living. Yet he had a clear vision of the perfect or near-perfect society and how it could be achieved. His utopia would be won only by revival of the

* "Our faith in legislation as the universal panacea for all the irregularities in human conduct," Stone emphasized, "tends constantly to carry legislation across the boundaries of that considerable area of human conduct which lies outside the province of positive law because it can only be suitably regulated and controlled by the conscience of the individual or the moral sanctions of public opinion." (H. F. S., "Obedience to Law and Social Change," *New Hampshire Bar Association Proceedings* [New Series], Vol. V, No. 3, 1925.)

latent decency in man. The institution for effecting this moral rebirth was the school. "The hope and safeguard of democracy is education," he proclaimed, "not that so-called education which would popularize learning at the cost of a sacrifice of standards, nor education in the narrow and technical sense, but the education which enlightens the masses as to the right relationship of the individual to the organization of society and inculcates a sense of individual responsibility for the preservation of that relationship on a sound basis of which law is only the outgrowth. In that type of education it is not only proper but necessary that our profession should exercise a guiding influence."[68]

CHAPTER SEVEN

# In Defense of Individual Freedom

## 1917-1920

When America entered World War I, Stone at once saw that it was "a war of nations, not merely a war between the military forces of nations. Until its conclusion," he wrote, "it will bring to bear ever-increasing stress on all the economic, moral, and intellectual forces of our national life."[1]

Stone was an interventionist. From the war's outbreak in 1914 he had been impatient with Wilson's "wait and see" policy. An ardent Anglophile, he never doubted that Germany was this country's real enemy. Shortly before war was declared he wrote an old friend: "I had thought for a time that we were going to get into the row, but I am losing hope. Germany will certainly be contented if she can sink our vessels without our doing anything about it, and apparently this country will be contented too."[2] As early as 1915 he had predicted the war would be a long one, but thought it "inevitable that Germany will be forced to seek terms of peace in the end."[3]

After 1917 he disliked doing "things which seem so relatively unimportant," while others gave their services. In the fall of that year he hoped that "another spring will see me in France in some capacity," though he doubted whether he was "fit for military service."[4] By September 1918, however, he did not know any valid reason why he "should not shoulder a musket and go with the rest if I pass the physical examination."[5] He felt "useless and helpless." "Apparently about all there is to do for an old duffer like me is to mind my own business and pay my taxes, if possible," he wrote despondently.[6]

Meanwhile Dean Stone felt uneasy lest standards of education "established through generations of painstaking effort" be seriously impaired. The Law School lost one-third of its students in 1917. The following year he anticipated a 50 per cent reduction in registration with a consequent loss of $45,000 in revenue from tuition alone. The first effect would be "the abandonment for the present of well-matured plans for the expansion of the school by additions to its faculty, which are of the first importance if it is to maintain its position as one of the leading law schools in the country." But "it has been and will be," he commented, "the settled policy of the School of Law to do its work as far as possible without interruption and to maintain without impairment its educational standard." The faculty, he said, "held steadfastly to the opinion that the maintenance of the educational work of the school was even more of a duty in time of war than in time of peace."[7]

The arrival of the military on the campus in 1918 roused mixed feelings. It was welcome financially, but Stone was quick to assess its deteriorating effects on standards. "The draft and the demands of the S.A.T.C. [Students Army Training Corps]," the harassed dean wrote his brother Winthrop in the fall of 1918, "are practically putting our Law School out of business."[8] Yet he felt obliged to stay on.

It seems to be definitely decided that I am to put in another year at Columbia. The authorities there feel that I am much needed there in order to keep things from disintegrating too much during the disturbing war conditions. My emotions over the matter are conflicting. It would certainly hurt me terribly to see the educational work of the school going to pieces so that it would not be in good position to build up when the war is over. It may seem egotistical for me to say it, but I think the fact is, the outcome is more dependent on me than anyone else. On the other hand, it makes me sad not to be having a more active part in this gigantic conflict. I am hoping to get something to do during the summer months which will be of service.[9]

In May 1918 Washington beckoned. The War Trade Board wanted him for a high post. Torn between a sense of patriotic duty and his obligations to Columbia, he decided to accept only government work that would not interfere greatly with his duties as dean. "If I were satisfied that I could do more good there than here," he wrote his brother Winthrop, "I would be inclined to do it, but I am not satisfied and I have a horror of getting into the game of drawing and filing documents, which seems to be overwhelming in Washington."[10]

In the late spring of 1918 an opportunity came to do war work without cutting all ties with the school. On June 1 he, along with Major Richard C. Stoddard* (chairman) and Federal Judge Julian W. Mack, were appointed to a special Board of Inquiry to breathe life into a liberalized policy toward the conscientious objector caught in the toils of Selective Service.

The Selective Service Act excluded from the draft "one who is found to be a member of any well-recognized religious sect or organization at present organized and existing and whose existing creed or principles forbid its members to participate in war in any form."[11] Omission of the non-religious category from those exempted by the Act made it necessary for the Adjutant General to issue instructions declaring that "'personal scruples against war' should be considered as constituting 'conscientious objections' and such persons should be treated in the same manner as other 'conscientious objectors.' "[12] The Act provided, however, that no person so favored "shall be exempted from service in any capacity," and by executive order, March 23, 1918, President Wilson designated several branches of war service as "noncombatant."

The special consideration thus accorded "conshies," popularly regarded as slackers, met with prompt and outspoken disapproval.† The *New York Times* reasoned that "a citizen's first duty" was to respond to the call of his country for military service, and this should not be shirked by the conscientious objector because the burden is thus made "heavier for his neighbor." "We should not ask about the sincerity of such a man," the *Times* commented summarily. "If he puts his belief into practice, we should either put him to death or shut him up in an asylum as a madman."[13] This small anti-war contingent, necessitating attention and supervision grossly disproportionate to any potential worth in the war effort, was a thorn in the side of the military. To save time and trouble, Army authorities and local draft boards defined exceptions to the Selective Service Act narrowly. The phrase "well-recognized religious sect" was given the most rigorous interpretation, and any who based conscientious objections on political rather than religious foundations got short shrift. Such objectors were either "shot to death by musketry," "imprisoned for long terms by court martial," or subjected to indignities and physical violence "by their more patriotic fellows."[14]

* Stoddard served until August 1918, when he was replaced by Major Walter G. Kellogg, also a lawyer in civilian life.

† Secretary Baker reflected the pressure of hostile public opinion in writing President Wilson, March 21, 1918: "We are now doing absolutely all that public opinion will stand in the interest of conscientious objectors and others whose views do not happen to coincide with those of the vast majority of their fellow countrymen." (*New York Times*, March 22, 1919.)

Neither the Articles of War, the draft law, nor congressional action, had provided for the Board of Inquiry. It was a presidential agency, and its job, as defined by the executive order creating it, was "to discover and weigh and measure the secret motives which actuated the objector to resist authority." The military had proved itself altogether unequal to the task.* If lawyers were to do better, they had to enter delicate and unfamiliar areas. "Really to know sincerity from insincerity requires what is meant by 'a searching of hearts,'" the *New York Times* editorialized on the Board of Inquiry's work, "a task recognized as beyond human ability."[15]

Nevertheless President Wilson's soul-searching inquisitors, all lawyers, fared forth without apparent misgivings. From June 1918 until the Armistice, they traveled constantly, visiting and revisiting army camps on both coasts and throughout the interior, listening to the often weird stories of drafted men who claimed to have religious or political scruples against fighting. Over a period of approximately six months, hearings were granted 2294 objectors, and of this number all but a few accepted noncombatant duty or farm furloughs. Looking back on this experience in 1944, Chief Justice Stone considered the effort "highly successful and that the whole problem was handled rather more skillfully than . . . in this war."[16]

Besides well-recognized religious sects, such as Quakers, there were others, some with ancient beginnings, with whom military discipline and the appeal of reason were equally ineffective. A negligible fringe in terms of the war effort, each member of this group was "supremely interested in the salvation of his own soul even though the world perish." To Stone these eccentrics presented "a depressing example of dense ignorance of what was going on in the world, and stolid indifference to those moral and political questions which were so profoundly stirring the minds and hearts of their fellow countrymen." But, he observed emphatically, they were neither "physical nor moral cowards."[17]

The Government faced hard alternatives: either inflict the extreme military penalty or devise ways of getting objectors out of military service. For Stone, the latter solution was so patently sound that the disposal of religious objectors could be swift and simple.

But the political, or non-religious, objectors could not be so easily handled, one reason being that they were interviewed as individuals, not in groups, as was the case with religious recalcitrants. Ernest L. Meyer, a non-religious objector who came under Stone's scrutiny,

---

* Under the Adjutant General's order of April 27, 1918, a camp commander might direct that conscientious objectors be tried by court martial, or he could credit the objector's sincerity and issue a noncombatant certificate. Those to whom no such certificate had been issued, and who were not to be brought to trial by court martial, fell within the purview of the Board of Inquiry.

wrote of this experience in his war diary.* Stone fired questions
"with the precision of hammerblows":

STONE: You are a member of no church?
OBJECTOR: No, sir.
STONE: Socialist?
OBJECTOR: I share many of their beliefs, but I am not a member of the
party.
STONE: What would you do if you were attacked, or a burglar entered
your house and tried to rape your wife or mother?
OBJECTOR: Resist him. Try to save my wife.
STONE: Then how can you maintain your position in opposition to war?
You sanction the use of force.
OBJECTOR: I see no analogy whatever in your comparison. I can't concede
that this is a defensive war. . . . You imply . . . one side is an innocent wife
or mother and the other side a fiend. I can't admit this. . . . I am dealing
with one individual. But in war we are dealing with nations. . . . America,
as the outstanding neutral, could have exerted enough pressure to bring
about peace without resorting to arms. . . .
STONE: Other means have been tried. They failed. . . .
OBJECTOR: They were not tried with the same vigor, the same sacrifice,
that we have mobilized in the war.
STONE: Your country made the choice. It is up to you to abide by it.[18]

Stone entertained a profound repugnance toward the refractory few
who refused to fight because "the war was the natural fruit of our
capitalist system." When these "glib talkers" confronted him he applied the law rigorously: "The uniform ruling of the board was that
the objector whose objection was directed exclusively toward this
war or the capitalistic war must nevertheless fight the battles of his
country."

In the mid-1930s after the Nye Committee disclosures of the munitions industry's fabulous war profits,[19] Fred Briehl, a political objector
who had been interviewed by Stone at Camp Riley, continued the
debate Meyer began in 1918. Writing Stone, now an Associate Justice,
March 2, 1936, the objector argued at great length to prove "I was
originally right, and you to the same extent were wrong. . . . If you
were wrong, then your 'sincerity' and not mine, should have been
questioned." Two days later the Justice calmly replied:

I think you misinterpret the action of the Commission [Board of Inquiry].
. . . The judgment . . . was not that you were insincere, but that your

* "Dean Stone was rubicund, smoothshaven, cheerful," Meyer is reported to
have said on one occasion, "a jovial good fellow in any other atmosphere, I
thought. And keen! Startling questions (easily uttered because of frequent itera-
tions, I believed) popped with disconcerting rapidity out of his mouth—several
times leaving me gasping weakly like a fish and chasing my poor brains in a jog
trot down a dusty, cloudy track." (Quoted in Norman Thomas, *The Conscientious
Objector in America* [New York: 1923], p. 114.)

objections were not of the character which we were authorized to deal with by President Wilson's order. We were authorized only to extend certain privileges to those men in the service who had conscientious objections to all war. I do not think I doubted then, nor do I doubt now, that you were sincere in your objection to the war in which we were then engaged.

I think I had few, if any, illusions about the war then, and so I am less disillusioned about it now than most people. Perhaps the only important way in which I differ from you and some others who refused to take part in the war is that I believe that inasmuch as I must live in and be a part of organized society, the majority must rule, and that consequently I must obey some laws of which I do not approve, and even participate in a war which I may think ill advised. I respect the views and opinions of those whose objections to all war, or to a particular war, are so great as to forbid their participation, but it has always seemed to me that those who take that extreme position should accept the consequences without complaint, just as arctic explorers should accept without complaint the severe cold of the arctic region. Organized society is as much a reality as ice and snow in the arctic. It must function by majorities. It contemplates that minorities who are against all war or a particular war may vote and speak against it, but it cannot admit of the right of minorities to resist it, and remain organized society. . . .

I respect your position. I do not presume to say that it will not ultimately be proved to be right, but it will probably be yet a long time before the world will accept that view, and in the meantime those who hold it must pay the price of martyrdom.*

Summing up the work of the board many years later, Stone observed:

The religious objectors definitely identified with a sect for which pacifism or non-resistance is an article of faith, did not present many difficulties. The cases of political objectors or those who, upon purely ethical grounds, felt that the state had no right to exact military service, were much more serious. In such cases we had no formal rules of procedure or standards for determining whether the objector was sincere. We usually allowed him to tell his story, asked him rather searching questions as to his background and experience, and as to the basis of his objections. In most cases we felt that objectors of this type were sincere, and when sincere they had as sound moral basis for their attitude as those who based their objections on religious dogmas.

Our real difficulties arose from the fact that we could relieve a drafted man from the duties of his enlistment only by recommending him for non-combatant service or for service on a farm, as prescribed by the President's order. Sometimes the objectors refused this method of escape. They were

* Justice Stone's reply did not satisfy Briehl who, on March 20, 1936, rebutted the Justice point by point. Meanwhile, Briehl published his first letter. This was too much. A polite letter from the Justice's secretary, March 23, 1936, terminated the "debate" for "reasons which you will readily appreciate."

court-martialed and in most cases sentenced to long terms of imprisonment in an army prison, usually Fort Leavenworth. Most of these men, but not a large number in all, were ultimately pardoned or their sentences commuted by presidential order after the Armistice. A surprisingly large number of objectors were persuaded, after talks with the board, to accept service. Among these was Sergeant York, who was a religious objector, but finally went to the front and became one of the heroes of the war.[20]

By late fall of 1918 the board had caught up with the examination of objectors at the army cantonments. Secretary of War Newton D. Baker, seeking advice, sent Stone all the records of conscientious objectors who had been court-martialed, either prior to or in contravention of the President's executive order of March 23. In his memorandum of December 8, 1918, Baker informed the Chief of Staff that "Judge Mack and Dean Stone would continue the inquiry . . . seeing all records of court martial in these cases . . . and . . . have access to all persons in this class whom they may elect to see in order that their work may be comprehensive, and that I may have a complete survey of the entire case."

This new assignment took Stone to Fort Leavenworth Disciplinary Barracks, where he spent three days of the New Year's vacation, "working sixteen hours a day." He and Judge Mack interviewed 350 objectors and submitted a preliminary report recommending that about 150 of these men receive clemency without delay.

On hearing of this last phase of the dean's war work, Columbia University's President Butler became much interested in the outcome. The educator confessed that "no one has less sympathy with these morally half-witted people than I have," but he wanted to be kept posted. On January 15, 1919, Stone submitted a report calculated to give the educator pause. He told of many cases in which it appeared that "the objectors, sometimes through misinterpretation of the orders of the President and the Secretary of War and sometimes through excess of zeal, had been improperly placed on trial by the military authorities." In all such cases he had recommended "immediate clemency, if the Board of Inquiry, after examination of the prisoners, found them to be conscientious in their objections."

"We have prepared a second report," Stone told Butler, "recommending most of the others for clemency in a reasonable time and certainly as soon as peace is declared."

### THE GRANITE MARKER
#### BETWEEN LIBERTY AND AUTHORITY

Stone's experience as a member of the Board of Inquiry convinced him that no single phase of the war had presented "so many questions

affecting the citizenship of our country requiring intelligent study."
A year after the Armistice he elaborated his own thoughts in a seminal
article, published in the *Columbia University Quarterly.*

Unlike President Butler, he did not consider conscientious objectors
as "cowards," "slackers," or "half-wits." Certain objectors had, he said,
adhered to their principles under circumstances where "the normal
man . . . might well have chosen active duty at the front as the
easier lot." Some men had, it is true, taken refuge among thorough-
going pacifists. He repudiated as fantastic the notion that the objector
was a modern saint. "At most," Stone observed, "he will be found
to fall into certain well-defined groups; not all of them will prove
to be saints, and relatively few of them will merit the extreme rigors
of military punishment at the hands of a wise and humane government." It seemed to him that, generally, they followed the god of
things as they ought to be while their brothers obeyed the god of
things as they are.

"When one realizes," he observed perceptively, "the seriousness of
their purpose and the power of their influence over the ignorant and
discontented, he can have no illusion that the mere application of
force to them or the forcible suppression of their incendiary utterances will bring any real solution of the problem which they create."
"All human experience teaches us that a moral issue cannot be suppressed or settled by making its supporters martyrs."

The challenge of the conscientious objectors is as ancient as society
itself. But the problem confronting Stone went far deeper: it involved
coercion of an unoffending citizen rather than the power of government to restrain the commission of unlawful acts. For him there
was a radical difference "between compelling a citizen to refrain
from acts which he regards as moral but which the majority of his
fellow citizens and the law regard as immoral or unwholesome to the
life of the state . . . and compelling him . . . to do affirmative acts
which he regards as unconscientious and immoral." The action of
government in the first situation "does not in most instances which
are likely to occur do violence to . . . conscience"; but, he concluded
emphatically, "conscience is violated if [the citizen] is coerced into
doing an act which is opposed to his deepest convictions of right
and wrong. . . . However vigorous the State may be in repressing
the commission of acts which are regarded as injurious to the State,
it may well stay its hand before it compels the commission of acts
which violate the conscience."*

In erecting this granite marker on the frontier between liberty
and authority, Stone grasped instinctively the generative power latent

---

* The idea embodied in this passage became the core of Mr. Justice Stone's
dissenting opinion in *Minersville School District* v. *Gobitis,* 310 U.S. 586 (1940).

in the free individual. Men are not mere ciphers arranged in a beneficent utilitarian equation. Human motivation comes from within.
National unity and power could not be attained by outraging the
conscience of individuals. He knew that American citizens would not
accept forced values as their own; that the vital spirit of unity is
largely lost through coercion; that such an imitation of national coherence must dissolve whenever crisis disturbs the social order.

"The ultimate test," Stone said, "of the course of action which
the State should adopt will of course be the test of its own self-
preservation." But he warned: "It may well be questioned whether
the State which preserves its life by a settled policy of violation of
the conscience of the individual will not in fact ultimately lose it
by the process. At least," he went on, "in those countries where the
political theory obtains that the ultimate end of the State is the
highest good of its citizens," society should act with extreme caution
in compelling conformity at the price of conscience.

"All our history gives confirmation to the view that liberty of conscience has a moral and social value which makes it worthy of
preservation at the hands of the State. So deep in its significance and
vital, indeed, is it to the integrity of man's moral and spiritual nature
that nothing short of the self-preservation of the State should warrant
its violation. . . . Every ethical and practical consideration . . . should
lead the State . . . to avoid the violation of the conscience of its
citizens."

Government must, however, be constantly on the alert to conditions
and forces that endanger national unity. The record of conscientious
objection in World War I furnished many lessons, particularly "for
those charged with the responsibility for public education and for
the dissemination of information on questions of public interest." As
for religious objectors, "many," Stone said, "were plainly fanatics, with
abnormal mental experiences, requiring the attention of the physician
or the psychiatrist." For these he held out slim hope: "Born under
different conditions and in different environment, and enlightened
by education, they would have been loyal citizens, the first to offer
their services to their country." Obviously it was futile in young
manhood to begin inculcating a sense of the reciprocal rights and
duties of citizenship.

Stone was hardly more sanguine as to the small knot of political
or non-religious war-resisters. "One can but wonder," he observed
soberly, "what forces are at work in our social and educational life
to produce the ill-balanced and distorted intellectual processes by
which these young men, in many respects intelligent, had worked
out their social philosophy. Neither family life, nor education, nor

contact with the world had given them the kind of intellectual
discipline and self-control on which all social cooperation must be
founded." Careful study convinced him that these young men were
the "natural products, if not the victims, of an educational system
which too often encourages dabbling in the social sciences and in the
problems of contemporary civilization without laying any adequate
foundation in historical study and without insisting on rigorous
method in the verification of data and in subjecting them to analysis.
Education had taught these men to read and to talk; it had stirred
their emotions and given them information and opinions on almost
every conceivable subject; but neither it nor the hard knocks of
experience, which were lacking in their lives, had ever forced them
to weigh evidence or to reach conclusions by the processes of
thought."

The very fierceness with which Dean Stone struck out at the alleged
progenitors of "false" social theories seems to warrant the inference
that in education, at least, he knew right from wrong. In his report
of 1917 to President Butler he had declared with well-nigh apoca-
lyptic assurance:

> I observe generally that the average college student of today has a radical
> tendency due, in part, no doubt, to the trend in that direction of our political
> thinking. This is a wholesome condition when it is based on accurate
> information and sound thinking, but I cannot avoid the conclusion that
> this tendency has been unduly encouraged by the fact that our colleges
> have attracted to their faculties a considerable number of loose-thinking
> sentimentalists who seem to be much more impressed with the dramatic
> quality of their utterances than influenced by the desire to arrive at the
> truth. In fact, I believe the most immediate problem of our educational
> institutions is to devise some method of attracting to their faculties a greater
> number of men of brains and balance.[21]

Seeking correctives for this "radical tendency," certain of his contemporaries had turned instinctively to force. Theodore Roosevelt
had suggested, among other things, that anyone who refused all
service should be "permanently sent out of the country as soon as
possible."[22] The sovereign head of Columbia University had commanded his academic vassals to maintain unalloyed patriotism. "So
long as the national policies were in debate," President Butler told
faculty members, "we gave complete freedom. . . . So soon, however,
as the nation spoke by the Congress and by the President declaring
it would volunteer as one man for the protection and defense of civil
liberty and self-government, conditions sharply changed. What had
been tolerated before became intolerable now. What had been wrong-
headedness was now sedition. What had been folly was now treason.

The separation of any such person from Columbia University will be as speedy as the discovery of his offense. This is the University's last and only word of warning. . . ."[23]

Dean Stone was as much disturbed by all such tyrannical outbursts as by the "loose-thinking sentimentalists" against whom they were directed. And when, in due course, Butler began to act on his warning of speedy separation, Stone demurred. He did more than that—and presumably in President Butler's presence. At the opening exercises of the University, September 1918, he made a full-dress plea for academic freedom.

Stone felt that in becoming a university professor one did not "forfeit his rights as a citizen or as a social being." The teacher, like others, must take his stand, and when he does, he should feel no restraint from academic hierarchy. "He must be and remain free, free to form and hold his opinions and free to express them without incurring the risk of loss of the privileges and emoluments of his position. Restraints upon the intellectual freedom of the university teacher, whatever their form and however plausible their justification, will inevitably impair confidence in its teaching and ultimately undermine and destroy its influence." Stone then undertook to draw that wavering line which separates the teacher from the propagandist.

"A freedom from control or restraint so untrammeled carries with it responsibilities, which, if not self-imposed, should be imposed by the force of enlightened university opinion." The instructor, Stone explained, "gains the ear of the public because he wears its mantle; and so long as he wears it a sense of loyalty and propriety will cause him to refrain from word or act which will make his university the subject of unseemly controversy or lower the respect to which it is entitled as a public institution charged with important duties and responsibilities."

He held "that the university professor should voluntarily renounce the role of propagandist and agitator. The university stands for scientific truth. Its attitude, if it would preserve its influence, must never be that of the partisan, but rather that of the judicially minded. The university professor, in acting the part of the agitator, inevitably subjects the university as well as himself to attack in a controversy in which it can with propriety take no part and to which it is powerless to offer a defense. In other words, the university professor, like the cleric and the judge, must give up some freedom of action because of his position—a restriction which is not imposed by law, or any formal rule or requirement, but which will be induced by a clear perception of the ethical obligations of his position, and controlled by both a sound common sense and a delicate sense of propriety."[24]

This statement raises some difficult questions. Freedom is restricted by "the force of enlightened university opinion." What if university opinion is not enlightened? Faculty members' sense of "ethical obligations" may vary greatly. Is "truth" or "propriety" the guiding rule? Who, in any case, is to decide when the limits of freedom are transcended?

The difficulties involved in applying Stone's principles were illustrated when J. McKeen Cattell became a victim of President Butler's crusade to make the University safe for democracy. On May 21, 1913, Stone had passed along to John Bassett Moore word of how "the University is seething over the proposed enforced retirement of Cattell (aged fifty-three) on a small pension. If the Trustees adhere to the announced purpose, I think there will be some interesting developments." In 1917, after twenty-six years of service, Cattell was fired because he had, among other things, written several congressmen on departmental stationery supporting measures to prevent sending conscripts to fight in Europe against their will. Despite the fact that Cattell had spent the week before his dismissal drawing War Department plans for the scientific selection of aviators, the Trustees unanimously found that he and a pacifist colleague, Henry W. L. Dana, had done grave injury to the university by their public agitation against the conduct of the war.*

Cattell brought a libel suit against President Butler and the Trustees for $115,000 and asked Dean Stone if he would give him advice on the legal questions involved. "It would not only be common decency but common sense," Cattell wrote, "for the Trustees to pay the pension due me. . . . Otherwise . . . a law suit will bring out facts concerning the President, the Trustees, and the University which will not be of service to them. I venture to consult you . . . in the hope that you may be willing to take steps that will result in a settlement without undesirable publicity."

Invoking considerations of propriety, Stone refused to be drawn openly into the controversy: "I think it quite important that you should have good legal advice. My relations to the University, however, are

---

* In the case of Cattell, however, Butler acknowledged an ancient vendetta: "For a number of years it has been the strongly held opinion of the Trustees that the interests of the University required the dismissal of Professor Cattell from its service." (Nicholas Murray Butler to the Special Committee of Trustees, Sept. 28, 1917.)

After investigation, the American Association of University Professors condemned President Butler and the Columbia University Trustees, saying: "It is a grave abuse of the power of dismissal, when administrative officers or governing boards attempt by their official declarations publicly to attach the stigma of treasonable or seditious conduct to an individual teacher because of acts of his which are in fact neither treasonable nor seditious." ("Report of Committee on Academic Freedom in Wartime," *Bulletin of the American Association of University Professors,* Feb.-March, 1918, pp. 45-46.)

such that there would, I think, be a lack of propriety in my undertaking to advise or act for you professionally. It seems to me, therefore, desirable from every point of view that you should consult someone who has no connection professionally or otherwise with the University."[25] Stone did not, however, stay out of the case. On the contrary, it was he who was instrumental in the settlement of Cattell's claims out of court. "Following the meeting of the Trustees yesterday," President Butler wrote Dean Stone, February 7, 1922, "at which Mr. Pine and Mr. Milburn made most complimentary statements as to your helpful mediation in the matter of Cattell, several Trustees asked me to write you on their behalf and to express their appreciation of your helpfulness in the matter."

"As you doubtless know," Stone replied on the 10th, "what I did was done at the request of several Trustees and in the hope that I might be of some service to the University."

The pressures of war-bred hysteria mounted. On January 7, 1920, the New York State Assembly suspended, by vote of 140 to 6, five duly elected Socialist members of that body, because of their political views. On the 13th the Association of the New York Bar of the City of New York staged a debate on the merits of the action. The central question at issue was: "If Socialists are permitted to vote, are they not permitted to vote for their own candidates?" The discussion continued into the small hours of the morning, when the Association, by a discouragingly narrow margin, passed a resolution denouncing the Assembly's action.*

In this battle of the lawyers Stone was on freedom's side, not because, as he said, of "any partiality for the Socialist program," but because basic principles of free government dictated this stand. Years later he pointed to that debate as a glorious example of how the Bar Association had spoken out against "a foul blow to representative government" and had exerted its influence in behalf of "those principles of government upon which this nation was founded."[26]

Shortly before the Assembly's decision, April 1, 1920, to oust the Socialists, Stone carried his defense of individual freedom onto the

* The Assembly, by secret vote, excluded Mr. Charles Evans Hughes and his Bar Association Committee from hearings before the Assembly's Judiciary Committee which took place between January 20 and February 5. In early March the committee voted that the Socialist members had not been "obedient to the Constitutions and laws of the United States and the State of New York, nor desirous of the welfare of the country, nor in hearty accord and sympathy with its government and institutions, and for said reason and also because of other facts and reasons, . . . they are . . . disqualified to occupy seats in the Assembly of the State of New York as members thereof." Proceedings of the Judiciary Committee of the Assembly of the State of New York in the Matter of the Investigation . . . as to the Qualifications of Louis Waldman, August Claessens, Samuel A. DeWitt, Samuel Orr and Charles Solomon, to Retain their Seats in Said Body. (*Leg. Doc.*, Vol. 2, No. 35, p. 4 *et seq.* [1920]; *ibid*, Vol. 3, pp. 2673, 2715.)

national stage. In February he joined a committee of protest against Attorney General A. Mitchell Palmer's "Red Raids" and, on behalf of the National Popular Government League, urged special investigation. This action led to the creation of a congressional committee to probe "charges of illegal practices in the Department of Justice." When the Sterling subcommittee met on February 1, 1921, a letter from Dean Stone was the first order of business. Translating his liberalism into basic constitutional principles, he wrote:

. . . It does not seem open to serious doubt that although there is no constitutional prohibition of the deportation of aliens within the United States, nevertheless an alien who has been admitted to the United States by the immigration authorities is a "person within the United States," and therefore entitled to the protection of the due process of law guaranteed by the Constitution to persons within the United States. It appears by the public admissions of the Attorney General and otherwise that he has proceeded on the theory that such aliens are not entitled to the constitutional guaranty of due process of law. Moreover, it appears from the reported decisions of federal courts that, in deportation proceedings taken by the Department of Justice under direction of the Attorney General, aliens have been deprived of such constitutional guaranties. It also appears that the agents of the Department of Justice, in violation of the express provisions of the statute, have arrested aliens in deportation cases without warrant. These undisputed facts would of themselves seem to require a thoroughgoing investigation of the conduct of the Department of Justice in connection with the deportation cases. Moreover, the statute authorizes the deportation of aliens because of their political opinions and confers on administrative officers the power to deprive persons within the United States who are aliens of their liberty without the ordinary safeguards which are given to those who are charged with crime. The reason why these safeguards are provided for those charged with crime is not because they are criminals, or probable criminals, but because sound public policy requires that every individual who is deprived of his liberty should have the protection of those safeguards. It is therefore very much to be hoped that any such investigation will not only reveal fully the facts with respect to the violation of constitutional safeguards and statutes by the agents of the Department of Justice in the administration of the deportation laws, but that such investigation will result in legislation more adequately protecting aliens or those alleged to be aliens, but who may be citizens of the United States, from the arbitrary exercise of power by administrative officers.

It is inevitable that any system which confers upon administrative officers power to restrain the liberty of individuals, without safeguards substantially like those which exist in criminal cases and without adequate authority for judicial review of the action of such administrative officers will result in abuse of power and in intolerable injustice and cruelty to individuals.[27]

Stone was as skeptical of "radicals" as Nicholas Murray Butler, or A. Mitchell Palmer. But the impact of their obviously self-defeating devices moved him to advocate other remedies. Force could not muzzle Socialists, tame teachers, or make fighting men of pacifists. The deepening social tension these attempts exposed could be lessened only by illuminating vast areas of human ignorance. "We shall not find the answer," he wrote, "by shutting our eyes to the facts or by persuading ourselves that our duty is done when we have made superficial appeals to patriotism and to loyalty to American institutions."

"The only methods which hold out promise for the triumph of democratic institutions over the assaults now directed against them," are, he maintained, "firm but impartial adherence to the law by those in authority, and ceaseless and untiring efforts to educate and enlighten these men and especially the class to whom they make their appeal, together with the fullest discussion and most searching analysis of the doctrines which they preach." Education must be deep as well as broad: "Before we can persuade the conscientious objector to accept our views of the duties of citizenship we must understand his views and know the forces at work in American life which produce them."

The educational program needed as a corrective could not be entrusted to "sentimentalists," who spawned "loose-thinking" radicals, or to teachers having the authoritarian outlook of a Palmer or Butler. In national crisis, when leaders in high administrative offices, on the campus, and in the legislature were confused, Stone kept cool. He spoke out bluntly against President Butler's preference for the witch-hunt. In the postwar frenzy, when all the vaunted values for which the war had allegedly been fought seemed to vanish, he denounced "intolerable injustice" in high places and demanded due process of law for aliens as well as citizens. In the very arena where its exercise was considered most heavily freighted with danger to the established order, he extolled the "moral and social value" of freedom.

CHAPTER EIGHT

# The Drive for Social Justice

## 1912-1923

During the period of Stone's deanship, the law and the courts, as at no previous time, were subjects of popular discussion and criticism. There had been a significant shift of stress from legal justice to social justice. Implicit in an ever-growing body of legislation was the realization that government must keep order not only physically but socially. Statutes, giving expression to this realistic social outlook were enacted, but judges, imbued with the relentless spirit of individualism, often construed them away or set them aside as unconstitutional. Such blind application of legalistic concepts in the face of necessary social and economic change stirred angry protest.[1] Stone was profoundly disturbed. Criticism of the New York Court of Appeals was "so loud, so ill tempered, and so misguided, as to startle those who have respect for and faith in our institutions."[2]

A welcome opportunity to illuminate the problem and perhaps allay popular clamor came in January 1914, when he was scheduled to give the Hewitt lectures at Cooper Union. But these were broken off after the first lecture by a virulent attack of typhoid, which laid him low for the remainder of the academic year. "I have been on the shelf since January 30 and am still very weak and helpless," he wrote John Bassett Moore, May 6, 1914. It was not until February of the following year that the series was completed.

What troubled Dean Stone especially was the "political aspiration" called "social justice." When conceived of as a "political theory of social welfare" or "as a political war cry," he disclaimed any interest in this "fantastic" social fad. He was very much concerned when it was coupled with "the notion that judges, in the administration of common law rules, and especially in formulating new rules of law, should consciously endeavor to mold the rules of law to conform to their own personal notions of what is the correct theory of social organization and development, even though the result should be in many cases to disregard or overturn established rules of law." The Hewitt lectures were given in the conviction that ill feeling might be ameliorated if certain fundamental notions about law and its administration could be made "part of the intellectual equipment of every intelligent citizen."[3] It was a large and demanding order, the more so because he tried to make the lectures interesting to a popular audience, and at the same time scholarly enough to avoid being trashy.

Public discussion had recently centered on the celebrated Ives decision, which invalidated the Workingmen's Compensation Act of 1910. The theory underlying the legislation, the court said emphatically, "is not merely new in our system of jurisprudence, but plainly antagonistic to its basic idea."[4] Stone sympathized with the plight of the injured workman. He was certain that such economic loss "should not fall upon the employee in the trade, but should be added to the cost of production."[5] Yet he endorsed the Ives decision on the theory that the statute did "deprive the employer of property without any common law liability on his part, and the mere fact that the deprivation . . . was economically desirable, did not constitute the taking due process of law."[6] He also agreed that "the proper method of securing the economic benefits of workmen's compensation . . . is 'by the orderly process of constitutional amendment rather than by making a universal test of the right to take private property for the supposed economic advantage to result therefrom.' "[*][7]

Stone had stated his position more incisively in 1912 on the Tenement House case, in which an apartment house owner objected to having the strict provisions of the Tenement House Act of 1901 apply to him, and the court sustained his objections.[8] The decision was bitterly attacked by Edward T. Devine, Columbia University sociologist and editor of *The Survey*. "Another bad decision," Devine wrote. "The fundamental remedy lies not in amendment, but . . . in a process of education through which it will eventually be brought home to judges and their successors that such blundering with human lives . . . is not good law any more than it is good economics, philosophy and morals."[9]

Stone attacked Devine's editorial as "typical of much of the criticism of our courts appearing in current newspapers and magazines. . . . The view that it is possible to base judicial decisions upon some vague notion of social justice," he reminded the editor, "finds frequent expression in these days of hasty and ill-considered criticism. Social justice may mean anything, and therefore, as a basis of judicial decision, means nothing, . . . it is usually used as a term descriptive of the particular remedy which the critic of courts desires very much, but is unable to obtain from the courts by the application of his particular theories of judicial legislation. Abstract justice, or social justice, cannot exist under a system administered by mere man, apart from that approximate justice which is administered by our courts, according to a system of rules and principles. Not abstract justice, not social justice, therefore, should be our quest, but justice according to law; and, in order that justice according to law may approximate

---

[*] The speaker did not pause to tell his audience that the ruling was largely ignored in other jurisdictions. He did not call attention to a decision of the United States Supreme Court upholding federal workmen's compensation for employees of interstate carriers (Second Employers' Liability Act cases, 223 U.S. 1 [1912]). Nor did he point out that five state courts—Kansas, Ohio, Washington, Wisconsin, and Massachusetts—approved workmen's compensation legislation within a year after the Court of Appeals nullified the New York statute. However, the lecturer did call attention to the fact that, among 749 opinions handed down by the New York Court of Appeals in 1911, only the Ives decision had stirred the febrile pens of ardent social reformers. "Certainly . . . the volleys of criticism which have been directed toward the Ives case . . . [were]," Stone concluded, "entirely disproportionate to any practical inconvenience which flowed from that decision." But there were some 60,554 victims of industrial accidents in 1911, many of whom received no compensation largely because the employer was able, thanks to the court's ruling in the Ives case, to invoke common law defenses which Stone himself considered anachronistic.

abstract justice, let us direct our criticism of the courts toward the rules and principles of decisions, not toward the intelligence or motives of the judges, and let us value the correctness of their decisions by the skill and accuracy with which they apply those rules and principles."

"The School of Law, in which I have the honor to be a teacher," Stone went on, "is much engaged in the criticism of judicial opinions. Neither teachers nor students consider that in so doing they are guilty of any disrespect to the courts, or that they act in contempt of the institution which is vital to the perpetuation of a free government. In the discussion of judicial opinions, however, the following canons are carefully observed:

1. That all criticisms should be intelligently directed toward the rules and principles which must necessarily govern judicial decisions.

2. That such criticism should be fair and made with respect for the courts, as the best instrumentality for the administration of justice which humankind has as yet devised.

3. That abstract or social justice as a test for the correctness of judicial decisions is absolutely without value.

4. That the fact that one or many members of the community who very much desire the establishment of a legal principle are actuated by good motives does not establish that the principle is sound, or will, in the generality of cases, promote justice.

"Do you not think, Mr. Editor," the Dean asked, "that *The Survey* might properly and wisely adopt these canons of criticism?"[10]

For Stone, legal change was a process by which governing rules come to slow maturity. The legislator and the judge play their respective roles. The legislator is concerned with what is good public policy and must necessarily "seek to ascertain the opinion of the community" of which he is a representative and to which he is responsible. But not even the legislator has *carte blanche*. Besides constitutional restriction, he must be wary lest he jeopardize respect for law in giving legal sanction to a moral precept which long experience has not yet crystallized into a "settled principle of social conduct." The judge's function is even more circumscribed: "to ascertain whether the facts proved in the case . . . are controlled by rules of law which may be found in the precedents." If legal rules can be found to fit the facts at bar the judge is bound to apply them "regardless of his personal notions of what may be 'social justice.' "[11]

The main purpose of Stone's reply to Devine, as well as of his Hewitt lectures, was to prove that the "impractical aspirations" then parading under the sleazy banner "social justice" were "political war cries," not valid "principles of judicial decision." In the "fantastic" drive to achieve it, agitators were undermining popular faith in legal justice and substituting for it "the notions of social and political quacks." To restore public confidence, he advocated, among other things, "more exacting requirements for admission to the bar which conform to sound educational standards, and the stimulation and preservation in every possible way of the professional spirit and corporate feeling of the bar."[12] There is no hint in Stone's Hewitt lectures of the bold hypothesis Louis D. Brandeis propounded a year later, that the waning respect for law, lawyers, and judges was clear evidence of failure to "keep pace with the rapid development of the political, economic, and social ideals." There is no suggestion that the disturbing effects of specialized law practice might be overcome by broader education—"by study undertaken preparatory to practice—and continued by lawyer and judge throughout life: study of economics and sociology and politics which embody the facts and present problems of today."[13] This was precisely the remedy Devine recommended, so one may infer that Stone at this time took no stock in it.

The Hewitt lectures, published in book form in 1915 under the title *Law and Its Administration*, received both favorable and unfavorable comment from the reviewers. "The author of the lectures before us," one writer commented with enthusiasm, was neither an unfair critic nor an unmeasured eulogist of our legal system. The book demonstrated "clearly that a true reformation even of our procedural defects is not to be effected by legislative waving of a magician's wand, but by the slow process of stimulating in the public mind the love of justice, of educating it as to the nature of law and the grave importance of delegating its administration only to those who are fit to bear that responsibility"[14]—that is, to lawyers and judges.*

Another reviewer called the book "decorous and unexciting," an indictment of "those perverse infidels who would push the fallible methods of modern science into law and religion"; dedicated to the "pious aim" of strengthening "the traditional American faith that God can govern his chosen people only through a constitution, courts, and lawyers"; a rebuke to the "adherents of sociologic jurisprudence who would make judicial decisions in regard to large public questions depend upon the fallible and sometimes hasty human sciences of sociology and economics."[15] In the same vein was a review that said Dean Stone was not "thoroughly acquainted with present-day social philosophy. . . . He would improve the machinery of law and make it more efficient, but he seems to think that nothing else is really needed. . . . To be more efficient in doing the old things," the writer com-

---

* Outlining the essential requirements of effective law reform, Stone had observed: "Law should be reformed by lawyers, for they have the knowledge, experience, and special training essential to the task of planning reforms and carrying them out, provided they are inspired with the sincere desire to correct the faults and abuses of an existing system."

mented scornfully, "is . . . cold comfort to those who have seen the inadequacy of doing some of these at all."[16]

An opportunity to give further exposition to his thought came in 1916, when Truxton Beale, editor of a volume to be called *Man versus the State,* invited Dean Stone to write an introduction to Herbert Spencer's chapter, "The Sins of the Legislators." Taking issue with Spencer's central theme, Stone declared: "The promotion of social efficiency through natural selection, when applied to modern social life, is not inconsistent in principle with the exercise of social prophylaxis through legislation. . . . The fact is that under modern social conditions benefits are not always conferred upon either individuals or groups in accordance with merits, and the unfit do survive in fact and perpetuate their species to become sources of weakness to the social structure." Nevertheless, "Spencer's vigorous warning" did furnish "food for thought and will perhaps ·inspire with caution the zealous advocates of such sweeping legislative changes as are involved in the many proposals for the various types of pension law, and minimum-wage statutes, and modern legislation of similar character." Furthermore, Spencer's indictment of the sins of legislators, resulting from failure to prepare for the lawmaking task, required, in Stone's opinion, "no modification or restatement." Indeed, he traced the "growing lack of that respect for law which must be at the foundation of every adequate and efficient legal system" to the sins Spencer had excoriated.

"The drawing of a legislative act," Stone wrote, "requires exceptional training, experience and skill. . . . No legislation can be enacted which does not have its effect, and oftentimes a serious effect, upon the existing law, written or unwritten, or both. He who thus undertakes to interfere with our complex legal system should not only know the exact legal situation to be affected by the proposed legislation, both historically and as a matter of existing law, but he must know how the desired change can be accomplished by correct legal methods without the enactment of provisions which conflict with or do not harmonize with existing law intended to be preserved."

Believing that mechanical defects in law and lawmaking, rather than the failure of courts to make legal justice coincide with social justice, were the major causes of trouble, Stone became, in 1911, a member of the New York City Bar Association's Watchdog Committee on the Amendment of the Law. Largely through the efforts of a group at Columbia University, Congress was induced to set up an agency to assist in the drafting of bills. Dean Stone took pride in the fact that in 1913 the Columbia group helped to frame the amendment correcting the Ives decision. All this was helpful but not enough. The very mass of judicial decisions, combined with the annual torrent of new statutes, ruffled the calm faith of the legal profession that all was well with the common law.

By 1921 the dimensions of the problem had grown enormously. Stone noted "the tendency of society to become stratified into more or less distinct and permanent social classes, the tendency for the social position of the individual to become static, . . . the growing complexity of social, industrial, and commercial relationships, . . . changes entailing social, economic, and political consequences, raising new problems requiring the application of study and scientific methods to their solution. . . . I have never been able," he said of the common law, "to regard it as having reached perfection or as a fixed and changeless system. . . . The difficulty in the past has been that the lawyer has not felt under any social or business necessity of making his product fit the wearer of it. In a society organized on aristocratic lines our profession may for a very considerable time maintain itself without minding whether the shoe pinches or not. But in a democracy such as ours, the lawyer must not only know where the shoe pinches, but must endeavor to make a shoe that fits."[17]

Law could be stretched or shrunk to regulate the new activities of communities just as shoes can be modified to fit feet. An occasional shrill complaint was no more evidence of a need for a different system of law than a blister proved that men should wear wings instead of shoes. The common law could be made to work in the twentieth century if its doctrines were clarified, simplified, and adjusted here and there to relieve growing pains. In 1923 he went further and listed "failure to appreciate the social and economic significance of facts or the relation of law itself to social well-being . . ." among the influences affecting ". . . adversely the judicial declaration of law." Then no price seemed "too large for the preservation and perpetuation of a great system of law."[18]

Unrest and dissatisfaction within the profession thus coincided with popular agitation for reform. After World War I, Stone's constructive energies went primarily into improvement of the law from within. Between 1920 and 1922 he kept a file labeled "Anachronisms"—startling examples of legal rules out of joint with the times. By the end of his deanship he was inclined to give more sympathetic consideration to "sociological jurisprudence," the purpose of which, as he saw it in 1923, was "to establish in our legal thinking that trinity of juridical theory—logic, history, and the 'method of sociology'—as the source of all true legal doctrine." Though the methods of sociology were no longer shocking, these were still not applicable to genuine reform:

It is not a novel idea that in declaring law the judge must envisage the social utility of the rule which he creates. In short, he must know his facts out of which the legal rule is to be extracted, and in a large sense they embrace the social and economic data of his time. . . . But can we in any proper sense speak of the application of this principle as a "method"? . . . At most it warns the judge and the student of law that logic and history cannot, and ought not, have full sway when the dynamic judgment is to be rendered. It points out that in the choice of the particular legal device determining the result, social utility, the mores of the times, objectively determined, may properly turn the scale in favor of one and against the other; and it should lead us as lawyers and students of law to place an appropriate emphasis on the study of social data and on the effort to understand the relation of law to them, because by that process we may lay the foundation for a better understanding of what social utility is and where in a given case the path of social utility lies.[19]

"Social engineering" was useful, but it offered no royal road to reform. The real problem was adoption of some device whereby the development of the common law "may be more systematic and more scientific and whereby the law may free itself of its centuries of accumulations of anomaly and of rules and technique, the reason for which has disappeared or been forgotten, without loss of its vitality and its adaptability to each particular case as it arises."[20] This was not a job for sociologists. Rather, law school teachers must come forward with a solution free from the difficulties inherent in both codification and sociological jurisprudence.[21]

In 1915 the Association of American Law Schools had formed a Committee on the Establishment of a Juristic Center, to which Stone was named. War intervened, and the committee was virtually inactive until 1919. Then, after two years of study, the committee concluded, and persuaded the members of the association to agree, that "an authoritative restatement of the law" would best accomplish the aim of improving the law by "utilizing American legal scholarship for the purpose of carrying on constructive scientific work, primarily directed to the clarification and simplification of the law and its better adaptation to the needs of life." It was also the conviction of the committee that "such a work could only be undertaken, with reasonable hope of success, by a permanent organization composed of the leaders of the profession on the bench, at the bar, and in the schools."[22] At the 1921 meeting of the association, the committee was empowered "to invite the appointment of similar committees" by other lawyers' organizations "for the purpose of creating a permanent institution for the improvement of the law."[23]

In May 1922 a Committee on the Establishment of a Permanent Organization for the Improvement of the Law was created. During the rest of the spring and summer Stone spent a great amount of time on committee work, serving as a "critic," attending meetings, and reviewing the memoranda of "reporters" engaged full time on the project. On January 11, 1923, the committee issued a call to leading lawyers, judges, teachers, and representatives of professional groups for a meeting to be held in Washington, D. C., on February 23. It was now recognized that dissatisfaction with the administration of justice was "dangerous" because "it breeds disrespect for law . . . the cornerstone of revolution." Moreover, discontent was not confined to that "radical section of the community which would overthrow the existing social, economic, and political institutions."[24] To allay unrest from whatever quarter, the committee proposed "to survey the entire field of Anglo-American law, to discover basic principles, and to state the rules which had been generally worked out in the different states."[25] Addressing the Association of the Bar of the City of New York shortly before the Washington meeting, Dean Stone outlined what the restatement must accomplish:

> It must state in detail and with precision accepted rules and doctrines, eliminating or modifying the rule or doctrine not supported by reason or adapted to present-day social institutions and needs; . . . it must avoid the formal statement of the law as a closed system, clearly leaving open for future statements, on the basis of judicial decisions as they are rendered, the rules governing the new and unforeseen situations with which the law must hereafter deal as they arise. And finally there should accompany such a restatement, preferably in a separate document, a comprehensive annotation showing the origin and history of each rule and doctrine dealt with in the primary restatement, indicating conflicts of authority and, in the case of conflict or in the case of precepts modified or eliminated, the reason for the adoption of the rule actually incorporated into the restatement.[26]

"I suppose no one would deny," Stone observed, "that a statement of law thus prepared would be the most important and useful law book published since the compilation of the Digest."

Out of the Washington meeting came the American Law Institute. Contrary to Stone's recommendation,* the Institute overwhelmingly decided to issue the judicially honored private law rules without seeking legislative sanction. "If the work is so well done," the *American Bar Association Journal* observed, "that it commends itself to the judgment of the profession sufficiently to be cited in briefs and arguments of counsel and to be quoted with approval by the courts of last resort, it thereby will become a part of the law of the land. If the work is

---

* With legislative sanction, Stone wrote W. D. Lewis, Oct. 24, 1922, "the restatement would at once have an authority which a restatement not so sanctioned and approved would not possess and at the same time would not fetter the courts as would a formal legislative code. It would give to the courts greater freedom in adopting the rules laid down in the restatement and at the same time would leave them free to deal with those cases when they inevitably arise which are not covered by the restatement and which, on the other hand, has not generally been deemed compatible with a formal legislative code."

poorly done so that it does not meet with the approval of the bar and the bench, it will come to naught."[27] Experience proved that Stone put his finger on the difficulty the "Restatement" would encounter.[*] "Not intended to be a substitute for the cases but only to clarify them," Thurman Arnold remarked in 1935, "it therefore becomes only an additional source of argument."[28]

Enthusiasm born of the Restatement effort persisted.[†] The labor lavished upon it has been described as one of "three main areas of public policy activity" which "in the first half of the twentieth century . . . gave to the bar some sense of nation-wide corporate purpose."[29] For Stone this was only a by-product, not the central task, of the Institute. The job to which he conceived that body dedicated and to which he devoted himself was that of enabling "the common law to live on and do its appointed work as a vital and energizing force in Western civilization."[30]

Thus the period of Stone's deanship was a time of intellectual turmoil, of increasing awareness that, without considerable modification, the common law system of justice could not survive. The system was imperiled from without as well as from within. The problem, as he conceived of it, was to find ways of enabling the law to cope with the impact of industrialism without doing violence to the genius of the common law, or to his own intellectual and political inheritance.

In 1912 he derided social justice as "absolutely without value" as "a test for the correctness of judicial decisions."[31] Three years later he denounced its proponents as calamity howlers, attempting "to formulate law on the basis of the legislator's view of what is sound public policy based upon his observations of social conditions."[32] In 1923 he recognized that sociological jurisprudence need not be tied inextricably to the political aspirations of captious "do-gooders." Sociological jurisprudence had a contribution to make—in checking the actual

---

[*] Mr. Justice Branch of Stone's native New Hampshire saw the problem that had led to Stone's suggestion. "Probably," he said in 1936, "few courts will overrule their prior decisions because they find that the Institute is against them." See H. F. S., "The Common Law in the United States," in *The Future of the Common Law* (1937), p. 152.

Felix Cohen's judgment was more harsh. "The 'Restatement of the Law' by the American Law Institute," he wrote, "is the last long-drawn-out gasp of a dying tradition. The more intelligent of our younger law teachers and students are not interested in 'restating the dogmas of legal theology.'" ("Transcendental Nonsense and the Functional Approach," *Columbia Law Review*, June 1935, p. 833.)

[†] Stone was not always happy with what was being done. On March 23, 1926, he wrote John Bassett Moore: "The Institute is putting out restatements which to me are shocking in their lack of sound scholarship and of a knowledge of the more elementary principles of English common law. I have recently indulged in a sharp correspondence with them [especially Wm. Draper Lewis] on the subject, but I think it makes no more effect than does rain on a duck's back."

operation of legal rules, in measuring their effectiveness in controlling human behavior, in ascertaining the facts of "social utility." "But," he insisted, "we must have other resources if we are to make of the common law the great and abiding system which it may become."[33] For these he looked primarily to the American Law Institute. The "Restatement" would serve as a point of departure: "It would create a comprehensive and flexible scheme whereby our law might move at once in the direction of enlightened and considered reform with the best expert assistance. . . . It would be free from those exigencies which in America seem inevitably attached to efforts at reform carried on under the direction of public officials and which are inimical to scientific investigation and collaboration."[34]

In 1915 courts may not have been considered the only organs of government having the capacity to govern, but they were for Stone the most trustworthy agencies. Implicit in his analysis was narrow construction of the Constitution and a limited role for the legislature. Criticism of law and its administration was the special province of an inner sanctum and should be directed primarily to rules and principles of decision. But a shift had occurred even before he quit the Columbia Law School. Stone "was considerably affected," Thomas Reed Powell, the dean's Law School colleague, has explained, "by the personal and intellectual quality of the man who advanced various views. He had no respect for Devine, a professor of sociology at Columbia, and Devine's criticism of the Ives case influenced Stone to support or apologize for it and minimize it in his Carpentier [Hewitt] Lectures. However, when [Frank] Goodnow and [Joseph] Chamberlain (Columbia Law School professors) criticized the Ives decision, Stone with his respect for them was ready to consider their views calmly and to give weight to the fact that they held them."[35]

"I should be surprised," Justice Stone wrote in 1938, "if there were not a good many things in Law and Its Administration with which I do not agree today."[36]

Even as modified, Stone's position fell short of the reliance liberals normally place on government as an instrument of social and economic betterment. He felt that lawyers need not become crusaders in the conventional sense. But the time had come when they could no longer rest content to be good technicians, skilled in the practice of their profession and interested only in technical improvement. Now more than ever, their interest and training must be extended into fields where the law touches good citizenship. "Logic and history are not the keys which alone will set free the vital spirit of the law." There must also be "resort to a complete, accurate, and sympathetic survey of the social and economic facts to which rules of law must apply. Let us hitch our wagon to a star, but let us remember that it will function as a wagon only by permitting its wheels to roll on the solid structure of Mother Earth."[37]

Despite the apparent stodginess of Stone's Hewitt lectures, they afford a clue to the sophistication he later manifested as a Supreme Court Justice. In 1915 he vehemently denounced the view that mere wish to establish a desirable social and economic theory was enough to validate it as the law of the land. As a Supreme Court Justice, he was equally harsh in his attack on the notion that distrust of a social theory embodied in legislation was enough to condemn it as unconstitutional. Thus views formerly seen as denoting a reactionary bias became in later years a powerful liberalizing force in constitutional interpretation.

CHAPTER NINE

# Breaking with Academia

## 1921-1923

Stone's resignation from the Columbia Law School was long in the making. Yet it could hardly have been foreseen even by himself within five years prior to his departure. In 1915 his salary had been "fixed" at $12,000* "for the express purpose," as President Butler reminded him in 1918, "of having you withdraw from active private practice."[1] "If I were to do this over again," Stone replied, "I should prefer to make my separation from practice more abrupt and complete. . . . At the present time I should be quite willing to have my name withdrawn from the firm if in your judgment or that of the Trustees such a course is desirable or preferable."

"My principal interest in life and my only ambition," he went on, "is to do the work of a law teacher in this school, and it seems to me that given good health and the kind of support which the school deserves in the matter of appointments and salaries (to my associates) that I ought to be able to render increasingly valuable service to the University for the next twenty years."[2]

---

* In his letter of Jan. 30, 1915, Butler had written: "The purpose of this action is not only to give material expression to the confidence which the Trustees have in you and to the satisfaction with which they have followed your work, but also, in accordance with the tenor of our recent conversations, to enable you to devote yourself wholly to the work of the Law School and to feel free from the necessity of taking on professional work and obligations outside the University."

Here was the rub, at least in part. The Law School had made remarkable progress under Dean Stone's leadership. In 1908 registration had dwindled to 257. By 1915 it had risen to 334. The school's annual income was $90,000. Expenses amounted to only $40,000, leaving a surplus of $50,000. Yet President Butler had been inconsiderate of Stone's persistent efforts to secure salary increases and larger appropriations for the library. Finally Stone proposed to donate a part of his own salary in order to insure increases for Professors Nathan Abbott and Young B. Smith. He would do this, he told Butler, "with the expectation that it would not in any way affect or diminish the service which I am rendering to the University." By making a gift of this kind he would, he thought, "most effectively contribute to the loyalty and *esprit de corps* of our teaching staff."[3]

The idea did not appeal to Butler. Instead he suggested it would be "wiser and more in the interest of sound University policy if you were to withdraw your name from the firm with which it has been so honorably associated."[4] This suggestion apparently got Stone's back up. For though he had offered to do this very thing, the dean now decided, upon "reflection," that the decision should wait "until we can see a little more clearly what is likely to happen." "If the turn of the Law School should come to make sacrifices I am obviously the one to make them, because under present conditions I could probably suspend my work here temporarily and make my living, and it would be difficult for some of the other men on the faculty to do it. So long as I have a nominal connection with a firm like mine I could always return to it and make a substantial professional income."[5]

Butler was evidently not wholly satisfied with the Law School's progress. Refusal to approve Stone's budget proposals for the most essential purposes, including library, salaries, and the law review, reflected his displeasure. He was disinclined, however, to have this out with Stone face to face. Instead he sent him an oblique telegram that evoked Stone's pointed response:

I shall have to confess that until I read your telegram it had not occurred to me that it [the school] had steadily declined in authority and importance. When I have recalled its condition and general reputation not so many years ago, I have been encouraged to believe that at least until we entered the war we had made some progress in the direction of making our school stronger and more influential and more worthy of its position in a great University and this without any increase in our faculty.

I realize of course that one may be so close to a situation that he does not see it in its proper perspective and that perhaps is my own position. . . . I should have been gratified if you had long since advised me of your views that our school was on the decline so that the whole matter might have been taken up and discussed by the faculty and Trustees. I hope that this will now be done.[6]

Butler quickly changed his tune. Within a month the Trustees' Committee on Education raised the salary scale from $6000–$7500 to $6000–$10,000. Walter Wheeler Cook's call to the faculty at $10,000 was approved, along with a salary increase for Young B. Smith. Stone was elated. "For the first time since I became connected with the school," he wrote the President, "I feel that we have the assurance of stepping into the first position among the law schools of the country."[7]

But this glow of satisfaction did not last. President Butler, believing the degree Juris Doctor objectionable both in principle and in practical working, continued his opposition to a proposal very close to Stone's heart. The dean, with equal persistence, continued to press his case for it. It would be awarded, he said, primarily in recognition of "a dissertation showing originality and making a substantial contribution to legal science."[8] Butler's argument that if the degree of doctor of law were instituted no logical objection could be interposed to the later establishment of the degree in architecture, business, engineering, education, and so on, seemed unconvincing.

In May 1922 Stone restated his case in crisp terms:

I have had considerable correspondence during the past year with men who desire to do research work in law but in every case they have made it perfectly clear that they were only interested in a doctorate in law. One of our own men is going to Yale next year to work for that degree because we do not offer it. It will be a real misfortune if we are obliged to leave this field of educational endeavor to other schools which are really not any better equipped, and probably not as well equipped, to do it as we are.[9]

The conclusion of Stone's letter gave Butler a real opening: "I hope some way will be found to develop research in law in this school without placing us at too great a disadvantage with respect to our principal competitors." Butler replied with evident relish. He shared "to the full" Stone's "desire to go forward with the better organization of advanced instruction and research in law as rapidly as possible," and added:

Meanwhile . . . please do get rid of the notion that you have "competitors." There are no such things in university organization and life. This is particularly true of Columbia, which is in a class by itself. If any student wishes to go elsewhere, let him, since we have far more than we can properly care for. We shall do our best if we frame our own policies as we think best, and leave the field free for others to do the same.[10]

Stone had to recant, and he explained rather lamely that "the idea . . . which I wish to convey is that as University work is now organized . . . I do not believe that we can stimulate research work in law here without an appropriate degree administered in such manner as to attract the students who would naturally do this type of work."[11]

The conflict was finally resolved in 1923, when the Trustees decided to limit doctorates to "the four traditional academic groups and the four historic university faculties of law, medicine, theology, and philosophy."[12] After twelve years of struggle, the capstone had finally been placed upon the "era of legal scholarship."

Meanwhile developments within his own faculty were making Stone's life difficult. Walter Wheeler Cook, whom Stone had added to the faculty in 1919, soon began to expound an approach to the law that smacked of faddish sociological jurisprudence. And when, in the spring of 1921, another major addition to the faculty was under consideration, smoldering discontent erupted. Among the candidates under consideration was Professor Herman Oliphant of the University of Chicago. "Radicals" Cook and Underhill Moore, claiming Oliphant as their own, used aggressive tactics to win his appointment. This prompted Young B. Smith to warn Stone:

> I believe I state the truth when I say that both Cook and Moore feel very sincerely that the best way to make Columbia the leading law school in the country is to startle the profession into a state of admiration and wonder by something new and unique. As they see it, an economic interpretation of the law, expressed in scientific terminology, should be our program. To accomplish their purpose, two things are necessary.
>
> *First,* to recruit to the faculty teachers with similar views. Their enthusiasm to annex [Robert L.] Hale, to call [Manley] Hudson, and finally to elect Oliphant at any cost are manifestations of this desire.
>
> *Second,* to get control of the courses which afford the best opportunity for impressing the student body with the new learning. This is the reason for their drive to have you turn the Personal Property over to Cook. You must not forget that in the estimation of these reformers many of your views about law are unsound.

Smith wanted the "reformers" contained, not exterminated or silenced. "No one appreciates more than I the real value to our organization of both Cook and Moore. Their radical ideas constitute an excellent tonic for the intellectual liver, but as a steady diet they are simply impossible." Smith urged Stone to hold firm until the conservative forces could be rallied:

> In my opinion it would not only be unwise, but a real loss to the school for you to abandon your work in the first year. Furthermore, I feel confident that this is the view of the decided majority of your colleagues, and I sincerely hope that you will stand by your position that any radical change in our program of work ought to be postponed until [Ralph W.] Gifford and I are back. At that time I believe we will dispel Oliphant's possible illusion that the Columbia Law Faculty is composed of Cook and Moore.[13]

Well aware of the problem, Stone made clear his purpose to maintain a balance between the old and the new:

I think you have sized up the situation correctly. I very cordially agree with you, too, that the ideas that Cook and Moore hold about law are valuable as a tonic to our intellectual liver. I am distinctly for it—that was why I wanted to bring them here—and I am still for it, but I do not wish to make the diet of the Law School all tonic and no old-fashioned corned beef and cabbage. As liberals, they ought to feel the same way and be willing that the patient should have a little corned beef and cabbage, but I am beginning to fear that they really wish to cut that out of the diet.

What I would like to arrange for is to have Cook give a course in the first year where he would have full opportunity to expand his ideas, but I believe it would be a very great mistake, both educationally and also a mistake of policy, not to preserve the traditions of law as it has come down to us in the books and in the courts. It is a mistake educationally because unless our students thoroughly grasp and master the approach of courts and lawyers to the law as we find it in the books they will be at a disadvantage in their practice. It is a mistake of policy because, rightly or wrongly—very possibly wrongly—the public will get the impression that we are a group of doctrinaires without any close attachment to our common law and equity system. . . .

The point about Personal Property: it is, . . . as I some time ago discovered and as Cook has discovered . . . a fine medium for getting into the student's head some fundamentals, and I have been using it for that purpose with what seems to me very considerable success.' . . .

You know how, when Cook and Moore get their minds made up that they want something, they are not at all backward about insisting on getting it. In fact, I think if they had displayed a little more of the first principles of courtesy, they might have had what they want already.

As matters now stand, however, I think I shall stick to my guns for another year. And then the faculty can have all my courses if they want, to do what they please with.[14]

Stone seemed to be as much disturbed by the manners and judgment of the newcomers, by their undue haste, their determination to get their ideas entrenched at all cost, as by their "radicalism." In a letter of recommendation several years later he noted:

Walter Wheeler Cook, about whom you inquire, is almost, if not quite, a genius. . . . If he were quite content to work up . . . ideas and let others do the work of organizing and building up any kind of an institution for law study which would use his ideas, he would undoubtedly make important contributions to legal science.

Continuing, Stone observed:

. . . he had, I think, very exceptional opportunity to do the very thing that he is most interested in both at Yale and Columbia, but failed to do it, very largely, as I see it because of his inability to adjust himself to existing conditions or to take himself such a part in the work of organization as to make it effective. During his connection at Columbia I realized to the fullest the contribution he might make and did all in my power to aid and facilitate his making it, but, becoming impatient because his views were not followed more promptly and effectively than was possible under the circumstances, he threw away the golden opportunity.[15]

## THE PLAGUES OF ADMINISTRATION

Besides the strain of coping with the "soreheads," as Smith described Cook, Moore, *et al.*, Stone found himself more and more frustrated by the details of administration. His office was the hub of Kent Hall. Problems ranging from the hours the building was to be open to major decisions of educational policy had to be channeled across the dean's desk. As the school grew in size and importance, the mass of trivia to be attended to increased proportionately.

Stone was a good administrator. He had the two prime requisites for the job: the ability to get along with people and the capacity to produce effective action. "He could accomplish a great amount of work without wearing," his secretary observed, "and never became ruffled or irritable."[16] To the mechanics of his job he added human understanding and warmth. Extremely approachable, he was willing to take the time necessary to explore students' problems, both great and small. Nevertheless he profoundly resented the time administration increasingly absorbed at the expense of more worth-while duties— teaching and research. He deplored the modern tendency to establish administration as the end rather than the means of education. "Administration is a necessary evil to be tolerated and justified only so far as it makes more potent the educational influence," he said.[17] The administrator should have only the narrowest functions in university life.*

The growing tendency to measure a university in terms "of buildings and equipment and administration" indicated "a lack of appreciation of the true function of the university as a center of intellectual and spiritual influence." To him nothing seemed "more important than that every administrative officer of the university should realize that his is a position subordinate to that of the teacher and the scientific investigator, and that his success will depend not on the number of reports he makes or calls for, or the blanks which he prepares or the documents which he files, but upon the ease and directness with which

---

* "Administration, with a large A," he wrote Dwight Morrow, Jan. 25, 1927, "has to my mind been the bane of American education." A college, Stone went on, "doesn't need very much administration anyway, but what it does need is a man who knows what scholarship means and what it can be made to mean in the lives of young men who come to it. That was what made Amherst mean so much to you and to me; that was the chief thought of men like Garman, Morse, Derwald, Olds and some of the others. They needed mighty little administration to carry that thought into execution and all that was needed then or is needed now can be carried on by some college officer much subordinate to the President."

he aids the bringing of the teacher and the scholar into contact with the receptive mind of the student."[18]

The relatively low estimate he placed on the importance of administration, combined with his natural distaste for it, soon loomed quite large among the factors leading to his resignation. When in 1919 he was suggested as a possible candidate for the presidency of the University of Wisconsin, he commented: "I think it quite unlikely that I would give up the work of a law teacher to accept the presidency of any institution."[19]

## PRESIDENT BUTLER'S 1922 REPORT

Until 1922 Dean Stone and President Butler, though frequently in disagreement over matters of university policy, had worked together harmoniously on a professional basis. But that year Butler included in his annual report some provocative statements about legal education:

That legal education has fallen into ruts and that it has never been subjected to critical examination from the standpoint of educational principle, is generally admitted. In fact, legal education has been treated too largely as a matter of law and too little as a matter of education. . . .

Law schools in the United States have, ever since their establishment, been cast in a common mold. They have slavishly imitated the program of instruction and the methods of teaching followed in one or two of the older and more influential law schools, and there has been no such searching criticism of either the program of study or the methods of instruction as has been the case with letters and with science. Such critical examination should be no longer delayed, and Columbia University may render a distinct service by undertaking it. A great teacher does not of necessity leave behind him a great school. If it be true that an institution is but the lengthened shadow of a man, one must be certain that the man who hopes to build an institution really casts a shadow. Many powerful personalities come and go in the fields of higher and professional education without contributing in any important way toward the permanent character and influence of the institutions which they have served. Imitation is no doubt sincerest flattery, but critical examination of proposed courses of action and of the principles upon which these rest, is wiser than imitation. . . .

That the conventional discipline of law students in private or municipal law is too narrow and too technical is now quite generally admitted. The study of Blackstone, some time since abandoned, had its advantages. Not infrequently under conditions as they now exist a practicing lawyer has had some years of professional experience before he gains a clear idea of the relations between law and ethics, economics, and social science.[20]

The comment was so pointed that Chief Judge Hiscock of the New York Court of Appeals, speaking at the Columbia Law Alumni meeting, tried to answer Butler's criticism. Stone thought Hiscock had read too much into the report. It was always his policy not to "show resentment even if you feel it."[21] Stone wrote Butler:

At the conclusion of his address I told him [Hiscock] that I was quite sure that your discussion of the Law School in your report was not intended as criticism of it; for, of course, while I realize that this school, like most educational institutions, is not perfect, I believe you know how seriously and earnestly we are trying to make it in every respect a stronger and better school.

Nevertheless, I know that a good many people prominent as judges or in the legal life of the state have had a similar interpretation of the views which you express, and we are in the somewhat unfortunate position of having people rush to our defense. This, of course, gives me some concern and at some convenient time I would like to come in and talk with you about it.[22]

Butler's reply was ambiguous:

I would not worry about the matters set out in yours of the 18th. As a matter of fact, the passages in my Report on legal instruction and research are the outgrowth of our own personal discussions on those subjects. If they have the effect of holding up your hands in bringing about such study of existing conditions and of future possibilities as will enable you to make the Law School still more effective, well and good. The comparative excellences of the best form of American legal training are so marked and so widely recognized that no one need hesitate to point out ways and means by which they may be still further improved.[23]

Later, when Judge Benjamin N. Cardozo sought clarification, Butler tried to back water:

I am particularly proud of the humane and progressive spirit which, under the leadership of Dean Stone and his admirable body of associates in the Law Faculty, has animated and is now animating our own Law School. The observations on legal teaching and research that were contained in my last Annual Report were the outcome of conferences with Dean Stone himself, and of discussions as to what we could do to strengthen his hands and still farther extend the influence of the Law School.

Butler then interjected a point on which he had recently taken Stone to task.

The imitative instinct is similarly strong in the field of legal education itself, and it has been quite customary for one law school to look over its shoulder to see what another law school was doing, and to imitate it, rather than to examine the problem *de novo* and find the solution for it. . . .

Fortunately, under Keener, and then still more largely under Stone, we have come a long distance toward our conscious goal. On the other hand, as I go about the country, I see and hear very distressing things as to both judicial and legal competence. Not long ago I sat in a more than usually important court in another state and listened to the conduct of a trial in which serious issues were raised. I came away with a feeling that if justice were done, it would be by accident or by the mysterious workings of Divine Providence, rather than by any measure of competence on the part of the judge or opposing counsel.[24]

As it finally took shape, the crucial issue between Stone and Butler was whether law should be taught as a natural science or as social science. Butler, an inveterate mossback, in effect joining forces with the "wild horses"[*] on the Law School faculty, thought the relationship between law and economic and social experience was being inadequately demonstrated in even the best law schools. He wanted the connection between law and ethics and economics thoroughly explored. He therefore accused schools that taught strictly by the case method, Columbia included, of "imitating" and of failing to examine critically their outmoded teaching techniques. Removing Blackstone from the law curriculum was a mistake, Butler believed; no attempt was now being made to integrate legal principles with the facts of modern life.

Stone, on the other hand, considered the primary purpose of legal education the training of the student's mind. The law was not a social science but a body of abstract doctrines to be applied to human activity. Students should learn the fundamentals of the social system in college and leave the law schools free to concentrate on inculcating mental habits that would enable them to use the law as an instrument of social control. Students should be taught how to find the law, and, with reasonable intelligence, they then should know what to do with it without having someone else feed them ideas on the "ethical" or "sociological" use of the law. In using the case method, law schools were not being imitative but were utilizing the system recognized as best for legal instruction. The case method was not a method of learning law by memorizing facts and doctrines of leading precedents. "It is a method of law study in which emphasis is placed on the student's gaining his knowledge of legal principles by his own effort from original sources in judicial opinion, and in which the mere acquisition of knowledge is subordinated to the development of the student's capacity to deal with the material with which the lawyer deals when he prepares an opinion or briefs a case."[25]

Similarity of teaching technique did not mean that the schools were unimaginative or uncritical in formulating their policies. The "organization and content" of Columbia's courses were, as Stone pointed

---

[*] When Huger W. Jervey, Stone's successor as dean, resigned, the Justice wrote him a consoling letter (May 15, 1928) in which he said: "I don't see how a man who is not entirely well could stand the strain of trying to drive that team of wild horses at Columbia."

out, "quite different" from those of other institutions. It was, for example, one of the few schools that had an effective introductory course. Columbia had added professors to the faculty who emphasized the sociological approach to legal education.[26] Butler was nevertheless unhappy. He wanted the law itself treated as a social science.

Though Butler claimed that his conclusions were the outcome of discussions with Dean Stone, his remarks and later correspondence between the two men belie this statement. He did not get his ideas on "imitation" from Stone. Nor did his implied criticism of the case method come from Stone. Butler's observation that "one must be certain that the man who hopes to build an institution really casts a shadow," was made with the knowledge that Stone had serious intentions of resigning.* The dart of personal attack was further sharpened by the comment: "A great teacher does not of necessity leave behind him a great school."

Stone chose to put the best face possible on the President's pointed pronouncements. In sending a marked copy of the report to John Bassett Moore, he commented: "Just what this means I think neither he nor anyone else could say with certainty, except that those outside the University and some in other departments of the University construe it as being unfriendly to the Law School. I doubt whether that was intended to be the effect."[27]

On receiving a copy of Butler's letter to Cardozo, however, Stone wrote the President a long statement outlining the reforms needed in legal education and suggesting that the members of the bar the President had observed with such dismay were undoubtedly products of the low-grade law schools. "It would be a fortunate thing if this type of school would imitate the schools of the first class," he wrote, and pointed to Columbia as a notable example:

I do not think their primary difficulty is that they are imitative of the particular type of education maintained by any given school or schools; in fact, critical examination of what is going on at Columbia, for example, and has been going on for some years, would demonstrate conclusively that it is not imitating any other school. For instance, here you will find a closer alliance between law and the social sciences than exists in any other American institution; you will find greater liberality in the offering of public law, of Roman law, of civil law, legal history, and jurisprudence; both the organization and content of our courses are quite different from that of any other institution; in our attitude toward the introductory courses in law and in the effort to introduce the student at the outset to fundamental legal conceptions we are developing along lines different from that of any other institution so far as I know, and I believe in better lines. . . .

* The President did not ordinarily write his report till the end of June. On June 16, 1922, Stone wrote Butler of an offer from a downtown firm.

With respect to the case system it would be a mistake to call this an imitation just as much as it would be a mistake to say that our science departments were imitative because they use test tubes similar to those in use in other scientific schools. We are using the case system here and will undoubtedly continue to use it because we are convinced that it is the best method of instruction in any subject of intellectual inquiry.[28]

In his 1923 report, published after Stone left, Butler had the last word:

The thoroughly grounded lawyer of the next generation must have a much firmer hold on economic law and economic fact than has seemed necessary in the past. He will have to be familiar not only with the decisions of the courts but with the recorded experiences of the economic and social life of modern peoples. . . . It will be the task of the Faculties of Law and Political Science to see to it that the new opportunity which has been created be made use of to the full.[29]

Stone might have adopted this statement as his own. In his own report he conceded that "we have failed to recognize as clearly as we might that law is nothing more than a form of social control intimately related to those social functions which are the subject matter of economics and the social sciences generally." But Stone saw, as Butler apparently did not, that legal study was threatened with "educational nostrums" prejudicial to sound grounding in the law:

Professional training, especially in law, is in very real danger from a kind of competitive zeal which has for some years adversely affected undergraduate education in colleges and universities. The desire to do something distinctive, to give some evidence of originality, to attract public attention, or to secure patronage, has led from time to time to the presentation to the public of numerous educational nostrums, as improvements upon the old educational fundamentals or as dispensing with them as relatively unimportant. "Point of view" on the part of the student or the callow instructor, on occasion, seems to be more important than the formation of educational experience and intellectual capacity on which one may build the superstructure from which with years and experience he may hope to have a "point of view." "Openness of mind," it would appear, is more to be desired than the development of the mind's capacity to lay hold of the fundamentals of human knowledge and experience, and to organize and use them with discriminating intelligence.[30]

## THE PARTING OF THE WAYS

Along with the policy differences between them, there was a rather more personal area of disaffection.* This was touched off by Stone's

* John Bassett Moore conjectured that "jealousy was the cause of Butler's generally disaffected attitude" toward Stone. (John Bassett Moore to H. F. S., Dec. 29, 1923.)

"Your diagnosis of the case is, I think, correct, although it seems remarkable to

letter of June 16, informing the President of a downtown offer. Stone wrote:

I have just received a very pressing invitation to join one of the largest and best-known law firms of the city as a full partner, to assume direction of all their important litigated matters with opportunity to appear in person in the various courts of the country in such of those matters as I may select. The financial return would be very large—seven or eight times my present salary, at least.

While the financial advantages of the position are of the least concern to me, the great professional opportunity as well as the opportunity which it presents to make a more adequate provision for my family and to provide a future for my sons, one and possibly both of whom may study law, makes me feel that I should give the matter serious consideration. It goes without saying that whatever I do, I shall not relinquish my work here without giving the fullest opportunity and ample time to make some suitable disposition of it.

On the merits I am very much in doubt, with, however, strong inclinations to decline the offer, flattering as it is and exceptional as its possibilities are. On the other hand, when I contemplate that action, there are two aspects of the matter which are of great weight with me: One is the very strong impression that I have that I have already made such contribution as I am probably able to make to this school, and that in the next fifteen years, by mere force of circumstances, I should be marking time a good deal more than I have in the past ten; and that possibly the appointment of a new man with a wider range of scholarship than mine to my professorship and the selection of one of my associates as dean would result in more being built on the foundation which I have been trying to lay here than would be the case if I remained here; that in short I have gotten my growth here and that taking a long view of the situation the school would be better for a younger growing man in my place.

The other consideration is the enormous amount of time which I am perforce compelled to use up in the attention to petty administrative details. I may be mistaken about it but I feel very strongly that I have capacities which could be better employed, and yet I do not see under our organization how the use of a great deal of time in this way by the head of the Law School, whoever he is, can be avoided. Day after day my working hours are consumed in interviewing students, attendance upon committee meetings, and the attention to petty office detail which, it seems to me, I should be using in law study and in real scholarly or professional work of some type,

---

me that a man in such an important position should be affected by such petty considerations." (H. F. S. to John Bassett Moore, Jan. 7, 1924.)

The truth is that Butler, panting for the Presidency or some other high political office, was consumed by jealousy as he saw members of his own faculty tapped for positions that in some ways eclipsed his own. When Moore was elected a judge of the Permanent Court of International Justice he declared that it was a "damned shame that Root was not on the Court instead." (John Bassett Moore to H. F. S., Dec. 29, 1923.)

which would involve growth and professional progress. I am often oppressed by the feeling that in a few years more my work will be done and that I will not have accomplished as a lawyer or a teacher or a writer what I should have accomplished; and yet no one realizes better than I how much the personal touch is necessary in connection with these relatively unimportant matters if the school is to go ahead on the lines on which it has been progressing.

Aside from this feeling that it has not been possible for me to make use of my time to the best advantage, my association here has been most delightful and satisfactory in every respect, and I should give it up only with genuine regret and upon the conviction that it was the wise and appropriate thing to do under all the circumstances. I shall hope to come to a decision within the next two weeks. . . .

Before that period was up Stone wrote Underhill Moore: "For ten days past I have been struggling with an offer to go downtown with one of the big firms at an income which looks like $100,000 a year or more, and I have about decided to turn it down. I suppose most people will think me crazy if I do it and perhaps I am."[31]

Meanwhile President Butler, professing "the greatest possible concern," addressed to Stone an earnest plea to reconsider. He spoke of how the school "under your leadership was steadily forging to the front," of its "repute for productive scholarship, for high standards and well-balanced conception of law." "You occupy one of the commanding positions in the legal life of the country," etc., etc. When Stone decided to stay on, Butler expressed "profound satisfaction," and assured him that the decision was the right one "from the standpoint of your highest interest and your largest usefulness." Next day the President informed Stone that the Finance Committee of the Trustees had "unanimously voted to increase your salary from $12,000 to $15,000, effective July 1, 1922, as a mark of the University's appreciation of your decision to remain in its service despite most tempting and attractive professional and financial invitations to return to the bar."[32]

Stone was both nettled and embarrassed. The unsolicited salary advance intimated that money was his primary motivation. Obviously troubled, he tried to make it clear that the Trustees' action was "a very great surprise." He would consider it "as an expression of confidence which I value quite beyond my power of expression."[33]

In another year it became quite clear he had had enough of academia. The end came on February 21, 1923, when he sent President Butler a long and gracious letter of resignation to take effect not later than September 15, 1923. His resignation was promptly accepted.

Various factors contributed to Stone's decision. The relative weight given them seems not to have been altogether clear in his own mind.

For one thing, he found "all the petty details of law school administration rather boring." "To tell the truth," he wrote a few years afterward, "that was what drove me out of the business."[34] He was,
moreover, "thoroughly disgusted with the petty bickerings which go
on in the life of a university,"[35] It was not so much his objection to
the ideas entertained by the "soreheads," though he did query both
their ideas and their methods. It was rather his native inability to
tolerate or deal with personal squabbles. In reply to Garrard Glenn's
observation, "You and John Bassett Moore are lucky to have left the
cloisters before the emergence in public life of the Tugwells, Moleys,
Berles, and Franks," Stone commented in 1934, "I share your views
on some of the professor gentlemen. It was just such fellows as they
that drove me out of the teaching profession."[36]

Not entirely absent from the considerations leading to his resignation was the fact that Dean Stone "always cherished an exceedingly
low opinion"[37] of President Butler. As early as 1913, after many bouts
with the president, he had not been "any too confident or happy about
the future."[38] He felt contempt for his shallow righteousness and
ubiquitous currying of favor with "the great." In 1937 a former law
clerk who had joined the Columbia Law School faculty sent Stone a
caricature of the "well-known educator" and expressed the hope that
"you will derive as much pleasure from contemplating it as I do from
hearing you discuss the subject."[39]

"The luminous countenance of the famous man confronts me as I
write," Justice Stone replied in mock appreciation. "It is a masterpiece,
and I am grateful to you for sending it. I am bound to say, however,
that it seems to bring a discordant note into the calm and peaceful
atmosphere of our library, and I am looking for a really suitable place
to hang it. What do you think about some place in the basement?"[40]

Money was a factor, though not a major one, in his resignation.
Not long before he left Columbia he was asked point-blank by a
friend why he devoted so much time to the deanship when he could
make so much more money, with less effort, in the actual practice of
law. His answer came without the slightest hesitation. "I am interested
in law as law. Money, as money, does not particularly appeal to me.
All I want is enough to support my family and give my children the
advantages of an education."[41] It was primarily his talents, not his
pocketbook, that Stone wanted to enrich and employ. He thought he
had capabilities which were being frustrated on Morningside Heights,
and he wanted greater scope. If he did not break away now, he would
be too old to blaze new trails.

The decision had not been an easy one. Members of the faculty and
of the Board of Trustees expressed genuine regret at his going. On
December 19, 1923, more than a thousand educators, members of the

bar and bench, and persons prominent in other fields honored him at a testimonial dinner at the Waldorf "in appreciation of Dean Stone's services to Columbia Law School and of his character, vision, and learning." President Butler and former ambassador John W. Davis were the principal speakers. The committee on invitation included such notables as Benjamin N. Cardozo, Frederic R. Coudert, Paul D. Cravath, William Nelson Cromwell, Edward R. Finch, William D. Guthrie, Frank H. Hiscock, Charles Evans Hughes, Irving Lehman, Herbert L. Satterlee, and Royall Victor.

On this occasion, President Butler praised Stone highly. He mentioned particularly the "notable additions to the teaching staff," plans for strengthening and developing larger opportunities for research. "To fill Dean Stone's place," Butler concluded, "is one of the most difficult academic tasks imaginable."*

John Bassett Moore, who could not be present, wrote a long letter[42] of appreciation:

There is no one to whom honor could more fitly be shown by the alumni of the Columbia Law School than to the great teacher and able administrator who is now retiring from its service. What he accomplished for the school is a matter of common knowledge, but the public has little opportunity to grasp the varied elements of personality that combined to produce such a result. . . . While giving to his students, in full measure, the benefit of his profound and comprehensive knowledge of legal principles, he was also a wise and sympathetic counselor, thoroughly human and helpful in his attitude, always patient and tolerant, seeking for qualities of strength to commend and develop rather than for weaknesses to expose and censure. . . .

Judged by skill and power in imparting knowledge, Mr. Stone belongs, as an instructor, in the highest rank. The notion that one teacher is as good as another is as preposterous as would be the supposition that one lawyer, or one general, or one artist is as good as another. I hazard nothing in saying that among all the teachers of law in the United States during the past fifty

* Through no effort on his own part, Stone's influence continued at the Columbia Law School for years after his resignation. Members of the faculty and President Butler himself freely turned to him for counsel and advice. On September 12, 1927, his successor, Dean Huger W. Jervey, wrote: "I still have an ineradicable feeling that you are Chief of the Columbia Law School and I am Vice-Regent. Therefore, Chief, I report to you."

When Dean Jervey resigned for reasons of health, President Butler solicited Stone's advice as to a successor. Stone's answer "in substance" was that if the responsibility "were mine I would appoint" Young B. Smith. This produced a row among some of the irreconcilables, especially Oliphant, who wrote Stone several times, suggesting that it was on the Justice's advice that Butler had appointed Smith without consulting the faculty. Smith himself believed this. On April 25, 1928, he wrote Stone: "It is needless for me to say that I appreciate deeply your recommendation to the President that I be appointed dean. It will always be a source of inspiration to me that you had enough faith in me to make the recommendation and should I be chosen I shall endeavor to justify your confidence."

years, those who deserve to [be] put in the same class with Mr. Stone can be numbered on the fingers of one's hands.[43]

But he belongs to a yet smaller group. One may succeed as a teacher but fail as a practitioner. The demonstration Mr. Stone has given of capacity for both careers is but an additional proof of his genius for the law. Nor did his contact with the practical side of his profession render him insensible to the need of the progressive adaptation of rules and methods to the changing conditions of the times. Always open-minded, he illustrated the truth that an instructed, enlightened conservatism, not readily deceived by superficial appearances, is an aid rather than a hindrance to real progress. . . .

I desire only to add that Mr. Stone has held up to the students of the school an exalted standard of personal character and conduct. In the course of a long and intimate association with him I have never known him to be influenced in his work by any narrow or selfish consideration. . . .*

In what Stone later called his swan song at Columbia, he said:

Law is neither formal logic nor the embodiment of inexorable scientific laws. It is a human institution, created by human agents to serve human ends. The attainment of its ultimate end and its successful administration, whether in the field of constitutional law or of private law, must depend in large measure upon the sympathetic popular understanding of its essential aims and of the more fundamental notions which underlie it. Is it too much to expect that with so much of achievement to our credit, we may include in our aspirations the hope that in the University and the Law School something more may be done to humanize law and lawyers, something accomplished to clothe the bare skeleton of legalism with the grace and dignity and beauty which are rightly attributes of the most sacred aspiration of mankind, the aspiration for the realization of justice on earth?[44]

Though Stone, in later years, looked back with pleasure and satisfaction on his Columbia Law School work and associations, there were apparently never any regrets. "Between ourselves," he wrote Young B. Smith in 1925, "I have never regretted leaving. It was a wise decision. Long tenure as the head of any institution tends to emphasize his faults and minimize his strong points, and in that situation a change is good both for the individual and the institution."[45]

* Stone, deeply touched, wrote John Bassett Moore, Dec. 24, 1923:

"I want to thank you for the very fine and very generous (all too generous) letter which you wrote to Judge Finch and which was read at the dinner the other evening. I would like to think that it is all true, but I must make some allowances for your generosity and for the friendly feeling which I know you have always had for me and which I value more highly than I can say.

"But I can say this, that if you had made a study of my life and my inmost thoughts and had endeavored to express with precision and accuracy what has always been my ideal of work and conduct, you could not have expressed it more completely or more accurately than you stated my supposed accomplishments in your letter."

CHAPTER TEN

# Law and Order
# in the Department of Justice

## 1924-1925

On June 20, 1923, Stone sailed with his family for Europe, where they spent the summer traveling through Italy, Switzerland, Holland, and England. In mid-September he took up his duties with the leading Wall Street firm of Sullivan and Cromwell. After long months of trying to decide whether or not to head their litigation department, Stone was destined to give only six months to big-time law practice. By early April 1924 he was in Washington to begin an uninterrupted public career.

### THE SHADY SIDE OF LAW AND PROPRIETY

Harry M. Daugherty's ouster from the Attorney General's office in March 1924 did not occur suddenly, without warning. Lurid tales of his exploits had long concerned even the shabby politicians of Harding's administration: all night poker-and-liquor parties with the "Ohio gang" at Howard Mannington's "little green house on K Street," the meeting place for shady barons of industry, captains of bootleg and highjack; lucrative traffic in Department of Justice liquor permits, the "deals" handled by Jess Smith, Daugherty's valet, chargé d'affaires, and buffer; William J. Burns' "shadowing" of congressmen who dared expose, or had exposed, the Harding scandals; stock-market speculations by the Attorney General himself under an assumed name, and so on. Mark Sullivan, no unfriendly critic, wrote: "The mere fact that Daugherty had such associations was enough to disqualify him. Those associations were a sign that Daugherty had not the sort of standing that the head of the Department of Justice ought to have."[1]

Instead of choosing a "best mind" for the Department of Justice, President Harding had been content "to choose merely a best friend."[2]

After Coolidge became President on the death of Harding, Daugherty was the only major figure implicated in scandal who held on to the bitter end. Navy Secretary Denby quit under clouds of suspicion and distrust. Colonel Forbes, once chief of the Veterans' Bureau, was trying to disable the proceedings of the grand jury convened to indict him. Albert B. Fall, sulking on his New Mexico ranch, awaited the day when he must answer for his sins as Secretary of Interior. Obviously Daugherty, the very symbol of political iniquity, could not escape. By 1924 Senate investigators were hot on his trail.

Harding's former political mainstay was now the Achilles' heel of Coolidge's regime. "Everyone in administration circles shivers when Daugherty's name is mentioned, no matter in what connection," the Republican *Boston Herald* reported, February 16, 1924. Nevertheless the taciturn Chief Executive, described by Daugherty as a man of "peaceful instincts,"[3] shrank from demanding his Attorney General's scalp. But on March 1, when the Senate passed Brookhart's resolution[4] calling for investigation of Daugherty and his bedraggled department, Republican politicians were frantic. They feared what the probe might uncover and dreaded even more the political consequences of Coolidge's delay in removing him. Daugherty had custody of the very records the Brookhart Committee needed to prove the charges made against him. Though the Attorney General had invited investigation, when he was asked to open Department files he refused, asserting that "I had in mind an investigation which would be conducted in a judicial manner. . . . To permit a general fishing expedition among the files of the Department by a representative of your committee with power to withdraw from the files such papers and documents as the examiner might choose would lead to endless confusion."[5]

Having kept Daugherty on out of fear, the President now threw him out in a panic and covered his belated action with a flimsy pretext.[6] On March 27 Coolidge wrote Daugherty: "I do not see how you can be acting for yourself in your own defense in this matter, and at the same time and on the same question acting as my Attorney General. . . . These two positions are incompatible and cannot be reconciled. I am sure that you will see that it is necessary for me to have the advice of a disinterested Attorney General. . . ."

The next day the Attorney General resigned.

### A MAN EMINENTLY QUALIFIED

Among those suggested for the vacancy were Judge William S. Kenyon of the Federal Court of Appeals in Iowa and Chief Justice Arthur P. Rugg of the Massachusetts Supreme Court. Stone, almost unknown except in educational and legal circles, did not figure in press speculation. But the President had been considering him for weeks before the embattled Attorney General stepped out. Coolidge had talked with Stone's Amherst College classmate, New York Congressman Bertrand H. Snell, about the embarrassing situation in the Attorney General's office. One day when they were on the presidential yacht *Mayflower* for a weekend the matter was gone over at length.

"I told him," Snell recalled years later, "that I personally liked Harry Daugherty, but under the circumstances I doubted if he could keep him as Attorney General"—a conclusion the President had now reached. Snell then suggested a man "eminently qualified" for the post. "I told him every good thing I knew—all I dared to—about Doc Stone—that he was a man of unblemished character, not a flaw in his work, one of the outstanding lawyers in the country." No comment from Mr. Coolidge.[7]

In late February or early March, when Stone was leaving his office for the day, the telephone rang. The voice was that of the President, whom he had not seen for some years, asking him to Washington for a conference the next morning. Surmising a discussion as to the selection of counsel for the oil cases then pending, the lawyer was surprised when the President sounded him out as to nominees for Attorney General. Several weeks passed; apparently the subject was dropped.

Meanwhile Snell saw Coolidge two or three times a week on legislative matters. "Nearly every morning when I was there I brought up the question of Stone's appointment." "Silent Cal" remained silent. One day, as Snell's hopes were fading, the President asked, "How do you know that Stone would take the job if it was offered to him?" Snell replied that he did not know. "Perhaps you had better go and find out," Coolidge suggested.

Snell brought up the matter of appointment during a visit to Stone in New York, but the Wall Street lawyer demurred. He explained the recent resignation as dean of the Columbia Law School, his lucrative practice in Sullivan and Cromwell, and his desire to capitalize on his years of study and work in the law. Snell persisted. If Stone went to Washington as Attorney General he would be even better able to capitalize on previous experience. But the difference between a $100,000 practice and a $12,000 Cabinet salary, even with an auto thrown in, made Stone hesitate. He could not make up his mind on the spot, but said as Snell was leaving, "I doubt if any man ought to decline a call from the President of the United States to an important government position."

Snell conveyed these sentiments to Coolidge, with his own belief that Stone would not decline the position if it were offered. "I knew Coolidge well enough to know that when you had said enough you had better stop."

On April 1 the President again called Stone to the White House for breakfast. There he met Senators Lodge, Curtis, Watson, Moses, Lenroot, Cummins, and a few others. After the legislators left, Coolidge took Stone to his study on the second floor, lit a cigar, and smoked in silence for some minutes. "Well," Coolidge finally commented in his accented nasal twang, "I think you will do."[8] Stone told the President, "I feel it is my duty to accept it."[9]

Later that day Snell was called by White House secretary Bascom Slemp. "Well, Bert," said Slemp, "you have made an Attorney General, and I'm sending the newspaper boys up to you to get an interview, as you seem to be the only man around here who knows Stone intimately and can answer questions in regard to him." "Bascom, what do you mean?" asked the astonished Congressman. Slemp was equally surprised. "Don't you know that Stone was appointed Attorney General this morning? Didn't the President tell you that when you were here this morning?" Amazed that the President should not have informed him of the appointment, Snell later asked Coolidge, "Why didn't you tell me that you had appointed Doc Stone Attorney General when I was in here the other morning right after you had made the appointment?" "Well, I thought you would find it out," the President replied.[10]

"I have nothing to say," Senator Smith W. Brookhart, Iowa insurgent and chairman of the committee investigating the Department of Justice, said in answer to questions from newspaper reporters; and the committee's "prosecutor," Senator Burton K. Wheeler, also in the dark, stated: "I cannot comment on Stone's appointment because I never heard of him before."[11] Scantily informed newspapermen fell back on friendship and common New England heritage triumphant over politics. Stone and President Coolidge, the *Boston Evening Transcript* reported on April 3, "had a common environment in their early years. . . . Both were small-town boys. Both married girls from their own stratum. Both men went to Amherst College, too." Some were reassured that the lawyer's library included the "philosophical writings of Herbert Spencer." One paper noted that "the appointee earns $125,000 a year in private practice, is an Easterner, a 'big business' attorney."[12] "Liberals" also found satisfaction: it was recalled that "when A. Mitchell Palmer perpetrated his greatest 'red' raid . . . this sterling New Englander from New Hampshire, with the blood of the Puritans in his veins," wrote a strong letter to the Senate Judiciary Committee in protest.[13] The portrait was blurred, but the *Washington Star* reconciled it all by describing Stone as "honest, able, loyal—a level-headed, brainy conservative-progressive."[14]

The Attorney General's friends were not surprised. A few of them had written urgent letters to the President: "Appoint Harlan Fiske Stone, former Dean of Columbia University Law School, to the ex-

*"Restored"; Clubb in the Rochester, N. Y., American, April 5, 1924*

alted office of Attorney General. . . . He is the very man needed in this hour. His appointment will go a long way towards restoring confidence and ending the surreptitious and insidious forces that now disturb the orderly current in the life of our country."[15]

Stone's friends and Amherst neighbors took the event as fulfilling their hopes and expectations. "What would they say—Ed Clark, Olney Gaylord, and the rest of Mill Valley?" a boyhood friend wrote. "Probably what the rest of us Amherst town folks and the rest of us Amherst alumni are saying. It is fine that you are able to live up to what your good father and mother deserved of you. Pity it is that they are not here to see it."[16]

There were many outpourings of warm sentiment and generous good will, as well as the earnest approval of such hardheaded lawyers as Charles C. Burlingham and such sedate newspapers as the *New York Times.* "Nothing could have happened to give me greater satisfaction," Burlingham wrote on April 3, "than your nomination. It has cleared the political atmosphere like a northwest wind. . . . With my mind's eye I see you sitting on the extreme left of the C. J. in one of those capacious chairs which the conformation of your body requires."

"In nominating Mr. Stone," the *New York Times* editorialized, "the President has taken a man about as far as possible from the type of the preceding Attorney General. In character, in legal attainments, in the approval of his brethren of the bar, in physical vigor and ability to cope with the severe labor which will be laid upon him in the Department of Justice, Mr. Stone is unusually well qualified."[17]

Clearly the President had acted on the basis of substantial considerations. "Mr. Coolidge was moved," the *Dallas Morning News* observed, "by the desire to get clean outside of the orbit of horse-swapping politics and find a man whom he knew he could rely upon. It looks like he succeeded in both objects."[18]

In the Senate were rumblings of doubt, especially from those who hoped the administration would respect the claims of geography. Senator Hiram Johnson of California dubbed Stone a "child of the prosperous East." "To whom are the deflated farmers of the West to look for support of their case?" he wanted to know.[19] Kansas' Senator Capper, grieving that the President had not appeased the farm bloc by appointing Judge Kenyon, echoed the *New York World's* dictum that "business does not suffer from the substitution of Stone for Daugherty."[20] "This appointment still shows that big business controls the White House," Senator Pat Harrison of Mississippi growled. The Senate Judiciary Committee promised to look into Stone's "Wall Street connections." All this only confirmed the general belief that the President had made a "judicious choice." On April 4 the committee approved, and in executive session three days later the Senate, with only a few senators present and after perfunctory discussion, confirmed Stone as Attorney General of the United States.

Reached by a reporter at his home on Riverside Drive, on April 7, Stone seemed more willing to talk about the fishing prize he had won over the weekend than of his Cabinet post. In reply to a question whether he would propose an immediate reorganization of the Department of Justice, he said that "it would be improper to talk without full knowledge of the conditions."[21]

After a short chat with the President on April 9, the new appointee was ready for work. "Where is the Department of Justice?" he asked the police sergeant as he left the White House. After receiving directions, Stone walked alone to his office on Vermont Avenue.

## EVERYTHING TURNS ON MEN

The Attorney General was hardly settled at his desk when speaking invitations descended upon him. His preference was to decline; the duties of his office were heavy, and he lacked the knack for public discoursing. "I am not a popular speaker," he told the wife of a former Law School colleague who asked him to address a New York women's club.[22] And, refusing to meet Clarence Darrow in public debate, he wrote, "I have what is perhaps . . . the most difficult office in the Government and I find it very absorbing."[23] But the day after taking office he accepted Mrs. Herbert Hoover's request to address the Women's National Committee on Law Enforcement and used the occasion to declare what might be expected under his leadership.

"There is nothing," he said, "quite so vital to the future well-being of this republic as that its laws should be enforced and respected. And by that I mean. *all* its laws. And that statement too is not applicable alone to those enemies of society who violate the law for personal gain or advantage; it applies to all of the agencies of law enforcement and to the Government itself." To make punishment of disobedience "swift and sure" was, he agreed, a "high ideal"—one which could not, perhaps, be realized. "But, after all, it is well to have the ideal." "Now," he concluded, "I think you will understand and appreciate that it's much more important that I should be engaged in the business of law enforcement than that I should spend much more time talking about it. A loaded desk awaits me over at the Department of Justice, and I am going back to it without delay."[24]

Certain distractions were, however, unavoidable. Persistent calls kept up from the Brookhart Committee for the files Daugherty had stubbornly retained. Taking the initiative, the new Attorney General visited the committee five days after he assumed office and tried to work out an understanding with the investigators. Whatever the precise arrangement, Stone left the Senate Office Building "smiling and . . . in the best of humor." "I think there will be no further trouble about obtaining the information we desire from the Government records," Senator Brookhart told reporters.[25]

But Stone and the committee were actually working at cross purposes. The Attorney General wanted to cooperate because he desired to have the findings grounded in fact. The investigators, aggressively led by Senator Wheeler, relished that blissful twilight zone between truth and fiction. Stone saw the committee's attempt to uncover previous wrongdoing for what it was—a "political backfire, hastily publicizing charges, . . . thus doing relatively more harm than good to the clean-up cause it professed to serve."[26]

Stone's willingness to cooperate did not succeed. As the investigation wore on, the proceedings became more and more bizarre. If Daugherty and his cohorts had associated, Senator Wheeler explained, with "crooks and criminals and divorcees and that class of people," the Committee had no alternative but to call these people as witnesses.[27] And yet Wheeler was not entirely sympathetic with Stone's suggestion that credible witnesses, persons who knew the facts, be called if possible. On June 13 Stone wrote Senator Brookhart a very pointed letter suggesting that it was time to call members of the Justice Department who knew of the transactions under inquiry. "In a number of instances," he asserted, "certain inaccuracies have crept into the testimony, and in others . . . a false impression may well have been created because important facts having a bearing on the inquiry have not been testified to at all." The public interest, the "interest of both your committee and of this Department, requires full and accurate information." He not only gave the names of employees and officials he wanted called as witnesses, but also assigned Warren Grimes of the Justice Department to keep him posted on the committee's findings. One day Grimes was called to testify as to a case he had handled. Wheeler, extremely sensitive to any reflection on the legitimacy of the committee's purpose, or on the reliability of witnesses previously called to testify, brow-beat Grimes so that even Senator Moses was moved to object.[28]

Nevertheless Stone had made his point: "I think the testimony of all members of the Department was very effective. Certainly the newspaper reports indicated that we still have a Department of Justice whose officials know what it is about."[29]

Shortly after taking office, Stone sought advice from Felix Frankfurter. In response, the Harvard law professor sent a copy of a recent letter of his to Walter Lippmann, then in charge of the *New York World*'s editorial page. "The key to Stone's problem," Frankfurter had told Lippmann, "is, of course, men. Everything is subordinate to personnel, for personnel determines the governing atmosphere and understanding from which all questions of administrative organization take shape." The letter had been written, Frankfurter told the Attorney General, "with never a thought that it would see your eyes."[30]

"I have followed almost exactly the suggestions contained in your letter to Lippmann," Stone replied.[31]

Speaking at the annual meeting of the American Bar Association in July 1924, the Attorney General made personnel his central theme. Lawyers, he said, seek "to improve the law by a better formulation of it." Their objective is "to remove obscurity . . . and increase its certainty." The lay public is motivated "by hue and cry for a victim. . . . The action demanded is the wreaking of vengeance." Neither approach went to the heart of the problem. Harry Daugherty showed that an "impassible gap" lay between law as "a mere statement of rules of conduct and the effective translation of those rules and the actual control of human action. . . ." Daugherty proved that the most important step toward law enforcement was "improvement in the training, character, and morale of those to whom its administration is primarily committed."[32]

To Stone this meant gradual recruitment of men of integrity in key posts.

### THE DAYS OF "OLD SLEUTH" ARE ENDED

The Bureau of Investigation had long been a target for harsh criticism. Headed by William J. Burns, former chief of the Burns Agency, the Bureau had become a private secret service for corrupt forces within the government itself. Included among the special agents were some with criminal records. Bureau badges and property had been issued to persons not employed by the government. Working as confidential agents and informers to "frame" evidence against personal enemies of the Harding administration, these specialists were commonly referred to as "dollar-a-year men."

"When I became Attorney General," Stone recalled in 1937, "the Bureau of Investigation was . . . in exceedingly bad odor. The head of the Bureau was under violent attack, and, as the records of the Department disclosed in official communications passing between former Attorney General Wickersham and President Taft, had himself participated in serious infractions of law and obstructions of justice. The Bureau was filled with men with bad records, and many of them had been convicted of crime. The organization was lawless, maintaining many activities which were without any authority in federal statutes, and engaging in many practices which were brutal and tyrannical in the extreme."[33]

Stone was less concerned with finding proof of past abuses, grave as these were, than with establishing standards for the future. Taking Scotland Yard as his model, he singled out three main qualifications for a successful police organization: "(1) that the organization itself should be law abiding; (2) that all appointees should be men of intelligence and some education; (3) that they should be subjected to a thorough course of training for their work."[34]

The barriers against abuses had to be erected within the Department itself. "I am firmly of the opinion," Stone said, "that officials of the Department of Justice can more effectively perform their duties by acting the part of gentlemen than by resorting to tactics of a different character. The work of gathering evidence and of conducting litigation should be done in a gentlemanly way." Bureau agents must be "impressed with the fact that their duties require the gathering of evidence of violations of the federal statutes and that it logically follows that they must not be guilty of violations of law in gathering evidence upon violations of law, for the respect to which they are entitled as law-enforcement officers can only be obtained by their strictly observing the rights of citizens and the law of the land."[35]

To Stone, Burns embodied all that was unhealthful, undesirable, and inexcusable in law administration. Though the Attorney General was under constant pressure to remove him, it was not until May 9 that Burns was called to the Attorney General's office and told that his resignation was desired. The idea did not appeal to Burns; he had no intention of resigning.[36] "Perhaps you had better think that over," Stone suggested as Burns was leaving. It took only one night for Burns to think it over.[37]

"I am in no hurry to select Mr. Burns' successor," Stone announced, "because I want just the right man for the job. Until I find that man, I intend personally to supervise the Bureau."[38] He began searching the field for a person with police experience who was not steeped in the "more usual police tradition that it takes a crook to catch a crook, and that lawlessness and brutality are more to be relied upon than skill and special training."[39]

"I don't know whom to trust; I don't know any of these people," the Attorney General confided to John Lord O'Brian, prominent Washington attorney.[40] For several weeks Stone had been considering J. Edgar Hoover, a young lawyer who had been Burns' secretary and executive assistant. One morning he asked Mrs. Mabel Walker Willebrandt, an Assistant Attorney General, about Hoover. She told him that she "regarded Hoover as honest and informed and one who operated like an electric wire, with almost trigger response." "Everyone says he's too young," the Attorney General responded, "but maybe that's his asset. Apparently he hasn't learned to be afraid of the politicians, and I believe he would set up a group of young men as investigators and infuse them with a will to operate independent of congressional and political pressure."[41]

On May 10 Stone asked Hoover to serve as acting director with the understanding that the appointment was temporary, effective until such time as the Attorney General could find the best possible man for the job. Not only was Stone cautious in making the appointment temporary; he also required Hoover to report directly to him.[42]

Hoover, aged twenty-nine, agreed to accept the post if Stone would give him authority over hiring and let him take only educated and honorable men, divorced from partisan politics. "Young man," Stone replied, "I wouldn't let you take the job under any other circumstances."[43]

After discussing what policies were henceforth to be followed, the Attorney General put his ideas in a six-point memorandum of May 13. Five related directly to personnel.

1. The activities of the Bureau are to be limited strictly to investigations of violation of law, under my direction or under the direction of an Assistant Attorney General regularly conducting the work of the Department of Justice.

2. I desire that the personnel of the Bureau be reduced so far as is consistent with the proper performance of the duties.

3. I request that you go over the entire personnel of the Bureau, as conveniently as may be done, and discontinue the services of those who are incompetent and unreliable.

4. I, some time ago, gave instructions that the so-called "dollar-a-year" men" should be discontinued, except in those cases where the appointees are in the regular employment of this Department. Please see that these instructions are carried out with all convenient speed.

5. Until further instructed, I desire that no new appointments be made without my approval. In making appointments, please nominate men of known good character and ability, giving preference to men who have had some legal training.

6. I am especially anxious that the morale of the Bureau be strengthened and I believe that a first step in that direction is the observation of the foregoing suggestions.[44]

Hoover thereupon began examination of the Bureau's personnel files. Numerous changes were soon in process. Systematic inspection of all field offices was effected by Department representatives instructed to inform the field personnel of the new policies adopted and the requirements set as standard conduct. In accordance with Stone's explicit order, all special agents were given courses of instruction upon their appointment and before being assigned to field duty.[45] Qualifications for the accounting unit and the force of special agents were raised so as to exclude from consideration any applicants without legal training or a knowledge of accounting.[46] Uniform efficiency reports were instituted, and each special agent rated within thirty days after a new assignment. A printed form of investigative report was adopted and instructions issued to improve the writing of these. Identification records of the former Bureau of Criminal Identification in the Department of Justice, together with the records of the International Association of Chiefs of Police, were consolidated in the Division of Identification. And to all this was added an over-all bureaucratic improvement—the simplification of paper work.

Efficiency increased impressively. The grand total of fines and recoveries in the last six months of 1923 amounted to $200,281.89. For the last six months of 1924 these rose to $320,179.78. The grand total of imprisonments under the Thefts and Frauds Division for the last six months of 1923 was 269 years. For the same period of 1924 it rose to 443 years, 4 months, and 289 days.

Though quite responsive to his chief's ideas, Hoover's action was not always as drastic as Stone thought proper. Hoover had given one agent a last chance by transferring him to a new location. The agent was a relative of a powerful political boss, and shortly after the change had been effective a congressional leader stormed into Bureau headquarters, demanding that the transfer be canceled forthwith. The irate congressman was soon face to face with Stone and the acting director. At the Attorney General's request, Hoover stated the facts, giving names, dates, and places, while the incensed congressman paced the floor. When Hoover finished, Stone remarked, "I am not sure, Mr. Hoover, that you haven't made a mistake. I think you should have fired the agent."[47]

At the end of seven months Stone sized up his acting director as "a man of exceptional intelligence, alertness, and executive ability." Believing that Hoover gave "far greater promise than any other man I had heard of," Stone appointed him director of the Bureau effective December 19, 1924.[48]

Throughout his short service as Attorney General, as well as during his many years on the Supreme Bench, Stone observed "young Hoover" with keen interest. The director of the FBI, in turn, continued to keep his chief on a pedestal. "The Chief Justice," Hoover wrote in 1946, "has been to me an ideal. . . . He is in fact the real father of the Federal Bureau of Investigation as we know it today."[49]

In April 1933 it was rumored that Hoover would be replaced by one of the old type, more amenable to political influence. Stone spoke out strongly against this and wrote of Hoover's work: "He removed from the Bureau every man as to whose character there was any ground for suspicion. He refused to yield to any kind of political pressure; he appointed to the Bureau men of intelligence and education, and strove to build up a morale such as should control such an organization. He withdrew it wholly from its extra-legal activities and made it an efficient organization for the investigation of criminal offenses against the United States."[50]

Stone could not, of course, keep abreast of the huge organization Hoover later built up, but he remained sure that the FBI was "far more efficient than any other police organization in the country." However, he wrote, "personally, I have been sorry to see [the Bureau] get the great publicity which it has received, and I only hope that the ultimate effect will not be to break down its morale. One of the great secrets of the success of Scotland Yard has been that its movements are never advertised. It moves and strikes in the dark, and in consequence is more efficient both in its internal organization and its relation to criminals than would otherwise be possible."[51]

From the day he made Hoover acting director, Stone foresaw other dangers: "There is always the possibility that a secret police may become a menace to free government and free institutions because it carries with it the possibility of abuses of power which are not always quickly apprehended or understood; . . . it is important . . . that its agents themselves be not above the law or beyond its reach."[52]

## WAR TRANSACTIONS SECTION

When Stone took office, the War Transactions Section of his Department was notably chaotic and inefficient. Established in 1922 to prosecute businessmen who had defrauded the government on World War I contracts, the section lived in conflict and hostility. Congressional conscience was sensitive to wartime frauds, but legislators held the purse strings so tightly as to cripple the section in doing its work. Considering it "one of the worst political sink holes in the Government,"[53] Stone struck at the root of the trouble—men.

"I am going to need an Assistant Attorney General at no distant date," he wrote Paul Shipman Andrews on April 21, 1924. "You are the type of man I would like to see in the place. It is worth doing, even if some sacrifice is required. Think it over and tell me how you feel about it." On June 2 Andrews took the oath of office. Stone also persuaded Jerome Michael to leave his New York law practice. "I know of nothing that would make me happier than the privilege of being associated with you and helping you in any way I can in the great public service that you have undertaken."[54] In midsummer Michael and Andrews, well known to Stone as student editors of the *Columbia Law Review*, became co-directors of the War Transactions Section.

"When I took charge," Andrews has written, "there was no docket or list of the cases. . . . There was no way of telling whether other cases were in default or about to become at default. There were a number of good lawyers . . . to be sure, but everybody seemed to be working in a watertight compartment of his own; . . . the section had no competent leadership whatever. . . ." The co-directors were to provide leadership rather than drastic house-cleaning. As to pending cases, Stone felt it "was best to keep in charge the same men who had originally brought them. If they did not succeed there could be no hue and cry that failure was due to change of personnel."[55]

Andrews, a Republican, and Michael, a Democrat, at once began recruiting top-flight personnel. Twenty-seven attorneys were then working in the section, some of them plainly not up to Stone's standard. To find replacements letters of inquiry went out to leaders of the legal profession and law school deans. "As a matter of self-defense against too much political pressure," Andrews has recalled, "we included in the letter a statement of the kind of man we required, which, as one reply from a friend of mine put it, was so high that if they could have found a man to meet the requirements they would have started grooming him for the Supreme Court of the United States!"[56]

Stone's prestige meant that the type of man most wanted could be attracted to government service under him for salaries much lower than they got in private practice. Within a year forty-four lawyers, in addition to the ten retained, were in the section. Among them was Alexander Holtzoff (now judge of the United States District Court). When Andrews told Stone that Holtzoff had accepted the appointment the Attorney General beamed. "Well, the Department of Justice is certainly looking up when we can get a man like Alec Holtzoff to come down."[57]

By September, Andrews and Michael had achieved a semblance of order. But only five months then remained before all fraud crimes committed prior to February 12, 1919 (three months after the Armistice), fell under the statute of limitations. If Stone had headed the Department earlier, his reforms would have been more productive. He had to make the best of a bad situation and actually did succeed in transforming the War Transactions Section from a "serious liability" into "a substantial asset" to the Republican party.[58]

### CLEANING OUT THE ATLANTA PRISON

Another trouble spot was the Atlanta federal penitentiary, where Mrs. Willebrandt, whose responsibilities included the Bureau of Prisons, had long suspected official irregularities. The key man was Heber Votau, Supervisor of the Bureau of Prisons, a retired missionary in India and brother-in-law of President Harding. Sentimental and inefficient, knowing little of "what it was all about," as Mrs. Willebrandt put it, Votau made it easy for politicians to use the Bureau of Prisons for patronage. After getting Votau's resignation, Stone began an investigation of the prison itself on a plan, conceived by Mrs. Willebrandt, of "committing" as prisoners hand-picked agents of the Bureau of Investigation. Their worm's-eye view soon produced all the evidence needed.

In December 1924 certain long-awaited changes occurred. The first official to leave was D. J. Allen, purchasing agent for the penitentiary.

The resignation of A. E. Sartain and his deputy, L. J. Fletcher, followed quickly. On suspicion that prison chaplain Thomas P. Hayden had turned over to Sartain cash obtained from bootleggers doing time in Atlanta in exchange for soft prison assignments, Hayden too was forced to go. A grand jury was quickly impaneled to present evidence gleaned by Justice Department investigators. Three days later Sartain and Fletcher were arrested on charges of asking for and receiving bribes amounting to $5000 and $2500 respectively, from one prisoner. Later they were convicted and locked up in the prison they had corrupted.

Stone did not come out of this shake-up unscathed. Prison officials—notably one gentleman from Idaho—used political influence with William Randolph Hearst to turn the heat on the Attorney General and Mrs. Willebrandt. Headlines and editorials denounced "the espionage system it employed against its own trusted employees." Deciding that it would be unfair to other officials and prisoners and their families to expose the wretched conditions discovered, Stone got Mrs. Willebrandt to relate the facts to Hearst privately. Shortly thereafter that crusade died out.

From most quarters Stone's action received high praise. Congressman Fiorello La Guardia (later Mayor of New York City) rose on the floor of the House and said that he had such confidence in the Department of Justice as to be convinced that it was finding the facts in the only way possible in order to make a real clean-up. The esteemed *Louisville Courier-Journal* commented on December 22: "In the presidential campaign, Mr. Davis [Democratic candidate for President] was on no point more effective than when he insisted that 'the springs of justice had been poisoned' while Daugherty was Attorney General, that justice had become a 'subject of barter,' and that the machinery of the Attorney General's office . . . had been perverted into a means of protecting lawbreakers and persecuting lawkeepers. More than once since Mr. Stone became Attorney General he has taken action that proves the charge made by Mr. Davis. And it matters not to Mr. Stone that the policy he is pursuing vindicates the position of Mr. Coolidge's campaign opponents in the presidential race. The vigilance of the present Attorney General reassures the country that once more the office he holds is in honest and efficient hands."

## ATTACKING LAW ENFORCEMENT
## AT THE GRASS ROOTS

In the shake-up Stone initiated in his own office, he was able to keep close tabs on what went on. This was harder when he went out to the grass roots of the Justice Department hierarchy—the district attorneys. Though responsible for seeing that they performed their duties efficiently, the Attorney General did not have power to remove them for not doing so. Such power belonged to the President alone; only the assistants could be discharged by the Attorney General. With a President who liked to "keep peace" with politicians, the position of a district attorney was so secure as to make the work of a conscientious Attorney General difficult. Stone's problem was further complicated by the fact that he took office in the heyday of that masterpiece of mass folly—Prohibition. The U. S. district attorney, to supplement his meager salary, was often tempted to take protection money from aggressive and lawless operators.

Stone waded into this miasmic situation cheered by the ideal of law enforcement "without fear or favor." Soon after taking office he added the sword of fact to his armament. At his request Mrs. Willebrandt prepared a memorandum for each federal district in the United States, giving names of officials, docket conditions, pending cases, the number of judges, and other statistics, together with confidential notes as to complaints and lax law enforcement. Stone, most enthusiastic about the usefulness of this statistical data, ordered the memorandum printed and mailed to all U. S. attorneys with an urgent request for cooperation. "Well," Stone chuckled, "these facts will put U. S. attorneys on their toes, and bring politicians out in the open, and lay the foundation for our demands to clean up the dockets."[59]

Reaction was explosive and immediate. Some judges registered objections with Chief Justice Taft, others wrote the Attorney General, complaining that the distribution of such a document was in fact criticism of them. U. S. district attorneys protested bitterly; some gave out interviews, while others stormed the Department of Justice.

The first to fall victim in Stone's clean-up campaign was John T. Williams, U. S. district attorney in San Francisco. Appointed by Daugherty, with the approval of Senators Hiram Johnson and Samuel Shortridge, Williams' energy had won from Mrs. Willebrandt her recommendation for a salary increase in 1923. His good fortune took a sharp turn for the worse the next year when Professor James M. Hyde of Stanford University charged that Williams gave protection to the "biggest importers of liquor and the chiefs of the bootlegging industry."[60]

Hyde's report stimulated Stone himself to start an investigation. On June 7 he telephoned Williams and reported the charges against him. After reading off dates and incidents the Attorney General warned: "I'm giving you a chance to resign and make your own explanation of your resignation, but if you don't, I will file charges that you are unfit to hold public office."[61] The three hours the Attorney General gave Williams to get out was time enough.

The day Williams resigned, Sterling Carr. Stone's classmate at Columbia, was appointed U. S. district attorney by Federal District Judge John S. Partridge, under a provision of the law that required a court appointment to fill the unexpired term of a district attorney. Soon thereafter things began to happen. Oblivious to the amenities which Stone now recognized as a necessary ingredient of party government, Carr, a Democrat, pursued his duties vigorously—"without fear or favor." Zealous administration of the law and politics could, he believed, be kept separate—each, as it were, in watertight compartments. To Carr any deference to politics evinced weakness on the part of the administrator. Little did Carr realize how wrong he was.

On August 6, a month after Carr's appointment, Senator Shortridge telegraphed Stone of the trouble caused by Carr's political naïveté: "Resignation of Calif. man who received appointment at my suggestion was demanded by Carr without any previous notice to me or reason given me therefor to date. Request by Carr for appointment of Whalen was sent to you and promise to Whalen of such appointment made by Carr without any consultation with me as to my desires. . . . Am greatly embarrassed and do not appreciate being put in a position of merely approving or objecting to Carr's appointments when am not accorded slightest privilege of suggestion or consultation by him concerning same before his recommendations are made."

Not only had Carr undertaken to change his deputies without senatorial consultation, but he also objected to what Stone described as the "established custom" of the Department, namely, that he obtain from the California Senators approval of his recommendations for personnel changes. Explaining his position, Carr wrote the Attorney General: "I understood . . . that the office was to be run without political affiliations of any kind and I was informed that such were your wishes. . . . If I have to go to the Senators for endorsements for my deputies—and thereby bring into the office the very political influences which I wish to keep out, and which are so undesirable for the proper administration of justice—my hands will be so tied that I can do nothing. . . . I do not desire to stay in the office and be subject to the political influences which have—and are still trying to surround it. . . ."[62]

Stone advised calm reason. "If it comes to a difference of opinion about what ought to be done, I expect to back you up in every reasonable way and place you in the position to meet the responsibility which has been placed on you."[63] At the same time he asked Carr to adopt a more worldly attitude. "The best interests of the United States, which we both have sworn to uphold and support, must be our guide. Where those interests are concerned, I do not intend to give ground.

However, tact, consideration of the sense of dignity of others and recognition of the fact that we have to live under a system of party government, are considerations which we must not leave out of account. As long as we can catch more flies with honey than vinegar, let's use the honey, but continue to go after the flies."[64]

Stone's opinion of Senator Shortridge "wholly conformed" to Carr's, but he realized that nothing could be gained "either by you and certainly not by me, by placing the Senator in a position where he is compelled to fight in order to 'save his face.' " "Do whatever is needful to enable him to 'save his face' short of yielding the main point, namely, that you are to be free of political domination in appointments and management of your office," Stone suggested.[65]

The high road of reform was far more difficult to travel than Carr realized, as Stone tried to make clear: "The situation in San Francisco is only one of many where I must travel the difficult path involved in getting rid of an unsatisfactory U. S. attorney and getting a satisfactory man in his place. Ultimately this will involve the presidential appointment of a U. S. attorney and his confirmation in the Senate. I do not want to fail in these confirmations because senators feel that I haven't been sufficiently mindful of senatorial etiquette. . . . If you have my end of the situation in mind and also have in mind the fact that it will be to your own advantage not to place the Senator in a position where he is forced to carry on open warfare, that is all I ask. You are quite free, so far as I am concerned, to follow the dictates of your own judgment and conscience."[66] By the end of September, Carr could report that matters were "ironed out nicely" with Shortridge.[67]

Stone's difficulties were partly of his own making. He simply refused to be governed strictly by the demands of partisan politics. Wherever two men were equally able, he consistently chose Republicans, though he considered it an unfortunate practice. However, insisting on personnel of high caliber, he not infrequently recommended Democrats, sometimes unwittingly. In explaining to Hugo L. Black the latter's appointment as Assistant Attorney General in Alabama, he said: "My position is clear. I would rather have a competent Republican doing this job; but if I can't get a competent Republican, I want a competent Democrat. You go back and do the job. I will make only one request, that you accept a salary for your services. Our salaries are not large and will not be fair compensation for you, but I cannot approve of anyone working for the Government without compensation."[68]

Nor was Stone deterred from swinging the ax by protests from politicians. Of all the personnel changes he effected, the removal of Walter D. Van Riper, assistant district attorney for New Jersey, was the most widely publicized as well as the most controversial. Among the complicating factors were Van Riper's powerful political connections. As the number one protégé of Senator Walter E. Edge of New Jersey, he had been nursed to full political maturity under the tutelage of U. S. District Attorney Walter G. Winne, a Daugherty appointee sponsored by Edge. Apparently acting on the assumption that Van Riper was not in sympathy with prohibition enforcement, Mrs. Willebrandt, as chief prohibition officer, had instructed Winne that prohibition cases were to be handled by two specified assistants and not by Van Riper.

This order appears to have been observed until December 15, 1924, when a Hudson County grand jury began hearings on the state's exposure of a Weehawken rum scandal. This case involved some of the biggest operators in state and county politics. A newspaper report that the federal authorities were prepared to investigate the same charges evoked from Mrs. Willebrandt a prompt telegraphic reprimand to Winne: "In spite of announcements from this Department that we will not usurp a prosecution apparently proceeding vigorously by the state authorities, the press announces that Van Riper is to present evidence in the Weehawken case to the federal grand jury. If the only evidence in your possession is what the state is acting on, do not present it to the federal grand jury until the state is given time to act. If any different evidence indicating violations of federal laws is furnished you, immediately notify this Department, but Van Riper must not handle this case."[69]

Outraged by this reference to Van Riper, Senator Edge immediately announced that he would have this out with the Attorney General himself, and on December 16 he, Van Riper, and Winne conferred with Stone. Confident that it would result in complete exoneration, Edge and Van Riper agreed to an investigation. These hopes were disappointed. Stone's action was so strong as to surprise even Mrs. Willebrandt. He told Van Riper to "discontinue all participation in the work of the office of United States Attorney. . . . The particular counts against you are grave indeed and amount to what I consider a gross disregard of the Government's interests in the handling of the duties of your office. Your explanations of these delinquencies do not, in my opinion, place your case in any more favorable light. . . . I have tried to be both painstaking and patient in this matter and have given consideration to all of your explanations and statements in our various conferences and in the letters you exhibited to me. In view, however, of my official duty, I can take no other step than the above."[70]

Van Riper replied in detail, denying all charges and refusing to resign. Without further explanation, Stone fired the Assistant District Attorney.

Quite apart from the specific situation in New Jersey, Mrs. Willebrandt has expressed the belief that the established Wet routine in New Jersey was "to please the Drys by filing cases, and take care of the Wets by never bringing the cases to trial." "If that is true," Stone commented, "where we have now the responsibility of enforcing the Constitution (including the Eighteenth Amendment), then in a less spectacular way it is equally true with anti-trust laws, customs, tax, and other laws which political constituents in an area don't like."[71]

While the Van Riper affair raged in New Jersey, Robert O. Harris, an aged gentleman with an impressive past, was fighting a losing battle to hold his post as U. S. district attorney in Boston. A man of culture and refinement, Harris had been accused by the Massachusetts Anti-Saloon League of being lax in enforcing the Prohibition laws. In fact these responsibilities had been left to his assistant, "called, and lovingly so, by every bootlegger in Boston—Joe."[72]

Objections to Harris's mismanagement had been accumulating in the Justice Department since 1922. On the advice of Senator Lodge, Stone requested Harris to reorganize his office and discharge his assistant. If Harris failed "gracefully to acquiesce," Lodge, on whose recommendation Harris had been appointed, suggested that both men be asked to resign. In an interview with Stone, Harris emphatically refused to do either.[73] The Attorney General persisted in trying to avoid a showdown.

"I think it would be only an act of kindness to Judge Harris," he wrote a Boston lawyer, "to persuade him that he should retire from his present office without the necessity of my asking the President to remove him. That, however," Stone advised, "is a matter for his friends to consider."[74] Instead of a peaceful resignation, the Department of Justice received refusals to resign, accompanied by countercharges and numerous open letters. At Stone's request, the President removed Harris in early December.

So deftly did Harris play the double game as champion of Right and victim of Wrong that certain members of the Boston bar took up arms in Harris's behalf. Stone rejoined: "My judgment is based on an observation of the functioning of Harris's office . . . and on two interviews with him. . . . It is perfectly apparent to me what the difficulty is. . . . Old age is affecting him seriously, and my observation of him leads me to the definite conclusion that he is not competent to handle any business of importance. The difficulty with the situation seems to be that a great many of Harris's friends . . . are not as familiar with his work as I am, and are thinking of Harris as he was perhaps ten years ago."[75]

"You will understand, of course," Stone wrote a few days later, "that I have made no point about his integrity. About his ability to do his present job I think I know more than they because I know what he has actually been doing and failing to do. . . . I think if they spent a few days in examining our office files, they would be amazed at the patience and tolerance with which I have dealt with this matter."[76]

As early as September, Stone had been considering the replacement of Harris. But Senator Lodge urged him to bide his time until after the November election. Meanwhile Lodge died, and William M. Butler, chairman of the Republican National Committee, was appointed to fill the vacancy. Frederick Huntington Gillet was elected senator. Action was further delayed when the Senators proved unable to agree on a choice. By early December conditions were critical. "It isn't simply that important litigation is at a standstill," Mrs. Willebrandt informed Stone. "The serious phase of the situation is that defendants are pressing their advantage and fixing . . . cases so that the evidence will be lost. . . . Cannot something be done to impress the President with the emergency of the situation . . . which is fast becoming intolerable?"[77]

Stone's patience had already worn thin. Writing Charles F. Choate, Jr., of the Boston bar, November 20, he had said: "I suppose our system of securing appointments of federal officials is the wise one, taking into account all the difficult types of personalities which may head the different departments of the Government. I may say, however, in connection with this matter that if the authority had rested wholly with me this situation . . . would have been cleared up and progress would have been made toward a more efficient administration of the law many months ago."

### THAT THORN IN THE FLESH—POLITICS

Stone clearly understood the rules of the political game. Replying to Charles D. Hilles, chairman of the Republican National Committee, regarding a complaint on the appointment of Democrats, Stone outlined his stand:

When I assumed my official position it was my understanding that all matters of patronage were to be taken up with the Senators of the respective states, confirmation by the Senate being necessary in many appointments, and that the Senators were in touch with the state organizations and were authorized to speak. . . .

In the matter of any appointment, and especially major appointments, I am desirous of getting the views of anyone who feels any especial interest in appointments to be made. That is of course especially the case with those who are influential in the political organization of my own state.[78]

Stone apparently disagreed with Hilles only in thinking that the public interest and the party's fortunes were inextricably joined. "I am deeply desirous of securing the best possible man," he told Hilles, "not only because it is a public duty imposed upon me, but because I believe that thereby the greatest service will be rendered to the country and to the President, and to our organization."[79]

Throughout his tenure Stone was hampered by political obstacles both in making policy and in implementing it. Mrs. Willebrandt was not far wrong in imputing the degeneration of law enforcement to political factors. In a letter to Joseph M. Steele, president of the Law Enforcement League of Philadelphia, she stated her views in plain terms.

In most states United States attorneys are hard-working and faithful officials, but as a matter of fact, there are nine or ten of them, whom, if I had the power, I would summarily remove because of their inactivity or political evasiveness in enforcing prohibition statutes.

I have in no uncertain terms called these instances to the attention of the person who is delegated to act [Assistant Attorney General Rush Holland]. In most cases, I have met with the information that a senator or a political situation prevented any change. . . .

Remember, your senators and your state politicians put and maintain your federal appointees in office. . . . Pennsylvania is one of the worst states in the Union as far as prohibition enforcement is concerned. . . .

The answer is in the way the law-enforcement machinery, both state and federal, is under political control—it's a case in Pennsylvania of political strangulation all down the line.[80]

In the midst of the political campaign that fall Samuel Untermyer, New York lawyer and special counsel of the Couzens Committee (investigating the Internal Revenue Division of the Treasury Department), released her confidential letter of July, in a furious attack on the administration. Untermyer charged that Coolidge, by his refusal to take action against incompetent or corrupt district attorneys, sanctioned the national scandal which had flourished under the aegis of the Harding administration.[81]

This happened while Stone was on a speech-making tour for President Coolidge. On his return, within a week after the letter's publication, the Attorney General went immediately to the White House for a conference with the President. In reply to reporters eager for a statement on Untermyer's charges, he was somewhat evasive. "I am sorry that I was in the West when Mrs. Willebrandt's letter was made public," he said. "I could have furnished the proper reply—that is, that steps have already been taken to alter the situation in any place where there is indifference to prohibition enforcement."[82] Since the letter was written, six district attorneys had in fact resigned and four more had been asked to.

Fearing this incident might embarrass the Attorney General and the President, Mrs. Willebrandt expressed her regret. "Rather than give me the slightest word of condemnation," she recalled, "he told me to go right on 'plugging at 'em.' "[83]

## APPLYING THE SOLVENT OF COMMON SENSE TO COMPLEXITY

It is difficult to imagine an Attorney General's path more thickly strewn with obstacles than was Stone's. He took over at a time when, as the late Robert Jackson once said, "the country felt actually unsafe because of the misuse that had been made of its powers."[84] Stone's problem was complicated quite apart from the outright dishonesty of his predecessor. He was responsible for the enforcement of national prohibition. He was also entrusted with enforcement of anti-trust legislation in an era when the grain of economic development ran against it.

The very nature of the Volstead Act invited a commingling of politics and law administration. When to this bootleg profits were added, the result was a huge mess of legal-political corruption. That Stone did not blink the difficulties confronting him is the more remarkable in that he was not himself a dry. But he was impatient with anyone who refused to cooperate. In a statement that suggests the theory of the judicial function he later crystallized as a Supreme Court Justice, he declared:

If you ask me whether I favor this or that law, and whether the one is as worthy of being enforced as another, I answer very frankly I do not consider that to be the concern of the Attorney General. Those are considerations to be addressed to Congress to guide it in determining what laws it shall enact and what penalty it shall fix for their violation; but not to the law-enforcement officer to determine what law he shall enforce. If violation of the federal law occurs, and there is a reasonable probability that prosecution will succeed, then it is his duty to act without fear, without favor, and without oppression to secure its enforcement.[85]

A major difficulty in enforcing prohibition lay in the fact that the act permitted small fines in lieu of jail sentences. In practice such fines were merely a tax on wealthy liquor syndicates for the privilege of doing illegal business. Jail sentences were more effective restraints both substantively and as examples to other lawbreakers. Stone therefore recommended that penalties for first violators be substantially increased[86] and urged that the limited staff devote its energies to the big offender:

There are many complaints that the money made in illegal traffic is going back into dirty politics and corrupting law administration at the source. That, of course, is the thing which it is important to stamp out. In doing this you will find, I believe, that it is much the better to attack the large conspiracies which violate the law and get the offenders in a single indictment and prosecution which will break up their traffic, rather than to push for convictions of single petty offenders.[87]

Stone's efforts achieved notable results. After eight months in the Attorney General's chair he reported that the average jail sentence for prohibition offenders had increased from twenty-one days in 1923 to thirty-four days in 1924; that the annual aggregate amount of revenue from fines, forfeitures, and penalties had been increased from $5,832,389 in 1923 to $7,487,235 in 1924; that 46,609 criminal cases arising under the Act had been terminated, an increase of 3879 over the previous year.[88] According to Mrs. Willebrandt, if Stone "had remained in the office of Attorney General for five years, enforcement of the Eighteenth Amendment would have become as respected a field of federal law enforcement as other federal laws." From her many discussions with Stone she believed that that was also his view.[89]

Stone was equally optimistic as to the possibilities of enforcing the anti-trust laws. Speaking before the American Whig Society of Princeton University in January 1925, he said: "I am firmly convinced that at no time since the [Anti-Trust] Act was passed has there been so great a need for its vigorous enforcement as now. . . . The decrees entered against the great combinations in the past must be translated into practical results. The defendants who have been found to have violated the statute must, in spirit and in practice, conform to the decrees and to the law. No new methods of circumventing freedom of commerce must be permitted to gain a foothold in our industrial life."[90]

But such sentiments ran counter to the temper of the times. Opposition to the Sherman and other anti-trust laws was almost universal. American Federation of Labor President Samuel Gompers then saw the Sherman Act as threatening to curb production and prevent distribution of goods in interstate commerce.[91] Commercial interests naturally opposed the intrusion of the "white ants of politics" into business regulation.[92] In his 1924 annual report Stone declared that the Department of Justice "considers that its duty requires it to invoke the Anti-Trust Act in every situation, however novel, which appears to come fairly within the spirit or intendment of the Act."[93] The

*Journal of Commerce* disagreed, saying: "If all laws were administered in this way, the result would inevitably be to keep the business world in a constant state of disturbance, with resulting impossibility of doing anything. . . . The country at large does not want experimentation and 'activity' under the Anti-Trust Law. It wants the formulation of a reasonable and consistent policy designed to safeguard the average man. . . ."[94]

It is not surprising that Stone failed to attain distinction as a trust-buster. Anti-trust prosecutions are not brought overnight. Some cases require years of preparation before the Government can make an effective showing in court. Nevertheless, in January 1925, thirty-three cases were pending before the Department which required actual trial or had already been submitted and were awaiting decision, and twenty-one cases were in a stage where civil or criminal proceedings were imminent. This total of fifty-four cases was a larger number than had been pending at any one time since the Sherman law was passed. Thus, despite all handicaps, the Anti-Trust Division of the Department during Stone's administration was far from defunct.

Since Stone served less than a year, his accomplishments naturally fell short of the goal. His achievements were rendered less spectacular by his temperate methods and by the limitations imposed on his actions. The Attorney General cannot summarily remove presidential appointees confirmed by the Senate. For the removal of U. S. district attorneys he had to convince the President and have the order issued by him—no easy task with a man of President Coolidge's stamp. To get rid of questionable prohibition agents who collected the evidence for U. S. attorneys to present to the grand jury, he had to appeal to Secretary Andrew W. Mellon, since prohibition enforcement was under the Treasury Department. Mellon paid "no attention to the appointment of agents or to the executive who supervised them." Once after a conference with Mellon in which Stone protested the type of agent employed, the Attorney General commented in disgust: "Law enforcement agents shouldn't be under *that* man."[95] He did not say that Department.

In pursuit of his purpose to recruit men of integrity and responsibility, Stone exercised both patience and consideration. He would get misfits quietly to resign and thus avoid public controversy. His way was neither swift nor drastic. Anyone inclined to measure success in terms of the number of persons fired may look on his Attorney Generalship with disappointment. Mrs. Willebrandt, a sympathetic co-worker, has written: "I think he was seriously hampered by not cleaning out his own Department more fully and more promptly." She was referring especially to the lawyer in charge of personnel, Rush L. Holland—"a politician pure and simple."[96]

Stone did not come to the Attorney Generalship experienced in the management of a public law office. But the practice he had gained, as Dean of Columbia Law School, in judging the abilities and character of men, proved of great value in reorganizing the shabby Department of Justice. Lacking the procedural legerdemain of an experienced bureaucrat, he sought to restore the integrity of his Department and of the law by improving personnel. The problem was not technical but human. No paper panaceas would suffice. Leadership, and leadership alone, could stir the driving desire to enforce and obey the law. The inspiration needed was of a very special kind.

"To work under him," Paul Shipman Andrews has recalled, "was a lesson in leadership, in kindliness, in how to administer an office. . . . He never 'breathed down the backs of our necks'; but he was always on hand and available if we wanted help or advice." Stone had unusual ability to stimulate those around him to do better work, not because he had the authority to require it, but because he had the ability and personality to inspire it. His very presence made people resolute to be their best selves: "He was a delightful person to talk to; a conversation with him was not a monologue on his part but rather a process of drawing out, so that you felt yourself talking better than you knew how. You came away stimulated and inspired."[97]

Stone was not a crusader; he was a craftsman. Less political in his outlook than most appointed public officials and more practical than most critics of corruption, he poured the oil of calm, reasoned judgment on the turbulent waters of 1924-25. Thus his first public office as Attorney General became a major step toward his career on the Supreme Bench.

<br>

CHAPTER ELEVEN

# Grooming for the Supreme Court

## 1924-1925

<br>

Other shortcomings of Stone's predecessor may be discovered by thumbing the pages of the U. S. Supreme Court Reports. With Daugherty as Attorney General, one notes that where the Government was a party, it usually was represented by specially appointed counsel. The Department of Justice was a sort of "sailor's snug harbor" wherein a congressman or senator might get shelter and a salary, on an *ad hoc* or permanent basis, for his professionally unsuccessful constituents. Briefs were poorly prepared and sloppily argued. This practice, politically profitable but governmentally disadvantageous, was discontinued by Stone. Under him, the Government's law business was handled by the permanent legal staff, and in major cases the brief presented by the Attorney General himself.

"It has not been usual for Attorneys General to argue cases for a good many years," Stone wrote his sons, December 4, 1924, "but it has seemed to me desirable to revive the tradition." He went on to tell of a case he had just argued in the Supreme Court that presented a novel constitutional question. "The President pardoned a man sentenced to prison for contempt of court. Under the Constitution he is authorized to grant 'pardons and reprieves for offenses against the United States.' The question was whether a contempt of court is an offense against the United States. There is some interesting legal history back of the expression. I contended that the President had the power."

The events culminating in the case had their origin before Stone took office. Philip Grossman, a liquor dealer in contempt of court for ignoring a restraining order served on him for violating the Volstead Act, had applied for a pardon. Twice rejected by Harding, he succeeded in having Assistant Attorney General A. T. Seymour repeat the recommendation to President Coolidge. Returning Seymour's letter transmitting the application, Coolidge scrawled at the bottom: "I do not wish pardon. Fine should be paid and sentence commuted."[1] Grossman then paid the fine and was free, not having served any jail sentence.

Coolidge's commutation order would have ended the matter had not Chicago Federal Judges Wilkerson and Carpenter interpreted the President's action as a slur on the judiciary. "The power to punish for contempt," they ruled, "is inherent in and essential to the very existence of the judiciary. If the President is allowed to substitute his discretion for that of the courts in this vital matter, then truly the President becomes the ultimate source of judicial authority. Such a holding would be a distortion of that cardinal principle of American institutions that the executive, legislative, and judicial branches of Government are coordinate and proudly independent."[2] Committed to jail, Grossman appealed. The case came to the Supreme Court in December 1924.

Stone was intrigued by the issues. "If the Court would permit it, and I can find the time to do it, I would be interested in arguing in behalf of the power of the Executive," he wrote.[3] But as Attorney General he was in a dilemma. On the one hand, having recommended clemency in his capacity as legal adviser to the President, he had to uphold executive authority. On the other hand, the authority of a federal court was being flouted, and it was his duty as Attorney General to safeguard the judiciary. To reconcile this ambiguity, he appeared as *amicus curiae* before the Supreme Court, arguing his case against his own special assistants!

The crucial constitutional issue was the scope of the President's prerogative in its relation to the fundamental principle of separation of powers. Stone conceded that unlimited exercise of the pardoning power did tend to nullify powers rightfully belonging to the judiciary. "The fair question," he argued, "is whether he [the President] may thwart the exercise of judicial power to punish offenders . . . by granting pardons. The answer is that the Constitution does establish a system of checks and that the pardoning power does furnish a potential check upon some judicial actions. If the President abuses this power he may be impeached."[4]

Contending that Grossman's offense was "simply a disobedience of a valid order of the court just as the ordinary crime is a disobedience of a valid law," Stone summarily concluded: "The power to grant pardons has been entrusted to the President and has not been entrusted to the courts."[5]

A unanimous bench, speaking through Chief Justice Taft, accepted this doctrine, and *Ex parte Grossman* became a leading constitutional case illustrating the principle of separation of powers. That same doctrine was later upheld in *McGrain* v. *Daugherty.*

It is ironical that litigation growing out of the rampant activities of the Brookhart Committee should establish once and for all the power of Congress to compel testimony. It is ironical, too, in view of the skepticism with which Stone regarded that committee's procedures, that it should have fallen to him as Attorney General to uphold that power before the Supreme Court.

In seeking incriminating evidence to condemn Stone's predecessor, the Brookhart Committee met with Daugherty's obstinate resistance. Nor was the committee more successful in trying to induce his brother, Mally S. Daugherty, to come to Washington with certain records of the Midland National Bank, of which he was president. The committee then went to meet Mally on his own ground. April 11, 1924, two days after Stone assumed office, the investigators were in Washington Court House, Ohio, Harry Daugherty's home town. This shift showed firm determination to get at records that might prove that Daugherty had taken bribes while Attorney General. But instead of records the committee faced a showdown. When the committee opened for business four men, identifying themselves as Mal Daugherty's attorneys, filed into the hearing room and announced that neither their client nor any other official of the Midland Bank would testify, nor would any of the bank's records be placed at the committee's disposal.

"I guess that makes the issue clear, gentlemen," the committee chairman remarked plaintively.

"Let me say to you gentlemen," Senator Wheeler broke in, "that we, of course, expect to proceed with contempt proceedings. . . ."

"We anticipated that would be the course," Daugherty's counsel observed with airy confidence.[6]

Contempt proceedings against Daugherty were voted by the Senate on April 26, but before he was arrested Harry's agile brother had secured a writ of habeas corpus·from the Cincinnati district court. The judge used the occasion to deliver a stern lecture denouncing power in the Senate to compel testimony as a particular form of legislative tyranny:

> The modern menace of tyranny is from the legislative branches of government, both state and federal, and from no other. The tendency of legislatures to grasp power beyond the constitutional limit is obvious and notorious. . . . I know it is said this power is necessary in aid of legislation. I deny the necessity. Convenient, at times, it may be; but necessary never. . . . An alleged necessity has, throughout all time, been the apology for wrong.[7]

The Daugherty brothers had thwarted the designs of the Senate—but not for long. On June 5 that body adopted a resolution requesting the Attorney General to bring the case before the Supreme Court. Stone was ready and willing. Nearly a month earlier he had advised Senator Brookhart that the Department of Justice would use every proper effort to defend and protect the interests of the Senate in the matter, and he appointed Colonel William T. Chantland of his Department as his special assistant, assigned to help the committee and to act as liaison between the Department and the committee.

At Senator Brookhart's request, Stone urged the Court to advance the case on its docket. The argument was set for December 5, 1924.

Daugherty's counsel argued that the Senate, when acting in its legislative capacity, had no power of arrest to compel testimony:

> The Senate can compel testimony only in cases where it has judicial power specifically granted by the Constitution. Any argument which begins with an assertion that citizens owe a duty to give testimony and thereupon asserts that Congress, or a branch thereof, may enforce this duty by its own processes, will result in nullifying the express division of powers among the three branches of government. . . .
> Congress, under the federal Constitution, has only those powers which are granted to it. . . . Not even when Congress is given an express power can that power be exercised in derogation of the express guaranties of individual liberty. . . . If Congress has no such power where there is a specific grant, certainly Congress cannot destroy personal guaranties through any implied grant incidental to the general power to enact laws.[8]

Testimony could be compelled, Daugherty's lawyers argued, through the judicial process *only* in cases where Congress clearly indicated the legislation it contemplated and where such legislation required testimony from the individual in question. By giving the case this posture, the lawyers could argue quite persuasively that the resolution authorizing the Brookhart Committee contemplated no such legislation:

> The personal cast of the resolution, the inability of the committee to do anything except to try the facts concerning the charges contained in the resolution, and the total inability of the Senate to use the findings of the investigating committee for any purpose other than to pillory Harry M. Daugherty before the American people, clearly demonstrate that the proceeding is an attempt to usurp the judicial function.[9]

To uphold the Senate's investigative power, Stone invoked Chief Justice Marshall's historic decision in *McCulloch* v. *Maryland* (1819). Congressional power to compel testimony and the production of evidence, he argued, is derived from "the well-settled rule of unexpressed power necessary or proper to the exercise of express powers, being recognized by the courts as necessarily a part of the constitutional grant." The power of each House of Congress, he pointed out, "was asserted from the beginning, not because it was exercised by the House of Commons in England, but because it is 'necessary or proper for carrying into execution' the powers vested by the Constitution in Congress, and each House thereof."[10]

As to the relationship between the subject of investigation and contemplated legislation, Stone stated:

> Each House has power to do whatever is customarily required to enable it intelligently to participate in the making of laws. Such implied power cannot be reserved to the states, respectively, or to the people, for it can only be exercised by the House itself. If it be not vested in such House, it exists nowhere. That it does exist in each House, and constantly has been exercised for nearly a century past, is abundantly demonstrated.[11]

In closing, the Attorney General put the question squarely to the Justices:

> Can it possibly be said that the discovery of any facts showing the neglect or failure of the Attorney General or his assistants properly to discharge the duties imposed upon them by law cannot be and would not naturally be used by Congress as the basis for new legislation safeguarding the interests of the Government and making more improbable in the future the commission of any illegal or improper acts which might be shown to have been committed in the past?[12]

When the decision finally came down in 1927, Stone himself was a Supreme Court Justice. Though unable to participate in the case, he had the satisfaction of seeing his brief accepted by a unanimous bench.

While the case was in progress, Alfred A. Wheat, special assistant to the Attorney General, had lamented: "I wonder if any really beneficent law ever was or ever will be passed as the result of information obtained by subpoenas and threats of imprisonment and wrung from intimidated persons in the presence of reporters, photographers, and a claque." " 'The art of our necessities,' " he quoted, " 'is strange that can make vile things precious.' "[13] The art of democratic necessities is indeed strange, especially in light of the subsequent activities of some congressional investigating committees. A wide gulf separates inquisition from investigation. Whatever the technique employed, all such inquiries are under obligation to Harlan Stone for the opportunity to pursue their vastly divergent ways.

These were not the only headline cases Stone argued. On November 5 he wrote his sons of plans to take part in *United States* v. *Chemical Foundation, Inc.*, "one of the big cases growing out of the war." This litigation, like *McGrain* v. *Daugherty*, was the child of scandal. "Nothing in any oil transaction, not even the acts of Albert B. Fall," one newspaper commented, "has any more sinister aspect than the transaction" involved in the Chemical Foundation controversy.[14]

During World War I, the Alien Property Custodian, in accordance with the "Trading with the Enemy Act," seized, in the name of the United States Government as trustee, approximately six thousand German-owned dye patents then leased to various companies in the United States. On February 25, 1919, A. Mitchell Palmer, the Alien Property Custodian, without express authorization from Congress, without advertising for bids or conducting a public auction (as specified by Congress in the event that the President did not direct otherwise and give his reasons for so doing\*), and without having appraised their value, sold these patents to the Chemical Foundation, Inc. Not until one week after the sale was authorized, however, did the Foundation receive its charter of incorporation. In the meantime Francis P. Garvan, president of the Chemical Foundation and also a member of the Custodian's advisory committee which had recommended the sale, became Alien Property Custodian. Ramsey Hoguet, patent attorney in the Custodian's office at the time of the sale, became

\* When President Wilson left for Versailles, he designated Frank L. Polk, counselor for the State Department, to act for him in the matter. Polk signed the executive order approving the sale. But the Government contended that Polk could not lawfully do so, for the following reasons: (1) The President had designated Polk as an individual, and hence no executive power was vested in him (Polk) to prescribe the manner of sale; (2) Polk signed the executive order authorizing the sale (at the behest of Palmer) *after* the President had already returned from Europe and consequently was in a position to act for himself in the matter. Polk's power to act, however, was upheld by the Supreme Court.

the patent attorney of the Foundation; Joseph H. Choate, Jr., counsel for A. Mitchell Palmer when he was Custodian, became the Foundation's legal adviser. It was said by the Government's chief prosecutor that a lawyer named Squires had been given the opportunity to examine all the patents and make a list of the ones that should be seized in the event of war. By the end of 1922 the Chemical Foundation had accumulated over a million dollars under this arrangement.

When the Republicans came to power, Harry Daugherty, prompted by a plea from the former German owners of the patents, sniffed on the trail of his Democratic predecessors. His well-trained nose soon led him to the office of the Alien Property Custodian, where he found something to bark at. In 1922 he brought suit before Judge Morris in the district court at Wilmington, Delaware, against the Chemical Foundation Corporation for return of the patents to the United States Government, contending that the sale was invalid.[15] Judge Morris dismissed the suit, and the appeal was set on the docket of the Circuit Court at Philadelphia for November 1924.

Those who foresaw a dramatic legal battle were not disappointed. That the Attorney General himself would present the Government's case was enough. "It was the first time," the *Philadelphia Record* commented, "an Attorney General has appeared in the local United States courts since Attorney General Wickersham argued a case here during the Taft administration."[16] With Stone were Solicitor General James M. Beck and Special Prosecutor Colonel Henry W. Anderson of Virginia. The Foundation retained veteran Boston lawyer Moorefield Storey. On November 10 the arguments began.

"Mr. Storey," one paper reported, "moved the speaker's rostrum flush up against the judge's bench, in order that he might be heard, but many times his voice dropped to a whisper and even the judges had difficulty in hearing him." But no one could miss the lawyer's overtones as he pictured the looting of factories, warehouses, and châteaux in France by the Germans, who "carried off wives and daughters of the French and Belgians." There was, Storey asserted, "no power on earth to prevent [the patents] getting back to their German owners"—that "powerful confederation of German scientists" could afford at any time to outbid the Chemical Foundation. And here, said Storey, was the United States Government, seeking to confiscate the property of honorable American business.* While castigating Daugherty for instituting the proceedings at the request of the Germans, the lawyer praised his own clients as "men of high standing

* Actually, the government did not seek to "confiscate" the holdings of the Foundation. As Stone made clear, the Government intended to give full credit to the Foundation for proper expenditures, though not for the excessive profits made.

in the business and financial world, [who] should not be branded with the mark of having committed an unlawful act." "The Foundation held these patents in trust for the benefit of the people of the United States," he concluded. "It has faithfully discharged that trust."[17]

While Colonel Anderson replied, Stone sat at the counsel table making notes. Finally the Attorney General delivered a powerful summation, consuming two full hours.

"I have no apologies to make for continuing this case," he countered in reference to Storey's implication of collusion between Daugherty and the Germans. "It will be a dark day for this Republic when public officials charged with public duties and responsibilities can do acts disclosed by this record, without any consequences to them and those who claim under them. It will be a sadder day if the Attorney General of the United States, in the face of this record, did not present the matter in court, and ask relief for the United States."

On the vital issue of patents' ownership, Stone's answer to Storey was that Congress alone had power to determine the disposition of seized enemy property:

We are told that this suit is brought in the interests of the Germans. It is quite possible that Congress may determine to return this property, or the proceeds of it, to the private owners from whom it was taken. It has that power. It had been expressly reserved. The power to make the final disposition of this property Congress has reserved to itself.

Whether or not that occurs is not the responsibility of this appellee. It is not the responsibility of the Attorney General; it is not the responsibility of this court. . . . It is . . . the power and authority of Congress to deal with this property as it sees fit.[18]

The Alien Property Custodian occupied as to the patents the same fiduciary responsibility that a common law trustee holds for any kind of property. Thus the Custodian had committed a breach of fiduciaryship, not only in selling the patents for less than their fair value, but in selling property that had not been appraised. "Who shall say that these men have the right to throw this property away?" Stone demanded. Contending that the Chemical Foundation was anything but a charitable trust, Stone lashed out at Garvan and Hoguet for violating their public trust:

If the gentlemen active in the concoction of this scheme can come here and argue that they performed their duties to the United States, and at the same time performed their duties for the corporation, I will not question they hold that opinion, nor will I question their opinion that they can substitute their will for that of Congress; but we do question their power to make a sale [such] as this, and [do] most earnestly maintain that they were bound to recognize the sacred obligations imposed upon them as public

officials. . . . These men violated these laws in being interested in a corporation to which they sold the patents. If there was nothing else in the case,
how can a court of equity uphold this transaction?[19]

In the course of his argument Stone took satisfaction in reading to
the court from John Bassett Moore's recent address on how the fiduciary principle had been lost sight of in the administration of alien
property. In the Chemical Foundation case that principle, he wrote
Moore, "had been ultimately translated into the practice of patriotism
for profit. . . . You would hardly believe that such things could happen
in our Government."[20]

The Court of Appeals, unimpressed by the Attorney General's argument, affirmed the Delaware district court's dismissal of the suit.[21]
Appealed to the Supreme Court, the case was decided after Stone
himself had been elevated to that august tribunal. Again the Government lost,[22] partly, Stone believed, because counsel did not argue
the case along the lines he had laid down in Philadelphia. Several
years later he wrote:

> Government counsel in that case insisted on trying to win it on farfetched
> constitutional grounds, although it was demonstrable from the record, the
> statute, and elementary principles of law that the property was held in a
> trust capacity, and that the Alien Property Custodian and other Government
> officers to whom the guardianship was entrusted had been guilty of grave
> violations of their trust; and the Government was the proper party to demand
> an accounting. I was never satisfied with the outcome in these matters.[23]

### THE POLITICAL POT BEGINS TO BOIL

In June 1924 the Attorney General and Mrs. Stone went to his Amherst reunion and from there to Yale, where he received an honorary
LL.D. and delivered a "real highbrow"[24] address.* The couple then
visited Cleveland to view the nomination of Calvin Coolidge.

The July Convention signaled the start of a heated campaign.
Though Stone tried to remain aloof from political entanglements, he
inevitably became embroiled. "The political pot is boiling in lively
fashion," he noted in September. "Up to the present I have taken

* The address, delivered June 18, 1924, was entitled "Some Phases of American
Legal Education." What Stone said on this occasion made it clear that the views
he had expressed nearly a decade earlier, in his book *Law and Its Administration,*
had undergone change. "Our most distinguished and capable teachers of law
now recognize," he observed, "that we can no longer deal with law as though it
were a hermetically sealed compartment of social science, to be explored and its
principles formulated without reference to those social and economic forces which
call law into existence, and from which law must derive its form and substance if
it is to serve adequately its purpose." (*New York Law Journal,* Oct. 25, 1924,
p. 340.)

no part in the campaign, believing that actions speak louder than words, especially in the case of one of the main actors in the political moving pictures."[25] However, demands for his services began pouring in, "all interesting, some disgusting."[26] And there were some he could not ignore. "It seems particularly appropriate that the Attorney General speak out in view of the attacks on the Department of Justice during the last year," John Q. Tilson, Speaker's Bureau chairman of the Republican National Committee, wrote him. Stone tried to beg off. "It is very difficult for me to devote much time to campaign speaking in view of the burden of work there is in this Department."[27] His excuses were unavailing. Having entered the Cabinet as Daugherty's successor while the entire country was forming an opinion of the Coolidge administration, Stone was a key figure in its defense. The obligation he owed to his party was as inescapable as that which the party owed him.

By mid-October his itinerary was settled—one address in Des Moines (Oct. 24), another in Philadelphia (Oct. 29), and another in Boston (Nov. 1).

The campaign of 1924 was a three-cornered struggle among President Coolidge, John W. Davis, the Democratic nominee, and Robert M. La Follette, the Progressive party candidate. Whatever the strict party differences between Coolidge and Davis, on the broad questions of protecting the nation's welfare and institutions they were firmly of one and the same mind. La Follette, on the other hand, represented a trend that his antagonists said would "disrupt the fundamental organization and administration of many of the national institutions. In fine, it was a battle between right, which believes in our national ideals, and wrong, which believes in disruption and discontent."[28]

There was not much danger that La Follette would be elected, but there was concern among both Democrats and Republicans lest the election be thrown into the House of Representatives.* In Congress. as constituted by the 1922 election, the balance between Democrats and Republicans was almost even, and it was felt that the Progressives might conspire with the Democrats to deadlock the election in the House and force the Senate to elect Charles R. Bryan of Nebraska, the Democratic vice-presidential candidate—supposed for campaign purposes to be a wild-eyed radical—dumping the deadlocked conservatives Davis and Coolidge in the process. Republican orators saw two choices open to the voters: election of Coolidge by the people or

* This belief was shared by members of all parties, including Franklin D. Roosevelt, who had run for Vice-President on the Democratic ticket in 1920. "I have a hunch," he wrote a friend in October 1924, "that Davis' strength is really improving, but I still think his election will go into the House."[29]

election of Bryan by Congress. It was, they said, "Coolidge or Chaos."
Said the *New York Herald Tribune*:

> A vote for La Follette is a vote for Bryan.
> A vote for Davis is a vote for Bryan.
> A vote for Coolidge is a vote for Coolidge.[30]

On October 22 the Attorney General left Washington for the Middle
West. After spending a day in Indiana, looking over possible sites for
a federal prison for women, he went to Des Moines, where he made
a major address on the 24th. There were in addition five "spur of the
moment" speeches. He gave a non-political talk at Drake University
Chapel and met various Des Moines luncheon clubs. At an afternoon
meeting he spoke to Republican women, and in the evening at the
local bar association dinner.

The central issue of the campaign, Stone told his principal Des
Moines audience of eight thousand, was whether Calvin Coolidge
should be elected President or whether the election and organization
of the government should be controlled by a defeated minority. The
third party, he said, did not seriously contemplate the election of its
own candidates. It sought rather to draw enough strength from the
Republican and Democratic parties to prevent any candidate from
obtaining 266 votes in the Electoral College. The election would thus
be thrown into the House of Representatives as constituted by the
1922, rather than the 1924, election. There the vote for President
would be by states, each state delegation casting a single vote in
accordance with the majority will of each delegation. At least five
state delegations, Stone conjectured, would be deadlocked over the
presidential candidates and would be unable to vote in the House
election. From the remaining forty-three states no candidate would
be able to draw the twenty-five votes (a majority of the states) necessary to elect a President. "No President could be elected by the
methods prescribed by the Constitution, and when that happens, the
third party will have achieved its great purpose." This, Stone said, was
a serious situation:

> It is serious because any proposal made in the name of popular rule to
> defeat the will of the people and to control the election and the Government
> in this country by a minority is a perilous enterprise. History has taught us
> over and over again that minority control of Government in a democratic
> country means chaos, and in all history I know of no attempt at such control
> comparable with this one, unless it be the minority rule of the Soviet
> Government in distracted Russia.

Equally subversive, if not more so in Stone's mind, was La Follette's
Supreme Court proposal. The American revolution, he told his Des
Moines audience, had brought home to the founding fathers the ne-

cessity of a strong central government endowed with sufficient power to conduct its foreign relations and control domestic interests national in character. This strong central government had to be created, however, by the action of thirteen independent states, each of which, for most purposes, was politically sovereign. It was desirable that these states should retain their sovereignty to provide for their local self-government. The framers of the Constitution therefore had to create two independent and sovereign governments, each supreme within its own field. The federal government was one of delegated powers. As to the states, the Constitution provided "first by implication and then later on by the express provision of the Tenth Amendment, that all powers not delegated expressly or by fair implication to the National Government, should be deemed to be reserved to the states." The Progressive proposal, Stone said, would give Congress power "to wipe out every vestige of state sovereignty and all the reserve powers of the states."

Another problem had challenged the founding fathers: what legal restraint was to be exercised over these governments if either exceeded its constitutional powers? "The novel arrangement under our Constitution," Stone explained, "was the provision, embodied in it by clear implication, that where the state government encroaches upon the powers of the federal government, or vice versa, the rights of each may be authoritatively determined by the Supreme Court." This implies the power of the Supreme Court "to declare law of either the federal or state government to be unconstitutional and void if it runs counter to the provisions of the Constitution." Allowing Congress to re-enact a law which the Supreme Court had declared unconstitutional would, Stone said, be allowing Congress totally to usurp state sovereignty at its own discretion. With La Follette's proposal

in force we would cease to be a national federation of states with sovereign powers vested in federal government for the purpose of conducting national affairs and with sovereign powers in the state government for the purpose of administering local self-government. We would have created in Congress a centralized political organization not unlike that of the Roman Empire, where the central government, at first Republican and later Imperial in form, drew to itself the actual regulation and control, in minute detail, of every function of local government within the Empire.

The practical consequences of such a development would be unfortunate in the extreme: "I ask whether you, as citizens of the sovereign State of Iowa, are prepared to relinquish to Congress the power at will to withdraw the rights of your citizens from the protection of your own state government guaranteed to it by the Constitution of the United States?" Stone thought not.

The Progressive proposal, the Attorney General contended, would also disrupt the constitutional separation of powers among the executive, the legislative, and the judicial branches of the Government. By overriding the pronouncements of the Supreme Court, "Congress might destroy, even to the last vestige, all the powers now residing in the judiciary and in the executive."

Finally, the Progressive proposal would enable Congress by a single act of legislation to wipe out American civil liberties. The Constitution, Stone emphasized, guarantees to every citizen "those privileges and immunities which, placed beyond attack and destruction by either the legislative or the executive branch of the Government, constitute the protection and the guaranty of civil liberty." Thus, from various angles, the Progressive proposal constituted a "complete departure from all the fundamental principles embodied in the Constitution, and its practical effect amounts to an abolition of constitutional government in the United States." Disguised as an attack on the Supreme Court, La Follette's proposal would destroy "at one stroke all the principles which are fundamental to any constitutional government."

The address was, as Stone said, of "a serious character and rather dull but the people seemed to like it."[31]

On the 29th the Attorney General talked to the Union League Club in Philadelphia. Here his speech was also well received. He was less pleased with the reception in Boston. "It was too late in the campaign," Stone thought, "and they were more interested in the 'hot air' type of speech."[32] In the Hub city the Attorney General himself lowered the tone of his appeal. In a brief impromptu talk delivered at a large Negro meeting late in the evening, he fiercely assaulted La Follette's Supreme Court proposal. Playing fast and loose with the facts of constitutional history, he said:

> No one knows better than the Negro citizens of our country that the Supreme Court has always been the bulwark of the oppressed. Under it the colored race has been protected in the rights obtained since the abolition of slavery. But I wonder if you realize what this La Follette plan would mean. It provides that if Congress once passes a law and the Supreme Court declares it unconstitutional, Congress by repassing the law can work it into the law of the land and the Court is powerless to prevent it.
>
> Now you know what Congress can do and what it has at times attempted to do. You know that a Democratic Congress is always dominated by the Southern Democrats, the traditional foes of your race, who have fought steadily against the advancement of the colored people. Do you want to put your brothers and sisters in the Southland under the absolute power of such a Congress? Do you want to destroy the protection the Supreme Court has given you? I believe not.[33]

All this was demagogic and completely out of character for Stone. He was at his best in more informal talks, especially those concerning the work closest to his heart—the Department of Justice. It was on this subject that he "produced enthusiasm that was real, that was spontaneous, and that reflected deep feeling." Speaking without excitement, the Attorney General had created "the impression that in the Justice Department at Washington, things are all right."[34]

For Stone, Coolidge's victory represented a "fine outcome," "a triumph of decency and straightforwardness over a mudslinging campaign." The election would do much to "set the country on the path which it should travel in the next few years." And though he himself had had enough of political life, he wrote his sons, November 5, he felt that "the job was worth doing for a time at least, and so I shall stick to it for the present."

On November 18 he wrote them: "The President evidently wants me to continue in my present position, so that I am likely to be here for some time to come." By December 4 events had taken a turn that promised to keep him in Washington indefinitely. In a postscript to a letter to his son Marshall he scribbled:

*Confidentially* there is much prospect that I may go on to the Supreme Court by the first of the year. Both the President and the Chief Justice have talked about it and I think it is likely to happen if the President can get a new Attorney General to his liking. He thinks he has the man although he is reluctant to take him in my place. But he also feels that I am the man he wants on the Court. I have some doubt about taking it but it is a place of great dignity and public usefulness—a life position. The salary is not large but I think we can get along comfortably with such other income as I have. Please do not mention this until the matter is ended or becomes public.

It became public January 5, 1925. Meanwhile, he contemplated the prospects with mixed feelings. It was not easy to relinquish the high professional rewards now assured him in law practice. He and his wife had recently furnished a very attractive New York apartment, and this meant they would have to give it up. But there were compensations for the Stones in Washington. In mid-December he wrote of an overnight party on the *Mayflower:* "There were about sixteen people in all; several Senators and their wives included. We were the ranking guests. So I had the honor of taking Mrs. Coolidge out to dinner and Mother was taken out by the President."[35]

Meanwhile the Attorney General had been figuring somewhat in the papers. Headlines told of his "disposal" of U. S. attorneys "who do not perform well." Also newsworthy was his "cleaning out of some office-holders at the Atlanta Penitentiary who were not doing their duty."[36] Certain headline cases were on their way to the Anti-Trust Division. Among those tagged for prosecution was Andrew Mellon's industrial stronghold, the Aluminum Company of America. On October 7, at the peak of the presidential campaign, the Federal Trade

Commission had issued a preliminary report on the company's activities since 1912. The report charged, among other things, attempts to gain tariff protection, suppression of independent rolling mills, and virtual control of 90 per cent of all known bauxite deposits in America.*

When questioned by newsmen, Stone pledged an investigation, but said he could take no action until the Commission submitted its findings to him.[37] On October 17, after ten days of feverish activity, the Commission, hastening to put the responsibility in the Attorney General's hands before election day, had finished its report and certified it to the Department of Justice.[38] But for the next three months the matter was, to all intents and purposes, forgotten. During the presidential campaign the White House kept an embarrassed silence. Secretary Mellon volunteered no information, and his fellow Cabinet officer, Stone, followed suit. It was not until February of the following year that the Attorney General, having made a thorough study of the Trade Commission's report, transmitted his findings to the Commission.

It is apparent . . . [he declared] that during the time covered by your report, the Aluminum Company of America violated several provisions of the decree [dissolution decree of 1912]. That with respect to some of the practices complained of, they were so frequent and long continued, the fair inference is the company either was indifferent to the provisions of the decree, or knowingly intended that its provisions should be disregarded, with a view of suppressing competition in the aluminum industry.

"Having . . . practically complete control of the sources of supply of the raw materials," Stone concluded, "it is in a position to and does control the domestic price of sheet aluminum to utensil manufacturers." He was still unable to proceed with a suit, however, since the information in the report covered only the period through 1922. Not knowing whether the practices complained of were still in effect, he wrote: "In order that the Department may act with full knowledge of the course of conduct of the company up to the present time, I have instructed that the investigation of the facts be brought down to date by the Department of Justice."[39]

* Arthur V. Davis, president of Alcoa, made the following statement to an agent of the Federal Trade Commission:

"The company really consists of A. W. Mellon and R. B. Mellon. Of course, A. W. Mellon resigned as a member of the Board of Directors when he went into the Government, and we now have six directors instead of seven. When he has finished his work in Washington he will again become a member of the Board of Directors.

"The Aluminum Company of America has an authorized capitalization of $20,000,000, all common stock, of which there is outstanding $18,729,600. Of this amount . . . at least . . . 60 per cent of the total outstanding, is owned by the Board of Directors, Maria T. Hunt, and A. W. Mellon." (*New York Times*, Oct. 8, 1924.)

Here Stone's part as Attorney General in the aluminum affair ended. A month earlier President Coolidge had nominated him Associate Justice of the United States Supreme Court.

CHAPTER TWELVE

# Sham Battle in a Real War

### 1925

On January 5, 1925, the press announced the news that Attorney General Stone would succeed Associate Justice Joseph McKenna, who was retiring after twenty-seven years on the Supreme Court. "President Coolidge certainly started the New Year off right," the *Washington* (D.C.) *News* editorialized on January 7. Throughout the country newspapers hailed Stone's appointment, describing him as practical and level-headed, well equipped for his job, a brilliant addition to the Court. Even his physical vigor and relish for work were commented upon. His friends were of course jubilant, and many congratulatory letters mentioned that they had felt since college days that he would attain this prominence. The appointment was also well received by judges and members of the bar.

"You have every qualification," Judge Learned Hand commented, "are as nearly fitted for the job as a man can be by training, by experience and by character. I am especially delighted to have there a man who will continue the scholar's background which Holmes has furnished."[1] Judge Benjamin N. Cardozo called the choice "ideal." "You will make a great judge," he said.[2] "We must console ourselves," William Nelson Cromwell wired his departing law partner, "with the reflection that we surrender you to the unparalleled tasks of the present and future which will make you the John Marshall of the twentieth century." To Stone had come the privilege, Cromwell said, "of elevating the law and guiding our nation not only in the strong simple likes of its Founders but in the marvelous and diversified paths which this century has developed."[3]

The decision to don judicial robes was hard to make, and not altogether free from sadness. He hated to leave the work undone in the Department of Justice. He was sorry to drift away from old friends in New York. "To a moderate degree," he was sorry not to make the money which awaited him on his return to Sullivan and Cromwell. The sacrosanct solemnity that hovers over the august tribunal may have caused momentary pause. "Perhaps later on," he wrote an old friend, "you will come over here and take a look at me sitting in a black robe as solemn as though I never heard one of your off-color stories."[4] These were small matters compared with the work of the Supreme Court of the United States. After careful and somewhat hurried reflection, it seemed to him, as he said, that "refusal to accept an appointment to the Court was one which I could not justify either to myself or my family."[5]

Stone took his appointment, along with the plaudits accompanying it, in stride. He and the country at large assumed that the Senate's approval would be routine. "Your confirmation will no doubt be made speedily," Justice Sutherland assured him, "and we shall be working together within a few days."[6] Stone began at once to wind up his affairs as Attorney General.

"You have, doubtless, before this received the news of the change in my fortune," he wrote his sons on January 9, four days after his nomination was announced. It was likely, he thought, to be confirmed the next week. "This means," he went on with mixed feelings, "several important changes in my life. We will become permanent residents of Washington; give up our New York associations; accept the rather meager pay of a Justice of the Supreme Court instead of the rather substantial income which I could make in practice. On the other hand, there will be the opportunity to do work of great importance and of scholarly interest. Incidentally, there will be occasional leisure during the summer holidays at least."

### WAS STONE KICKED UPSTAIRS?

As Stone's nomination was referred to the Senate Judiciary Committee, various sour notes were heard. Because of his policy of enforcing the law "without fear or favor," especially his "overzealous" activity in purging the Justice Department of corruption and his efforts to enforce the anti-trust laws, it was suggested that he was being "kicked upstairs." "Honest, capable, and irreproachable public servants," a union journal noted, "who nevertheless make themselves *persona non grata* are frequently 'elevated' in order to end activities obnoxious to those invisible forces which control Washington."[7] One paper wondered "whether political pressure of the machine variety" had influenced the President "to create a vacancy in his Cabinet at this time."[8]

Surely Stone's task of cleaning up the Justice Department could not have been completed, and it was wondered whether Stone "by any chance is being eased out of the Cabinet . . . to make room for one who will play the game more to the President's desire?"[9] Attorney

General Stone's activities "have not made the head of President Coolidge lie any easier at night," the *Chattanooga Times* remarked.[10]

Other speculations on the Coolidge strategy centered on the Attorney General's well-known determination to enforce the anti-trust laws. Large business interests, the *New York Commercial* observed, had long been confident that the President would not interfere with their programs of industrial consolidation. Stone's activity in the Justice Department threatened to plunge the government into extensive anti-trust litigation and thus arouse the antagonism of business. "By elevating Mr. Stone to a woolsack on the supreme tribunal," this paper reasoned, "Mr. Coolidge has protected business from disturbing litigation or the threat of such litigation, has saved the administration from the charge that it has betrayed the confidence of business, and at the same time has extended the amende honorable to an old friend."[11]

Other papers shaped and sharpened the hypothesis. The *Johnstown Democrat* noticed particularly Stone's plan to prosecute the Aluminum Trust of which Secretary of the Treasury Andrew Mellon was "the uncle and most of all the other relatives." "Attorney General Stone," the *Democrat* observed, "would keep the Republican leaders at Washington on pins and needles. There would be no telling where he would break out next. As a result, there is nothing to do but promote him."[12]

Stone himself believed the aluminum empire was getting too many favors because of Secretary Mellon's position in the administration and that the Secretary himself was utterly indifferent to the obligations his high office imposed.[13] "I feel sure," Mrs. Willebrandt has observed, "Justice Stone *was* 'kicked upstairs' to the Supreme Court. I feel confident that he thought so too. When he told me of the offer, it was with a sense of regret, because, as he said, 'I like doing this job. It needs to be done and I've only just gotten started.' "[14]

Whatever Stone's inner feelings were as to the explanation of his promotion, he never committed himself. Many years later Sterling Carr, mildly resenting William O. Douglas's appointment to the Supreme Court as an alleged attempt to halt or slow down an SEC investigation of TransAmerica Corporation, the Giannini colossus, chided his law school classmate: "Douglas is not a man they could pull down or handle, and so the only way to get rid of him . . . is to promote Douglas with honors. If you will recall," Carr commented slyly, "another such instance came about in the not very distant past —even though you won't admit it."[15]

On the record, Stone's investigation of the Aluminum Company was neither more nor less than would have been expected of any Attorney General. The matter did not originate with him. Having received the

Federal Trade Commission's complaint, he was obliged to investigate with a view to bringing charges. The real puzzle may be why the Federal Trade Commission released its report one month before election day, not Stone's decision to follow it up.

Still other influences, some rather conflicting, are supposed to have fixed the President's choice. "I rather forced the President into his appointment," Chief Justice Taft wrote his brother in July 1925. "The President was loath to let him go, because he knew his worth as Attorney General, but I told him . . . that he was the strongest man that he could secure in New York that was entitled to the place."[16] President Nicholas Murray Butler, in his *Autobiography* (published in 1939), claimed special credit for putting Stone on the Court. Butler did in fact confer with the President and mention Stone's name, along with those of William D. Guthrie and Benjamin N. Cardozo, as "worthy of consideration." But the educator's talk with the President occurred after December 4, when Stone himself informed his son Marshall that there was "much prospect" that he would go on the bench.* Dubbing Butler's claim "all nonsense," Stone explained: "I was appointed the day that Justice McKenna retired and my appointment had been agreed upon some days in advance before his retirement was made public, and I am quite sure before Butler heard of the retirement. Incidentally President Coolidge[17] didn't have to ask Butler whom to appoint, and he had almost as little regard for President Butler's opinions as he did for Chief Justice Taft's, who I see also claims the credit or discredit for my appointment."[18] "I doubt," Stone commented emphatically, "whether the responsibility for my appointment weighs very heavily on either of them."[19]

It seems not improbable that Coolidge's decision to appoint Stone

---

* On December 9, 1924, Butler wrote Coolidge:

"Ever since my last visit to the White House I have been thinking anxiously over one of the most important questions upon which you touched, namely, the sort of men who might be available in this state, if in the not distant future appointment is to be made to the United States Supreme Court.

"To the best of my knowledge and belief there are three outstanding names: William D. Guthrie, who is in the very first rank of members of the bar; Benjamin Nathan Cardozo, who as Judge of the Court of Appeals in this state has won for himself a position of exceptional distinction; and Attorney General Stone.

"The Attorney General you know all about, and for that very reason may well hesitate to take him from the post he now occupies. On the other hand, it would, I fancy, be somewhat easier to get an Attorney General than to find the equal of Stone for a Supreme Court Justice. All his associates here have always regarded him and have spoken of him as temperamentally a judge. He wears his legal learning lightly, and he is as open-minded and fair as he is solid and substantial in character. If Mr. Guthrie be thought a little too old, and if Judge Cardozo's religious and racial associations be felt to be, as conditions are at present, an insuperable objection, then I should think that the Attorney General is in a class by himself. Moreover, he is only fifty-two years of age, and ought to have twenty or twenty-five years of good service ahead of him. . . ."

was prompted by three considerations: his record, marked by fear-
lessness and independence, as head of the Department of Justice,
achievements that excited the admiration even of its traditional critics;
his political services during the 1924 campaign; and personal friendship.

### THE OWNBEY RUCKUS

On January 17 Stone added this cryptic postscript to a letter written
his son Marshall: "A man named Ownbey, whom I walloped in a law
suit in the Supreme Court some years back, is objecting to my confirmation. He is, I think, partly crazy and partly crooked. Nothing to
it, I think, although it will delay my confirmation."

Described picturesquely as a "veteran Indian scout" who still bore
the scars of prairie life,[20] Ownbey had a very sad story to tell. In
February 1915 while he was general manager of the Wooten Company, the J. P. Morgan estate had brought action in the District Court
of Colorado for the appointment of a receiver and for an accounting
of the affairs of the company. A receiver was accordingly appointed,
but while testimony was still in progress the Morgan interests began
foreign attachment proceedings in Delaware against Ownbey's stock
in the Wooten Company, a Delaware corporation. Judgment was
obtained against Ownbey in the Superior Court of Delaware for
$200,165, collectible only from the attached shares of Wooten Com-
pany stock.

As soon as Ownbey learned of this writ of foreign attachment, he
retained counsel in Wilmington, announcing that he owed nothing
and would make full defense. Then the plot thickened for, under the
Custom of London Law, which governed foreign attachment proceedings in Delaware, Ownbey was required to post special bail before
entering a defense in the Superior Court. Such bail was to be sufficient
to cover a possible judgment against him in an amount to be determined by the court. Ownbey's bail was fixed at $200,000. Since he
was unable to post that amount the Delaware Superior Court refused
to permit appearance of his counsel.[21]

"The courts," Justice C. J. Pennewill ruled, "are clearly of the
opinion that in a foreign attachment suit against an individual, there
can be no appearance without entering special bail; indeed, the entering of such bail constitutes the defendant's appearance."[22] This decision was affirmed by the Delaware Supreme Court. Never permitted
to appear in his own defense before either of these courts, all Ownbey's
shares of Wooten Company stock were subsequently awarded to the
Morgan estate, by whom they were sold for $41,000.

Undaunted, Ownbey's lawyers removed the case on certiorari to the

United States Supreme Court and laid down a constitutional broadside against the Delaware foreign attachment law. The Delaware statute, they argued, deprived their client of his property without due process, "the essential elements" being the "right to appear and to be heard in the defense of the action in which Ownbey's property was attached." They contended, moreover, that the Delaware statute deprived Ownbey of the equal protection of the laws, since "he was debarred from appearing and defending without first giving special bail, whilst under the express terms of the statute a foreign corporation may appear and answer without the necessity of giving bail."[23]

It was to defend themselves against these constitutional salvos in the United States Supreme Court that the Morgan executors retained the New York firm of Satterlee, Canfield and Stone. Stone himself prepared the brief, and on November 18, 1920, presented it in oral argument.

By a long survey of American and British precedents, he sought to prove that the Delaware practice of requiring bail, both in actions of debt and in proceedings begun by foreign attachment, was a settled procedure of the common law, having "its origin in the Custom of London." Invoking leading Supreme Court decisions, he observed: "A process of law is due process if it can show the sanction of settled usage in this country and in England." He quoted as especially apt the Court's language in *Murray* v. *Hoboken Land and Improvement Company* (1856): " '. . . We must look to those settled usages and modes of proceeding existing in the common and statute law of England, before the emigration of our ancestors, and which are shown not to have been unsuited to their civil and political condition by having been acted on by them after the settlement of this country.' "[24]

The Supreme Court's decision was a complete victory for Stone and the Morgan executors. Seven Justices, with only Justice Clarke and Chief Justice White dissenting, held that the Delaware foreign attachment statute neither contravened the due process clause of the Fourteenth Amendment, denied Ownbey equal protection of the laws, nor abridged his privileges and immunities as a United States citizen. The Delaware process, the Court decided, gave Ownbey a chance to appear and make defense conditioned only upon his giving security to the value of the property attached. A denial of due process, Justice Pitney ruled, "must be determined not alone with reference to a case of peculiar hardship arising out of exceptional circumstances, but with respect to the general effect and operation of the system of procedure established by the statutes. . . . The due process clause does not impose upon the states a duty to establish ideal systems for the administration of justice, with every modern improvement and with provision against every possible hardship that may befall."[25]

In 1925 Ownbey's query, whether in the light of Stone's defense of the Morgan interests he was a "fit man" to sit on the Supreme Court, seemed empty. Lawyers were completely mystified. Willard Saulsbury, who had represented the Morgan interests throughout, described Ownbey's attack as founded on "ignorance and prejudice."[26] Louis Marshall, Ownbey's lawyer in the Supreme Court, labeled as preposterous the charge that Stone had been guilty of any misconduct in representing the Morgan interest. Yet Senator Lee S. Overman of North Carolina, much troubled by this charge, sought advice from J. W. Bailey, a Raleigh attorney.

"A lawyer is expected to represent his clients," Bailey informed the Senator, "and I do not know that in all the history of jurisprudence, an instance can be found where a lawyer was criticized for invoking every available law in behalf of his cause. If the Custom of London was applicable to the Ownbey case that was the fault of the law, and not the lawyer. . . . Lawyers are not the judges of the righteousness of the law."[27]

"Stone regarded the Ownbey case," Professor Noel T. Dowling of the Columbia Law School has recalled, "not only as an interesting episode in his own practice but as an important event in constitutional law." In his oral argument before the Supreme Court he "tried to get the Justices to see that in the exercise of their power of judicial review they would have enough to do in respect of new legislative ventures without going back and reagitating the validity of *old* methods, especially when those old methods were sanctioned by ancient usage." The correction of old methods and processes, Stone thought, ought rather to be left to the legislatures.[28] Herein he adumbrated what was to become a major theme in his constitutional jurisprudence.

"Do not worry about the Ownbey matter," Stone wrote a friend. "It is mostly newspaper talk and cheap politics. I have paid absolutely no attention to it. . . . By another week I shall be 'Mr. Justice.' "[29]

The Attorney General was mistaken. On February 5 Senator Tom Heflin of Georgia, "a notorious blatherskite," "a high-hatted, long-tail-coated windbag," held the floor for two and one-half hours, objecting to Stone's confirmation.[30] Having earlier described Ownbey as "one of the torchbearers of American civilization penetrating the wilderness of the West," the Senator cried: "It appealed to me when this man with tears in his eyes told me about this dreadful case. I said, 'They may not have heard you out yonder; they may have adhered to some sort of technicality in the Supreme Court which has done you a grave injustice, but I will tell the story of your case to the Senate and to the country.' "[31]

Finally Senator Thaddeus H. Caraway of Arkansas succeeded in interrupting Heflin's tirade: "Let me ask the Senator . . . if his activities in the case referred to render Mr. Stone unfit to serve on the bench, then ought the others who recognized the constitutionality of the Delaware statute to be impeached?"

"I would not go quite that far," Heflin ventured, "but I will tell my friend that if I were President I would not hesitate to accept their resignations." Laughter on the floor and in the galleries rose to such a pitch that the chair called attention to the Senate rule against manifestations of approval or disapproval.[32] Besides Heflin, no one except Senator Overman took stock in Ownbey's charges.

### THE WHEELER CASE

The objections raised against Stone as to the Ownbey case obscured other charges, banked hotter fires that had been smoldering since Stone became Attorney General. Among the many unpleasant legacies bequeathed him was the so-called Wheeler case. On April 8, 1924, about the time Stone took office, an indictment had been returned against Senator Burton K. Wheeler by a federal grand jury at Great Falls, Montana, charging him with practicing law as a senator before an agency of the Government, and with conspiracy to defraud the Government.* After his election to the Senate but before his induction into office, the indictment alleged, Wheeler had received compensation for services to be performed in appearing before the General Land Office of the Interior Department on behalf of one Gordon Campbell. The Senator did not deny his receipt of $10,000 from Campbell, but alleged that it was paid him for legal services performed in Montana. The indictment, Wheeler further contended, was an act of Republican political revenge. In bringing the Montana action in April 1924, Attorney General Daugherty was merely trying to discredit him as prosecutor for the Brookhart Committee, then investigating the Justice Department.†

Simultaneously with the Montana proceedings, the Senate made its own investigation of the charges against Wheeler. After extensive

---

* The relevant statute (Section 113, Penal Code of the U.S.) allegedly violated reads: "If two or more persons conspire either to commit any offense against the United States or to defraud the United States in any manner or for any purpose, and one or more of such parties do any act to affect the object of the conspiracy, each of the parties to such a conspiracy shall be fined not more than $10,000, or imprisoned not more than two years, or both."

† Wheeler's view of the matter is endorsed to some extent by Mrs. Willebrandt. "I think there is not the slightest doubt," she wrote, "that Daugherty broke the Wheeler case prematurely in order to *discredit* Wheeler in his charges against Daugherty and Harding." When rumors broke that Wheeler was about to "blow the lid off" the Harding administration, "Daugherty came to the Department, summoned Burns and other investigators and the U.S. attorney, and worked feverishly with Rush Holland and other political appointees to bring an indictment against Wheeler *before* Wheeler brought his whispered charges out in the open."

hearings, the committee, under the chairmanship of Senator William E. Borah, issued a report completely exonerating Wheeler of all the charges pending against him in the Montana courts. In Wheeler's mind, as well as in that of his friends, this action confirmed his suspicion that the Montana indictment was in fact "one of the darkest pages in American history."[33]

Attorney General Stone was under no illusions as to what motivated the charges against Wheeler. It was soon apparent to him that the prosecuting zeal displayed by Daugherty and his cohorts could not be wholly attributed to an unbiased desire to administer justice and uphold the law. Stone, like Wheeler, regarded the indictment as a "part of a political fight," as "*an improper* use of the federal process to serve a political purpose."[34] At the same time, Wheeler's connection with Campbell's attempt to obtain valuable leases under questionable circumstances was not, in Stone's mind, entirely free of suspicion. The Senator had helped Campbell, constituent or client, to get oil leases from the Department of the Interior; he had been paid by Campbell for services, whether as lawyer or as senator.

Soon pressures began on the Attorney General from two sides. Cabinet officers, the Postmaster General, the Secretary of the Navy, and Republican leaders in the Senate urged him to do something about the Wheeler prosecution. The Senator's friends and supporters, on the other hand, organized as the Wheeler Defense Committee, prodded Stone to drop the case.[35]

"Everyone to whom the undefiled administration of justice is a truly sacred interest," Professor Felix Frankfurter, a member of the Wheeler Defense Committee, wrote the Attorney General glowingly, "must be grateful to you for the retirement of Burns, for the termination of the 'dollar-a-year man' privilege, and above all, for your personal assumption of the direction of the Bureau of Investigation. . . . It is a very heartening thing, if I may say so, that you have taken personal charge of the immediate chief problem." In his second and last paragraph Professor Frankfurter expressed the "hope" of "some of us" that "other officers of the Department of Justice will follow Burns into retirement if there are no other facts behind the indictment of Wheeler than those which have been submitted to the Borah Committee."[36]

The Attorney General was "grateful" in reply, but suggested that the Borah Committee in exonerating Wheeler may not have been Simon pure. "I think it would be well to suspend judgment about the Wheeler indictment. A senatorial committee is not just the place to determine the guilt or innocence of a man charged with crime."[37]

Though confessing that his first communication may have "bordered upon the impertinent," Frankfurter did not let up. He insisted that the

Wheeler indictment was so "egregiously suspicious" that "we are entitled to have . . . the quickest and most authoritative disposition [of the case] by the Department of Justice."[38] Again Stone's reaction was courteous and incisive: "There is only one question presented to me, and that is whether I should allow the law to take its course in the customary manner, or whether I should do something to interfere."[39] In his mind, it was bad practice for the chief administrative law officer to interfere with the usual course of the administration of the criminal law—especially at a time "when the Attorney General had been publicly charged with such personal interference."[40]

In his next letter Frankfurter told the Attorney General what to do: "either dismiss the indictment and the officers of the Department who procured it under such unseemly circumstances, or advise the public promptly that the Senate Committee has wholly misconceived the case and misrepresented the evidence."[41] Stone had other ideas and minced no words in stating them:

> I have a strong impression that the public interest requires that cases in which there is a widespread public interest and about which there is a radical difference of opinion should be left to the decision of the courts, who alone have the authority and power to determine the question of guilt or innocence, let the result affect whom it may. In other words, I think it more important that the ability and authority of the courts to pass upon the guilt or innocence of persons charged with crime should be vindicated than that I should shape my course with respect to the particular reputation which I may establish for courage or disinterestedness.[42]

Frankfurter, at last, seemed content to let Stone run his Department in his own way; acknowledgment merely thanked the Attorney General for his letter. But a day or so later Stone made a speech before the Columbia Law School alumni. The *New York Times* report suggested that either the speech had been garbled or the speaker hadn't known what he was talking about. As Frankfurter related the *Times* report to Stone, the Attorney General had said:

> Under our system there reposes in the courts the duty to define the law. It is not for the Attorney General or others in authority, especially in such cases as there may be great public interest, to proceed in such a manner as to intrude upon this function of the courts and thwart the ends of justice.*

---

* The prepared copy of Stone's speech on this occasion reads: "Our system reposes on the courts the authority, the duty, and the capacity to declare what the law is, to determine the rights of litigation, to determine the guilt or innocence of those charged with crime. It is not for the Attorney General, it is not for any other officer or for any other body, to usurp that function of the courts, or to interfere, by his or their action, in cases of public interest about which there may be differences of opinion, so as to thwart the ends of justice as administered by the courts."

"You surely need not be reminded," the Harvard professor wrote, "that the power to *nol-pros* is as legitimate a part of the administration of the law as the power to prosecute." Yes, Stone replied tolerantly; he knew the "power and duty of prosecuting officers. . . . I have approved a considerable number of motions to *nol-pros* since I came into office."[43]

Though well aware that such inflexibility in the discharge of his responsibilities as he saw them might affect his reputation, he kept his own counsels. In the midst of this rapid fire with Frankfurter, he wrote an old friend: "I will probably be the most unpopular Attorney General the United States ever had, for you know that one of the jobs of the Attorney General is to refuse to do things that a lot of people are very anxious to have him do. The consequent disappointment often produces acute distress."[44]

Stone was less impressed with the Senate's exoneration of Wheeler than were the Senator's supporters. For him this tactic represented an effort to forestall criminal action in Montana until public opinion could be influenced in his favor by vote of the Senate. At the same time the Attorney General doubted whether the proceedings in Montana were sufficient to cover the case. He ordered a new investigation to proceed in Washington under the direction of Assistant Attorney General William J. Donovan. Donovan was told to make a thoroughgoing study of the entire transaction, both in Montana and in Washington, D. C., and on the basis of this investigation make recommendations.[45]

Donovan began his work in September 1924 and submitted his report about December 1; it convinced Stone that "there were facts in the case which indicated that it had a much wider scope than the subject matter of the indictment obtained in Montana," that Campbell's promotional schemes "involved primarily the securing, fraudulently, of oil and gas prospecting permits on public lands in Montana, and that the most important element in them was the validating of these permits by the Interior Department and the approval of assignments of these permits by the executive officers of the Interior Department at Washington."* Wheeler had been involved in these transactions. "In fairness to him and with a view to the due and orderly administration of justice," Stone gave instructions early in December that the entire matter should be submitted to a grand jury

* Wheeler believes that some one "lied" to Stone. "He [Stone] and I afterwards became very good friends," Wheeler has written. "I think he was an honest, honorable, able man, and I believe that the only way you can account for the handling of the case against me after he became Attorney General was that he was lied to by the people in the Department." (Burton K. Wheeler to A. T. M., Dec. 5, 1950.)

in the District of Columbia. The hearing was set for February 2, 1925.[46]

Meanwhile Wheeler's indictment in Montana was hanging fire. A demurrer to the indictment and a motion to transfer the trial to Wheeler's home town had long delayed proceedings, and various Montana judges had disqualified themselves from hearing the case. Repeated efforts of both the Government and Senator Wheeler to obtain an early trial had been frustrated by the requirements of Wheeler's campaign for the vice-presidency on the Progressive party ticket in 1924, the exigencies of his wife's confinement, or difficulties of Montana court procedure.[47]

Stone had been in the crossfires of this political battle throughout the nine months of his Attorney Generalship. When he refused to yield to fierce pressures from members of the Wheeler Defense Committee, its vice-chairman, Basil Manly, charged that the Department of Justice had remained tainted under Stone with the mephitic atmosphere of Daughertyism. "Contrary to popular opinion," Manly wrote, "Attorney General Stone made practically no change in the personnel of the Department of Justice after assuming office on April 7, 1924."[48] Stone could hardly have failed to realize that still another action against Wheeler would arouse powerful opposition to his confirmation. But rather than stand back safely he walked straight into the line of fire. On January 16, in the midst of the Ownbey ruckus, the Attorney General dispatched a letter, marked "Personal and Confidential," to Wheeler's counsel, Senator Walsh of Montana: "I have endeavored to communicate today with Senator Wheeler but find that he is out of the city. It is important that he should be advised of certain facts at once, and am communicating directly with you as his colleague and counsel."

Stone went on to say that evidence had been brought to his attention which he felt duty bound to submit to the federal grand jury in Washington, D. C. It seemed probable that such evidence would be submitted to that jury early in February, but Stone intended, he wrote Wheeler's counsel, "to instruct counsel for the Government to request the jury to permit Senator Wheeler to appear before that body if he should so desire and be given the opportunity of testifying in his own behalf." As was usual in such cases, Senator Wheeler would have to sign a waiver of immunity. "I would greatly appreciate your advising him of my intention," Stone concluded, "and also your letting me know as conveniently as possible whether he wishes to avail himself of this privilege."

Senator Walsh's first reaction was cordial. "I thank you very much," he replied on January 17, "for sending me the letter concerning the contemplated proceedings involving Senator Wheeler. Your courtesy in the matter is much appreciated." To progressive senators on Capitol Hill, however, Stone seemed to be turning the knife in an old political wound. He appeared to be going out of his way to persecute, under the guise of unswerving justice, a man whom they thought had performed a great and needed public service in waging war on Daughertyism.[49] A week later Senator Walsh, now in a bellicose mood, told newspaper reporters he would oppose the Attorney General's confirmation to "the last ditch."

On January 19 Walsh wrote Stone for more information about the Washington proceedings. Calling attention to a press announcement of the Department's intention of "dismissing the indictment in Montana and having him [Wheeler] indicted in the District," Walsh wrote, "If that procedure is to be pursued, I shall be very thankful to be advised of it."

"There has never been any indication," Stone replied January 22, "that the indictment of which you speak should be *nol-prossed*. As to 'having him indicted' in the District of Columbia, I am certain that it is unnecessary for me to assure you that it is not the policy of this Department to indict or 'have indicted' your client or any other person." Repeating his offer to permit Senator Wheeler, under waiver of immunity, to testify on his own behalf before the Washington grand jury, his letter concluded: "I can well understand the inconvenience to counsel for Senator Wheeler if obliged to proceed to Montana and at the same time to be concerned with the proceedings pending here. I should be very glad, therefore, if it will better suit your convenience, to direct that the District Attorney in Montana consent to a continuance of the above motions pending the determination of the proceedings before the grand jury in this District."

In the late afternoon of January 22 Walsh called on Stone at the Department of Justice. It was unfair, the Senator protested, to try his client so far removed from his own vicinage. Because of the bias of juries in behalf of the Government, a fair trial could not be obtained in Washington, he said. Stone disagreed. Three considerations had led him to insist on an inquiry in the District of Columbia: the proposed investigation involved defendants other than Senator Wheeler and concerned transactions occurring within the District and constituting a different offense from the one charged in Montana; the facts in Washington merited a broader inquiry than had been involved in Montana; and, finally, the proceedings in Washington could be carried on under the immediate direction of the Justice Department, to avoid any coercion or unfairness in the inquiry.

"I recognize my obligation to the defendants in this case," Stone wrote, "as in all others. The proceedings will be conducted with scrupulous care to safeguard the rights of all possible defendants but without sacrifice of the interests of the Government."[50]

On January 24, two days after his meeting with the Attorney General and five days after the Judiciary Committee had recommended Stone's confirmation, Senator Walsh made a speech on the floor of the Senate that sent cold chills down Republican backs. Stone's nomination, the Senator demanded, should be referred back to the Judiciary Committee for complete reconsideration. Speaking in executive session, his remarks were said to be characterized by extreme bitterness. Democrats and Republican insurgents were agreed that Stone's part in the Wheeler incident did warrant further study.

The press, however, was still solidly behind Stone. "All the presumptions are," one paper observed, "that he acted from a strong sense of duty, with entire disregard of all consequences personal to himself." A politician in his place "would have pigeonholed the entire affair, or left it to his successor." He was "all the better judge, but the poorer intriguer for place."[51]

On January 26 Stone revealed his innermost feelings on the matter to his old friend, Luther Ely Smith:

By now, if you are reading the newspapers, you will, I think, be able to form some judgment of the real motive which has been holding up my confirmation. A good deal of pressure has been brought on me to drop the Wheeler case, which I am not inclined to do, especially as an investigation develops the need of a broader inquiry than that involved in Montana. Confidentially, you may be interested to know that this inquiry shows that a crime has undoubtedly been committed here in an effort to defraud the United States. The evidence of it which would have to be submitted to a grand jury will implicate Senator Wheeler. I have given instructions that this evidence be submitted next month. In order that the proceedings may be conducted with perfect fairness to him, I have given instructions that he be permitted to appear before the grand jury and give any testimony he may desire, provided only that he waive immunity. If that action on my part keeps me off the Supreme Court, I am content to accept the result, although it will be a sad day for our country if such a thing can happen.

Senator Walsh's blast on January 24 had thrown Republican leaders "into a panic."[52] Immediately following the Senate session that day, Senators Charles Curtis of Kansas, William M. Butler of Massachusetts, James E. Watson of Indiana, David A. Reed of Pennsylvania, and Thomas Sterling of South Dakota conferred with the President at the White House. After stating briefly what had taken place in the Wheeler matter, Stone expressed his confidence that if the facts were presented to the Senate, it could not reject his nomination. In any event, he was prepared to stand or fall on the facts, and he suggested further that if the Judiciary Committee should invite him to appear and make a statement, he would take the unprecedented step of appearing before it, provided it was a public hearing. The Attorney General's suggestion was endorsed by all present. On Monday, January 26, the New York *Sun* announced:

President Coolidge informed Republican leaders of the Senate today that he would not withdraw the nomination of Attorney General Harlan F. Stone to be Associate Justice of the Supreme Court, but that he had no objection to the Senate referring the nomination back to the Judiciary Committee for a more complete inquiry into Mr. Stone's reasons for asking Senator Burton K. Wheeler of Montana to appear before a federal grand jury.

That same day Senator Curtis in executive session moved that Stone's nomination be sent back to committee, and the Senate unanimously endorsed his proposal.

### COMING OFF WITH FLYING COLORS

Before the committee on January 28, Stone opened with a concise statement of the history of the Wheeler case and of his reasons for ordering the Donovan investigation and the Washington proceedings. After quoting his entire correspondence with Senator Walsh, he closed with a statement cheered by newspapers throughout the country:

The course pursued by the Department of Justice since this matter has come under my observation has been, I believe, in full accord with both the letter and spirit of the Constitution and laws of the United States and with the highest conception of the due and orderly administration of justice. For it I accept full personal responsibility.[53]

On completion of his statement, Stone was subjected to a lengthy cross examination. Most of the questions, chiefly from Senators Walsh, Overman, and Reed of Missouri, concerned Montana trial procedure and the federal court system. Apparently their main purpose was to prove that the U.S. district attorneys in Montana had been responsible for any unreasonable delay in Senator Wheeler's trial, or that the Attorney General had not done everything possible to expedite proceedings. By the end of the questioning it seemed evident that any delay in the trial was due to Wheeler's interposed demurrer to the indictment and motion to transfer the trial from Great Falls to Butte.

Stone also stuck to his declared position that the proceedings scheduled for the District of Columbia could be better conducted there than in Montana. Not least among the reasons that had led him to initiate proceedings in Washington was, he said,

the very grave concern I had that the processes of the courts and the agencies of the Government should not be used oppressively. I do not mean in saying that to criticise at all what has taken place in Montana, but there have been charges and countercharges in the proceedings in Montana, and I have felt that if there were any further proceedings in these matters they should be conducted in such a way that I had personal assurance that such criticisms could not be justly made.[54]

Thereupon Walsh proceeded to imply guilt by association. Following the line laid down by the Wheeler Defense Committee, the Senator ran through an elaborate listing of all the important officials

*Berryman in the Washington, D.C.,* Evening Star, *January 29, 1925*

in the Justice Department appointed by Daugherty and retained by Stone. Only at this point did the Attorney General show signs of losing his temper:

SENATOR WALSH: . . . Is Mr. Rush Holland still in the Department of Justice?

ATTORNEY GENERAL STONE: He is.

SENATOR WALSH: He was an appointee of Mr. Daugherty's?

ATTORNEY GENERAL STONE: I believe so.

SENATOR WALSH: He was raised with him at Washington Court House in the State of Ohio?

ATTORNEY GENERAL STONE: I could not answer to that. But I do not think it has anything to do with the matter under inquiry.

SENATOR WALSH: Well, of course there may be different views about that.

ATTORNEY GENERAL STONE: Well, I have a very positive view about it, and I am stating my view.[55]

Shortly thereafter Senator Henry F. Ashurst of Arizona took over the questioning. Had the Attorney General, he wanted to know, ever made a statement to the effect that if he had been Attorney General, the Wheeler indictment in Montana would never have occurred? After four emphatic "no's" Ashurst still persisted.

SENATOR ASHURST: . . . you do not remember saying that?

ATTORNEY GENERAL STONE: I remember positively that I did not say that. . . . I also have a very distinct recollection as to what I did say.[56]

Most of the questions were technical, picayune, and unimportant, apparently designed "to bait the Attorney General into some indiscreet action or statement."[57] He could not be baited; his replies were forthright, courteous, and cooperative. At four-thirty p.m., after nearly five hours, the questions petered out and the hearing was adjourned.

Stone's appearance before the Judiciary Committee was a complete success for the Republican party and a personal triumph for himself. By that same token, it was a boomerang for Senator Walsh. The Attorney General came off, Chief Justice Taft reported, "with flying colors and left Walsh with a great deal of explaining to do."[58] "The coyotes have been trying to bite me," Stone wrote, "but I think they have only broken their teeth."[59] "I did not foresee that they would deliver themselves into my hands quite so completely."[60] The country seemed delighted, and the papers had, he said, "praised me far beyond my deserts."[61] Said the *New York Herald Tribune* on January 29:

The Attorney General lived up to his high reputation. He confirmed every conviction of his rare qualifications for the Supreme Court bench. He displayed clearness, calmness, courage and, incidentally, a calm contempt for the petty politics being played against him.

Even the *New York World,* on January 30, while maintaining its reservations about the Wheeler charges, applauded Stone's performance:

Of the personal courage and good faith of Attorney General Stone his appearance before the Senate committee leaves no doubt. There by every ordinary sign was a straightforward public servant who had tried to do his duty without fear or favor. . . . Mr. Stone's qualifications for the Supreme Court . . . remain as they were when he was first nominated: unusually complete for high judicial office.

Stone's friends marveled at his steadfastness of purpose in the face of what Chief Justice Taft described, in a letter to Stone on January 29, as an "outrageous attack on you in the Senate and the malevolence or foolishness of those who are taking part in it." "I am glad to note," the Chief Justice applauded, "that you don't give an inch to any of them." Taft especially deplored the fact that Borah and Walsh used "their position as members of the Judiciary Committee and members of the Senate to further their conduct of Wheeler's defense and to attempt to frighten the administration and you by a threat against your confirmation."*

"Neither Mrs. Stone nor I are worried a bit about this matter, annoying as it is. I never slept better. I think one could afford to be personally defeated on such an issue if the people were made to realize how far the Senate has really gone in allowing itself to interfere with the processes of justice in order to protect one of its own members."[62]

The Judiciary Committee, in executive session, on February 2 recommended Stone's confirmation to the Senate. Though Borah and Walsh were supposedly unconvinced, it was understood, the *New York Times* reported, that they would interpose no further objections.

February 5 was, for Senator Walsh, a day of atonement. "Mr. President," he announced on the floor of the Senate, "the Attorney General enjoys a deserved reputation for justice, for probity, and for high character; I would not have anybody understand that I question that in any particular. . . . I have the very highest esteem for the Attorney General. The very excellent opinion I formed of him by reason of my connection with him, brief as it was, before this time, was confirmed by his demeanor before the Committee on the Judiciary."[63]

Senator Norris, however, rang changes on the theme that Stone, as former counsel for the House of Morgan, had by that fact alone become enslaved by those predatory interests. He intended to vote against confirmation, the Nebraska Senator announced, because the American people in the 1924 election had indicated their preference for a Vermont farmer rather than a Morgan lawyer as President of the United States. "They did not know then," Norris said, "that instead of putting in the White House for four years an executive who repre-

---

* Taft described Wheeler as "a vicious man, a man irresponsible, and with a very bad reputation in Montana"; "clear up to his armpits in doing the very thing he is charged with." (W. H. Taft to Robert A. Taft, Jan. 25, April 26, 1925.) But Wheeler was ultimately acquitted in both Montana and in the District of Columbia. The persons with whom Senator Wheeler was entangled—Gordon Campbell and his fellow conspirator, Edwin Booth, Solicitor for the Department of Interior—were found guilty.

Fifteen years earlier, when his own Secretary of Interior, Richard Ballinger, was involved in similar irregularities, Taft had been more indulgent. Nor in this instance was President Taft's own conduct beyond reproach. (See my *Bureaucracy Convicts Itself* [New York: The Viking Press, 1941].)

sented the Morgan interests, their action meant putting on the Supreme Bench for life another attorney of Morgan & Co."

In closing, Norris waxed hotter: "With Morgan & Co.'s attorney on the Supreme Bench, with the Sugar Trust running the Attorney General's office, with the railroads themselves operating the Interstate Commerce Commission, with the greatest reactionary of the country sitting on the Federal Trade Commission, tell me—Oh, God, tell me!— where the toiling millions of the honest, common people of this country are going to be protected in their rights as against big business."[64]

Senator William E. Borah of Idaho took the trouble to reply. "I want to call to the attention of my friend, the Senator from Nebraska," Borah retorted, "the fact that in my opinion the Attorney General is one of the most liberal-minded men who has been in the Attorney General's office for many years. He is not only a man of extraordinary ability, but he is a man of liberal mind and of a high sense of public duty, and the deepest regret I have in seeing him advanced to the Supreme Bench is that he is leaving the Attorney General's office, where I think he has been doing splendid work ever since he has been there."[65]

Senator Norris was engaged in a real war, a conflict he continued with renewed vigor in his battle of 1930 against Charles Evans Hughes' confirmation as Chief Justice. Hughes resented the "Wall Street" label. Stone, on the other hand, was completely unmoved. "I have always been sorry," he commented lightheartedly many years later, "that I didn't have the Morgan House for my clients more than I did. They were good clients."[66]

Stone was confirmed on February 5 by a vote of 71 to 6. Even Senator Kenneth McKellar of Tennessee, Senator Reed of Missouri, and Senator Borah, who had opposed his action in the Wheeler case, voted for confirmation, while Senators Wheeler and Walsh abstained.

The Attorney General submitted his resignation to President Coolidge on February 28, having delayed action to clear matters in the office and await Charles Beecher Warren's confirmation as his successor. Meanwhile warm words of welcome came from all the Justices. "The slavery of it is sometimes depressing," McReynolds wrote, "but there are compensations."[67] Columbia Law School colleagues and former students anticipated that his opinions would "rival those of Holmes and Brandeis."[68] Even Morris R. Cohen who, in 1915, had written a "rather angry review" of Stone's Hewitt lectures, Law and Its Administration, recanted. In the years since, Stone had, Cohen wrote, "displayed a remarkable capacity for appreciating new facts and for adopting sound, established principles for dealing with new situations."[69]

The unforeseen delay in the Senate's confirmation, though annoying, worked no hardship on the Court. The Justices were then in recess and not scheduled to meet again until March 2.

That day Coolidge wrote:

My dear Mr. Attorney General:

As it is by my appointment that you are leaving the office of Attorney General for that of Justice of the Supreme Court, I cannot appropriately express regret other than to say that I have put you on the Supreme Bench because I thought it would promote the public welfare, while I am parting with you as my legal adviser, a member of the Cabinet, with a distinct sense of personal loss. You have discharged the duties of Attorney General in a way that has commended itself universally to the good opinion of the people of your country. I wish to thank you for this service and commend you for the self-sacrifice you were willing to make in becoming Attorney General, and now in accepting an office which carries with it a life tenure. Your resignation is accepted to become effective immediately upon your assuming the duties of a Justice of the Supreme Court of the United States.

In the interval between confirmation and going on the bench, the Stones enjoyed their first vacation since he assumed office. In late February they joined Secretary and Mrs. Hoover on a twelve-day yachting and fishing trip among the Florida Keys.

"We had a wonderful time," Stone reported to his sons, "and I got more rest than I have had since I left New York last year. . . . I am now busy cleaning up my desk preparatory to going on the bench on Monday. . . . There will, I suppose, be a brief ceremony of swearing me in. I wish you could be present."[70]

## PART THREE

# Finding His Niche

## CHAPTER THIRTEEN

# The Nineteen-Twenties

Washington was astir with the approaching inauguration of President Coolidge and his self-dramatizing running-mate, Charles G. Dawes. Two days before the ceremonies got under way a distinguished crowd gathered in the old Senate chamber of the Capitol to witness the induction of Harlan Fiske Stone, President Coolidge's only appointee to the Supreme Court. The courtroom was filled at noon, March 2, 1925, when the Justices, led by Chief Justice Taft, filed in. The brief ceremony was the first order of business.

"His induction," eyewitness Noel T. Dowling observed, "was simple and brief. Immediately after the Court convened the Chief Justice announced the appointment and the clerk read the commission. Mr. Stone, who had remained in the background and almost out of view, stepped forward and stood beside the Chief Justice while the latter administered the oath. He then went to the seat assigned by custom to the junior associate at the extreme left of the bench. The Court turned to its regular work, and Mr. Justice Sanford, sitting on the far right as the next junior associate, began the delivery of an opinion. In all, less than five minutes had been consumed."[1]

The turnover in the post of Attorney General was so rapid as compared with the time it took to get a case before the Supreme Court that one counsel, trying to catch up with developments, asked the Justices' permission to change "Attorney General Daugherty" to "Attorney General Stone" on his papers. When Chief Justice Taft pointed out that Stone was then seated at his extreme left, the attorney moved to substitute the name of Attorney General Charles Beecher Warren. Mr. Warren, the Chief Justice pointed out, had not yet been confirmed. While the attorney cogitated on what to do next, Taft, "restraining with difficulty his famous chuckle, suggested that perhaps it would be safer if the Court itself made the substitution."[2]

Stone entered the national stage midway in the roaring twenties, a confused, tumultuous era somewhat offensive to his Puritan inheritance. It was a decade pre-eminent for exploitative large-scale business; its leaders preached the "Gospel of Goods." "Canonization of the salesman" was seen "as the brightest hope of America."[3] The absorbing ambition was to make two dollars grow where one had grown before, to engineer, as utilities magnate Samuel Insull put it, "all I could out of a dollar"—that is, get something for nothing. All this ran counter to Stone's faith in the "old-fashioned virtues of thoroughness and fidelity to the day's task."[4]

As Dean of the Columbia Law School, Stone had been unwilling to relax standards even to accommodate returning veterans. Later on, he quoted with approval Justice Holmes' pronouncement that "it was a good thing for us in our college days that we were all poor." One who has all "the luxuries of life poured into a trough for him at twenty" is hindered, not helped.[5] In recognizing the nation's inheritance as rooted in classical antiquity and European culture, in prizing "spiritual values above the material," Stone's innermost persuasion clashed with the callous exaltation of the dollar. He had demanded educational institutions "devoted to teaching its students how to live rather than how to make a living."[6]

The materialism which Stone condemned was but a single aspect of a more general manifestation of disillusionment with fervid idealism at both the national and international level. After Wilson's quixotic national tour had failed to rally America to the League of Nations, the range of America's international outlook contracted perilously. Dollar diplomacy sloughed off the President's cosmic dream as the flag followed the dollar into Haiti, Guatemala, and Nicaragua. Outside the Western Hemisphere, America wanted to be let alone, but was nevertheless entangled. Squabbles with European allies over war debts continued futilely. Secretary of State Charles Evans Hughes blithely ignored communications from the League, but he astounded the world by his proposals for disarmament at the Washington Naval Conference in 1922. A similar flash of empty optimism led to the Kellogg-Briand Pact of 1928, forswearing war as an instrument of national policy. Falling in with the trend of the times, a cartoonist of the era depicted the "typical" American family addressing Mars, the god of war, with the emphatic injunction, "You're fired."[7] America wanted peace, but, characteristically, its nominal leaders thought this precious goal, like prosperity, could be attained through sheer force of confidence.

In domestic affairs the people were restless, confused, and undirected, their leaders smug and complacent. After the 1920 presidential election, in the glow of victory, the guardians of "normalcy" released from prison conscientious objectors incarcerated under Woodrow Wilson's regime of New Freedom. Hysterical fear of the "red menace" declined after 1920, but hostility to radicals and progressives continued. Two men who offended as foreigners and radicals were convicted of murder on flimsy evidence in the face of worldwide protest. Twenty-four states enacted criminal-syndicalism or criminal-anarchy laws. The renascent Ku Klux Klan, straying from its native Southern haunt, "flourished like a green bay tree," and garnered in the Northeast and Midwest an all-time peak of six million members.[8] Silver-tongued William Jennings Bryan led the forces of obscurantism to a last-ditch forensic defense of "the story of Divine creation as taught by the Bible."

As never before, the businessman's philosophy was dominant and pervasive. Man's ultimate goal was material prosperity, "a full belly, and a warm hut." When Sinclair Lewis defined Babbittry as the ambition to be "rich, fat, arrogant, and superior," business leaders gleefully acknowledged the portrait as their own and rushed to its defense. "Was Babbitt so evil a thing?" Nation's Business wanted to know. The answer was self-evident. God and Babbittry had made the U.S.A. "the richest nation in history."[9] This "must have been . . . the intent of the Creator of all things," a prosperity spokesman mused, "in implanting deep in human nature the mighty motive of selfishness, and the constructive assertion of the right of private-property."[10] "I have come to the conclusion," a Chamber of Commerce writer avowed weightily, "that industry is the fundamental basis of civilization."[11]

And yet social and political prospects for divinely blessed Americans were not unclouded. Behind the rosy façade of stock prospectuses and bankers' optimistic tales of fabulous prosperity ahead lurked a sense of profound uneasiness. Impoverishment and wretchedness continued to darken the glow around the plump picture of plenty painted by those possessing it. "There has been a tendency," Brookings Institution economists cautiously observed, "at least during the last decade or so, for the inequality in the distribution of income to be accentuated"; in the golden year of 1929, practically 60 per cent of American families were barely above the subsistence level.[12]

Ugly hints of mob rule clouded the industrial horizon; "radicalism" threatened to dominate the thinly populated ranks of organized labor. Similar false doctrines were said to be rampant in the faculties of colleges and universities. "One great issue confronts the world today," a magazine editorial noted. "It hardly needs comment or rather it defies comment. Strike after strike warns us of a tremendous industrial upheaval threatening the world. When Russia began it, we thought we were safe, but now we are not so sure. Capital and labor are engaged in a great struggle, and tangles of red tape on the one hand and stout 'Red' threads on the other tie the whole world together, not for brotherhood, but for strife."[13]

Despite Woodrow Wilson's vigorous crusade to spread democracy, it was still suspect in America as carrying within it the seeds of its own destruction. Echoing the fears Chancellor James Kent voiced a century earlier, Charles N. Fay told the business community with resignation that "wage-workers will usually constitute the majority of voters in free, civilized countries like ours, . . . and they will be employed by you because they have not initiative enough to be employers themselves. So too, in politics, they will be voters, steered by politicians, because they have not initiative, or time, or brains enough to study policies, and make up their minds for themselves, how to vote."[14]

Some suggested that the brainless masses could be prevented from becoming the tool of conniving political demagogues only if their waking hours were fully occupied in keeping body and soul together. That is why emphasis had to be put upon "work—more work and better work, instead of upon leisure."[15] "They have for the most part," President John E. Edgerton of the National Association of Manufacturers reported, October 1929, "been so busy at their jobs that they have not had time to saturate themselves with false theories of economics, social reform, and of life. They have been protected in their natural growth by absence of excessive leisure and have been fortunate not only in their American-made opportunities to work, but in the necessities which have compelled its reasonable indulgence." "Nothing breeds radicalism more quickly," President Edgerton said, "than unhappiness, unless it is leisure. . . . As long as people are kept profitably employed, there is little danger from radicalism."[16]

The same idea was given a sardonic twist by Samuel Vauclain, Baldwin Locomotive Works chief, who suggested that the automobile had saved the United States from revolution by giving industrial workers "a glorified rattle" to occupy their spare time. "A man who keeps at work to support a car," one editor commented smugly, "will have little time to give revolutionary impulses to his mental flywheel."[17] Perhaps the automobile had forestalled revolution. In any event, the progressive upsurge, which before World War I had pressed corporations in legislative halls and fought them in the courts, now seemed dormant. The people were hardly aware of politics as they swung frantically from one fad to the next. Politics, they seemed to agree, must be subordinated to economics, and this meant no tinkering with economic laws. "Legislation won't prevent it," became axiomatic. To any reformer foolish enough to believe in the "patented lawmaking pill,"[18] ridicule provided sufficient answer.

Politics in the eighteenth-century sense of political economy was scorned. Office-holding was still what it had been a half-century earlier—"*prima facie* evidence of littleness."[19] "What we need," avowed Henry Ford, the modern Hercules of rugged enterprise, "is a strong man in this country to send all these politicians packing." A new order, a special governing elite, was envisioned to replace the corrupt, inefficient politician.

The theology of profits, the subordination of politics to economics,

a theory of constitutional interpretation that considered "certain fundamental social and economic laws . . . beyond the right of official control"[20]—all these were firmly enthroned. Two years after former
Senator George Sutherland of Utah spoke these words, he was an
Associate Justice of the United States Supreme Court, enforcing this
political dogma as the law of the land. But even as industrial leaders
rejected regulation and control, they warmly embraced the usual
gratuities and government action against interlopers, especially organized labor. Business demanded, and got, tariff protection; abroad,
business interests were guarded by the State Department and protected by Marines; aviation and shipping enterprises were sustained
by government subsidies. In 1921, when the wheels of industry turned
more slowly, its leaders quickly identified the cause. "All authorities
and members of all parties, groups and schools of thought agree,"
the New York *Journal of Commerce* asserted confidently, that "internal revenue duties . . . are a chief cause of business depression and
disturbance and that they must be revised."[21] Industrial magnate
Andrew Mellon, in the role of Cabinet officer, responded quickly by
steadily reducing taxes, especially in the higher brackets.

Yet the bounties and protection industrial magnates gladly accepted
in their own behalf were vociferously denied to labor and agriculture.
When farmers, trapped in poverty and depression by the assumptions
of divine economic providence, attempted to procure legislative relief,
*Iron Age* accused them of "unsporting instinct" in "grumbling over the
consequences of the mismanagement of their business of the corn-
grower."[22] Spokesmen for business regarded labor with special hostility. But organization was not taboo among industrialists and businessmen. Trade associations flourished, fair trade laws were promoted
by desperate retailers and government agencies. Industrial cartels
formed at an accelerated pace. Chain stores struck hard at the individual storekeeper's traditional control of retail trades. Many thought
the day of trustbusting had passed. "When business cures its own
abuses"—that, Herbert Hoover said emphatically, "is true self-
government."[23]

Hoover soon emerged as the decade's incarnation of Prosperity and
symbol of Efficiency. In various respects he appealed to the dominant
motif of American life. He was a "success"—a self-made millionaire;
he was a humanitarian—he had fed Europe's starving; he was an
engineer—a great administrator, the high priest of efficiency. Though
such extreme reactionaries as William Howard Taft distrusted his
"progressivism," Hoover was in fact eminently safe politically. As
Harding's Secretary of Commerce, he was destined to make his mark
as a leader of the burgeoning forces of efficiency in the war on waste.
Later Hoover presided over the Conference on Unemployment, called

by President Harding to advise on the "national emergency." This emergency, the Conference reported, "is primarily a community problem."[24]

Industrial leaders had found special satisfaction and encouragement after 1920 in the political complexion of the national administration. "God is still in His Heaven," N. A. M. President Edgerton noted in 1924, "and there is in the White House a man whose essential qualities of mind and soul, and whose unswerving attachment to the fundamentals of free government are going to be demanded by an awaking people in the next President of the United States."[25] Edgerton was a good reporter. The people demanded a leaderless nation,[26] and they got exactly what they asked for. In succession Harding and Coolidge occupied the Presidency as spectators, while businessmen molded the country to their heart's desire.

Stone himself was a devout Republican, a grateful beneficiary at the hands of the national administration. Yet, in certain important respects, he was at odds with the trend of the time. He not only singled out certain perils endangering our tradition, but also stressed the humanistic values necessary for maintenance of its integrity. American tradition, as he interpreted it, had "exalted spiritual values above the material." "It presupposes enough at least of intellectual repose, if not leisure, to admit of some cultivation and appreciation of literary and artistic excellence." "If our Puritan inheritance for a time gave to it a somber, austere tinge," he observed in 1927, "it added also something of simplicity, of dignity, and a sturdy integrity. Those of us who cherish that tradition and who scan the changing scene of our American life, cannot, I think, feel wholly free of concern at the diminishing strength of those elements in it which tend to perpetuate that tradition or ignore those manifestations of present-day civilization which are so destructive of intellectual repose and of that dignity and simplicity of life. Nor may we disregard as of little moment the growing disposition, even among educated men, to emphasize the material rather than the spiritual measure of accomplishment."[27]

Stone's Republican allies, including his good friend, Herbert Hoover, were inclined to count the nation's blessings statistically—"nine million more homes with electricity, six million more telephones, seven million radio sets, and the service of an additional fourteen million automobiles," all accomplished under the aegis of Republicanism from 1921 to 1928.[28] In noting our great "scientific discoveries and the ingenious application of scientific knowledge to the control of natural forces," Stone wondered about "the social changes they are bringing and their ultimate effect on human conduct and on man's spiritual nature and aspiration":

They have brought to great numbers of people a prosperity and leisure unknown before, but it remains to be seen whether they are to bring a corresponding capacity for the right use of wealth and leisure. We are propelled through space with higher velocity and with greater ease than ever before, . . . but we cannot say that our movements are more purposeful, or affect more favorably our lives or those of our fellows.

When a people is largely engaged in the expansion of business and the accumulation of wealth, attention must be more and more directed to the procedures by which profits may be made and conserved. . . . The goal [extension of our control over matter] once gained enlarges the opportunity and stimulates the inclination for physical activity as an end in itself, hence we see the progressive development of a civilization in which movement is more characteristic than reflection, and which counts its most striking achievements in terms of speed and of time and space.[29]

Stone, unlike some other high-ranking Republicans, stressed the "more durable satisfaction"—the joy of "putting forth all one's powers for the attainment of a worth-while end." He placed highest value on "some conscious contribution, however small, to the age-long process of improving man":

If we take the long view of man's rise from savagery through barbarism to civilization and of the progress of civilized man to ever higher moral and intellectual planes, the things which seem to us most important in everyday life sink into insignificance. Wealth, power, the struggle for ephemeral social and political prestige, which so absorb our attention and energy, are but the passing phase of every age; ninety-day wonders which pass from man's recollection almost before the actors who have striven for them have passed from the stage. What is significant in the record of man's development is none of these. It is rather those forces in society and the lives of those individuals, who have, in each generation, added something to man's intellectual and moral attainment, that lay hold on the imagination and compel admiration and reverence in each succeeding generation.[30]

The spirit which Stone deplored found its most marked manifestation in "the cramped mind of the clever lawyer, for whom intellectual dignity and freedom had been forbidden by the interests which he served."[31] In his 1924 report as Dean of the Columbia Law School, Stone had criticized the "tendency to make isolated studies of various legal devices without reference to the more significant social functions which they serve." He advocated the study of law as involving "a method of social and economic control," requiring not only "good mental discipline," but also "a thoroughgoing knowledge of the social functions with which the law deals."[32]

Cloistered after 1925 in the nation's highest court, not so free as before to express himself publicly, he voiced in private a harsh judgment of the American bar. "I have no hesitation," he wrote in 1926, "in saying to you [President Butler], although I should not feel free to say it for publication, that I think the legal profession, as a whole, presents a very sad spectacle. I fear that it has become so legalized and commercialized in its higher strata and has so little professional and public spirit throughout that it is lagging behind the other professions. Sometimes I feel that I would like to be free from the restraints of public position just long enough to say a few very disagreeable, but nonetheless true things about the present condition of our bar."[33]

Within the Supreme Court of the United States a pliant acquiescence in the "natural" scheme of things—that profitable pattern ordained by business and its lawyer adjuncts for their own benefit, was the order of the day. Nor was this result accidental. William Howard Taft had often gloried in having been able, as President, to appoint six men to the Supreme Bench in four years, with the happy consequence that President Wilson, in twice the time, could appoint only three. Taft criticized Wilson severely for his "subservience to labor-union domination," for his appointment of "many persons of socialistic tendency." The former President denounced Wilson's "latitudinarian construction of the Constitution" as tending "to weaken the protection it should afford against socialistic raids upon property rights." In his opinion, two of President Wilson's appointees, Louis D. Brandeis and John H. Clarke (he was apparently satisfied with Justice McReynolds), represented "a new school of constitutional construction, which, if allowed to prevail, will greatly impair our own fundamental law." As four of the incumbent Justices were beyond the retiring age of seventy, and as it seemed not unlikely that the next President, like Taft himself, would use the appointing power to further his own political views, there was "no greater domestic issue [in the 1920 election] than the maintenance of the Supreme Court as the bulwark to enforce the guaranty that no man shall be deprived of his property without due process of law."[34]

As Taft had foreseen, the Court's reconstitution followed on the heels of Harding's election. By 1923 four of the nine Justices—Sutherland, Butler, Sanford, and Taft himself as Chief Justice—had been appointed by the Republican President. With Van Devanter, McReynolds, and the infirm McKenna (whom Stone replaced), these four new judges heightened the rigidities of constitutional interpretation. The genial Chief Justice, described by his biographer as "conservative, if not reactionary,"[35] thus won his ambition to preside over a court that could be counted on to go down the line for big business. Soon after his appointment the Chief Justice announced at a conference of the Justices that he "had been appointed to reverse a few decisions," and with his famous chuckle, "I looked right at old man Holmes when I said it."[36]

The groundwork had already been laid. A generation earlier the "rule of reason" had tamed the Sherman Anti-Trust Act. A statute intended to be a sword against monopoly had been converted into a shield to thwart public regulation and a weapon for industry to wield in its war on organized labor. Exercising the power of a super-legislature over both nation and states, the judiciary achieved unprecedented pre-eminence. Up to 1925 the Court had set aside only fifty-three congressional acts as unconstitutional. In the 1920s it handed down twelve, or nearly one-fourth as many, of these adverse rulings. The Court's power was augmented by the existence of two independent, logically exclusive, judicially created lines of precedent in every major area of constitutional interpretation. In a particular case, the Justices could go either way and fear no paucity of impressive authority. Little wonder that in the 1924 presidential campaign Robert M. La Follette, a life-long Republican and Progressive presidential candidate, could, by making an issue of the judicial veto over congressional legislation, attract four and a half million votes. The public, like former President Taft, was beginning to realize that the permissible scope of social and economic experimentation depended not upon the Constitution, but entirely "upon the Court's own discretion, and on nothing else."[37]

In this picture Stone was an enigma. Could he be counted on, as Senator Norris had argued, to support without question the "princes of privilege"? Would he follow unswervingly the dictates of Wall Street? Or would he become "a power on the Court" because of the confidence he might command from "colleagues of varying shades of opinion"?[38] Little or no light could be shed on these questions from Stone's experience or from his pronouncements. Constitutional law had not been his major interest or concern.

"I make no pretense to being an authority on the Constitution," the Attorney General had told an audience of Republican women in 1924. "Although I taught and studied law for a great many years, I only came incidentally, in my studies and in my instruction, upon the field of constitutional law. As a practicing lawyer I have had occasion to advise on constitutional questions, and occasionally to argue a case involving such questions, but that is far from making one an expert or one who may speak with authority on a subject of this kind."[39]

Those who had known him as a colleague at the Columbia Law School were optimistic. "The Court will be greatly improved," Professor Thomas Reed Powell predicted in a congratulatory letter, "both as a balance wheel and a lighthouse by adding to it your equilibrium and your lustre. I hope that you will be the medium by which those of your colleagues who need it will get more of the skepticism of Mr. Justice Holmes and more of the realism of Mr. Justice Brandeis."[40]

The *St. Louis Post-Dispatch* was less certain. "Whether his experience has given him that sympathy for the changing equities which are coming to life under new social aspirations—whether he has caught the vision of the new day which Brandeis . . . possesses and which sits like a halo on the white head of that youthful octogenarian Holmes—cannot be asserted."[41]

Against the background of a country in ferment, of leaders who would not lead, of entrenched privilege reinforced by a Supreme Court imbued with the dogmas of eighteenth-century individualism, how would Stone line up?

CHAPTER FOURTEEN

# Team Play

## 1925-1927

When Stone took his seat as an Associate Justice of the United States Supreme Court, that august tribunal possessed some of the attributes of a small claims court. The Justices held the power of life and death over crucial state and national legislation, often the final word in controversies between huge competing private interests, but they had almost no control over their own docket. A die-hard lawyer could appeal his client's claim no matter how picayune or devoid of public interest. This freedom of appeal had become a luxury the nation could ill afford. After World War I, a flood of cases growing out of wartime transactions, income tax, federal espionage, and prohibition litigation engulfed the Court. By 1925 the normal work had also vastly increased; each term cases were carried over to the next session. Matters of grave constitutional import bided their time while the nine Justices wrestled with a host of minor disputes. Some portion of the responsibility for failure to clear the cluttered docket could be laid to age and infirmity. But the basic cause lay in the enlargement of judicial tasks beyond the human powers of nine or any number of men to perform—especially if every case in the future, as in the past, was to be the concern of each judge.

Congress struck at the root of the trouble in February 1925 by restricting the right of appeal, by leaving to the Court's discretion what cases it would receive from the federal circuit courts. "The sound theory . . . of the new Act," Chief Justice Taft explained, "is that litigants have their rights sufficiently protected by a hearing or trial in the courts of first instance, and by one review in an immediate appellate federal court. The function of the Supreme Court is conceived to be, not the remedying of a particular litigant's wrong, but the consideration of cases whose decision involves principles, the application of which are of wide public or governmental interest. . . ."[1] It could not be said after enactment of the "Judges' Bill"[2] that the work of a Supreme Court Justice was any lighter than before—the job, even under the new procedure, taxed and still taxes the physical strength of its members, but after 1925 the work had less in common with the labors of Sisyphus, and the Court was soon able to keep abreast of its docket.

Taft lost no time in harnessing the energies and knowledge of the Court's newest and youngest member. Within a week after his induction the Chief Justice assigned him a bankruptcy case. Though the assignment called for the competence he had acquired as a teacher and writer on equity, Stone's first draft drew sharp comments. Justice Sanford felt so strongly that he threatened to dissent. Making the most of the critical comments, Stone revised his opinion,[3] and on recirculation Sanford decided to withhold his defection. The Chief Justice was highly pleased, and the other brethren agreed that the new version was a vast improvement. Somewhat inauspiciously, Stone had delivered, within six weeks of his oath of office, his first Supreme Court opinion.[4]

In mid-May the Stones took time out to go to New York and pack their belongings for the move to Washington. So much effort and money had been spent in establishing pleasant living quarters on Riverside Drive that the trip seemed "a good deal like going to a funeral."[5] On May 20, 1925, two big vans of possessions were on their way to the capital, part of the load for their apartment at 2400 Sixteenth Street and the rest for storage until such time as they could secure a house.

The new appointee was soon settled in the routine life of a judge, troubled only by Washington's postwar housing shortage. Crammed into a small apartment, he had no place to work apart from the living quarters. The Supreme Court had offices in the Capitol, but the Justices, except Sutherland and Sanford, preferred to work at home, and through the years much of the space allotted to the Court had been absorbed by legislators. Stone wrote the Chief Justice of "the difficulties" under which he labored in carrying on his work "for want of adequate office facilities."[6]

Stone's was not an isolated complaint. The Justices had long been aware of the need for increased efficiency, not only through greater use of certiorari* proceedings provided in the "Judges' Bill," but also through the creation of adequate physical working facilities. "We ought to have a building by ourselves and one under our control as the chief body at the head of the judiciary branch of the Government," the Chief Justice told Senator Curtis of Kansas. "There are many on the Court, who would not really enjoy the amplitude and comfort of such a building, but those of us who have responsibility ought to look after the welfare of those who come after us." Taft asked that "a special effort" be made "to secure proper chambers for our last Justice of the Supreme Court, Justice Stone."[7] Still without office space when the new term opened in the fall, the exasperated newcomer queried his chief on the possibility of evicting senators from the Court's ancestral property. Taft demurred. "It is a good deal easier," he pointed out, "to keep one Senator out than it is to put out one or more."[8] The upshot was that the Stones, after innumerable attempts to buy a suitable dwelling, decided to build a house of their own. In November they bought a 90-foot-square lot at the southeast corner of Wyoming Avenue and Twenty-fourth Street, just a block west of the Chief Justice's residence. "When we get money enough saved we will probably build a house," the Justice told his sons. "Whatever we do," he growled characteristically, "we will probably be stung by real-estate sharks and builders."[9] Meanwhile Stone worked in a basement room in the Senate Office Building.

Few people derive the lasting pleasure from house building that came to the Stones. Husband and wife participated in the plans and construction at every step. They wanted their house to express certain aesthetic standards as well as to fit their convenience and comfort. Lavishing attention on every detail, they finally handed architects Wyeth and Sullivan a complete scale of drawings, including size and arrangement of rooms, location of windows, wardrobes, fireplaces, and so on. The rooms were spacious, all beautifully lighted. "The interior arrangements," the Justice commented proudly, "are all the result of Agnes' planning. The architects have not changed in any particular the arrangements or the dimensions as Agnes planned them."[10]

Ground was broken in July 1926. That summer the Justice and his wife stayed on in Washington several weeks after the adjournment of Court to supervise the construction. Not satisfied to hire an architect and lodge full responsibility in him, they visited the site twice daily, making independent inspections, to see that everything met contract specifications. "Between the architects and ourselves," Mrs. Stone

* A writ used instead of error or appeal whereby the Supreme Court brings up a case from a lower court.

commented in 1950, "little was put over on us." The Stones moved in November 19, 1927, Mrs. Stone's birthday. The house cost close to $90,000, but the extra expense was worth the pleasure which they derived from the special features incorporated into the building, "because of our desire to combine both a country and city style residence."[11]

The Justice and his wife took great pride in their handiwork. "He was always telling people," Mrs. Stone has recalled, "that I drew the plans for the house." Gracious compliments came readily from colleagues and friends. "Stone's house is shaping up finely," Taft reported, "and I have no doubt he will have the handsomest of the judicial houses. His wife is an artist and something of an architect and she has worked out a very satisfactory plan."[12] The very spaciousness of the dwelling betokened heavier responsibilities ahead. After visiting the Stones in their new residence, former Columbia Law School colleague Nathan Abbott poured forth his feelings: "It seems so appropriate for you, and makes me confident that it is designed for the Chief Justice, unless you get bunkoed out of it by some unhappy shuffling of political cards, which God forbid."[13]

The library, a huge room occupying a wing of two stories, had been especially planned for the Justice's comfort. Though distinctly a workshop, it, like the rest of the house, reflected personality. On one side French doors opened upon a quiet, pleasant garden. The Justice derived boyish delight from the "secret" panel that could be swung open to afford access to the living room. Bookcases lined the lower walls. Above the level of the first floor, on four sides, were tall windows; favorite prints and portraits of famous jurists occupied the spaces in between. A balcony across the north end of the room over the secretary's office provided work space for the law clerk. The Justice sat at a large desk below in full view. In easy reach were bound copies of his own opinions, while the official reports were along a wall a good twenty feet distant. "The geographic location was not accidental," one of his law clerks has observed. "He had, . . . because he was human, a considerable preference for a collateral or dissenting opinion by Stone, J., to a square authority written by another."[14] The Justice's secretary worked in a partitioned section at the north end of the room, and a messenger stood ready to dispatch messages to colleagues, fetch weighty tomes from the Library on the Hill, and rush copy to the printer. "The new house is a joy," the Justice wrote shortly after the shift from Room 132, Senate Office Building. "The library where I spend most of my working hours when I am not in Court is especially attractive. It is so quiet and the light is so good that I feel like a different man."[15] Altogether the arrangements made for a happy integration of home life and work.

On the Court, as in earlier years, Stone's life was keyed to the rhythm of work. His day began early. By six-thirty or seven he was taking his daily walk. By eight-thirty or nine he was at his desk. Visitors were limited to the early morning or late afternoon, so as to leave the routine undisturbed. There were no self-created distractions, little lost motion, and a maximum of enjoyment. "I never had a job in my life which I did not enjoy," he said in 1941.[16] "From Stone," a law clerk has recalled, "I got vividly the feeling that a man's most lasting pleasure was doing the best he could with the job at hand; not just on his good days, but eight hours a day every day." He was so intent on the living present that he never worried over what the future might bring. "Sufficient unto the day is the evil thereof"—that was his working philosophy.[17]

Meeting deadlines conscientiously was almost a ritual. Unlike certain of his colleagues, he never held up opinions merely to polish the style or to bolster his reasoning with profuse documentation. Yet he took great pride in his work. When the proofs came in he went over them very carefully, making changes in the wording and sentence structure. Schedules, all the more rigid for being imposed by a New England conscience, demanded production at top speed. Opinions, written in longhand, so illegible that he sometimes had difficulty in reading them himself, poured forth from his library like power from a harnessed river. A law clerk, preceding him to Washington one year to prepare petitions for certiorari, accumulated what he thought was enough to hold the Justice "two or three days at the very least. But, as soon as I had the material piled up next to his chair, . . . he sat down and went through everything in a few hours. At first, I thought this surely must have indicated a most superficial examination, but I was to discover that the Justice did not miss anything. He simply worked with extraordinary speed."[18] His colleagues soon became aware of the new appointee's efficient dispatch of the task at hand. Within a month after his appointment he proudly reported: "I have just sent off my third opinion to the printer. They seem to meet with the approval of my associates, so that I feel I have made a fair start."[19]

If Court were sitting he left home about eleven-thirty carrying his lunchbox in the manner of a rural school boy. Court sat from twelve o'clock, adjourned one-half hour for lunch, and reconvened until four-thirty. On returning home about five, or reaching a good "stopping place" in his work, he took the usual exercise of the desk-bound public figure—a brisk afternoon walk. A favorite jaunt took him out Massachusetts Avenue to the Cathedral and back. Mrs. Stone frequently accompanied him, and when she was occupied, the law clerk went along. The Justice often worked on into the evening. The picture he liked to draw of himself—"tied to my oar even on Sundays and holidays"—mingled boasting and martyrdom.

The role of judge was highly congenial, not only because of his training and habit of hard work, but also because his temperament and cast of mind equipped him for it. His intellect was not the self-starting type, deeply absorbed in imponderables. He was content to deal with day-to-day issues. Proceed slowly, render judgment only after inquiry and careful "weighing of evidence"—this was the method he had imbibed at Amherst from Professor Garman. It had served him well as a law teacher. The transition from academic work to that of a judge was easy, but he felt keenly the loss of those moments of calm reflection and general reading which had become a part of his life at Columbia. Before he had been on the bench a year he sounded the note which was to become a refrain: "I regret that I am not a little less busy so that I could take the time to keep better informed about the social progress of this country. It is peculiarly a class of knowledge with which Supreme Court judges should be familiar. As it is now, by working steadily every day I am able to keep up with the work which is assigned to me and produce opinions which might and probably would be better if I had a little more leisure."[20]

Stone's first important opinions drew on his experience as Attorney-General. In 1925 the Government sought to enjoin twenty-two manufacturers of hardwood flooring—united in the Maple Flooring Manufacturers Association and controlling nearly 70 per cent of this commodity—from distributing to its members data concerning average costs and statistics reporting sales, prices, inventories, etc. Five years earlier, the Court had held similar activities by another trade association in violation of the Sherman Act.[21] Brandeis and Holmes had dissented because they felt that trade organization rationalized competition and eliminated waste. In the flooring manufacturers case, Stone followed their lead. The prices charged by members of this particular association were "fair and reasonable," in some cases lower than prices of competitors. To the Government's argument that the information supplied through the combination inevitably resulted in a common effort to maintain stable prices, Stone replied: "Persons who unite [in trade associations] are not engaged in unlawful conspiracies in restraint of trade merely because the ultimate result of their efforts may be to stabilize prices or limit production through a better understanding of economic laws and a more general ability to conform to them, for the simple reason that the Sherman Law neither repeals economic laws nor prohibits the gathering and dissemination of information."[22] No evidence had been produced showing that the published material was used by the association as the basis for fixing prices or for price maintenance. "Consequently," Stone contended, "the question which this Court must decide is whether the use of this material by members of the Association will necessarily have that effect so as to produce that unreasonable restraint of interstate commerce which is condemned by the Sherman Act." "We do not conceive," he said, "that the members of trade associations become . . . conspirators merely because they gather and disseminate information, such as is here complained of, bearing on the business in which they are engaged and make use of it in the management and control of their individual businesses." "Restraint upon free competition begins," he insisted, "when improper use is made of that information through any concerted action which operates to restrain the freedom of action of those who buy and sell." In Stone's view, "free competition" meant "a free and open market among both buyers and sellers. . . . Competition does not become less free merely because the conduct of commercial operations becomes more intelligent through the free distribution of knowledge of all the essential factors entering into the commercial transaction."[23]

Stone stated the nub of the decision in a letter to a former Columbia Law School colleague, Herman Oliphant. The Sherman Act, he said, "is concerned with the artificial kind of restraint which arbitrarily affects commerce by any kind of an agreement which affects its operation otherwise than by the dissemination of information which influences individual human action." The former type of restraint is to be distinguished "from the restraint which results from informed individual action. . . . Trade associations, like any other organized group of men, may be the cover for an agreement in restraint of trade. Or it may be an entirely legitimate activity in order to further the knowledge of the economics of a trade or business." Paraphrasing the result of the case, he added facetiously: "About all that was decided in the Maple Flooring case . . . is that while bricks may be made the instruments of murder, nevertheless the manufacture and sale of bricks is not illegal; but of course it does not follow from that that murder committed by the use of bricks is legal."[24]

In the preparation of his opinion Stone had solicited the Department of Commerce for information. Secretary Hoover responded with speeches and other materials, all emphasizing "the complete necessity for statistical services in the country as a basis of economic stability."[25] When Stone's opinions led to the same result, Hoover wrote enthusiastically: "I have found the two opinions of the most powerful interest and extraordinarily helpful. It is a great economic document."[26]

Dissenters Taft, Sanford, and McReynolds were highly skeptical.

They seriously doubted whether the association's vaunted competition among classes of products and in "services" did in fact establish the sovereignty of the consumer. "Why all this detailed interchange of information between competitors," said Justice Sanford, "if not *intended* to restrain competition. For much of it I can see no other purpose." The Chief Justice was also unconvinced, and crusty Justice McReynolds wrote a sulphurous dissent: "Ordinary knowledge of human nature and of the impelling force of greed ought to permit no serious doubt concerning the ultimate outcome of the arrangements. . . . Pious protestations and smug preambles but intensify distrust when men are found busy with schemes to enrich themselves through circumventions."*27

This, his first important opinion, evoked warm praise from Holmes and Brandeis and the acclamation of the others who voted with him. "Uncommonly good," Brandeis noted on his copy of the slip opinion. Holmes called it "good sense and good law." "A model opinion in every respect," Van Devanter applauded. "A good and useful job," Sutherland scribbled across the back of his copy. Even a dissenter had words of approbation. "Strongly and clearly put," Sanford remarked, "but I am not convinced."

The new Associate Justice maintained cordial relations, of varying degrees of warmth, with all his colleagues except McReynolds. With Holmes he formed a friendship in which admiration, respect, and affection were joined. The two jurists had much in common—a passion for legal scholarship, a liking for humor with a bawdy tinge, a delight in the arts, and a profound interest in history. At first Stone was wary of Brandeis, whose elaborately documented opinions seemed to him unduly ostentatious. Brandeis's stand in one case convinced him that the erstwhile People's Attorney was ready to use "bad economics to support bad law."28 In another he detected in Brandeis an unsportsmanlike quality, an element of trickery. The case had been decided without dissent and the opinion assigned to Stone. The Justice labored long and hard and was well pleased with the result. Brandeis did not concur; instead, much to Stone's surprise, he entered a well-reasoned dissent, arguing that the case should be dismissed for want of jurisdiction. The point had not been raised

* Many years later, in a letter to Justice Roberts (Nov. 10, 1944) concerning the Court's opinion in *Hartford-Empire Co.* v. *United States,* 323 U.S. 386 (1945), a complex anti-trust case involving monopoly based on abuse of patent privileges, Stone himself commented adversely on the work of trade associations in justification of a stringent decree against the organization tied up with the glass industry. "Nothing is easier," he said, "than to abuse statistics gathered by a combination or association of competitors, and the abuse may be very difficult to discover. Inasmuch as the defendants have flagrantly abused the privilege I lean rather strongly to saying that they may not re-establish any kind of an association or combination for gathering and disseminating them [statistics]."

by counsel, and Stone, unfortunately, had not considered it. The newcomer was understandably annoyed.

"Brandeis's action," Alfred McCormack recalled, "violated Stone's sense of team play. He felt that Brandeis, when he discovered a point that the Court had not considered, should have brought it to their attention or to that of the writer of the opinion, especially when the latter was a new Justice, with little experience in the intricacies of federal jurisdiction. His annoyance was not abated when it became clear, after long nights of research, that the position of Brandeis was virtually impregnable."[29]

At the outset Stone seemed attracted to the "solid virtues" of Taft, Butler, Sutherland, and Van Devanter. In Butler, these were lightened by a ready wit; in Van Devanter, they were combined with consummate craftsmanship and profound knowledge of the intricacies of judicial procedure. Sutherland, "a man of character and ability, an altogether pleasant associate,"[30] delighted Stone with his fund of Scotch stories.

Few Justices, perhaps none, ever found it possible to carry on harmoniously with Justice McReynolds. "He was," as Chief Justice Taft said, "inconsiderate of his colleagues and others and contemptuous of everybody. A fine-looking fellow, a man of real ability and great sharpness of intellect, he has been spoiled for usefulness."[31] When Stone first joined the Court, McReynolds tried to "ride" him. President Wilson's appointee liked brevity; Stone's rambling style offended his taste. "I think your conclusion is good," the cantankerous Justice wrote on the draft of an early opinion, "but I think you confuse the issue by too much detail. . . . Discuss the *essential* law point and no others." "Your opinion would be much better if only half as long," McReynolds complained on another occasion. "Think of the 10,000 who should read what you say."[32] "My observation," he counseled sagely, "has been that unnecessary discussion returns to plague." Stone never quite forgave him.

Justice Van Devanter was more sympathetic. When the novice fumbled in dealing with the technical details of Court procedure or had difficulty in parrying the thrusts of his critics, Van Devanter gave helpful counsel. On one occasion when two separate cases had been considered together, Stone either through unfamiliarity with judicial practice or mental lapse concluded the decision by affirming the trial court in both cases. Van Devanter set the matter straight by a short notation: "One suit should have been dismissed and the other affirmed." Even in disagreement Sutherland was deferential, sometimes acknowledging the superior force of Stone's argument. "I voted otherwise," the former Utah Senator noted on Stone's first excursion into the mysteries of the due process clause, "but

I shall not dissent." A little later Sutherland's praise was affirmative: "I was very doubtful about this, but you have put it convincingly, I agree." "I felt very strongly the other way," he scrawled on another draft, "but I shall quit."[33]

The Chief Justice went out of his way to cultivate the new brother and align him with the conservative majority. "Unanswerable," Taft noted on one of Stone's first opinions, "and . . . a most wholesome exposition of the way of the transgressor in equity. I felicitate you on the statement and reasoning."[34] When, within a few months after his accession to the bench, Stone felt hard pressed, the Chief Justice offered words of encouragement: "It only takes one year's experience to realize why we must have three months in the summer to recuperate. The truth is that during the nine months we are at work we never take an hour or day that we don't feel that we are wasting time in the effort to keep up. But," the Chief Justice added, "we are not resigning on that account, and we have got to face the music and I don't know anyone better able to do it than you are."[35]

Stone, in turn, was anxious to be helpful. This spirit of cooperation extended to the practical business of shaping opinions. During a bitter and violent strike between the St. Louis-San Francisco Railway and its employees, a strikebreaker was shot and killed by the workers. His family sued the railroad in the federal courts, claiming compensation under the Federal Employer's Liability Act. It was a routine case, and Stone's first draft dismissed the suit on the ground that the employer had no duty to provide guards for its employees under the conditions prevailing at its yards; certainly the railroad could not be held liable for failing to foresee circumstances necessitating a larger number of guards. The opinion was unanimous, and circulation of the draft evoked only Taft's comment. "I concur," he wrote, "but . . . I have a feeling that the R.R. company owed something morally under conditions like this to their strikebreakers." "You might add," he suggested, "that if in the contract of employment there had been a term that the railroad company would safely guard the men to their homes and back again, different questions might have been raised." Stone incorporated the suggestion in his opinion, without stating it quite so baldly. He put Taft's point this way: "Nor is there any evidence of such an undertaking [the employer's duty to guard strikebreakers] in the contract of employment."[36]

Toward other members of Taft's retinue Stone was equally cooperative. He was considerate of their judgments and seemingly desirous of winning their approval. Yet he remained essentially independent and open-minded, intent on learning his job. Before he was on the Court a year a case arose that proved his mettle. The principal question for decision was the right of the present holder of a patent to sue when the person from whom he had acquired it would not join in the suit voluntarily and could not be brought under the jurisdiction of the Court. At conference the Justices voted 7 to 1 to deny the suit, Stone alone dissenting. "I told them," Stone remarked to his law clerk, "that for three hundred years the courts have been struggling to give the right of suit to the real party in interest, and that our Court is now turning back the hands of the clock, but they were dead-set against me."[37] The fledgling jurist did not give up. Gathering the leading articles on "real party in interest" from a dozen volumes of the Columbia and Harvard law reviews, he took them to the Chief Justice. Along with these learned dissertations he submitted a memorandum summarizing his point of view and requesting reconsideration. Taft's draft opinion was circulated some time later, with the following note appended: "Dear Brethren: I think we made a mistake in this case and have written the opinion the other way. Hope you will agree. W. H. T."[38] The new Taft opinion became the decision of a unanimous court.[39]

Within a year after his appointment the newcomer rendered a special service to the Chief Justice in helping him to hammer out one of the most significant decisions in American history—*Myers* v. *United States.* "I never wrote an opinion that I felt to be so important in its effect," Taft said after handing down the 6 to 3 decision upholding the President's authority to remove a postmaster without the consent of the Senate.[40]

Since 1917 Frank S. Myers, postmaster at Portland, Oregon, had held office under an 1876 Act of Congress that prescribed that "postmasters . . . shall be appointed and may be removed by the President by and with the advice and consent of the Senate and shall hold their offices for four years unless sooner removed or suspended according to law." With more than a year of his statutory term still to run, the postmaster was fired by President Wilson without senatorial consent. To recover his salary for the unexpired portion of his term, suit was filed in the United States Court of Claims. This was turned down, and an appeal was made to the Supreme Court, arguing that his removal without the consent of the Senate violated the Act of 1876.[41]

Did the President have the exclusive power to remove executive officers of the United States whom he had appointed by and with the advice and consent of the Senate? Apart from the provision for impeaching civil officers of the United States, the Constitution was silent on the matter, and the Court had been extremely careful to refrain from espousing any definitive doctrine. Nor was it likely that a question so long mooted would now be decided unanimously, even by prolonged effort. For once Taft was resigned to a divided

Court. "It looks now," he wrote Stone, December 6, 1925, "as if we should stand 6 to 3, but if it were 5 to 4, I should be happy for my country that by even so small a margin we could prevent the excesses of congressional action." The controversy cut across the usual Court alignment. In the end, Stone ranged himself with the Chief Justice against the unusual dissenting team of Brandeis, McReynolds, and Holmes.

The issue was novel for the Court but not for Stone. When high-tariff senators had hounded President Coolidge to get rid of Tariff Commissioner William S. Culbertson, who had outspokenly denounced fellow commissioners for judging cases involving personal interests, Bascomb Slemp, Coolidge's secretary, had requested Attorney General Stone to advise the President on his power to remove Culbertson. In due course Stone had arrived at the White House armed with the opinion that counseled against any wholesale executive prerogative.

From information he had gathered, he concluded that "Mr. Culbertson was engaged actively in another function or employment, but that such employment did not involve or evidence any inefficiency, neglect of duty, or malfeasance in office, which, by the terms of the statute were alone made grounds for removal."* He therefore held that the statute did not authorize the President's removing Mr. Culbertson, and that "if the President possessed the power it was because he was clothed with executive power by the Constitution, which embraced authority to remove all appointive officers, regardless of any restrictions which Congress might interpose upon the exercise of such a power."[42]

In recalling the incident, Stone commented: "In view of the peculiar circumstances attending the request for this opinion I decided not to transmit it to the White House by messenger, as is the usual course. Instead I placed the opinion in my pocket, walked over to the White House, and asked for an interview with the President. As was his invariable practice with a member of his Cabinet, he saw me promptly, and listened without comment while I explained to him that I had prepared the opinion which he had requested, and had brought it in person as I thought that possibly he might wish to ask some questions about it. He did not take the opinion which I started to hand to him, but asked me to explain to him what its contents were. This I did very briefly, doubtless in a way which suggested that I thought that he desired to effect the

* Title 19, Section 91, U.S.C.A., declared that "No member shall engage actively in any other business, function, or employment. Any member may be removed by the President for inefficiency, neglect of duty, or malfeasance in office." One of the charges made against Culbertson was that he had been engaged as a part-time lecturer at Georgetown University.

removal, and that he needed to be cautioned; that if he did so he must accomplish it by the exercise of a constitutional power, which had often been challenged and was not free from doubt. When I had finished he said, bluntly, in substance: 'But I do not wish to remove Mr. Culbertson.' Then, no doubt, seeing the puzzled look on my countenance, he went on to say that complaints had come to him, from persons unnamed. . . . As I arose to leave I asked him if he wished to see or to keep the opinion, to which he replied, 'No, I do not want it.' "

Stone carried the paper back to his own office and deposited it in the files of the Department.

"The occurrence," Stone's comment continued, "left me with the strong impression that the President had no personal interest in securing Mr. Culbertson's removal, that the effort to enlist my aid in the undertaking did not originate with him, and that my action in the matter came to him as something of a surprise."[43]

Taft's approach to the issue in the Myers case was colored by different considerations. With painful White House experience still fresh in his memory, he squarely faced the issue which earlier courts had avoided.* Congress could not, he insisted, require the assent of the Senate to the removal of any executive officer appointed by the President with the advice and consent of the Senate. Article II, Section 1, by vesting the executive power in the President, gave him the power of appointing and removing executive officers. Express recognition of the appointing power in Article II, Section 2, reinforced this view on the well-approved principle that the power of removal of executive officers was incident to the power of appointment.† Congress could not limit the President's removal power of either high-level or inferior executive officers appointed with senatorial

* "I have been doing a great deal of reading in the Postmaster case on the question of the executive right of removal," Taft wrote Justice Butler, Sept. 16, 1925, "and the more I think it over, the stronger I am in the necessity for our reaching the conclusion we have. I agree that in the beginning it might have been decided either way, but it was decided in favor of the view that the Constitution vested the executive power of removal in the President, with only the exceptions that appear in the instrument itself. My experience in the executive office satisfies me that it would be a great mistake to change that view and give to the Senate any greater power of hampering the President and tying him down than they have under the view we voted to recognize as the proper one."

† "The executive Power shall be vested in a President of the United States of America," and (Section 2:) "he shall nominate, and by and with the advice and consent of the Senate, shall appoint Ambassadors, other public Ministers and Consuls, Judges of the Supreme Court, and all other Officers of the United States, whose Appointments are not herein otherwise provided for, and which shall be established by Law; but the Congress may by Law vest the Appointment of such inferior Officers, as they think proper, in the President alone, in the Courts of Law, or in the Heads of Departments."

consent by transferring this power elsewhere or by imposing qualifications on it. Finally, Congress could provide for the removal of
inferior executive officers by some lesser authority than the President, but only if it vested their appointment in the same lesser
authority.[44] For Taft the constitutional mandate that the President
"take care that the Laws be faithfully executed" was most significant
in that it "emphasized the necessity for including within the executive
power as conferred the exclusive power of removal." The President
should possess uninhibited removal power "in order to secure that
unitary and uniform execution of the laws which Article II of the Constitution evidently contemplated in vesting general executive power in
the President alone."*[45] To bolster these arguments, the Chief Justice
relied heavily on the congressional debates of 1789, when the executive
departments of Foreign Affairs, Treasury, and War were created. He
found support also in Jackson's protest message to Congress explaining
the reasons for removing Secretary of the Treasury Duane and in the
debates on the Tenure of Office Act of 1867.

Few cases have been the subject of such prolonged deliberation.
First argued in December 1923 and reargued in 1925, more than a
year elapsed before the decision came down on October 25, 1926.
Together, the four opinions occupied 243 pages in the official reports.
Taft had assigned the majority opinion to himself and worked on it
during the summer of 1925. His draft rambled through the history
of the removal power with reckless disdain for logical, sequential
ordering of arguments and events. Too distracted by administrative
duties to make the necessary revision, he sent his draft to Stone,
suggesting "that I may talk to you about it before circulation. . . .
Could you," he asked, "come to confer with Van [Van Devanter],
Sutherland, Pierce [Butler] and myself, say Sunday afternoon about
3:15?"[46] Following the conference, Stone, Butler, and Van Devanter

* The President, the Chief Justice reasoned, "must place in each member of
his official family, and his chief executive subordinates, implicit faith. The moment
that he loses confidence in the intelligence, ability, judgment or loyalty of any one
of them, he must have the power to remove him without delay. To require him
to file charges and submit them to the consideration of the Senate might make
impossible that unity and co-ordination in executive administration essential to
effective action. . . . The imperative reasons requiring an unrestricted power to
remove the most important of his subordinates in their most important duties
must, therefore, control the interpretation of the Constitution as to all appointed
by him." (Myers case, p. 134.)
   The wide scope of the opinion thus extended a direct and uninhibited presidential removal authority over all appointees named by him with the consent of
the Senate, whether or not engaged in administrative or non-administrative duties.
The Court even inferred that Congress could not restrict the removal of presidential appointees named *without* the consent of the Senate, although that point
was not at issue in the case.

took on the task of putting the Chief Justice's cumbersome handiwork in order.* Within a week a second version had been prepared. Stone was in agreement with the Chief Justice in his view that the Act of 1876 was unconstitutional, but disturbed by Taft's loose and disorganized argument, as well as by the preposterous length of the opinion.

For Taft, the absence of any constitutional distinction between officials serving the President in high-level posts and "inferior" officers only proved that all officers appointed by the President by and with the consent of the Senate were removable at the discretion of the Chief Executive. Stone disagreed. Such inferential reasoning based solely on surmise seemed inconclusive. He suggested that the Chief Justice might find support for wholesale removal authority over superior and inferior officers in the President's duty "to see that the laws are faithfully executed."† In response Taft added a paragraph showing the "good reasons" for extending the executive prerogative on this basis. Stone also found a way to buttress Taft's basic premise—that the power of removal is an inherent part of the constitutional grant of executive power. "As a mere matter of exposition of the written document," Stone explained, "the fact that the executive power was given in general terms with specific limitations, whereas the legislative powers were specifically enumerated, gives very great importance to the fact that there was no express limit to the power of removal either in the enumerated legislative powers or the enumerated restrictions on executive power."[47] Again Stone's idea was incorporated.

The most formidable obstacle Taft had to overcome was Chief

---

* "As I read it through," Taft wrote his brother Charles, Nov. 1, 1925, "it does not satisfy me, and I have had to do some more reading." What troubled him especially was "the plan or arrangement of the statement of the facts and the argument to sustain the conclusions. . . . That takes me rather more time than any other feature of a long opinion." The case occupied the Chief Justice "very intensely," he wrote Charles on Nov. 29, 1925, and "has been the occasion for my losing some sleep." And though the Justices who agreed with him had been of considerable help, he was "not quite sure" whether or not he had lost his "sense of proportion as to arguments in the pressure to state them all."

† "You seem to concede," Stone wrote the Chief Justice, Nov. 13, 1925, "that the power [of removal] must exist as to those to whom discretion is not delegated because no distinction is made between that class and the class to whom discretion is delegated. To my mind this implied concession is not necessary. It is the duty of the President to enforce the laws even though little or no discretion is involved. As Chief Executive he is entitled to faithful and efficient service by subordinates charged only with administrative duties. It is for that reason that the power is conferred and the duty imposed on him to exercise the power of removal, and that, to my mind, is just as *controlling* in the case of officers with little or no discretion as in the case of a cabinet officer. . . . I think there may be some revisions . . . so as to show that power and duty go hand in hand with respect to officers high and low in the executive branch."

Justice Marshall's famous dictum in *Marbury* v. *Madison:* "As the
law creating the office gave the .officer a right to hold it for five
years, independent of the Executive, the appointment was not rev-
ocable, but vested in the officer legal rights which are protected
by the laws of his country."[48] Stone thought that the best way to deal
with this proposition was simply to deny it. "I have some doubts,"
he commented, "whether the treatment of the language in Chief
Justice Marshall's opinion in *Marbury* v. *Madison,* entirely meets the
situation. I am not certain whether it would not be better to say
frankly that we do not agree with him and that in his *Life of
Washington* . . . he really agreed with us."[49] Once again Taft revised
the opinion.

With so many cooks at work, the judicial broth began to show
signs of spoilage. Arguments became scattered and unrelated, and
the ideas of individual Justices were left uncoordinated. As a corrective, Stone's law clerk, Alfred McCormack, remembered a device
he had used as editor of the *Columbia Law Review*—preparation
of a summary of the main points, use of these as topic sentences,
and rearrangement of material in logical order under these headings.[50]
The Justice's first impulse was that any such wholesale tampering
would involve *lèse majesté*. "I hope you will realize," Stone wrote
Taft, "that my suggestions . . . are due to the feeling that this is
one of the most important opinions of the Court in a generation
at least."[51] Taking the precaution of submitting a preliminary outline,
and pointing to several places where the writing was redundant
or the logic fumbling, Stone recommended not merely revision but
"a survey of the whole opinion from the point of view of the proper
emphases." "I . . . realize," he commented deferentially, "that it might
not be possible to carry out these suggestions in a way which would
be acceptable to you or to me either. If, however, you would like
to have me place these suggestions in more concrete form, I should
be very glad to attempt it in some detail and submit the result to
you."[52]

With Taft's approval Stone put his clerk to work with scissors
and paste. In a few days the reordered opinion was set in type and
sent to Butler and Van Devanter. A week later a revised draft appeared. Stone was still dissatisfied. As time went on, he began to question the Chief Justice's uncritical use of the maxim that the "power
to remove is incident to the power of appointment." In *United
States* v. *Perkins*[53] the Court had decided that Congress could
regulate dismissals by the head of a department in whom it had
vested the appointing authority. Taft had used the Perkins case
to strengthen his position, maintaining that it demonstrated the
maxim, and by a sort of *a fortiori* argument proved, that whom

the President hired he could fire. His exegesis made it clear, however, that Congress could avoid (in the case of inferior officers)
the whole problem of the locus of the removal power by the simple
expedient of lodging their appointment with someone other than "the
President by and with the advice and consent of the Senate." Still
worse, in Stone's view, Taft implied that the legislature itself could
participate in removals. Stone mentioned to Taft his "concern about
the possibility of misunderstanding by the casual reader of what the
Perkins case decided and of what our duty toward it is."[54] In a
special memorandum covering the point, he refuted the implication
that "Congress can lodge the power of removal in any body or in
any officer other than those on whom it might confer the power
to appoint. . . . To hold that Congress, by its own enactment, can
transfer any part of the power to remove, even an inferior officer,
to itself, or to either branch of Congress would be to establish a
check upon the admittedly constitutional power of the President without any express warrant in the Constitution itself and would run
counter to the principle of the separation of powers."[55]

To Stone, logical extension of the Perkins case seemed to threaten
the essentials of our form of government. The President is only the
titular head of his party, yet he is responsible for presenting a program of legislation and carrying it through. One of his greatest
weapons is patronage. The Perkins case might render the practical
outcome of the Myers case insecure by showing Congress how the
President's power over patronage could be minimized. Such wholesale
transfer of power from the executive to the legislature must somehow be foreclosed. Far from doing this, Stone saw Taft's use of the
Perkins case as undermining his own position.

"We say in the opinion that the power of removal was granted
to the President as a part of the executive power. By granting to
him the power of appointment and the executive power, we reach
the conclusion that there is vested in him the power of removal.
But Congress is given the power to provide for the appointment
of inferior officers as a part of its legislative power and by implication from the grant of this particular power Congress would undoubtedly have the power to say on what terms and conditions
the appointing officials could remove the officer appointed. I am
not quite sure that it follows by implication that Congress can withdraw from the President his executive power of removal in the
case of purely executive officers. Certainly, if it can, it would very
seriously impair his authority as an executive officer in just the
way you describe it. . . ."[56]

"Can you not," Stone asked Taft, "give your opinion all the vigor and effectiveness which it now possesses and at the same time avoid any pronouncement on this question?" Stone then proceeded to tell the Chief Justice how he thought this might be done. The relevant paragraph might be amended so as to read: "Even if the power of removal is incident to the power of appointment as a part of the executive power granted to the President, it is not incident to the power of advising and consenting to appointment." Taft's comment on the Perkins case, Stone persisted, could be amended to read: "These words [Article II, Section 2, the vesting of power to appoint in heads of departments, by congressional action], it has been held by this court, give to Congress the power to limit and regulate the removal of inferior officers by heads of departments when it exercises its constitutional power to lodge the power of appointment with them."

By such an amendment, Stone felt that the independent presidential power to remove inferior as well as superior officers would be sustained. "While we accept the general statement that the power of removal is incident to the power of appointment," his memorandum continued, "as so explained, we think it more accurate to say, in respect to the President's powers, that both appointment and removal are part of the executive power and are naturally united as appurtenant to it."

The Chief Justice was not quite convinced, but in the final draft, completed almost a year later, Taft considerably modified his handling of the Perkins case, contending that the Court "never has held, nor reasonably could hold . . . that the excepting clause enables Congress to draw to itself, or to either branch of it, the power to remove or the right to participate in the exercise of that power." Congress could not, for example, condition dismissal of inferior officers appointed by a department head upon Senate approval. "To do this would be to go beyond the words and implications of that clause and to infringe the constitutional principle of the separation of governmental powers."[57]

The Chief Justice was highly pleased. "I thank you for the trouble you have taken to help me in the Myers case opinion," he wrote Stone. "I agree that we have not had a case in two generations of more importance. . . . I have adopted your suggestions generally except when Van Devanter anticipated you. There may be one or two instances in which I rather preferred my own phrases where they were equivalent."[58]

When the dissents of Brandeis and McReynolds came in, another flurry of activity ensued in the Taft camp. As to McReynolds' screed, Stone commented, "I have very little to suggest." McReynolds "refers to the 'arbitrary' exercise of power of removal by the President as though the whole question is whether an arbitrary power of removal was given to the President or whether a reasonable power of removal or reasonable control of the power of removal was given to Congress. . . . The fact that this power, wherever it resides, may be used arbitrarily," Stone commented, "does not determine where it is lodged."[59] As for Brandeis's opinion, the basic difficulty, he told the Chief Justice, was that it proceeded "upon the basis of certain assumptions which are either not well founded, or, if granted, are inconsistent with the result for which it argues."[60] Brandeis contended, for example, that the President's power of removal "comes immediately from Congress." "This statement," Stone replied, "ignores the express language of Article II, Section 2: 'The President shall, by and with the advice and consent of the Senate, appoint [certain specified officers] and all other officers of the United States whose appointments are not herein otherwise provided for. . . .'" Brandeis's argument seemed to assume "that no power of removal was lodged with the President by the Constitution." "If the dissenting Justice makes this assumption," he observed, "it is quite unnecessary for him to write any opinion."[61]

"Both the dissenting opinions," he informed Taft, "have rather assumed that the people speak only through legislation, forgetting for the moment that the people spoke through the Constitution and that the legislative branch, as well as other branches of the government, have only such powers as were conferred . . . by the Constitution."[62] Brandeis, especially, had argued, by analogy from judicial deference to administrative interpretation of statutes, that the Court ought to give great weight to legislative construction of the meaning of the Constitution. "No such process of reasoning," Stone commented, "can be applied to a question of constitutional construction. Congress has no power to change the Constitution. Neither have Congress and the President acting together. Therefore, no more or greater weight can be given to their acquiescence in a particular construction of the Constitution than it is entitled to by its inherent merits."[63] Stone was also unsympathetic with Brandeis's "assumption that power of removal of inferior officers in the heads of departments, either with or without the consent of the Senate, is an adequate provision for the execution of the laws, without any reserve power in the President to remove inferior officers regardless of the consent of the Senate."[64] Fortunately for Taft, neither dissenter had elucidated the strong argument which Stone thought might be built on the Perkins case.

When the ridiculously long opinion* was finally completed and delivered, the Chief Justice felt "like a woman who has given birth to a large child."[65] Despite his failure to persuade three recalcitrant dissenters, he felt certain that executive prerogative had been firmly entrenched in an authoritative judicial opinion.†

Stone, apparently, never doubted the correctness of the "result," but to the very end he was "somewhat troubled" by a lingering doubt "as to whether we have adequately safeguarded the opinion against the attack which can be made upon the logic of it upon the basis of the decision in the Perkins case." Seeing the shoals ahead, he had attempted to convince Taft of the wisdom of confining the opinion to the narrow point at issue. "What I have in mind by these suggestions," he had tactfully insinuated, "is to so frame the opinion that we do not foreclose ourselves with respect to the power of removal except as it is actually involved in the present case."[66]

Stone pressed these views strenuously, but once his insistence evoked signs of the Chief Justice's displeasure, he assured him of continued loyalty. "This," Stone commented on his last remarks about the Perkins case, "does not affect in the slightest my views of the result, which upon historical and political science grounds, seems to me entirely correct."[67]

A dramatic sequel to the Myers case arose in 1935 when President Roosevelt, finding that Federal Trade Commissioner Humphrey's mind did not "go along together" with his own, summarily removed him.[68] The President's action had been based squarely on implications drawn from the Myers decision,[69] yet the four Justices who voted with Taft joined in a unanimous decision repudiating Roose-

---

* Taft's original rendition had been twenty-eight pages, but after Brandeis had filed a dissent of thirty-two pages and McReynolds had followed suit with forty-nine pages, the Chief Justice had had to double his in order to cover the points the dissenters insisted on developing, a few days before the opinion went down.

† Taft continued to express satisfaction with the decision after it had been delivered. "I am very strongly convinced," he wrote Thomas W. Shelton, Nov. 9, 1926, "that the danger to this country is in the enlargement of the powers of Congress, rather than in the maintenance in full of the executive power. Congress is getting into the habit of forming boards who really exercise executive power, and attempting to make them independent of the President after they have been appointed and confirmed. This merely makes a hydra-headed Executive, and if the terms are lengthened so as to exceed the duration of a particular Executive, a new Executive will find himself stripped of control of important functions, for which as the head of the Government he becomes responsible, but whose action he cannot influence in any way." As to the effect of the decision, the Chief Justice wrote Horace Taft, Oct. 28, 1926: "It curtails the power of the Senate and the power of Congress in erecting executive tribunals and boards that cut down the President's authority, and the members of such boards of course are strongly against the exercise of this presidential power. . . . The legitimate method of meeting the opinion, if contrary to popular view, is by amendment."

velt's action. Certain expressions in Taft's opinion did "tend to sustain the Government's contention, but these," the Court said, "are beyond the point involved and, therefore, do not come within the rule of *stare decisis.*"* "The narrow point actually decided," Sutherland observed, "was only that the President had power to remove a post-master of the first class, without the consent of the Senate as required by act of Congress." The Court did not make an about-face; it did not adopt the views of McReynolds and Brandeis. Justice Sutherland simply shifted the emphasis of the Myers decision from the "simple logic" of Article II—that the removal power is inherently "executive"— to the theory that a postmaster "is merely one of the units in the executive department and hence inherently subject to the exclusive and illimitable power of removal by the Chief Executive, whose subordinate and aid he is."[70] Stone could acquiesce in all this because the ruling of 1935 reiterated his views of November 13, 1925: "As Chief Executive he is entitled to faithful and efficient service by subordinates charged *only with administrative duties.*"[71] On the Humphrey case and Stone's position in relation to it, Marquis Childs has observed: "So the President fumed and Justice Stone had the cold comfort of saying 'I told you so.' For the question was at the center of his most cherished legal conviction. The earlier opinion had come when the Court was under the late Chief Justice Taft, and Stone had at that time stoutly opposed it. He had argued, in the privacy of the conference room, that the matter before the Court could be decided on a narrow point of law. In effect, he had said to the brethren: 'Look here, we don't have to stick out our necks on this one and tell the President in broad terms what he can or cannot do; if we do this now, the opinion is certain to haunt us later.' "[72]

For well over a year memoranda and counter-memoranda had passed between the Chief Justice and Stone. The newest Court member had helped to clarify Taft's conclusions and to steer him away from language and ideas conveying erroneous implications. Realizing that the Myers case was vital to his Chief, he did not press his views dogmatically.

Team play, the desire to maintain harmonious relations with Taft, may have deterred Stone from writing a concurrence. The very persistence with which he pressed his diverging views indicated an independence of mind that Taft deplored. The Chief Justice's ability to keep the new member in line on vexing social and economic issues had still to be tested.

---

* The policy of following previous decisions and precedents as authoritative and final.

CHAPTER FIFTEEN

# Facts versus Formulas

## 1927-1928

On the Supreme Court, after about 1905, a small group of Justices vehemently denied that the Constitution makes certain individual rights absolutely immune to governmental reform. But also on the Court, and usually in the majority, were Justices bitterly opposed to any government intrusion into areas hitherto ruled by private arrangements between men legally free and presumptively equal. At the foundation of their die-hard position lay unalloyed faith in free enterprise—which was, and is, considered the only true vehicle of progress. In America, they insisted, "the rights of private property" had been "established in the Constitution itself." The fundamental division of powers was not, as usually supposed, into executive, judicial, and legislative, but between the "voters on the one hand and property owners on the other, . . . with the judiciary as arbiter between them."[1] The Justices envisioned themselves in the service of a holy cause as old as the nation itself.

With the challenge of a continent before them, Americans had thrown off practically all government restraints on trades and callings. They had become free—free to govern themselves. In a system of small-scale enterprise, "liberty of contract" served well enough to guide the relations of buyer and seller, owner and employee, farmer and merchant. When that tradition ran into headlong conflict with inexorable economic tendencies inimical to its existence, lawyers and Supreme Court Justices, by skillful exegesis, molded the due process clause of the Fourteenth Amendment into a protective shield for private bargains. Thus the Amendment, intended primarily to secure the benefits of liberty to former slaves, set impassable limits on government interference in economic affairs. The simple contract between individual buyer and seller gave way under industrialism to bargains between the corporation and the individual worker. Yet the corporation was defined by the Court as a "person," thus preserving the fiction that the relationship was unchanged. Large-scale business organizations as well as individual enterprises were placed beyond the reach of legislative majorities.

In time laissez faire, interpreted as the absence of government restraint, produced the "strange combination of individualism as a pattern of belief and the corporation as the pattern of control."[2] Mere dogma, glorified in legend but not written into the Constitution itself, became the principal avenue to wealth and power. To give this dogma force and effect, various constitutional formulas were fashioned—"business affected with a public interest," "direct and indirect effects," and so on. Much of the first half of Stone's tenure on the Court was devoted to clearing these away, to persuading his colleagues to address themselves to realities.

Constitutional controversy was particularly rife over the requirement that a business, to be within the purview of government control, must be "affected with a public interest." Chief Justice Morrison R. Waite had introduced this concept into jurisprudence to validate government power over economic affairs. In the leading case of *Munn v. Illinois* of 1876 it was held that a state legislature could fix the prices charged for storage in grain elevators without violating the due process clause. On the basis of this principle the Court took judicial cognizance of the untoward social effects of private economic power.*

Inevitably, changes in the composition of the Court brought changes in interpretation. Long before 1923 slow strangulation had begun to beset the liberal doctrines of Chief Justice Waite. By sharply defining "business affected with a public interest," Chief Justice Taft limited the applicability of this standard. A "mere declaration by a legislature that a business is affected with a public interest," he commented, "is not conclusive." Such businesses must fall within three categories: public utilities carried on under the authority of a public grant of privileges; businesses traditionally regulated, such as inns and grist mills; and "businesses which though not public at their inception may be fairly said to have risen to be such and have become subject in consequence to some government regulation." These categories had all but crystallized, except so far as the third class presented a slight possibility of expansion—a majority of the Supreme Court so willing. The matter of determining the existence of "public interest" had always been "a subject of judicial inquiry."[3]

Justice Sutherland raised still another bar against governmental power. In the Minimum Wage case of 1923 he enforced the differentiation, insisted upon in Justice Stephen J. Field's dissent in the Munn case, between price-fixing and other aspects of the con-

* Also in *German Alliance Insurance Co. v. Lewis,* 233 U.S. 389 (1913), the Court, acknowledging that insurance was a business "affected with the public interest," noted that the price of insurance was not fixed by bargaining, but "in the councils of the underwriters," and that it was "illusory to speak of a liberty of contract."

tractual relation. Prices and wages, Sutherland said, are the very "heart of the contract," and relatively free from government control and regulation.[4] Flatly repudiating any distinction between different aspects of a contract, Justice Holmes observed: "If the public interest be established the regulation of rates is one of the first forms in which it is asserted."[5] Subsequently, in case after case, Holmes, Brandeis, and Stone vainly protested.

When in 1927 the Court, again speaking through Sutherland, set aside a New York statute limiting the mark-up on theater tickets to fifty cents above the price printed on the ticket, Stone, along with Holmes and Brandeis, dissented. Sutherland found the statute wanting on two scores: price-fixing makes such a drastic inroad on the property right that it can be justified only by unusual circumstances; the theater, not being a business "affected with a public interest," is not one in which such a regulation can be sustained. "Constitutional principles" must be "applied as they are written," Sutherland observed. "They may not be remolded by lawmakers or judges to save exceptional cases of inconvenience, hardship, or injustice."[6]

Stone conceded that the formula, "business affected with a public interest," had served as "a convenient expression for describing those businesses, regulation of which has been permitted in the past." But, he declared, "to say that only those businesses affected with a public interest may be regulated is but another way of stating that all those businesses which may be regulated are affected with a public interest. It is difficult to use the phrase free of its connotation of legal consequences, and hence when used as a basis of judicial decision, to avoid begging the question to be decided." In any event, a concept formerly utilized as a liberalizing principle was now given a restrictive connotation. What made the phrase so paralyzing in the hands of reactionaries was their "assumption that the category [the third mentioned by Taft] has now become complete or fixed and that there may not be brought into it new classes of business or transactions not hitherto included, in consequence of newly devised methods of extortionate price exaction."[7]

Stone also inveighed against Sutherland's notion that the price feature of a contract enjoys peculiar sanctity. "The constitutional theory that prices normally may not be regulated rests upon the assumption that the public interest and private right are both adequately protected when there is 'free' competition among buyers and sellers. . . ." But where this is not the case, a very different standard measures government price-fixing power. Ticket brokers, for example, enjoy "a virtual monopoly of the best seats . . . and . . . are enabled to demand extortionate prices of theater goers." State regulation may appropriately be substituted, he said, for the regulation of the "forces of competition" which no longer operate. "Self-interest," in the dissenter's view, "is not permitted to invoke constitutional protection at the expense of the public interest."[8]

"We should," Stone contended, "make searching and critical examination of those circumstances which in the past have been deemed sufficient to justify the exercise of the power [of state regulation] before concluding that it may not be exercised here." The "choice" between the economic ideas competing for recognition in this case "takes us from the judicial to the legislative field. The judicial function ends when it is determined that there is basis for legislative action in a field not withheld from legislative power by the Constitution as interpreted by the decisions of this Court."[9]

Stone had not reached this judgment easily. Three weeks before the decision came down he still had not made up his mind. "I voted the other way and am inclined to the same opinion still," he told Sutherland. "However, I will see what added light I can get."[10] The additional "light" shed by further exploration served only to confirm his initial judgment. "It seems to me," he wrote Holmes, "that Justice Sutherland has completely misapprehended the nature of the evil sought to be attacked by the state legislation.* It is, in effect, to break up a combination between managers and ticket brokers whereby the patrons of the successful plays are forced to pay for the losing ventures of the theatrical business. Of course, this particular kind of gouge does not superficially look like others which in the past have been thwarted by regulation which this Court has upheld, but it seems to me rather absurd for us to say that the state is powerless to meet the situation mainly because the rogues refuse to travel the road which the states have heretofore been permitted to close. In any event I am sorry to see any case decided upon the basis of such a phrase as 'affected with a public interest.' "[11]

"I don't feel so badly about the result in the ticket scalping case as I do about the reasoning which was used to support it," Stone commented informally. "I am anxious to see this Court, of all others, deal with realities rather than meaningless phrases."[12]

Holmes shared Stone's distrust of the majority's reliance on catch-

* Sutherland had dealt with the case as if it involved governmental price regulation when, in actual fact, the statute made no attempt to regulate prices. It merely required the sale price of tickets (whatever it might be) to be printed on their face and prohibited licensed ticket brokers from reselling at more than fifty cents above the printed price. The excuse for Sutherland's discourse arose from a section in the preamble of the statute declaring that the price or charge for admission to places of public entertainment was a matter affected with the public interest and subject to regulation because of the possibilities for fraud and coercion inherent in the business of ticket selling. (See Thomas Reed Powell, "State Utilities and the Supreme Court," *Michigan Law Review*, May 1931.)

words. Indeed, Sutherland's constitutional rigidities had driven the
Bostonian to write one of his most devastating dissents. "We fear
to grant power and are unwilling to recognize it when it exists,"
Holmes said. "I think the proper course is to recognize that a state
legislature can do whatever it sees fit to do unless it is restrained
by some express prohibition in the Constitution of the United States
or of the state, and that courts should be careful not to extend
such prohibitions beyond their obvious meaning by reading into them
conceptions of public policy that the particular court may happen
to entertain."[13]

Stone agreed that Holmes had written a fine essay, but he was
not quite satisfied. His reasons for writing a separate dissent (in which
Holmes and Brandeis concurred) indicate the similarity of thinking
between Holmes and himself, as well as the diversity of their methods:
"Of course, Holmes, as usual, went directly to the heart of the
matter. In view of what he had written I hesitated to write at all,
but it seemed to me that his opinion might not be understood or
at any rate not adequately understood by many lawyers, and therefore I thought it advisable to meet the majority a little more on their
own ground. Both he and Brandeis cordially agreed to this, so I
wrote what I had to say. A little too much perhaps, but nevertheless
it may be useful later on."[14]

For the time being these efforts were fruitless. Sutherland, joined
by five other Justices, held to the position established in the Minimum
Wage case. Legislative regulation of wages and prices "is not only
a more definite and serious invasion of the rights of property and
freedom of contract," he said, "but its exercise cannot always be
justified by circumstances which have been held to justify legislative
regulation of the manner in which a business shall be carried on."
To come within the regulatory scope of the phrase "business affected
with a public interest," the property "must be such or be so employed
as to justify the conclusion that it has been *devoted* to a public use
and its use thereby, in effect, *granted* to the public." "A theater is a
private enterprise," Sutherland concluded, and the ticket broker, a
mere appendage of the theater, is free from price regulation.[15]

So also was an employment agency—or so the Court held in 1928.
Employment and ticket agencies were equally brokers. In the Tyson
case, the majority of Justices reasoned, "we declared unconstitutional
an act of the New York legislature which sought to fix the price
at which theater tickets should be sold by a ticket broker, and it
is not easy to see how, without disregarding that decision, price-
fixing legislation in respect of other brokers of like character can
be upheld."[16] Sutherland's boldness in treating the ticket-agency
statute as a price-fixing measure now paid off. Sanford, who had

dissented in the ticket case, joined the majority because he was "unable to distinguish" the regulation of ticket brokers and employment agencies. To close the discussion once and for all, Sutherland snapped: "It is no longer fairly open to question that, at least in the absence of a grave emergency, . . . the fixing of prices for food and clothing, of house rental or of wages to be paid, whether minimum or maximum, is beyond the legislative power."[17] Such dogged adherence to formula shocked Stone. Holmes and Brandeis, equally aggrieved, but feeling that their usefulness had been somewhat impaired by repeated protests, stepped aside and let Stone write for all three.

"Ticket brokers and employment brokers are similar in name," Stone commented somewhat ironically. "In no other respect do they seem alike to me." If anything, employment bureaus were more appropriate subjects of government regulation, for "the state has a larger interest in seeing that its workers find employment without being imposed upon, than in seeing that its citizens are entertained." "To overcharge a man for the privilege of hearing the opera is one thing, to control the possibility of his earning a livelihood would appear to be quite another." The New York ticket agents exercised monopolistic powers over a "luxury"; their depredations affected "a relatively small part of the population within a comparatively small area of the State of New York." Their victims were not "necessitous." By contrast, employment agencies dealt with a necessitous class that was often dependent upon them for opportunity to earn a livelihood. Furthermore, relevant and easily available source material exposed far-reaching employment-agency abuses—extortionate fees, discrimination, misrepresentation as to conditions of work and terms of employment, fee splitting with foremen—almost a rascal's litany of wrongs against workers. The agency charged only the employee for a service valuable also to the employer. At every point within their operations, they chose to exact their tolls from the weaker party— to prey on individuals already, as idle men, in a relatively defenseless position. "We are not judicially ignorant," Stone commented, "of what all human experience teaches, that those so situated are peculiarly the prey of the unscrupulous and designing."[18]

Stone used this opportunity to probe further into the concept "affected with a public interest." "That phrase is not to be found in the Constitution," he said. "It has and can have only such meaning as may be given to it by the decisions of this Court." Turning again to Chief Justice Waite's broad construction in *Munn* v. *Illinois,* he insisted that Taft's third category was susceptible of well-nigh unlimited expansion and had, in fact, been enlarged by the Justices themselves. In a host of cases the Supreme Court had sustained regulation, even as to prices. Precedents established that "the economic disadvantage of a class . . . may alone be sufficient to give rise to the 'public interest' and to justify the regulation of contracts with its members." Thus, even on the basis of the Court's own decisions, private employment brokers were subject to price control. "Unless we are to establish once and for all the rule that only public utilities may be regulated as to price," he wrote, "the validity of the statute at hand would seem to me to be beyond doubt. Certainly it would be difficult to show a greater necessity for price regulation."[19]

Once granting, as the majority did, "constitutional power to regulate," Stone refused "to make a distinction based on no real economic difference." Perceiving no "controlling difference between reasonable regulation of price, . . . and other forms of appropriate regulation which curtail liberty of contract or the use and enjoyment of property," he denied that the abuses of job agents "are grounds for regulation, but not for price-fixing." "The Constitution does not require us to hold that a business, subject to every other form of reasonable regulation, is immune from the requirement of reasonable prices, where that requirement is the only remedy appropriate to the evils encountered." "Price," he observed, "is only one of the terms in a bargain."[20]

"As I read those decisions," Stone declared, "such regulation is within a state's power whenever any combination of circumstance seriously curtails the regulative forces of competition, so that buyers or sellers are placed at such a disadvantage in the bargaining struggle that a legislature might reasonably anticipate serious consequences to the community as a whole."[21]

The dissent ended with pungent protest against the usurpation of legislative prerogatives by the ruling judicial clique. He would be "the first to admit" that "there may be reasonable differences of opinion as to the wisdom of the solution here attempted. . . . But a choice between them," he wrote, reverting once more to the doctrine of *Munn* v. *Illinois*, "should be left where, it seems to me, it was left by the Constitution—to the states and to Congress."[22]

"This is admirable and sockdological," Holmes wrote on the back of his copy of Stone's dissent. "My only difficulty in marking my agreement is that I go further." Brandeis, with equal delight, commented, "Yes, indeed!"

Warm personal tribute came to Stone from Felix Frankfurter, who wrote, the "opinion will establish itself in history as one of the leading utterances upon the due process clause. You have made clear, with an explicitness not to be found in any other opinion thus far, the real meaning of the decisions of the courts in these recent price-fixing cases, namely, that if, since price regulation is the only effective means of regulation, there can be no regulation at all—a proposition as you so conclusively indicate, wholly without warrant either in the text or the implications of the Constitution. . . ."

"One can't help wondering," Frankfurter went on, "where all this will lead to. The decisions at this term, and particularly during the last few months, give one just ground for fear that the due process clause will be used as an instrument of restriction upon the area of discretionary power of the states over local matters, and whatever may not be susceptible of curbing through the due process clause will be restrained by the requirement of the 'equal protection of the laws.' "[23]

Some observers put the contrasting approaches of the majority and minority in the idiom of philosophy. "The majority opinion," Edwin W. Patterson said, "exhibits certain of the fallacies to which the rationalistic method leads—reliance on the application of concepts ('business affected with a public interest') and their application to new conditions by a process assumed to be purely deductive. Thus the employment agency is essentially a private business presumably because it has a shop that looks like a druggist's or a butcher shop. There is no consideration of the economic consequences of classifying a business as either private or public. The dissenting opinion tends to strengthen one's confidence in John Dewey's proposition that once you have the 'facts' before you the ethical problem of what 'ought' to be done becomes fairly simple."[24]

"I think all your comments very just and interesting," Stone commented on Patterson's analysis. "These regulations under the Fourteenth Amendment are peculiarly fact cases. The formulae which the Court has developed are really meaningless except as they are applied to particular facts."[25]

Law had become divorced from life. "One of the amazing things about our day and time," Professor Oliphant wrote apropos the unemployment agencies decision, "is the degree to which folks can get out of touch with the actual processes and problems of life. To say that for the state to attempt to remedy the abuses inherent in the employment agency situation is an arbitrary and unreasonable exercise of government power, represents an all but complete unawareness of what is actually going on about us."[26]

Stone agreed that judicial competency and education must go hand in hand. "One job I would like to see done," he told Oliphant, "is a thorough-going examination of the economics of the Supreme Court, in the light of the last developments of that science. . . . As the work of the Court goes on it will be increasingly working with problems of this kind, and it is tremendously important that . . . the judges should recognize that problem, and, that the various legal formulae which have been developed under the Fourteenth Amendment are meaningless except as judges know the economic problem involved."[27]

"If judges could have less reverence for the way in which an old doctrine was applied to an old situation," the Justice reflected, "the law might prove to be more flexible than it is. The fact of the business is, that the world has never, in its history, changed quite so rapidly as it has in your day and mine."[28]

Lawyers, quite as much as judges,* were responsible for the determined trend toward a sterile constitutionalism. Stone deplored "the hopeless narrowness of members of the bar who present cases of this character to us." Verbal logic chopping, with no apparent consciousness of relevant social and economic forces, was, he said, "about all we get. If anything appears in the opinion, it is because some member of the Court takes the time and energy to go on an exploring expedition of his own." Sorely needed was less preoccupation with labels and more meditation on realities. Perhaps there were signs that opportunity for such a blossoming was at hand.† "Fortunately," he continued, "we are catching up with our docket. If that should come about, some of us could become real students of the social

* Years later Stone, writing D. O. McGovney (Dec. 3, 1934), still thought "the Tyson and Ribnik cases may be used as horrible examples to show the unfortunate position in which a court may find itself if it attempts to write into the Constitution the particular social or economic philosophy in which the judges have been trained."

† What Stone appears to have overlooked is the fact that a majority of the Justices, Sutherland in particular, considered social and economic data irrelevant, indeed inappropriate, in the business of judging. On the mass of data and reports presented for the Court's surveillance in the Adkins case, Sutherland commented dryly: "We have found [them] interesting but only mildly persuasive." They were, he said, "all proper enough for consideration of the lawmaking bodies, since their tendency is to establish the desirability or undesirability of the legislation; but they reflect no legitimate light upon the question of its validity, and that is what we are called upon to decide" (pp. 559-60).

A considerable number of Stone's colleagues went so far as to object to his references to law reviews in his opinions. In the 1926 term Van Devanter cautioned him: "In your nolo contendere case please consider whether the long note (possibly more than one) ought to be omitted—whether it encourages an inadmissible use of notes. I thought of it when reading the opinion, but preferred to make no suggestion. Since then two of our brothers who were speaking of opinions in a general way referred to the use of notes and mentioned that opinion as going beyond what they thought proper in that regard. I merely suggest that you consider it and then do as you think best. As I recall the opinion the long note adds nothing to it." (The case was Hudson v. U.S., 272 U.S. 451.)

Van Devanter continued to query "the wisdom of reference to law reviews." Justice Butler, it has been said, never concurred in an opinion which cited a law review article. In the 1931 term Chief Justice Hughes also questioned this practice of Stone's in the latter's opinion in Shriver v. Woodbine Savings Bank, 285 U.S. 467. "An exception," Chief Justice Hughes suggested, "may possibly be allowed where the writer is a generally accepted authority."

and economic development of the United States, whether counsel are interested or not."[29]

Stone was also heartened by what he discerned as a developing trend in the nation's law schools, indicating a break with the rubrics of the past. "I think," he speculated, "the disposition of the faculty [at Columbia Law School] to slough off some of the old formulas and to take a more realistic view of the law and of the functions of law schools is one of the most hopeful signs in the field of education at the present time."[30]

Meanwhile, as "liberty of contract" and other power-crippling concepts continued to flourish, barriers against state legislative power matching those erected on "due process" were discovered in the commerce clause. When Pennsylvania attempted to protect poor and guileless immigrants from the frauds of unscrupulous steamship agents, the Supreme Court struck down the licensing statute as a "direct" state interference with foreign commerce forbidden by the Constitution. Another label was thus invoked to defeat the power to govern. In a forceful dissent, Stone queried this judicially created "test of the limit of state action." For him, the criterion "whether the interference with commerce is direct or indirect," like "business affected with a public interest," was "too mechanical, too uncertain in its application, and too remote from actualities, to be of value." "We are," he declared, "doing little more than using labels to describe a result rather than any trustworthy formula by which it is reached." The "national interest" comprehended in the commerce clause is the maintenance of "freedom of commerce across state lines." Instead of the "direct" and "indirect" abstraction, Stone urged pragmatic inquiry—recourse to reality. To determine whether the challenged statute infringes the "national interest" or "concerns interests primarily local," requires "a consideration of all the facts and circumstances, such as the nature of the regulation, its function, the character of the business involved, and the actual effect on the flow of commerce."[31]

Following his father's lead, Lauson Stone, then a student at the Columbia Law School, prepared a note on the case for the law review. "The opinion in the Di Santo case," Lauson wrote, "fails to do what nearly all previous cases have failed to do—define what is meant by the ever-recurrent words, 'direct burden.' The fact that there is not the slightest suggestion ventured as to how the Court reached its decision that the license law constituted a 'direct burden,' leads to the conclusion that, as intimated in one of the dissenting opinions, the Court, while purporting to give a reason, was, in fact, merely stating the result it was about to reach."[32]

The Justices were sharply divided on the primary division of authority between the national government and the states. Within each sphere they conceived of varying degrees of authority. Questions of kind and degree were fused with conflicts over social and economic policy. Athwart the power vortex stood nine men, at odds with themselves as to the role the Court should play in achieving proper balance between freedom and order.

As between the national and the state governments, the most vexing problem during these turbulent years had to do with governmental immunities from taxation. Through a long series of cases commencing with Chief Justice Marshall's decision in *McCulloch* v. *Maryland* the Court had established the proposition that the institutions and instrumentalities appurtenant to and forming any part of the governmental activities of the national or state governments were immune from taxation by the other.[33] For Marshall, the problem turned primarily on considerations of sovereignty. The function of the Court was to determine the existence or nonexistence of governmental power. That accomplished, the immunities doctrine applied automatically. The Court thus secured for itself authority to review cases of governmental tax exemptions, but the doctrine it had adopted imposed rigid limitations on the scope of judicial review.

To Stone, this excessive formulism, this facile "black and white" approach, again obviated any judicial attempt to get at the core of the matter—whether taxation by one government upon the instrumentalities of the other was of sufficient degree to imperil governmental functions. The first opportunity to develop his ideas came in *Metcalf* v. *Mitchell*. Here the Court was asked to determine the constitutionality of the federal income tax upon fees received by consulting engineers for advisory services to states or their subdivisions with reference to proposed water supply and sewage disposal systems. Speaking for a unanimous Court, Stone recognized the immunities doctrine as controlling, but queried whether "the effect [of the tax in question] is such as to bring it within the purview" of the past decisions forbidding inter-governmental taxation. It was not possible, he said, to describe "universally" the instrumentalities of either the state or the national governments that were exempt from taxation. Surely, not every person, because of some "dealings with the government," could be construed to be "an instrumentality of government within the meaning of the rule." "As cases arise . . . , it becomes necessary to draw the line which separates those activities having some relation to government, which are nevertheless subject to taxation, from those which are immune. Experience has shown that there is no formula by which that line may be plotted with precision in advance."[34]

Even when properly exercised, the taxing power of one government "unavoidably" must have "some effect upon the other." The true criterion of the limits of such "effect" is that "neither government may destroy the other nor curtail in any substantial manner the exercise of its powers." This standard was not to be applied blindly, exempting automatically all activities or instrumentalities of one government from taxation by the other. Consideration of facts and appraisal of the "degree" of interference were necessary. "The limitation upon the taxing power of each, so far as it affects the other, must," Stone insisted, "*receive a practical construction* which permits both to function with the minimum of interference each with the other; and that limitation cannot be so varied or extended as seriously to impair either the taxing power of the government imposing the tax . . . or the appropriate exercise of the functions of the government affected by it." Utilizing this criterion, Stone concluded that the tax in question was imposed on the income of one who in no sense could be considered an officer or employee of government. No agency of government was involved. Therefore it could not "be deemed to be an interference with government, or an impairment of the efficiency of its agencies in any substantial way."*[35]

Stone had won a battle, but not the war. In 1928, by a 5 to 4 decision, the Court, speaking through Justice Butler, set aside a Mississippi gasoline tax collected on sales to the Coast Guard Fleet and a Veterans' Hospital. The Justices again unequivocally applied the immunities doctrine. "Mississippi," they said, "may not lay any tax upon transactions by which the United States secures the things desired for its governmental purposes."[36] Stone and Brandeis concurred in a dissent written by Justice Holmes, and McReynolds dissented separately in an opinion with which Stone also concurred.†

The struggle was unending. Three years later the majority went to the lengths of holding that the federal excise tax was not applicable on sales of motorcycles by a manufacturer to a municipality.‡ "Where the principle applies," Justice Van Devanter asserted, "it is not affected

---

* Later on Stone attempted to clarify the ambiguous distinction between a state operating in a business capacity and exercising a governmental function. On March 10, 1936, he reminded his friend Sterling Carr: "You may have noticed *U.S.* v. *California* [297 U.S. 175 (1936)] in which I tried to elucidate further the theory of tax immunity of governmental instrumentalities and incidentally to lay the ghost of that distinction between state action in its sovereign capacity and in its private capacity."

† Holmes' dissent went directly to the point. As to Marshall's simplified doctrine, he commented: "In those days it was not recognized as it is today that most of the distinctions of the law are distinctions of degree." "The question of interference with Government," Holmes observed, following Stone's opinion in the Metcalf case, "is one of reasonableness and degree, and it seems to me that the interference in this case is too remote." (*Panhandle Oil Co.* v. *Mississippi*, pp. 223, 225.)

‡ While Brandeis concurred once more with Stone, Holmes acquiesced with the majority, believing that the decision in the Mississippi case was controlling.

by the amount of the particular tax or the extent of the resulting interference, but it is absolute." Wearily taking up the cudgels once again,
Stone vigorously attacked the immunities doctrine. "The practical
effect of enlargement is," he said in his dissent, "commonly to relieve
individuals from a tax, at the expense of the government imposing it,
without substantial benefit to the government for whose theoretical
advantage the immunity is invoked."[37]

Stone's persistence, though not immediately successful, was not in
vain. Largely through his efforts the Court had become conscious of
another useful tool for the attainment of judicial realism—the change
"from a [concept of] 'total failure' of power into an inquiry whether
the exercise of the power produces 'undue interference.' "[38]

In the procedural aspects of the law also, new frontiers were con-
quered, reforms made. In several states "declaratory judgment action"
promised speedier relief for litigants. When legislation empowering
courts, in a real controversy, to render a declaration of the rights of
the parties was challenged, Stone tried to persuade the Justices that
these functional and desirable judgment actions were "cases" or "controversies" within the meaning of Article II, Section 2, of the Constitution, and therefore within the Court's appellate jurisdiction. But, as
usual, he encountered resistance. Here too he faced stolid adherence
to unchanging dogma. In January 1927 the Court (in the Grannis
case) unanimously dismissed, for want of jurisdiction, a petition presented under the Kentucky Declaratory Judgment Act for the determination of rights under a Kentucky tobacco sales regulation statute.
Justice Sanford, relying on prior although not substantially similar
decisions, held that the United States district court, from which an
appeal had been taken to the Supreme Court, "had no jurisdiction to
entertain the petition for the declaratory judgment."[39] Inferentially it
appeared as though the Court were intimating that the declaratory
judgment procedure was unconstitutional because it did not present
a "case" or "controversy" within the meaning of the Constitution.

Stone acquiesced in the Grannis decision, but in the Swope case,
decided the same year, he upheld, for a unanimous Court, a special
procedure created under a Missouri statute for deciding the validity
of a local ordinance for improvement assessments and the amounts of
liens proposed to be applied under it.[40] The action in question, though
not characterized by Stone as a declaratory judgment action, possessed
all the attributes of such a proceeding.* He now suspected that the
earlier case had been incorrectly decided. "I think," he told the Chief

---

* "I was quite aware," Stone wrote Zechariah Chafee, Jr., April 29, 1939, "when
I wrote the opinion in the Swope case that we were reviewing a declaratory judgment, although it seemed to me more important in that case to describe accurately
what we were doing than to call it names."

Justice, "we will have, in increasing measure, statutes like those involved in both the Grannis case and the Swope case, and that we ought to be extremely cautious about limiting the utility of such statutes." He then suggested the possibility of reopening the question in the Grannis case. But Taft was inclined to "allow the thing to proceed just as it is until somebody raises the question again." Stone persisted, reiterating his conviction that whenever the question arose again it should be handled on its facts alone without the loose inferences of unconstitutionality which had been included in the Grannis opinion.* To this, Taft made no reply.[41]

A year later the question came up, collaterally, once more, in *Willing* v. *Chicago Auditorium.* Justice Brandeis, writing for the majority, asserted in dictum: "What the plaintiff seeks is simply a declaratory judgment. To grant that relief is beyond the power conferred upon the federal judiciary." Taft silently acquiesced despite his assurances of the previous year, and Stone again questioned the Court's denial of authority to accept cases arising under declaratory judgment measures. In his opinion, the constitutional prerequisites of "case" or "controversy" were fully met by such actions. "I concur in the result," he stated. "It suffices to say that the suit is plainly not one within the equity jurisdiction . . . of the Judicial Code. But it is unnecessary, and I am therefore not prepared to go further and say anything in support of the view that Congress may not constitutionally confer on the federal courts jurisdiction to render declaratory judgments in cases where that form of judgment would be an appropriate remedy, or that this Court is without constitutional power to review such judgments of state courts when they involve a federal question."[42]

Holmes joined in the opinion of Brandeis, but only because of his belief that prior decisions led to such a determination. "I do not care to join in the criticism of his [Brandeis's] opinion," he wrote on his copy of Stone's concurrence, "but I also regret his conclusion that we cannot render declaratory judgments—which, however, I thought had been stated heretofore."

Despite these rebuffs Stone persisted. In 1933 he wrote a friend: "You will be interested, if you have not already seen it, to take a look at my opinion, *Nashville, Chattanooga and St. Louis Railway* v. *Wallace*"—a decision accepting review of a case arising under the Tennessee Declaratory Judgments Act—"and compare it with my concurring —although in effect dissenting—opinion in *Willing* v. *Chicago Audi-*

---

* Stone's discomfort at the Court's fuzzy doctrinairism was expressed in a letter to W. W. Cook, May 2, 1927: "I don't mind saying, confidentially, that I was not a little troubled, when I came to the [Swope] opinion about some of the things that had been said (in prior discussions) about what is a 'case' or a 'controversy' or 'judicial power' within the meaning of the Constitution."

*torium. . . .* It is interesting to see that the views I there expressed have since become the views of the Court."[43]

For Stone the end result, not the rate of speed toward it, was the important consideration. "You, of course, will appreciate," he wrote Professor Edwin M. Borchard of Yale, February 10, 1933, "that I would have written a very different type of opinion in . . . [the Wallace case], if it had not been for past history and the necessity, wherever possible, of writing an opinion to which one's associates will agree. I fear that our trouble has been in the fact that too much attention has been paid to labels and too little to realities. It was for this reason that I did not use the words 'declaratory judgment' when I wrote the Swope case. It seems to me that now the way is open to deal with declaratory judgments like any others, to look at the facts and the law, and see whether as the statute has been applied a real controversy was developed."*

Given the make-up of the Court, it was inevitable that Stone would not write many majority opinions in the "big" cases. In the 1927 term Taft assigned Stone a minor case turning on the due process clause of the Fourteenth Amendment. Stone made the most of the opportunity. A Virginia statute tried to protect the state's important apple-growing industry from fatal rust prevalent among ornamental, but industrially insignificant, red cedar trees, by providing for the destruction of diseased cedars without any compensation to the owners except the cost of removal. Stone made this rather small case memorable as an exhibit of judicial deference to the legislative judgment on the relative worth of competing private interests.

Compared with the cedars of Virginia, the state's apple orchards represented large investments. Their extensive cultivation for domestic use and export had induced development of rail facilities and growth of subsidiary enterprise. The state's economy revolved about apple growing, and an appreciable portion of the working population depended on it for employment. Yet a single red cedar tree, infected with rust, within two miles of the fruit trees, placed in jeopardy the entire economy, delicately attuned to the welfare of the apple. Either the rust would destroy the orchards and disrupt the productive life of the commonwealth, or the infected cedars would have to be uprooted.

"The state," Stone commented, "was under the necessity of making

* The Wallace case had only extended the Court's jurisdiction to review declaratory judgments from state courts. "It is not quite true," Stone wrote Clinton Rossiter, April 12, 1941, "that the federal courts had power generally to render declaratory judgment before the enactment of the federal statute." (Public Law No. 343, Laws of 1934, Chapter 512.) "Before that there were several types of equity suits which were undistinguishable from declaratory judgments and therefore within the judicial power as defined by the Constitution. It required a statute to enlarge the authority of the federal courts to pronounce declaratory judgments in other cases."

a choice. . . . It would have been nonetheless a choice if, instead of enacting the present statute, the state, by doing nothing, had permitted serious injury to the apple orchards within its borders to go unchecked."

The circumstances posed an inescapable governmental choice, but did it follow that the state could impose the burden wholly upon the owners of the dangerous property? "When forced to such a choice," Stone maintained, "the state does not exceed its constitutional powers by deciding upon the destruction of one class of property in order to save another which, in the judgment of the legislature, is of greater value to the public. It will not do to say that the case is merely one of a conflict of two private interests and that the misfortune of apple growers may not be shifted to cedar owners . . . ; for it is obvious that there may be, and that here there is, a preponderant public concern in the preservation of the one interest over the other."[44]

Taft and his colleagues soon came to look upon Stone as a workhorse, an expert's expert. "With respect for one who can dance the sword dance," Holmes endorsed Stone's adroit manipulations of equity doctrine.[45] Possessed of an unerring instinct for the relevant facts, he could drive to the heart of tangled events in tort cases, in admiralty causes, and in patent disputes. Each patent case, involving the settlement of conflicting claims to priority of invention or the determination of whether there had been an invention, turned on unique facts. Legal guides were general, and, to make matters worse, "attorneys on both sides pressed many matters of no consequence on the mere chance that the judge might be misled by some of them into a decision in favor of one side or the other."[46]

In writing a patent opinion, the judge must at the very least acquire mastery of the vocabulary of the science contributing to the discovery. Stone went much further. His excursions into science usually began with a statement of the problem as it faced the supposed inventor, then a review of what had been done, what was wrong, and what was known about the subject. This approach illuminated the contribution of the "inventor" to the new product or process, and persuaded brethren, who confessed or feigned an inability to understand. "I agreed with all you say and some of it I understand," Sutherland noted on one such treatise. "Seriously," he added, "I think you have done a fine job." "I think I agree and should write 'yes' whichever way you came out," Holmes remarked in another scientific controversy.[47]

The case which won Stone his spurs as a patent expert concerned an inventor who had devised a substitute for animal glue through a process using starch with limited water-absorbing qualities. By degenerating the starch and combining it with water and alkali, he produced a substance "as good as animal glue." The alleged infringer,

Stone learned, had come upon untreated natural starch with similar absorption properties and, in combining it with water and alkali, had made a glue like the inventor's product. Obviously the mere use of natural starch did not make the patented process unique. But the patentee had attempted to protect his monopoly in another way. He had described his invention by its function. "Any glue," he said, "made of a starch base, whatever its composition, water absorptiveness or other properties, combined with three parts of water, as is animal glue used in veneering, and with alkali, which has substantially the properties of animal glue, or is as good as animal glue for use in the woodworking trades, is claimed as Perkins' glue." With other members of the Court, Stone shared the conviction that the patent monopoly was to be restricted sharply and protected only to the extent necessary to accomplish the constitutional purpose of patent—"to promote the Progress of Science and useful Arts." "A claim so broad," Stone observed, "if allowed, would operate to enable the inventor who has discovered that a defined type of starch answers the required purpose to exclude others from all other types of starch and so foreclose efforts to discover other and better types. The patent monopoly would thus be extended beyond the discovery and would discourage rather than promote invention."[48]

Stone's masterful handling of the case brought plaudits from all sides. Brandeis jokingly welcomed him to the "patent section" of the Court. "This is the first patent case that I have read with understanding," a former law clerk commented. "It makes me feel that you probably would have been as great a dean of the School of Chemistry as you were of the Law School, had you specialized in catalytic and oxidizing agents and water absorptivity and the viscosity of fluids, earlier in your career."[49]

By the end of his third term Stone had definitely made his mark. In the summer of that year he accepted the American Bar Association's invitation to address its semicentennial meeting in Seattle. Though the proprieties required him to discuss generalities, he nevertheless welcomed the opportunity to speak out. "This gives me a chance to say some things about the decisions under the Interstate Commerce Clause and the Fourteenth Amendment," he told his former law clerk, "although of course, I cannot enter into the controversial field."[50]

The address was a memorable one for unabashed optimism, if for nothing else. The Justice saw no necessary incompatibility between the Constitution and social requirements. The judicial aberration lay not in the Constitution but in men's minds. The fundamental law was, the speaker said, deep enough and flexible enough to accommodate changes and growth in the nation and yet preserve the spirit and import of free government. The Court's recent interpretations of "com-

merce" and "due process," characterized as "the most significant developments in the constitutional field" since the Civil War, were cited
to illustrate the point. Interstate commerce had been brought "completely within the power of the federal government." Here was an
"impressive record of the application cf constitutional principles to
the growing needs and interests of the expanding nation."

A similar transformation had occurred in the Court's interpretation
of the Fourteenth Amendment. It had been designed "as a guarantee
against the encroachment of the states upon the liberty of the individual." But "the constitutional requirement of due process did not
bind us rigidly to any rule of the past." The limitations embodied in
it were, he believed, "consistent with the enlightened progress of the
law." Yet Stone did confess that application of due process "affecting
all the varying situations which may arise in our present-day civilization, would give rise to strong differences of opinion, often resulting
in decisions by a divided Court." Interpretation of that vague phrase
ran naturally into the use of descriptive clichés, such as "business
affected with a public interest." Such formulas, the speaker said, were
meaningful only within the context of particular fact situations.

"The character of these differences," the Justice continued, "suggests the great importance, in applying the Fourteenth Amendment
to cases as they arise, of the Court's being fully informed as to all
phases of the particular social conditions affected, the evils supposed
to originate in them, and the appropriateness of the particular remedy
sought to be applied." Mindful no doubt of the Court's failure to
understand or investigate the fact situations in recent cases, Stone bore
down on the point: "Intimate acquaintance with every aspect of the
conditions which have given rise to the regulatory problems are infi-
nitely more important to the Court than are the citation of authorities
or the recital of bare formulas."[51]

Inferentially Stone's address struck at the very heart of the battle of
ideas being waged in the Court. The majority had failed to appreciate
the Constitution as a "continuing instrument of government" as well
as the judiciary's role in implementing it. In its zeal to protect property from legislative encroachments, it resorted to stultifying formulas identified as *the* Constitution. The Justices had subverted the
democratic process by substituting their own preconceived views for
those expressed by legislatures. This blindness in judges merely reflected the shortsightedness of the bar, whose members needed, as
Felix Frankfurter wrote Stone while the Bar Association address was
in preparation, "some education as to the conservative tradition which
lies behind the expressions of dissent."[52]

Deploring the formulism rampant at the bar and in the Court, the
Justice cautioned his audience of lawyers: "We ought not to be com-

pletely absorbed in the technique of the law. Who could listen to those inspiring addresses which we heard yesterday and for a moment suppose that law could exist and function separate and apart from science or from adequate understanding and appreciation of the significant facts of modern life which affect social right? The questions which come to us are rooted in history and in the social and economic development of the nation. To grasp their significance our study must be extended beyond the examination of precedents and legal formulas, by reading and research in fields extra-legal, which nevertheless have an intimate relation to the genesis of the legal rules which we pronounce."[53]

Stone's judicial reputation had now risen to such point that even the laity took special notice of it. An awakening nation began to appraise the Justice and it liked what it saw. "With respect to Justice Stone," Mark Sullivan commented, "it is appropriate to add that he is one of the very alert men in American public life today. In the judgment of many he is the most valuable recruit brought to public service in Washington since the Great War."[54]

CHAPTER SIXTEEN

# With Holmes and Brandeis

## 1927-1929

In 1921 it was generally believed that the new Chief Justice would be able to smile away the divisions within the Court, so common during the incumbency of Edward D. White. "Mr. Taft has such tact and good humor," the New York Tribune editorialized, "and has so unconquerable a spirit of fair play, that he is greatly beloved of his fellow citizens. With Chief Justice Taft as a moderator, it is probable that not a few asperities that mar the harmony of the celestial chamber . . . will be softened and that not quite so often in the future will the Court divide 5 and 4."[1]

In 1925 complacent indulgence screened deep rifts soon to appear. "Stone is an admirable addition to the Court as it is now," the Chief Justice wrote. "Holmes assures me that never before have they gotten along with so little jangling and dissension."[2] The prospect looked very bright indeed. "We haven't had many dissents," Taft reported, "and we have been pretty nearly solid in all cases."[3]

The Chief Justice's pressure for unanimity was felt by all—by Holmes and Brandeis as well as Stone. All recognized that if dissent was to be effective as a weapon for persuading colleagues, it must be charily used. Sometimes as many as three Justices would reluctantly go along with the majority because no one of them felt strongly enough about the issue to raise his voice in protest. It was not unusual for Justices to write on the back of circulated slip opinions: "I shall acquiesce in silence unless someone else dissents"; or, "I do not agree, but shall submit." Stone himself developed "a general disposition not to dissent" unless he felt "strongly on the subject."[4] In many letters written to other Justices about their opinions, he suggested modifications or shifts of emphasis that would make the opinion more acceptable to him. Usually he did not insist on his ideas, but, like the other Justices, went along in most cases for the sake of harmony.

When disagreement was strong the argument sometimes continued after the decision had been reached. On rare occasions the dissenters were able to swing the author of the opinion to their view—and by the force of arguments to bring the majority around to changing its mind. Stone was instrumental in one such shift. With Brandeis and Holmes, who had also disagreed with the decision in conference, he carried on the argument with the opinion writer, Justice Sutherland. The Justices had voted to set aside a zoning ordinance. Under Stone's persistent hammering, however, Sutherland began to doubt the correctness of his conclusion and asked for reargument. On the second hearing Sutherland changed his mind. The ordinance was upheld.[5]

During his first fifteen months Justice Stone moved cautiously, slowly cutting for himself a niche in the informal judicial hierarchy. By and large it was a period of self-immolation. Moderate by nature, he was prone where personal knowledge or conviction did not dictate an independent stand to resolve doubts in favor of the majority. Inclined initially to credit his colleagues with greater knowledge and less prejudice than they perhaps possessed, he was reticent about speaking up in separate opinions. Falling in with Taft's absorbing ambition to "mass the Court," he dissented only four times through the spring and fall of 1925.

Liberals, quick to judge men in stereotyped terms, were positive the "Wall Street Lawyer" would be in the Taft camp. In a *per curiam* decision of October 10, 1925, the Court had affirmed the decision of a lower federal court that the Arizona Minimum Wage statute was unconstitutional.[6] The worst fears of the liberals seemed to be confirmed. "He aligns himself with the majority without reservations," the *New Republic* lamented. "It is too early to assign him a durable place on the spectrum of the Court's range of social opinion. But one's expectations of him in this most vital field of constitutional determi-

nations ought not to be pitched high."[7] Harold Laski, sharing these
sentiments, expressed his anxiety to Holmes: "I was immensely interested to note that your colleague, Harlan Stone, had sided with the
conservative part of the Court."[8]

"Don't make a mistake about Stone," Holmes cautioned his correspondent. "He is a mighty sound and liberal-minded thinker. In the
case to which I suppose you refer he thought as I did, but also
thought that no countenance should be given to the notion that the
decisions of the Court were subject to a change of personnel and
therefore refrained from joining in my declaration."[9]

The harmony prognosticators foresaw in 1921 proved to be short-
lived. By 1925 the bench was entangled in the complexities of social
and economic policy. Before long, dissents outnumbered those of
Taft's predecessor. Almost a year to the day after Stone's appointment, the phrase "Holmes, Brandeis, and Stone dissenting" resounded
for the first time on the ears of the complacent majority. The following
week the same combination protested another decision. Significantly,
in each instance the conservative six ruled that state statutes had
passed the boundaries for regulatory legislation marked by the Fourteenth Amendment.

When Justice McReynolds found "arbitrary and unreasonable" an act
of the Wisconsin legislature that taxed as bequests all gifts made within
six years of death, Stone was dumfounded. "I cannot find out," he told
his clerk, "how my brethren get the standard that they are applying.
I think that six years is rather a long time for a conclusive presumption that a gift is in contemplation of death, but establishing a 'conclusive presumption' is only a way of saying that all gifts in that
period will be taxed." Trying to put himself in the position of the
Wisconsin lawmaker, he reasoned: "If . . . my object were to come
as near as I could to taxing the sum total of property passing
from Wisconsin citizens to their heirs, I don't know but that I would
decide on six years as the period that would give me the best and
fairest results. And if I did, I would not understand how a court
could have any basis for telling me I was unreasonable."[10] He prepared a dissent along these lines but was not satisfied that it conveyed
his thinking clearly. It was never published.

Stone shared Justice Holmes' indignation at the Court's indifference
to the reasonableness and intelligence of state legislatures. "In dealing
with state legislation upon matters of substantive law," Holmes wrote,
"we should avoid with great caution attempts to substitute our judgment for that of the body whose business it is in the first place."[11] In
another case, Justice Butler set aside a Pennsylvania statute forbidding
the use of "shoddy" in bedding as "purely arbitrary." Holmes, supported by Stone and Brandeis, replied pointedly: "If the legislature of

Pennsylvania was of opinion that disease is likely to be spread by the use of unsterilized shoddy in comfortables, I do not suppose that this Court would pronounce the opinion so manifestly absurd that it could not be acted upon. If we should not, then I think that we ought to assume the opinion to be right for the purpose of testing the law."[12] Such persistent dissent threatened to loosen Taft's grip.

Stone's implacable integrity and independence evoked no sympathetic response from the Chief Justice, who began to wonder whether the new colleague was entirely "safe." But in Holmes and Brandeis the newcomer found an approach to the law and a breadth of view upon which he could build his own. "Stone was always influenced by confidence in the integrity and capacity of others who espoused positions unfamiliar to him," Thomas Reed Powell observed. "It was his respect and liking for Holmes and Brandeis that turned him from earlier attitudes."[13]

The "hopeless" ones welcomed him to their ranks. Stone, in turn, took satisfaction and strength from their friendship and counsel. Together the Three Musketeers fought an unceasing battle against formalistic jurisprudence. In the 1927 term, they were together in dissent ten times. "It is a great comfort," Stone observed in June 1928, "that when one starts out to 'proclaim the truth' he can usually count on such staunch supporters as Justice Holmes and Justice Brandeis."[14]

Stone and Holmes, drawn by ties of personality, instantly "hit it off." Though he did not esteem the great dissenter in an altogether uncritical fashion, the resemblances between them far outshadowed their differences. With Brandeis his relationship was not entirely felicitous at the start, and the younger jurist felt obliged on occasion to disassociate himself from the strictures the crusading Justice leveled at the stuffy majority. "I wrote a brief dissent," he explained to a former law clerk, "only because I thought there were some expressions in Brandeis's dissenting opinion which were better left unsaid, although the logic of it and the authorities cited seem to me unanswerable."[15] Eventually, however, the prime wisdom of dissenters "standing together"[16] in the face of prolonged internecine judicial warfare convinced him that his fiery colleague deserved support.

"When I came to the Court from a Wall Street environment," Stone recalled in 1941, "I had no adequate understanding of the man [Brandeis] but close association with him soon made me realize his great qualities. I count myself particularly fortunate in having had such intimate associations with him and Justice Holmes—two of the great figures of our times."[17]

By the fall of 1926 Taft was already beginning to fear that he would not fill out the full decade. This was the more regrettable as he foresaw, with grave misgivings, "some questions coming before our Court for decision that I should like to take part in deciding."[18] Stone figured in the Chief Justice's dismal calculus. In 1926 he strayed from the majority no less than five times. Late in that term a case arose which left no doubt as to where he stood.

In 1921 the Bedford Cut Stone Company, producers of Indiana limestone, refused to renew contracts with their employees' union, the Journeymen Stone Cutters' Association. A strike by the union failed and was followed by a lockout. Intent on driving organized labor out of the industry, the producers organized "independent" unions. Negotiations over several years failed to restore the Journeymen Stone Cutters' Association to its old prerogatives, and the work of quarrying limestone was carried on almost completely by non-affiliated, "independent" union labor. The national union numbered no more than five thousand men, but their skill was in demand and the union remained strong in industrial cities using limestone for construction. At last, the national union decided to invoke that provision of its constitution which pledged members to refuse to "cut, carve, or fit any material that has been cut by men working in opposition to this Association." Orders were sent to the membership not to work on stone cut by non-union labor.

The Indiana limestone producers sent nearly 75 per cent of their product outside the state, where the effect of the union's order was felt. Immediately the producers sought an injunction against the union on the ground that the directive to its members was a restraint of interstate commerce prohibited by the Sherman Act. The district court refused to issue an injunction, and its decree dismissed the suit. On appeal, the Circuit Court agreed.

When the case reached the Supreme Court in 1927 the Justices split on the central issue, whether the acts of the union constituted an "unreasonable" restraint of interstate commerce. At conference, they voted 5 to 4 to uphold the injunction. Taft, Sutherland, McReynolds, Butler, and Van Devanter comprised the majority; Justice Stone voted with the minority. The almost certain possibility of a 5 to 4 decision sorely distressed the Chief Justice. Added to his aversion to dissents was his wish that the full prestige of the bench might meet this serious threat from organized labor. If the union's refusal to work were not declared illegal, Taft reasoned, "every national labor union could at once adopt it as a means of establishing a closed shop instead of an open shop in every center of business activity in the country."[19]

Holmes and Brandeis were intransigent. In conference the Chief Justice detected uncertainty in the votes of Sanford and Stone, and their wavering prompted him to center his attack on them. "Both of them are of course wide of the mark," the Chief Justice wrote Sutherland, "but we have to approach them according to their difficulties. Stone, it did not seem to me, was certain on the subject, and I don't think we ought to let up in seeking to have them take the proper view. . . ."[20] Immediately thereafter, Taft started a campaign of persuasion.

"My dear Brother Stone," he wrote, "I am quite anxious, as I am sure we all are, that the continuity and weight of our opinions on important questions of law should not be broken any more than we can help by dissents. . . . I write with reference to the decision in the Stone Cutters' Union. . . . Whatever you might think of this issue, freed from authority, as a matter of common law, it is here affected by the anti-trust law and the construction put upon it by us with reference to what constitutes a burden or restraint of interstate commerce. . . . My strong impression is that if you will read the case of the Duplex Printing Company, . . . *separate the facts and apply the decree* which was made in that case, you will reach the conclusion that it covers all over the Stone Cutters' Union case."[21]

In the Duplex case of 1921 to which Taft called Stone's attention, the Court had decided that sympathetic strikes, picketing, and the boycott of the products of a company were in restraint of interstate commerce and therefore illegal under the Clayton Act.* Justice Brandeis, joined by Holmes and Clarke, had entered a devastating protest. Brandeis, conversant with existing economic conditions and skilled in labor-management controversies, perceived the "unity of interest" throughout the union. The sympathetic strikers, he argued, "injured the plaintiff, not maliciously, but in self-defense. . . ." "May not all with a common interest," he asked, "join in refusing to expend their labor upon articles whose very production constitutes an attack upon their standard of living and the institution which they are convinced supports it?"[22] In the Bedford case, "unity of interest" among the strikers also appeared well established. "No outsider," he observed, "be he quarrier, dealer, builder, or laborer, was a party to the combination.

---

* The Duplex Company, one of four competing companies manufacturing printing presses, was the only one not unionized. Two of the other three companies notified the union that their labor contracts would be terminated unless the Duplex Company also met union requirements. A strike at Duplex met with no success; the company refused the union demand for both the eight-hour day and the minimum-wage scale. In a last desperate attempt to gain recognition at Duplex and maintain hard-won achievements elsewhere, the union boycotted Duplex printing presses. Justice Pitney expressed for the majority the view that no more was involved in the union's efforts to organize Duplex than a dispute between two individuals. From this standpoint the boycotters, "standing in no relation of employment under complainant, past, present or prospective," were not permitted by the Clayton Act "to make that dispute their own and proceed to instigate sympathetic strikes, picketing, and boycotting against employers wholly unconnected with complainant's factory."

No purpose was to be subserved except to promote the trade interests of members of the Journeymen's Association."[23] Taft feared the influence of Brandeis's logic on Stone and Sanford.

To reverse Stone's negative vote and to bring him in line with the majority, the Chief Justice resorted to an argument that judges have been loath to sanction, even by inference. "There are some [presumably Holmes and Brandeis] who have deep convictions on the subject of the law governing the relations between employer and employee, whether it involves interstate commerce or not. It is to be expected that in their attitude of protest in the past they should find distinctions enabling them to continue their attitude in cases presenting what are substantially the same issues." But Stone, the Chief Justice intimated, was not one of these. "With respect to those judges who have come into the Court since these decisions were rendered," he wrote suggestively, "I am sure it is not their purpose to depart from what has been declared to be accepted law."[24]

This communication found Justice Stone in a mood to listen. He would "go over the whole matter afresh, reading particularly the citations which you give in your letter." The decision of the five-man majority in the Bedford case would, he knew, "in its practical operation . . . preclude all strikes against non-union material under all circumstances except within the state." At first he thought that a case decided a short time after he came on the Court had disposed of the issues in favor of the Stone Cutters. When San Francisco's building contractors and supply dealers had combined to "put over" the open shop by requiring purchasers of building materials to obtain permits from a "Builders Exchange" and by refusing permits to builders who would not cooperate, the Supreme Court, employing the maxim, *de minimis non curat lex*, found no "substantial" violation of the Sherman Law. Stone had agreed with the result in that case, but he had disliked the rationale and was reluctant to employ it. On "the importance of avoiding dissents which do not seem necessary," however, Stone was in hearty agreement. "You know," he told the Chief Justice, "that I am not disposed to be opinionated or over-cocky about the opinions I do hold." But the acrid comments of his brethren, the heated arguments—all this had convinced him that the reasoning process had not been carried through, else the solution reached would be satisfactory to more members of the Court. He would, however, "examine the question anew in the light of the sharp difference of opinion which developed at our conference."[25]

The Chief Justice's reply to "My dear Judge Stone" was courteously formal: "I voted against the decision of the Court in [the San Francisco case], but I acquiesced because I considered it, on the statement of Justice Sutherland, a mere difference on my part in the matter of the significance of evidence, rather than any difference in principle between us. When the case is carefully read, it will be seen that it is a case of *de minimis* and a mere yielding to the opinion of the Court below in its conclusions of fact. It certainly did not embrace any such propositions as that which Mr. Justice Brandeis now advances. However, now that I have called your attention to it and pointed out what seemed to me the controlling considerations that should govern in the decision of this case, I shall not bother you further, unless, as you say, you come and talk with me about it, when I shall be glad to continue our discussion."[26]

To the bitter end Taft tried to placate the two fence-sitting justices, suggesting alterations in Sutherland's draft in order "to meet what will trouble Stone, and I think, too, will trouble Sanford."[27] Justice McReynolds also made one last desperate plea, appealing, as he thought, to Stone's innate conservatism. "Please don't think me presumptuous," he wrote. "Certainly I do not mean to be. All of us get into a fog now and then, as I know so well from my own experience. Won't you 'Stop, Look, and Listen'? In my view," he continued, "we have one member [presumably Brandeis] who is consciously boring from within. Of course, you have no such purpose, but you may unconsciously aid his purpose. At least do think twice on a subject—three times indeed. If the Court is broken down, then there will be rejoicing in certain quarters."[28]

Stone's reply was cordial but firm. "Of course I do not regard what you say as presumptuous," he wrote. On the contrary, he would give "serious thought" to it. At the same time he made it clear that, in his judgment, the majority rather than the dissenters were embarked on a radical course threatening to existing institutions. He had not been just "stringing along" unwittingly with a subtle traducer. His carefully considered stand had been dictated by reason and authority. "I am sure you will give me credit for being sincere in the views I express," Stone commented. "If I did not hold them strongly and believe that very many thoughtful men, trained in the law, would agree with them, I should not take the trouble to write any dissent." The majority had, moreover, made "some very serious mistakes . . . which would not have been made had it not been for the disposition of the majority to rush to conclusions without taking the trouble to listen to the views of the minority." In certain instances the opinion of the Court had rested "on propositions that are demonstrably not sound and lead to consequences which, it seems to me, we all ought to be eager to avoid. . . . Holding these views, it seems to me that I should express them, unless we are to depart from every tradition of the Court. Will you not do me the favor," Stone concluded, "to consider carefully what I have written, and then tell me frankly wherein you think I am wrong."[29]

McReynolds did not pursue the matter further. He, like the Chief Justice, must have considered Stone a lost cause. Taft voiced his bitterness the day before Sutherland delivered the opinion. "We have an important labor opinion to deliver which Sutherland wrote, and in which Brandeis has written one of his meanest opinions. Holmes sides with him, and while Sanford and Stone concur in our opinion, they do it grudgingly, Stone with a kind of kickback that will make nobody happy."[30]

Sutherland, for the Court, found the union's actions blameless unless they contravened congressional policy as embodied in the Sherman Law. As to this, he said, the refusal of the union to work non-union materials "necessarily threatened to destroy or narrow petitioner's interstate trade by taking from them their customers." "The opinion in *Duplex Co.* v. *Deering*," he commented summarily, "might serve as an opinion in this case." For Brandeis and Holmes the matter was not at all settled by earlier cases. "If, on the un-disputed facts of this case," Justice Brandeis wrote for the dissenters, "refusal to work can be enjoined, Congress created by the Sherman Law and the Clayton Act an instrument for imposing restraints upon labor which reminds of involuntary servitude. . . . I cannot believe that Congress did so."[31]

Stone, in his separate concurrence, left no doubt that he strongly disliked the result. "As an original proposition," he observed, "I should have doubted whether the Sherman Act prohibited a labor union from peaceably refusing to work upon material produced by non-union labor or by a rival union, even though interstate commerce were affected. In the light of the policy adopted by Congress in the Clayton Act, with respect to organized labor, and in the light of *Standard Oil Co.* v. *United States* . . . [and] . . . *United States* v. *American Tobacco Co.* . . . . I should not have thought that such action as is now complained of was to be regarded as an unreasonable and therefore prohibited restraint of trade. But in *Duplex Printing Press Co.* v. *Deering*, . . . these views were rejected by a majority of the Court and a decree was authorized restraining in precise terms any agreement not to work or refusal to work, such as is involved here. Whatever additional facts there may have been in that case," he wrote to explain his difference with Justice Brandeis, "the decree enjoined the defendants from using 'even persuasion'" to effect such an agreement. "These views," he concluded, "which I should not have hesitated to apply here, have now been rejected again largely on the authority of the Duplex case. For that reason alone, I concur with the majority."[32]

Torn between concurring on the basis of the injunctive decree in the Duplex case and following his natural inclination to dissent with Brandeis and Holmes, he adopted the former policy as the most feasible. His concept of jurisprudence and his human understanding of the Chief Justice's plight may have dictated his stand. But it may be that Taft had pressed his advantage too far and may have started Stone on an independent course that did not follow the dictates of the conservatives, the lofty line of Holmes, or the impassioned social crusading of Brandeis.* This experience must have emphasized in Stone's mind that Taft, quite as much as the dissenters, entertained "deep convictions."

Thereafter the relations between Stone and Taft cooled perceptibly. The Chief Justice no longer pursued the former law school dean with the ardor of a country swain. "I am not always sure," the Chief Justice observed, "how experience as the head of a law school and supervising a law journal helps in making a first-class judge. Stone is a good judge, but he will need longer experience."[33]

Stone now spoke for the majority less frequently. After the 1926 term, his second full year on the bench, the number of cases assigned him declined steadily, the low point being reached in the 1929 term when he wrote only seventeen majority opinions and announced individual views (often with Holmes and Brandeis) in nine cases.[34] Though dissenting sometimes seemed a dismal business, without "utility beyond enabling the dissenter to live comfortably with himself,"[35] the work as a whole was rewarding. When, in 1927, Sterling Carr suggested that he groom for the Presidency, the former dean replied: "I have a conscience, right or wrong, that I am fitted for the job which I am doing and am supremely interested in it, and when a man is in that situation, it is well for him to 'stick to his last.' If the Presidency of the United States were unanimously tendered to me I would hesitate to accept it, and if I did accept it, should do so with genuine regret."[36] Even dissenting served a beneficial purpose. "I always write a dissent with real reluctance," he commented, "and often acquiesce in opinions with which I do not fully agree, so you may know how strongly I have really felt in order to participate in so many dissents as I have recently. But where a prevailing view rests upon what appear to me to be false economic notions, or upon reasoning and analogies which will not bear analysis, I think great service is done with respect to the future development of the law, in pointing out the fallacies on which the prevailing

* Compare, for example, his concurring opinion in the Bedford Stone case with his remarks on the applicability of the Sherman Act to labor unions in *Apex Hosiery Co.* v. *Leader,* 310 U.S. 469 (1940), pp. 487-89 *passim,* when his views had matured.

view appears to rest even though the particular ruling made should never be overruled."[37]

Recent cases highlighted the "fascinating battle" that was being waged. Comfort came from the knowledge that there were those who studied the work of the Court with painstaking care and appreciated its significance. "We on the sidelines," a former law clerk wrote, "are confident as to where ultimate victory will be."[38]

Though the Taft-led wing continued triumphant, the future seemed quite unpredictable. "Safety and the preservation of a conservative majority in the Court," the Chief Justice's biographer tells us, "became an obsession with Taft as the final days approached. The most that could be hoped for, he wrote Justice Butler in the fall of 1929, 'is continued life of enough of the present membership . . . to prevent disastrous reversals of our present attitude. With Van [Van Devanter] and Mac [McReynolds] and Sutherland and you and Sanford, there will be five to steady the boat. . . . We must not give up at once.' " [39]

To Taft the whole world seemed engulfed in a whirlpool of radicalism. Even the Republican party had picked a man for the Presidency who needed to "remember the warning of the Scriptures about removing landmarks." In a senile rage the aging ex-President lumped his tormentors together. "The truth is that Hoover is a Progressive, just as Stone is, and just as Brandeis is and just as Holmes is."[40]

This haunting fear of progressivism had turned Taft away from what might have been a stimulating and courageous judicial career. Had he maintained the powerful position he had assumed in his Minimum Wage dissent of 1923,* he might have, with Stone's appointment in 1925, and the backing of Holmes and Brandeis (and probably Sanford), swung the Court along the lines that the Three Musketeers were so eloquently staking out.

By the spring of 1929 Stone had achieved a solid reputation, both on and off the Court, for durable workmanship. His likeness graced the cover of an issue of *Time* magazine with the caption: "Tackle, Guard, or Center—A Comfort to the Coach." "Scanning the bench," a Luce reporter wrote, "an inquisitive eye moving to the right, comes to rest upon a large man in the last high-backed chair. Attention is fastened by his breadth of black-gowned shoulder, breadth of forehead, breadth of jaw. Other Justices break in to ask attorneys questions, but this one sits silently intent upon the argument, his square chin cupped

---

* "It is not the function of this Court," Taft, joined by Sanford, had said in 1923, "to hold congressional acts invalid simply because they are passed to carry out economic views which the Court believes to be unwise or unsound." (Adkins case, p. 562.)

in his palm, his elbow propped on the table before him. His light blue eyes are small, concentrated, penetrating. His dark brown hair, quickly parted on the left, looks slightly disarranged."[41]

The *Nation* pointed to Justice Stone as one whom any judge might emulate. "A profound student of social life," the editor said, "who may be trusted to weigh wisely and comprehendingly the varied economic, political, and legal considerations that actually enter into the determination of the important questions faced by the Court, and to go skillfully through the necessary legal motions of making the decisions and rendering the accompanying opinions. He is of the stuff of which great Supreme Court Justices are made."[42]

CHAPTER SEVENTEEN

# Friend of President Hoover

## 1928-1932

After Stone's appointment to the Court he took little active part in politics or in the executive end of the Government. But as the occasion arose he exerted his influence to bring in competent personnel. In Coolidge's Cabinet he had tried hard to instill the idea of efficiency in administration. Though small success rewarded that effort, his respect for Coolidge rose steadily, finally reaching the point where he believed the Vermonter would have made "a great President if he had been more concerned with getting good men into the Government."[1]

On Silent Cal's last day in the White House, Stone called to say good-by and to wish him well.* The Justice ventured to express the hope that the President might ultimately return to Washington, perhaps as Senator from Massachusetts. Mr. Coolidge discussed the matter thoughtfully but said that changed conditions, and particularly the changed relationship of a President of the United States to his party and party politics, would make it exceedingly difficult and inadvisable for an ex-President to participate in the political life of the nation as a member of Congress. After an unusually long conversation on this and other subjects, the Justice, rising to leave, remarked that he was convinced that Mr. Coolidge's decision not to run again was a wise one.

---

* The taciturn Coolidge had recently delighted the Stones by accepting their dinner invitation. "It is unusual," the Justice wrote his sons, March 2, 1929, "for the President and his wife to go to a private house, and I believe they did it only once before during his administration."

Besides other reasons he was convinced that during the next administration the country would undergo the most serious economic and financial convulsion since 1873, that the President would carry a heavy burden—one that no man should be asked to bear who had passed through two successful terms. To all this the President replied in terse New England accents: "It is a pretty good idea to get out when they still want you."[2]

From the beginning Stone had supported Hoover, Coolidge's Secretary of Commerce, as the Republican presidential nominee. Friendly relations between them had grown out of their association in the Cabinet. Rising from humble origins to the top of their respective professions had developed in them sturdy regard for the traditional American virtues. Both sprang from obscure rural communities; as boys they had lived the simple life. Both had to make their own way, and in the course of making it they had enjoyed varied contacts and rich experiences. Their early life had not always seemed easy, nor did they always think of it as beneficial. In later years, however, each recalled his heritage with pleasure and satisfaction. When, during the middle twenties, these "self-made" stalwarts were thrown together in places of political power and influence, they discovered a mutually invigorating moral and intellectual kinship.

Socially, too, the Stones and the Hoovers had much in common. The Hoovers, who cared little for dining out or formal entertainment, often invited the Stones on short notice to gatherings small enough for stimulating intellectual conversation. The Justice and his wife enjoyed these impromptu visits. Hoover, "always loaded to the brim with information about the current economics of the country," liked to have "people around with ideas in their heads."[3]

By June 1928 Stone was confident that Hoover would be nominated. "A very fortunate outcome for the country, I think," he wrote. "The thing to do now is to get busy and elect him."[4] Stone's enthusiasm ran high. "Thursday evening," he wrote his sister shortly after the Republican Convention in June 1928, "we joined a party of friends of the Hoovers at their house and received the returns over the radio from the nominating convention. . . . We are a long ways now from the Harding regime, and if the people know what is good for them, they will stick to it [the Republican party]."[5]

Prevented by the usual proprieties from entering the campaign openly, Stone strongly urged family and friends to get back of the Republican candidate. "I hope you both registered and that you will vote for Hoover," he advised his sons. "I am increasingly convinced that it would be a mistake for the country not to elect him. There is a lack of issues between the two parties in any really political sense. Both parties have committed themselves for prohibition, and while there may be some revision of the laws on that subject, I am satisfied that the time is not yet, and the real question is, to which crowd are we willing to entrust the government. The more I see of Al Smith and his crowd, the more unwilling I would be to give them any opportunity to deal with it."[6]

Whenever a friend voiced doubt about Hoover, Stone hastened to the defense: "I have known Mr. Hoover and his family perhaps better than any other member of the Cabinet, and I am enthusiastically for his election to the Presidency. I do not know what past activities of his you refer to, but I know of none which are not admirable." Stone agreed that Hoover was not the "usual political type." The qualities of "independence and capacity," which politicians subjected to "a systematic course of defamation," made his claims to the Presidency, especially in a time of unparalleled complexity, all the stronger. "The next ten years in this country," the Justice prophesied, "will see the development of great economic problems and likewise social problems, having their sources in the economic development of the country. I have never met any man who had such a grasp on these problems as Mr. Hoover. That, to my mind, is the big and conclusive reason for his election."[7]

Stone sought to allay any fears that Hoover might inaugurate drastic reform. The notion that Hoover was a believer in "minute regulation of business by law" he dismissed as "a mistaken one, due to the fact that he has, by personal contact, so profoundly influenced business practices in one way or another. . . . It is important to remember," Stone added, "that he has always accomplished those results by inducing cooperation through personal leadership." Even the Hoover-instituted wartime controls had depended to a large extent on "methods of cooperation and not on any statutory enactment." Hoover had assured the Justice "in most certain terms, that such control by law could be justified only by the extraordinary conditions growing out of the war."[8]

On election night the Hoovers were at their Palo Alto home, but a little group of close personal friends—including, besides the Stones, the Vernon Kelloggs, the Adolph Millers, and the Mark Sullivans—gathered at the candidate's S Street house to listen to the returns. At eleven o'clock victory was certain; the only question was how great. The enthusiastic group then composed and sent off a telegram: "Yours is a deserved triumph. We know that your administration will be wise, capable and progressive. We send you affectionate regards, and salute you."

The expectations of friends and supporters exceeded all bounds. Stone called Hoover's election "a great triumph. He has a difficult task ahead of him, but I expect to see him acquit himself well."[9] William

Nelson Cromwell of Sullivan and Cromwell predicted that it would be "the most noteworthy administration since the Civil War, more beneficent for our people than that of any nation in the realm of civilization."[10] Intelligence had prevailed over Al Smith's "Rum, Raskob, and Raddio."[11]

Never before had "any President come into office so free to follow the dictates of his own conscience and judgment."[12] Stone was anxious to help in making the most of that opportunity. Less than a week after the election he offered his assistance: "If it is agreeable to you, I should like at some appropriate time to bring to your attention the names of some men who are worthy of consideration for a position in your Cabinet." The Justice disclaimed any personal interest beyond "the great desire I have to see your administration a brilliant success, and my thought that my own experience and my acquaintance with some of the individuals concerned might be of service to you in making a choice."[13]

To preserve intact the conventional judicial proprieties, Stone consistently refused "to be placed in the position of apparently seeking or urging an appointment." "I have seen Mr. Hoover since he came back to Washington," he wrote shortly after the election. "He seems in good health and spirits and he is tackling his new job in great shape. One result of my visiting him is that everyone who tries to get any influence on the new administration thinks that he can possibly secure it through me. I have many callers and many letters, to all of which I pay very little attention."[14]

There was no hesitation, however, in bringing influence to bear once the initiative was taken by the appointing authorities. To the innumerable requests that came to him from those seeking to enlist his support went this response: "For obvious reasons I am taking no active part in the selection of any federal officials. I take it that you will get your name before the President through the customary channels, and in doing so, you are at liberty to refer to me and I shall be glad to answer inquiries and be of assistance to you."[15] Stone held on to this technicality with bulldog tenacity. "In the coming administration, as in the past," he wrote a Wall Street partner, "I shall adhere strictly to my practice of not intruding my views unless they are sought. A President has a hard enough task to meet his responsibilities without the assistance of back-seat driving which he does not solicit. Therefore, I have made it a strict practice to say nothing until solicited, but, if invited . . . I should wish to be prepared."[16]

In late January the Justice went with the President-elect on a Florida cruise. Stone had not anticipated this "vacation south" with much relish. Mrs. Stone, who was staying with their six-month-old grandchild Doris while Marshall and his wife were on vacation, could not go along. The Justice regretted leaving his wife, and as the day of departure approached there was talk of canceling the trip. "I would back out of it," he commented consolingly, January 23, 1929, "were it not for the Hoovers. I want them to feel that we are *their* friends." The Justice was soon reconciled, however. "It has stormed for two days," he wrote Mrs. Stone from Miami, "so we have not attempted to fish but we have spent the entire day talking with Mr. H. about appointments, policies, and what not, and in going over his inaugural address. I think I have been of some help, which justifies my coming."

The trip was also worth while recreation-wise. Of his exploits as a fisherman Stone wrote a former student and fellow angler:

For three days we were down near Long Key on a yacht, and had wonderful sport sailfishing. The sailfish is the liveliest boy I have ever tackled other than a salmon. We used split bamboo rods of moderate weight, with a line which would hold a strain of about fifteen pounds. At the end of the line there is bent on a leader of piano wire with a heavy hook. The hook is baited with a strip from the side of a bonita, nicely trimmed so as to pass through the water like a moving fish. About seventy-five feet of line is paid out and the boat runs at a speed of five or six miles an hour. The sailfish has a long sharp bill and when he sees the bait he strikes it with his bill and then waits for developments. The trick is, as soon as he strikes, to pay out about sixty feet of line and then after a brief interval to strike him as hard as possible. He has a very bony mouth and the strike may merely result in scaring him so imperfectly that he will shake the hook free after a half hour of effort to get him in. As soon as he is hooked he runs and then leaps into the air, straight up, his full length, and dances along on his tail for about fifteen or twenty feet and then crashes down. While this performance goes on it is important to reel the line and keep it taut and make him come along toward you if possible. As soon as he is down he runs, often getting the leap several times before he is captured. As soon as he is down in the water and begins to tire, the trick is to reel him in and bring him as near the boat as possible. Several times before he is captured he will take long runs and leap again, but finally, after thirty minutes or more, it is possible to get him alongside and bring him in if, in the meantime, he has not shaken himself free or a shark has not overhauled and eaten him. I captured four sailfish, the most of anyone in our party.* The smallest

* In February 1930 the Justice again joined the Hoovers on a Florida vacation, this time accompanied by his wife. On fishing trips Mrs. Hoover and Mrs. Stone often went with the men or trailed them in a boat of their own. Presumably for no other purpose than to be helpful in case of a sure bite, the fishing club's manager accompanied the women. Mrs. Stone, suspicious that he might be inclined to lend a hand, told him emphatically, "If I get a bite, don't you dare touch my line." She got a bite—a sizable one. From dusk to moonrise, eight miles out in the Atlantic, she played her game while the men, who had come abreast, looked on with doubt and admiration. The Justice's catch of the previous year had numbered the "most of anyone in our party," but his wife did better still by hooking the largest sailfish of the season—sixty-six and one-half pounds on light

measured six feet six inches in length and the largest about a foot more. We did not weigh them, but they told us that they would weigh about sixty-five pounds. It is great sport, but still not quite equal to trout and salmon fishing in my judgment. . . .[17]

Stone and Hoover had more in common than piscatorial pursuits. Each in his own way symbolized a new and higher standard of political leadership—different indeed from the Harding holdovers who had surrounded them when they were both in Coolidge's Cabinet; different also from Wilson and his New Freedom crusaders. Both believed in efficiency; they shared a basic faith in the "good" man in politics.

Stone's concern for getting "good" men into government posts harmonized with the best traditions of party government. "In general, appointees should be of the same political faith as the administration appointing them, and they should not be appointed over any reasonable objection, having in mind the legitimate means and ends of party government. . . . But the appointments should not go as a reward for party service or be made either in the hope or expectation of such party service. . . ."[18] Hoover apparently agreed. "Friendship is not to be the controlling factor in making appointments," a Washington commentator wrote in 1929. "Friendship will be disregarded when it clashes with competency—that is, for the key places. Results are what we are after in this administration. Efficiency and 'the best available man for the job' regardless of his politics. . . That is the Chief's idea —and a noble one it is."[19]

The President-elect consulted Stone on possible appointees for the Departments of Agriculture and the Interior and for the Governorship of Puerto Rico. Men of high caliber who were willing to serve were scarce. "Mr. Hoover is making a genuine effort to bring in men of ability, courage, and independence," Stone reported, "but it is really extraordinary how few such men there are who are available. I sometimes wonder whether the tendencies of American life are not to make most successful men narrow specialists, unfitted to move in any but the narrow groove in which they have found their success."[20] "The critical positions in the new Cabinet," Stone said, "will be those of the Attorney General, the Secretary of State, and, of course, in view of recent history, it is important that the right men should be both in the Interior and Agriculture Departments."[21]

Stone himself figured prominently in pre-inauguration speculation as the most likely candidate for Attorney General or Secretary of State. "Very great pressure has been brought to bear on me," he wrote, "to take on this new work [Secretary of State], or other work which is by some counted more important and responsible in the executive branch

---

tackle. For this, the Long Key Fishing Camp Club awarded her a gold sailfish button.

of the government. Up to the present time I have resisted all these blandishments . . . [for reasons] quite apart from any balancing of personal advantages or disadvantages, which is repugnant to me."

It was a hard decision. In his perplexity Stone turned to his old law teacher, John Bassett Moore. "I need a bit of friendly advice which I think only you can give," he wrote, January 8, 1929. "I have an important question to answer. It is should I allow myself to consider giving up my present post to take the post of Secretary of State. My instinct and inclination are against it, although I know that the possibilities of public service and my readiness to tackle a new and difficult job argue for it. Will you let me have the benefit of your judgment?"

Moore replied January 9, stating his "predilection for a judicial career" and the "hope to see you Chief Justice rather than President."

"I am grateful for your letter," Stone replied, January 11. "You look at the situation just as I do. I have no ambition to hold political office or to secure advancement in either direction. I think nothing is more fatal to one's success and happiness than constant calculation as to what one is to get out of one course of action as against another way of personal aggrandizement. I am trying to view the whole matter in terms of opportunity for useful service. I think I know what I can do in my present post—quite apart from any possibilities of personal advancement. I could make the change now with every disposition on the part of the powers that be to return me to my present work in due time. But I know how uncertain any such prospect must inevitably be and I feel grave doubts whether a deliberate plan of that character is fair to the great institution of which I am a part." He hated "to contemplate the possibility that after four or eight years I might be forced to use such talents as I have for mere money-making alone."

Stone's firm decision did not halt Hoover's insistence, nor that of his friends. Carr, in particular, saw a Cabinet post—as Hoover and other politicians had seen it—as affording excellent opportunity to remove the judicial basket under which Stone's talent for political leadership was hiding. On January 26 Carr wrote about this at great length: "For some time a feeling has been growing in me that your great talents of leadership and ability to inspire confidence belong in a field of activity—particularly so at this time when the country is so in need of real moral leadership. . . . The more I think of it," Carr rambled on for nine handwritten pages, "the more convinced I am that you are the man. . . . You are too young, too energetic, too full of leadership —yes, too subject to the call of Fate to remain in the cloister." Carr, like Moore, took Stone's ultimate promotion to the Chief Justiceship for granted, but he still felt that his friend's "great God-given qualities" should be at the service of the executive rather than the judicial branch of government.

Stone absolutely refused to conspire with Fate. Expressing warm thanks for Carr's "long and interesting letter," he replied on February 12, "I could not leave my present position without abandoning responsibilities which, in the long run, are perhaps as important as any others that are likely to come to me. I owe something to the institution of which I am a part, and there are battles to be carried on here and won, as elsewhere. . . . All in all, it seemed to me that I would not be justified in dropping out."*

To ward off Hoover's "special drive" to induce him to take the post of Secretary of State, the Justice suggested his old Amherst friend and Englewood neighbor, Dwight Morrow. For reasons not altogether clear, Hoover refused to take Morrow from his post as Ambassador to Mexico. "I see by the papers," Stone wrote his wife on January 24, "that Hoover has definitely decided not to promote Dwight M. I do hope he isn't planning to make another drive on me. I would enjoy working with him . . . but I fear I could never be quite reconciled to giving up my present job."

Newspaper guesses linking the Justice's name with major executive posts tickled his vanity, but he was glad to see that "they seem to have subsided now and properly so, for I have never had any notion of deserting my present job for any other."[22]

Though the Hoovers were "terribly rushed in preparation for moving into the White House and getting ready for inauguration," the Stones continued to see them socially. The Justice and his wife were on hand for the big event. "Sunday was a beautiful day and everyone expected that Monday would be too, but we awoke to find it cloudy, and in the middle of the day drizzling rain, at times a downpour. I called on Mr. Hoover early in the morning and had a little talk with him; then we attended the ceremony in the Senate chamber at eleven

---

* Melville W. Fuller had expressed sentiments not unlike these when, in 1892, President-elect Cleveland asked him to resign from the Court and head the new Cabinet as Secretary of State. "I am convinced," the Chief Justice wrote Cleveland, "that the effect of the resignation of the Chief Justice under such circumstances [for the sake of the party and its leader] would be distinctly injurious to the Court. The surrender of the highest judicial office in the world for a political position, even though so eminent, would tend to detract from the dignity and weight of that tribunal. We cannot afford this." For the full text of Fuller's letter, see Willard L. King, *Melville Weston Fuller* (New York: The Macmillan Co., 1950), pp. 165-66.

Similarly, Chief Justice Morrison R. Waite had stoutly declined to permit his friends to advocate his nomination as Republican candidate for the Presidency in 1876. "I am one of those who know," he wrote, "that a Chief Justice cannot be a candidate for the Presidency without damaging the office he holds and himself too. . . . There ought to have been a constitutional prohibition against the political advancement of judges. . . . The Chief Justiceship is damaged if it is permitted to enter the political whirlpool." (Bruce R. Trimble, *Chief Justice Waite, Defender of the Public Interest* [Princeton, N. J.: Princeton University Press, 1938], p. 144.)

o'clock. Following the inauguration we went to the White House, where, with a considerable group of others in official life, and personal friends of the Hoovers, we had a buffet lunch and then sat in the President's stand to review the parade. After the parade we went back to the White House, where the Hoovers received a considerable number who had been invited for the occasion. It was well toward six o'clock before the day ended for us."[23]

Stone's refusal to be dislodged from his judicial post did not lessen the warmth of Hoover's friendship for him. After the new administration got under way the Justice frequently responded to the President's requests for comment on drafts of speeches and executive messages. When in 1931 Hoover was faced with the ordeal of preparing the address dedicating the Harding Memorial, he turned to Stone for help. It had to be a circumspect utterance. "In an address of this character," the Justice wrote the President, "you should aim at under, rather than over-statement."[24]

Justice Stone was also one of the first to be asked to join Hoover's pre-breakfast "Medicine-Ball Cabinet." Played on the White House courts, these games were initiated by the President's physician, Dr. Joel T. Boone, to keep his distinguished charge in good physical trim. But the medicine-ballers themselves saw these vigorous matutinal contests as further evidence of their chief's "efficiency." In this way the engineer-President could ensure early arrival of key administration figures at their posts. Stone himself soon perceived that these early morning sessions were more than setting-up exercises. "Mr. Hoover," he wrote, "is a man peculiarly dependent on his friends, and I think perhaps the gathering of them every morning and the exercise do him good, as they do me."[25]

Stone rode to the White House with various "Cabinet" members— Charles Evans Hughes, Jr., then Solicitor General, Attorney General Mitchell, or Dr. Boone. Years later young Hughes, recalling these contests, stressed the Associate Justice's considerateness toward others. "When Mr. Mitchell and I would call for him mornings, we could always discern dimly through the curtains the bulky shape of the Justice sitting just inside the front door, and he would be outside almost before our car had come to a stop. Whether this was to spare us delay, or to avoid disturbance of his household at an early hour, I cannot say; either way it was typical of him."[26]

Medicine ball, then the fashionable conditioner for statesmen, could be played with whatever degree of energy suited each player's age and physique. Justice Stone, in his stained and faded leather jacket, charged into every game with strength and determination. His large, muscular physique and zest for the sport made him a threat to other players. In the excitement of the contest minor injuries were suffered. The President was knocked breathless by a hard throw from Stone; the Ambassador to England, Hugh Gibson, suffered a like impairment, and a newspaperman, William Hard, strained a ligament in his right foot stopping one of the Justice's fast ones.* Associate Justice Harlan F. Stone, the *Washington Star* editorialized, "plays a lively game; and, recognizing that the judiciary is entirely independent of the executive, he shoots as hot ones at the President as he does at any other member of the 'Medicine Ball Cabinet.'" Stone was fifty-seven, Hoover fifty-five, yet it was the older man who left the impression of greater physical robustness and vigor.[27]

The wives of "cabinet members" were not long to be cut off from these pleasures. Justice Stone left home one day with no presentiment that his wife planned to follow him. "When the men's game was at its height," one paper reported, "with Justice Stone of the Supreme Court passing along a swift one from the President to his secretary, Newton, the women trooped out of the White House. Their cheers and comments from the sidelines caused considerable consternation, and when they produced a light rubber ball and staged a rival game the masculine players became entirely demoralized and welcomed the call to a breakfast of eggs, sausage and hotcakes in the basement dining room."[28]

However much the game aroused Stone's spirit of camaraderie, no flush of enthusiasm could break the reserve he deemed appropriate for a judge on the nation's Supreme Bench. "With all his affability and informality," Charles Evans Hughes, Jr., recalled, "there went a strict conception of what was becoming in and toward a Justice of the Court. While unfailingly friendly and companionable, he was never familiar. Nor was his bearing such as to encourage familiarity in others. There was an unostentatious but clearly perceptible reserve which drew a line beyond which only the most obtuse would have cared to venture. As to anything touching the Court, he was reticence itself, . . . never a word about the work of the Court or cases before it, or of comment upon any of his brethren." In this "intimate group," however, "there was nothing restrained about the conversation around the breakfast table. Justice Stone contributed much and interestingly to it."[29]

Nor did the President easily surrender his purpose to have the Justice in the new administration. In his inaugural address Hoover had included a proposal to reorganize and reform the judicial and law-enforcement system. The "initial paragraphs" covering this subject had been "suggested and contributed" by Justice Stone.[30] And at the very moment when the Justice rejoiced that the first rush of demands upon him was waning, Hoover approached him once more,

---

* Gibson and Hard were visitors, not regular members of the "Cabinet."

asking him to head the proposed Law Enforcement Commission. Stone tried to beg off, invoking considerations of propriety and the incompatibility of service on the commission with membership on the Court.

"President Hoover," the Justice told his sons a decade later, "became very much enamored of the idea that I should head the commission to consider and report on the Eighteenth Amendment [Wickersham Commission on Law Observance and Enforcement]. I was equally desirous of not serving in that capacity, partly because I was convinced that a political question of that character, with respect to which there were such violent conflicting opinions, could never be settled by a commission, and partly because I was convinced that the President would not accept any recommendation of the commission which did not further his political aims. . . . I tried to convince him that such a service on my part was incompatible with my position as a member of the Supreme Court, both because it would be too time-absorbing and thus prevent my doing my fair share of the work, and because I felt that discussions of my action as chairman of the commission might readily impair my public standing as a member of the Court."

"I was not at all disposed," the Justice continued, "to hazard such little reputation and public standing as I had by monkeying with the prohibition buzzsaw. It seemed to me at the time, as it has since, that the whole performance indicated a singular lack of appreciation on the President's part of the proper standing and function of the Court in our governmental structure. Subsequent events have proved how futile the commission idea was, since the report of the commission neither found support from the public or the President himself."[31]

Hoover would not take "no" for an answer; what he wanted was to have Stone take on the assignment and retain his position on the bench. If this were not agreeable, he wished the Justice to resign and accept the chairmanship. Failing to convince Stone, he took up the matter with Chief Justice Taft. "I have again this week, with the assistance of several of our best members of the bar," the President wrote Taft, April 7, 1929, "traversed the personnel of the bench and bar of the whole country, and I have not received a single suggestion of a man who, in the view of these helpers, can adequately undertake the job with any hope of its successful consummation and the necessary support of its conclusions by the public, except Justice Stone. The necessity to have ability, understanding, youth, energy, imagination, and established position of confidence in the country, eliminates name after name until we have no one left who is by any means available."

After a conference of the Justices, the decision was unchanged—

such service would not be compatible with Stone's position on the Court.

"The President is daft in respect to the qualities of our youngest member, Stone, because he has known him for a long time," Taft commented. Nor did the Chief Justice share the President's enthusiasm for Justice Stone's administrative ability. He told the President "that Stone did not have the qualities and that Stone would not retire, but he did not seem convinced."[32]

In Taft's opinion Justice Van Devanter was far better fitted than Stone for the newly created post and strongly urged his appointment.* Taft also suggested Justice Brandeis, who, like Van Devanter, had reached retirement age. Hoover stubbornly refused to consider any Justice but Stone. Only with the greatest reluctance did he finally accept the Court's and Stone's decision and turn elsewhere. On May 28, 1929, the President announced the appointment of George Wickersham as chairman of the United States National Commission on Law Observance and Enforcement.†

In the appointment of Wickersham, Taft believed the President was more fortunate than he realized. "I think it is an admirable appointment and that it is far and away the best he could do, . . . and he is so much better adapted to such a position than Stone that

---

* "The best man in the United States for the place," the Chief Justice wrote Robert A. Taft, March 17, 1929, "is Willis Van Devanter . . . and he will be seventy and entitled to retire this coming month of April. . . . The loss of Van Devanter to the bench I could not overestimate. He is a very remarkable man and admirably equipped to revamp the Criminal Code of the United States and put it into proper condition. I don't know anybody who knows more about it. The accuracy of his memory and its wide scope in such a subject offer an opportunity to the President that he does not appreciate. The truth is that Van Devanter has been very modest, and nobody knows the extent to which the whole Court are indebted to him for keeping the main line in reference to the condition of the law and their own decisions as well as the statutes. His weakness has been that he has been opinion shy, and while in conference he can deliver a conclusion that could be put by stenographic announcement right into an opinion, he never gets done looking over the various features that he would like to consider in an opinion, but he is very quick in the preparation of rules and in the organization and formulation of views of the Court into action." "I am afraid," Taft went on pessimistically, "that he [Hoover] will not value Van Devanter as much as he should. . . . I find it most awkward in dealing with a lawyer's question to convince a man who is not a lawyer and who has one lawyer to whom he looks for his judgment. If he talks with Stone, Stone will know what the real standing of Van is."

† The President's unenthusiastic acceptance of Taft's former Attorney General was premised upon more than disappointment at his failure to persuade Stone. When Stone's declination had become firm, the Chief Justice commented: "My impression is that Hoover is so much under the Progressive influence that it would be enough to be against George on account of his relation to me in the past, although I would think that George could put the thing through rather more promptly and effectively than any of them." (W. H. Taft to Robert A. Taft, April 7, 1929.)

I rejoice, although it is greatly to the disappointment of Mr. Hoover. George has more administrative ability in two minutes than Stone has in a much longer time, and then George's judgment is so much better than Stone's that I think Hoover is really to be congratulated, although he gnashes his teeth over the result."[33]

The Justice's friendship with the President attracted widespread attention even after speculation about the Cabinet posts subsided. Stone made no attempt to hide his enthusiasm for Hoover or his administration. Nor, apparently, did he avoid talking where his remarks might be overheard and repeated. "An admirable quality about the New Yorker and the former Dean of Columbia Law School," a columnist observed in 1929, "is that he does not care a tinker's dam about press criticism of a jurist's too active participation in politics any time and every time he thinks he can do a favor or lend a word of worth-while advice to a friend, even though the friend happens to be the head of another arm of our triangular checks and balances form of government. Whether he is right or wrong, he commands respect for going ahead when he thinks he is right."[34]

From the very day of Hoover's election, no high-level post could be vacated without a concomitant rumor that Stone would be drafted to fill it. Close friends of the Justice were certain that Hoover would appoint him Chief Justice if the opportunity arose.[35] Whispers of this were circulating during the spring and summer of 1929. On September 10 Justice Butler passed along to the Chief Justice a very disturbing rumor. "My Secretary," Butler wrote, "heard Sater, the Associated Press man, tell a group in the Clerk's office that the President has told the newspapermen that he intends to make Stone Chief Justice. Sater was not present on the occasion referred to. It seems to be unbelievable that Hoover would do that. There is no vacancy and he has no right to assume that there will be one during the present term of Presidency. We all hope and believe that there will be none. Moreover, there would be no reason for making the announcement now even if it is the present purpose to nominate Stone if and when there is opportunity.

"However," Butler continued, "there has been enough of publicity in reference to Stone's elevation—when taken in connection with the President's known desire to have him for Attorney General, Secretary of State, and head of the Law Enforcement Commission, to indicate that there is an understanding between them and a purpose—even with indecent haste—to reorganize the Court for the accomplishment of some purpose."

The Chief Justice replied laconically September 14: "What you say with reference to Stone's promotion to succeed me, I have no doubt has a good deal of truth in it, and it can hardly be called news."*

Whether or not rumor and the President's extravagant esteem aroused Stone's expectations, one cannot say, but we do know that it filled the ailing Chief Justice with painful apprehension. He felt that Hoover would be making "a great mistake, for the reason that Stone is not a leader and would have a good deal of difficulty in massing the Court. He may greatly improve, as doubtless he will, but at present I don't think there is anybody on the Court, except Stone, who would think that he is fitted for Chief Justice."[36]

Taft was also critical of the vast sweep of Stone's opinions. "He has great difficulty in getting his opinions through because he is quite disposed to be discursive and to write opinions as if he were writing an editorial or a comment for a legal law journal, covering as much as he can upon a general subject and thus expressing opinions that have not been thought out by the whole Court. He is a learned lawyer in many ways but his judgments I do not altogether consider safe, and the ease with which he expresses himself and his interest in the whole branch of the law in which he is called upon to give an opinion on a single principle make the rest of the Court impatient and doubtful. . . . Without impeaching at all his good faith in matters of that sort, we find we have to watch closely the language he uses."[37]

Taft, ever concerned lest a conservative majority on the bench be destroyed, wrote his brother Horace, December 1, 1929: "I think we could hold our six to steady the Court. Brandeis is of course hopeless, as Holmes is, and as Stone is. Should Stone ever have the administration of the Chief Justiceship, he would find himself embarrassed in respect to a good many principles that we have declared as the result of a great many years of careful declarations. However," he noted rather wistfully, "the only hope we have of keeping a consistent declaration of constitutional law is for us to live as long as we can, because should Hoover's administration continue, I do not doubt there will be an attempted revolution. . . ."

Taft's undertone of despondency disturbed his brother. On December 8 the Chief Justice wrote again: "You speak of my pessimism. I suppose I must have had reference to the situation in the Court.

* On May 12, 1929, the Chief Justice wrote his brother Charles: "I had a notice from the *Herald Tribune* this week that they had a report that I was going to retire in order that Stone might be appointed Chief Justice. I was only able to say that I had not known of it but that I could not otherwise deny it. There has been a good deal of an effort to boost Stone by complimentary articles in places where it would seem as if they had come from the same source. At least there are some of my brethren who insist that reading them between the lines, the information given must have come from 'home' sources. I don't know how true this is."

My feeling with respect to the Court is that if a number of us die, Hoover would put in some rather extreme destroyers of the Constitution, but perhaps we are unduly exercised, because of the conservative members of the Court we have six, and two of the remainder are Brandeis and Holmes. Brandeis is seventy-three and Holmes is eighty-nine. He enters his ninetieth year next month. I have no doubt there is persistent hope, especially by the younger crowd of college professors, that in some way or other Holmes will be continued on the Court while the rest of us die off." Bolstered somewhat by philosophical reflection, the Chief Justice continued: "The good luck of the Court in times past has been marked, and changes of a radical character have not been made all at once. More than that, when men are visited with the responsibility of change, they often find themselves rendered conservative by a fuller realization of the effect of the changes which when they haven't the responsibility they think they would make. . . ."

Failing in health, almost at the point of death, Taft did not sit with the Court after January 6, 1930. He resigned on February 3. "The great work of the Court," he wrote in reply to a consolatory letter from his colleagues, "will go on well without me."[38] The brief interregnum during which Justice Holmes presided as Acting Chief Justice provided a wholesome change of pace for Stone. "I really should have reported," he wrote glowingly to Felix Frankfurter on January 27, "on the admirable manner in which the young man is presiding over our Court. Conferences are a joy, and we are dispatching business with great rapidity."

In open Court, Monday, March 10, 1930, Holmes announced: "On Saturday, just as we were expecting him at a conference of the Justices, we were informed that our brother, Mr. Justice Sanford, had become unconscious pending a slight operation. Five minutes later we received word that he was dead. Thus suddenly the light of a faithful worker, who was born also to charm, went out. Afterwards came the news that the late Chief Justice had found relief from his hopeless illness in death. Such events must be accepted in silent awe."[39]

Since late January, Attorney General William D. Mitchell had known that the appointment of Taft's successor was imminent. Mitchell's choice, from the first, was former Associate Justice Charles Evans Hughes.* Not wishing to make the recommendation to the President without knowing that Hughes would accept, the Attorney General sought the assistance of Justices Van Devanter and Butler, who dined with Hughes in his New York apartment on January 28.

* Hughes had resigned from the Supreme Court in 1916 to run for President on the Republican ticket.

The Justices "came back to Washington convinced that he was willing and so informed the Attorney General."[40] The President then made known his intention to nominate Hughes at a breakfast conference with him the next day.

Hughes hesitated. "There are various reasons why you should not nominate me," he told the President. Being within a few months of his sixty-eighth birthday, Hughes thought of himself as "too old." Another reason was his reluctance to interfere with the career of his son, who had served less than a year as Solicitor General. "I was convinced," Hoover wrote Hughes some years later, "your sense of public service would compel you to accept, and I reported to the Attorney General that he could consider it settled if Mr. Taft felt he must retire."[41]

Taft's resignation no sooner reached the President than speculation arose as to his successor. The *New York Times* noted a "widespread report that Associate Justice Harlan Fiske Stone of New York would be the new Chief Justice." The "widespread report" had its source in Presidential Press Secretary George Akerson, who "tipped off" press corps friends. "Exactly an hour later, just long enough for the correspondents to rush off inside dope messages to their papers and for one local Washington paper to prepare an 'extra' layout announcing Stone's appointment," Akerson appeared and said that Charles Evans Hughes, Sr., had been named.[42] In the interim newsmen had gone to Stone's house, trying to wheedle confirmation of the original announcement out of the Associate Justice or his secretary. Even his loyal secretary, who had served Stone for nearly five years, was in the dark and thought the Justice was being unduly reticent. "It irked me," she recalled, "to have him tell me, each time I'd ask, that so far as he knew he was not to be Chief Justice. The newspapermen also thought we were being secretive. I told him as much, and he countered: 'Well, I'm afraid they will be disappointed if they expect it to happen.' I thought he was holding out on me until he and Brandeis had a telephone conversation in which he said: 'I think it will be the man from New York.' And then I knew he was not to have the post."[43]

Within five hours after receiving Taft's resignation Hoover submitted the name of Charles Evans Hughes as Chief Justice. The President had expected to withhold announcement until his regular press conference the following day, but "the change in this intention was brought about by the feeling that if it were published throughout the country that Justice Stone would be elevated to the head of the Supreme Court the situation might become embarrassing."[44]

The reactions to the Hughes nomination in the press on February 4 were conflicting. The *Baltimore Sun* said Hoover "gave Washington the biggest surprise of his administration," observing that the President maintained "utmost secrecy" about Taft's successor. But the United Press reported that Taft's personal physician stated that the Chief Justice had been asked beforehand to approve Hughes' appointment, and had done so with pleasure.* Capitol newsmen, caught off balance by their hunches and by the press secretary's tip, were thoroughly confused. So also were White House advisers. Working together they tried to re-evaluate the events immediately preceding February 3, 1930.

"It was said by close associates of the President," the *Times* correspondent wrote, "that his choice of Mr. Hughes for the highest judicial post in the nation was no case of snap judgment. The impression prevailed, when the nomination was sent to the Senate, that the President had made up his mind to appoint him between the time this afternoon when the resignation of Chief Justice Taft was handed to him . . . and the few hours thereafter when the nomination was transmitted." "President Hoover knew, when Mr. Taft went to Asheville, N. C., on January 14," the *New York World* declared, "that his condition would prevent his return to his duties in the Court." The *Baltimore Sun* was less dogmatic: "To prepare for possible eventualities Mr. Hughes was invited to breakfast privately with the Hoovers, only a few days ago. It is assumed that the President conditionally tendered the Chief Justiceship to the New Yorker. . . . No member of the White House staff, it appears, had an inkling that Mr. Hughes would be appointed, although his name was mentioned in many quarters among the possibilities." The President's own press secretary, however, had had more than an inkling that Stone would be named.

In the face of this strange turn of events Stone maintained at least the appearance of calm detachment. "The next morning," his secretary recalled, "I made some caustic remark about President Hoover's action, and all he said, with no seeming rancor, was: 'Well, I am sure Mr. Hughes will make a very fine Chief Justice.'"† "I think," she

---

* Taft's endorsement of Hughes suggests that in the Chief Justice's mind the latter could be counted upon, as Stone could not be, to oppose a "latitudinarian construction of the Constitution," and invoke it against "socialistic raids upon property rights."

† Stone had made a somewhat different estimate of Hughes' qualities on his appointment to the International Court. "I see that Mr. Hughes has finally been selected as a judge of the Permanent Court," he wrote John Bassett Moore, Sept. 11, 1928. "This is to me a rather surprising episode. Nevertheless, there is much to be said in support of the choice, although I do not think his judicial qualities are his strength. He has a vigorous personality, great intellectual power, and great prestige, all of which will be of value in the new position."

John Lord O'Brian tells a story that spells out what Stone may have had in mind. Hughes' confirmation had been hanging fire for several days. In the late afternoon of the very day the Senate confirmed the nomination, O'Brian called at the Justice's house. A newspaper with big headlines announcing confirmation

concluded, "that was the first time I felt any real affection for him and realized what a truly great man he was. It was a keen disappointment which he took on the chin."[43]

Stone's congratulatory letter went out promptly, on February 4: "Please accept my heartiest congratulations on your appointment as Chief Justice of the United States and my good wishes for long and useful service as the leader of the Court. We will be welcoming you soon to a round of hard work which is never ceasing, but which never fails of interest, and with which you fortunately are well acquainted."

Stone's family and friends marveled at his remarkable control. Some ten days after the nomination the Justice and his brother Lauson, walking in New York, were offered an afternoon paper with a large picture of "the man from New York" carrying the banner headline: "Hughes, the new Chief Justice." Lauson glanced at his brother to ascertain his reaction and was amazed to see his face wreathed in smiles. "Humph," Stone said, chuckling, "there's many a slip 'twixt the cup and the lip."[45]

For over two decades the story has persisted that Hoover had made up his mind to appoint Stone when someone (supposedly Joseph P. Cotton, his Undersecretary of State) reminded the President of the "deep political debt" the party owed Charles Evans Hughes for his help in the 1928 election campaign. It would be a fine political gesture, this strategist reasoned, to offer Hughes the post on the theory that he would decline. Acting on this hunch, Hoover telephoned Hughes and tendered him the Chief Justiceship. As the conversation proceeded, Hoover blanched; his jaw dropped. The President hung up, visibly shaken. "Well, I'll be damned. He accepted."[46] This seemed the perfect illustration of the old Yankee story of the man who aimed to blow medicine down the horse's throat through a straw, but the horse blew first.

Some years later when Chief Justice Hughes read published accounts of this tale he was greatly disturbed. It was not, however, until publication of *The Nine Old Men*, by Pearson and Allen, in 1937, one year after Stone had lambasted his reactionary colleagues in his AAA dissent (to Hughes not only patently wrong but "unduly theatrical"), and only two weeks after President Roosevelt—his convictions reinforced by this dissent—had launched his plan to pack the Court, that the story first came to Hoover's attention. On February 19, 1937, the ex-President "voluntarily" wrote Hughes an indignant and em-

---

had just been placed at the entrance as Justice Stone opened the door and greeted his visitor. "Well, of course that is an excellent appointment," the Justice commented. "But it is my observation that men rarely change their economic views after sixty." (A.T.M.'s interview with John Lord O'Brian, June 29, 1954.)

phatic denial of it, but went no further than to discredit the authors who spread "a purported [telephone] conversation of mine with Joe Cotton." Hughes replied the next day, calling Hoover's attention to the fact that the story had first appeared in *The New Yorker* under the authorship of the well-known biographer Henry F. Pringle, who, interestingly enough, made no mention of a telephone conversation. "Mr. Hoover, according to the best information," Pringle had written, "desired to promote Associate Justice Stone, his close friend. He confided this to the late Undersecretary of State Cotton, who said that it was out of the question to pass over Mr. Hughes. But Hughes, he added, would not accept. He was earning enormous fees in private practice. Besides, Charles E. Hughes, Jr., would have to resign as Solicitor General if his father became Chief Justice. 'Offer it to Mr. Hughes,' suggested Cotton. 'He'll decline and then you can pick Justice Stone.' "*

On February 25 Hoover made another attempt to smooth the Chief Justice's ruffled feelings. But as in his earlier communication, his most emphatic denial was that "The whole story falls to the ground from the fact that no telephone conversation as to your appointment as Chief Justice ever took place." Hoover's lengthy letter does no more than say that he had not discussed the subject with Cotton after his conference with Attorney General Mitchell on January 29.[47] Furthermore, support for the "Joe Cotton story" is contained in Justice Butler's letter of September 10, 1929, to Taft and the Chief Justice's reply three days later. Even then Hoover's intentions with respect to Stone and the Chief Justiceship could, as Taft said, "hardly be called news."†

Stone's friends were bitterly disappointed. "Nothing could have surprised or astonished us more than the news in this morning's journals," John Bassett Moore wrote, February 4. "I also dislike the marks of prearrangement which the transaction bears upon its face. Yesterday evening the expressions in the press, as far I saw them, were unanimous in the view that age formed a bar in this particular case. Public opinion is not always wrong, and opportunity to express itself may be very salutary. Another phase which I most strongly reprobate is the

---

* After reading the Pringle "Profile," Hughes had "thought of writing to Mr. Hoover about the matter but decided not to do so in view of the possibility that the inquiry might be embarrassing to him." (C. E. Hughes to his son, Feb. 20, 1937.) May not one infer that, initially, Hughes was inclined to credit the story?

While Pringle was preparing his biography of Taft, Hughes' son and daughter expressed to Pringle "the desire that this story should be eliminated." (C. E. Hughes to C. E. Hughes, Jr., Feb. 20, 1937.) As no reference is made to it in the published biography, Mr. Pringle apparently was convinced that the story was not authentic. Walter H. Newton, Secretary to President Hoover, 1929-33, is also on record against it. See Newton's letter, *New York Times,* Dec. 18, 1938.

† See pp. 274-75.

restoration to the Court, with the reward of the highest position in it, of a former member who left it in order to run for political office."*

Nor were Stone's reactions those of a man who never considered himself in the running. "I am too familiar with the history of this country and of the Court," he replied to a former law school colleague's word of commiseration, "to have any illusions about appointments to high office. There are so many contending forces which control the matter that one who goes regularly about the business, without permitting himself or his friends to urge his claims, may well be passed by. Further, one should recognize that there are others who, in point of long distinguished public service, have claims which could not be urged on my behalf.† After all, being Chief Justice of the Supreme Court is a good deal like being Dean of the Law School— he has to do the things that the janitor will not do. The post never enlarges the occupant's individual capacity for judicial work, and it may diminish it."[48]

In a letter to his sons the Justice admitted his own "candidacy": "There was, of course, some mention of my name in connection with the post, as I suppose was inevitable, because of my close acquaintance with the President. Many people seem to feel that such appointments are made as a mark of personal favor, which, of course, is not, and should not be, the case."[49]

Through all his replies ran the somewhat rueful note that "one's

* The day before John Bassett Moore had sent the following letter to the President: "Sterling integrity, ability of high order, learning in the law, and judicial experience, together with industry, patience, and a strong assurance of length of service, constitute an ideal combination for the post of Chief Justice of the United States. This unusual combination is found in Justice Harlan F. Stone, whom I have known from his youth up."

Mr. Justice Holmes did not share Moore's view that Hughes' resignation from the Court in 1916 to run for the Presidency disqualified him for the Chief Justiceship. On Feb. 27, 1930, Holmes wrote: "As to Hughes, I was more pleased by his appointment than I could have been by any others. . . . I don't so much mind Hughes' having left the bench and coming back. Lots of our judges have had the presidential bee, and as to appointments by way of promotion I should adopt no formula." Holmes spoke of Hughes as "an old friend" and expressed "great satisfaction" that he had been "confirmed by the Senate as C.J." (*Holmes-Laski Letters*, Vol. II, pp. 1224, 1226, 1227.)

† What those claims were are detailed in Albert Shaw's long congratulatory letter of Feb. 5, 1930, to the new Chief Justice: "Your hearty support, in 1928, of the Republican situation, along with your firm refusal to be the candidate yourself, contributed greatly to the success, in the convention and at the polls, of the Hoover movement. . . . In the years lying immediately ahead of us I think that we need a sense of order and stability to govern our economic and social transition even more than we need strength in the Executive Department or new laws on the statute books. In short, I think we need wisdom at the apex of our federal judiciary system, for reassurance as we go forward, more than we need anything else in our mechanism of government. . . . What some people call 'liberalism' would not be in the interests of the people, but exactly the reverse."

capacity for useful work bears very little relation to high dignity that may be showered upon him. . . . So I shall be contentedly sawing wood at the old stand."[50]

Professor Frankfurter, who visited Stone shortly after Hughes' appointment, went away much impressed by the Justice's "philosophic mood about recent events." "It requires a good deal of wisdom," Frankfurter wrote, "to detach one's self as you were detached, although there are not many things that make for less serenity of mind than to nurse a concrete ambition. Most people who think hard about these matters looked to you as the next Chief Justice, and I could not help but feel invigorated to find that you have such a spacious outlook on the whole situation."[51]

"It has always been a part of my deliberate policy in life," Stone replied, "never to nurse concrete ambitions beyond endeavoring to do the particular job I have to do as well as I can. I believe it is the real secret of a happy life, or at least as near as we ever come to its secret."[52]

This extraordinary tale of abortive political strategy is still current and credited. Mr. Hoover has refused to dispel the mystery.* In reply to an inquiry as to whether he had offered the posts of Secretary of State and the Chief Justiceship to Stone, he would not elaborate or grant an interview. "The Secretary of State offer is true," the former President responded cryptically, "the other is not."[53] "Akerson's blunder has never been fully explained," Hughes' sympathetic biographer, Merlo J. Pusey, concluded lamely.[54] Certainly Mr. Pusey does not explain it.†

---

* Former President Hoover's account of the bitter controversy roused by Hughes' nomination is laconic: "Upon the death of Chief Justice Taft, with the general approval of the country, I nominated Charles E. Hughes for Chief Justice. Because of some old grudge, Senator Borah opposed the appointment, but Hughes was confirmed nevertheless." (*The Memoirs of Herbert Hoover, 1920-1933* [New York: The Macmillan Co., 1952], p. 268.)

† A perceptive reader of these pages, and one very close to Stone, writes: "As I read the story of Hughes' appointment as Chief Justice, I cannot help surmising that the clue to what happened lies in the relations of Attorney General Mitchell and Justice Butler. It may be imagined that Butler, aware of the "danger" that H.F.S. would soon become Chief Justice, went to work on Mitchell in various ways and succeeded in convincing him that Hughes would be the best appointment, with the desired result that Hoover, too, was persuaded. It is not necessary to suppose that Hoover ever promised the appointment directly or indirectly to H.F.S. His embarrassment about commenting on the matter may be due to the fact that his change of mind, while involving no broken commitments, was a rather public one associated with private intrigues which went on prior to Taft's admission of his inability to continue. The possibility that Hoover had some rather old commitment to Hughes cannot be altogether ruled out though this seems inconsistent with Hoover's account of his choice of Hughes. I think that what Hoover said about the appointment must be taken as true; it is behind the things unsaid that one may suspect maneuverings of the kind I have suggested."

One need not linger over the embellishments of the story—the telephone call or Akerson's alleged misstep, etc.,—nor even credit the implication that Hoover offered the post to Hughes with the expectation that he would decline. The evidence demonstrates that President Hoover, along with other competent observers, believed Stone qualified. Chief Justice Taft and Justice Butler, among others, confidently believed that Hoover intended to elevate him. For some reason—Hughes' service to Hoover and the party in the 1928 campaign, the fear of what "some people call 'liberalism,'" or whatever—he changed his mind at a late hour.

Meanwhile the country sank deeper into the throes of economic depression. With a view both to his own interests and to the economic safety of the nation, Stone continued his study of economic conditions and of investment trends. He deplored the President's failure to come to grips with the crisis. Hoover seemed not to understand the tragic threat either to his own political future or to the country's welfare. Writing from Europe, July, 1930, Stone commented: "The political situation doesn't look so good partly because of things Hoover could not control and partly because of some that he could. Mr. [Adolph] Miller of the Federal Reserve Board who is traveling with us thinks we are in for a considerable period of depression with possible further slumps; so investors should be cautious."[55] In early August 1930 Stone made specific complaint. "The President has signed the tariff bill, a mistake, I think."[56]

The situation grew more hopeless with each passing month. "There is, of course, ground for pessimism," Stone wrote in late December. "The magnificent economic system which we had thought had been created so that it was impervious to slumps and reactions has been found more vulnerable than most people thought. . . . That we will get going again in some fashion I have no doubt, and that we will achieve a certain prosperity again in due course is, I think, very certain. But we are not likely to see another such boom as followed the war in your day and mine.

"Politically," the Justice continued, "we are certainly in a bad way. The President seems to get off on the wrong foot when he tackles any political problem; the politicians have no use for him, and the vast number of people who are not politically minded, but who supported him for the nomination and election, have either lost interest or been alienated. Anti-prohibition sentiment has grown enormously, as was indicated in the election."[57]

To promote the "natural healing processes," the President indulged in pep talk, deprecated any thought of government interference. "We cannot legislate ourselves out of a world depression," he said, refusing to call a special session of Congress in 1930. "We can and will work ourselves out,"[58] if "we just keep on giving the American people a chance."[59] The American people got their first chance in the 1930 congressional election, and gave a resounding vote of no confidence. "The election returns make the Republicans feel pretty glum, and they ought to," Stone reported. "Of course, the financial slump is, I suppose, primarily responsible, but there are other things which I believe could have been avoided. It is going to be a very difficult time for the President these next two years."[60] And Stone agreed that the untoward prospect was caused by lack of leadership.

When the jittery President took bold government action, as in his egregious order of July 1932 commanding General Douglas Mac-Arthur to disperse the Bonus Army, the political repercussions were even more disastrous. "I was out of the country when it occurred," Stone recalled years later, "so I never understood what led to such an inept performance." Stone saw Hoover's action for what it was—"a colossal political blunder."[61] He agreed with William Allen White's remark that Hoover had "a gift" for making political mistakes.[62]

Inaction alone practically ensured the President's defeat in 1932. At first the Justice entertained the hope that the Democrats would exhibit political ineptitude equaling Hoover's and thus enable the Republicans to snatch victory from the jaws of defeat. But Republican ineptitude was hard to match. "Just now," Stone noted, in April 1932, "the government seems to be in the throes of economizing and about the only idea that anyone seems to have is to take the economy out of poor underpaid employees."[63]

Gone, almost to the vanishing point, was the unbounded enthusiasm with which he had supported the Republican candidate in 1928. As the campaign progressed he followed the maneuvers of the major candidates—"an interested spectator on the sidelines during such time as I am not busy grinding the weekly grist of Court work."[64] Meanwhile his friends once more pressed him to make a bid for the nomination. In mid-January 1932 an old college friend, Grosvenor Backus, wrote him about a letter he had received, which concluded: " 'I think Hoover is the most tactless individual and poorest politician we've had for President yet. I wish you would have Justice Stone nominated, so that there would be no doubt, in any minds, of integrity and sense.' Will you," Backus inquired, "accept the nomination?"[65]

Republican prospects were waning rapidly. The Republican party had "laid down with the covetous international bankers," Sterling Carr commented, "and cannot get up without the fleas of sin." The conviction that Hoover was finished deepened. Carr urged Stone to stir the President from his lethargy for one last push. "What we need today is moral leadership of real he-man character and the dragging of the people back on to the right track and train of thought. Why don't you talk to the President and see if you cannot bring him to see the light?" Make him see, Carr suggested, that he must re-establish himself in the hearts of the people by vigorously aligning "the forces of the federal government behind a big clean-up."[66]

"What you say about the situation and about the part the President might play is all too true," Stone replied, "but I doubt if he has any faculty for playing that kind of role. As for myself, I only give advice when it is asked, and the little I have given is not generally followed. The distressing thing about the present situation is that Roosevelt is, so far, in the lead of all other Democrats. He seems to be an utterly impossible man for President of the United States, and yet he may be elected almost by default unless the Democrats utterly wreck their opportunities, or conditions very much improve between now and election day. Of the latter I do not think there is much hope, but as to the former," he chided his Democratic friend, "the resources of our Democratic brethren are infinite."[67]

By the middle of May the political horizon bore unmistakable signs of Republican disaster. "This is certainly a sad and pessimistic world hereabouts, and New York is even worse," Stone observed. "The Grand Old Party would certainly be in for a sound licking if the Democrats had any real gumption, but they haven't, so I don't know what we can look forward to." As world-wide economic depression worsened and gloom spread over the nation, Stone became increasingly critical of the administration's complacency: "Life goes on much as usual in Washington. The nation's capital has been spared the distress and panic of the country because nearly everyone is on government salary and people are less affected by conditions than elsewhere."[68]

The Stones were soon off for a flying trip to Scandinavia where "one could still find traces of medieval grandeur and meditate on the changes in the course of the world's progress economic forces have wrought."

"I see," the Justice wrote to his son Lauson, June 23, 1932, from Sweden, "that the Republicans have nominated H. H. and straddled the liquor question. Sweden seems to have settled the problem by making mild beer and light wines easy to get and limiting the purchase of spirits with meals or from government agencies. I wish we could find a like solution, but I doubt if it would work with our people who are less law-abiding and less civilized than the Swedes."

Just before the election a correspondent submitted to the Justice a prognosis which the Justice accepted as his own: "It looks as though people this year [are] fiercely agin. Despite the stock-market flurries, trade really doesn't move substantially, and if that holds— as it is likely—'til election an adverse vote against the administration is highly probable. From a long-term point of view that seems to be most desirable. No wonder so wise and disinterested a Republican as Dwight Morrow thought a year ago it would probably be a good thing for the country to have a Democratic administration. And the pity of it all, when one thinks of the vast good will with which the President came in and the succession of opportunities he passed up. I think the crux of his difficulty is that he is still operating on economic principles which he was taught at Leland Stanford and which doubtless he found vindicated in his business experience in the undeveloped countries of Australia, and China and Siberia. What's been happening in the United States is, I believe, that the 'inarticulate major premises' of economics under which we have been operating for generations no longer fit our needs and the transforming forces that govern us."

"Your analysis of the political situation . . . agrees with mine," Stone said in reply. "The truth of the business is that we are in a sad state politically as well as economically, and if, as a result of the approaching election, the air is cleared somewhat, it will be a very fortunate thing."

Nevertheless the Justice continued to assist the Republican standard bearer throughout the 1932 campaign. Late in the struggle a presidential secretary submitted a speech,* asking Stone to "make such comment and suggestions as occur to you and return as soon as possible."[69] "I am with the President 100 per cent in this address," the Justice replied. "It is altogether admirable."[70] He was still banking on the "many things that might happen," but by mid-October all hope had practically vanished: "The forces on which I counted to elect the Republican ticket seem to me not to be manifesting themselves as much as I had expected. For one thing, Roosevelt is making a much stronger campaign than I had expected, and for another, the resentment against the Republican administration is even deeper than I had supposed."[71]

The defeat, though regrettable, was not without its bright side. "I cannot see in Roosevelt and his entourage any improvement over

* This is, perhaps, the President's address of October 12 before the American Bar Association on the occasion of the dedication of the new Supreme Court building. "We have long recognized," Mr. Hoover said, "that certain functions in our economic life are affected with a public interest, which requires that their activities shall be in some measure controlled by government, either state or federal, in protection of the citizens. In that situation we have sought to find a bridge between these controls and the maintenance of that initiative and enterprise which assures the conduct and expansion to perfection of these functions." Justice Stone could easily endorse such sentiments.

Hoover," Stone wrote shortly after the election. "Nevertheless the overturn may not be without benefit. It is at least important for the party in power to know that if it is not alive to realities, it is likely to be chastened at the polls."

Depressed economic conditions had played a major part in the GOP's smashing defeat, but Stone attached some of the blame to Hoover himself. In a world that was so obviously "in a bad way" the President had failed to meet the need for more constructive leadership. "I was not surprised," Stone wrote Carr. "I have seen it coming for two years at least. The depression, undoubtedly, accounted for it to some extent, although I am not convinced that it interposed insuperable obstacles, if the Progressive elements in the country had had greater faith in Hoover—and by Progressive I do not mean extremists—but those who realize we are in a changing world and that old formulas will not solve our problem."[72]

The President perhaps did not deserve such faith. He had come into office under no obligations to the hack politicians or the stand-patters. "I cannot escape the feeling," Stone wrote his brother Lauson, December 2, 1932, "that if he had disregarded the political hacks and followed his own instincts to do the right thing by the great mass of people who elected him, that the result might have been different notwithstanding the depression."

But this realistic estimate did not mar their friendship. As soon as things settled down after the election, the defeated President, wanting to get away from Washington for a few days' fishing, urged the Stones to spend the Christmas holidays with him and his wife on a southern cruise. Stone did not relish the idea, for it would preclude his greatest joy—spending the Christmas holidays with his sons. Besides, the trip meant taking "time I can ill afford to spend in elegant leisure because of the Court work I have to do."[73] There was also the probability that one of Hughes' innovations, designed to speed the work, might break in. "The scheme of having only two weeks' recess," he complained, "does not work very well, at any rate, it does not work well for me."[74] But he managed, despite the abbreviated recess, to take another Florida cruise with the Hoovers.*

"Mrs. Stone and I have just been off for a short cruise with President and Mrs. Hoover," he reported to Sterling Carr. "He seemed really to be relieved that he is approaching the day when he will not have the responsibility of office. He seemed to be more like his old self than I have seen him since he took the Presidency, and it really

---

* During the years when Taft was Chief Justice, it was easier to go on these trips. Then the Court heard arguments for three weeks and recessed for three weeks, thus giving two Saturdays without conferences.

seemed like old times to go away and fish without any thought of politics or official responsibilities."[75]

In early February the Justice and his wife gave a dinner for President and Mrs. Hoover and all the Medicine Ball crowd and their wives. Anyone who had played at any time was on hand, including Alexander Legge, who came from Chicago, and two others from New York—making a party of thirty-three. Foolish presents were presented; Commodore Ernest Lee Jahncke was court martialed. There were songs, good food, and fine conversation.[76] Helen E. Boone, wife of the White House physician, regaled "Cabinet" members with lines more or less inspired by Coleridge. Beginning with Justice Stone, her doggerel told how her husband had dragooned each player into the game:

> He was the White House doctor,
> And he stoppeth one of three,
> A Justice of the Supreme Court,
> Who was on his way to tea.

> "What wantest thou?" the Justice said,
> With a glitter in his eye,
> "To join the President's Medicine Ball,
> Before the sun is high."

Former Solicitor General Charles Evans Hughes, Jr., and his wife returned to Washington for the festivities. There was a stanza for him too:

> Charles Evans Hughes the Junior
> He loved to try a case.
> But soon resigned his job, to make
> For his Pa-Pa a place.

Mrs. Boone's good-natured spoofing ended on a solemn note:

> We'll miss our morning exercise,
> And the comradeship it brought.
> We'll ne'er forget the happy hours.
> We give them many a thought.

> A Toast, to our Beloved Chief,
> And to his Ladye fair—
> "Luck, happiness and health supreme"
> We hope you both may share.

As a climax the President was given a silver cigar box decorated with a picture of the Medicine Ball court, the White House in the distance. It was a hilarious evening. "I think," the Justice commented soon after, "the Hoovers had the most amusing time they have had since he became President."[77]

Later on the Hoovers gave a farewell White House party. Stone returned home sobered and contemplative. He had thoroughly enjoyed the free and easy exchange with the President and other top-ranking Republican officials. His influence on policy and personnel had served to compensate, at least partially, for the frustrations of a chronic dissenter. He opened the wide doors of his library and stood, opera hat tilted back on his head, gazing out at the full moon. His law clerk had worked late that night, and as he descended from his balcony perch, Stone turned to him and said: "Well, I guess I'll not be at the White House again for some time."[78]

The Stones never became reconciled to the new order. They attended, as usual, the 1933 inauguration exercises in the Senate Chamber. But, instead of staying on to hear the New Deal President's address, they went with other friends to the train to see the Hoovers off. "I shall never forget," the Justice's widow recalled many years later, "the expression on Mr. Hoover's face."[79]

HARLAN STONE, AGED FIVE

AGNES HARVEY, AGED THREE

AGNES HARVEY AND HARLAN STONE IN 1892

JUNIOR AT AMHERST COLLEGE, 1893

DEAN AND MRS. STONE WITH THEIR TWO SONS, 1910

THE STONE FAMILY IN 1914
*Standing, left to right:* Richard (son of Winthrop), Winthrop, Margaret (Winthrop's wife), Helen Stone Willard, Agnes, Harlan, Lauson, David (son of Winthrop); *seated on step:* Lauson (son of Harlan), Mrs. Stone, Mr. Stone, Luthera Willard (daughter of Helen), Marshall (son of Harlan)

ON A FISHING TRIP AT PYRAMID LAKE, NEVADA, 1933

*Left to right:* Herbert Hoover, Ray Wilbur, Jr., Ray Lyman Wilbur, Stone

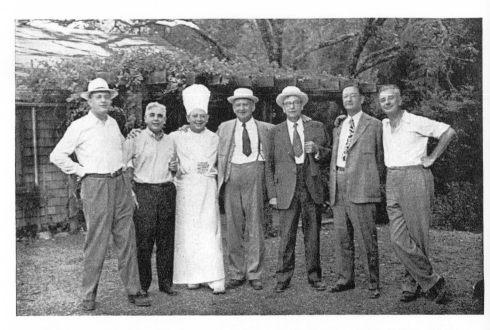

SONS OF THE VINE IN THE SANTA CRUZ MOUNTAINS, CALIFORNIA, 1941

*Left to right:* Chaffee E. Hall, Farnham P. Griffiths, Dr. George Selleck, Sterling Carr, Stone, Carl R. Ganter, Dr. Raoul Blanguie

BRINGING HOME HIS CATCH ON THE OPENING DAY OF THE TROUT SEASON,
LONG ISLAND COUNTRY CLUB, APRIL 6, 1924 (*Underwood and Underwood*)

IN COOLIDGE'S CABINET, ATTORNEY GENERAL STONE AND
SECRETARY OF STATE CHARLES EVANS HUGHES, 1924 (*Acme*)

WITH HIS PREDECESSOR, ASSOCIATE JUSTICE JOSEPH MC KENNA, 1925 (*Acme*)

SUMMER COTTAGE AT ISLE AU HAUT, MAINE

RESIDENCE AT 2340 WYOMING AVENUE, WASHINGTON, D.C.
*(Tenschert Studio)*

WITH JUSTICES HOLMES AND BRANDEIS IN 1930 (*International News*)

THE NEWLY APPOINTED CHIEF JUSTICE WITH HIS GRANDSONS, PETER, FOUR,
AND HARLAN, SIX, AT THE BROOKLYN HOME OF HIS SON LAUSON

BEING SWORN IN AS CHIEF JUSTICE OF THE UNITED STATES BY
WAYNE HACKETT, U.S. COMMISSIONER, ROCKY MOUNTAIN
NATIONAL PARK, COLORADO, JULY 3, 1941

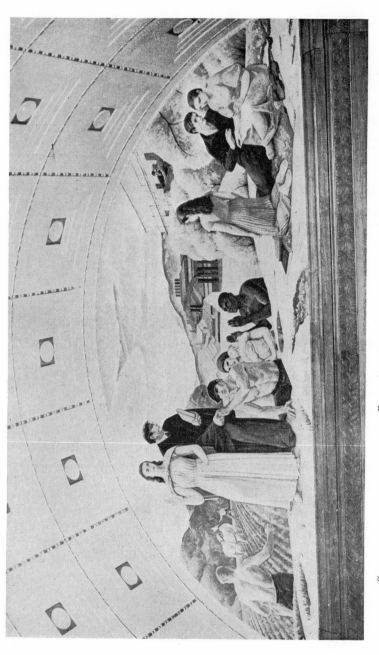

MURAL, "THE TRIUMPH OF JUSTICE," BY LEON KROLL IN THE DEPARTMENT OF JUSTICE BUILDING. STONE WAS THE MODEL FOR THE FIGURE IN JUDICIAL ROBES (*Acme*)

CHIEF JUSTICE STONE AND HIS BENCH, 1941 (© *Bachrach*)

HARLAN FISKE STONE, 1941 (*New York Times Studio*)

# Upholding the Power to Govern

## CHAPTER EIGHTEEN

# Rehearsal

## 1930

The shadow of Franklin Delano Roosevelt on politics has almost hypnotic fascination. But the very pervasiveness of his personal influence after 1932 is apt to obscure prior events, which, if explored, might illuminate the complex pattern of the so-called New Deal years.

Every literate American is familiar with President Roosevelt's epic struggle to "pack" the United States Supreme Court. But not many remember that President Hoover had also been suspected of these dangerous thoughts. Few now understand that in 1930 Hoover provoked a fierce political contest, foreshadowing the 1936 impasse between Court and Congress, as well as F. D. R.'s crusade of 1937 to bring the judiciary into line with the basic necessities of the modern state.*

That 1930 uprising began with Hoover's appointment of Hughes as Chief Justice. Three months later it showed up again in the President's abortive nomination of Judge John J. Parker as Associate Justice. These appointments, coinciding with economic depression and endemic unemployment, poured new freshets into the swelling demand for reform. Hoover was unable to measure the proportions of the disaster, much less formulate a policy that would stem it and so appease the rising tides of public indignation. Both Republican insurgents and Democratic liberals were in revolt against the stale sham of normalcy; and though GOP stalwarts still held fast in the Senate, a small contingent of progressives was militant and outspoken. While the President peered in vain for the corner around which, he said, prosperity was lurking, the 71st Congress mirrored only too clearly the public's restless temper and itch for a change. Recent Supreme Court decisions served to accentuate the "radical"

* There is quite a difference between a President's exercising his constitutional duty in filling vacancies on the bench and high-handed intervention to make the Court's views conform to a particular set of social and economic values, which President Roosevelt attempted in 1937. But that difference becomes rather technical if the President, as the insurgents in 1930 firmly believed, selects men for the Supreme Court in order to give scope to his own and his party's economic and social predilections.

spirit. The name "O'Fallon," in particular, had become a rallying point.

Valuation of public-utility property for rate-fixing purposes had long been a vexing public issue. Now it had become a bone of contention between the divergent wings of the Court. Chief Justice Taft disliked the whole problem and candidly confessed his incompetence, but he commented: "We have some experts on our Court. One is Pierce Butler, the other is Brandeis."[1] The "experts," unfortunately, were in complete disagreement. Butler, as a railroad attorney, had argued successfully that "reproduction cost" was the correct basis of valuation. On the Court, with the aid of like-minded colleagues, he elevated this theory to the status of a constitutional directive. "It has failed," Brandeis had countered, bitterly assailing this "good times" formula, "to afford adequate protection either to capital or to the public. It leaves open the door to grave injustice."[2] The famous O'Fallon Railway rate case of 1929, featuring these judicial differences, drew national attention, especially the dissenting opinions of Stone and Brandeis.[3]

Under the Transportation Act of 1920 railroads earning more than 6 per cent of their valuation were required to pay half the excess into a fund administered by the Interstate Commerce Commission for the benefit of less prosperous roads. Administration of this provision demanded a rate-base determination for each road, but the act gave the Commission no clear guide. Section 15a directed the ICC to "give due consideration to all the elements of value recognized by the law of the land for rate-making purposes"—hardly a precise formula. The railroads, of course, were interested in as high a valuation as possible, in order that their earnings would not exceed the 6 per cent limit. In the inflation of the 1920s this meant valuation weighted toward "reproduction cost"—that is, on the current, higher cost of replacing the total investment. One observer believed that such a formula would increase the valuation of the nation's railroads 10 billion dollars,[4] thus enabling the roads to charge higher rates without approaching the 6 per cent level set by Congress.

In the O'Fallon case the majority of the Commission had found that "the value of the property of railroads for rate-making purposes . . . approaches more nearly the reasonable and necessary investment than the cost of reproducing it at a particular time."[5] Had this view prevailed, the total of the original investment plus subsequent investments would have been below the inflated "reproduction cost" rate and the road's profits would have had to remain lower to avoid Government expropriation. But the railroad experts, falling back on precedent, denied the Commission's view; so did a majority of the Supreme Court. Relying on the "reproduction cost" rule, adopted by the minority of the ICC, they successfully argued that income in excess of 6 per cent had not been earned and therefore the Commission could not collect the payments it sought.

Justice McReynolds, speaking for the Court and following the ICC minority, ruled that in determinations of the Commission's majority sufficient weight had not been given the principle of "reproduction cost." In a masterful dissent Brandeis depicted the practical difficulties of applying this rule, as well as the fallacy of attempting to use "market value" primarily in the determination of earnings without weighing other considerations affecting "valuation" for rate purposes. Stone and Holmes joined in the dissent, and Brandeis and Holmes, in turn, concurred in Stone's persuasive exposé. By utilizing the very premise of the Court's majority, he uncovered grievous flaws in the reasoning. The Commission had, in fact, received evidence as to the present reproduction value of the small road's property; it had given "proof of reproduction cost all the weight to which it was entitled on its merits. . . . Had the Commission not turned aside to point out in its report the economic fallacies of the use of reproduction cost as a standard of value for rate-making purposes, which it nevertheless considered and to some extent applied," he commented discerningly, "I suppose it would not have occurred to anyone to question the validity of its order."[6]

This Court, Stone concluded, "has said that present reproduction costs must be considered in ascertaining value for rate-making purposes. But it has not said that such evidence, when fairly considered, may not be outweighed by other considerations affecting value, or that any evidence of present reproduction costs, when compared with all the other factors affecting value, must be given a weight to which it is not entitled in the judgment of the tribunal [the ICC] 'informed by experience' and 'appointed by law' to deal with the very problem now presented."[7]

For Stone the case raised issues of statutory interpretation and judicial power rather than differences of social and economic policy. The small block of vociferous insurgents in the Senate who opposed Hughes' confirmation made no such distinction. For them, the majority opinion in the O'Fallon case was but the reflection of economic and social preference. The addition of Hughes to the High Court would, they thought, serve only to entrench outmoded economics.

Even more distasteful to them was Justice Sutherland's subsequent ruling in the Baltimore Street Railways case that a rate permitting the company to earn only 6.26 per cent on its investment was "confiscatory." The Three Musketeers again protested. Realizing that hyper-inflated values, based on purely hypothetical reproduction cost in terms of 1930 prices, would impose crushing tolls for essential services, Brandeis contended that the only equitable and safe foundation of value was original cost plus prudent investment. Stone, agreeing with Brandeis, elaborated the argument in a separate dissent. The depreciation allowance necessary "to replace all the elements of a composite property purchased at various times . . . is," Stone declared, "a question not of law but of fact."[8] Apparently hopeful of persuading the obdurate brethren to reconsider, he circulated a memorandum calling attention to "aspects of the present case which should be argued and considered before we can arrive at the conclusion that the rate upheld by the state court is confiscatory."* "The Fourteenth Amendment," he reminded them, "no more guarantees to a public service company the right to earn the unnecessary cost of capital invested in an uneconomic financial structure, than that it be permitted to earn any other unnecessary expense of an uneconomically managed business. . . ." If the Baltimore Street Railways experienced financing difficulties upon a return of 6.26 per cent, "it is not because the permitted return is too low, but because there is doubt whether it will be earned. Doubt of the capacity of the business to earn the permitted return but reflects doubts upon the correctness of the assumed valuation." More was involved in the case than met the eye. "The cost of capital for many public service companies," Stone wrote a Columbia Law School friend, "is enormously increased by faulty financial structure, which no doubt has played a part in determining what is an adequate return on their property."[9] "These are times when we need to be more economists than lawyers," he commented.[10]

"I have just finished," Professor Frankfurter wrote Stone, January 13, "the reading of the January 6th batch of opinions . . . and I find I am deeply in your debt—all of us are, who really care about our constitutional system and your Court, and are apprehensive over the prevailing trend to read personal limitations of outlook or economics into the Constitution. Only such dissenting disavowals as the youngest and the two oldest members have been giving will help soften the mischief of 'self-inflicted wounds' of which Hughes spoke in his work on the Supreme Court."†

* It was not until twelve years later that Stone found an opportunity to set forth his flexible approach to rate-making problems. "Writing for the Court in *Federal Power Commission* v. *Natural Gas Pipeline Co.* (315 U.S. 575, p. 586) in 1942, he held that the 'Constitution does not bind rate-making bodies to the service of any single formula or combination of formulas.' They are free, he asserted, to make the 'pragmatic adjustments which may be called for by particular circumstances.'" (Herbert Wechsler, "Stone and the Constitution," *Columbia Law Review*, Sept. 1946, p. 780.)

† "In three notable instances," Hughes wrote in *The Supreme Court of the United States* (p. 50) "the Court has suffered from self-inflicted wounds." The three cases referred to are: *Dred Scott*, 19 How. 393 (1854), *Knox* v. *Lee*, 12 Wall. 457 (1872), and *Pollock* v. *Farmers' Loan and Trust Co.*, 157 U.S. 429 (1895).

In the backwash of public resentment against these rulings, President Hoover nominated Hughes (who, along with John W. Davis, had been of counsel for the railroad in the O'Fallon case) to succeed Chief Justice Taft. On the surface the President's choice seemed admirable. An eminent Wall Street lawyer and man of unquestioned integrity, Hughes, as Associate Justice from 1910 until 1916 had demonstrated qualities of judicial statesmanship. As Secretary of State, he had given dignity, even distinction, to Harding's shabby administration. Yet the nominee had been strangely apprehensive when the President broached the appointment. "I don't want a fight over the nomination," Hughes had told the President. "If you are convinced that the nomination will be confirmed by the Senate without a scrap, I will accept it. But I don't want any trouble about it."[11]

Hoover gave calm and confident assurance that there would be no trouble, and it looked at first as though he might be right. Senator George Norris, insurgent Republican and chairman of the Senate Judiciary Committee, told reporters "that favorable action would be taken at the regular meeting of the committee, to be held next Monday."[12] But, oddly enough, the committee recommended confirmation a few days later by a split vote of 10 to 2—Norris himself was one of the dissenters. For reasons still unclear, the Nebraska Senator changed his mind and declared himself ready to lead the opposition. On February 10, 1930, Norris took the Senate floor to announce the committee's decision and the reasons for his dissent.

President Hoover had unwittingly cleared the way for a significant and meaningful debate on the role of the Supreme Court in American politics. What qualities, if any, other than honesty and membership of the bar, should be required of one appointed to the Nation's highest bench? Is the appointee's intellectual outlook relevant? If so, how can it be fitted into the ambiguous precepts of constitutional interpretation? This time, unlike the 1925 fight over Stone's confirmation, there were no diverting side issues—no Ownbey affair, no Wheeler case— to obscure these basic questions.

Hughes' confirmation was objectionable on two grounds: Senator Norris questioned the propriety of the former Justice's return to the bench after resigning in 1916 to essay presidential politics; and, more important, he believed "we have reached a time in our history when the power and influence of monopoly and organized wealth are reaching into every governmental activity." "Perhaps," the Senator explained, "it is not far amiss to say that no man in public life so exemplifies the influence of powerful combinations in the political and financial world as does Mr. Hughes."[13]

"All men, whether on or off the bench, are human," Norris continued, "and it is only natural that those who have always been connected with monopoly, who have always been serving powerful industry and great combinations, should be even unconsciously influenced in their very nature and at least partially controlled by such associations. . . . In my judgment men should not be elevated [to the Court] . . . who have lived this one-sided life, and where the men who toil and the men who suffer have not been within the vision of the person who is to be elevated to the position of supreme and final arbitrator."

"I am aware," the Senator concluded somewhat apologetically, "that it will be said that I should not oppose the confirmation of Mr. Hughes simply because I do not agree with him on these great fundamental issues. . . . Nevertheless, I am not willing that this program should be carried out and brought further to its ultimate fruition by any vote of mine."*

"We, in passing upon these nominations," Senator La Follette said, "are filling the jury box which ultimately will decide the issue between organized greed and the rights of the masses of this country. If that be the situation, the Court is responsible for it."[14]

No longer circumspect, lest they discredit the orthodox theory that judges exert only judgment, not will, Hughes' critics stated flatly that they would have to explore Supreme Court appointments because the Court itself had become a power group. Why, the Senators fumed, should discussion of the nominee's fitness be confined to the legal aspect? "Can it be true," Senator Tom Connally of Texas asked, "that in passing upon the competency of a man to sit upon this or any other court the mind of the Senate is to be closed to all questions except that of the character of the appointee and whether or not he is versed in law?"[15]

Featuring the Court's recent rulings in the O'Fallon and Baltimore Street Railways cases, the Senate aired for the first time the private opinions of a Supreme Court nominee. These decisions were cited as examples of a long-range trend, illustrating how "the Supreme Court in recent years has gone far afield from its original function and has constituted itself a court in economics and in the determination of social questions rather than in the interpretation of statutes passed with reference to the Constitution itself."[16]

---

* Norris's opposition was to Hughes' economic and social views; he conceded his "great talents as a lawyer." Indeed, it was because of the distinction Hughes had achieved that the Senator was unusually circumspect. This was one of the few occasions, perhaps the only one, in which he took the trouble to write out the speech he intended to make in the Senate, "so that there could be no possible misunderstanding or misinterpretation of my words." (*Fighting Liberal: The Autobiography of George W. Norris* [New York: The Macmillan Co., 1945], pp. 373-74). Apparently Norris never recanted, though he did praise some of Hughes' opinions, attributing these to the fight he waged in the Senate against the Chief Justice's confirmation. (See Alfred Lief, *Democracy's Norris* [New York: Stackpole & Hecht, 1939], p. 381.)

The insurgents pointed out that the Court had become "a great political body, appointed very often through political influence, passing on political questions, fixing policies for the people, legislating when they should leave that to Congress."[17] "The Supreme Court," said Senator Wheeler, "is not only determining legal questions but it is likewise determining the great economic questions." Senator Borah went even further. "Under the Fourteenth Amendment the Supreme Court of the United States, as to most questions of a nature similar to the one which the Court passed upon in the railway case, becomes really the economic dictator in the United States." Senator Norris stated the issue bluntly: "We have a legislative body, called the House of Representatives, of over four hundred men. We have another legislative body, called the Senate, of less than a hundred men. We have, in reality, another legislative body, called the Supreme Court, of nine men; and they are more powerful than all the others put together."[18]

The main burden of it all was that the Justices had virtually annexed the power of a super-legislature. In determining controversial social and economic policy, they had been guided by political considerations rather than the Constitution. Judicial aggrandizement had thus carried the Court to the point where legal competence was only one—and perhaps not the most important—test of fitness for judicial service. Hughes was opposed because his appointment would presumably reinforce what Senator Dill of Washington had described as "a judicial system of law that is fast bringing economic slavery in this country." "If the system of judicial law that is being written in defiance of state legislation and of congressional legislation is continued," the Senator observed prophetically, "there is no human power in America that can keep the Supreme Court from becoming a political issue, nationwide, in the not far-distant future."[19]

Hughes' confirmation by 52 to 26, with 18 not voting, was almost anticlimactic. But the senatorial inquisition was not finished. To fill the vacancy created by the death of Justice Sanford, President Hoover nominated John J. Parker, North Carolina Circuit Court Judge. As a North Carolina Republican, Parker's nomination had been urged on Hoover as a "master political stroke."

Again the President's political stratagem went awry. Parker failed to win Senate confirmation, largely because of his alleged conservative opinions, particularly in labor cases and his attitude on civil rights for Negroes.[20] In a halting attempt to console him, Stone wrote: "I don't know of anything that gives less satisfaction than a letter such as I am writing now. Yet I don't feel like going away for the summer holiday without letting you know how sorry I am that you received the treatment, at the hands of the Senate, which you did.

It was an unhappy combination of circumstances which brought about the result, such as has happened more than once in the history of the country. But you have the consolation of knowing that what the Senate does or fails to do cannot affect your capacity to do good judicial work, and to increase the good reputation which you have established as a Judge."[21]

Stone attributed Judge Parker's rejection, in part, "to the debate and hard feeling that was stirred up over the Hughes nomination." Parker was, he said, "the unfortunate victim of the circumstances which have developed this issue, for he is really a very decent sort of a chap."[22]

Following Parker's defeat,* generally interpreted as a blow at conservatism, President Hoover nominated Owen J. Roberts of Philadelphia. Roberts had made a national reputation as prosecutor in the Teapot Dome scandal. Confirmation followed quickly and liberal spirits rose again.†

The progressive campaign waged against Hughes had been exploratory and educational. Accepting confirmation as a foregone conclusion, the insurgents merely had wished, as Senator Dill said, "to place in the Record . . . a warning, . . . to call the attention of the people of this country to the fact that if they would free themselves and have justice at the hands of their Government they must reach the Supreme Court of the United States by putting men on that bench

---

* A few years later Stone's temper rose sharply when Pearson and Allen asserted in The Nine Old Men, without qualifications: "Stone had warned Hoover against the appointment of John J. Parker." "My attention has just been called," the Justice wrote Parker, Jan. 31, 1937, "to a statement appearing in a recent scandal book to the effect that I warned President Hoover against your nomination. The impression created is that I was opposed to it, which is quite a mistaken one. It is true that I warned him that there might be opposition of the character which afterward developed, in the hope that he would take precautionary measures to forestall it. I have always thought if that had been done that the outcome might have been different. Having had some experience with the difficulties of judicial decisions on labor problems I perhaps appreciated it more than others." Stone had, in fact, supported Parker for Attorney General in a memorandum of Feb. 14, 1929. "He is a man of vigorous, attractive personality," Stone had written Presidential Secretary Lawrence Richey, "is said to try cases very well and, on the whole, made a favorable impression on me as a man of character and ability." Destiny, however, pointed to William D. Mitchell, whom President Hoover nominated for the post.

† Stone appraised Roberts, whom he knew only by reputation, as a very good man. "He is a hard worker, has a good mind, and has had a wide range of experience," he wrote his sons, May 15, 1930. "I should expect him to deal in the liberal way with important constitutional problems, because he has the type of mind that would take in all aspects of a problem." A few less sanguine voices were raised. "What his [Roberts'] constitutional background is," Learned Hand wrote H.F.S., May 29, 1930, "I don't know, but we must live in hopes. Just at present it ain't so promising; but the flag will fly while the Three Musketeers remain on the job. Thank God for that."

who hold economic theories which are fair and just to all, and not in the interest of the privileged few."[23]

"We all realized from the very beginning," Senator Norris commented, "that we had no hope of victory. . . . Yet we feel justified in having taken up the time of the Senate . . . to call to the attention of all our liberty-loving citizens the terrible condition that confronts us." The insurgents had fought this battle in "a conscientious belief that . . . profit will come perhaps even to the Supreme Court if they will read the debates of the Senate, and if the majority members of that Court will even read the dissenting opinions of their brethren, Brandeis, Holmes, and Stone."[24]

In this respect, the debates afforded a dramatic prelude to the more stirring events of 1936 and 1937. The questioning senators did not insist that Supreme Court Justices become crusading liberals. Rather, they directed their fire against those constitutional rigidities which suggested that the founding fathers dictated cramping judicial decisions and that judges must not tamper with their handiwork. The senators urged only that the Court take to heart the avowed principles of judicial self-restraint, and one commentator ventured the opinion that Hughes would be "a better Chief Justice for the experience" to which he had been subjected.[25] The opposition aimed more at the Supreme Court itself than at the particular men nominated for it. "The attack centered," the staid *Washington Star* commented, "on the Court itself."[26] By calling public attention to the Court's discretionary power, the senators hoped to destroy "the 'hush-hush' that has protected"[27] that institution.

"The debates," Stone observed, "really have, I think, a great deal more significance than many people think, and reflect the deep concern of a good many people over what they conceive to be the tendency of the Court to enlarge its powers, and to read into the Constitution* and laws of the United States the social and economic philosophy of the Court or a majority of it."[28]

Nor had the effort been exerted in vain. At long last even professors of constitutional law were alerted to the fact that the business of judging involves lawmaking, even constitution-making. In the introduction to his 1930 edition of *The Constitution and What It Means Today*, Professor Edward S. Corwin asserted: "Judicial review, [far]

* "What is there in the Constitution," the *Baltimore Sun* asked, Feb. 13, 1930, "that gives any guidance as to whether 5, 6, or 8 per cent is a fair return on public-utility property? . . . And what is there that sheds any light on the question of whether utilities shall be valued for rate-making purposes at what they originally cost, or what it would cost to reproduce them at current prices? There is not a shadow of a clue. The issues involved must be settled by the application of highly controversial economic theories." At the request of Senator Carter Glass of Virginia, the *Sun* editorial was reprinted in the *Congressional Record*, Vol. 72 (1930), p. 3553.

from being an instrument for the application of the Constitution, tends to supplant it. In other words, the discretion of the judges tends to supplant it." The identical disclosure came more tersely that same year from the Harvard Law School. "The Supreme Court," Professor Felix Frankfurter said, "*is* the Constitution." "Let us face the fact that five Justices of the Supreme Court *are* molders of policy, rather than impersonal vehicles of revealed truth."[29] The Senate debates had driven home the fact that judicial decisions threatened to make government impossible.

Shortly after Hughes' confirmation Professor Frankfurter discussed "recent events" with Justice Stone and went away impressed by "the statesmanlike interpretation that you placed upon the outbursts in the Senate and in the country."[30] Stone interpreted the Senate fight not as a personal attack on Hughes but as evidence of "wholesome interest in what the Court was doing." "I wonder if you read the debates in the *Congressional Record* over the Hughes nomination," Stone asked a former law clerk. "There were some pretty severe things said about the Court and for the first time since the Dred Scott decision there were extended debates over the opinions of the courts. The O'Fallon case and the Baltimore Railways case seem to incite the most interest."[31]

"I often wonder," he wrote John Bassett Moore somewhat later, "whether people at large will ever grasp what is going on in the work of our Court. . . . I have always believed, though, that in the long run the tendencies of its work would not go unnoticed. Consequently, I was not as surprised as some at the outburst over the Hughes nomination, although its suddenness and violence was a little startling. The curious thing about it is, though, that there are a good many who are playing the role of statesmen who, I think, have missed its significance completely."[32]

Frankfurter kept Stone posted on political trends. He interpreted the increasing number of requests coming to him for articles and addresses on the Court as manifestations of a growing interest in the issues raised by recent decisions. "I quite agree with you," Stone replied. "There is a very surprising but I think wholesome interest in what the Court is doing, and a disposition to study and discuss it with real intelligence. What troubles me most about it is that some of the people who ought to be quickest to see this and most prompt to give present tendencies a different trend, seem not to appreciate the situation. I think one aspect of the matter which is not adequately understood is that it is not *a contest between conservatism and radicalism, nearly so much as it is a difference arising from an inadequate understanding of the relation of law to the social and economic forces which control society.*"[33]

"A lot of people," Stone continued suggestively, "think law, especially in our Court, is a system of mathematics. Sometimes, though, I think if it were applied with scientific precision that we might come out better than we do. . . . Why don't you write a restrained, considered article," he suggested, "dealing with the whole matter?"*

The article Justice Stone wished to have Frankfurter write came out in *The Forum*, June 1930. It seemed odd to Professor Frankfurter that Hughes, or anyone else appointed a Supreme Court Justice, should have expected, or even desired, immunity from public exploration of his views. "Surely the men who wield the power of life and death over the political decisions of legislatures and executives," Frankfurter wrote, "should be subjected to the most vigorous scrutiny before being given that power. Public opinion, the President, and the Senate should all have a lively understanding of what the appointment of a Supreme Court Justice means. . . . It is not good, either for the country or the Court, that the part played by the Court in the life of the country should be shrouded in mystery." In support of his thesis, Frankfurter quoted Justice Brewer's "memorable words" of 1898: " 'The time is past in the history of the world when any living man or body of men can be set on a pedestal and decorated with a halo.' "[34]

Justice Stone, praising the article as an "excellent job," inquired: "Where did you find that statement of Justice Brewer's?† It is something I have been saying often of late, but I didn't know I had such eminent backing."

Stone made no predictions as to how the 1930 appointments might affect judicial decisions. "Such appointments are often a lottery," he

* At the same time Stone recommended Judge Proskauer's recent article in *Harper's* (April 1930) on the dissenting opinion as "good and very instructive." The Justice had written Proskauer, March 21, 1930: "Somehow, dissenting opinions always seem to me a dismal business. When I do it I feel somewhat as the smart youth ought to feel when he proclaims his opinion, which has not proved convincing to older and wiser men. This feeling has kept me silent sometimes when I had the inclination to speak, but I soon found that when I remained silent, despite strongly held convictions the other way, I was not altogether happy with myself. As I have to live with myself for some time, I hope, I have come to the conclusion that I ought to do it on amicable terms. Your paper will serve a very useful purpose in enlightening many people who think that a judicial decision ought to be as certain and free from differing opinions as the solution of a mathematical problem—in fact, though, I believe the mathematicians cannot always agree."

† "It is a mistake to suppose," Brewer said, "that the Supreme Court is either honored or helped by being spoken of as beyond criticism. On the contrary, the life and character of its Justices should be the objects of constant watchfulness by all, and its judgments subject to the freest criticism. . . . True, many criticisms may be, like their authors, devoid of good taste, but better all sorts of criticism than no criticism at all. The moving waters are full of life and health; only in the still waters is stagnation and death." (David J. Brewer, Lincoln Day Address of 1898.)

commented later on. "It is very difficult to predict from a man's past experience just what he will do as a Supreme Court judge. Independence of mind and intellectual integrity are of first importance, as well as some understanding of the social and economic forces which dominate the world. If, in addition to that, the man chosen has learning and great capacity for the grinding work of the Court, the appointment will be a fortunate one."[35]

The lawmakers of 1930 had raised a warning flag. In the years ahead the Court would continue its role as supreme arbiter of state and national policy at its own risk. Hereafter any persistent disregard of the enlightened principle of judicial self-restraint seemed almost certain to jeopardize both its power and prestige. Far from opposing critical scrutiny of the Court and its judgments, Justice Stone welcomed it as "wholesome"—perhaps as necessary to ward off an embarrassing impasse between Court and Congress. The power to govern was needed, as never before, and yet the effectiveness of that power—even its existence—turned absolutely on the votes of nine men appointed for life and politically responsible to no one.

Could the Constitution be made to function, and thus meet the requirements of modern government? Or would it, as Al Smith suggested, have to be "wrapped up and put on a shelf for the duration of the crisis?" What was the Court's proper role in the fierce power struggle characteristic of every free society? Had it, along with Congress and the President, a constructive part to play in satisfying human aspirations for freedom?

CHAPTER NINETEEN

# The Votes Count

## 1930-1931

As the 1930 term opened, certain commentators cast doubt on the forebodings of senators who had opposed the new Chief Justice's confirmation. "It will be remembered," one observer noted, "that when Justice Stone was appointed by President Coolidge, similar objections were raised against him by the 'liberals' in the Senate. But it has so turned out that on questions where there is a cleavage between what may be loosely termed as conservatives and liberals, Justice Stone has more often adhered to the views expressed by Justices Brandeis and

Holmes. And thus far it may be observed that every opinion rendered by Chief Justice Hughes has been in favor of what might be termed the 'liberal' viewpoint."[1]

Stone's own outlook became increasingly identified as "liberal." In certain quarters it was equated with the point of view voiced in the *New Republic* and the *Nation*. Though these sprightly weeklies, of which he was an avid reader, found few occasions to admire his craft in tax decisions, his skill in applying equity doctrine, or his mastery of the science underlying patent matters, they sometimes featured his dissents in cases dealing with basic social and economic issues. Food for thought as well as encouragement came also from the law schools—from Thomas Reed Powell and Felix Frankfurter at Harvard, from Robert L. Hale and Milton Handler, a former law clerk turned teacher, at Columbia.* Powell's caustically humorous thrusts amused him and he sometimes showed them "to one of my brethren who has preserved a sense of humor."[2] The Justice glowed under the paeans of congratulations pouring in from Professor Felix Frankfurter. By 1930 Frankfurter's communiqués appeared with such regularity that if no word had come from Cambridge on a Wednesday following the delivery of opinions on Monday, the Justice was apt to ask his law clerk for explanation.

"I always ask myself after leaving you," the Harvard professor wrote, "why we cannot have enough like you on the Court to prevent some of the foolishness, particularly of recent years. For the Lord knows that you don't want to turn the country upside down, or prevent men from earning an honest or even profitable living, or make any other inroads on what may be called old-fashioned Americanism. But somehow or other, high intelligence, awareness that judges are profoundly important, even more than legislators—all these seem to be rare qualities for five men to have all at one time! And so I conclude, sufficient unto the day is the goodness thereof, and express gratitude that you are where you are."[3]

Stone's Republican convictions were strong. His social and economic views were in general accord with those of his right-wing colleagues. As a Supreme Court Justice, however, he was now usually joined with Holmes and Brandeis. The explanation was the simple one he

---

* After Karl Llewellyn's path-breaking lectures on "Law and Its Study" appeared in 1930, Stone wrote him, Jan. 6, 1931, suggesting that he put the lectures in permanent form. The "philosophical aspects of the law" should be annotated, he said, by "some examples, horrible and otherwise, of how courts have actually proved your point. . . . In fact, I should like to send copies to some of my associates, even though they might be shocked at the idea that things are to be learned by men in their exalted position from mere professors." The Llewellyn lectures, entitled *The Bramble Bush*, were published in 1930 for the use of Columbia Law students. The point for which Stone might have cited familiar examples appears in Llewellyn's discussion of the doctrine of precedent, pp. 64-65.

had elaborated during the Senate fight against Hughes: the contest within the Court arose out of fundamental differences as to the relation of law and of the judicial process to "the social and economic forces which control society." Stone believed profoundly in the correctness of his judicial approach and expressed cold contempt for formalists, "for people who think law, especially in our Court, is a system of mathematics."[4] Still there were moments of doubt. A persistently obstructive role made him uncomfortable. "It is good to know," he replied to one of Frankfurter's effusions, "that independent minds see something in my position. Otherwise, I should have the kind of fear that I used to have when I went into the trial of a case, feeling that the other side had no case and knowing that such was likely to be a dangerous situation for my client."[5]

The narrow margin separating the Court's divergent wings made the votes of the newcomers crucial. Stone himself speculated on how "changed personnel" would affect judicial decision and avidly read the Chief Justice's American Bar Association address that summer, which stressed the importance of preserving the rights of the states from federal encroachments.[6] But this served to confuse rather than clarify. "I did not observe," Stone commented, "that he mentioned his role in the . . . recent Missouri Insurance Co. case,* as exemplifying his advice."[7] Justice Butler had also made weighty pronouncements. In an address delivered in St. Louis, he had "decried any disposition of judges to write their own personal views into the Constitution so as to uphold unconstitutional legislation, and had asserted the duty of judges to confine themselves to applying the law of the Constitution 'as it is written.'" "Thus," Stone quipped, "we live and learn." He surmised that what Butler meant to say is that "nothing is easier for a Justice than to profess not to do that which he does."[8]

Stone's first assignments under the new Chief Justice included several technical cases. "I rather enjoy writing a patent opinion as an intellectual exercise," he commented at the end of the 1930 term, "although I often think it is a futile line of business compared with some of the other cases we have."[9] As an ally of Holmes and Brandeis in dissent, he had, from the first, indicated a strong interest in the techniques of dealing with constitutional issues and utilized every op-

---

* The Chief Justice had concurred in an opinion by Justice Butler in which an insurance company escaped state taxation on the theory that the Constitution requires that in ascertaining the taxable net worth of its assets, tax-exempt bonds must be excluded from the computation. "That conclusion," Stone wrote in dissent, "appears to me to open a new and hitherto unsuspected field of operation for the immunity from taxation enjoyed by national and state securities as instrumentalities of Government, and to accord to their owners a privilege which is not justified by anything that has been decided or said by this Court." (*Missouri v. Gehner*, 281 U.S. 314 [1930], p. 322.) Stone was joined by Justices Holmes and Brandeis.

portunity to round out his conception of the judicial process. *Per curiams*—cases disposed of without opinion—were kept under close surveillance and frequently used as precedents. Ever alert to the dangers of a "little loose talk" in opinions, he regarded "the old practice of overruling in silence or . . . attempting to get around the difficulty by refinements and thin distinctions . . . almost as mischievous as the original fault."[10] He was careful to square his own decisions with the precedents or to slash the earlier doctrine inconsistent therewith. But the extent to which he was allowed to do this depended upon the willingness of the brethren to cooperate. They did not always agree that an outworn principle should be openly discarded. When this happened, Stone chafed.

Conspicuous examples of his judicial technique appeared in cases on constitutional immunity from taxation of federal and state instrumentalities. From the outset he had doubted whether corollaries of the doctrines of *McCulloch* v. *Maryland* and *Collector* v. *Day*[11] did not unduly interfere with the reasonable exercise of governmental power. Chief Justice Marshall, he said, had dealt "with the whole question as an infringement of sovereignty and had treated the sovereignty infringed as though it were that of a government wholly foreign to the taxing government. . . . And thus . . . he left out of account the necessity of making the two governments function together as part of one system."[12] By the time Stone reached the Court the immunity doctrine had been carried so far as seriously to curtail the sovereign taxing power of both governments.

Less than a year after taking his seat, he delivered the opinion of the Court in *Metcalf & Eddy* v. *Mitchell*, which held that consulting engineers employed under contract by a state, or its subdivisions, to advise them, but whose work was not continuous or permanent, were not exempt from national income tax on their compensation.[13] When, three years later, in *Macallen* v. *Massachusetts*, the Court held that a state tax on corporation franchises measured in part by net income, which included income from United States bonds, was unconstitutional, he, joined by Justices Holmes and Brandeis, dissented vigorously.[14]

After Hughes and Roberts joined the Court, the Justices were called upon in *Educational Films Corporation* v. *Ward* to consider the validity of a state franchise tax measured by net income as applied to a corporation deriving income from a federal copyright. The statute was upheld, the case being distinguished from Macallen because the legislation in this instance did not give any indication that it was "specifically intended" to reach income from tax-exempt sources.[15] Justice Stone spoke for the Court, with Justices Sutherland, Van Devanter, and Butler in dissent. Stone interpreted this decision as taking a "backtrack on the Macallen case," indicating that "the world does move after all."[16] This virtual overruling of precedent, without forthright acknowledgment of what had been done, aroused critical comment. Professor Thomas Reed Powell lampooned the majority in a lengthy "imaginary judicial opinion."

"Our problem," Mr. "Justice" Powell declared, "has been less what we should decide than what we should say in our opinion. There is of course a long line of authority which sanctions the decision now rendered. Our only difficulty has been that of determining whether to confess frankly that the minority of the Macallen case has become a majority or to take advantage of the opinion in the Macallen case to confine that decision to grounds not inescapably available here. Upon due reflection we have decided to avoid frankness and to take advantage of the lack of frankness in the opinion in the Macallen case."[17]

Powell's forthright "judicial opinion" gave Stone "a good laugh." "I should have preferred to have written your opinion," Stone told him, "than the one which will actually appear in the books." But a serious note permeated his drollery. "Had I done so," Stone explained, "I should have been in a minority of two or three, instead of a majority of six. Someone else would have written the opinion and, I fear, would have said some approving words (what I have carefully avoided in this and other cases) of doctrine, about which the less said the better, unless it is to be flatly disapproved. In other words, you will see that I proceed upon the theory, which I am willing to admit may be a mistaken one, that the large objective should be kept constantly in mind and reached by whatever road is open, provided only that untenable distinctions are not taken, and that I am not, in the process, committed incidentally to the doctrine of which I disapprove or which would hinder the Court's coming out ultimately in the right place. All of this proves that the university professor is the only free man who can develop legal doctrine in his own way and travel the road he chooses in accounting for his conclusions."[18]

In the Educational Films case, the vote stood 6 to 3. A year later the Macallen decision was further undermined in *Pacific Co.* v. *Johnson.* But Stone, speaking for the Court, still felt impelled to distinguish the badly shaken precedent.[19] Again he was confronted with the "practical" necessity of placating a majority, which included McReynolds. While preparing the opinion, he brought persistent pressure on the Chief Justice to agree to a flat statement overruling the Macallen case. "Following our conversation this morning," he wrote the Chief Justice, January 29, 1932, "I drafted the insert which is attached to . . . the enclosed copy of the opinion." (The insert had been included at Hughes' insistence, incorporating a nonexistent distinction.) "After thinking it over, I decided to omit it from the circulated opinion, because it seemed to me that we ought to avoid the perpetuation of such narrow distinctions, if possible. It is too much like that one in the *Macallen Co.* v. *Massachusetts* to secure a different result. I, of course, recognize that I made one very much like it, *ex necessitate*, in the Educational Films case, but now I think there is an opportunity to get rid of it. I hope you agree. But if not, if the necessity arises, we can fall back on this distinction to bring the present case under the Educational Films case, but I think that would be a misfortune."

Hughes apparently equivocated but leaned toward the inclusion of the fine-spun distinction. When Sutherland's dissent came in, forthright and hard-hitting as usual, Stone took up the question again. "I quite agree," he commented, "with his [Sutherland's] statement that the Macallen case ought to be overruled, and I hope that it will be possible for me to add at the end of my opinion the following: '*Macallen* v. *Massachusetts*, so far as inconsistent with this opinion, is overruled. . . .' Everything," he went on, "now depends on Mr. Justice McReynolds, from whom I have not heard."[20]

On March 22 Stone circulated another memorandum suggesting explicit destruction of the authoritative force of the earlier decision. "I think this should be done in justice to Massachusetts," he contended, "so that it may be left free to tax corporate franchises measured by non-taxables, as California is permitted to do by this decision." "I agree," Hughes scrawled on Stone's memorandum, "but should not press for a statement to that effect if it was not supported by a majority." Without Hughes' active support—which was not forthcoming—Stone could muster no more than four Justices for his position. Accordingly, no statement expressly repudiating the Macallen decision appears in the official report.

"I am still a bit puzzled," Stone wrote, "to know how the Court ever brought itself to put the kibosh on the Macallen case. Its performance in that direction is almost as marvelous and difficult to understand as some of its others with which I do not agree. I feel fairly well satisfied with the opinion of the Pacific Company case, except that it should have had added at the end a single sentence, stating that the Macallen case is now overruled. However, I think that fact will penetrate even the dullest intellect." "I hope," he went on, "Massachusetts will now have the courage to enforce the law overruled in the Macallen case and see what happens."[21] It seemed "a pity to draw fine distinctions in order to save any part of the Macallen case, but one must deal with situations as he finds them." "It seems," the Justice had earlier written Thomas Reed Powell, "that it will not do to let the bar understand that our decisions are not the product of rigid logic."²² Such subterfuge was not easily executed. To maintain the semblance of consistency in this particular area, the Justices had, Stone suggested, to rival the "artistic excellence of the circles cut by a dog when he chases his own tail."²³

Despite failure to win a specific overruling of the tenuous Macallen precedent, the Pacific Company decision raised Stone's spirits. Previously he had doubted the effectiveness of dissenting opinions and expressed reluctance against appearing so often in the role of dissenter.* Now, at long last, the Court began retracing its steps, returning to the very positions he had espoused in dissenting opinions from the start. His convictions as to the rightness of his views thus reinforced, he could not remain silent. "I must either speak," he told John Bassett Moore, "or leave the Court."²⁴ Henceforth "the desire to preserve intellectual integrity" would be his "main motive for continuing to say my say." "Incidentally," he added, "I think it inspires a little caution on the part of some of my brethren, but not many."²⁵

Encouragement in his new resolve came, as usual, from the law schools. In response to Stone's apology that one of his dissents merely reiterated earlier views, Frankfurter wrote: "For Heaven's sake, don't get the notion that you are 'repeating the old story' or, in the alternative, that it does not need to be repeated. After all, you are an educator, even more so on the Supreme Court than you were off it. . . . The whole nation is your class. . . . Don't let yourself get weary of well-doing."²⁶

Stone utilized every opportunity to persuade members of the Court to a more forthright recognition of the doctrinal implications of current decisions. Even when the prospect seemed well-nigh hopeless, he urged his colleagues to clear out the dead wood left in their paths. "I am very sorry," he informed Justice McReynolds, "to see the matter settled without some reference to the Billings case which seems to me to be overruled in principle by the present decision and your view in Blodgett v. Holden."²⁷ By and large his efforts seemed to fall on barren ground.

Before the end of Hughes' first term as Chief Justice, Stone was convinced that "the prediction so freely made last spring that a new era in the history of our Court was dawning seems not to be fully realized."²⁸ His misgivings also included Justice Roberts. The most

---

* "It is a rather interesting fact," he commented in a letter to John Bassett Moore, Oct. 18, 1930, "that the only regret that has grown out of my judicial career up to the present is for my failure sometimes to speak out instead of remaining silent. I have so often differed with the Court and said so, that I have felt under some restraint to pass in silence expositions with which I did not agree where only matters of statutory construction were involved, but I am not at all sure that this is good practice."

important opinion delivered in the 1930 term revealed to Stone the disaffection of the new Associate Justice.

With the support of Brandeis and Holmes, Stone dissented forcefully from the Court's ruling that the ICC had no control over the disposition of a $9,000,000 fund collected from security owners in the Chicago, Milwaukee and St. Paul Railroad during the reorganization of their company—the then largest bankruptcy in history.[29] As the directors demonstrated their incompetence and the once proud St. Paul Railroad staggered into receivership, the bankers appeared on the scene with their trusty vassals, the lawyers. Together they worked out a scheme for re-establishing the railroad under a new company and mapped out the strategy for putting this plan into effect, including the all-important feature of control remaining in the hands of the bankers until the new company took over. The attorneys were most helpful, selecting the court and the judge who could be relied on to appoint the "right" receivers. They assisted in the establishment of "reorganization committees," ostensibly to represent the various classes of security holders, actually minions of the bankers. An eminent Wall Street lawyer was the chief draftsman of the "Reorganization Agreement" binding the bankers and the reorganization committees created to re-establish the company. This plan was swiftly approved by the federal court, over the loud protest of "independent" reorganization committees representing an obdurate minority of security owners who would not submit to the bankers.

The imprimatur of the Interstate Commerce Commission was not so easily obtained. After exhaustive investigation and hearings, the Commissioners, in the words of their dissenting chairman, Joseph B. Eastman, found "themselves faced with the alternatives of either approving a poor plan or compelling the negotiation of new agreements with the likelihood of further considerable delay and expense in taking the railroad out of receivership. In this dilemma they choose approval of the plan as the lesser evil in the public interest."[30] Although the Commission reluctantly sanctioned transfer of the St. Paul property to the new company and the issuance of new securities in accordance with the plan, it retained for further scrutiny the bankers' proposals for distributing funds composed of contributions from investors.

The prospective beneficiaries of this lush fund, the bankers, their lawyers and reorganization managers, accepted the major part of the Commission's order and consummated the reorganization. Next they denied that the ICC had any power to condition its sanction for this reorganization plan upon later approval of the reorganization fees. Private investors had lost half a billion dollars in the long-drawn-out collapse and reorganization, but this did not prevent tedious argument for control of the funds from which fees were to be paid.

In the High Court, the New York corporation counsel who had figured prominently in the case since 1925 gave place to another, John W. Davis. To bolster their theory of the control of reorganization fees, the lawyers argued that the Reorganization Agreement was but a private contract between individuals to which—by its terms—the reorganized railroad was not a party. None of the bankers, they argued, was a party to the ICC hearing, "although, the bankers and their lawyers were the persons who started and conducted that proceeding, and the new company was simply a technical device in their hands."[81]

The Wall Street lawyers persuaded a majority of the Supreme Court. Arrangement for payment of the special fund of expenses incurred and services rendered "in formulating and bringing out an approval of the plan" were, in Mr. Justice Sutherland's words, "matters in which the private parties alone were concerned."[32] By its condition, the ICC sought to control a contract not a part of interstate commerce "to which the carrier was not a party, in which the carrier had no enforceable interest, and which was not within the purview of the regulating power of the Commission."[33] The original lawyer's technicality—"the simple expedient of so arranging the reorganization plan that reorganization managers may retain and disburse, from the moneys paid in by the old stockholders . . . such amounts as may be required for reorganization expenses"[34]—so swayed a majority of the Court that it failed to discern the realities of the case.

The question before the Court, Justice Stone said in dissent, was whether the statutory provisions of the Interstate Commerce Commission could be avoided. Could "an issue of securities to defray excessive reorganization expenses" be withdrawn from the control of the body authorized by Congress? The majority of the Justices said "Yes." The astuteness of the bankers' lawyers in the drafting of the document had, they ruled, effectively deprived the Commission of power to enforce necessary public safeguards. By the Court's decision, the reorganization managers of the St. Paul secured a million and a half dollars for themselves, and a half-dozen New York law firms received an amount estimated by one of the managers to be in the neighborhood of a million dollars.[35]

Stone, joined by Brandeis and Holmes, forced his colleagues and the country to face up to facts ignored in the "Alice in Wonderland" majority opinion. St. Paul's investors, they pointed out, "inevitably uninformed," like thousands of other security holders, concurred in the "plan presented to them by the reorganizers because of lack of information and lack of any practical alternatives."[36] Through "legal forms" and "technical distinctions" six Supreme Court Justices had lost sight of the controlling consideration, that the St. Paul's "bankers, the present reorganization managers, were active in bringing about the receivership and have since dominated the reorganization." Even more shocking, the majority accepted the contention that the contract for the disposition of the special fund "was a mere private agreement unrelated to the issue of securities."[37] These, Stone said, were "technical distinctions" which "ought not to affect the authority of the Commission." As he saw it, the Commission's central concern for a secure, healthy, viable national transport network, gave it a primary interest in enhancing and protecting the marketability of railroad securities. Failure to attract new capital threatened the "permanency and stability" of the whole system.

"No one familiar with the financial and corporate history of this country," he wrote, "could say that railroad credit and the marketability of railroad securities have not been profoundly affected . . . by the numerous railroad reorganizations in the course of which junior security holders have found it impossible to save more than a remnant of their investment, and that only by the assumption of a heavy burden of expense, too often the result of wasteful and extravagant methods of reorganization."[38]

Not only had a responsible, recognized leader of the bar concocted the technical formula masking the operation of the bankers, but, in violation of the first tenets of equity, attorneys had challenged the condition imposed by the ICC "only after the reorganization had . . . become an accomplished fact by [their] . . . taking the benefit of so much of the order as suited [their] . . . purposes." Such questionable practices, Stone wrote wrathfully, failed "to conform to those elementary standards of fairness and good conscience which equity may always demand as a condition of its relief."[39] This ground alone justified a refusal to assist the bankers.*

United States Circuit Court Judge George W. Anderson praised Stone's dissent as "powerful and convincing," and criticized the majority opinion as calculated "to unduly cripple the Commission in the performance of its absolutely necessary functions and duties."[40]

"I am glad you liked my opinion in the St. Paul case," Stone replied. "One never knows how far he should go in setting up his own views as against those of the majority, but I have learned from experience that I lead a happier life when I have voiced my convictions. In this case it seemed to me important because I think it is still possible to accomplish something by legislation, notwithstanding the suggestion in the opinion of the Court that the control of abuses in railroad reorganization is beyond the power of Congress."[41]

"I hope when you have opportunity," Stone wrote John Bassett Moore February 13, 1931, "you will take a look at some of my remarks

---

* Following Stone's decision, Congress amended the statute giving the Interstate Commerce Commission power to scrutinize the fees paid to lawyers.

in the opinion which I sent you dealing with the St. Paul reorganization. With railroad receiverships actually impending and proposed consolidations which will require bankers' financing, the decision of the Court leaves us in a somewhat unfortunate situation, the more so as the majority opinion plainly intimates that power cannot constitutionally be conferred on the Interstate Commerce Commission to deal with the subject of reorganization expenses even when the expense fund is raised from stockholders of the old company through the issue of securities by the reorganized company, an interstate carrier."

"Only your dissent helps to assuage my feelings about the decision in the St. Paul Reorganization case," Frankfurter wrote. "If in these days of new types of casebooks one were to get out readings on unreality *versus* realism in law, I don't believe one could find better material than the majority opinion and your dissent. That such a formal device as was invented by some lawyer (I suspect it was Swaine) to circumvent control by the Interstate Commerce Commission of abuses in reorganization schemes through excessive fees should not only prevail with the Court, but should be elevated to the august level of constitutional right, would be ludicrous indeed were it not so tragic. That such things can come to pass and find in the American Constitution a shield will, I suspect, furnish the future historian of the United States not a little material for an understanding of the social development in this country.

"This is why your dissent is so deeply important. It is at once luminous, balanced, and devastating. Judging by reality and morality, each of your grounds is, I believe, conclusive."[42]

Later on Frankfurter told Stone that Swaine thought the Court's ruling "of doubtful value."[43] "That nugget of wisdom from Swaine is too good," Stone commented. "I am surprised, though, that he thinks it is of 'doubtful value' to include in a book on corporate reorganizations the Court's approval of his clever scheme. Can it be that in retrospect it looks to him to be just a little too clever?"[44]

As the first term under Chief Justice Hughes wore on, the nation's press noted significant shifts in the Court's alignment.[45] Three widely noticed cases provided fresh material for prognosticators. With the Court divided 5 to 4, the new liberal majority of Stone, Brandeis, Holmes, Hughes, and Roberts prevailed in two. In the third, Roberts joined the conservatives. When the constitutionality of the Indiana chain store tax came up for decision the constitutional views of Stone, Brandeis, and Holmes were in the ascendancy. Roberts wrote the Court's opinion, sustaining an occupational tax on retail establishments graduated according to the number of stores under single ownership.

"The record shows," he said, "that the chain store has many features and advantages which definitely distinguish it from the individual store."[46] Stone concurred heartily in the use of the doctrine of "classification based on reasonable differences," though, with Holmes, he seriously doubted the beneficial results of such laws. "I am very strongly inclined to the view that the Tax Act dealt with in that case and other similar cases is unwise legislation," he wrote, "but . . . I am inclined to leave the question of the wisdom or unwisdom of such legislation to the legislators, whose business it is to decide."[47]

There were other bright spots. On the very last day of the term the new liberal majority invalidated Minnesota's notorious "gag law." Here the Chief Justice led the former dissenters in a landmark decision, fusing the constitutional restrictions of the First and Fourteenth Amendments.[48] But in this sensitive area of civil liberties the new alliance lacked solidity. In the famous MacIntosh and Bland cases,[49] it split, Roberts joining the conservatives to render a decision denying the right of conscientious objectors to American citizenship, which, as the Baltimore Sun said, made "the nation safe for morons."[50] This was offset, however, by another 5 to 4 decision, which gave Brandeis his first opportunity to write a majority opinion upholding the constitutionality of state economic regulation. Here the Court sustained New Jersey legislation regulating commissions paid fire-insurance agents.[51] Since the majority included Hughes and Roberts, the inference was that they agreed with the former dissenters as to the validity of price-fixing statutes.

Alignment of the most recent appointees with the so-called liberals to uphold economic regulation and set aside the Minnesota "gag law" seemed to herald a new day. "Recent developments have indicated," a law review commentator observed optimistically, "that our economic organization has not the skill of conveniently curing its ills. Governmental aid appears inevitable. Man is not born into our society free of economic constraints. Legislation relaxing them may more likely be an enhancement of than a restriction upon the 'liberty of contract.' The Court is not to stand in the way of experimentation. The addition of two vigorous thinkers to the bench has carried the day for pragmatism and liberal tolerance of legislative experiment with control for the purpose of advancing a larger capacity for individual freedom."[52]

By and large the year's work afforded reason for encouragement. "I have been busy, as usual, grinding out opinions," Stone told Cromwell of the Wall Street firm. "In the three weeks' recess, which just ended, I have finished and printed seven, which is about as much as one ought to think of doing, and which, confidentially, is rather more than anyone else on the Court has done."[53] When, at term's end, he considered the year's work—twenty-four opinions, twenty-two being for the Court—his mood was hopeful.

"I am busy winding up the work of the term," he wrote. "On the whole it has been an interesting one although, due to change in the personnel of the Court, I have not found it necessary, in the words of the old hymn, to 'raise my Ebenezer' in protest at some of the atrocities committed by the majority on the minority, chiefly because I haven't been so often with the minority."

"Both Justice Holmes and Justice Brandeis," he continued cheerfully, "went away looking extremely well. They made a remarkable record, going through the year without [writing] a single dissenting opinion. I wonder when that has happened before. It looks now as though I should be able to join them by another year, on the assumption that most times we will be in the majority and, if not, the Chief will pull the laboring oar."[54]


CHAPTER TWENTY

# The Judicial Rift Deepens

## 1931-1932


The contrast between the new Chief Justice and his predecessor was sharp. "As Chief Justice," Stone recalled, Taft "was extremely generous in the assignment of cases, often keeping for himself some of the least desirable ones in order to treat his brethren fairly."[1] His successor was guided by a different principle. "I think I am not likely to get many cases of large public interest," Stone commented, "but I can get a good deal of fun out of a good technical problem when some fortunate accident brings it my way."[2]

"When Charles Evans Hughes is a liberal," a close observer of the Court's work noted, "he proclaims it to the world. When he is a reactionary, he votes silently and allows somebody else to be torn to pieces by the liberal dissenters. . . . One can only wonder what the reputation of Mr. Hughes would be, if, in the fifty-one cases in which he helped to create a reactionary majority, he had exposed himself sixteen times to the dissenting logic of Mr. Justice Stone. . . . Not once has he [Stone] had an opportunity to analyze an opinion written by the Chief Justice himself."[3]

Insult was added to injury when Hughes began writing a large share of the liberal dissents. In *United States* v. *Macintosh*, for example, involving a delicate area of civil liberties in which Stone was particularly anxious to get his views on record, he had been prevented from doing so. "I prepared and printed my own [dissent]," he wrote, "but did not circulate it, awaiting further developments. It turned out that the Chief Justice wanted to have his say and, sensing a possible feeling that the publication of another dissent would not be wholly appreciated, I withdrew my own."[4]

Undaunted, Stone continued to dispatch his assignments with customary alacrity. "I congratulate you," the Chief Justice wrote him. "Incidentally, I don't seem to be able to keep you busy. I shall try to do better next time."[5]

The heavy allotment of tough cases was a recognition of Stone's powers. Denial of the opportunity to write for the Court in important constitutional rulings was also a tribute, as it reflected Hughes' "recognition that Justice Stone's opinions would withstand any later attempts to diminish them by artificial distinctions."[6] Conscious, perhaps, that disappointment over not being offered the Chief Justiceship might color his thinking, Stone suspended judgment. When he grumbled, his spleen was vented on the highly paid lawyers, the prima donnas of the bar, whose arguments often obfuscated what they should have clarified. "Damn it," he would say, "that opinion I just wrote will make more for the petitioner's lawyer than I get paid for a whole year's work on the Court. If I'm going to have to keep on doing all the work on these complicated cases which the lawyers don't understand and don't give me any help on, I think I'll go back to practice and write the briefs instead of the opinions. If I have to do the attorneys' work for them, I might as well get paid accordingly."[7]

Other Justices also had difficulty adjusting to the new regime. Accustomed to Taft's leisurely yet efficient procedures, they rankled under the pressure. At times personal relations among certain justices became embittered. Cold, formal politeness replaced the confidence and warm friendliness of the early years under Taft. Outwardly Stone himself remained jovial, but this was not always true of his colleagues. "That was the dullest argument I ever heard in my life," he remarked one day after the Justices filed from the courtroom. "The only duller thing I can think of," McReynolds snapped, "is to hear you read one of your opinions."[8] Stone could remain calm because the basic source of his malaise lay less in the quality of friendship he had with the majority than in a disturbing, inner sense of futility. "They have been seven mighty busy and interesting years," he responded to a congratulatory wire from the Columbia Law Faculty on the anniversary of his elevation to the bench. "Whether they have been useful or not my grandchildren will know. I fear I never shall. I never had any doubt about the usefulness of my work as a teacher, but sometimes I feel, with respect to my present job, that I might just as well be practicing law in Wall Street, or sitting under a coconut tree on a sunny beach in the South Sea Islands. However," he added characteristically, "I do have lots of fun."[9]

By Christmas of 1931 events had proved Hughes and Roberts to be unreliable members of the so-called liberal majority. In conference the veil of liberalism, imputed or feigned, was dropped. Optimism, born of their arrival, faded as the newcomers displayed resemblances to their predecessors, Taft and Sanford. Two decisions involving ICC orders made it clear that the addition of Hughes and Roberts had not overnight transformed the minority of Stone, Holmes, and Brandeis into a permanent majority. In one case, carried over from the Taft regime, a small switching line complained that big trunk lines took an unfair share of joint-haul rates. The ICC agreed and ordered division of the rate on a new basis more favorable to the little railroad. Its order, dated November 5, 1927, was to take effect as of August 6, 1927, and to operate until changed by the Commission. In 1928 the Supreme Court decided that the ICC lacked power to issue retroactive rate orders.[10] All ICC orders must be made effective no sooner than thirty days after issuance. Accordingly, the Commission modified its first order, to make it binding as soon as legally permissible. After a four-year legal duel the High Court ruled that the rate division never became effective because the Commission had not specified a date, thirty days after its promulgation, when it should go into operation. Stone made no effort to disguise his impatience. This shabby technicality, he observed for the dissenters, "would not . . . occur to anyone unfamiliar with legal niceties."[11]

In the second case the ICC had painstakingly investigated the apportionment of freight-car rentals on the nation's railroads. Each car-owning line was obviously entitled to a reasonable rental. The Commission held that such costs would be more equitably divided among car-users if short-line roads, performing time-consuming terminal services, were permitted two days' free use of rented cars. The exemption period coincided with the two days' "free" time allowed shippers to load and unload cars that the terminal roads received from and returned to the trunk lines. But Mr. Justice Sutherland, for the majority, declared the provision for "free" use so "arbitrary" as to violate the Fifth Amendment.[12]

Stone again "said a few kind words" for the Three Musketeers. As he saw the problem, the ICC order had little or nothing to do with final compensation for owners of borrowed freight cars. "Instead of abandoning the *per diem* system altogether for the benefit of the comparatively few roads prejudiced by it," he commented, "the Commission lightened its burden upon them by a rule of thumb no more crude or arbitrary than the principle of *per diem* itself." As to this parody of the judicial process, Stone observed sharply: "The Fifth Amendment does not command the impossible. A remedy may, and, in the present case, must be shaped to meet the evil."[13]

Even students of the Supreme Court were aghast at such judicial imperviousness to facts. A letter from a judge, passed along to Stone by a close friend, stated that he was "impressed" by the dissents and "could not understand how it was that the Chief Justice and Justice Roberts failed to agree with Stone." Expressing deep concern for the future, this profoundly troubled correspondent observed: "At the time when the liberals were rejoicing over the apparent shift of opinion in the Court from the conservative to the liberal side, I was afraid that the rejoicing might not be well founded. The distressing thing to me is that it seemed as if the intelligence of the Chief Justice and Justice Roberts would save the situation in many instances, but now there seems to be little certainty that this will be the result."

Unable to satisfy himself as to what lay back of the car-hire case, Professor Frankfurter pressed Stone for an answer. "You asked me a difficult question," Stone replied, "but the following is my analysis:

"First, there is a background, possibly more or less subconscious, that·the Commission ought to be held in check. Second, there is the tendency of the human mind, and especially the human minds engaged in the work of our profession, to fit any new situation into familiar categories. Of course, if the statute compelled every landlord to allow two months' free rent on his lease, in the absence of some very special circumstances, that would look like a taking of the landlord's property. Two days' use of a railroad car, rent free, superficially, has a similar appearance. The 'logical' conclusion follows. . . . Finally there is a tendency of a certain type of mind to become closed the moment it has formed a conclusion and announced it, . . . especially where business and economic problems are involved, rather than those having a moral and emotional content. . . . The tendency once a conclusion [is] reached never to revise it cannot be left out of account in predicting our future work."[14] "Of course," he continued, "a little wholesome skepticism might prevent such conclusions. In fact it was such skepticism which led to my taking the case up. There was little in the argument or briefs to emphasize the fact that the car-hire arrangement under inquiry was in fact a division of joint transportation costs, although it became clear enough on scrutiny of the report of the Commission and the evidence in the case."*

* Two years later the Court, under the leadership of Justice Roberts, again threw obstacles in the way of administrative action. "It's a great pity," Walter

Justice Sutherland, sometimes with the support of Hughes and Roberts, proved himself "quite capable of putting the blind eye to the telescope where that serves his purpose."* A striking example was *First National Bank* v. *Maine* where the Court went the full length of declaring that stock of a domestic corporation, owned by non-resident stockholders, had no situs for taxing purposes at the home of the corporation, and this in terms broad enough to preclude any taxation of stock held by foreign stockholders in American corporations.

In a biting dissent, and with tongue in cheek, Stone observed: "Recognizing that responsibility must rest primarily on those who undertake to blaze a new path in the law, to say how far it shall go, . . . I am not persuaded that either logic, expediency, or generalizations about the undesirability of double taxation justify our adding to the cases recently overruled, the long list of those which, without a dissenting voice, have supported taxation like the present. . . . Only by recourse to a form of words—saying that there is no taxable subject within the state, by reason of the fictitious attribution to the intangible interest of the stockholder of a location elsewhere—is it possible to stigmatize the tax as arbitrary."[15]

This tax case left one close student of the Court with conflicting emotions. He could think of nothing "funnier," or "more naïve in the books, than to insist in one part of an opinion that respect for the processes of logical thinking requires a decision, and yet fundamentally to base such a decision on the purest kind of a fiction." "You

---

Gellhorn wrote H.F.S., Feb. 14, 1934, that "Justice Roberts was suffering from one of his astigmatic spells. Your opinion, if it could only have been substituted for his, would have been a boon for administrative bodies. Your realistic discussion of the 'open chapter in the record of corporate concentration' surely points the path to sound consideration by the Court of practical problems." The case was *Arrow-Hart & Hegeman Electric Co.* v. *Federal Trade Commission*, 291 U.S. 587 (1934).

"It does seem," Stone replied on April 14, "that Courts, in interpreting statutes defining the powers of administrative bodies, ought to use the same ingenuity to make a system work that they display in other fields of law. I think the day may come when a decision like that in the Trade Commission case will be deemed as archaic as some of Lord Coke's whimsicalities."

* Stone made this characterization of Sutherland with special reference to *District of Columbia* v. *Colts*, 282 U.S. 63 (1930), in which Sutherland had "stated that reckless driving was an indictable offense at common law and, therefore, was not a petty offense such as could be tried without a jury; notwithstanding the constitutional requirement for a jury trial." "This was urged," Stone reported to John Bassett Moore, May 27, 1931, "as *historical* support for the decision in the case, that a present-day charge for reckless driving of an automobile must be by jury, although it was pointedly called to his attention that there was no such offense at common law." Sutherland had taken this stand in the face of "a statute of George III, adopted before the Revolution, making reckless driving an offense punishable by imprisonment and triable *before a magistrate without jury.*"

will perhaps be amused to know," Stone replied, "that I wrote the dissent in the Maine tax case practically as is before receiving the prevailing opinion, which shows that I know my psychology."

The same judicial subterfuge was exhibited in crucial social and economic issues. As the wheels of industry turned more slowly under stoical "natural" laws, various states sought to correct the disharmonies between production and consumption. Attempting to inject a modicum of reason into the competitive economy, Oklahoma enacted a statute requiring a certificate of "public convenience and necessity" of anyone wishing to enter the ice business. In no uncertain terms, six Justices rode roughshod over this modest essay in regulated economy.

"The control here asserted," Justice Sutherland fumed, "does not protect against monopoly, but tends to foster it. The aim is not to encourage competition, but to prevent it." The business of manufacturing, selling, and distributing ice, he ruled, "is a business as essentially private in its nature as the business of the grocer, the dairyman, the butcher, the baker, the shoemaker or the tailor. . . ."[16] The Chief Justice and Roberts agreed.

But did the Constitution provide an absolute right to engage in certain kinds of enterprise? "The notion of a distinct category of business 'affected with a public interest,' employing property 'devoted to a public use,'" Brandeis and Stone responded, "rests upon historical error. . . . The true principle is that the state's power extends to every regulation of any business reasonably required and appropriate for the public protection." "Under certain circumstances," the dissenters asserted, "free competition might be harmful to the community and . . . , when it was so, absolute freedom to enter the business of one's choice should be denied."[17]

Brandeis and Stone vigorously protested the galling premise that, in the midst of depression, the old and tried laissez-faire virtues were working out the divine harmony of the spheres: "The people of the United States are now confronted with an emergency more serious than war. Misery is widespread, in a time, not of scarcity, but of over-abundance." Unemployment on an unprecedented scale, catastrophic price declines, and tremendous economic losses had led "some people" to believe "that the existing conditions threatened even the stability of the capitalistic system." "Increasingly," the dissenters observed, "doubt is expressed whether it is economically wise, or morally right, that men should be permitted to add to the producing facilities of an industry which is already suffering from over-capacity."[18]

The triumphs of science—the material basis of social life—had been achieved by bold, painstaking experiment. Why should not the same technique be open to use by government to meet the paradoxical challenge of depression in the midst of plenty? One of the "happy incidents" of federalism, the dissenters reminded their conservative brethren, permitted "a single courageous state" to try out novel social and economic ideas without endangering the nation. In ruling out an experiment, the majority had taken upon itself "a grave responsibility." "This Court has the power to prevent experiment," Brandeis commented. "But in the exercise of this high power, we must be ever on our guard lest we erect our prejudices into legal principles. If we would guide by the light of reason, we must let our minds be bold."[19]

"Yes, I joined with Justice Brandeis in his opinion on the Oklahoma Ice case," Stone wrote John Bassett Moore, March 29, 1932. "While I doubt the wisdom and efficacy of much attempted regulation of business, I think those are questions to be determined by the legislature and not by the Supreme Court. I have never been able to persuade myself that the Fourteenth Amendment was ever intended to preclude the legislature from regulating business where regulation could not be said to be palpably arbitrary and unreasonable. The whole history of the regulation of business by statute or public control, dating back some centuries before there was a constitution, indicates so plain a recognition of this power and the propriety of its exercise, that it has always seemed to me to be going very far to say that the Fourteenth Amendment was devised to prevent it."

"The attitude of the Court, expressed in *Munn* v. *Illinois*, seemed to me altogether sane and defensible," Stone went on. "Since that time the Court has been engaged in building up a wholly artificial conceptualism about what kind of business could and could not be regulated. In one case in which I dissented,[20] the Court held that the business of running a cotton gin could be regulated in Oklahoma because it resembled the business of running a grist mill in more or less medieval times. But as the general use and commercial distribution of ice was not known in the time of Lord Hale, and since any effective regulation of the business as conducted in Oklahoma involved curtailment of free competition, the statute was held to be unconstitutional. All of this seems to be very remote from the realities and from any sensible interpretation of the Fourteenth Amendment, even though, if I were a legislator in Oklahoma, I might, and probably would, vote against any drastic regulation of the ice business."

Brandeis and Stone had uttered a timely warning. All over the country people demanded action; Oklahoma was simply trying to move faster than the storm. If under judicial fiat affairs stood as they were, ruled by eighteenth-century insights, the prognosis was simple. "It was a matter of idle hands, then hunger, then chaos."

All was not gloom, of course. Stone relished work that others shunned and often found reward in the lavish praise that came to him. He was especially adept at income-tax controversies, and his settlement of heated disputes between taxpayers and Government more frequently than not resolved trying problems in favor of the Treasury. But he scouted the idea that government briefs exhibited "any excessive persuasiveness." "The fact is," he commented, "that so many fantastic claims are urged by ingenious tax lawyers in behalf of taxpayers that a low percentage of successful applications . . . by taxpayers is to be expected."[21] His complete command of the subject enabled him to solve questions baffling to government experts and highly paid tax attorneys alike. Stone took peculiar satisfaction from beating the experts at their own game.

"I remember," one of his law clerks has recalled, "his struggling with a case I could not fully understand then or now." After stating the respective positions of the taxpayer and the Treasury in this case, Stone wrote: "We think that neither the Government nor the petitioner has chosen the correct method of restating the account."[22] Then he proceeded to open up the problems in an entirely fresh way. Chief Justice Hughes was pleased. "Yes Sir!" he agreed emphatically, "I am glad you were able to work it out." A few days later Stone glowed with pleasure when his law clerk told him that one of the lawyers in the Solicitor General's office had remarked: "I never was satisfied with the analysis we made of the case. But darned if I could figure out a better one. It took Stone to do it."[23]

At times Stone delighted in exposing his stodgy brethren. On occasion he buried a sly dig at the majority, as in the Maine tax case. Yet the majority's very persistence sometimes drove him to distrust his own reasoning. Perhaps he had missed a step in the process or selected a premise that sent him hurtling into an intellectual *cul de sac.* If men of the caliber of Hughes and Roberts did not agree with him, how could he be sure of his position? More and more he relied on correspondents in the law schools and drew wisdom and inspiration from Holmes and Brandeis.

## CHAPTER TWENTY-ONE

# Rewarding Friendships—
# Holmes and Cardozo

## 1932-1933

Justice Holmes, completing his ninety-first year, was wont to jest about his age and addressed Stone familiarly as "sonny" or "my lad."[1] "My boy," he would often say, "when you're as young as I am. . . ." Yet behind this banter there was, as someone has observed, "a serious concern lest he outstay his competence on the Court, as others before him had done."[2]

In the summer of 1931 Holmes had a "bad spell." His friends noted marked change. "Confidentially," Frankfurter wrote Stone, September 30, "you will find Holmes physically weakened since you saw him last. . . . The sheer physical machinery is not what it was—though his brain and spirit are as alert, comprehensive, and acute as ever. One thing I have noticed in him—a show of confidence and encouragement seems to be more vitalizing and refreshing to him than it ever has in the past. . . . I know how much real comfort and joy you have given him, and your capacity for giving these to him, and I thought I would whisper these remarks in your ear. He is, of course, the same old soldier, and goes to the task as he did to the field of battle seventy years ago."

Waning strength caused the great dissenter to fall behind. The terse, handwritten bravos sent Stone on the backs of draft opinions bore signs of physical deterioration. At length the time came, just before opinion day, January 5, 1932, when the aged jurist knew he could no longer keep step. The opinion at hand had challenged the vigor of the Court's acknowledged tax authority. Even he had worked it out only after rejecting the theories of both Government and taxpayer. Habit more than muscle directed the hand as Holmes scrawled in pencil across Stone's draft opinion: "*Quicquid solvitur solvitur secundum modum solventis*,"* and then translated, "As this is your opinion, I suppose the conclusion is right and say yes without verification."

* Literally, "Whatever is solved is solved according to the manner of the one who solves it." The case was *American Hide & Leather Co.* v. *United States* (1935).

By January all the brethren realized that Holmes could no longer do his full share, or anything near it. A majority of the Justices then asked the Chief Justice to request Holmes to resign. Stone took no part in this decision. If ever he regretted the loss of the Chief Justiceship, he must have then been grateful that Hoover, for whatever reason, passed him by. On January 12, 1932, Stone wrote Frankfurter:

> As you read your evening paper today, you will appreciate the feeling of sadness which has weighed upon me in the last few weeks, and especially since Sunday, when Justice Holmes concluded to terminate his long period of service on the bench. As you probably know, he has been in failing health since last summer, and those of us who knew him best and saw him frequently became aware that the time would not be long when he would have to give up his work. On Sunday he had a talk with the Chief Justice and at the conclusion of it sat down and wrote the letter of resignation which you will have seen in the paper.* It is as characteristic a thing as he ever did in his life.
>
> Yesterday Justice Brandeis was ill and did not attend Court, and so after the adjournment I asked Justice Holmes to ride down with me for his last Court attendance. I found him in good spirits and treating the march of events in his true philosophical spirit. In this, as in everything else, he is the gallant gentleman, facing the future with equanimity and taking a just, although characteristically modest, pride in the past. I stopped for a little chat with him again tonight on the way down from Court and found him in good form. What a career of public service, and what a gallant, noble ending of it!

Thus passed from the Court "one of the greatest men who ever sat upon it, and one of the greatest men and most beautiful characters it has been my privilege to know."[3]

The association with Holmes had been fruitful on both sides. By the time Stone came to Washington, Holmes was already poignantly feeling the loneliness of old age—if only, as he said, because there are so few with whom one can exchange memories. Stone gave with grace and energy a friendship that was more than formal. In making the elder jurist feel that he was significant for him, Stone helped to bridge the gulf between the sixties and the nineties.

Holmes gave as well as received. His exceptional culture, wide reading, and philosophic bent enthralled the junior Justice. "He has the soul of the artist and poet," Stone wrote, "a keen and incisive mind, enriched by a lifetime of reading, study, and experience, a keen sense of humor, as well as sparkling wit and a beautiful prose style, peculiarly adapted to the revelation of the process of legal thought, without . . . excessive definition."[4] Any lull in judicial routine would more

---

* Hughes performed the unpleasant task of requesting Holmes' resignation on January 11, 1932.

than likely find the two Justices together at the red brick house on I Street, talking "about anything in the world except our daily labor." These "jaws" ran the full gamut of human experience. Some years after Holmes' death Stone was asked why he did not write his reminiscences of Holmes. "I'll have to wait," Stone replied with a chuckle, "until I have a male secretary."[5]

Every anniversary was marked by warm words of affection. "You may be sure," Holmes replied to one of these notes, "that the feeling of companionship is reciprocated and that I count it an added happiness to have you with us. I shall try to cling like a barnacle for a little longer, not without occasional misgivings, but encouraged nevertheless. If a man can only be old *enough,* age will take the place of accomplishments, but I need two or three years more for that. It is pretty good sport trying to add them in such company."[6]

On occasion Stone pulled all stops from his New England reserve. "I am open to congratulations as one of the most fortunate of men," he wrote on Holmes' ninetieth birthday, "for tomorrow . . . I add another to the golden years of my association with you. You are a constant source of inspiration to me. When the task seems irksome and my best efforts futile, I recall the serenity with which you meet each day, the problems which it brings—never giving yourself concern as to the outcome if you have given your best. So I bend myself to the task with renewed confidence, even though I know my best will never equal your worst."[7]

Through Stone's correspondence with Holmes and in his comments to others about his doughty colleague runs the suggestion that the younger judge revered Holmes as he had once revered the common law. It had been given to Holmes, as one of the rare figures of the common law, "to give a new direction to the law and to breathe into it a new vitality." Proud of his friendship with the older jurist, Stone took precious time from an unremitting schedule to write three closely typed pages for a correspondent who wished to eulogize the great Justice before a St. Louis civic group.

"Justice Holmes has a rather curious New England inheritance," Stone wrote, "intermingled with something which is not New England at all. His outlook on life, I think, is very typical of that distinguished group of New England men, typified by his father, by Emerson, and the so-called Concord School of Philosophy. But there is very little puritanism in his make-up, and added to the New England strain are characteristics of the gallant gentleman, a man of the world. He is not at all religious in the ordinary, accepted use of that term. He would disclaim being religious at all. But in the unyielding fidelity to truth, to right conduct, to the tolerant treatment of his fellow men, he is essentially religious. Add to this the soul of the artist and you have the principal characteristics of the man."[8]

Holmes was equally generous. He saw Stone's opinions as clear, direct, and incisive. They did not often disagree, but when they did Stone had his reasons, "although they may not have been good ones."[9] "We are so seldom on opposite sides of the fence," Stone wrote Holmes, December 21, 1928, "that I hate to break a good precedent. I withdraw from the debate before I am beaten," he added diplomatically, "but as is the way of humankind, cling to my error."

In methods of work the two Justices were poles apart. "I hate facts," Holmes boasted.[10] Preferring to formulate "general propositions," he resisted grubbing among the authorities to bolster his case. Dissenting opinions afforded peculiar pleasure, one suspects, because in preparing them he could forego the dreary recital of facts and soar beyond them into the rarefied realm of philosophy. Stone thoroughly enjoyed his colleague's jocular dispatch of weighty issues; he reveled in the spirited and often brilliant shafts at the recalcitrant majority.

Whenever Stone returned from conference with the air of a man bursting with a good story, his law clerk knew what was coming. "Well," the Justice would begin, "the old man is still the keenest one of the lot." He would then tell of a long wrangle over a case and of how Holmes, growing weary, would settle back for his afternoon nap. Suddenly he would open his eyes and launch into a summary of the issues so lucid and persuasive as to carry the entire bench with him. "A grand old man," Stone would say. "He punctured their arguments like a bubble." "Holmes and Butler had another spat today," the Justice reported one day on returning from conference, and then regaled his law clerk with the story of a case, hotly debated at several sessions, in which Holmes and Butler carried the opposing arguments. When Butler's position finally triumphed with only Holmes dissenting, the victor turned to Holmes and said with utter gravity: "I am glad we have finally arrived at a just decision." "Hell," Holmes snapped, "Hell is paved with *just* decisions."[11]

Stone admired and enjoyed his colleague's craftsmanship but always felt a certain uneasiness about his facility in getting out an opinion. A difficult case begun on a Saturday night would, more than likely, be finished by Tuesday morning and a printed draft in circulation. "This is a pretty good opinion on the point that he decides," Stone remarked on one of these, "but the old man leaves out all the troublesome facts and ignores all the tough points that worried the lower courts." "I wish," he once said in grudging admiration, "I could make my cases sound as easy as Holmes makes his."[12]

"Are you not treating this point rather lightly?" he would ask.[13] In a price-fixing case, for example, Holmes told Stone that "in spite of Brandeis's exhortations, I do not intend to write. I have said my say." "But," he went on, "I thought I should say this: 'Of course I yield to the authority of decided cases, and although I thought that this case might be distinguished from its predecessors, it is for the authority that established the precedents to say how far the violet rays of the Fourteenth Amendment reach. . . . I am rather pleased," he added, "with this innuendo of 'violet rays.' " "I like your phrase," Stone replied, "and would like to join you in it, but I hesitate merely because there are so many solemn-minded people, unembarrassed by any sense of humor, who might feel that we were treating lightly and irreverently a very serious matter. I shall, of necessity, touch the susceptibilities of such people often enough, so that I hesitate to do it unnecessarily."[14]

In dissent Stone felt obligated to answer directly the arguments of his opponents and thus keep pure the stream of doctrine. In the employment agency case, for example, Holmes expressed dissatisfaction with Stone's dissent, preferring his own forthright position that "a state legislature can do whatever it sees fit to do unless it is restrained by some express prohibition in the Constitution. . . ." Stone's painstaking alignment of the precedents to support his arguments and his reworking of the sociological materials supplied by Brandeis seemed to Holmes wasted effort. "Why not say," Stone countered, "that you would go further than I and refer to your dissent in the Tyson [ticket-scalping] case, but that you think I go far enough to demolish the majority or words to that effect? Of course, with respect to your views in the Tyson case, I agree with them, but I think it advisable to meet the majority on their own ground."[15] And this Stone did with marked effectiveness.*

In 1930 the Court denied, under the due process clause of the Fourteenth Amendment, state power to levy inheritance taxes on the credits, bonds, and notes of a resident not within the jurisdiction of the taxing state. In a much-quoted passage, Justice Holmes exploded: "As the decisions now stand, I see hardly any limit but the sky to the invalidating of those rights [of the state] if they happen to strike a majority of this Court as for any reason undesirable."[16] Stone applauded this somewhat injudicious outburst. He could understand how the great dissenter did not want "to detract from its force by dealing with any of the technical aspects of the matter." Yet his col-

---

* "No comment on Mr. Justice Sutherland's elaboration [in the Tyson case] of the words 'affected with a public interest,' " Thomas Reed Powell wrote, "could be more cruel than to place his discourse in juxtaposition with Mr. Justice Stone's elucidation of its question-begging meaninglessness." ("State Utilities and the Supreme Court, 1922-1930," *Michigan Law Review*, May 1931, p. 836.)

league's opinion failed to satisfy. "That was my only excuse," he explained, "for writing anything, but I am inclined to think a valid one. You know well enough how many there are in our profession who would look at that aspect of the matter rather than the larger one dealt with by Mr. Justice Holmes."[17]

Without recourse to Stone's more tedious procedures, Holmes usually reached the same result. "One of the curious things about him," Stone remarked, "is that he seems to have an intuitive sense of the possibilities of entirely new problems which have year after year been presented to him in his daily work as a judge. He reads no newspapers and, so far as I know, none of the current journals of opinion. He takes no time for search and study of current economic and social problems, as does Justice Brandeis, and yet both arrive at the same point, Justice Holmes, it would seem, almost intuitively, Justice Brandeis as the result of exhaustive study of the problem." Stone's procedures, like those of Brandeis, were painstaking. He nevertheless greatly admired this aspect of Holmes' judicial personality. "It is this quality of intuitively grasping the essence of a problem," he wrote, "realizing that it is not necessarily like old and familiar ones, and that a constitutional system must give some play for dealing with such problems, which lies at the root of his distinguished contribution to jurisprudence."[18]

In many ways Holmes was the kind of man and judge Stone himself wanted to be. In an address prepared but never delivered, he paid tribute to Holmes and his jurisprudence:

Profound student of the history of the law, it was for him more than the legal archaeology which so often passes for legal history. In it he discerned the processes, which he revealed with perfect clarity, by which the common law, if it is to fulfill its mission, is always adopting new principles from life.

Mr. Justice Holmes steadily gave evidence of his conviction that the judicial method by which the common law is drawn from life is equally adapted to the interpretation of a written framework of government. But he was aware that the problems with which it must grapple where constitutional rights are at stake involves the consideration of social values which are absent when only the rights of individuals are to be adjudicated. In solving them the court must mediate between the conflicting interests of the individual and the expressed will of an organized society by giving a content with some degree of permanence to an instrument of government "intended to endure for ages to come and consequently to be adapted to the various crises of human affairs." The dangers which he discerned in the performance of so momentous a task are that interpretation may result in meticulously framed rigid rules, rather than in the establishment of standards as the measure of constitutional power, of the reasonableness of official action, of continuing validity when applied to changing social and economic conditions, and that in the appraisal of social value in determining whether they are without or within the constitutional protection we mistake the familiar for the necessary.

Holmes had, Stone agreed, rightly conceived the task of government as that of "effecting the peaceful accommodation of the clashing interests of society." Legislation is "the resultant of conflicting demands of self-interest, of all the multiple elements of a complex society." Public investigation, debate, and the sense of fair play which attend lawmaking are restraints on majority action. But beyond the specific restraints on governmental action, constitutional government "contemplates a minimum of individual right beyond the reach of governmental power." To this extent constitutional government restricts majority rule. And, in cases actually before it, it is the duty of the Court to say what that minimum is. But "the very vagueness of the penumbra which envelops "liberty," "property," "equal protection," "due process," and the like, leaves the judges "some freedom of choice as to standards marking the limits of governmental power." "It is a fundamental tenet of the Holmes philosophy," Stone wrote, "that the choice should be governed by considerations of public policy, and that these should envisage all the elements of a constitutional system which undertakes to curtail democratic action." Courts are, within these limits, "constitution makers, just as in other circumstances . . . they are legislators in the choice of the possible common law rules which they adopt."

The latitude within which Courts may make law is, however, relatively narrow. Reconciliation of conflicting social and economic interests is committed primarily to legislatures.* For the discharge of this task, they are equipped, as Courts are not, with facilities for study, investigation, and appraisal of those interests. They are also dependent on popular election for continuance in office. Sensitive to popular temper, they are free, as courts are not, to revise or repeal earlier statutes. And legislatures, as well as courts, are sworn supporters of constitutional rights. Courts have, on occasion, been alert to these facts. In deference to them, they have sought to safeguard the democratic process by declaring that all statutes are presumed to be con-

---

* Stone elaborated his thought on this point in a letter to Perlie P. Fallon, Dec. 27, 1939: "A friend said to me recently, the problem for the judge is not whether the judges made law, but when and how much. Justice Holmes said 'they can do so only interstitially, they are confined from molar to molecular motion,' or as another has said, the legislature makes law wholesale, judges retail. It all comes to this: that judges must make some law out of existing materials and with due deference to the presuppositions of the legal system of which they have been made a part. It is a difficult system to operate and can only be done successfully through the exercise of wisdom, of which the Lord knows we all have too little."

stitutional and that the burden rests upon him who attacks a statute to establish its unconstitutionality beyond all reasonable doubt. "But," Stone added,

notwithstanding this precaution, the experience of the past one hundred and fifty years has revealed the danger that, through judicial interpretation, the constitutional device for the protection of minorities from oppressive majority action, may be made the means by which the majority is subjected to the tyranny of minority. It was the lasting contribution of Justice Holmes that he saw clearly that the danger arose, not from the want of appropriate guiding formulas for the exercise of the judicial function, but from the judicial distrust of the democratic process, and from the innate tendency of the human mind to apply subjective rather than objective tests of the reasonableness of legislative action. . . .

Speaking on his own, Stone concluded:

It is plain that unless government is to be left stripped of all power to solve, by democratic means which the Constitution has provided, the terms which beset the modern state, the courts cannot act as the arbiters of such differences of opinion by the simple expedient of adopting its own preferences of those which the Constitution has sanctioned. There is a difference between determining whether the legislative cure of a social ill is wise, and in determining whether legislatures, in believing it to be wise, are so unreasonable as to place their action beyond the constitutional power. The one which is essential to the performance of the legislative function in a democracy is committed by the Constitution to Congress and the state legislatures, and it is the other which alone has been reserved to the courts. In recognition of this difference by the courts and their studious observation of the narrow limits which circumscribe the performance of the function of judicial review of legislation, Justice Holmes found the hope of reconciliation of the need for democratic solutions of the clashing social interests with constitutional restraints on legislative action.*

Much of what Stone wrote about Holmes' constitutional jurisprudence was applicable to himself. Indeed, he had presented the core

* This was to have been the opening lecture for the academic year 1938-39 on the Holmes Foundation at the Harvard Law School, established by Mr. Justice Holmes. Judge Learned Hand was to have followed Stone with three general lectures. (J.M. Landis to H.F.S., May 24, 1938.) With his eye, as usual, on the really important events, Stone accepted quite promptly. "I shall make the jump," he wrote Dean Landis, June 7, 1938, "and plan to give the dedicatory lecture in the Holmes series."

That summer he made a rough draft of his talk, excerpts from which are quoted in the text. Meanwhile Hand backed out, pleading he had nothing worth while to say. "It became clear to me," he wrote Stone, August 9, 1938, "that I could never spin out three lectures before the term opened in October. . . . The more I tried the less there was. . . . It was like retching on an empty stomach. Maybe I could have squeezed out one lecture, but that was the limit. How do these birds do it? I'll tell you one way: they repeat themselves, like the conversations of an affectionate old couple."

of these ideas two years earlier in his Harvard Tercentenary address.[19]

Stone tended to gloss over or obscure basic philosophical differences. Holmes saw the world in process of constant change, not necessarily for the better nor for the worse. "The inevitable is not wicked," he said.[20] Social institutions, in his view, were not susceptible of great change at human hands. They were altered through the years, sometimes in response to mass pressures, but he never called this progress. Holmes dubbed himself a "bettabilitarian"—"one who thinks you may bet more or less on the universe."[21] Man could not greatly affect his social environment by social changes embodied in legislation, but one could "bet" about it. Dubious as to the results of such innovation, he nevertheless did not resist legislative experimentation. At the basis of his skepticism was a feeling of the utter futility of human tinkering.

Stone's misgivings about legislative remedies for contemporary social ills sprang more from his reluctance to concede the wisdom of altering a social structure he felt basically sound. Innate conservatism, deep-rooted individualism, led him to a policy stand not unlike that of Holmes. They agreed on the necessity of social and economic experimentation. Holmes said, "They can't do it, but let them try." Stone said, "They should not do it, but judges are not the ones to oppose."

Holmes was a realist who made his world ideal. "A man," he said, "may live greatly in the law as well as elsewhere; . . . there as well as elsewhere his thought may find its unity in an infinite perspective; . . . there as well as elsewhere he may wreak himself upon life, may drink the bitter cup of heroism, may wear his heart out after the unattainable." He knew and loved the "secret isolated joy of the thinker."[22] The acerbic searchlight of intellect was turned on all that came within his ken as a judge, to reveal in the passions, foibles, and hopes of men the unspoken major premises of the law. Yet he did this not to change the world in any particular direction, but solely as a member of a "little army of specialists" in the "service of Truth, their only queen."[23]

Neither Stone nor Holmes was "attempting to do anything socially."[24] "He is spoken of as a liberal, as, indeed, I am in these degenerate days, but neither of us," Stone commented, "are liberals in the sense, for example, . . . that Judge Brandeis is. He [Holmes] has almost nothing in common with the group of people in this country and abroad who are commonly known as liberals. He is in no sense a reformer, and I think has never been very vitally interested in reform movements or had anything in common with leaders of such movements. What has identified him as a liberal in the public mind is his attitude toward constitutional questions, which leads him to so interpret the Constitution, as he would say, 'to give opportunity for play of the joints,' which includes scope for liberal programs as well as others. . . . He does not reject legislation dealing with current social and economic problems on the assumption that he knows more about it than the legislature, or that the Constitution prohibits it merely because he does not like it or would not vote for it if he were a legislator. He believes profoundly in the freedom of the human spirit and in the freedom of thought and opinion. He indulges in no presumption that any provision of the Constitution was intended to curb or circumscribe either of them."[25]

Love of struggle, of superlative achievement, of civilization, gave impetus to Holmes' effort. He held to these values with little or no sympathy for the democratic passion of moral improvement. Stone cared more than did his colleague for the world that is, and entertained greater faith in man's capacity for legal and constitutional betterment. His dissenting opinions reveal him as the skilled craftsman, exploring dark corners in the law with an eye to improvement. He was not content merely to expose and deplore; he took positive and well-considered steps to correct judicial shortcomings that disabled the Constitution as a "continuing instrument of government."

Stone felt called upon to demonstrate to the profession and to the public that constitutional salvation lay in a reinterpretation of existing principles. As he saw it, his "mission on the Court" was "to show the profession that by use of accepted doctrine and technique, wise and honorable applications of the Constitution may be effected."[26] The older jurist was less painstaking, more cavalier. As to Stone's more precise analysis, Holmes once remarked: "I only think the Fourteenth Amendment so remote from this case—that I wonder that you have taken such pains to fasten it down."[27] Such tedious undertakings were not for Holmes. Nor did it lie within the ken of a doctrinaire liberal. This was the job for a conservative in the Burkean sense of that much abused tag.* In particular, Stone set for himself the special task of correcting the Court's besetting sin—its tendency to damage itself by overreaching its power. He attempted to effectuate Holmes' philosophy as to the place of the Court in a democratic society. Deeply disturbed by the conflict between the people's elected representatives and the Court, he strove to bridge that gap by rigorous delineation of the judicial function.[28]

Holmes' claim to pre-eminence rested on other grounds. Like John Marshall, he had the happy faculty of developing a subject in a single stroke. Stone put it this way: "The power and brilliancy of his statement has rather obscured from view his close thinking, his knowledge

---

* "A state," Burke wrote, "without the means of some change is without the means of its conservation. Without such means it might even risque that part of the Constitution which it wished most religiously to preserve." (*Reflections on the French Revolution* [New York: Merrill Co.; Maynards English classics series], p. 10.)

of history, and the fundamentals of the society in which we live, which constituted the real groundwork of his opinions and which, in the long run, will insure their permanent value."[29]

The qualities setting Holmes apart were those of "judicial caution and self-betterment which attend judicial detachment." Self-searching had enabled him "to realize that some of his most closely held convictions might not be "ultimate truth, and that others might differ from them without casting doubt on their sanity or rationality." "This," Stone said, "was the great service of his judicial life."[30]

Toward the end, as his powers began to fail, Holmes relied implicitly on his younger colleague. The quality in Stone that particularly impressed Holmes was the rugged New Hampshire jurist's capacity for intellectual growth. Never stunted by interminable controversy, nor stultified by prolonged labor, his work, as Holmes saw it, was clear, vigorous, hard-hitting.* "Who am I to say yes or no to these masterpieces of the human intellect?" Holmes wrote in the margin of a 1931 opinion. "I bow my head and accept the biddings of the master."[31]

Stone regretted that this "wonderful man" could not have stayed

---

\* Stone liked to think that the elder jurist reciprocated his admiration. Observing the high value he placed on Holmes' friendship, the late Harold J. Laski, a close friend and long-time correspondent of Holmes, apparently told Stone of the flattering comments the great dissenter put in his letters about his colleague.

From early 1935 on, Stone kept after Laski. "Don't forget sometime to send me those letters of Justice Holmes," he pleaded, November 19, 1935. On February 29, 1937, Laski mentioned "those extracts I sent you last summer from O.W.H.'s letters," and whetted the Justice's burgeoning interest by sending him this alleged item of September 6, 1932: "Stone grows all the more. There is something massive about him, and a power of energy in his thinking. He and Brandeis give me comfort such as I have rarely known."

"I never received the letter which you mentioned enclosing other abstracts," Stone complained, February 3, 1937. "In fact, I wrote you a couple of times since I was in London, but never heard from you. If it is not too much trouble I wish very much that you would send the extracts again." "I prize the quotation [that of September 6, 1932] more than I can say."

When these tidbits did not arrive Stone asked Felix Frankfurter to remind his good friend Laski. With no way out, and to save face at whatever cost, Laski, it seems, sat down and fashioned a score of excerpts, all dated and presumably authentic. The heading above the list reads: "Excerpts from letters written by Justice Oliver Wendell Holmes to Professor Harold J. Laski, Devon Lodge, Addison Bridge Place, London, W.14, England, who is in possession of the originals."

"I know that for long months," Laski wrote apologetically, January 27, 1938, "there have been arising in your heart deep suspicions that this was never going to arrive. Here it is and I am sure you will understand that the job of going through nearly 600 letters has really been a heavy one, and that leisure has not come too easily to complete it."

Stone was elated: "I do not know when I have been so touched." The Justice picked out one of the more extravagant excerpts and quoted it back to Laski. "My children will be glad to have these excerpts, and will thank you for them,

on the bench until his ninety-first birthday. But the old man's health was so precarious that it might any day decline "so that he could not have written the beautiful letter he wrote on resigning." Stone dropped in to see him as often as he could, "to pass the time of day with him and to cheer him up. He really needs little of the latter on account of his cheerful outlook on life, of which he well knows little remains to him."[32]

When the end came, three years later, Stone experienced "a real wrench." "My relations with him have been so delightful during the last ten years," he wrote, "that they have formed a most interesting and important chapter in my life."[33]

From the first Stone had thought the man appointed Holmes' successor "should be one of first-class ability, no matter where he comes from, and also a man who has had a few ideas since 1870."[34] When consulted by President Hoover, he wrote an old friend, "I mentioned Cardozo, Learned Hand, and Newton D. Baker as examples of men conspicuously fit for the place."[35] Cardozo, the urbane Chief Judge of New York's Court of Appeals, was the leading contender, but Stone feared they would not get that type of a man.

To the President, initially at least, the new vacancy seemed a good opportunity to redress the heavy Eastern representation by appointing

---

as I do," Stone said. "If it could ever be possible for me to have one of the original letters, it would be one of my most valued possessions."

Laski could no longer continue the hoax. Not a single one of the excerpts Laski sent appears in the published *Holmes-Laski Letters* (edited by Mark DeWolfe Howe, with a foreword by Felix Frankfurter). Nor did Laski take the trouble to include the few references Holmes did make to Stone. Suspicion that Laski faked these alleged excerpts is strengthened by a comparison of dates. Passages from Holmes' letters purporting to comment on Laski's reflections on Stone are not responsive to anything which recently received Laski letters had dealt with. Also there is flat contradiction in the estimate Holmes gave Laski of Hughes in his letter of February 27, 1930 (Vol. II, p. 1227. See also pp. 1224 and 1226). The alleged excerpts Laski sent Stone read:

"*Jan. 15th, 1930:* Stone would, I think, make a great Chief Justice. I should have liked it ten years ago; now I am too old. But he is a man of despatch, he knows the world, and he can take a detached view. And he is as straight as a die. His courtesy to me may affect my judgment—one clings to one's friends. But he has helped to make the Court a happy place to me in a special way.

"*Jan. 4th, 1932:* Stone thinks I underestimate Ames. But we both agree in putting Thayer above him, and he spoke of Thayer's piece on Marshall as you would have wished to hear him speak. I like him for many qualities, not least because his heart is warm and is not allowed to grow cold. He feels what he writes, but he thinks as he feels. He would have made the best Chief of my time. I must not comment on what you say of Hughes; but you will infer that I do not blame you for being emphatic. We both belong to the Stone age."

"It seems to me quite clear," Mark DeWolfe Howe writes, "that Laski sat down and manufactured for Stone's satisfaction the string of compliments. . . ." (Howe to A.T.M., April 30, 1954.) The Laski thus self-revealed was the man who for nearly two decades continued a warm and intimate correspondence with Justice Holmes.

a Western or Mid-western lawyer. Hughes, Stone, Brandeis, and Roberts were all Easterners; the Chief Justice and Stone, New Yorkers. Hoover queried the political wisdom of adding to the New York contingent. At the crucial moment Stone told the President that he would resign to ease the political problem so that the nation might have the benefit of Cardozo's great learning.*

Reports of Stone's gesture reached the press with dramatic effect, but still Hoover delayed. On several occasions, after a medicine-ball session, the Justice seemed distressed by the President's apparent willingness to "satisfy the supposed sectional requirements of the present emergency."[36] "One day," his law clerk has recalled, "he said that the current was running swiftly in the direction of Judge Orie L. Phillips. He requested me to dig out all of Judge Phillips' opinions and to give him a memorandum about them."[37] Through Brandeis, Stone obtained a memorandum on Phillips from a mutual friend, which "proves to the hilt what was to be expected from a young man of our generation who got his law in a correspondence school, and whose strong allegiances are with the Elks." He also received a *St. Louis Post-Dispatch* editorial on the jurist from Professor Frankfurter. All expressed the point of view Stone had consistently held—that the appointment of Cardozo would be the wisest from a strictly political point of view. Hoping they would "do good," the Justice sent them on to the President. "While I can hope," Stone said, "I do not expect." "Just why the opportunity to do an outstanding and fitting thing should seem so unattractive," he commented, "I do not understand."[38] The more the appointment was delayed, the more discouraged Stone became.

* "When President Hoover had under consideration the appointment of a successor to Justice Holmes," Stone recalled in 1939, "I was apprehensive lest a selection should be made which would emphasize the Court's conservative tendencies. . . . Feeling that they were already overemphasized, I feared that great public harm might result and that some sort of an explosion would occur not unlike that which actually took place after the decisions in the AAA case and the Tipaldo Women's Wage case. In a conversation with President Hoover, intended to emphasize both the importance of the appointment and Judge Cardozo's fitness, I intimated to him that if he feared criticism because of the addition of a New York man to the Court, when there were two other New Yorkers already there, I would be willing to retire from the Court. . . . I deserve no credit for the suggestion. I had some thought of retiring at that time because I felt that mine was a voice crying in the wilderness so far as the tendencies of the Court were concerned, and I had numerous opportunities to do other worth-while things." (H.F.S. to George S. Hellman, Nov. 30, 1939.)

Stone's support was rooted in mutual respect and confidence born of long-standing friendship. "I follow the work of the Supreme Court in these days with a more personal and intimate kind of pleasure than ever before," Cardozo had written Stone, March 22, 1928, "and with a subconscious sense of pride that one whom I hold to be a real friend is carrying forward its great traditions." Stone reciprocated Cardozo's friendship and respect and never regretted the major role he played in influencing President Hoover to make the appointment.

In one of his discussions with the President, Hoover mentioned an objection made in an influential quarter that the judge was not "socially" acceptable, that Cardozo was a Jew. "I told the President," Stone reported, "that he could assure the objector that the latter would never have a chance of being accepted as a member of the Century Club, to which Judge Cardozo had belonged for many years."

"I am as much in the dark as you are about the probable appointment to our Court," Stone told an old friend on the day Holmes' successor was named, "but I am apprehensive of the outcome."[39]

When, at last, Hoover yielded and sent Cardozo's appointment to the Senate, February 15, 1932, Stone was overjoyed. "The appointment is so obviously non-political that it will, paradoxically enough, be of great political advantage to the President. But, of course, that is always good presidential politics." It was, he said, "due more to the logic of the situation than anything else, and the fact that the President gave himself time really to survey the situation and learn all that was involved in it." "Perhaps," he added modestly, "I was in some measure responsible for its being dealt with in that way."[40]

Stone had a very special reason for backing Cardozo. He was grateful for a "fresh mind" and welcomed a recruit to his side of the great constitutional debate. "I feel quite sure," Stone predicted, "that his tendency will be to look upon the controversial questions which come before our Court almost as I do, although, of course, I realize that he may not always take the same slant. With his point of view and his rich experience, he will bring great strength to the Court. . . . I am very happy about it."[41]

"Hope you come soon," he wrote Cardozo, February 15, 1932. "We have been saving up some interesting cases for you."

From the beginning Stone and Cardozo were closely associated. The new Associate Justice lived only a block and a half from Wyoming Avenue, and the two men consulted frequently about pending cases, often exchanging memoranda. Among the cases Stone might have been "saving" was *Crowell* v. *Benson*, construing the Longshoremen and Harbor Workers' Compensation Act. At the time of this decision the Court consisted of eight justices. At conference they had split 5 to 3, Roberts siding with Stone and Brandeis. In short order Hughes rattled off an opinion that gave the dissenters their sole chance for rebuttal during eight terms of Court. The Chief Justice contrived his decision carefully. To give the flavor of friendliness to workmen's compensation and other administrative machinery, he devoted nearly three-fourths of his discussion to fending off phantom attacks upon the constitutionality of the administrative process. When he settled down to deciding the crucial issue, however, his position became crystal clear.

"There can be no doubt," he asserted early in the opinion, "that the

Act contemplates that as to questions . . . within the purview of the Act, the findings of the deputy commissioner, supported by evidence and within the scope of his authority, shall be final."[42] But the Chief Justice then discovered a species of "jurisdictional" or "constitutional" facts, which, like questions of law, the Court and not the commissioner, finally must determine. In Hughes' judgment, these must be decided on the basis of new evidence presented in court at a new trial rather than upon the record compiled by the administrative officer. He then made it appear that only this construction of the Act saved its constitutionality. Such interpretation, the dissenters believed, rendered the Act altogether "unworkable."

Stone and Brandeis had apparently cooperated in delaying delivery of the decision, hoping to wear down the Chief and force a modification of his opinion, or perhaps to obtain reargument after Cardozo joined the Court. "At the conference," Stone wrote Hughes, December 18, 1941, "I expressed doubt as to the construction given to the statute by the majority of the Court, which doubt still persists. I am holding your opinion for some further study on the point." In connection with his dissent Stone wrote Brandeis: "Even if the considerations which seem to weigh heavily with the Chief Justice require limiting the power of the commissioner, it does not follow that [the Court] should destroy his power as a collector of evidence. It would certainly be easier to construe [the Act] as requiring the Court to review that record even though it reviewed the evidence, than to construe it as the Chief Justice does. . . . You might make even more of this point."[43]

Neither the Act nor the Constitution commanded an interpretation prohibiting the commissioner from "performing all the functions of a special master." In other words, judicial scrutiny of administrative proceedings should be in the nature of a review of the record in that hearing, not a new trial in which evidence was received by the Court. "If that much of the Act were saved," Stone commented, "it could be made . . . workable."[44]

Brandeis had little opportunity to make capital of Stone's suggestions, as Hughes, weary of temporizing, wrote them identical letters, February 22, 1932, setting the decision's delivery for the following day. "I have no changes to propose," he wrote impatiently. "Justices Van Devanter, McReynolds, Sutherland, and Butler advise me that they have none, and that they will adhere to that opinion. It is their desire as it is mine—the case has been pending so long—that the decision should be announced at once."

Brandeis's painstaking dissent candidly exposed the practical effect of requiring a court trial *de novo* of fact issues canvassed thoroughly in the administrative proceeding. This process, the dissenter wrote, "will, I fear, gravely hamper the effective administration of the

Act. . . . Persistence in controversy will be encouraged. And since the advantage of prolonged litigation lies with the party able to bear heavy expenses the purpose of the Act will be in part defeated."[45]

Stone, in correspondence with friends, was sharply critical. "*Crowell v. Benson,* and some others which are on their way, are no surprise to me, but they do make me sad. . . . Notwithstanding all my years of teaching, I never realized what a treacherous and generally undependable instrument the human mind is, until the last six years."[46] "The Chief is getting concise," Stone said sarcastically of Hughes' rambling and largely irrelevant discourse. "Whenever I read one of his opinions I feel as if I'd been through a cyclone with everything but the kitchen stove flying in my face."[47] This biting indiscretion, picked up and reported in a Washington gossip book, was not calculated to foster wholehearted cooperation.

The congeniality between Stone and Cardozo, on the other hand, was evident from the start. Holmes' successor made his judicial debut in dissent. "Justice Cardozo's opinion was a gem," Stone exulted. "It afforded a very interesting contrast with the method and style of the prevailing opinion. He was a good deal troubled at the thought of starting his career with us by writing a dissenting opinion, but I think I persuaded him, if he needed any persuasion, that the way to happiness and a good night's sleep, is at least to agree with yourself."[48]

Yet the new Associate Justice did sometimes hesitate. In a highly controversial case, involving application of federal income tax to profits from the leases on state lands, Cardozo joined Stone's blast at the majority's decision exempting the leases from federal taxes as state instrumentalities; but he abstained from approving Brandeis's stern lecture, supported by Stone and Roberts, on the uses of *stare decisis* in cases involving constitutional issues. "I think Justice Cardozo did not join in Brandeis's opinion in the Coronado case," Stone explained, "because he felt sensitive about appearing too much in the role of a dissenter before he had put down an opinion for us."[49] Of Cardozo's eventual stand, however, there was no doubt. "He has courage and sees clearly, and I am sure will have faith and ultimately he will bring us to better days."[50]

In Washington, Cardozo found himself in a circle quite unlike the congenial aura of his New York court. Temperaments, accustomed to command, and never gentle, had been rubbed raw by the constant wrangling. "I have no doubt," Stone observed, "that he misses the atmosphere of the New York Court of Appeals and that he finds the present one a bit harsh."[51] In the circumstances, it was understandable that a novice might pause. Nor were biting comments confined to the Four Horsemen.* On occasion Stone himself had held off from one

* Butler, McReynolds, Sutherland, and Van Devanter.

of Brandeis's smarting indictments of the majority* in which "some expressions" were used "which were better left unsaid, although the logic of it and the authorities cited seemed to me unanswerable."[52]

In 1932, however, not even Cardozo's appointment to the Court was enough to lift Stone's spirit. The majority's usual disposition to give scant weight to legislative judgment when dealing with constitutional issues carried over into its conduct of every-day court work—interpreting and applying valid statutes.

The extent to which the majority undertook to defy manifest congressional purpose appeared strikingly in a case upholding an injunction against the oleomargarine tax despite explicit command of the federal taxing statute. "No suit for the purpose of restraining the assessment or collection of any tax shall be maintained in any court," the Act said.[53] But Justice Butler found that "special and extraordinary facts and circumstances" made Congress's prohibition "inapplicable." Brandeis joined Stone's brief dissent, which pointedly observed that the Act "cannot rightly be construed as permitting the present suit, whose sole purpose is to enjoin the collection of a tax. Enacted in 1867, this statute, for more than sixty years, has been consistently applied as precluding relief, whatever the equities alleged."[54] "The net result of that decision," Stone wrote, "is to authorize, if the Court is so minded, an injunction in any case where the tax is burdensome." A more elaborate dissent had been discarded because, "after all is said and done, the only objection to [what the Court did] . . . is that Congress has said in unmistakable terms that it shall not be done."[55]

Another of Stone's opinions, this time for the Court, restricted the power of federal courts to interfere by injunction with the collection of local taxes where state procedure afforded protection for the claimed federal right. "The scrupulous regard for the rightful independence of state governments which should at all times actuate the federal courts, and a proper reluctance to interfere by injunction with their fiscal operations," Stone observed, "require that such relief should be denied in every case where the asserted federal right may be preserved without it."[56]

But even occasional success did not affect his deep-seated despair. Friends and correspondents, noting his discouragement, tried to buck him up. "If ever your work seems endless and sometimes thankless," Carr wrote encouragingly, "just believe that it is appreciated by the profession as a whole and through it by people generally with whom the profession discusses the situation. You are steadily becoming

---

* The case was *Quaker City Cab Co.* v. *Pennsylvania*, 277 U.S. 389 (1928). Brandeis stressed the difference between a business carried on in corporate form and the same business carried on by natural persons as "justifying the legislature in classifying the former to their disadvantage for purposes of taxation."

stronger and stronger in the minds of the people as a whole as the coming leader of the liberal forces. Now that Justice Holmes has left the bench that feeling will become more profound. I am surprised how often lawyers express that view to me."[57]

Still the Justice would not be consoled. "The American Bar Journal," he complained, "which purports to give an account of the current doings of the Supreme Court has reported no case in which I have dissented this term. . . . You have more faith in the possibility of educating the bar than I have. I think, as a whole, it is the least educable body we have. I doubt whether many of them read dissenting opinions, or are particularly interested in them."[58]

A Harvard law teacher agreed that the bar was intractable. In "the Bourbon tradition—they not only learn nothing; they forget nothing." "But you are writing for many others," he countered, "for the law teachers, and if you think they don't need it you are greatly mistaken. Apart from all else, they need encouragement against, and liberation from, the inert influence which leaders of the bar directly and indirectly exert upon law schools. . . . Secondly, you educate students and the younger bar. Thirdly, it is more and more important to enlighten as you do the other departments of the social sciences and the influence that they exert upon the young and opinion generally. Finally, of course, there is the lay public and the lay press which . . . are interested in the work of the Court as never before . . . because of the increasing awareness that the Court touches daily the lives of people as never before."[59]

"May I say that you seem to get stronger all the while," Judge Learned Hand wrote, January 15, 1932, "and I adjure you not to be dissuaded from keeping your side vocal. Some day, with God's help, it will have a larger representation, but meanwhile, you must nail your colors to the mast, even though there be only two of you on the raft."*

By this time Stone's ability to marshal facts, and through them explore basic issues, rivaled that of Brandeis. He was especially and justly proud of his devastating dissent in *Heiner* v. *Donnan.* Here the majority held a federal statute imposing death duties on all gifts made within two years of death "arbitrary," "capricious," and afoul the Fifth Amendment. Speaking for the Court, Justice Sutherland evoked the sympathetic image of "the young man in abounding health, bereft of life by a stroke of lightning within two years after making a gift," whom the statute "conclusively presumed to have acted under the

---

* Efforts to bolster courage and confidence were still in order nearly two years later: "While all of us continue to be unhappy that some of your strong opinions are in dissent instead of being for the Court," Walter Gellhorn wrote, April 12, 1934, "nevertheless it is encouraging to observe how many of the views once expressed by you in dissent are now finding their way into majority opinions. That must give you a great deal of satisfaction."

inducement of the thought of death, equally with the old and ailing who already stand in the shadow of the inevitable end."[60] Stone's analysis of 102 cases in which the Government attempted without aid of the presumption to prove that gifts were made in contemplation of death completely demolished Sutherland's fabric of unreality, demonstrating how successfully wealthy old men evaded federal estate taxes by distributing gifts.*

The history of taxation had long been, to no small extent, a battle of wits between skill in devising taxes and astuteness in evading them.[61] Estate-tax authorities were especially troubled by difficulties growing out of the vague phrase "in contemplation of death." Finding it impossible to isolate gifts designed to elude the tax collector, Congress in 1924 imposed a tax on all gifts, irrespective of date or motive, at a rate equal to those under the estate tax. "The inclusion of this provision," the Ways and Means Committee of the House reported, "will prevent most of the evasion and is the only way in which it can be prevented." But the Supreme Court closed off this one possibility. The Act was arbitrary and unreasonable, the Justices said, because it might apply to gifts made with no thought of death or taxes.

The device chosen by Congress to garner this revenue seemed to Justice Stone well adapted to the legitimate object of reaping the full harvest of the estate tax. "The difficulty," he observed dryly, "of searching the motives and purposes of one who is dead, the proofs of which, so far as they survive, are in the control of his personal representatives, need not be elaborated. As the event has proved, the difficulties of establishing the requisite mental state of the deceased donor has rendered the tax on gifts in contemplation of death a weak and ineffective means of compensating for the drain on the revenue by the withdrawal of vast amounts of property from the operation of the

---

* "In 20 cases involving gifts of approximately $4,250,000, the Government was successful. In 3 it was partially successful; and in 78 involving gifts largely in excess of $120,000,000, it was unsuccessful. In another the jury disagreed. In 56 of the total of 78 cases decided against the Government, the gifts were made within two years of death. In this group of 56 donors, two were more than ninety years of age at the time of death; ten were between eighty and ninety; twenty-seven were between seventy and eighty; six were between sixty and seventy; six were between fifty and sixty; and only one was younger than fifty. There was one gift of $46,000,000, made within two months of death by a donor seventy-one years of age at death; one of $36,790,000 made by a donor over eighty, who consulted a tax expert before making the gift; one of over $10,400,000 made by a donor aged seventy-six six months before death; and one by a donor aged seventy-five at death, in which the tax assessed was over $1,000,000. There was one other in excess of $2,000,000; 5 others largely in excess of $1,000,000; 4 others in excess of $500,000; 13 in excess of $250,000; and 14 in excess of $100,000. The value of the gifts was not shown definitely in 3 cases; 12 involved gifts totalling less than $100,000. In the remaining 22 cases the gifts were made more than two years before the death of the donor." (*Heiner* v. *Donnan,* pp. 343-45.)

estate tax." Denial of the Act's validity, Stone concluded, "seems to me to rest on no substantial ground and to be itself an arbitrary and unreasonable restriction of the sovereign power of the Federal Government to tax, for which neither the words of the Fifth Amendment nor any judicial interpretation of it affords justification."[62]

Correspondents acclaimed Stone's dissent as a "judicial masterpiece." Justice Brandeis, who joined in it, was uncommonly enthusiastic. "It must be a pretty good opinion," Stone told his clerk. "I can't remember Justice Brandeis ever having been so flattering before."[63]

"They know not what they do," Professor Frankfurter groaned. "I suppose some of your brethren would be shocked to hear that they will bear not the least responsibility for what they may regard, and eventually may well be, too drastic action 'on the Hill.' That's why an opinion like yours is so profoundly important. It helps to save the Court from too comprehensive condemnation for its obscurantism in the delicate and awful task of wisely distributing the tax burdens in our complicated society."[64]

"The story of the old boys from seventy to ninety," Stone replied, "who gave away their fortunes and succeeded in beating the government was almost comical, if it were not for the tragedy which such things spell for government." But it was an "old story." "I suppose most lawyers will think I should have shut up after the Schlesinger case,* but it seemed to me worth while to demonstrate all the technical fallacies which entered into that decision, which were implicit, of course, in what Justice Holmes said, but not too obvious to the casual reader."[65]

The fulsome praise Stone's opinion evoked, combined with its intrinsic excellence, made the dissent stand out as the high spot of a dreary term. Long afterward the Justice identified the law clerk of that year by saying, "Let's see: You were with me when we did *Heiner* v. *Donnan*, weren't you?"[66] Nevertheless, the term left Stone unusually disconsolate. New and disturbing proof had been added to that rapidly accumulating since 1890, that the Supreme Court suffered most from "self-inflicted wounds."†

* See Chapter XVI, p. 253.

† "Look at the somewhat iconoclastic book, *Government by Judiciary*, by Louis B. Boudin," the Justice wrote a correspondent, April 16, 1932. The author's strictures were harsh, Stone agreed, but he could point to specific passages where the book had landed telling blows.

Stone called specific attention to Volume II, page 542 and following, especially the notes on page 544, also pages 548 and 549 and footnotes on the latter. On page 543, the author quoted a line from Hughes' book, *The Supreme Court of the United States*, pp. 52-53: "Stability in judicial opinions is of no little importance in maintaining respect for the Court's work." From this Boudin concluded that in any situation where the Chief Justice was bound to choose between recognizing the power to govern and the maintenance of "stability in judicial opinions" and

"My work is done," he commented wearily, May 25, "and we are packing our bags for a brief sojourn abroad. Twenty-nine opinions of all kinds is my record of this year, most of them uninteresting and unimportant, but as Justice Cardozo says, the votes count."[67]

CHAPTER TWENTY-TWO

# Judicial Advocacy, Pro and Con

## 1932-1933

The political scene shifted swiftly. Two months after Roosevelt's inauguration Stone reported: "To judge by the rapidity of changing events, as many decades might have passed."[1] This implied stricture of the Hoover regime did not mean that Stone was a New Dealer. But he did deplore GOP standpattism. The economic disaster and pervading social unrest, he felt, demanded prompt and courageous action, and he encouraged Republican bigwigs to support the administration's desperate effort to achieve economic recovery. "It is not only good citizenship, but good politics," he wrote, "for members of our party to support the administration and to strengthen its hand in any effort it may make to get control of the present situation. In fact, I am very strongly of the opinion that whether Congress votes it or not, the new President can exercise a very great degree of control if he has the courage and the will to do it and acts promptly as soon as he takes office. Unless he gets that kind of control in the first six months of his administration, he will be ruined in my judgment."[2]

F.D.R. rose to the challenge with alacrity. Personifying the confidence Hoover preached and blithely innocent of the complexities before which economists trembled, the President plunged dynamically

---

"respect for the Court," Hughes would take the latter course. It seemed extraordinary to the author that with "all the fuss raised about Mr. Hughes' views when he was nominated for the Chief Justiceship, it never occurred to anyone to inquire into the views held by him" on this subject.

The author of *Government by Judiciary* also took issue with the view that judicial decisions were becoming more "liberal." He was of the opinion that "our progressives are again doomed to disappointment." Of two things Mr. Boudin was certain: judicial decisions were dictated by chance, by the calendar, "by the *class* or *type* of men who administer judicial power, rather than by the Constitution"; that "there is a steady course of absorption of power by the United States Supreme Court at the expense of all other departments of government and of the people themselves."

into the work of reconstruction. Washington was "like a hospital," he commented gleefully, and "many of the patients came from Wall Street." Even Henry Ford conceded it was "up to the Government" to bail the nation's banks out of their financial morass.[3]

Stone did not approve the rush of innovations in toto. "Some of them, such as the economy measures," he wrote Hoover, May 2, 1933, "are very welcome, but others, such as the thirty-hour week and the move to revive foreign trade, seem irreconcilable."[*] In December the Justice noted with consternation "the disposition of the administration to trifle with the currency," and predicted a "battle royal" unless the President receded (which seemed to him not impossible) from the "extreme position which he has been taking."[4]

"There is a very strong impression here among competent observers," he reported, "that if the administration took a definite stand in favor of stabilization at almost any ratio, we would make a start toward revival of business, despite the added costs which have been loaded onto industry by the various rehabilitation measures."[5]

Among the measures Stone approved were those "the President is taking to balance the budget and to attend to other pressing matters affecting the Government. It seems to me that he has made a very good start and that if he can get most of his measures through before Congress begins to get out of hand, we may make some progress in getting the country going again on an even keel. I certainly wish him well."[6]

An invigorating spirit was also spreading to the capital's social life;

---

[*] Stone, like Hoover, had thought the return of prosperity was somehow dependent on Europe. By January 1932 the United States seemed "about as far down in the dumps as it has ever been." "I think I can see signs of a possible turn in the tide," he commented, "but I have little faith that it will become actual until the European situation is more settled." (H.F.S. to William Nelson Cromwell, Jan. 5, 1932.)

Stone spelled out his views thus: "I have often thought, in these years since the war, how differently the whole picture of the debt situation would appear if, in the negotiations for settlement, the European statesmen had planted themselves squarely on a single proposition, namely, that the repayment of their debt to us could not be guaranteed with certainty and regularity, except through the delivery of goods here or credit for goods delivered elsewhere, the same way in which the debt was created. That would have brought our protectionists to face the facts at the outset and would have necessarily resulted in some more flexible method of treatment than was actually provided for in the settlements. Finally, the last proposition made to us—that we acquiesce in omission of the next installment of the debt by France and all the others, without any showing or offer to show that those installments could not be met—was, to say the least, inept, and discloses a singular lack of knowledge of popular sentiment here. If they could have expressed a willingness to pay the next installment, as Italy evidently intends to do, it certainly would have paved the way to a more considerate reception of their main, and the really important proposition, that the whole debt problem now be examined in the light of realities." (H.F.S. to John Bassett Moore, Nov. 23, 1932.)

the Justice endorsed that too. "Last week we made our bow to the Roosevelts. Instead of the usual formal stand-up party when the Court greets the new President, we were invited for tea and had a very pleasant call. Both the President and Mrs. Roosevelt have an easy manner and quite attractive personalities. I can imagine that his path will be smoother than was Hoover's because of difference in personality. The latter found it difficult to meet people casually."[7]

This mild social revolution disturbed certain Justices. "I am not sure but what the pillars of the Constitution will fall," Stone remarked with simulated gravity. "Some of my brethren seemed to think so. Called upon to give such profound thoughts as I had on the subject, I said that I thought it would probably not affect our opinions and that beyond that I was not particularly interested."[8]

Exciting as the New Deal was in its beginnings, it had not yet touched the work of the Court, and nothing filled the void left by Hoover's absence in Stone's daily routine. "There have been busy moments for us," he remarked nostalgically, "although some of the activities of other days seem to have vanished—medicine ball, for instance. Now I content myself with daily setting-up exercises and an early morning walk before breakfast. But more than that I miss the old crowd. We gathered up the remnants for a little dinner party recently. . . . Very naturally the Hoovers were the leading subject of conversation. Alas," he wrote, "most of the party have left town by now and the Stones remain, hanging like the last leaves on the tree."[9]

On the Court his feeling of isolation grew. Picayune assignments, and the Chief Justice himself, added to his dissatisfaction. Discontent finally developed to such a point that he considered returning to law practice. Certain friends, carried away by political ambitions for the Justice, encouraged the move.

By December 1932 it was clear that "Hoover would have no more chance in 1936 than the proverbial snowball." "You would be the ideal candidate," Carr suggested, "one around whom all factions of the party could rally." Stone might be, it was thought, in a more advantageous position to win the Republican nomination off the Court. "While practicing in New York," Carr prognosticated, "you would of necessity be occupying a more or less public position through the character of business that would come to you. That, coupled with a reasonable adherence to political activities, would keep you in the forefront of the profession and afford the necessary publicity. There is no outstanding lawyer at the New York bar today, and the opportunity for you there is wonderful; and then, if the future should hold for you still greater honors, it would give to the people of this country a leader such as is more badly needed than ever before in our times."[10]

"There was genuine depression that year," his 1932 law clerk has recalled. "Whether he ever seriously thought of quitting I am not certain—but I do remember once (in the midst of *Puerto Rico* v. *Russell & Company*[11]) he threw down his pencil and said, in substance: 'I don't know why I bother with this instead of taking on a man's size job like reorganizing the railroads.'"[12] The reactionary course of judicial decisions, the prospect that the Court under Hughes' leadership would not follow the course Stone had set, forced him to think that he might be happier and his life more constructive in other fields. Close contact with politics in high places did not, however, whet ambition for a political career.

"You are quite right in saying that there will be an entirely new political picture in the next four years," the Justice commented on Carr's prognosis, "but having seen it all at close range, I cannot say that I am interested in it." "I might be interested," he added, in what seems to be an afterthought, "in going back to practice law in New York, as I suppose I could do at any time."[13]

John Foster Dulles's invitation to return to Sullivan and Cromwell was awaiting acknowledgment. "You certainly put a very difficult problem up to me," Stone replied, January 6, 1933, "especially because I think I realize what I could do in the New York setting, and how much I would enjoy doing it. But after thinking the matter over, with what seems to me adequate deliberation, I have come to the conclusion that I would not be justified in making any change. A decision either way must necessarily involve some regrets, but I cannot persuade myself that I ought to abandon the path on which I have started." Nearly three months later Dulles was "still mourning because I don't come back to New York."[14]

Judge Learned Hand, hearing that Stone might drop his judicial robes, strongly discouraged the idea: "If it is not impertinent to say so," Hand wrote, "I think you are going from strength to strength; your friends ask nothing more than that you should continue as you are now doing. The job is a big one, and men who attend to it grow with it. Besides, it seems to me that your views are likely to prevail in the not too far distant future, if you will only stick. I don't count too much on this burst of speed which the new 'Great White Father' has shown, but it is pretty clear that any appointments he is likely to make will turn out to be on your side rather than that of the present majority. That is not to be sneezed at."[15]

All such reassurances helped to compensate for "the bricks that are heaved at us."[16] Nevertheless the behavior of Hughes and Roberts continued to rankle. "Our Constitution is so simple and practical," the smiling new President had declared in his inaugural address, "that it is possible always to meet extraordinary needs by changes in emphasis and arrangement without loss of essential form."[17] F.D.R. might have cited the shifty judicial behavior of Hughes and Roberts in illustration. No consistent principles seemed to govern either of the most recent appointees. Indeed, the Chief Justice served under two flags. By placating both wings, he apparently hoped to avert an open break.

Hughes' split personality was especially conspicuous in cases involving the powers of administrative agencies. In *Crowell* v. *Benson*, for example, he spoke for the reactionaries and evoked the vehement protest of Stone, Brandeis, and Roberts.* To close students of the Court, this alignment of the Chief Justice with the mastiffs seemed incredible. "Before I had read the opinion," Professor Frankfurter commented, "I could hardly have believed that disciplined legal minds would reach the conclusions which the majority reached."[18] Later on the Chief Justice joined Stone and Cardozo in dissent when the majority, including Roberts, struck down a Virginia statute authorizing the state highway commissioner to order elimination of railroad grade crossings without giving the roads notice or opportunity for hearing. Justice Roberts, even more unsure of his ground than the Chief Justice, could write opinions on both sides of basic issues. "We are under a Constitution," one might have observed, parodying a famous dictum, "but the Constitution is what Hughes and Roberts say it is." Because of their vacillation, no clear-cut alignment was possible. Opinions veered now to a latitudinarian interpretation, now to the narrow, strict construction dear to bitter-end conservatives.

Many shared Stone's dissatisfaction. "I have been very much disappointed that Justices Hughes and Roberts have not joined with you and Justice Brandeis in your recent dissents," Professor Jerome Michael wrote, March 26, 1932. "I am puzzled by them. Apparently they are likely to view questions involving personal rights such as freedom of speech and of conscience pretty much as you and Justice Brandeis do, but they do not see economic issues the same way."

For Stone, the constitutional battle had two fronts. Against the Van Devanter-Sutherland faction, he waged a full-scale war of ends. In the camp of liberal dissenters, there were skirmishes over means.

Holmes once characterized Brandeis as an "upward and onward fellow." The accumulated lore of family background, wide reading, prodigious energy, and a keen mind, had developed in him a rigorously consistent set of social beliefs. In 1912 he had been recognized as one of the leading spokesmen of the "New Freedom." Nor were his convictions lightly held. Whenever he was convinced that he was 51 per cent correct, he then clung tenaciously to his beliefs and fought for them savagely. This was particularly true of his devotion to littleness, his mistrust of industrialization, born of the unique mixture of the pre-1848 German liberalism of his parents and profound knowledge of the

* See Chapter XXI, p. 337-39.

mysteries of corporate finance. On this and other subjects his writings carried vehement assurance, rivaling "the pronouncement of a believer in the Ptolemaic astronomy that the new Copernican world will not do."[19] Even Brandeis's warmest friends saw him as a proud, imperious man.* A peremptory note sometimes crept into his judicial opinions. Confident of his principles, he would attempt to convince all and sundry by flooding them with massive documentation, much of it strangely absent from the briefs submitted to the Court. In this respect, Brandeis's methods differed from those of both Holmes and Stone.

While Holmes would uphold legislation as not unconstitutional, Brandeis upheld it as constitutional and desirable. The latter's social and economic beliefs sometimes erupted in dissent as masterful social and economic discourses on the problem at hand. Brandeis's colleagues, even those most sympathetic with his stand, could not fail to see this. "I told him once," Holmes wrote, "that when he had strong economic, etc., convictions I thought that he sometimes became the advocate and ceased to be detached—but it isn't often."† "I don't think an opinion should be like an essay with footnotes," Holmes observed, "but rather should be *quasi* an oral utterance."[20]

Similarly Stone's disagreements with Brandeis were mainly procedural. Even when he agreed with the result, he sometimes found himself at odds with Brandeis on the form and content of the opinion. Elaborately annotated opinions seemed to him pretentious and made him suspicious. "I have read every one of these cases," he once commented in reference to one of Brandeis's long footnotes, "and not one of them supports his proposition."[21]

The differences between Stone and Brandeis were highlighted in *Liggett v. Lee*. Here Hughes and Roberts transferred allegiance from the "liberal" coalition which two years before had upheld the Indiana chain store tax,‡ to strike down a substantially similar Florida enact-

---

* "He gives orders like an omnipotent Sultan," Harold Laski wrote of Brandeis's Zionist activities. "Moreover he treats his fellow Zionists who differ from him almost as criminals." Laski found Brandeis a very difficult person— "intransigent and dominating, and unnecessarily prone to read evil motives into obvious actions. . . . I did not realize before how curiously suspicious a nature Brandeis has. He is extraordinarily profound in his insights, but, I should have said, not quite human in his contacts, with the result that he does not always see round a subject." (*Holmes-Laski Letters*, Vol. II, pp. 1298-99, 1302.)

† Taft also thought that Brandeis's judicial decisions were "much affected by preconception." "His preconceptions," the Chief Justice wrote Henry Taft, Oct. 26, 1926, "are as marked in one way as those of McReynolds in another, and neither he nor McReynolds exercises any such influence on the Court as does Van Devanter."

‡ The opinion was by Justice Roberts. The new dissenters, led by Sutherland, let the cat out of the bag, very much as Holmes, Brandeis, and Stone had done, when outvoted, in earlier cases. Said Sutherland: "The decisions have depended not only upon the varying facts which constituted the background for the par-

ment.[22] Brandeis, implacable foe of "bigness," entered a heavily documented dissent and sent it to Stone, inviting concurrence. "Your opinion," Stone replied March 1, 1933, "is a very interesting and powerful document." He expressed wholehearted agreement with Brandeis's customary use of the presumption of constitutionality, but the "rest of it goes further than I am inclined to go, because I do not think it necessary to go that far in order to deal with this case."

Nor was Stone content to dispose of his misgivings by generalization. "Specifically, my hesitation in joining your opinion is due to the following: I think you are too much an advocate of this particular legislation. I have little enthusiasm for it, although I think it constitutional. In any case I think our dissents are more effective if we take the attitude that we are concerned with power and not with the merits of its exercise. . . . Inquiry must be made whether the condition imposed [by the statute] is unconstitutional, and that requires examination of the question whether it is unduly discriminatory, because its method of graduation is unreasonable. My preference is to deal with the latter question as the more immediate, and as requiring no departure from the method of treatment employed in the earlier cases."

"I understand," he concluded, "Justice Cardozo is writing something on this line and I am inclined to go along with him if his development accords with my notions." In the end, Stone concurred with Cardozo. The opinion was most unusual in that its treatment of Brandeis, also dissenting, was almost as harsh as its condemnation of the majority.

Stone's failure to join Brandeis reflected the former's theory of what his function was as a dissenting judge. In dissent, Stone was intent on using his judicial talents within the conventional framework. He tried to force his brethren to live up to the oft-repeated pretensions of constitutional adjudication. He concurred with Cardozo because he was anxious to get before the profession a demonstration that "by use of accepted legal doctrine and technique, the Constitution may be made to fit our social and economic system."[23]

"Stone," Judge Learned Hand observed, "was a much more detached nature than Brandeis—more 'judicial' and reliable. However, Brandeis was a great innovator, most of the time in good causes."[24]

Justice Stone took seriously the "aphorisms of his trade." To him this meant thorough probing of ambiguous statutes for the "intent of Congress"; it meant according legislation he distrusted full benefit of the "presumption of constitutionality." When the Court struck down legis-

---

ticular legislation under consideration, but also, to some extent, upon the point of view of the courts or judges who have been called upon to deal with the question." (*State Board of Tax Commissioners* v. *Jackson*, 283 U.S. 527 [1931], p. 550.)

lation Brandeis favored in terms of sound public policy, the erstwhile
People's Attorney did not hesitate to take on the role of advocate and
utilize the Court as a forum to persuade others of its wisdom—a practice Stone deplored. Holmes, initially unfavorable, could put aside his
prejudices to sustain legislation without ever relinquishing his doubts,
and produce an opinion so cryptic as to leave his position unclear. On
this score, Stone often found Holmes' opinions inadequate. He never
accepted the modern industrial corporation uncritically as representing
what for Holmes was "one of the greatest forms of human power."
Nor did he share Brandeis's deep-seated enmity toward industrial bigness. Yet the former law school dean matched the People's Attorney
in his hostility toward business leaders who played fast and loose with
the moral obligations imposed by their positions of trust. It was always
a mystery to him "why we treat commercial crimes, and especially
frauds of a peculiarly despicable character, as leniently as we do,
and why, by way of contrast, the English courts have always been as
commendably stiff-necked as they appear to be."[25] Small wonder that,
in 1932, when George Washington Hill, president of the American
Tobacco Company, rode into the greatest economic debacle in history
on the crest of fabulous personal profit, the restrained New England
Justice sharply reminded business managers of their "duties as
fiduciaries."

The tobacco industry had not felt the pinch of economic depression.
In contrast with the poverty of the growers and the meager profits of
the distributors stood the alluring "composite return of 15.95 per cent
on net investment in the depression year of 1930."[26] Meeting after this
extraordinarily good year, the American Tobacco Company's board of
directors "considered and passed upon the adequacy of the compensation which its members were then receiving for their services to the
corporation, and the necessity of conferring further benefits on themselves in order to insure the continuance of those services."[27]

This was but the consummation of a plan the directors had initiated
in 1912 under a by-law authorizing six senior officers to divide among
themselves 10 per cent of any annual profit in excess of that earned
by the company. Since 1921, $10,000,000 had been thus distributed.
President Hill, in addition to his regular salary of $168,000 and a
special cash "credit" of $273,000, received in 1930 a profit-sharing
bonus bringing his total compensation for the year to more than
$1,278,000. Apparently even these rewards were insufficient to supply
management incentive.

Under a so-called "Employees Stock Subscription Plan," 56,712 unis-
sued shares of stock with a market value of $112 a share were sold for
$25 a share as a result of the 1931 meeting to persons selected by the

directors. Bonuses allotting 32,370 of these "employees" shares to officers brought Mr. Hill $1,169,280, while five vice-presidents divided nearly a million and a half.

Called upon "to account for their stewardship," these gentlemen sought absolution in stockholder approval of their nefarious "Plan," with no more than a hint that top management was to be blanketed into an "employees" stock bonus system. To say that this hint, "addressed by men in the position of trustees to their beneficiaries, gave warning of the wholesale gratuities which the directors subsequently bestowed upon themselves," irate Justice Stone growled, "would be extravagant." In effect, the directors' scheme requested "the stockholders to confer plenary authority on them to formulate a plan and to carry it into execution without any disclosure of its provisions." These well-laid plans had been foiled when Richard Reid Rogers, New York attorney and owner of four hundred shares of class B common stock, sued to enjoin transfer of the stock.

The case slowly worked its way to the Supreme Court, where Chief Justice Hughes and Justice Roberts and the four "reliables"—Butler, McReynolds, Van Devanter, and Sutherland—evaded the issue. Both federal and state courts "as a general rule," Justice Butler said for the majority, "decline to interfere with or control by injunction or otherwise the management of the internal affairs of a corporation organized under the laws of another state but will leave controversies as to such matters to the courts of the State of the domicile."

The Justices had "for the first time" held that "a federal court should decline to hear a case on the ground that it concerns the internal affairs of a corporation foreign to the state in which it sits." What is more, this innovation was achieved in the face of "peculiarly cogent reasons" why the federal courts should decide "cases like the present." Stone felt outraged. "The Court has decided today," he summarized ironically, "that its discretion requires it not to decide the tobacco case. As my discretion does not work that way, I took the liberty of committing the indiscretion of saying why."[28]

Far-flung activities of large corporations frequently, as in the case of the American Tobacco Company, rendered the legal home of business "neither the place of its real corporate life nor the home of its officers and directors." Rights of stockholders, steadily whittled down by the transfer of de facto control over gigantic financial structures to a handful of insiders, could be wiped out by the procedural complexities consequent upon restricting stockholders' suits to the state of the corporation's domicile. Such rights as stockholder-owners still possessed could be protected effectively only if the law permitted suits to be brought "where necessary parties and witnesses may be found, rather than in the place of the technical corporate domicile." The depression showed just how much the national welfare was tied up in the activities of the managers of integrated, multi-state industrial enterprises. "Extension of corporate activities, distribution of corporate personnel, stockholders, and directors through many states, and the diffusion of stock ownership, separated from corporate management," Stone noted (citing the then recent book by Berle and Means, *The Modern Corporation and Private Property*), "make the integrity of the conduct of large business corporations increasingly a matter of national rather than local concern."

Joined by Brandeis, Stone exposed the unquenchable greed of the American Tobacco executives and disclosed prior secret stock bonuses and cash "credits," awarded without the "knowledge or approval of its stockholders." "Perhaps," he observed privately, "the most astonishing manifestation of our times is the blindness of those who have the big stake in our present system. . . . It is the story of the Bourbons over again."[29]

The case exhibited but another facet of the general social malaise revealed by the stock-market crash and the ensuing economic chaos— the faithlessness of the great financial leaders to their trust. Bearing down on the major point, Stone conceded that the management had been skillful. Their initiative and enterprise had, it was true, helped to produce fabulous profits, but the directors were not dealing with the stockholders "at arm's length." These men were fiduciaries. "We need not conjecture," the Justice commented sharply, "whether, if the directors had had the hardihood to disclose in advance the benefits which they were to award to themselves, the stockholders would nevertheless have given their approval. Nor is it important that these directors have successfully managed the corporation and that under their direction it has earned large profits for its stockholders. Their business competence did not confer on them the privilege of making concealed or unauthorized profits or relieve them of the elementary obligation which the law imposes on all corporate directors to deal frankly and openly with stockholders in seeking their consent to benefit personally by reason of their relationship to the corporation."

To call their disingenuous proposal a "Plan," would be a perversion of language. In fact, "no plan of sufficient definiteness to comply with the New Jersey statute was ever submitted to the stockholders for their approval." The meeting of share owners represented nothing more than the rubber stamp of "proxies selected by the management of the corporation for the occasion." All this was in plain violation of the most elementary responsibilities of men occupying positions of trust.

Stone expressed his position bluntly. The American Tobacco shareholders were entitled, he said, to read that proposal "in the light of the fundamental duty of directors to derive no profit from their own official action, without the consent of the stockholders, obtained after full and fair revelation of every circumstance which might reasonably influence them to withhold their consent. . . . They were entitled to assume that the proposal involved nothing which did not fairly appear on its face and above all that it was not a cloak for a scheme by which the directors were to enrich themselves in great amounts at the expense of the corporation, of whose interests they were the legal guardians."

The most notable aspect of the majority opinion, endorsing this managerial greed, was its ironically sensitive regard for the jurisdiction of state courts and the evident desire to be restrained in the scope given diversity of jurisdiction. A close student of the Court speculated on "how it must have pained the moral nature of the Chief to be prevented by technical 'jurisdictional' requirements from expressing his moral indignation at the facts you set forth in your opinion."

"It proves," Professor Frankfurter observed, "that obstructions and difficulties, unreason and injustice, inhere not in the Constitution and in our legal conception, or in the operating ideas of lawyers but are referable to the equipment of particular men, and therefore demonstrate that we ought not to throw out the baby with the bath, we ought not to make inroads upon our constitutional structure but ought to be zealously alert in the choice of those whom we entrust with the administration of our laws or our lawmaking."

Stone's opinion was even more significant, perhaps, as a penetrating "diagnosis of modern business abuses," prompting one observer to wish he could write a series of studies entitled "Enemies of Capitalism." Said he: "Instead of dealing with Marx, Lenin and Co., I should analyze the Charles E. Mitchells, the Samuel Insulls and Co., and include therein one George W. Hill."

Though the Associated Press sent out a full report of Stone's opinion, only one paper—the *St. Louis Post-Dispatch*—published it. The *New York Times* on January 24 had a meager and somewhat garbled report on the financial page. "I would like to think this is only lack of news sense," the Justice commented somewhat sardonically, "but evidently that sense was not lacking to the Associated Press. Perhaps it may have been overborne elsewhere by a sense of the benefits to be received by Lucky Strike advertisers." Despite such private censorship, news of Stone's dissent circulated rapidly.

"The sad part of the majority opinion," a former law clerk wrote, January 25, 1933, "is its far-reaching effects. It has been impossible to curb the greed of the states in their competition for the lucrative corporation business and the taxes accruing therefrom. So long as the courts of the nation were open to the stockholder, he could receive some measure of protection despite the unsocial character of the legislation in force in such states as Delaware. One cannot effect a very exalted jurisprudence from the judiciary of a state which has statutes of this character upon its books!"[30]

Requests for copies of the opinion soon exhausted Stone's personal allotment, indicating that the tobacco company's stockholders recognized that the indignant dissent had poison in it. This may have been understood dimly even by Hill himself. In any event, the *New Republic* believed that the Justice's exposé alone had moved the magnate to announce "the surrender of his heavy stock allotment."[31]

"It is rather amusing," Stone commented, "that after all the years of criticism the solid brass of the gentleman in question was penetrated. His public statement made it appear that it was the plan for the stock allotment to employees that was assailed. Whereas it was the failure of the directors and high officials to reveal their share in it to stockholders, in seeking their consent, which was the subject of criticism. What a pity it is that responsible and honest businessmen cannot be made to realize that such people are far greater enemies of capitalism than Lenin and his associates!"[32]

When, in an attitude of abject conversion, Hill piously scheduled a stockholders' meeting to consider "the acts of the management in awarding remuneration to the officers and directors of the company for the past fifteen years,"[33] Stone, with many others, assumed ratification of the directors' actions would be "easy." Later he was encouraged by reports that they were sending out special delivery repeat requests for proxies. Frankfurter passed along news from Connecticut's Governor Cross about " 'some stockholders in the American Tobacco Company who tell me that they are now carefully scrutinizing the material which the company is sending them.' "[34] On April 5, 1933, "George Washington Hill got his ratification at last, but not without a sizable dissent. Perhaps," Stone wrote, "the leaven is working."[35]

Hill's bold raids came up for Supreme Court examination again in 1933. This time the lavish cash bonuses were questioned. "I have seldom planted any ferment that worked better than the Tobacco case dissent," Stone exulted while the second case was under consideration.* "I suspect it may even have some effect on some courts."[36] He

---

* In reinforcing the disclosures then being made in testimony before the Senate Banking and Currency Committee, Stone's opinion presumably influenced the enactment of the Securities Act of 1933 (Public Law No. 22, 73rd Cong.). "Of course," Stone wrote Frankfurter, May 15, 1933, "the Stock Exchange should require precise information as to the total distribution made to officers and directors. The fact that it has never done so shows how little it performs what should be its real function to protect adequately those who deal in securities sold under its auspices. Many years ago after I had unearthed a series of shockingly fraudulent performances by members of the Exchange, which should have been known to the Governors of the Exchange, I told the latter that the survival of the Exchange would depend primarily on their own willingness to take proper measures to protect adequately the interests of those who availed of its facilities."

was right. This time his brethren unanimously* pronounced Hill's cash gratuities "so large as in substance and effect to amount to spoliation or waste of corporate property."[37]

In midsummer George Washington Hill gave up. At his prompting, suits based on Stone's dissent were settled. Fellow officers and directors returned their shares and accepted a plan substantially reducing their "extra" compensation. That Hill, after reading Stone's dissent, "promptly surrendered his stock" seemed to the Justice, "the greatest tribute ever paid my literary powers."[38]

"Certain it is," Stone's law clerk has recalled, "that he put his whole heart into a job like the dissent in *Rogers* v. *Guaranty Trust;* and he said over and over, while it was being written, that it was by such practices of businessmen who forgot they were trustees, rather than by socialist theories, that the system of free enterprise would be brought down."[39]

Increasingly the Court became the subject of critical comment, and the Chief Justice was represented as resenting close scrutiny of the Court's doings. In passing along this gossip to Stone, Frankfurter commented: "Why people should resent constant criticism upon their labors—particularly people who have ultimate power—I have never been able to understand. But perhaps the answer is that they *have* ultimate power."[40] Now, more than ever, it was in the Chief Justice's interest to preserve the fiction that judges exert only judgment, not will. "If only the theological tradition were not so strong upon our profession," Frankfurter opined September 28, 1933, "or rather if it did not lie so heavily upon some of its leading ministers like the Chief [Hughes], then there would be more forthrightness in opinions—things would be called by their right names instead of pretending that it is all a logical unfolding and that cases inconsistent with each other can be reconciled."

It was on this fortress of judicial pretense that Stone continued to direct his fire. In a long series of opinions he proved "that abstractions and difficulties, unreason and injustice, were not in the Constitution, . . . but are referable to the equipment of particular men."[41] Nor was his effort wholly ineffective. After the triumph in the Minnesota Moratorium case of 1934,† Sterling Carr asked whether "a great light did not dawn upon Chief Justice Hughes from the Rogers case." "I think you have hit upon a great truth," Stone replied. "The gentleman in question is too intelligent not to know when he gets off on the wrong foot. What was said in the Rogers case and some others has brought home the danger of doing that."[42]

---

\* Justice Roberts took no part in the decision or consideration of the case.
† See Chapter XXIII, pp. 360-65.

Only the most obtuse could fail to see that the Court was deeply mired in politics. For one of Stone's most prolific correspondents, the old plaint "They know not what they do" now became a persistent refrain. This had been the subject of comment in one of Professor Frankfurter's visits with Stone in the spring of 1932. "I refuse to prostitute the office which I hold by playing politics," the Justice told the Harvard Law professor. "That's the attitude," Frankfurter commented in an appreciative note, "that makes the Supreme Court for me a truly venerated institution. We must indeed fight to have at least a majority so conceive their function."[43] To this cause Stone was now increasingly dedicated.

CHAPTER TWENTY-THREE

# *Tenuous Victory*

## · 1933-1934

In the fall of 1933 Stone's foreboding gloom gave way to a craftsman's sense of a great task ahead. "I have been literally on the jump since we reached Washington the last of September," he wrote Carr. "At that time I had examined three hundred applications for certiorari, and have gone over a hundred or more since. We have also had two weeks of argument, with an unusually difficult lot of cases, and in the last two weeks I have turned out three opinions dealing with unusual and difficult subjects. The Supreme Court is not yet in the NRA, so far as hours of labor and pay are concerned."[1]

Nights were also full. "It looks as though we would be out every evening this month: two Embassies, the White House, and three private parties are on the list this week."[2] He still missed Hoover, but now thought of his old friend as a private citizen or Cabinet member, not as President. "I walk by the S Street house almost every day," he wrote Hoover, "and wish that its old occupants were back in it. We will give them a housewarming whenever they choose to come."[3]

The growing professional eminence of his sons—Marshall, a mathematics professor at Harvard, and Lauson, a rising New York lawyer—helped to lift Stone's spirits. In 1933 both the Justice and his son Marshall were elected to the American Academy of Arts and Sciences. "Marshall," his father wrote proudly, "lately made an address before the Academy which caused a good deal of comment among the scientific men. It was, I suppose, on a mathematical subject. He hasn't yet told me."[4]

Other prospects had brightened as well. Stone foresaw the end of prohibition and approaching opportunity to indulge his skill as a connoisseur of fine wines. "I imagine you will have a merry Christmas in San Francisco," he suggested to Carr, "although I suppose repeal of prohibition will not make such a difference to San Franciscans." Repeal, however, had not brought "better days" to the District of Columbia. "Unfortunately, we are still under the dry law in Washington, a survival of pre-Volstead days. As far as I can observe, no one pays any attention to it except Supreme Court Justices, so you see my last state is worse than my first." For a time Stone feared, and not in jest, that Congress would keep the capital dry "as a political sop." "But if we should ever be free men," he told his friend, "I would like very much to *purchase* some well-selected California wines." The very subject roused tender memories of "before the drought." "My recollection is that California used to produce excellent wines of the claret, burgundy, Moselle, and Chablis type. I distinctly do not wish you to give yourself any trouble about it, but in your travels you may hear of something good or learn of producers of a good quality of wine who have eastern representatives from whom I can secure a supply, if the better days come."

By late January the liquor bill was past Congress and ready for the President's signature. "The estimate is," the one-time Attorney General wrote, "that in about two weeks we will be living in a free world again. It hardly seems possible that after all these years one can take a glass of wine and not be a criminal. What a performance we have been through, and I am wondering whether, in our eagerness to get the country out of the depression, we are not doing things which will seem equally foolish ten years hence."

Though repeal did not take effect immediately, Stone pushed plans to restock his cellar. "You can have the wine reserved," he told Carr impatiently, "so that we will be sure of it, and the moment I get word you can ship it on."

At long last the ban was lifted, and Stone did secure some California wines. "Saturday evening," he hastened to relate to Carr, "we had the luxury of giving a dinner to twenty-two people, with wine on the table. It seemed like old times."[5]

Repeal of the Volstead Act was not the only significant reform under way. A hundred days of the New Deal had encouraged people in all walks of life to lift their heads in hope and look to the future. But the long road uphill was tortuous; swift congressional achievements had not yet brought relief from the ravages of depression years. The state legislatures also had to tackle tangled problems of jobless workers, debt-ridden farmers, and bankrupt business. Over all this unprecedented outpouring from the legislative mill, both national and state, loomed the lethal threat of unconstitutionality.

Four Justices were set on freezing the *status quo*. With occasional help from Hughes and Roberts, they had built up a frowning wall of precedents limiting, restricting, or destroying the power to govern. "Freedom of contract" was still "the general rule and restraint the exception."[6] This meant in practice that government had no power to fix minimum wages for women, or to regulate exploitive private employment agencies, or to protect the public from greedy theater-ticket scalpers; even in an emergency "more serious than war," government could not regulate and control persons who wished to enter a business already suffering from over-capacity.[7] Individuals were free to act against the general welfare; government was not free to act for the general welfare. The Constitution barred such action, the Justices declared solemnly, not the Court.

Justice Holmes had exploded this myth as early as 1905, when he accused his colleagues of enforcing as fundamental law Herbert Spencer's dogma that liberty is measured by the "relative paucity of restraint" that government places on the individual.[8] In case after case, Holmes, Brandeis, and Stone had riddled the vacuous and stale assumption that "natural" economic arrangements ("laws") are so implicit in men's acts as to be beyond constitutional power and control. Yet the barrier of restrictive decisions was built even higher. Purporting to carry more than merely constitutional authority, laissez faire was proclaimed as the basic reality of social progress itself. "To sustain the individual freedom of action contemplated by the Constitution," Justice Sutherland had pontificated in the District of Columbia Minimum Wage case, "is not to strike down the common good but to exalt it; for surely the good of society as a whole cannot be better served than by the preservation against arbitrary restraint of the liberties of its constituent members."[9]

By querying all such assumptions and devices, by boldly proclaiming that "new conditions impose new requirements upon Government and those who conduct Government,"[10] F.D.R.'s swift innovations stiffened and angered judicial reaction. Stone himself was not uncritical of the new regime. He scored Roosevelt's failure to recommend "legislation of any kind" in his 1934 message to Congress. "It was," Stone noted, "merely a report of what he had been doing, with the evident hope and expectation that it would be approved by Congress and that Congress would keep hands off until he could do some more—a strange governmental situation for the United States of America." Congressional abdication and concentration of power in the hands of "one man" gave him "some concern about the political future of this country." But he added, "I am not saying that there is any different or any better method which could have been pursued in this crisis."[11]

Stone knew that quick, effective action must be taken to lift the country out of depression—perhaps necessary also to avert drastic change. He had long recognized standpattism as playing into the hands of revolutionaries. Now, even in rural areas, law and order ran neck and neck with riot and anarchy. Formerly prosperous Midwestern states such as Minnesota had seen annual cash income of farmers fall in 1932 to an average of $141. That same year more than one-half of the state's farms were mortgaged or foreclosed. "The situation produced a general outcry for relief," one observer reported. "In isolated instances mobs of farmers took the law into their own hands and prevented foreclosure sales by force."[12] These sporadic outbreaks indicated the trend and force of feeling among the debtors, and Minnesota's wheat growers made every effort to impress their plight on the state's lawmakers. "When the legislature assembled, a caravan of two or three thousand farmers descended upon St. Paul from southern Minnesota, in an astonishing array of antediluvian automobiles, and swarmed over the capitol, making demands and threats and uttering dire predictions." Three weeks later the Governor addressed an uproarious gathering on the steps of the capitol: "I want to say to the people of Minnesota that if the legislature—the Senate in particular—does not make ample provision for the sufferers in this state . . . I shall invoke the powers that I hold. I shall declare martial law. A lot of people who are now fighting the measures because they happen to possess considerable wealth will be brought in by provost guards. They will be obliged to give up more than they are giving up now."

The Governor ordered sheriffs "to refrain from proceeding with all foreclosure sales until after the legislative sessions." In due course, a bill modeled on New York's postwar Emergency Housing Act, giving courts power to postpone mortgage foreclosures, was passed without a dissenting vote.[13] Debtors now hastened to bring their holdings under its protection, while creditors challenged in the courts this statutory readjustment of the terms of their contracts.

The first test case under the Act concerned one Blaisdell and his wife, who were struggling to pay off a mortgage on their fourteen-room house by letting rooms and keeping boarders. The state's highest court did not question the legislature's action in bowing to desperation.* "The members of the legislature," it observed, "come from every community of the state and from all the walks of life. They are familiar with conditions generally in every calling, occupation, profession, and

---

* The State Supreme Court declared the Governor's executive order unconstitutional.

business in the state. Not only they, but the courts, must be guided by what is common knowledge. It is common knowledge that in the last few years land values have shrunk enormously. Loans made a few years ago upon the basis of then going values cannot possibly be replaced on the basis of present values. We all know that when this law was enacted the large financial companies, which had made it their business to invest in mortgages, had ceased to do so. No bank would directly or indirectly loan on real-estate mortgages . . ."[14]

On November 8 and 9, 1933, in faraway Washington, the case was argued in the Supreme Court, and on January 8, 1934, the Justices sustained the Act, 5 to 4. Chief Justice Hughes, taking advantage of his prerogative, assigned this strategic majority opinion to himself.

The Minnesota statute seemed to fly in the face of the Constitution's categorical imperative—that no state shall pass any law "impairing the obligation of contracts" (Article I, Section 10). Nevertheless the Chief Justice upheld the act by distinguishing between the *obligation* of contract and the *remedy* given by the legislature to enforce that obligation. In short, he tried to demonstrate that the moratorium did not really impair the *obligation* of Minnesota mortgages; the statute only modified the remedy. Article I, Section 10, is qualified, Hughes argued, "by the measure of control which the state retains over remedial processes," and the mortgage contracts themselves are subject to the "reservation of the reasonable exercise of the protective power of the state," which is "read into all contracts as a postulate of the legal order."[15]

The Chief Justice went out of his way to consider the relation of emergency to power. "Emergency does not create power," he said. "Emergency does not increase granted power or remove or diminish the restrictions imposed upon power granted or reserved." Specific constitutional requirements, such as the representation of each state by two senators, are plainly distinguishable, he noted, from the constitutional provisions against impairing the obligation of contracts. The former provision is not affected by emergency; the latter is. "While emergency does not create power, emergency may furnish the occasion for the exercise of power."[16]

It was this line of reasoning that opened the way for reactionary attack. The priestly dogma of Sutherland's jurisprudence knew no such loopholes, and he took this occasion to say so. "I can only interpret what is said," the dissenter remarked scornfully, "as meaning that while an emergency does not diminish a restriction upon power it furnishes an occasion for diminishing it; and this, as it seems to me, is merely to say the same thing by the use of another set of words, with the effect of affirming that which has just been denied." Sutherland was especially vehement in opposing Hughes' "adaptative" theory of the fundamental law. Invoking historical evidence, he concluded: "The foregoing leaves no reasonable ground upon which to base a denial that the clause of the Constitution now under consideration was meant to foreclose state action impairing the obligation of contracts *primarily and especially* in respect of such action aimed at giving relief to *debtors in time of emergency.*"[17] War constituted an emergency, justifying legislative modification of rent leases, to be sure, but ruinous economic depression was not a comparable holocaust. This was no occasion for slackening the stubborn "strength of the fabric" woven by the Fathers.[18] The aging justice had seen "economic emergencies" before: "The present exigency is nothing new. From the beginning of our existence as a nation, periods of depression, of industrial failure, of financial distress, of unpaid and unpayable indebtedness, have alternated with years of plenty."[19]

Two hundred billion dollars of private credit had been destroyed, a total national income had been reduced from over eighty billions to under forty billions. But to this Supreme Court Justice all such cataclysmic economic chaos was nothing new. Now, as always, recovery must be achieved by "self-denial and painful effort." As the "snapper" to his forthright dissent, the former Utah Senator challenged: "If the provisions of the Constitution be not upheld when they pinch as well as when they comfort, they may as well be abandoned."[20]

Cardozo and Stone read the Chief Justice's first draft with misgivings so serious that each considered writing a concurring opinion. The former actually prepared a draft, and Stone submitted a long memorandum. In conflict were two fundamentally different conceptions of the Constitution. For Sutherland, a Constitution, in essence, limited rather than granted power. For him, a Constitution that "grows or changes with every passing popular pain, ceases to exist." The views of Stone and Cardozo, on the contrary, resemble Jefferson's. Jefferson believed that "to lose our country by a scrupulous adherence to written law, would be to lose the law itself, with life, liberty, property and all those who are enjoying them with us; thus absurdly sacrificing the end to the means."[21]

Their approach was also in the tradition of Marshall and Holmes. The opening paragraph of Cardozo's undelivered concurrence quoted Marshall's famous dictum: "We must never forget that it is *a constitution* we are expounding," a constitution "intended to endure for ages to come, and, consequently, to be adapted to the various *crises* of human affairs."[22] Cardozo also included the bold note Holmes struck in 1920: "The case before us must be considered in the light of our whole experience and not merely in that of what was said a hundred years ago."[23] The Minnesota statute, Cardozo admitted, "may be inconsistent with things" which the men of 1787 believed or took for granted, but "their beliefs to be significant must be adjusted to the world they

knew. It is not . . . inconsistent with what they would say today. . . ."
For them as for us, Cardozo suggested, "the search was for a broader
base, for a divison that would separate the lawful and forbidden lines
more closely in correspondence with the necessities of government."

Cardozo did not undertake to square the Minnesota statute with the
literal requirements of Article I, Section 10. He did not rest his case
in favor of the moratorium on "the distinction between right and remedy with all its bewildering refinements." The more general provisions
of the Fourteenth Amendment were seen as pointing the way "toward a
rational compromise between private rights and public welfare." "A
promise exchanged between individuals," he concluded, "was not to
paralyze the state in its endeavor at times of direful crises to keep its
life-blood flowing."

Cardozo's attack on Justice Sutherland's deep-freeze dogmas was
equally forthright. "A gospel of laissez faire—of individual initiative—
of thrift and industry and sacrifice—may be inadequate in the great
society that we live in to point the way to salvation, at least for economic life. The state when it acts today by statutes like the one before
us is not furthering the selfish good of individuals or classes as ends
of ultimate validity. It is furthering its own good by maintaining the
economic structure on which the good of all depends." The Chief
Justice took over this idea almost verbatim.

Stone also threatened to speak out independently if certain of his
points were rejected. "I have taken more than the usual time to study
your opinion," he wrote, December 13, 1933, "because of the great importance to the public and to the court of the questions involved." Like
Cardozo, he wished to elevate the tone of the opinion and focus the
argument on the merits of the case: "I am not inclined to join in so
much of the [opinion] . . . as states that the relief afforded could only
be of a temporary character. . . . I think we should be meticulous in
not making pronouncements with respect to cases other than that
before us. Moreover, the statement itself, without definition, has not
very much meaning. We may yet have to deal with cases where the
moratorium is for longer periods and where the law itself is made
applicable for longer periods than those involved in this case; whether
they could be regarded as temporary or not is, of course, a relative
matter, and other and controlling considerations might come in. Therefore, it seems to me that we should leave ourselves absolutely unham-
pered by pronouncements which might be taken to affect situations
not presented to us in this case."*

---

* Hughes disregarded this suggestion; it may be that he was looking ahead too.
Test cases involving NIRA and the AAA loomed on the horizon. Emphasis on the
temporary character of the Minnesota legislation might, if the Court's approach in
the Blaisdell case proved embarrassing, provide a dignified, unhurried retreat. Be-

Continuing, Stone wrote: "I think the part of the opinion which discusses what the Court has sometimes treated as a distinction between obligation and remedy is somewhat confusing and, to some extent, obscures the point with which we have to deal in the present case. The distinction . . . comes to nothing more than a question of degree, and the net result of the cases seems to be unreasonable. Our present case has no complications of this character, since the statute does cut down both obligation and remedy to a material extent, and the sole question is whether private parties, by their contract, may tie the hands of the state so that it is powerless to deal with a problem vital to the Government itself. I think the opinion would gain in power and directness if the discussion of the right-remedy phase were very much condensed or relegated to a footnote."

Why not, Stone suggested, erect the opinion on more realistic foundations? "We are . . . confronted with a problem permeating the entire economic structure, of which Chief Justice Marshall probably never had any conception. A generation or more ago the state was concerned principally with problems affecting the moral and physical well-being of society. When its concern for public morality had led a state to a judgment different from that which had formerly prevailed, this Court could not say that it exceeded constitutional limitations in curtailing a grant to indulge in public lotteries, even though lotteries had long been accepted as legitimate activity. Today, when the whole economic structure of society is threatened with widespread foreclosures, the state has afforded a measure of relief which tends to prevent the impending ruin of mortgagees, as well as mortgagors, and to preserve the stake of the former as well as of the latter in land mortgages, viewed as a form of investment security. . . . It is, I think, desirable to emphasize the special character of the mortgage situation as affects both mortgagors and mortgagees, to show that, looked at collectively, the legislation protects the interest of both and harms neither. Once conceded, as it must be, that the contract clause is not an absolute and unyielding restriction upon the state, such legislation is demonstrated to be so reasonable in character as to be plainly within state competency."

The Chief Justice's opinion, as finally announced, included long pas-

---

fore the year was out, the Chief Justice found occasion to use his previously prepared defense. An Arkansas statute, unlimited in duration, exempting the avails of all insurance policies from seizure for debts, was unanimously held invalid. Hughes noted that the Arkansas legislation made no attempt to discriminate among debtors on the basis of need, or to limit the sacrifice of contract rights. He distinguished the Blaisdell statute principally on the ground of its temporary nature, which brought from Sutherland the tart observation that "we do not possess the benevolent power to compare and contrast infringements of the Constitution and condemn them when they are long-lived or great or unqualified, and condone them when they are temporary or small or conditioned." (*Worthen Co.* v. *Thomas,* 292 U.S. 426 [1934], p. 435.)

sages[24] from the Cardozo draft opinion and from Stone's memoranda. But he kept intact the legalistic logomachy about emergency power, thus exposing himself to Sutherland's broadside. From Cardozo came the verbal formulation of the Court's recognition of "the necessity of finding ground for a rational compromise between individual rights and the public welfare"—the passage that commentators praised as embodying juristic statesmanship. But Hughes retained the stultifying arguments to which Stone and Cardozo objected. So equivocal a result dissatisfied Stone. "Probably if I had been doing the writing, I should have presented the matter in somewhat different form," he remarked to a friend. "Just between ourselves I feel it was too long and discursive."[25] Believing that the Court had really done nothing more than it had in the Rent cases,[26] Stone felt that the Chief Justice's views could have been expressed more forthrightly.

When Stone at last gave up any idea of a concurring opinion, his law clerk, Howard C. Westwood, and his secretary, Miss Gertrude Jenkins, were distressed. Miss Jenkins later recalled that "Stone was inclined, at first, to write a concurrence, stronger than the majority opinion written by Hughes, C.J. He changed his mind and wrote the memorandum, taking it down personally to the Chief. . . . As it [Hughes' opinion] was rewritten incorporating H.F.S.'s views, it was accepted by Brandeis and Cardozo, who, with Stone, thought Hughes' opinion [as originally circulated] was poor."

Stone himself may have regretted his hesitancy to speak out. "The opinion [Hughes'] was given such widespread publicity, and C.E.H. praised so highly, one article likening him to Marshall," Miss Jenkins recorded, "that I think H.F.S. was cured and will write his dissents and concurrences in the future, for all his hesitation to do so."

While Minnesota's mortgage-ridden farmers won success in preventing foreclosure sales, disgruntled dairymen in Wisconsin, Illinois, and New York were protesting the baneful effects of that implacable "natural law"—supply and demand. Marauding bands of Wisconsin dairy farmers blocked farm-to-market roads and stopped the movement of milk to cities. Individuals, acting in a concerted "strike," dumped their milk rather than sell it at the going price. The spirit, if not the action, of "agricultural rebellion" reached out to New York dairymen, and they held back "only to give the legislators a chance to move in their behalf."[27] The same pressures that led to moratorium legislation in Minnesota moved the New York Assembly to approve a milk-control law, setting up a board to establish minimum retail prices. Acting promptly, this board pegged the price at nine cents a quart. In the face of this statute, Leo Nebbia, an obscure Rochester grocer, sold two quarts of milk and a five-cent loaf of bread for eighteen cents. The state courts upheld his conviction under the Act, and he appealed to Washington.

As in the Blaisdell case, the verdict was 5 to 4, the Chief Justice and Justice Roberts aligning themselves with Stone, Brandeis, and Cardozo to sustain the statute. Here, at last, was an opportunity to correct the restrictive "business affected with a public interest" barrier, as well as to break through the impassable wall Justice Sutherland and his followers had raised against price-fixing. Stone's dissents in the Tyson and Ribnik cases might well have served as the opinion of the Court. It did not, however, work out that way.

The Chief Justice assigned this crucial case to Justice Roberts, who, "in effect," merely restated the doctrine found in "Justice Stone's dissenting opinions."[28] "The deflation of the once mighty concept of public interest is almost wholly Stone's work," Walton Hamilton wrote, "yet, when the time for the final blow came, another Justice was appointed to say that it had all been an historical error."[29]

Justice Roberts' opinion begins by noting the New York joint legislative committee's "radical" assertion that "milk is an essential item of diet," and further that for New York the milk industry "largely affects the health and prosperity of its people." Admittedly, the industry was not a public utility, nor a monopoly, yet it had been much regulated. "But if, as must be conceded, the industry is subject to regulation in the public interest," Roberts commented, paraphrasing Stone's remarks in the Ribnik case, no "constitutional principle bars the state from correcting existing maladjustments by legislation touching prices." In a frontal attack on a basic taboo of Sutherland, Justice Roberts continued: "The thought seems nevertheless to have persisted that there is something peculiarly sacrosanct about the price one may charge for what he makes or sells, and that, however able to regulate other elements of manufacture or trade, with incidental effect upon price, the state is incapable of directly controlling the price itself." "This view," he commented, returning to Chief Justice Waite's liberal doctrine in *Munn* v. *Illinois,* "was negatived many years ago."[30]

Gone also was Chief Justice Taft's restrictive interpretation of "business affected with a public interest." The concept which Chief Justice Waite had used to broaden the scope of state regulatory power, and correspondingly narrow judicial review, had been converted by the Taft Court to enlarge its own power at the expense of the legislature. Now it was as clear for Roberts, as it had been for Stone, "that there is no closed class or category of businesses affected with a public interest." "The phrase . . . can, in the nature of things," the Court now observed, "mean no more than that an industry, for adequate reason, is subject to control for the public good." It was merely "the equivalent of 'subject to the exercise of the police power.'" Stone's dissenting taunt to the majority in the Tyson case—"Self-interest may not be constitutionally protected at the expense of the public interest"—now carried the weight of constitutional authority. In Roberts' words: "The Constitution does not secure to any one liberty to conduct his business in such fashion as to inflict injury upon the public at large, or upon any substantial group of people."[31]

McReynolds met this liberal challenge head-on. To him, "former decisions" clearly proved the unconstitutionality of the milk-control law. It had not been supposed "since the adoption of the Constitution" that the dairyman's business was "clothed with such a public interest that the price of his product . . . could be fixed by state regulation." "Constitutional guaranties," the Tory rhetoric ran, "are not to be 'thrust to and fro and carried about with every wind of doctrine.' They were intended to be immutable so long as within our charter. Rights shielded yesterday should remain indefeasible today and tomorrow. Certain fundamentals have been set beyond experimentation; the Constitution has released them from control by the state. Again and again this Court has so declared."[32]

For McReynolds, as for Sutherland, constitutional principles and economic theory made for a fundamental law that might either "pinch or comfort." The troubles of New York milk producers stemmed, Justice McReynolds held, from the "human tendency to raise too many heifers" when prices were high. After the onset of depression, consumers lacked money to buy milk, and farmers, consequently, were impoverished. "Naturally," he commented, "they became discontented." But any legislative effort to relieve the inevitable working of economic laws was bound to be "futility." Our basic charter of government was equally rigid. "The adoption of any 'concept of jurisprudence,'" McReynolds warned, "which permits facile disregard of the Constitution as long interpreted and respected will inevitably lead to its destruction."[33]

This encouraging judicial resurrection of 1934, this refusal to permit "private parties," as Stone put it, to "tie the hands of the state so that it is powerless to deal with a problem vital to government itself," seemed to exemplify Mr. Dooley's famous dictum that the Supreme Court follows the election returns.

For the time being it appeared that a constitutional crisis, brewing since 1920, might be averted. The Blaisdell and Nebbia decisions, widely read as showing the Supreme Court's stand on crucial New Deal legislation, gave liberals fresh hope. Upholding Minnesota's moratorium on mortgage foreclosures, Chief Justice Hughes, with substantial help from Justices Stone and Cardozo, had supplied the theoretical foundation on which the New Deal was building. Changed economic and social conditions had led, Hughes noted, to "an increased use of the organization of society in order to protect the very bases of individual opportunity."

Justice Roberts took an even more exalted view of public power, national and state. "This Court," he wrote in the Nebbia case, "from the early days affirmed that the power to promote the general welfare is inherent in government."[34] Such ringing words instilled confidence in the most skeptical New Dealer. "As it stands," wrote the *New Republic's* Washington reporter, "the [Nebbia] decision has created the popular impression that the Supreme Court sees no unconstitutionality in the Roosevelt program."[35] Other commentators went further, anticipating that judicial review itself might soon fall into "innocuous desuetude."[36] Optimistically, many thought the Court had foreshadowed "a change from an era of laissez faire to an era of government regulation."[37]

Sutherland, apparently accepting this view, looked gloomily at the "gradual but ever-advancing encroachments on the sanctity of public and private rights."[38] For McReynolds prospects were equally bleak. But did not New Deal critics and sympathizers alike miss the real point of the judicial upset? What had been disrupted was not the formal provisions of the Constitution but only four Justices' views of economic and social policy, and the two main barriers which these Justices had fashioned to safeguard that policy. Certain observers, along with Justice Stone, knew that nothing very drastic had taken place. "This decision," a Philadelphia attorney said of the Nebbia case, "is important not because it enunciates new principles of constitutional law, but because it applies existing principles in a different way, and marks distinctly a change from recent conceptions of due process."[39]

Stone advanced a similar view: "I am glad that you have taken the trouble to remind people that there were some of us to whom the doctrine announced in *Nebbia* v. *New York* was not a novel one, although I confess that I could never hope for such a sweeping repudiation of the Tyson case and those like it. All in all, it makes an interesting chapter in legal history."[40] As to the Blaisdell decision, he remarked: "The case is not so novel or far-reaching as the press seemed to think."[41] "It was a case of great interest and importance," Stone agreed, but even the lawyers who argued it "seemed not to grasp its significance." "One hearing the words of the Honorable James M. Beck," he wrote, "would think the pillars of the Constitution were falling. As a matter of fact, the Court decided nothing more than it decided in the Rent cases quite a number of years ago, and all that it did decide might have been said in much less compass than it was."[42]

Nor did the views reasserted in 1934 have any assurance of permanence. Opponents of the New Deal legislative program were encouraged by Chief Justice Hughes' stress on the *emergency*. Justice Roberts' opinion also suggested that the Court's repudiation of its self-made role as censor of state and national legislation was not complete or final. "The function of courts in the application of the Fifth and Fourteenth Amendments is," Roberts said, "to determine in each case whether circumstances vindicate the challenged regulation as a reasonable exertion of governmental authority or condemn it as arbitrary or discriminatory."[43] Judicial review remained as a useful gun behind the door and might again serve to usurp sovereign authority.

The prognosticators of 1934 might have done better if they had paid more heed to the fact that Hughes, ignoring Stone's protest, had stressed the emergency provision in the Minnesota moratorium act. They would have done still better if they had known that primary credit for judicial recognition of "increased use" of the "organization of society" to protect the "very bases" of individual opportunity belonged not to Chief Justice Hughes but to Justices Stone and Cardozo.

In retrospect the Blaisdell and Nebbia cases proved once more that judicial interpretation does not and cannot eliminate the bias of the interpreter. The twisting course of decisions from 1930-1934 makes it plain that the key to the immediate future lay locked in the law-laden bosoms of Mr. Justice Roberts and Chief Justice Hughes. As the Court met the pressures of the time, it would still have alternative precedents between which to choose.

CHAPTER TWENTY-FOUR

# Power and Duty in the Modern State

## 1934

On Sunday, March 5, 1933, President Roosevelt called a special session of Congress. "Must" legislation soon began rolling out almost without dissent, adding vast powers to those the President had already assumed. As Congress responded to his bidding and passively awaited the next command, events gave our politics the aspect of an alien order. One man held the center of the stage, one man had power— no one seemed able or willing to oppose him. Government, drawing to itself far-reaching authority, entered fields hitherto left completely to state or local government; Congress began to exercise control over commerce and industry formerly wielded by private syndromes of wealth. Regulations issuing from the national Capitol displaced the unfettered discretion of individuals.

Stone found little satisfaction in the New Deal. "I do not wonder," he wrote Hoover, "that you find present-day doings subject both for comment and for reflection. I try to look at it all philosophically, but confess that the uncertainty as to the future, which seems as great now as it has been at any time in the last year, gets on my nerves."[1] Sharing the prejudices against Rooseveltian concoctions common to many good Republicans, the Justice joined in ridiculing the "professors" and the "Brain Trust." "We are indeed," he remarked to a law school classmate, "in a theoretical mess, or a mess of theorists."[2] But Stone's basic criticism probed beneath the superficial foibles and petty mistakes so much the butt of the Old Guard. "I am wondering how you feel about this present day and age," he asked "an old-fashioned Democrat." "Much of it seems incredible to me and especially our departure from traditional *methods* of dealing with public questions."[3] Fundamentally, he thought New Dealers prone to invoke the coercive sanctions of the community before allowing the intelligence and public spirit of responsible individuals opportunity to provide an enduring corrective.

He did not, however, consider it "incredible" for Government to attack the evils uncovered by the Senate Banking and Currency Committee's probe into the financial affairs of the Morgans, the Mitchells, the Wiggins, and other prominent Wall Street figures. "Of course," Stone commented sympathetically, "not a thing has come out that I have not expected, and I expect some others if the investigation is diligent enough and sagacious enough to see the true significance of the wily acts of some of those who infest the Wall Street jungle. But the general public and some others who ought to have been aware of what is going on are surprised and horrified."[4] In an attitude of "I told you so," he recalled the series of "shocking fraudulent performances" he had unearthed a few years before.* Since the Stock Exchange had done nothing to set its own house in order, Stone heartily approved the administration's measures to regulate the securities market.

With the passage of the NIRA and the departure from the gold standard, the first phase of the New Deal had been accomplished. Though modest in scope, thoughtful persons soon began to wonder whether freedom and democracy could survive even this amount of government regulation. Even if the capitalist system came through the economic distress, could it endure political control with all its baneful consequences? When in 1934 the patient seemed likely to survive, legislators and others began to argue with the doctor.

* For Stone's views, see the American Tobacco case, Chapter XXII, pp. 351-56.

"It seems clear," Stone wrote Hoover in the Spring of 1934, "that the honeymoon is over and that we may witness the beginning of real political discussion." This was very good news to Hoover, since the former President felt sure that New Deal policy marked a long step down the road to "regimentation," "planned economy," "despotism," and so on, to ruthless ruin. Hoover, still titular head of the Republican party and the opposition's major spokesman, developed this surmise in a manuscript and sent it to Justice Stone for comment.

Stone's reaction was of the "yes and no" description: "With the main theses of this paper I fully agree. The principle of individual liberty which has hitherto been regarded as an indispensable factor in our polity should be preserved. It can be preserved only by a system which gives some scope for altruistic, non-compulsory cooperation, and which affords opportunity for rewards for service, through a reasonable maintenance and protection of property rights. I fully agree with the arraignment of the present regime for its reckless disregard of these values. This is the strongest part of the paper. I think even more could be said about present tendencies to depart from traditional forms of democratic government under the Constitution."[5]

Stone deplored the "steady absorption of power by the President, the failure of Congress to perform its legislative duties, the absence of debate in Congress and of open public discussion of public problems, the creation of drastic administrative procedures without legislative definition and without provision for their review by the courts." These, the conservative Republican judge told Hoover, constitute "an even greater menace than the program for whose advancement these sacrifices have been made." Stone also endorsed the former President's emphasis on the value of human liberty, but wondered whether Hoover realized the true dimensions of the problem. The size and power of the modern corporation, sometimes surpassing those of the state governments, and able on occasion to challenge national authority, required positive governmental safeguards to secure individual liberty. Circumstances had transmuted the issue of liberty *versus* authority into the problem of "responsible use of power"—the power of individuals and groups as well as of official government. Perhaps the basic flaw in Hoover's thinking was his failure to appreciate "the perpetual, and to some extent, irreconcilable conflict between the demands of individual liberty and the necessities of an increasingly complex civilization, in which every individual and every group within the state becomes increasingly interdependent with every other."

"There was," the Justice explained, "undoubtedly much larger scope for individual liberty in the state which Jefferson contemplated than there is in the civilization which we have actually developed in this year of our Lord." The nation then consisted of small, independent communities. Actions of an individual in the next state, or even the next county, had little effect "on Jefferson and his neighbors." "Personally," Stone commented emphatically, "I like the Jeffersonian state better, but I have to recognize that because I live in a highly industrialized modern state, in order to make the system work I have to suffer restrictions on individual liberty, which Jefferson would probably have regarded as intolerable." The Justice went on to cite illustrations of the way industrial civilization infringed on human freedom, and therefore required more rigid government:

> Because certain manufacturers in Detroit have enjoyed freedom to flood the country with automobiles, I have lost freedom in the use and enjoyment of the streets and highways. Because other manufacturers have demanded and secured the benefits of a protective tariff, my freedom as a consumer of foreign goods has been curtailed. The railroad builders and operators, the big businessman—and some little ones—the shippers of merchandise in interstate commerce, have all suffered similar restrictions on their freedom of action.

The pertinent question in 1934 was whether America must prove Jefferson's phobia that freedom and urban industrialism are necessarily incompatible. Stone did not think so. Nor was he sure that freedom would be the possession of men in twentieth-century America if Government simply abstained from regulating their affairs.

Reform was essential. Restraints, both unnecessary and unbearable in Jefferson's Garden of Eden, must now be accepted as prerequisites of a system of "ordered liberty." Industrialism had produced a new level of human dependence and interdependence. The connecting lines of interest ran across all boundaries, political and geographic, to tie the nation into a sensitive whole:

> Today what the Wall Street banker does may have serious consequences on the fortunes of the cotton planter in Mississippi and the farmer in Iowa. The textile manufacturer of New England is at the mercy of the employer of child labor or underpaid labor in the South. He must either yield to the pressure or abandon his business, with all the consequences to his employees and to his community—unless, perchance, the freedom of action of the employer of child labor is to some extent curtailed in the interest of the larger good.

The depression itself contained persuasive arguments for enlarging the area of Government power:

> Now, at the end of an era of extraordinary industrial expansion and prosperity, we have been made suddenly aware that we have multiplied and improved the instruments and methods of production beyond our powers of consumption; that the distribution of wealth created by our extraordinary

capacity for production is not such as to enable consumption to overtake or even keep pace with production; that our financial system, the creation and use of credit, upon which modern civilization increasingly depends, is maladjusted and honeycombed with grave abuses, and that our foreign trade is shrinking and can be regained, if at all, only after years of effort.

Surely, Stone suggested, the community, through agencies of public control, must take account of any drastic change that places the individual at the mercy of forces beyond his control.

Hoover maintained that the economic crisis was somehow the inevitable consequence of World War I and European in origin. Stone questioned this hypothesis:

It is undoubtedly true that the World War and world disorders which have followed it have played a part in this unhappy outcome, but there will be other wars and new clashes of the economic interests of nations. Even without them it seems almost inevitable, without some correction or control of the forces which have produced our present situation, history will in due course repeat itself, but with the difference that the ensuing crisis will be more acute than the present one has been, with even graver political and social consequences.

For the questions he raised, however, Stone had no easy, doctrinaire solution.

The conflict between individual freedom and the private interest which it envisages, with the public interest, is never-ending. The line of battle shifts and will inevitably continue to shift as civilization becomes more complex and the interest of the whole becomes increasingly sensitive to the mistakes or misdeeds of the few.

Social problems make unending demands on intelligence. "Some adjustments" must be made "between the demands of individual liberty, and those of the larger social good."

The issues cannot be settled by an appeal to the eighteenth-century philosophy of individualism in the abstract, for that philosophy cannot be completely adapted to the twentieth-century state. The demands of the two must, to some extent, be accommodated, but with full realization of the values which that philosophy can contribute to present-day society.

Unprecedented social and economic changes raised major questions that "statesmanship must attempt to answer." It must ask itself "what reforms are necessary to prevent recurrence of present-time evils, and, second, how can these reforms be effected with the least impairment of individual liberty?"

"Reforms of the first magnitude" were in order. Nor could these be made "without such radical departure from the essential qualities of a free society as is now contemplated." Among other things, the banking

and credit systems should be "thoroughly reformed." To prevent recurrence of deep-seated depression, a basic departure from laissez-
faire economics was essential. "A possibly more doubtful question, but
still one which cannot be summarily dismissed," was whether some
method must not be found by which "the flow of production may be
more closely related to consumption,* and by which industry may be
given an opportunity, within reasonable range, to be marked by administrative procedure under law, of stabilizing itself." Such reforms
necessarily "involve some restraints on freedom of action of the individual."

Mere verbal lamentations over freedom's fate could not make the
people forget that Roosevelt had acted to bring about necessary correctives. And Hoover's failure to come to grip with realities led the
Justice to question the wisdom of publishing the manuscript:

> If published in its present form, at the present time, there is a real risk
> that it will be misinterpreted and that it will be severely assailed as "stand
> pat" in its philosophy and outlook. The country is convinced that the time
> has come for sweeping reforms, and that these are being, and will be, re-
> sisted for selfish reasons by those who have an excessive stake in things as
> they are or have been in the past. People expect that objection will be made
> to such reforms on the ground that they infringe the principle of freedom of
> the individual. Even the man in the street is aware that every important
> reform in the past seventy-five years has been resisted and assailed as an
> infringement of individual liberty.

Acrimonious debate had attended the establishment of the Interstate Commerce Commission, workmen's compensation, the Sherman
and the Clayton Acts. Though "attacked in legislatures, in public
prints, and in the courts on the ground that they were encroachments
upon the American system and a curtailment of the freedom of action
of the empire builders who had made America," all were now accepted as an essential part of our constitutional system. Stone antici-

---

* On December 17, 1935, Richard B. Scandrett, Jr., wrote Justice Stone that
"the great difficulty lies in the stubborn unwillingness of a large number of businessmen to admit and face the basic economic problem which requires the transforming of the potential consuming capacity into an actual purchasing power."
"You are right," Stone replied, December 20, 1935. "There is no doubt that the
problem of the hour is the reconciliation of the principles of liberty with the type
of economic society we have constructed, and that we shall have to find a way of
securing a better distribution of income if we are to maintain it. Yet, I can see
no recognition of this truth on the part of any important Republican leader. My
one feeling is that we have sat asleep at the switch again until the train passed by.
"It is true enough that one of the grave faults of the Roosevelt administration
is its administrative incapacity, its lack of financial foresight, and its reckless disregard of the most elementary principles of justice in dealing with great public
problems. This may overturn them if they lose popular favor in the next six
months as rapidly as they have in the last six. But the Republicans are doing little
to improve their opportunity."

pated that Hoover's attack on the New Deal would be placed in "the same category as these earlier pronouncements."

Now the people are disposed to endure the evils of the administration program in the hope that they may bring a better day, freed from the dangers from which we are now suffering. To accomplish that end they are in the mood to make any necessary sacrifices, but I think they would be overjoyed if someone could point the way to accomplish it without the sacrifices of liberty which they are being called on to make.

Hoover's failure to realize that the New Deal was in response to genuine social wrongs endangered the very freedom he sought most eagerly to protect, provoking Stone to throw out as his final dictum:

If it is thought that . . . reforms are not needed, the time is not yet ripe to assail the program which the administration has sponsored. The time for that will come only when we are more prosperous. It may then succeed, and all programs for any extensive reforms be abandoned, but with, I fear, grave consequences in the future.

As Stone had foreseen, the seed broadcast in the former President's manuscript, published under the title *Challenge to Liberty*, fell on barren soil.* Following the 1934 elections the Justice wrote a close friend: "I would like to show you a criticism and prediction which I wrote to one of my Republican brethren with respect to the Republican attitude. It is completely confirmed by what I read in the papers this morning. As I read the returns they do not represent complete satisfaction with the New Deal, so much as they do a realization that our Republican brethren have nothing constructive to offer, and that the people are willing to take their chances with Roosevelt a while longer."[6]

Stone was much concerned about the role the legal profession had played in bringing the country to its present condition. In case after case he had seen eminent members of the bar serving as adjuncts to great corporate power or as midwives, bringing to fruition the most nefarious schemes of corporate finance. His knowledge of these interrelations antedated the disclosures made in 1933 by the Senate Banking and Currency Committee. In 1926 he had declined to write a paper on the American bar, explaining "that if I wrote a worth-while article, which really expressed my views . . . I should be under the necessity of saying a good many caustic things about the American lawyer and American bar organization." "The leading lawyers," he

---

* Hoover's tract provoked exactly the reaction Stone predicted. "Mr. Hoover," one critic wrote (and many others sounded the same note), "desires freedom for the bankers, for the privateers of finance, and for the great captains of industry, and he desires freedom for them to do as they please. He has overlooked the freedom of the man and woman whose toil makes capital possible." (Wayne C. Williams to the editor, *Washington Post*, Oct. 1, 1934.)

wrote the editor of *Harper's*, "are men of high character, distinct intellectual power, great skill, and devoted to the practice of their profession. Their success is measured by the profession and the public very largely in terms of their professional income. You will rarely find their services enlisted in any case which does not involve substantial professional remuneration, and almost never on the unpopular side of a case involving human rights and personal liberty."[7] The bar had "in a real sense become commercialized."[*] "Rights of property" which Stone had debunked as a dangerous fiction in 1915, had triumphed over human rights and now claimed first allegiance from the most eminent figures of the American bar.

The task he had declined to undertake in 1926 Stone welcomed in 1934. That spring he accepted the University of Michigan's invitation to receive an honorary LL.D. and take part in the exercises dedicating the law school's new quadrangle. "I suppose you will feel," Dean Bates's letter said, "that you must avoid discussing anything controversial which might come before the Court; but every thoughtful person is interested in some of the larger aspects of the transitional period through which we are passing." Stone hardly needed to be prodded. "Lawyers have become such literalists nowadays," he replied, "that they need to be reminded that the business of interpreting the Constitution is not quite like that of interpreting a contract to be performed within the year in which it is made."[8] Here was an oppor-

---

* The full text of Stone's letter reads:

"I have no hesitation in saying to you, for your own information, that as I see it the great mass of the membership of the American bar falls into three well-defined classes: (although, of course, there are notable exceptions to the generalization).

"There is a limited number of the entire membership of the bar, found principally in the larger cities, who are counted as its leaders. They are men of high character, distinct intellectual power, great skill, and devoted to the practice of their profession. Their success is measured by the profession and the public very largely in terms of their professional income. They would admit to you in private conversation that the great mass of the membership in the bar was unworthy of its best traditions, but they have little interest in raising its standards, in improving its membership, or in improving the administration of the law in any substantial way. You rarely find their services enlisted in any case which does not involve substantial professional remuneration, and almost never on the unpopular side of a case involving human rights and personal liberty. In these respects they have broken with the tradition of the bar of fifty to one hundred years ago. Some inquiry should be directed to the cause of this, and in trying to ascertain whether the bar has not, in a real sense become commercialized, even though it has preserved in this stratum its tradition of professional skill, integrity, and fidelity to clients.

"A second class is made up of the great number of members of the bar who, though personally honest, regard their profession in the light of a business or trade. They do not even make an ideal of good workmanship; any kind of professional training which will secure admission to the bar is good enough for them; any kind of a brief for which the client will pay is good enough to be submitted to the court. The public would be amazed if judges of experience in

tunity to spell out ideas that had been building up through the years. Here was a chance "to point the way" to social betterment "without the sacrifice of liberty" demanded by the New Deal.

When the pace of Court work slackened he buckled down to writing. By early June the job was finished. An unvarnished indictment of lawyers' neglect of public duties, the address went to Dean Bates with an apology for its challenging tone. "If after you read it, you want to withdraw your invitation, I will be sick or make any other necessary excuse."[9]

Bates, apparently, liked the Justice's dynamite, and on June 15, 1934, Stone delivered the major address dedicating Michigan's magnificent law building—"a unit completely organized and equipped for the training of lawyers."

The speaker recognized at the outset that "the towering edifice of business and industry . . . had become the dominating feature of the American social structure." Setting his speech in the grim perspective of 1934, he turned quickly to the class that had sapped or raised (depending on one's viewpoint) the edifice—the investment bankers and executives. What had seemed the "impregnable fortress of a boasted civilization" had developed "unsuspected weaknesses." Interwoven throughout the address were the twin themes of the irresponsibility of the men controlling powerful economic aggregations and the failure

---

appellate courts would state frankly how often the administration of justice fails and clients' rights are forfeited by the sloppy methods and incompetence of this type of practitioner.

"The third class is made up of those members of the profession who are without moral character or standards, who regard the license to practice as a license to prey on the community.

"Both the second and third classes have been enormously increased in recent years, through the development of our so-called system of legal education and the unwillingness of the bar as a whole to insist upon more exacting requirements for admission to it. The legal profession has lagged far behind the medical profession in these respects. Bar organizations have generally taken only a perfunctory interest in the real problems of the profession. They have been chiefly organizations which, when not given over to petty politics, have been devoted to honoring the leaders of the profession and to describing in sonorous phrases the noble traditions of the bar and the perfection of the common law. Most of the inspiration for reform has come from the teachers in the law schools, but until recently they have wielded slight influence, and movements toward reform in bar organizations have been of a perfunctory character and usually fall into the hands of those who are more interested in the self-advertising to be gained from them than in real accomplishment.

"From the foregoing you will see how difficult it is to get the right man to write your article. If he is influential, you are likely not to get very much of an article; if he is critical, he is likely not to be influential." See Louis D. Brandeis, "The Opportunity in the Law" (1905) and "The Living Law" (1916), reprinted in *Business—A Profession* (Boston: Hale, Cushman & Flint, 1933); also *Other People's Money and How the Bankers Use It* (Washington, D. C.: National Home Library, 1933).

of the legal profession to rise above its basic, narrowly defined ideal of loyalty to private clients.[10]

In the struggle "unique in our history, to determine whether the giant economic forces which our industrial and financial world have created shall be brought under some larger measure of control," the legal profession had not measured up to its responsibility.

What, he asked, had led the lawyer to forsake his traditional role as guardian of the common welfare, to become primarily the spokesman for vast, but nonetheless particular, private interests? Critically, Stone asked why "a bar which has done so much to develop and refine the technique of business organization, to provide skillfully devised methods for financing industry, which has guided a world-wide commercial expansion, has done relatively so little to remedy the evils of the investment market; so little to adapt the fiduciary principle of nineteenth-century equity to twentieth-century business practices; so little to improve the functioning of the administrative mechanisms which modern government sets up to prevent abuses; so little to make law more readily available as an instrument of justice to the common man."

Lawyers still cited as objects of emulation "the great figures of the law [who] stir the imagination and inspire our reverence according as they have used their special training and gifts for the advancement of the public interest." "Yet," Stone declared, "candor would compel . . . us . . . to admit that in our own time the bar has not maintained its traditional position of public influence and leadership." Instead of responding to a vastly changed social and economic context, the bar had accentuated certain traits identified with rugged individualism to the detriment of an interdependent society's urgent demand for a broad public spirit. Conventional legal ethics embodied "generalizations designed for an earlier era," and ignored the "more fundamental consideration of the way in which our professional activities affect the welfare of society as a whole." While zealously guarding elementary tenets of the lawyer's code, such as fidelity to the private interests of clients, the practitioner became ever more oblivious to his public functions.

Modern practice itself was not calculated to inspire a sense of public interest and responsibility. No longer a solo operator whose clientele cut across class and occupational strata of the community, the modern practitioner was a specialist, "the proprietor or general manager of a new type of factory, whose legal product is increasingly the result of mass production methods." More often than not, the "law factory" became an adjunct of a great commercial banking house, dependent upon this connection for the constant flow of legal business onto the firm's assembly line. Society put its premium, not upon public service, but upon the tangibles one could acquire in the struggle for existence. Small wonder that the learned profession of an earlier day had become "the obsequious servant of business," "tainted with the morals and manners of the marketplace in its most anti-social manifestations."

The law schools, far from providing a corrective, exaggerated the evil by unduly stressing "proficiency," by overlooking the "grave danger to the public if this proficiency be directed wholly to private ends without thought of the social consequences." Expert legal scholarship, which might otherwise have given balance to the law student's mental diet, persistently delved into the past. There was little or no "reflection upon the relationship of law to the social and economic forces which produce it." In short, both training and experience taught the lawyer to regard himself as a "technician rather than an originator of [social] policy," giving rise to the impression that "the lawyer existed to serve and not to counsel his clients."[11]

By thus tolerating the corruption of its standards, the bar itself had aggravated the economic plight of the United States. "I venture to assert," the Justice predicted, "that when the history of the financial era which has just drawn to a close comes to be written, most of its mistakes and its major faults will be ascribed to the failure to observe the fiduciary principle, the precept as old as holy writ, that 'a man cannot serve two masters.' More than a century ago equity gave a hospitable reception to that principle, and the common law was not slow to follow in giving it recognition. No thinking man can believe that an economy built upon a business foundation can long endure without some loyalty to that principle. The separation of ownership from management, the development of the corporate structure so as to vest in small groups control over the resources of great numbers of small and uninformed investors, make imperative a fresh and active devotion to that principle if the modern world of business is to perform its proper function. Yet those who serve nominally as trustees, but relieved, by clever legal devices, from the obligation to protect those whose interests they purport to represent, corporate officers and directors who award themselves huge bonuses from corporate funds without the assent or even the knowledge of their stockholders, reorganization committees created to serve interests of others than those whose securities they control, financial institutions which, in the infinite variety of their operations, consider only last, if at all, the interests of those whose funds they command, suggest how far we have ignored the necessary implications of that principle. The loss and suffering inflicted on individuals, the harm done to a social order founded upon business and dependent upon its integrity, are incalculable."

In deploring the unholy alliance of lawyers and industrial financiers,

Stone's Michigan address is among the first pronouncements on the trusteeship theory of business enterprise. He proclaimed that the great power held by individual businessmen as chiefs of far-flung, integrated industries carried concomitant duties toward the public whose very lives depended upon the skillful and faithful administration of these economic giants. Comparing the struggle for effective control over the aggregates of private power with the post-revolutionary campaigns for the Bill of Rights, the speaker said: "It was no more vital to that day [in the 1790's] that free speech should be preserved than it is to our own that those who act as fiduciaries in the strategic positions of our business civilization should be held to those standards of scrupulous fidelity which society has the right to demand."

Any interference with the operation of the natural laws of greed, would, he knew, be challenged as subversive of liberty. Yet the damage done to society by the businessman's unthinking exercise of power had been so manifold in its evil ramifications that Stone was led to question the wisdom of untrammeled economic liberty. "In a changing economy," he observed, "mere material gain to the individual may not in itself be the social good it was once conceived to be." American society, with its peculiar emphasis upon "material gains," especially needed the restraining influence of a responsible, intelligent social leadership. "For as our conception of what is reward is less related to the social welfare," he observed perceptively, "the problem of bringing individual conduct into harmony with the demands of society becomes more acute."

Stone, in 1934, like Brooks Adams and Louis D. Brandeis in 1913, did not consider the businessman a trustworthy repository of social power. The industrial elite's failure in 1929 had been as conclusive as it was colossal. Surely the task of social reconstruction could not be entrusted to the profit-grabbing and power-hungry. Distrusting over-all governmental authority, he sought, as he had told Hoover, a system giving "some scope for altruistic, non-compulsory cooperation." In the interest of preserving freedom he relegated the "coercive power of the state" to the enforcement only of those responsibilities which individuals could not or would not undertake to meet themselves. The policeman's "night stick," he observed, is not "our most potent civilizing agency." "Unless the urge to individual advantage has other curbs, unless we may have recourse to other forces of social betterment, and unless the more influential elements in society conduct themselves with a disposition to promote the common good, society cannot function." Guardianship of the public interest must, therefore, be entrusted to organizations outside the formal structure of the political organization and also independent of the overwhelming pressure for private gain. By turning too readily to government for the solution of our difficulties, we surrender the potential "free offering of good citizenship, forgetting that in doing so we give first place to the policeman's club."

In the face of these serious strictures leveled against the profession, Justice Stone still put his trust in lawyers. The job which businessmen had proved themselves incompetent to discharge had to be shouldered by these corporate "servants." Stone thought that lawyers could devise a political and ethical framework adequate for the control of new social forces despite their corporate ties. The legal profession could be stirred from lethargic veneration of the past by "data patiently assembled and organized so as to show with the powerful impact of revealed truth the extent to which devotion to private interests has obscured our vision of the public welfare." Once aroused, lawyers would possess both the spirit and the power to achieve necessary reforms. The same process of economic concentration by which the bar lost independence had brought these indispensable technicians to a position where the possibilities of their influence "are almost beyond calculation."

The chief burden of Stone's plea was the creation of a cadre of devoted individuals, functioning at the center of a delicate and crucial sector of the national life, dedicated to placing the public interest above the particular interests they represented and from which they gained their livelihoods. "Just as the lawyers of 1790 to 1840 took a leading part in fashioning the country's ideals to suit political change, so we must now shoulder the task of relating them to business and economic change."

If effective, this would mean revolution, a radical turnabout in the relation of lawyers to their corporate clients and to the public generally. For the leadership necessary to bring about this transformation, Stone looked to "a new force in American legal life"—a source so stimulating to his own judicial statesmanship—the law teachers. Formerly contenting themselves with the necessary work of analysis, clarification, and statement of legal doctrine, they had recently "expanded their inquiries to embrace the relation of law to the social forces which create it, and which in turn it is designed to control." Already "they are beginning to turn their attention to the bar as an institution, seeking to gain an informed understanding of its problems, to appraise the performance of its public functions, and to find ways of stimulating a more adequate performance of them." Law teachers had a record of public service and had demonstrated capacity to arouse the bar on questions of reform. "It is they," he observed hopefully, "who today represent the most cohesive, disinterested, and potent single force operating within the profession to establish its public relationships on a higher plane." In their hands lay the power to mold the aspirations of younger lawyers—to fire in them the ideals of the past, and to relate those ideals meaningfully to the problems of the present.*

Stone's address was generally recognized as a trenchant and forthright analysis of a very timely subject. "Amidst the serenity and detachment that grace the life of United States Supreme Court Justices," the *New Republic* commented, "one of them has written a document that has the quality and importance of a state paper."[12]

In response to William D. Mitchell's praise, the Justice revealed the inner urge that had moved him to make this pronouncement. "One in my position hesitates to say anything outside of a judicial opinion, but the subject of this address had been festering in my insides long enough so I had to get it out."[13]

The acclaim was not unanimous. Harold Laski queried Stone's optimism. "Having been made a dependency of the business empire," Laski wrote, the legal profession had "to adapt its habits to the standards of its protector."[14] "You may be right in your conclusion," Stone replied. "Certainly the more recent history of the legal profession seems to indicate that yours [socialism] is the only solution, and yet it seems almost the counsel of despair, if the profession can be made to function properly only by detaching it wholly from the profit motive. That is equivalent to saying that it is impossible to train any considerable group of men for the bar who will place the moral and intellectual values in life above greed. One illusion to which I have clung is that it is possible. . . . Notwithstanding all the discouragement, I still have hope. I am almost compelled to have it, for if I am wrong, then it would seem that there is little hope for the improvement of the race through the processes of education."[15]

The Justice also discovered that his harsh words had not stirred "any great enthusiasm among my practicing brethren."[16] "No one, un-

---

* On the ambitious program laid out for the law schools, Walter Gellhorn, himself a law teacher, was less sanguine than Stone. "In the midst of a plethora of timid, inconsequential utterances about the purging of the bar," Gellhorn commented, "it is indeed refreshing to read your forthright statement of the fundamental disharmony between the lawyers' work and the public interest." But could the task Stone cut out for the law schools be effectively discharged? The emphasis was still on training proficient craftsmen, with the inevitable implication that the prizes of a lawyer's life go to the most skillful. "We have yet to develop," Gellhorn wrote, "adequate consideration of the different channels in which proficiency may be utilized; and it is only sporadically and as individuals that we suggest, as you observed, that the satisfying prizes need not always be material ones." (Walter Gellhorn to H.F.S., Nov. 20, 1934.)

"The law school group," Stone agreed, "is not a perfect instrument, but where will you find such? In this as in most other constructive efforts, we must use the instruments we have. Just at the moment, I don't think much reliance can be placed on the practicing bar, but if they are once stirred up they will do plenty." (H.F.S. to Duane R. Dills, Dec. 3, 1934.)

fortunately," William D. Guthrie observed, "can read Mr. Justice Stone's address without the impression that he has come to believe that the profession in the United States has of recent years greatly deteriorated, and fallen morally and intellectually to a low and deplorable state. . . . I do not hesitate to affirm," he wrote indignantly, "that the facts would not warrant the indictment, disparagement, and condemnation of the American bar as a whole which the address of the learned Justice seems to imply, even if unintended by him." The Wall Street lawyer immediately confronted the "learned Justice" with the latter's highly favorable appraisal of the bar in the Hewitt Lectures of twenty years before. For this champion of business nothing had changed; Stone's 1915 estimate still applied. "In my judgment, there continues to be . . . a considerable body of lawyers conspicuously fitted, by character and attainments, for the practice of their profession. . . . They still constitute," Guthrie challenged, "the true representatives and leaders of the profession in the United States." "I believe," he went on, "a large majority in the profession have not become and never have been . . . 'obsequious servants of business,' and . . . are not 'tainted,' . . . 'with the morals and manners of the marketplace in its most anti-social manifestations' or otherwise."[17]

Stone had done more than impugn the good name of the lawyer. "Subversive doctrines," Guthrie told readers of the *Fordham Law Review*, "are being taught and advocated. Ancient principles are at stake." "False prophets" were leading the nation "from the long tried old order . . . to national socialism, the repudiation of standards and obligation heretofore upheld, the leveling of classes, the destruction of property, and the overthrow of our federal system designed to be composed of sovereign and indestructible states." "If these problems are to be wisely, justly, and providently solved," he warned, "it will be predominantly under the guidance of the legal profession and in accord with long tried and honest standards, heretofore observed, and constitutional principles, heretofore revered, and with just and equal laws in accord with these true standards and principles."[18]

"What a dismal performance it is," the Justice commented on the 1934 meeting of the American Bar Association, in an oblique answer to Guthrie. Earle W. Evans, sidestepping the "controversy" of the New Deal, urged members to take up a "crusade" against a few "lawyer criminals" as the way to "restore the profession to its proper place in public esteem."[19] The official organ of the bar, as such, became greatly incensed over the obscure lawyer who cheated a client out of a few hundred dollars,[20] but looked the other way when an eminent member of the bar devised schemes such as the St. Paul railroad reorganization plan.

Despite serious misgivings, Stone's faith in the American bar remained unshaken.* "We are on the eve of a change," he noted October 9, 1934. "I really believe that the law schools will take the lead and ultimately turn the tide in another direction."[21]

CHAPTER TWENTY-FIVE

# Straws in the Wind

## 1933-1935

The farflung legislative program initiated by F.D.R. posed constitutional issues calling for creative judicial statesmanship of a high order. Cases might originate in the lower courts, but it was not until they reached the Supreme Court that their decision was felt. "The most futile job I have to do," Judge Learned Hand wrote Stone, February 6, 1934, "is to pass on constitutional questions. Who in hell cares what anybody says about them but the Final Five of the august Nine of whom you are one? However, there is always talk, talk about everything and anything, from defense of laissez faire in the guise of an Old Tory, to speaking with the beatified and radiant face turned toward the New Deal, in the guise of a child of light, Filius Aurorae. . . . Personally, the Filii Aurorae make me actively sick at my stomach; they are so conceited, so insensitive, so arrogant. But on the whole the Old Tories are intellectually so moribund, that as a mere matter of my own personal conceit, I can't flock with them. They seem to me as persons more fit associates for a gentleman, . . . but they are so stupid and emit such dreary, hollow sounds."

"You write in a very pessimistic vein," Stone replied, February 7, "one which I can often duplicate in these days, for I feel just about as far from the 'children of light' as I do from the Tories, and as having about as much influence on the world as one of my favorite clams in the clam flat at Isle au Haut. However, my vote still counts

---

* In 1934 this may have seemed a vain hope. In 1950 "it appeared that events might be maneuvering lawyers back toward a greater position of constructive public influence." As an indicator of the possible trend, Willard Hurst quoted Robert T. Swaine, counsel for the bankers in the St. Paul case and historian of the famed New York Cravath law firm: "It behooves all of us who render 'specialized service to business and finance' to seek such solutions of the legal problems of our clients as are compatible with the changing social concepts and as will avoid the abuses of economic power to which our profession too often contributed in past decades." (Willard Hurst, *The Growth of American Law*, pp. 355, 356.)

one." Hand's reply was prompt and emphatic: "Yes, your vote still counts one, and it counts for much more than one. What you are doing really does matter. You must not have the idea that it doesn't."[1]

The Supreme Court, sometimes through decisions of a scant majority, had attained for itself such pre-eminence in politics that it could deny important powers to both state and nation on principles nowhere found in the Constitution itself. It could and did allocate powers as between state and nation, or between Congress and the Executive.* In this way the Court could and did exert control over the economic and social policy of the country. "It sat," Robert H. Jackson wrote, "almost as a continuous constitutional convention, which, without submitting its proposals to any ratification or rejection, could amend the basic law."[2] But in the process of annexing power, at the expense of both national and state authority, the Court had left intact precedents on the basis of which the entire New Deal program might be sustained,[3] whether it was erected on the commerce or the national taxing and spending power.[4]

The Minnesota moratorium and Nebbia milk decisions "held out," as President Roosevelt said, "a glimmer of hope that the Supreme Court would take a broad view of the Constitution, which would permit its adaptation to the various crises of human affairs."[5] But even in these cases the shift of a single Justice would have meant that the Constitution was inadequate to cope with pressing needs. And those already casting a nostalgic eye backward to the good old days fondly hoped that the Supreme Court might again prove itself an impregnable "bulwark of defense against unsanctioned theories."

New Dealers hesitated to face the real constitutional bout. "One of the deepest weaknesses of the administration in Washington, ever since the Agricultural Act and the Recovery Act went into effect," the *New Republic* noted, November 15, 1933, "has arisen from its fears that these laws, or parts of them, would be declared unconstitutional if allowed to be tested in the courts." For this reason General Hugh Johnson, the administrator, hesitated to prosecute violations. "I pointed out," Harold Ickes recorded, October 2, 1933, "that there would be more likelihood of getting a favorable opinion from a court while public enthusiasm for the Code was running high than after a cold sweat had begun to break out."[6] But the administration continued to temporize. "Why can't we have a decision on NIRA?" an impatient student of constitutional interpretation asked Felix Frank-

---

* The Court, moreover, had the authority not merely to apportion power between state and nation, but also between public and private government. As life became more complicated it became more apparent that there is not more or less government. "There is always," as one writer has said, "just about so much, and the real question is, Who is doing it? If the government does not, or cannot, somebody else will." (Charles P. Curtis, Jr., *Lions under the Throne*, p. 50.)

furter in the spring of 1934. "Why are you so anxious for a decision," the circumspect Brain Truster replied, "until you are sure of getting the right one?" "The one NRA case that has come up has been postponed, at the urgent request of the Government," Justice Stone noted in May 1934.[7] In December he wrote: "We have been getting our first grist of New Deal cases. There will be many more to follow. The laxity with which the Government is proceeding in carrying out the legal details of the New Deal have been pretty shocking."[8]

The delay was both unusual and embarrassing. Previously, controverted laws of crucial importance had been swiftly subjected to the judicial test.* The overhanging threat of unconstitutionality hampered enforcement, made officials timorous and violators contemptuous of the law. The administration was urged to slough off all doubt and march on to Armageddon. "Liberals," Thurman Arnold observed, "have become so firmly convinced that anything they want is unconstitutional, that they entertain the same constitutional doubts as the conservatives."[9] Naturally the opposition, interpreting vacillation as a sign of weakness, cheered the judicial lag.

Stone deplored the "agitation for haste in decision of constitutional cases. It is a good deal more important," he wrote, "that they should be decided right than in a hurry. I think the practice which permits the Supreme Court to bring up such a case on certiorari directly from the district court is a good one, but I should deplore any direct appeal to the Supreme Court. The public little realizes how much is accomplished by passing through an intermediate court—the clash of counsel, the preparation of briefs and judicial decision, before the case comes to the Supreme Court often does much to clarify the question, and the minds of courts and counsel in dealing with it. . . . Where it facilitates decision, the Supreme Court can issue its certiorari in the district court, as it did in some of the cases involving various phases of the Gold Clause, but unless such special circumstances exist I am inclined to believe that the cause of constitutional government will be best served by their going through the regular routine."[10]

On November 6, 1934, Erwin N. Griswold (now Dean of the Harvard Law School) expressed his concern over the Court's denial of certiorari. "The figures show that last term less than one petition out of six was granted, as against about one out of five for several preceding terms. Why should the Court deny certioraris, and then not have enough cases to fill its sessions? I think I could name twenty cases last term," Griswold challenged, "in which certiorari was denied, in

---

* The Adamson Eight Hour Law, for example, went into effect January 1, 1917. Within ten days its constitutionality had been argued in the Supreme Court; by mid-March a decision upholding the Act had been rendered. (*Wilson v. New*, 243 U.S. 332 [1917].)

which a decision by the Court would have been a matter of public concern."

Stone's reply, November 9, 1934, was somewhat oblique: "I am glad to see that you are interesting yourself in the principles which are supposed to control the grant of certioraris. I have opinions, but there is not much I can say on the subject."

Meanwhile, without benefit of constitutional baptism, a far-reaching reorganization of national life had taken place. Commerce, banking, currency, bankruptcy, agriculture, labor—all underwent drastic changes under the impetus of a swiftly fashioned, sprawling recovery program.

Storm warnings might have been read early in the 1934 term when the Court raised a doubt about the milk-control law approved in the Nebbia case. Stone and Cardozo joined in a half-hearted concurrence that hardly did justice to the depth of their convictions.[11] Certain observers thought this cautious withdrawal may have been inspired by the solid opposition of the American Liberty League. "It is no secret in Washington," a New York Times reporter wrote, "that the criticism the court received for its [liberal] decision in the Minnesota moratorium and New York milk cases, criticism not only from the bar but from the bench as well, penetrated under the judicial robes."[12] In letters to close friends Justice Stone complained of the timidity manifest in the opinions of brothers Hughes and Roberts. "I am inclined to think," he wrote apropos of one opinion in which Roberts and the Chief Justice joined, "that even more exasperating than the judge who lacks ability to deal adequately with important questions is he who has a real intellectual equipment but who is afraid to trust it at critical junctures."[13] Major cases illustrating this troublesome defect were soon forthcoming.

The Supreme Court swung the ax vigorously at the New Deal for the first time on January 7, 1935. By a vote of 8 to 1 it chipped out the section (9c) of the National Industrial Recovery Act under which Congress had delegated to the President power to regulate petroleum shipments. The case, Panama Refining Co. v. Ryan, had been argued on December 10, 1934, under circumstances that augured ill for the administration. The Panama Refining Company had challenged the validity of executive orders issued under NIRA prohibiting the shipment of "hot oil" (oil exceeding quota limits) across state lines. Early in the argument government counsel disclosed that criminal penalties attaching to violation of the relevant code provisions had been inadvertently omitted from the executive order. Judicial curiosity was immediately aroused. Concern deepened when opposing counsel bitterly complained that his client had been arrested, indicted, and held several days in jail for violating this nonexistent "law." In fact, his client had seen only one copy of the code, and that was in the "hip pocket of a government agent sent down to Texas from Washington." Pressed by the Justices for light, government counsel finally admitted that there was no practical way for a private citizen to learn the content of these executive orders or when they were issued.[14]

From this point on it was difficult for the Government to get on with its argument that Congress could constitutionally empower the President to ban in his discretion "hot oil" from interstate commerce. Hughes and seven other Justices held Section 9c invalid as an unconstitutional delegation of legislative power to the Chief Executive. Congress, they said, established no "primary standard," thus leaving "the matter to the President without standard or rule, to be dealt with as he pleased." For the first time the maxim *delegata potestas non potest delegari,* a principle not found in the Constitution, formed the basis of judicial decision overthrowing an act of Congress. Only Justice Cardozo dissented.[15]

"It is a rather extraordinary situation," Stone wrote his brother. "Executive orders, purporting to have the force of law, violation of which was a crime, not being published or authenticated in any way so that those charged with criminal offenses could tell whether or not their acts were prohibited. Strange doings!"[16]

Stone's failure to register a separate dissent or at least a concurrence "bewildered" certain of his friends. Denouncing the Chief Justice's opinion as "worse than antediluvian," Professor Karl Llewellyn took the former Columbia Law School dean sharply to task: "You are a lawyer; you are a statesman; you have vision, and you know the hamstringing power of unfortunate judicial language and fool judicial theory, and yet you concurred."

"I sympathize with your feelings," the Justice replied somewhat lamely. "I waited until the last moment, thinking that the dissent might produce something I could agree with, or that someone would be willing to join me in a concurrence placed upon less rigid grounds. Failing both, it seemed to me advisable, by remaining silent, to save my powder for where it would do more good." "You know," he added, "if I should write in every case where I don't agree with some of the views expressed, you and all my other friends would stop reading them."[17]

Public interest ran at high pitch. Speculation was especially keen as to the outcome of cases that would test the constitutionality of Joint Resolution No. 10 of June 5, 1933, banning the so-called Gold Clause from all existing contracts of public or private debt. In the future, all such contracts must be "discharged upon payment, dollar for dollar, in any coin or currency which at the time of payment is legal tender for public and private debts." No legislation had ever made such drastic inroads on property rights. From this date on, assuming the Joint Resolution's validity, the entire debt structure of the country would be at the mercy of a legislative majority. In deference to public impatience as to the outcome, Chief Justice Hughes took the unprecedented step of announcing on two successive weeks that an opinion would not be forthcoming. "I did not like the communiqué procedure," Justice Stone wrote, "and hope that we will have no more of it, but other important cases are coming and now we will be embarrassed whether we follow the procedure or not."[18] When, on February 18, 1935, no contrary word was issued, everyone knew that the Gold Clause cases had been decided.

The atmosphere in the crowded courtroom was tense. The fate of a hundred billion dollars in public and private contracts turned on these decisions. As in the Minnesota moratorium case, the issue boiled down to the question whether private parties by their contract can tie the hands of government to deal with a problem vital to the existence of the State itself.

As to private bondholders, the Court upheld national power by a vote of 5 to 4, disposing of the matter by regarding such contracts subject to the constitutional power of Congress "to coin money and regulate the value thereof."[19] Quite different, however, was Hughes' approach to holders of Liberty Bonds, containing the government's promise to pay in United States gold coin of the present standard of value. Employing John Marshall's classic technique in *Marbury* v. *Madison*, the Chief Justice first delivered a lecture on constitutional proprieties. " 'The United States are as much bound by their contracts as are individuals,' " he said quoting Chief Justice Waite in the Sinking Fund cases ( 1878 ). "We conclude that the Joint Resolution of June 5, 1933, insofar as it attempted to override the obligation created by the bond in suit, went beyond the congressional power."[20]

From this language one might have thought that the Court demanded that the United States treat its own debts on a footing different from all other obligations in the country. But not so. The Chief Justice decided that the Court was powerless to do anything for the victims of the injustice exposed by his reasoning. The Liberty Bond holder was entitled to no more than the promised gold coin was worth in terms of the purchasing power of dollars. No proof was offered that the plaintiff had sustained a loss entitling him to sue for damages. On the contrary, internal changes in the price level had enhanced the commodity power of the dollar. Payment of his full claim would not be, the Chief Justice declared, "recoupment of loss in any proper sense but an unjustified enrichment."[21]

Justice Stone, no less than Hughes and the dissenters, was shocked by the Government's repudiation of its promise to liquidate Liberty

Bonds in gold. "The Gold Clause cases," Stone's law clerk of 1935 recalled, "were perhaps the best example of the insulation of the Justice from the man."[22] He had taken pains to dispose of his Government bonds before the case reached the Supreme Court. Now, sorely troubled by the Government's action, he vowed never again to buy securities from a government so faithless to its obligations. Yet he alone of the nine Justices took the view that congressional power to regulate the value of money might extend to abrogating gold clauses in public as well as private contracts.

"As much as I deplore this refusal to fulfill the solemn promise of bonds of the United States," Stone wrote in a concurrence, "I cannot escape the conclusion, announced for the Court, that in the situation now presented, the Government, through the exercise of its sovereign power to regulate the value of money, has rendered itself immune from liability for its action. To that extent it has relieved itself of the obligation of its domestic bonds, precisely as it has relieved the obligors of private bonds."[23]

As in so many other cases, Stone again made it clear that he felt the Court should judge only the question before it, not "needlessly intimate any opinion" on imaginary questions.* He insisted that, upon concluding that the plaintiff had suffered no damage, the majority opinion should have terminated without attempting to "prejudge the rights of other bondholders and of the Government under conditions which may never occur." Impatiently he declared that it would "not benefit this plaintiff, to whom we deny any remedy, to be assured that he has an invaluable right to performance of the Gold Clause." "It is unnecessary, and I think undesirable," Stone commented, "for the Court to undertake to say that the obligation of the Gold Clause in government bonds is greater than in the bonds of private individuals, or that in some situation not described, and in some matter and in some measure undefined, it has imposed restrictions upon the future exercise of the power to regulate the currency."[24]

Stone's distaste for the Chief Justice's dialectics is quite evident in the official reports. In letters to family and friends, his annoyance and the reasons for it are unmistakable. Writing to John Bassett Moore, he said: "There has seldom been any great question before the Court about which the public seems so ill informed, and certainly none which was more disagreeable to decide. To countenance the repudiation of solemn obligations is abhorrent to me, but to say that the Government's power to regulate currency and fix the value of

---

* Stone's view that it was unnecessary to say whether or not the Joint Resolution would be constitutionally applied to the obligations of the United States was later expressed in Smyth v. United States, 302 U.S. 329 (1937).

money can be set at naught by public or private contracts is equally distasteful."[25]

"It is well to remember," he wrote his sons, "what most of the papers seem to have missed, that there is no opinion of the Court in the Government Bond cases. The Chief Justice wrote one, in which three of his brethren concurred; I wrote another, and the dissenters wrote another,* so the Court has not declared, decided, or adjudged that the Government is bound by the Gold Clause. Besides my desire not to agree to an opinion which seemed to face both ways, you will see that there was method in my madness.† My opinion has been a good deal commented upon in the papers in this part of the country. The *Washington Post* ran a long editorial on it, and several of the New York papers have mentioned it. . . . So I feel well satisfied with my somewhat anomalous position in agreeing with the result in the Government Bond case, but not with the reasoning of my brethren."[26]

Justice Stone was not alone in taking exception to the Chief Justice's gift for posing "polar opposites."‡ Judge Hand congratulated Stone "on being the only one who intellectually 'comes clean,' " and he added: "Unless I misconceived it [Hughes' opinion in the Perry case]

---

* It seems not unlikely that Justice Stone felt some sympathy with Justice McReynolds' dissent. Much aroused, the dissenter delivered an extemporaneous speech, twenty minutes of which the *New York Times* called "scorn and indignation." The Constitution "is gone," the Justice said. "In one breath it is said that Congress has no power to repudiate a government obligation. In the next breath, it is said, it is true you have but sixty cents and you were promised a dollar, but Congress made it unlawful for you to accept what you contracted for. . . . Congress made it unlawful for you to accept what is due you. And since it is unlawful, there is no damage. . . . Here we have a monetary system the extent—I almost said wickedness—of which is almost beyond comprehension. . . . No such power was ever granted by the framers of the Constitution. It was not there then. It was not there yesterday. It is not there today. . . ." (*New York Times*, Feb. 19, 1935.)

† Stone had not only prevented a bad decision from going down in the record as the opinion of the Court, but also got his own views out in the open.

‡ "He could," Thomas Reed Powell wrote, "pose polar opposites without confessing that they were opposites, but he would leave it clear what the Court was deciding." ("Charles Evans Hughes," *Political Science Quarterly*, June 1952, p. 172.)

For what Stone described as "a beautiful piece of dissection," see Henry M. Hart, Jr., "The Gold Clause in United States Bonds," *Harvard Law Review*, May 1935. "The Court," Hart said, "violated two of its most frequently repeated canons of constitutional decision. It decided a constitutional question when it was not necessary to do so; and it permitted that question to be raised by a litigant who was able to show no interest in its outcome. Probably also it violated a third, and much more important, canon by deciding a constitutional question which upon the facts was not presented for decision." Throughout the article Professor Hart invoked Justice Stone's "trenchant refutation" to underscore the "apparent inconsistencies" in the Chief Justice's language.

Justice Stone himself encouraged commentators to speak out. In response to a congratulatory note from Assistant Attorney General John Dickinson, he wrote, Feb. 20, 1935: "I hope someone will undertake the task of showing the steps by

it means that though Congress may not repudiate the promise, it may make reception of performance unlawful. . . . How it is a counter-weight to this pettifoggery to preserve some kind of obligation living in a new *jus gentium*, I can't see. The honor of the United States may be saved that way, but I don't relish that sort of honor. . . . What you said was refreshing, honest and direct. Everybody dealing with a sovereign knows he is dealing with a creature who can welch if he wants to welch. To trick up a lot of international stuff as though it were law frankly makes me puke, as dear old Holmes used to say."[27]

This decision, as much as any single ruling in American history, revealed the judiciary's awesome power. "A difference of one vote," President Roosevelt remarked somewhat later, would have invalidated "the chief foundations of the whole recovery program," returning the country to the "pre-existing chaos in foreign exchange and domestic currency," enriching the "favored few" at the "expense of the general public."[28] Discomfiting forebodings may have been in the President's mind even before the decision came down. "This evening," Stone commented shortly after the Gold Clause cases had been argued, "the Court goes to the White House to the judicial dinner. I suspect we will be as popular there as a skunk in a hen house."[29]

Before the dust thrown up by the Justices over "gold" had fairly settled, the Court made headlines again in its 5 to 4 decision scuttling the recently enacted Railroad Retirement scheme, requiring the carriers to subscribe to a pension plan for superannuated employees. Mr. Justice Roberts, switching again to the right, riddled the statute with constitutional objections. Writing for the majority, he brushed the legislation aside contemptuously as based on "the contentment and satisfaction" theory of social progress. "Is it not apparent that they [pensions] are really and essentially related solely to the social welfare of the worker and therefore remote from any regulation of commerce as such?"[30] the Justice asked. Congress might, he agreed, require out-right dismissal of all aged workers, but it could not give them pensions.[31] Congressional effort to compel railroads to pension off older workers must fail for want of any relation between the pensioning system and the efficiency or safety of the national rail network.

On all sides Justice Roberts' opinion signified that he was lost to the New Deal. Nor was this all. His opinion reinforced the doubts of those who questioned "the capacity of Court and Constitution to satisfy the needs of our national life." "One wonders how many more

---

which the first conclusion in the Perry case opinion was reached, and of comparing them with the steps by which the conclusion in *Norman v. B. & O. R.R.* was reached. No doubt many may think my position in the Norman case was wrong, but I have the comfortable feeling that I shall be under no necessity of explaining what it is." Dickinson's article, "The Gold Decisions," appeared in the *University of Pennsylvania Law Review*, April 1935.

such decisions," the *New Republic* asked impatiently, "touching the very foundation of national power in a modern industrial society, can be absorbed without destroying the very Constitution the odd man on the Court thinks he is preserving."*

The Railroad Retirement Act was admittedly "a bad one." "If I had been a member of Congress," Justice Stone observed, "I am certain I should have voted against it, but to say that it is beyond the range of constitutional power puts us back at least thirty years. A bad matter was made worse by the cocksure assumption that we could determine judicially that there was nothing for the congressional judgment to act upon. How arrogant it must well seem to those unaccustomed to judicial omniscience in the interpretation of the Constitution."[32]

As in the Minnesota moratorium case, the Chief Justice had been prompted to broaden the base of his opinion, this time a dissent,† by a carefully reasoned memorandum from Cardozo and Stone. "What is the distinction," they asked in a letter to Hughes, "between compensating men who have been incapacitated by accident (though without fault of the employer), and compensating men who have been injured by the wear and tear of time, the slow attrition of the years? What is the difference between replacing worn-out machinery and replacing worn-out men? Is not each a legitimate incident of the business? In that view what is left of the argument of Roberts, J., that the Government should instruct the railroads to dismiss their superannuated workers without payment or pension, throwing them out helpless into the world?"[33] In accordance with the Cardozo-Stone letter, Hughes pointedly observed in dissent: "The fundamental consideration which supports this type of legislation is that industry should take care of its human wastage, whether that is due to accident or age. That view cannot be dismissed as arbitrary or capricious. It is a reasoned conviction based upon abundant experience. The expression of that conviction in law is regulation."[34]

---

* This unsigned editorial speaks of the "reckless irresponsibility of the majority opinion," and credits Justice Roberts with writing "the most persuasive brief of our times in favor of government ownership of railroads." Commenting on the editorial, Stone wrote Frankfurter, May 21, 1935: "It gets at the kernel of the matter."

† Hughes noted the most ominous aspect of the opinion: "The majority finally raise a barrier against all legislative action of this nature by declaring that the subject matter itself lies beyond the reach of the congressional authority to regulate interstate commerce. In that view, no matter how suitably limited, . . . or how appropriate the measure of retirement allowances, or how sound actuarily the plan, or how well adjusted the burden, still under this decision Congress would not be at liberty to enact such a measure. . . . I think that the conclusion thus reached is a departure from sound principles and places an unwarranted limitation upon the commerce clause of the Constitution." (Railroad Retirement case, p. 375.)

Taken together, the Panama Refining and the Railroad Retirement cases clearly forecast the New Deal's doom. The blow fell May 27, 1935, "Black Monday," when the NIRA (symbolized by the Blue Eagle) and the Frazier-Lemke Act,[35] were guillotined out of the recovery program. That same day the President received a severe personal setback in the Court's didactic ruling that he had exceeded his authority in summarily firing Federal Trade Commissioner William E. Humphrey.[36] What was most discouraging of all to New Dealers was that the Court was unanimous in all three.

"When the Justices filed into the courtroom on May 27, 1935," one observer noted, "they were looking cheerful. Particularly, it was pointed out, Chief Justice Hughes, McReynolds, and Stone. The Chief Justice had every right to be pleased. The Court was going to deliver a unanimous opinion. McReynolds may well have been pleased, because it was going to be unanimous against the New Deal. Why did Stone look pleased? Perhaps it was the cherry blossoms outside."[37]

NIRA, the "heart and core" of the recovery program, represented the culmination of the longed-for day of cooperation between government and business. With its enactment Administrator Hugh S. Johnson had envisioned the golden dawn of a new era. "First and foremost," he observed, it is "a contract to divide up the existing work in such a way as to put hundreds of thousands of new names on the payroll and then raise the wage scale high enough to give all workers a living wage for the shorter shift. . . . Their own profits will come back and we shall be on our way back to the kind of a country that we knew in happier years."[38]

After delaying nearly eighteen months, the Department of Justice had chosen to stake the Blue Eagle's life on a case exhibiting the most extreme features of the law—its application to the "live poultry" industry in New York City. The casualness with which Assistant Attorney General Robert Jackson explained how the Schechter case was chosen suggests that his Department's pursuit of the poultry slaughterers was not altogether disingenuous. "The case was far from ideal as a test case," Jackson commented, but "as the Schechters were carrying it to the Supreme Court, there was no real choice but to make it the test case there."[39]

The Schechter Brothers, wholesale poultry dealers in Brooklyn, were charged with violating NRA's Live Poultry Code as to minimum wage and maximum hour requirements, and in giving special treatment to preferred customers. Government counsel sought congressional authority under the commerce clause to regulate the Schechter's business. The Court, speaking through the Chief Justice, denied this. The Act was also found to be wanting as an unconstitutional delegation of legislative power.

"In determining how far the Federal Government may go in controlling intrastate transactions, upon the ground that they 'affect' interstate commerce," Hughes began, "there is a necessary and well-established distinction between direct and indirect effects. The precise line can be drawn only as individual cases arise, but the distinction is clear in principle," and "must be recognized as a fundamental one, essential to the maintenance of our constitutional system. Otherwise . . . there would be virtually no limit to the Federal power, and for all practical purposes we should have a completely centralized government."[40]

Stone and Cardozo, in a separate opinion written by the latter, agreed with the Court's disposition of the case. But they chose to stress the "delegation running riot" feature of the Act. If NRA prevailed, "anything that Congress may do within the limits of the commerce clause for the betterment of business may be done by the President upon the recommendation of a trade association by calling it a code," they said. Nor could they find any support in the commerce clause "for the regulation of wages and hours of labor in the intrastate transactions that make up the defendants' business." Without characterizing all production as "local," Stone and Cardozo rejected "a view of causation that would obliterate the distinction between what is national and what is local in the activities of commerce." At the same time they seemed wary of accepting Chief Justice Hughes' view that the distinction between direct and indirect effects is one of kind rather than of degree. The concurrence was more inclined to follow Judge Learned Hand, who said in the lower court's decision of the case that American society "is an elastic medium which transmits all tremors through its territory; the only question is of their size." To this Cardozo and Stone pointedly added: "The law is not indifferent to considerations of degree."[41]

Close friends of the so-called liberal Justices were shocked and puzzled. "Let not the Court be o'er proud," John Bassett Moore commented chidingly. "Let me say I am not disposed to be 'o'er proud,'" Stone replied somewhat apologetically. "While I did not see how I could come out any differently from what the Court did, I nevertheless realize that in many respects industry in the United States has become national and that the power ought to reside somewhere to treat some features of it at least nationally. But I did not see how even with a flexible Constitution, flexible-minded judges could quite stretch it to the point requisite to sustain the Government in the Schechter case. The general sloppiness of everything that has been done in connection with this effort is disheartening. Let us hope that Congress will now undertake to do its job and that ultimately we may find solutions of what in any aspect must be regarded as serious problems."[42]

At the end of the term Stone found himself sorely troubled by the high barriers he had helped to erect against national power. "We are getting new doctrine now," he observed dourly, "faster than I can absorb it."[43] The power-stifling formulas marshaled against the New Deal were both old and new. To slaughter the Blue Eagle the Court raised the classic injunction against delegated powers. For ammunition against the Act based on the commerce clause, the opinion ran all the way back to 1895; to *U.S.* v. *E. C. Knight* and Chief Justice Fuller, whom Stone characterized as "the most prolific dispenser of Obiter our Court has had."[44] The difference, if any, between the Schechter case and the Knight case (in which the "direct, indirect" distinction first appeared) was, at most, only one of degree. Had the Court been so inclined, it could have destroyed all such power-crippling precedents with the same constitutional scythe, for in between the two decisions lay impressive precedent to sustain congressional authority.[45]

Throughout the 1934 term, one venerable principle had remained strangely dormant. "It is but a decent respect due to the wisdom, the integrity, and the patriotism of the legislative body, by which any law is passed," Mr. Justice Washington had commented in 1827, "to presume in favor of its validity, until its violation of the Constitution is proved beyond all reasonable doubt."[46] No technical rule, this fundamental precept, so indispensable to the maintenance of the separation of powers, was woven into the very fabric of constitutional government. Now, as "the rights of Government to protect individual citizens from aggregations of private economic power were being gradually whittled away,"[47] this universally accepted doctrine hardly received lip service.

At his famous eighty-five-minute press conference on May 31, President Roosevelt intemperately denounced the Court's "horse and buggy" definition of interstate commerce and called on the people to meet squarely the issue whether the country was going to recognize power in the Federal Government to control economic conditions which needed control, or turn back to eighteenth-century state functions.[48] From the Schechter opinion he concluded that of five major divisions of national economic activity—manufacturing, mining, construction, farming and transportation—only one, transportation, could be regarded as "directly" affecting interstate commerce. "Does this decision mean," he queried, "that the United States Government has no control over any national economic problem?"

The Court seemed to be in the grip of rigid, sterile conceptualism. Even Stone and Cardozo, though they stood slightly to the side in the Schechter case, did not disavow the lengths to which the Court had gone to make certain that nothing approaching NRA would be tried again. Stone recognized "the necessity of national authority to deal with national problems," but balked at the obliteration of state control of internal affairs implicit in NRA. Disagreement with Hughes boiled down to distaste for the verbal device the Chief Justice employed in defining the reach of congressional authority. Nor were the commentators blind to the "aid and comfort" Stone had given this "social setback of fifty years."[49] Correspondents expressed disappointment; law school teachers encouraged him to speak out against the power-stifling trend.

"I thought the decision in the Railroad Retirement Act was the worst performance of the Court in my time," Stone said in reply to a prod from Thomas Reed Powell. "I judge you think the later one with respect to NRA was not much better. The result in the latter is one in which I can take no comfort, for I think I am as aware as anyone that the power to deal with industry, which has now become national, in a national way, should reside somewhere. According to such light as I have been able to get, the only way in which it can be dealt with adequately would require departure from our traditional distinction between the control of national interests which we call interstate commerce, and local interests which we call intrastate commerce, to such an extent as practically to end the local control of business by the states. Learned Hand, in his opinion in the Schechter case, seemed to me to put the matter very well without resorting to mechanical distinctions between action affecting commerce 'directly' and 'indirectly.'"

"I hope," the Justice told Powell, "you will cut loose and tell us what you think."[50]

Powell did so with a vengeance. Comparing the NRA to the remedies of a medicine man, he wrote: "To some of the members of the Supreme Court many legislative remedies seem but the counsel of quackery. Others are more tolerant toward experiment even when their faith is frail. When all are united in proscribing a prescription when there is no doubt that the patient is in grievous need, then we may well infer that confidence in the physician is not unduly great." As for the Chief Justice's Schechter opinion, it could be summed up by saying: "We think this goes altogether too far."

Powell went on to query the heavy responsibility the judiciary had thus shouldered. Charging that the Justices had assumed capacity to deal with the most delicate and complicated issues of modern life in terms of legal categories, he urged the "need of light from greater breeds without the law," especially from the economists. "Lawyers should be humble," he said, "when they realize how many of their craft pronounce pontifical conclusions with all too little sign of mastery of the elements of the problems that the conclusions seek to solve."[51]

Though Stone confessed shock at Powell's "exposure of the lack of substance in the Schechter opinion," he shared the educator's misgivings. The case involved complicated economic issues, transcending the bounds of law, and these, he agreed, were "not so simple as they seem to some minds. If they seemed as puzzling as they do to me, perhaps there would be greater disposition to let legislatures struggle with them."[52]

Chief Justice Hughes had for some time been credited with harboring a "chilly resentment against being watched to see what the Court was doing."[53] Stone did not share this distaste for comment on the Court's decisions: "I have no patience with the complaint that criticism of judicial action involves any lack of respect for the courts. Where the courts deal, as ours do, with great public questions, the only protection against unwise decisions, and even judicial usurpation, is careful scrutiny of their action and fearless comment upon it. I feel this more strongly now that I have had some years' observation of the judicial process behind the scenes." "No amount of criticism," he agreed, "will affect the courts today, but it is likely to have a profound effect on the courts of the next generation."[54]

In deciding New Deal cases the Court had obviously discarded its own cautious tradition against advancing to meet constitutional issues. Justice Roberts had not been content to cripple the railroaders' pensions on due process grounds—a defect that might easily have been overcome by corrective legislation. He went on to deny any rational relationship between pensions and interstate commerce, thus forestalling all valid congressional action in the field. Not satisfied, in his Schechter opinion, to throw out NIRA on the ground of improper delegation of power, Chief Justice Hughes also condemned it as an unwarranted effort to control intrastate commerce. To students of constitutional law, the Court's eagerness to anticipate basic problems in double-barreled opinions suggested motivations other than faithful enforcement of the Constitution.

One writer suggested that the Justices were bent on converting the "direct" and "indirect" formula into a sort of due process clause protective of state power.[55] Commenting on the current tendency, Professor Frankfurter remarked: "Constitutional theory and practice of a century and a half unite in protest against such advisory pronouncements" unnecessary in deciding a case. There is "logical difficulty," Frankfurter conceded, "when a decision is rested upon two constitutional grounds, in singling out either one as unnecessary," but he suggested that the Court confine itself to the decision of the lesser constitutional issue—"that which involves a narrower circumscription of congressional power."[56]

Stone was not fully convinced. He could not shake off the belief that the Railroad Retirement and Schechter decisions raised a purely technical problem of the proper method of dealing with cases standing on "two constitutional legs." "I think," he wrote Frankfurter somewhat defensively, "I have gone as far as anyone to insist that we ought not to decide constitutional questions unnecessarily,* but your discussion raises some questions for the answer of which a guiding principle must be found. Where a case stands on two constitutional legs, the sufficiency of both is fully argued, and the Court is agreed that neither is adequate to support it, which one shall it saw off? How shall the matter be resolved if the members of the Court are not agreed as to the choice? . . . These questions are food for thought and perhaps for further discussion in the law journals."[57]

Such advice pouring in on Stone from the law schools no doubt reinforced his independence, giving him, as he expressed it, "food for thought." It is doubtful, however, whether their effort alone could have moved him to the forthright stand he finally took in the climactic year 1936. His own colleagues had to prove unmistakably the truth of Frankfurter's and Powell's contentions.

On November 15, 1935, Stone spoke, apropos of pre-decision maneuvers in *Colgate* v. *Harvey,* of the new ideas that came to him "in the light of recent history." That same day he wrote Powell: "Judges ought to be more prayerful. I am going to develop the habit and pray that I may avoid deserving the hiding you gave one of my brethren in your law review article.† When we attempt to be God, or even to do the job of the legislature, the reduction of what we do to its lowest terms is very revealing and in the long run, I hope, is going to be very useful."[58]

*Colgate* v. *Harvey* apparently marks the turning point in Stone's judicial thinking. In this case, he observed, "The Court handed down an opinion in which, for the first time in its history, it gave vitality to the privileges and immunities clause of the Fourteenth Amendment, holding that it was a restraint on state taxing power where interstate transactions were concerned. To me this was a rather shocking extension of judicial power, with little to warrant it."[59] How could the Court ignore a half century of precedents and rule that the right to carry on business across state lines is a "privilege and immunity" of citizens protected by the Federal Government? How could this long-neglected clause of the Fourteenth Amendment be refurbished so as to restrain the power of states to tax the income of a citizen derived from

---

* "You will perhaps recall," Stone wrote Irving Brant, Oct. 6, 1937, "that I declined to participate in unnecessary constructions of the Constitution which are made in the opinions in the Government Gold Bond case and in the Guffey Coal Act case."

† Apparently a reference to Powell's attack on Chief Justice Hughes' Schechter opinion in the *Harvard Law Review* article, Dec. 1935, p. 193.

Also useful and revealing was the Frankfurter and Landis "Review of the Business of the Supreme Court for the 1934 Term." These writers had taken the Court to task for failure to state reasons for granting certiorari, and warned of the importance of not deciding unnecessary constitutional questions.

sources outside the state, when no such limitations stemmed from that Amendment's "equal protection" clause?

"My last opinion," the Justice reported, "a rather elaborate dissent on constitutional questions, is now being printed. I wrote the dissent two weeks ago with such effectiveness that the writer [Sutherland] of the opinion of the Court has had to revise it extensively and rely on new and seldom mentioned provisions of the Constitution to support his position."[60]

Stone's dissent was sharp: "If the exemption does not merit condemnation as a denial of the equal protection which the Fourteenth Amendment extends to every person, nothing can be added to the vehemence or effectiveness of the denunciation by invoking the command of the privileges and immunities clause." Such restrictions upon local policy, such subordination of state power to individual interest, "could be justified only by a pointed command of the Constitution of plain import."[61] All this seemed self-evident to the dissenter but, as Stone commented to his friend Powell, "I am only a voice crying out in the wilderness."

Moreover, this gratuitous disinterment of the privileges and immunities clause in the face of a half century of precedent to the contrary was effected by methods exemplifying reactionary desire to build up not a rational, consistent body of constitutional law, but rigid doctrinal bulwarks against effective government.

The full measure of the power-crippling effect of *Colgate* v. *Harvey* could be seen only when that decision was placed alongside others in which congressional regulation was at stake. Contemporaneously almost every assertion of national power, predicated on the assumption that economic forces had made the country a single unit, was resisted as an alleged invasion of state domain. In these circumstances, it seemed "almost playing with destiny to deny freedom to the state in such an exercise of the taxing power of Vermont as the Court condemned."

Nor was this all. "The full story," Stone wrote, "of how it was brought about is even more shocking. The Court suffered in this case, as it has in a good many recent ones, from an overstimulated inventive genius. If the opinion had rested on the equal protection clause it would have merely added another bad decision to a considerable group. Evidently that idea, after it was developed, was found not to be very satisfactory, and so resort was had to the privileges and immunities clause as a happy afterthought. This way of dealing with constitutional questions is even more alarming than the results themselves."[62]

"If the inventor," Stone added, "would only sponsor his invention in public, I think I could write a really effective dissent." But prudence, as usual, warned Hughes against any "unnecessary exposure to attack."[63] Sutherland, not the Chief Justice, wrote the majority opinion.

Stone continued to brood over the majority's handling of the Colgate case. Four years later when the Court flatly overruled it, he "shed no tears."[*] Then, Justice Roberts, mourning the triumph of Stone's views, circulated an opinion in which he said that the ill-fated case was decided after the fullest consideration. "In this statement I think your recollection is at fault," Stone promptly challenged. "For the Court to set aside the course of judicial decision for a half century and decide for the first time that the privileges and immunities clause afforded protection to property rights not growing out of any relationship between the citizen and the national government, and without a word of discussion in conference, seemed to me then, as it does now, not to be full consideration or, indeed, any consideration worthy of the name, in view of the importance of the subject."[64] Justice Roberts revised his dissenting opinion, omitting the statement to which Stone objected.[65]

Stone was on solid ground. On February 4, 1936, perceiving the full impact of *Colgate* v. *Harvey* and sensing its historic importance, he recorded:

This case was argued on October 14 and 15, 1935. The briefs made some mention of the privileges and immunities clause, but that clause played no part of any significance in the argument. The reliance of counsel was placed wholly on the equal protection clause and that alone had been considered by the Supreme Court of Vermont.

At conference on the following Saturday, the case was presented by the Chief Justice, in his usual fashion of greatly over-elaborating the unimportant details of the case and disposing, by *ipse dixit*, in a sentence or two, of the vital question. He thought that there would be no want of equal protection if the income were exempted of investments required to be in property or mortgages within the state; but that since the statute permitted the loans made there to be withdrawn from the state and used for purposes outside the state, this was clearly a denial of equal protection. The argument under the privileges and immunities clause he thought unworthy of consideration. The other judges acquiesced in this conclusion, without discussion, except Justice Brandeis, Justice Cardozo and myself. Justice Brandeis contented himself by stating that he thought there was no denial of equal protection. I combatted, in a few sentences, the idea that the classification was not a permissible one, even though some loans might be made within the state for use or purposes without the state, pointing out that it did not appear that there were any such and that in any case the exemption of income from loans made within the state at 5% or less would favorably affect interest rates within the state. Justice Cardozo merely stated that he agreed with the views I expressed.

* "If *Colgate* v. *Harvey* was not stillborn, it has been certainly short-lived," Stone wrote a former law clerk, Alexis Coudert, Feb. 6, 1940, "and I shed no tears over it."

There was no discussion of the privileges and immunities clause by anyone.

The writing of the opinion was assigned to Mr. Justice Sutherland, who promptly circulated an opinion. . . . I at once circulated a dissent containing so much of the dissenting opinion as was ultimately published down to the end of the paragraph numbered I.* This evidently jarred the determination of the majority judges to rest the case on the equal protection clause alone, and resulted in conferences between the Chief Justice and Justice Sutherland. On the following conference day, at the end of our two weeks recess, Justice Sutherland asked that the opinion go over and announced that he would re-circulate. When the second edition appeared, it rested the case heavily on the privileges and immunities clause, although the matter had not been presented or considered in conference, and never was so presented or considered. I at once added paragraph 2 of my dissenting opinion, after which Justice Sutherland's opinion was again revised and circulated. The privileges and immunities clause thus entered into a new phase without ever having been discussed or without having received the consideration of the Court in conference, and was resorted to to support a decision because the majority had been unable to support it adequately on the grounds originally agreed upon.

Stone made no bones as to the majority's underlying motivations and freely expressed his indignation. "It just seems as though, in some of these cases," he commented February 17, 1936, apropos of *Colgate* v. *Harvey*, "the writer and those who united with him, didn't care what was said, as long as the opinion seemed plausible on its face."[66]

Differences in the councils of the Supreme Court merely reflected the clash of forces raging in the country. And if Stone's dissenting opinions manifested (as they certainly did) increasing vehemence, the reason may be that none of his colleagues foresaw more clearly the disaster that might follow in the wake of judicial decisions warped to satisfy the purblind demands of practical politics.

Stone felt profoundly his responsibility, but now, as always, it must be discharged in his capacity as a judge. On general grounds of propriety, he had usually shied away from extra-judicial appearances. Now there were special reasons why he did not wish to encourage any publicity or seem to do so.† For, once again, Stone's friends were boosting him as the ideal candidate for President on the Republican ticket in

* Herein Stone denounced the "equal protection" basis of the Court's opinion, arguing that the Vermont statute must be upheld, "unless, as we profess not to do, . . . we are to sit as a super-legislature, or as triers of the facts on which a legislature is to say what shall and what shall not be taxed." Brandeis and Cardozo concurred.

† "I decided not to make the address at the Bar Association," the Justice wrote Karl Llewellyn, May 9, 1935. "There were a number of reasons, only one of which I will state. . . . You may have observed the political gossip which has been going around the country about me. It seems to me indispensable that I should neither encourage nor seem to encourage it by any public appearance."

1936. "It is a good thing for a Supreme Court Justice to keep out of politics," Stone wrote Sterling Carr, who since 1927 had been steadfastly trying to get Stone to run, while Stone had as steadfastly refused. "I can think of no more discouraging task," he had commented, "than being a candidate for President. It seems to me one sees human nature at its worst and its lowest." Furthermore, history had proved to him that it was not good politics "to take a man off the Supreme Court and make him a candidate for anything."* Finally, his brief spell as Attorney General raised doubts whether professional politicians would "favor or support me."[67]

When in May 1934 the *Detroit News* mentioned the Justice as "the logical candidate," one warm supporter wrote him "that the suggestion is a very popular one in Michigan. You would, I am sure, turn this state back in the Republican column by a big majority." When other papers carried the "news," a chorus of cheers went up from former students and well-wishers. "What an opportunity to give a little of ourselves to you," one enthusiastic correspondent wrote. "The start has been made and you'll be moving into the White House." So far as Stone was concerned, the presidential boom fell absolutely flat. "My hat fits just as well this morning as it did before that screed was published," he commented.[68]

Certain friends, alert to the pitfalls of politics, reinforced the Justice's misgivings. "Every now and then," one wrote, "your picture appears in the papers, and there was some statement that you were going to run for President. I am pretty sure you won't be so foolish. I am confident you are going to be Chief Justice and would have been before this but for the fine Italian scheming of that old scamp, Mellon."[69]

The Justice absolutely refused to encourage or even to recognize the move to draft him. Moreover, he disliked being placed in a position where people could say that he shaped opinions to build popular support for personal political ambitions. Yet, far from waning, speculation on Stone as presidential timber attracted official notice. In 1935 W. Kingsland Macy, New York State Republican chairman, proclaimed the need for "a man of the type of Justice Stone." "There is not in the country a better man for President than Justice Stone," Mark Sullivan wrote. About the same time William Allen White, believing that "the sun has set forever on the Coolidgian era," expressed the conviction "that Stone would make an ideal candidate."[70] Quick to perceive his party's predicament, Stone remarked: "No one knows better than I that this is

---

* "I have never thought," Stone wrote Sterling Carr, May 29, 1934, commenting on Justice Hughes' resignation in 1916 to accept the Republican nomination for the Presidency, "that it did Mr. Hughes' long-run reputation any good, although he has rendered distinguished public service and now sits in the position of Chief Justice, which he doubtless never would have occupied if he had stayed on the Court."

merely the counsel of desperation." GOP leaders were simply making "a belated effort to liberalize the Republican party."* They had done nothing to indicate that "the party had any constructive program to do anything more than balance the budget and then go back to the good old times of '29 and before."[71] "Someone," he said, "must point out to our Republican brethren the futility and lack of substance in their lip service to abstract notions of individual liberty." "The great problem," as he saw it, was "reconciliation of the need of individual liberty with the needs of organized society."[72]

Stone was now being pushed from all sides. As if to prove that the Court's primary function was political, Republican friends, betraying their pose as objective defenders of the Constitution, urged Stone to doff judicial robes and run for office. At the same time others were spurring him to use his judicial position in such a way as to make effective government possible, and thus avert or discourage more radical measures.†

In March 1935 Stone completed his first decade as an Associate Justice. During that time he had eleven law clerks, each staying with him about a year, as is customary. One Sunday evening they assembled from all directions to celebrate his anniversary. As a memento of the occasion the law clerks gave him a handsome silver bowl with an engraved inscription, followed by all their names. "We had a merry time," Stone reported to his sons, "full of interesting reminiscences, and recalling many pleasant associations. It was one of the happiest occurrences of my life."[73]

In early May he went to the *Harvard Law Review* dinner and made a brief speech. At midnight he took the train to New York and arrived in time to have breakfast with his son Lauson and to salute his first grandson, Harlan Fiske II. He was back in Washington early enough to send to the printer an opinion he had written on the train. It was "a fairly strenuous excursion, but worth all the trouble."[74]

The administration's reaction to burgeoning judicial pre-eminence, especially to the unanimous Schechter decision, had been uncompromising. Close friends of the so-called liberal Justices (including those out of sympathy with the New Deal) were shocked and puzzled. Stone, trying to console one of his critics, wrote: "I think I discern

---

* As the national nominating convention date approached, Stone continued to follow Republican strategy with a skeptical eye. "The political pot seems to be boiling very hard now," he wrote Sterling Carr, April 16, 1936. "Everyone here is very much for Landon (Alf. of Kansas), and many are busy trying to persuade their friends that he is a great man, which he well may be. But people hereabout seem to know very little about him. I am not persuaded just now that he or any other Republican candidate in sight can win unless the picture changes very much."

† "The fools," Frankfurter wrote Stone, Aug. 1, 1935, "if they only knew, they would realize that this man in the White House is one of the best chances there is for maintaining the essentials of the old capitalist, i.e., competitive system."

signs of returning sanity and that the Constitution may not be as badly manhandled as some of the Brain Trusters have thought. If the Court will only stick close to the cases actually presented and will not 'slop over' in the business of opinion writing, I shall have confidence in the outcome."

Ten years of immersion in the battle of ideas had reaffirmed his resolve to follow an independent course. This was a time when wise men, and courts especially, should not be pushed off their feet by the emotions of the moment.[75] As a judge he would refuse to play God—or politics. He would put behind him all thought of a political career and strike a bolder, more independent note in his judicial opinions. He was now ready to use the powder saved "for another time." The occasion was at hand.

CHAPTER TWENTY-SIX

# Outraged Plea
# for Judicial Self-Restraint

## 1935-1936

One of the planks in the platform on which F.D.R. was elected—a commitment equal in emphasis to the Democratic candidate's campaign promise to balance the budget—was his solemn vow to restore agricultural prosperity. The measure designed to do this—the famous Agricultural Adjustment Act (AAA)—levied a processing tax on basic commodities such as wheat, corn, and cotton. From the funds thus accumulated, money was paid out to farmers as inducement to reduce their acreage. Here, at long last, was a self-financing scheme to subsidize farmers, similar to the protective tariff that had long subsidized industry.

The program had been in operation two and half years before it reached the Supreme Court. On December 9, 1935, in the courtroom of the new Supreme Court Building* a huge crowd collected to hear

* The Justices began the October Term in the new building. The last argument in the old courtroom had been heard in May 1935. Though Stone had had a part in the planning, he was disappointed in the outcome. Specifically, he found the lighting, the acoustics, and the library accommodations wanting. "A day or two ago I visited the Supreme Court building into which I suppose we will move some-

argument on the AAA. "All day, every day, the courtroom was filled to capacity, even including standing room."[1] Those who came in the expectation of witnessing a display of histrionics were not disappointed. Attacking the Act's constitutionality was Philadelphia's most eminent lawyer, George Wharton Pepper. He was perfectly cast for the role. "I have tried very hard to argue this case calmly and dispassionately," he told the Justices, "because it seems to me that this is the best way in which an advocate can discharge his duty to this Court. But I do not want your Honors to think my feelings are not involved and that my emotions are not deeply stirred. Indeed, may it please your Honors, I believe I am standing here today to plead the cause of the America I have loved; and I pray Almighty God that not in my time may 'the land of the regimented' be accepted as a worthy substitute for 'the land of the free.' "[2]

The former Senator's prayers were soon answered. Within a month, on January 6, the Court announced its decision. Justice Roberts spoke for the majority. The vote was 6 to 3, Brandeis, Cardozo, and Stone dissenting.

The keystone of AAA, the processing tax, could not be upheld as a tax. "The word has never been thought to connote the expropriation of money from one group for the benefit of another," the Court ruled.[3] If valid, the exaction could be supported only as an exercise of the disputed power to tax and spend for the "general welfare." Yet, through many administrations, regardless of party, appropriations of money had been made to accomplish purposes not identified with those Congress is authorized to promote under its other powers.* Hamilton had upheld this view in his famous Report on Manufacturers,† and Justice Roberts emphatically embraced the Hamiltonian doctrine. At first

---

time next year," he wrote his sons, May 24, 1935. "It is a very grand affair, but I confess that I returned from my visit with a feeling akin to dismay. The place is almost bombastically pretentious, and thus it seems to me wholly inappropriate for a quiet group of old boys such as the Supreme Court of the United States. In my brief inspection I discovered many inconveniences, due to bad plans and lack of criticism of the plans by the people who are to use the building. It seems a great pity that the United States should spend $10,000,000 upon a building, constructed to last forever, but exhibiting such grave faults." In later years the Justice modified his views.

* Several Presidents, however, following the Madisonian interpretation, had vetoed appropriations they believed to be unconstitutional. See James F. Richardson, *Messages and Papers of the Presidents*, Vol. I (Madison), pp. 584, 585; Vol. IV (Polk), pp. 610, 618, 620; Vol. V (Buchanan), pp. 599, 601.

† "It is therefore, of necessity, left to the discretion of the National Legislature to pronounce upon the objects which concern the general welfare, and for which under that description, an appropriation of money is requisite and proper. And there seems to be no room for a doubt, that whatever concerns the general interests of learning, of agriculture, of manufactures, and of commerce are within the sphere of the national councils, as far as regards an application of the money." (*The Works of Alexander Hamilton*, Lodge ed., Vol. IV, pp. 151-52.)

glance this would seem to settle the case in favor of the AAA. Not so, for at this point Justice Roberts' reasoning took a sharp, almost devious turn. In words reminiscent of Chief Justice Taft and *Bailey* v. *Drexel Furniture Company*, the Justice contended that the AAA was really not a tax at all. It was part of a plan to control agricultural production. So the Court had to do more than consider the tax; it had to pass on the constitutionality of the regulatory plan.

Again one might have supposed that the Court would be in favor of AAA, for if Congress has the power to levy and collect taxes and spend money for the general welfare beyond its specifically granted powers, as Hamilton had held and as the Court had just agreed, why could it not require that money be spent for the purpose of curtailing agricultural production? The AAA did not simply offer a conditional grant to farmers; it required them to sign a contract to reduce acreage before they got the money.

Here was the rub. Congress could give the money to the farmers unconditionally, but it could not make conditional offers to them to do something—in this case reduce their acreage—because this would be to give Congress control over subject matter that it could not reach directly. The AAA must fall, Roberts ruled, because "it is a scheme for purchasing with federal funds submission to federal regulation of a subject reserved to the states. . . . The Congress cannot invade state jurisdiction to compel individual action; no more can it purchase such action. . . . It must follow that it may not indirectly accomplish those ends by taxing and spending to purchase compliance."

But why *must* this follow? Roberts' answer is unmistakably clear. "If the Act before us is a proper exercise of the federal taxing power, evidently the regulation of all industry throughout the United States may be accomplished by similar exercise of the same power." The United States would be "converted into a central government exercising uncontrolled police power in every state of the Union, superseding all local control or regulation of the affairs or concerns of the states." Congress would "become a parliament of the whole people subject to no restrictions save such as are self-imposed."

Roberts' probe into congressional motives thus discovered that the AAA was not a taxing measure at all but a disingenuous disguise for the regulation of agricultural production, an invalid invasion of the reserved domain of the states:

From the accepted doctrine that the United States is a government of delegated powers, it follows that those not expressly granted, or reasonably to be implied from such as are conferred, are reserved to the states or to the people. To forestall any suggestion to the contrary, the Tenth Amendment was adopted. The same proposition, otherwise stated, is that powers not granted are prohibited. None to regulate agricultural production is given, and therefore legislation by Congress for that purpose is forbidden.

Justice Roberts thus placed the taxing and spending provisions in a special category, doing for Congress's power to tax and spend what Justice Day had done in 1918 for Congress's power to regulate interstate commerce.[4] In both instances the judiciary wrote the word "expressly" into the Tenth Amendment. "It is an established principle," Justice Roberts concluded, "that the attainment of a prohibited end may not be accomplished under the pretext of the exertion of powers which are granted."

Such drastic restriction on the scope of the national taxing power was a far cry from Justice Stone's views. Some years before, New Dealers, mapping legislative strategy for proposed social security laws, "drew courage" from his informally expressed confidence. "I had said to him, in the course of a social occasion," Secretary of Labor Frances Perkins* recalled, "that I had great hope of developing a social insurance system for the country, but that I was deeply uncertain of the method since, as I said laughingly, 'Your Court tells us what the Constitution permits.' Stone had whispered, 'The taxing power of the Federal Government, my dear, is sufficient for everything you want and need.' "[5]

Justice Stone's dissent, largely written on New Year's Day, 1936, directed attention to "the pivot" on which the decision of the Court was made to turn—that a levy unquestionably within the taxing power of Congress may be treated as invalid because it is a step in a plan to regulate agricultural production and is thus an infringement of state power. Here, at last, was the opportunity to use his powder "where it would do the most good," and he rose to the occasion with unprecedented vehemence. The intramural judicial war, developing since 1930, now reached its climax. Six Justices, including Hughes and Roberts, were solidly united against the power to govern. Stone's dissent, therefore, not only attacked the majority's view of the taxing and spending power, but blasted judicial usurpation as such.†

The power to use money for the general welfare, the dissenter began, is a substantive power, granted "in specific and unambiguous terms," and therefore equal in force to any other enumerated power. It, like Congress's authority to coin money or declare war, comes within the

---

* "Miss Perkins," Stone wrote his sons, January 11, 1934, "I admire greatly for her capacity and wisdom. She is the first real Secretary of Labor the country has ever had."

† Justice Roberts strongly resented the vehemence of Stone's dissent. He complained to the Chief Justice, but Hughes refused to intervene in the matter, merely suggesting that the aggrieved Justice might discuss the matter with Brandeis. Perhaps at his prompting, Stone softened the tone of his original draft somewhat, but Brandeis had approved Stone's unrevised version, saying: "I join in a fine job."

general proposition that the powers of Congress carry with them a choice of means for their execution. It comes also within the proposition that such power and such means enjoy supremacy over any conflicting state power whatsoever. The majority opinion, Stone asserted, reverses "the time-honored principle of constitutional interpretation that the granted power includes all those which are incident to it." The majority opinion, he charged, subjects a grant of power "to limitations which do not find their origin in any express provision of the Constitution and to which other expressly delegated powers are not subject."

Nor could the traditional presumption of constitutionality be effectively sidestepped by a display of "coercive effect which rests on nothing more substantial than groundless speculation." It is, Stone said, a "contradiction in terms to say that there is power to spend for the national welfare, while rejecting any power to impose conditions reasonably adapted to the attainment of the end which alone would justify the expenditure." Any such gratuitous, inconsistent limitation would lead to the most absurd consequences: "The government may give seeds to farmers, but may not condition the gift upon their being planted in places where they are most needed or even planted at all. The government may give money to the unemployed, but may not ask that those who get it shall give labor in return, or even use it to support their families. It may give money to sufferers from earthquake, fire, tornado, pestilence, or flood, but may not impose conditions— health precautions designed to prevent spread of disease. . . . All that, because it is purchased regulation infringing state powers, must be left for the states, who are unable or unwilling to supply the necessary relief."*

There were, Stone conceded, "widely held and strongly expressed differences of opinion on the wisdom of the Agricultural Adjustment Act." But, however a judge may feel about legislation in terms of policy, such views should not be permitted to influence his consideration of the Act's validity. Courts are properly concerned not with matters of policy but of power. Even in this narrow province, they should be deferential to legislative findings of fact out of which controverted statutes emerge.

Justice Roberts had raised the specter of "legislative power, without restriction or limitation," "vested in a parliament . . . subject to no restrictions except the discretion of its members." But, Stone countered, consider the status of judicial power. Precisely because it is unfettered,

* Justice Stone tersely stated the point six months later: "Persuasion, coercion, if you please, is inseparable from the granted power and an incident of it, and that incident is included in the grant. Does not all this mean that whatever the effect, if the payment is persuasive or coercive, 'the tail goes with the hide' and is within the constitutionally granted power?" (H.F.S. to Robert L. Hale, June 1, 1936.)

he insisted, judicial responsibility should be discharged with finer conscience and humility than that of any other agency of government.[6]

Of course "governmental power of the purse" was, as Stone conceded, fraught with frightening possibilities of abuse. But the majority's inference that such power, unless judicially limited, might be put to undesirable and constitutionally prohibited ends "hardly rises to the dignity of argument." "So may judicial power be abused," he commented curtly, and continued his blast:

A tortured construction of the Constitution is not to be justified by recourse to extreme examples of reckless congressional spending which might occur if courts could not prevent [it]. . . . Such suppositions are addressed to the mind accustomed to believe that it is the business of courts to sit in judgment on the wisdom of legislative action. Courts are not the only agency of government that must be assumed to have capacity to govern. Congress and the courts both unhappily may falter or be mistaken in the performance of their constitutional duty. But interpretation of our great charter of government which proceeds on any assumption that the responsibility for the preservation of our institutions is the exclusive concern of any one of the three branches of government, or that it alone can save them from destruction, is far more likely, in the long run, "to obliterate the constituent members" of "an indestructible union of indestructible states" than the frank recognition that language, even of a constitution, may mean what it says. . . .

The redundancy embodied in the Tenth Amendment—"powers not delegated are reserved"—had long been conspicuous in the armory of judicial devices for defeating national power. Justice Stone had been troubled by the inferential sanction Chief Justice Hughes gave this notion in his Schechter opinion; he went out of his way to discredit it in the AAA dissent. Several weeks later he was still pondering the subject: "Have you ever found in your researches in our constitutional history," the Justice asked Charles A. Beard, "any indication that the framers of the [Tenth] Amendment intended the reserve powers of the states to constitute a limitation of the power of Congress?"[7]

Beard's research served only to confirm Stone's conviction that they had not so intended.[*] "I have always held," the Justice wrote the his-

---

* When Madison presented the amendment to Congress, it read: "The powers not delegated by this constitution, nor prohibited by it to the States, are reserved to the States respectively." (*Annals of Congress*, Vol. I, pp. 453, 458-59.) On August 18, 1789, Mr. Tucker moved to add "expressly" so as to make it read "The powers not expressly delegated by this constitution." Mr. Madison rose to the floor and objected to this amendment, because it was impossible to confine a government to the exercise of express powers; there must necessarily be admitted powers by implication, unless the Constitution descended to recount every minutia. He remembered the word "expressly" had been moved in the Convention of Virginia, by the opponents of ratification, and, after full and free discussion, was given up by them, and the system allowed to retain its present form. Mr. Sherman agreed,

torian, "that the framers of the Constitution intended to create a strong government, adequate to deal with every situation. I think they would have been surprised, even after the Tenth Amendment, to learn that the Constitution reserved a legislative field to the states. It granted power to the National Government and, in the vernacular of the farmer, 'the tail goes with the hide.' "[8] The Tenth Amendment, framed, as John Marshall said, "for the purpose of quieting the excessive jealousies which had been excited,"[9] was quite innocuous, unusable even as a means of limiting the implied powers "without smuggling into the text what was not there—the word 'expressly.' "[10] In 1936 six Supreme Court Justices, bent on slaying the New Deal, had performed precisely this feat, doing then what the first Congress, after due consideration, had specifically refused to do.

This latest step in the Court's annexation of areas in which the Justices could "romp at will" provoked prompt reaction, especially among legislators and students of the Constitution. Another significant item had been added to the list of functions that neither the Federal Government nor the states could effectively exercise. "What we face now," Dean Lloyd K. Garrison said, "is the question, not how governmental functions shall be shared, but whether in substance we shall govern at all."[11]

Building on Stone's dissent, Democratic legislators and others denounced the Justices for usurping powers of Congress, for substituting their individual views on basically political issues for those of the people's elected representatives. "Never before," Professor Howard Lee McBain declared in a popular article, "has a dissenting minority gone quite so far toward calling into question the motives of the majority and clearly implying that they have abused their judicial prerogative."[12]

"I thought your article in yesterday's *New York Times* very interesting and able," Stone wrote his former Columbia University colleague, but "perhaps I should enter one disclaimer. I do not question the motives of my brethren, and did not intend to do so in the vigorous language which I used in my dissenting opinion. I do question a method of thinking which is perhaps the greatest stumbling block to the right administration of judicial review of legislation." Continuing, Stone stated his position:

We see it frequently enough in the common untrained mind, which is accustomed to think that legislation which it regards as bad or unwise must

---

arguing that "corporate bodies are supposed to possess all powers incident to a corporate capacity, without being absolutely expressed." (*Ibid.*, p. 790.)

A few days later, Mr. Gerry again proposed to add "expressly" to the amendment. On a roll call vote, his motion was defeated, 32 to 17. (*Ibid.*, p. 797.)

necessarily be unconstitutional. Where there is a choice of interpretations of a constitutional provision, such a habit of thought is very likely to make a choice of the interpretation which would lessen the possibility of enacting a bad law. The difficulty with this method is that lessening the power to enact bad laws likewise lessens the power to enact good ones, and the judgment of what is good or bad, which is essentially a legislative function, is likely to be affected by the passions and prejudices of the moment. Such an approach to constitutional construction tends to increase the dead areas in the Constitution, the lacunae in which no power exists, either state or national, to deal with the problems of government.

There was nothing personal in these intracourt battles. "The fact that we have intellectual differences," Stone explained, "has not yet made us uncivilized."[13] Stone queried not the motives of his associates, but rather their conception of the judicial function. "If judges can be brought to understand," he told McBain, "what I conceive to be the true nature of the judicial function, I can think of no institution likely to be of more enduring value."[14]

Two days later McBain expressed regret for having drawn "from your words a deduction as to motives which you did not intend." On second thought, however, the Columbia professor stood by his guns. The implications he had found in Stone's words had been spelled out only after very careful thought, and they still seemed "not unreasonable." "Frankly I do question the motives of your colleagues," McBain reiterated. "Their motives are so inextricably interwoven with their thought processes as to reveal themselves without their even being conscious of the revelation."

Stone seemed ill prepared to continue his disclaimer. Earlier he had been inclined to hold to the implicit faith in the honest intention of judges that he had voiced in his Hewitt lectures of 1915. In his letter to McBain on January 28, 1936, only a trace of that faith remained. "In the long run, I do not suppose it makes much difference whether unfortunate interpretations of the Constitution are purposeful or only the product of muddy thinking and the subconscious force of unrecognized prejudices."

Stone's forthright attack on judicial autocracy, his fervent exposition of "the true nature of the judicial function," were welcome grist for the New Deal legislative mill. The President did not for the time being give way to any lurking impulse to upbraid or declare war on the judiciary, as he had done in the ill-tempered interview following the unanimous Schechter decision. "It is plain to see," Ickes recorded, January 24, 1936, "that from what the President said today [at Cabinet meeting] and has said on other occasions, that he is not at all averse to the Supreme Court declaring one New Deal statute after another unconstitutional.* I think he believes that the Court will find itself pretty far out on a limb before it is through with it and that a real issue will be joined on which we can go to the country."[15]

"We were," the President commented later on, "stopped short and thrown back in our efforts . . . to serve obvious national needs. The whole line of decisions cast a deep shadow of doubt upon the ability of Congress ever at any time to protect the Nation against catastrophe by squarely meeting modern social and economic maladjustments."[16]

Depression-ridden farmers, however, were not so cool and collected. "This decision," a Great Plains wheat grower said, "works great hardship, particularly on the farmers of this Northwest which was hit by drought, and many a farmer who tried his best all his life has defeat staring him in the face."[17] "Mr. Justice Roberts," a Richfield, California, man commented, "after discussing the general welfare clause right up to the point where his conclusion must be that the Act is constitutional, dodges the point and says it invades states' rights. Yet it is impossible for any state legislature to regulate farm production in other states, so the majority decision strikes out of the Constitution the welfare clause so far as it applies to farmers."[18] This same correspondent expressed "heartfelt thanks to the Illustrious Three who feel that national welfare requires that farmers have similar rights to banking and commerce."

Both lay and professional opinion ran overwhelmingly in Stone's favor. "Despite all," one law professor wrote him, "history remains the ultimate tribunal. There votes are not counted but arguments weighed and so your dissent will take its place with the great moral pronouncements of your Court." Congressional critics felt "particularly indebted" to him "for the brilliantly forceful and persuasive assignment of reasons . . . for affirming the constitutionality of such farm legislation."[19] "As in the law schools, so throughout the country," the editors of *Fortune* summarized, "was Mr. Justice Harlan Fiske Stone's dissenting AAA opinion greeted as better law and better logic than the majority opinion written by Justice Roberts."[20] Using the AAA opinions, the *New Republic* staged a running debate between Justices Stone and Roberts. In this format, too, Stone had the last word.[21] One of the most carefully reasoned attacks on the majority opinion was Irving

---

* "There isn't any doubt at all," Ickes recorded a week later, "that the President is really hoping the Supreme Court will continue to make a clean sweep of all New Deal legislation, throwing out the TVA Act, the Securities Act, the Railroad Retirement Act, the Social Security Act, the Guffey Coal Act, and others. He thinks the country is beginning to sense this issue but that enough people have not yet been affected by adverse decisions so as to make a sufficient feeling on a Supreme Court issue."

Brant's *Storm over the Constitution*. Soon after Brant's book appeared Brandeis wrote Stone expressing the "wish" that "the fairies would make our junior from Pennsylvania [Roberts] read it."[22]

The Old Guard was much heartened by this most recent assertion of judicial power to scuttle the New Deal. "Thus far," Raoul E. Desvernine, American Liberty League vice-president, wrote in 1936, New Dealers "have met with an unsurmountable obstacle. . . . The judiciary has again proved itself to be the bulwark of defense against the subtle and skillful manipulation of democratic processes to achieve unsanctioned theories."[23] Justice Stone's opinion, the League's court of last resort announced, is "contrary to established constitutional law in respects that have been thoroughly recognized since the very foundation of the Republic."[24] Desvernine's conception of the true nature of the judicial function was quite different from Stone's:

> To confuse, as Mr. Justice Stone in the Hoosac Mills case did, *judicial* action with *governing* action under our system is to display an absolute lack of appreciation of the true nature of our judiciary. Our judiciary does not *govern* in any sense of that word, it simply rationalizes and validates our conduct with constitutional concepts. It performs an act of comparative analysis in comparing a legislative enactment, or an executive action, with the Constitution and determines if they gibe. It is the searching Conscience of Americanism.[25]

Mildly amused by such notice from a "rival tribunal," the dissenting Justice chose to regard it as evidence that official defenders of the faith needed the "aid and comfort" of outside support.[26]

The political overtones of the case were generally recognized. At a Cabinet meeting on February 14, 1936, some "interesting gossip" was passed along by Attorney General Cummings. "He said," Ickes recorded, "there was a report to the effect that Chief Justice Hughes was willing to go either way in the AAA case." "The Chief Justice does not like 5 to 4 opinions," Cummings told fellow Cabinet members, "and if Justice Roberts had been in favor of sustaining AAA, the Chief Justice would have cast his vote that way also."[27] The story seems incredible. Even more so is Chief Justice Hughes' casual disposition of the case in conference. In a memorandum of February 4, 1936, Stone wrote:

> This case was argued on December 9 and 10, 1935, and brought up at conference by the Chief Justice on the following Saturday. In presenting the case he recommended that the statute be overturned for improper delegation. He recognized that by the August 1935 legislation, Congress had adopted the rate and method of taxation as promulgated by the Secretary of Agriculture, but that in his judgment the Act of the Secretary of Agriculture was an illegal act and was not capable of ratification. After a painful elaboration of these ideas he concluded by saying that if we were to come to the

merits he thought that the AAA was a regulation of agriculture within the states and an invasion of the reserved power of the states. In putting forth this idea he emphasized the fact that contracts were taken by the Secretary to restrict production. There was no suggestion of coercion and no analysis of the relation of conditional grants or the contracts to the spending power.*

Each of the judges, except Brandeis, Cardozo, and myself, expressed objection to resting the case on unconstitutional delegation, but accepted without discussion his suggestion that the AAA was unconstitutional regulation of agriculture. Justice Brandeis passed. I pointed out that under the Chief Justice's decision in the Goodcell case† we had a case of a defective tax and a curative statute, and that we plainly could not overturn the statute on grounds of improper delegation without in effect overruling the Goodcell case, which I thought sound in principle which should be adhered to. Discussing the merits, I stated that I thought that there was nothing coercive about the AAA legislation; that gifts upon condition which were consistent with a national purpose were within the spending power and not infringements of reserve power of the states.

Justice Cardozo contented himself with saying that he agreed with my views, and the Chief Justice stated that he was willing to put the case on the ground of unconstitutional regulation, and called for a vote.

Thus the main question in the case was decided practically without discussion and with no analysis or consideration of the relation of conditional gifts for a national purpose to the spending power conferred upon Congress.

On the following day Justice Brandeis announced to the Chief Justice that he agreed with Justice Cardozo and me.

The opinion was written during the first week of recess. It was circulated late Saturday evening of that week. I spent the Sunday (December 29th) in Boston, found the opinion on my desk on my return the following day. I spent the day in getting out an opinion for the Court on which I was working, and on Tuesday took up the writing of the dissent. I discovered that the

* Merlo J. Pusey, in his biography *Charles Evans Hughes* (Vol. II, p. 745), tells us that Stone's "brethren of the majority felt that his words were unduly theatrical because of the narrowness of the difference between the two groups. Stone himself recognized that 'the power to tax and spend' could not be used to coerce action left to state control." The biographer does not, however, suggest any circumstance that may have stimulated the dissenter's histrionics, nor does he point out that "the narrowness of the difference" between the majority and the minority—indeed the point on which the case turned—had not been discussed in conference at all. But clearly the "differences," far from being narrow, involved not only the nature and scope of the congressional taxing and spending power, but also sharp divergence as to the scope of judicial power and the role of the Court in a free society.

† In *Graham v. Goodcell*, 282 U.S. 409 (1931), Hughes ruled that Congress could by a later amendment retroactively correct a defect in a taxing scheme without "violating any substantial equity." The original AAA delegated to the Secretary of Agriculture the power to set tax rates for processors. After the Panama Refining and Schechter cases, also after the facts giving rise to the Butler case, Congress adopted the Secretary's rates as its own. "Any defects there may have been in the manner of laying the tax by the Secretary," Stone observed in his Butler dissent, "have now been removed by the exercise of the power of Congress to pass a curative statute validating an intended, though defective, tax."

Library was closed on that afternoon (the day before New Year's Day) and also on New Year's Day, so that I was unable to obtain books. I managed to get an opinion which went to the printer's on Thursday and was circulated on Friday. This produced a large number of amendments to Justice Roberts' opinion, which was read at conference on the following day, Saturday. He did not recirculate.

Opinion and dissent were both produced in conjunction with other work of the writers during the two weeks' recess, in which there were two holidays, Christmas and New Year's.

The whole history of the case was characterized by inadequate discussion and great haste in the production and circulation of the opinions.

The AAA decision thus stands as but one more example, and a striking one, of Arthur Twining Hadley's proposition that "democracy was complete as far as it went but constitutionally it is bound to stop short of social democracy."[28] Nor were the Court's disabling vetoes confined to national legislation. Justice Roberts' opinion suggests deep attachment to the traditional conception of states' rights. It should be noted, however, that almost simultaneously with the AAA ruling he formed a part of the same majority in *Colgate* v. *Harvey* which reversed decisions of sixty years' standing, and introduced a construction of the privileges and immunities clause "pregnant with heretofore unimagined limitations upon state power."[29] These decisions are consistent in that both were dictated by the conviction that, "in the shackling of all governmental power, both state and national, lies the salvation of the nation."[30] What the most alert commentators did not know were the lengths to which Chief Justice Hughes and his colleagues had gone in both the AAA case and *Colgate* v. *Harvey* to achieve this result.

Respectful silence now "ceased to be a virtue," and Stone willingly endorsed a characterization of him which said: "A very moderate person is now a very wrought up one."[31] Back of Stone's AAA dissent lay the fervent hope that it might provoke "a wide, dispassionate discussion among thinking men, and especially students of government, as to what the judicial function may rightly be."[32]

"You do not dislike the AAA any more than I do," he told a Wall Street lawyer. "That perhaps was what made me emphasize the fact that our function is not to get rid of laws merely because we don't like them. If that were the criterion, I should have been on the other side."[33] In his view, "we are clutched in the dead hand of economic theories of a century ago" unless "legislators are free to deal" with economic questions.[34]

Stone felt that the Court was set on a course calculated to destroy the very institutions the die-hard majority sought so stubbornly to preserve. "You may be interested to know," he wrote a correspondent, "that I think, and I also believe, that my opinion in the AAA case was the conservative one."[35]

Both New Dealers and Old Guard misunderstood his position and regarded his forthright denunciation of judicial usurpation as whole-hearted sanction of Roosevelt's entire legislative program. He was dubbed a "liberal" and included in the exclusive Holmes-Brandeis category. Stone profoundly disliked this label. It had, he said, "a connotation which ought not to be applied to a judge."[36] Nor was this his only reason for not wishing to accept the plaudits now so freely bestowed upon him. "Where one is outvoted two to one," he remarked, "one should be humble and skeptical of his own judgment."[37]

Some Democrats went so far as to suggest the Justice as F. D. R.'s running mate in 1936. How far they were from the mark is indicated by an incident that took place shortly after the AAA decision came down. Stone, Henry Wallace, and James Roosevelt sat discussing public affairs at the home of a mutual friend. Wallace and young Roosevelt blithely assumed that Stone was at least sympathetic to the administration's policies, if not a New Dealer. The conversation flowed on; the Justice listened silently, thoughtfully. Finally he shot out: "My duty as a judge is simple and explicit. It is to see that the Constitution functions. It is not for the judge to approve or disapprove social policy in his decisions." As for the New Deal, he added, "it is only a question of time before many of these things will have to be scrapped."[38]

Both sides overlooked Stone's special sensitiveness to the judicial wisdom exhibited during those all-too-brief interludes in American history when the Court lived up to its non-political tradition. One such interlude was during the Chief Justiceship of Morrison R. Waite, whose opinion in *Munn* v. *Illinois* was the high point of a career devoted to keeping the Court out of politics. For Stone, Waite was the only man holding the office of Chief Justice "who had really measured up to it since Taney's time."[39] Waite exemplified the "judicial self-restraint" which Stone considered "fundamental to the preservation of constitutional government and to the satisfactory functioning of our Court." "The power of courts to declare a statute unconstitutional," the AAA dissenter declared, "is subject to two guiding principles which ought never to be absent from judicial consciousness." One is that courts are concerned only with the power to enact statutes, not with their wisdom. The other is that while unconstitutional exercise of power by the executive and legislative branches of the Government is subject to judicial restraint, "the only check upon our own exercise of power is our own sense of self-restraint. For the removal of unwise laws from the statute books appeal lies not to the courts but to the ballot and to the processes of democratic government."*40

With anti-judicial feeling at a new high, Chief Justice Hughes suddenly interrupted the New Deal's headlong rush down the steep decline leading to the lethal chamber of the judiciary. Departing abruptly from recent majority practice, the Court upheld the highly controversial TVA by confining itself to the specific program challenged, the sale of power from Muscle Shoals Dam.41 At least one close observer believed that the Justices had also intended to invalidate this bold innovation: "After the preliminary line-up on the TVA case must have revealed itself in the court, Stone talked about the Court's attitude toward New Deal legislation with an alarm concerning the future which would have been illogical, or at least unlikely to manifest itself, if the Court had then swung even in part from the trend revealed by the AAA decision. . . . But public reaction against the Hoosac Mills decision persuaded the Court to follow precedents and uphold the TVA."42

The favorable outcome received warm approval in many quarters. "We have finally disposed of the TVA case," Stone wrote Sterling Carr, February 21, 1936, "and there seems to be more satisfaction with the result than in the case of the AAA."

Soon, however, the Court made good once more, as to both state and national power, Thomas Jefferson's bitter remark: "It is the office of a good judge to enlarge his jurisdiction." In the Great Northern Railways case, the Justices, "for the first time," set aside "a tax as a violation of the Fourteenth Amendment on the ground that the assessment on which it is computed is too high, without any showing that the assessment is discriminatory or that petitioner is in any way bearing an undue share of the tax burden imposed on all property owners in the state."43

The Court's next blow at Roosevelt's recovery program was the Guffey Coal case, in which five Justices destroyed the administration's desperate attempt to salvage NRA remedies for the distressed bituminous coal industry. In the teeth of congressional declaration that the Guffey Coal Act's price-fixing and labor provisions were separable, Sutherland held that they were united inextricably, and therefore must stand or fall together. They must fall, he ruled, because the labor provisions here, like those involved in the Schechter case, bore no "direct" relation to interstate commerce. Mining is a local matter; chaotic labor relations therein might conceivably affect interstate commerce, but

* Compare Chief Justice Waite's words of 1876 in *Munn* v. *Illinois:* "We know that this [legislative power] is a power which may be abused; but that is no argument against its existence. For protection against abuses by legislatures the people must resort to the polls, not to the courts."

they affect it only indirectly and are therefore beyond congressional power.

In a concurring opinion Chief Justice Hughes charged that Sutherland had been mistaken in denying the separability of price-fixing and hours of labor regulation. But he apparently agreed with Sutherland's contention that mining is not commerce; he apparently agreed that the distinction between direct and indirect effects is a difference of kind rather than of degree. "If the people desire to give Congress the power to regulate industries within the state, and the relations of employers and employees in these industries," Hughes observed, "they are at liberty to declare their will in the appropriate manner [that is by constitutional amendment] but it is not for the Court to amend the Constitution by judicial decision."

In his dissenting opinion Justice Cardozo, joined by Brandeis and Stone, was able, ironically enough, to draw substantial support from earlier rulings of the Chief Justice himself. "What the cases really mean," Cardozo said, "is that the causal relation in such circumstances [where consideration of degree is involved] is so close and intimate and obvious as to permit it to be called direct without subjecting the word to an unfair or excessive strain. There is a like immediacy here."[44]

Thoughtful observers were astounded by the Court's apparent determination to build an impassable blockade against the power to govern. How could one explain the meandering course of judicial decision after 1930? Stone expressed his views in answer to an insistent query from Frankfurter:

It seems that you have been trying to find an answer to a question which continually recurs to you, as it does to me. I don't know that I shall ever reach a satisfactory answer, but perhaps it can be summed up in two phrases which you have doubtless heard me repeat before: lack of vision and the unwillingness of certain gentlemen to trust their own intellectual processes.

Just why we should be afflicted as we are just at present is another question, but I think there has never been a time in the history of the Court when there has been so little intelligible, recognizable pattern in its judicial performance as in the last few years. Take, for example, as simple a matter as the presumption to which we occasionally pay lip service in favor of the constitutionality of a statute. It would be interesting to have some of your bright young men discover how often in recent years it has been relied upon and repudiated by the same judge. . . .[45] It just seems as though, in some of these cases, the writer and those who united with him didn't care what was said, as long as the opinion seemed plausible on its face, if not compared with any other. The worst of it is that the one [Hughes] that you find it most difficult to understand is the one chiefly responsible.[46]

The Chief Justice's concurrence in the Guffey case was a special source of discouragement, prompting Professor Karl Llewellyn to suggest that the materials for creative judicial statesmanship would have to be sought elsewhere.

"When the time comes," he wrote apropos the Cardozo-Stone dissent in the Guffey case, "and the attitude you express becomes a majority attitude, the case should be clear, with the first victory, that (1) a whole new line of doctrine, and perhaps even (2) a whole new body of recorded precedent come into alternative being together." Llewellyn went on:

The first is the more important. It can be done by regularly insisting on the growth-process in the constitutional field, rehearsing in full the prior lines of growth—in distinction to Sutherland's powerful and baleful attempt to get back to pure original intent in the Guffey case. And another feature which I hope you may find wise is the building together of the series of dissents by taking every opportunity, in any of them, *to rely on any of the prior* ones—not merely on prior majority opinion. This last point seems to me vital, to give your new and sound doctrine body and power—opinions should rely on the whole series of the dissents—which will be vastly easier if they are concatenated in advance. . . .

I know no series of opinions bunched within a couple of years which shows anything like so coherent a development as these dissents of yours.[47]

"I think your suggestion that we cite our own dissents is an interesting and amusing one," Stone replied. "There are no doubt some who think that is the only authority we have to go on. Trying to build good law is something like the task of Sisyphus, was it not, who, in rolling the stone up the mountain slipped back more than he advanced. Certainly I have taken a long slide downward this year. One of the problems of future jurisprudence will be how to make a Court stay put where it really has made an advance."[48]

Nor was the paralyzing effect of Hughes' effort confined to his dissenting and concurring opinions. The Chief Justice could be as harmful to a broad construction of the Constitution when writing for a liberal majority as in dissenting from it. There is hardly a case (Blaisdell being a notable exception) where he could speak for the Court without rousing the so-called liberal Justices to protest, qualify, or disclaim the narrowness of his position.[49]

Quite apart from the unpopularity of the decisions themselves, the majority's slipshod methods in striking down New Deal enactments *seriatim* without bothering, as Stone put it, to "rake after the cart," were rapidly undermining the Court's prestige. "I can hardly see the use of writing judicial opinions," the Justice exploded, "unless they are to embody methods of analysis and of exposition which will serve the profession as a guide to the decision of future cases. If they are not better than an excursion ticket, good for this day and trip only, they do not serve even as protective coloration for the writer of the opinion and would much better be left unsaid."[50] Stone went so far as to accuse his colleagues of writing "for morons," expressing the conviction that no trained lawyer "will swallow such buncombe."[51]

In the case to which Stone was explicitly referring, six Justices—Hughes, Roberts, Sutherland, McReynolds, Butler, Van Devanter—went to the rescue of J. Edwards Jones, a Wall Street promoter, decreeing that the SEC was powerless to compel Jones to produce his books and papers. The Commission's action, Sutherland declared heatedly, was wholly "unreasonable and arbitrary. It violates the cardinal precept upon which the constitutional safeguard of personal liberty ultimately rests." Three Justices—Brandeis, Stone, Cardozo—taking quite a different view, said: "The rule now assailed was wisely conceived and lawfully adopted to foil the plans of knaves intent upon obscuring or suppressing the knowledge of their knavery."[52]

"I suppose it was not very important whether Mr. Jones should be compelled to answer, in a public hearing, surrounded by all the safeguards of the Constitution," Stone wrote of the majority opinion. "But the Court's setting aside the plain command of Congress, without reference to any identifiable prohibition of the Constitution, and with only the support of platitudinous irrelevancies, is a matter of transcendent importance."[53]

The reactionary Justices, fulfilling their reputed role as the last bulwark of embattled privilege, seemed intent on perverting the Constitution's most explicit, power-giving language. Federal bankruptcy authority, they ruled, could not be employed to rescue local governments from staggering burdens of debt. Governmental power over devastating social maladjustments fell between the slats as the recalcitrant Justices widened the gap between state and national governments. "Keep this up," the *St. Louis Star-Times* editorialized indignantly, "and nothing will be left of the Constitution."[54]

Stone was alert to these pressures as well as to his responsibility as a judge. In due course, the explanation he refused to give Professor Frankfurter for the Justices' suicidal disregard of our fundamental law, he put in a candid and revealing dissent. In June 1936, the majority, despite all the misery of depression, followed Sutherland's reactionary Minimum Wage decision of 1923—that no valid state action could deprive employer and employee of the "equal right to obtain from each other the best terms they can by private bargaining." Stone, joined by Brandeis and Cardozo, in *Morehead* v. *Tipaldo*, bitterly assailed the majority's deification of the private-wage bargain: "The liberty which the [Fourteenth] Amendment protects is not freedom from restraint of all law or of any law which reasonable men may think an appropriate means for dealing with any of those matters of public concern with which it is the business of government to deal. There is grim irony in speaking of the freedom of contract of those who, because of their economic necessities, give their services for less than is needful to keep body and soul together."

As to why Supreme Court Justices approved such a seemingly preposterous result, Stone suggested: "It is difficult to imagine any grounds, other than our own personal economic predilections, for saying that the contract of employment is any the less an appropriate subject of legislation than are scores of others, in dealing with which this Court has held that legislatures may curtail individual freedom in the public interest."

Nor was Stone content, as in the AAA dissent, to confine his attack to the constitutional aspects of the majority opinion. Besides reiterating the charge against judicial fiat, he queried the majority's Spencerian assumptions: "We have had opportunity to learn that a wage is not always the resultant of free bargaining between employer and employees; that it may be one forced upon employees by their economic necessities and upon employers by the most ruthless of their competitors. We have had opportunity to perceive more clearly that a wage insufficient to support the worker does not visit its consequences upon him alone; that it may affect profoundly the entire economic structure of society and, in any case, that it casts on every taxpayer, and on government itself, the burden of solving the problems of poverty, subsistence, health, and morals of large numbers in the community."

There was much in the judicial habit of mind, but nothing in the Constitution, that prevented government from trying to solve social and economic maladies, responsibility for which had shifted increasingly from the individual to government. The "vague and general pronouncement" of the Fourteenth Amendment was a "limitation on legislative power," not a "formula for its exercise." In words reminiscent of Justice Holmes' classic Lochner dissent of 1905, Stone scathingly denounced substitution of political dogma for the Constitution: "It is not for the courts to resolve doubts whether the remedy by wage regulation is as efficacious as many believe, or is better than some other, or is better even than the blind operation of uncontrolled economic forces. The legislature must be free to choose unless it is to be rendered impotent. . . . The Fourteenth Amendment has no more embedded in the Constitution our preference for some particular set of economic beliefs than it has adopted, in the name of liberty, the system of theology which we may happen to approve. . . . We should . . . leave the selection and the method of the solution of the problems . . . where it seems to me the Constitution has left them, to the legislative branch."[55]

Though such "eternal emphasis on the obvious" had now become "a bit tiresome," he had taken this occasion to speak out again because he considered it "important not to let these matters go by default." What spurred him especially was the Chief Justice's curious dissenting technique—that of limiting the objections he leveled against the majority to alleged differences between the New York law involved in the Tipaldo case, and the District of Columbia statute upset in the 1923 Minimum Wage decision. Hughes upheld the New York statute but refused to reject the earlier case as a viable precedent. He dissented from the majority opinion because there were "material differences in the cases presented." The effect was to leave all judicial bridges intact.

"I agree fully with what you say in your opinion," Stone had written the Chief Justice, May 26, 1936, "except the rather oblique implication . . . that if the distinction between the statutes is immaterial the Adkins case should be regarded controlling authority. Perhaps you will feel like eliminating or modifying the sentence so as to remove the implication, in which case I shall join in your opinion. However, as I am writing a brief memorandum stating my belief that I think the decision should rest on broader grounds, I will make my agreement with what you have written evident if you prefer not to change your opinion."

"I am quite willing," Hughes replied, "to omit the sentence to which you refer: 'Unless this distinction be treated as immaterial, the Adkins case should not be regarded as a controlling authority.' "[56]

To Stone it seemed "a sad business to stand only on differences of the two statutes, especially after all the Court has decided and said on this subject in the past three years." He could not understand why "the Chief Justice felt it necessary to so limit his opinion."[57] It seemed a pity that such an imposing façade should rest upon such a slender foundation.

Various cases decided since 1923, notably *Nebbia* v. *New York,* had removed the cloak of sanctity, the special immunity against government regulation, that Justice Sutherland had claimed for the price and wage provision of private contracts. More recent precedents, not the discredited 1923 Minimum Wage decision, should have served the Court as controlling. Surely the verbal gymnastics devised by the majority and accepted by Hughes to avoid recognizing *Nebbia* v. *New York* as the controlling authority deserved more careful scrutiny. "I hope you will read, with some care, all the opinions in the Minimum Wage case," Stone wrote Irving Brant, an editorial writer on the *St. Louis Star-Times.* "The technique of all three is quite interesting, although of course, it is not a subject for popular editorial writing."[58] Undeterred, indeed "properly spurred," by the Justice's suggestion,

Brant wrote an editorial demonstrating that the Court itself had strikingly proved Professor Corwin's revealing thesis of 1934—that the Supreme Court, in deciding major constitutional issues, often has wide choice among conflicting precedents.[59]

But Brant's editorial, though illuminating, had missed the point. "My remarks as to a choice between conflicting precedents," Stone wrote the newspaperman, "were directed to an interesting bit of technique in the Court opinion, which stated that the Court could not consider overruling the Adkins case because the petitioners for certiorari had not asked for it." "I know of no rule or practice," Stone had written in his dissent, "by which the arguments advanced in support of an application for certiorari restrict our choice between conflicting precedents in deciding a question of Constitutional law." "Of course," he told Brant, "the conventional rule where precedents conflict, is to choose the later one. But if that be discarded the judge cannot well avoid making a choice, and in making it he is bound to exercise his judgment as to where social advantage lies, not in the sense of following his own economic predilections, but in seeking to ascertain objectively the mores of the time."[60]

"We should follow our decision in the Nebbia case," Stone had pleaded in dissent. Irving Brant expressed the nub of the matter: "Because five is a larger number than four and for no other reason, the law is unconstitutional."[61]

The "battalion of death" had at last gone too far. Even a conservative correspondent spoke of the decision as "a ton of straw on the broken back of a camel." The five had demonstrated anew "the resources of unreason and folly." "The majority decision," the *New York Times* editorialized, "will leave the states at sea regarding how they are to deal with the exploitation of women in industry." The *Washington Post* saw the implications as "far reaching indeed." "Two weeks ago the Court decided, in its opinion on the Guffey Coal Act, that Congress has no authority to regulate wages in 'purely local' undertakings. Now, it has denied to the states even the right to prescribe minimum wages for women and children." The power necessary to deal with social and economic problems had been "impaled on two horns of a legalistic dilemma," and the *Washington Daily News* ventured to ask "the majority as they leave for their recess, to give some little thought . . . to the question of where we go from here."[62]

Relegation of millions of women to "wage slavery" raised doubts in the minds of the most obtuse reactionaries. *Kiplinger's Letter* reported that the decision "has had big effect in causing criticism of the Court in quarters formerly defensive of it." "Admittedly a shocking blow to enlightened conservatives," the *Boston Herald* called it. The most obdurate partisans now feared the consequences of judicial obscurantism. The rationale of the Tipaldo decision, that chaos and chaos alone is constitutional, the magazine *America* warned, "plays into the hands of radical change."[63] William Allen White, himself a Republican, pronounced the decision "tragic." "No other agency than government," he averred, "can bring justice into the relations of those who work with the machines and those who own the machines."[64] Congressional Republican wheel-horse Hamilton Fish was "frankly shocked" by this "new Dred Scott decision."[65] "The worry has begun," Arthur Krock noted.[66] Increasingly, GOP hosannas to America's House of Lords gave way to the chant, "Something must be done."

Stone followed events with cheerful satisfaction. "It is rather amusing," he wrote, "to have the Republicans, as well as the Democrats, expressing doubts about the wisdom of the Minimum Wage decision. Fortunately it is a subject which everybody can understand and perhaps there will be some who will begin to wonder whether the dissenters are so extreme as they thought."[67] This most recent example of "government by judiciary" had made "even some of the Republican leaders doubt whether they could completely swallow all that the Supreme Court does."[68] "It seems to be dawning on a good many minds," Stone told Brandeis gleefully, "that after all there may be something in the protest of the so-called liberal minority." "Yes," Brandeis replied, noting the same outraged phenomenon, "the consternation of the enemy is encouraging."[69] Proof of the pudding came a fortnight later when the 1936 Republican National Convention repudiated *Morehead* v. *Tipaldo* and went on record for re-enacting the law without a constitutional amendment.*

Within one short term the Court had woven a constitutional fabric so tight as to bind political power at all levels. In their desperate attempt to stop Roosevelt and preserve "rugged individualism," the judges themselves had advanced civic education, disabusing even the most credulous of the belief that court decisions are "babies brought by constitutional storks."[70] Thrusting themselves into the vortex of a raging political controversy, they abandoned traditional judicial caution and indulged in a "form of indecent exposure."[71] The Justices themselves made clear what they sought most anxiously to disguise— that judicial decisions are, in fact, born out of the travail of economic and political conflict.

"We finished the term of Court yesterday," Stone wrote his sister, June 2, 1936, "I think in many ways one of the most disastrous in its history. At any rate it seems to me that the Court has been needlessly

---

* "We pledge ourselves . . . to support the adoption of state laws . . . to protect women and children with respect to maximum hours, minimum wages, and working conditions. We believe that this can be done within the Constitution as it now stands." (Republican Party Platform, 1936. *New York Times*, June 12, 1936.)

narrow and obscurantic in its outlook. I suppose no intelligent person likes very well the way the New Deal does things, but that ought not to make us forget that ours is a nation which should have the powers ordinarily possessed by governments, and that the framers of the Constitution intended that it should have. Our latest exploit was a holding by a divided vote that there was no power in a state to regulate minimum wages for women. Since the Court last week said that this could not be done by the national government, as the matter was local, and now it is said that it cannot be done by local governments even though it is local, we seem to have tied Uncle Sam up in a hard knot."

Stone had responded magnificently to the need for judicial pronouncements "in the Holmes tradition." In various areas of constitutional interpretation he had in a single term stripped from judicial decisions the façade of impartiality—the guise of the logical imperative. In doing this his purpose was not to destroy but to restore and vitalize. His dissenting opinions provided sorely needed education in the conservative tradition.

In this uphill struggle Brandeis and Cardozo had been staunch allies. "Their great legal knowledge, skill, resourcefulness, and steadfastness," Stone said, "have been a consolation to me in this term, as indeed they have been in all the earlier ones. Mine would be indeed a forlorn task were it not for their constant insistence on deliberation and adherence to the highest and best traditions of the judicial office."[72]

With the mask of judicial objectivity—Stone called it "protective coloration"—removed, government by judiciary became a crucial public issue. Thoughtful men began to wonder whether government adequate to cope with a complex industrial civilization was compatible with judicial review. Few had foreseen the tremendous popular outburst that followed the AAA and Tipaldo cases. Fewer still believed that public resentment could seriously alter the attitude of the judiciary, entrenched for life on the nation's highest Court. Yet, in the spring of 1936, Congress in response to popular sentiment introduced over a hundred bills and resolutions whittling down the power of federal courts. Unless the Justices themselves lifted the judicial blockade, it seemed not unlikely that judicial interposition against the power to govern was in for drastic diminution. During far less trying times Chief Justice White had admitted that the Court "relaxed constitutional guarantees from fear of revolution." History might now repeat itself.

CHAPTER TWENTY-SEVEN

# Law as an Instrument
# of Creative Justice

## 1936

After the Court became the focus of bitter controversy, Stone became more reluctant than ever to accept speaking invitations. Events alone served to underscore his stock reply: "It is impossible to discuss any question of general interest without committing some kind of judicial indiscretion."

But there were exceptions. When Harvard University, celebrating its Tercentenary, asked him to join Lord Wright, Master of the Rolls, Sir Lyman Duff, Chief Justice of Canada, Sir Frank Gavan Duffy, Chief Justice of Australia, and other eminent jurists and scholars in a discussion of the future of the common law, the Justice, with his sure eye for the really important events, accepted. "I should like to have part in the Harvard celebration, as I regard it a very great event," he wrote Roscoe Pound, dean of the Harvard Law School, January 17, 1936. "Yes," he reported to his sons in mid-March 1936, "I finally consented to make the address at Harvard, foolishly perhaps, because I am too busy to think much about what I should say until the term ends. It is a distinguished occasion, and if I can get my mind working I ought to have something worth while to say."[1]

The apparent narrowness of the assigned subject troubled him. "If I confine myself strictly to the topic," he commented, "it will not bring into play my range of thinking during recent years, which has been concerned with public law questions."[2]

"Don't bother about detailed exploration of the common law and its fate in this country," Professor Frankfurter suggested. "Any number of people could do that. . . . What is needed is a powerful and philosophic stream of reflection regarding the underlying attitudes and procedure of the lawyer trained in the common law traditions, in formulating and adapting the body of accommodations which constitute the law for a dynamic federated society like ours. . . . Give us," Frankfurter advised, "the distillation of your nearly forty years' unique experience in the law."

"I shall not spell out in detail the considerations that made you and not another [presumably Chief Justice Hughes] our choice as the legal spokesman for this country," Frankfurter went on. "Certainly, no one else so happily synthesizes the four great aspects of our profession—the law teacher, the private practitioner, the law officer, the judge—as you do."[3]

Characteristically, as the delivery date approached, Stone tried to beg off. "The pressure of work just now is so great," he pleaded, "that I am unable to give any attention to the preparation of a suitable address." Dean Pound adamantly held the Justice to his promise and offered to supply a working memorandum. Stone took up the offer gratefully but admonished Pound to remember "I have to be cautious about keeping away from subjects which come within the field of controversy which, from time to time, centers upon our Court."[4] As he prepared to leave Washington for the summer, a lengthy memorandum arrived from Cambridge. Stone assured Pound that it "fits very neatly into a rough scheme which I have laid out for my talk."[5] But the memorandum did no more than supply a point of departure—the idea that "one of the most significant features of the development of the common law in the United States is the working out of a public law on common law lines."[6]

The finished product appears as a highly personal document, as a crystallization of Stone's mature reflections on the manifold sources of law, on the relative claims of tradition and change, on the creative role of the judiciary in the lawmaking process. Ignoring Pound's long historical excursions, Stone addressed himself at once to the question of "what the judicial function involves." The common law tradition embodies "the generative principle" necessary for the correction of current shortcomings in judicial interpretation. And the Justice's address makes clear what his work on the Court demonstrated—that a "progressive science of law" might have been easily achieved but for the three-front war waged by Old Guard judges. The legislation they could not overrule, they had construed so narrowly as to defeat its purpose. They had hamstrung administrative agencies by parsimonious construction of their powers. They had, by recourse to abstract formulae, erected unprecedented constitutional barriers to political change. Frustration of the power to govern had been conspicuous in cases involving statutory construction no less than constitutional interpretation. By construing statutes narrowly, without real regard to intentions, judges sometimes obstinately obstructed the democratic will.

As he spoke, Stone's listeners may have recalled his recent tangle with Justice McReynolds over the meaning of the "commodities clause." McReynolds had refused to admit that business between two subsidiaries of United States Steel, one a railroad and the other a steel plant, came within the prohibition of the Interstate Commerce Act forbidding shipment of goods owned by the railroads on their own lines. To Stone it was obvious that such interpretation overlooked the legislature's attempt "to withhold from every interstate rail carrier the inducement and facility for favoritism and abuse of its powers as a common carrier, which experience had shown are likely to occur when a single business interest occupies the inconsistent position of carrier and shipper." "One is at a loss to say what scope remains for the operation of the statute," he exclaimed. McReynolds had reduced the law "to a cipher in the calculations of those who control the railroads of the country."[7] Here, surely, was a striking example of a statute "looked upon as in the law but not of it, a formal rule to be obeyed . . . but to be obeyed grudgingly, by construing it narrowly and treating it as though it did not exist for any purpose other than that embraced within the strict construction of its words."[8]

Equally fresh in the speaker's mind was Mr. Justice Roberts' unfeeling emasculation of the Federal Trade Commission's powers over industrial mergers. Here was another example of a Justice taking refuge in "literalism" to defeat clear legislative policy. The FTC had begun investigation to determine whether to order a holding company to sell its stock in two competing firms. Before the Commission could complete its inquiry, the company brazenly merged its subsidiaries. Though no court would tolerate such subversion of its jurisdiction, Roberts blandly held that the Commission could issue no order against the company, because the statute did not expressly forbid mergers, but only the holding of stock in competitors.

"I am unable," Stone wrote in dissent, "to construe so narrowly a statute designed, as I think, to prevent just such suppression of competition as this case exemplifies." "Even if the question were a new one in this Court," he continued, "no plausible reason has been advanced for interpreting this remedial statute as though it were a penal law. The Clayton Act was designed to prevent abuses growing from deficiencies due to the generality of the Sherman Act. It sought to accomplish that end by conferring upon the Commission the power to strike at specific practices. In this, as in most schemes for regulation by administrative bodies, there must be a balance between the general and the particular. When the courts are faced with interpretation of the particular, administration breaks down and the manifest purpose of the legislation is defeated unless it is recognized that, surrounding granted powers, there must be a penumbra which will give scope for practical operation. In carrying such schemes into operation the function of courts is constructive not destructive, to make them, wherever reasonably possible, effective agencies for law enforcement and not to destroy them."[9]

In contrast with his reactionary brethren, Stone knew that society must inevitably turn from "the law book" to the legislatures. Yet judges, including certain of Stone's colleagues, refused to believe that a statute, no less than a judicial precedent, "is a declaration and a source of law, and a premise for legal reasoning." Conceiving of their role as "preservative" rather than as creative, misjudging the adequacy of precedents to fit law to "the way of life of a people," they could not accept Stone's "ideal of a unified system of judge-made and statute law woven into a seamless whole by the process of adjudication." They demonstrated "genius," Stone commented plaintively, "for the generation of new law from that already established," but the "common law courts have given little recognition to statutes as starting points for judicial lawmaking comparable to judicial decisions."

Modern courts had been peculiarly reluctant to consider legislative standards of conduct as capable of delineating new obligations and conferring new rights. When confronted with legislative controls designed to harness the forces of industrialism, judges tended to regard their task in Blackstonian terms.* They conceived of their function as that of "finding law" in the precedents, not realizing that they could find in the books no adequate pattern into which new experience could readily be fitted. To ward off judicial hostility, to remove constitutional doubt, legislators revived the ancient practice of stating in the statute itself the reasons for its enactment. The New Deal had made conspicuous use of this device. Far from resenting this practice, Stone accepted it as a substantial aid to judicial interpretation. If continued, it might well lead to recognition of the power of judges to extend the written law to cases plainly within its reason and spirit, and thus restore to courts a privilege they "renounced only because they have mistakenly regarded statutory enactments as in some degree less a part of the law than their own decisions."

Almost from the beginning of his judicial career Stone had demonstrated consummate ability to work with statutes. He had a real talent for breaking the crust of verbiage in which statutes are encased and for tracking the thread of purpose through section after section, in search of the meaning which the legislature attempted to express. Better than most, he could articulate a complex series of enactments into a comprehensible, rational whole.[10] His work as a Supreme Court Justice illustrates what the history and principles of the common law taught—that statutes embodying "social policy . . . are as significant and rightly

* Commenting on James M. Landis's essay, "Statutes as Sources of the Law," Stone wrote: "The chief reason why we have dealt with statutes so ineptly has been the survival of the Coke-Blackstone tradition that the common law was a complete and perfect system, to which statutes are but alien intruders, to be dealt with as narrowly as possible. We are getting away from that idea somewhat, but not far enough." (H.F.S. to James M. Landis, June 8, 1936.)

as much a part of the law, as rules declared by judges." "A statute is not an alien intruder in the house of the common law, but a guest to be welcomed and made at home there as a new and powerful aid in the accomplishment of its appointed task of accommodating the law to social needs."

At the very base of the traditional common law theory lies the principle of *stare decisis*. This is, Stone agreed, ordinarily a "wise rule of action." It gives to our institutions a certain stability and continuity of great practical worth. But there is no need for rigid and mechanical observance of the rule. On the contrary "its strength is derived from the manner in which it has been forged from actual experience by the hammer and anvil of litigation, and . . . the source of its weakness lies in the fact that law guided by precedent which has grown out of one type of experience can only slowly and with difficulty be adapted to new types which the changing scene may bring."

Querying the basic assumptions that prevented judges from making the law "progressive," especially their facile reliance on precedent, Stone wondered "whether continuity of legal doctrine is worth the price which, in some periods of our legal history, we have paid for it." What troubled him especially was the "habit of mind with which judges and lawyers approach the decision which no precedent necessarily controls." Nowhere was this more apparent than in their hostility to administrative tribunals. Here indeed was "an interesting parallel to their attitude toward other forms of external change." Instead of accepting administrative agencies as "inspiration to the performance of creative service," the profession saw in this new method of control, as in social legislation, no opportunity "except for resistance to a strange and therefore unwelcome innovation."

Though well aware that rapidly multiplying boards, bureaus, and commissions threatened to upset the traditional separation of powers, Stone accepted them as necessary to deal with the complexities of modern life. They provided highly technical expert services to government which courts could have offered, "if at all, only more tardily and with far greater difficulty." Little was to be gained, in any event, from "futile resistance to the inevitable."

Stone's critical appraisal of judges in 1936 recalls Justice Holmes' characterization of them a generation earlier. He, like Holmes, saw judges as naive, simple-minded men, obtuse to the inevitability of change, distrustful of innovations emanating from non-judicial sources.[11] In cases involving constitutional issues, they construed their function narrowly as that of laying "the article of the Constitution which is invoked beside the statute which is challenged and . . . [deciding] whether the latter squares with the former."[12] Stone knew that, whether the judge was attempting to square a controverted statute with the Constitution or with precedent, judicial interpretation so mechanical and superficial would "become at last but a dry and sterile formalism." It did not need to be so rigidly confined. "If, with discerning eye, we see differences as well as resemblances in the facts and experiences of the present when compared with those recorded in the precedents," Stone observed, "we take the decisive step toward the achievement of a progressive science of law." The "most critical and delicate operation in the process of judicial lawmaking" occurs in the case which is not directly and necessarily controlled by precedent. Here the danger lies in finding "analogies and resemblances which will serve as a superficial justification for the extension of a precedent to sets of facts whose social implications may be quite different from any which the precedents have considered."

"It is just here," the speaker commented, "within the limited area where the judge has freedom of choice of the rule which he is to adopt, and in his comparison of the experiences of the past with those of the present, that occurs the most critical and delicate operation in the process of judicial lawmaking. Strictly speaking, he is often engaged not so much in extracting a rule of law from the precedents, as we were once accustomed to believe, as in making an appraisal and comparison of social values, the result of which may be of decisive weight in determining what rule he is to apply. The law itself is on trial, quite as much as the cause which is to be decided. . . . The skill, resourcefulness and insight with which judges and lawyers weigh competing demands of social advantage, not unmindful that continuity and symmetry of the law are themselves such advantages, and with which they make choice among them in determining whether precedents shall be extended or restricted, chiefly give the measure of the vitality of the common law system and its capacity for growth."

Measured by the rigorous test of actual achievements, the common law simply had been "unable to keep pace with the rapid [social and technological] change." The failure was due, however, not to any inadequacy inherent in the law. It was due rather to judges' misconception of law and of their relation thereto. It was due to "outgrowths of a legal philosophy which was too little concerned with realities, which thought of law more as an end than as a means to an end, and assigned to the judicial lawmaking function a superficial and mechanical role, very largely unrelated to the social data to which the law must be attuned if it is to fulfill its purpose. Pursued to its logical end, such a philosophy could lead only to sterility and decay." Therefore, in drawing on what he modestly called "my somewhat exhausted repertoire of legal ideas,"[13] and applying them to the current crisis, the Justice did not lose "faith in the capacity of the common-law system to find adequate solutions of the problems of public and private law in a rapidly changing order." "There is nothing," he said with great conviction, "either in the spirit or the technique of the common-law method of expanding and applying judge-made law which need stand in the way of the creative development of doctrines and princi-ples adequate to all the demands which may be made upon them and suitable to the judicial interpretation of the prohibitions of the Con-stitution which will enable that instrument to operate as a workable chart of government, responsive to social and economic conditions."

In condemning the negative approach to the judicial process, in according government a relatively larger role, free from constitutional restraints judicially imposed, Stone ran head-on into one of our most cherished American ideals—government of laws and not of men—the common law doctrine, supremacy of law. How could adherence to these ancient shibboleths be squared with the relatively limited role accorded judicial review? His answer turns in part on the proposition that neither the ideal nor the doctrine precludes government action. On the contrary, the framers, with "extraordinary prescience," formu-lated an instrument intended to be " 'adapted to the various *crises* in human affairs' " and therefore singularly free from "embarrassingly meticulous" directives. Apart from a few precise and relatively non-controversial provisions, the Constitution did no more than set a standard for the application of principles. The "chief and ultimate standard" which "the great constitutional guarantees and immunities of personal liberty and of property" exact "is reasonableness of official action and its innocence of arbitrary and oppressive exactions. They are not statements of specific commands. They do not prescribe for-mulas to which governmental action must conform. There is little in the spirit and tradition of the common law to induce us to attempt to reduce the constitutional standard of reasonableness to a detailed formulation of definite propositions. There is neither scope nor his-torical support for the expansion of the constitutional exaction of reasonableness of official action implied in the use of the phrases 'liberty,' 'property,' 'due process,' 'unreasonable,' and the like, into a body of detailed rules attaching definite consequences to definite states of fact."

Thus, for Stone the Constitution was not a body of hard and fast precepts to be handed on and followed from generation to generation. It was rather "an indication of starting points for legal reasoning and of a technique for developing it, expressing the ideal of a reasonable exercise of the powers of politically organized society." For him con-stitutional law was "pre-eminently a system built up by gradual ac-cretion of special instances." This "essential element," which it shares with common law, enabled modern society to resolve clashing inter-ests within the constitutional framework. The essential continuity was not that of "rules" but of "aims and ideals," allowing government "to continue to function and to perform its appointed tasks within the bounds of reasonableness." In determining whether official action passes these bounds, the judge must look beyond both precedent and Constitution. He must open his eyes "to all those conditions and circumstances within the range of judicial knowledge." "The common law technique does not rule out but requires some inquiry into . . . social and economic data." The descriptive facts about society and existing legal rules constitute the configuration into which the new step must be fitted if it is taken.

Even assuming that all such factors are taken into account, when the judicial process is brought to bear on a constitutional issue there is still the question of whose standard of reasonableness is to be applied. Stone's answer at Harvard seems to take a more charitable view of his colleagues' position than he did in his AAA and Tipaldo dissents. "Whether the constitutional standard of reasonableness of official action is subjective, that of the judge who must decide, or objective in terms of a considered judgment of what the community may regard as within the limits of the reasonable, are questions which the cases have not specifically decided." What follows, however, must have come as a slap in the face to his more reactionary brethren: "Often, these standards do not differ. When they do not, it is a happy augury for the development of law which is socially adequate. But," he added pointedly, "the judge whose decision may control government action . . . must ever be alert to discover whether they do differ and, differing, whether his own or the objective standard will represent the sober second thought of the community, which is the firm base on which all law must ultimately rest." If there exists, as it did in 1936, a wide divergence between what the political organs of government consider socially desirable and what the Justices are willing to allow, crisis is inevitable.

It is apparent that Justice Stone, speaking in 1936, entertained far different ideas about the nature of law, the scope of the judicial function, and the relation of law to social well-being than did Dean Stone in 1915, the Hewitt Foundation lecturer, or even the same Dean some years later in the vanguard of the movement that led to the American Law Institute.

The Justice's individualistic streak, however, remained basic. He still discussed constitutional law as essentially the imposition of restraints on government. By 1936, however, personal predilection for freedom from socially imposed restrictions had been muted by an appreciation of the threat to liberty from private power, from groups other than government. Intricately organized society required curbs on individual and group tyrannies as well as against the arbitrary power of government. "There comes a point in the organization of a complex society where individualism must yield to traffic regulations, where the right to do as one will with his own must bow to zoning ordinances, or even on occasion to price-fixing regulations."

By 1936 Stone had come to place reconstruction of the law at least on a par with economic recovery. With uncanny insight as to what was in store, and in sharp contrast with his outlook in 1915, he urged judges to take the lead in adapting law to social realities and thus head off popular reprisals against the judiciary.* Unlike Sutherland, *et al.*, he did not regard statutes as embodying "the prejudice or the mere whim or caprice of the moment."[14] Against the dominant trend he came down hard on the idea that an administrative system devised to safeguard enlarged concepts of the public interest was any more a "government of men" than the common law rule of judges. Finally, he exploded the fiction that judges do not make law, but only discover and declare existing law.

"We are coming to realize more completely that law is not an end, but a means to an end—the adequate control and protection of those interests, social and economic, which are the special concern of government and hence of law; that that end is to be attained through the reasonable accommodation of law to changing economic and social needs, weighing them against the need of continuity of our legal system and the earlier experience out of which its precedents have grown; that within the limits lying between the command of statutes on the one hand and the restraints of precedents and doctrines, by common consent regarded as binding, on the other, the judge has the liberty of choice of the rule which he applies, and that his choice will rightly depend upon the relative weights of the social

---

* Nor was the Justice hopeless as to the future. In a letter written the President of Harvard College, Sept. 8, 1936, at the request of President Conant, to be filed with other similar letters and opened at the celebration of the Four Hundredth Anniversary, Stone said: "The last century has witnessed striking social and economic changes in American life, but relatively few important changes in law and government. So far as one can now foresee an uncertain future, I should think it unlikely that another century would pass without a marked shift in emphasis in those interests upon which the activities of government center and without profound changes in the methods, if not the structure of government itself. I take this opportunity to record my belief that the happiness and well-being of generations yet unborn will be best and most certainly secured if those changes are brought about within the framework of the constitutional government which we have set up and in conformity to its principles. I conceive those principles to envisage a national government rendered strong and competent by the wise exercise of those powers expressly granted to it by the Constitution and all others, which in the light of the Constitutional purpose, may be reasonably implied from those granted, but subject to the restraint of those guarantees of liberty and justice embraced in the Constitutional bill of rights. That such may be the path of law and government in the United States is my most cherished hope. Despite the doubts and uncertainties of the moment I have faith that such the course will be."

and economic advantages which will finally turn the scales in favor of one rule rather than another. Within this area he performs essentially the function of the legislator, and in a real sense makes law."

Extreme as this position may appear, one should not conclude that Stone's judicial philosophy was yet fully developed. In later years when this passage was construed as equating judicial lawmaking in constitutional and common law fields, he took exception and drew a distinction. In common law, the judge has a choice of rules and must arrive at an independent judgment on desirable social policy. In passing on the constitutionality of statutes, however, he is relieved of that duty. Here "legislative views of social policy should prevail."[15]

The Harvard address includes no discussion of the vital individual liberties of speech, press, and religion. His attitude at this time is perhaps best characterized by his reaction to "loyalty oaths" required of teachers in the District of Columbia. "In my ignorance I thought all such issues as dead as the Dodo." Later he enunciated the doctrine that the Court should subject legislation restricting civil liberties to "more searching judicial inquiry."* Stone also leaves unanswered the question of how a judge should interpret specific constitutional prohibitions when they conflict with pressing social needs. In view of his memorandum to the Chief Justice on the Blaisdell case, suggesting that the proscription of the contract impairment clause might be reduced to a requirement of reasonableness, the inference is that any constitutional clause must give way at last to the "sober second thought of the community."

Well aware of the potential impact of his words, Stone insisted, over Pound's objection, that the address be published in the *Harvard Law Review*, prior to its appearance in the collection of papers read at the Harvard celebration. "I hope I did not go out of bounds in pressing him to do this," the Justice told Frankfurter, "but I do feel strongly that it is hardly worth while for me to take the trouble to make speeches unless what I say can be made available to the bar generally and particularly to its younger members. Clerks in offices and law students see the *Review*, but they would not be so likely to see a volume of speeches sold only by subscription and probably not otherwise available."[16] Nor would Supreme Court Justices—the most crucial target—be likely to encounter the Justice's pronouncements unless they were currently published.

The Justice "has uttered a clear warning," Irving Brant wrote, "to the reactionaries who would use the courts to stop progress. His speech was a warning that the judiciary itself is on trial, and that it must either adjust itself to the modern world or be broken by its inability to do so."[17] In this context the Harvard address may be regarded as

\* See Chapter XXXI.

a timely reiteration of his AAA caveat that courts are not the only agencies of government that have the capacity to govern. Here was a considered effort to make judges see judicial interpretation as requiring above all the subordination of personal preference to the demands of social reality. Some observers regretted that he had not borne down harder on the necessity of "divorcing the question of distribution of power under the constitution from emotion." "If I were a free man," the Justice wrote one troubled correspondent, "I should have liked to develop it much more than I did."[18]

"I have nothing personally against the world in which I grew up," Stone explained. "That world has always made me very comfortable. But I don't see why I should let my social predilections interfere with experimental legislation that is not prohibited in the Constitution."[19]

Even as Justice Stone spoke, the judiciary stood on the brink of disaster.

CHAPTER TWENTY-EIGHT

# Showdown

## 1936-1937

In June 1936, with popular feeling rising to the point of exasperation, the constitutional crises reached the explosive stage. "The way out will be found shortly," the *St. Louis Star-Times* predicted, "because it must be found."[1] The forebodings Senate insurgents had voiced in 1930 were completely vindicated. The Supreme Court's usurpation of power was the issue of the hour.

The ill-fated Court-packing proposal did not come, as generally supposed, as a bolt from the blue. At least two years before its announcement the President had begun to suspect that a majority of the Justices would continue to treat the Constitution as a device for preventing action rather than as an instrument of progress. In early January 1935, when it looked as if the Justices might vote against the government in the Gold Clause cases, the President* had sug-

---

* At a Cabinet meeting, December 27, 1935, the President "had a good deal to say about what the Supreme Court is likely to do on New Deal legislation." Ickes recorded, "Clearly it is running in the President's mind that substantially all of the New Deal bills will be declared unconstitutional by the Supreme Court." The President suggested three ways of meeting this eventuality: "(1) by packing the Supreme Court, which was a distasteful idea; (2) by trying to put through a

gested that "the number of Justices should be increased at once so as to give a favorable majority."[2] Prospects for obtaining a favorable majority through the normal process of retirement were slim, despite the fact that several members of the bench were well past the retirement age. Hughes, McReynolds, and Sutherland were in their seventy-fifth year; Van Devanter was seventy-eight, Butler seventy-one, and Brandeis past eighty. None had intimated his intention to quit. Hoover's appointment of Cardozo in March 1932 had been the last for almost five years, and some observers began to suspect, in Robert H. Jackson's phrase, that the Court had "declared the mortality table unconstitutional."

Nevertheless the President preferred to delay action until "forced" by public opinion. "He wants to be pushed," one commentator observed. "It is better strategy, politically, to let a universal popular exasperation set the forces of reform in motion."[3]

Following the AAA decision, a legislative ground swell mounted rapidly. "This detached group," Representative Walter M. Pierce of Oregon said of the Court majority, "did not hold that the Triple A Act was in contravention of the rights of man or the laws of God, but it did say that by its passage the Congress had interfered with the rights of the states. What an arbitrary, unjust, and reactionary opinion it seems to those of us who hold that the minority opinion is more logical, more legally sound, more just, and more helpfully constructive in a changing social order."[4]

At any time up to June 1, 1936, the Court might have retreated and thus avoided a showdown. The New York Minimum Wage opinion, handed down that day, convinced even the most reverent that five stubborn old men had planted themselves squarely in the path of progress.[5] "How much longer," Pennsylvania's Senator Guffey wanted to know, "will we let the Supreme Court sanctify the sweatshop and pervert democratic processes?" "Nine black-robed fates," exclaimed Texas Representative Oliver H. Cross, smash "into unconstitutional fragments every law of Congress tending to establish economic and social justice. . . . Truly the alias for this country's Nemesis is the Supreme Court." The Texas legislator anticipated that Congress, "aroused to a sense of its patriotic duty," would "dethrone this judicial

---

number of amendments to the Constitution to meet the various situations; and (3) by a method that he asked us to consider very carefully." This was a constitutional amendment giving the Attorney General the right, if he has any doubt of the constitutionality of a legislative act, to apply to the Supreme Court for a ruling, that ruling to state specifically in what respects the act was unconstitutional. Then, if the next succeeding session of Congress, with this opinion of the Supreme Court before it, should re-enact that statute, it would, by that fact, be purged of its unconstitutionality, and become the law of the land. (Harold Ickes, *Secret Diary* . . . , pp. 494, 495.)

oligarchy and issue another proclamation of emancipation that will wipe out this 'no man's land' of sweatshop slavery."[6]

Nor were the militant lawmakers wholly without press support. A small but vocal group of newspapers took up the cry: "Curb this Court before it destroys the nation." We must bring the Justices down from "the pedestal of fetish and deal with them as men and not supermen."[7]

Various remedies were open. The President and Congress might limit the jurisdiction of the Supreme Court, or increase the number of judges so as to override the current arrogant majority, or compel judicial retirements, or sponsor constitutional amendments limiting the Court's power. After the sweeping decisions of May 1935, certain writers revived T. R.'s remedy of 1912—recall of judges and of judicial decisions. "We know," one writer commented perceptively, "that it is difficult to strip the ermine from judicial shoulders. . . . The worshipful attitude of the people toward the courts must be changed through education."[8]

As five or six recalcitrant Supreme Court Justices were chiefly responsible for the crisis, the simplest remedy lay with the personnel of the Court itself. Nor were these grim defenders of the *status quo* unaware that stern measures were in the making. Liberty League officials and spokesmen anticipated Court-packing as a distinct possibility well in advance of the 1936 elections. In September, United States District Judge Merrill E. Otis noted that at least two bills to increase the number of Supreme Court Justices had been introduced in Congress.[9]

Though many congressmen urged that something be done, they were uncertain what to do, not quite sure whether the trouble was traceable to the Constitution or to judges "callously insensible to the needs and demands of our people."[10] The President and his party were uncertain too—at least as to the politically feasible remedy. "If these problems [social and economic] cannot be effectively solved by legislation within the Constitution," the 1936 Democratic party platform said, "we shall seek such clarifying amendment as [we] . . . shall find necessary, in order adequately to regulate commerce, protect public health and safety, and safeguard economic security. Thus we propose to maintain the letter and spirit of the Constitution."[11] Throughout the campaign Democratic orators muted the discord between the Court and the New Deal, giving the public no hint that President Roosevelt would, if re-elected, wage an all-out war on the judiciary. The Constitution and the Supreme Court were not brought into the campaign as an issue, Harold Ickes commented, "because the groundwork had not been laid."[12]

At the first Cabinet meeting following the President's electoral avalanche, "there was a good deal of discussion" about the judiciary. "I think," Ickes noted, "that the President is getting ready to move in on that issue."[13] A few weeks later the Chief Executive told George Creel that if the Supreme Court set aside the Wagner Labor Disputes Act, the Social Security Act, and other measures designed to promote the general welfare, "Congress can enlarge the Supreme Court, increasing the number of Justices from nine to twelve or fifteen."[14]

While all this was going on, Stone was absent from the scene. On October 12 he was stricken by a devastating attack of bacillary dysentery, picked up shortly after his return from a fine vacation. For six of the nine weeks that he lay ill at his Washington home he was literally fighting for his life. Much of that time he was hardly rational, without a scrap of energy to devote to anything but the struggle for existence. "It laid me low," the Justice wrote. The experience was especially "hard work for one who is accustomed to always being well and working at top-speed."[15]

During these trying days, none of Stone's colleagues was more attentive than Chief Justice Hughes. One day as he was leaving, Hughes talked to Mrs. Stone of the heavy drain of her husband's long and serious illness on their financial resources, and bespoke his readiness, if necessary, to come to their assistance. "I shall not try to see you today," the Chief Justice wrote December 20, "but I want you to have this word of rejoicing in your steady and satisfactory progress toward recovery and in the prospect of your enjoyment of the warm sunshine of the South. Don't try to come back too soon—we need you—but we need you in full vigor."

On December 20 the Stones left for Sea Island. The Justice was moved in a wheel chair from the car to the train, and this was almost as insufferable as the illness itself. In the warm Georgia sun, under the watchful ministrations of Mrs. Stone, his health improved rapidly. Medical and nursing care of the first order were lavished on him, of course, but Stone credited his recovery "above all to the good judgment, resourcefulness, and eternal vigilance of Mrs. Stone as commander-in-chief."[16] During convalescence a daily tonic of egg yolk and brandy became a favorite medicine, but as he grew stronger he also grew more alert. One day after downing the prescribed remedy he suspected that his wife might be using his "best brandy." This upset him. Fine liquor, he protested, was "just wasted" on his insensitive palate. Soon he began to take walks, and by easy stages went back to his regime of two miles a day. In late January 1937 he was back in Washington, completely restored "to my usual good health, and so far as I can see, with many years of hard work ahead of me."[17]

Though somewhat fearful that his mental powers had been sapped by long illness, he plunged, February 1, into the usual routine.* "I am busy writing opinions for the first time during the present term," he reported happily. "It is like learning to walk again, but I think I shall manage it." "Now that I have got it going," he wrote a week later, "I think my intellectual apparatus will work as well as usual, and ought to keep running for sometime past seventy."[18]

New Dealers, who had suspected that Stone's illness might encourage further reaction, hailed his recovery as reinforcing their program. "I hope that your return may help in avoidance of that crisis in government which you saw in the future, a year ago," Irving Brant commented, February 2, 1937. Brant was concerned, "merely because I see values in the Court that are in danger of being lost if the issue becomes catastrophic."[19]

Evidence that corrective plans were in the offing might have been gleaned from the words of sweet reasonableness the President addressed to Congress in his 1937 State of the Union message:

During the past year there has been a growing belief that there is little fault to be found with the Constitution of the United States as it stands today. The vital need is not an alteration of our fundamental law but an increasingly enlightened view with reference to it. Difficulties have grown out of its interpretation; but rightly considered it can be used as an instrument of progress and not as a device for prevention of action.

With a better understanding of our purposes, and a more intelligent recognition of our needs as a nation, it is not to be assumed that there will be prolonged failure to bring legislative and judicial action into closer harmony. Means must be found to adapt our legal forms and our judicial interpretation to the actual present national needs of the largest progressive democracy in the modern world. . . . We do not ask the courts to call nonexistent powers into being, but we have a right to expect that conceded powers or those legitimately implied shall be made effective instruments for the common good.[20]

"It is possible to interpret these paragraphs as a warning to the Court," the *New York Herald Tribune* commented editorially, January 7, 1937. "But the good temper and restraint of the whole passage seems to us such a vast improvement on the 'horse and buggy episode' . . . that we prefer to accept it as the promise of new wisdom rather than as an exhibition of old wounds."

---

* Stone's friends were much concerned about his refusal to be more careful of his health. G. H. Backus, among others, urged him, Dec. 6, 1937, to take time off so as to keep in "the pink" and do his job better. "I am not one to commend the present incumbent of the White House as a good example for anyone—least of all for a man of your wisdom, character, and patriotism. But he does seem to have some glimmering of the value of frequent and well-placed vacations. If poor old Hoover had taken things the way your former pupil [F.D.R]—I will not say disciple—does, he probably would have been impeached for being absent from his command during battle."

F.D.R. could not be sure, even when backed by an impressive electoral mandate, that the Court would give ground. In no mood to take chances, the President awaited the propitious moment. Early February 1937 seemed well-nigh perfect. The election had gone his way overwhelmingly. Congressional opinion seemed overtly hostile to the Court. "The boys on Capitol Hill have their knives out, and how they do ache to use them," one news commentator reported.

On February 5, at the very peak of his popular and congressional prestige, the President sent a message to Congress proposing a drastic shake-up in the judiciary. In a word, the solution was to give a Supreme Court Justice, past age seventy, six months' time to retire. If he failed to do so he could continue in office, but the Chief Executive would appoint an additional Justice—presumably younger and better able to carry the heavy load. As there were six Justices in this category, F.D.R. would have at once six appointments to make. "Life tenure of judges, assured by the Constitution," the President explained, "was designed to place the courts beyond temptations or influences which might impair their judgments; it was not intended to create a static judiciary. A constant and systematic addition of younger blood will vitalize the courts and better equip them to recognize and apply essential concepts of justice in the light of the needs and the facts of an ever-changing world."[21]

In presenting his proposal the President gave no hint of wishing to stem the tide of anti-New Deal decisions. He tendered the hemlock cup to the elderly jurists on the elevated ground that they slowed the efficient dispatch of judicial business. His appeal was slick, his timing shrewd. "Can it be said," the President observed, "that full justice is achieved when a court is forced by the sheer necessity of keeping up with its business to decline, without even an explanation, to hear 87 per cent of the cases presented to it by private litigants?"[22]

Since 1932 Stone had "heard much talk about increasing the membership of the Court if it didn't do 'right.' "[23] Nothing had come of it, partly for want of a "popular slogan which would pungently express grievances and aspirations." In the Minimum Wage case of 1936 Stone himself unwittingly supplied the perfect warcry—"economic predilections." "As soon as you made that crack in your dissent it became evident that it was just what was needed," a Washington attorney wrote. "It was far superior, from the standpoint of a slogan, to anything Justice Holmes ever said; his remark about Herbert Spencer's social statics was too highfalutin. Despite the syllables in 'economic predilections' the words themselves have a splendid sound and they are sufficiently esoteric to belie argument."[24]

Though seemingly favored by the gods, the President's reorganization proposal immediately ran into obstinate public opposition. Overnight Supreme Court Justices were once more pictured as demigods far above the sweaty crowd, abstractly weighing public policy in the delicate scales of law. Constitutionality was talked about as if it were a tangible fact, undeviating and precise rather than a majority of the Justices' "current theory of what ought and what ought not to be done under the Constitution."[25] The same congressmen who, prior to F.D.R.'s message, had demanded the scalps of reactionary Justices, now, "shocked beyond measure," turned upon Roosevelt in an attitude of anguished surprise. Closing ranks with bar associations, the newspapers lined up heavily against "Court-packing."*

Anyone who could read knew that the nine Justices were not nine vestal virgins of the Constitution. Yet, through the years, and despite increasing evidence that judicial interpretation, not fundamental law, shackled the power to govern, the American people had come to regard the Court superstitiously as the symbol and strength of their freedom.† They were sure that it provided an impregnable barrier against any risk of dictatorship and personal government. "The President wants to control the Supreme Court" was hammered home incessantly. If the plan were accepted, the anti-New Deal press averred, "not a thing would stand between the ambitions of an unscrupulous man . . . in becoming absolute dictator of this country."[26]

Roosevelt's disingenuous argument for Court reform lent credence to the charge.‡ "Because he is adroit and not forthright," William Allen White reflected, "he arouses irritating suspicions, probably need-

---

* Through much of the opposition's talk ran the inference that the number nine is sacred, perhaps fixed by the Constitution itself. Quite the contrary is the case. The number of Justices was changed from six in 1789 to five in 1802; to seven in 1807, to nine in 1837, to ten in 1863, to seven in 1866, and to nine again in 1869.

† Opponents of the New Deal had deliberately whipped up an emotional frenzy about "The Constitution." While the American Liberty League was in the formative stage, W. H. Stayton circulated a "confidential memorandum" among its founders which said: "However strong and however efficient such an organization may be, it will have great difficulty in accomplishing its work unless it has a moral or emotional purpose, and thereby creates a moral or an emotional issue. Nor do I believe that many issues could command more support or evoke more enthusiasm among our people than the simple issue of the 'Constitution.' The public ignorance concerning it is dense and inexperienced, but, nevertheless, there is a mighty, though vague, affection for it. The people, I believe, need merely to be led and instructed, and this affection will become almost worship."

‡ On the ethics of "Court-packing," the President entered an angry defense: "If by that phrase, . . . it is charged that I wish to place on the bench spineless puppets who would . . . decide specific cases as I wished them to be decided, I make this answer: that no President fit for his office would appoint, and no Senate . . . confirm, that kind of appointees to the Supreme Court. But if . . . the charge is made that I would appoint . . . Justices worthy to sit beside present members of the Court who understood those modern conditions, that I will appoint Justices who will not undertake to override the judgment of the Congress on legislative policy, . . . then I say that I and with me the vast majority of the American people favor doing just that thing—now." (Fireside Chat, March 9, 1937.)

less, about his ultimate intentions as the leader of his party and the head of the Government." Even the President's warmest supporters resented his shiftiness. "Too clever, too damned clever," remarked the pro-New Deal *World-Telegram*.[27] "I do not entirely favor the President's plan," Professor Ralph Fuchs of Washington University Law School explained. "It is tricky, and perhaps dishonest. I should greatly have preferred to see him propose an amendment to the Constitution, or, if that is impractical, to say honestly that he wanted more Justices to give the Court a liberal balance."[28]

Roosevelt, quick to sense that his initial approach had been a major blunder,* moved closer to the real issue on March 4, when he likened the Judiciary to an unruly horse on the government gang plow, unwilling to pull with its teammates, the Executive and Congress.[29] As he saw it now, the crucial question was not whether the Court had kept up with its calendar, but whether it had kept up with the country. In a nation-wide Fireside Chat on March 9, the President shed the cloak of sophistry. Drawing heavily on Stone's dissenting barbs, he explained:

> The Court has been acting not as a judicial body, but as a policy-making body. . . . That is not only my accusation. It is the accusation of most distinguished Justices of the present Supreme Court. . . . In holding the AAA unconstitutional, Justice Stone said of the majority opinion that it was a "tortured construction of the Constitution." And two other Justices agreed with him. In the case holding the New York Minimum Wage Law unconstitutional, Justice Stone said that the majority were actually reading into the Constitution their own "personal economic predilections," and that if the legislative power is not left free to choose the methods of solving the problems of poverty, subsistence, and health of large numbers in the community, the "government is to be rendered impotent." . . . In the face of these dissenting opinions, there is no basis for the claim made by some members of the Court that something in the Constitution has compelled them regretfully to thwart the will of the people.[30]

The President's frankness came too late. The "big lie" he had promulgated on February 5 dogged his path to the end. Every segment of society soon joined in the struggle.

Though Stone's position throughout remained somewhat equivocal, he opposed Court-packing. First of all, he scored the approach; he disliked F.D.R.'s tactics. "You can rest assured," he told Grosvenor Backus, February 12, 1937, "that those who assert that age has affected the work of the Supreme Court, or that it does not do its work with

---

* "I made one major mistake when I first presented the plan," Roosevelt later commented. "I did not place enough emphasis upon the real mischief—the kind of decisions which, as a studied and continued policy, had been coming down from the Supreme Court. I soon corrected that mistake—in the speeches which I later made about the plan." (*Public Papers and Addresses*, Vol. VI, p. lxv, 1941.)

the highest degree of efficiency of any Court in the world, cannot get to first base." The Justice deplored the President's recklessness in dragging the Court into politics: "Between ourselves, the recent proposals about the Supreme Court are about the limit. To see it become the football of politics fills me with apprehension."*

"Granting all the faults that are attributed to the Court," he wrote, "it still embodies in its traditions and habits of work, and in the performance of its functions essential to our form of government, values which are inestimable. I fear that in the emotional stress of the moment these may be sacrificed."[31] Despite unpardonable excesses, his faith in judicial review remained unshaken. Since he did not wish the Court to relinquish or lose power, wanting only to eliminate abuses, he saw "no satisfactory solution for our problem except in the character of the judges appointed to our Court."[32]

Roosevelt's proposal had still other shortcomings: it would hamper the Court's work. "If the change should be made," the Justice commented, "I fear that there would be a loss of efficiency. The intimate conference which ought to be carried on in the decision of the important questions which come to the Court, would be increasingly difficult with increasing size. It would be a serious loss to the continuity and thoroughness of the work if every member of the Court did not participate in a case, as has been the practice of the Court throughout its life."[33] Finally, Stone believed such drastic reform unnecessary. For him a point not sufficiently emphasized in the debate was summed up in Lincoln's aphorism: "Nothing valuable can be lost by taking time." Mistakes in the development of the law have a way of "rubbing themselves out in time, and if we have made mistakes . . . as most institutions do, I have no doubt that time will correct them long before the country will come to any major disaster."[34] "Time irons out a great many difficulties," he reiterated, "and I have no doubt that the Court situation would have righted itself if the President could have possessed himself in patience for a reasonable time."[35] "Congress might grow reckless with the backing of a packed Court, and the country would be flooded with bad laws,"[36] he said. Worse still, adding to the number of Justices by political maneuver would "decrease faith in the constitutional decisions of the Court just at the moment when they become worthy of faith."[37]

Decline of judicial prestige was already evident in the testimony of those opposing as well as of those favorable to the plan. Stone was much chagrined that "those, who by training and experience, are

---

* Stone deeply resented F. D. R.'s intrusion of political controversy into the sanctity of judicial life. On March 6, 1936, he wrote Felix Frankfurter: "Naturally these are unhappy days for me, but I don't see that there is much I can do except to keep sawing wood, although I can say that I do now have regrets that I did not yield, some years ago, to my inclination to seek other occupation."

qualified to speak," should need the reminder to "act like scholars and not like politicians."[38] The testimony of Court-packing professors* simply boiled down to the proposition that they did not "believe in a Constitution, or in those orderly processes through which alone a Constitution can function."[39] He was especially distressed over the "antics of men who ought to know better, men who seem to think that because the Court has made some mistakes that they ought to be corrected by another and graver one. I am beginning to think that all my life I have greatly overestimated the capacity of the human mind to deal with novel problems."[40] "It almost makes you wonder, whether the democratic form of government can permanently endure, and whether we will not ultimately go the way that so many European countries seem to be going now."[41]

Yet Stone's own experience had convinced him that something must be done to break the constitutional log-jam. He scored Court-packing but did not oppose all correctives. "The real issue," he told a friend, "is one of methods of correcting an evil, and what price we are willing to pay to do it in a hurry. Those who know their history and the course of events in the life of this Republic will, I think, reach the conclusion that the price is too high to pay merely to gain a solution in a hurry, which ultimately may prove to be no solution at all."[42] He was certain that an amendment compelling retirement at seventy-five could be "promptly passed, and would solve all our troubles."[43]

The discussion itself was welcome. On March 12, three days after the President's Fireside Chat, Stone commented: "We are certainly getting a thorough airing and if we can come through all this discussion without serious loss of the prestige of the Court the result may be good. I think the popular impression—certainly among intelligent people in the eastern part of the country—is that the Court has misused its powers. Assistant Attorney General Jackson yesterday gave a powerful exposition of this view before the Senate Judiciary Committee, and there is too much truth in it for the comfort of those

---

* "Recent discussion of the Court and Constitution," he wrote John Bassett Moore, Sept. 8, 1937, "has revealed abysmal depths of ignorance in quarters where it would seem that we are entitled to look for knowledge and intelligence. The new Dean of the Harvard Law School [James M. Landis] in a widely quoted speech gave the impression that the proposal to give the Court power to declare laws unconstitutional was twice rejected by the Constitutional Convention. I doubt whether he really intended to give such an impression, but his language was not well chosen to describe the proposal to give the Court revisory power over legislatures acting in a legislative capacity, which was the only such proposal. In the numerous speeches dealing with the power of the Court to declare laws unconstitutional I have seen no reference to the judiciary article which gives the Court appellate jurisdiction in cases 'arising under the laws and Constitution' of the United States, or any adequate reference to the historical background of the judicial power or to the numerous discussions of the subject penned by competent hands."

responsible for the Court's action in recent years. But I think there is also a strong popular feeling that correction ought to be secured in some other way which would not look so much like expecting the Supreme Court to get its law from Presidential messages."[44]

The Justice himself was more deeply involved than he realized. One enterprising editor went so far as to disinter and reprint his address of 1928 before the American Bar Association as shedding light on the issue. Herein Stone had explained the Court's pre-eminent position in terms of "firm adherence to its established tradition of judicial independence." Even the unjust and unreasonable attacks on the Court had, he said, left "no scar," concluding that "the only wounds from which it has suffered have been . . . 'self-inflicted.' "[45] In 1928, as now, he feared repetition of judicial mayhem, and did his best to prevent it.

As time went on Stone gave some evidence of enjoying the ruckus: "Roosevelt is giving the Court a lively time, but for the most part I am sitting pretty. I have said nothing which I have to unsay, and nothing which has drawn serious criticism from either camp in the fight."[46] "Justice Stone," the "Washington Merry-Go-Round" reported, "is pleased and openly defiant." It may be that he considered F.D.R.'s assault "just retribution for recent Supreme Court waywardness."[47] He did indicate sympathy with Erwin N. Griswold's sentiments. "I think I am against it," Griswold wrote, "but it is terribly close. . . . In spite of my opposition to the particular plan, I find myself not displeased that the President has raised the issue. Perhaps I take a sort of sadistic delight in just retribution. But more particularly, I hope some people may see the seriousness of what has been done by courts, and that the public may have some understanding that the task is not to lay the statute beside the Constitution and see if one squares with the other."[48]

Stone wanted to avoid personal entanglement in this explosive political struggle, but the President's evolving strategy had catapulted him into the center of conflict. That the President had drawn his "best ammunition" for the March 9 Fireside Chat from Stone's dissenting opinions to show how inadequately the Court had met its obligation to keep the Constitution functioning, deeply troubled the Justice. "The place to which we have come is very distressing to me," he lamented, "the more so because it might have been avoided, and with a little forebearance on all sides would have been, without any ultimate loss to the country."[49] But, now the issue had arisen, he depreciated precipitate action. "The notion that this thing must be done or we bust is all nonsense," he said.[50]

F.D.R.'s opponents could not resist the temptation to enlist Stone openly as an authoritative spokesman on their side. Suggestions kept pouring in from friends that he make his position clear. "If it is a proper question for a citizen to ask, and for a member of the Supreme Court to answer," Columbia University Professor Douglas W. Johnson wrote, probing circumspectly for Stone's opinion, "I should like to know to what extent, if any, the refusal of the Supreme Court during the last fiscal year to hear 717 petitions for review out of 867 presented, was due to lack of time because of a crowded calendar?"[51]

"I am very glad to answer the questions," Stone promptly responded, "on the understanding that I am not to be quoted. The reason for my wish not to be quoted at this time is not because I have any objection to the facts becoming known, but because I do not wish to be put in the light of participating in the present controversy." After making clear his opposition to the President's plan, Stone supplied Johnson with four closely reasoned pages of "facts" leading to the conclusion that "rejection of certiorari applications is not for lack of time to deal with them." Indeed, in denying numerous petitions for review, the Justices were but carrying out the mandate of Congress in the Judiciary Act of 1925 "that the Supreme Court ought to devote itself to the consideration of cases involving important public questions, that its time and energy ought not to be absorbed in hearing and deciding cases merely to provide an unsuccessful litigant with further opportunity for delay, or to give him another chance, or where the issue is not doubtful or has plainly been considered and adequately dealt with by a competent appellate tribunal." "In my opinion," the Justice declared, "it has made the mistake of being over-generous . . . but it is of course better to err in that direction than in the other."[52]

Johnson thanked Stone for his "more than generous response," but he was unwilling to let the matter rest. "It seems to me," he wrote the Justice, "that the President, whether misinformed or misinterpreting data given him, has painted a most misleading picture." The Attorney General had stressed, among other things, the enormous number of pages the Justices must read before refusing certiorari. "Is it true," Johnson wanted to know, "that the Justices must read all of every application and supporting papers? Cannot a Justice, like Walter Hines Page, tell an egg is rotten without eating all of it?"[53]

The Justice agreed that the case had been misrepresented: "With the skill which comes from knowledge and experience it is possible to come to a satisfactory conclusion without the enormous amount of reading which has been suggested." To reinforce the point, Stone enclosed excerpts from congressional reports and debates, quoting as the most "authoritative" source Senator Albert B. Cummins, chairman of the Judiciary Committee, to show that the Supreme Court, in rejecting the vast majority of applications for certiorari, was doing no more than was expected by the sponsors of the 1925 Judiciary Act. "I can see no objection to making any use of the facts which you see fit," the Justice told Johnson.[54]

Ammunition was not enough; Johnson wanted to have Stone known as an avowed opponent of Court-packing. "The strong language you have used in certain dissenting opinions has naturally led some of your friends, and me among them," the correspondent suggested, "to surmise that you might be sympathetic with the President's action."[55] It seemed only fair that an authoritative source of facts, having direct bearing on this important public issue, be made known.

The Justice, having generously fed the fire, now tried to bank it. "I do not care to engage in any public discussion," he replied, "or to have my views quoted for the purpose of influencing current discussion. But I have no hesitation in saying, for your own personal information, that I think the present proposal is too high a price to pay for the correction of some decisions of the Court which I, in common with a great many others, think unfortunate. In any case, I see no urgent need for haste. Our resources for dealing with pressing problems of government by constitutional methods are by no means exhausted. Time irons out many of the difficulties of constitutional construction. If we are not willing to wait for that, the Constitution itself points the way for their removal."[56]

Johnson, sensing in Justice Stone a repressed desire to spike the embattled project, pressed him "to let the American people know the views of one whose opinions have been cited repeatedly in support of the President's proposal."[57] Stone finally gave tentative permission to the drafting of a letter asking Senator Burton K. Wheeler to call the Justices, especially Mr. Justice Stone, to testify, reserving "judgment as to the wisdom of our participating in controversy." "That will depend," he said, "on views expressed in conference with associates and our joint decision as to what is the advisable course."[58] Four days later a draft letter making Stone's position clear was ready for release. "I can state with assurance," the letter said, "that while Justice Stone feels very keenly that some decisions of the Supreme Court have been unfortunate, he regards any proposal to alter the membership of the Court with a view to affecting its decisions as both unnecessary and dangerous."[59]

"Cannot approve," the alarmed Justice wired. "I wish, quite as much as you," he wrote in explanation of his seeming about-face, "that my views on this question could be known without the kind of embarrassment to the Court, and the storm of public debate and criticism, which would inevitably follow their publication, but in which I could take no part. Fairness to my associates, also, I think, requires that I should not do anything either directly or indirectly which would put on them

the onus of entering a field of debate which up to now they have refused to enter." "If I were to make any statement," he went on, "it
should be done directly, by making a public statement. . . . Approval
by me of any method by which my views were brought before the
public by indirection would be subject to possible criticisms which
the more direct method would not merit—all of which proves that the
job of being a Supreme Court Justice is not free from its difficulties
and embarrassments. One must remain silent under unfair and unjust
criticism and various types and degrees of misrepresentation, relying
only on his published opinions as giving the measure of his views and
of his intelligence and character."[60]

A week later the Justice seemed more relaxed, more inclined to
minimize his involvement in this unseemly controversy: "I go my way,
doing the day's task, and render unto Caesar the things that are
Caesar's, by letting the political arm of the Government decide
whether they want six new judges or are content with nine."[61]

Throughout the furor, that select group which knew most about the
situation, the Justices themselves, kept silent. No one doubted where
they stood, or that they held the trump card in this political game.
The problem was to get them into the fray without offending their
professional dignity and their alleged remoteness from political controversy. Senator Burton K. Wheeler, leader of the opposition to
F.D.R.'s plan, hesitated to consult members of the Court on a purely
political matter. The Senator knew personally only one Justice, and
as the hour approached of his appointment with Justice Brandeis,
known as the most fastidious stickler for proprieties on the bench,
Wheeler grew increasingly apprehensive. The interview had hardly
begun, however, before he realized that his anxiety was altogether
groundless. "Why don't you confer with the Chief Justice?" Brandeis
suggested. The Senator demurred, explaining that he did not know
Hughes. "Well," Brandeis said reassuringly, "the Chief Justice knows
you and knows what you are doing."[62]

The Chief Justice's judicial statesmanship was at stake, and he knew
it. When the President's proposal was announced, Secretary Ickes
wrote in his diary: "What a blow this will be to the prestige of Chief
Justice Hughes, who has had a chance during the last four years to
make a high place for himself as one of the great Chief Justices in
American history, but who has not shown either the strength or the
adroitness to control his court and make it an instrument for social
and political progress!"[63]

With Brandeis's endorsement, Hughes plunged into the struggle
with alacrity. Events moved swiftly. Though the Senator did not reach
him until Saturday, March 20, the Chief Justice was able to prepare
a long and closely reasoned document for presentation to the Judiciary

Committee the following Monday, March 22. "The baby is born," Hughes said with a broad smile as he put the letter into Wheeler's hand late Sunday afternoon.[64]

The Chief Justice's cold statistical analysis scotched the President's allegation that the Justices were not abreast of their docket. "The Supreme Court is fully abreast of its work," Hughes wrote. "There is no congestion of cases upon our calendar. This gratifying condition has obtained for several years." "An increase in the number of Justices would not," he said, "promote the efficiency of the Court." As to the suggestion that an enlarged Court hear cases in divisions, the Chief Justice ventured the opinion that such a course might run afoul the constitutional provision for "one Supreme Court." "The Constitution does not appear to authorize two or more Supreme Courts or two or more parts of a Supreme Court functioning in effect as separate courts."*

Finally the Chief Justice managed to convey the impression that the entire Court endorsed his statement. Ignoring the customary disavowal of authority to speak for members of a body not consulted, he was "confident that it is in accord with the views of the Justices." He admitted, however, that "on account of the shortness of time, I have not been able to consult with members of the Court generally." Only Justices Van Devanter and Brandeis specifically endorsed his letter.[65]

The Chief Justice's biographer censures Hughes for not consulting his colleagues before releasing the letter: "Considering the delicacy of the issue, Hughes' action with the approval of only two of his eight colleagues was certainly a tactical error."[66] But was it? If the Chief Justice had consulted all his colleagues, they would have been divided. In that case, there might have been no letter, or at least a very different one. Later on Justice Stone tried to set the matter in perspective:

> In the interest of accuracy, and to avoid the perpetuation of a mistaken impression, may I say that . . . the Justices other than those named in the letter did not join in the expression of the opinion [that the Constitution does not authorize two or more Supreme Courts or two or more parts of a Supreme Court functioning in effect as separate courts]. The fact is that I did not then, and do not now, approve of such an extra-official expression on

* Whether Hughes' words constitute an advisory opinion remains a moot question. In any event, the Chief Justice seems not to have been hampered by his own earlier condemnation of advisory opinions from the Court. Discussing Justice Johnson's favorable response, on behalf of a unanimous bench, to a request from President Monroe for an extrajudicial opinion on internal improvements, Hughes remarked in his book, The Supreme Court of the United States (pp. 30-31): "This, of course, was extra-official, but it is safe to say that nothing of the sort could happen today. The Court has rejected the overtures of the Congress for opinions on constitutional questions in the absence of a real case or controversy to be decided."

a constitutional question by the Court or its members. Justice Cardozo, with whom I discussed the matter, was of the same view.

I first learned of the Chief Justice's letter when a copy of it was printed in the newspapers shortly after its date. I was not consulted in connection with its preparation. Justice Cardozo told me that he was not. I have never formed any opinion on the constitutional point in question or discussed it with any members of the Court.

There was no reason of which I am aware why all the members of the Court should not have been consulted in connection with the preparation of a document which purported to state "the views of the Justices," or for expressing the views of Justices who for any reason could not be consulted. Although the Court was then in recess, all its members were in the city. They could have been brought together for a conference on an hour's telephone notice, or less. Throughout the recess Justices Sutherland, Cardozo, and myself were in our homes, which are within five minutes' walk of the residence of the Chief Justice.*

Court-packing opponents, working to bring the full weight of the Court's prestige to bear against Roosevelt, lost no time capitalizing on the Chief Justice's letter. Read by Senator Wheeler before the Senate Judiciary Committee's first public session on the Court bill, March 22, 1937, the Hughes statement heaped fuel on the fires of controversy raging in the press. Wheeler immediately drew the inference that whatever the Court's differences on other matters, they were unanimous on the Chief Justice's letter.

Despite the false use to which the Hughes letter was put, Stone kept silent. After the furor died down, however, he stood ready to dispute any implication that he had approved it. "I should perhaps have put the matter in its proper light at the time," he told Justice Frankfurter in 1939, "but it did not occur to me that such an expression of opinion would, in the circumstances, be attributed to members of the Court who were not consulted, and it seemed to me undesirable that the Court or its members should, at that stage of the Supreme Court controversy, be subjected to any additional publicity."

But Stone had, in various ways, allowed himself to be drawn into the fight. At a Sunday evening conference on Supreme Court appointments the Justice told the President that the crying need was for more Justices who not only shared the philosophy of Holmes, Brandeis, and Cardozo, but who were able to express it in written opinions, and thus bear their share of the Court's work and help educate the people and

---

* When Frankfurter and Shulman's revised casebook on *Federal Jurisdiction and Procedure* appeared in 1939, it contained a note on the Hughes' letter implying that it represented the position of all the Justices. Stone immediately wrote Frankfurter this letter (Dec. 29, 1939), stating his objections. "The fact of the matter is," Frankfurter wrote A.T.M., March 3, 1953, "that it was a prearranged correspondence—Stone wrote me in order to put the matter on record in a very formal fashion."

especially the lawyers of the country.[67] Nor was Stone's interest confined to Supreme Court appointments. He talked and wrote to friends with customary candor on other phases of the conflict. The cool reception he accorded the Chief Justice's letter soon leaked out, and this, too, indirectly implicated him.

On Sunday morning, March 21 (the day Hughes' letter was turned over to Senator Wheeler), Irving Brant had called at 2340 Wyoming Avenue and found Alfred Lief there "sounding out" the Justice's willingness to sign a protest against the President's bill. After he refused to do so on the general ground that he did not think it proper for members of the Court to take part in a political controversy, there was no reason for Lief to bring up a specific matter such as the Hughes letter. It was not until he read his newspaper the following morning that Stone learned the purpose of Lief's call.* "As it was a three-cornered conversation," Brant wrote Stone later on, "I relayed word of his [Lief's] errand to the White House. It made a nice commentary on Mr. Hughes' statement that he had not had time to submit his letter to all his colleagues." "I, too, was amused when Lief's errand became manifest," the Justice replied. "I had supposed that he came in just for a social call. Later he wrote to ask whether it was true that I had been asked to sign the Chief Justice's letter. I replied† by saying merely that I did not know of it until I read about it in the papers."[68]

Wheeler later denied acquaintance with Lief and suggested to Brant that the Chief Justice must have sent Lief to see Stone.‡ "Absurd," Stone snorted, "I don't know Lief very well, but I don't think he would misrepresent the facts, and the Chief Justice knows well that he can find out what I think any time by asking—sometimes he finds out without asking."[69]

Stone's ambivalent attitude toward Court reform, his opposition to packing, while admitting the need for some change, placed him in a peculiar position. His refusal to speak out publicly and his eagerness for private conversation so obscured his stand as to make him useful to both sides. He explained at the outset that he did not wish to be

* Years later Brant recalled the incident and remembered Stone's remark, "I really couldn't make out what that young man came here for." "My impression is," the newspaperman suggested, "that Senator Wheeler sent him here to ask you to join in a statement against the Court." "It was very strange," Brant commented in a letter to A.T.M., July 22, 1951, "that Stone did not know that he had been asked to sign something of the sort."

† "Numerous people," Stone had written Lief, April 2, 1937, "who have no connection with the Court have called on me and asked me to sign statements, either separately or with the Court as a whole. In each instance I have declined the invitation and in most instances referred the inquirer to the Chief Justice."

‡ Evidently Stone and Brant thought Lief came as Senator Wheeler's emissary. "The odd way Lief kept mixing questions to me about Wheeler with questions to Stone about joining in a protest left no doubt in my mind at the time that he had come at the request of the Senator," (Irving Brant to A.T.M., July 22, 1951.)

quoted, "because I do not wish to be put in the light of participating in the present controversy." Yet he talked freely thereafter to Irving Brant,* and encouraged Brant's attempt to sell F.D.R. a modified Court-reform bill compelling retirement by constitutional amendment.[70] Those portions of the bill providing regular pension allowance for retired Justices would, he believed, prove a feasible solution of the current difficulty.† Everything Stone told Brant, even on highly technical matters, was immediately passed on to F.D.R. himself or to advisers such as Thomas G. Corcoran.‡

Stone's views also served the opposition. In some quarters he was credited "with having a hand in knocking down some of the contentions which were raised in its [the Court plan's] favor."[71] "He counseled delay," Congressman Emmanuel Celler reported. "He said that

* The Justice got a "great kick" out of reading Brant's peppery editorials and welcomed an opportunity for a "quiet evening so we can discuss the state of the nation in general and of the law in particular." (H.F.S. to Irving Brant, May 24, 1937.) Stone's readiness for talk with Brant may be explained in terms of the newspaperman's unusual grasp of the issues. "He writes," Stone said, "about the Constitution and Court matters with more grasp and understanding than any other editorial writer in the country. While I am unable to follow him in his evident belief that the President's program is desirable, I would not deny that it could have been solved, and probably still could, without breaking up the household furniture." (H.F.S. to Luther Ely Smith, April 29, 1937.)

† Those close to Stone gained from him the distinct impression that Hughes and Roberts might, without any threat of Court-packing, "switch" their votes. If this did not occur, Stone thought a sound retirement plan might turn the trick. Indeed the impasse between Court and Congress might never have developed had not several Justices, due for retirement, elected to remain on the bench. As to the reason for this "stubbornness," Stone frequently cited the unhappy experience of Justice Holmes, whose compensation Congress had reduced after his retirement in 1932. This put all Justices on notice that they could not rely upon the congressional promise, under the act of April 10, 1869, "that any judge of any court of the United States, who, having held his commission as such at least ten years, shall, after having attained the age of seventy years, resign his office, shall thereafter, during the residue of his natural life, receive the same salary which was by law payable to him at the time of his resignation." (R.S. Sec. 714; U.S. Code, Title 28, Sec. 375.) Congressional action in Holmes' case meant that Justices of the Supreme Court did not have the privilege accorded judges of the lower federal courts— retirement as distinguished from resignation. This situation was remedied by the act of March 1, 1937 (C. 21, 50 U.S. Stat. 24; U.S. Code, Title 28, Sec. 375 a. 26), which gave Supreme Court Justices "the same rights and privileges with regard to retiring, instead of resigning," as that granted other federal judges. Within a year two Justices, Van Devanter, in June 1937, and Sutherland, in January 1938, left the bench.

‡ Stone wrote Luther Ely Smith, June 4, 1937, suggesting that he put Brant onto the Court's shenanigans in *Railroad Commission* v. *Pacific Gas & Electric Co.*, 301 U.S. 669 (1937). It was, he said, "more than the usual rate case." One week later, the Court's action in this case, a 4-to-4 stalemate affirming a reactionary lower court opinion, formed the basis of Brant's argument to F.D.R. against appointing Senator Robinson, ex-utilities lawyer, to the Supreme Court. (Irving Brant to F.D.R., June 12, 1937.)

time settles many things, that in due course the problem of the Court would settle itself. While he did not indicate it in so many words, the fair implication of his language was plain—two, if not more, of the Justices would retire—if the retirement bill were passed; I asked 'within what period?' and he responded, 'Six months to a year.' "[72]

The Chief Justice's letter and the press campaign of education had put severe crimps in Roosevelt's ambition to overhaul the Court; but they had not erased the fact that many people considered change necessary. "The troublesome thing to overcome," Stone commented, "is that practically all the witnesses on both sides of the question concede that the Court has been very narrow in its interpretation of constitutional questions and that there is need of some kind of reform."[73] Senator Wheeler himself admitted judicial shortcomings.* As if to confess their "guilt," penitent Justices began undermining their recent handiwork, even as the fight raged about them. The first tower to fall was the most recent, *Morehead* v. *Tipaldo,* which had set aside the New York Minimum Wage Law.

Justice Roberts' contribution to this strategical about-face in the Washington Minimum Wage case has been immortalized by the somewhat scurrilous comment, "A switch in time saves nine." Everything he subscribed to now, he had not only rejected the previous June, but as late as October 12, when New York's petition for rehearing of the Tipaldo case was denied. Chief Justice Hughes' part in the upset, on the other hand, was praised to the skies. "The Chief Justice read the opinion confessing error," Robert H. Jackson wrote in 1941. "But his voice was one of triumph. He was reversing his Court, but not himself. He was declaring in March the law as he would have declared it the previous June, had his dissent been heeded."[74]

It was not, however, quite that way, as Stone made clear in a letter to his sons, April 1, 1937. In the Tipaldo case, he explained, "the Chief Justice wrote an opinion saying that the New York statute was distinguishable in some of its features from that one before the Court in the Adkins case, and that the Adkins case consequently was not controlling. I wrote an opinion stating that while I agreed that there were the distinctions pointed out by the Chief Justice, I nevertheless thought that it should be placed on broader grounds, namely that due process had nothing to do with wage regulation wherever at least there was a serious legislative problem presented. In October the Court denied a motion for reargument of the case. Monday the

---

* "There is a wrong way and a right way to correct those evils. The wrong way is to pack the Court—the right way is to amend the Constitution." (Radio address, March 10, 1937, in *Congressional Record,* Vol. 81 [1937], Appendix, p. 581.)

Chief Justice wrote the opinion, overruling the Adkins case and adopting the views expressed in my opinion of last June."*

In the Washington Minimum Wage case Hughes went out of his way to deplore "exploitation of a class of workers who are in an unequal position with respect to bargaining power and are thus relatively defenseless against the denial of a living wage." "We think," Hughes announced for the Court, "that the decision in the Adkins case was a departure from the true application of the principles governing the regulation by the state of the employer and employed." "The liberty safeguarded," he now explained, "is liberty in a social organization which requires the protection of law against the evils which menace the health, safety, morals, and welfare of the people. . . . The community is not bound to provide what is in effect a subsidy for unconscionable employers."[75] Though all this seemed a far cry from the stand he had taken a year earlier in the Tipaldo case, the Chief Justice was at pains to deny any suggestion that F.D.R. provoked the shift and to explain that the case had been argued and a decision reached some time before the President announced his Court plan.† Commentators were not, however, impressed with the technical basis on which the Chief Justice rested his claim. "We are told," a skeptical paragrapher noted, "that the Supreme Court's about-face was not due to outside clamor. It seems that the new building has a soundproof room, to which the Justices retire to change their minds."‡[76]

On the same day that the Hughes-Roberts switch won judicial sanction for the minimum wage, a chastened Court unanimously approved broad extensions of national power.§ A new Frazier-Lemke Act regarding farm mortgages found unwonted favor with the Justices;[77] while Justice Stone upheld the National Firearms Act, a penalizing license tax so stiff that it made small weapons traffic prohibitive. "In-

---

* The Washington Minimum Wage case was argued in Stone's absence, Dec. 16, 17, 1936, but his vote was necessary to a majority as the judges were otherwise divided 4 to 4. "He did participate in the decision, and it is not uncommon for a Justice who did not hear the arguments to participate in the decision of the case." (E. P. Cullinan, Assistant to Clerk of Supreme Court, to A.T.M., July 14, 1951.)

† This is literally true, but one may suspect that rising anti-Court sentiment, along with the election returns, quite apart from any specific proposal to pack it, may have influenced judicial decision.

‡ At least one of the Justices was not thus sealed off. Justice Roberts, on January 29, 1954, told Senators considering the proposed anti-Court Packing Amendment, that he was "fully conscious of the tremendous strain and threat to the existing Court" inherent in Roosevelt's plan. It was, he said, "a political device to influence the Court." (Hearing before a Subcommittee on the Judiciary. S.J. Res. 44, p. 9.)

§ Two decisions written by Justice Cardozo indicated the Court's more liberal attitude toward state regulation and taxation. See Highland Farms Dairy v. Agnew, 300 U.S. 608 (1937), dismissing petition for injunction against a state milk-control law in advance of application to petitioner; and Henneford v. Silas Mason Co., 300 U.S. 577 (1937), sustaining a "use" tax levied by a state on articles purchased beyond its borders.

quiry into the hidden motives which may move Congress to exercise a power constitutionally conferred upon it," Stone announced triumphantly, "is beyond the competency of Courts."[78] Without a dissenting voice, he sanctioned the collective bargaining provisions of the Railway Labor Act, even as to so-called "backshop" employees not directly engaged in interstate activities. Congress could now require railroads to bargain with their employees' chosen representatives without infringing "liberty." "The Fifth Amendment, like the Fourteenth," Stone declared for the Court, "is not a guaranty of untrammeled freedom of action and of contract. In the exercise of its power to regulate commerce, Congress can subject both to restraints not shown to be unreasonable."[79]

"This has been an exciting week," Stone reported. "On Monday the Court upheld the constitutionality of the collective bargaining provisions of the Railway Labor Act. I wrote the opinion. It was fairly good as written, but it was mangled somewhat in order to meet the wishes of some of the other Judges. It finally won concurrence of the entire Court." Stone rejoiced to see the Court on "more solid ground," though he felt "unhappy about the tortuous path which has been pursued to arrive there." Just what effect "all this will have on the President's pending proposal remains to be seen. I am fearful, though, that the dissent of the four so-called conservatives, expounding their views of a rigid and changeless Constitution, apparently to be applied always in the same way, no matter how much the subject matter to which it is applied may change, will stimulate the criticism of the Court and give emphasis to the demand that it be reformed."[80]

The really big issue facing Court and country still remained unresolved. What would be the fate of the Wagner Labor Relations Act? A year earlier national authority over the employer-employee relation was still under the judicial ban, and social security at best highly suspect on constitutional grounds. Would the Justices now permit the national government to substitute law for naked force in labor relations? Five cases were argued February 10 and 11, 1937. Condemnation of the Act by the Liberty League's Committee of Fifty-eight had stiffened employer resistance. Meanwhile, the famous sit-down strikes occurred in Detroit. Industrial peace—or war—seemed to hang in the balance when, on April 12, 1937, Chief Justice Hughes put forward, in the Jones & Laughlin Steel case, a broad and encompassing definition of interstate commerce and claimed for Congress the power to protect the lifelines of national economy from private industrial warfare. Arguments that had proved effective in the Schechter and Guffey Coal cases were unavailing. "These cases," the Chief Justice commented summarily, "are not controlling here." They were not controlling because he now chose to consider that "fundamental" distinction between "direct and indirect effects" as one of degree rather than of kind. They were not binding because he now minimized the point much stressed in the Schechter case, namely, that the "fundamental" nature of the distinction between direct and indirect effects of intrastate transactions upon interstate commerce arises from the fact that it is "essential to the maintenance of our constitutional system."[81] Since interstate commerce was now seen as a "practical conception," interference with that commerce "must be appraised by a judgment that does not ignore actual experience." Somewhat disdainfully the Chief Justice now declared that, in light of the industry's "farflung activities," it was "idle to say" that interference by strikes or other labor disturbances "would be indirect or remote. It is obvious that it would be immediate and might be catastrophic."

"We are asked to shut our eyes to the plainest facts of our national life," the Chief Justice continued, "and to deal with the question of direct and indirect effect in an intellectual vacuum. . . . When industries organize themselves on a national scale, making their relation to interstate commerce the dominant factor in their activities, how can it be maintained that their industrial labor relations constitute a forbidden field into which Congress may not enter, when it is necessary to protect interstate commerce from the paralyzing consequences of industrial war?"[82] Nor was the Chief Justice's sweeping doctrine applicable solely to large-scale industries, such as steel. He proceeded immediately to apply the same doctrine to two small concerns, a trailer company and a men's clothing manufacturer.[83]

The Chief Justice's colleagues naturally supposed that the man who took a position apparently so completely at odds with his earlier pronouncements must have seen a "new light."[*] "Every consideration brought forward to uphold the Act before us was applicable to support the Acts held unconstitutional in cases decided within two years," Jus-

---

[*] But in confronting his own handiwork the Chief Justice was less embarrassed than generally supposed. Unlike Justice Sutherland, he had never said, in so many words, whether the "direct-indirect effects" formula meant a distinction of degree or of kind. But in joining Justice Roberts' AAA opinion, and in subscribing to Justice Sutherland's unequivocal views in the Guffey Coal case, he clearly indicated his belief that to sustain national regulation of agriculture and manufacturing would be tantamount to destruction of the federal system. In his Guffey Coal concurrence, the Chief Justice went so far as to suggest that: "If the people desire to give Congress the power to regulate industries within the state, and the relations of employers and employees in those industries, they are at liberty to declare their will in the appropriate manner, but it is not for the Court to amend the Constitution by judicial decision." The conclusion seems inescapable that if it was a part of the Constitution on May 18, 1936 (when the Guffey Coal case was decided), that Congress could not regulate the employer-employee relationship in industry, then the Constitution was in that respect amended on April 12, 1937, when the Jones & Laughlin case was decided. (See E. S. Corwin, "The Court Sees a New Light," *New Republic*, Aug. 4, 1937, p. 355.)

tice McReynolds growled in dissent. The report Stone sent off to his sons on April 15 indicates substantial agreement with his irascible colleague: The Wagner Labor decisions "seem popularly to be regarded as very revolutionary, and perhaps they are in view of the decision of the Court in the Guffey Coal Act case. As a matter of fact, it has been well understood for many years that the power to regulate commerce not only involves the power to regulate the commerce itself, but to regulate things materially affecting commerce. The Sherman Act, which gets its only constitutional sanction from the commerce clause, has been applied to manufacturers and to their employees, and to the employees in mines. It has been applied to the employees of the building trades in San Francisco, and of the limestone quarries in Indiana. The National Government has regulated transactions on the Chicago Grain Exchange because of its effects on interstate commerce, and has authorized the regulation of intrastate rates of interstate carriers where the rates were so low as to threaten their successful operation in interstate commerce."[84]

"Of course," the letter continued, "in order to reach the result which was reached in these cases last Monday, it was necessary for six members of the Court either to be overruled or to take back some things they subscribed to in the Guffey Coal Act case. But as I did not join in those statements, I had nothing to take back. Whether it is wise for the National Government to enter this field is a question with which I am not concerned, but it seems clear that under these decisions the National Government can exercise some control over the relations of employer and employee and hold both to a larger degree of responsibility in conducting their labor relations."

For those bent on spiking the President's plan the Hughes and Roberts switch came in the nick of time. But Stone was wary of rejoicing at the first sign of change; he had seen sudden conversions before. It was ironical, too, that Hughes, in choosing to assign the Jones & Laughlin case to himself, should have taken a plum that rightfully belonged to Cardozo, whose Carter case dissent had spelled out the basic ideas of the new majority.* The glory of announcing the extremely popular

---

* Samuel Hendel gives this appraisal: "When the pressure for innovation became great, and the risks to the nation and to the Court itself apparent, reluctantly at first, but increasingly [Hughes] went along with change. Having sedulously sought to protect the precedents of the Court, sometimes at the risk of offending logic, he witnessed and often participated in the shattering of one precedent after another. He stood thus as a kind of heroic and, in a sense, tragic figure, torn between the old and the new, seeking at first to stem the tide but then relentlessly caught up and moving with it." (*Charles Evans Hughes and the Supreme Court* [New York: Columbia University Press, 1951,] p. 279.)

Irving Brant insists that the Chief Justice wished, above all, to be known as a "liberal," and his prerogative in assigning opinions, in speaking for the Court himself whenever he was with the majority, or passing the task along to one of his

pro-New Deal decisions was, as someone has suggested, the psychological price of Hughes' and Roberts' conversion. "A synthetic halo," a lifetime student of the Court commented June 2, 1937, "is being fitted upon the head of one of the most politically calculating of men."

Others shared these feelings. "Hughes and Roberts," Irving Brant wrote, "bend with the *hurricane* of public opinion, but *in lesser* winds stand with the reactionary four." Their build-up as liberals continued as they read opinion after opinion overturning their own work, while Stone, Brandeis, and Cardozo were virtually ignored. "The three liberals," he noted, "are not being allowed to speak for the Court because the two liberals-by-compulsion fear what they might say, or begrudge them credit for their consistent stand."[85]

In the parade of cases, exhibiting the Constitution reinvigorated, Stone delivered the opinion in only one major case. He made the most of his opportunity. In upholding Alabama's unemployment compensation tax, he said: "There is no warrant in the Constitution for setting the tax aside because a court thinks that it could have drawn a better statute or could have distributed the burden more wisely. Those are functions reserved for the legislature." "A tax," Stone observed, "is not an assessment of benefits. It is . . . a means of distributing the burden of the cost of government. The only benefit to which the taxpayer is constitutionally entitled is that derived from his enjoyment of the privileges of living in an organized society, established and safeguarded by the devotion of taxes to public purposes."*

---

associates, made this quite easy. In a perceptive article Brant tells how this self-portrait was executed. (See Irving Brant, "How Liberal Is Justice Hughes," *The New Republic,* July 21 and July 28, 1937.)

Brant got support for this interpretation from Justice Stone. In a letter of August 2, 1952, to A.T.M., Brant wrote: "While I was engaged in the research for those articles, in June of that year, Stone passed through St. Louis and stopped at the house of Luther Ely Smith, who invited a few people in to see him. I told Stone that I was making a study of Hughes' record and methods but said nothing about the intended use of it. He then told of the Chief Justice's system of assigning the writing of the Court's opinions to other judges when he was a member of a conservative majority and knew there would be a dissent. Stone said: 'He has never given me a chance to tear him to pieces.'" Stone told Brant that "Hughes often took the lead in conference on the reactionary side, and then voted with the liberals if they had a majority without him." "In quantity," Brant commented, "not much came from Stone, and he had nothing to do with the inception of the articles. But his remark about Hughes' assignment of opinions was the key to the whole enigma."

* Explaining his approach to Noel T. Dowling, May 28, 1937, the Justice wrote: "One of the important puzzles [in the Alabama Unemployment Compensation case] was whether to treat it as a regulation and pursue lines followed in the Employers Liability Cases [223 U.S. 1 (1912)] or to treat it as a tax. After going over the whole ground, it seemed to me there was a good opportunity to treat the whole problem purely as one of taxation, and in that connection develop some tax ideas a little further than they had been carried. A somewhat novel question was that of the relationship of burdens of the taxpayer to the benefits of the expenditure

Nor had Alabama unconstitutionally abdicated power to the national government. On the contrary, Stone drew an impressive picture of the possibilities of national and state cooperation in the expanding field of social insurance: "The United States and the State of Alabama are not alien governments. They coexist within the same territory. Unemployment within it is their common concern. Together the two statutes now before us embody a cooperative legislative effort by state and national governments, for carrying out a public purpose common to both, which neither could fully achieve without the cooperation of the other. The Constitution does not prohibit such cooperation."[86]

The New Deal's judicial field day wound up with Justice Cardozo's opinions upholding the social security taxes and the old age pension system.[87] These decisions threw into the shade, but did not expressly overrule, the AAA and Railroaders' Retirement cases. Nor had the Chief Justice's Jones & Laughlin opinion explicitly undermined the Schechter and Guffey Coal precedents. Though these reactionary pronouncements lay lifeless in the books, their ghosts still walked.

All these pro-New Deal decisions struck at the very heart of F.D.R.'s Court-packing plan. Yet the fight straggled on. On May 18, 1937, the day the Judiciary Committee was to vote on the President's bill, F.D.R.'s case was further undermined by Justice Van Devanter's announcement that he would retire June 1. One close observer suggested that "it was so perfectly timed as a strategic move that it seems unlikely to have been accidental."[88] Senator Borah, among others, had impressed upon Van Devanter "the great service he could render the cause by stepping down."[89] Those close to the White House said that the Van Devanter resignation "had been engineered by Chief Justice Hughes, Senator Wheeler, and Van Devanter, with Justice Brandeis helping."[90] Brandeis was also under pressure from the administration to quit. Stone was not privy to these maneuvers. "I did not know of it [Van Devanter's retirement] until the announcement, but it did not take me entirely by surprise."[91]

The Justice's resignation evoked in Stone mixed feeling. He remembered this die-hard's helpful advice when he first came to the bench. "But I always felt," he wrote his children some years later, "that he conceived it his duty to declare unconstitutional any law he particu-

---

of proceeds of the tax. I found little on this until I happened to remember that I had dealt with it a couple of times in *Nashville, Chattanooga & St. Louis Ry.* v. *Wallace* [288 U.S. 249 (1933)] and *Carley & Hamilton* v. *Snook"* [281 U.S. 66 (1930)].

"The constitutional power to levy taxes," Stone had held in the Wallace case (p. 268), "does not depend upon the enjoyment by the taxpayer of any special benefit from the use of funds raised by taxation." In the Carley case (p. 72), Stone could find "nothing in the Federal Constitution" to require a state to apply vehicle registration fees so as to benefit those who paid them.

larly disliked, which to my mind is a fatal way of interpreting an instrument of government which must envisage the possibility of difference of opinion about social and governmental questions."[92] Nor was Stone certain that F.D.R. could be relied on to make a wise choice of a successor. "I am fearful," he wrote Felix Frankfurter, May 28, 1937. "I have not much faith in appointing men because it is thought they will vote in a particular way. All that I would ask is that the appointee

*"Spring Practice"; Hungerford in the Pittsburgh* Post Gazette, *April 1, 1937*

have integrity, intelligence, and sound legal knowledge, and that he have some appreciation of the world in which we live." "How I wish," he added in pencil as an afterthought, "it would be you!"

All hope for the ill-fated plan faded in midsummer when, at the height of the battle, Senator Joseph T. Robinson, F.D.R.'s floor leader, collapsed in the Senate. For years Stone had been "dreading Robinson's appointment more than anything else that might happen."[93] As the Arkansas Senator's death released the President from pressure to appoint a Southern conservative to the Van Devanter vacancy,* the need for drastic reform became less urgent.

Whether moved by the 1936 election, the CIO "sit-down" strikes, by fear of the President's attack, or by new insight into their own functions, the Court by rapid strides brought the Constitution up to date. F.D.R.'s major premise, that the judicial function in the constitutional field is essentially political, was thus confirmed by the Justices themselves. The President, with strangely ironical results, had his way. This "clear-cut victory on the bench," the President believed, "did more than anything else to bring about the defeat of the plan in the halls of Congress." The "great solvent, Time," had, as Stone predicted, done its work. It may be doubted, however, that time alone was the crucial factor. "It would be a little naïve," F.D.R. wrote later on, "to refuse to recognize some connection between these 1937 decisions and the Supreme Court fight."[94] One surveying the entire battle may find it difficult to conclude (despite Chief Justice Hughes' words to the contrary) that these reversals and new interpretations were unrelated to the President's bold determination to reorganize the judiciary.† A gen-

---

* In 1932 it had even been rumored that President Hoover, in deference to political considerations, would appoint Robinson to the seat vacated by Holmes! (Robert L. Hale to H.F.S., February 13, 1932.)

† In an effort to prevent repetition of the 1937 Court fight, and to remove the Court permanently from the political arena, Senator Butler of Maryland in 1953 introduced a joint resolution proposing a constitutional amendment fixing the composition and jurisdiction of the Supreme Court. On May 11, 1954, after a desultory debate in which only a handful of Senators participated, the Senate approved the proposed amendment by a vote of 58 to 19, deleting only the provision concerning the ineligibility of Justices to become President or Vice-President. Approval by two-thirds of the House of Representatives and three-fourths of the state legislatures is necessary before the amendment becomes effective.

The Butler amendment seems to rest on three assumptions: (a) Supreme Court Justices can do no wrong, cannot abuse their power. Many dissenting opinions, the most notable being Stone's AAA dissent, refute this view. (b) The Court has not been in politics, except as drawn in by the political organs of government. (c) The proposed amendment, by increasing their independence, would keep the Justices out of politics. There is little in American history to bolster any of these assumptions. In the past, moreover, as during the administrations of Jefferson, Jackson, Lincoln, and the two Roosevelts, when judges, ignoring their professed "self-restraint," interposed the judicial arm to impede democratic solution of vital issues of the day, the power of Congress to determine the size of the court and control its appellate jurisdiction, has proved to be a useful gun behind the door.

eration earlier, Theodore Roosevelt said: "I may not know much law, but I do know that one can put the fear of God in judges."[95]

By the spring of 1937 Hughes and Roberts had learned the lesson Holmes, Brandeis, and Stone had long been trying to teach—that the majority's recalcitrance imperiled the very things these lions of the law thought they were safeguarding.

The truth Stone had voiced in 1936 was vindicated. Judges could recast their habits of mind. Without change in personnel, the Court saw fit to let the Constitution function as a workable charter of government. But would the recent gains hold? As the term ended, Stone was not sure: "Let us hope that when we get back to work next fall, the Court question will have subsided, and that the reformation that seems to have been accomplished proves to be a permanent one."[96]

## PART FIVE

# *Consolidating Victory*

## CHAPTER TWENTY-NINE

# Old Wine in New Bottles

## 1937-1938

When the Court reconvened in the fall of 1937 Stone was dismayed to find that the bench was just as much a bone of contention as when the Justices had adjourned in June. "We need a season of peace and quiet," he said again in October. But this was not to be.

The spotlight now turned on F.D.R.'s first judicial appointee, zealous New Deal Senator Hugo L. Black. The new Justice joined the Court on October 5, 1937, with the flames of debate licking at the fringes of his robe. As the term opened the first order of business was to consider politically inspired attacks upon his right to sit. The Court curtly repulsed these in a *per curiam* opinion,[1] but no one could doubt that the Justice's performance would be closely watched.

Though the 1937 revolution had eliminated the judge-made constitutional obstacles that previously prevented the law from moving forward along lines Stone had espoused, the Court's load had not been lightened. Between headline-catching cases, the same run-of-mill issues had to be ground out. From the outset of the term Stone found himself in a "jam of work" as the burden shifted increasingly to the younger judges. Justice Cardozo was now too ill to carry on; McReynolds had passed his seventy-sixth birthday "going strong," Stone reported, in response to talk about the testy Justice's retirement. Hughes and Butler remained at their posts, though they, along with Brandeis, must have flagged in trying to maintain the Court's swift pace. Fear that the "Nine Old Men" might founder despite the Chief Justice's boast of efficiency plagued Stone through the 1937 term. Even his congratulatory note to the New Deal Justice, though cordial enough, conveyed an undercurrent of concern, a hint to Black as to how he might best contribute to the Court's work: "Greetings and good wishes on your ascending the Areopagus. The life has some dull moments but it has its compensations. Despite all the criticisms that have been leveled against it, the Court is a great tribunal doing its work with extraordinary thoroughness and fidelity and the preservation of most of its traditions is worthy of our best efforts. If at any time I can be of any assistance to you in the process of your getting into the new work, do not hesitate to call on me." "Since that day more than twelve years ago, when I met you as Attorney General," Black replied graciously, "you have had no warmer admirer than your Alabama Assistant to the Attorney General. It will be a most happy experience to serve with you on the Court. Your letter added much to the joy of my appointment and confirmation, and I shall seek your counsel before the Court convenes."[2]

Stone's plea to the new Justice on the score of tradition was unavailing. Black had hardly settled in his chair before he struck out furiously in a long dissent to a *per curiam* decision, blasting the "reproduction cost" theory of rate-making valuation, and chiding his more seasoned brethren for returning to the District Court a rate case begun in 1931 solely because cost data used in the lower tribunal's ruling were obsolete.[3] Stone himself, with little enthusiasm for the *per curiam*, pointed out how "logical application of what we say might lead to a situation where a rate case could never be ended because of the necessity of finding reproduction value at the precise moment when the decree was entered."[4] On reading Black's unprecedented dissent, however, he saw he had more to worry about. "I am a good deal troubled," he wrote Hughes, "by the dissenting opinion which Justice Black has just circulated in the Indianapolis Water Company case. He states a good deal which counsel did not take the trouble to present. If true, it requires either a different result or, to say the least, a radical change in the presentation of the matter in the Court's opinion. I see in Justice Black's dissent the handiwork of someone other than the nominal author,* and I think if the opinions should go out in their present form that important consequences may result. In view of his criticisms, I should like to have the case reargued or, if not, then I should like to have it to go over so that I could make a more adequate study of the whole case."[5]

Justices of long service, recalling but one instance of a dissent to a *per curiam*,† were amazed at their junior colleague's brashness. Stone, in particular, feared that Black's slashing method of disposing of matters in any way he thought desirable would again focus critical public gaze on the Court. Despite Stone's plea, the Chief Justice's inexorable timetable did not afford time to reconsider the case. The decision came down January 3, 1938.

Back in 1928, amid his grimmest battles with Sutherland's formalism, Stone could say confidently with reference to the Fourteenth Amend-

---

* One can only wager a guess as to whom Stone had in mind. "Some astonished persons, admitting the strength of his [Black's] opinions," Charlotte Williams observed, "suggested that perhaps he did not write them, and Washington rumor pointed to New Dealer Thomas Corcoran as the 'ghost.'" (Charlotte Williams, *Hugo L. Black*, pp. 82-83.)

† Since 1938 the practice of entering extended dissents to *per curiams* has become quite common. See *Keenan* v. *Burke,* 342 U.S. 888 (1951), and *New York* v. *United States,* 326 U.S. 572 (1946).

ment that "there is general agreement that arbitrary and unreasonable legislation is forbidden." He still held this belief, but did his brother Black? The new Justice dissented from a decision invalidating California's tax on out-of-state reinsurance premiums—a case Stone regarded as plainly calling for exercise of nullifying judicial power because these transactions were wholly foreign to that state. Stone might have overlooked mere differences of opinion on the validity of state legislation, but when the former New Deal Senator entered the tradition-encrusted field of constitutional exegesis, it seemed as if generations of judicial interpretation had gone for naught. Citing Stone, Brandeis, and Cardozo as authority for periodic re-examination of constitutional precedents, the dissenter called for reconsideration of a long line of decisions blanketing corporations into the inclusive protection given "persons" by the Fourteenth Amendment.[6]

Black's revolutionary dissents "really startled" Stone. As he saw it, the rules of the game as well as tradition demanded that such radical change be approached "gradually and by intimation." A polemic, however vigorous, was not enough to change the course of fifty years. Such procedure might, in the end, involve the Court in very serious difficulties. Stone and others had been put to very great trouble in extricating the Court from the position to which extreme interpretations of the Fourteenth Amendment had carried it. Justice Black's novel use of this and other Amendments would create a new impasse. Black was a potentially powerful and resourceful ally, but he should, Stone thought, keep his views within the bounds of accepted judicial technique. With help from someone steeped in the mores of judging, Black might, however, serve his cause as well on the Court as he had served it in the Senate.[7]

"Do you know Black well?" Stone asked Frankfurter, February 8, 1938. "You might be able to render him great assistance. He needs guidance from someone who is more familiar with the workings of the judicial process than he is. With guidance, and a disposition to follow it until he is a little·surer of himself, he might do great things. I am fearful though that he will not avoid the danger of frittering away his opportunity for judicial effectiveness by lack of good technique, and by the desire to express ideas which, however valuable they may be in themselves, are irrelevant or untimely. There are enough present-day battles of importance to be won without wasting our efforts to remake the Constitution *ab initio,* or using the judicial opinion as a political tract."*

* The "great assistance" Stone thought Frankfurter might render Black took the form of a long memorandum. "Writing in the same spirit and for the same academic purpose as I would were I writing a piece as a professor in the *Harvard Law Review,*" Frankfurter pointed out: Judges "cannot escape the responsibility of filling in gaps which the finitude of even the most imaginative legislation renders

Bloody but unbowed, Black silently withheld approval of Stone's notable opinion in the Carolene Products case, which included the now famous footnote adumbrating the Court's function in scrutinizing statutes curbing personal and political freedoms.* A month later, when Stone laid another studiously fashioned brick on the foundation he had been patiently rearing since 1926, looking to the opportune and appropriate moment when *Collector* v. *Day* could be eased painlessly out of the law, the Court's New Dealer again struck out for himself, boldly insisting that this venerable landmark be leveled on the authority of the Sixteenth Amendment.[8] In short, before Black was halfway through his first term he had committed, in Stone's eyes, two major sins—flagrant disregard of customary procedures and undue emphasis on the political aspects of the judicial process. After less than eight months on the bench, the first New Deal Justice had rolled up eight solo dissents, the highest total of the term.†

Throughout F.D.R.'s battle to pack the Court Stone had been certain that a constitutional amendment compelling retirement of federal judges "would solve all our problems." Black's shenanagins now turned his attention to the qualifications of the judges soon to be appointed. This must have been on his mind when a discerning student of constitutional interpretation, querying the minority rule implicit in judicial review itself, suggested a much more drastic remedy for Court troubles.[9]

"I quite agree," he wrote Max Lerner, "that all restraints on govern-

---

inevitable. And so it is that even in the countries governed exclusively by codes and even in the best of all codes there are provisions saying in effect that when a controversy arises in court for which the code offers no provision the judges are not relieved of the duty of deciding the case but must themselves fashion the law appropriate to the situation.

"So the problem is not whether the judges make the law, but when and how and how much. Holmes put it in his highbrow way, that 'they can do so only interstitially; they are confined from molar to molecular motions.' I used to say to my students that legislatures make law wholesale, judges retail. In other words they cannot decide things by invoking a new major premise out of whole cloth; they must make the law that they do make out of the existing materials and with due deference to the presuppositions of the legal system of which they have been made a part. Of course I know these are not mechanical devices, and therefore not susceptible of producing automatic results. But they sufficiently indicate the limits within which judges are to move. . . .

"I think one of the evil features, a very evil one, about all this assumption that judges only find the law and don't make it, often becomes the evil of a lack of candor. By covering up the lawmaking function of judges, we miseducate the people and fail to bring out into the open the real responsibility of judges for what they do, leaving it to the primary lawmaking agency, the legislature, to correct what judges do if they don't like it, or to give them more specific directions than what they so often do by what is put on the statute books."

* See Chapter XXXI.

† Justice Butler also wrote eight dissents, while the other members wrote the remaining nine recorded during the term.

ment are, in a negative sense, a form of 'minority rule,' in that they prevent or check majority action. Paradoxical as this may seem, it nevertheless finds its exemplification in the Constitution, and has some force even without the aid of judicial review. What else is the veto power or the electoral college, or the reserve powers of the states, if they are given any particular efficacy in the affairs of government? Whether these restraints are desirable, and if so how their boundaries should be marked, are questions about which opinions may differ. . . . The present-day problem of government is how to make the mechanism function adequately." "The truth of the business is," the Justice concluded, "that the particular system is not as important as the people who work it. If our judges were selected with the same care and with the same reference to the particular type of function they perform, as in the case of the English judges, I believe the problem of judicial review would not give us very serious concern."[10]

His correspondent was not convinced that "the problem of judicial review comes down to a question of the careful selection of judges." He agreed that "if we had judges like Holmes and Brandeis and Cardozo and yourself, we should have no problem of judicial review." But the very mention of those names gave some measure of the difficulty. "A system is not satisfactory if only an extremely unusual personnel can make it work well," Lerner retorted. Stone did not capitulate but he seemed disinclined to continue the discussion: "Of course I am not so naïve as to suppose that all the difficulties of judicial review can be solved by a cautious and careful selection of judges. Nevertheless, the system could be immensely improved and I would like to see it tried."[11]

Stone favored promotion of judges from lower federal courts or state supreme courts, men with training in the juridical craft.* "Those who so lightly suggest that legal knowledge and experience are of little importance to a judge," he wrote, "must be ignorant of the vast amount of litigation which comes to our Court which cannot be solved by recourse to a 'social point of view' or by any means other than the use of skill born of knowledge and experience."[12] The Justice, along with other eminent lawyers, mistrusted the President; they were convinced that he tended to concentrate unduly on the political aspects of judging, ignoring craftsmanship.[13] Stone even suspected that F.D.R. "ap-

* Black soon confirmed Stone's misgivings. In reply to a draft memorandum on *Adam* v. *Saenger*, 303 U.S. 59 (1938), submitted by Black, he pointed out certain technical pitfalls. "There are . . . difficulties with writing the case in the way you have," he wrote Black, Jan. 26, 1938. "It is usually inadvisable to write a case reversing a state court on points involving state law which were not considered or decided by the court below. . . . It is much safer to review the federal questions decided below, leaving it to the state court, after the case goes back, to apply the Texas law. If the Texas court commits mayhem, the case can be brought to us again. But if we deal with points of Texas law, the Texas court can say that we went completely off the reservation. . . ."

pointed Black in a fit of pique."[14] Such distrust was momentarily allayed when on Justice Sutherland's retirement in January 1938 the President promoted his Solicitor General, the sober, steady Stanley Reed. "I am quite happy about Reed's appointment," Stone wrote. "He is honest, straightforward, and a hard worker, and I think a good lawyer. The Court ought to get many years of good service from him when he settles into the new job. Meanwhile, work is piling up and I am under the painful necessity of doing my work in a hurry."[15] Stone mixed nostalgia with doubt in the note he sent Frankfurter on Justice Sutherland's retirement. "Will [Thomas Reed] Powell now bind all Sutherland's opinions into a separate volume of interesting historical material now obsolete?"[16] he wondered.

In the fall of 1937 the Justice began taking early morning walks with Marquis Childs, correspondent of the *St. Louis Post-Dispatch*. As they strolled, Stone spoke freely of his concern for the Court as an institution. Drawing illustrations from decisions coming down currently, Stone cited Black as an example of the sort of judge F.D.R. might continue to appoint. The walks continued morning after morning, and on January 22, 1938, the results of the newspaperman's gleanings were published.

"The *Post-Dispatch* has been privileged," Childs' article began, "to gain an inside view of the Court and of the concern for its future of the members who feel keenly the importance of its integrity and continuity. Their concern at this time is over the kind of appointments that are to be made in the Court. . . . A new man on the bench who has had no judicial experience and only a comparatively limited legal experience is not a help to his colleagues in the first two or three years."

The prospect was frightening. F.D.R., ironically enough, now had it in his power to bring about the very fault—a crowded docket—for which he had unjustly censured the "old men" in his famous message of February 1937. "Court-packing based on political partisanship," the article argued, "is no enduring cure for the old evil of deciding cases according to economic predilection." For this there are two possible remedies: abolish the Court entirely; or acknowledge the fallibility of human institutions and, in the proper time and in the proper way, fill judicial vacancies with men of highest capacity. In Childs' column, Stone's anti-Court packing theme song rang out strong and clear: "It is necessary to have some patience in dealing with human institutions. If the old majority on the Court was 'wrong,' it was certainly no remedy to appoint a new majority that would be 'right.' It is not enough to vote 'right'; one must be sufficiently skilled in the law to state convincing reason why one is 'right' or the opinion will have no weight."

"Fine," Stone commented on reading the article, "just what is needed to educate the public. But why," he asked, "don't you publish something of the sort in a magazine having national circulation?" Childs had that very thing in mind but knew that the article would be far more acceptable if he could cite an authoritative source for his information. Of course Stone could not fill that need. "I suppose," the Justice suggested, "you can find a formula."[17] The upshot was publication, in May 1938, of the article, "The Supreme Court Today" in *Harper's*. Here the author spoke in behalf of "those Justices who are just now gravely concerned for the future of the institution of which they are a part." Pulling no punches, Childs told of the Alabaman's "lack of legal knowledge and experience, deficiencies in background and training" that led him "into blunders which have shocked his colleagues." To make matters worse, Black was "unable to carry his share" of the Court's work, and "several opinions he has written have been rephrased by other members of the Court and . . . subsequently released with something less than satisfaction." As in the newspaper version, the central theme stressed the continuing value of judicial self-restraint.

"Of course the Court must pass on large constitutional issues from time to time," the author reasoned. "But it is the contention of those who are most concerned with keeping the judiciary within its proper function that this should be done with great caution and extreme reluctance. Whenever it is possible to avoid passing upon the constitutionality of a law the Court should avoid it. For the longer the law is seen in relation to the whole legal structure and fabric of society, the easier will be the task of the Court when finally it is necessary to decide the basic issue." "It is just here," Childs concluded, "that Justice Black has most distressed certain of his colleagues on the bench. It is as though, a comparatively inexperienced player, he had stepped into a fast game, say tennis or pelota, and, ignoring the rules, made vigorous passes at every ball with a piece of board."

Before 1937 laws were declared unconstitutional when there had been no call on the Court to do more than interpret a minor point of law or procedure. It was this habit, Childs pointed out, "that first gave rise to the hostilities between the Court and the President." Could anyone believe that the author of the AAA dissent would approve similar behavior in judges taking their cues from the White House? If it was wrong for a majority opposed to the New Deal to translate their "economic predilections" into law, why was it not "equally wrong for other men to vote another set of 'economic predilections?'" "Repeatedly in his dissents," Childs reminded the reader, "Justice Stone rebuked the majority for over-stepping their function as judges." It would be a great mistake for the President or anyone else to assume that Stone could or would welcome a colleague who "voted right." He had always shunned political tags, as inapplicable to a judge. He especially deplored that Holy Grail of politics, "liberal."

One could hardly have anticipated the explosive force of Childs' article. When Justice Stone's private ruminations were translated into popular language, hypersensitive New Dealers even suspected the Justice of a "deliberate effort to inspire a new attack on Justice Hugo Black."[18] Furthermore, Childs' criticisms were so pointed and so well informed as to make it virtually certain that he had an "inside" informant. Speculation on the identity of the loquacious insider soon became rife. Hughes' quotable remarks on "judicial temperament" at the annual Law Institute dinner were promptly linked to the *Harper's* blast at Black, but this hypothesis was authoritatively squelched.[19] Snoopers finally discovered that the newsman had been accompanying Justice Stone on his daily walks.

One day, soon after the article appeared, Childs got a frantic phone call from Justice Stone's secretary, Miss Gertrude Jenkins. "I am calling from a pay station. Reporters are hounding me. What shall I say?"

"Deny everything," Childs said.

"I always told the Judge he talked too much," Miss Jenkins lamented, hanging up the receiver.

She then told newsmen: "The Justice will not comment on the reports that he is one of the sources for material used in the magazine article referred to. You may say as coming from his office that he was not the source of the material in the article and that any statement that he was is unwarranted." Childs also insisted that "Justice Stone is not a source of material which appeared in the article. . . . My information came indirectly from persons close to the Supreme Court but not from any Justice."[20] "But all Washington newspaperdom," *Newsweek* reported, "knew that, in private, Childs had named Stone as his source."[21]

After issuing the denial, Stone gave weight to popular suspicion by abruptly terminating his strolls with the harassed author. "Childs and Stone are acquainted," one reporter commented. "The Justice is somewhat expansive, and it is no secret that he has been deeply concerned over institutional problems which the Court has faced. He may have expressed to Childs concern over the possibility that Justice Black would expend his energy on objectives which could not be attained instead of on those which could." This, he wrote in partial mitigation, is a "far cry from imputing to Black a lack of 'legal craftsmanship.' "[22] Yet even scholars have taken the article as an out and out attack on Black's judicial competence.[23] This derogatory charge, not Stone's sober concern for judicial self-restraint, received the most public attention, provoking a minor tempest in the press. Black's critics had nursed rather than forgotten their grievance, and scores of newspapers reprinted Childs' statements impugning the Justice's competence.

"Justice Black has had legal training enough," his adherents retorted indignantly. "What he needs is a course in hallowed platitudes."[24] Black's worst sin, Walton Hamilton commented, was that "he regards the sacred cows as ordinary heifers; finds it impossible to accept verbal symbols as realities; refuses to metamorphose the actual question to be resolved into an esoteric issue at law; and fails to appreciate the pomp and circumstance of circumlocution by which the processes of justice are kept decorous. And the Supreme Court, like any other savage tribe, demands of its members a reasonable conformity to its folkways."[25]

Black did not, however, escape the fires of controversy unscathed. Even his supporters were inclined to accept Max Lerner's appraisal: "Black has become a judicial crusader before he has come to maturity as a judge."[26] It was doubted, moreover, whether Black's small stint of fifteen Court opinions* was "a full term's work for an able-bodied Justice." Blaming Hughes for the paucity and scant interest of Black's assignments, Hamilton explained: "Accordingly his [Black's] talents have found their readiest outlet in dissent." "I think you can well take satisfaction in the Walton Hamilton article," Stone wrote Black, June 8, 1938, "although probably it is a good rule for us on the Court to discount about 50 per cent or more of everything that is said about us, good and bad. Even if the discount is too great, it helps keep our feet on the ground and our eye on the ball."

Amid this angry backwash of controversy, this unseemly probing into responsibility for published charges against a colleague, no one could have been more surprised and discomfited than Stone himself. He had intended no personal attack, but he did hold in highest regard the common law and its procedures. In his Harvard Tercentenary address, he had pointed out, as we have seen, that "its method of marking out, as cases arise, step by step, the line between the permitted and the forbidden, by the process of appraisal and comparison of the experiences of the past and of the present, . . . is as applicable to the field of public law as of private."[27] Black's bravura challenges to entrenched precedents, his cavalier disregard of judicial tradition, were mistakes, errors a trained jurist such as Cardozo would not make. Stone apparently did not realize that few other people would be able to appraise his anxiety as anything other than a naked charge of incompetence.†

* During the 1937 term Stone and Black each wrote 26 opinions. The difference is, however, that 23 of Stone's were for the Court, while Black turned out only 15 Court opinions, writing for himself alone in the 11 others.

† "What he [Stone] said," Irving Brant wrote Black, May 10, 1938, "did not remotely support the statements made by Mr. Childs. He said he was concerned over the possibility that you would expend your energies on objectives which could not be attained, instead of concentrating on those that could be. Not the slightest question was raised as to your knowledge or ability. The Childs article, I presume,

"Stone had no such intention," Marquis Childs wrote in a considered appraisal some years later.[28] Rather he wanted to draw public attention to a new danger, to still another deviation from the tried and sure path of judicial self-restraint, by simply asking which judge, the spectacular, irrepressible Black, or the patient, hard-working Reed, represented the type F.D.R. would elevate, as Brandeis, Hughes, Butler, McReynolds, and Cardozo departed. So engrossed was he in this uncertain prospect, and so genuine was his friendly attitude toward Black himself, it did not occur to him that by personifying the evil he might be considered guilty of a foul blow.

Whatever the message Stone tried to convey, it evaporated completely in the shocked reaction to his alleged breach of judicial etiquette. "Honor among judges dictates that they must not talk about one another to outsiders," the *Nation* declared gravely, adding that Childs' accusation, true or not, had "not made matters any easier for the Justices themselves."[29] "It should have been fairly clear," another commentator for the same journal wrote, "that an article purporting to reveal 'the inner workings of the Court,' and purporting to represent Justices as lamenting professional unfitness on the part of another Justice, would be calculated to recoil."[30]

Having recently exposed the Four Horsemen's enthronement of their "personal economic predilection" as equivalent to the Constitution, Stone could have little patience with this same approach in the case of Black. On the other hand, constitutional reconstruction was far from complete, even in Stone's more restricted view of what needed to be done. If possible he wanted Black as a comrade in arms, and in that role wanted him as effective as possible. Black put Stone in the awkward position of defending precedents at which he had been whittling away for years with a view to their ultimate demise. Originally forced on him by the Old Guard, this method had now become endemic, an unchanging essential of the judicial process, linked by him to judicial self-restraint. Somewhat like a general who thinks the next war will resemble the last and plans accordingly, Stone thought Black should shape his technique to fit the judicial war of attrition he had fought. Black, of course, refused to do this, and so in the main did the other new judges who came on the bench during Roosevelt's second term.

Amid Black's gyrations, the Justices "put down the most important opinion since I have been on the Court." It was not, however, a case likely to attract public attention. "The *New York Times*," Stone ex-

is a composite of information given him from various sources and his own deductions, but I can assure you that if it is based in any part on statements made by Justice Stone, he has completely twisted their implications." "I can assure you," Black replied calmly, May 20, "that I am not disturbed in the slightest by the matter to which you referred."

plained, "did not even mention it," since it dealt with fairly uninteresting procedural, rather than substantive issues.* Replying to Stone's gentle prod, Arthur Krock commented apologetically: "If the Supreme Court, like so many other arms of the government, had a publicity agent, eight days would not have passed before the importance of its decision in the Tompkins case became known. . . ."[31]

In this notable decision Stone's own reluctant vote helped to deal "sudden death" to the doctrine of *Swift* v. *Tyson*, a precedent adhered to consistently in federal courts since 1842. In that case Justice Story ruled on the meaning of Section 34 of the 1789 Judiciary Act directing federal judges to apply "the laws of the several states" to cases coming before them which involved suits between citizens of different states. National tribunals, Story ruled in construing the Act, were obliged only to follow local statutes, being free in disputes involving the unwritten law to base decisions on their own independent judgment as to the principles of general law. "It never has been supposed by us," he declared, "that the section did apply, or was designed to apply, to questions of a more general nature . . . where the state tribunals are called upon to perform the like functions as ourselves, that is, to ascertain upon general reasoning and legal analogies, what is the true exposition of the contract or instrument, or what is the just rule furnished by the principles of commercial law to govern the case."[32] Story believed this approach would make for uniformity, that states would defer to federal judges in evolving a consistent commercial code. While federal courts embraced Story's plan without reservation, states persisted in local peculiarities in their own courts. The result was separate versions of unwritten law as between state and federal court in the same area, often involving rights of action and claims. Litigants were thus confronted with two systems of "common law." Serious injustice was often suffered as a decision one way or the other depended upon whether a state or a federal court had jurisdiction.†

---

* "Stone was astonished that the bar and the public at large did not immediately understand the great significance of the Tompkins case. The case received practically no publicity until after Stone . . . pointed out the effect of the case." (Louis Lusky to A.T.M., Sept. 12, 1952.)

† Story had apparently misinterpreted congressional intent. Charles Warren's extensive examination of the legislative history of Section 34 of the Federal Judiciary Act of 1789 led him to conclude: "The chief and only real reason for [the enactment of Section 34] . . . was to afford a tribunal in which a foreigner or citizen of another state might have the law administered free from the local prejudices or passions which might prevail in a state court against foreigners or non-citizens. The federal court was to secure to a non-citizen the application of the same law which a state court would give to its own citizens, and to see that within a state there should be no discrimination against non-citizens in the application of justice. There is not a trace of any other purpose than the above to be found in any of the arguments made in 1787-1789 as to this jurisdiction. The idea that a federal court in a state was to administer any other than the law of that

Until 1938, despite vigorous protests from Holmes and Brandeis, *Swift* v. *Tyson* remained undisturbed. Story's decision stood as the sturdy trunk of a tree having all the force and vigor of ruling law. Nor had Stone been able, as in certain other areas, to set ideas to work like termites hollowing out its core. Brandeis's long-awaited chance to destroy this intolerable invasion of state independence arose out of a freak accident to Harry Tompkins, who was struck by the door of a passing freight car while walking alongside the Erie Railroad tracks in Pennsylvania. A jury, instructed in "general" law by a New York federal judge, awarded him $30,000. The railroad contended that Pennsylvania law did not permit a trespasser to recover such damages. Apparently Tompkins' suit reached the Justices "just when the Court was ready to blow a doctrine that never should have been into kingdom come."[33] "If we wish to overrule *Swift v. Tyson*," Chief Justice Hughes announced as he laid the case before the conference, "here is our opportunity."[34]

Only Butler and McReynolds demurred, so Hughes put Brandeis, leading opponent of the old rule, to writing an opinion. In due course a draft circulated, choking off *Swift* v. *Tyson* root and branch by denying the constitutionality of its construction of Section 34 on the ground that Congress lacked authority to permit federal courts to ignore state rules in diversity cases.* Stone quickly approved the veteran's work, but, "upon reflection," informed him: "One part of your opinion in *Erie Railroad* v. *Tompkins* gives me some concern. You say in effect that there is no constitutional power in Congress to require federal courts to apply rules of law inconsistent with those in force in the state, unless Congress is acting under one of the substantive powers granted to the national government. This may be so, but I hesitate to say it, partly because it is unnecessary to do so, and the matter is not, in my mind, entirely free from doubt—the power may be implicit in the judicial sections. And I am also apprehensive of a doctrine which

---

state or were to discriminate in *favor of a non-citizen* and *against a citizen,* or to administer law as an entirely free and independent tribunal, never appears to have entered the mind of any one." (*Harvard Law Review,* Nov. 1923, p. 83.)

\* It is sometimes claimed for Justice Black that his dissent in *New York Life Insurance Co.* v. *Gamer,* 303 U.S. 161 (1938), anticipated and pointed the way to the majority's decisions in *Erie Railroad* v. *Tompkins.* The truth is that the whole question of the law applicable to diversity cases was much in the air during January and February 1938. The Gamer case was argued January 13 and decided February 14. The Tompkins case was argued January 31, but no decision came down until April 25. By the time Black had written and circulated his Gamer dissent, however, a conference decision had already been reached in the Tompkins case. Stone wrote Black, Feb. 11, 1938, that he could not agree with the Gamer dissent because Black had not stated Montana law as it was. He agreed that Montana courts might adopt Black's view but said, "I understand that the basis of our decision in the Pennsylvania railroad accident case is that we follow local law when it is well enough defined so that we know what it is."

would require this Court constantly, without any aid from Congress, to draw the line between the rules of law applied by the federal courts which are substantive and those which are procedural." "Could you not," he asked Brandeis, "eliminate the paragraph or rephrase it so that we would not be taken as deciding the point in advance?"[35]

Troubled by similar doubts, Justice Reed entered a concurrence: "To decide the case now before us and to 'disapprove' the doctrine of *Swift* v. *Tyson* requires only that we say that the words 'the laws' include in their meaning the decisions of the local tribunals."[36] Stone could not accept this solution. In his mind it was equally important to avoid breaking another of his judicial tenets—that of adhering to *statutory construction*. Unless there were grave errors of constitutional significance in the accepted interpretation, he would not upset a rule accepted by Congress for ninety-six years. These two principles, avoidance of unnecessary constitutional issues and adherence to time-honored statutory construction, each in itself a vaunted signpost on the road of self-restraint, stood in the way of the solutions offered.

Stone was vexed. *Swift* v. *Tyson* had been an "erroneous" decision. It had, however, governed the federal courts for almost a century. It had to be obviated, yet neither of the solutions presented (i.e., the theory of "misinterpretation" by the former court, and the invalidity of the action by Congress) was satisfactory. Was there another approach?

Reed's opinion made it highly desirable to find a constitutional peg for the majority's decision. "In view of the long history of our support of *Swift* v. *Tyson*," Stone wrote Brandeis after comparing the two opinions, "I realize the force of the constitutional aspects of the case as an impelling reason for overruling *Swift* v. *Tyson* and the long line of cases which have followed it. Nevertheless, I think it is important that we should not discuss the constitutional question unless we definitely conclude that without it we would not overrule the precedents of one hundred years. I therefore suggest that the second sentence on page 7 of your opinion be rephrased as follows: 'If only a question of statutory construction were involved we would not be prepared to abandon a doctrine so widely applied throughout nearly a century. *But the unconstitutionality of the course pursued* has now been made clear and compels us to do so.' "[37] The revision Stone suggested rested on the astonishing premise that the prior decision in *Swift* v. *Tyson* was unconstitutional. So vital did Stone regard this suggestion that he threatened to write a separate opinion if Brandeis did not acquiesce: "If you prefer not to make the change, or find it inconvenient to make it, I will concur with a sentence making plain my position that I come to the constitutional question only because otherwise I should, as Mr. Justice Holmes said, leave *Swift* v. *Tyson* undisturbed, but without allowing it 'to spread the assumed dominion into new fields.' "[38] In short, Stone now urged his colleague to reinforce the constitutional basis for deserting *Swift* v. *Tyson.*

Brandeis adopted Stone's suggestion verbatim, following it with his own discussion of the constitutional reasons for the decision that federal courts must honor state law whether declared by the legislature or by the highest state courts. "There is no federal general common law," he announced. "Congress has no power to declare substantive rules of common law applicable in a state whether they be local in their nature or 'general,' be they commercial law or a part of the law of torts. And no clause in the Constitution purports to confer such a power upon the federal courts."[39] The inference was that Congress had no authority to define the law to be applied in diversity cases.

"The 'unconstitutional' course referred to in the majority opinion," Justice Reed observed, "is apparently the ruling in *Swift* v. *Tyson* that the supposed omission of Congress to legislate as to the effect of decisions leaves federal courts free to interpret general law for themselves."[40] In other words, the concurring justice regarded the Court's discussion of congressional power as dictum and viewed the decision as based on Brandeis's reasoning, stating in effect that it was an unconstitutional assumption of power for the Court alone to authorize federal judges to make unwritten law independently of state decisions.

Stone hastened to lay his dilemma before Professor Frankfurter. "Certainly the Tompkins case was a remarkable performance," he exclaimed. "I haven't gotten over my own surprise at it."* But "we were confronted with a statute which had been construed and applied for a hundred years, during which it had often been the subject of debate in Congress. We have often refused to disturb statutory construction, especially in procedural matters so long settled." Stone excused this flagrant departure from normal practice by advancing his own constitutional reason for doing so. "The only possible justification" for repudiating the century-old line of decisions, he said, "is that the Court itself has been acting unconstitutionally. See Justice Holmes' famous dissent in the Black & White Taxicab case, where he said: 'If I am right, the fallacy has resulted in an unconstitutional assumption of powers by courts of the United States which no lapse of time or respectable array of opinions should make us hesitate to correct.' Beyond this, of course," Stone said, "it was unnecessary to go.† I should have

---

* In this opinion Stone sharply criticized Brandeis and the majority for gratuitously advancing the position that federal courts lacked power to issue declaratory judgments.

† "I agree, of course," Stone wrote Justice Roberts, Jan. 3, 1941, apropos his opinion in *Sibbach* v. *Wilson & Co.*, "that Congress cannot declare the substantive law of a state, but I do not think it is at all clear that Congress could not apply (enact) substantive rules of law to be applied by federal courts. I think that *Erie Railroad Co.* v. *Tompkins* did not settle that question, notwithstanding some unfor-

liked to have said that, and that it was unnecessary to say how far or to what extent Congress might legislate, but," he explained, "I thought enough was written without my risking the final result by putting in my oar."[41]

Once the Justices settled down to peaceful coexistence with the New Deal the focal point of controversy shifted from constitutional power to considerations of the scope and limits of its exercise. Here, too, significant differences emerged between the "liberals" of the old Court and the new appointees. In general, Stone and Brandeis were unwilling to go the limit in construing statutes so as to find justification for everything the newly created administrative agencies wanted to do. The prime bone of contention was enforcement of the Wagner Act—a novel national labor policy commanding employers to keep hands off and pledging government aid to workingmen's efforts at self-organization and collective bargaining.

Enforcement started off well. The Act survived the constitutional ordeal in 1937, and in 1938 the judges unanimously approved Justice Stone's decision giving the National Labor Relations Board authority to uproot company-dominated unions.[42] But after the easy questions were answered, Stone's alignment with Chief Justice Hughes became a source of concern to New Dealers. A series of cases, decided against labor, with Stone's support, over strong protests from Black and Reed, caused Irving Brant to urge on the President the importance of building up a court of judges who combined the New Deal point of view with "a thorough grounding in the philosophy of the law they are

---

tunate dicta in the opinion. Certainly ever since the Judiciary Act of 1789, federal courts under the authority of that Act have applied their own substantive rules of equity which often differ from state rules in that field. I anticipate that we will have to say, at no very distant date, whether *Erie Railroad Co.* v. *Tompkins* has changed that. I do not know how that question should be decided, but I am anxious to avoid saying anything that will foreclose the question. I think you could omit it or that you could merely say that Congress has not undertaken to declare the substantive law of the state, etc., etc." See *Guaranty Trust Co.* v. *New York,* 326 U.S. 99 (1945).

For the difficulties encountered by federal judges in administering the deceptively simple rule laid down in the Tompkins case, see Charles E. Clark, "State Law in the Federal Courts: The Brooding Omnipresence of *Erie* v. *Tompkins,*" *Yale Law Journal,* Feb. 1946, esp. pp. 280 ff. Judge Clark sets out four of the "most striking illustrations to date of cases where the simple rubric of the intolerability of competing systems of law applicable to the same facts is not adequate." Clark's criticisms are polite, but they mince no words as to the resentment he feels at being forced to "prostitute" his intellectual capacities, at being held in "bondage" to outmoded, bizarre, or erroneous state decisions which state courts themselves will not, in every case, follow. Circuit Judge John J. Parker regarded the Tompkins decision as a mistake when made, but in 1949 observed that unification of American common law under the aegis of *Swift* v. *Tyson,* the restatements and uniform state laws had gone so far that "whether the Court was right or wrong in overruling *Swift* v. *Tyson,* the time had arrived when the action did not make very much difference." (*American Bar Association Journal,* Jan. 1949, p. 19.)

called on to expound, and a sufficient deference to it to win the sympathy of the more liberal members of the central group," such as Justice Stone.[43] Brant saw how opposing individual methods made it "difficult to obtain the combined value of Black's economic acumen and Stone's legal philosophy." Someone was needed to close the gap.

The opportunity to do this came in July 1938, when Justice Cardozo died after a long illness. Stone had expressed a desire to see Professor Frankfurter on the bench. Realizing F.D.R.'s tendency to give special weight to the advice freshest in his mind, those close to the White House who shared Stone's view made sure of having him talk to the President the last possible moment before the appointment was to be announced. At Brant's suggestion, the President sent for the Justice. Stone advised the Chief Executive to waive the geographical considerations usually brought to bear on Supreme Court appointments and appoint Frankfurter.

"Of course, Mr. President," Stone said in substance, "you could get a very good man from every judicial circuit in the country and thus constitute a Supreme Court of character and ability. But you could not get a distinguished Court that way because you cannot find a distinguished judge or lawyer in every circuit. . . . The Supreme Court ought to be a distinguished Court." In conversation with Harold Ickes later on, Roosevelt "kept referring to what Justice Stone had said to him," proving to Ickes "that Stone had made a great impression on his mind."[44]

Naturally the appointment of his old friend in 1939 pleased Stone. He had always greatly admired the Harvard law professor's legal scholarship, and the appointment helped relieve his mind of some of the worries he had about Black's lack of judicial orthodoxy. "I don't know what all the considerations were which led to the appointment of Frankfurter rather than someone from the Far West," the Justice wrote Sterling Carr. "I do know that Frankfurter is eminently qualified."[45]

In 1935 Professor Frankfurter had urged on Stone the wisdom of the very course of restraint Justice Black treated with such slight respect. Before long, however, the former law teacher demonstrated that he too rated consistency as no more than "the hobgoblin of little minds." Indeed his judicial commission seemed but a license to continue with greater authority the discussion of constitutional questions for which he had become known as a teacher. Thus when the majority ducked reconsideration of the old doctrine of "reproduction cost" in rate-making, the new Justice, much to Stone's dismay, rushed out a concurrence to do battle with the devil. "I am satisfied," Stone wrote him, "that in the near future *Smyth* v. *Ames* [source of the "reproduction cost" rule] will be overruled. I think it is going to come naturally and more easily if we withhold our attack until we have a case where the issue is raised and unavoidable. After all, *Smyth* v. *Ames* isn't as old as *Collector* v. *Day*, and I have disagreed with the latter for a good many years, but I thought it wiser not to say so until the Graves case two weeks ago, and then I found all but two of my colleagues went along with me. It seems to me the effect of reviving the question now will be to stir new resistance on the part of some of your colleagues and to put others, contrary to the fact, in the attitude of supporting *Smyth* v. *Ames*."[46]

Stone's suggestion that judges should conduct themselves with more restraint than teachers fell on barren soil. "I should be suppressing a deep conviction," Frankfurter replied adamantly, "if I said nothing about Reed's opinion."[47]

If the new Justice had been commissioned to mediate between Stone and Black, especially on labor matters, he was quite unsuccessful. The sit-down strikes of 1937 frightened Stone, bringing out his innate conservatism. He was much too astute, however, and far too sure of the Wagner Act's constitutional foundation, to make a direct attack on labor's new charter. But more than any of his New Deal colleagues, Stone demanded fair and impartial administration of the Act, and by fairness he meant that the NLRB should approximate Court procedures. Such an independent stand put him out in no man's land, where he could be raked with crossfire from opposing forces in conference and in other pre-decision discussion. On the one hand, fidelity to firmly held conceptions of national power—upholding NLRB jurisdiction over intrastate activities affecting interstate commerce in the Fainblatt case —aroused McReynold's wrath. "This subversive doctrine," the shackled spokesman of the Old Guard sputtered, "brings within the ambit of federal control most if not all activities of the nation; subjects states to the will of Congress; and permits disruption of our federated system."[48] But Stone's "splendid service" in widening the reach of the NLRB was marred for his younger brethren, Black and Frankfurter, by pointed hints to the Board that its procedures could be improved.

When the celebrated Fansteel case, testing reinstatement rights of sit-down strikers, reached the Court, Stone sided with Hughes and the majority in denying such rights to strikers discharged during the dispute. The Chief Justice, however, drew no distinction between workers fired in the heat of controversy and those fired after settlement. Therefore Stone wrote a separate concurrence, holding that the fourteen men not discharged while the strike was in progress lay in "the Board's discretion, not ours."[49] If the employer wanted to be absolutely certain of nullifying the Board's authority to reinstate strikers he would have to cut them off the payroll while they were on strike. Stone's insistence on respect for Board authority seemed to pro-labor observers diabolically inspired. "This is to elevate sheer abracadabra to the dignity of a criterion of what will promote collective bargaining and peaceful industrial relations," certain commentators charged. "The Chief Justice's opinion gives the employer in the heat of the strike a provocative verbal weapon. Mr. Justice Stone's opinion compels him to use it."[50]

Detractors, aided and abetted by leading newspapers and publicists, branded the Board a "kangaroo court," a "drum-head court martial," and charged that "an employer has as much chance before that Board as an aristocrat had before the French tribunes of the Terror."[51] Stone, apparently undisturbed, coolly absolved an employer from the charge of refusing to bargain, so long as his workers did not issue unmistakable invitations to the conference tables. "While the Act," he declared, "makes it the employer's duty to bargain with his employees, . . . it imposes no like duty on his employees."[52] Frankfurter took no part in the case but predicted that the press would invoke the Court as authority that the Act was jug-handled. Such political implications left Stone unmoved. "It seems to me of some importance in the circumstances of this case," he informed his critic, "that the employees were under no duty to act, for this gives force to the suggestion that the employer is under no duty to do anything until the employees in person, or through an authorized representative, ask him to bargain."[53]

Court personnel, meanwhile, underwent another important change when Justice Brandeis was succeeded by William O. Douglas. Stone greeted the appointment with "high hopes." "I could wish he had been seasoned in active practice a little more," the older Justice commented, "but he has great capacity to learn and comes on the Court at a fine age. What would it not have meant to me if I could have had the years between forty and fifty on the bench?"[54] Douglas, however, experienced the same rigorous impartiality of Stone's approach in 1940 when an employer subverted collective bargaining by negotiating individual contracts with his employees. In the National Licorice Company case Stone drove home the point that employers "cannot set at naught the National Labor Relations Act by inducing their workmen to agree not to demand performance of the duties which it imposes."[55] Douglas agreed wholeheartedly but pressed for outright abrogation of the illegal contracts as "fruit of the company-union tree."[56] Justice Stone stood firm; the Labor Board as well as the employers must be held to the strict letter of law. Denying Douglas's contention, he pointed out that the individual workers who gained rights by these contracts had not been given an opportunity to be heard by the NLRB. "We are laying out the lines on which other cases in the future must proceed," he reminded his colleagues, "and in those cases, it may be of the greatest importance that the Board's order should not purport to determine anybody's rights except those of parties before it."[57]

Stone was no less a stickler for observance by the Labor Board of legal niceties than vigilant in requiring employers to live up to bargaining agreements. They must, he insisted, give solid evidence of their good faith by signing union contracts even though neither the Board nor the Supreme Court could point to any specific statutory authority for commanding such action. He went along with Douglas's formula governing employer accountability for virulent anti-union campaigns conducted by his subordinate supervisors. Such drives, he agreed, need not be inspired or directed by the company president or board of directors to be completely effective against unionism.[58] But having surrendered so much, he could not be persuaded to approve an NLRB cease and desist order which enjoined violation of the Wagner Act "in any manner." Such sweeping commands were not purely hortatory, for disrespect of Board orders could be punished. The Act was not intended to hang like Damocles' sword over every employer guilty of a single violation, so that, having once refused to bargain, he must conduct his labor relations faultlessly in the future or face a summons for contempt.[59] The Labor Board, Stone reasoned, was like a court of equity—having found acts constituting one unfair labor practice, it was free only to restrain that practice and other related unlawful acts. This interpretation ran the risk of putting employers in a position to tie up organization drives endlessly. Stone hedged against this possibility by saying that the employers' conduct might be judged in the context of the whole case to determine whether prior orders had been violated.*

Finally, he took on the entire group of New Deal Justices—Frankfurter, Black, Reed, Douglas, and Murphy†—dissenting for himself and Hughes in two cases decided in April 1941. In the first, Stone displayed his continued attachment to the stand he had taken in an earlier dispute with Douglas against permitting the Labor Board to affect rights of persons and groups not participating in its proceedings. The epithet "company" attached to the word "union" was not for him a signal to give the Labor Board *carte blanche.* Therefore NLRB certification of a CIO affiliate rather than an independent union at the Pittsburgh Plate Glass works suffered a fatal defect, he maintained, because of its failure to afford the "company" union, the Crystal City Glass Workers, an "'appropriate hearing.'"[60] In the second, he fought another round in his struggle against the disposition of the new Justices to give the broadest possible scope to the remedial powers of the NLRB. The issue was whether the specific language of the Wagner Act empowered the Board to compel employers to hire, with back pay, men whom it

---

* In 1946, in a concurrence, Stone explained that his 1941 decision did not deny the Board all authority to enjoin interference "in any manner," but simply that the propriety of such an order depends upon the circumstances of each case. See *NLRB* v. *Cheney California Lumber Co.,* 327 U.S. 385 (1946).

† Frank Murphy was appointed in January 1940 to succeed Justice Butler, who died in November 1939.

had refused to employ at all on account of their union affiliations. "Reinstatement," Frankfurter wrote for the majority, "is the conventional correction for discriminatory discharges. Experience having demonstrated that discrimination in hiring is twin to discrimination in firing, it would indeed be surprising if Congress gave a remedy for the one which it denied for the other." Stone dissented. Though he could find authority for letting the Labor Board require employers to sign union agreements, he could find no hint in the legislative history of the Wagner Act that Congress or any member of it empowered the Board to force the hiring of strangers with back pay—a power "few courts had ever assumed to exercise or had been thought to possess." "Authority for so unprecedented an exercise of power is not lightly to be inferred."[61]

Unquestionably, Stone's "conservative" decisions in this pre-eminently crucial area of statutory construction aided and abetted the continuing campaign of vilification against the Wagner law.* "The recalcitrants today," commentators observed, "only infrequently launch direct attacks upon the acknowledged objectives of the Act. . . . Instead they seek to destroy public confidence in the statute by assailing the methods of its administration."[62] Stone knew this, but he would not give up essentials to either side. He refused to yield an inch to McReynolds' fuming, and he would not shape opinions to pander to "liberals." He remained unshaken in his belief that NLRB powers were, like a court's, limited strictly to adjudication of rights of persons heard by it, and he worked hard to keep remedial sanctions within bounds set by the plain meaning of words. Precisely because he recognized Congress had given the Board broad authority, he deemed its procedures important. "Most of the decisions of the Board involve discretion which is to be exercised by it alone and not the courts," he observed. "For that reason the only substantial right of the litigant before the Board is, in most cases, the right to invoke the exercise of that discretion upon a full and fair consideration of all the relevant evidence." This, he said, in a sentence that did not escape his sharp-eyed brethren, is the most important, "if not the only safeguard," of personal rights in administrative proceedings.[63]

"It is not the province of the Court to do that which Congress has failed to do," he reiterated. New Deal Justices showed little or no

* By 1939 some thought that the Supreme Court had "accomplished by construction much of what groups unfriendly to the Act have been seeking by amendment." (See Note, Problems of the National Labor Relations Board, a collection of articles on the major labor cases appearing in the *International Juridical Association Bulletin,* issued by the American Association for Economic Freedom, Washington, D. C., 1939.) And as they emphasized: "Far from accepting these judicial amendments as an accomplishment by indirection of the results demanded by the proponents of amendment, . . . the latter have sought to utilize the decisions as a source of renewed strength for their drive upon the Act."

greater aptitude for mastering this elementary tenet of Stone's judicial creed than certain members of the old Court. "I have had a fairly tough winter," he reported, April 17, 1941. "I have been resuming some of my law-teaching experience but with students not as receptive as some that I have known."[64] For him no single case was more important than the development of consistent patterns for restrained exercise of judicial power. In the new Court, as in the old, he was much concerned that his decisions should square with existing law. Before 1937 his insistence that the issue be narrowly defined and the decision confined to it had served very well his drive to safeguard the Constitution as an instrument of power. Then, he attempted to restrain his more conservative brethren from following objectionable old doctrine to the bitter end. In 1937 the Washington Minimum Wage decision discarded laissez faire as the cardinal tenet of constitutional construction, releasing pent-up judicial energy for reform that did not quickly spend itself. Thereafter, Stone pursued a similar course of restraint in an effort to preserve the Constitution as an instrument of rights. His belief in slowly narrowing and clarifying doctrine, the chief basis of his quarrel with Black, became, Allison Dunham observes, "a 'retarding' skill rather than an 'advancing' skill as it had been under the old Court. This is not to say it was unsound under the new Court, but its effect was to hold the new Court back, which was unacceptable to many of them."[65]

During most of Stone's first ten years on the bench he had striven constantly against reactionary efforts of the Four Horsemen to embroil the Court in politics. It was now evident that in the years ahead he would have to strive against the politically slanted crusades of the New Dealers. A judge, Stone believed, has no right to be doctrinaire and has no unfettered commission to read his preference into the Constitution. The primary obligation of a judge is to be faithful to the charter of government he expounds. Sutherland's dogmatics crippled that charter's inherently broad powers; Black's creed ignored its few, but nonetheless real, restraints.* Both adopted "a fatal way of interpreting an instrument of government," which must, if it is to endure, "envisage the possibility of differences of opinion about social and economic questions."[66]

At an Amherst reunion in June 1939, Stone's classmate Wallace Kemp asked, "Doc, are you a *liberal*, opposing the *conservatives?*" The answer came without an instant's hesitation. "No, Wallace, I believe in conserving the Constitution as a living instrument."[67]

---

* Black, his most authoritative biographer observes, "sees the social point of a case, its implications to the lives of people, in a flash; and he has the energy and the ability to devise ways—new ways if need be—of serving what in his conception is the largest good. . . . His significance as a Justice is that he knows what to do with the power thus given him." (John P. Frank, *Mr. Justice Black*, p. 139.)

CHAPTER THIRTY

CHAPTER THIRTY

# The Shifting Battle Line

## 1938-1940

For years Stone had complained of being kept on short rations. After it had become apparent that his constitutional views were more in accord with the mavericks, Holmes and Brandeis, than with those of the solid majority, practically all his assignments dealt with "technical questions requiring careful handling," cases dealing, as he said, with "more or less intricate and obscure questions which require thought and careful statement." The experience was not without its rewards. One of the rare joys of such cases occurred when the preparation of an opinion carried him deeply into abstruse subjects, such as medieval French law. Eventually, however, he despaired of writing endless patent cases in which the judge "must combine all the talents of the mathematician, the physicist, and state his conclusions with the subtlety of a serpent." The effort seemed futile, the only result being "that one man gains a few more dollars and another loses them."[1]

"It is bad enough to have to write them without being obliged to read them," he said capriciously. "Why," he wondered, "should one read such trivia?"[2]

He felt much the same way about his annual output of perplexing tax cases. These, he said, "surpass chess," but were "of no earthly importance to anyone except the litigants, and then only as the result is measured in dollars." As "an implement of decision," he commented fatalistically, "I serve the functions of a dice box."[3]

Caught and confined, with few opportunities (except as he spoke out in dissent) to exercise a constructive influence, he sometimes accounted for the niggardly quality of his assignments by attributing to Chief Justice Hughes a fear that he would be too plain-spoken, or that his solid craftsmanship would be more than a match for the Chief Justice's subtle attempts to destroy it through artificial distinctions. Nor did the "shift in emphasis" in constitutional interpretation that occurred in the spring of 1937 end his personal purgatory. The clouds parted slightly, however, in the new year. "With Sutherland off the Court," he reported fulsomely, "I have been getting rather more interesting opinions."[4] Even then the Chief's bounty was uncertain. Justice McReynolds had, it seems, imbibed enough new learning to displace Stone occasionally when Hughes was handing out assignments. To Stone's former law clerk it was quite a spectacle to see McReynolds faithfully following Stone's ideas in a tax case.* "I should have thought," Louis Lusky remarked, "the Chief Justice might have allowed you the satisfaction of writing the opinion yourself, but on past performance, I suppose it was not to be expected. At all events, you have the satisfaction of knowing once again one of your opinions has become the law of the court."[5]

By 1939 another factor operated to give Stone enlarged opportunities for self-expression. "The Chief," Stone wrote, June 6, "has gotten to the point where he will have to let up a little, but I doubt whether he will or, perhaps, even can. We are as we are."[6] Thus, for various reasons, Justice Stone himself began to play a role as the Court's spokesman.

Presented, for the first time in his judicial life, with an opportunity to express his own deep-seated convictions, he began to demonstrate that the authentic foundation of constitutional jurisprudence rests upon a clear understanding of the nature of our constitutional system and of the role of the judiciary within it. In a federal system where political power is divided between the national government and the states, and where representation in all governments is impossible, protection of individual freedoms from arbitrary government cannot always be adequately preserved by the usual political processes. Political restraints on the actions of the national government, affecting the entire nation, can be effectively achieved by the citizens of the states through representation in Congress. But the citizens of some states cannot possibly check the excesses of others through the medium of congressional restraints. Here was a power vacuum which the Supreme Court must fill. In the momentous years from 1937 to 1939 Stone reached fairly definite conclusions as to how this task should be discharged.

In the process, his insistence on interposing judicial power where the operation of political processes provided inadequate protection moved Justice Black to charge him with precisely the same disregard of the Court's proper role that Stone had brought against the die-hard Justices in 1936. Unlike Justice Black, Stone refused to rely on political checks alone. The proper functioning of the judicial process required clear perception as to when politically discriminatory action must be invalidated. Only through the complementary operation of the political and judicial processes could free government be made secure. To heighten this perception Stone devised a series of standards by which the Court could determine when judicial intervention was necessary in

* The case, *Guaranty Trust Co.* v. *Virginia*, 305 U.S. 19 (1938), involved double taxation of income from a trust. McReynolds cited Stone's *New York ex rel. Cohn* v. *Graves*, 300 U.S. 308 (1937), and adopted the rationale of Stone's concurrence in *Safe Deposit and Trust Co.* v. *Virginia*, 280 U.S. 83 (1929), to justify limiting the Court's intervention to prevent double taxation.

three of the most controversial areas of national power—commerce, labor, and taxation.

The main constitutional peg on which the New Deal had hung much of its regulatory legislation was the "commerce clause." Since 1887 it had been one of the most important "power" clauses in the Constitution. Judicial interpretation had not produced a smooth, undeviating flow of opinions. The Justices featured troublesome distinctions about subjects "national in scope" vis-à-vis those of a "local nature," and made obscure references to "direct" and "indirect" effects. Until the smashing victories following the "revolution" of 1937, these and similar refinements had enabled the Court to establish a no man's land where neither state nor national regulation was permissible.

Stone had long been anxious to make the pragmatic approach to the commerce clause. In 1928 he had insisted that "the function of the Court must . . . be to prevent discrimination and the erection of barriers against interstate commerce, but upon careful scrutiny of every relevant fact and circumstance, to save to the states the regulation and control of all interests peculiarly local which do not infringe the national interest in maintaining untrammeled the freedom of commerce across state lines."[7] His Di Santo dissent in 1927 had already indicated his purpose to throw the light of factual investigation into this controversial area of constitutional law. Deploring the stand-pat use of the inconclusive and unrealistic "direct-indirect" formula, he then urged "consideration of all the facts and circumstances, such as the nature of the regulation, its function, the character of the business involved, and the actual effect on the flow of commerce."[8]

Meanwhile changed circumstances injected new complexities. The rapidly developing economic pattern of society during the twenties and thirties and the mounting costs of local government increased the pressure upon state legislatures to enact measures regulating and taxing various aspects of interstate commerce. With the expansion of congressional authority under the commerce clause the Court, by 1938, was faced with the issue not only of the degree of permissible state legislation in the commerce field, but also of the role of the Court in adjudicating state interferences with interstate commerce. It was at this juncture that Stone got his first opportunity to reconsider the whole problem.

In 1933 the legislature of South Carolina had decreed that trucks exceeding 90 inches in width and 20,000 pounds in weight were prohibited from using state highways. Over the objections of interstate truckers and the Interstate Commerce Commission, Stone, speaking for a unanimous Court, upheld the legislation in the Barnwell case.

Determination of the "national interest" was, he conceded, a "legislative, not a judicial function, to be performed in the light of the congressional judgment of what is appropriate regulation of interstate commerce, and the extent to which, in that field, state power and local interests should be required to yield to the national authority and interest." The Court's function was to carry out these policy determinations. In the absence of national legislation, it was limited to "the inquiry whether the state legislature in adopting regulations . . . acted within its province, and whether the means of regulation chosen are reasonably adapted to the end sought." Regulation of motor vehicles moving in interstate commerce is, Stone held, within the province of the state, and, from an examination of "the whole record," the Court could not say that "the legislative choice is without rational basis." Highway rules were of such nature that they applied equally to interstate and intrastate traffic and thus possessed a built-in factor "against their abuse."[9]

"So long as the state action does not discriminate," Stone observed, "the burden is one which the Constitution permits because it is an inseparable incident of the exercise of a legislative authority, which, under the Constitution, has been left to the states." "The commerce clause, by its own force, prohibits discrimination against interstate commerce," and is applicable "when state legislation nominally of local concern is in point of fact aimed at interstate commerce, or by its necessary operation is a means of gaining a local benefit by throwing the attendant burdens on those without the state." "It was to end these practices," he observed, "that the commerce clause was adopted."[10]

In the achievement of this objective, Stone claimed for the Court a positive role. As in the Carolene Products case, he used a footnote as the vehicle for propounding somewhat novel views as to the complementary doctrines of political restraints and judicial review.

"State regulations affecting interstate commerce," he wrote, "whose purpose or effect is to gain for those within the state an advantage at the expense of those without, or to burden those out of the state without any corresponding advantage to those within, have been thought to impinge upon the constitutional prohibition even though Congress has not acted." A distinction must be drawn between judicial acceptance of congressional action, enacted in the national interest and subject to the political restraint of voters within the states, and state "regulation . . . of such a character that its burden falls principally upon those without the state," that is, "legislative action . . . not likely to be subjected to those political restraints which are normally exerted on legislation where it affects adversely some interests within the state."[11] Where institutional political restraints are incapable of correcting palpable discriminations or measures creating competitive disadvantages, the Court must intervene to protect the citizens of other states.

Favorable comment from the other Justices was unusually profuse.

"A job admirably done, wise and well said," Brandeis scribbled on the slip opinion. "Well done," the Chief Justice said. Justice Black was pleased as well as helpful.* Especially enthusiastic words came from Frankfurter, who predicted that it would become as much of a classic with students of constitutional law as *Gibbons* v. *Ogden.*

Under the doctrine of political restraints featured in the Barnwell opinion, the Court must intervene "whenever it sees that the state measure is such that to a certain extent it places an economic burden upon those not represented in the legislature." The Justices must determine "whether the national interest in commerce has been subordinated by those bent upon local gain."[12] This case was hardly ensconced in the official reports before Stone considered how the same doctrine might apply to state taxation of interstate commerce.

A New Mexico publishing company, selling advertising space outside the state, had sued to recover a state privilege tax levied upon gross receipts received from the sale of advertising space by those engaged in the business of publishing newspapers or magazines, on the grounds that it ultimately imposed an unconstitutional burden on interstate commerce. The tax was upheld, despite the dissents of Butler and McReynolds, on Stone's reasoning that "we think the tax assailed here finds support in reason, and in the practical needs of a taxing system which, under constitutional limitations, must accommodate itself to the double demand that interstate business shall pay its way, and that at the same time it shall not be burdened with cumulative exactions which are not similarly laid on local business." As with state regulation of certain aspects of interstate commerce in the absence of congressional legislation, there were areas of permitted state taxation. The Court would intercede, however, whenever state taxes were such that they "have placed on the commerce burdens of such a nature as to be capable, in point of substance, of being imposed . . . with equal right by every state which the commerce touches, merely because interstate commerce is being done, so that without the protection of the commerce clause it would bear cumulative burdens not imposed on local commerce." Gross receipts taxes, even though non-discriminatory, were generally of such a nature, and their multiplication, he asserted, "would spell the destruction of interstate commerce and renew the barriers to interstate trade which it was the object of the commerce clause to re-

---

* Black had questioned Stone's use of the subjective word "reasonable" in the last paragraph of his original draft, which had read: "The regulatory measures taken by South Carolina being reasonably adapted to the exercise of an authorized legislative power. . . ." Grateful for the suggestion, Stone acknowledged that it was "a good one." The revised paragraph begins: "As the regulatory measures taken by South Carolina are within its legislative power . . ."—in order to obviate any misconstruction that "judges are to substitute their views of reasonableness for those of the legislature." (H. F. S. to Hugo L. Black, Feb. 11, 1938.)

move." But the mere fact that a tax is labeled a "gross receipts tax" did not require a "rigidly logical application" of the cumulative burden doctrine, "Practical rather than logical distinctions must be sought" in balancing "the opposing demands" that commerce should bear its share of local taxation and that it shall not, on the other hand, be subjected to multiple tax burdens.[13]

The multiple burden test was in effect an application in the tax field of the principle enunciated in the Barnwell decision. As in the former case, it justified judicial intervention to protect interstate commerce from locally imposed, politically irremediable burdens.

Not all the brethren accepted Stone's doctrine. Justice Black, in particular, objected to judicial intervention in matters primarily political. "Only Congress," he said, "has the power to formulate rules, regulations and laws to protect interstate commerce from *merely possible future unfair burdens*."[14] Stone had an opportunity to answer Black's complaint a year later, when the Court invalidated a Washington tax on the gross receipts of a dealer shipping fruit from the state in interstate commerce.

"For more than a century," he explained, "it has been recognized that under the commerce clause, Congress not acting, some protection is afforded to interstate commerce against state taxation of the privilege of engaging in it. . . . During that period Congress has not seen fit to exercise its constitutional power to alter or abolish the rules thus judicially established. Instead, it has left them undisturbed, doubtless because it has appreciated the destructive consequences to the commerce of the nation if their protection were withdrawn."[15] Justice Black, convinced that Stone projected the judicial function into a province essentially legislative, stood firm. If any relief is to be had against state laws interfering with interstate commerce, except those patently discriminatory, he argued in dissent, it must be gained through the action of Congress, not at the hands of the Court.

The climax in the evolution of Stone's theory was reached in 1940 when he sustained a New York City sales tax levied upon the sale of Pennsylvania coal in New York, over the dissents of Chief Justice Hughes and Justices Roberts and McReynolds. New York taxed every sale within the city, a sale being defined as "any transfer of title or possession or both," and it fell equally upon interstate and intrastate transactions. Of the tax in question Stone said, "Equality is its theme." Resting his decision "on a practical judgment as to the likelihood of the tax being used to place interstate commerce at a competitive disadvantage," he carried judicial inquiry beyond a mere consideration of discrimination.[16] At the same time he subtly injected his political restraints doctrine, pointing out that the burden of the tax lay not only upon those outside of New York but also on the voters within. This tax was therefore excluded from the category of taxes in which the onus falls primarily on those unable politically to rectify their grievance.*

Stone's ideas were triumphant, but the battle he had initiated more than a decade earlier against mechanical jurisprudence continued.

"The net result of my reflections," he wrote, "is that in the past the Court has probably been too doctrinal and has relied upon judicially contrived formulas as exact rules of decision, rather than upon an analysis of the facts and circumstances of each case, to see whether there really is any burden on interstate commerce distinguishable from the tax burden which may fall on all goods in the state of origin or of destination, both before and after their interstate journey. Of course, in addition to this, there are certain types of taxes which hit the operation of transportation or the goods themselves which could be the means of destroying commerce while in the course of transportation, and which it cannot be assumed that Congress intends to permit. I am inclined to think that if we approached each case in a more practical and concrete fashion and with less deference to formulas and doctrines we would do a better job and avoid making the commerce clause the source of special privileges which benefit particular individuals in such fashion as to amount to no more than subsidies of interstate commerce at the expense of the state taxing power."[17]

His work of "gentle education" had not been without effect. It had served to sharpen the perceptions of the Justices to the complexities of the problem. Practical considerations of "competitive disadvantage," of "multiple burden," and so on, were not only criteria for judging, but also a reminder that the Court and Congress must play complementary roles in the maintenance of the federal system. But his views were still not altogether acceptable to all members of the Court. Rumblings of discontent rose on all sides. It began to appear as though his doctrine would soon run into stormy weather.

Trouble was brewing also in the ever-controversial field of labor. Here, too, the battle line was shifting. By 1940 unionism, under the auspices of the Wagner Act, had achieved unprecedented strength. Then, just as public agitation over sit-down strikes had subsided, the Court was faced with the question whether the Sherman Act outlawed such violent union activity. A series of disputes in the Apex Hosiery Mill finally culminated in a Supreme Court decision of 1940.[18]

In 1937 union men not employed at the Philadelphia mill seized the factory and held it for several weeks, three times refusing to open the gates to permit shipment of finished stockings into interstate markets.

---

* Stone cited as forbidden taxes those which "discriminate against the commerce, or impose a levy for the privilege of doing it, or tax interstate transportation or communication or their gross earnings, or levy an exaction on merchandise in the course of its interstate journey. Each imposes a burden which intrastate commerce does not bear. . . ."

Afterward plant owners sued the union under the Sherman Act for treble damages amounting to more than $700,000. Partisans of capital felt certain that conduct so "outrageous" must be illegal. Labor leaders, on the other hand, followed the case closely, hoping the Supreme Court, with five Roosevelt appointees, would hold the Sherman Act inapplicable to trade unions. Exercising the Chief's prerogative because both Hughes and McReynolds were in dissent, Stone assigned this thorny case, bristling with emotional pitfalls for the unwary, to himself.

In Stone's mind the Apex strikers' acts constituted "a lawless invasion of petitioner's plant and destruction of its property by force and violence of the most brutal and wanton character." Strong personal feelings did not, however, disturb his balanced view of law. Unquestionably the strike had affected interstate commerce, putting it plainly within reach of congressional authority "if Congress has seen fit to exercise it." But had Congress, in fact, done so? "The prohibitions of the Sherman Act were not stated in terms of precision or of crystal clarity," Stone observed. "In consequence of the vagueness of its language, perhaps not uncalculated, the courts have been left to give content to the statute."[19]

Since prior decisions had settled that labor unions were "to some extent and in some circumstances" subject to anti-trust law, it was now too late to argue for labor's exemption. Nor had Congress, despite much political prodding, corrected this construction. This failure was, in Stone's view, "persuasive of legislative recognition that the judicial construction is the correct one." It was also too late to insist on the employer's right to buy labor at the lowest price which defenseless, unorganized individuals would accept. In passing the anti-trust act, Congress had aimed at the "prevention of restraints to free competition in business and commercial transactions which tended to restrict production, raise prices, or otherwise control the market to the detriment of purchasers or consumers of goods and services." The Court, Stone said, never applied the law unless it "was of opinion that there was some form of restraint upon commercial competition in the marketing of goods or services."* Common law, prior to 1890, had given "restraint of trade" a well-understood meaning, and although, as Stone said, "a combination of employees necessarily restrains competition among themselves in the sale of their services to the employer, yet such a combination was not considered an illegal restraint of trade at common law when the Sherman Act was adopted, either because it was not

---

* Some experts have criticized this statement. Charles O. Gregory, for example, says it is not true that the boycott cases involved any market restraint, but it is clear Stone did not say they did. He wrote only that the Court "was of opinion" that such boycotts restrained the market, a qualification Gregory does not quote. (See his *Labor and the Law*, p. 258.)

thought to be unreasonable or because it was not deemed a 'restraint of trade.' "[20]

The Justice went further: "Since in order to render a labor combination effective it must eliminate the competition from non-union made goods . . . an elimination of price competition based on differences in labor standards is the objective of any national labor organization."[21] Nothing in the Sherman Act prohibited it, and in other legislation, such as the Fair Labor Standards Act, Congress had sanctioned such restriction of competition. The Supreme Court had taken the vague and ill-defined Sherman Act—born of indignation at business trusts—and, without considering the applicability of the "rule of reason," had turned it against labor. Such discriminatory construction could no longer be tolerated.*

The Justices ought to look at union restraints in the light of the rule of reason. Tested by "an impartial application of the Sherman Act to the activities of industry and labor alike," the Apex strike, Stone concluded, was not illegal. "So far as appears the delay of [mill] shipments was not intended to have and had no effect on prices of hosiery in the market." Prevention of interstate shipments of stockings was but a consequence of a strike planned to achieve union recognition.[22]

Nor did violence alter application of the Sherman Act. Statutory provisions aimed primarily at prevention of practices inimical to commercial competition do not extend to the policing of interstate transportation, a matter properly within the scope of local officials.

Justice Douglas, like Frankfurter, had anticipated that certain pitfalls might beset the opinion writer. Regarding earlier decisions as just so much "obstructive material" to "get over or around," Douglas queried whether Stone's draft opinion had effectively handled the Bedford Cut Stone and Duplex cases. "My thought," he said, "goes back to the talk you and Frankfurter and I had after the argument in Apex. I vividly recall that discussion and your statement of the reasons why you felt that those cases should have gone the other way and why in the Bedford case you felt yourself bound by the precedent of Duplex. I shared your views then, as now. I think the Duplex and Bedford cases were decided wrongly. I am apprehensive that, contrary to your intentions, this draft would be taken to mean an implicit approval of those cases. This may not be (and probably is not) the occasion to repudiate them," he added. "Perhaps my difficulty could be handled by some

* "The statement in the Apex opinion that the applicability of the rule of reason to restraints effected by labor unions 'was not considered' meant 'was not discussed,'" Stone told James Landis, April 11, 1941, "although I am quite sure it was literally true in the Bedford case. This appears more fully from footnote 25 appended to the statement. I have never thought that Pitney, by his reference to public policy in the Duplex case, had in mind the rule of reason as it had been developed in connection with common law restraints of trade."

express reservation. But I would leave it entirely to you for the discovery of some facile way of depriving the supporters of the Duplex and Bedford cases of any comfort in this opinion."[23]

Stone then made his point explicit: "The only significance of the two cases for present purposes is that in each the Court considered it necessary, in order to support its decision, to find that the restraint operated to suppress competition in the market."[24] But he would go no further: "I do not wish in this case either to approve or disapprove of decisions in the Duplex Printing and Bedford Stone cases. . . . In my concurring opinion in the Bedford Stone case I expressed my disapproval, and in footnotes 24 and 25 I think I have made plain to those who read with discernment the objections to the decisions in those cases."[25]

A majority of the Justices received Stone's finished opinion enthusiastically. "Powerfully constructive—indeed creative," one commented. "Not only have you my vote, but I'd like to stuff the ballot box." "A superb job of analysis and reconstruction," Douglas exulted. "This is unquestionably the best job ever done in the history of the Court on the Sherman Act. I congratulate you and am proud to join with you in this historic opinion."[26] Justice Black characterized Stone's "exposition of the underlying philosophy of the Sherman Act [as] the clearest and soundest that has been written."[27]

But in some circles the decision was accorded quite different treatment. Columnist David Lawrence saw it as part of a pro-CIO plot, though no CIO affiliate was involved. "What the decision of the New Deal majority really means," he asserted, "is that the Supreme Court has one set of harsh rules to apply against industry and business and another to apply leniently against labor unions."[28] "The Supreme Court," the *Washington Star* pontificated, "in its decision in the Apex Hosiery case, has enunciated what is indeed a strange doctrine of constitutional law—that the most wanton kind of lawlessness on the part of a labor union . . . is beyond the reach of any federal statute."[29] Such unrestrained comment was the more remarkable in the face of the Justice's express declaration that Congress was empowered to regulate labor strife such as the Apex strike. "Being a judge," he reflected calmly, "is a hard life."[30]

Though AFL spokesmen hailed the decision as a "complete vindication for labor" and CIO counsel saw it as a "notable victory," the reaction among labor sympathizers was divided. Some regretted that the Sherman Act had been retained as a potential weapon against unions; while others rejoiced at finding "strong ground for the belief that the shocking inequality of fifty years' standing in the Act's application to capital and labor has at last been leveled off."[31] Something of the same confusion marked Thurman Arnold's reaction. The New Deal's trustbuster, then waging a campaign against union abuses, said the opinion sustained every one of the actions he had brought. The following day, however, he dropped prosecution of the Teamsters' Union officials, apparently because of the Apex decision.[32]

Law review writers could not understand Stone's treatment in the Apex decision of the four labor boycott precedents—Danbury Hatters, Duplex Printing, Bedford Cut Stone, and the second Coronado case. He had taken all four decisions, with their diverse facts, as illustrating his proposition that the Supreme Court had never applied the Sherman Act to labor unions unless it had been of the opinion that union activities had affected commercial competition.* Professor Lehan Tunks called the Apex decision "a new federal charter for trade unionism," but added: "One has the alternative of believing what Mr. Justice Stone says as distinguished from what he cites. Nearly every Supreme Court decision which he rallies to his support . . . can be impeached. Yet the language of the decision gives the unmistakable impression of laying a new foundation for future labor cases under the Sherman Act."[33] Others said Stone's treatment of the precedents did no more than pay lip service to the principle of judicial self-restraint.

"Justice Stone would have made it easier for himself and for the bar in general, to say nothing of employers and unions," Charles Gregory wrote, "if he had simply declared that in the past the Supreme Court had fostered incorrect views about the application of the Sherman Act to labor unions and is now starting afresh with the correct view. Almost everything he says in his opinion about Congress's real intentions in the Act seems extraordinarily lucid. He gets into hot water only when he tries to reconcile his views with previous decisions of the Court."[34]

---

* Roscoe Steffen was particularly skeptical of Stone's emphasis on "commercial competition," labeling it the "new test" of anti-monopoly law violations. "The basic philosophy of the present Court is thus clear enough," he declared. "It is concerned with commodities, prices, and free business competition and only reluctantly, if at all, with services, wages, and labor combinations in restraint of trade. So far so good. But in evaluating such a policy it must be remembered that the Court is construing a statute. In a democratic system it is the Court's function—more or less scrupulously—to do the legislative bidding, be it good or bad, rather than to carry out its own bias in favor of one view or another. Nor is it any concern of the Court what cases are prosecuted under the statute. Probably no member of the Court more fully appreciates this than Mr. Justice Stone." ("Labor Activities in Restraint of Trade: The Apex Case," *Yale Law Journal*, June, 1941, p. 795ff.)

Judge Learned Hand, a few months later, somewhat sardonically dubbed the price competition test a "new contribution" and followed it, reluctantly, if one may read between the lines, to sustain union boycotts in a service industry where no effect on price was shown. See *United States* v. *Gold*, 115 Fed. (2d) 236 (1940).

Stone clarified his position some years later in a letter to Robert H. Jackson (June 8, 1945): "While it is true that the opinions mainly discuss competition in price, I think the opinion, read as a whole, makes it plain that any restraint of competition in the sale, marketing, or transportation of goods, either in or affecting interstate commerce, violates the Act."

Such commentary, however, went somewhat wide of the mark. Stone had not been so ambitious. "The Court was dealing only with *one* of the conditions," a former clerk of the Justice explained, "not *all* the conditions, deemed essential for bringing the Sherman Act into play. Therefore the only *necessary* operation for this Court was to determine whether any earlier decisions were in conflict with what the Court was now holding to be a necessary condition for invocation of the Sherman Act. . . . Stone was not concerned with affirming or denying any other aspect of the earlier cases."[35]

The law clerk's comment many years later was less charitable: "His method of distinguishing the four labor boycott cases—by imputing to the earlier Court a factual finding that the restraints in question operated to suppress competition in the market—made it possible for him to avoid overruling them 'on the law.' But by leaving open the question whether the Apex Court would have made a similar finding on similar facts, he rendered it impossible for anyone to say whether the earlier cases were still good law in the sense that the same facts would again produce the same decisions. This sort of thing makes life very hard for a practicing lawyer, and may be a high price to pay for an appearance of consistency."[36]

Later on, writing Dean James M. Landis of the Harvard Law School, Stone frankly admitted that the "opinion left some matters vague and uncertain, in that it did not attempt to commit the Court on any matters unnecessary for the decision." This he defended as "good judicial practice especially desirable in this particular field where so much has already been said which isn't so, and where dicta to which the Court might agree today would not be followed tomorrow." He "had not thought" that he "attempted to reconcile the Duplex and Bedford cases with anything." Since the Apex case presented no question under the Clayton Act there was no occasion for such a reconciliation. "For the purposes of the Apex case it was only necessary to refer to them to show that in both cases the Court had relied upon restraints of competition as the basis of violation of the Sherman Act." His sole purpose, he said, was to point up the fact "that the Apex case, which gave great emphasis to the doctrine of common law restraints of trade as the foundation of the Sherman Act, did not foreclose consideration of certain aspects of that doctrine which were involved in the Duplex and Bedford cases but not discussed in the opinions in those cases."

"That I did the job rather badly," he concluded, "seems evident both from what you have written and also from an article by Professor Roscoe Steffen recently appearing in the *Yale Law Journal*. However, anyone who attempts to write an opinion in this field without writing a treatise has his work cut out for him."[37]

A federal indictment of "Big Bill" Hutcheson, president of the Carpenters' Union, arising out of an unseemly jurisdictional squabble between AFL carpenters and machinists over construction jobs at the Anheuser-Busch brewery in St. Louis, brought the issue of the vitality of the labor boycott cases to a head. The company surrendered to the machinists and promptly faced a strike and picketing by the carpenters and a press campaign urging a boycott of Anheuser-Busch beer. If the old boycott cases were still valid, it looked as though the union had violated the law. Six Justices, however, thought otherwise, and the Court's split gave Stone another opportunity to exercise the Chief's prerogative. His assignment of the opinion to Justice Frankfurter brought on a remarkable debate. The former law professor pressed for a comprehensive statement of the relation of labor to the anti-trust laws in one sweeping opinion, while Justice Stone held out for a more cautious, empirical approach, keeping the old line of precedents behind the door—just in case.

"By a process of construction never heretofore indulged by this Court," as Justice Roberts put it for the dissenters, Frankfurter evolved an ingenious method for getting around objections to a flat overruling of the boycott cases. Reading the applicable statutes in what someone has called "a spirit of mutilating broadness," he discovered a congressional intention in the Norris-La Guardia anti-injunction statute to repudiate the construction put on the Clayton Act by the Duplex and Bedford Cut Stone cases. The Court was not overruling these boycott precedents, he declared, insisting that Congress had expressed its mind with new clarity and had indicated that it wanted a different construction.[38] On its face, the Norris-LaGuardia Act simply took from federal courts their powers to issue injunctions in certain kinds of labor disputes, while the earlier Clayton Act had removed the taint of illegality under "any federal law" from a restricted list of union activities. "It would be strange indeed," Frankfurter contended, "that although neither the Government nor Anheuser-Busch could have sought an injunction against the Acts here challenged, the elaborate efforts to permit such conduct failed to prevent criminal liability punishable with imprisonment and heavy fines." He refused to believe that Congress had intended conduct allowable on the equity side of the Court to be "the road to prison."[39] Stone demurred, fearing that this novel approach would "stir up controversy in the Court."[40] He knew, as Walton Hamilton had pointed out just before the case came to the Supreme Court, that "the Norris-La Guardia Act has solved one problem by creating another, for employers denied injunctions are now suing for damages."[41] It was at least conceivable that Congress had intended to punish as criminal, after a jury trial, labor activities not subject to the more summary injunction. "The indictment," Stone pointed out, "fails to state an offense, and this without our resorting to the Norris-La Guardia Act." "If you wish to write, placing the case on the ground which I think tenable and desirable," he told Frankfurter, January 20, 1941, "I shall cheerfully join you. If not, I will write a few observations for myself," applying the logic of the Apex opinion.

Frankfurter objected that the ground on which Stone suggested that the case be put would also create controversy. The vice, as he saw it, was that the Chief and Roberts talked about the secondary boycotts in the Duplex and Bedford cases with all the undefined and conflicting meanings attached to those phrases. He preferred to apply the exact language of the Clayton Act as illumined by the Norris-La Guardia Act.[42]

When the older judge stood firm, "inspired by the assumption that I could write an opinion without reliance upon the Norris-La Guardia Act which our brethren could not plausibly challenge,"[43] Frankfurter, calling Stone to his defense, cited the passages on creative statutory construction in the 1936 Harvard Tercentenary address. He regarded the use of the Norris-La Guardia Act in interpreting the antecedent Duplex case and Clayton Act as an example of the judicial technique Stone had formulated at Cambridge. Suspecting, perhaps, an unvoiced objection behind Stone's refusal to approve his views, he asked if the Norris-La Guardia Act was not a powerful indication of how Congress thought the Clayton Act should be construed.

Stone's oblique reply revealed still another reason for his reluctance. His allegiance to the boycott cases was now sealed by vanity as well as principle. "It has seemed to me that the Norris-La Guardia Act was possibly a springboard from which we might overcome Duplex, but here again Duplex has been so long on the books that I feel such a course embarrassing in view of what was said in the Apex case on the same subject, and in any case it seems to me not good judicial practice to overrule cases, especially not involving constitutional questions, where there is a fairly plain way to deal with the case without overruling." "You hit a body blow," he went on, "when you quote my favorite author against me. But apart from my desire to pursue the peaceful rather than the warpath, I have the uncomfortable feeling that the quotation does not fit the situation created by the passage of the Norris-La Guardia Act. I suspect that Roberts could make a much more powerful showing than he has that the Norris-La Guardia Act was a compromise by which the proponents of the bill gained much and the opponents yielded something but not all."[44]

At this latter observation Frankfurter lashed out fiercely, claiming personal knowledge as to the drafting and the passage of the Act. He refused to regard this legislation as a compromise of conflicting viewpoints and maintained that correction of the Duplex and Bedford constructions was its chief objective. As any further argument must seem to question Frankfurter's knowledge or his candor, direct debate came to a halt.

Stone did, however, forward a rough sketch of his proposed concurring opinion. He divided the allegations of the indictment into two heads—one charging restraints on interstate commerce arising from the strike and picketing, the other alleging such restraint in the attempt to boycott Anheuser-Busch beer. "It is a novel proposition," he commented on the first charge, alluding to the recent cases protecting picketing as a form of speech, "that allegations of local peaceful picketing of a manufacturing plant . . . accompanied by announcements that the manufacturer is unfair to organized labor is a violation of the Sherman Act" whatever its intent. The acts of the carpenters, he said, amounted to no more interference with interstate business than is "incidental to every strike causing a shut-down of a manufacturing plant whose product moves in interstate commerce or stopping building operations where the builder is using materials shipped to him in interstate commerce." The carpenters' boycott, unlike that of the Danbury Hatters, did not confront Anheuser-Busch customers with "any concerted action or refusal to patronize." The mere publication of the notice was "an exercise of the right of free speech guaranteed by the First Amendment." As the clincher, he added that the strike against Anheuser-Busch, being a strike by its employees, was "a labor dispute between employer and employees within the labor provisions of the Clayton Act as they were construed" in the Duplex case.[45]

Frankfurter's broken field running through the statutes received a more critical reception from the public and scholars than the Apex decision.[46] Commentators, reflecting community alarm, declared that the decision "virtually took organized labor entirely out from under the Sherman Act" and threw to the winds the leash Stone's Apex reasoning kept on unions, which would have permitted the Court to intervene when their practices resulted in actual market restraints. To avoid penalties of the Sherman Act, unions had only to employ means within the Norris-La Guardia Act. Both points troubled Stone. He opposed the Hutcheson opinion, he told Dean Landis, "because I think it is rather extreme statutory construction, but more particularly because it seems to have discarded the Apex case by refusing to apply it to a case to which it seemed fairly applicable."[47]

Public sentiment generally echoed Roberts' blistering dissent. "Resurrecting a rejected construction of the Clayton Act and extending a policy strictly limited by the Congress itself in the Norris-La Guardia Act," he charged, amounted to "a usurpation by the courts of the function of the Congress not only novel but fraught, as well, with the most serious dangers to our constitutional system of division of powers."⁴⁸ With this warning from Justice Roberts, so reminiscent of the challenge flung before the Four Horsemen by Stone, Brandeis, Holmes, and Cardozo, the newly liberalized Court had come full circle.

Another area in which Stone had long been deploring undue extension was that of the governmental tax immunities. By recourse to abstraction the Justices had unnecessarily restricted the taxing power of the government imposing the tax. Since 1926, when he wrote *Metcalf & Eddy* v. *Mitchell,* he had had no occasion to voice his views, for the Court or in dissent, on one of the most important aspects of this problem—tax exemption of government workers' salaries.⁴⁹

Meanwhile he had been laying the groundwork for future limitations on the doctrine of reciprocal immunity of official salaries. In 1937, when Irving Brant editorialized on the subject, Stone hastened to set him straight. The doctrine he pointed out, was "bound to become more important before a great while." "Chief Justice Marshall," he told the newsman, "invented the doctrine that neither state nor national government could cast any tax burden upon the activities or instrumentalities of the other." Stone saw "some ground in reason" for such a rule, but protested that steady extensions of it had so enlarged the scope of immunities that vast amounts of purely private property and many significant economic activities had been left virtually tax free. "I have always felt," he went on, "that everything needful would have been accomplished had Marshall merely declared that neither government can adopt a tax which discriminates against the other, and that in the absence of discrimination either government is free to lay such taxes as it pleases regardless of its effect upon the other. The result would be that each government, like everyone else, would have to pay its way without special favors from the other. But to Chief Justice Marshall everything was either black or white."⁵⁰ This curbstone opinion, making discrimination the sole test, went far beyond anything Stone had uttered or ever would utter from the bench. It was itself a sort of "black or white" rule.

Stone had already held that state-owned industry was not immune to regulation under the paramount national power to regulate commerce.⁵¹ He was now determined that the numerous new state and municipal enterprises in competition with private business bear a share of the cost of government. The loss of revenues suffered by the Federal Government through enforcement of the immunity doctrine was in itself a most persuasive argument for limiting it. "The National Government has never been very alert on this subject," he told Brant. "The Attorney General, so far as I know, has seen fit to intervene but once in state taxation cases, objecting to a state tax on gasoline sold for the use of the government, apparently unmindful of the enormous amount of revenue which it loses through the expansion of the immunity of state instrumentalities."[52] The Justice went even further. He wanted the Justice Department to take a stand against extension of the federal immunity.[53] In 1937 and 1938 when the Justice Department took the position that only discriminatory taxes laid by one government on the activities of the other were unconstitutional, Stone could hardly have been surprised.

Suddenly the mash of ideas brewing in his Metcalf decision began to spill over into the Court's opinions. Chief Justice Hughes contributed to the ferment by upholding a West Virginia privilege tax on income earned by a contractor from work on federal dams and locks in the Dravo case. Somewhat belatedly, the Chief Justice recognized that Stone's Metcalf opinion had been "a pivotal decision."[54] While drafting another opinion upholding congressional authority to tax profits of private oil companies from state-leased lands, Hughes recanted his stand in the 1932 Coronado case and sent Stone the good news. "I have reached the conclusion," he wrote, February 23, 1938, "that . . . these cases should be overruled and I have written accordingly."[55]

But Hughes had not "pushed back the frontiers" as Stone had hoped. Instead of bringing order out of the chaos, instead of establishing the immunities doctrine on its original basis, the Chief Justice merely prevented another extension of the theory because no "substantial burden" on functions of local government could be deduced from the incidence of these taxes. The Court, under Hughes' leadership, had "missed a great opportunity." "The net result of what we have done," Stone commented, "is merely to put all the opinions in a pot and stir them up and insist that the soup is clear."

Aside from the exemptions accorded government bonds and interest, government-owned property and the salaries of persons directly employed by government, he thought it impossible "to establish by any process of logic a line between the things which have been held immune from taxation and those that have not." "It would have been better," he declared, "to have done over again what I thought I had done in the Metcalf & Eddy case, namely, point out that logic offers no solution; that the business of increasing immunity by insisting that the burdens of a tax imposed by one government are passed on so as to affect another necessarily results in such a constant increase of immunities of the one government as to break down the taxing power of the other. Once this is recognized the effect is to set limits to any expansion of the early cases which were recognized in the case of officers, public property, and public bonds."[56]

By this time the Justice had begun to reappraise what he had told Brant earlier in the year concerning the true scope of intergovernmental tax immunity. He would limit the scope of the immunities concept to the prevention of the destruction of, or direct interference with the functions of, the government affected by a tax. "In the Brush case," he wrote, "the dissenters [Roberts and Brandeis] thought that there should be no immunity except where the tax law was discriminatory, which," he cautioned, "would go further than anyone has ever suggested, and would wipe out even the limited class of early cases of immunity to which I refer."[57] One friendly critic deplored the fact that Stone had not written the Dravo opinion. What the Chief Justice had said was "not even a potpourri, it's just a hodge-podge." "There was a chance," he continued, "to rationalize the mess into which the Court has got—to put some things on one side of the line and other cases on the other, to wrest some order out of the chaos of cases." The opportunity to do just that arose sooner than could have been hoped for.

Shortly thereafter Stone was assigned the Gerhardt case, which raised the question of the Government's authority to tax the income of an engineer working for the bi-state Port of New York Authority. The assignment to Stone had been purely gratuitous. "Chief Justice Hughes had been absent from the conference, or had not participated in it, and McReynolds had dissented," Stone's law clerk recalls.* "That left it up to Brandeis to assign the opinion, and he gave it to Stone."[58]

Here was a long-awaited opportunity, and the Justice set to work with a will "to clear away some of the underbrush and bring the case

---

* Much credit for the Gerhardt opinion belongs to Stone's law clerk, Louis Lusky, whose thirty-two page memorandum sharpened the tenets of the Metcalf opinion. "I think you *must*," Lusky wrote, "point out the differences between state and federal immunity; revive old doctrine by asserting that the federal immunity rests entirely on the power and intent of Congress; recall that the doctrine of state immunity was designed to prevent *destruction* of the states, and insist that it be applied only where destruction, as opposed to mere burden, is possible; and resuscitate the dictum of the Metcalf case, that state immunity is a function of two factors: the importance of the state activity protected and the probability that the tax burden in question will fall on the activity."

It has been said that Stone was "a great absorber of other men's ideas, but short on recognition." "I think this is a fair statement, if properly understood," Lusky writes. "It is true that he [Justice Stone] was very willing to adopt good ideas wherever he found them, and it is also true that he generally set them forth as his own, often without acknowledgment of the source. There is no basis for any implication, however, that this was due to a desire to pre-empt the credit for them. For one thing, a statement by the Justice ordinarily carried more weight when he made it as his own than when he cited someone else's opinion to substantiate his own. A citation of authority often implies a partial disclaimer of responsibility. Another consideration is that some types of citations were resented by other members of the Court. . . . Furthermore, I have little doubt that Justice Stone very often was unconscious, at the time he set an idea on paper, that he had taken it from someone else. He had made the idea his own by adopting it, and it just didn't seem important to him that someone else had thought of it first." (Louis Lusky to A.T.M., Oct. 13, 1952.)

closer into line with the ideas which I think Marshall held in this field, without interposing any obstacle to further limitation if that should seem desirable."[59]

"It was held," in *McCulloch* v. *Maryland*, Stone began, "that Congress, having power to establish a bank by laws which, when enacted under the Constitution, are supreme, also had power to protect the bank by striking down state action impeding its operations; and it was thought that the state tax in question was so inconsistent with Congress's constitutional action in establishing the bank as to compel the conclusion that Congress intended to forbid application of the [Maryland] tax to the federal bank notes."[60] The acts of Congress, passed within its constitutional power, being supreme, it lay within the prerogative of the national government to decide whether a federal instrumentality which it had created would or would not be immune, either expressly or by implication, from state taxation. The basis of federal immunity was the power and intent of Congress, rather than the federal function involved.

After thus reverting to the original progenitor of the immunities doctrine, Stone then proceeded to sweep aside the accumulated bric-a-brac that had hidden the clear course for so long and set forth his own doctrine. Chief Justice Marshall had recognized, Stone explained, a "clear distinction" between the extent of the power of a state to tax federal agencies and that of the national government to levy on state instrumentalities. Marshall was careful to point out "not only that the taxing power of the national government is supreme, by reason of the constitutional grant, but that in laying a federal tax on state instrumentalities the people of the states, acting through their representatives, are laying a tax on their own institutions."[61] Consequently, the possibility of abuse through federal taxation is subject to powerful "political restraint."

This approach fitted in perfectly with Stone's theory of the relation of the judicial function to the political processes. After *Collector* v. *Day* in 1871 the taxing power of the Government became subject to an implied constitutional restriction. Stone left this restriction standing, but confined it severely. The reasons for doing so were self-evident.

Since 1871 states had embarked on a variety of undertakings unknown in 1789, including management of businesses and performance of functions formerly operated exclusively by private individuals. Taxes on such new functions might, in fact, be passed on to the state itself, but to attain the basic constitutional purpose of the implied immunity, Stone argued, "it is not ordinarily necessary to confer on the state a competitive advantage over private persons in carrying on the operations of its government." If every federal tax on some new form of state activity were to be set aside as an infringement on state sovereignty, national taxing authority would be severely crippled. Non-discriminatory income taxes, hitting private citizens and Port Authority employees alike, "could by no reasonable probability be considered to preclude the performance of the function which New York and New Jersey have undertaken, or to obstruct it more than like private enterprises are obstructed by our taxing system." Thus the tax was valid because it did not threaten any function "essential" to the continued existence of the state government.[62]

Butler and McReynolds dissented, but their standpat position was no longer important. Argument took a new turn in Justice Black's concurring opinion—in its own way as subtle and suggestive as any Stone had written in the field.

Black willingly subscribed to what Stone called the "chief reason" for his decision—the obligation of a citizen who draws his income from a state to support the United States and pay federal income taxes as does every other citizen.[63] But the concurring Justice based his support of the result on Congress's power under the Sixteenth Amendment to tax incomes "from whatever source derived."* Black objected strenuously to the Court's presuming to distinguish "essential" from "non-essential" state functions; his sole point was that no constitutional dispensation from non-discriminatory federal income taxes existed no matter what the relationship between the taxpayer and state government.

Stone, however, apparently interpreted Black's opinion as demanding outright abolition of all state tax immunities. Withdrawing from the line he had taken with Irving Brant, he told Black he was not willing to go so far, and insisted on maintaining the difference between "essential" and "non-essential" government activities "in view of the seriousness of adopting a rule which would leave the states wholly at the mercy of an aggressive Congress." "If," he asked the New Deal Justice, "you . . . reject the idea that there can be to any extent an implied immunity of state governments, on what clause of the Constitution do you rely when you say that the discriminatory tax is valid?"[64]

His colleague's reply was not a model of candor. Dodging the point of the question, he believed it "would be far more serious to have such state activities as this Court deems 'non-essential' placed in such a position that they might be injured." "Leaving only those state activities to be taxed which could be done by private enterprise," he contended,

---

* Black rather ignored the "difficulties" in the way of his interpretation, to which Stone called attention. (H.F.S. to H. L. Black, May 18, 1939.) One year after the adoption of the Sixteenth Amendment the Supreme Court had declared the sole effect of the new Amendment was to relieve income taxes of the constitutional apportionment requirement. See *Brushaber* v. *Union Pacific Railroad Co.*, 240 U.S. 1 (1916); see also *Evans* v. *Gore*, 253 U.S. 245 (1920). Cf. Stone's comment in *Metcalf & Eddy* v. *Mitchell*, 269, U.S. 514 (1926), p. 521.

"would single them out for tax purposes which could conceivably result in wholly depriving them of the support against discrimination resulting from a general and uniform tax." "Income taxes alone are involved in this case, and my references are to them," Black pointed out.[65]

"Strictly entre nous," Stone wrote Frankfurter after the decision came down, "I wrote for a minority of the Court, which I am afraid would have remained a minority if I had written on any other lines. . . . I did not mind Black's concurrence, in fact, I made some suggestions for it which he adopted."* "I was only sorry," he concluded, "that he did not recognize a little more explicitly that I used the phrase 'essential governmental function' more narrowly than he seemed to think."[66]

The decision offers a good illustration of Stone's judicial technique. Not willing to overrule old precedents and established traditions with one sweep of the pen, he worked slowly but doggedly toward the elimination of ancient but dubious dogma, building deliberately, and acclimatizing his brethren to each forward move until the moment arrived to thrust the keystone into place. The task of the writer in the Gerhardt case, he wrote, "was to avoid the extension of precedent and dicta of over one hundred years . . . and at the same time succeed in getting four judges to agree." It had been, he proudly conceded, "something of an achievement to make the opinion the opinion of the Court." He was certain, too, "that it was a considerable step in the right direction," since there was "nothing in it to preclude taking another step whenever the Court is so minded." Revealing his own philosophy, he concluded: "The task of a judge is to decide right the case before him. If, in addition, he can expose the nature and limits of the doctrine of unhappy precedents, without approving them, and point the way to their further limitation, he accomplishes more than usually falls to his lot."[67]

But new concepts are not absorbed by nine men at the same rate of assimilation, and on the very day that *Helvering* v. *Gerhardt* came down, Justice Roberts delivered a tax immunity opinion which upheld the power of Congress to tax receipts of athletic contests at state universities. The Court split wide open. Only Hughes and Brandeis joined in the opinion without qualification. Athletic contests were not, Justice Roberts said, so much an essential of state government as to be exempt from the burden of a non-discriminatory tax. He distorted this conclu-

---

* Stone was successful in getting Black to state in his opinion that both were agreed "a citizen who receives his income from a state owes the same obligation to the United States as other citizens who draw their salaries from other sources or the United States and pay federal income taxes." (H.F.S. to Hugo L. Black, May 20, 1938.) He was not able to budge Black in his belief that *Collector* v. *Day* should be re-examined in the light of the Sixteenth Amendment.

sion by relying upon the old distinction between "governmental" and "proprietary" functions, a distinction which Stone thought he had eradicated by intimation in the Gerhardt decision. Stone concurred with the result but felt that the case should have been dismissed since the district court, under congressional enactment, had no jurisdiction to entertain suits brought to restrain the collection of a tax. Black and Reed also concurred, the former denying any sanction to "the reasoning of the Court on the question of state immunity from interference by federal taxation." Butler and McReynolds, of course, dissented.[68]

The Gerhardt case threw grave doubts on *Collector* v. *Day* and other precedents, and Justice Roberts' subsequent opinion muddled the law completely, leading Thomas Reed Powell to observe: "I am now teaching intergovernmental relations between 11 and 12, and before I make any statement on Monday, I always take out my watch to see what time it is in order to know whether I am safe in making the remark."[69]

With the whole question of the tax liability of official salaries up in the air, the climax came quickly. In the following term Solicitor General Jackson filed an *amicus* brief in the O'Keefe case, on behalf of New York's authority to tax an attorney for the Federal Home Owners' Loan Corporation. Tactically the contention came with better grace from federal authorities when they could argue for extension of state, rather than federal, taxing power. But New York immediately saw the implication, and its Solicitor damned the challenge to traditional immunity as "wholly impertinent."[70] The latter rested the state's claim on the fact that the HOLC had "all the earmarks of a regular private business corporation" and performed a "proprietary," not a "governmental" function.

Every constitutionally created federal agency, Stone replied in a sweeping opinion for the Court, is a national instrumentality; Congress decides whether and to what extent its creatures shall be free from taxation. In the absence of congressional command, "it is in order to consider the nature and effect of the alleged burden, and if it appears that there is no ground for implying a constitutional immunity, there is equally a want of any ground for assuming any purpose on the part of Congress to create an immunity." "The only possible basis for implying a constitutional immunity," he continued, "is that the economic burden of the tax is in some way passed on so as to impose a burden on the national government tantamount to an interference by one government with the other in the performance of its functions."[71]

Correlating his discussion of this test of taxation by one government of the salaries of employees of the other, he noted that some economists maintain that income taxes would require government to pay higher wages, but not all agree, and the formula "cannot be judicially assumed." "The theory, which once won a qualified approval, that a tax on income is legally or economically a tax on its source," he said flatly, "is no longer tenable." The burden laid on governments by such taxes, if any, "is but the normal incident of the organization within the same territory of two governments, each possessing the taxing power." It made no difference whether the income taxed was that of a state or a federal employee—in both cases the past exemption had been based on "untenable" assumption, and, as a result, the venerable *Collector* v. *Day*, establishing immunity for state officers, and the recent Rogers case, confirming it for federal employees, must be overruled, "so far as they recognize an implied constitutional immunity from income taxation of the salaries of officers or employees of the national or a state government or their instrumentalities."[72]

In thus cutting out dead precedents, the O'Keefe opinion went considerably beyond Stone's decision of the prior term. By emphasizing the interference doctrine as the sole constitutional test, it consolidated the previous year's inroads, making explicit what Gerhardt had implied —that government employment was no refuge from taxes.

Justice Frankfurter praised the outcome highly—but dimmed the moment for Stone by adding, after the fashion of the professor in a seminar, a few words of his own. The new jurist's concurrence was not entirely superfluous; he would add another decision, *Dobbins* v. *Erie County*, to the list of superannuated precedents. To complete his effort, dissenters Butler and McReynolds consigned *Brush* v. *Commissioner* to constitutional limbo.

But was Justice Stone entitled to cut four notches in his gun after the O'Keefe case, as these Justices thought, or only two, as he stated in his opinion? The Dobbins case, for example, had invalidated a state tax laid directly on a federal office, though measured by the salary of the incumbent. As Stone understood immunity, such a tax might still be unconstitutional. In any case, innate caution led him to think judges should "hear argument in a specific case before expressing an opinion." He had purposely written the O'Keefe case as "narrowly" as he could. "I think it of importance," he told Frankfurter, "that we proceed to effect as widely extended a reform as the present one in just this way, step by step, if possible." He very much wanted his opinion that of the Court. "As the matter now stands," he reminded the concurring Justice, "unless the Chief Justice comes in, it will require agreement by all those who voted to reverse in order to get an opinion of the Court. . . . If that cannot be accomplished," he exclaimed somewhat petulantly, "it would perhaps be as well to settle the matter by announcing our vote, without opinion, as the Court did in the Prohibition cases."[73]

It was a great triumph, yet congratulations from the law clerks who had been with him through the long struggle did not seem to exhilarate him. "In the space of only a few years," Walter Gellhorn commented cheerfully, "you have gotten your Court to reverse a trend. One could almost present this subject on a chart, with the line ever ascending nearer to the true goal—until, by golly, it arrived there."[74] Truly, Stone now occupied the position of Powell's candid sham jurist—preferring always to confess that cases had not been overruled. "I cannot say that I am happy in having a part in overturning a doctrine as long followed as that of *Collector v. Day*," he replied to Gellhorn. "But it had so little to support it and the tendency has been so strong in the past to extend it that it seemed as though there was nothing else to do."[75]

Thirteen years had elapsed since Stone's first suggestion of pragmatic inquiry into the immunities doctrine. Gently leading his brethren after him, step by step, he had substantiated Taft's early comment that one had to be "careful" of Stone's opinions.

CHAPTER THIRTY-ONE

# The Core of Free Government

## 1938-1940

Like the opposition party that finally wins an election, a Supreme Court Justice faces new difficulties the moment his dissents become the law of the land. Once the balance has shifted, the precedents are no longer decisive. New cases, in fresh areas of controversy, probe for the limits of the Justice's now dominant philosophy and compel him to give content to the general principles he has declared. So it was with Justice Stone and his colleagues after 1937, when time began to establish the objectives of Mr. Roosevelt's Court reorganization plan.

The most puzzling aspect of the new order was that justice now appeared two-faced. The "enlightened Court" bowed in case after case to legislative judgment on the reasonableness of this or that commercial tax or regulation, assailed under the due process clause. At the same time it warded off legislative encroachments on personal and political liberties. Where official action trenched on those individual rights which history has proved to be the indispensable conditions of a free society, the Court explicitly disclaimed any initial disposition to hold either that the legislature was really seeking its avowed objective or that the means employed were appropriate.[1]

Had not the Justices become ensnared in what Judge Learned Hand has described as a "logical dilemma"? Had they not overlooked the fact that in America "property itself is the matrix, the seed-bed, which must be conserved if other values are to flourish"?[2] As Judge Hand noted in 1946, "It began to seem as though, when 'personal rights' were in issue, something strangely akin to the discredited attitude toward the Bill of Rights of the old apostles of the institution of property, was regaining recognition. Just why property itself was not a 'personal right' nobody took the time to explain; and perhaps the inquiry would have been regarded as captious and invidious anyway; but the fact remained that in the name of the Bill of Rights the courts were upsetting statutes which were plainly compromises between conflicting interests, each of which had more than a merely plausible support in reason. That looked a good deal as though more specific directions could be found in the lapidary counsels of the Amendments than the successful school had been able to discover, so long as the dispute turned on property."[3]

Imputing his own ideas to Stone, Judge Hand declared that the core of Stone's constitutional jurisprudence was acceptance of the presumptive constitutionality of legislation, whether it affected economic activities or specific guarantees of personal freedom. He believed, Judge Hand contends, in "even-handed application" of the due process clause, "since only by not intervening could they [judges] hope to preserve that independence which was the condition of any successful discharge of their duties."[4]

It is difficult to square Judge Hand's interpretation with Stone's record, or with that of the Court itself. At the very moment the Justices abandoned guardianship of economic interests, they seemed ready to shoulder a special responsibility for speech, thought, and religion. Having surrendered the heavy responsibility of passing on the wisdom of social and economic policy, they were soon faced with the question whether judicial self-restraint was equally applicable to the review of legislation infringing those freedoms that had come to be thought of as "implicit in the concept of ordered liberty."[5]

"It is the paradox of the period, if paradox it be," Herbert Wechsler has written, "that new areas of constitutional protection were emerging even as the power to govern was being sustained. Justice Stone's part in this branch of the development was . . . commanding."[6] Just as he had led the battle for judicial self-restraint in cases involving social and economic legislation, so it was he who, with the "casualness of a footnote"[7] (to use Justice Frankfurter's somewhat derogatory language), suggested a formulation that ultimately flowered into the so-called doctrine of "preferred freedoms."

In the otherwise obscure case of *United States* v. *Carolene Products Co.*, decided in 1938, Stone wrote these lines into the body of his opinion for the Court:

Regulatory legislation affecting ordinary commercial transactions is not to be pronounced unconstitutional unless in the light of the facts made known or generally assumed it is of such a character as to preclude the assumption that it rests upon some rational basis within the knowledge and experience of the legislators.

He would not go so far as to say that no economic legislation would ever violate constitutional restraints, but he did suggest confining the Court's role strictly. Attached to this proposition was the famous footnote four:

There may be narrower scope for operation of the presumption of constitutionality when legislation appears on its face to be within a specific prohibition of the Constitution, such as those of the first ten amendments, which are deemed equally specific when held to be embraced within the Fourteenth.

It is unnecessary to consider now whether legislation which restricts those political processes which can ordinarily be expected to bring about repeal of undesirable legislation, is to be subjected to more exacting judicial scrutiny under the general prohibitions of the Fourteenth Amendment than are most other types of legislation. . . .

Nor need we enquire whether similar considerations enter into the review of statutes directed at particular religious . . . or national . . . or racial minorities . . . whether prejudice against discrete and insular minorities may be a special condition, which tends seriously to curtail the operation of those political processes ordinarily to be relied upon to protect minorities, and which may call for a correspondingly more searching judicial inquiry.[8]

The first draft of the second and third paragraphs of this historic note was written by Stone's law clerk, Louis Lusky.* Stone "adopted it almost as drafted," Lusky has recalled, "simply toning down a couple of over-emphatic words."[9] The opinion was then circulated. Chief Justice Hughes was "somewhat disturbed" by Lusky's language. "Different considerations may apply," the law clerk's draft of the first paragraph said, "and one attacking the constitutionality of a statute may be thought to bear a lighter burden, when the legislation aims at restricting the corrective political processes, which can ordinarily be expected to bring about repeal of undesirable legislation."

"Are the 'considerations' different, or does the difference lie not in the *test* but in the nature of the right invoked?" Hughes asked.[10]

---

* It was not unusual for Stone to allow his law clerks to use footnotes as trial balloons for meritorious ideas. "I have always been very proud of these contributions," Lusky wrote. "They are my contributions only in a limited sense. The ideas originated with me, but they became important only because the Justice adopted them as his own. It would be a great mistake indeed to suppose that any law clerk ever got anything into the Justice's opinions which he didn't want there himself. He could not be pushed or persuaded against his own judgment." (Louis Lusky to A.T.M., July 28, 1952.)

"You are quite right," Stone replied somewhat ambiguously. "I wish to avoid the possibility of having what I have written in the body of the opinion about the presumption of constitutionality in the ordinary run of due process cases applied as a matter of course to these other more exceptional cases. For that reason it seemed to me desirable to file a caveat in the note—without, however, committing the Court to any proposition contained in it. The notion that the Court should be more alert to protect constitutional rights in those cases where there is danger that the ordinary political processes for the correction of undesirable legislation may not operate has been announced for the Court by many judges, notably Chief Justice Marshall in *McCulloch* v. *Maryland*, with reference to taxation of governmental instrumentalities."[11] As it later developed, the difference in Stone's mind lay in both the "test" and the nature of the right involved.

This embattled footnote* of three paragraphs contains a corresponding number of ideas. The first suggests that when legislation, on its face, contravenes the specific constitutional negatives set out in the Bill of Rights, the usual presumption of constitutionality may be curtailed or even waived. The second paragraph indicates that the judiciary has a special responsibility as defender of those liberties prerequisite to the purity of political processes. The Court thus becomes the ultimate guardian against abuses that would poison the primary check on government—the ballot box. It must protect those liberties on which the democratic effectiveness of political action depends. The third para-

---

* In 1949 Justice Frankfurter flatly denied the propriety of the phrase "preferred position" and deplored use of a footnote as the "way of announcing a new constitutional doctrine." "This is a phrase," he said somewhat contemptuously, "that has uncritically crept into some recent opinions of this Court. I deem it a mischievous phrase, if it carries the thought, which it may subtly imply, that any law touching communication is infected with presumptive invalidity. . . . I say the phrase is mischievous because it radiates a constitutional doctrine without avowing it. Clarity and candor in these matters, so as to avoid gliding unwittingly into error, makes it appropriate to trace the history of the phrase 'preferred position.'" In the course of his detailed exploration Justice Frankfurter himself appears to have glided "unwittingly into error" in stating that the preferred freedoms doctrine (erroneously equated with presumption of unconstitutionality of legislation which touches the First Amendment freedoms) "has never commended itself to a majority of this Court." "I think my brother Frankfurter," Justice Rutledge wrote in dissent, "demonstrates the conclusion opposite to that which he draws, namely, that the First Amendment guaranties of the freedoms of speech, press, assembly, and religion occupy preferred position not only in the Bill of Rights but also in the repeated decisions of this Court." See *Kovacs* v. *Cooper*, 336 U.S. 77 (1949), pp. 90, 95, 106.

In the Dennis case (1951), Justice Frankfurter confessed his error: "In reviewing statutes which restrict freedoms protected by the First Amendment, we have emphasized the close relation which those freedoms bear to maintenance of a free society. . . . Some members of the Court—and at times a majority—have done more. They have suggested that our function in reviewing statutes restricting freedom of expression differs sharply from our normal duty in sitting in judgment on legislation."

graph suggests a special role for the Court as protector of minorities and of unpopular groups peculiarly helpless at the polls in the face of discriminatory or repressive assault.*

The footnote clearly manifested Stone's growing concern for civil liberties and his conviction that the Court was under particular responsibility to protect them. "I have been deeply concerned," he wrote Judge Irving Lehman the day after the decision came down, "about the increasing racial and religious intolerance which seems to bedevil the world, and which I greatly fear may be augmented in this country. For that reason I was greatly disturbed by the attacks on the Court and the Constitution last year, for one consequence of the program of 'judicial reform' might well result in breaking down the guaranties of individual liberty."[12]

Here, obviously, was a fertile field for creative judicial statesmanship. In his Gerhardt and Barnwell opinions, Stone had adumbrated the doctrine of political restraints.[13] The Carolene Products footnote seemed but a logical corollary. If the political processes cannot be depended upon to provide protection against legislation restricting, say, the right to vote, freedom of speech, religion, and assembly, or against statutes directed at discrete and insular minorities, the courts are under special obligation to scrutinize the infringements.† One commentator has described Stone's basic thought in these words:

> I am first of all a man of reason. I believe in reason and its power in the market place of discourse. I am also a democrat. I believe that our governments are to be run by the governed. Therefore I shall use my great power as a Supreme Court Justice sparingly, but I shall use it when it is necessary to preserve the democratic process or to protect those injured by unreason under circumstances where political processes cannot be relied on to protect them.[14]

* Lusky, in his article "Minority Rights and the Public Interest," omits paragraph one completely from his discussion. Lusky's former law partner, George D. Braden, reasoning both from the contradictory nature of the ideas and Lusky's omission, surmised that Hughes wrote the paragraph. "My guess is," Braden observed in his article, "The Search for Objectivity in Constitutional Law," "that Chief Justice Hughes added the paragraph to protect some theory he had which he thought the citations to his opinions demonstrated."

† Braden's article also suggested that Stone was "addressing himself to a problem arising out of the use of the presumption of constitutionality as a means of forestalling due process clause attacks on economic legislation. His problem was to make the presumption stick in economic cases without being plagued by it in civil liberties and similar cases. Accordingly, he suggested by typical judicial indirection that legislation restricting political processes and legislation directed at 'discrete and insular' minorities should not have a favorable presumption of constitutionality to protect the legislation against attack. His expressed reason for the latter half of this was that political processes 'can ordinarily be expected to bring about repeal of undesirable legislation,' but that minorities such as racial and religious groups are subject to prejudice 'which tends seriously to curtail the operation of those political processes ordinarily to be relied upon to protect minorities.' "

Stone was quick to disavow his own pioneering in this field. The groundwork had been laid in the earlier opinions of Holmes, Brandeis, and Hughes;[15] the real pathbreakers were Cardozo and Holmes.* Stone mentioned certain of the latter's opinions as indicating that "he thought that the judge should not be too rigidly bound to the tenet of judicial self-restraint in cases involving civil liberties."[16] Even after the Carolene Products footnote had been formulated, Stone tried to reassure a worried champion of civil liberty by citing Justice Cardozo's opinion in *Palko* v. *Connecticut*, as illustrating "what the Court had been doing in recent years to iron out difficulties in the way of effective protection of freedom." Cardozo had spoken of the "social and moral values" of freedom of thought and speech as existing on a "different plane" from the other rights set out in the first eight Amendments. "Of that freedom," Cardozo observed, "one may say that it is the matrix, the indispensable condition, of nearly every other form of freedom." These rights are, he said, "the very essence of a scheme of ordered liberty."[17] With reference to Cardozo's formulation, Stone commented: "I am not sure but that it [the application of special constitutional safeguards necessary for protecting individual freedoms] will be worked out about as well now as if a new amendment were drafted."[18]

Further evidence of the Court's opportunity for creative endeavor was forthcoming that same year, when the Justices honored the CIO's challenge of Mayor Hague's power to close Jersey City's public parks and streets to public meetings on the mere opinion of the Director of Public Safety that his refusal would prevent "riots, disturbances, and disorderly assemblage." Speaking for the Court, Justice Roberts asserted the right of citizens of the United States to discuss union organization under the Wagner Act.† This, he held, is a "privilege and immunity" of citizens of the United States. Stone took a broader view. Freedom of speech and assembly is more than a privilege or immunity peculiar to United States citizenship which is secured to citizens of the United States by the privileges and immunities clause of the Fourteenth Amendment. "It has been explicitly and repeatedly affirmed by this Court, without a dissenting voice," Stone wrote, "that freedom of speech and of assembly for any lawful purpose are rights of personal liberty secured to all persons, without regard to citizenship, by the due process clause of the Fourteenth Amendment."[19]

Following the authoritative lead of Justice Samuel F. Miller,[20] he

* Professor Frankfurter contended that Holmes "attributed very different legal significance to those liberties of the individual which history has attested as the indispensable conditions of a free society" and "was far more ready to find legislative invasion in this field than in the area of debatable economic reform." (See his *Mr. Justice Holmes and the Supreme Court*, p. 51.)

† Hughes approved Roberts' position on the merits and agreed with Stone as to the state of the record. McReynolds and Butler wrote separate dissents.

spoke out strongly against all attempts to revive this "privileges and immunities" clause from constitutional limbo.* Having just overcome judicial censorship of state economic legislation via the due process clause, the Justice was understandably reluctant to permit the same issue to arise anew under privileges and immunities. "I should have no difficulty," he told Irving Brant, "in agreeing that public discussion of the Wagner Act was a privilege of United States citizenship protected by the privileges and immunities clause if the record had supported our decree on that theory. But it did not, and I am not willing to relinquish any protection to personal liberty afforded by a clause [due process] of the Fourteenth Amendment in the hope that some other clause may be made to serve. The more so when that can be accomplished only by enlarging the privileges of U.S. citizenship (including privileges of property) at state expense."[21]

In his Hague opinion, as in the Carolene Products footnote, Stone made two points crystal clear: the safeguards for freedom embodied in the First Amendment are firmly anchored in the due process clause of the Fourteenth Amendment; and the Court henceforth would subject legislation restrictive of personal freedom to "more exacting judicial scrutiny." He was beginning to claim for the Court a special responsibility for safeguarding the political processes. For unless it stepped in, interferences with this primary mechanism for obliging government to control itself might render free government a sham.

Stone's special concern for civil liberties may not have registered with some observers because in earlier years circumstances had conspired on several occasions to misrepresent his views to the public. And before 1940 the Hague and Carolene Products cases were the only ones in which he had spoken out on civil liberties during his fourteen years on the bench. Privately, however, he had thrown his weight on freedom's side as occasion demanded. The yellow journals screamed the day after his forthright law clerk, Walter Gellhorn, having witnessed high-handed police "protection" against "radical" demonstrations around the Japanese Embassy, testified for the defendants. Not quite sure what his Chief's reaction would be, Gellhorn reported the

---

* Stone's reluctance to ground the decision in "privileges and immunities" may be traced to his dissent in *Colgate* v. *Harvey*, 296 U.S. 404 (1935). In a footnote to his opinion in the Hague case, Stone said: "If its restraint upon state action were to be extended more than is needful to protect relationships between the citizen and the national government, and if it were deemed to extend to those fundamental rights of person and property attached to citizenship by the common law and enactments of the states when the Amendment was adopted . . . it would enlarge Congressional and judicial control of the state action and multiply restrictions upon it whose nature, though difficult to anticipate with precision, would be of sufficient gravity to cause serious apprehension for the rightful independence of local government. That was the issue fought out in the Slaughter-House cases, with the decision against enlargement."

incident to the Justice with misgiving. But Stone shrugged it off calmly.[22] In the middle thirties the Justice ridiculed movements then current to require loyalty oaths of teachers. Logical consistency, he blurted out to a Senator's devoutly patriotic wife, demanded that each teacher renew her pledge daily before undertaking classroom duties. He considered this movement "so silly that it will fall of its own weight, unless too much is made of it by the university people."[23]

A few years later he was much less certain. "Well, I see," he wrote Dean Young B. Smith, "that Mr. Nicholas Murray Butler has discovered that true academic freedom is identical with that of a citizen of the German Reich—the freedom to do what he is told by his Führer and entourage. I hope someone will be found in Columbia University to give the nonsense the excoriation it deserves."[24]

On the Court, however, Stone had failed to express individual views even at the risk of appearing inconsistent. At the very outset of his judicial career he had left the impression that he agreed with the conservative majority in the controversial Gitlow case. Benjamin Gitlow circulated Communist literature and was convicted of violating the New York Criminal Anarchy Act of 1902. The argument of his counsel that the New York statute deprived him of liberty without due process of law by unreasonably restricting freedom of press evoked from the Court its first announcement of the proposition that freedom of speech and of the press, protected by the First Amendment from abridgment by Congress, "are among the fundamental personal rights and 'liberties' protected by the due process clause of the Fourteenth Amendment from impairment by the States." But the Court, apparently rejecting Holmes' "clear and present danger" test, held that the New York act, as applied to Gitlow, did not unduly restrict freedom of press and was therefore valid. Holmes and Brandeis dissented. Stone, though a member of the Court when the case came down, did not participate. Through an oversight he was nevertheless credited with having joined the majority.[25]

"The Gitlow case was argued before I went on the Court," he explained in 1941, "and I had no part in it. The Reporter omitted to state that fact in his report of the case and, due to my inexperience, I neglected to see that he did so. I have always regretted the oversight."[26]

Two years later another opportunity came to put his views on record. Then, Anita Whitney, a member of the Communist Labor party, convicted and sentenced under California's Criminal Syndicalism Act, sought review by the Supreme Court. Miss Whitney claimed that the statute violated the Constitution. The Justices, in an opinion by Sanford, rejected her plea and confirmed the state court's sentence. Holmes and Brandeis concurred in the result, the latter taking the occasion to state in memorable words the sanctity of the constitutional protection afforded freedom of speech and press.[27] Stone joined the majority when the opinion was revised to meet his objections. In Sanford's draft the majority had been content with the statement that freedom of speech is not absolute and might be limited by making it a crime to form or join syndicalist groups. "You should mention the fact," Stone wrote Sanford, May 13, 1927, "that the legislature declared in enacting the Act that the Act was necessary to the public peace and safety, etc.; that this declaration was not challenged by the defendant and therefore we cannot say that there was not a proper basis for the exercise of the legislative judgment. I would like to leave all reasonable scope for upholding freedom of speech against purely arbitrary legislation aimed at only fanciful evils. I think we can do that by giving the benefit of every presumption to the legislature unless the contrary fact is proven."

Actually it is hard to ascertain the difference between his stand and that of Brandeis and Holmes, except on the basis of a suspicion that they were willing to relax a standard he thought it vital to maintain undiluted. Had he been more desirous of "leaving all reasonable scope" for free thought than of preserving doctrinal consistency, he might have joined their concurrence. Perhaps his experience with political agitators as a member of the Board of Inquiry during World War I made him characterize as "real" those evils Holmes and Brandeis cast aside as purely "fanciful."

A few years later the Justice appeared, without explanation, on opposite sides in cases dealing with the right of pacifists to become naturalized Americans, voting in *United States* v. *Schwimmer* to deny the right, and dissenting with Hughes, Holmes, and Brandeis in *United States* v. *Macintosh* to affirm it. Again Stone had some explaining to do. "My participation in the Macintosh case did not indicate any change of view on my part, although here again the record on its face is against me," he later pointed out.[28] Holmes had rained ridicule on the Schwimmer majority for ruling that a woman applicant nearly sixty must swear to bear arms in defense of the United States. "So far as the adequacy of her oath is concerned," the dissenter observed, "I hardly can see how that is affected by the statement, inasmuch as she is a woman over fifty years of age, and would not be allowed to bear arms if she wanted to."[29] Stone joined the majority's narrow interpretation because he thought Miss Schwimmer's past "behavior" indicated a disposition to resist wartime acts of Government and to encourage others to do so.

Because of the narrowness of Justice Butler's opinion, however, Stone sought modifications. He was especially anxious to overcome the "impression," created by Holmes' scorching dissent, "that we are assailing mere opinions not likely to result in action." Accordingly he advised Butler to leave out any reference to "feelings of dislike and distrust," because such expressions suggested that "we are actuated by feelings of prejudice." Shift the emphasis, he told Butler, from Rosika Schwimmer's noxious "opinions" to her radical "behavior."[30] The majority's revised opinion said that pacifists "encouraged disobedience in others." This, in itself, evidenced want of "attachment to the principles of the Constitution." Butler incorporated Stone's suggestions side by side with his original inquiry into the propriety of the applicant's opinions and beliefs, but the resulting combination of ideas was exceedingly awkward, to say the least.

Stone's friends and former colleagues were incredulous. "Was the *United States Daily* correct in not including your name among those dissenting in the Schwimmer case?" Robert L. Hale inquired. "It is hard for me to believe. . . . You certainly do not share his [Butler's] views that persons make dangerous citizens because they have beliefs which differ from yours."

"No, I did not dissent," Stone replied. "I agreed with everything Justice Holmes said, but thought it not quite applicable to the situation created on the record. The situation, as I read it, places an affirmative burden on the applicant to show that his conduct is such as to evidence attachment to the Constitution. On the record presented to us it was fairly inferable that the petitioner would refuse obedience to the Constitution and laws enacted under it requiring citizens of the United States to support and maintain a war; and would encourage such disobedience in others.* That being the case, it seemed to me that the applicant did not show attachment to the principles of the Constitution. . . . The question was not merely, as Justice Holmes seemed to think, that the applicant was a person who believed that the Constitution could be improved. Such persons, if they are willing to obey it until such time as it is changed by the prescribed procedures, may become good citizens and be attached to the principles of the Constitution. When their objections carry them further than that, I think Congress, rightly or wrongly, has prescribed that they should not be admitted."[31]

Ignoring all such refinements, conservative and liberal sources alike lambasted the decision. One writer said that Butler's opinion turned altogether "upon the applicant's views, opinions, and beliefs." "The law is the law," the *New York Times* mused with an air of bewilderment, but "it is a little anomalous that a country which has renounced war should exclude from its citizenship a person whose chief offense is her

---

* On the record presented to the Circuit Court of Appeals and thence to the Supreme Court, such inferences could only have been drawn from Madame Schwimmer's expressed opinions about war and pacifism. The appeals were heard on a stipulation of facts which said: "The testimony at the hearing of the petition shows that the petitioner is qualified for citizenship except insofar as the *views* of the applicant set forth in the foregoing agreed statement of facts may show that the applicant is not attached to the principles of the Constitution. . . ." (Quoted in Henry B. Hazard, "Supreme Court Holds Madame Schwimmer, Pacifist, Ineligible to Naturalization," *American Journal of International Law*, July 1929, p. 629.)

opposition to war." The *Nation* labeled the decision "Treason to Conscience," adding that it "puts an indelible stain of disloyalty to American precedents, principles, and ideals upon the names of William Howard Taft, Justice Butler, and every one of the judges who laid down this doctrine."[32]

These were the reactions of persons and journals whose opinions Stone respected. And it is fair to surmise that doubts may have been raised as to the wisdom of his acquiescence in Butler's opinion even as revised.

The Schwimmer opinion spurred immigration officials to even greater efforts to ensure the political orthodoxy of applicants for citizenship. Prospective citizens were asked absurd questions, which, being honestly answered, resulted in their rejection because they would not swear in advance to support every war, however unjust. Several cases testing the more rigorous policies were on their way to the Supreme Court when, in October 1930, Stone sent a long handwritten letter to John Bassett Moore asking for comment on the Schwimmer decision. "It would be a great help to me," the Justice said, "if I could (because of your wide experience in dealing with questions affecting citizenship and naturalization) know just how much force you would give to the phrase in the statute 'attached to the principles of the Constitution.' "[33]

Judge Moore's reply minced no words. He was quite "unable to accept the views laid down by Mr. Justice Butler" and, apparently, considered these indistinguishable from Stone's. "I had always regarded freedom of thought and of speech not only as the very cornerstone of our liberties but also as the first condition of progress in religion, in science, and in government. I could not forget that our own independence and form of government were founded in revolution, and as regards our national defense, and the defense of our institutions, I could not help feeling that if this was in a pre-eminent sense 'the home of the brave,' it was due to the fact that it was also 'the land of the free,' it being as natural to love a government that assures us liberty as it is unnatural to love a government that oppresses us."

Coming down to Stone's technical query, the meaning of the phrase "attached to the principles of the Constitution," Moore pointed out that it required the Court to make only a limited inquiry into the morals and character of the applicant. "By what authority," he asked, "can a court assume to set up, under the mere prescription of an oath, an inquisition into beliefs and to censor the thoughts and prescribe the views which persons seeking citizenship must or may not hold?" "Pacificism," this leading authority on international law declared, "has never been considered illegal or *unconstitutional*. It will hardly be pretended that believing in or teaching pacifism either is immoral, or is inconsistent with attachment to the 'principles' of the Constitution or with a good disposition toward the order and happiness of the country." Moore did not subscribe to pacifist doctrine, yet he believed that "its adherents not only are qualified for citizenship in the sense of the Act of 1906, but that they also constitute the great body of those who pay to the cause of peace and its promotion more than an emotional, unthinking, shallow lip service. As such they perform a useful service in counteracting the general tendency to violence which has so ruthlessly held sway during the past fifteen years."[34]

Moore's letter apparently shook the Justice's confidence in his policy of reticence. Once again he regretted not having stated his views. In writing Moore, Stone was not only trying to reassure himself as to the wisdom of his stand in the Schwimmer case, but was also thinking of a case then on its way toward decision—that of a Yale divinity professor, Clyde Macintosh, who, on the ground that he would not swear beforehand to support every future military adventure of the United States, lost his bid for naturalization. Stone prepared, but did not deliver, a dissent. Taking his cue from Moore, he pointed to the similarity of the naturalization oath and that prescribed by the Constitution for federal officers: "It comes as a surprise, after the lapse of one hundred and forty years, to learn that Congress, by prescribing the same oath as prerequisite to citizenship, has authorized an inquisition into the beliefs of applicants for citizenship, censored their thoughts, or prescribed for them the views which they, more than persons seeking public office, must or may not hold."

In the Schwimmer case, the undelivered Macintosh opinion said, "the proven conduct of the applicant, quite apart from her opinions and theories, supported the District Court's inference of her want of that attachment to the principles of the Constitution which the Naturalization Law requires. . . . Here, the applicant stands ready to take the statutory oath as it is written."

"The construction of the statute by the opinion of the Court," Stone concluded, "as requiring applicants for citizenship to promise unconditionally to bear arms in some future hypothetical war, and authorizing their exclusion on the basis of their views and opinions, wholly apart from their behavior, seems to be a strained and unnatural one, not consonant with its words or history."[35]

Stone's draft opinion did not go down, however, as Hughes' willingness to distinguish the Schwimmer case and treat it as standing on its own "special facts" enabled Stone to join Holmes and Brandeis in the Chief Justice's dissent. "Sensing a possible feeling that the publication of another dissent would not be wholly appreciated," Stone explained, "I withdrew my own."[36] Once more Stone had an excuse for not stating "succinctly" his peculiar stand—that Miss Schwimmer was denied citizenship not for her opinions but for her past behavior.

Moore made his disgust over the Macintosh ruling known immediately. "Yesterday," he wrote Stone, May 26, 1931, "I read with real grief the decision in the naturalization case; a decision having, in my opinion, no foundation in law, and involving the exercise of a narrow, tyrannical, inquisitional supervision over personal beliefs. Most fully do I agree with the declaration that it 'is not within the province of the courts to make bargains with those who seek naturalization'; and for the very same reason the courts commit a bald usurpation of power when they go outside the terms and well-styled interpretations of old statutes in order to force those who seek naturalization to make extra-legal bargains with them."

Why was Justice Stone at such pains to maintain a distinction seemingly so tenuous? The reasons may have been his instinctive distrust of radicals and agitators. Writing in 1919, he suggested that their "muddle-headed" thinking was produced by a "variety of causes," but listed "false social and political theories" among the "most frequent."[37] Rosika Schwimmer was cut from the same cloth as the proud political zealots Stone had encountered in camp after camp during World War I. Pacifists refused, sometimes on political grounds, to use force on behalf of their government. As a Supreme Court Justice, he could do no more for Miss Schwimmer than he had for political recalcitrants as a member of the Board of Inquiry in 1918. A religious dissenter such as Professor Macintosh, on the other hand, could enlist his support.

As to the effect of Stone's experience in reviewing cases of conscientious objectors, Justice William O. Douglas has written: "I know from what he told me that it was for him a moving experience. Perhaps he learned from the quiet Quakers, or from those who are more impassioned, the full meaning of religious freedom. Perhaps he saw in the deep, burning eyes of some of the two thousand drafted men whom he interviewed the message that there are some who will die rather than bear false witness to their religion."[38]

These naturalization cases disturbed Stone profoundly. Invoking technical reasons for not speaking out in the agitators' behalf, he sometimes seemed to grasp at straws. In the case of Marie Bland, another pacifist seeking citizenship, decided with the Macintosh case, he argued that because she refused to take the oath exactly as written, the Court could not assist her. A separate concurrence was written along this line, but as no one, including members of Sutherland's majority, thought this fact significant, Stone abandoned it and joined in Hughes' brief dissent.[39] The same pattern reappeared in *Hamilton* v. *Regents of the University of California*, where the Court held that the state might require students attending the state university to take military drill in spite of religious scruples.[40] Justice Butler, speaking for the Court, featured the Schwimmer and Macintosh cases as supporting precedents.

Stone, though wanting to go along with the majority, was discomfited. "I wish very much," he wrote Justice Butler, November 28, 1934, "that I could persuade you to drop from your opinion . . . the references to the Schwimmer case and the Macintosh case. Neither case has very much to do with the question presented to us now, and the present case does not need their support. I do not deny the truth of the quotations from these opinions. My only feeling about them is that they unnecessarily rub salt into the wounds of a great many very worthy people who, I am convinced, dwell on a higher spiritual plane than I do, and I am not at all sure that another generation may not conclude that their views about war are a great deal wiser than my own. The subject with which we are called upon to deal is a delicate one, and I feel that we ought to avoid causing any unnecessary irritations so far as is reasonably possible."

Justice Butler refused to budge. "Admittedly the Schwimmer and Macintosh cases as to the points on which they are here cited accurately state the law," he wrote Stone. "I fear failure now to cite them might, because of the difference on other points reflected by the dissenting opinions, be misunderstood to the detriment of the law."[41]

Justice Cardozo also had misgivings and stated them in a six-page memorandum. Uncertain as to "whether it is wise to circulate it," he temporized. "All through the land," he wrote Stone, "conscientious and high-principled young men—for ethical if not religious reasons—are opposed to military training. I think it oppressive to make them submit to it in these times of peace, though I am satisfied the state has the power to be oppressive if it chooses. The opinion of the Court seems to be quite without sympathy for their attitude. But I suppose it is best to keep one's mouth shut when in doubt."[42]

In the end, however, Cardozo's memorandum went down as a concurring opinion. Stone, along with Brandeis, joined in it. Justice Stone had again missed an opportunity to speak his own mind. As his letter to Justice Butler indicates, the policy of "remaining silent" still seemed the wiser course.

Stone never quite subdued the nagging disquiet caused by parting company with Holmes in the Schwimmer case. Yet to his dying day he maintained that there was a difference between her case and that of Professor Macintosh.[43] Naturalization involves the assumption of obligations as well as the entry upon privileges, he reasoned. Therefore the authorities, bound by an act of Congress, were justified in ascertaining whether the applicant was frank in claiming to assume those obligations. "He found it almost impossible," Louis Lusky observed, "to admit that he had changed his mind about anything he had said in an opinion, . . . with resulting lack of clarity."[44] To the very end he could admit no more than a regret that he had not made his position clear. "I have always thought that the Schwimmer case was correctly decided but not for the reasons stated in the opinion. These cases later attracted attention," he explained in 1941, and "I have naturally regretted that I did not write my own opinions in both of them."[45]

At intervals over a period of twenty years Stone had wrestled earnestly with the paradox of liberty and authority at this most sensitive level. The battle was never fought to a finish. The ghosts of old decisions continued to rise up and haunt him. Until 1940 he, somewhat like the Court itself, seemed to be keeping open two lines of approach. The showdown came in the spring of that year. Then, in flat contradiction to the "preferred position" he and other Justices had indicated for freedom of thought and belief, all his colleagues approved the compulsory flag salute required of Jehovah's Witnesses. It was a crucial decision. At long last Stone spoke out—alone.

In 1936 the Gobitis children, aged twelve and ten, had refused to join other pupils in the flag salute, as ordered by the Minersville, Pennsylvania, School Board, and they were expelled from the town's grammar school. Their refusal did not mean that they were unpatriotic or that they did not love their country. It simply meant that, as they read the Scriptures, the flag salute violated the Biblical injunction against bowing down to a graven image. Their father's suit to obtain readmittance reached the Supreme Court just as World War II threatened. The nation was already in the throes of hectic preparation. Moved, one suspects, by considerations of time and circumstances, eight Justices, speaking through Justice Frankfurter, found the School Board's prescribed ceremony rationally related to the purpose of fostering national unity—"the basis of national security," and "an interest inferior to none in the hierarchy of legal values."[46]

The basic issue was not new for either Stone or Frankfurter. In his memorandum of September 18, 1918, to Secretary of War Newton Baker, Frankfurter had said that "conscientious objectors, whether sectarian or individualistic, . . . who stand in uncompromising opposition [whether to combatant or noncombatant service] should be convicted and confined." "I suggest," Frankfurter wrote, that "these absolutists be turned over to the Fort Leavenworth authorities for treatment." Stone, on the other hand, held that "all human experience teaches us that a moral issue cannot be suppressed or settled by making its supporters martyrs."[47] Justice Stone adhered to this belief in the Jehovah's Witnesses cases. Earlier in the 1939-40 term Chief Justice Hughes' hint from the bench during argument that Jehovah's Witnesses could not invoke the free-speech protection because what they said was offensive to Catholics, had stirred him profoundly.[48] "I suppose," he wrote John Bassett Moore while the Gobitis case was under consideration, "there are limits beyond which personally offensive free speech cannot be pressed, but there would not be much necessity for free-speech protection if it extended only to those things we like to hear."[49] At conference, however, he reserved his vote.

By the time the case reached the Justices, April 21, 1940, this issue had been before them three times. In each instance they had disposed of the matter by *per curiam* opinion, for want of a substantial federal question. As late as April 17, 1939, Justice Stone joined his colleagues in denying appeal from the Supreme Court of California, upholding the flag salute.[50] When it became evident that Stone would dissent in the Gobitis case, Justice Frankfurter was astonished and dismayed. In a five-page letter he elaborated the consideration he had given this "tragic issue," all the more delicate for him in that it involved a "clash of rights, not the clash of wrongs." "For resolving such clash we have no calculus," Frankfurter commented. "We are not exercising an independent judgment; we are sitting in judgment upon the judgment of the legislature."

"Nothing has weighed as much on my conscience, since I have come on this Court, as has this case," the Court's spokesman wrote Stone. "All my bias and pre-disposition are in favor of giving the fullest elbow room to every variety of religious, political, and economic view." Frankfurter's stand was more soul-wrenching in that it entered "a domain where constitutional power is on one side and my private notions of liberty and toleration and good sense are on the other. . . . I want to avoid the mistake comparable to that made by those whom we criticized when dealing with the control of property. . . . My intention . . . was to use this opinion as a vehicle for preaching the true democratic faith of not relying on the Court for the impossible task of assuring a vigorous, mature, self-protecting, and tolerant democracy by bringing the responsibility for a combination of firmness and toleration directly home where it belongs—to the people and their representatives themselves." In all this, Frankfurter thought he was but following Stone's pointed admonitions about judicial self-restraint. "I have tried in this opinion really to act on what will, as a matter of history, be a lodestar for due regard between legislative and judicial powers, to wit, your dissent in the Butler case."

Nor was this the only case in which Stone had stated the guiding rule Frankfurter thought he was following: "I am aware of the important distinction which you so skillfully adumbrated in your footnote four (particularly the second paragraph of it) in the Carolene Products Co. case. I agree with that distinction; I regard it as basic. I have taken over that distinction in its central aspect in the present opinion . . . by insisting on the importance of keeping open all those channels of free expression by which undesirable legislation may be removed, and keeping unobstructed all forms of protest against what one deems invasions of conscience, however much the invasion may be justified on the score of the deepest interests of national well-being."

"We are not," Frankfurter emphasized, "the primary resolver of the clash." He was concerned lest we "exercise our judicial power unduly, and as though we ourselves were legislators by holding with too tight a rein the organs of popular government."[51]

Stone simulated embarrassment at being confronted by an antagonist who cited his own words against him. But, he retorted, any "vulgar intrusion of law in the domain of conscience," as in this case, imposes on the Court a larger responsibility than in legislation dealing with the control of property. "I am truly sorry not to go along with you. The case is peculiarly one of the relative weight of imponderables and I cannot overcome the feeling that the Constitution tips the scales in favor of religion."[52]

For Justice Frankfurter the great lesson of the controversy over the Supreme Court in 1937 was that Judges may not interpose personal valuations in any sphere of judicial competence. "The precise issue," in the Gobitis case, was "whether the legislatures of the various states and the authorities in a thousand counties and school districts of this country are barred from determining the appropriateness of various means to evoke that unifying sentiment without which there can ultimately be no liberties, civil or religious." The Court must defer to local authority, Frankfurter insisted. "To stigmatize legislative judgment in providing for this universal gesture of respect for the symbol of our national life in the setting of the common school as a lawless inroad on that freedom of conscience which the Constitution protects, would amount to no less than the pronouncement of pedagogical and psychological dogma in a field where courts possess no marked and certainly no controlling competence." The essence of Stone's Carolene Products footnote was that

Except where the transgression of constitutional liberty is too plain for argument, personal freedom is best maintained—so long as the remedial channels of the democratic process remain open and unobstructed—when it is ingrained in a people's habits and not enforced against popular policy by the coercion of adjudicated law.

At the end Frankfurter threw down the very caveat Stone had hurled at his colleagues in 1936. "To the legislature no less than to courts is committed the guardianship of deeply cherished liberties."[53] Stone's first thought was to follow his usual pattern in cases of this sort—merely note dissent without supporting reasons. "Partly out of urging on my part and partly because he felt rather strongly," his law clerk, Allison Dunham, recalls, "he finally decided to write his dissent."* But he delayed so long that his dissent circulated only after most of the Justices had signified adherence to Frankfurter's opinion.

On the day the Gobitis case was to come down he was told that Frankfurter planned to read his opinion in full.† "He began to think of reading his opinion also," Dunham recalls. "During the course of the morning it became clear that he was getting more and more worked up. At Court time, when the opinions were read, Frankfurter, to our surprise, did not read his but merely announced the result." By this time Stone was so agitated he could not change his plans. When his turn came, he sat forward in his seat and, in a manner rare for him, read with fervor and emotion.[54]

"History teaches us," he said, "that there have been but few infringements of personal liberty by the state which have not been justified, as they are here, in the name of righteousness and the public good, and few which have not been directed, as they are now, at politically helpless minorities."[55] The Pennsylvania law did more than prohibit the free exercise of religion. In the name of national unity, it sought to coerce the Gobitis children to express a sentiment they did not entertain, in violation of their deepest spiritual convictions. The flag salute requirement could not stand, even though it be thought to enhance the interest of national unity.

Where there are competing demands of the interests of government and of liberty under the Constitution, and where the performance of governmental functions is brought into conflict with specific constitutional restric-

---

* "Dunham had fierce feelings on the subject," Justice Frankfurter commented in an interview, April 7, 1953. "Stone took weeks to decide." But Dunham rejects any implication that he had "any effect" on Stone's initial decision to vote against the majority. The former law clerk is inclined to think that "the law clerk was not important in the decision-making process which Stone went through in making up his mind." "My recollection," he observes, "is that when I talked to him before the conference he had even then made up his mind to vote as he did. . . . My influence, if any, in the Gobitis case was in inducing Stone to write a dissent as distinguished from noting his dissent." (Allison Dunham to A.T.M., June 26, 1952.)

† Stone, along with Brandeis, had been instrumental in fixing the custom of reading a brief summary in each case, rather than giving the opinion at length from the bench.

"I have omitted to tell you about the change which has gradually taken place in our practice of oral delivery of opinions," Stone wrote Frankfurter, March 17, 1938.

"At the outset, I should say that I have long felt that the elaborate oral delivery of opinions was a great waste of time, without any compensating advantage to the Court, and that the practice was especially bad when, as in the case of some notable dissents, the dissent delivered had no relationship to the written dissent which had previously been circulated among the members of the Court. There has, I think, always been a feeling on the part of some members of the Court that the business of delivering opinions orally was overdone, but there have always been some members who have been strongly opposed to any serious restriction of the practice.

"Some time ago a number of us adopted the practice of merely announcing the

tions, there must, when that is possible, be reasonable accommodation between them so as to preserve the essentials of both; . . . it is the function of courts to determine whether such accommodation is reasonably possible.

Granted that national cohesion is a desirable social end,

there are other ways to teach loyalty and patriotism which are the sources of national unity, than by compelling the pupil to affirm that which he does not believe and by commanding a form of affirmance which violates his religious convictions. Without recourse to such compulsion the state is free to compel attendance at school and require teaching by instruction and study of all in our history and in the structure and organization of our government, including the guaranties of civil liberty which tend to inspire patriotism and love of country. I cannot say that government here is deprived of any interest or function which it is entitled to maintain at the expense of the protection of civil liberties by requiring it to resort to the alternatives which do not coerce an affirmation of belief.

Loyalty is a beautiful idea, the dissenter said in effect, but you cannot create it by compulsion and force.

Stone did not, of course, insist on religious freedom as an absolute. "Government has a right to survive and powers conferred upon it are not necessarily set at naught by the express prohibitions of the Bill of Rights." A pacifist could be made to fight, though a wise state might attempt accommodation to his scruples. A man could be forbidden to do many things dictated by his private conscience. But great care must be exercised in adjusting the necessary functions of government to the legitimate demands of freedom, so as to "preserve the essentials of both." There was no occasion for weighing the regulation to see if it could be valid under any conceivable state of facts. The Minersville School Board had struck at the vitals of liberty; its patent destruction of religious freedom could not survive judicial inquiry, and no niceties of judicial self-restraint should keep the Court from saying so:

The guaranties of civil liberty are but guaranties of freedom of the human mind and spirit and of reasonable freedom and opportunity to express them. They presuppose the right of the individual to hold such opinions as he will and to give them reasonably free expression, and his freedom, and that of

---

name of the case, the way in which it came to us (certiorari, appeal, certificate, etc.), the precise question presented, and the decision. This takes about two minutes. We have gradually gained recruits. Those who preferred the old method became somewhat conspicuous if they indulged in long oral discourse, and have gradually curtailed their own performance. The result has been that on the last few opinion days following recesses, delivery of opinions has occupied only a brief time, twenty minutes or so. One day the docket broke down because the Clerk did not realize that most of the day would not be consumed with the delivery of opinions.

"Thus, by force of example, there has come about a reform which it seemed impossible to establish by any formal action."

the state as well, to teach and persuade others by the communication of ideas. The very essence of the liberty which they guarantee is the freedom of the individual from compulsion as to what he shall think and what he shall say, at least where the compulsion is to bear false witness to his religion. If these guaranties are to have any meaning they must, I think, be deemed to withhold from the state any authority to compel belief or the expression of it where that expression violates religious convictions, whatever may be the legislative view of the desirability of such compulsion.

Far from being free to wash its hands of such questions by deferring to legislative judgment, or by applying the usual presumption of constitutionality, the Supreme Court had a positive duty, enjoined by the Constitution itself. Though America's fundamental law may embody no particular economic theory, it does contain explicit protections for personal liberty. These the Court is bound to enforce. No legislative evaluation of national unity could override safeguards the Constitution places around religious freedom. "The framers were not unaware," Stone said, "that under the system which they created most governmental curtailments of personal liberty would have the support of a legislative judgment that the public interest would be better served by its curtailment than by its constitutional protection." The positive terms of the Bill of Rights made it inconceivable that "they intended or rightly could have left any latitude for a legislative judgment that the compulsory expression of belief which violates religious convictions would better serve the public interest than their protection." The very terms of the Bill of Rights preclude "any reconciliation of such compulsions with the constitutional guarantees by a legislative declaration that they are more important to the public welfare than the Bill of Rights."

Nor could judges avoid expressing an independent judgment on the wisdom of legislative policy in conflict with the Bill of Rights, even if the political process remained unimpaired. "Where all the effective means of inducing political changes are left free from interference," Frankfurter had argued, "education in the abandonment of foolish legislation is itself a training in liberty. To fight out the wise use of legislative authority in the forum of public opinion and before legislative assemblies rather than to transfer such a contest to the judicial arena, serves to vindicate the self-confidence of a free people."

"I am not persuaded," Stone replied, "that we should refrain from passing upon the legislative judgment 'as long as the remedial channels of the democratic process remain open and unobstructed.' This seems to me no less than the surrender of the constitutional protection of the liberty of small minorities to the popular will."

Jehovah's Witnesses were an unpopular religious minority, subject to prejudice which tended to curtail the operation of corrective political processes. Under the rule suggested by the third paragraph of the Carolene Products footnote, the Court is the ultimate "resolver of the clash." If the Justices stood aloof, as the majority opinion held, numerically inconsequential groups might find themselves helpless victims of overpowering prejudice. Such minorities have a claim to be heard, a claim honored in the Constitution. All acts infringing their rights must be subjected to "searching judicial scrutiny."

Nor was tolerance a luxury to be enjoyed only in untroubled times; it is "needed most, and most urgently, . . . in times . . . when the nation is subject to extraordinary stress."[56] Answering Frankfurter's argument that liberty is best maintained when it is ingrained in a people's habits, and not enforced against popular policy by adjudicated law, Stone wrote:

The Constitution expresses more than the conviction of the people that democratic processes must be preserved at all costs. It is also an expression of faith and a command that freedom of mind and spirit must be preserved, which government must obey, if it is to adhere to that justice and moderation without which no free government can exist.

Stone's emotions rose to heights he seldom exhibited. Later in the day he became somewhat ashamed and rather regretted having read his dissent at length. But he had made a profound impression. "Not only sensible, but courageous," Thurman Arnold wrote the dissenter. "When a liberal judge holds out alone against his liberal brethren," Benjamin V. Cohen remarked, "I think he ought to know when he has spoken not for himself alone, but has superbly articulated the thoughts of his contemporaries who believe with him in an effective but tolerant democracy." A former law clerk, who had toiled over the American Bar Association's *amicus* brief in behalf of the Gobitis children, wrote him: "It certainly took me down a peg to see with how much more insight and skill you were able to expound the same position after working only a few days at the most." For this erstwhile co-worker, Stone's opinion combined "the grace of Holmes, the solidity of Brandeis, and a certain hard-hitting subtlety and economy of language which you have made your own. And beyond that, it must have required some courage to print such an opinion in times like these."[57]

The dissenting Justice also drew praise from some who had never screwed up enough courage to congratulate a judge. "My admiration for one who could not be swayed by the passions of the time from a proper evaluation of the worth of human freedom got the best of me," a timorous correspondent commented. In Massachusetts, where the issue had not yet been settled, citizens were urged to ponder Stone's dissent "before making any more religious martyrs out of children."[58] Clergymen from a variety of denominations saw "grave error" in the majority stand. John Haynes Holmes, chairman of the American Civil Liberties Union, said Stone's dissent would "rank as one of the great dissenting opinions in American history."[59]

Press comment was highly favorable. One hundred and seventy-one leading newspapers promptly condemned the decision; only a handful approved it. The *St. Louis Post-Dispatch* called it a "terrible decision." "We think this decision of the United States Supreme Court is dead wrong," the *Post-Dispatch* editorialized. "We think its decision is a violation of American principle. We think it is a surrender to popular hysteria. If patriotism depends upon such things as this—upon violation of a fundamental right of religious freedom, then it becomes not a noble emotion of love for country, but something to be rammed down our throats by the law." "The Court," the *Miami Herald* asserted, "cannot stop these people from believing in their strange doctrine."[60]

All such press support demonstrated to Justice Stone that "there are many who set high value on civil liberties and are deeply concerned by our decision."[61] Few shared the *Boston Herald's* conviction that "a strong declaration [by the Supreme Court] as to the importance of national cohesiveness is timely."[62] Even the Catholic journal *America*, voice of the Jehovah's Witnesses' principal target, took exception to the idea that "patriotism can be taught by an enforced flag salute."[63] Liberals far and wide, including some with whom Frankfurter had worked shoulder to shoulder before coming to the Court, deplored his "judicial self-restraint," regretted his misguided attempt to fortify national unity at the cost of freedom. "First and foremost," Harold Laski wrote Stone from London, "I want to tell you how right I think you are in that educational case from Pennsylvania and, to my deep regret, how wrong I think Felix is. That was a noble decision, nobly written."[64] The Court itself is verging on hysteria, the *New Republic* commented, when it "says in effect that we must imperil religious liberty in the interest of the American state, which is worth preserving because it guarantees religious liberty. . . ."[65] "The spirit now shown toward 'communists,'" John Bassett Moore observed, "is of a piece with that which is requiring children in the schools daily to salute the flag. I am sorry to see Frankfurter acting as the mouthpiece of such measures, which are likely to create disloyalty more than to promote loyalty."[66]

Certain correspondents marveled at the "staunchness" of Stone's associates in withstanding the force of his reasoning.[67] But the Justice himself felt somewhat crushed by his failure to wean anyone from the majority. To a federal circuit court judge who was "a good deal moved," he replied: "One of the difficulties with the opinion is that it is not moving enough."[68] "I am sorry," he told a law clerk, "that the opinion in the Flag Salute case did not draw at least one 'just' man to its support. However, as you know, I do not mind standing alone if I must."[69]

In certain quarters Stone's temerity stimulated ugly reaction. A Boston veterans' organization called for his resignation. "In dissenting on that decision," its resolution read, "you simply gave a bad example and encouraged more pupils to refuse to salute the flag. One might gather also from your action that you are either a radicle [sic] or a disciple of that so-called religion."[70]

In the wake of the Court's stamp of approval of the compulsory flag salute, religious bigotry and fanatical, unthinking patriotism became rampant. Jehovah's Witnesses, it was said, "don't believe in Religion; to them Religion is a Racket of making money by selling Judge Rutherford's volumes."[71] Vigilante committees took it upon themselves to enforce respect for the flag by violent means. Between June 12 and June 20, 1940, hundreds of attacks on the Witnesses were reported to the Justice Department for possible action by the FBI. At Kennebunkport, Maine, Kingdom Hall was burned. At Rockville, Maryland, within twenty miles of the majestic Supreme Court building, police joined a mob attack on a Bible meeting. At Litchfield, Illinois, a crowd of a thousand townsfolk milled around sixty canvassing Witnesses, burning their tracts, overturning their cars. At Connersville, Indiana, the Witnesses' attorney was beaten and driven out of town. At Jackson, Mississippi, a veterans' organization banished the Witnesses and their trailer houses from the city.[72] Similar incidents occurred in Texas, California, Arkansas, and Wyoming. The Department of Justice traced this wave of violence directly to the Court's decision in the first Flag Salute case.[73]

The Court itself thus became a weapon in the struggle for men's minds. By its approbation, "foolish" laws become somewhat less so; novel restraint, lodged in the structure of government, had become "constitutional." With the blessing of an authoritative Supreme Court judgment, the country's local school officials tightened up on the flag salute requirement.[74] In several states the lower courts treated recalcitrant Witnesses' children as delinquents and confined them to state reform schools. After the Supreme Court's decision, trial court rulings were speedily reversed in Stone's own native New Hampshire.[75]

"It would be a mistake," the *St. Louis Post-Dispatch* commented soberly, June 10, 1940, "to attribute these outbreaks of violence against religious minorities solely to the United States Supreme Court's opinion upholding the compulsory flag salute in public schools. . . . Yet there can be little doubt that most unfortunate decision will be an encouragement for self-appointed guardians of patriotism and the national moralists to take the law into their own hands."

Although no "just" man could be weaned from the majority to support Stone's dissent, it soon became apparent that the majority was not as cohesive as the vote—and Justice Frankfurter's opinion—seemed to indicate. Two years later, perhaps assisted by public reaction to the decision, certain members of the majority, reconsidering their votes, helped to bring about one of the most dramatic reversals in the Court's history.*

Commentators disagree as to the role Stone assigned the judiciary in the rarefied area of civil rights. One writer gives him special credit for "developing a rationale justifying a larger scope of judicial intervention in those cases in which alleged impairment of basic civil liberties was involved."[76] Judge Learned Hand denies that Stone made any such distinction. It needed little acquaintance with Stone's "robust and loyal character," Judge Hand wrote in 1946, "to foretell that he would not be content with what to him was an opportunistic reversion at the expense of his conviction as to the powers of a court." Judge Hand is certain that Stone never meant to insist that the courts have a wider latitude for enforcing their own predilections when concerned with "personal rights" than when concerned with property itself.[77]

In 1940 the Bill of Rights, especially the guarantee of freedom to the human mind and spirit, loomed large in Stone's constitutional jurisprudence. "Justice Holmes' opinions," he told an inquiring student, "indicate that he thought that the judge should not be too rigidly bound to the tenet of judicial self-restraint in cases involving civil liberties, although so far as I know he never formulated the distinction. You will find my formulation of it in a footnote in *United States* v. *Carolene Products Company*."[78] The "preferred position" of the freedoms guaranteed against infringement by the First Amendment† derived not only from the specific constitutional injunction against their infringement but also from their elevated rank in the hierarchy of

* See Chapter XXXVI.

† In setting aside a Texas statute preventing labor organizers from soliciting union membership without first obtaining an organizer's card, Justice Rutledge, building on Stone's Carolene Products footnote, said: "The case confronts us again with the duty our system places on this Court to say where the individual's freedom ends and the State's power begins. Choice on that border, now as always delicate, is perhaps more so where the usual presumption supporting legislation is balanced by the preferred place given in our scheme to the great, the indispensable democratic freedoms secured by the First Amendment. . . . That priority gives these liberties a sanctity and a sanction not permitting dubious intrusions. And it is the character of the right, not of the limitation, which determines what standard governs the choice." See *Thomas* v. *Collins*, 323 U.S. 516 (1945) pp. 529-30.

A statute which Stone considered "invalid on its face" was at issue in *Lovell* v. *City of Griffin*, 303 U.S. 444 (1938). Here a unanimous Court held invalid the requirement of a license for the distribution of pamphlets to be issued at the sole discretion of a municipal officer. Also a state statute which forbade peaceful picket-

values. Presumption of constitutionality—a practical rule of government holding that the people and their representatives should be allowed to correct their own mistakes wherever possible—simply does not apply in a situation where, for one reason or another, the legislature cannot be expected to correct its mistakes. In such a case the Court must, under the philosophy embodied in the second and third paragraphs of the Carolene Products footnote, assume responsibility for the result. Guardianship of corrective political processes was a special function of his Court. It must be alert to legislative intrusions that prevent the effective operation of free government; it must extend its benefits to the novel, the unpopular, the unorthodox. "If only popular causes are entitled to enjoy the benefit of the constitutional guaranties," he observed, "they serve no purpose and could as well not have been written."[79]

"There must be reasonable accommodation between the competing demands of freedom of speech and religion on the one hand, and other interests of society which have some claims upon legislative protection," Stone wrote in an unpublished opinion. "To maintain the balance between them is essential to the well-ordered functioning of government under a constitution. Neither is absolute, and neither can constitutionally be made the implement for the destruction of the other." And, as he never tired of reminding his brethren: "That is where the judicial function comes in."[80]

CHAPTER THIRTY-TWO

# Coming into His Own

## 1937-1940

Between 1937 and 1941 Stone's cup brimmed over with personal gratification. During these years the public and private fortunes of the entire family flourished. By this time prospering investments, carefully managed, put him on the road to becoming a millionaire.

---

ing for purpose of notifying the public of the facts regarding a labor dispute is "invalid on its face." See *Thornhill* v. *Alabama*, 310 U.S. 88 (1940).

Writing Justice Murphy, April 14, 1940, in connection with his opinion in the Thornhill case, Justice Stone observed: "The question which troubles me is whether you should treat the statute as void on its face or void only as applied to this particular petitioner. . . . Perhaps it comes down to a matter of use of words, but as I understand it when a statute is void on its face we mean that it can never be applied to anyone under any circumstances."

Stone had not suffered from the crash of 1929. "I saw the financial storm coming from afar and had all sails furled," he wrote in October 1929, "so it did me no particular damage."[1] Six months before the collapse he had "felt uncertain about the market and what to choose." "It seems to me," he commented, "that we are bound to have a serious slump if this sort of thing [the continuous advance in stock prices] keeps on much longer, and then the man who has conservative securities with an obligation on the part of somebody to pay him an income is likely to have the advantage."[2] The Justice not only came through the crash virtually unscathed, but during the depression years, he knew what and when to buy. "I am inclined to agree with Professor Kemmerer," he had suggested to his son Marshall, "that in the present uncertainty it is probably wiser to invest one's money, as far as may be, in property other than credits payable in money. Probably the best example of that kind of investment is productive real estate."[3]

"Don't speculate," he had warned in 1925. "There is only woe in that process; but when you make investments, it is a good plan to buy at favorable prices."[4] By 1939 the wisdom of this advice had been proved many times over.

Stone's prosperity cannot be explained solely in terms of wise financial management. In Washington the New England Justice became noted for his "little economies." When the weather was fair he would walk rather than ride, take a streetcar in preference to a taxicab. Rather than pay for the *Washington Herald* he would take home the discarded Court paper. Once, while lunching near the Capitol, he ordered a sandwich made with raisin bread. On discovering that this cost five cents more he asked why. "Raisin bread costs more," the waiter informed him. Carefully scrutinizing his sandwich, the Justice remarked, "I can only find three and a half raisins and I don't think they're worth a nickel." No electric light could burn for an unnecessary quarter hour. Generous in replenishing his wife's wardrobe, he insisted on wearing his oldest suits as long as possible, while new ones of excellent quality hung idle in his closet. An expensive tie was an unconscionable extravagance. "I count on my nephews and my sons," he remarked jocularly, "to see that my neckties conform to the proper standard by sending me some of their own discarded ones." Asked one day about the cost of his judicial robe and whether he wore ordinary clothing beneath it, he pointed to a cartoon hanging in his office, depicting two Justices in conversation, one saying, "Confidentially, I haven't worn pants in years. They bother me."[5]

The Justice's sons, Marshall and Lauson, rising steadily in their respective fields, won public recognition. The year 1937 was a banner one. Mrs. Stone, eminent in the philanthropic field, also won recognition for her painting. Lauson joined another lawyer to form the New

York law firm of Ignatius and Stone. Marshall became a professor of mathematics at Harvard. Generally known as a distinguished mathematician, he was elected in 1938 to the National Academy of Sciences, and a few years later became a member of the American Philosophical Society. "In a good many parts of the world," Stone commented expansively, "I am known, if at all, as Marshall's father—about as gratifying a distinction as I ever expect to have. In fact, I am a good deal 'set up' over both my boys."[6] Stone himself came in for special notice, in April 1939, with his election to the American Philosophical Society, founded by Benjamin Franklin, the oldest learned organization in this country. At about the same time he became an honorary member of the English Society of Public Teachers of Law, which included a short list of outstanding men—Lord Atkin, Justice Farwell, the Lord Chancellor of England, Lord MacMillan, and the late Justice Holmes. All in all there was every reason for contentment. "I have," the Justice mused more than once, "the best job in the world, a good family, and a good house. What more could anyone want?"

Stone had always regarded family as his first and most important consideration. "Nothing upsets me so much as illness in my family," he told a former Wall Street associate. "In fact, it is about the only thing that seems to unfit me for the day's job."[7] In trouble, he was the rock of comfort to whom all members of his family turned for sage advice. No request, no news of misfortune, ever failed to evoke from him appropriate action or soothing words, as occasion demanded. In intimate relationships, as in other aspects of his life, understanding, sobriety of judgment, kindness, predominated. "I am indeed sorry for the news which your letter brings me," he wrote his sister on one occasion, "and I can appreciate just how disturbed and wrought up you must feel. . . . But let me beg of you to realize that worry and yielding to your emotions are not going to help. One of the inescapable obligations of family life is the necessity of bearing with fortitude the mistakes of those that are near and dear to us. . . . In the long run I think it is never best for us to let any number of mistakes alienate us from those that are ours, because after all that is about all we have in life. . . . Write me how things develop."[8]

Though he found a fishing cruise with President Hoover glamorous and exciting, as we have seen, if it meant forgoing a visit with his sons and their families over a holiday, he was much discomfited. "I would much prefer a little party with you," he said when plans for a Hoover trip were finally set.[9] Later on he made no bones about preferring his children's company to that of an evening with the New Deal President, and he complained bitterly when a White House engagement prevented him from making the most of an overnight visit from Lauson.

Despite his unflagging attention to his family, so-called New England reserve seemed to cut him off from intimate association even with them. "When he visited my family," Lauson recalls, "he would pick up a book or a magazine and read for hours, while the conversation went on around him." The same could be said of his sons' visits home, paid after many earnest pleas in weekly letters for a longer stay so father and son could see each other and talk. Even with his wife he was, at times, reticent and often noncommunicative. When she shared his walks, they went on in thoughtful silence or else discussed small matters of mutual interest. "Sometimes," she recalls, "I used to say that if I wanted to find out 'the news' I had to invite good friends to dinner to hear it."[10]

Father Stone, Lauson observes, did not seem to be very fond of small children. During boyhood the sons saw their father only on Sundays, and often on those days the hard-driving dean and practicing lawyer had serious adult work to do. On "Mother" fell the major responsibility for their care and discipline. When the youngsters became restless in the crowded compartment of a European train, their little legs dangling over the edge of a narrow seat, Stone would cry plaintively, "Mother, can't you stop the boys from wiping their feet on my clothes?" Stone, apparently, found it difficult to adjust his interests to those of a small boy. In their early years his sons dreaded those rare occasions when their father was disposed to spend time with them. "Mother," Lauson would ask, "do I have to walk with father and Professor [Underhill] Moore? They talk about nothing but law." Later on father and son talked joyfully of little else. Meanwhile, however, Stone could not understand why his sons did not manifest greater interest in his burgeoning public career. In early 1926 the Columbia University Law School unveiled a portrait of the former dean, by then an Associate Justice of the Supreme Court. Though Marshall and Lauson, now aged twenty-three and twenty-two respectively, were in New York, neither took the trouble to attend the ceremonies. The Justice was bitterly disappointed. "I had hoped," he wrote reprovingly, "that you boys would go over to see the picture presentation and give me a report. . . . I sometimes wonder if you will attend my funeral."[11]

Nevertheless Stone watched the progress of his sons closely, giving careful consideration to the details of their development, taking pride in every forward step. In later years the same attention was lavished on his two grandsons. Once, when Lauson's wife was in a quandary as to whether her son, Harlan II, had enough playthings, the Justice offered friendly counsel: "According to my observation most children of the present generation have altogether too many playthings. The object of children's playthings is not primarily to amuse them, but to develop them mentally and physically. For that reason playthings which invite them to use their hands are much more worth while than mechanical toys, which seem so much more amusing to older people. The only worth-while playthings that Marshall and Lauson had were the tools and materials out of which they built things—battleships, cranes, engines, carts and what not. They never seemed to tire of them and they did not have such a surfeit of things that they did not prize them."[12]

From the time his sons completed college and were ready for careers, he took an active, vocal interest. Anxious, almost overweening, in his desire to see them succeed, he often regretted that they did not have opportunity to acquire the valuable training of "responsibility, work in cooperation with others," with "definite duties to perform," such as he had had in his home life on the farm. He missed no opportunity to further their interest. In 1932, knowing that Marshall would welcome an opportunity to spend a summer in California, he passed the word along to the Chairman of the Board of Trustees at Stanford University, a former Medicine-Ball Cabinet member. "You see," the Justice reported to Marshall, "I am not letting the grass grow under my feet in working in your interest."[13]

In 1920 he had created a trust fund for his sons with the definite purpose of giving them economic security during the years when they were establishing themselves; his primary purpose was to enable them to take on family responsibility which might otherwise have been difficult under existing economic conditions.* It was, as he said, "the result of a carefully thought out plan on my part that I would rather extend this assistance to you now than leave you a larger amount when the times comes for me to pass on, and when it might be of comparatively little service to you."[14]

Any important event in the boys' lives brought forth a letter of advice and, one supposes, a good deal of talk too. In the end he left it to them to accept or reject his counsel, but he definitely threw his weight into the scales, making it impossible to ignore him. When Marshall completed his studies at Harvard with a reputation as a "most brilliant student of mathematics,"[15] Stone inquired carefully into his son's professional prospects, seeking directly the advice of his

---

* "The trust fund," Marshall comments, "was not sufficiently large to give Lauson and me economic security in the sense that either of us could have lived on the income. The fund was set up essentially to guarantee our education, and it was dissolved in the mid-twenties, being distributed to Lauson and me. This assistance from our father removed certain worries from our minds and, above all, permitted both of us to assume with fewer misgivings the responsibilities of marriage, as we both did at the age of twenty-four. As my father thought it wise, he added to this initial financial assistance, so that we both have every reason to feel grateful without ever having been induced to rely unduly upon his generosity and without ever having become dependent upon it."

teachers, Osgood and Birkhoff. Thereafter he used his connections to get information not available to the young mathematician about intimate conditions at various institutions and poured out detailed instructions for success in an academic career: "Don't overload yourself with teaching. I think it very important that you keep yourself free to develop your capacity for research and publication. There is everything in forming the habit when one is young. I have seen so many men in academic life who had put off publication until it became practically impossible for them to do it. They seemed to get some sort of complex which paralysed their writing hand. I think it is because they did not start young."[16]

Marshall had read his first paper before the American Mathematical Society at nineteen. As the flow of publications continued unabated the Justice commended each achievement and reported it all to colleagues and friends, along with the incidental accomplishment that Marshall "read Tolstoi in the original Russian for amusement." Marshall's mind and work moved in a sphere close to Stone's original interests, but he took great pleasure in pretending that his son's achievement soared beyond his understanding. When, in 1932, Marshall presented "with love and respect" the "first fruit of several years of study," Stone described his son's work—*Linear Transformations in Hilbert Space and their Applications to Analysis*—as "six hundred and twenty-one pages of perfectly non-understandable material so far as ordinary mortals are concerned."[17] Receiving the book with "joy and paternal pride" and with reverence for its abstruse contents, the Justice praised every point at which his experience permitted comment, right down to its "beautiful printing job." He could readily appreciate "how much thorough and painstaking work" went into this theoretical development of one of the essential mathematical tools of atomic physics. "Fine accomplishment," he exulted. "It will add to your already excellent reputation as a scientist." "I liked very much your foreword, both the ideas it expresses and its beautiful English, with the possible exception of your use of the word 'splendid.' However, I imagine there are many who would not agree with that idiosyncrasy of mine. The omitted chapter on applications of your abstract theory would have interested me most of all, because I am such a hopeless utilitarian."[18]

Thereafter a copy of this recondite volume, always at hand on his work table, had to be exhibited to each and every visitor. Once when his son's mathematical prowess was mentioned in a column, the Justice explained: "I suppose he must have heard somewhere of my bragging and hastened to get it into print."[19] But as the newsman knew the Justice quite well, it is more than likely his information came direct. Stone's letters to friends telling of Marshall's invitation to Russia in 1935 to read a paper before a mathematical congress, his year at the Institute for Advanced Study at Princeton—"to make an investigation of linear representations in abstract space—whatever that is"[20]—fairly burst with parental pride. On occasion the Justice thought Marshall was inclined to exclude all other interests in life. In 1934 he was pleased to note that "you are beginning to think a real vacation is worth while. It is!" he declared emphatically. "When you get a chance, drop in to see *One Night of Love*, Grace Moore's movie— much better than its name."[21] At one point only did Marshall give him real concern. The youthful educator left Harvard in 1930 for promotion and a lighter teaching schedule at Yale. Two years later he was considering a return bid to Cambridge. "You, Marshall," the Justice wrote sternly, "are getting to the time in life when you should not be making many more changes, and you will give serious consideration this time to the problem, where you are going to spend the rest of your life. I should like to talk it over with you."[22]

The Justice watched the career of his younger son with equal concern. Following in his father's footsteps, Lauson brought himself into an area where the father felt technically competent to give helpful advice. When, as a Harvard undergraduate, Lauson did especially well in courses related to the law, his father was much gratified, and once it was decided that he would follow a legal career, he pressed the young man to enter Columbia Law School, arguing that the faculty possessed sounder views, even if they were not so well known as men in the same fields at Harvard. He pointed also to the advantage of studying law in New York, the city with greatest opportunities for young lawyers. During law school years, when certain courses gave trouble, Lauson was urged to submit specific questions. The Justice even offered to rummage through his papers for his own student notes. "I am anxious to know how you came out in your mid-year's examinations," he wrote, and added a word of caution: "You must not allow yourself to think that the *Review* work or your connections would save you if you turned in a poor paper." "There is nothing like having members of your family win distinction and get items in the paper," he commented on reading of his son's election as president of his class. "Very good, Lauson, but remember," he went on, "the responsibility inherent in such recognition."[23]

In 1927 Lauson was selected revision editor of the *Columbia Law Review*, and in December of his third year he was among those recommended by the faculty to serve as law clerk to Justice Stone. This pleased the Justice greatly, but he had misgivings as to whether this was the advisable thing for Lauson to do. "No doubt a man who spends a year with me has an interesting and useful experience," he wrote Wilbur Cummings of Sullivan and Cromwell. "It is especially valuable to those men who have planned to do teaching or legal writing and is useful to the man who expects to practice. I think Lauson exaggerates its utility to him somewhat."

"As I see him," the Justice continued, "what he needs more than anything else is the discipline of a well-organized office. That I cannot give him, partly because I haven't the organization and partly because that discipline doesn't function as well in the relations of a grown-up son and his father as it does when he is dealing with comparative strangers."[24] Stone much preferred to have Lauson take a position in the office where he was to do professional work, thinking he would promptly adapt himself to its environment, respond to its discipline, and soon exhibit a real capacity for growth—the big thing in an office.

As graduation time drew near, Lauson, exhibiting an independent streak, proceeded to interview law offices without consulting his father. "There are some tips I would like to have given you, both about the offices to visit and the attitude which I think a young man should take in seeking a job in a law office," the Justice wrote with a trace of chagrin. "To my mind, salary plays altogether too large a part in the choice of offices with the young fellows. Of course, I have no objection to the young man's taking it if he can get it, but salary ought not to have the slightest influence on his choice of an office. The place to be chosen is the place that is well organized, has plenty of business, and affords the young man opportunity to grow and develop in his chosen firm. When you are in such a place income takes care of itself, and it is a lot more important to be in a position where you can earn income according to your merit than it is to secure a place which gives a tempting return at the start and never produces much more."[25]

Entering Stone's old firm of Sullivan and Cromwell at his father's prompting, Lauson received a word of warning and a thoughtful recipe for success:

You will have the advantage, which is also a disadvantage, of being among friends. This means that there will be a disposition to help you, but it is of course one that you must not presume upon. Make it a point to learn all you can about office organization; how a law business is conducted; how records are kept; papers filed; clients handled. . . . Learn how papers are served; calendars answered; records looked up and where public offices are located. Remember, that what makes a young fellow valuable in an office is his ability to look after details systematically and with promptness. The men above you will be delighted to find someone who will be eyes and memory for them. Promptness and diligence are qualities which help win recognition.[26]

After a few years Lauson, chafing under the confinements of a large law firm, broke away from Sullivan and Cromwell to enter a well-established smaller practice. There, Stone reported, he enjoyed "his associations much more than he did the treadmill, departmentalized work he had done with my old office. In my day it was not quite so much departmentalized and we tried hard to keep it from becoming so."[27] Once in independent practice, Lauson took an active interest in civic affairs in New York City, and was named to the Board of Higher Education, which supervises the city colleges, and later on to the administrative committee of Brooklyn College.

In 1940 Lauson found himself in the middle of a fight that attracted national attention. The Board of Education had engaged Bertrand Russell to teach mathematics and philosophy at City College, but before he could take up his duties the educator was bitterly attacked as not fit to teach young people because of his unorthodox views on love and religion. The affair profoundly aroused the Justice's interest, moving him to make heated protest. "I don't suppose anyone would have ever thought anything about it," he remarked, "had not Bishop Manning started his crusade. He really came into prominence some centuries too late. He would have been a perfect flower of the period of the Inquisition, when no one was permitted to have any but 'correct,' 'moral,' and 'orthodox' ideas." "I suppose," he continued, "if you had anticipated all the row you might have selected, instead of Russell, a man less likely to be subject to controversy. But, having selected him, and the criticisms leveled at him having nothing to do with the subjects which he was to teach, it seems to me you did quite right to stand pat."[28]

Much was made of the attack on Russell as an attempt to subvert academic freedom, but once the fight moved into the courts Lauson and his father saw something more at stake than "Russell's peculiar philosophy." "I don't know what the statute says about the appointment of an alien or other technical objections raised in the opinion," Stone commented somewhat scornfully on the decision of the New York Supreme Court setting aside Russell's appointment, "but the thought that courts can review the wisdom and policy of action of the Board of Education and substitute their own judgment for that of the Board is shocking." "The real issue," he reminded Eugene Meyer, publisher of the *Washington Post*, whose paper had defended Russell, "is whether courts should substitute their judgment, which is expert only with respect to matters of law, for the judgment of administrative boards and officers, who have important functions to perform, for which they are supposed to have special training and experience, and who should be free to exercise their own judgment within the province which is particularly theirs. It is a form of dictatorship to which democratic society is exposed more than it has been to any other." All in all, it was for Stone "a sad chapter in the fields of law, religion, and education."[29]

Mrs. Stone's full life won her handsome recognition also. High tributes greeted her efficient management of the Instructive Visiting Nurse Society of Washington, which, for many years, she had served as president. In 1940, on the organization's fortieth anniversary, Mrs. Roosevelt, speaking over a national radio hook-up, commended the society and Mrs. Stone. "Mother responded over the radio," Stone reported. "All very good and very successful. I was permitted to stand up and let the audience greet me as 'Mrs. Stone's husband,' and won proper applause when I said that was my proudest position. If I had known in advance what was planned I would have let you know, but Mother, of course, kept it all under her hat."[30]

Several dark clouds, however, obscured his generally pleasant prospect. For one thing, domestic politics, nationally in Democratic hands since 1932, profoundly distressed the Republican Justice. He blew hot and cold on particular aspects of the New Deal. Sometimes, as in the recession of 1937, he deplored the "failure of national government to secure national acceptance of any intelligent economic program in time to avert a crisis in government." In the fall of 1937 he went so far as to advocate extreme corrective measures to "redress the unequal distribution of national income." It was then difficult for him to see how "we can maintain a stable capitalistic system without greater purchasing power, or how that can be attained without the development of a low-priced economy with stability of wages or increase enough to redress the unequal distribution of national income. So far as I can see the effort to raise prices, which has seemed to be the aim of the government, is not getting us anywhere."[31] More often than not, however, he criticized the administration's specific projects, and his confession of November 1937, "I do not care so much for the New Deal," could hardly have come as a startling revelation.[32] The far-flung welfare programs were criticized as sapping the vitals of American greatness—individual independence, thrift, self-reliance. The people, losing respect for themselves, had come to believe that they had rights, rather than reciprocal rights and duties.

"It is essential," he told a friend, "that we maintain sufficient faith in ourselves to make sacrifices to preserve our self-government and, if necessary, to fight for it." On this score he found something to admire in Nazi Germany. "The only Western nation that has taught that doctrine to its people," he commented in June 1940, "is not a democracy but the totalitarian state of Hitler." "For the past ten years," his letter continued, "the only emphasis in public discourse has been upon rights and privileges of the citizen. There has been nothing to suggest that he has duties and that sacrifices may well be worth while to preserve what we have and particularly to maintain our democracy. This applies as well to capital as to labor."[33]

As Hitler and his fascist entente dominated foreign news, Stone's attention was drawn increasingly to international affairs. His thinking, somewhat like that of the late Senator Arthur H. Vandenberg,[34] underwent radical transformation. In the late thirties Stone was isolationist, inexperienced in the field of foreign affairs, fiercely suspicious and sharply critical of things on which he was not fully informed. His views appear to have been influenced by the late nineteenth-century liberalism of his former law school teacher, John Bassett Moore, now a judge on the Hague Tribunal. Each bolstered the other's tendency to be wistful about the simple past and resentful of the responsibilities of the present. "I wonder whether we shall ever see a world such as we enjoyed for the thirty years or so which preceded the great war," Stone wrote nostalgically in the fall of 1938. While never clear-cut as to what policy should be followed, Stone, nevertheless, was almost invariably antagonistic to administration action. America's fumbling with peace after World War I had disillusioned him and left him extremely distrustful of the capacity of any American government to conduct foreign relations intelligently. "I have much fear," he commented, "that there is a disposition in high quarters to take a hand in European affairs and see that they are settled properly. I fear that disposition more than I can say, when I recall how we settled matters by our last appearance there."[35]

Though underestimating the threat, strength, and aspirations of the Third Reich, he condemned the Munich Conference as "the greatest disaster to the world since 1914. Perhaps I am mistaken about this too," he wrote, "but time will tell, and judging by the performances in Vienna in the last two days and Hitler's speech in the Saar, the time will not be long."[36] And yet when official American spokesmen, trying to arouse an apathetic nation, lashed out at the totalitarian menace to world peace, he became profoundly irritated. "I wish I could exclude from my horizon the sad spectacle of three important officers of our Government hurling Billingsgate at the Nazis in the best Nazi style," he commented when the President, Secretary Ickes, and Senator William King of Utah denounced German atrocities against the Jews in 1938.[37] Even if he had sympathized with the substance of their pronouncements, he would nevertheless have insisted that government officials maintain self-imposed silence in the circumstances then prevailing.

As tension mounted in 1939, the foreign sphere became "most distressing," especially as Stone was still inclined to blame the United States. "It may seem an extreme statement to you," he wrote Moore, March 6, 1939, "but I really think that we are the biggest menace to the peace of the world just now. Quite possibly Hitler and Mussolini would be if they had the resources really to carry on a large-scale and long-time war, but as I see the situation, they are not likely to be in that position for a very long time to come. Meanwhile our public pronouncements by various high officials of the Government help them to maintain their position at home and to build up a war spirit. We ought to adopt as a motto 'Keep our mouths shut and our powder dry.'"

Stone and Moore were especially hostile to prominent Republicans who lent themselves to F.D.R.'s efforts to consolidate public opinion against totalitarianism. Henry L. Stimson, "embittered by his previous and openly confessed failures, as a soldier and then as a diplomatist, to 'make the world safe for domocracy,'" Moore exploded, "pants to try it again, even if we should have to sacrifice our last man, spend our last dollar, eat our last rat, and then leave the devastated lands to the rehabilitation of despots."[38]

In April 1939 Stone reiterated his "sense of uneasiness about our foreign relations, and about our public declarations with respect to them." He believed that "all public assaults on the dictators are politically useful to them at home." "My friends in Congress," he reported, "tell me that the country is strongly for a 'mind your own business policy.' But if we continue not to pursue it I am wondering where ultimately we will land." Four days before the Nazis marched on Poland, Stone still distrusted America's "so-called neutrality" policies. He still saw no reason to bring the Western countries into an alliance for common defense. "It is a mystery to me," he declared, "how one can justify 'support' to any of the parties to the European quarrel. I am for staying at home in a political sense and keeping our powder very, very dry."[39]

Once war broke out, however, he could see no satisfactory "midground between the maintenance of our rights as neutrals, as they have been defined by international law, and a complete and absolute stay-at-home policy, involving an embargo of all our shipping wherever there is even the remotest possibility of supplies reaching the belligerents either directly or by trans-shipment." "We would thus surrender," he observed, "all of our rights as neutrals in the hope of avoiding war by keeping out of trouble." He did not favor such a policy, for he thought the original neutrality law "foolish" in surrendering American rights and as tying "our hands in times of peace without adequate appreciation that when war occurred we would probably wish to pursue some other policy." Yet it seemed to him that "repeal of the embargo after war is declared, in order to aid one of the belligerents, was a breach of neutrality." "The net result," he complained, "will probably be that we will neither stick up for our rights as neutrals nor succeed in avoiding the clashes which put us into the last war." As he held no strong brief for one side or the other in this strictly "European" conflict, he was amenable to humanitarian proposals to mitigate the misery of the millions under Hitler's heel, and pressed his university friends to find suitable places for academicians who had fled Germany because they would not "distort science to fit the Hitler ideas of the German race."[40]

"I think our friends the British ought to be mindful of the effect of the action they take from time to time on the oppressed peoples of Europe," he commented on the blockade during the height of the Battle of Britain. "They should be astute to lose no opportunity to put the onus on the Germans, and I believe they could so maneuver their forces that Western Europe would get food from the United States without benefiting the Germans or, if it did, they could then cut off the supply, placing the responsibility where it belongs."[41]

It is difficult to discover on the basis of these sporadic and somewhat dogmatic pronouncements just what Stone really thought about foreign affairs. Certainly he liked to fulminate, but after his fulminations have been written off, one might expect to find some kind of guiding thread. Existing materials fail to disclose it. A study of the Justice's methods of handling problems in his own domain shows clearly that one cannot expect his judgment to correspond precisely to his feelings. In fairness, his comments should be taken for what they were—"loose observations of one occupied with other matters, and perhaps not competent to speak on the subject at all."[42]

CHAPTER THIRTY-THREE

# Dissent Ascendant

## 1938-1940

As the Justice began his vacation in June 1940 the "generally parlous state of the world" haunted him. Violent public reaction to the Gobitis decision, popular acceptance of the "indispensable man in government" obsession, along with what he considered the rapid degeneration of American virtues, produced "only sad reflections." "What has become of the sturdy common sense which once characterized popular thought?" he pondered dolefully.[1] Overshadowing all other issues, international and domestic, was the third-term bogey. That Herbert Hoover, as late as February 1940, once again appeared to him fit presidential timber suggests the measure of Stone's desperation. He thought "the country would do well for itself if it made him President in the present juncture," but he was realistic enough to suspect that "there isn't a ghost of a chance."[2]

The 1940 presidential race absorbed his attention more than any since 1920. He would sometimes stay up late into the night, listening to speeches. As the campaign neared the end he wistfully sensed alarm among New Dealers because of "the drift which seems to have set in strongly for Willkie."[3] The outcome, though not altogether unexpected, was a bitter disappointment.

In identical letters to his sons and Sterling Carr on November 7, Stone poured out the "grave concern" he felt over the "continuance in office of a single party for twelve years by such a preponderant vote." He had thought the election "would be closer and that there was a possibility of an overturn." "I should feel differently," he explained, "if this administration were more disposed to take the people into its confidence in advance of action, and if it were disposed to exercise a more scrupulous self-restraint in seeking power and in exercising that which it has." He feared "the decadence of party government," deplored the "weakness of the Republican party and the supineness of the Democratic party." In bold contrast was the continuing vitality of party government in England, "where under the stress of a great war, the Prime Minister feels bound at frequent intervals to submit to inquiry, criticism—and rebuke, if thought proper."[*]

One star brightened the generally dark horizon—Wendell Willkie and his determination to "take active leadership of the Republican party and keep our domestic issues before the country." "The party," the Justice observed, "has needed that kind of leadership for a long time, and if the country is convinced that it is wholly divorced from finance capitalism, which has given business in this country such a black eye, much good may come out of it." Still grumbling, he settled down "to a quiet (?) life, subject only to the ministrations of Mr. Hitler."[4]

Such quiescence did not continue. Within a few months "the unique

---

[*] Breach of the venerable third-term precedent stirred sober thoughts: "I am rather inclined, as I have been in the past," he wrote Young B. Smith, Oct. 5, 1940, "to believe that a single term of, say, six years is better than our traditional two-term practice. The only point that troubles me about it is that with a fixed single term a President loses some measure of party control, but he usually loses that in the second term unless he is running for the third, and the practice of shaping all national policy during the first term in order to secure a second is pretty bad. In those respects I think the parliamentary system has some advantage over our own. The party leader maintains his influence with his party in order to avoid an unfavorable vote in Parliament and the consequent ouster from office. How this element of party control can be introduced into our system without the evils which flow from the effort to secure a second or third term, to say nothing of a fourth or fifth, is something of a problem."

event in American history, inauguration of a President for a third term," intensified somber forebodings. Attending this "grim ceremony," the Justice read the reactions of onlookers as in accord with his own: "The crowd seemed apathetic. I could not quite make out whether it was because of the solemn feelings over the war, or, what I suspect is more likely, a subconscious realization that this may make great changes in our history." "It seemed as though people wondered whether they had done the right thing," he mused. "I suspect they will wonder more before we get through our present trouble." The Stones went to the White House for a buffet luncheon, but declined an invitation to sit in the President's box to watch the parade. Soon after lunch they went home and "settled down to work."[5]

The election results were not, however, wholly of evil omen. Now alerted to the menacing specter of nazism, the Justice began to strike a more belligerent note in his comments. "Perhaps," he said, "we can take some comfort from the fact that the election serves notice on our foreign friends, and enemies as well, that we are going to be a united country and that we are not inclined to back down in the face of threats of force."[6] American interests could best be defended, he believed, by assisting Great Britain's struggle. Yet a lingering grudge over the ingratitude of the Allies after World War I died hard. "I have no illusion that when our present troubles are over and England has triumphed—if she does triumph," he wrote, "that she will be any more appreciative of our efforts than she was after the last war. But to my mind that is wholly irrelevant to our present problem, and that is, how shall we best defend ourselves against the forces that are breaking down liberal government wherever and whenever they can?" Now, far from begrudging assistance to England, his criticism was that the United States would not do enough. "We should not delude ourselves with the prevalent talk about our doing everything short of war," he observed. "We have been in the war now for some time, and the question is, being in it, how shall we best conduct ourselves to protect our own interests. So far as I am now able to see ahead," he went on somewhat ambiguously, "we shall best do that by giving such support as we can. I am most troubled by the fear that we shall not do our best in that direction."[7]

Justice Stone had a special quarrel with the New Deal on the score of its continuing disservice to the Supreme Court. Several retirements were in the offing, and he was still apprehensive that any appointments made by President Roosevelt would confront him with the unhappy prospect of "working very much alone in the remainder of my years."[8] "During most of my service," he had written in 1938, " the Court has been manned by able lawyers, whether we always agreed or not, and all have contributed their share to the work of the Court, and have been of great aid because of their legal knowledge and experience. The prospects for the continuance of that relationship do not seem very good just now."[9] The appointment a year later of William O. Douglas, a former student at the Columbia Law School, as successor to Louis D. Brandeis, had roused mixed feelings. The President's choice pleased him, of course, but when "I found one of my recent pupils sitting on the other end of the bench—then I knew it was time to reminisce."[10]

Soon his "young and energetic associates" were making him "hump to keep up with them." Nor did it appear likely that he would ever be able (or willing) to absorb "some of the new ideas."[11] "These are tough times for old boys like me," he would say. "I am undecided whether to settle down in Maine as a lobster fisherman or just raise huckleberries in the summer and hell in winter. What do you recommend?"[12] Any serious suggestion, however, that he would soon go on the shelf evoked prompt negative reaction. A law clerk's innocent remark that "you've had a grand career" drew from him the protest that "it sounds a little like an obituary, or an editorial on my retirement. No doubt our old friends, the *New Republic* and the *Nation*, after boiling me in oil, will use similar language."[13]

Despite his doubts about the vastly changed judicial terrain, majority opinions increasingly embodied the legal philosophy stated in his Harvard Tercentenary address of 1936. "Probably no man in the history of the Court," a former law clerk suggests, "has lived to see so many of his dissenting opinions become the law of the Court."[*14] In two terms, 1937 and 1938, one hundred and eighty cases were reversed, several of which were landmark decisions. Stone himself thought it would be "an interesting study" to see how many of his own dissenting opinions "now represent the law," adding as a qualifier, "I do not flatter myself that the change was due to the force of the opinions, but to the force of the events."[15]

Brandeis's retirement in February, 1939, and McReynolds' retirement the next year, suddenly left Stone Senior Associate Justice. To him this seemed "almost incredible, though an unavoidable reality."[16] Within two years after this last survivor of the hardy crew that had battled the New Deal left the scene, the Justices completed the job of bringing the commerce clause into line with the ringing dissents of Stone, Holmes, Brandeis, and Cardozo. The Court's blessings on the Fair Labor Standards Act of 1938, forbidding shipment in interstate commerce of goods produced under proscribed wages-and-hours

* His exuberance should be tempered by Justice Brandeis's record. The Roosevelt Court overthrew thirty-two precedents; Stone had participated in thirteen of these decisions, dissenting in ten. Brandeis took part in twenty and made protest in seventeen.

standards, came as a sort of long-last confirmation of Hamilton's dictum that "a Constitution cannot limit a nation's needs."

In a case of such moment, one might have guessed that Chief Justice Hughes himself would speak for the Court. Hitherto he had instinctively recognized those "occasions when an opinion should carry the extra weight which pronouncement by the Chief Justice gives."[17] Surely the Darby case was such an occasion. One suspects that Hughes ignored his usual procedure and assigned the writing of this crucial opinion to Stone because of the doubts he entertained as to the Act's constitutionality. For one thing, the undefined phrase, "production *for* commerce," which Congress had used to delimit the scope of the Act, Hughes considered too vague to be valid in a criminal statute. "In attempting to give some appropriate content to this loose phrase," the Chief Justice wrote, "I think that the test should be as objective as possible and should not be centered on the mere *intent* or *expectation* of the employer apart from the usual and normal course of business or actual transactions." "Even with the best possible test," he told Stone, "the statute is a highly unsatisfactory one and as it is a borderline case, I should prefer not to write."[18]

Nor could the Chief Justice accept the unqualified definition of the commerce power required to sustain the Wages and Hours statute. For him, "regulate" meant "facilitate," "promote," "advance," "foster"; only incidentally did it comprehend "restrain," "control," or "prohibit." He agreed that the power "to protect interstate commerce"[19] was plenary. But his understanding of the nature and scope of "commerce" and of the power to regulate it was a far cry from John Marshall's grand conception laid down in *Gibbons* v. *Ogden*. There the great Chief Justice had boldly sketched this binding tie of Union as the authority to govern commercial intercourse among the states, characterizing the constitutional grant as "sovereign," "complete," "plenary," "absolute," and of the same scope as if it were vested "in a single government," and therefore utterly unaffected by the coexistence of the states. Regulation signified the authority "to prescribe the rules by which commerce is to be governed," and extended to all "that commerce which concerns more states than one." Apart from certain specific constitutional prohibitions, such as that barring discriminatory preference for the ports of one state, the "sole restraints" on congressional exercise of this fundamental power were political—those "on which the people must often solely rely, in all representative governments."[20]

All but ignoring Hughes' refinements in the great commerce cases decided since 1935, Stone went all the way back to *Gibbons* v. *Ogden*. The definitions he fashioned for the key words "power" and "regulate" carry the majestic sweep of Marshall's classic decision of 1824.

The Darby opinion, Stone explained to Professor Noel T. Dowling, was designed "to make two things clear, namely (1) that the commerce power of Congress is not restricted to intrinsically harmful commodities, and (2) that the motive of Congress in passing commerce clause laws is none of the Court's business."[21] Thus for the first time since Marshall, the Court said flatly that Congress "is free to exclude from commerce articles whose use in the states for which they are destined it may conceive to be injurious to the public health, morals, or welfare."[22] Manufacture of goods, Stone agreed, is not commerce, but their shipment is, and the power to regulate is the power "to prescribe the rule by which commerce is governed. It extends not only to those regulations which aid, foster, and protect the commerce, but embraces those which prohibit." Quoting Chief Justice Marshall, he held that the power "is complete in itself, may be exercised to its utmost extent, and acknowledges no limitations other than are prescribed in the Constitution."

Nor is congressional action a "forbidden invasion of state power merely because either its motive or its consequence is to restrict the use of articles of commerce within the states of destination." "The motive and purpose of a regulation of interstate commerce," Stone said, "are matters for the legislative judgment upon the exercise of which the Constitution places no restriction and over which the courts are given no control. . . . Whatever their motive and purpose, regulations of commerce which do not infringe some constitutional prohibition are within the plenary power conferred on Congress by the commerce clause."[23]

No mention is made of Marshall's doctrine of political restraints as a corrective for abuses of power. As Stone afterward explained, his opinion had been "deliberately fashioned on the model of Justice Holmes' dissent in *Hammer* v. *Dagenhart*."[24] Stone, like Holmes, could not understand how the commerce clause, which admittedly empowered Congress to prohibit interstate traffic in diseased livestock, lottery tickets, adulterated and misbranded articles, women for immoral purposes, intoxicating liquors, stolen motor vehicles, kidnaped persons, and convict-made goods,[25] could be construed so as to nullify a law prohibiting trade among the states in commodities manufactured under substandard conditions of labor or by children. The contrary ruling in *Hammer* v. *Dagenhart*, decided twenty-two years before over what Stone called "the powerful and now classic dissent of Mr. Justice Holmes," could no longer stand. The reasoning and conclusion of the Court in the Dagenhart case, Stone said, "cannot be reconciled with the conclusion which we have reached, that the power of Congress under the commerce clause is plenary to exclude any article from interstate commerce subject only to the specific prohibitions of the Constitution."

"*Hammer* v. *Dagenhart*," he wrote, "has not been followed." It was an "aberration" resting on the unacceptable judicial refinement that "congressional power to prohibit interstate commerce is limited to articles which in themselves have some harmful or deleterious property —a distinction which was novel when made and unsupported by any provision of the Constitution." "The conclusion is inescapable," he announced, "that *Hammer* v. *Dagenhart* was a departure from the principles which have prevailed in the interpretation of the commerce clause both before and since the decision and that such vitality, as a precedent, as it then had has long since been exhausted. It should be and now is overruled."[26]

The Darby opinion did more than vindicate Holmes. Stone had waited nearly five years for an opportunity to read out of constitutional jurisprudence that mainstay of laissez faire—"dual federalism"—the notion that the Tenth Amendment sets an independent limitation on the powers of Congress. "I have been thinking for some time," he had written Charles A. Beard apropos of Justice Roberts' use ( or misuse) of that Amendment in the AAA decision, "that the time might be opportune to say something in an opinion about the historic aspects of federal power. I think I shall improve the first opportunity to do something of the kind."[27] In the interim the Carter Coal case had strengthened the impression that Congress could not, without unconstitutionally invading the reserved powers of the states, govern the relations of industrial employers and employees. That difficulty remained even after the Jones Laughlin decision. The principal barrier against congressional regulation of the economy—that the relation of employer and employee is "local," and therefore beyond the reach of national control—had yet to be expressly removed. The opportunity to repudiate the theory that the very existence of the states limits national power finally came in the Darby case.

In a now famous passage, Stone wrote:

> Our conclusion is unaffected by the Tenth Amendment. . . . The Amendment states but a truism that all is retained which has not been surrendered. There is nothing in the history of its adoption to suggest that it was more than declaratory of the relationship between the national and state governments as it had been established by the Constitution before the Amendment or that its purpose was other than to allay fears that the new national government might seek to exercise powers not granted, and that the states might not be able to exercise fully their reserved powers. . . . From the beginning and for many years the Amendment has been construed as not depriving the national government of authority to resort to all means for the exercise of a

granted power which are appropriate and plainly adapted to the permitted end.[28]

Stone also laid to rest Chief Justice Hughes' objections that the statute was too indefinite: "One who employs persons, without conforming to the prescribed wage-and-hour conditions,* to work on goods which he ships or expects to ship across state lines, is warned that he may be subject to the criminal penalties of the Act. No more is required."[29]

Douglas and Black also had reservations. Stone's original version, especially his defense of the minimum wage established by the law, they considered open to the construction that "had *we found* the wage rate 'unfair or oppressive,' we would hold that the law offended the due process clause." They would not agree to any such inference. "In fact," Black commented, "so far as the due process clause of the Fifth Amendment is concerned, I am unable to see its application to an act properly coming within the commerce power."[30] "I did not suppose," Douglas had written on the draft, "that such an issue ever brings the Fifth Amendment into play. But perhaps I misunderstood." At their request Stone deleted his statement that a minimum wage of less than $600 for a full year's labor cannot be assailed as unfair or oppressive.

In the end the Court's endorsement of the Fair Labor Standards Act was unanimous. Several of his brethren—Black, Douglas, Frankfurter—had nothing but praise for Stone's opinion. Reed, too, was enthusiastic: "It has been a long journey, but the end is here. We should have overruled Hammer years ago. Maybe it would have saved the Civil War as Judge Lovett said."† Reluctantly, it may be inferred, Hughes scribbled on the final draft of Stone's opinion: "I will go along with this."

The press generally interpreted the decision as "clearing away the last legal doubt about major New Deal reforms." Many papers noted how the long struggle for a child labor amendment had been brought to a successful close by the Court itself. The *St. Louis Star-Times* welcomed the decision as further evidence of the Court's "determination to permit the democratic processes to operate free from the autocracy of judicial tyranny." Even the staid *New York Times* approved this "historic decision."[31]

Stone accepted the *Times'* characterization as apt. The opinion was

---

* In a companion opinion Stone approved the methods of the Wages and Hours Administrator in setting minimum wages for employees engaged in production for commerce. See *Cotton Mills* v. *Administrator*, 312 U.S. 126 (1941).

† Judge Archibald Lovett, counsel for Darby, had argued that if the Court upheld the Wage-Hour Act, it would show that the Civil War was unnecessary because the only thing needed would have been a pre-Civil War act that said no goods produced by slave labor might cross state lines.

"at least of interest," he said, "as it puts fairly, and explains the whole relation of the National Government to interstate commerce, and shows that the conception of it now applied by the Court was that applied by Marshall and has continued to be the rule of the Court, except for the single aberration* in the Child Labor case."[32]

But there had been other aberrations both before and after the Child Labor case, as certain discerning newspapers pointed out. The "old Court" had obscured, if it had not destroyed, the historic Constitution. Even after Chief Justice Hughes' 1937 opinion upholding the NLRA a complete return to Marshall seemed slightly revolutionary. "The change that has been effected," the *Washington Post* noted, "is scarcely less significant than it would have been if accomplished through a constitutional amendment." With the Darby case the Government "emerged as a government of almost unlimited powers in the economic and social field." The *Wall Street Journal* also recognized how the Court had "proceeded to wipe out its own previous decisions," to give Congress sweeping power, and greeted the decision somewhat regretfully "as indicating a permanent federal power over local conditions of employment and the maintenance of national wage levels to which the low-wage areas will have to adjust themselves as best they can." Certain editors in these so-called low-wage areas lamented that states' rights were now dead—"as dead as the gallant boys from North Carolina who fell on the scarred slopes of Gettysburg. . . . Now the states, like the Negro in the Dred Scott decision, have no real rights which the Federal Government is bound to respect."[33]

The sweeping nature of the decision dampened Stone's own pleasure in his achievement. The Justice felt "that not everyone will like the Wages and Hours decisions. . . . It seems to be the fate of the judge that he can never please more than fifty per cent of his customers, and sometimes not even that."[34] Perhaps his satisfaction was also tempered by personal distaste for a national minimum wage. A staunch belief in the tried and sure virtues of individual effort, thrift and enterprise, had never wavered. "There is a good deal in what you say," he had told Sterling Carr in 1940, "about a 'back to the land movement' for the unemployed. It would at least keep them busy and help them to keep body and soul together and would be better for them and the country than having them sit around in idleness complaining because the Government doesn't do more for them."[35]

Stone's constitutional principles, not his views on public policy, prevailed in the Darby case. Shortly after the decision came down, and with specific reference to the Wages and Hours Act, he commented,

---

* The Justice's statement is not strictly accurate. Surely the old Sugar Trust case —*U.S.* v. *E. C. Knight,* 156 U.S. 1 (1895)—of evil memory, is an equally notable aberration.

"The truth is that I feel obliged to uphold some laws which make me gag."[36]

The ascendancy of Stone's jurisprudence was largely a mute triumph. In the Court's leftward swing, Brandeis and Stone found themselves in the center and "blessed with cases which might once have gone to McReynolds and Butler."[37] Nevertheless Stone's personal satisfaction was great, and when the new Court took positions he had unsuccessfully advocated in conference, he went out of his way to make known his own contribution. "Brandeis's opinion in the Mitchell case," he wrote Frankfurter, March 7, 1938, "reaches finally a result which I tried very hard to have the Court adopt in the La Franca case, 282 U.S. 568 (1931), which he cites.* It finally puts to rest that 'old Man of the Sea,' the Coffey case, 116 U.S. 436 (1886)." Robert H. Jackson, in his account of the 1937 Court-packing battle, failed to mention the fact that Justice Stone's opinion in *United States* v. *Lowden* had in effect done away with the reasoning and decision in the Railroad Pension case. Promptly setting the matter straight, Stone wrote: "This opinion will serve both as a footnote and a headstone for the earlier case."[38] There was also satisfaction in the fact that the Lowden case had removed the constitutional gloss that, back in 1931, brought about judicial approval of the nefarious St. Paul railroad reorganization scheme.

Stone realized that the changes wrought were not traceable solely to himself. And when Justice Douglas, wanting in one instance to leave no one in doubt as to the source of views now in the ascendancy, specifically identified him as the real pathbreaker, he demurred. "It has been customary heretofore," he wrote apropos of Douglas's draft opinion in *Olsen* v. *Nebraska*, "not to mention by name Justices who are still living and sitting on the Court. For that reason I think it would be better to refer to the dissenting opinion in *Ribnik* v. *McBride* without naming the writer."[39]

The period 1937-1940 was, as Stone said, "one of the most interesting of our history, a time and a subject which will occupy the minds of historians much in the future."[40] Writing at the end of 1941, Professor Dowling discerned "five pieces of tracery" in the emerging pattern of Stone's constitutional jurisprudence. In the economic area, Stone insisted that there was a minimum of justification for interposing judicial judgment against legislative appraisal of a given situation and prescription of a remedy. There should be tolerance even for govern-

---

* In *United States* v. *La Franca*, the Court ruled that an unsuccessful criminal trial for violation of the Prohibition Laws constitutes a bar to imposition of civil penalties on the same facts. Stone did not dissent. Brandeis's 1938 decision, *Helvering* v. *Mitchell*, 303 U.S. 391, permitted the Government to collect civil penalties for income-tax evasion after an attempted criminal prosecution had resulted in acquittal.

ment price control. In certain circumstances reliance should be placed on the normal political restraints to prevent abuse of legislative power, thus obviating the reason and necessity for judicial intervention. At the same time he maintained that reliance on political processes imposed a special responsibility upon judges to apply more rigorous "scrutiny" to government restrictions upon those processes, such as legislative restrictions on the dissemination of information, voting, and peaceable assembly. More recently he had turned his attention to interests of higher value, as in his dissenting opinion opposing legislative exaction of the flag salute.[41]

Professor Dowling's analysis of the Justice's "methods" elicited grateful response. "Your article in the *Columbia Law Review*," he wrote the author, "gave me great satisfaction because you give the reader some idea of some of the more important things which I have been trying to do all these years. . . . I am grateful to you for tying the threads together so that others can see perhaps what they were not aware of as the opinions were handed down."[42]

In March 1940 the Justice completed a decade and a half on the bench. Frankfurter used the occasion to tell Justice Stone's wife* what her husband's work had meant to Court, country and to him personally.

For fourteen years, I have cherished this as a signal day in the Court's, and therefore the country's history. I did so as an outsider, as a student of the Court's work. And now has been added a year's intimate knowledge of what it means to have Harlan Stone on the Court—above all the privilege and joy of being a colleague. From the day I came on—a callow freshman— he has indeed been a warm-hearted brother, putting his experience and understanding and encouragement freely at my disposal. Long—very long may the country and I be able to enjoy him where he now is.[43]

Justice Brandeis, in retirement, also marked the date. "Your steady growth throughout the fifteen years," he wrote in one of his characteristically cryptic notes, March 1, 1940, "makes me hope that you will give to the Court at least ten years more."

"They have been fifteen happy years," Stone remarked in his reply, "mainly because you and a few others whose opinions I value have seemed to think they were worth while. As for the rest, satisfaction has come from the inner consciousness of doing the best I could, whether it was very good or not."

Increasingly, Stone's work attracted public notice. "After more than fifteen years on the highest bench," one newspaper commented, "he is now regarded as the Court's most lucid spokesman for the 'liberal'

---

* In addressing Mrs. Stone, Frankfurter explained that he merely recognized "where sovereignty lies."

doctrine of constitutional interpretation. . . . Decriers of the 'New Court,' like Wendell Willkie, who bewail that 'Mr. Roosevelt has won,' neglect to add that Justices Holmes, Brandeis, Stone, and Cardozo blazed the trail for recent 'revolutionary' majority opinions. Some of the most important of those opinions were delivered before Mr. Roosevelt had made a single appointment to the bench."[44]

In 1939 Alfred Lief proposed to select and edit Stone's leading opinions under the title *Public Control of Business*. Lief's previous collections of Holmes' and Brandeis's opinions had been successful, yet Stone was dubious about the appeal of a book embodying his own. "I don't know whether they will prove to be worth assembling," he said. "The enthusiasm of my publisher and his staff for the forthcoming volume mounts each time we discuss the project," Lief reported reassuringly. Swallowing doubts, Stone assisted Lief in the choice of cases and afterward made suggestions concerning the notes and biographical sketch.* The editor, in his selections, made special effort to eliminate "features forbidding to the layman," his purpose being to reach "a large number of businessmen and teach them 'the new relationships of law and industry.'" Later on he told of an encouraging advance sale. On the very eve of publication, however, Stone was incredulous: "Just why anybody should want to pay money for my opinions remains something of a mystery to me."[45]

Stone's misgivings seem in the main well grounded. "The attempt to turn Mr. Justice Stone into Essayist Stone does not come off," Walton Hamilton said in a perceptive review. A trick that scored for Holmes and Brandeis refused to serve Stone. The reasons were quite apparent. Unlike Holmes or Brandeis, Stone was no virtuoso. "As a member of the orchestra his solos," the reviewer said, "even when his part is dissonance, are inseparable from the unfinished symphony." Nor was this to his discredit. If Stone suffers by comparison with Holmes and Brandeis, it is because he, unlike them, seldom undertook to do more than deal narrowly with the question which he had to decide. If his opinions refused to be made over into "essays in the grand manner, Stone is not of lesser stature than Brandeis or Holmes. If he resists where they yield to translation, it is because he is rather more of the judge." This was, the reviewer concluded, "an admirable tribute to the self-restraint which Stone commends to his Court."[46] Though the Justice thought Hamilton's review "perhaps over-generous," he accepted it as "an excellent job, one in which I take some satisfaction for it seems to me that he realized better than any of my

* A pre-publication publicity slip, leaving the impression that Stone was bringing out his own opinions, touched his delicate sense of propriety, and he wanted it "clearly understood that what you are publishing is your own child, except for the opinions I wrote, for which, of course, I assume full responsibility."

academic critics the limits which I have set for myself in judicial writing."[47]

Appreciation of these self-imposed limits provides the clue to an understanding of Stone's enduring work as a judge. The subject was one to which he referred frequently in judicial opinions and informal conversation. Again and again he emphasized his ideal of sticking close to the case to be decided, not by closing his eyes to the implications—however far-reaching—of the views expressed, but by scrupulously refraining from broadening the scope of the results envisaged by the enunciation of sweeping generalizations. The "limits" Stone had in mind are illustrated in *United States v. Morgan.*

In this case, decided at the very end of the 1938-39 term, the appellees were operators of market agencies in the Kansas City Stockyard. They contended that a procedural error in the conduct of a hearing by the Secretary of Agriculture rendered his rate order not only void but irremediably void, so that the market agencies were conclusively entitled to the charges paid into court pending judicial review of the order. The Court, speaking through Justice Stone, looked at the problem in a different way. The purpose of the statutory plan of regulation, he explained, was to assure just rates and charges, and the judiciary should not make itself an instrument of injustice by refusing to the Secretary opportunity to reconsider the rate order in a properly conducted proceeding. As to the relationship that ought to exist between courts and administrative agencies, he stressed the

cardinal principles which must guide us to our conclusion. The one is that in construing a statute setting up an administrative agency and providing for judicial review of its action, court and agency are not to be regarded as wholly independent and unrelated instrumentalities of justice, each acting in the performance of its prescribed statutory duty without regard to the appropriate function of the other in securing the plainly indicated objects of the statute. Court and agency are the means adopted to attain the prescribed end, and so far as their duties are defined by the words of the statute, those words should be construed so as to attain that end through coordinated action. Neither body should repeat in this day the mistake made by the courts of law when equity was struggling for recognition as an ameliorating system of justice; neither can rightly be regarded by the other as an alien intruder, to be tolerated if must be, but never to be encouraged or aided by the other in the attainment of the common aim.\*[48]

In an address of 1939, Solicitor General Robert H. Jackson cited this opinion and concluded: "I venture to assert that . . . hostility to the work of another agency of Government is not the spirit of the Constitution or the framers or the judges of the early period of our consti-

---

\* Justices Butler, McReynolds, and Roberts dissented. Stone furthered this concept in his famous wartime opinion, *Yakus v. United States* (1944).

tutional development. It is the opinion of Mr. Justice Stone, with its warning against regarding another agency of Government as 'alien intruder,' that captures the spirit of the founders."[49]

In its results, Stone's steadfast adherence to the principle of judicial self-restraint was calculated to endear him to the White House and the coterie around it. But only a few New Dealers, Maury Maverick for one, acclaimed him wholeheartedly. "An ideal court," Maverick commented in 1939, "would be composed of men of the general stamp of Justice Stone—men who did not allow their personal views and prejudices to influence the opinions they wrote."[50] On all sides he was acclaimed as "one of the most capable members of the Court."[51] After Justice McReynolds' retirement, Stone, as senior associate, was given a "trial run" as Chief Justice. When a majority split away from Hughes, Stone assigned the opinions; when the Chief disqualified himself, Stone presented cases to the conference. "I am as busy as I can be," he wrote John Bassett Moore, "trying to grind out opinions and to get the members of the Court to pull in harness."[52]

Stone was now recognized as the intellectual leader of the Court's center. At the height of his powers, and reassured by the triumph of his method, he resorted increasingly to trying out constructive ideas. Little wonder, then, that public attention should have promptly focused on him when Chief Justice Hughes, shortly after administering F.D.R.'s third oath of office, decided to lay down his heavy burden.

PART SIX

# Chief Justice

———

## CHAPTER THIRTY-FOUR

# Burdens
# John Marshall Did Not Know
## 1941

On June 2, 1941, Chief Justice Hughes, aged seventy-nine, wrote President Roosevelt that "considerations of health and age make it necessary that I should be relieved of the duties which I have been discharging with increasing difficulty." Accordingly he advised the President of his intention to retire, effective July 1. The Chief had had a hard winter, Stone told his family, "due to the fact that his own strength is failing somewhat and to Mrs. Hughes' illness. I think he would have resigned earlier in the year had the President filled McReynolds' place, so that he could have left the Court with only one vacancy."[1]

McReynolds' seat had been vacant since February. Senatorial and other pressures coincided with the President's desire to appoint Senator James F. Byrnes of South Carolina, but announcement of the crusty Justice's successor had been allowed to drag along because of the President's desire to have Byrnes remain in the Senate to assist with important matters of legislation until that session of Congress ended.* Then with the unexpected retirement of the Chief Justice, creating two vacancies, the public was again alerted to the baneful potentialities of Court packing.

Speculation as to Hughes' successor centered almost entirely on Attorney General R. H. Jackson and Associate Justice Stone. Commentators saw various factors pointing strongly to Stone. Each passing day brought the United States closer to the brink of war, and the President was working with typical vigor to cement national unity in the international crisis. To have a Republican as Chief Justice would be "good strategy." In the eyes of close observers this was a fitting reward for the uphill battle Stone had fought in behalf of the power to govern. At the peak of the Court fight White House confidant Tom

---

* It was not until June 25, 1941, that Byrnes was commissioned to succeed McReynolds.

Corcoran had been anxious for Roosevelt to establish a personal relationship with Stone and thus put him in line for Chief Justice.[2] "If and when President Roosevelt appoints his Six Young Men to the Supreme Court," Pearson and Allen had noted in 1937, "the new Chief Justice of that reorganized institution will be the man who has watched the present judiciary battle with more than a twinkle of amusement in his eye—Justice Harlan Fiske Stone."[3]

Effective prosecution of the Court's work demanded that the President act promptly. Since January cases had been stalled by 4-4 conference votes, which added to the Court's burden, to say nothing of the resulting inconvenience to litigants.* "A certain gentleman in California is about to be hanged," Stone wrote his sons, April 25, 1941, "because this Court, by reason of a 4 to 4 vote, was unable to disturb his judgment of conviction. I am quite sure that he will think Mr. Roosevelt owes it to him to appoint a judge who could sit in and decide his case."

Much that F.D.R. had fought for was accomplished. Now the crying need was revitalized judicial independence and internal cohesiveness. Stone might effectively harmonize the disparate elements within the reconstituted Court and thus prepare for the trying years ahead. "Mr. Justice Stone eminently merits the post, and the nation eminently merits a Mr. Chief Justice Stone," the *Christian Science Monitor* observed, June 7, 1941. His appointment would bring added prestige and influence to the Court at a time of impending national crisis. Others reported a feeling among presidential advisers that Roosevelt "would be making a mistake in not giving public recognition to Stone's distinguished service."[4]

Would the seemingly impossible happen? Stone had not wooed presidential favor. In 1941 it was almost too much to expect that the New Deal President would remember the Republican Justice who had unintentionally given him such powerful weapons against the recalcitrant majority. In fact, there was much in Stone's activity during the interim calculated to displease F.D.R. Stone had continued to hew an independent line; he had been hard-set against interposing anybody's "economic predilections" into judicial decisions—Justice Sutherland's, F.D.R.'s, or even his own. Certain former law clerks, cherishing the hope that their chief might succeed Hughes, followed Stone's recent opinions with mixed feeling—rejoicing in their vigor and honesty, yet with a twinge of regret that a few of the punches could not have been pulled.[5] "Whatever the rest of the world may think," Stone commented, "Washington is under no illusion that I am a new dealer."[6]

* Automatic affirmance of the lower court is the rule in such cases, with leave to apply for rehearing.

Some thought he had put himself forever out of the running by his indiscreet remarks about Justice Black. "To add to the warmth of his relations with the Roosevelt administration," Marquis Childs remarked ironically, "several papers printed the story that the President had been flunked out of Columbia University Law School by Stone when he was dean there."[*7] Many thought the President could not bring himself to name a Republican. "Jurists and lawyers generally agree now," an anti-New Deal columnist commented, "that if the President, putting from his mind all thought of politics, prejudice, and personalities, should desire to fill Mr. Hughes' place with the best-equipped man, he would designate Justice Harlan Fiske Stone. But he is not expected to do that."[8] "We all think you should be C.J.," Charles C. Burlingham wrote, June 9, 1941, "but who can predict what F.D.R. will do? He has not the faintest idea of what goes to make a judge. 'Views' are all he seems to value. Even if R.H.J. [Robert H. Jackson] should say to him 'Stone is the man,' he could not be sure what F.D.R. would do."

The belief that the choice of Stone would be astute politics spread beyond the columns of those who distrusted or hated "that man" in the White House. "The Attorney General," the *St. Louis Globe-Democrat* speculated on June 9, "is generally considered a whacking good lawyer. He has had an extensive practice before the Supreme Court. Yet it would appear far wiser in the President to raise Justice Harlan F. Stone or Justice Owen J. Roberts to head the bench. Both are Republicans, but have been aligned with the liberal wing of the Court and thus should appeal to Mr. Roosevelt. . . ."[†] The *St. Louis*

---

* On April 2, 1937, Stone had inquired of Dean Young B. Smith: "Can you sometime tell me the real facts about F.D.R.'s [law school] career? Did I condition him?"

"Our Bulletin," Smith replied, April 5, 1937, "shows that you were Adjunct Professor of Law during the academic year of 1904-05 and taught the first year course in Criminal Law and the second and third year courses in Equity. The Rules of the Faculty . . . permitted a first-year student to elect the course on Constitutional Law, . . . in place of the course on Criminal Law. President Roosevelt elected to take the course on Constitutional Law, in which he received a Pass. Consequently, he did not take your first year course on Criminal Law. During President Roosevelt's second and third years in the school (1905-06, 1906-07), you were not teaching in the Law School.

"He entered the school in the fall of 1904 and remained here for three years. There is a variety of grades in his record, ranging from B to F. His deficiencies were in the first and third years. It should be stated, however, that his record contains a notation that during his first year he had seventy-three absences, forty-five of which were excused on account of illness. During his second year, he had thirty-five absences, ten of which were excused. . . . Under the rules of the school at that time, he was eligible to return and complete the requirements for the LL.B. degree, but he did not do so."

† This observation seems to overlook Justice Roberts' conspicuously "illiberal" stand in the Butler and Tipaldo cases.

*Post-Dispatch* swelled the refrain: "Would it not be the statesmanlike thing to go outside New Deal circles, especially for the new Chief Justice? Taft's elevation of Justice White, a Southern Democrat, to head the Court in 1910, suggests how eminently fitting it would be for Mr. Roosevelt now to rise above party, for example, by promoting Justice Stone, now the senior member with sixteen years of distinguished, stalwart service to his credit. . . ."[9]

Meanwhile Stone calmly went on planning his summer vacation. "We are just about finishing up the term's work," he wrote an old friend, "and while we are not definitely settled about our summer plans, we expect to leave here about the middle of June for a stay of a few weeks in Colorado, going on from there to the Coast, and ultimately coming back to Maine for a course of my usual late summer diet of lobsters and certioraris."[10]

Shortly after receiving Hughes' resignation F.D.R. invited him to lunch for discussion of his successor. Hughes "strongly recommended Stone." The President's suggestion of Attorney General Jackson also received the Chief Justice's approval, but Hughes felt that "Stone's record gave him first claim on the honor."[11] Later F.D.R. sent for Justice Frankfurter, because Hughes had told him that the former Harvard law professor "knew more of the history of the Court and its needs than anyone else." The President greeted him cordially but soberly, Frankfurter recalls, refraining from talk until the waiters had finished laying out their lunch at his desk. Plainly he had something serious preoccupying his mind. As soon as they were alone he opened up, proceeding in the most businesslike manner to pose two questions. "First," he asked, "is there any reason for naming a new C.J. at once, or wouldn't it do just as well to let it run along, since the Court has adjourned, 'til the fall?" Frankfurter gave him the reasons "why it would be very bad not to make a prompt appointment—the need of a head, even in vacation time, that Stone would *de facto* be head 'til the place was filled, that it would be unfair to him to have him act and then not name him; *per contra*, a new man ought to be broken in and not start the new term with the summer accumulations, green and unprepared." Without comment, the President went at once to his second question: "As between Stone and Bob Jackson, whom would you make C.J.?" "I wish you had not asked me that question," Frankfurter replied. "Why?" queried the Chief Executive. "Because on personal grounds I'd prefer Bob. While I've known Stone longer and our relations are excellent and happy, I feel closer friendship with Bob. But," he went on, "from the national interest I am bound to say there is no reason for preferring Bob to Stone—quite the contrary. Stone is senior and qualified professionally to be C.J. But for me the decisive consideration, considering the fact that Stone is qualified, is that Bob is of your political and personal family, as it were, while Stone is a Republican."

"Now it doesn't require prophetic powers," Frankfurter told the President, "to be sure that we shall, sooner or later, be in war—I think sooner. It is most important that when war does come, the country should feel that you are a national, the Nation's, President, and not a partisan President. Few things would contribute as much to confidence in you as a national and not a partisan President than for you to name a Republican, who has the profession's confidence, as Chief Justice."

F.D.R. listened patiently but made no comment. Nevertheless Justice Frankfurter left the President confident Stone would be named. "Be prepared to be C.J.," he told his colleague the next day, but "Stone professed skepticism."[12]

The Justice's misgivings were not wholly groundless. In discussing Court matters with Attorney General Jackson, the President had often said that he wanted to put Jackson in the center chair. There had been no commitment, however, and when F.D.R. found himself confronted, in the spring of 1941, with an unexpectedly difficult situation, he called in his Attorney General and said: "I have to make these two Court appointments. I'd like to see you Chief Justice, but is this the time? I've had a talk with Hughes. He questions whether at the present juncture one not having judicial experience should be appointed. I have a feeling I should name Stone." The President's logic seemed unanswerable. Republican representation on the Court had been reduced to Stone and Roberts. If, in one vacancy, the President put his Attorney General, and in the other the Democratic Senator who had been his floor manager at the recent Chicago national convention, neither of whom had an hour of judicial experience, the President thought it would not be well received by the country, especially in view of all the recent wails about Court-packing. Jackson heartily agreed* and said he would be glad to see the veteran Associate Justice elevated.[13]

Even as the matter of Hughes' successor was being weighed in the press and the White House, Stone refused to think of himself as in the running. "You have no doubt read the news of the Chief Justice's retirement," he wrote. "There is much talk about his successor, who I think is likely to be Attorney General Jackson. He is young, able, and has rendered great service, political and otherwise, to the administration, and is naturally indicated for the appointment. There is some talk about me, inspired mainly by friendship and generosity. I am

---

* Jackson was quite content, he recalled several years later, to fill, as an Associate Justice, the Hughes vacancy, to which the President appointed him in July 1941. (Interview with A.T.M., May 15, 1950.)

indifferent to it all."[14] His primary concern was "lest the President delay appointment of somebody else until October."[15]

In advance of the event the Justice discounted the importance of the post as he had done in 1930 after Hughes' designation. "I have no personal interest in it," he wrote his family, June 4, 1941, "beyond hoping that we will get a good C.J. who is able to carry the heavy burden which he will have to carry in these troubled days." To him, being Chief Justice still seemed a good deal like being the dean of a law school—"he does what the janitor is unable or unwilling to do." "I am much more interested," he said, "in studying the cases and writing opinions than I am in doing administrative work of any kind."[16]

Roosevelt, as if to refute the charge that he made loyalty to the New Deal a primary qualification for the Supreme Bench, selecting "his Justices not so much for their intellectual and legal attainments as for their complete acquiescence in his political philosophy,"[17] passed over his popular Attorney General and sent Stone's name to the Senate on June 12, 1941. The highest judicial office in the land, which had eluded him in 1930, came from a Democrat, from a man toward whom he had no sense of fealty.

When the news broke, the nominee had already learned of the President's intentions from Jackson. To avoid an avalanche of publicity he went to the home of his son in Brooklyn. It was a setting that pleased him profoundly. "Few men ever become Chief Justice," he afterward wrote his family, "and that you were present when that event took place in my life will always be a great satisfaction to me."[18]

For one who professed to regard the office as somewhat beneath the janitor's, Stone's reactions were strangely sober. "I don't know whether one should feel gratification at assuming such large responsibilities," he said. "It is the kind of recognition any man would appreciate, but the responsibility is so great that it doesn't create any sense of elation."[19] The next morning he went to Lauson's law office on lower Broadway, pockets bulging with letters and telegrams of congratulation. Sitting at a long table in the firm's library, he asked for a secretary and plunged immediately into dictating replies. The gist of them all was that he hoped he would prove worthy of the honor which had come to him.[20]

Seldom has a presidential appointment evoked such a wave of public approval.\* The President's action was, Archibald MacLeish said, "so clearly and certainly and surely right it resounded in the world like the perfect word spoken at the perfect moment." Morris

---

\* Of the numerous editorial comments noted, only one, the *Macon* (Ga.) *Telegraph*, June 16, 1941, disparaged the appointment, on the grounds that Stone had become a "New Dealer."

R. Cohen expressed "the satisfaction which the great body of American citizens feel that their chief judicial officer is a man who realizes both the necessity for governmental regulation of our complex economic life and the need for safeguarding the rights of individual conscience —that even an alien is a person and entitled to the protection of civilized law."[21]

"As happy and fortunate an act as any by the President in his three administrations," exclaimed the *Springfield Republican.* "As Cardozo was the one jurist in the country to succeed Holmes," observed the *St. Louis Post-Dispatch,* "so was Stone the one jurist to follow Hughes."

His appointment serves the cause of national unity, commented the *Rocky Mountain News,* explaining that "even die-hard Bourbons will applaud the appointment."[22]

"Last week," *Time* magazine summarized, "the U.S. realized how much it liked the idea of a solid man as Chief Justice to follow Charles Evans Hughes. And solid is the word for Chief Justice Stone—200 lb., with heavy, good-natured features and a benign judicial air. On the bench, Frankfurter moves around and makes notes; Douglas looks restless and bored; Murphy stares pensively under his bushy eyebrows; Black smiles enigmatically to himself; but Mr. Justice Stone, leaning forward impassively, his grey hair falling over his forehead, is almost as impressive a figure of justice as were Taft and Hughes before him."[23]

Many observers emphasized the non-political quality of the President's deed. But his choice was highly political in the best sense of the word, and he made the most of it, as Hoover had done in naming Cardozo as Holmes' successor. Patently calculated to boost the President's prestige, Stone's appointment had precisely that effect. Conservatives found their faith restored. "On this date I acquire new hope for my country," Arthur Krock wrote Stone, June 12, 1941. "There is some balm in Gilead after all," Gifford Pinchot acknowledged somewhat grudgingly. Presidential supporters, whose allegiance had been strained by past judicial appointments, now closed ranks solidly behind him. Old, deep wounds seemed to heal as political foes exchanged kind words. Stone's own middle position was highlighted by the qualified compliments he received from opposing partisan groups—from Alf Landon of Kansas and Senator John H. Bankhead of Alabama. To some the selection symbolized the "American way"—a great dissenter becoming, without influence or conniving, the leader and spokesman for the majority.[24] Stone had, in short, "done nothing to win the job except to deserve it."[25]

Lawyers swelled the chorus of praise. Stone's elevation was "so manifestly appropriate as to cause no disappointment to any other aspirant." For the legal profession, the President's action simply put the official seal on a universal private judgment. "It was the best possible selection that could have been made," Dean Henry M. Bates of the Michigan Law School summed up. "No other man in the country possesses such a combination of exceptional vigor and clarity of mind, broad and varied experience . . . as that which the new Chief Justice brings to his great office."[26]

Judges on all levels of the federal hierarchy found F.D.R.'s selection to their liking. Concealing a wealth of tribute in the aloof style that had won him the political sobriquet "Chillie Charlie," Hughes wired on June 12: "I am greatly pleased." From an old warrior came a message so sincere it did not need the aid of words. "My thoughts you have known," Brandeis wrote. "To have the office go to the most deserving must encourage the whole country."[27] Privately, the aging dissenter could hardly restrain his enthusiasm.* "Aren't you delighted with what the President has done in elevating Justice Stone to the Chief Justiceship?" Brandeis inquired of a visitor. "No other President has performed such a signal service." When reminded that President Taft, a Republican, had promoted White, a Democrat, to be head of the Court, he replied: "But White cannot be compared to Stone."[28] Another associate now on the sidelines, George Sutherland, sent a word of advice. "You are shouldering this great and most responsible burden at the most critical period in our history. Hold the scales level," Sutherland admonished. "I think you will."[29] "The President's great stature loomed to full height when he named you as Chief Justice," New Deal Justice Frank Murphy said.[30]

"This will put an end to all talk of retirement, won't it?" Learned Hand asked. "It is an enlistment for the duration of the war. You know, far better than I can, how much you have taken on, but your friends will be relentless that you shall keep on the firing line, while you can keep on your pins."† Later Judge Hand made a more formal statement: "It is our immense good fortune that at so critical a moment in our history there should have succeeded as the head of our judicial hierarchy a man whose moderation, modesty, and wisdom have always saved him from the vanity of the doctrinaire and the impertinence of the dogmatist. We rightly trust him not to be dazzled by immediate apparent gains; not to forget that in the end man can

* Elizabeth Brandeis Raushenbush, a daughter of the Justice, wrote H.F.S., Oct. 1941, after her father's death: "You doubtless know, as I do from conversations over the years, how warmly Father felt about you. I trust you also know of his keen satisfaction (expressed to me last summer) at your designation as Chief Justice."

† Hand acknowledged his debt to Stone: "I personally can never forget that to you I owe that 'step' as the English say, which has made so much difference in my life." In December 1924 Stone, as Attorney General, had recommended Judge Hand's promotion from U.S. District Court, Southern District of New York, to U.S. Circuit Court, 2d Circuit.

be tamed and societies can be fashioned only as they are satisfied that the voice of the law is made up of many voices, voices that no longer speak, voices that are not of the market-place, the rostrum, nor the halls of debate."[31]

Though most congratulatory notes were in dead earnest, not a few must have brought a smile to their recipient. There was an invitation from "one justice to another" to sit with the police court of Richmond; another bore admiration from a practicing lawyer for Stone's judicial performance, "although once, many years ago, you refused to permit me to enter the Columbia Law School because I was a woman." Still another reported enthusiasm among all kinds of people in the small town where she vacationed. Most of them, she said, "would never have credited the New Deal with that much sense. Of course," she added, "this is Vermont." Stone's appointment was also in some respects a social promotion. A Washington hostess assured the new Chief "this matter of protocol is all nonsense . . . to settle it once for all—you are going to take precedence and we are all going to continue dining happily together!" "All Morningside is proud and happy," prestige-hungry Nicholas Murray Butler gushed, adding that the appointment "gives to Columbia three holders of that great office, John Jay, Hughes, and yourself."[32]

The public hubbub over his appointment heightened his modesty, offended his sense of dignity. "I am pursued by reporters and photographers until I am nearly worn out," he wrote. "If you see a photograph of me in the bath tub don't be surprised."[33] The flood of publicity also quickened his native humility. "No man could merit all the generous things that are just now being said about me," he told a correspondent, "but they are at least something to live up to."[34] In the midst of the excitement he received a cablegram from England announcing his election as Honorary Bencher at Lincoln's Inn to fill Justice Holmes' place. "This gives me" he said, "the first kick I have gotten from all the recent uproar."[35]

After all allowances are made for public disposition to lionize the "successful" man, one thing stands out: Stone had long shown qualities of leadership. Time had at last confirmed the intimations of high accomplishment friends and colleagues had discovered many years before.

"Dear Harlan Stone," his Amherst public school teacher familiarly addressed him. "This is a voice out of the past, from one who remembers you as a boy with great potential ability, the boy of all others who came under my care, most likely to attain great position. To say that I am delighted with the great honor which has been conferred upon you and which I am sure is richly deserved, is to express my feelings mildly. Although our lives have been far apart, I have always read with interest what has been said of you in the press and have taken great pride and pleasure in your career. I should have been much disappointed had you not received the nomination when Chief Justice Hughes resigned. With warmest congratulations and regards. Your boyhood's friend and teacher, Jessamine Dixon Walcott."[36]

Besides personal tribute, homage was also paid the institution he now headed. In the hundreds of letters and telegrams that poured in ran the sobering undercurrent that the people looked on his appointment as a first step in restoring the judiciary to its former dignity and proper place in public confidence. Dean Griswold of the Harvard Law School had pressed Stone's appointment on F.D.R. because it "would go far toward preserving the confidence of the public in the integrity and impartiality of the courts." "Sometimes in my darker moments," he wrote the new Chief Justice, "I find myself fearing that this is going to be one of the problems of the next few years."[37]

The same thought was also uppermost in the minds of certain of Stone's colleagues. Associate Justice Jackson saw the need for leadership "in the direction of amendment of doctrine rather than toward destruction of institutions" and the desirability for a symbol of "stability as well as of progress" as the prime reasons for Stone's elevation: "It was the indispensability of this kind of assurance that made the succession of Harlan F. Stone to the Chief Justiceship not only appropriate but well-nigh inevitable if the interest of the judiciary as an institution were to be fostered."[38] But even the friendliest observers, mindful that there could hardly be any rapid escape from the problems which had beset the Court, were not quite certain that Stone was to be felicitated upon the advancement. Some queried whether even Stone's great abilities were equal to the job before him. "You have through your years on the Supreme Court hit the nail on the head more often than anyone else," Judge Augustus N. Hand told the new Chief, "and I know well enough that you should have the appointment—certainly a reward at last for conspicuous merit. Whether in these revolutionary times you can establish any predictable system of law in what seems to me a great present confusion I have no idea and some doubt, but whatever may be the result of your efforts, you have my congratulations and best wishes in your deserved office."[39]

Lawyers, law students, judges, Medicine-Ball Cabinet members, congressmen, Amherst classmates, diplomats, childhood acquaintances, Isle au Haut neighbors, artists, politicians, friends, and the man in the street—all agreed that this was the "best possible" appointment. Even before formal confirmation, Stone had received enough enthusiastic senatorial congratulations to leave no doubt of the outcome. When his name came up for Senate consideration in the late afternoon of June 27, 1941, Senator George Norris, last of the tiny contingent of progressives who had fought Stone's original appointment in 1925, made the only speech: "I am now about to perform one of the most pleasant duties that has ever come to me in my official life when I cast a vote in favor of his elevation to the highest judicial office in our land. . . . When Mr. Justice Stone was appointed an Associate Justice of the United States Supreme Court many years ago, I opposed the confirmation of his nomination and voted against it. In the years that have passed I became convinced, and am now convinced, that in my opposition to the confirmation of his nomination I was entirely in error. . . . It is a great satisfaction to me to rectify, in a very small degree, perhaps, the wrong I did him years ago."

The Senate's presiding officer posed the question: "Will the Senate advise and consent to the nomination of Harlan F. Stone to be Chief Justice of the United States?" After a brief pause he answered: "Without objection, the nomination is confirmed."[40]

Certain New Deal insiders had been so convinced that Jackson would be named that this turn of events left them piqued, incredulous. They circulated a rumor that Stone, with only one full year to serve before reaching retirement age, would take office with the understanding that he would soon resign to make way for the promotion of Associate Justice Jackson. "Had any suggestion of such agreement been made to me, I should have declined the appointment," Stone commented when the rumor was revived in 1943.[41]

Hughes' resignation left only Stone and Roberts as reminders that there had been other Presidents to name Supreme Court Justices. These two holdovers from the Coolidge and Hoover administrations were surrounded by men who had made their way to the bench through faithful and unremitting service to the New Deal. Upon completing the roster with the appointment of James F. Byrnes and Attorney General Jackson, the President wanted to make the swearing in a notable ceremonious event and proposed that all three take the oath of office in Washington. Berating the idea as "advertising," Stone turned thumbs down on the request. However, the new Chief Justice willingly gave in to the President on a minor point. Roosevelt asked that he not take the oath of office until the day the resignation of Chief Justice Hughes took effect on July 1. This, the President thought, "would please Mr. Hughes."

When the Senate confirmed the nomination Stone was at Estes Park, Colorado, where, in his own cottage at Sprague Lodge,* he was sworn in, July 3, 1941; the oath was administered by Wayne H. Hackett,

---

* "I saw Stone recently at Estes Park, Colorado," William Hard commented in a feature article in *Reader's Digest*, Aug. 1941. "He was proceeding up a hill with that heavy rolling walk of his, the walk of a football guard on a muddy field. The hotel clerk looked at him massively climbing and said: 'He's the biggest shot we ever had here and demands the least attention.'"

Commissioner of Rocky Mountain National Park, in the presence of Mrs. Stone and a few Park officials. One of the Chief Justice's first extra-official duties was to lead the nation in a Fourth of July pledge of allegiance over a transcontinental network. In choosing this simple rustic setting, so reminiscent of Calvin Coolidge in the Vermont farmhouse ceremony of 1923, Stone may have proved that his own grasp of the dramatic in the American tradition was at least equal to that of the President's.

Immediately on taking office, he sat down and wrote notes to the President and the former Chief Justice. Both letters, characteristically New England in understatement and emphasis, leave no doubt that Harlan Stone had become the steward of the Constitution and the law. "I thank you for the confidence you have shown in me," he told the President. "It will be my high endeavor in the days to come to justify that confidence by the adequate performance of the trust imposed on the Chief Justice by the Constitution and laws of the United States." His letter to Hughes bespoke appreciation for the extra-official responsibilities of the great office: "When I reflect upon the fact that I have taken the oath as your successor, and upon the great service which you have rendered the country and the Court, I bow my head in humility and pray that I may in some moderate degree prove worthy to be your successor. In the last few days," he went on, "beset on every side by a publicity-mad world, I am beginning to realize as I had not realized before that you have borne, and I must bear with such equanimity as I can, some burdens which John Marshall did not know."

CHAPTER THIRTY-FIVE

# The Wild Horses

### 1941-1942

What was the new Chief Justice's conception of his office? Some idea of what Stone thought Hughes' successor should be can be gleaned from an article he wrote before his promotion to the center chair.[1] A new Chief should, of course, carry on in line with the "historic shift of emphasis in constitutional interpretation" achieved under Hughes; he should view the Constitution as "an enduring instrument of government." Prompt consideration and disposition of the Court's business would be in the future, as in the past, highly important, but that standard must be supplemented by another, set for the Court by the "precept and example" of the new Chief himself —speed in disposing of cases must be sacrificed in order to allow "painstaking consideration by every Justice." Even though time might be lost, each Associate Justice had a right to expect from the Chief "full exposition of the questions involved in all matters awaiting decision." Stone said he could not exaggerate "the effect on the efficiency and morale of the Court, of . . . adequate presentation and full consideration under the guidance of a Chief Justice fired by a passion for the prompt and faithful performance of the work of the Court."

On the matter of "massing the court," Stone thought there was a line beyond which the Chief Justice could not, with propriety, press for compromise. He might seek unanimity by removing doubts and misunderstandings "so far as that could be accomplished by exposition and discussion at conference." But unanimity purchased at the cost, "either for himself or others, of strongly held convictions" was not worth the price. A Chief Justice should recognize the "part played in the development of law by the dissenting opinion."* A line could be found for dissent without anarchy, for judicial harmony consistent with principle. Actually it was asking too much to expect the Chief Justice to achieve complete unanimity. After all, he was little more than the "titular leader among equals." He must be friendly to all, partial to none, provoking no resentments and cherishing none. No differences of opinion, however strong, must be allowed to disturb that relation. Finally the Supreme Court itself was "greater than the individuals who happen for the moment to represent it." As the human vessel of Court tradition, the Chief Justice must be jealous of its dignity and prestige and ever "aware that these will not endure without the single-minded devotion of its members to the faithful performance of the high duty committed to it by the Constitution."

On this platform, Harlan Fiske Stone took office as the twelfth Chief Justice of the United States.

The reconstituted bench went to work without ritual. Refusing to make any ceremony of his ascension to the Chief Justiceship, he asked Roberts, as senior Justice, simply to announce Hughes' retirement and his own elevation. Having already taken the oath, the new Chief would then announce the appointment of Justices Byrnes and

* "If there are differences of opinion in the court," he wrote Admiral Joseph Strauss, May 5, 1937, "it is a great safeguard for the future that those opinions should be fully expressed. In the long history of constitutional interpretation dissenting opinions have often ultimately become the law of the Court, and in other instances have served as a check upon the doctrines adopted by the Court.

"The strongest guarantee for the permanent survival of a system of government based on a written constitution, interpreted by a court, is that its pronouncements be supported by written opinions, freely examined and criticized by the members of the Court who do not agree with them."

Jackson.* "I took my seat last Monday," the Chief Justice wrote his sister, October 12, 1941, "before a great audience which included Marshall and Lauson and their wives. The ceremony was brief, partly due to the death of Justice Brandeis the day before."

Hughes' retirement marked the end of an era. As one writer observed, Hughes "put great emphasis on the outward forms." His opinions were read from the bench with an impressive air enhanced by his full beard. In conference he was precise, formal, a stickler for punctuality, for keeping the Court up to schedule, for etiquette.[2] Stone had no flourishes, no pretense—no beard.

By 1941 President Roosevelt had exceeded George Washington's record for Supreme Court appointments, selecting seven Justices and a Chief Justice in the space of four years.† What did judicial restraint mean in this altered context? Stone himself had maintained that judges were obliged to decide cases according to their own judgment as to "the mores of the times," objectively determined, using the statutes as if they were common-law decisions, as crystallizations of policy, as starting points for legal reasoning. But when his brethren on the left began to do just that, the yawning theoretical gap between Stone and the New Deal emerged. The new Chief Justice's "objective judgment" on the mores of the day was vastly different, and seemingly more conservative. Worse still, New Dealers were themselves torn by sharp differences. Disappointing the fond expectations of F.D.R.'s enemies, the new Justices, who were supposed to look on the Court as part of a "three-horse team driven by public opinion," were anything but a collection of "yes men," and no basic core of philosophy or of legal doctrine was in sight around which a solid majority could be rallied.‡ It seemed certain that at least a bare majority—Stone,

* The question whether all three should take the oath a second time had been carefully canvassed. "Mr. Cropley, with his usual thoroughness," Stone wrote Roberts, "has been searching all the precedents for our seating of the new Justices, October 6th. So far as he can ascertain Chief Justice Taft is the only Chief in recent years who was appointed in midsummer. He took the oath immediately in order to deal with pending matters requiring his signature as Chief Justice, but on taking his seat at the opening of Court his appointment was announced by Mr. Justice McKenna, who administered the oath again. So far as Cropley can ascertain the oath has never been administered a second time in the case of any Justice of the Court. You will remember it was not in the case of Justice Black." (H.F.S. to Owen J. Roberts, Sept. 27, 1941; Owen J. Roberts to H.F.S., Sept. 30, 1941.)

† Hugo L. Black, Oct. 1937; Stanley F. Reed, Jan. 1938; Felix Frankfurter, Jan. 1938; William O. Douglas, April 1939; Frank Murphy, Feb. 1940; Byrnes and Jackson, 1941.

‡ But this was not yet apparent to the nation. The appointments of Byrnes and Jackson seemed to many commentators the final brick in the creation of the New Deal Court. "Unlike the retiring Chief Justice," United States News commented, June 13, 1941, "the new head of the Court also will find no sharp divergence of opinion among his colleagues." Similarly the Washington Post, June 13, 1941, foresaw "for years to come" a "virtual unanimity on the tribunal."

Roberts, Reed, Frankfurter, and Byrnes—would not be led astray by
the visions of social theorists. It was Stone's task to provide leadership
for "a new unity in Supreme Court doctrine, based on a clearer philosophy of government than has yet been expressed in the swift succession of decisions rendered by a Court standing in the shadow of
political change."[3]

The 1941 term opened most auspiciously. During the first week the
Justices reheard cases on which the Hughes Court had divided 4 to 4
the year before, and disposed of more petitions for review than they
had ever been called on to handle at the opening of a term. "I was
fearful that we might not get through," Stone recounted. "In order
to accomplish it I had one extra conference and began an hour earlier
on two other days, and last night at six o'clock the job was done."
His feeling of personal satisfaction was heightened because "all this
was accomplished without foreclosing desirable discussion or curtailing
adequate consideration of the questions on which we had to pass."

Berryman in the Washington, D.C., Evening Star, June 1941

"There is a good deal which has to be done by the Chief Justice which doesn't make any public showing," he commented, "but it is important for the Court because on this depends the speed and regularity of its performance." Measuring himself against the requirements of the job in the first few weeks, he felt confident that he would settle into the routine of the work and get on with it very comfortably.[4]

Despite his concern lest the Justices fail to keep abreast of the docket, the Court's procedures under his leadership became noticeably more relaxed. As the brethren turned to opinion writing, the Chief sent the most recent appointees, Byrnes and Jackson, a memorandum stressing the desirability of having opinions ready for consideration at the conference following each recess. Each could contribute much to the dispatch of business by prompt examination and return of circulated drafts. To forestall disagreements and embarrassment akin to that Brandeis had caused him in 1926,[*] he pointed out that one who voted with the opinion writer but disagreed with his reasoning "should promptly notify the writer to that effect."[5] A letter went out to Byrnes, admonishing him that the memorandum was "not to be taken as any suggestion that opinion writing should be hurried." As the new Justice was then working on the first big constitutional case of the term —Edwards v. California—one may fairly assume that Stone had this case particularly in mind.

Of all the states none had been so plagued as California by the drift of indigent migrants. To protect herself from economic disaster the legislature passed an act making the transportation of such persons across state lines a crime. When the Edwards case was discussed in conference, it seemed to certain Justices, including Byrnes, that "few things could more fittingly be described as a 'privilege of a citizen of the United States' than the privilege of moving without restraint through the states."[6] For Justice Douglas, too, the California act clearly abridged a "fundamental right," protected by the privileges and immunities clause of the Fourteenth Amendment against state interference. Such legislation, Douglas said, would "introduce a caste system utterly incompatible with the spirit of our system of government. It would permit those who were stigmatized by a state as indigents, paupers, or vagabonds to be relegated to an inferior class of citizenship."[7]

Justice Jackson, taking much the same position, disliked Chief Justice Stone's suggestion that California's ban against admission of hapless migrants be invalidated under the commerce clause. "The migrations of a human being," Jackson said, "of whom it is charged that he possesses nothing that can be sold and has no wherewithal to buy, do not fit easily into my notions as to what is commerce." He, like Douglas,

* See Chapter XIV, pp. 219-20.

favored resting the decision on the privileges and immunities clause of the Fourteenth Amendment. Why, Jackson wondered, has the Court always hesitated to give any real meaning to this clause?[8]

This was not the first time that the Court had tried to use this clause. It had been invoked in 1935, at a time when the Hughes Court was casting about for new constitutional barriers against state legislation born of the New Deal. Its use now might lead to untoward consequences of still another sort, unleashing perhaps a veritable flood of national legislation. The Chief Justice was concerned, as he had been earlier, and wrote Byrnes:

> The Edwards case . . . involves some difficult problems, the adequate disposition of which will require a considerable examination of the opinions going back to the Slaughter-House case. While I do not wish to obtrude my views, I hope, if you decide to rest your decision on the privileges and immunities clause that the opinion will consider and deal with points which seem to me important. They are:
>
> 1) As the Court has often declared, experience has demonstrated the unwisdom of departing from the sound judicial policy of not deciding constitutional questions unnecessarily, or placing decision on novel constitutional doctrine when it may rest as well on long-accepted constitutional principles.
>
> 2) As the Court has held over and over again the right of the individual, whether a citizen or not, to pass from state to state is within the protection of the commerce clause and the due process clause of the Fourteenth Amendment.
>
> 3) To bring such rights within the protection of the privileges and immunities clause involves a construction of that clause which has been repeatedly rejected for more than half a century and requires an extension of the clause in a way which, in the future, and with a changed complexion of the Court, might well expose our constitutional system to dangers to which it has been exposed in the last fifty years through the over-expansion and refinement of the due process and equal protection clauses.

Citing his own dissenting opinion in *Colgate* v. *Harvey* and concurring opinion in *Hague* v. *C.I.O.*, the Chief Justice told Byrnes that if he wished to discuss the matter further, "I am at your service at any time."

Whether or not there was further discussion one cannot say, but Byrnes did change his mind. "Inasmuch as the enclosed opinion embodies a theory other than that which I approved at the conference," Byrnes wrote his colleagues, "I think it appropriate to indicate some of the reasons which have actuated me in relying upon the commerce clause instead of the privileges and immunities clause of the Fourteenth Amendment, as a basis for the invalidation of the California statute." At the time of the conference Byrnes was under the impression that the Court, in at least one case, *Crandall* v. *Nevada* (1867), had held moving without restraint throughout the states to be a privilege of a citizen of the United States. But after making the sort of historical investigation the Chief Justice had suggested, he discovered that the Court had left the constitutional basis of its decision "wholly uncertain." Though that case had been decided before adoption of the Fourteenth Amendment, the Court had not referred to the immunities clause (Article IV, Section 2) of the original Constitution. Later on the Court, citing the Crandall case, had placed foremost among the privileges of national citizenship "the *limited* privilege of interstate travel for the purpose of transacting business with the Federal Government." This was the way the matter stood until the Fourteenth Amendment and the Slaughter-House cases (1873), in which the Court had drawn a sharp distinction between rights of state citizenship and rights of national citizenship. The latter were relatively small in number, and, as Byrnes pointed out, if the Court now included interstate travel among the privileges of national citizenship, a long line of precedents would have to be overruled. He wanted to avoid this as well as inevitable controversy among the Justices on the issue of "due process against privileges and immunities."

"Basing this opinion on either of these two clauses would probably result in varying concurring opinions," he observed. "I think it desirable to avoid this in view of the fact that the decision affects similar statutes in many states." For all these reasons, Byrnes concluded, "I have deemed it best to rely upon the commerce clause. I do not think the soundness of this constitutional basis can be questioned. As a practical advantage—it would grant protection against such statutes to many persons who are not citizens of any state or of the United States; but who are lawfully in this country."[9]

The reaction of Byrnes' colleagues to his somewhat ponderous explanation of change of front gave a hint of what was in store for Stone's Court. In arriving at a unanimous agreement that the California statute was unconstitutional the Justices divided three ways. Douglas wrote a concurring opinion in which Black and Murphy joined, and Jackson concurred alone. One cheering sign, however, was Byrnes' intimation of his agreement with the philosophy of the Chief Justice. In buttressing his opinion he apparently accepted the political restraints doctrine Stone had enunciated in the Barnwell case. The indigent non-residents were deprived of the opportunity, the Justice observed, "to exert political pressure upon the California legislature in order to obtain a change in policy."[10]

As the decision came down Stone believed he was "getting the job organized so that . . . it will run on smoothly if I can get my team of wild horses to pull together." In an optimistic vein he predicted: "We shall reduce our docket very materially soon. I have some difficulties in making my brethren agree, but inasmuch as the most rabid disagreement occurs among the newer appointees of the Court, there is no serious cleavage between the old and the new which might create an unfortunate impression."[11] The Chief Justice might also have noted that his colleagues divided along no clear-cut political lines.

Commentators and members of the bar generally took a less sanguine view. "The time has passed," one national opinion journal commented in early December 1941, "when a pleader before the Supreme Court could concentrate his arguments on four or five justices in confidence that he could count the others already with him. The 'nine old men' divided almost invariably according to their adherence to liberal or conservative tradition. Now that the new Court is altogether liberal, its members in practice are asserting the highly individualistic traits characteristic of liberalism."[12]

Dead-set against the dry rot of mutual agreement, the Justices displayed, in Court and out, their scant regard for tradition. For once it was clear that Supreme Court Justices were not free from the perplexities of mind and heart that beset all thinking men. On the day the Edwards decision came down the *Wall Street Journal* noted the "tendency to fall into clamorous argument even on the rare occasions when they agreed on the end result." For the *Journal* this typified the "friskiness" of the nine young men comprising the "New Deal Court." "The traditional liberalism of men like Chief Justice Stone and Justice Frankfurter," this paper said, "is being left behind, as the Young New Dealers step out with a new brand of liberalism."[13]

The Chief Justiceship added heavily to the demands on Stone's energies. He told friends of how he was "saving" himself by declining to go out in the evening more than twice a week.[14] Besides backbreaking administrative duties, his new position carried with it such honorary posts as Chancellor of the Smithsonian Institution, vice-president of the National Red Cross, and chairman of the National Art Gallery. All this sometimes interfered with the primary work of judging. He complained about "interruptions" and the "amount of work which was unexpectedly dumped on me."[15]

Soon after entry of the United States into the war, the Chief's life was further complicated by Justice Roberts' assignment to the Pearl Harbor probe and Justice Byrnes' increasing attention to economic planning. "I am struggling along with the work of the Court as best I can, with one and a half men away," Stone wrote early in 1942. "Roberts has returned from Hawaii, but I think he is still busy preparing his report. I am hoping that we shall get him back on the job again soon."[16] When the Justice finally returned to the fold the Chief complimented his work. "It is altogether a thorough document," he said of the Pearl Harbor report, "ably dealing with one of the most unhappy episodes in our history. I am glad to see that it is being well received as a difficult task, adequately performed."[17]

Aside from his failure to "mass" the Court in *Edwards* v. *California,* Stone's methods and ideas seemed, at first, to be winning support. The new Chief's first decision, sustaining Alabama's sales tax on materials purchased by a United States government contractor even though the burden of the tax was passed on directly to the federal treasury via "cost-plus" contracts, had the backing of the entire bench. The enhanced price of government purchases, Stone said once again, "is but a normal incident of the organization within the same territory of two independent taxing sovereignties."[18] In another opinion the Justices unanimously joined him in authorizing a state to require a permit for the transportation of intoxicating liquor across its territory. The Chief Justice sustained the requirement as affording local officials opportunity to ensure that the liquor crossed their state without diversion. "Such regulations, in the absence of supervening congressional action," did not "forbid or preclude the transportation, or interfere with the free flow of commerce among the states beyond what is reasonably necessary to protect the local public interest. . . . It does not violate the commerce clause." This time even Justice Black went along, though Justice Jackson, concurring in the result, inveighed against Stone's theory as one that "adds another to the already too numerous and burdensome state restraints of national commerce and pursues a trend with which I would have no part."[19]

Despite these successes the term was hardly under way before commentators noticed that the new Court "as shaped by Franklin D. Roosevelt in the course of natural appointments, is not a collection of rubber stamps. It is not deciding every case from a New Deal point of view."[20] In the *Los Angeles Times* and Harry Bridges contempt cases Black, Reed, Douglas, Murphy, and Jackson set aside the convictions as an invasion of freedom of speech, while Stone, Byrnes, and Roberts joined Frankfurter in upholding the lower courts, because "our whole history repels the view that it is an exercise of one of the civil liberties secured by the Bill of Rights for a leader of a large following or for a powerful metropolitan newspaper to attempt to overawe a judge in a matter immediately pending before him."[21] At the term's end 5 to 4 decisions totaled sixteen; one or more of the Justices had disagreed with his colleagues in 36 per cent of the cases.[22] The Chief Justice himself once more became prominent in dissent, leading the protest against a five-judge ruling that inspection of renovated butter by federal agents barred similar state regulation and against another forcing New York to recognize Soviet confiscation of former czarist properties.[23] He noted disagreement again when a bare majority refused to reconsider and overrule the famous wiretapping case.[24] Stone played no favorites in his twenty-two minority opinions. In the course of the year he lodged at least one dissent against opinions by each of his colleagues except Justice Murphy.[25]

A striking manifestation of the attitude of the Court, in contrast with that of the Chief Justice, was its opinion holding that a so-called New York labor organization, which collected money for beating the drivers of trucks coming into New York from New Jersey, was not amenable to the Anti-Racketeering Act of 1934. Stone's long and vehement dissent attracted widespread attention.

The acts of which the union members had been found guilty were not in dispute. "They . . . lay in wait for trucks passing from New Jersey to New York," the Chief Justice observed, "forced their way onto the trucks, and by beating or threats of beating the drivers procured payments to themselves from the drivers or their employers of a sum of money for each truck, $9.42 for a large truck and $8.41 for a small one, said to be the equivalent of the union wage scale for a day's work. In some instances they assisted or offered to assist in unloading the truck and in others they disappeared as soon as the money was paid without rendering or offering to render any service."[26]

Speaking through Justice Byrnes, the majority did not deny that payments were obtained by violence or threat of violence, but held that Congress had intended to exempt such militant labor activity by forbidding application of the 1934 Act to "the payment of wages by a bona fide employer to a bona fide employee." The tactics of the teamsters were not, Byrnes said, "the activities of predatory criminal gangs of the Kelly and Dillinger types" at which the Act was aimed. On the contrary, they were "among those practices of labor unions which were intended to remain beyond its ban." "Congress plainly attempted," the majority concluded, "to distinguish militant labor activity from the other and to afford it ample protection." "This does not mean," the opinion added, "that such activities are beyond the reach of federal legislative control. Nor does it mean that they need go unpunished. . . . The use of the violence disclosed by this record is plainly subject to the ordinary criminal law."[27]

The Chief Justice, dissenting alone, considered the majority's reading of the Act tortured and unjustified; worse still, an encouragement of racketeering. He saw violation of the statute in the very purchase of immunity through payments, "even though the defendants stood ready to unload the trucks in the event that they were hired to do so." Elaborating his thought, he said:

Unless the language of the statute is to be disregarded, one who has rejected the proffered service and pays money only in order to purchase immunity from violence is not a bona fide employer and is not paying the extorted money as wages. The character of what the drivers or owners did and intended to do—pay money to avoid a beating—was not altered by the willingness of the payee to accept as wages for services rendered what he in fact intentionally exacted from the driver or owner as the purchase price of immunity from assault, and what he intended so to exact whether the proffered services were accepted or not. It is no answer to say that the guilt of a defendant is personal and cannot be made to depend upon the acts and intention of another. Such an answer if valid would render common law robbery an innocent pastime. For there can be no robbery unless the purpose of the victim in handing over the money is to avoid force. . . .

It is a contradiction in terms to say that the payment of money forcibly extorted by a payee who is in any case a lawbreaker, and paid only to secure immunity from violence, without establishment of an employment relationship or the rendering of services, is a good faith payment or receipt of wages.

Nor was it conceivable that Congress intended to exempt any such extortionists:

When the Anti-Racketeering Act was under consideration by Congress, no member of Congress and no labor leader had the temerity to suggest that such payments, made only to secure immunity from violence and intentionally compelled by assault and battery, could be regarded as the payment of "wages by a bona fide employer" or that the compulsion of such payments is a legitimate object of a labor union, or was ever made so by any statute of the United States.[28]

Stone's characterization of the truckers as "victims" and the unionists as "extortionists" indicated his growing alarm. This demonstration of New Deal thought toward social tension in the nation he dejectedly described as "a rather interesting manifestation of the Court toward current-day problems."[29] As Associate Justice he had approved giving peaceful picketing constitutional sanction under the rubric of free speech, and therefore immunity to state infringement by statute or by common law.[30] He joined in upholding state control, however, where peaceful picketing* was enmeshed in violence.[31] As Chief Justice his votes in labor cases indicate a tendency to retreat from earlier positions.[32] As the national economy moved from labor abundance to labor scarcity, his reservations, reinforced by a wave of strikes in mushrooming defense industries, seemed well founded. Observers now saw him standing to the right of center. As views formerly voiced in dissent came to prevail, "liberalism" had to be preserved rather than won.

"These are certainly troubled days," he had written Sterling Carr, October 31, 1941. "A good many of the President's labor chickens are

---

* Stone differentiated the various connotations in the word "picketing." "It may mean . . ." he commented, to Robert Jackson, March 5, 1942, "the mere exhibition of a sign or banner, or it may be associated with varying degrees of violence, force, coercive, oppressive or annoying conduct, which, in my view, may be regulated by the state, which may also suppress the use of the banner or sign if it is intimately associated with other conduct which the state may pronounce unlawful."

coming home to roost just now, and if he doesn't stiffen up his back and act promptly we will be in serious trouble. Labor certainly is badly led. When one considers all that has been done for labor by legislation and the heavy burdens and restrictions that have been put upon employers without any corresponding obligation on the part of labor, its leaders are singularly irresponsible. They are likely to get a reaction in this country which will surprise them."

The reaction he foresaw was touched off by the Anti-Racketeering decision, which moved the press to denounce once more the "New Deal Supreme Court and some of its surprising, not to say astonishing, decisions." "The one it handed down last week," a Michigan paper commented, "was just about the limit, and beyond."[33] Hailing Stone's "biting dissenting rebuttal," the press reported "consternation" among "deeply shocked" congressmen.[34] Inasmuch as the issue turned entirely upon the revision of the Anti-Racketeering bill in 1934 by the House Judiciary Committee, Merlo J. Pusey, associate editor of the *Washington Post*, went to members of that committee and asked what their intent had been. The Court's opinion "is a ridiculous misconstruction of the law," they said. Every member of the 1934 Judiciary Committee who was still in Congress—Democrats, New Dealers, and Republicans alike—told Pusey that the Court misconstrued the law, and that Stone's dissent was "100 per cent right."[35]

The Chief Justice's mail bag bulged with letters praising his "wise and courageous" dissent. Editorialists, far and wide, could not find "anything other than racketeering of the most brazen sort" in the teamsters' activities. Others interpreted the decision as illustrating the "strange thesis that a labor organization can do no wrong."[36]

The majority was, however, not without defenders. The *Wall Street Journal*, though roundly condemning the "thoroughly reprehensible" practice whereby the union "effectually establishes at the borders of New York City a toll gate with the union in the role of collector," believed that the majority's refusal to intervene was "based on sound reasoning." Seizing upon an aspect of the case generally overlooked, the *Journal* warned against using any stick to beat a dog. Punishment of the teamsters was clearly "a job for a police court," the *Journal* said. "As the majority points out, this and other restrictive union labor rules were well known to Congress at the time the Anti-Racketeering Act was passed, and Congress in that Act did not specifically forbid them. Therefore it must have intended to leave them unaffected. The Court here refuses to stretch the meaning of a law beyond its intent. It has checked an attempt by federal law-enforcement authorities to act without a clear legislative mandate to cover the action. One may hope that our courts will continue along that salutary line of reasoning."[37]

The Chief Justice had lost a legal fight but had won a moral victory. Commentators, recalling his lone dissent in the Flag Salute case, again portrayed him standing alone for what he believed to be right. "He has earned," one writer said, "the gratitude of all law-abiding citizens, including that great majority of the workingmen themselves who deplore lawlessness within their fold."[38]

Meanwhile the quickened sense of judicial responsibility for freedom, stressed by Stone, had encouraged various minorities to stand up for their rights. Increasing insistence that constitutional guarantees, traditionally enforced only against governments, be expanded so as to protect the individual against oppression by private groups, had prompted Frank Murphy, when Attorney General, to re-examine federal responsibilities. The upshot was the creation, February 3, 1939, of the Attorney General's Civil Rights Section in the Department of Justice. Back of this move was Murphy's recognition that infringement of liberty by private forces may require the positive intervention of government. The first aggressive step in this direction was taken in Louisiana, where, during the lurid post-Huey Long era, reform politicians, fighting fire with fire, stole primary ballots and counted them for their own political stalwarts. Relying on Sections 19 and 20 of the old Enforcement Act of 1870, the fledgling Civil Rights Section prosecuted corrupt election officials. Voters in a primary election for federal office, it was contended, had a right to have their ballots counted honestly.

Such bold action flew in the face of the Court's contrary ruling twenty years previously in the controversial Newberry case, a decision that had left an intolerable gap in congressional protection of national elections.[39] Passing over the Newberry decision, generally regarded as holding primaries immune from any federal control, Stone upheld congressional authority "when, as in this case, they are a step in the exercise by the people of their choice of representatives in Congress." For him, the provisions of Article I, Section 4, authorizing Congress to regulate the time, place, and manner of holding elections for senators and representatives, were not dry bones set forever in an eighteenth-century context. In the circumstances of 1787 the framers could not, it is true, have thought of or intended that the word "election" include a primary. But in the light of the great purposes they had in mind such considerations are irrelevant. "The free choice by the people of representatives in Congress," Stone declared, "was one of the great purposes of our constitutional scheme of government." Such a scheme obviously presumed that ballots cast would be fairly counted. Viewing the Constitution as "a continuing instrument of government" intended to endure "for the indefinite future and in all the vicissitudes of the changing affairs of men," he ruled that the word "election" contemplated the entire mechanism by which the people registered their choice.[40]

The test was one of fact. Writing Justice Douglas, April 29, 1941, Stone put the matter thus: "The Constitution guarantees the right to participate in the choice of representatives, and it isn't important whether the effort to participate would or would not be successful. But in order to invoke the constitutional protection and to bring the case within the statute, participation in the primary must be a participation in the choice. If the primary had no more effect on the election than a Gallup poll, calling it a primary would not bring the voter in such a primary within the constitutional protection. If, however, the primary is either by law or in fact influential upon the election, then I think that failure to count the vote is an infringement of the right whether the vote if counted would have changed the result of the primary or not, because it is a denial of the right to participate in the procedure of choice, which is what the Constitution guarantees."

The case came within the statute if participation in the primary was in fact participation in the choice. Moreover, in Stone's mind, this was the conservative course. Article I, Section 4, coupled with the "necessary and proper" clause,* empowered Congress to take over completely the regulation of federal elections to the exclusion of the states. "Such an expedient," he said, "would end that state autonomy with respect to elections which the Constitution contemplated that Congress should be free to leave undisturbed, subject only to such minimum regulation as it should find necessary to insure the freedom and integrity of the choice."[41]

The Justices unanimously supported this portion of his opinion, but three colleagues—those most eager to advance civil rights—Black, Murphy, and Douglas, did not agree that Congress in a statute enacted long before primaries were known in American politics, had exercised its great power in regard to them. As they saw it, Section 19, which forbade under heavy penalties two or more persons to "conspire to injure, oppress, threaten, or intimidate any citizen in the free exercise or enjoyment of any right or privilege secured to him by the Constitution or laws of the United States," did not apply to primaries. In Douglas's view Stone was broadening the rights of primary voting at the expense of another civil right—that of a criminal defendant to have the crime with which he is charged clearly defined. He was extending the penalties of 1870 to the conduct of primaries "by adding

* Article I, Section 8, Paragraph 18, of the Constitution authorizes Congress "to make all laws necessary and proper for carrying into execution" express powers, such as that of regulating the conduct of elections in Article I, Section 4.

inference to inference," and in so doing "left the safety zone of interpretation of criminal statutes."* "Civil liberties are too dear," Douglas
wrote, "to permit conviction for crimes which are only implied."[42]

Stone was not dissuaded. Viewing the broad purposes of the old
statute in much the same spirit as the Constitution, he applied the
liberal techniques of statutory construction he had advocated at Harvard in 1936. "If a right secured by the Constitution may be infringed
by the corrupt failure to include the vote at a primary in the official
count," he said, "it is not significant that the primary, like the voting
machine, was unknown when Section 19 was adopted."[43]

From the standpoint of vindicating congressional authority over
elections, the Classic opinion is clearly among the most important
judicial pronouncements since the adoption of the Civil War Amendments. Such judicial statesmanship, fusing what someone has styled
"the genius of the Constitution and the ingenuity of judges," enabled
the Court to make a fresh approach to injustices sanctioned under
older ways of thinking.[44] Under this ruling the Justice Department
was given both a sword and a shield for safeguarding civil rights.[45]
One commentator has spoken of the Classic opinion as opening
"breath-taking constitutional vistas." It brought closer to realization
the demand that constitutional rights be protected from abuse of
private power. "The doctrine asserted in the Classic case," he wrote,
"is a broad formula that must cover . . . freedom from vicious private
interference with political education and the formation of opinion,
and freedom from economic obstacles in its expression."[46]

Built on new insight, Stone's opinion, in Holmes' phrase, had "poison
in it." In the minds of some liberals his language suggested that the
Court would uphold federal laws abolishing the poll tax. "Accept the
plain meaning of these words," Irving Brant said of his opinion, "and
the argument that the anti-poll tax bill is unconstitutional vanishes
into thin air."[47] "It is clear that the Chief Justice was not being precise," Virginia's Attorney General Abram P. Staples commented in
Senate hearings on an anti-poll tax bill. Though the witness did not
take the trouble to mention the cases Stone had cited, his distortion

* But see Hines v. Davidowitz, 312 U.S. 52 (1940), in which Black's majority
opinion invalidated a state alien registration law on the ground that a federal act
had occupied the field. Stone objected that this conclusion was drawn "from vague
inferences as to what Congress might have intended if it had considered the matter
or by reference to our own conceptions of a policy which Congress had not
expressed and which is not plainly to be inferred from the legislation which it has
enacted." In the judgment of Professor Noel T. Dowling, "the apparent inconsistency disappears when it is remembered that the Classic case was concerned
with the protection of those interests which he thinks the Court should be more
willing to safeguard than in other fields." ("The Methods of Mr. Justice Stone in
Constitutional Cases," Columbia Law Review, Nov. 1941, p. 1177.)

was used with such compelling effect on legislators that Irving Brant conferred with the Justice himself.[48]

"One of the members of the Senate Judiciary Committee told me that he had heard it said a dozen times in the Committee," the newspaperman reported, "that you wrote inadvertently when you referred to the power of the states under Article I, Section 2, being restricted by the power of Congress under Section 4."

"I never wrote anything inadvertently in my life," Stone told Brant emphatically. "I knew that the opinion in the Classic case would be a bitter pill. I am used to having my words distorted by those who do not like them. I make a practice of citing cases in the body of an opinion, instead of in footnotes, in order to make them part of the opinion."

In answer to Brant's suggestion that the Classic case overruled the Breedlove case,* Stone remarked: "I believe the Court should correct its own errors, even when I help to make them. I had not studied the history of the suffrage clauses of the Constitution at the time of the Breedlove case. When the Classic case came to us, I made a thorough study of the clauses dealing with federal elections and came to the conclusion that the purpose was to give the Federal Government power over the whole electoral process."[49]

As had the Gobitis dissent, Stone's Classic opinion stimulated a flood of speechmaking invitations. He rejected them all. "It is important to the preservation of the appropriate influence of this Court," he wired, declining one invitation, "that anything I do or say on civil liberties should be restricted to the performance of my judicial duties."[50]

Once again his reticence may have helped create misunderstanding. For disunity among the New Deal Justices had now reached such a point as to arouse national concern. "Those bozos," an eminent federal judge said of them, "don't seem to comprehend the very basic characteristic of their job, which is to keep some kind of coherence and simplicity in the body of rules which must be applied by a vastly complicated society."[51] Academic critics and others felt that the Justices' fervor had persuaded them that the Court had not only veto power over legislation they disliked, but also the power to do what the legislature ought to have made clear.[52] At times Stone's judicial conference, run as a university seminar, must have taken him back to those trying days just before he resigned the Columbia deanship, when certain instructors embroiled him in harassing wrangles.

Retrospectively the conservative Justices began to take on new

---

* In *Breedlove* v. *Suttles,* 302 U.S. 277 (1937), in an opinion by Justice Butler, a statute providing for the collection of a poll tax of one dollar, as a prerequisite of the right to register and vote, was held not to violate the "equal protection" and privileges and immunities clauses of the Fourteenth Amendment.

stature in Stone's eyes. In the memorial address he prepared on Justice Van Devanter this die-hard Justice stood as a symbol of reserve, of dignity, of thoroughness, of judicial independence. Formerly he had come in for serious censure*; now he was seen as living up to the "high conception of the function of a Justice of this Court." He had been, Stone said, "a tower of strength," and thus provided a "good text to preach from." In conference, when Van Devanter's turn came to present the case in hand, "no point was overlooked, no promising possibility left unexplored." To a Chief Justice harried by eight very expressive judicial personalities, even Van Devanter's written opinions became "models of judicial exposition, never discursive, redundant, or sprinkled with irrelevant citations." "They gave a hint," Stone said, "but only a hint, of the painstaking care which in fact he gave to their preparation." Opinions such as Van Devanter's bolstered the "true source" of the Court's strength and influence—"public confidence in the thoroughness, integrity, and disinterestedness with which it does its work."[53]

At the end of his first term the Chief Justice nevertheless felt considerable satisfaction. "It has been a busy term and on the whole a successful one," he believed. "The Court has done some things it shouldn't have done and I think will not be likely to repeat them, which means that the disciplinary force of the institution is getting in its work." Despite differences of view, vigorously expressed in the opinions, the spirit of the Court was good and the relations of its members altogether friendly. "That makes life easier for me," the Chief Justice said, "even though sometimes matters do not go as I could wish and as I think competent critics may think they should have gone."[54]

There was also satisfaction in the fact that Stone's "wild horses" had valiantly matched the Hughes record. After hearing all cases ready for argument, the Court adjourned in early June, having disposed of 1168 cases, which exceeded by 183 the total considered in the last year of Hughes' regime.[55] "Work of the past year has presented some other interesting features," Stone told the Judicial Conference dryly—a surprising number of dissents had come from a bench "composed almost entirely of judges appointed by one man, selected, many thought, largely for their devotion to the New Deal philosophy of

* At the height of the Court fight Stone had described Van Devanter as the commander-in-chief of judicial reaction, mapping strategy instead of writing opinions. (Irving Brant to A.T.M., July 22, 1955.)

In general, however, Stone always had a high regard for Justice Van Devanter. His criticisms of the old Court were centered on McReynolds and Butler. Van Devanter's tendency to write opinions on subjects in which he was a highly qualified specialist naturally diverted Stone's criticism to the others, who were more vociferous as leaders of the reactionary majority.

government."[56] The Chief Justice knew the public expected an explanation and he did not blink at the facts: "Any high expectations that the Justices of the newly reorganized Court would have minds with but a single thought and hearts that beat as one were speedily dissipated. There have been quite a number of 5 to 4 decisions and a goodly number of dissents—more in fact than during any recent years, but not as many, I believe, as at some other periods in the Court's history."*

Times had changed. Conflicts during the decade of the 1930s were the result of legal lag—the Court was unable to adapt itself readily to changing conditions. Those of the early 1940s (apart from certain accidental factors of personality) were the result of "polarization" —the development of divergences of view in response to the impact of social events that Justices, though marching under the liberal banner, felt compelled to appraise in different, sometimes highly individualistic ways. In this transformed context Stone was still a robust defender of the dissenting opinion.

A seasoned veteran in the battle of ideas, he did not now disown the primary instrument used in the long campaign he had waged against recalcitrance. Dissent served one of the "most important objects of opinion writing." It tended to break down a "much cherished illusion of certainty in the law and of the infallibility of judges," and gave "some assurance to counsel and to the public that decision has not been perfunctory." Beyond that, "a considered and well-stated dissent sounds a warning note that legal doctrine must not be pressed too far." Minority protest had a function in the rational process of judging. It implied "willingness to take and give friendly, impartial criticism, a manifestation in its best sense of the common effort of judges to develop law dispassionately." In his Court, he boasted, conflict represented intellectual, not personal, differences.

---

* If Stone meant to refer to dissents in Hughes' Court, he was wrong. Neither the number nor the proportion of dissents was ever so high in Hughes' regime as in the 1941 term, when 59 non-unanimous opinions comprised 36 per cent of the total opinions and drew 160 dissenting votes. (See C. H. Pritchett, *The Roosevelt Court*, Table I, p. 25.)

CHAPTER THIRTY-SIX

# In the Saddle

## 1942-1943

When the Justices convened in the fall of 1942 they faced unprecedented problems. Many of these grew out of the wartime activities of military and civilian officials—the trial of German saboteurs, the prosecution of alleged Nazi propaganda agents, restrictions on American Japanese, and the power of draft officials to determine conscientious objection to military service.[1] Still other issues, touching the fundamentals of American society and government, awaited decision: the scope and nature of the right of trial by jury received searching consideration in two cases; a majority upheld the right of a Communist to American citizenship and sustained a novel anti-trust suit against the American Medical Association for blocking group health plans.[2] Also growing out of the war was the fact that Stone's Court had to carry these burdens one judge short. In October 1942 Justice Byrnes left the bench to become F.D.R.'s deputy commander on the home front.

"All of us part with you reluctantly and with regret," Stone wrote on behalf of the Court. "We are reconciled to your going only by the realization that you are moved by a sense of duty to render a needed service of public importance in a time of great national emergency." Byrnes' reply was equally warm: "I shall always treasure your generous words of esteem and affection. . . . They encourage me to hope that I may still continue to enjoy your companionship."[3]

Byrnes' chair remained vacant half the term. Meanwhile Charles C. Burlingham did what he could to get Judge Learned Hand named to the post. Stone was highly sympathetic but was held back, as usual, by considerations of propriety. "Despite your persuasive plea," Stone wrote Burlingham, November 14, 1942, "I feel that I should not volunteer my advice on the matter of judicial appointments. However, my scruples are no longer of importance because inquiry has been made of me. I stated very emphatically my view that the appointment . . . would greatly strengthen the Court and that I should be made very happy by it. I suspect, however, that the age question stands in the way." Burlingham was doubtful, too, suspecting that the President might pass over the distinguished Circuit Court judge and name another professor. "What is it that makes F.D.R. so partial to professors?" Burlingham asked bitterly. "He started his first term with Warren of Cornell, then Moley and Tugwell and the rest, some of whom favored saving by spending, killing the pigs and plowing up wheat. Then he brought others into the Treasury and then he began to fill the courts with them." "Professor folks are all right," Stone replied tolerantly, "but we don't need too many of them, at least unless they have been seasoned by some of the hard knocks that one gets out of the practice of the legal profession or the business of judging."[4]

In Wiley Rutledge, the man F.D.R. finally named to Byrnes' chair, the President got a professor and Stone got a seasoned judge. But the Chief Justice's enthusiasm was not unbounded. "I shall be glad to have a new judge to take over [Byrnes'] share of the work," he commented. "From all that I know of him he is a rather promising man, but only time will tell whether he will fulfill the promise." Newspaper reports that Rutledge was Stone's candidate were mistaken. "There is nothing in it," he said. "The President made the appointment without even consulting me."[5]

At about this time rumors became current again that Stone's elevation to the Chief Justiceship had been part of a deal whereby he agreed shortly to resign in favor of Justice Jackson. Sterling Carr eagerly caught every published item and promptly passed it along. "It is an old game to chisel the office holder if you want his place," Stone observed, "and some of the New Deal boys are especially skillful at it. Of course, no sensible man wishes to overstay his time in any office, but my present inclination is to choose the time of retirement for myself, without the aid of any interested parties."[6]

Despite all handicaps and momentary irritations, 1942 was Stone's most triumphant term as Chief Justice. More than a score of major decisions came down, and, what is more, he had the satisfaction of seeing his views vindicated in the two major areas of his constitutional jurisprudence: national power and civil rights. In two landmark cases, opposite sides of the commerce power-states' rights coin were delineated in unanimous decisions.[7]

After the sweeping pronouncements upholding New Deal legislation enacted under the aegis of the commerce clause, it was difficult to establish the point at which the Court might be expected to call a halt. One discerning commentator saw the Court's most recent constructions of the commerce power as "a matter of degree" without any logical stopping place.[8] In 1941 Justice Stone himself had sounded the death knell of dual federalism. The Tenth Amendment, he had stated, was but a truism; all powers not delegated are reserved. Stone's opinion had been greeted, as we have seen, with cries of despair. The

Court had forsaken the states; the line between matters local and those of national concern had been erased; all power now lay within easy reach of a power-hungry central government. Reflective students of the Constitution wondered whether the Justices could prevent Congress from using its power completely to obliterate state control over its own affairs. Early in 1943 critics of the Court thought that the unanimous decision of *Wickard* v. *Filburn* furnished a negative answer.

Roscoe Filburn ran a small farm in Ohio; his primary business was raising chickens. Each year he planted some acres of wheat for his livestock and poultry. He accepted an Agricultural Marketing Agreement allotment of 11.1 acres, but actually planted 23 and raised 239 bushels in excess of his assigned quota. The penalty provisions of the Act were invoked by the Secretary of Agriculture, and suit was brought to collect the fines.

Filburn's defense seemed unanswerable. Federal regulation was unconstitutional, he said, because he had grown the wheat for his own chickens, not for an interstate market. Farmer Filburn's objection posed a hard problem. After argument in the spring of 1942 five Justices (Jackson, Murphy, Roberts, Byrnes, and Frankfurter) requested reargument.* For one thing, the farmer's lawyer had given them little help on the real issues, and they feared that "most of the Government men feel too sure of the Court to bother with enlightening it."[9] Black and Douglas saw no difficulty; for them there were no limitations on the commerce power save those few explicit restraints in the Constitution. Like John Marshall, they held that the supremacy clause swept before it any objection that Congress had invaded the preserve of the states when the matter regulated touched the national interest in commerce. If the Black-Douglas theory of the national commerce power were accepted, Jackson wondered whether the Court had any function. He, like Stone, refused to go that far; he was inclined to distinguish congressional enactments regulating commerce from those controlling "activities that are neither interstate nor commerce [which] are regulated because of their *effect on interstate commerce.*"[10]

In language reminiscent of the Old Guard, Jackson poured out his doubts: "The Constitution drew a line between state and federal power and here Congress wants to cross that line admittedly. I suppose that before we give it our approval there must be some finding that it is warranted by facts and conditions. Otherwise, the federal compact was pretty meaningless if Congress is to be sole judge of

---

* Justice Reed took no part. The Chief Justice, Black, and Douglas were "for prompt disposition of the case, not reargument." Stone was willing, however, to defer to the request of those who needed more time. (Memorandum re *Wickard* v. *Filburn*, May 27, 1942.)

the extent of its own commerce power. As you have well pointed out in the Darby case, sometimes the Court has been required to determine the facts that carry federal power across the line; sometimes administrative bodies do it; sometimes Congress has done it— but only, I think, where the effect was obvious to the naked judicial eye. If I am wrong about the proposition that whereas regulation of interstate commerce itself requires no justification beyond the will of Congress, but regulation of what is neither interstate nor commerce does depend on at least a reasonably probable effect of some kind, not too indirect, remote or trivial, then we have no function but to stamp this Act O.K." Urging reargument, Jackson confessed that "if a completely baffled mind can be called an open one, mine is."[11]

For all his doubts, Jackson had put his finger on the core of the matter—the Court's power to inquire into the factual justification for congressional control over acts not interstate and not in themselves commerce, but which affect commerce. After a second hearing the Chief Justice assigned Jackson the task of justifying federal intrusion into Filburn's chicken yard. The farmer could be penalized, the Court held, for his non-quota wheat even though he never intended it to reach the market or leave his farm. "Such wheat," the majority ruled, "overhangs the market and if induced by rising prices tends to flow into the market and check price increases." Even "if we assume that it is never marketed," the Court reasoned, "it supplies a need of the man who grew it which would otherwise be reflected by purchases in the open market. Home-grown wheat in this sense competes with wheat in commerce."[12]

The worst fears of calamity howlers seemed to have been borne out. Federal bureaucrats now stood between the farmer and his chickens; national agents took over where few state authorities had dared to enter. Small wonder Stone's correspondents were so much disturbed. The Chief Justice, however, had no misgivings. Jackson's opinion stemmed directly from two decisions handed down before he came on the Court. One was the Shreveport case, written by Associate Justice Hughes, which determined that Congress could, if it saw fit, regulate the intrastate rates of railroads where they had a substantial economic effect upon interstate rates. The power to regulate a wholly intrastate matter was said to be due to the fact that it had an important influence on interstate rates, which were within the jurisdiction of Congress.[13] Later Chief Justice Taft had upheld congressional regulation of the Chicago Board of Trade.[14] The practices there were admittedly intrastate but nevertheless subject to the regulation of Congress because they affected interstate commerce. "It was the same reasoning which was used by Jackson," Stone explained, "to sustain regulation of the wheat quota." The Chief Justice conceded that this might "seem like an extreme application of the rule, but it seems to me clearly within it, and like other things committed to Congress, can be reformed or adjusted only by appeal to the ballot."[15]

In *Wickard* v. *Filburn,* national power was sustained even though it reached subject matter normally thought of as lying within the state's domain. Two months later California's far-reaching agricultural regulations came before the Court for adjudication. Would the same Justices also throw out California's Agricultural Prorate Act as a burden on interstate commerce?

California farmers grew nearly all the raisins consumed in the United States. About 90 per cent of the annual product was shipped interstate. Under the Prorate Act a state-sponsored monopoly was given control of all marketing for California raisins, and growers were required to comply with its rules. By these regulations the raisin crop was handed over to a central committee for marketing. The grower was permitted to sell only 30 per cent of his crop in the open market; the remainder was divided into surplus or stabilization pools from which the committee controlled the flow of raisins into the interstate market so as to raise and maintain prices. Three questions were at issue: whether the marketing program set up under the Prorate Act was rendered invalid (1) by the Sherman Act, (2) by the federal Agricultural Marketing Agreement Act of 1937, or (3) by the commerce clause. In keeping, perhaps, with the ascendancy of national authority in this area, the lower court resolved all these issues against the state. But the Justices upheld the California Act unanimously.*

* While the Justices were unanimous on the merits, they were divided on a thorny jurisdictional problem. At one stage it was proposed to remand the case to the district court for detailed findings as to facts supporting the Court's jurisdiction. Stone prepared such an opinion but withdrew it. (Memorandum re: *Parker* v. *Brown,* Oct. 21, 1942.)

When his brethren proceeded with the plan, he wrote a dissent: "I think that, without further delay, we should decide the question presented by this appeal, whether the court below was right in enjoining the enforcement of the California Agricultural Prorate Act as unconstitutional.

"I do not doubt that pleading and proof establish threatened irreparable injury to respondent's business through petitioner's enforcement of the Act which, if enforced, would have prevented respondent from marketing any part of the 1940-41 raisin crop. It affirmatively appears that since the trial he has marketed some of his crop but still has on hand a part of it. It is plain that unless the decree below was wrong on the merits respondent is entitled to the continued protection of the injunction against prosecution by state authorities for marketing some of his crop *pendente lite* and to be protected from such prosecutions for the marketing of what remains.

"On the argument here petitioners repeated admission of their pleading that they propose to prosecute violations of the statute and it seems evident that respondent, if he is prevented from marketing the rest of his crop by threats of prosecution, is without any remedy in damages. The threat of injury is aggravated by our action, after the case has been twice argued here, in vacating, without

The Sherman Act had no application, the Chief Justice ruled, because that law made no mention of the states. "In a dual system of government in which . . . the states are sovereign, save only as Congress may constitutionally subtract from their authority, an unexpressed purpose to nullify a state's control over its officers and agents is not lightly to be attributed to Congress." Since the Sherman Act did not mention the states, it must be "taken to be a prohibition of individual and not state action."[16]

Nor did California's plan run afoul of the federal agricultural program. By adopting the Agricultural Marketing Agreement Act, Congress had not completely occupied the legislative field. The very fact that the Secretary of Agriculture saw harmony between the scheme he administered and California's prorationing plan showed that Congress had not intended to exclude the states altogether.

Finally, the lower court's judgment that the California arrangement interfered with interstate marketing was mistaken. The regulation of raisins before they were ready for shipment out of state might properly be described as a local activity. Courts were not, however, confined to so mechanical a rule. Summing up, the Chief Justice said: "When Congress has not exerted its power under the commerce clause, and state regulation of matters of local concern is so related to interstate commerce that it also operates as a regulation of that commerce, the reconciliation of the power thus granted with that reserved to the state is to be attained by the accommodation of the competing demands of the state and national interests involved."

"Such regulations by the state are to be sustained, not because they are 'indirect' rather than 'direct,' . . . not because they control interstate activities in such a manner as only to affect the commerce rather than to command its operations. But they are to be upheld because upon a consideration of all the relevant facts and circumstances it appears that the matter is one which may appropriately be regulated in the interest of the safety, health, and well-being of local communities, and which, because of its local character and the practical difficulties involved, may never be adequately dealt with by Congress."

With these decisions Stone's bench turned the old Court's no-man's-land—an area immune from all government regulation—into a neutral zone within which either state or national government could control

---

decision on the merits, the injunction under whose protection respondent has acted in marketing his crop."

Somewhat later the Justices came around to the Chief's position. In conference they reached an agreement that the opinion should not debate the question of the equity jurisdiction, but that the dissents of those who thought there was no equity jurisdiction should be noted. (Memorandum for the Members of the Court, Dec. 30, 1942; cf. *Parker v. Brown*, pp. 349-50.)

economic affairs largely free of judicial interference.* The Constitution left "wide scope for local regulation." At the same time, it gave due regard to the paramount "national interest in the regulation of commerce by a single authority," so as to maintain the free flow of commerce—"the principal objects sought to be secured by the commerce clause." But judicial review was not a dead letter. When Congress or the states attempted to regulate within this shadowy area, the Court would adjudicate validity upon "consideration of all the relevant facts and circumstances."

The Chief Justice's most notable victory was yet to come. Since 1940, when the first Flag Salute decision came down, Jehovah's Witnesses continued to press their claims so furiously that Stone suggested they "ought to have an endowment in view of the aid which they give in solving the legal problems of civil liberties."[17] Like "many of the other pests in the world," they were seen as "performing a useful service by making us face the issue again of freedom of speech." "I am afraid," he had commented somewhat dejectedly, "we did not face it too well, but the final decision is not yet."[18]

In June 1942 the ubiquitous Witnesses came again to the Supreme Court in *Jones* v. *City of Opelika* and two companion cases. These, it was said, represented but a "logical extension" of the principles on which the decision in the Gobitis case had been based.[19] All three concerned the validity of municipal ordinances imposing a license tax on the privilege of selling books and pamphlets on the streets or from house to house. The municipalities argued that the Witnesses' sale of tracts and pamphlets could be taxed as is any other commercial activity. In opposition, representatives of the sect claimed protection under the First Amendment, made applicable to the states by the Fourteenth, and urged that the ordinances were a forbidden interference with fundamental religious freedoms.

In an opinion by Justice Reed the Court ruled that these sales partook "more of commercial than religious or educational transactions." When "proponents of religious . . . theories use the ordinary commercial methods of sales of articles to raise propaganda funds," Reed observed, "it is a natural and proper exercise of the power of the state to charge reasonable fees for the privilege of canvassing." Chief Justice Stone again dissented, urging that the Witnesses were "peripatetic religious propagandists" engaged in the non-commercial, nonprofit activity of disseminating religious ideas.[20]

---

* A Court majority deliberately created, over Stone's protest, a "twilight zone" between state and federal governments in connection with certain types of "maritime" employees, so that those of doubtful status could receive workmen's compensation from either state or national funds without regard to constitutional limitations on the respective jurisdictions. See *Parker* v. *Motor Boat Sales, Inc.*, 314 U.S. 244 (1942); *Davis* v. *Department of Labor*, 317 U.S. 249 (1942).

Black, Douglas, and Murphy, in a remarkable about-face, recanted their earlier votes. "Since we joined in the opinion in the Gobitis case," they said in an unprecedented joint statement, appended to Stone's dissent in *Jones* v. *City of Opelika*, "we think this is an appropriate occasion to state that we now believe that it was also wrongly decided. Certainly our democratic form of government functioning under the historic Bill of Rights has a high responsibility to accommodate itself to the religious views of minorities however unpopular and unorthodox those views may be. The First Amendment does not put the right freely to exercise religion in a subordinate position. We fear, however, that the opinions in these and the Gobitis case do exactly that."[21]

Several months before the Opelika decision came down the West Virginia State Board of Education adopted a resolution requiring the flag salute of pupils and teachers. Refusal to comply was made an act of "insubordination," and insubordination meant expulsion. Under the compulsory school attendance law an expelled child became automatically a delinquent, and both he and his parents were subject to prosecution.[22]

Given hope, perhaps, by the Opelika dissent, one Walter Barnette and several other Witnesses brought suit in the summer of 1942 to enjoin enforcement of the regulation, claiming that it denied them and their children the free exercise of religion guaranteed by the Fourteenth Amendment. With rare prescience, a three-judge district court disregarded precedent and granted the injunction. "Ordinarily we would feel constrained to follow an unreversed decision of the Supreme Court . . . whether we agreed with it or not," Circuit Court Judge Parker commented. "The developments with respect to the Gobitis case, however, are such that we do not feel that it is . . . binding authority. . . ." Under such circumstances, the judges believed, "we would be recreant to our duty as judges if . . . we should deny protection to rights which we regard as among the most sacred of those protected by constitutional guarantees."[23]

As the Barnette case proceeded to the Supreme Court for review the district court's estimate of the situation was further reinforced. Justice Byrnes, a member of the majority in the Opelika case, was succeeded by Justice Rutledge. Four days after the new Justice took his seat the Supreme Court granted certiorari in *Murdock* v. *Pennsylvania*, another case involving a license tax on Witnesses' missionary activities, and ordered reargument in *Jones* v. *City of Opelika* and the two companion cases. In May 1943 the four dissenters and Justice Rutledge reversed the decision in the Opelika case and decided all four cases in favor of the Witnesses. "Freedom of press, freedom of speech, freedom of religion, are in a preferred position," Justice Douglas declared for the majority in the Murdock case.[24] Justice Frankfurter, joined by Justices Reed and Roberts, dissented.*

In the Barnette case the Court voted 6 to 3 that the West Virginia State Board of Education's regulation was an unconstitutional invasion of the religious rights of a minority. Justice Jackson, drawing heavily on Stone's Gobitis dissent, endorsed "preferred freedoms" for the Court in the strongest terms:

> Much of the vagueness of the due process clause disappears when the specific prohibitions of the First [Amendment] become its standard. The right of a state to regulate, for example, a public utility, may well include so far as the due process test is concerned, power to impose all of the restrictions which a legislature may have a "rational basis" for adopting. But freedoms of speech and of press, of assembly, and of worship may not be infringed on such slender grounds. They are susceptible of restriction only to prevent grave and immediate danger to interests which the state may lawfully protect.[25]

As the Court's spokesman, Justice Jackson stressed the judicial duty Stone had steadfastly maintained alone: "The very purpose of a Bill of Rights was to withdraw certain subjects from the vicissitudes of political controversy, to place them beyond the reach of majorities and officials and to establish them as legal principles to be applied by the courts." Disputing Frankfurter's judgment on the overriding importance of national unity, Jackson added a wrinkle of his own. "If there is any fixed star in our constitutional constellation, it is that no official, high or petty, can prescribe what shall be orthodox in politics, nationalism, religion, or other matters of opinion or force citizens to confess by word or act their faith therein. If there are any circumstances which permit an exception, they do not now occur to us."[26]

Stone concurred wholeheartedly in the result, but expressed doubt about certain things Justice Jackson said along the way. He did not approve the suggestion that ours is a "government by consent of the governed, and the Bill of Rights denies those in power any legal opportunity to coerce that consent."[27] "Undoubtedly," he commented, "the Government may coerce citizens to obey constitutional laws, whether they consent or not, but it may not coerce expressions of opinions either by suppressing them or compelling them, because such acts of government come within the prohibitions of the First Amendment."[28] The Chief Justice also objected to Jackson's reference to

* What Frankfurter said was presumably inspired and reinforced by Stone himself. "Not long ago," Frankfurter wrote, "we were admonished that 'the only check upon our own exercise of power is our own sense of self-restraint. For the removal of unwise laws from the statute books appeal lies not to the courts but to the ballot and the processes of democratic government.'" These, of course, were the ringing words of Stone's dissent in the Butler case. Frankfurter also cited the Carolene Products Co. footnote to bolster his argument.

mob violence following the Gobitis decision. "It is quite possible," he wrote, "that the Legion and other similar-minded organizations would have produced similar disorders" had the decision gone the other way. "That should not affect our judgment, and if it doesn't, is it worth repeating?"

In words reminiscent of the objections Justice Van Devanter raised against Stone's use of law review references, the Chief Justice also expressed "revulsion of feeling" at quotations in footnotes from the *Saturday Evening Post*, Merwin K. Hart, and General Van Horn Mosely. "You should go over the footnotes with care," he advised Jackson, "to see whether they really measure up to the dignity which should characterize an opinion of the Supreme Court of the United States." Stone admonished his colleague to stick to his knitting and criticized aspersions on the wisdom or educational utility of the required flag salute. "Our only concern," he said, "is whether their method of dealing with it violates constitutional limitations."[29] On balance, however, he agreed that Jackson had done a "good job."

In a short concurrence that elicited Stone's warm approval Justice Black said: "The ceremonial [flag salute], when enforced against conscientious objectors, more likely to defeat than to serve its high purpose, is a handy implement for disguised religious persecution."[30] "I wish to express my personal appreciation for your concurring opinion," Stone wrote, April 1, 1943. "The sincerity and the good sense of what you have said will, I believe, make a very deep impression on the public conscience. It also states in simple and perfectly understandable form good constitutional law as I understand it."

"All's well that ends well," Stone commented in reply to a congratulatory note, "but I should like to have seen the case end well in the first place without following such a devious route to the desired end."[31]

"The truth is," he wrote, "the Court before 1938 committed itself to the view that the restrictions of the First Amendment were imposed on the states by the Fourteenth. It did this under the leadership of Holmes and Brandeis and with the plaudits of the 'Children of Light.'* It is a view which cannot be reconciled with the notion that the states are free to pursue their own notions of policy hostile to freedom of speech and religion. I had no part in this but I see no adequate ground for overturning it now or for saying that compulsory participation in a ceremony and a forced declaration contrary to religious beliefs is not infringement of freedom of speech and religion."[32]

In terms of the quantity of work accomplished as well as the com-

---

* Compare with Justice Frankfurter's account of the origins of the "mischievous phrase"—"preferred" freedom. *Kovacs v. Cooper*, 336 U.S. 77 (1949), p. 90. Frankfurter is at special pains to disassociate Holmes from the doctrine.

plexity of the issues handled, the 1942 term has gone down as among the most spectacular so far in American history. The Court ran on later than usual and some of the most important cases came down at the last session on June 21, 1943. "I did some forty-six opinions of all kinds," Stone wrote proudly, "a good stout year's work."[33] High standards were also maintained. He was especially proud of his opinion in a case involving a seemingly trivial matter—forfeiture by California officials of an illegally used fish net. Since the net was seized at sea the real issue concerned state authority in offshore waters as opposed to the admiralty jurisdiction of federal courts.[34] To bolster his conclusion that California could rightfully seize the net, "the Chief Justice ransacked the law of maritime forfeitures from the time of Edward the First in England, cited the American Colonial and Confederation precedents, colony by colony, and maritime treatises; examined the history of the English Court of Exchequer; and for good measure analyzed the laws of all our present states to show what their statutes said as to the forfeiture of a fish net."[35]

Stone carried this load because he wanted his Court to keep abreast of its docket, as it had done under Hughes, and he wanted the work done well. The attempt to achieve this twofold objective with the bench over which he presided imposed an unprecedented burden. Besides being one judge short during much of the term, forcing others to make extra effort, all the Justices, except Stone and Roberts, were comparatively inexperienced. It was also a young Court. The Nine Old Men in 1937 had averaged seventy-two. In 1943, when F.D.R. made his last judicial appointment, the age level fell to an average of fifty-six. Nor was this all. Certain Justices seemed unable to rise to the Chief's standards. Stone "spared" Rutledge by taking the load on himself. The new Justice, perhaps puzzled as to the real reason for his niggardly assignments, chose to put the best construction on it.

"I do not want to allow the end of my first term here to pass without expressing to you my deep and sincere appreciation for the very great kindness and courtesy which you have shown to me in my period as a novitiate," he wrote his Chief, June 21, 1943. "You have been more than easy upon me in assignments and, frankly, I have something of a feeling that I have not done my full share here this spring, certainly not as much of the total load as I had hoped to be able to carry, and I am afraid that a very considerable part of this has fallen upon your own shoulders."

The Chief Justice's frank estimate of his junior colleague was revealed almost unconsciously in his reply on June 24. "The matter of assignments is a most perplexing and difficult task with the Chief Justice. There are so many and competing angles which have to be recognized. I have long thought that a new judge beginning the work of the Court should be put at his ease in taking on the work until he is thoroughly familiar with it. I have much hope that next year we will have the experience, which we have not had for some years, of a court working through the term without changes. It will be amazing how much better we can do our work and how much more easily we can carry it on under these conditions."

Other factors complicated Stone's task. Colleagues who might have been expected to carry more than a proportionate amount of the work were hampered by their zeal for self-expression. Concurrences and dissents cut into time that might otherwise have been spent on less personalized work. Brethren who found it "very hard to be unanimous on any subject" made for trouble from another side. It "has involved," Stone said, "our having reargument in quite a number of cases and of course much opinion writing."[36] The rate of disagreement had continued to climb so that by the end of Stone's second term as Chief Justice nearly half the decisions provoked dissent—a situation, the *Newark Evening News* remarked, that "is bewildering and does not add to the prestige of the Court." "The entire term of the court has been a disgrace to the judicial history of this country," another newspaper commented in disgust, "and perhaps the longer it remains on vacation the better it will be."[37]

Justice Frankfurter's well-known temperament, among the various causes of delay, wore increasingly on the Chief Justice. Insatiable curiosity and philosophical bent led the former law teacher to explore byways far removed from the issues to be decided, with the result that arguments were impeded, conferences prolonged, and opinions delayed. An habitué of the university seminar, he could not forgo its methods even in the formal forum of the courtroom. One day when a lawyer was arguing an important tax case under the usual limitations of the time set for argument, Frankfurter leaned back nervously in his chair and inquired, "And what is your philosophy of administrative law?" Fortunately, and of necessity, counsel turned off this invitation to expatiate.

It was far more difficult to quench irrelevant curiosity in the more informal councils of the conference and in the preparation of opinions. The versatile Justice, in pursuit of irrepressible intellectual interests, often put off writing his opinions only to find himself rushed at the end of the term and constrained to join with other "ten o'clock scholars" in prolonging the term for a week or more. At times, particularly when conferences held on till a late hour, Stone became considerably annoyed. Nor were such irrelevancies and irresponsibility confined to the conference. On occasion they manifested themselves in opinions, as in the patent case of *Marconi* v. *United States*.

In this complex technical field Stone had long been a recognized expert. He not unnaturally assigned the case to himself. His colleagues heaped high praise on the resulting opinion. "This is a magnificent job," Justice Douglas wrote on the slip opinion. "We owe you a real debt for the great effort and work which it entailed." Even Justice Rutledge who dissented "in part" described Stone's opinion as "a magnificent job." Yet Justice Frankfurter used this as an occasion for personal comment about judicial competence. "To find in 1943," Frankfurter wrote in a wordy dissent, "that what Marconi did really did not promote the progress of science because it had been anticipated is more than a mirage of hindsight. Wireless is so unconscious a part of us, like the automobile to the modern child, that it is almost impossible to imagine ourselves back into the time when Marconi gave to the world what for me is part of the order of our universe. And yet, because a judge of unusual capacity for understanding scientific matters is able to demonstrate by a process of intricate ratiocination that anyone could have drawn precisely the inferences that Marconi drew . . . the Court finds that Marconi's patent was invalid although nobody except Marconi did in fact draw the right inferences that were embodied into a workable boon for mankind."[38]

"I thought your opinion in this case fine—for some other case," Stone wrote somewhat facetiously. "The Court has hard enough times defending its decisions without having attributed to it things which it does not decide. . . . I hope that upon reflection you will conclude to eliminate or modify the sentence . . . 'And yet because a judge . . .' etc."[39] The sentence was not omitted. As a result Justice Rutledge, though agreeing with the dissenter that "the judgment should be reversed insofar as it holds Marconi's broad claims invalid," refused to join Frankfurter because, as he told Stone, "I cannot quite swallow the manner of Frankfurter's opinion."[40]

In these continuous squabbles subsidiary issues took on exaggerated importance. Sometimes certain Justices dropped everything to write full-length opinions where their original thought had been to dispose of the matter in a brief *per curiam*. The Chief Justice welcomed movements for compromise, but he could not consistently press others to go along. Furthermore, his own methods, so stimulating to his younger brethren, also encouraged a clash of attitude that sometimes led to acrimonious controversy. "The drive of the work, the zest of inquiry, the pride in the craft," as Walton Hamilton has observed, "all make for heat."[41] But in a larger sense the novel and complex nature of the issues, rather than the personality and methods of the Chief Justice, generated intracourt differences. Disputes, hard to decide in the hustings and legislative halls, could not be expected to find easy solution in the judicial forum. Differences here, as elsewhere, were but a normal, healthy part of decision-making in a free society. The

Supreme Court has rarely been able to resolve really fundamental issues. In all our great debates preceding crystallization of majority sentiment, its rulings have usually proved no more effective, as Stone said, than a boy's mud dam on a rain-swollen creek.

What bothered him was the needless obstacles his colleagues placed in the way of getting the job done. At times their quarrelsome factions created in him the attitude of the Massachusetts judge who resigned because he could not decide against both parties. His only recourse—highly unsatisfactory at best—was to do the work himself. "I have had much difficulty in herding my collection of fleas," he complained somewhat irreverently, "and they have been so busy disagreeing with each other that I have found it necessary to take more opinions than I really should."[42] He had come through the term unfatigued, but confessed: "I do crave change and relaxation so, as David Harum says, 'I can liberal up my mind.' "[43] One might think he would tire of leading such a court; paradoxically, however, the violent disputes only made him the more loath to quit.*

"Sometimes I am tempted to try retirement myself," he wrote, "but I don't know just how well I would like it—with more real work to my credit or discredit during the last term than in any year of my life."[44]

CHAPTER THIRTY-SEVEN

# The Stampede

## 1943-1944

As his seventy-first birthday approached, the Chief Justice's friends took it on themselves to ward off recurrent rumors of his retirement. Through their good offices it was widely reported that Stone thoroughly enjoyed the work and seemed to be having the time of his life. "Chief Justice Stone in very recent months has shown new force and vigor in behalf of the dignity of the Court," one paper said. He is giving the judicial process "the vitality of old teachings that justice is not at the disposal of partisans. . . . He is a judge who endeavors not to seem 'liberal' but just."[1] The passage of another year aroused only a twinge. "I can't say," he responded to a congratulatory message,

---

* Such an attitude was not unprecedented. Chief Justice Taft expressed much the same feeling shortly before his retirement.

"that birthdays stir my enthusiasm as they once did, but I am happy that my friends still find them the occasion for saying what I fear are sometimes over-generous words to me."[2]

Despite advancing years, perhaps because of them, he was still being asked to take on outside tasks. A few months after his birthday a bid came from Hugh Gibson of Doubleday, Doran to write a book on a subject of abiding interest. "I have often thought that I would like to do a life of George Mason," Stone replied, "because I have believed him to be one of the fruitful minds of the Revolutionary period, and less seems to be known of him than the other great figures of the time. But," he added, "the load of work which a Chief Justice has to carry is too great for me to consider taking on anything in addition, and so it would be out of the question before I retire, and it will then probably be too late for me to take on a new enterprise."[3]

The heavy load of judging and administration became, more than ever, a monotonous refrain. He told his friends of how he had gone through the "throes" of the Judicial Conference and summer's accumulation of certioraris by holding the brethren in evening session until at last, "between seven and eight o'clock of Saturday, October 9th, the job was done." Thereafter he had to keep "on the stretch" to get out opinions and attend to "the numerous other responsibilities which seem to descend like a flood on the Chief Justice."[4]

Adding to his already "inhuman" burdens, the divisive forces building up since the Court's reconstitution in 1941 now settled like a cloud over judicial deliberations. Nothing could restrain his "wild horses," and the New Deal Judges gave tongue to their sharp disagreements. As personalities were traded in the oral delivery of opinions, the smoldering fires of controversy, long at work in the conference, erupted into the open.

The public breach first appeared January 3, 1944—a day of memorable dissents. Of fourteen cases, the judges were unqualifiedly unanimous in only three, handing down twenty-eight full-dress opinions, not to mention four taciturn notations of grudging concurrence or partial disagreement. Two cases brought five judges into action and provided the most exciting scuffle of the term—Justice Black's verbal flogging of Mr. Justice Frankfurter. "Although I entirely agree with the Court's judgments and the grounds on which they rest," Black wrote in a curt concurrence, "I find it necessary to add a few remarks in order that silence may not be understood as acquiescence in the views expressed in the dissenting opinion of Mr. Justice Frankfurter." "For judges to rest their interpretation of statutes on nothing but their own conceptions of 'morals' and 'ethics,'" Black continued somewhat self-righteously, "is, to say the least, dangerous business."[5]

At first blush a dissent from a dissent seems a novelty, but not for these tradition-smashing Justices. The former Harvard law professor was again the target when a majority ruled that the Federal Power Commission need follow no particular formula or method in rate-making so long as the result appeared "reasonable and just"—a ruling that prompted three dissents and evoked a concurrence from Black and Murphy for no better purpose than to denounce "what is patently a wholly gratuitous assertion as to constitutional law in the dissent of Mr. Justice Frankfurter."[6]

Leading members of the New York bar were profoundly distrubed. In a letter to the *New York Herald Tribune* a correspondent who identified himself as "member of the Supreme Court Bar" focused attention on the "unhappy state of the Court" by listing the number of the day's dissents: "Murphy, 5; Black, Reed, and Frankfurter, 4 each; Roberts, 3; Douglas 2; Stone, C. J., 1; Rutledge, 1." "It is not to be expected," this anonymous writer commented, "that the Justices will always agree, but there seems to be a growing tendency to disagree; and if this is not checked the effect on the public will be unfortunate, making for doubt and uncertainty and a lack of respect and a loss of confidence in the Court. It is one of the essential functions of a Chief Justice," the correspondent went on, "to persuade his associates not to insist on differences which can be adjusted. . . . One of the least desirable practices that has grown up in the Supreme Court in recent years is the concurring opinion in which a Justice who agrees with the decision but is dissatisfied with the language of the opinion or its implications insists on expressing himself in his own words. In this last batch of decisions two of the Justices have indulged themselves in concurring opinions criticizing the approach and attitude if not the character of one of their colleagues. This breach of judicial propriety is in violation of the high tradition and dignity of the court."

The writer went on to chastise the Justices for failing in their obligation to keep the law clear "so that the whole body of citizens may know what it is and what it will continue to be." Without reserve, he condemned the "turnabout" of Black, Murphy, and Douglas in the Jehovah's Witness case. "One would think," he commented somewhat acidly, "that in cases involving the Bill of Rights a judge would know his own mind in 1940 as well as in 1943." Drastic shifts and disagreements would lead the public to suspect what the writer himself believed —that law, constitutional law in particular, was a matter of individual opinion. Implying that the Justices were duty-bound to guard their terrible professional secret, this stern critic concluded that "the Supreme Court is not a mere judicial tribunal of nine men; it is a co-ordinate branch of our Government charged with grave responsibilities and endowed with great authority and power. Personal differ-

ences should be confined within the council chamber and not proclaimed from the bench."

Side by side with this harsh rebuke the *Herald Tribune* pontificated
editorially on the Court's "obligation to produce a coherent doctrine,
a clear interpretation of the law of the land." "In the interests of the
people, who must know the law to abide by it, one may hope," the
editorial suggested, "that this trend will be reversed—and speedily."[7]

The Chief Justice's reaction to these diatribes was mixed. He welcomed criticism on the vice of concurring opinions, one may be sure,
and resented quite as much as the correspondent the unworthy comments his colleagues made about each other in judicial opinions. But
he rejected the imputation that it was his duty as Chief to gloss over
principle or muddle otherwise clear-cut positions for the sake of
maintaining the appearance of harmony. From long experience he
realized how a solid-looking precedent may turn out to be a weak
reed. Under Taft and Hughes basic disputes, since they were neither
spelled out nor ironed out, had smoldered beneath the surface.

The Chief Justice "didn't absolutely know" who wrote the *Tribune's*
broadside, but he had "suspicions."[8] Without revealing the identity of
the author he suspected, he rapped out a memorandum to the brethren
setting forth his own thoughts.

I do not know who the authors are, but they are evidently friends of the
Court as an institution. Their articles seem well intentioned and merit our
prayerful consideration.

I do not find myself in full accord with them, but I desire to make the
following comments. The right of dissent is an important one and has proved
to be such in the history of the Supreme Court. I do not think it is the appropriate function of a Chief Justice to attempt to dissuade members of the
Court from dissenting in individual cases. Nevertheless I feel free to say that
there is considerable scope for judicial self-restraint in the matter of dissents,
lest its usefulness and effectiveness be impaired by its abuse. It is not necessary to play every fly speck in the music. Not every difference of opinion
calls for a dissent, and there are many cases where the settlement of a rule
is more important than that it be settled one way rather than another, or
that different modes of settlement be emphasized. Dissent is of little worth
unless it is read. The more numerous the dissents, the more trivial the matters with which they deal, the less likely are any to be read, and the more
the public is likely to gain the impression that we are obsessed with triviali-
ties rather than the larger issues which the Court is called on to decide.

It is one of the oldest and, until recently, one of the most honored traditions of the Court that its opinions be written by a single judge. It is for
this reason that the writing of the opinion is assigned to a particular judge
only after conference, so conducted that he may be fully informed as to the
individual views of the Justices. It is for this reason that any member of the
Court is entitled to ask the writer of the Court's opinion to modify it, and

that both should seek some accommodation of their diverse views before separate concurring opinions are written. Adherence to this practice has tended to give coherence to the work of the Court, to make the effect of its decisions readily ascertainable and understood, and to command the respect of the public, which may readily be lost by over-emphasis of differences of opinion which do not produce differences in result.[9]

Stone then communicated with the person he suspected of "putting the heat on his Court." "I read your piece in the *Herald Tribune* about the unhappy state of the Court, and found myself in substantial agreement with it," he wrote Charles C. Burlingham, January 15, 1944. On one point only did Stone take issue—the writer's suggestion that Cardozo's placid administration of the New York Court of Appeals might be considered a model for the Chief Justice of the United States. "I doubt if Cardozo ever did more than to encourage proper judicial self-restraint in the matter of dissents," Stone said, "or that he would have gotten very far with some of my associates. Our trouble really comes from the persistent use of the concurring opinion."

"Truth, like murder, will out," Burlingham replied, January 18. "As I was gunning for Black, Murphy, and Douglas I hoped to keep out of sight. I confess," he explained, "that I have regretted my reference to Cardozo and the functions of a C.J. I strongly believe in dissents if they are on important questions, and I always thought that Rugg, C. J. [Supreme Judicial Court of Massachusetts], was wrong in trying to suppress them. I agree with you that Cardozo had a wholly different problem in Albany from yours in Washington. In fact, Cardozo himself was one of the most frequent dissenters in the S.C., was he not?"

The New York lawyer also explained how he had come to write his "superficial" letter: "My pet aversion is the concurring opinion. But while I had my pen in hand I thought I'd express a few other prejudices. I have a strong aversion to Black because he sat silent in the Senate and permitted Borah to state that he had never had anything to do with the Ku Klux Klan. I am told he is very smart and very diligent. Maybe so! I was vexed by the two concurring opinions *slating* Felix. It may be that he has brought it on himself by previous opinions prevailing, dissenting, or concurring. Another thing I touched on was the shift of Black and Douglas from their position in Gobitis. You stood firm and the majority came to you. Felix stood firm and lost out. There was nothing new to persuade Black and Douglas to shift. They just shifted."

Burlingham's somewhat petulant communication reflected the widespread uneasiness among lawyers. The eight Roosevelt appointees, once accused of being rubber stamps in faithful service of the New Deal, were now being castigated for making a sort of judicial hash of the law.[10] Formerly it was high praise for a judge to be told by a colleague that he had handled "a difficult job with great skill," that he had made a contribution to the law by "steering between two lines of authority and distinguishing the case in hand from the situation presented in each."[11] By and large the new bench preferred to choose openly between opposing precedents or wipe out both and start afresh. Such boldness shocked even a sophisticated lawyer such as Burlingham. As one writer sized up the issue, critics of the new order "long for a single authoritative opinion, and they regard any dissent as smelling of heresy or disloyalty." They did not realize that "compromise is as alien to the feelings of the judicial process as what Solomon offered to do with the baby was to the feelings of the mother"; they pressed for perfect unanimity, thus losing sight of "the very basis of the judicial process."[12]

Law as a stabilizing influence had not lost its mystic tinge. Even before Burlingham voiced his alarm Justice Frankfurter sounded a warning. "Law as a living force in society," the Justice had written his Chief, "must make adaptations and from time to time slough off the past, but . . . law implies certain continuities, or, at the very least, a permeating feeling that stability as well as change is an element in law. Past decisions ought not be needlessly overruled. If this is done with sufficient frequency, the whole notion of law is discredited. . . . Am I wrong," he asked, "in finding at present a too eager tendency not merely to bring the law into conformity to our present needs but gloatingly to show up the unwisdom, if not injustice, of our predecessors? If such an attitude is good for society then I wholly misconceive the notion and the function of the law."[13]

Justice Roberts shared Frankfurter's concern and he gave their complaint authoritative stamp in a dissent that has been labeled "the strongest words ever delivered from the Court."[14] In an obscure admiralty case the Chief Justice had written the majority opinion, employing his favorite technique of trimming authority to meet his own needs. Protesting against such piecemeal repudiation of precedent, Roberts, joined by Frankfurter, poured out his dissatisfaction with the whole trend of decision since his propitious "switch" in 1937. Almost point for point from the lips of a Justice of the Court itself came the same indictment Burlingham and others had leveled against Stone and his unruly bench. The practice of reversing cases wholesale confused litigants and the lower federal courts. Under these circumstances, Justice Roberts exclaimed, "the law becomes not a chart to govern conduct but a game of chance; instead of settling rights and liabilities it unsettles them." This, however, was only a minor result. "The more deplorable consequence," the Justice declared, "will inevitably be that the administration of justice will fall into disrepute.

Respect for tribunals must fall when the bar and the public come to understand that nothing that has been said in prior adjudications has force in a current controversy."[15]

But had not Roberts himself become famous as "a man of many minds?" Had he not participated in that historic switch that was supposed to save nine? "Of course the law may grow to meet changing conditions," he went on more tolerantly. "I do not advocate slavish adherence to authority where new conditions require new rules of conduct. But this is not such a case." Finally, directing an ironical shaft at the Justices who changed sides in the Jehovah's Witnesses cases, the dissenter proposed an extreme, even a fantastic, solution: "The tendency to disregard precedents in the decision of cases like the present has become so strong in this Court of late as, in my view, to shake confidence in the consistency of decision and leave the courts below on an uncharted sea of doubt and difficulty without any confidence that what was said yesterday will hold good tomorrow, unless indeed a modern instance grows into a custom of members of this Court to make public announcement of a change of views and to indicate that they will change their votes on the same question when another case comes before the Court. This might, to some extent, obviate the predicament in which the lower courts, the bar, and the public find themselves."[16]

Publicists marveled at the tone of Roberts' lecture. "No layman," the *St. Louis Post-Dispatch* commented, "would dare denounce the present Court as capricious, but that is just what is done by these two members."[17] "Feeling must be running high," a *New York Times* writer observed, "for the phraseology of the attacks upon legal and economic theories clearly demonstrates no momentary judgment, but instead a carefully measured criticism, motivated by an unconcealed impatience or anger." He discerned a fairly solid block of Justices on the Court's left, led by Black "with Chief Justice Harlan F. Stone sometimes joining in," though he "is not invariably in this camp. . . . Nearly always, this group firmly insists on individual rights when it comes to questions of civil liberties, property and patent controls, and similar broad issues." This side, "stands as a phalanx; the other shifts its formations." The remaining judges, Frankfurter, Jackson, Reed, and Roberts, could not be catalogued "as a distinct faction"; even to "label them individually is a difficult and sometimes a confusing task."[18]

It remained for Justice Jackson, however, to hurl at his colleagues precisely the charge that President Roosevelt had brought in 1937 against the die-hards of 1936. With the unqualified support of Justices Frankfurter, Reed, and Roberts, Jackson accused a majority that included the Chief Justice of legislating, of elevating its own judgment of public policy as a substitute for that of Congress. In this case the

Court had taken upon itself the exercise of "discretion" toward the undoing of a holding company. "We have been unable to find that Congress ever has announced a legislative policy such as the Court announces," Jackson declared. "The Court is not enforcing a policy of Congress; it is competing with Congress in creating new regulations in banking, a field peculiarly within legislative rather than judicial competence."[19]

But after the Court-packing fight and all that it revealed as to the nature of judging, how could any body of sincere and discerning critics, whether on or off the Court, reasonably expect the Justices to stick rigidly to the letter of the basic document? How could they expect the Court to solve hard puzzles as to " 'big' or 'little' business and such matters without being influenced by personal inclination, even predilection?" "Perhaps," one commentator noted with reproving understatement, "the law interpreters would follow their 'economic predilections,' a practice which Mr. Stone warned against some time ago but which seemingly has not been repudiated by every member of the lofty bench."[20]

All such arraignment nettled the Chief Justice, though privately he tried to minimize the "internecine war." "Only New Dealers involved," he commented in a family letter, "so I am more or less on the side lines." "You no doubt have heard something of the feud which the newspapers say is developing among the New Deal members of the Court," he wrote an old friend. "Fortunately . . . I have no part in it."[21] Amid unprecedented troubles Stone tried desperately to achieve that peace of mind Lucretius expressed:

> 'Tis sweet to stand upon the shore,
> And watch the waves in wild commotion,
> And to enjoy it all the more,
> Because you are not in the ocean.[22]

The Chief Justice could not, however, disguise his genuine concern. A trusted off-court friend had pointedly queried his capacity for judicial leadership; Justice Roberts had bitterly assailed his judicial methods, and his erstwhile supporter, Felix Frankfurter, had joined in the blast. Quarrels heretofore kept within the secret confines of the conference had erupted into formal opinions. Well aware that his reputation as Chief Justice was on trial, the thought that "no Chief Justice [had] ever labored under the difficulties which descend upon me from day to day" became a recurring motif in his correspondence.[23]

Nor is there convincing evidence that the Chief Justice proved especially adept in smoothing troubled waters. On the contrary, after the furor born of Justice Roberts' Mahnich dissent died down, Stone continued to nag Brother Frankfurter's defection in supporting it. The

*Berryman in the Washington, D.C.,* Evening Star, *February 1944*

latter stuck to his guns. "It was with much sadness that I joined," he explained, March 18, 1944, "but as you so often say, one has to live with himself. Not a bit more than you, do I believe that 'it is a sin against the Holy Ghost ever to overrule a case.' That never has been, is not now, and never will be my outlook on law. I am sorry to remain impenitent about Mahnich and I am encouraged therein by comments that have come to me from people entitled to speak in this field who no more want to grind the faces of the poor than you or I do. In any event," he concluded, "if I know the tradition of this Court it is to speak one's convictions even though it involves disagreements with one's seniors and betters—always provided it is done within the limits of courtesy."

To confirm his position, Frankfurter passed along several articles from the *New York Law Journal* on the history of dissent in the Supreme Court. Once again the Chief Justice seized the opportunity to needle his colleague: "As is pretty well known, I do not believe in dissenting just for the sake of dissenting or overruling just for the sake of overruling. But there are occasions which call for both lines of effort, and no doubt I shall do my share in the future as in the past." A short time afterward, with the Mahnich dissent still rankling, he sarcastically twitted Frankfurter for throwing a shadow on his departed judicial ancestors. "I am inclined your way in *Union Broker-age Co.* v. *Jensen,*" he commented suggestively. "The only point that gives me trouble is that . . . you, in effect, overrule *International Text-book Co.* v. *Pigg,* and I have been so recently admonished not to overrule cases that I am a bit scared."[24]

Burlingham's letter, Roberts' and Frankfurter's dissents, the excitement they stirred both within and without the Court—all this had an effect that attempted humor could not conceal or erase. There is no evidence, however, that the Chief Justice steered his course in deference to the charge that his Court was sapping the foundations of society. Whenever he faced the necessity of cutting dead wood out of law, he cast about briefly for some reasonable means of accomplishing the end and then went straight ahead. Among the cases decided during this term, none illustrates judicial forthrightness better than *Smith* v. *Allwright,* which pronounced the doom of the white primary.

In 1935 Justice Roberts and all his colleagues, including Stone, had held in *Grovey* v. *Townsend* that primary voting was not a constitutional prerogative but a privilege of party membership. Thus, by delegating primary elections to the Democratic party, Texas had, under this decision, found a valid way around the constitutional injunction against suffrage discriminations based on race or color. In 1941 Stone, without expressly saying so, flouted the basic reasoning of the Grovey case. In his famous Classic opinion he ruled that participation in preferential primaries was a right secured by the Constitution. Thus, with the unqualified adherence of Justice Roberts, and without discussing *Grovey* v. *Townsend,* Stone had circumspectly brought traditional Southern election customs to the brink of destruction. More alert than Justice Roberts, commentators knew that another precedent, and a very recent one, had been relegated to the scrap heap. "The Grovey case," one writer said about the revolutionary effect of Stone's Classic opinion, "had an air of finality about it until the successful prosecution . . . of a group of Louisiana primary election officials for violation of the Civil Rights Act."[25]

The Allwright case, twice argued, November 1943 and January 1944, consumed nearly five months. Decision came quickly in conference on January 16, a few days after the second argument. Eight judges agreed that the Classic case had spelled ultimate destruction of the implacable barrier the Grovey case had put in the way of Negro suffrage. Great difficulties were experienced, however, in getting out an opinion, partly because the Justices were somewhat leery of openly discarding still another landmark of the old Court.

Without thought of possible untoward consequences the Chief Justice appointed Justice Frankfurter the Court's spokesman. Immediately some other judges had misgivings, and Justice Jackson spelled these out to the Chief, January 17, 1944:

I hope you will forgive me for intruding into the matter of assignments, the difficulties of which I feel you generally resolve with wisdom and always with fairness, but I wonder if you have not overlooked some of the ugly factors in our national life which go to the wisdom of having Mr. Justice Frankfurter act as the voice of this Court in the matter of *Smith* v. *Allwright*. It is a delicate matter. We must reverse a recent, well-considered, and unanimous decision. We deny the entire South the right to a white primary, which is one of its most cherished rights. It seems to me very important that the strength which an all but unanimous decision would have may be greatly weakened if the voice that utters it is one that may grate on Southern sensibilities. Mr. Justice Frankfurter unites in a rare degree factors which unhappily excite prejudice. In the first place, he is a Jew. In the second place, he is from New England, the seat of the abolition movement. In the third place, he has not been thought of as a person particularly sympathetic with the Democratic party in the past. I know that every one of these things is a consideration that to you is distasteful and they are things which I mention only with the greatest reluctance and frank fear of being misunderstood. I have told Mr. Justice Frankfurter that in my opinion it is best for this Court and for him that he should not be its spokesman in this matter and that I intend to bring my view of it to your attention. With all humility I suggest that the Court's decision, bound to arouse bitter resentment, will be much less apt to stir ugly reactions if the news that the white primary is dead, is broken to it, if possible, by a Southerner who has been a Democrat and is not a member of one of the minorities which stir prejudices kindred to those against the Negro.

I have talked with some of them [the other Justices] who are still in the building, and they feel as I do.

I rely on the good understanding which I have always felt existed between us and upon our mutual anxiety for the welfare and prestige of the Court to excuse my intrusion in a matter which, having spoken my piece, is solely for your judgment.

Stone retreated at once, withdrawing the case from Frankfurter and reassigning it to Reed.

Though *Grovey* v. *Townsend* was obviously doomed, Reed immediately came under pressures to adopt one device or another for mitigating the storm of resentment certain to be aroused in the South and elsewhere. Uneasy lest the Court be accused of a disingenuous discarding of the Grovey case, Justice Frankfurter suggested an elaborate funeral. For him, Grovey was not a case eroded by time or whittled away by subsequent decisions. He saw no escape from a frank reversal of judgment by the Court. The Court should not, he thought, draw an inference against Grovey which in Classic it was careful to withhold.

Another Justice doubted whether this was not an appropriate occasion to apply the rule limiting the effects of a reversal to its future operation.* "Whatever may be the merits of the rule," Reed argued in a memorandum to the brethren, "it does not seem to me that the disadvantages arising from the overruling of *Grovey* v. *Townsend* are sufficient to call for its application here."† Reed preferred to say that the Justices were simply "recognizing" that Grovey had been dead since the Classic case. Engaging in some rather shameless double talk, he declared: "The fusing by the Classic case of the primary and general elections into a single instrumentality for choice of officers has a definite bearing on the permissibility under the Constitution of excluding Negroes from primaries. This is not to say that the Classic case cuts directly into the rationale of *Grovey* v. *Townsend*. This latter case was not mentioned in the opinion."26

The leopard, Reed would have one believe, had not changed its spots; Stone's Classic opinion had not changed the actual character of primary elections and so had not made the exclusion of Negroes "any more or less state action." But there was no blinking the fact that Stone's recognition in 1940 of "the place of the primary in the electoral scheme" indicated his belief that the Grovey decision had been erroneous. "I think your opinion in this case is good," the Chief Justice told Reed. "You have handled a thorny matter very skillfully."27

In the end the Justices aligned themselves as they had originally voted, except that Justice Frankfurter, perhaps convinced that his approach to the Grovey reversal was more likely to forestall recrimination, tersely concurred in the result. Roberts, forced to watch the cruel mangling of his Grovey opinion, refused to submit in silence to any implication that by agreeing to Stone's Classic opinion he had helped undo his own handiwork. A major aspect of Stone's judicial statesmanship—his deliberate sapping of unyielding precedent—came in for plain-spoken denunciation. Objections that had been somewhat veiled in Roberts' Mahnich dissent now came out in the open.‡

* Reed does not name the Justice originating this suggestion, but for a somewhat similar position, see Justice Jackson's opinion in the Southeastern Underwriters case.

† In this undated memorandum for the conference Reed pointed out: "So far as the recovery of damages is concerned, they can be recovered only where refusal of a right to vote has taken place. These must be very limited in number. In all likelihood, they would be small in amount. I take it that criminal prosecutions might be brought also only against those who had actually refused a ballot to Negroes. These must be very limited in number."

‡ Roberts knew his brethren thought he had been duped in the Classic case. In his Mahnich dissent (p. 108) he had said: "There has been some suggestion that the holding in the Pinar del Rio case to which I have referred crept into the opinion by inadvertence. But I cannot assume any such thing in view of the proverbial care which all the Justices exercise to prevent expression of opinion on questions not necessary to the decision of a case. The decision must be taken at face value as the expression of the views of all the members of the Court." Taken

"Not a fact differentiates [the Grovey case] from this except the names of the parties," Roberts exploded. "It is suggested that *Grovey* v. *Townsend* was overruled *sub silentio* in *United States* v. *Classic*. The case is not mentioned in either of the opinions in the Classic case. If this Court's opinion in the Classic case discloses its method of overruling earlier decisions, I can only protest that, in fairness, it should rather have adopted the open and frank way of saying what it was doing than, after the event, characterize its past action as over-ruling *Grovey* v. *Townsend*, though those less sapient never realized the fact." "The instant decision," he fumed, "tends to bring adjudications of this tribunal into the same class as a restricted railroad ticket, good for this day and train only."[28]

Outwardly Stone took all such fulminations calmly and sat back to await more considered reaction. "I hope you are gratified," he wrote Reed, April 5, 1944, "at the reception which most newspapers have given your opinion in the Smith case. I am glad to see that such papers as the *Washington Post* recognize it is sometimes our duty to do away with a bad precedent and that this was one of those times. As for myself," he continued, defending his own methods, "when I wrote the Classic case I was convinced that the Court would one day feel compelled to do what it did do Monday, and I certainly should have felt that I did not do my duty as a judge had I not joined in your opinion."

Perhaps judges, such as those on Stone's Court, who work in the intense light of public scrutiny perform differently from those whose comings, goings, and chance remarks are not blazoned on the front pages. However that may be, Stone's bench, right down to the end of the term, was plagued and perplexed by what was essentially a public relations question having little direct bearing on legal issues. How could they change the law gracefully amid the hubbub incited by their continued wrangling? The most dramatic illustration of the troubles confronting the Chief Justice and his Court was yet to come—the Southeastern Underwriters case, involving anti-trust prosecution against 196 fire-insurance companies engaged in a rate-fixing combine.

Back in 1869, in *Paul* v. *Virginia*,[29] the Court had repulsed an effort to invoke the commerce clause against the exercise of state power and had held that the states could regulate insurance because it was not commerce. Succeeding Justices had faithfully adhered to that decision.

seriously, of course, this would apply with force to Roberts' own position in Classic.

The decision to overrule *Grovey* v. *Townsend* had been reached sometime before the opinions came down in the Mahnich case, January 31, 1944, a circumstance that caused one commentator, following *Smith* v. *Allwright*, to observe: "I think I know now from what decision Mr. Justice Roberts dissented in the Mahnich case." (Alexander Pekelis to H.F.S., April 4, 1944.)

On this understanding a vast and complicated structure of state regulation of insurance had grown up. On this understanding, too, the Sherman Act had been passed. Congress had not seen fit to regulate insurance, and the direct question of federal authority in this field never came to court. Since 1937, however, the expansion in the scope of the commerce clause by judicial interpretation made it evident that Congress could exercise extensive powers over the insurance business. In effect, Congress had been misled by *Paul* v. *Virginia* just as federal judges had been led astray by *Swift* v. *Tyson*. Should the Justices now disabuse the legislators, apply their matured concepts of commerce to insurance despite the legal confusion that such a decision would probably engender, or should they fly in the face of their own beliefs, hold fast to *Paul* v. *Virginia*, deny Congress's power in order to avert temporary chaos? Or perhaps they could take a middle ground—hand down an advisory opinion upholding congressional power, coupled with a refusal to apply the Sherman Act because Congress could not have intended in 1890 to regulate what it firmly believed it could not control.

The opinions, prevailing and dissenting, circulated originally in March, and much effort went into their revision. In mid-May one Justice, foreseeing possible embarrassment in abandoning time-honored constitutional doctrine, proposed a compromise *per curiam* decision. Justice Black objected immediately. Like judges of an older school, he did not hesitate "to correct a century of error." Nor did he fear probable repercussions. "Upon consideration," he wrote Stone, "I have reached the conclusion that we should not decline to decide this case on the ground that only four members of the Court believe that Congress has power under the commerce clause to regulate the business of insurance when its activities are conducted across state lines. . . . Since Congress has made six members of this Court a quorum, it undoubtedly contemplated that four should render judgments. . . . Much as I deplore the necessity for four to three decisions, I am not ready to subscribe to a disposition . . . which would hereafter be cited as a precedent to preclude statutory interpretations by a majority of the Court quorum."[30]

Even if a *per curiam* opinion proved feasible, one determined judge, like Black, could spike the plan by following the now-established practice of lodging a lengthy dissent, which others would feel constrained to answer. The Chief Justice, though apparently undecided in his own mind as to the best course, suggested a compromise. "I think I would be willing," he wrote the brethren, "to join in the following *per curiam*, which it seems to me tells all that the public is entitled to know about the case, if we do not put down opinions":

The Court is of the opinion that this question of statutory construction cannot be decided without raising questions of constitutionality and more particularly the power of Congress and of the states under the commerce clause in relation to the business of insurance. For any view concerning these constitutional issues there is wanting a majority of the entire Court. The Court is of the opinion that constitutional issues of such gravity ought not to be decided by less than a majority of the entire Court, the more so since decision would involve overruling in principle decisions of this Court which have long been accepted as authoritative. We are therefore constrained to leave the judgment of the District Court undisturbed.

Justice Douglas, he announced, would circulate another short draft giving his views. "As at present advised," Stone informed his colleagues, "I would be inclined to join in any of these proposals, but I am not yet committed to any."

Frankfurter promptly accepted Stone's draft but objected to any revelation of individual sentiments in a *per curiam*. From Justice Roberts, sulking on the sidelines, came a reaction that perhaps demonstrated to all the folly of the proposed compromise. "As I did not participate in the decision of the case," he wrote Stone, "I do not care to express any opinion as to propriety of handing down the *per curiam* in question. I should tell you, however," he continued, removing all doubt as to his real position, "that if this *per curiam*, or any other like it, is handed down I should like a notation to be added as follows: 'Mr. Justice Roberts took no part in the consideration or decision of the case and did not vote for this opinion or participate in its formulation or promulgation.' "[31]

In the face of this uncompromising reaction the objections to Douglas's more extreme proposal—to let the public know the true nature of the disagreement—were so plain that his effort fell flat. Black's full opinion came down on June 5, 1944, accompanied by separate dissents from the Chief Justice, Frankfurter, and Jackson.

"Commerce is interstate," Justice Black began, citing the weighty authority of Chief Justice Marshall, "when it 'concerns more states than one.'" "No commercial enterprise of any kind which conducts its activities across state lines has been held to be wholly beyond the regulatory power of Congress under the commerce clause. We cannot make an exception of the business of insurance." Black was equally forthright in holding the Sherman Act applicable to insurance: "Congress wanted to go to the utmost extent of its constitutional power in restraining trust and monopoly agreements." The fear, so troublesome to several of his colleagues, that the decision would throw the insurance business into turmoil by invalidating state regulation, Black cast aside lightly as "exaggerated."[32]

Justice Jackson, dissenting in part, admitted that insurance is commerce "in fact," but adhered to the doctrinal "fiction" that it was not. Arguing that Congress had not included insurance in the scope of the Sherman Act, he contended that, in view of the long history of state regulation, the legislature, not the Court, should take the first step in nationalizing insurance controls.* Both the Chief Justice and Frankfurter admitted that acts of interstate commerce incidental to the insurance business and the business itself insofar as it "affects interstate commerce" are subject to "appropriate exercise of federal power." But such questions, the Chief Justice insisted, are not before us. "We are not concerned here with the power of Congress to do what it has not attempted to do, but with the question whether Congress in enacting the Sherman Act has asserted its power over the business of insurance. . . . The questions here are whether the business of entering into contracts in one state, insuring against the risk of loss by fire of property in others, is itself interstate commerce; and whether an agreement or conspiracy to fix the premium rates of such contracts and in other ways to restrict competition in effecting policies of fire insurance, violates the Sherman Act." The District Court below had answered both questions in the negative. "I think that its answer is right," the Chief Justice said, "and its judgment should be affirmed."

"What you and Justice Jackson have written on the subject," Black said after he had read the dissenting opinions, "leaves me with the distinct impression that seven, not just four, members of the Court believe that Congress has power under the commerce clause to regulate the business of insurance when its activities are conducted across state lines." As he saw it, "disagreement really rests on differing views as to the applicability of the Sherman Act."[33]

Stone could not agree. He dissented "both on principle and in view of the permanency which should be given to the construction of the commerce clause and the Sherman Act." Clinging to the venerable precedent established by *Paul* v. *Virginia,* he tried to reconcile his stand with the Court's recent pronouncements by pointing to Congress's vast powers to deal with those aspects of insurance that affect interstate commerce. There was no inconsistency, he argued. Writing fire-insurance contracts in itself was not commerce in the constitutional sense. Nor was it within the meaning of the Sherman Act. "The congressional power to regulate does not extend to the formation and performance of insurance contracts save only as the latter may affect

---

* Justice Jackson's remarkably candid opinion deserves more extended treatment than can be given here, for it introduces a new factor in the equation of judicial restraint—the notion that in certain instances, at least, the Court ought to await legislative action before undertaking to revise obviously outmoded constitutional concepts. As the author of *Wickard* v. *Filburn*, he entertained broad views on the reach of congressional authority.

communication and transportation which are interstate commerce or may otherwise be found by Congress to affect transactions of interstate commerce. And even then, such effects on commerce as do not involve restraints in competition in the marketing of goods and services are not within the reach of the Sherman Act."

Lest he seem to lend support to critics who upbraided his Court for playing fast and loose with precedents, he was careful to point out that the mere fact that an ancient authority had been scuttled was not "in itself a sufficient ground for declining to join in the Court's decision. This Court has never committed itself to any rule or policy that it will not 'bow to the lessons of experience and the force of better reasoning' by overruling a mistaken precedent."*

Whatever its merits, Black's bold course was inexpedient. In the years since the Court had held that insurance was not commerce, vast effort had gone into the development of schemes of state regulation and into the organization of the insurance business in reliance on the permanence of the existing scheme of state regulation. "Overturning the precedents of seventy-five years governing a business of such volume and of such wide ramifications," the Chief Justice reasoned, "cannot fail to be the occasion for loosing a flood of litigation and of legislation, state and national, in order to establish a new boundary between state and national power, raising questions which cannot be answered for years to come, during which a great business and the regulatory officers of every state must be harassed by all the doubts and difficulties inseparable from a realignment of the distribution of power in our federal system."† Seeming to overlook his famous dictum that the Court is not the only agency of government with the power to govern, his opinion concluded: "These considerations might well stay a reversal of long-established doctrine which promises so little

---

* "This is especially the case," he had written in an early draft, citing a long series of cases, "when the meaning of the Constitution is at issue and a mistaken construction is one which cannot be corrected by legislative action. There are few Justices who have sat on this Court, and none on the Court as it is now constituted, who have not for these reasons participated in decisions overruling earlier decisions."

† Underlying Stone's anxiety was the suggestion he had expressed in his Barnwell decision as to the slowness of Congress to act in situations demanding uniform regulation of commerce. Here, as in *Parker* v. *Brown*, where there was an opportunity for concurrent regulation by both Congress and the states, he preferred to substantiate existing state regulation until such time as Congress would legislate to control those aspects of insurance falling within its commerce power, instead of leaving an unregulated "no man's land" in which confusion and hesitancy would be rife. However, his dire foreboding proved to be groundless. Following the Court's decision Congress passed the McCarran Act permitting the states to continue to regulate and tax the business of insurance in spite of its interstate character. In *Prudential Insurance Co.* v. *Benjamin*, 328 U.S. 408 (1946), the Court abandoned its traditional view that federal and state control over commerce are mutually exclusive and sustained the Act.

of advantage and so much of harm. For me these considerations are controlling."

Stone's views as to the scope of the commerce power had been brewing since the Schechter decision of 1935. He did not then "see how even a flexible Constitution and flexible-minded judges could quite stretch it to the point requisite to sustain the Government in the Schechter case."[34] A line could be drawn between matters properly within the sweep of the commerce power and those legitimately the exclusive concern of states. But where? Cardozo had not succeeded in formulating it to Stone's satisfaction in 1935. One by one, the barriers fashioned by the old Court against complete federal control over the economy had been sloughed off. On several occasions Stone had attempted to work out a distinction that would mark what he believed to be the great divide in the federal system—the boundary of federal power and states' rights. The "only real basis" for the Schechter decision, he wrote in a labor case of 1939, was that the effect on interstate commerce of the poulterers' business was "so tenuous, speculative," and "remote" that the regulation of its practices could be said "to be in reality only a regulation of local industry rather than of commerce."[35]

These words, written into the original version of Stone's Fainblatt opinion, evoked prompt objections from Justice Frankfurter, on the ground that in the future lawyers might be encouraged to argue that the effects of unfair labor practices were "tenuous, speculative, or remote." More pointed objections came from Justice Black: "I am not in accord with the conclusion reached in the Schechter case on this point or with the language used in reaching that conclusion. This sentence would in my judgment imply an approval of that decision, and I do not wish to approve it even by implication." "Perhaps," Stone explained somewhat dejectedly, agreeing to delete the sentence, "I am a little tender due to the fact that, remaining silent in the Schechter case, I have felt that the only tenable reason supporting it has never been adequately expressed. Perhaps even that is not worth while."[36]

Stone's own opinion in the Darby case indicated that the last bulwark of federalism had been destroyed. Little in the opinion points the other way. But there were significant omissions. In retrospect, his silence regarding the doctrine of political restraints, coupled with his intimation that the judiciary still had "to determine whether the particular activity regulated or prohibited is within the reach of the federal power," and his failure to cite Marshall's sweeping definition of "commerce," hint at a reluctance to be pushed all the way down the ramp to complete acceptance of unfettered congressional sway over the national economy.

Late in 1943 the Chief Justice was still trying to distinguish the

Schechter decision. In the Yakus case, which tested the validity of the Emergency Price Control Act, Justice Roberts said that comparison of "the so-called standards prescribed in the National Industrial Recovery Act" with those of the Emergency Price Control Act, and perusal of what was said in the Schechter case, left "no doubt that the decision [in Schechter] is now overruled."[37] The Court, however, disagreed, and Stone this time hit on something solid: "The present statute [Emergency Price Control] is unlike the National Industrial Recovery Act of June 16, 1933, . . . which proclaimed in the broadest terms its purpose 'to rehabilitate industry and to conserve natural resources.' That Act prescribed no method of attaining that end save by the establishment of codes of unfair competition, the nature of whose permissible provisions was left undetermined. It stated no standards to which those codes were to conform. The function of formulating the codes was delegated, *not to a public official responsible to Congress or the Executive,* but to *private individuals engaged in the industries to be regulated.*"[38]

This explanation won Frankfurter's hearty approval: "I'm glad you did it this way," he affirmed.

But New Dealers seemed never to know when to stop; administrators kept pressing at the margins of power, pushing deeper and deeper into formerly sacrosanct preserves. Since the gates opened in 1941, Stone himself had participated in decisions extending congressional control, under the commerce clause, to regulation of the hours and wages of custodial workers in metropolitan office buildings; to regulation of grain a farmer grows on his own land to feed his own livestock; to the labor relations of small factories in the backwaters of trade. Now certain New Deal Justices demanded authority to govern all contracts made across state lines. Moreover, an honored constitutional dogma, jettisoned by less than a majority of the entire Court, colored consideration of the insurance case, a concern especially evident in the dissenting opinions. Yet no Justice expressly alluded to the subject. Privately, however, Stone said that the insurance decision was "unfortunate"—"especially as only four members of the Court took the prevailing view."

"A number of times since I have been on the bench," he commented, "I would have been willing to have been one of five to overrule a decision, but not one of four."[39] Chief Justice Marshall's Court, in the face of an embarrassing situation caused by the temporary absence of two Justices, asserted that it would not decide any case involving a constitutional question unless a majority of the whole Court should concur. Marshall could and did resolve his difficulty by directing "these cases to be reargued at the next term, with the expectation that a larger number of judges may then be present."[40] The dilemma facing Stone's

Court could not be relieved so simply. Reed and Roberts had disqualified themselves, and, barring replacements, the Court would continue to be without a clear majority. One may also query the wisdom of the majority ruling in the face of contemporaneous evidence that at least five, if not six, Justices did not solidly support Black's broad interpretation of the commerce clause.*

For the friends of "freedom" who had fought the good fight against the New Deal, the insurance case caused consternation. In 1944 the hated New Deal, in abeyance at the White House, anathema on Capitol Hill, and dormant in the country at large, lived on in the United States Supreme Court. The irreconcilables spoke a bitter tongue. "An unsettling decision," the *New York Times* commented, June 8, 1944, on the Underwriters case. "Its practical effect is the same as if Congress had just passed a sweeping new piece of legislation. Once more the Supreme Court has acted, in effect, like a third legislative house."

"When the United States Supreme Court doffs its black robes Monday," the *Houston Post* announced forebodingly, "it will go with less popular admiration and respect than any previous Supreme Court has enjoyed within the memory of living men. In this body of jurists the majesty and the dignity and the prestige of the nation's highest tribunal has hit an all-time low." The American Bar Association broke out in a veritable rash of critical comment. The tendency to ignore precedent (dubbed "The New Guesspotism") came in for special censure. As in Jefferson's time, the Constitution had again become "a mere thing of wax in the hands of the judiciary."[41] Even Thomas Reed Powell, no hide-bound defender of reaction, took up the cry. "Who can tell what

---

* The same issue as to the reach of the commerce power was also raised in *Polish National Alliance* v. *NLRB*, 322 U.S. 643, (1944). The basic question was how the NLRB derived its jurisdiction over the labor relations of the Alliance, a fraternal society conducting an insurance business. "As we have held over and over again," Stone wrote Frankfurter, May 16, 1944, "the relation of any local, non-interstate commerce business to interstate commerce—such [as a] strike in the business [that] would affect the commerce—gives the Labor Board jurisdiction. Such I think, is the relation of the Polish Alliance to interstate commerce. So the Board found, and consequently it had jurisdiction. Unfortunately, Brother Black and his associates take a different view, with which you and I do not agree. . . . In substance, it is that the Board found that the insurance business is commerce; that strike in the insurance business obstructs the commerce; and that it is not necessary to go further to support the Board's jurisdiction." In the disposition of the case, the Justices considered again whether they should hand down full opinions or a *per curiam*. "I do not object to the *per curiam* stating . . . the position of a given number of members of the Court, however much I may disagree with it. Unless we are prepared to go that far, it seems to me that we cannot avoid putting down all the opinions. In the present posture of the case, I would prefer to have them go down, stated in shorthand fashion, than to have them elaborated." This compromise also failed, and in the resulting line-up the dissenters of the Underwriters' case won over Justice Reed and, inexplicably, Justice Rutledge, who sided with Black. Roberts, perhaps fortunately for the composure of his brethren, again did not participate.

other landmarks will be similarly obliterated? Where shall confidence be placed?" he asked plaintively.[42]

Criticism boiled down to three basic charges: the Justices were hopelessly split among themselves, and continuous disagreement on vital issues threatened the Court's authority and prestige;[*] the Court had, by systematically disregarding its own precedents and by constantly changing its theories, confused rather than guided lawyers and lower courts; the Court did not confine itself to the interpretation of the law as it is. "The majority of the new appointees," the *New York Times* commented editorially, "came to the Court . . . apparently under the theory that their function was not so much to know and apply the law as it stands, or in case of doubt to interpret it objectively, but to apply a new 'social philosophy' in their decisions."[43]

Stone's Court was not, however, without its defenders. A few discerning observers recognized that the Justices since 1941 had been dealing with "very tough legal problems" rather than "with run-of-the-mine cases that are easy of solution." Cases interpreting constitutional provisions could not be, in the nature of things, as predictable as those in private law.[†] Why shouldn't the Supreme Court, an organ of high policy in a society moving rapidly to a "new social order," reflect differences widespread among the people? Walton Hamilton asked. "If often its conduct has not been in accord with our angelic notions," he suggested tolerantly, "the reason is that the public is let in on the performance.[‡] I wonder if any other agency of state—the Executive Office, the State Department, the High Military Command, the Maritime Commission, the War Production Board—could under a like scrutiny exhibit either more brotherly restraint or a more conscientious regard for the general welfare."[44]

But there was no denying the fact that concern for the future of the Court enveloped the very deliberations of the Justices themselves. Jus-

---

[*] "In the interests of democracy at war," Arthur Krock wrote sardonically, "dissenting brethren should disagree in silence, or at least eschew personalities." (Quoted in Alexander Pekelis, *Law and Social Action,* p. 195.)

[†] "We can hardly expect the people to be forever ruled by decisions which seem to them unjust," Kenneth C. Sears commented, "merely to uphold the rule of *stare decisis* and thereby to make it possible for lawyers to advise their clients with greater accuracy. Such rigid conception of a judge's duty in constitutional law could cause revolutions." ("The Supreme Court and the New Deal—An Answer to Texas," *University of Chicago Law Review,* Feb. 1945, pp. 177-78.)

[‡] The unkindest cut occurred when Drew Pearson, in his broadcast on March 12, 1944, "predicted" with the confidence and accuracy of an insider that the Court would hand down a split decision in favor of the Government in the Underwriters case. This was not the only instance in which he apparently established a pipeline with the Justices' conference room. Before the Harry Bridges deportation case, Pearson not only "predicted" that the Court would reverse the California Supreme Court decision judging Bridges guilty of contempt, but named the dissenting Justices.

tice Roberts put one aspect of this concern into his *Smith* v. *Allwright* dissent: "It is regrettable that in an era marked by doubt and confusion, an era whose greatest need is steadfastness of thought and purpose, this Court, which has been looked to as exhibiting consistency in adjudication, and a steadiness which would hold the balance even in the face of temporary ebbs and flows of opinion, should now itself become the breeder of fresh doubt and confusion in the public mind as to the stability of our institutions."[45] Nor was Roberts alone in feeling that disregard of the past had perhaps gone too far. "Unless the assumption is substantially true," Justice Jackson told the American Law Institute, "that cases will be disposed of by application of known principles and previously disclosed courses of reasoning, our common law process would become the most intolerable kind of ex post facto judicial lawmaking." Jackson urged "moderation in change," being certain "that no lawyer today feels such assurance that a pat case will bring him victory or defeat as lawyers once felt."[46]

The Chief Justice himself was profoundly distressed, not so much because of actual disagreements as by his colleagues' "newsy proneness" to disagree.* "I have had a tough year because of the disagreements among several of my brethren," he commented at the term's end. "Fortunately, I seem to be outside the fights, and my personal relations with all the members of the Court are good. But, of course, publicly aired disagreements do not add to the reputation of the Court or aid it in doing its work."[47]

What "really shocked" the Chief Justice were "the misleading, not to say completely inaccurate, statements" appearing in the press. And for this he had at least a partial explanation. It was "due to the fact that the Court is constantly dealing with more and more technical and complex questions than perhaps ever before in its history, and the layman who undertakes to comment on it is often undertaking to write about something which he does not understand."[48] To remedy this he urged newspapers to retain a competent professor of constitutional law to read and criticize their stories before publication. Lawyers and laymen alike might then rely on press accounts as confidently as the British depend on the London *Times*.

It was not that the Chief Justice resented criticism. What he did object to was reporting that explained the Court's business in terms of

* Professor Noel T. Dowling of Columbia Law School recalls a conversation with the Chief Justice after the Underwriters decision: "I told him that I was trying to write a story about the Court in which I planned to say that a certain decline in the institutional responsibility of the Court was shown by, and possibly was the result of, everybody writing his individual views on record. To all of which Stone replied, 'Not me! And I would not have discussed this matter today except for so many new and unsettled questions coming on at once.'" (Noel T. Dowling to A.T.M., Nov. 12, 1952.)

personalities, as if to imply that such factors alone divided the judges and accounted for their decisions. Excessive dramatization of judicial decisions reacted within the Court itself. Before the 1944 Judicial Conference for the Fourth Circuit, Stone poured out his innermost thoughts and pleaded for restraint. Judges, he told the conference, are peculiarly "subject to popular misunderstanding." There are "few public servants whose official actions are so exposed to misinterpretation." "I read and hear in these latter days much that seems to suggest that precedent counts for little in present-day judicial administration," the speaker observed a bit sadly. Of course no appellate court worthy of the name "would be content to perpetuate its recognized mistakes," but "it is the unusual exception rather than the rule," the Chief Justice maintained, "that courts do not look to precedent as an aid if not the guide to decision. The habits of thought which have guided the development of the law for a thousand years are not put aside overnight. Judges whose decisions are reviewed by the Supreme Court and lawyers who practice there will make a very great' mistake if they believe that precedent may be safely ignored or that decision there will be distilled from the circumambient air." "Take a second cup of coffee and reserve judgment," Stone cautioned his judicial hosts, when you read in the morning paper that "some judge or court has done a palpably absurd thing" or that "the courts have now abandoned all the ancient landmarks."

If differences were more frequent now than formerly, there was a good reason for them, quite apart from considerations of personalities. The questions for decision facing his Court were novel as well as complex and raised unfamiliar issues of "peculiar delicacy and difficulty." Taking the "long view," the Chief Justice was not alarmed that they should stir up differences "stoutly held and stoutly maintained." Such differences were not to be deplored. On the contrary, they represented "the mode by which the common law and the law of the Constitution have been developed in the past. If the law as it is being shaped today is to stand the test of time, and if it is to satisfy the demands of sound theory and practical utility, it is important that it be exposed to the most searching examination and criticism."[49]

The view he expressed in 1937 was still his conviction in 1944: "None of our institutions is above criticism, and the right to criticize is perhaps all in all most essential to the well-being of our country."[50]

CHAPTER THIRTY-EIGHT

# A Stabilizing Influence

### 1944-1945

The Roosevelt administration remained a thorn in Stone's side. Wrangling within the Court, though troublesome, could be endured. What soured him most was the virtual breakdown of the two-party system. F.D.R.'s election to a fourth term in 1944 roused apprehension of something bordering on disaster. "We have an unusually large and tough docket this year," he wrote in November. "It seems that all the New Deal laws and New Deal agencies are continually getting themselves tied up in knots which we have to untangle if possible. I hoped they might get a setback in this last election, but evidently the country desires to encourage them. But I am sure it will get enough of it before the business is finished."[1]

Innate distrust of the New Deal commingled with a feeling that recent Court trends had betrayed the basic value of a free society went into the eulogy of Mr. Justice Sutherland which he delivered in December. The assignment, though a "bit delicate," was carried off with credit to Sutherland's memory and to his own feelings.[2] One suspects that experience with the jurisprudence of New Deal justices served to preclude censure of his former colleague's unilateral constitutionalism.

As was perhaps natural, Stone's encomium soft-pedaled Sutherland's responsibility for the well-nigh disastrous impasse of 1936. The lawyers and judges who fashioned a twilight zone immune to invasion by either national or local government were not to be condemned as "malevolent." The real villain in the play was Blackstone, who had given to both bench and bar artificial notions of the law, which, when applied to constitutional interpretation, cast the Constitution as a mechanical and inadequate instrument of government.[3] As to Sutherland's attempts to confine government to the narrowest course, Stone refused to pass judgment. "It is too soon, and we are perhaps still too close to the smoke of battle," he suggested, "to see clearly or to say with omniscient finality precisely how the great constitutional issues of that period should have been decided."[4] Despite all that had happened since 1937, overwhelmingly vindicating Stone's earlier positions, he would not deny the validity of Sutherland's position. "Who would be so rash," he asked, "as to say now . . . that Justice Sutherland's influence will not continue, perhaps in greater measure than today, to play its part in directing the current of our legal thinking?" "In any event, wise men will not doubt that the viewpoint which he so ably represented must be reckoned with in the formulation of constitutional principles by a tribunal which must determine the boundaries and distribution of power under a federal constitutional system."

The sobered Chief Justice could not now depreciate Sutherland's well-known views on "ill-considered experimentation"—dangers inherent in "encroachments of government on the freedom of the individual"—which Sutherland thought it was the design of the due process clause to prevent. Nor would he discount the value of his former associate's emphasis on the "constitutional protection of the few from the tyranny of the many." Indeed, the "greatest problem" of contemporary constitutional construction loomed as one of balancing the competing demands that "constitutional sanctions shall safeguard the individual from the abuse of power by the majority," against the equally cogent imperative that such sanctions must not "clothe the individual with power to restrict unduly the welfare and progress of the community as a whole."

Stone used this occasion to explain his Court's meandering course, more particularly, its inability to coalesce around fixed doctrines. His colleagues of 1944 had a much more thorny task adjudging fundamentals because, unlike Sutherland, they could not fall back on any doctrinaire theory or fixed formulas as guides. "Sound legal principles adequate to meet all the vicissitudes of human experience," the Chief Justice observed, "never sprang full-fledged from the brains of any man or group of men. They are the ultimate resultant of the abrasive force of the clash of competing and sometimes conflicting ideas—ideas which are rooted in different experience and different appraisals of all the multifarious interests which it is the concern of government to foster and protect." Court debates no longer lagged a generation or more behind the times; judges, immersed in realities, kept argument right up to snuff. The Constitution itself lay posited within their own awesome power.

Encroachment of government into domains formerly immune had proceeded too far, and Stone firmly believed that reaction was well overdue. In the process of retracing judicial steps, Justice Sutherland's judicial labors at least served to underscore the elementary requirements of good manners. "The time will come," he predicted, "when it will be recognized, perhaps more clearly than it is at the present, how fortunate it has been for the true progress of the law that at a time when the trend was in the opposite direction, there sat upon this bench a man of stalwart independence, and of the purest character, who, without a trace of intellectual arrogance, and always with respectful toleration for the views of colleagues who differed with him, fought stoutly for the constitutional guaranties of the liberty of the individual." As one who had contributed greatly to the destruction of the protective barriers Sutherland strove to place around the threatened, property-owning minority, Stone could go no further. After all, the very core of his own judicial philosophy—that the Court's function is one of weighing competing interests, accommodating the Constitution to them—precluded "blacks and whites," the crystalline principle of Sutherland's constitution. But as one "who sometimes differed" radically with Sutherland, he could and did remind his younger colleagues of their predecessor's inborn generosity of feeling.

In a final passage the Chief again struck a note in defense of his own Court, hinting that even in this age, though Sutherland was gone, there were Justices marked by the same "integrity and sturdy independence," the same "devoted loyalty to a great task." "Let our memory of him," he asked the public and the bar, "remind us that these, rather than unanimity of thought and opinion of those who must shape the course of law, are the indispensable qualities of the judge, without which justice will not prevail."

Stone's apparent nostalgia for the values Sutherland cherished aroused similar sentiments in others. "The dear old boy was about as much apart from me as anyone could be—just as he was from you," Learned Hand commented on the Chief Justice's address, "but he had what I like to think both of us have, and those Heralds of Brighter Vision seem so seldom to have: a sense that this is a world of doubt and surmise where in the end we can have a civilized society only by 'live and let live.'" "The time will come," Hand predicted, "when people will recognize this again—though God knows after how much agony—and those of us who have kept the faith will be forgotten."[5]

A month later Stone experienced the ordeal of yet another presidential inauguration. "On the 20th," he related phlegmatically, "I attended the Inauguration and administered the oath to the President. I thus have the undesired distinction of being the first Chief Justice to swear in a President for a fourth term. I hope no other will ever have it." The experience left Stone profoundly disconsolate. "About all I can do in my remaining years," he wrote, "is to try and make apparent some of the things that in days of yore made the Court great. But I confess I am very lonesome."[6]

Less than four months later both the Court and the country were profoundly shaken by President Roosevelt's sudden death. The news broke just as the Chief Justice was preparing to leave the Court for home at the end of the day. Hardly had he entered the threshold when he was off to the White House in response to urgent phone calls. There, in the presence of Cabinet members and congressmen, he swore in the new President. Later he rode on the somber funeral train to the burial at Hyde Park. "It is gradually becoming known," he revealed to his son Marshall, "that Roosevelt has not really been himself much of the time since sometime last summer."[7]

That same week Stone heard President Truman address a joint session of Congress. "He is creating, I think," the Chief Justice commented, "a favorable impression as being a man of common sense, simple, erect, and modest." "Truman's succession," he thought, "may well mark the end of one epoch and the beginning of another."[8]

But a new occupant in the White House did nothing to smooth troubled waters in the councils of the Supreme Court. In the turmoil of a swiftly changing era, when tried and trusted values were being subject to heavy assault, solid citizens, Stone among them, sought solace in those elements of American culture which manifested an image of rock-ribbed strength. "Give us all a beacon of light," Sterling Carr had beseeched the Chief Justice, "a ringing statement of Americanism and real democratic government . . . that will rekindle the faith and hope in the hearts of many who now against their own will are doubting." The head of a bench of "wild horses" was unable to comply. Instead of the encouragement his friend sought, he sent an opinion showing "how extensively the country is being run by administrative agencies under rules which they make for themselves without authority from anybody."[9]

In certain areas government by administrators was all but established, since the judiciary had progressively narrowed the extent to which it would curb their actions. Stone had gone along with this development in the old Court, fostered it in fact, because he had felt that expert boards and authorities could lay claim quite as much as judges to competence in their special fields. But a remarkable series of cases in the spring of 1945 brought into sharp focus the Court as arbiter between the convolutions of the administrative process and the individual. The Justices naturally varied among themselves as to when a case contained such an issue and precisely what the courts should do about it.

Litigation of such disputes sometimes assumed novel forms, as when the State of Georgia, led by its astute Governor, Ellis Arnall, shot that hoary issue of Southern politics, freight-rate discrimination, into national prominence by asking the Supreme Court's permission to file an original complaint charging a conspiracy among certain railroads to keep Southern tariffs above the competitive level.* As a political de-

* "The Supreme Court is granted original jurisdiction in cases in which a state shall be a party"—Art. III, Sec. 2 (2), of the Constitution.

vice calling attention to the drastic stunting of the Southland's economic growth by discrimination, his suit undoubtedly made sense. Legally, however, in seeking relief through the anti-trust laws, it encountered a most troublesome obstacle—the "villainous" railroads charged rates no higher than those approved by the Interstate Commerce Commission as "just and reasonable." Against this, the state claimed that the combination of railroads had conspired to manipulate rates within a zone sanctioned by the ICC, to Georgia's detriment, and demanded an injunction against the conspiracy.

In an area of plenary congressional power, in which an administrative agency had been created to carry out the will of the legislature, did the state have recourse to protect its citizens from an alleged economic injury? Was this a matter for the Supreme Court, in its discretion, to handle at all, or should it be remanded to other forums? The case raised political considerations so explosive as to lead certain Justices to conclude that Georgia's grievance was remediable only by Congress, not the courts. If the Justices accepted the case at all, they would be put in the position of having to pass on the wisdom and fairness of the national rail-rate structure.

Such considerations made the case a difficult one. Initially the Chief Justice headed a majority that agreed the problem could be disposed of by permitting Georgia, without prejudice, to prosecute a claim in any federal district court where the state could acquire jurisdiction over the defendant railroads, with leave to appeal later the questions of law to the Supreme Court. He prevented this easy solution, however, by the gratuitous suggestion he made in circulating a *per curiam* to this effect: "I raise again the question whether it would not be the wiser course to give Georgia her day in Court as it requests, with opportunity to show whether the conclusions expressed in this opinion may be wrong."[10] Other Justices, taking up the suggestion, upheld Georgia's petition. When the majority decided that the Supreme Court should hear the plea, Stone, now among the dissenters, shifted from a position of recommending its remittance to a federal district court without an opinion on the jurisdictional question, to one of outright opposition. Thus the Chief Justice found himself on the short end of another 5 to 4 decision.

The majority, composed of judges from the South, Far West, and Midwest, argued that nowhere else could Georgia bring so many of the defendant railroads into court. They saw the alleged conspiracy operating to keep Georgia's economy in a state of arrested development, held in bondage to Northeastern financial centers. The Court must intervene, they said, because "the Interstate Commerce Act does not provide remedies for the correction of all the abuses of rate-making which might constitute violations of the anti-trust laws." Stone and his northern colleagues found grave objection to the suit. Georgia's petition openly assaulted the rate structure carefully erected by the Interstate Commerce Commission in pursuance of policies laid down by the national legislature. In Stone's opinion the suggestion that the Court had been persuaded to accept, that it could enjoin "the alleged conspiracy to fix rates without regard to . . . whether the Commission finds them to be lawful or unlawful, is an invitation to a course of the veriest futility." Real success for Georgia could "only mean the breakdown of the unified system of fixing rates by Commission action, which Congress has ordained." When citizens of Georgia had failed to bring the action, the only other proper party was the Federal Government. It, not the state, stood in relation of *parens patriae* to the people of Georgia; it alone had the power to protect them and the rest of the national population from violations of federal laws. "To permit a state to bring a Sherman Act suit in behalf of the public is," Stone reasoned, "to fly in the face of the national policy established by Congress that the Federal Government should determine when such a suit is to be brought and how it should be prosecuted." The last reason for entertaining the suit had disappeared when the Justice Department filed an *amicus* brief supporting Georgia's claim. "If it believes that the alleged conspiracy exists and should be stopped by the remedial action of courts, without resort to the Commission," the Chief Justice commented, "it should . . . proceed to remedy in the usual manner the grievances of citizens of the United States including citizens of Georgia."[11]

Stone took a somewhat different position in the case of a Negro railroad fireman, Bester William Steele, caught between the upper and nether millstones of administrative process and restrictive union practice. By the terms of the Railway Labor Act the fireman was required to bargain through the Brotherhood of Locomotive Firemen and Enginemen, a union barring Negroes from membership. Following statutory procedures to the letter, the railroads and the Brotherhood amended previous agreements so as to cut down employment opportunities for Negroes, denying them promotion, paring their seniority rights, in order to eliminate them entirely from the jobs. Within the administrative framework envisaged by the basic statute there was no impartial forum to adjudicate the objections of minorities to agreements thus consummated between the authorized bargaining unions and the employers. The Alabama Supreme Court, dismissing Steele's suit, construed the Railway Labor Act as handing over to the Brotherhood unlimited power to fix rates of pay and working conditions for the craft as a whole, even at the expense of non-union minorities. In this situation, Stone observed, "constitutional questions arise."[12]

In the course of answering them, the Chief Justice, prodded by a correspondent, built upon an idea inspired by his own Classic opinion. Apropos of the latter case, Alexander Pekelis had written the Chief Justice of how, throughout the sprawling expanse of our national economy, individuals exercise what is tantamount to a governmental function. Against such private power groups, Pekelis suggested, our basic law injects the requisites of due process, "lest constitutional guarantees be unduly confined to the relatively narrow field of official government."[13] Translating this concept into economic terms to fit the case of the Negro fireman, Stone reasoned that when legislative policy invests great private economic power with discretion over its internal affairs, it imposes the corresponding duty that such authority be exercised in accordance with historic notions of fairness implicit in the Constitution. The Railway Labor Act, he affirmed, imposed on the authorized bargaining representative "at least as exacting a duty to protect equally the interests of the members of the craft as the Constitution imposes upon a legislature to give equal protection to the interests of those for whom it legislates." The Act, relating only to employer-employee relations, failed to supply an effective procedure for the administrative alleviation of Steele's grievance against the union. Therefore the only remedy for a "breach of the statutory duty of the bargaining representative to represent and act for the members of a craft is of judicial cognizance." An injunction and award of damages would issue, he held.[14]

As the Steele case moved toward final decision Justice Jackson compared Stone's reasoning with the line he was taking in a dissent in another case, to which the Chief had pledged his support. "I agree with all that you have said and am delighted at the way you have said it," Jackson wrote, December 1, 1944. "One thing only occurs to me. There may be to superficial readers, who constitute the greater number, an apparent conflict between your position in this case, that the minority is entitled to representation and to jobs, and the position we take in the Labor Board case that the National Labor Relations Board cannot punish the employer for joining in a contract which denies these."

The Wallace case, to which Jackson referred, arose out of a closed-shop agreement under which an independent union refused, after winning a certified election, to admit CIO members. Requiring their dismissal by the employer seemed to raise the very constitutional issue brought out by the Alabama Supreme Court's disposition of the Steele case. Stone told Jackson he had considered the wisdom of discussing the Wallace situation in his Steele opinion, but "concluded it was better to let the matter rest until the whole business was straightened out." "I count on you to draw the distinction in what you say in the Wallace case," he added.[15]

Upholding the order of the NLRB which had required reinstatement of the discharged employees after damning the action of the employer as an unfair labor practice, the majority's spokesman, Justice Black, who had separately concurred in the Steele case without opinion, dealt only briefly with constitutional problems. In his view the employer was flagrantly guilty of having pursued a policy aimed at defeating the CIO. This, and not the independent union's discrimination, was the vice of the case, justifying the Labor Board's punitive action against the employer.

Jackson concentrated the dissenters' fire on the NLRB's total lack of statutory authority to hold an employer responsible for reprehensible admission policies of a union that the law compelled him to recognize. The basic tenet upon which the courts were to rest their decisions in this area of individual rights and collective representation, he asserted, was legislative policy. The Steele case "arose under the Railway Labor Act, which contains no authorization whatever for a closed shop." But in the Wallace case, in which the Wagner Act was at issue, "we deal with a minority which the statute has subjected to closed-shop practices. Whether the closed shop, with or without the closed union, should or should not be permitted without supervision is in the domain of policy-making, which it is not for this Court to undertake."* In contrast to the railroad case, the inclusion by Congress of a closed-shop feature in the National Labor Relations Act indicated legislative policy to permit "each union to control its own admissions to membership," thereby effectively proscribing judicial or administrative intervention.[16]

Shying away from the charge of "judicial legislation" of which the majority opinion fairly shrieked, Stone indicated his complete agreement with Jackson's interpretation of the National Labor Relations Act. "Not only is there no statute purporting to regulate the conduct of the union," he asserted, "but there is a positive statute authorizing the employer to enter into closed-shop agreements."[17] No doubt Stone and Jackson did not wish at this late date to throw constitutional shadows on the Wagner Act. They wanted to slap down an outrageous imposition on an employer. The hapless administrators had picked on an innocent bystander in spite of statutory language and policy incon-

---

* The dissenters' attempted distinction of the Steele case has been criticized as "not unqualifiedly true" by some who thought that to square the NLRA with the Fifth Amendment the Act must be construed as forbidding such discriminatory admission practices. "If the NLRA means, as the dissenting Justices seem to imply, that a majority union may lawfully exercise congressionally granted powers so as to combine the closed shop with the closed union—it raises a substantial issue of due process." (See E. Merrick Dodd, Note, *Harvard Law Review*, Feb. 1945, p. 448.) Justice Jackson's dissent in the Wallace case hinted that the Board might get at the practice another way—withholding certification to closed-shop unions until it received guarantees as to future conduct.

sistent with the idea that the employer was empowered to police union policies. In the last sentence of his opinion Jackson expressed the key to the dissenters' view of the case—condemning the NLRB action as a "very unfair construction of the statute to the employer."[18] He thus understated Stone's wrath at the Board for "dragooning the employer into the agreement and then penalizing him because he yielded."[19]

Under the New Deal labor statutes unions now possessed and exercised power over jobs that had long been wielded exclusively by employers. Such far-reaching union authority disturbed the Chief Justice. Consciously or not, Stone and his most sympathetic colleagues balked in current labor cases. Feeling that unions had too much power, they refused to extend earlier positions favoring organized labor's claims. Sometimes they were hard put to distinguish the nuances of the majority's thinking. Stone's Apex Hosiery dictum that the Sherman Act still embraced unions "to some extent not defined" had been effectively undercut by the Hutcheson case. On June 18, 1945, the Court handed down two opinions that further construed the fine lines of reasoning flowing from that decision. In an 8 to 1 decision, it determined that a union agreement with manufacturers and contractors in New York City not to work on electrical equipment shipped in from outside violated the Sherman Act, since prices and market control as well as conditions of employment were involved. "Finding no purpose of Congress to immunize labor unions who aid and abet manufacturers and traders in violating the Sherman Act," the Court admitted that the same union activities "may or may not be in violation of the Sherman Act, dependent upon whether the union acts alone or in combination with business groups." The desirability of the union exemption alone, it declared, was a "question for the determination of Congress."[20]

The Court, speaking through Justice Black, used this same sweeping criterion in *Hunt* v. *Crumboch,* holding—in the face of an acid dissent by Justices Jackson, Roberts, Frankfurter, and the Chief Justice—that a union had not violated the strictures of the Sherman Act although it had practically driven an interstate trucker out of business by refusing to enroll his employees in its ranks and by applying pressure on his customers to refrain from dealing with him. The majority's conclusion that the union did no wrong, Justice Black maintained, followed naturally from the Hutcheson case, holding that the Clayton Act grants workers "an absolute right" to work or cease working according to their own judgment. "That which Congress has recognized as lawful," he told his brethren, "this Court has no constitutional power to declare unlawful, because of a belief that Congress has accorded too much power to labor organizations."[21] For the dissenters such drastic action was plainly "a direct destruction of competition in interstate commerce as an end in itself," thus meeting Stone's Apex test for a violation of the Sherman Act. "The reasons given in the Apex case that there was no restraint of competition in that case," Stone pointed out to Jackson, minority spokesman in *Hunt* v. *Crumboch,* "are really strong reasons for saying that there was an unlawful restraint in this case."[22]

Certain commentators were quick to credit Stone and Frankfurter with having created the very condition of which they now complained. But, in his own eyes, Stone did not deserve the sarcastic compliment Professor Corwin paid him for dissenting with Jackson. "While the Chief Justice's and J. Frankfurter's discontent at this decision does them credit," Corwin wrote, "it must be remarked that having been respectively the spokesman for the Court in the Apex and Hutcheson cases, their claim on one's sympathy is not great."[23] Others, noting a difference between the two cases, supported Stone's claim to consistency. "The Supreme Court has done the labor unions a real disservice in vesting them with the worst curse of modern times—too much economic power over others," Charles O. Gregory observed. "If the Supreme Court abandoned its unfortunate doctrine established in the Hutcheson case and adhered faithfully to the best of what Justice Stone said in the Apex case, it could even yet achieve substantial justice under the Sherman Act."[24]

During this term "a shocking and revolting episode in law enforcement" focused intra-Court controversy once more on Stone's Classic opinion, revealing further shifts among the Justices. Six judges upheld the indictment of Claude Screws, a Georgia sheriff, on charges of having deprived a Negro prisoner of his constitutional rights by brutally beating him to death. A wide gulf separated minority and majority on the question whether the Georgia sheriff's conduct constituted "state action" proscribed by the Fourteenth Amendment and Section 20 of the Federal Criminal Code.* The dissenters denied that the words "under color of any law" had ever been intended to apply to a case where a state officer acted in violation of state law. "The truth of the matter is," they wrote, "that the focus of attention in the Classic case was not our present problem." Stone's opinion, they said, "assumed quite needlessly" that the Civil Rights Act was co-extensive with the Fourteenth Amendment.

* Section 20 of the Criminal Code (18 U.S.C.A., Section 242) reads: "Whoever, under color of any law, statute, ordinance, regulation, or custom, willfully subjects, or causes to be subjected, any inhabitant of any state, territory, or district to the deprivation of any rights, privileges, or immunities secured or protected by the Constitution and laws of the United States, or to different punishments, pains, or penalties, on account of such inhabitant being an alien, or by reason of his color, or race, than are prescribed for the punishment of citizens shall be fined not more than $1000, or imprisoned not more than one year, or both."

Justice Douglas, who had dissented from Stone's opinion in 1940 now rose to its defense. "The Classic case," he wrote, "was not the product of hasty action or inadvertence. It was not out of line with the cases which preceded. The Classic case formulated a rule of law which has become the basis of federal enforcement in this important field. The rule adopted in that case was formulated after mature consideration. It should be good for more than one day only." If, as the dissenters maintained, the statute was designed to embrace only action authorized by the state in violation of the Fourteenth Amendment, he went on, "the words 'under color of any law' were hardly apt words to express the idea."[25]

For a second time Douglas and Black reversed themselves to make common cause with Stone in defense of civil liberty, but at the price of an interpretation of the civil rights statute that made its effective use as a guarantor of individual rights doubtful. Douglas had insisted in 1940 that the crime of depriving a person of his constitutional rights was so vague and uncertain as to be invalid unless the right asserted appeared plainly in the Constitution. To remove this doubt, he sent the Screws case back for a new trial, instructing the trial judge to submit to the jury the question whether Sheriff Screws had "willfully" denied his prisoner constitutional rights. The Chief Justice, meanwhile, had moved closer to Douglas's original position, conceding some soundness to his objections. The "all-embracing" definition of the Civil Rights Act, he now contended, "includes every act which may ultimately be determined to be a deprivation of constitutional right and refers the reader to a comprehensive law library in order to ascertain what they are. Such a statute," he declared, "must be deemed to be void for vagueness and uncertainty, save only as it can be interpreted to give fair definition in some ascertainable way to the acts which are deemed to be violations."[26] He therefore accepted Douglas's construction of "willfully"—a requirement that no conviction could be had under the Civil Rights Act except for acts which the defendant knew or ought to have known were violations of the Constitution. He accepted this construction, even though it precluded a workable distinction between cases like Classic, involving the transgression of specific constitutional provisions, and cases like Screws, denying rights protected by the due process clause only. "Although it will leave mighty little scope for its application," Stone wrote, "I am inclined to think that I should not object very seriously to such a treatment of a statute which omits all definitions of the criminal acts which it punishes."[27]

Frankfurter, Jackson, and Roberts rejected Douglas's construction, being certain that the statute was void because of vagueness. "It is as novel as it is an inadmissible principle," they wrote, "that a criminal statute of indefinite scope can be rendered definite by requiring that a person 'willfully'* commit what Congress has not defined but which, if Congress had defined, could constitutionally be outlawed."[28]

During most of the term no public event so dramatic as the Burlingham letter of the previous year disturbed the judicial atmosphere, yet the course of justice was far from smooth. The Court surpassed its own record for disagreement. In the 162 majority opinions announced, it cast a total of 231 dissenting votes. The Chief Justice himself dissented 29 times, more than anyone else, except for Roberts' unparalleled 53.† Schismatic factors produced a veritable stream of split decisions, of which 27 were 5 to 4 rulings, almost doubling the previous year's total. By a one-vote margin the judges held Western Union messengers exempt from child labor provisions of the wages and hours law; invalidated a Texas statute requiring a license before a union agent could address a meeting; ruled that conscientious objectors could be barred from law practice; forbade revision of a National Labor Relations Board order after Court review, even though the Board had erred; and permitted a patentee to obtain a sub-patent on an integral part of his invention with the avowed intention of suppressing use of that part so as to protect his broader claim.[29]

"The work has been heavy and the gyrations of my brethren have not made it any lighter," Stone commented gloomily. In addition to routine work, petitions *in forma pauperis*,‡ the brunt of which fell primarily on the Chief, rose phenomenally. The Court disposed of over 107 such pleas directed against the Warden of the Illinois State

---

* The ultimate outcome of the case was disappointing to liberals; upon remand, a second Southern jury refused to convict, gagging on the "willful" requirement. See R. K. Carr, *Federal Protection of Civil Rights*, pp. 114-15.

† Since the 1940 term the number of dissents assumed a disturbing upward trend: 1940 term—110; 1941 term—158; 1942 term—165; 1943 term—186; 1944 term—231. The number of dissents by each Justice in the 1944 term were as follows: Roberts, 53; Stone, 29; Black, 28; Frankfurter, 22; Rutledge, 22; Murphy, 21; Douglas, 21; Jackson, 18; Reed, 16. That Reed was somewhat of a "swing man" is indicated by the fact that Black, Douglas, Murphy, and Rutledge dissented as a unit seven times, and Stone, Roberts, Frankfurter, and Jackson stood together in dissent six times. (*United States Law Week*, June 26, 1945, pp. 3493-94.)

‡ *In forma pauperis* petitions (pleas from persons without funds, usually inmates of prisons seeking review of their convictions on the ground that some step in the trial violated due process) are often crudely typewritten papers prepared by the prisoners themselves. "When I first came on the Court," Stone wrote J. P. Comer, Feb. 6, 1946, "*in forma pauperis* cases were treated rather lightly, but during Chief Justice Hughes' time and my own, we have examined them with great care. They are mostly chaff, but occasionally we find some grains of wheat in the chaff and those cases we assign counsel, pay expense of printing the papers, and hear the case. This has occasionally resulted in unearthing grave abuses in trial courts which deprived the petitioner of his constitutional rights." One of the legacies of the Hughes' regime was a vast increase in the number of these petitions, stimulated by the Chief's interest in them. During Stone's first year as Chief he examined personally the records of 178 cases, 58 more than were filed the previous term.

Penitentiary alone. As to reports of his resignation, he blandly retorted that he hadn't given it any thought. "I am too busy," he remarked. When rumors began to circulate about his "being tired," he snorted: "I am only tired of some of the unfortunate stuff I see in the newspapers. No doubt they are inspired by thoughts of who will get my place."[30]

The deep personal rivalries of his colleagues were muffled, confined to conference, provoking no repetition of the outspoken denunciations of the 1943 term. Then, at the very end, the bench was rocked from within by a rancorous quarrel over the most delicate of all judicatory subjects—judicial disqualification.

Since the reconstitution of the Court in 1941 the Justices had been increasingly touchy on this matter. With three former Attorneys General and a former Solicitor General on the bench, the Court was constantly in danger that important government litigation could not be heard for lack of the statutory quorum of six Justices.* The situation had come to a head in the North American Company case of 1943, a constitutional appeal from an SEC ruling under the so-called "death penalty" clause of the Public Utility Holding Company Act. Stone announced his disqualification at the time certiorari was granted, "on the assumption that we had a full court to deal with the case."[31] Douglas, as onetime SEC chairman, was also ineligible. After the case came up for oral argument Reed and Jackson made known their disqualification. At this juncture the quorum question came forcibly to the attention of Congress. The legislature made no provision for the North American case, but passed a bill that enabled the Justices to transfer the earlier Alcoa case to the Circuit Court of Appeals for the Second Circuit for final review.† The Chief Justice was much disturbed that litigants, otherwise entitled to it, could not have their day in Court. His concern grew as more cases involving features of the

---

* On December 8, 1941, the Court was obliged to dismiss appeals in *Chrysler Corporation* v. *United States* (joined with *Commercial Credit Co.* v. *United States*, 314 U.S. 583), explaining that it lacked a quorum. A year later the Court Clerk notified Government and Alcoa counsel that the long-drawn-out anti-trust suit against the aluminum monopoly could not be heard. (*United States Law Week*, Dec. 8, 1942, p. 3173.) Investigation leading to this prosecution had been started by Stone during his administration of the Justice Department in 1924-25. Despite the passage of time, he thought that his connection with this controversial case as Attorney General had been so intimate for a time it was undesirable that he should sit in the case. When the case reached the Supreme Court in 1942 it had also implicated Justices Murphy, Reed, and Jackson.

† The bill provided that appeals taken to the Supreme Court from district courts in cases where the United States was a complainant must be remanded to the proper Circuit Court of Appeals for decision in the absence of a quorum. (H.R. 3054, 78th Cong., 2nd Sess., 58 Stat. 272 [1944].) The United States was not the complainant in the North American case, so the law did not apply. The Alcoa case was transferred, June 12, 1944, 322 U.S. 716.

holding company law were filed.[32] Should not this consideration, he wondered, overbalance those that moved him initially to announce disqualification? As no former law partner or client was present in these cases, he now saw no reason to disqualify himself. When he broached the matter in conference, however, Justice Roberts objected to his sitting on the ground that similar issues were raised in all the cases, and that if he were disqualified in the one, he ought not to sit in judgment on a related case. Roberts' suggestion, apparently querying the Chief Justice's honor and implying that he would discuss in an opinion the propriety of Stone's sitting, brought on a heated debate. The accusation so angered the Chief that he had his clerk prepare a memorandum of cases on which Roberts had sat although his old firm or former clients were involved.[33]

Roberts' attack, especially its accusative tone, also annoyed certain of Stone's colleagues. "Apropos the discussion in conference Saturday," Justice Rutledge wrote, "I want to add to you personally what I thought it as well for me not to say under the circumstances of that discussion, namely: I think it is outrageous for anyone to suggest that there is any valid reason, or semblance of one, why you should not sit in either of the cases, or both, according to your own preference and decision. It is even more outrageous," he continued, "to suggest writing to discuss your action, whether the decision is one way or some other. And I, for one, think that if any member of the Court should assume to do this, all other members—again including yourself or not, solely as you might wish and decide—should reply in an opinion which would leave no doubt about the matter." Rutledge said he "ordinarily would venture no suggestion" as he thought "the whole business is purely one of taste, not of law or morals," but "since the circumstances have made it necessary for you to have counsel, I want you to have no doubt as to my views or position."[34]

"Thank you for your kind note about the troublesome holding company cases," Stone replied warmly. "They have annoyed us so long that I think we may have all lost a little sense of proportion, but I am greatly troubled by the fact that suitors who have come to our Court who are entitled to be heard cannot be heard. It would seem to me that the simplest solution would have been to have heard the case which I am free in every possible aspect to hear, and leave the other alone." Roberts' remarks seem to have brought Stone's stubborn streak to the fore. As there was objection to his proposed course, he concluded, "I think I shall be willing to be the goat and sit in them both, although it is a very embarrassing situation for me."[35]

Action on these cases was deferred while tempers cooled, and certiorari was ultimately granted on June 5, 1944. Though Stone had determined his course, the disputed cases stood in abeyance another year. On May 28, 1945, the Court ordered them set for argument on October 8, 1945.* "Chief Justice Stone made it known," the *New York Times* reported, May 29, "that he had decided that he was eligible to sit." Just as Stone announced his recantation the bench was confronted by a brash petition for a rehearing of the inflammatory coal miners' portal-to-portal pay case, which the Court, affirming the Circuit Court of Appeals, had decided 5 to 4 in the union's favor.[36] The coal company's petition for rehearing alleged that Justice Black, one of the majority judges, should have stayed out of the case because the mine union's claim was presented by Crampton Harris, the Justice's law partner in a short-lived practice twenty years before.

The original Jewell Ridge case had been bitterly contested within the confines of the conference room. Legally and economically the issues had been troublesome. Tempers, frayed by the vexing term, had been at the breaking point. The first untoward development had found Justice Reed first agreeing with, and then turning away from the judges, including Stone, who were opposed to travel-time pay. The consequent change in the result had required reassignment of the case by Justice Black.[37] Loss of victory by such a turn may have nettled the dissenters. Stone, convinced that coal miners' contracts fixed a "high wage" that included compensation for travel, had thought the new majority's conclusion an "injustice."[38] Justice Jackson, in his dissent, quoting Senator Black by name, had sought to prove that Congress had not contemplated use of the Fair Labor Standards Act to alter collective bargaining agreements where the hours worked were less than forty and the wages set were above the minimum. In effect accusing Black of abandoning the position he had taken as a legislative sponsor of the wage-hour law, the dissenter had thrust an intolerable burr under Black's saddle. "The very page from which the dissent quotes," the outraged former Senator had protested, "negatives the inference which the dissent draws from my single sentence which the dissent does quote. If the dissent does go down as now printed, it will not be a fair representation of the true facts."[39] The minority, unperturbed, had retained the disputed quotation.

In this atmosphere of acid disagreement the Jewell Ridge Coal Corporation's petition for a rehearing precipitated what has been called the "greatest fight in the nation's highest and most secret judicial conference room."[40] In presenting a *per curiam* opinion to the conference denying the Jewell Ridge petition, the Chief Justice, to the surprise of the brethren, suggested that a statement be included to

---

* The North American case was decided April 1, 1946; but the Engineers Public Service Co. case dragged on. Its reargument was ordered June 10, 1946, and finally, on October 20, 1947, the case was remanded to the district court with directions to dismiss as moot.

the effect that no question of disqualification is ever open for consideration by the Court. Such a proposal Justice Frankfurter said, raised 'a
"brand-new matter," and Black insisted on denial of the petition
without any explanation.

The question was a delicate one. Since disqualification was a matter
of personal decision, with no specific rule to cover the matter, the
petition had to be denied. The difficulty arose in the phrasing of the
denial. A flat refusal of the petition, as Black desired, would have
implied approval by the whole Court of his having sat, a position
inconsistent with the absence of any rule on the subject and one to
which none of the dissenting Justices in the original case were willing
to give "blind and unqualified approval."[41] The most feasible way out
of the predicament, Stone surmised, would be a colorless explanation
of the absence of any Court rule on the subject. By such a method no
approval or disapproval of Black's action, either implied or expressed,
would be given.

The depth of feeling, heightened to fever pitch by the unrelenting
tensions of an arduous term, could not be placated by compromise.
Black suspected that behind the maneuvers of the dissenters lay a
desire to put his actions in an unfavorable light. The disposition of
the petition thus took on for him overtones of a fight for personal
vindication. At conference on June 9 argument grew so heated that
the Chief Justice accepted Murphy's suggestion that final decision be
postponed one week. Several days later Stone proposed a compromise
per curiam he thought "all could join without embarrassment." "This
Court," his brief opinion read, "is without the authority and does not
undertake to pass upon the propriety of the participation, by its members, in the decision of cases brought here for review."[42] Such an
announcement would, of course, at the very least imply neutrality on
Black's conduct in the Jewell Ridge case. But Black still preferred
ambiguous silence. "If the per curiam goes down in this case, as you
have today suggested," he responded to the Chief's memorandum,
"please put the names of the Justices who agree to it, and leave
mine out."[43] Those who sided with Black on the merits of portal-to-
portal pay also lined up with him against the per curiam.

Although Stone now must have perceived that any such opinion
would arouse Black's ire, he continued to press for a statement. Taking
advantage of a technicality in Court rules, by which a petition for
rehearing is addressed only to judges adhering to the protested decision, he redrafted his per curiam so that it would require the assent
only of the dissenters in the original Jewell Ridge case. "If our brethren
are unwilling to declare that this Court is without authority to pass
upon the propriety of Justice Black's sitting" in the Jewel Ridge case,
he wrote, "the least we can do is say something like the following:

'The Chief Justice, Justice Roberts, Justice Frankfurter, and Justice Jackson, who dissented from the opinion of the Court in this case, do not pass on the petition for rehearing, and they do not pass upon the propriety of the participation by any Justice of the Court in the decision of this case.'" The Justices named promptly accepted.[44]

At a final conference on June 16 Jackson made it evident that he was in no way willing to imply approval of Black's role. "Mr. Justice Black became very angry," Jackson declared later, "and said that any opinion which discussed the subject at all would mean a declaration of war." The flames had swept beyond control, and Jackson decided then and there "that I would not stand for any more of his bullying and that, whatever I would otherwise do, I would now have to write my opinion to keep self-respect in the face of his threats."[45] Frankfurter agreed and joined in Jackson's brief concurrence annexed to the simple denial of the petition, handed down on June 18.

"Since announcement of a mere denial of this petition for rehearing might be interpreted to rest upon any one of several grounds," Jackson wrote in part, "I consider it appropriate to disclose the limited grounds on which I concur.*

"The unusual feature of the petition in this case is that it suggests to the Court a question as to the qualification of one of the Justices to take part in the decision of the cause. This petition is addressed to all of the Court and must either be granted or denied in the name of the Court and on the responsibility of all of the Justices. In my opinion the complaint is one which cannot properly be addressed to the Court as a whole and for that reason I concur in denying it.

"No statute prescribes grounds upon which a Justice of this Court may be disqualified in any case. The Court itself has never undertaken by rule of Court or decision to formulate any uniform practice

---

* The denial, and Jackson's concurrence, were hidden under a series of important full decisions that day, and the world at large was left unaware of the deep rift until June 10, 1946, when Jackson, from the War Crimes Trials in Nuremberg, cabled statements about the Jewell Ridge flare-up to the House and Senate Judiciary Committees, the latter of which was considering President Truman's nomination of Fred Vinson for Chief Justice after Stone's death.

Insisting that the practice of ex-law partners of Justices trying close cases was bringing "the Court into disrepute," Jackson averred that if Harris's appearance without Black's disqualification were "ever repeated while I am on the bench I will make my Jewell Ridge opinion look like a letter of recommendation." (*New York Times*, June 11, 1946.)

When asked about the incident following Jackson's heated blast, Black refused comment. "I haven't made a statement of any kind to the press since coming up here. I don't expect to make any now."

Recognizing that dissents and disagreements were to be expected from among the Justices, the *Times* on June 12 editorially deplored the publicity given to this affair and commented: "It seems to us that Justice Jackson has committed an error in taste and that Justice Black has committed the worse offense of lowering judicial standards."

on the subject. . . . It appears always to have been considered the responsibility of each Justice to determine for himself the propriety of withdrawing in any particular circumstances. . . . There is no authority known to me under which a majority of this Court has power under any circumstances to exclude one of its duly commissioned Justices from sitting or voting in any case."[46]

In this showdown Stone backtracked. "The Chief Justice told me," Jackson stated later, "that at his age he did not want to be in the war which was threatened and withdrew his proposed opinion and kept silent."[47]

Afterward, when commentators pointed out that the Chief Justice himself had sat in cases involving the interests of persons as close to him as Crampton Harris to Black, Stone, repeating earlier explanations, carefully distinguished his own situation from that of his colleague.[48] In the Jewell Ridge case a petition for rehearing had been entered, premised upon the failure of Black to disqualify himself. Some explanation of the inability of the Court to act on such a motion was obviously necessary. It was the Chief Justice's attempt to achieve an impartial handling of the problem that had run headlong into a most explosive situation.

The Chief Justice recognized that such disputes as the one involved in the Jewell Ridge case more often than not were grounded in real difficulties. Without posing as oracles of the Constitution, without ceremonial, the Justices attempted to work out a new alignment and distribution of powers within the federal structure and among the Departments of the Government itself. "Congressional legislation of the past ten years," Stone wrote, "has entered new constitutional fields and created new problems, the nature of which is not always fully understood by the bar and is altogether mysterious to the public. All this has put a great strain on the Court as an institution."[49]

Stone attributed much of his difficulty to a "bad press." Popular journals were given to overplaying divisions among the judges, evaluating and explaining them in personal terms. Some observers, taking the longer view, considered Stone's Court head and shoulders above any within recent times. "The Court today is in the most creative period in its history," Max Lerner wrote at the end of this strife-torn term. "There is a good deal of talk about conflicts on the Court, but they are conflicts between men who—although they might deny it—share many common basic premises which the members of the Court did not share ten years ago. . . . They have thought carefully how men's rights can best be safeguarded and have debated it openly in their opinions, and have done it with so much ability as to keep the respect of every decent group."[50] "It seems at least possible," Professor Kenneth Sears added more cautiously, "that the Supreme Court, as constituted from 1937 to 1945, will be regarded as one of the greatest in the history of the Court."[51] Some commentators acclaimed Stone's leadership, insisting that he played an ameliorative role.

The Chief Justice himself rose above petty personal animosities. "I hope I am still not uncivilized," he told a correspondent who wanted to know if a 1936 disclaimer of rancor between the Justices held good in 1944. "But at any rate I am on good terms with all my associates— even though I do not always agree with them."[52] "Preserve your temper," he had counseled himself as well as others, "keep the discussion on a high plane, so that everybody is aware that you are fighting for principle and not because you are angry or vindictive."[53] "He has never sought to govern his fellow justices," the *Washington Post* observed on the twentieth anniversary of his elevation to the bench. "But he has brought to their deliberations an atmosphere of tolerance and friendliness which has served to temper the vigor of their intellectual differences."

Amid such vexatious disputes Stone's spirits were lifted somewhat by the tributes coming to him on this anniversary. Relieved for the moment of profound concern for the institution he led, he enjoyed a delightful evening at a dinner with all but two of the law clerks who had worked for him.[54] Since 1925 they had been selected by him annually from a group nominated by Dean Young B. Smith and Professor Noel T. Dowling of the Columbia Law School, and they represented a cross-section of America—different faiths, social backgrounds, social philosophies. "I do not object at all to having a man who has some of the so-called progressive ideas about law," Stone had informed Dowling, "provided it is tempered and restrained by a thorough knowledge of technique." But he did demand a "capacity to be receptive of my own ideas at least to the extent of being open-minded enough to ascertain whether they may possess some merit." "A man to be a good law clerk for me has to be a sort of paragon," Stone once said. "He should know more law than I do, be able to read proof and get stuff ready for the printer, which I am unable to do at all with any skill or success. He should also have sufficient command of English to get all the rough spots out of my opinions, to say nothing of supplying numerous other qualities which judges are supposed to possess and seldom do." "Above all," he had to be "a man who loves to work."[55]

After twenty years' experience with the young men from Columbia Law School, the "most impressive thing" about the assemblage was "the uniform excellence of the men, and the great assistance they have all been to me through the years. I honestly don't believe that there is any other law school in the country that could have done so well."[56] That evening he was in high glee. Not a few former clerks noted his spirit and vigor and expressed the opinion that he would have many years on the Court.[57] His perception was as keen as ever. In answering one of the multitudinous congratulatory letters and telegrams, he bantered: "It is good to have your letter remembering my twenty years on the treadmill, or, as I suppose Learned Hand would say, 'twenty years shoveling smoke.' "[58]

Rumors of his imminent retirement evoked strong conviction that the Court needed him, as never before, as a balance wheel. "For God's sake, don't do it," L. L. Coryell, Sr., had written, November 21, 1944. "People all over this country love you. I can imagine your aggravation and irritation, but for heaven's sake, don't leave us." Judge Learned Hand made the same plea. "Brother," he said, "I like to think of you as keeping the faith in which we were both reared. Often I wonder how you can do it, but for the love of God, hold the fort, and remember that we watch you with joy."[59]

Stone confessed that the internecine feuds of his brethren weighed upon him. But, like Taft in 1929, he quietly dismissed the thought of retiring. "The delicacy and difficulties of the situation in the Court," he explained, "seem to make it desirable for me to contribute such stabilizing influence as I can until conditions are somewhat better."[60]

CHAPTER THIRTY-NINE

# Inter Arma Silent Leges

## 1942-1943

A few months after Stone's Chief Justiceship began, war pointed up the sharp dilemma of a nation in crisis seeking to uphold and enforce constitutional limitations. In this country the Constitution rather than government is supreme. War recurrently put this faith to the acid test. In 1920 Charles Evans Hughes had queried whether "this Republic could survive another great war even victoriously waged."[1] No such dismal reflections troubled Chief Justice Stone in December 1941.

His first reaction to Pearl Harbor was prosaic, familiar. By chance he had dined on the evening of December 6, 1941, with the Australian Minister. They both thought that Japan would probably strike "at any moment." "Sure enough," Stone wrote, "they did it within twenty-four hours." Like other Americans, the Chief Justice wondered why, "if our people here in Washington felt it so strongly, our Army and

Navy commanders at the Philippines and Hawaii were not a little more awake."[2]

Stone was an enthusiastic onlooker when Britain's war leader, Winston Churchill, in heroic endeavor to cement an Anglo-American alliance, addressed a joint session of Congress. "You will be amused, I think," the Chief Justice wrote Sterling Carr, December 18, "to read the enclosed clipping from the *New York Times* recounting how Churchill and I gave the V signal to each other across the Senate rostrum." "I was the only one in the Senate chamber sufficiently on his toes to read his salute," Stone boasted. Churchill's speech was "one of the greatest I ever heard. I think it will do more to clear the cobwebs out of our brains and make us understand the nature of our job than anything that has taken place in a long while."

During the early months of all-out war Stone became increasingly alarmed by the administration's failure to arouse any genuine war fever among the people. "From my closet," he observed, "it seems that this country is too apathetic and too little ready to realize that freedom is gained and retained only by sacrifice, and that the time has now come for sacrifice, else we will cease to be free men." Washington was "a perfect bedlam; everybody getting in everybody else's way, and I sometimes wonder whether we *will* ever get down to business enough really to fight this war."[3]

"It is incredible to me," he wrote several weeks later, "that a country which has been so strong and self-reliant in all its history should be so incredibly bungling, as it seems to be. It needs a kind of leadership which seems to be wholly lacking."[4]

Despite the "painful surprises and experiences" he knew were in store, Stone did not for a moment doubt the ultimate outcome. Turning his attention to war's aftermath, he gave much thought to the post-bellum mistakes of World War I and how a repetition of these might now be avoided. "There is considerable danger," he wrote Herbert Hoover, February 21, 1942, "that history will repeat itself when this war ends." He wondered whether "we will then be really in a position to say as much about the peace as we were at the end of the last war." The prospect was all the darker for him because in foreign affairs, as on the domestic front, he distrusted New Deal politicians and their leader. "A great mass of people are dissatisfied with the conduct of the war," he observed in November 1942, "and with the disposition of the present administration to yield everything to labor."[5] The administration's penchant for secrecy in the conduct of foreign relations also disturbed him profoundly. "I do not see," he remarked, "how we can formulate a foreign policy and gain the necessary support for it unless the people are informed as to what issues are at stake and how we propose to deal with them."[6]

To make matters worse, he saw his own Court aiding and abetting what he considered to be the President's autocratic pretensions. *United States* v. *Pink* had dealt with the validity of an assignment of czarist properties to the United States under the Litvinov agreement of 1933.* Justice Douglas, speaking for the Court, held that recognition of Russia and the Litvinov assignment made the Russian decrees binding on property located in New York. Stone regarded the opinion as establishing these propositions:

1) That the President can, by executive agreement, alter the rights of individuals and states in pursuance of a national policy adopted in the conduct of foreign relations.

2) That the Litvinov assignment constituted such an agreement.

3) That the agreement by implication altered our domestic law so as to require a state having property of Russian nationals within its territorial limits to recognize and apply the confiscatory decrees of the Soviet Government applicable to that property and to require the State to turn the property over to the United States as assignee and successor of the Russian Government.[7]

Stone, joined by Roberts, dissented vigorously. "I assume for present purposes," he wrote, "that these sweeping alterations of the rights of states and of persons could be achieved by treaty or even executive agreement although we are referred to no authority which would sustain such an exercise of power as is said to have been exerted here by mere assignment unratified by the Senate." "Recognition, like treaty making," he went on, "is a political act, and both may be upon terms and conditions. But that fact no more forecloses this Court, where it is called upon to adjudicate private rights, from inquiry as to what those terms and conditions are than it precludes, in like circumstances, a court's ascertaining the true scope and meaning of a treaty."[8]

For expert comment on his stand he turned to John Bassett Moore. "Absolutely correct," Moore said of his dissent. "In time of war, private rights, including those in property, are always subject to arbitrary violations or abridgment, but the courts are not supposed to cooperate in it. They are useless, or perhaps worse than useless, when they do."[9]

Nor was Moore the only authority to express abhorrence. To Professor Edwin M. Borchard of Yale the Pink decision meant that

---

* The bare facts of the Pink case were these: In 1918 and 1919 the Soviet Government nationalized the property of Russian insurance companies, wherever situated. In 1931 the New York Court of Appeals directed the Superintendent of Insurance, who had satisfied policyholders and creditors, to dispose of the remaining assets of the First Russian Insurance Company to foreign creditors. (In the *Matter of the People*, 255 N.Y. 415, 175 N.E. 114.) The United States in 1933 recognized the Soviet Government and under the so-called Litvinov assignment became assignee of Soviet claims in the United States. The United States thereupon sued the Superintendent of Insurance of New York to recover the assets.

"executive agreements are interchangeable with treaties and can do exactly what a treaty could do. It enables the President, in fact, to set aside a statute of Congress or a treaty at his will, so that we have already become a potential dictatorship."* "I am not surprised that the decision . . . is having some serious consequences," Stone responded. "The surprising thing to me has been how few there are, both within and without the Court, who realize its possibilities for mischief. Its fallacies will be seized upon as a ready means of enlarging executive power beyond, I think, anything that the Constitution ever contemplated."[10]

The damage done was not, however, beyond repair. "Notwithstanding the aid given in the Pink case," Stone wrote Borchard a few months later, "I cannot believe that the drive underway to by-pass the Senate by substituting the executive agreement for treaties will ultimately succeed if the Senate,† the bar, and especially those concerned with international law, do their full duty."[11]

During the first six months of the war Stone's day-to-day feelings oscillated according to the tenor of news from the front. In late February 1942 he feared that victory's fruits would be snatched from the United States either by repetition of its failure to join a postwar international organization, or by a combination of Great Britain and Russia, which could dictate the terms of the peace. Rather pessimis-

---

* "I am much distressed about the opinion of the Court in *United States* v. *Pink*," Edwin M. Borchard wrote Stone, February 9, 1942. "For fifteen years we refused to recognize Soviet Russia on the ground mainly that they had no respect for private property and confiscated it. During all this time Secretaries of State repeated the remark that a country which failed to observe its international obligations could not be recognized. After the Litvinov assignment . . . this administration undertakes to insist on the validity of Soviet confiscations not merely in Russia but *mirabile dictu* of property located in the United States. This is a reversal with a vengeance."

There were, in fact, notable precedents for the Court's decision. Besides *United States* v. *Belmont*, 301 U.S. 324 (1937), there was *United States* v. *Curtiss-Wright Export Corp.*, 299 U.S. 304 (1936). In the latter case Justice Sutherland, taking sharp exception to Woodrow Wilson's dictum of 1908, said: "A political society cannot endure without a supreme will somewhere. Sovereignty is never held in suspense. When, therefore, the external sovereignty of Great Britain in respect of the colonies ceased, it immediately passed to the Union." Of this case Stone wrote Edwin Borchard, February 11, 1942: "I have always regarded it as something of a misfortune that I was foreclosed from expressing myself in . . . the Curtiss-Wright case . . . because I was ill and away from Court when it was decided." Stone had also been unable to participate in a similar case, *United States* v. *Chemical Foundation*, 272 U.S. 1 (1926), because as Attorney General he had argued the case before the Supreme Court.

† The opinions in the Pink case figured in 1953, when Senator Bricker of Ohio introduced a Joint Resolution, bringing the power of the President to make executive agreements under legislative control. After months of acrimonious debate the Senate rejected the proposal by a roll call vote of 60 to 31. (*Congressional Record*, Feb. 26, 1954.)

tically he thought that America's contributions would not be sufficient to win a commanding place at the peace table. To him, Hoover had sounded the clarion call for the peacemakers. "The nation needs now, as it never did before, wise counsel," the Chief Justice wrote, commending the former President's major speech at the Waldorf. "It is because your address was full of good sense and practical wisdom that it has heartened many people."[12]

A few months earlier the Chief Justice had agreed to read in manuscript the Hoover-Gibson book, *The Problems of Lasting Peace*—a catalogue of historical antecedents written across a schoolboy's map of prewar Europe. Stone gave the manuscript long and careful consideration all the more willingly because he believed strongly that an international program should be put forward "long enough in advance of peace so that people can be thinking about the problems which it discusses."[13]

Hoover and Gibson had, he said, made "a substantial contribution to sound American thinking." And yet what they offered was a corrective of the American approach to the Versailles Conference instead of light on the problems that would later confront the United States. Stone's notes and queries—"some random observations," he called them —lent a touch of realism to the discussion. Sore spots that have vexed international politics since the successful conclusion of World War II were clearly anticipated. Germany, he said, would be the "immediate and preliminary" question at the peace conference. Along with a "definite program for sustaining her economically," steps "must be taken to prevent re-establishment of military power such as launched her on her present militaristic career." Japan with her dense population would be a "constant threat to peace" unless her "natural energy and capacity, her need for markets and sources of raw materials," were satisfied. Solution of those and many other pressing problems required over-all organization.

But any scheme for world peace, he told Hoover, built upon the "military and economic domination of the world" by the most powerful of the Allies, would be illusory. Multifarious factors, including the spectacular rise of Russian might, a swiftly changing Orient, with the possibility of "the white race wholly eliminated from the Far East," the "strong protectionist sentiment," the erection of trade barriers "to preserve an illusory temporary prosperity after the war"—all these precluded permanent settlement based on any sort of modern Pax Romana. "Regimes which are sustained by force," he said, "are usually ended by it." Of course victory by the free nations augured well for peace, but, he cautioned, their cooperation in this effort "might be embarrassed by Russia's disposition to spread her peculiar doctrines

in other countries." "That may well prove to be," he added prophetically, "a source of danger to the other countries and a source of
irritation which may well threaten the future peace of the world."

The opposite tack—"establishment of a peaceful world by means
other than world domination by the victors"— was also doomed to
failure, Stone believed, unless a fulcrum was provided for the release
of national pressures through the give and take of discussion.* The
problem was basically political. At bottom, peace rested upon the self-
restraint of the dominant nations, within whose grasp lay the choice
of the olive branch or the sword. Paper declarations of the type
epitomized by the Kellogg-Briand Pact, pious and empty protestations
against aggression, were but shadow-boxing with world peace. "Peace
cannot rise above its source in the will to peace of the dominant
nations," he contended, "and the successful prevention at the peace
table, and later as they arise, of the stresses and irritations which
produce war."

Ethical resolutions for peace were not enough. Its effectuation
through the medium of institutional arrangements was essential. The
League had failed because "it was made and intended to be made
the implement of power politics conducted principally by England and
France after the peace, much as they had been conducted by them
before." Its machinery, or something like it, ought, however, to be
available after the peace, "not with the illusion that it will compel
European powers to behave when they do not wish to behave, but as
the useful implement for removing sources of irritation and facilitating
understanding and mutual accommodation if such is their will and
desire."

In the context of world politics Stone sounded the keynote of his
constitutional jurisprudence—"self-restraint," respect by the powerful
nations for the rights of others, and the creation of the machinery for
making effective the will to peace through continuing alleviation of
the tensions and irritations certain to arise at the end of the war.
Restraint, give and take, discussion, compromise—the very elements
that governed his own personal relations as well as his jurisprudence
—were fundamentally the elements upon which international peace
had to be buttressed.

Stone's first Court term as Chief Justice made a decided difference
in his standing before the world. "He is more than Chief Justice of
the United States, exalted as that title may be," Professor Dowling
wrote in 1941, "he is in a large sense the exponent and exemplar of
that 'ordered liberty' which needs to be replenished and quickened

---

* For Stone, a permanent court added "very little" to the idea of a league, which
he regarded as a forum for removing "sources of irritation and facilitating understanding and mutual accommodation."

lest it, too, like the form of government of which Lincoln spoke, be in danger of perishing from the earth."[14] It may be that Stone himself had unconscious appreciation of the demands of his new office when in the spring of 1942 he turned down the British Ambassador's invitation to visit England during the summer. "I have had a hard year and have a hard one ahead of me," he explained, "and any rest I get will be in July before the grind of certs begins. A trip to England just now would not be very restful, and I think I owe it to the Court and to the job generally to stick to it."[15] Very shortly events ratified his resolution to follow the path of duty.

On June 27, 1942, as the battlefield fortunes of an unprepared nation showed signs of improvement, popular confidence in the ability of political leaders to protect those at home was rudely shaken. On that date the American people learned that two weeks earlier a German submarine had risen to the surface within a few hundred feet of Amagansett Beach, Long Island. In the darkness of night a small boat had put in to shore and landed four young men, all graduates of a German sabotage school near Berlin. Dressed in the uniform of the German marine infantry, they changed quickly to civilian clothes and proceeded to New York City, carrying a supply of explosives, fuses, incendiaries, and various other gadgets of sabotage. Four nights later an equal number of classmates, similarly garbed and equipped, landed from another U-boat at Ponte Vedra Beach, Florida. Soon they too, dressed as American citizens, were on their appointed mission to various parts of the country. Thanks to the alertness of a coast guardsman and the thorough follow-up by the FBI, all the would-be saboteurs were in custody within two weeks after their landing.

Acting hastily, as if to make an example of these bold invaders, President Roosevelt appointed, on July 2, 1942, a military commission of seven Army generals to try the saboteurs, vesting it with extraordinary discretion over procedure and directing it to transmit the record of the trial "directly to me for my action thereon."[16] By Proclamation, the President also closed the courts of the United States to "all persons who are subjects, citizens, or residents of any nation at war with the United States . . . and who during time of war enter or attempt to enter the United States . . . and are charged with committing or attempting . . . to commit sabotage."[17] Trial by military commission commenced July 8, in strict secrecy; the commission issued only an uninformative daily communiqué. Without a hitch, the insistent demands of the leaders for "justice" appeared certain to be quickly satisfied.

Public sentiment, however, seemed to favor giving the Nazis a judicial hearing before they were shot. Behind the scenes two Army colonels, Kenneth C. Royall and Cassius M. Dowell, appointed by the President to defend the Germans, worked feverishly to obtain for them the benefits of a civilian trial, while preparing for and continuously defending the accused before the commission. The Chief Justice's son, Lauson, then an Army major, was called into the case to assist Colonel Royall and to investigate the legality of the military trial. Within a day his researches led him to *Ex parte Milligan*, a post-Civil War case that raised the question of the validity of a military trial of persons apprehended far from the scene of actual battle, and the availability of a writ of habeas corpus.[18] At this point defense counsel began efforts to get a court hearing on the claim that the saboteurs were entitled to a civil trial. Fearing that his activities might disqualify the Chief Justice if the case should get to the Supreme Court, they took Lauson off the constitutional issues.

Counsel for the defense resolved to make an attempt to obtain a writ of habeas corpus in order to test the validity of the saboteurs' detention and trial by military rather than the civilian authorities; they were determined to have the Supreme Court pass on the question. Colonel Royall went to see Justice Roberts, who was immediately interested and seemed to feel that perhaps something should be done. A few days later arrangements were made to have the colonels go up to Roberts' Pennsylvania farm, where Justice Black was also to be. Shortly thereafter Royall and Dowell, together with Attorney General Francis Biddle and Judge Advocate General Myron C. Cramer, flew up in the plane of Undersecretary of War Robert P. Patterson and spent several hours with the Justices. Before their arrival Roberts had called Stone to request authorization for the two Justices to bring the entire Court together if they thought that should be done. Before the colonels returned, it was agreed that the Court should be convened the following Wednesday.[19]

For the first time in twenty-two years the Court broke its summer recess. While the scattered jurists hurried back to Washington, their decision to meet was a carefully kept secret. Officials were startled by the announcement on the afternoon of July 27. "Decision to seek recourse in the Supreme Court did not meet popular approval in Washington," the *New York Times* reported July 28. "On the contrary, there is great dissatisfaction here with the length to which the [military] trial has already proceeded. . . . On all sides hope was expressed that the Supreme Court would make short work of the move."

The *Times* had put it mildly. The next day Representative Emmanuel Celler, in an interview, bluntly summarized congressional sentiment: "Our people are of the opinion that the eight Nazi saboteurs should be executed with all possible dispatch. . . . They are confident that the military tribunal will decree their death. Any interference with that trial by civil court would strike a severe blow to public morale."[20]

The Court convened on July 29. Justice Douglas, traveling from the

West Coast, had not yet arrived; Justice Murphy, resplendent in Army uniform, had returned from maneuvers in North Carolina, but decided not to sit in the case. Before argument could begin a preliminary hurdle had to be cleared. The Chief Justice, then staying with Lauson at the home of a friend and cognizant of his son's connection with the case, felt misgivings.[21] Though both Colonel Royall and Attorney General Biddle had urged him to sit, the Chief Justice wanted their views made a part of the record:

"I am informed that my son, who is an officer in the Army, was assigned to participate in the defense," the Chief Justice said, addressing himself to the Attorney General. "Of course if that fact were regarded as ground for my not participating in the case, I should at once disqualify myself. In order that I may be advised and that the Court may be advised whether he has participated in this proceeding and what his connection with the case is, I will ask you, if you are so advised, to state, so that it become of record."

"May it please the Court, and Mr. Chief Justice," the Attorney General responded, "the counsel for the prosecution and the defendants are agreed that your son, Major Lauson H. Stone, did not in any way participate in these habeas corpus proceedings. He assisted defense counsel in the presentation of the case before the Military Commission, under orders. He in no way worked on the proceedings or did anything in connection with the proceedings before this Court, and therefore counsel for both sides join in urging, Mr. Chief Justice, that you sit in this case."

"Does counsel for the petitioners concur in that statement?" the Chief Justice asked.

"We do," Colonel Royall answered.[22]

There was still a possibility that the Justices might balk at the threshold of this dramatic plea for habeas corpus on the ground that proper steps had not been taken to bring the case within their jurisdiction. The legal routine ordinarily required to take such a case to the Supreme Court could not have been completed in a few days, but Colonel Royall had made elaborate efforts to do so. Justice Frankfurter proceeded to subject his former student to a merciless examination on the niceties of federal procedure. After explaining what he had done, the lawyer finally commented somewhat helplessly, "As a practical matter, this was all that we could do."[23]

"Do you mind spelling that out?" Frankfurter asked.

"The Military Commission," Royall said, "started its sessions on the 8th day of July and counsel were appointed a few days before that and were under orders to take part in the proceedings before the Military Commission, which they did. It has been impossible, as a physical matter, to do anything but attend to those hearings, until the evidence stopped. I think no one would deny that who knows the circumstances. As soon as the evidence closed, even prior thereto, we made an effort to present this matter in the best and quickest way possible.

"The order appointing the Military Commission," Royall continued, "provides for no review in the ordinary sense. That is, between the time the commission takes its action and the time the Executive acts there is no period which anyone could safely count on between the conclusion of the hearing before the commission and the execution of any sentence that might be imposed; and it is apparent that it would have been impossible, even in the matter of preparing papers, if nothing else, to have followed anything other than this procedure."[24]

"Why could not the appeal have been perfected before the Circuit Court of Appeals?" Frankfurter asked. "Judge Morris' denial was at eight o'clock last night, or probably thereafter," the Army lawyer responded. "The commission meets again tomorrow to dispose of this matter, at least to hear our arguments, and then to dispose of it as it sees fit."[25]

The stark fact behind Royall's frenzied maneuvers was his suspicion that the decision of the Military Commission would not be communicated to defense counsel but would be submitted to the President for his approval, and that after consideration by the President the sentence would be carried out without defense counsel even being advised. Hence his haste to get before the Supreme Court questions only that tribunal could answer finally. "Clearly," Lauson Stone later commented with marked restraint, "judicial process would appear to be wanting in some respect if sentence had been carried out before the question had been determined by the Court."[26] Apparently Royall's sense of urgency became infectious. In any event the Justices concluded that the issues were important enough to warrant prompt decision without interference from any delaying technicalities. They acceded to Royall's request that they hear argument while his assistants scurried around the lower courts perfecting one phase of the appeal.

Actually the cases came before the Court in two ways. As the opinion shows,[27] the petitioners sought leave to file petitions for habeas corpus in the Supreme Court after such petitions had already been denied by the United States District Court for the District of Columbia. At this point there was some question as to whether it would be an unconstitutional exercise of the Court's original jurisdiction to decide the case.[28] The Attorney General, however, did not contest the Court's jurisdiction, and consideration of the question was deferred. While the argument was proceeding before the Supreme Court, petitioners hurried to perfect an appeal from the District Court to the United States Court of Appeals for the District of Columbia, and then applied for certiorari before judgment, which the Supreme Court granted. Thus both phases of the case were heard and decided together.*

"Had it not been for the urgency of the case and the necessity of prompt decision," the Chief Justice observed later, "we would, I assume, neither have entertained the petitioners' motions in our Court or jumped the Circuit Court of Appeals, but would have allowed the cases to take their usual course through application to the District Court, appeal to the Circuit Court of Appeals, and certiorari to our Court."[29] As a matter of fact the final steps were accomplished only a few minutes before the Court met on July 31 to announce its decision.†

"Thus," Professor Robert Cushman pointedly commented, "the Court's jurisdiction caught up with the Court just at the finish line."[30]

The decision itself, a cryptic *per curiam*, upheld the jurisdiction of the Military Commission to try the Germans and announced that an opinion would be filed later.‡ Within a few days sentences of death had been carried out against six of the Nazis and a seventh had been given a life sentence.§ As had been feared, the Military Commission

---

* At the conclusion of the case Lauson Stone recorded: "Colonel Royall had taken with him a draft petition of habeas corpus, and it was agreed that the papers would have to be completed and filed before the Court convened. At first the Attorney General showed signs of resisting at every turn but then became cooperative apparently on the theory that Colonel Royall would get the case into the Court somehow. . . . At first Colonel Royall thought a direct writ would lie in the Supreme Court. Later he and the assistants to the Attorney General worked it out that, having applied first to Black, temporarily designated as a Circuit Judge in the absence of the Chief Justice, and Black having declined singly to issue the writ, the Court could then entertain the writ in the exercise of its appellate jurisdiction. Two days before the Court hearing, Justice Roberts sent Colonel Royall a phone message citing *Marbury* v. *Madison*—thus indicating that he doubted the Court's direct jurisdiction. Accordingly, it was decided to prepare petitions to a district judge, have him sign orders denying them, then file copies in the Circuit Court, and file notices of appeal therefrom; also to file both original writs in the Supreme Court, reciting the denial by the district court, and also to apply for certiorari. Tuesday Colonel Royall went to see District Judge Morris, who heard both Colonel Royall and Biddle, after which the judge decided to deny the petitions. After dinner and about 8:30 p.m., Captain Hummel took the papers to the judge and he signed them. The next morning before Court opened the papers were filed and copies certified for the Court, and notices of appeal, etc., were filed." (Lauson H. Stone to A.T.M., June 27, 1952.)

† Justice Frankfurter disliked the implication that the Justices took extraordinary action. For him the reason which persuaded the Court to entertain the saboteurs' pleas was that "we had no judicial choice, i.e., we cannot refuse to entertain a duly filed application in order to decide whether we have jurisdiction to pass on such an application." It may be, however, that the Court had appellate jurisdiction from the beginning. See *Ex parte Siebold*, 100 U.S. 371 (1880), pp. 374-75.

‡ The procedure adopted was not unprecedented. In *Ex parte Milligan* the order of the Court was entered on April 3, 1866, and the opinion of the Court was delivered the next term, on December 17, 1866.

§ The eighth, George Dasch, who did not appeal to the Supreme Court, was given thirty years at hard labor.

did not communicate its decision to defense counsel, and they learned of the executions from the press.[31] Meanwhile the Chief Justice returned to his summer headquarters at Peckett's on Sugar Hill, New Hampshire, to write the Court's opinion.

Stone had begun study of the case even before the special Washington session. At his request, his law clerk, Bennett Boskey, had forwarded the presidential order directing trial by military commission, a copy of the Constitution, and copies of relevant statutes, including provisions of the Articles of War authorizing trial by commission rather than by jury. "Both briefs have done their best to create a sort of legal chaos," Stone complained as he settled down to work. "I certainly hope the military is better equipped to fight the war than it is to fight its legal battles." Not unlikely, his annoyance arose as much from an aching back as from the inadequacy of the briefs. During the time he was writing the saboteurs' opinion he suffered from a severe attack of lumbago; the pain was so bad that at one point he cautioned Boskey not to cram the "cert" bags as they had to be carried to his cottage by hand.[32]

As Stone saw it, the case had two aspects. The first concerned the claim of the saboteurs that they were entitled to jury trial in civil courts since they were captured outside the war zone. "Congress, having legislated over the entire field," Colonel Royall had argued, "and the civil courts functioning in this territory, it is unnecessary and contrary to our theory of government to appoint a military commission to do what Congress has clearly indicated should be done by the criminal courts."[33] The second aspect concerned the question whether F.D.R.'s order establishing the military tribunal departed from the requirements laid down in the Articles of War.

Though handicapped considerably by lack of library facilities and dependent on his clerk to document his conclusions, the Chief Justice made great progress with the first point while in New Hampshire.* "What I need most," he wrote Boskey as he plunged into the opinion, "is material to show that petitioners are unlawful belligerents in the International Law and Law of War sense, which would bring them within the jurisdiction of military tribunals, which the Commander-in-Chief under the Constitution and Article XV of the Articles of War

---

* Throughout the entire vacation Stone had found little opportunity for untroubled recreation. "We had a pretty strenuous summer," he wrote Charles Evans Hughes, Sept. 25, 1942. "First came an urgent request from the President for me to take up and solve the rubber problem. . . . Then came the Saboteur cases. . . . Then came a lame back, which finally incapacitated me for three weeks, due as near as I can find out to a combination of an extremely cold Pullman car on the way from Washington to Sugar Hill, after the strenuous days here during the Saboteur trials, followed by two strenuous days climbing over mountain trails. One at seventy or thereabouts really should be a little more discreet than at twenty-one, but I find that difficult."

may set up for their trial independently of the Fifth and Sixth Amendments." On such ground, he thought, their case could be distinguished from *Ex parte Milligan*, where the accused was neither a belligerent nor associated with the armed forces of an enemy. Later on he asked his law clerk to concentrate on "the reconciliation of the broad language of the Fifth and Sixth Amendments with the continued execution of the powers conferred by the Constitution before amendment to try military [offenses] . . . without a jury." The Court in some cases, he thought, had "given a restricted meaning to 'Crimes' as used in the Amendments. . . . The Amendments apply to all trials in the courts but were not intended to end trials by military commissions or require the latter to use a jury."[34]

Stone soon satisfied himself that the alleged citizen among the saboteurs need not be given special consideration because he had associated himself with German armed forces, thus becoming an enemy belligerent liable to be tried as such under the law of war. One point troubled him, however. "If Haupt is a citizen," he asked Boskey, "does that not make out a charge of treason as to him which the Constitution requires to be tried by the civil court?" Further reflection led him to conclude that Haupt's real offense was entering this country as an unlawful belligerent for a hostile purpose—"which constitutes a violation of the law of war but . . . may fall short of giving aid and comfort to the enemy." "The two offenses," he said, "are distinct and the same set of circumstances may support independent prosecutions for both."[35]

In concert, he and Boskey searched "through all the intricacies of the Constitution, the Statutes of the United States, the Articles of War, and the unwritten law of war." It was certainly, as Stone said, "a mortification of the flesh."[36] But he was assisted considerably throughout by the feeling, general among the Justices, that the opinion was rightly his and that it, like the decision announced in July, should be unanimous. At least for the moment the Court was enjoying the "peacefulness of being at war."[37] Even Justices often in disagreement expressed the strong hope that there would be only one opinion—Stone's. But the drive for unanimity limited and conditioned what could be said. The opinion simply had to be cut to the bone.

Stone returned to Washington on September 14, 1942, with the first part of his opinion pretty well in hand. But he had been unable to resolve satisfactorily the questions raised by the saboteurs' contention that the Military Commission and the President had not complied in several respects with the Articles of War. The more he dug into the case, the more puzzled he became by the possibility that F.D.R. had not followed the Articles. Boskey's memorandum on Articles 46 and 50½, pointing to the opposite conclusion, was not persuasive: "I am sorry to say it fortifies the conclusion which I reached in Washington that the President's order probably conflicts with the Articles of War."[38]

Among other things, the President's order establishing the tribunal had permitted five members to decree death where the Articles required unanimity. The order also provided that "such evidence shall be admitted as would, in the opinion of the President of the Commission, have probative value to a reasonable man." Although Articles 46 and 50½[39] ordered the "reviewing authority" to refer the trial record to a staff judge advocate or to the Judge Advocate General before final action, the executive order had commanded the commission to transmit its record directly to the President. Stone first considered dismissing the objections arising from the presidential order as "premature," since the Military Commission had not reached a verdict at the time of the Court's deliberation in July. However, it seemed "almost brutal to announce this ground of decision for the first time after six of the petitioners have been executed."[40] Justice Frankfurter reinforced his disinclination to follow this course. "If a legal right exists," Frankfurter wrote, "to say that it is prematurely presented when as a practical matter there would be no later time for presenting it—for dead men can present no legal claims—is to bring the law into disrepute and to make a mockery of justice." Nor would it help to decide the case as though the President had complied with the Articles. "There can be no doubt that the President did *not* follow the scheme of review under II G of the Articles of War. He has not said so in so many words, but as judges we ought not to be blind to that of which we have no doubt as men."

A possible resolution of the impasse was that these Articles of War were never intended to bind the President. "I am happy to say," Stone commented, "that I have found more to support the legislative construction of Article 46, which you favor, than I had expected to find in view of the dearth of such material in the Government's brief." Items of legislative history and administrative practice before and after the adoption of Article 46, he said, supported the view that the President was not restricted by the requirement that the record be submitted to the Judge Advocate General prior to final approval of the commission's decision. The same idea was inherent in executive construction, "although," Stone added, "I am frank to say that I can find such construction, if at all, only in the Presidential Order. But even that does not say that the review by staff judge advocate or Judge Advocate General is to be dispensed with. I find a pennyweight also in the ineptness of the language of Article 46, if it is to be taken as requiring the President to prescribe regulations for himself." He was not, however, wholly convinced by these findings. "I cannot say," he wrote, "that I am overenthusiastic about them in their totality."[41] "I have some difficulty in concluding that 46 does not apply," he had told Boskey on September

5, 1942, "when the President is the reviewing authority or that 50½ applies to courts martial and not to commission, or that these two conclusions are altogether harmonious."

The secrecy surrounding the trial* and F.D.R.'s review sorely nettled the Chief Justice. He did not feel happy in giving such proceedings a clean bill of health, for the Court did not know even then whether the President and the commission had ruled for or against the saboteurs on the procedural points raised in their petition for habeas corpus. Neither the surviving saboteurs nor anyone else outside the Executive could have access to the trial record so as to lay a factual foundation for habeas corpus. "My most serious difficulty," he wrote Frankfurter, September 16, "I passed over *sub silentio,* in order to avoid indecent exposure of some very worthy gentlemen. It is this. If the surviving petitioners were to renew their application tomorrow and we agreed with their construction of the Articles, I do not see what possible factual basis we would have for setting them free." For the Court to pass on the Articles, when it was under no obligation to do so in July, was "a pretty large dose for a court to swallow."[42]

Still on the fence, shortly after returning to Washington, Stone laid his dilemma before the brethren. "I have no doubt of the correctness of our decision not to sustain any of the petitions for habeas corpus," he wrote. "The precise ground on which it should be put presents a question of some delicacy and difficulty to which the Court, I think, should give rather careful consideration. I have expounded the matter in both aspects as fully as possible, merely as an aid to our discussion and conclusion."[43]

In a separate memorandum he explained the difficulties he had been having with the Articles, laying out the courses open to the Court and the "embarrassments" inherent in each:

In presenting the case at conference, immediately following the argument, I expressed doubts as to the construction of those Articles and stated that if it were necessary to decide the point I should not be able to decide without further investigation; that in my opinion it would be unnecessary to decide it; and in fact would be improper to do so since there were no facts disclosed on the record of the habeas corpus proceedings which drew in question the construction of the Articles. On that record we could not know what the judgment of the Military Commission would be, whether it would

* The Court had taken the steps noted in the *Supreme Court Journal* for Wednesday, July 29, 1942: "The motion for an order directing the Clerk of this Court to impound certain portions of the record and to hold the same for the exclusive use of the Justices of this Court is granted."

The *Supreme Court Journal* for Friday, July 31, 1942, however, contains the following: "The order of July 29, 1942, directing the Clerk to impound the record of the proceedings before the Military Commission in the above-entitled cases is hereby modified and the Clerk is directed to return said record to counsel."

convict or not, or if so whether it would be unanimous. The President's Order did not foreclose review by the Judge Advocate General or by a staff judge advocate appointed by him for that purpose, and we could not say in advance that the President would not direct whatever review the Articles might require. Consequently the construction of the Articles were not before us on the pending applications for habeas corpus, which were directed solely at the right to detain petitioners for trial.

The obvious disadvantage of placing decisions on that ground was, of course, that our determination might not finally dispose of the case and that in the course of further proceedings before the Military commission or the President events might occur which would afford a basis for testing the construction of the Articles in a later habeas corpus proceeding, on application either to the district court or to us. But even so, that could not have been a ground for deciding in the present proceeding questions which had not been brought before us and might never be.

I understood this view to be acceptable to the conference and necessarily so since the conference did not attempt to pass upon the construction of the Articles in question or to say that the contentions made by petitioners with respect to them were wrong. In preparing the draft *per curiam* I accordingly included one paragraph stating that the Court did not pass upon the construction of Articles 46 and 50½, in the absence of a decision by the commission or action of the President requiring their construction.

At conference the following day the Court struck this paragraph from the *per curiam*. This action has left me in doubt as to how the Court intended the opinion to be written—whether (a) it should decline to pass upon the Articles in question on the ground that their construction was not before us or, in the alternative, (b) it should construe the Articles contrary to the contention of the petitioners. These are the only possible alternatives. But in the present posture of the case the adoption of either involves the Court in some embarrassment to which I invite your attention.

Ground (a) was and is a perfectly tenable legal ground of decision, wholly consistent with our *per curiam*. The embarrassment arises only from the fact that the announcement that we have left the construction of Articles 46 and 50½ undecided is now made for the first time after six of the petitioners have been executed and when it is too late to raise the question in their behalf. Two have survived, but as to them we do not know whether decision of the Military Commission was unanimous; we do not know what method of review of the judgment was adopted by the President. If they were to renew their application for habeas corpus tomorrow their petitions would necessarily lack any factual basis for the construction of the Articles in question. And even if we knew those facts now, the knowledge would not alter the record on which we acted and on which our opinion must be written.

But whenever the facts do become known, as they ultimately will, the survivors, if still in prison, will be in a position to raise the question. If the decisions should be in their favor it would leave the present Court in the unenviable position of having stood by and allowed six men to go to their death without making it plain to all concerned—including the President—that it had left undecided a question on which counsel strongly relied to secure petitioners' liberty.

If we adopt alternative (b) and construe the statute against the petitioners' contentions, we are deciding a proposition of law which is not free from doubt upon a record which does not raise it. In short, we are rendering an advisory opinion. If we had put down a full opinion dealing with that point on the day Court adjourned, there would have been no possible basis or excuse for our discussing it. But whatever opinion we write now is written upon the same record and involves the same difficulty. No subsequent event which we know or can know judicially affords any added justification for our writing a legal essay on the meaning of Articles 46 and 50½. This Court has always frowned on the practice of writing advisory opinions. I am especially reluctant to see it adopt the practice in the circumstances of this case.[44]

With his memorandum went alternative drafts of his opinion labeled "A" and "B," reflecting the ideas sketched above.

Apparently no one, except perhaps the Chief Justice himself, was much impressed with the argument that by construing the Articles the Court would be rendering an advisory opinion; the Justices were more sensitive to his suggestion that a decision labeling the saboteurs' appeal as "premature" would look foolish, and worse, if announced after six men had been electrocuted. In short, the course Stone favored was not "good judicial diplomacy."[45] Their own involvement in the trial through their decision in the July hearing practically compelled them to cover up or excuse the President's departures from customary procedures. A finding that the Articles did not apply to the President or that he had complied sufficiently with them grew out of the circumstances of the case. Even Stone, whose mind had wavered on the construction to be given the Articles, was persuaded eventually that the Court could not act solely on the basis of the record, but must in the interest of justice take into account the public knowledge that the drastic sentences had been carried out.

Stone's handling of the case at both stages received high praise from his colleagues. But as was so often the case, agreement on the major issue did not preclude sharp conflict on subsidiary questions. At this point pressures for unanimity failed, and the bench split down the middle on the meaning of the Articles. As Murphy had disqualified himself, there was not a majority for either of the opposing views. If possible, it was important to have but one opinion. Accordingly, Stone's suggested construction of the Articles was pared to the marrow. Without going into the reasons, his opinion merely indicated that some Justices thought the Articles did not apply to the presidential Military Commission convened to try the admitted enemy invaders, while others believed that the President had made an allowable interpretation for this type of case.[46] Thus the Justices avoided all decision on the question of Congress's power to restrict the President's authority to conduct military trials, as to which the Court had divided in the Milligan case.

Negotiations among the Justices on these and other points consumed nearly a month. When the opinion in *Ex parte Quirin* came down on October 29, 1942, many observers were puzzled by the reticence with which it pronounced judgment on the President's order banning the saboteurs' resort to the civil courts. "It is urged," Stone wrote, "that if they are enemy aliens or if the Proclamation has force, no court may afford the petitioners a hearing. But there is certainly nothing in the Proclamation to preclude access to the courts for determining its applicability to the particular case. And neither the Proclamation nor the fact that they are enemy aliens forecloses consideration by the courts of petitioners' contentions that the Constitution and laws of the United States constitutionally enacted forbid their trial by military commission. As announced in our *per curiam* opinion, we have resolved those questions by our conclusion that the commission has jurisdiction to try the charge preferred against petitioners."[47]

This "somewhat cryptic" explanation, Stone commented privately, "was the result of patient negotiations to get the Court to agree unanimously to rejection of the argument that access to the Court by the prisoners could be denied."[48] At the request of certain of his brethren he deleted the much stronger statement that "even though guilty they [the saboteurs] were entitled to be tried by a tribunal and by laws which the Constitution has prescribed as the means of determining their guilt."[49] "There were so many eggs in the case which I felt it necessary to avoid breaking," he explained, "that I am afraid the opinion was not good literature. I hope you noticed that the opinion flatly rejected (as unobtrusively as possible) the President's comment that no court should hear the plea of the saboteurs. That, I thought, was going pretty far."[50]

The Chief Justice was dissatisfied with the newspaper response. "An interesting feature of the case," he wrote John Bassett Moore, "which was not commented on by the newpapers, was the President's Order prohibiting any court from listening to the saboteurs." Moore could hardly have failed to note the overtones. The Chief Justice wanted the Court's opinion to be recognized as a striking demonstration that the law of the land still governed and that the jurisdiction of the courts was not ousted no matter what the President proclaimed. Unfortunately the brethren had persuaded him to tone down his distaste for F.D.R.'s ban to such point that many publicists overlooked this aspect of the opinion. Moore, however, was not deceived. "Probably," he commented sarcastically on the President's order, "this was designed to impress upon Hitler our superior conception of the independence of judicial tribunals and of the oath the judges take to administer justice impartially, without fear or favor. I have the impression that courts martial are required to hear both sides."[51]

The crusty old scholar's remark was justified. Although there was precedent for the view that courts may be closed in time of war to civil suits by enemy aliens, there was none, in Stone's opinion, to prevent their recourse to the law to defend themselves against prosecution. It seems not unlikely that F.D.R.'s distrust of the judiciary still lingered. By letting events take their course, by enlisting the independent support of the judiciary, the President might have strengthened his own policy. As it was, he gave Stone and others on the bench an opportunity to assert their independence of the Executive.

Lawyers and others hailed the Court's action as vindicating the American tradition of liberty. "Your handling of the saboteurs' case has excited our admiration," Charles C. Burlingham wrote Stone. "The idea of the whole Court hearing the application was a fine conception —yours no doubt—and the conduct of the hearings, the argument of Royall, the prompt and unanimous decision—all made us proud of our country and the law."[52] "The picture of the highest court in the country convening specially to hear and pass upon the lawfulness of the trial of avowed enemies of the nation," one writer observed, "presents a sharp contrast to the practices prevalent in the land whence they came."[53] Other commentators in legal periodicals were willing to excuse the relaxation of standards in the procedure by which the saboteurs were brought to book on the ground that "in wartime quick justice and absence of delay are essential."[54] The case boiled down to this, Professor Cushman commented: "The Supreme Court stopped the military authorities and required them, as it were, to show their credentials. When this had been done to the Court's satisfaction they were allowed to proceed." Such action, in his judgment, was "a wholesome and desirable safeguard to civil liberty in time of war. . . ."[55]

Public acclamation could not, however, hide the fact that the Court had been somewhat in the position of a private on sentry duty accosting a commanding general without his pass. Conscious of the realities of the situation, Stone strove manfully to put into his opinion all possible safeguards for individual freedom—to make it something more than "a ceremonious detour to a predetermined goal."[56] While writing, he was spurred to even greater caution by Attorney General Biddle's offhand comment of July 31. The military trial and the procedure in the Supreme Court regarding the saboteurs "clarified" the situation concerning future cases, Biddle said. "He did not believe," the New York Times had reported, August 13, "that lower civil courts would accept petitions by such prisoners, in view of the Supreme Court ruling upholding presidential power to establish military commissions. Future saboteur trials would be held 'very promptly' before a military commission or a court martial . . . and the whole matter would be more or less 'routine' now."

"That interview of Biddle's was most unfortunate, if true," Stone snorted. "I hope it was not true; at any rate he will get very little comfort out of the opinion." But the fact remained that certain of his colleagues thought "the civil safeguards of the Constitution . . . irrelevant to military affairs in the actual conduct of war."[57]

The practical effect of judicial intervention, as Biddle's statement emphasizes, was to put the stamp of approval on military trials for a wide variety of wartime offenses. The bench had exercised its ultimate power of review, even suggesting the possibility of judicial review in the trial of "war criminals." Yet the Court, confronted by the practical difficulties of staying the executive hand until the case could be brought before it, had to use makeshift procedures. This was no strident challenge hurled at the President for daring to meddle with the judiciary. However one looks at it, approval of presidential and commission action after the fact, in ignorance of what had taken place, was stiff medicine. To Stone's chagrin, perhaps, the judiciary was in danger of becoming part of an executive juggernaut.

The question of the power of the military authorities to try enemy belligerents and the problem of the relationship between military and civil courts did not again come before the Court until after the war. By that time the Justices were somewhat bolder in sticking to their accustomed ways of doing business.

Shortly after the Japanese surrender a special military commission was established under General MacArthur's command to try the "Tiger of Malaya," General Yamashita, for crimes committed during Japanese occupation of the Philippines. As it later turned out, the elaborate charges preferred against him at the trial boiled down to an accusation that as commander of enemy troops he had violated the law of war by "permitting them to commit" brutal atrocities. No attempt was made to show that he personally participated in or authorized such crimes. On this charge he was found guilty and sentenced by the Military Commission to death. Once again diligent Army lawyers hastily carried an appeal from the military tribunal to the civil courts, seeking review first in the Supreme Court of the Philippines and then the Supreme Court of the United States.

The Justices did not, as in the Saboteurs' case, drop everything to hear Yamashita's appeal. Instead they calmly issued a stay, halting all proceedings until they had settled the appeal.[58] After argument, the spirit of business as usual reigned in the Court's inner councils. Nearly a month elapsed before a decision came down. Wiseacres among Government attorneys, confident of the ultimate outcome, explained the delay in terms of the Chief Justice's efforts to whip stray dissenters into line. Some observers felt that what was revealed on decision day confirmed this conjecture.

On or about January 22, 1946, Stone circulated a first draft grounded firmly in the Articles of War and the Court's power to review military proceedings on application for a writ of habeas corpus. In a case like Yamashita's, "the courts may inquire whether the detention complained of is within the authority of those detaining the petitioner." Judges may also examine the accusations against him to make certain they add up to a violation of the law of war. The Articles of War did not apply to a military commission trying offenses against the law of war by enemy combatants; errors, if any, were subject to correction only by higher military authorities, "which are alone authorized to review their decisions."*

Justice Reed, although agreeing in part, objected that the Articles plainly did apply. Moreover the Chief had not, he said, met the point that the Geneva Convention required trials of prisoners of war to be conducted exactly as trials of military offenders in American forces.[59] Reed's difficulties, however, were easily met. Almost immediately Stone circulated a revised version pointing out that the Geneva Convention made use of the Articles mandatory only in trials of prisoners of war for crimes committed as prisoners, not as active combatants.

The Chief Justice ran into more serious trouble when the dissents came in. As the draft stood, it did not even mention the Fifth Amendment, and Justice Rutledge took the unequivocal position that introduction of damaging evidence by deposition in violation of the 26th Article of War, the reception of atrocity accounts at second or third hand, and the commission's denial of time to prepare a defense—these could be sanctioned only if the Court held that "an enemy belligerent in petitioner's position is altogether beyond the pale of constitutional protection." "The Court does not declare expressly," he commented, "that petitioner as an enemy belligerent has no constitutional rights, a ruling I could understand but not accept. Neither does it affirm that he has some, if but little, constitutional protection. Nor does the Court defend what was done. I think the effect of what it does is in substance to deny him all such safeguards. And this is the great issue in the cause."[60] Stone attempted to meet Rutledge squarely on the "great issue" by adding three pages exploring his contentions.

Departing from the thesis that the judges had no power to review military proceedings, the Chief Justice in a revised draft compared the military commission to an expert administrative body that received all evidence and in its own discretion gave effect only to such material as

---

* The language of Stone's first draft was incorporated in the opinion without change.

had probative value. In the usual administrative case, he reasoned, the only complaint one may make is that such evidence "is prejudicial in the sense that it has been unfairly appraised or has been considered or given weight when it is entitled to none." Yamashita's lawyers did not contend, he emphasized, that the entire body of evidence, even excluding objectionable portions, was insufficient to sustain the verdict. Defense counsel, moreover, had lost their opportunity to gain more time for preparation by failing to renew their request for a stay at the proper time. "In all this," he concluded, "we are unable to find any denial of a fair trial or of due process."[61]

Justice Black promptly objected because, he said, the discussion "leaves these implications: (1) It would not violate the Federal Constitution to use in a judicial trial the same evidence on which Yamashita was convicted. (2) If we thought the commission had failed to give counsel adequate time to prepare a defense, we would invalidate the trial as a violation of due process." "Both these implications," he went on, "rest on the premise that the due process clause applies to military trials of enemy combatants for their conduct in waging war against us. This seems to me to be inconsistent with the rest of the opinion. Furthermore, if we are to apply the judicial concept of a 'fair trial' I should be inclined to agree with the dissents." Without the addition, Black interpreted the opinion to mean that "we denied the petition because the military authorities, in the absence of conflicting treaty or law, had the power to fashion their own rules for determining whether enemy combatants had violated military standards for battle conduct. The additions place us in the attitude of defending the commission's action rather than saying that it is beyond our powers of review. I hope you will see fit to omit the addition."[62]

The quickest way to resolve their outstanding differences, Stone told Black, would be for him to circulate his own memorandum or to make concrete suggestions for alterations, adding, "if I were to eliminate the new material, I would probably lose some of my own troops."*[63]

Under pressure to achieve unanimity among the majority Justices,

* Reed, too, had objections calculated to reinforce Black's theory that military proceedings were final, and he continued to press the point that the Articles of War forbade the reception of the kind of evidence used against the Japanese general. Pleading the gravity of the situation, Stone begged Reed to re-examine his analysis of the Articles. "You are the only one who has expressed any doubt on the subject," he wrote, Jan. 31, 1946, "and it seems to me crystal clear that the limitation in Article 25 (barring depositions in capital cases) cannot apply to trials of enemy combatants for violations of the laws of war. Perhaps you have overlooked the fact that the Articles permit the use of the military commission for trials of our own armed forces, and those associated with them, and to such a trial, of course, the limitations of 25 would apply." Reed reconsidered and withdrew his objection the same day in the interest of solidarity and at the price of the excision of the Chief Justice's effort to keep judicial strings on the proceedings of military commissions. (Stanley Reed to H.F.S., Jan. 31, 1946.)

Stone capitulated. "To accommodate my opinion to the views of some of my brethren," he explained in a memorandum for the entire bench, he had deleted discussion of the Fifth Amendment and substituted instead, these sentences: "For reasons already stated we hold that the commission's rulings on evidence and on the mode of conducting these proceedings against petitioner are not reviewable by the courts, but only by the reviewing military authorities. From this viewpoint it is unnecessary to consider what, in other situations, the Fifth Amendment might require, and as to that no intimation one way or the other is to be implied. Nothing we have said is to be taken as indicating any opinion on the question of the wisdom of considering such evidence, or whether the action of a military tribunal in admitting evidence, which Congress or controlling military command has directed to be excluded, may be drawn in question by petition for habeas corpus or prohibition."[64]

As in the Quirin case, the Court was faced essentially with the problem of the extent of its review over determinations of military tribunals established under congressional enactment. Conceding that Congress could constitutionally authorize the creation of such tribunals, Stone pointed out that "it must be recognized throughout that the military tribunals which Congress has sanctioned by the Articles of War are not courts whose rulings and judgments are made subject to review by this Court." "They are tribunals whose determinations are reviewable by the military authorities either as provided in the military orders constituting such tribunals or as provided by the Articles of War." "Congress," he asserted, "conferred on the courts no power to review their determinations save only as it has granted judicial power 'to grant writs of habeas corpus for the purpose of an inquiry into the cause of restraint of liberty.'" For this reason "we conceive here only the lawful power of the commission to try the petitioner for the offense charged. . . . We are not concerned with . . . [his] guilt or innocence. . . ."[65]

On the "great issue" in Yamashita's appeal the opinion was all but silent. Some commentators have taken the view that it represents "a complete, as well as completely *silent*, retreat" from the doctrines of the Saboteurs opinion, and cite Justice Rutledge's dissent for authority. In the majority view, Rutledge wrote, "the action taken here is one of military necessity, exclusively within the authority of the President as Commander-in-Chief and his military subordinates to take in warding off military danger and subject to no judicial restraint on any account, although somewhat inconsistently it is said this Court may 'examine' the proceedings generally." As a realistic interpretation of what the Court had done, it is difficult to quarrel with Rutledge's statement that "the difference between the Court's view of this proceeding and my own comes down in the end to the view, on the one hand, that there is no law restrictive upon these proceedings other than whatever rules and regulations may be prescribed for their government by the executive authority or the military and, on the other hand, that the provisions of the Articles of War, of the Geneva Convention and the Fifth Amendment apply."[66]

Justice Murphy's dissent, however, registers an altogether different conception of how much and how little of its traditional scope of review the Court had saved. "This Court fortunately has taken the first and most important step toward insuring the supremacy of law and justice in the treatment of an enemy belligerent accused of violating the laws of war," he declared. "Jurisdiction properly has been asserted to inquire 'into the cause of restraint of liberty' of such a person. . . . Thus the obnoxious doctrine asserted by the Government in this case, to the effect that restraints of liberty resulting from military trials of war criminals are political matters completely outside the arena of judicial review, has been rejected fully and unquestionably."* The majority opinion itself relied heavily on *Ex parte Quirin* to sustain the conclusion "that Congress by sanctioning trials of enemy aliens by military commission for offenses against the law of war had recognized the right of the accused to make a defense. . . . It has not foreclosed their right to contend that the Constitution or laws of the United States withhold authority to proceed with the trial." This assertion is carefully qualified throughout, limiting the scope of judicial inquiry to that appropriate to review by habeas corpus—an examination of "the lawful power of the commission to try the petitioner for the offense charged."[67] In the circumstances in which it was drawn, the opinion's nebulous reference to the Fifth Amendment denies rather than affirms the Court's authority to interfere further with the proceedings of military commissions.

Stone's opinion walked a tightrope between the affirmation of a narrow scope of judicial review by way of habeas corpus and the view that action of military commissions was under no circumstances within the Court's power. "The most unqualified recognition of the subordination of the military to law should, of course, be made," Justice Frankfurter advised while the opinion was still in the plastic stage. "But under our Constitution, all branches of government are subject to law. That includes this Court. Accordingly, this Court must observe the bounds of its authority. Nothing is more incumbent on us than to

---

* For evidence that Murphy's distinction was meaningful, even to members of the Court who disagreed with him in 1946, see *Johnson v. Eisentrager,* 339 U.S. 763 (1950), where Justices Black, Douglas, and Burton argued in dissent that American courts can exercise the power of granting a writ of habeas corpus whenever any United States official illegally imprisons any person in any land governed by the United States, such as occupied Germany.

observe the settled limits of our reviewing power by habeas corpus. Needless to say, that writ is basic to the safeguarding of liberty—but liberty is not safeguarded by a misuse of the writ." The Chief Justice, moved in part by practical considerations, avoided all such high-sounding sentiments. But he did not succeed in achieving unanimity.

"After Chief Justice Stone had read the opinion of the Court on that fateful Monday morning," Yamashita's lawyer, Frank Reel, recalled, "Mr. Justice Murphy and Mr. Justice Rutledge* read their dissenting opinions in tones so bitter and in language so sharp that it was readily apparent to all listeners that even more acrimonious expression must have marked the debate behind the scenes. Justice Rutledge commenced his statement by saying: 'Not with ease does one find his views at odds with the Court's in a matter of this character and gravity. Only the most deeply felt convictions could force one to differ. That reason alone leads me to do so now, *against strong considerations for withholding dissent*'—and, as he uttered the last clause, Rutledge carefully turned and nodded in the Chief Justice's direction."[68]

Difficulties abounded even among the brethren who agreed with the Chief Justice, and kept him fully occupied. A driving force shaping his opinion was the desire to have it the only expression for the majority side. To the very last, he was in danger of losing one or more of his supporters. Without recourse to any glittering patina, he succeeded in holding the majority to the theory that military trials can be reviewed within sharply etched limits of habeas corpus. To uphold the military, however, required a strained interpretation of the Articles of War. Here the Chief Justice led a divided Court into obscurity, paying the price that one must always pay for artificial unanimity. Yamashita's chief counsel may seem justified in his description of the Court's opinion as "a patchwork of ideas and statements, pieced together to satisfy the divergent views of men who were seeking to find 'good' reasons for a politically expedient result."[69] Overlooked is the fact that in both the Quirin and Yamashita cases, Chief Justice Stone stood by his dictum of 1936: "Courts are not the only agency of government that must be assumed to have capacity to govern."[70]

* The Chief Justice was much troubled by Rutledge's defection. On April 21, 1946, the day before he died, Stone had spoken of the difficulties "to which the Court had lately been put by Justice Rutledge's failure to read carefully what he [Stone] had written on a case up for decision." (Marshall Stone's memoranda of December 1954.) The evidence points strongly to *Yamashita* as among the cases Stone had particularly in mind.

Justice Rutledge was also disturbed by his inability to go along with Stone. The day after the Chief Justice's death he spoke of how he had been "saddened by the fact that more and more we had come to vote differently on many matters." "I am not altogether clear," Rutledge added, "about the reason for this." (Wiley Rutledge to Luther Ely Smith, April 23, 1946.)

CHAPTER FORTY

# Freedom Versus Survival

## 1943-1944

Shortly after Chief Justice Stone had succeeded in fashioning a judicial bulwark for those rights* which constitute "the very essence of a scheme of ordered liberty,"[1] the Court's positive duty to protect those rights ran headlong into the preponderant needs of a nation at war.

Three months after the attack on Pearl Harbor, General J. L. De Witt, military commander of the Western Defense Command, issued a proclamation, pursuant to a Presidential Order and ratified by a congressional statute, establishing a curfew for all "alien Japanese, all alien Germans, all alien Italians, and all persons of Japanese ancestry" resident within specified military zones along the West Coast.[2] Two months later 112,000 persons of Japanese ancestry, two-thirds of them United States citizens by birth, were removed from their homes and properties to "assembly centers," and then to "relocation centers." These restrictions on Japanese residents of the Pacific states were justified in military orders as necessary to protect Army and Navy facilities, as well as industries and public utilities, from sabotage in the event of a Japanese invasion of the mainland.

Were a citizen's rights to live peaceably in his own home, to go and come as he might choose, to pursue an occupation undisturbed, any less expendable than freedom of religion? Was an Army General's estimate of the necessity for curbing these fundamental rights immune to "searching judicial scrutiny"? Answers to these questions were forthcoming early in 1943.

In *Hirabayashi* v. *United States* an American citizen had disobeyed both the curfew edict and an order to report to an assembly center preparatory to evacuation. With great caution the Justices, looking only at the validity of General De Witt's order of March 24, 1943, directing all "persons of Japanese ancestry" to remain in their homes from 8 p.m. to 6 a.m., refused to consider the detention order.† Though

---

* See Chapter XXXVI.

† Hirabayashi had been indicted and convicted on both counts: The district court had imposed separate sentences of three months each on the defendant, to run concurrently. Since that was the case, the Chief Justice reasoned, "it will be unnecessary to consider questions raised with respect to the first count [failure to report to an assembly center] if we find that the conviction on the second count, for violation of the curfew order, must be sustained." (Hirabayashi case, p. 85.)

such drastic invasion of the rights of United States citizens was unprecedented, the Chief Justice required only that "those charged with the responsibility of our national defense have reasonable ground for believing that the threat is real."[3] This test, while giving great latitude to military discretion, was also designed to keep the door ajar for judicial intervention.

Stone, however, saw no occasion to override the judgment of a military commander preparing to meet imminent invasion. The General, he thought, could rightly have concluded that the Japanese in the country, whether citizen or alien, constituted a menace because of their group solidarity and their cultivation of Japanese institutions and traditions. Aware, moreover, of the obvious difficulty, or indeed impossibility, of immediately separating the loyal from the disloyal, the Court upheld the curfew on an emergency basis. "Whatever views we may entertain regarding the loyalty to this country of the citizens of Japanese ancestry," the Chief Justice ruled, "we cannot reject as unfounded the judgment of the military authorities and of Congress that there were disloyal members of that population, whose number and strength could not be precisely and quickly ascertained."[4]

General De Witt's method of thus appraising the danger of sabotage among the Japanese was accepted, rather than approved, "in the light of facts of public notoriety." "Distinctions between citizens solely because of their ancestry," Stone asserted, "are by their very nature odious to a free people whose institutions are founded upon the doctrine of equality." "These considerations would be controlling here," he continued, "were it not for the fact that the danger of espionage and sabotage, in time of war and of threatened invasion, calls upon the military authorities to scrutinize every relevant fact bearing on the loyalty of populations in the danger areas." "We cannot say," he observed, "that these facts and circumstances, considered in the particular war setting, could afford no ground for differentiating citizens of Japanese ancestry from other groups in the United States. . . . We cannot close our eyes to the fact, demonstrated by experience, that in time of war residents having ethnic affiliations with an invading enemy may be a greater source of danger than those of a different ancestry."[5]

Justice Douglas, himself a resident of the West Coast, objected strenuously, not because he wished to have the Court "sit in judgment on the military requirements of the hour," but because he wished to eliminate from Stone's draft "any suggestion of racial discrimination." Part of the Chief's reasoning, he protested, "implies or is susceptible to the inference that the Japs who are citizens cannot be trusted because we have treated them so badly they will seize on this way to get even. 'Racial solidarity' and lack of 'assimilation' do not show lack of loyalty as I see it," he observed. Such circumstances may, he agreed, "give rise to conditions that may breed disloyalty. But that is quite a different matter." Loyalty being "a matter of heart and of mind, not of race," isolation of a single group for special treatment was without warrant. The curfew could be justified as a temporary expedient only because "the exigencies of war and the necessities of quick action in defending the nation against invasion do not necessarily permit time to sort out the sheep from the goats."

"Is it not necessary," Douglas asked the Chief Justice, deviating from the narrow area of review acceptable to the majority, "to provide an opportunity at some stage (although not necessarily in lieu of obedience to the military order) for an individual member of the group to show that he has been improperly classified?" "Otherwise," he commented, "if the military commander knows there are only 10 per cent of the group who are disloyal he can nevertheless hold the entire group in confinement for the duration without any opportunity on the part of the 90 per cent to prove that they are as loyal to the United States as members of this Court."[6]

Douglas's revolt put Stone in a difficult situation because some Justices in the majority insisted that the opinion be written in such a way as to suggest that all avenues of legal relief were foreclosed to the Japanese evacuees, who were herded into War Relocation Authority compounds. Stone tried to placate the rebellious Justice by adding the following reservation to his opinion:

We need not now attempt to define the ultimate boundaries of the war power. Nor do we have any occasion to decide whether circumstances and conditions which may have arisen since petitioner's disobedience of the curfew order, which are not before us, would afford a basis for judicial inquiry as to petitioner's loyalty or as to any other fact having a bearing on the danger of espionage and sabotage. Whether or to what extent such issues could be adjudicated in the courts, and whether the courts could provide a procedure for determining the loyalty of individual members of the group of citizens of Japanese ancestry, are questions which are likewise not before us in this case. We intimate no views concerning them.[7]

Stone's attempt to meet Douglas's objections was unavailing. Only the first sentence of the Chief Justice's statement survived. One Justice, feeling that it was a great mistake, in terms of both judicial administration and civil rights, to yield so much, went so far as to say that if he were the Commanding General he would not allow these men to go back even if the Court should establish their loyalty. Also, he was irreconcilably opposed to Douglas's invitation to the internees to bring a thousand habeas corpus suits in the district courts.

Stone, following his own methods, refused to discourage Douglas's inclination to publish his concurrence. "I am anxious to go as far as I reasonably can to meet the views of my associates," he wrote his former law student, "but it seems to me that if I accepted your suggestions very little of the structure of my opinion would be left, and that I should lose most of my adherents. It seems to me, therefore, that it would be wiser for me to stand by the substance of my opinion and for you to express your views in your concurring opinion as you have already done."[8]

Douglas made one further attempt to reorient the majority opinion. "The nub of the matter," he wrote, "is that I could not go along in an affirmance of the judgment below except on the assumptions (a) that the group treatment was temporary; (b) that the individual must have an opportunity to be reclassified as a loyal citizen."[9] As he suspected, this injection was "too great a gap for us to bridge"; his ideas could not prevail against a majority who declined to interpose judicial road-blocks in the way of those politically empowered to prosecute the war.

Stone's final opinion sustaining the curfew contains a description of the war power that, in the very breadth of its terminology, makes manifest the limits of judicial review in this area.

The war power of the National Government is "the power to wage war successfully." It extends to every matter and activity so related to war as substantially to affect its conduct and progress. The power is not restricted to the winning of victories in the field and the repulse of enemy forces. It embraces every phase of the national defense, including the protection of war materials and the members of the armed forces from injury and from the dangers which attend the rise, prosecution, and progress of war. Since the Constitution commits to the Executive and to Congress the exercise of the war power in all the vicissitudes and conditions of warfare, it has necessarily given them wide scope for the exercise of judgment and discretion in determining the nature and extent of the threatened injury or danger and in the selection of the means for resisting it.[10]

At the suggestion of one of the war hawks the Chief Justice appears to have sanctioned shrinking judicial review of the war power almost to the vanishing point. "Where, as they did here, the conditions call for the exercise of judgment and discretion and for the choice of means by those branches of the Government on which the Constitution has placed the responsibility of warmaking, it is not for any court to sit in review of the wisdom of their action or substitute its judgment for theirs." To hold other majority Justices who wanted it made unmistakably apparent that the decision was exceedingly narrow, he added: "We decide only the issue as we have defined it—we decide only that the curfew order as applied, and at the time it was applied, was within the boundaries of the war power."[11]

Despite this attempt at qualification, the Chief Justice's sweeping language stimulated Murphy and Rutledge to dissociate themselves from the idea that military acts are not subject to the same review the courts give other acts of government. "While this Court sits," Murphy declared, "it has the inescapable duty of seeing that the mandates of the Constitution are obeyed. That duty exists in time of war as well as in time of peace."[12] "I have had more anguish over this case than any I have decided, save possibly one death case in the Court of Appeals," Rutledge had told Stone. He had decided to cast his lot with the majority even though "hesitant about accepting" the stringent modifications offered by other Justices.[13] At the last moment his fear of the implications of their statements led him to speak out cautiously: "The officer of course must have wide discretion and room for its operation," he said. "But it does not follow there may not be bounds beyond which he cannot go and, if he oversteps them, that the courts may not have power to protect the civilian citizen."[14]

Douglas, of course, was not silenced, and his concurrence suggested that Hirabayashi might test out his loyalty in an independent habeas corpus suit. One Justice, somewhat exasperated—especially after the Chief Justice, while trying to placate divergent views, had carefully confined judicial approval of the exercise of military authority—scribbled on the back of his copy of Stone's opinion: "For the life of me, I cannot see why this should not satisfy everyone. It will—all who are guided by reason." From the moderate Reed, privately, came the comment that best exemplified the considerations uppermost in Stone's mind: "You have stated a very difficult situation in a way that will preserve rights in different cases and at the same time enable the military forces to function." It was, as Reed said, "a thankless job" and in his judgment Stone had "done it well."[15]

Reaction to the decision throughout the nation was predominantly unfavorable. Civil rights had been circumscribed. The curfew for Japanese citizens had been sustained, as one writer saw it, "because the Court found that it had 'some relation' to the winning of the war, because the Court would not 'sit in review of the wisdom' of administrative action, because the Court could not say that the Government 'did not have ground for believing' the curfew was necessary."[16]

Some questions the Court had not discussed in Hirabayashi came up forcibly later in *Korematsu* v. *United States* and *Ex parte Endo*. Fred Korematsu's appeal from a conviction for disobeying the order excluding all persons of Japanese ancestry from Military Zone No. 1 on the West Coast was utilized by his attorneys as an opportunity for attempting to secure judicial examination of the entire program for the Japanese—exclusion from designated areas, detention in assembly centers, and evacuation to relocation camps. By this time, however, it was understood that such wartime controls would soon be drastically modified, if not abandoned.* Proceeding slowly, ignoring the innate relation of exclusion to the whole resettlement program, the majority ruled that they need consider only the validity of exclusion. "In the light of the principles we announced in the Hirabayashi case," Justice Black wrote, "we are unable to conclude that it was beyond the war power of Congress and the Executive to exclude those of Japanese ancestry from the West Coast war area at the time they did." Exclusion from a critical area, "no less than curfew, has a definite and close relationship to the prevention of espionage and sabotage," he observed, and ". . . when under conditions of modern warfare our shores are threatened by hostile forces, the power to protect must be commensurate with the threatened danger."[17]

As national victory over both Japan and Germany appeared to be certain, the Justices' individualistic tendencies reasserted themselves in force. Three of them were no longer content to sanction all military decisions unquestioningly. Together they confronted Black with an unusual dissenting combination, representing each of the major blocs on Stone's bench. Roberts, alone as usual, inveighed against deciding the case on the theory that Korematsu had been given free opportunity to go anywhere in his native land except designated areas, when, in fact, he faced detention in a "concentration camp." Murphy, turning sharply on his erstwhile leader and comrade, denounced Black's opinion as "legalization of racism." The third dissenter, Jackson, felt that he had been led down the garden path in accepting Stone's Hirabayashi decision. "In that case we were urged to consider only the curfew feature," he complained indignantly. "We yielded, and the Chief Justice guarded the opinion as carefully as language will do. . . . The Court is now saying that in Hirabayashi we did decide the very things we there said we were not deciding. I think we should learn something from that experience."[18]

Black, moreover, faced possible disagreements in his own camp. He had to walk carefully because he knew that Douglas and Rutledge had only reluctantly adhered to Hirabayashi. As usual, the Chief Justice did not want the opinion to infer that the Court was deciding any more than that the power existed and that it had been "reasonably" exercised. In an early draft Black had said: "Nothing short of apprehension of the gravest imminent danger to the public safety can constitutionally justify either curfew or detention at assembly centers." "I think you should qualify this sentence," Stone suggested, "so as to show, as we were at pains to show in the Hirabayashi case, that it is not our apprehension or our judgment of the gravity and imminence of the danger which governs, but that of the military authorities

* On March 11, 1943, the director of the War Relocation Authority first suggested repeal of evacuation and exclusion orders.

charged with the responsibilities in the premises, provided only there is a basis for their judgment. Knowing your attitude about these matters, I am sure you will agree that it is important for us to make it plain that we do not impose our judgment on the military unless we can say that they have no ground on which to go in formulating their orders."[19]

The Chief Justice also insisted that the opinion consider only the constitutionality of Korematsu's detention at the assembly center, the sole ground upon which the indictment had been based, rather than scrutinize the entire governmental program. In an unprinted (and undelivered) concurring opinion, he set forth the reasons why "we are not free to decide petitioner's main contention that a relocation order applied to him would be unconstitutional." "Petitioner," he pointed out, "has not been convicted of violating a relocation order and in fact has never been subjected to such an order. He has been convicted of violating an Act of Congress which penalizes his disobedience of an [assembling] order which in effect required him, pending further orders, to enter and remain in an assembly center within the military zone where he then resided." Entrance into an assembly center did not automatically presume "detention under a relocation order," the Chief Justice told the opinion writer. "Many who were sent to the assembly center were not sent to relocation centers, but instead were released and sent out of the military area. We cannot say that petitioner would not have been released, as others were." Therefore, he told Black, "it seems plain that we have no constitutional question presented to us with reference to the . . . relocation step, but that we do have to determine whether the temporary segregation in an assembly center . . . is an unconstitutional detention."[20]

Black revised his opinion so as to refute the dissenters' objections.

On the same day the Korematsu case was decided the Justices considered the validity of a relocation and detention order.[21] With war pressures subsiding, the Court unanimously scuttled the confinement of loyal citizens in the desert compounds of the War Relocation Authority. Miss Mitsuye Endo was ordered released from a relocation center not on any constitutional ground but because the legislation and the executive orders underlying the entire evacuation program had made no mention of such detention.*

* Douglas, writing for the Court, stated: "In interpreting a wartime measure we must assume that their purpose was to allow for the greatest possible accommodation between . . . liberties and the exigencies of war. We must assume, when asked to find implied powers in a grant of legislative or executive authority, that the lawmakers intended to place no greater restraint on the citizen than was clearly and unmistakably indicated by the language they used." Finding that neither the congressional act nor the executive orders establishing critical areas on the coast "use the language of detention," he affirmed that "Mitsuye Endo is entitled to an

How did the Court define the scope of its power to review military acts impinging on civilian life? One tie binds the majority opinions: the Constitution commits warmaking to Congress and the President; judges must construe the exercise of such power as they do other delegated authority, with full cognizance of its special characteristics. In these cases Stone applied his usual criteria of judging. Since the Court's task was to pass on the validity of the power exercised, not on the "rightness" or "wrongness," the wisdom or unwisdom, of specific governmental action, he avoided constitutional issues wherever possible and confined the Court's opinion rigidly to the issue presented by the record. Aware of the responsibilities faced by Congress and the President and the sweeping constitutional mandate supporting them, he construed the scope of judicial power narrowly. But in war, as in peace, it was still appropriate for the Court to inquire "whether, in the light of all the relevant circumstances preceding and attending their promulgation, the challenged orders and statute afforded a reasonable basis for the action taken. . . ."[22]

Wartime conditions inevitably circumscribe individual freedoms. Spelling out the paramount considerations of nation vis-à-vis citizens under war conditions, he commented:

If it [were] an appropriate exercise of the war power its validity is not impaired because it has restricted the citizen's liberty. Like every military control of the population of a dangerous zone in wartime, it necessarily involves some infringement of individual liberty, just as does the police establishment of fire lines during a fire, or the confinement of people to their houses during an air-raid alarm—neither of which could be thought to be an infringement of constitutional right. Like them, the validity of the restraints of the curfew order depends on all the conditions which obtain at the time the curfew is imposed and which support the order imposing it.[23]

The opinions evoked sharp response. Among the Justices, the focal point of criticism was the charge that the Court "had validated the principle of racial discrimination in criminal procedure and of transplanting American citizens"* so that "the principle," Justice Jackson exploded, "then lies about like a loaded weapon ready for the hand of any authority that can bring forward a plausible claim of an urgent need."[24] Blessed with the perception of hindsight, most postwar com-

---

unconditional release by the War Relocation Authority." Justices Murphy and Roberts concurred separately, each resting his opinion on the alleged existence of a constitutional question which the Court "endeavors to avoid." (Endo case, pp. 300, 304, 308.)

* The majority, however, had been careful to point out that the restrictive measures had not been predicated "in the nature of group punishment based on antagonism to those of Japanese origin," that the "temporary exclusion" was bottomed on military determination "that it was impossible to bring about an immediate segregation of the disloyal from the loyal." (Korematsu case, p. 219.)

mentators have concluded that the exclusion and confinement of Japanese Americans was a blunder—an unnecessary one at that. "The sober fact is," a moderate critic observed, "that neither on the West Coast nor in the Hawaiian Islands was one single Japanese, citizen or non-citizen, convicted of one single act of sabotage in the entire course of the war.* Had the authorities stopped short with the curfew order of March 24, making violations of it subject to close military detention, every actual necessity would apparently have been met."[25] "No matter how narrowly the rule of proof is formulated," Eugene Rostow commented, "it could not have been satisfied in either the Hirabayashi or the Korematsu cases." "Despite the careful language of the Chief Justice," he continued, "these cases treat the decisions of military officials, unlike those of other government officers, as almost immune from ordinary rules of public responsibility."[26] "The worst single wholesale violation of civil rights of American citizens in our history," the American Civil Liberties Union said of mass evacuation.[27] Government policy toward the Japanese, another commentator said, "cut more deeply across those basic rights than has any government regulation thus far attempted."[28]

"Many factors indicate that the Court should have sharpened, rather than relaxed, its vigilance in considering the constitutionality of evacuation," a careful student declared. "Notable among these factors were the extreme gravity of the civil liberties deprivation; its racial character; the fact that people were condemned en masse rather than according to the principle of individual liability; and the belief held by many that evacuation was the result of public pressures and racial animosity rather than the result of carefully conceived military policy."[29]

Critics also deplored what was conceived to be a tendency to subordinate the civilian to the military authority. "Military discretion beyond the limit of tolerance in a democracy," reminded one commentator of George III, who, in rendering "the military independent of, and superior to, the civil power, incited the colonists to revolt."[30] "Japanese Americans were the immediate victims of the evacuation. But larger consequences are carried by the American people as a whole. Their legacy is the lasting one of precedent and constitutional sanctity for a policy of mass incarceration under military auspices. This is the

---

* Sabotage there may not have been, but subsequent events lend credence to the Government's emergency action in 1942. "That there were members of the [relocated] group who retained loyalties to Japan," the majority opinion in the Korematsu case asserted, had been confirmed by investigations made subsequent to the exclusion when it was ascertained that "approximately five thousand American citizens of Japanese ancestry refused to swear unqualified allegiance to the United States and to renounce allegiance to the Japanese Emperor, and several thousand evacuees requested repatriation to Japan." (Korematsu case, p. 219.)

most important result of the process by which the evacuation decision was made. That process betrayed all Americans."[31]

In the light of these decisions it is clear that the Constitution tips the scales in favor of authority, and thus furnishes adequate power for any emergency—even global war. War subsumes to its purposes the entire Constitution and all organs of government, including the Supreme Court. In time of international conflict or civil strife the power-generating provision is that designating the President as Commander-in-Chief. Such a grant, great as it is, is not unlimited. The Constitution assumes that he, as a politically responsible civilian executive, will exert an overriding supervision of the military. Congress, too, has ample opportunity to vindicate the civilian character of free government. In time of war the stakes are high. The two political branches had opposed strict construction, since error might mean death for some individuals or defeat for the nation as a whole. Clearly, the Justices did not wish to obstruct prosecution of the war. Nor did they completely ignore those rights that constitute the very bases of any system of ordered liberty. They were confronted with Lincoln's poignant dilemma: "Must a government of necessity be too strong for the liberties of its people, or too weak to maintain its own existence?"[32] In the circumstances, it is understandable that the judges avoided the risk of rendering it too weak.

The sharp dissents in the Korematsu case plainly indicated that war-born subordination of judicial power to military expediency would soon end. Three Justices, at least, were growing restive, perhaps apprehensive, lest judicial review atrophy in idleness. Their next brush with military law, as applied to American citizens, brought forth decisive revival of judicial authority over the acts, even the wartime acts, of Army commanders.

The question decided struck close to the bench itself—whether military tribunals in Hawaii could supersede civilian courts in dispensing justice to civilians. Martial law, purporting to set up complete military government, was declared in the Islands a few hours after the attack on Pearl Harbor. Thereafter justice with a khaki tinge enlivened Island life. Two victims of swift, rough military law appealed to the courts for aid, and after some delays their cases were decided by the Supreme Court in January 1946.

Justice Black's four-man majority opinion, claiming support from the constitutional history of the nation, affirmed that the phrase "martial law" in the Organic Act establishing government for Hawaii, "while intended to authorize the military to act vigorously for the maintenance of an orderly civil government and for the defense of the Islands against actual or threatened rebellion or invasion, was not intended to authorize the supplanting of courts by military tribunals." The opinion, though invoking the Organic Act for Hawaii, was actually buttressed on the deeper constitutional conviction that no circumstances except "the establishment of a military government over recently occupied enemy territory" could ever justify substituting military for civil courts. Maintenance of the courts is "indispensable to our system of government," he declared. "They were set up by our founders to protect the liberties they valued."

"Our system of government," Black concluded, "clearly is the antithesis of total military rule, and the founders of this country are not likely to have contemplated complete military dominance within the limits of a Territory not recently taken from an enemy. They were opposed to governments that placed in the hands of one man the power to make, interpret, and enforce the laws."[33]

The Chief Justice disagreed and outlined his position in a memorandum sent to Black before the case came down. Diverging from Black's attempt to set strict limits upon martial law where the Constitution did not so command, Stone wrote: "I have no doubt that martial law could be constitutionally imposed in appropriate circumstances which would authorize the closing of the courts and the substitution of some kind of military justice adequate to the situation." The case presented "primarily a question of interpretation of the statute which authorizes the imposition of martial law." For its disposition, "I do not think we have to state what the constitutional limits of martial law are, or to define martial law, for all purposes, with precision." The object of martial law "defines its limits. I should not be prepared to say that under no circumstances, when the public safety and order require it, the military, having authority to apply martial law, could not set up courts and try offenses. But it is enough for present purposes, even assuming danger of invasion, that there is no public necessity of creating military courts when the civil courts are open and able to function." From the depths of his own convictions as to the role of the Court, and in light of the limited considerations which the instant case demanded, he concluded:

It seems to me that when Congress adopted this provision it adopted and emphasized the limitation upon the extent to which martial law can be applied by limiting it to those cases where it is needful in the interest of public safety and good order. That idea, fully developed, decides the case. As background material your emphasis on the early history of the country, both judicial and military, upon the importance of keeping the courts open, plus the cases in this Court dealing with the subject, gives broad support for such a construction of the statute. At the same time that construction does not render it impossible in time of great emergency to afford through martial law a means for adequately protecting the public safety. Such a treatment

of this case does not deny authority to Congress and the Executive to authorize martial law in appropriate cases. But it does restrain the military in the
execution of its authority.[34]

Stone, unable to persuade Black and the majority, embodied the
substance of these views in a concurring opinion.

As in calmer times the Justices split widely. But the Chief Justice,
throughout, hewed to the line he had consistently applied since that
far off day in March 1925 when he had followed Chief Justice Taft
out through the curtain to take his seat on the Supreme Bench. In
war, as in peace, the Constitution was a flexible "instrument of government"—it both grants and limits power. Power and rights must be
balanced. To achieve this delicate equilibrium the political and judicial
processes must be so integrated as to preserve those inextricably
related values—the public good and private rights. The core of Stone's
wartime jurisprudence was still the same as that which had prompted
him eight years earlier to uphold the assertion of national authority
over the economic life of the nation.

CHAPTER FORTY-ONE

# Palladium of Freedom

## 1944-1945

During World War II civil liberty enjoyed "a vitality which even the
optimist had hardly dared hope for."[1] In this area the Justices made
good the proud American boast that "men are not subjected to criminal
punishment because their conduct offends our patriotic emotions."[2]
Judicial review, which in the eyes of many critics lay prostrate before
military authority, proved quite supple in coping with civilian threats
to freedom of speech, press, and political beliefs. A majority of the
Court, and especially the Chief Justice, showed themselves decidedly
hostile to government attempts to convict George Sylvester Viereck,
a Nazi propagandist, for concealing information while registering as a
foreign agent. Viereck had freely admitted that he served the German
Government and listed among his activities everything for which he
was paid by the Nazis. He had omitted, however, to disclose private
ventures in propaganda, much of which aped the Nazi line. As Stone
saw it, Viereck's conviction could stand only if failure to disclose
propaganda activities on his own account had been made criminal by

the registration statute—a point of construction the Chief Justice decided in the defendant's favor.

The case was further discolored, in Stone's opinion, by Prosecutor William Powers Maloney's inflammatory summing-up appeals to the jury: "This is war. It is a fight to the death. The American people are relying upon you ladies and gentlemen for their protection against this sort of a crime, just as much as they are relying upon the protection of the men who man the guns in Bataan Peninsula, and everywhere else. They are relying upon you ladies and gentlemen for their protection. We are at war. You have a duty to perform here. As a representative of your Government I am calling upon every one of you to do your duty."[3]

Speaking for the majority in a 5 to 2 decision, the Chief Justice denounced the prosecutor's emotionalism as "an appeal wholly irrelevant to any facts or issues in the case, the purpose and effect of which could only have been to arouse passion and prejudice." "At a time when passion and prejudice are heightened by emotions stirred by our participation in a great war," the Chief Justice said, "we do not doubt that these remarks addressed to the jury were highly prejudicial, and that they were offensive to the dignity and good order with which all proceedings in court should be conducted."[4]

Justice Frankfurter had urged the Chief Justice to tone down his rebuke, but Stone was hot under the collar because he had "the impression that misconduct like that of the prosecuting attorney in this case is pretty frequent in the federal courts, and is almost certain to occur if the case happens to be an important one where the Government sends a prosecutor who has gained a reputation for getting verdicts."[5]

A few weeks before, Stone had seized the opportunity to tell a gathering of federal judges of their duty "to see to it . . . that the emotions of war are kept out of the courtroom, that all cases should be tried without the passions and prejudices that are aroused by a war."[6] He wanted to elaborate his statement from the bench. Justice Frankfurter also advised against this, and the Chief, not wishing to "overplay a good tune," yielded. Instead he quoted Justice Sutherland's ten-year-old admonition to prosecutors, which was even headier than what he had proposed to say.*

Viereck's career had aroused intense emotions, and the Court's decision elicited a great deal of comment.† Editorialists, by and large,

* "The United States Attorney," Sutherland had said, "may prosecute with earnestness. But, while he may strike hard blows, he is not at liberty to strike foul ones." (*Berger* v. *United States,* 295 U.S. 78 [1933], p. 88.)

† "The case made hot news copy and editorial writers had great sport canonizing or damning Stone or Maloney. Shortly after Stone's punch Attorney General Biddle shifted Maloney to other work." (Wesley McCune, *The Nine Young Men,* p. 155.)

cited Stone's opinion as pointing up "the strongest contrast that could be drawn between the Nazi and American ways of life," and characterized the decision as a "test case of democracy." Many took the middle-road position, saying that while it was "lamentable that this recognized enemy provocateur should go free of punishment," still "we glory in a judicial system that meticulously serves justice, despite the pressures and emotions of war." Even those editors who had been highly critical of the Court took "particular pleasure in echoing a layman's hearty amen to the Viereck decision and to the Court's observations with respect to the conduct of the trial."[7]

Others saw the matter in a different light. The *Chicago Times* scored Stone's opinion as giving support to "ballyhoo," as calculated to make Viereck "a martyr of Department of Justice persecution." "Let's Try Viereck Again, Not Reward That Nazi," the *Philadelphia Record* clamored. Still others wondered whether the decision meant "that democracy, in the midst of a world war, is unable to protect itself against those who would destroy it from within." As to this Raymond Moley, at least, had no doubts. Stone's opinion had proved to him that "there will be no breakdown of civil rights during the present war." The Viereck decision had confirmed and deepened the court's role as the palladium of the people's freedom. "The Chief Justice," Moley observed, "reminded us that we can fight and die, if need be, for republican institutions without suspending them here at home."[8]

The Chief Justice also received letters reflecting the partisan feelings Viereck had stimulated. A war mother in Massachusetts told him how his Court had "set a new low in patriotism." Another woman correspondent accused him of setting "the devil himself free to do what he pleases and to work against us." Contrariwise, one writer, who called himself "America First and proud of it," attacked Viereck's prosecutor, informing Stone that "it is about time we prosecuted the Smear Campaigners and the borers from within, especially men like Maloney."[9] Only one correspondent deserved more than mere acknowledgment. "I have for more than twenty-five years held George Viereck in great contempt and thus feel all the prouder as an American of the decision you recently delivered in his case," Alfred A. Knopf wrote. "It should hearten all Americans, I think, to realize that in the midst of total war our highest court can still show such consideration for the rights of a member of even the most unpopular minority." "Thank you for your kind letter, which I greatly appreciate," Stone replied. "I am quite sure that you realize that the judicial task is not always an easy one."[10]

A far more controversial task lay immediately ahead in *Schneiderman* v. *United States*. Here the Court was called upon to decide whether the citizenship of Communists can be revoked on the ground that they favor overthrow of the Government by force and violence. Twice argued before the Supreme Court, the case had hung fire for four years. Wendell Willkie's appearance in the high Court as Schneiderman's counsel underscored the political dynamite in his appeal. Government efforts to make Communist activity ground for denaturalization affected perhaps a handful of American citizens. After Russia's entry into the war on the side of the United Nations, however, the asserted principle seemed internationally indiscreet. In any event, the Justice Department successfully delayed argument through the 1941 term.

The Chief Justice's annoyance at political tinkering with the business of his Court is evident in the memorandum he circulated on April 18, 1942. "The Government, for reasons which are obvious, has found it embarrassing to proceed with this case at the present juncture and has secured several postponements, the last one on consent of Mr. Willkie. While I should be glad to have the case postponed by agreement of counsel, my own view is that the Court cannot rightly force its postponement over Mr. Willkie's objections."

For Stone the case called up an issue that he had never fully resolved—how far did the statutory requirement of "attachment to constitutional principles" authorize the Justices to ignore that other American precept, freedom to think and act politically as one sees fit? Since 1918 he had been confronted by various radical programs calculated to destroy law enforcement and orderly government. Political objectors to World War I had personified the dilemma; so had Rosika Schwimmer. William Schneiderman, erstwhile Communist candidate for Governor of Minnesota, presented the same grim threat to American institutions. Carefully, soberly, the Chief Justice outlined at conference a view of the naturalization statute that would permit the Government to rid the nation of such agitators. "Your exposition of Schneiderman was masterly," one Justice commented enthusiastically. Nevertheless a majority, speaking through Justice Murphy, said that mere evidence of active Communist party membership did not give "clear, unequivocal, and convincing" proof of a naturalized citizen's lack of attachment to principles of the Constitution. "Under our traditions, beliefs are personal and not a matter of mere association," Murphy declared. "Men in adhering to a political party or other organization notoriously do not subscribe to all of its platforms or asserted principles."[11] Murphy avoided discussing what to Stone was the heart of the case—"attachment to the principles of the Constitution." That is, whether petitioner, in securing his citizenship by naturalization, had fulfilled a condition imposed by Congress, that during the five years preceding his application "he has behaved as a man . . . attached to the principles of the Constitution of the United States, and well disposed to the good order and happiness of the same." "You must lay it out in your dissent with all the powerful detail with which you stated the case to us," a colleague had written the Chief Justice encouragingly. Whether prompted by this suggestion or not, Stone's dissent is perhaps the bitterest he had written since 1936.

"My brethren of the majority do not deny that there are principles of the Constitution," he observed sarcastically. "In the absence of any disclaimer I shall assume that there are such principles and that among them are at least the principle of constitutional protection of civil rights and of life, liberty, and property, the principle of representative government, and the principle that constitutional laws are not to be broken down by planned disobedience. I assume also that all the principles of the Constitution are hostile to dictatorship and minority rule; and that it is a principle of our Constitution that change in the organization of our government is to be effected by the orderly procedure ordained by the Constitution and not by force or fraud."[12]

The question of Schneiderman's opinions was not at issue, "save as they may have influenced or may explain his conduct showing attachment, or want of it, to the principles of the Constitution." And "such attachment or want of it is a personal attribute to be inferred from all the relevant facts and circumstances which tend to reveal petitioner's attitude toward those principles." Turning to the aspirations of the Communists, the Chief Justice continued:

It is not questioned that the ultimate aim of the Communist party in 1927 and the years preceding was the triumph of the dictatorship of the proletariat and the consequent overthrow of capitalistic or bourgeois government and society. Attachment to such dictatorship can hardly be thought to indicate attachment to the principles of an instrument of government which forbids dictatorship and precludes the rule of the minority or the suppression of minority rights by dictatorial government.

Stone supported these conclusions by recourse to official Communist pronouncements. "Methods repeatedly and systematically advocated in the Communist party literature . . . include first a softening-up process by which the breakdown and disintegration of capitalistic governments was to be achieved by systematic and general resort to violation of the laws, and second, the overthrow of capitalistic governments by force and violence." In support of all this, the Chief Justice's opinion carried heavily documented footnotes together with an appendix containing a three-page extract from Lenin's *State and Revolution*. Citing Marx and Engels' *Communist Manifesto* of 1848 as "the fountain head of Communist principles," he noted Engels' forthright announcement that "Revolution is an act in which part of the population forces its will on the other parts by means of rifles, bayonets, cannon, i.e., by the most authoritative means." Once the revolutionaries are triumphant, "the conquering party is inevitably forced to maintain its supremacy by means of that fear which its arms inspire in the reactionaries." Under such a government, Stone observed, citing Stalin's *Theory and Practice of Leninism*, "there can be no talk of 'freedom' for everybody. The dictatorship of the proletariat is incompatible with the freedom of the bourgeoisie."[13]

Justice Rutledge, looking beyond the case at bar, saw in Stone's position dire implications: "Immediately we are concerned with only one man, William Schneiderman. Actually, though indirectly, the decision affects millions." Rutledge depicted how this was so. If a man's citizenship can be taken away, after "nothing more than re-examination upon the merits of the very facts the judgment [granting citizenship] established," then "no citizen with such a threat hanging over his head could be free." "If he belonged to 'off-color' organizations or held too radical or, perhaps, too reactionary views, for some segment of the judicial palate, when his admission took place, he could not open his mouth without fear his words would be held against him. . . . Such a citizen would not be admitted to liberty. His best course would be silence or hypocrisy." "This," Rutledge concluded, "is not citizenship."[14]

Such considerations, however telling, seemed to be lost on the Chief Justice and his fellow dissenters, Frankfurter and Roberts. Undaunted, they stuck resolutely to their view that adherence to communism was ample cause to revoke a former alien's citizenship. The Communist party stands opposed to every principle on which the Constitution rests. "It would be little short of preposterous," Stone argued, "to assert that vigorous aid knowingly given" to such a party "is compatible with attachment to the principles of the Constitution." "A man can be known by the ideas he spreads as well as by the company he keeps." Yet the Court's opinion "seems to tell us . . . that the trier of fact could not 'impute' to petitioner any genuine attachment to the doctrines of these organizations whose teachings he so assiduously spread. It might as well be said that it is impossible to infer that a man is attached to the principles of a religious movement from the fact that he conducts its prayer meetings, or, to take a more sinister example, that it could not be inferred that a man is a Nazi and consequently not attached to constitutional principles who, for more than five years, had diligently circulated the doctrines of *Mein Kampf*."[15]

Back of the heat in these lines lay the unmistakable feeling that the majority did not give a rap for the law but fashioned an opinion out of whole cloth to meet the exigencies of international politics. Both Murphy and Stone expressly disavowed any connection between this case and American-Soviet relations. But why had Murphy, as Attorney

General in 1939, permitted the prosecution to proceed if, as he now intimated in the opinion, the statute never authorized such a suit? What had happened between the Nazi-Soviet Pact of 1939 and 1943 to cause his change of heart? "What is plain as a pikestaff," a colleague told Stone, "is that the present war considerations—political considerations—are the driving force behind the result of this case. It is very painful for me to say so, but I do not think there is the slightest doubt that if the same kind of a record had come up with reference to a Bundist, the opposite result would have been reached." After two arguments and nearly a year's deliberation, the majority opinion boiled down, in Stone's judgment, to a decision that "the Court at least ought to treat Communists more tenderly than Congress and the statutes had done."[16]

Nor can the minority be held to have avoided completely the influence of "political considerations." "I strongly hope," one Justice wrote Stone, "that you will begin your opinion by saying . . . that this case has nothing to do with the conduct of the war, with our relations with Russia, with one's past or present view regarding the Russian political or social system; that it has to do, on the other hand, with the conception of American nationhood and the relation of the principles of the Constitution to that nationhood." When Stone promptly adopted the suggestion, Murphy did not let this implied slur pass in silence. He swiftly added to his opinion a statement agreeing "with our brethren of the minority that our relations with Russia, as well as our views regarding its government and the merits of communism, are immaterial to a decision of this case."[17]

Comparisons with the Soviet Union were inevitable. The Chief Justice must, a colleague insisted, convey the idea that "Congress has the right to exact from aliens, to whom the privileges of citizenship are granted, attachment to the principles of the Constitution of the United States as much as the U.S.S.R. has the right to exact, and has exacted, devotion to its principles from Russian citizens." "At the core of the whole question," he said, "is whether attachment to the principles of the Constitution precludes political attachment to another independent political society, whether it be that of Russia or of Great Britain or of Germany." In fact, for this Justice, "the essence of this case is the very simple vindication of the old truth that one cannot serve, in thought and feeling and action, two independent masters."

The press comment, though somewhat reassuring, was by no means unanimous in praise of the Chief Justice's scorching dissent. The *Washington Star* considered the majority's ruling "extraordinary" and said that Stone's "sharp" protest was "in line with the practical judgment of the American people." The *Macon Telegraph* joined the Chief Justice in ridiculing the "idea that a man did not subscribe to the doctrine of a party which he had voluntarily joined. . . . We can only infer that Murphy and his associates are moved by political considerations, as usual." The *Norfolk Virginian-Pilot* was less certain that the Chief Justice was on the right track. "By reasoning" similar to Stone's, the editor commented, "the Italian Fascist state has canceled the citizenship of Italian Free Masons. We prefer Justice Murphy's dictum that where two interpretations of an organization's program are possible, the one reprehensible and a bar to naturalizations and the other permissible, a court in a denaturalization proceeding . . . is not justified in canceling a certificate of citizenship by imputing the reprehensible interpretation to a member of the organization in the absence of overt acts indicating that such was his interpretation.'" "Seven million naturalized citizens of the United States are more secure in their rights, and the principles of the Constitution are more firmly established," the *Chicago Sun* declaimed, "because of a decision handed down this week by the United States Supreme Court."[18]

Other editors hailed Murphy's opinion as "based on decency and common sense, even though so splendid a liberal as the Chief Justice joined a minority of three dissenting from the decision." "Socially, we may look askance at a man because of the company he keeps, but legally, we can impose no hardships on him because of his beliefs, or his associations, until action, or the immediate threat of it, subjects him to the rigor of the law."[19]

The Chief Justice could find little comfort in such press reaction. Private citizens, however, were laudatory. To a Pawtucket woman the majority of Justices "show all too plainly the pernicious influence of the New Deal."[20] "His [Schneiderman's] oath was a false oath," said another, "taken so that he might establish himself as an American citizen for the sole reason and purpose to be free to advocate a different form of government in our United States, under our constitutional guarantee of free speech."[21] "Did Schneiderman's acts in the United States indicate that he worked 'to form a more perfect union'? Did he work to 'establish justice'? Did he try 'to insure domestic tranquility'?" still another critic of the majority decision asked. "If you have time and the inclination to read my dissenting opinion," Stone responded, "you will see what I thought was the appropriate answer to your questions."[22]

The question one of the Justices had speculated about at the time of the Schneiderman decision—what sort of treatment might be accorded a naturalized member of the defunct Bund—actually did arise a year later. Far from turning tables, the Court unanimously set aside the denaturalization of a German-American citizen accused of continued allegiance to the German Reich. Justice Frankfurter's draft opinion made no mention of the Schneiderman decision. "I am with you in Baumgartner," Stone wrote, "notwithstanding Murphy's lament that you do not cite the Schneiderman case." But, he suggested, "if it would appease him, I would not object to saying that there was a lack in Baumgartner of the clear and convincing evidence which some members of the Court thought was present in the Schneiderman case."[23] Frankfurter repaired the oversight, but the damage had been done. The original omission stimulated Murphy to concur separately so as to announce expressly that the Schneiderman rule "is equally applicable whether the citizen against whom the proceeding is brought is a Communist, a Nazi, or a follower of any other political faith."[24]

At the same time a majority, including the Chief Justice, gave strong support to free speech in wartime, effectively halting prosecutions under the Espionage Act of 1917 for attempts to obstruct the draft or stimulate disloyalty in the armed forces by dissemination of propaganda. In the first such prosecution to reach the Supreme Court in World War II, the defendant, a native-born citizen, circulated scurrilous and vitriolic attacks on England, the Jews, and F.D.R., depicting the war as a great betrayal and urging its conversion into a race war against Asiatics. But, the Court said, "unless there is sufficient evidence from which a jury could infer beyond a reasonable doubt that he intended to bring about the specific consequences prohibited by the Act, an American citizen has the right to discuss these matters either by temperate reasoning or by immoderate and vicious invective."[25] Reed, Frankfurter, Douglas, and Jackson dissented.

In another 5 to 4 decision a year later, the Justices threw out the Government's prosecution of twenty-five German-American Bund leaders. This time, however, the Chief Justice led the dissenters.

The majority credited the petitioners' claim that the Bund, alleging that certain sections of the Selective Service Act were discriminatory and unconstitutional, had counseled refusal to do military service until a test case was brought and the Act's validity established. Stone cast this view brusquely aside. "There is no freedom to conspire to violate a statute with impunity merely because its constitutionality is doubted." For him the only substantial question for decision was whether the jury could rightly find that the Bund did in fact counsel evasion. "The conclusion seems inevitable," he wrote, "that petitioners, by counseling Bund members to refuse to do military duty, counseled evasion of military service, and that the jury's verdict of violation of Section 11 [of the Selective Service Act] is therefore sustained by the evidence."[26]

Government prosecutors fared little better in their efforts to bring to book on charges of treason Anthony Cramer, a naturalized American and old acquaintance of the Nazi saboteur Werner Thiel, who had befriended the German after the latter's notorious arrival on American shores by submarine in June 1942. Responding to a message from

Thiel, Cramer met him several times in New York, where, under the alert eye of FBI agents, he took Thiel's funds for safekeeping and notified friends of Thiel's presence in this country. All this he did, or so he insisted, for "old times' sake," though he admitted suspecting that Thiel had been sent to the United States on a mission for Germany. The only overt acts proved against him by two witnesses were the meetings with the saboteur; these acts were innocent if unexplained, as the FBI men had been unable to eavesdrop. A jury, however, found him guilty of treason in "adhering to enemies" of the United States.

When Cramer's appeal reached the Supreme Court, the Justices at first were all but agreed that the Government had improperly introduced damaging evidence, making a new trial imperative. After lengthy discussion at conference centering on the question whether it would be desirable "to pass on the substantive question of treason," they decided to dispose of the case on the evidence without interpretation of the constitutional provision governing treason trials.* Some of the brethren were of the opinion that it was well to dodge the constitutional point for the time being rather than arouse "a close division on an important question in the middle of the war."[27]

The Chief Justice, however, could not acquiesce. If Cramer were retried, no doubt he would appeal again, and the Court would then be forced to rule on the constitutional issue. Therefore he thought it "wise to decide the question now so that the jury might be properly instructed on a new trial."[28]

The Chief Justice set forth the dilemma: "We are forced to decide whether the overt acts charged must, by themselves, standing alone, manifest a treasonable purpose."[29] Objecting to any interpretation of the treason clause that would require the overt act in itself to reveal the treasonable intentions, he wrote Douglas:

> It seems to me that one of the great difficulties in the adoption of such a test of the overt act is the extreme difficulty in its application, and that in cases of giving aid and comfort to the enemy, especially here at home, there would be almost no overt acts which, unexplained by other evidence, would indicate the treasonable purpose. The effect of such an interpretation would be to emasculate the treason provision except in cases of levying war where in some but not all instances the warlike act would itself evidence the treasonable purpose.[30]

The difficulty affected more than this case. "If the offense is treason but the overt act cannot be proven as required by the Constitution," he speculated, "could Congress enact a statute which would punish

---

* Article III, Section 3, says: "Treason against the United States shall consist only in levying war against them, or in adhering to their enemies, giving them aid and comfort. No person shall be convicted of treason unless on the testimony of two witnesses to the same overt act, or on confession in open court."

it if the act charged is in fact and law treason? Punishment is forbidden by the Constitution unless it is proven in the manner provided by the Constitution. That would seem to exclude the possibility of Congress's providing by legislation for the punishment of acts constituting treason as defined by the Constitution, without meeting the constitutional requirement as to overt acts." "I think it would be difficult," he concluded, "for Congress to provide a punishment for Cramer if we hold that the overt acts charged do not meet the constitutional test."[31]

Stone's interpretation did not pass unchallenged. "After sleeping on and pondering much over your memorandum," one Justice wrote, "this is what comes up. Wise old Ben Franklin convinced the Constitution makers that 'prosecutions for treason were generally virulent,' and perjury too easily made use of against innocence . . . and so the Constitution makers decided that it is not enough to prove treasonable agreements, you must also prove 'an overt act,' and, what is more, you must prove it by two witnesses." Admittedly, the same Justice wrote, this view "makes it extremely difficult to prove treason, but that is precisely what Franklin meant to accomplish and what he persuaded the Constitution makers to enjoin."

Meanwhile the majority in favor of reversing Cramer's conviction merely on the evidence was crumbling. Justice Black, who had started to write the reversal, came to the conclusion that "if a conviction is not to be sustained on evidence such as the Government produced here, I doubt if there could be many convictions for treason unless American citizens were actually found in the Army of the enemy." "From the way the case was argued," Black explained, "I gathered the impression that there had been an inexcusable accumulation of evidence concerning the conspiracy and activities of the saboteurs. The Record in my judgment does not sustain such a conclusion. . . . Reading the entire Record has left me with the impression that Cramer was given a fair trial. Able counsel appointed for him took advantage of every point that could be suggested in his favor. After such a trial, the jury found him guilty of treason, and the examination I have made has led me to conclude that the jury's verdict was justified by the evidence."[32]

After some delay the Court ordered reargument on the constitutional question.[33] When, a year later, they finally reached a decision, a five-judge majority ruled that the Government had not made out a case under the constitutional standard of proof for treason—testimony from two witnesses to the same overt act of treachery.

Government power, checkreined on every occasion when it conflicted with the exercise of freedom of expression and political belief, now found its ability to prosecute for treason drastically curtailed.

"Never before [had] the Court had occasion to review a conviction. In the century and a half of our national existence not one execution on a Federal treason conviction had taken place."[34] The Cramer decision left that record unchanged. "The sum total" of the rulings to date, one writer concluded, "is the near elimination of treason from the calendar of provable crimes under the Constitution."[35]

Some measure of the total effect of the Court's work may perhaps be gained by comparing what it permitted the Government to do with Mr. Justice Sutherland's earlier statement of what the Government might do in wartime. Sutherland's 1931 pronouncement, then considered extreme, said:

> To the end that war may not result in defeat, freedom of speech may, by act of Congress, be curtailed or denied so that the morale of the people and the spirit of the Army may not be broken by seditious utterances; freedom of the press curtailed to preserve our military plans and movements from the knowledge of the enemy; deserters and spies put to death without indictment or trial by jury; ships and supplies requisitioned; property of alien enemies, theretofore under the protection of the Constitution, seized without process and converted to the public use without compensation and without due process of law in the ordinary sense of that term; prices of food and other necessities of life fixed or regulated; railways taken over and operated by the Government; and other drastic powers, wholly inadmissible in time of peace, exercised to meet the emergencies of war.[36]

Though the Court under Chief Justice Stone did not invalidate congressional attempts to punish "seditious utterances," it placed considerable obstacles in the way of the first part of Sutherland's statement. The second portion, however, dealing with wartime curbs on property rights, obviously does not begin to catalogue the vast economic controls the Government exercised during World War II. In passing on measures designed to effectuate regulation of business, the Justices were even called upon to sanction congressional curtailment of their own power and to square government action to safeguard the national welfare with the traditional demands of procedural due process.

Under the Emergency Price Control Act of 1942 Congress established an Emergency Court of Appeals, granting to it exclusive power to enjoin orders issued by the Office of Price Administration (OPA) and to determine the validity of regulations issued by the Price Administrator. There could be little protest so long as cases came to that court, but the OPA Administrator was empowered to prosecute violations of his regulations in any federal district court or state court in the country. In such trials the issues were immediately reduced to questions of guilt or innocence of the acts charged; the defendants were denied the opportunity to raise any question as to the validity of the regulations under which they were being tried. In the leading case on this issue, Albert Yakus, a wholesale meat dealer in Massachusetts, was haled before a United States District Court, convicted, and sentenced to a fine and imprisonment for violation of an order establishing maximum beef prices, an order he had not protested in the statutory manner through appeal to the OPA Administrator and the Emergency Court of Appeals.*

The narrow question at issue was "whether the validity of a regulation may be challenged in defense of a prosecution for its violation although it had not been tested by the prescribed administrative procedure and complaint to the Emergency Court of Appeals." Asserting that "Congress has constitutional authority to prescribe commodity prices as a war emergency measure, and that the Act was adopted by Congress in the exercise of that power," Stone sustained the procedural sections of the statute under the constitutional power "to prescribe the jurisdiction of inferior federal courts, and the jurisdiction of all state courts to determine federal questions." Congress could, he said, remove equity jurisdiction to restrain enforcement of price regulations from the District Courts and confer it exclusively upon the Emergency Court of Appeals and the Supreme Court. It could also remove from the lower courts "power to consider the validity of a price regulation as a defense to a criminal prosecution for its violation." The validity of the Administrator's regulations should not be subject to attack in lower court proceedings, "at least before their invalidity had been adjudicated by recourse to the protest procedure prescribed by the statute."[37]

In reply to the charge that Yakus had been deprived of due process of law guaranteed by the Fifth Amendment, the Court pointed out the existence of the "grave danger of wartime inflation and the disorganization of our economy from excessive price rises." Incalculable harm might result, it was suggested, if enforcement of the nation-wide price regulations were "delayed or sporadic," or were made ineffective by injunction "in advance . . . of final determination of their validity." The system of splitting judicial review of the validity of regulations from cases involving their enforcement did not offend against due process, Stone ruled, "so long as it affords to those affected a reasonable opportunity to be heard and present evidence."[38]

The Chief Justice was at pains to confine the issue narrowly. Since Yakus had not tested the validity of the beef regulation under which he had been imprisoned, the Court need do no more than pass on the due process sanctity of OPA's procedural system. "Only if we could

* Previously the Court had upheld the exclusive jurisdiction of the Emergency Court of Appeals to consider the validity of OPA regulations. (*Lockerty v. Phillips,* 319 U.S. 182 [1943].)

say in advance of resort to the statutory procedure," he commented, "that it is incapable of affording due process to petitioners, could we conclude that they have shown any legal excuse for their failure to resort to it or that their constitutional rights have been or will be infringed."[39] When and if such constitutional questions arose in the proper cases, the Court gave notice that it stood ready to determine whether fundamental rights had been abrogated.

Justice Rutledge, ignoring the Chief Justice's qualifications, vigorously attacked the decision* as a departure from settled principles:

> It is one thing for Congress to withhold jurisdiction. It is entirely another to confer it and direct that it be exercised in a manner inconsistent with constitutional requirements or, what in some instances may be the same thing, without regard to them. Once it is held that Congress can require the courts criminally to enforce unconstitutional laws or statutes, including regulations, or to do so without regard for their validity, the way will have been found to circumvent the supreme law, and what is more, to make the courts parties to doing so. This Congress cannot do. . . . Whenever the judicial power is called into play, it is responsible directly to the fundamental law and no other authority can intervene to force or authorize the judicial body to disregard it. . . .
>
> This is not merely control or definition of jurisdiction. It is rather unwarranted abridgement of the judicial power in the criminal process.[40]

Justice Roberts' quarrel with the majority was even more pronounced. "I am sure that my brethren, no more than I, would say that Congress may set aside the Constitution during war," he commented. "If not, may it suspend any of its provisions? The question deserves a fair answer. My view is that it may not suspend any of the provisions of the instrument. What any of the branches of government do in war must find warrant in the charter and not in its nullification, either directly or stealthily by evasion and equivocation."[41]

Again the exigencies of a national emergency had swept the once revered maxim, "freedom of contract," out of the Constitution. More important still, the Court had, certain observers charged, by validating

---

* "Just at the time the Yakus case was decided," Harvey C. Mansfield writes, "the Banking and Currency Committees of the two Houses were considering the renewal of price-control legislation. Mr. Justice Rutledge's dissenting opinion focused congressional attention on the procedural provisions of the Act, and it soon became apparent that the law would be changed. . . . As finally enacted [58 Stat. 632, c. 325, Laws of 1944], the extension act . . . permitted a defendant in either criminal or civil proceedings, upon good cause being shown, to file a complaint in the Emergency Court of Appeals challenging the validity of the regulation he was charged with violating. Upon such a filing, the enforcement court was authorized in its discretion to stay the execution of judgment in its proceedings until the validity question was settled. It was also flatly provided that a determination of invalidity would be a defense to charges of prior violations." (A Short History of OPA [Office of Temporary Controls, Office of Price Administration, 1947], p. 277.)

OPA's procedural system, destroyed "the distinction between 'jurisdiction,' which in the case of the national courts Congress *is* entitled to regulate, and 'judicial power,' which these courts theoretically receive from the Constitution itself, and which has heretofore been generally deemed to be beyond the reach of serious legislative curtailment." "Congress," these commentators believed, "had obviously invaded the very core of 'judicial power,' the power and duty of deciding cases in accordance with the standing law of which the Constitution is a part, and an irrepealable part."[42]

In the minds of these commentators, judicial review, that unique bulwark of American freedom, had at last been successfully assaulted. At war the Government, it seemed, possessed power of tyrannical dimensions, enabling it to conduct its battles constitutionally with small regard to the welfare of the individual. Just as property rights had been curtailed in depression, just so the Court seemed to have decided that in time of war even the most precious and jealously safeguarded personal rights were subject to "some infringement."[43] What the critics overlooked is that liberty is not absolute. Even in his most forthright assertion of the judicial duty to protect it, Stone had conceded that the freedoms recognized as necessities in peace are "infringeable" in war. "Government has a right to survive," he said, "and powers conferred upon it are not necessarily set at naught by the express prohibitions of the Bill of Rights."[44]

The Court had not abdicated, as critics of these decisions supposed. Even in the Yakus case—supposedly the most extreme example of judicial deference—Stone declared emphatically that "though the statute should be deemed to require it, any ruling at the criminal trial which would preclude the accused from showing that he had had no opportunity to establish the invalidity of the regulation by resort to the statutory procedure, would be reviewable on appeal on constitutional grounds."[45]

The Court was still the palladium of freedom; the great barriers of the Constitution had not been set at naught. Rather the Justices had simply enforced what the founders must have realized intuitively— that "a Constitution cannot limit a nation's needs"; that constitutional restrictions have much less force when their applicability "must be judged wholly in the context of war."[46] Emergency too plain for argument—war—unleashes reserves of power undreamed of in peacetime.

Wary of "petty judicial interpretation," which so often spells "serious danger to the country," the Court construed the Constitution as a grant of power, no less than a bulwark of freedom. "A weak and vacillating policy," Judge John J. Parker has observed, "would have been a national calamity. On the other hand, a failure to preserve constitutional rights because of the pressures of war might well have resulted in our losing the very things we were fighting for.* There was no weakness or vacillation, and there was no failure to protect fundamental rights."[47] At the same time there was full recognition that "the final cause of law is the welfare of society."[48]

With the life of the nation at stake, Stone and his bench exhibited no "mawkish sentimentality," no quixotic chivalry about the judicial function. Considering the power inherent in the Constitution and the unstatesmanlike conduct of the judiciary in World War I, the amazing thing is not that so much freedom was sacrificed on the altar of military necessity during World War II, but that more was not. Even in the time of greatest stress, the Justices upheld the citizen's liberty to think, speak, and act to an extent that the nation at peace has sometimes felt it could ill afford to maintain. In this realm Stone's Court almost brought a miracle to pass.

CHAPTER FORTY-TWO

# Proprieties

Through the years the Court had built up certain canons of judicial conduct. While retaining office, a judge should not undertake major additional functions even though these might be of great and commanding importance. The work of judging required absolute dedication, undivided attention. To these proprieties Stone adhered strictly.

There were, however, several extra-judicial tasks imposed on the Chief Justiceship by statute. "To my certain knowledge," Bennett Boskey has written, Stone "found high satisfaction in his duties as chairman of the Board of Trustees of the National Gallery of Art." This gave him the opportunity to put to practical use his long-standing interest in the arts and brought him personal gratification above and beyond that which could be obtained from his judicial office alone. He also enjoyed his duties as chancellor of the Board of Regents of the Smithsonian Institution.[1] These two extracurricular activities carried

---

* On September 20, 1810, Jefferson wrote: "To lose our country by a scrupulous adherence to written law would be to lose the law itself, with life, liberty, property, and all those who are enjoying them with us; thus absurdly sacrificing the end to the means. . . . The line of discrimination between cases may be difficult; but the good officer is bound to draw it at his own peril, and throw himself on the justice of his country and the rectitude of his motives." (*Works*, Vol. 11, pp. 146, 149.)

little risk of involving the Court in unseemly political controversy or in the kind of idle gossip that might detract from its stature and dignity.

Few Justices have taken the judicial office more seriously or suffered more distress when indiscretions, whether his own or others', turned the spotlight of noxious publicity on him. The campaigning congressman who invited himself to join Stone's early morning walk and then set a camera trap for the party caused acute embarrassment. Self-glorifying litigants, politicians, or misguided friends who got him improperly entangled aroused similar emotions. In 1928 New York's Mayor Jimmy Walker, after conferring with him on an application for stay of an injunction affecting New York's subway fare, gave newspapers a composite photograph because the Justice had refused to pose with him.* Stone was enraged. "One would think," he said, "that I had presented the subways to Mayor Jimmie and he was carrying them back to New York in his pocket."[2]

The results were not always happy even when his guard was up. "Every time I make a speech or an address," he told Karl Llewellyn, October 28, 1934, "I repent it in sackcloth and ashes." His rule was to accept a speaking invitation only when the occasion afforded opportunity—as in the Harvard University Tercentenary celebration or dedication of the new University of Michigan Law School Quadrangle —to take "some part in an important event in the legal life of the country in view of my associations with it in various capacities."[3] On such occasions he habitually prepared a full and carefully worked out draft of his address. The chances of a slip or ill-advised remark were thus reduced to a minimum.

Absolute dedication to his work sometimes manifested itself in unusual ways. Behind his most conspicuous "indiscretions," as in his

---

* On May 4, 1928, Stone wrote an explanatory note to "my associates on the Court": "No such photograph was in fact made of me. Recognizing the impropriety of having any part in such publicity, I declined an invitation to be photographed and remained inside my house. The photograph which was published is a newspaper snapshot of me taken four years ago on the White House steps when I was appointed Attorney General, and evidently inserted in the present photograph for publicity purposes. . . . The only action taken by me (after consultation with the Chief Justice) is disclosed in the enclosed copy of a letter to counsel for the Interborough."

The whole episode, quite apart from the composite photograph taken of Stone, ruffled Chief Justice Taft. On May 6, 1928, he reported the incident to his son, Robert A. Taft: "The Mayor came down here and had an interview with Judge Stone as if he was the most important feature in the situation, having announced that he was going to run for the mayoralty on the platform of a five-cent fare. The New York papers and the counsel seem to be more interested in publicity than they are in the consideration of the issue. They played a dirty trick on poor Stone. . . . It was an outrage, but it seemed better to say nothing, although Stone wrote a letter to his colleagues to explain that it was a fraud."

correspondence with Douglas W. Johnson on Court-packing and his talks with Marquis Childs on Justice Black, lay ulterior motives, an irrepressible desire to shape the course of public affairs constructively. Well aware of the urgent need for better public understanding of the Court's work and realizing the large contribution which news-papermen, such as Irving Brant and Arthur Krock, might make to that understanding, it was perfectly natural that a man of Stone's wide experience and shrewdness should, on occasion, be "guilty" of some indiscretion. For these, as we have seen, he paid a heavy price.

Meticulous in small things, Stone's extreme sensitivity should have led to caution in conversation. Yet he was quite free in his comments to all kinds of people, sometimes even with newsmen. In utilizing their columns as purveyors of his ideas, he cherished the illusion that "if you treat them all right they'll give you a break."[4] And, despite the words of Charles Evans Hughes, Jr., about the Justice's circumspect conduct as a member of the Medicine-Ball Cabinet, the fact remains that Stone loved to talk. The internal pressure to discuss things of a confidential nature with a small, understanding audience was great. But his discriminating sense of the proprieties evoked conscious effort to circumscribe the audience, the occasion, and the subject. He seemed not to realize that others might be much less sensitive.

Sometimes even a close friend abused his confidence. Edward Bruce, head of the Public Works Art Project, let it be known that he had consulted the Justice about his right to finance government work with Carnegie Endowment funds. Stone was furious and stated his objections at length:

First, I was not aware that in our recent conversation you were seeking, or that I was giving any legal advice. I recall that subject and I turned it aside with the observation that it was probably a matter which would not give you any occasion for worry. I had no thought of giving any advice on the subject; I examined no statutes, made no inquiry as to the circumstances of the receipt and expenditure of the money, and entered into none of the other considerations which you, as a lawyer, know must form the basis for any legal opinion or advice. So if you are relying on my passing remark as "advice," I beg you not to do so.

Second, and more important, is the fact that I can think of few things more discreditable to a federal judge, short of some kind of dishonesty, than for him to assume to give any advice on a legal matter in controversy be-tween two government officials, or more humiliating than to have it publicly proclaimed that he had done so.

I doubtless have become sensitive to the kind of unfortunate publicity which most public officials have to suffer here in Washington, and I have certainly received rather more than my fair share of it. But the fact is that one in my position is peculiarly exposed to irresponsible criticism, and peculiarly disabled from answering it. It is for that reason, I suppose, that I would never think of quoting in the public prints any statement of a friend without asking his permission, and in view of the difficult position in which I am situated I feel entitled to ask that of those who have respect for that position to say nothing of my friends.

I take it for granted that you had no thought of doing me any injury. I greatly admire your work, both as an artist and in carrying on so successfully your present activity with the Government. I want to help you in both, in ways that are open to me. I value your friendship. For all these reasons, in the future please do not make life more difficult for me by giving me any kind of newspaper publicity. As to the past, forget what has happened and throw this into the scrapbasket.[5]

Feeling hemmed in, both on and off the bench, it was not unnatural that the loquacious Justice should have been quite relaxed with his law clerks. These young men had, he assumed, "reached man's estate and had a reasonable amount of experience." Of course they "would refrain from commenting about their observations which come from intimate association into which they are invited." By 1937 he knew that such implicit trust was misplaced. Glancing over recent publications purporting to interpret the Court to the public, he noted "many unfortunate statements, most of them either untrue or so distorted as to convey a wholly erroneous impression." He knew, too, that practically all such "tittle-tattle" was traceable directly or indirectly to the young men who served the Justices. So far as it related to him personally he was unconcerned, but when Court gossip took the form of "an attempt to report alleged statements of mine or report supposed opinions of mine about my colleagues it is embarrassing and troublesome." "It tends," he said, "to degrade the Court and its members in the minds of many thoughtful people."[6]

The Justice himself had unwittingly contributed to this result. Repeated warnings from his wife and secretary had little effect. He had to learn the hard way.

More than once his indiscretions rose up to trouble him. During Taft's judicial regime he had generously responded to the query Frederick William Wile addressed to the Justices asking for information about their reading habits, and he deplored Taft's uncooperative reply as "damned nonsense." "You'd never have gotten such a letter from me," he assured the journalist emphatically. The reluctance of his colleagues to speak out, Stone suggested, "may be that they haven't any reading habits." In 1939 Wile proposed publication of the incident in his autobiography. Stone, now a bit wary, felt the story should not be told. "Many things can be said well enough in private conversation, but they take on a somewhat different complexion recorded in print."[7] The imbroglio over the Childs article about Justice Black the year before had driven that lesson home to him so firmly that he would never forget. But before these scars had properly healed, he was caught up in another painful situation.

On May 2, 1939, the news columns of the *Washington Post* blared forth the announcement: *"Associate Supreme Court Justice told Georgetown University law students and faculty members last night he agrees with 'most, if not all' of the administration's program to curb monopolies."* This startling headline had been fashioned from Stone's comment, the night before, on an innocuous speech made by anti-trust lawyer Wendell Berge about nothing more controversial than the legal profession's changing attitude toward public service. The newspaper's report completely unsettled Stone's equanimity. Berge and his chief, Thurman Arnold, were also embarrassed. They could not accept Stone's alleged support, since the *Post's* garbling of his extemporaneous remarks might easily lead to his disqualification in several crucial anti-trust cases then pending. Hurried conferences with Stone and the crest-fallen *Post* editor resulted in a correction appeasing Stone's scruples.[8]

At one of Mrs. Stone's "At Homes" a few months later the bumptious Mr. Arnold thumped his host on the back and said triumphantly, "No other Justice has ever commended my anti-trust program publicly." Stone laughed heartily but soon turned grave, and took this opportunity to tell how the Attorney General's determined drive to enforce the Sherman Act had played hob with his investment portfolio. To avoid holdings in corporations involved in government litigation, he had instructed his broker to sell certain stocks. The broker had complied and had given Stone a list of his new securities, but, the day after, Stone had read that the Justice Department had instituted proceedings against the very company in which his funds had been reinvested.[9]

Stone was very careful to see that his investments were not with companies likely to be involved in government suits. "On more than one occasion, he sold substantial investments in order that he would not have to disqualify himself." And "once he had sold them he felt that he could not thereafter purchase the same securities."[10] The responsibility to disqualify or "recuse"* himself rests on the judge alone,

---

* Technically a justice is never "disqualified"; he "recuses" himself, as the following colloquy between the Chief Justice and Representative Hobbs shows:

MR. HOBBS: Mr. Chief Justice, I notice you have used the words "disqualification" and "disqualify." Is there not a distinction to be drawn?

CHIEF JUSTICE STONE: Well, of course there is this distinction: I do not know how far it applies to the Supreme Court, but it does to other courts. There are many cases, or some cases in which the lower court federal judges are forbidden by statute to sit.

MR. HOBBS: But that is not true of any case in the Supreme Court?

CHIEF JUSTICE STONE: I think not; at least, I do not recall any at the moment. There are many cases, however, where the district judge, if he is the right kind of

and one of the duties of Stone's law clerk was to alert him to any circumstances that might suggest disqualification. Though Stone set a high standard—serving, indeed, as a model for the most fastidious[11]— it is difficult to extract from his practice the maxims he applied.

Stone often refused to sit because a member of his old firm of Sullivan and Cromwell was counsel in the case. He did not, however, stay out of every litigation in which a member of this firm appeared.[12] Though himself careful about abstaining from government cases begun during his brief tenure as Attorney General, he thought it permissible for a Justice who had served in that office to sit in cases to which he was connected by nothing more than "mere *pro forma* relations which an Attorney General often has with cases in the Department of Justice."[13] No mechanical rule of thumb indicated the proper course. Each situation had to be carefully weighed and decided on its own merit.

After much soul-searching, he recanted disqualification in the Securities and Exchange Commission cases, from which he had felt barred because Sullivan and Cromwell represented the North American Company at the time he was a partner. "As a youngster in the office," he explained, "I ran errands for it. It was one of our important clients after I became a partner in the firm."[14] Two weeks before the decision came down he thought that "because of my peculiar relation to the case it would probably be better for me merely to concur in the result."[15] In the end, however, he joined the Court's opinion, explaining that he had announced his disqualification on "the assumption that we had a full Court that would be able to deal with the case."[16] Had he not participated, the case would have been dismissed for want of a quorum.*

Judges of his Court declined to sit, he said, if they had "anything substantially to do with the case before it reached the Supreme Court."[17] At times, however, the reason he assigned for recusing himself appeared quite "unsubstantial." In certain cases he would simply

---

judge, would not sit, and his view that he would not sit should be respected, I suppose. I used the term generally as referring to either class of cases where the judge felt that he should not sit. . . .

MR. HOBBS: But it is "recused" rather than "disqualified."

CHIEF JUSTICE STONE: Yes; you are quite right.

MR. HOBBS: And, therefore, it is left entirely to the sound discretion of any Justice of the Supreme Court? . . . But he recuses himself and is not disqualified?

CHIEF JUSTICE STONE: Yes.

("To Change the Quorum of the Supreme Court of the United States," *Hearings before the House Judiciary Committee*, June 24, 1943, pp. 31-32.)

* Stone had followed the rule of necessity. "Although a judge had better not, if it can be avoided, take part in the decision of a case in which he has any personal interest, yet he not only may, but must do so if the case cannot be heard otherwise." (F. Pollock, *First Book of Jurisprudence* [6th ed., 1929], p. 270.)

say, "The petitioner is an old acquaintance of mine and I have been entertained on various occasions at his house,"[18] or "I prefer not to participate in these cases."[19] A Supreme Court Justice, like Caesar's wife, must be above suspicion.[20] To be balanced against qualms of conscience was the judge's obligation to keep himself qualified in as many cases as possible. The requirements of propriety in a legalistic context, though not easily ascertained, are simple compared with the standards of fitness circumscribing the political and non-political judicial service.

Early in our history the appointments of Justices Jay and Ellsworth as foreign ministers stirred heated Senate debate. "This was breaking in upon what I would have a fundamental principle," Chief Justice Marshall's close friend and brother-in-law, Joseph Hamilton Daveiss, declared, apropos of Jay's ambassadorship; "you ought to insulate and cut off a judge from all extraneous inducements and expectations; never present him the jora* of promotion; for no influence is more powerful in the human mind than hope—it will in time cause some judges to lay themselves out for presidential favor, and when questions of state occur, this will greatly affect the public confidence in them, and sometimes deservedly."†[21]

---

* Probably a misspelling of the obsolete word "jure," defined in the New English Dictionary as "a just privilege, a right."

† Nevertheless several Justices, notably David Davis and John McLean, openly entertained presidential ambitions. Davis eventually won a seat in the Senate and resigned from the Court to fill it. President Grant appointed Justice Nelson to represent the United States in the arbitration of the Alabama Claims with Great Britain in 1871. Five Justices served on the Electoral Commission that resolved the disputes arising in several Southern states over the 1876 presidential campaign—a purely political creation for the decision of a political question. Justice Stephen Field served on a commission for the revision of state laws named by the Governor of California. In 1897, Chief Justice Fuller and Justice Brewer accepted appointment as boundary arbitrators between Venezuela and British Guiana. Justice John M. Harlan was one of the arbitrators in the Fur Seal Arbitration. In later years, however, President Wilson acquiesced unhesitatingly in Chief Justice White's opinion that the proprieties precluded Brandeis's service on a commission to settle a border quarrel with Mexico. Later on, Wilson entertained equally strong qualms about disturbing Brandeis's judicial work for the sake of the war effort. Chief Justice Taft, apparently, shared White's views and carried the Court with him on a strict policy against off-Court assignments.

Associate Justice Hughes thought it "best for the Court and the country that the Justices should strictly limit themselves to their judicial work," but yielded in the summer of 1911 to the invitation of the importunate Taft to serve on a commission to determine second-class postal rates. In 1916 Hughes surrendered to his party's presidential "draft." As Secretary of State, he prevailed on President Harding and the German Government to name Justice Day to the American-German claims commission. In 1930 he undertook settlement of the century-old border quarrel between Guatemala and Honduras, sitting as president of the Special Boundary Tribunal. Justice Owen J. Roberts served on the Mexican Claims Commission, and Justice Willis Van Devanter served as an arbitrator in our controversy with Great Britain growing out of the seizure of the ship *I'm Alone*.

Justice Stone embraced Daveiss' injunction with great determination. "It has been a long tradition of our Court," he wrote Newton D. Baker, October 24, 1931, "that its members do not serve on committees or perform other services not having a direct relationship to the work of the Court." A judge's duties should not be interrupted or diluted by any other activity, even if the added job would put his feet on the road to the White House. As we have seen, Stone scotched all attempts to persuade him to run for office, and considered even speculation on the matter as prejudicial to his position. Though courteous to his old friend Sterling Carr, who in 1940 was still thinking of him as the Dark Horse, he was quite brusque that same year with other correspondents. "It is always a pleasure to hear from one of my old students, even though the subject of the letter is one which I do not feel free to discuss and in which I take no interest at all," he told an admirer who, in 1940, had found him "easy to sell" as next President of the United States. Apologizing for having to neglect his correspondence "in order to get out some opinions," the Justice's letter concluded: "That is a subject in which I have a deep and abiding interest."[22]

Presidents, too, often showed a "lack of appreciation" of the "proper standing and function of the Court in the governmental structure,"[23] as Chief Justice Taft said of President Hoover when the latter was so insistent on having Justice Stone serve as chairman of his Law Enforcement Commission. Under President Roosevelt there were repeated calls for extra-judicial assistance of various kinds. In the autumn of 1939 President Roosevelt invited Justices Stone and Frankfurter to accompany him down the Potomac on the presidential yacht,[24] taking up with them his "dilemma" over the refusal of Congress to appropriate money for housing a hundred thousand new Army and Navy recruits. At a press conference a few days later F.D.R. told newsmen he had authorized these Departments to incur deficits for the needed barracks, and let it be known he had discussed the matter with Stone and Frankfurter.* The President's critics were quick to exploit the incident. Representative John Taber, the economy-minded

---

* The special dispatch, *New York Times*, Oct. 4, 1939, reads:

"President Roosevelt disclosed today that he had ordered the War and Navy Departments to ignore statutory prohibitions against budgetary deficits growing out of unauthorized expenditures for army and navy housing, hospitalization and the reconditioning of obsolete vessels.

"After discussing the matter, involving an apparent conflict of laws, with two Supreme Court Justices and the Controller General, the President said that he had decided to anticipate Congressional approval of expenditures necessitated by the limited emergency program calling for 100,000 more soldiers, sailors and marines and the recommissioning of a hundred World War destroyers for patrol duty. . . .

"Mr. Roosevelt did not disclose whether Associate Justices Harlan Stone and Felix Frankfurter had expressed any opinion on the wisdom of his course when he discussed the legal conflict with them on a week-end cruise down the Potomac River. He did claim support for his action in an informal opinion he said was given

Republican Appropriations Committee member, upbraided the Chief Executive for his devious tactics, and, by implication, scored the Justices for their indiscretion.* In all such situations, the old saw, "Least said, soonest mended," was the crux of Stone's policy, but this incident disturbed him so much that he wrote Taber, denying any indulgence "in the luxury of extra-official advice on any legal matters."[25]

"I will admit that my statement was intended as an absolute and direct criticism of the Chief Executive," the crusty legislator had written on January 9, 1940. "There was no criticism in what I said of the Justices, although frankly, it is my opinion that a Justice of the Supreme Court who places himself in a position where the Chief Executive can give out the kind of statement that he did with reference to you and Mr. Frankfurter, would be subject to the same kind of criticism. I wonder, do you not agree with me?" Apparently the Justice did. Firmly resolved never to go on another "social" cruise with the President,† he instructed his wife to be ever-ready with a prearranged out-of-town engagement should another invitation come.[26]

Close relations between the President and a Supreme Court Justice during the Hoover regime was one thing, under F.D.R. quite another. Considering the kind of person Stone was, it is inconceivable that he would, on his own initiative, raise controversial political questions with any Chief Executive. It is equally inconceivable that he would not interject comments or offer his opinions on matters of public policy at the early morning sessions of the Medicine-Ball Cabinet. After 1940 Stone resented the uninhibited way in which certain of his colleagues dabbled in politics. "During my first year with the Judge," Allison Dunham has written, "the medicine ball sat on the corner of his desk.

---

to him by Controller General Fred H. Brown, with whom he discussed the question just before his press conference today.

"Mr. Roosevelt appeared to think there was nothing unusual in the fact that he had discussed apparent legislative conflicts with Supreme Court Justices. He was casual in recalling his conversation with them on the subject and said that both had agreed the situation came within the category of a prescribed course in all law schools—a course he termed conflict of laws. . . ."

* Frank R. Kent wrote Stone, Oct. 20, 1939, in response to Stone's complaint against his column entitled *Why Not Ask Congress?* (*Baltimore Sun*, Oct. 11, 1939): "On October 3, the President told the reporter that he had discussed this subject with the Justices and that they had 'agreed' that there was a 'conflict of law,' which he interpreted as meaning he could go ahead." "It was he [the President]," Kent wrote again three days later, "who deliberately created the impression that he had asked and gotten advice from you." "I think," Kent suggested, "that if the Justices feel aggrieved at being put in this position it is the President with whom they should take it up, not me. He did it."

† "I recall very well the incident," Stone's son Lauson writes, "at least I remember Father's account of it within a day or two after it happened. I do not think that Father was completely sure whether or not the other Justice said something to F.D.R. which might have provided some basis for F.D.R.'s claim that he had some advice." (Lauson H. Stone to A.T.M., Feb. 24, 1954.)

The press at the time was full of stories about Justice Douglas and Justice Frankfurter going over to the White House to see F.D.R. and advise him. Occasionally Stone would grumble about the Court participating in such affairs, and when he did I would always look at the medicine ball and kind of jokingly say, 'Well, here is the medicine ball.' He always rose to the occasion and insisted that the medicine ball was purely an athletic undertaking, which it may have been. At any event, when I returned after the summer recess, the medicine ball was no longer located on his desk. . . . I could never determine why he moved the medicine ball—unless it was because of the current political implications."*[27]

Understandably, F.D.R. had little use for off-the-bench service from members of the old Court. But after reconstituting the judiciary, and with the outbreak of World War II, he found it difficult to believe that he had cut himself off irrevocably from close advisers merely by assigning them to the Supreme Court. James F. Byrnes barely got started as an Associate Justice before the President began to draw heavily on his time and energies. As early as December 30, 1941, Stone complained that Byrnes was "devoting a large part of his time to assisting the President with current legislation"; and after Pearl Harbor, Roosevelt, much to the annoyance of the Chief Justice, appointed Justice Roberts to head the commission of inquiry into the disaster. The outside activities of Byrnes and Roberts gave Stone serious apprehension lest the work and reputation of the Court suffer.[28] With one hundred and thirty million people in the United States to draw from to do these jobs, it seemed to him "as though the Court might have been left alone."[29]

After 1941 the responsibility for preserving the judiciary's integrity and independence—in a real sense the obligation of every Justice— fell heavily on Stone as Chief Justice. In declining Senator Styles Bridges' invitation to a testimonial dinner to be tendered him by the six New England states, the Chief Justice explained:

If I followed my own personal inclination I should accept at once. But there are other considerations which make me hesitate to do so.

The Court, as you know, has of late suffered from overmuch publicity. After all, its only claim to public confidence is the thoroughness and fidelity with which it does its daily task, which is exacting enough to demand the undivided attention of all its members. The majority are new in their positions and not too familiar with the traditions of the Court, which have stood

---

* "I am inclined to think," Lauson Stone writes apropos of Dunham's implication that his Father may have given advice during Hoover's administration of the type he later criticized, "that anything Father may have said or done was in the line of conversation rather than advice. . . . I also suspect that the removal of the medicine ball was a result of Mother's housecleaning and not an indication of any change in Father's thinking." (Lauson H. Stone to A.T.M., Feb. 24, 1954.)

it in such good stead during the 150 years of its history. The upshot of all this is that I am anxious to see the Court removed more from the public eye except on decision day, as soon as possible—to imbue its members by example and by precept with the idea that the big job placed on us by the Constitution is our single intent in life and that, for the present, public appearances and addresses by the judges and the attendant publicity ought to be avoided.

Perhaps not irrelevant to this is the feeling which I entertain that a judge can never do more than his duty and that he ought not to be publicly praised because he has not done less. In that respect the Chief Justice does not stand on any different footing from the other members of the Court, and I confess that I shrink from being selected to be the recipient of public praise, for doing or trying to do the same thing which my colleagues are doing. I fear the effect of such an appearance on morale, which can only come with team-work and single-minded devotion to the work in hand—all of which I am anxious to stimulate just now.[30]

Stone's determination to keep the Court out of the public eye, except on opinion day, never wavered. "Chance and fate have placed me at the head of a great institution which at the moment is in real danger of losing its proper influence and prestige," he told an old Columbia University colleague. "I think everything I have should be devoted to avoiding such an unhappy possibility."[31] Such dedication meant that he must refuse to take on other tasks materially detracting from his ability to work "long hours pretty continuously" at the job of being Chief Justice. "I have accepted the office," he reiterated, "and acceptance necessarily carries with it the obligation on my part to give whatever of time and energy are needful for the performance of its functions."[32]

Stone's feelings were strongly aroused in 1942 by Justice Murphy's decision to enter into military service. "I learn from the paper that you yesterday took the oath as Lieutenant Colonel in the Army," he wrote Murphy, June 11, 1942. "In that connection have you considered the effect of 5 United States Code [provision prohibiting holding more than one remunerative federal office at a time] upon your office as a Justice of the Supreme Court?" Later on, Congressman Celler (a former Stone student) raised with the Chief Justice a number of questions relating to Murphy's status, principally, "Can Justice Murphy legally enjoy the dual role of a judge and a commissioned officer of the Army?"[33]

"I can only say that Mr. Justice Murphy did not bring to my attention or to that of the Court his intention to seek a commission in the Army," Stone replied. "My first information on the subject came from newspaper reports published after the Court had adjourned for the summer. No action, formal or informal, has been taken by the Court or by me with respect to the matter."[34] "I was very reluctant to enter into any discussion of the matter with him," Stone told his colleagues, passing on Celler's inquiry and his own reply, "but I felt I could not rightly ignore his letter."[35] Whatever may be thought of its propriety in other respects, Murphy, apparently, had violated no statute in accepting an Army commission.

During the war years he felt more than ever obliged to avoid off-Court assignments threatening the slightest involvement in politics. In the early summer of 1942 Stone's firm resolve faced a formidable challenge. A rancorous quarrel had developed in the administration's handling of the nation's rubber supply. Conflicting methods of making rubber synthetically sharply divided F.D.R.'s subordinates, pitted farm-bloc congressmen against the powerful oil industry, and irritated the general public. The President sought to take these perplexing questions out of politics by naming an investigating commission so thoroughly respectable that few would dare dispute its findings. As he saw it, the recommendations of a beloved elder statesman could restore peace among his feuding aides, placate Congress and the citizenry. In this dilemma the President turned somewhat jauntily to Chief Justice Stone:

July 17, 1942

My dear Chief:

I have a problem in this rubber matter, as you know. It is extremely difficult for me, with a million other problems mostly military and naval on my hands, to spend even the three or four days which are, in my judgment, essential to obtain a true picture of the facts.

These facts relate not only to consumption, production, etc., but also to certain scientific processes of which I do not consider myself competent to judge.

Nevertheless, I would rather have a non-scientist review these things for me than a chemist or a manufacturer. And I find it difficult to get anybody within the administrative structure of the Government to look at the whole picture from an outside, non-sectional, and non-political basis.

Therefore, I have readily concluded that the most available and the most useful person I could call on for this short task is none other than your good self.

I am wondering if you would care to undertake this at your convenience? I do not think it should take more than four or five days in Washington—and it need not be official in any way—merely a helping hand, a summary, and a verbal suggestion or recommendation.

I could let you have any of my youngsters to do footwork or a gathering of information for you—somebody like Judge Rosenman, for example, though I would want you to feel fully free to ask for anyone's help you desire.

As I said before, there is no immediate hurry about this, though it would be best, in my judgment, for me to take some kind of action within the next two or three weeks.

I hate even to break in on your vacation for a few days, and I hope you will forgive me for turning to you in time of need. I think it is wholly ethical work for the Chief Justice!

The President's request rubbed Stone the wrong way. What service did F.D.R. really want from the Chief Justice? Even without investigation, Stone knew what common sense would say: "We need rubber to win the war; we must conserve in every possible way what we have; and increase the supply of synthetic rubber by any practical means, favoring the method which would least disturb priorities without wasting time in speculation as to the most ideal method; and finally put the whole matter in the hands of some one of commanding ability and large experience, with full authority to act." Why, he wondered, should it be necessary "to tell a school boy, much less a great government, such obvious things."[36]

Determined not to hire out his "good self" even for a few days, Stone, then on vacation in New Hampshire, pondered his reply, writing and rewriting, discussing its form and content with an intimate friend. "Can't find any holes in it," he commented finally to his wife and sent it off to Washington.

July 20, 1942

Dear Mr. President:

I have your letter of the 17th inst. Personal and patriotic considerations alike afford powerful incentives for my wish to comply with your request that I assist you in arriving at some solution of the pending rubber problem. But most anxious, not to say painful, reflection has led me to the conclusion that I cannot rightly yield to my desire to render for you a service which as a private citizen I should not only feel bound to do but one which I should undertake with zeal and enthusiasm.

At the outset, I may say to you in confidence, that during the administration of your predecessor in office, when I was an Associate Justice, I felt obliged to decline a somewhat similar request for reasons which are for me as persuasive now as they were then. Apart from the generally recognized consideration that it is highly undesirable for a judge to engage actively in public or private undertakings other than the performance of his judicial functions, there are special considerations which I think must be regarded as controlling here.

Although it can by no means be certain, I assume that I would have no occasion to pass upon proposals involving questions of constitutional power or other questions which would be subject to review by the courts. That, of course, would be plainly inadmissible. But the rubber problem must be solved in the first instance by executive and legislative action, having important political implications, not to say repercussions. Any findings that I might make (which, unlike judicial findings, could not be restricted to evidence appearing of record), and any action I might recommend, if adopted, would almost certainly become the subject of political attack.

A judge, and especially the Chief Justice, cannot engage in political debate or make public defense of his acts. When his action is judicial he may always rely upon the support of the defined record upon which his action is based and of the opinion in which he and his associates unite as stating the ground of decision. But when he participates in the action of the executive or legislative departments of government he is without those supports. He exposes himself to attack and indeed invites it, which because of his peculiar situation inevitably impairs his value as a judge and the appropriate influence of his office.

We must not forget that it is the judgment of history that two of my predecessors, Jay and Ellsworth, failed in the obligations of their office and impaired their legitimate influence by participation in executive action in the negotiation of treaties. True, they repaired their mistake in part by resigning their commissions before returning to their judicial duties,* but it is not by mere chance that every Chief Justice since has confined his activities strictly to the performance of his judicial duties.

I hope, Mr. President, that you will fully understand how deeply I regret my inability to render this service for you, and that it is only a sense of public obligation transcending all personal considerations, which prevents. I console myself by the assurance that there are others, *not judges,* more capable than I, of doing this particular task, on whose disinterestedness and patriotism, you and the public can rely.†

On July 23, 1942, news leaked out that Roosevelt had named Stone rubber czar. The following day reporters who called the Chief Justice at Peckett's drew a curt response. Refusing to elaborate, he told them all: "I have not accepted and do not intend to."[37] Newspapers the next morning reported that F.D.R. at his press conference the day before denied that he "had asked the jurist to head up a survey of the complicated rubber situation, as had been reported." The President admitted he had recently consulted the Chief Justice, but when asked whether he intended to request him to take on the assignment "the President stated that he doubted it."[38] Less than a week later the President's contradictory note went to the Chief Justice: "I have care-

* Stone's exact meaning is not clear. Jay returned to the Chief Justiceship and resigned only after his election as governor. Ellsworth gave up his judicial post while still on duty in France, but apparently for reasons of health rather than scruples about the propriety of his dual role.

† Bennett Boskey, Stone's law clerk at the time, comments: "Actually I think the Justice had very little taste for undertaking this particular non-judicial task, though had he been merely a private citizen he might have felt obliged to accept. But he was careful not to base his refusal on any ground of personal disinclination. In its setting I think he saw the President's request as an effort on the part of the Executive—and a rather improper effort—to obtain some judicial sugar-coating for recommendations that, however necessary, might be distasteful to a large segment of American business. Justice Stone had no wish to be used for such a purpose, no matter how laudable the President's general objective might be. What he did was to make use of the opportunity to give expression to the principle he believed so important to assert at that time." (Bennett Boskey to A.T.M., Dec. 18, 1953.)

fully read your letter, and, honestly, I must admit that you are so persuasively right and correct that I cannot let the case 'go to the jury.' I
fully understand—and I hope to see you soon."[39]

Stone said nothing publicly or to the President to clarify the situation. Instead, he wrote him a friendly letter: "I cannot tell you the
sense of relief I feel at your assurance that you do understand my
scruples. No one realizes more that I how much you are entitled to
ask for assistance in carrying the heavy burden which rests upon you
and no one could regret more than I that I am not free to give it."[40]

Newspapers praised Stone's "blunt" refusal. "Last week our beloved
President got his comeuppance," the *Emporia Gazette* editorialized,
July 30, 1942. "It was a glorious thing for the country," the *Lynchburg
News* said. "Chief Justice Stone has acted to restore to the Supreme
Court some of the honor in which it was held before politicians, high
and low, made it a football of politics, or sought to use it to further
their own political and personal interests." "Chief Justice Stone has
shown the best kind of judgment," the *Washington Post* commented,
"in refusing to lend the weight of his authority to an inquiry into
matters on which he is not equipped to speak with authority." "To
have acted differently," one columnist wrote, going to the heart of
the issue, "would have encouraged a practice that already has de-
tracted from the dignity of the Court."[41]

Even after returning to Washington from his vacation the Chief
Justice continued to feel nettled. He let friends know the facts and
made certain that the whole story would someday become fully
known.*

Apparently F.D.R. did consider the Chief Justice's reasoning "persuasively right and correct." At any rate, when the President wished

* At Mrs. Stone's Monday afternoon tea on October 13, 1942, Professor Noel T.
Dowling queried the Chief Justice on F.D.R.'s reported request and the President's
later denial. "Come in here and I will show you something," the Chief Justice said.
"At that," Dowling has recalled, "we went to his chambers, where from some papers
on his work table he picked out several and handed them to me."After reading
the exchanges between Stone and F.D.R., Dowling observed: "These papers are
important, especially your letter, and they ought not to stay buried in your files."
"Yes, I think they are important," Stone commented. "I hope that what I wrote
to the President will be known someday. Maybe I'll give you a copy of the correspondence later on. I'll think about it." (Noel T. Dowling to A.T.M., Nov. 22,
1950.)
That is the way the matter stood until 1945. "You will remember a certain
letter which I wrote to President Roosevelt a couple of years ago," the Chief Justice reminded Dowling, June 23, 1945. "I think that the time has come when you
can have a copy of it if you still desire it. If so, I will look it up in the fall when
I get back." Dowling, of course, wanted the correspondence, and it was sent to
him on Oct. 24, 1945, in an envelope marked "Personal and Confidential." "I hope
you find it interesting," the Chief Justice commented suggestively.

Justice Byrnes' service as presidential assistant, the Justice resigned from the Court, October 1942, so as to accept the post of Director of Economic Stabilization. "I am sorry to lose you from the Court," Stone told his departing associate, "but I'm glad you can make up your mind whether you want to be a judge or something else."[42]

Executive raids on the Supreme Court for administrative talent were thus temporarily halted, but that tribunal was not the Chief Justice's only concern. Judges of lower courts, on their own initiative and in response to executive recruiting, also deserted for more active service elsewhere on the home front. Stone fought the tendency as best he could in talks to judges at judicial conferences, stressing the importance of balance between war front and home front, and the necessity of keeping the courts functioning smoothly. "If there be any judges in this country who find that their judicial duties are not sufficient to keep them occupied," he told District of Columbia judges, "I have the means of giving them all the work that they can possibly do by assigning them to other districts, and it is judicial work and the kind that they are fitted to do."[43]

Personal aversion to outside assignments became a handy weapon in a struggle to keep the judiciary intact. As a result, the Chief Justice himself was forced to renounce opportunities for doing things he he wanted to do and which in no way conflicted with his obligations to the Court. "I am doing all I can by way of precept and example to counteract the unfortunate tendency of federal judges including those of my own court to dilute their judicial influence and efficiency by engaging in extra-judicial activities," Stone responded to an invitation to become honorary president of a proposed scholarly legal association. "I know that you will rightly say 'this is different' but the question is whether they will see the difference. I fear not—and I do not wish to take the risk."[44]

The Chief Justice was equally adamant against extra-judicial service whether the initiative came from the President or Congress. In 1943 Congress proposed a War Ballot Commission to be named by the Chief Justice. As the bill came on for debate, Senator Arthur H. Vandenberg thought it wise to sound out Stone's willingness to handle this latest assignment to the political hot corner.[45] Stone responded:

I have your letter of the 20th instant, inquiring whether the Chief Justice of the United States would be likely to honor a request that he associate himself with the administration of the proposed law for the establishment of the United States ballot commission either as its chairman or by designating its members.

In response I feel free to say, for myself only, that I regard the performance of such a function as incompatible with obligations which I assumed with the office of Chief Justice and as likely to injure my usefulness in that office.* It is enough to say, without more, which might be said, that action taken by the Chief Justice in connection with the administration of the proposed legislation might become subject to review in the Court over which he presides and that it might have political implications and political consequences which should be wholly dissociated from the duties of the judicial office. For that reason and for that only, as at present advised, I should feel obliged to decline such a request if made.[46]

In deference to these objections, the legislation was altered.

Teamwork between the Michigan Senator and the Chief Justice was equally successful in heading off a congressional move to place Stone at the head of the Atomic Energy Commission. "My impression is that you have a general objection to any such activities," Vandenberg wrote, September 21, 1945. "If you would care to indicate your point of view to me, I shall be glad to act in the premise as I did before." Stone replied in the usual vein, repeating his conviction that the duties of a Supreme Court Justice are "difficult and exacting"—"in a very real sense a 'full time job.'" This time he bore down harder, hoping that "the federal judges who are gallivanting about the country, seeking to do glamour jobs at the expense of their judicial work . . . will read and ponder it."[47]

Such unswerving devotion to duty and to principle sometimes aroused genuine regret. As to possible service on the Atomic Energy Commission, Stone wrote: "This is a matter that I should be much interested in, although I have no illusions about the willingness of Congress to accept any solutions which I might conclude were the proper ones."[48] However, his resolve not to allow himself to be diverted remained unshaken. Lest an acceptance be misinterpreted, he declined, a few weeks later, President Truman's offer of appointment to the panel of judges of the Hague arbitrations.[49] The likelihood of service being quite remote, this was an extreme example of reticence even for Stone, and it was so intended. "It is perhaps too much to expect that my own course will persuade others to take a more common sense view," he explained. "But at least I can keep trying."[50]

Yet Stone's views on the propriety of extra-judicial work for judges, which must have been known to President Truman, did not dissuade the President in 1945 from naming Justice Robert H. Jackson American Prosecutor at the Nuremberg War Crime Trials. Stone was deeply

---

* John Bassett Moore applauded the Justice's refusal to serve as "judicial umpire" in the matter of military voting. "I can well recall," Moore wrote, Nov. 28, 1943, "the night when, in a telegraph office in Felton, Delaware, I heard the announcement that the electoral commission had, by a vote of 8 to 7, given a decision in favor of seating Hayes as President of the United States. In the cry immediately heard of fraud triumphant in a presidential election, the Justices of the Supreme Court came in for special censure because of their judicial station."

disturbed, and he let his views be known. When President Truman named former Attorney General Francis Biddle American representative on the panel of judges to try the war criminals, the Chief Justice expressed his disapproval of the entire proceedings by refusing Biddle's personal request to swear him in. "I did not wish," he explained, "to appear, even in that remote way, to give my blessing or that of the Court on the proposed Nuremberg trials."[51]

Insult seemed to be added to injury when *Fortune* magazine, in December 1945, carried an article which Stone read as stating that Justice Jackson appeared for the United States Supreme Court at a meeting of four Allied delegations. "This statement," he wrote to the editor, "seems to suggest that the Supreme Court of the United States was represented at the meeting in question and that it is participating or has in some way participated in the movement which brought about the trials. For your information, but not for publication as coming from me, I would like to advise you that the Supreme Court had nothing to do, either directly or indirectly, with the Nuremberg Trials, or the governmental action which authorized them. I was not advised of Justice Jackson's participation until his appointment by the Executive was announced in the newspapers."*

"So far as the Nuremberg trial is an attempt to justify the application of the power of the victor to the vanquished because the vanquished made aggressive war," he explained, "I dislike extremely to see it dressed up with a false façade of legality. The best that can be said for it is that it is a political act of the victorious States which may be morally right, as was the sequestration of Napoleon about 1815. But the allies in that day did not feel it necessary to justify it by an appeal to nonexistent legal principles. As a practical matter, it seems to me that the difficulties and uncertainties of saying who is the aggressor under the conditions which produce modern war should make us hesitate to lay down for the future a principle which would always require that question to be answered by the victor."[52]

All wars are in fact aggressive. The real source of authority is "the

---

* William D. Geer, in his reply on Jan. 10, 1946, to Stone's letter of Jan. 2, pointed out that the sentence in the *Fortune* article from which the Chief Justice drew his unhappy inference reads: "There met in London four Allied delegations, British, French, Russian, and, for the U.S., Supreme Court Justice Robert H. Jackson." Might not over-sensitivity explain Stone's failure to read the well-placed comma? "I think you can take it for a fact," *Fortune* editor Herbert Solow writes, "that Mr. Stone was sent proof, that this was what we call lock-up proof, that a lock-up proof is identical with what appears in the magazine, and that Mr. Stone did fail to notice a comma which was actually there." (Herbert Solow to A.T.M., Jan. 20, 1954.) "I wonder," Lauson Stone comments, "if he [the Chief Justice] did not purposely overlook the comma in the *Fortune* article in order that he might have a basis to make his views known." (Lauson H. Stone to A.T.M., Feb. 24, 1954.)

power of the victor over the vanquished." "It would not disturb me greatly," he wrote, "if that power were openly and frankly used to punish the German leaders for being a bad lot, but it disturbs me some to have it dressed up in the habiliments of the common law and the Constitutional safeguards to those charged with crime.* It looks as though we were committing ourselves to the proposition that the outcome of every war must be that the leaders of the vanquished are to be executed by the victors."[53] Just how, he wondered, is this new rule of law to be applied between the Russians and Finns, or the Russians and the Japanese, the Russians having entered the Japanese war in violation of the treaty of non-aggression? "Fortunately," he said, "I do not have to settle these questions."

But he did continue to speculate about them. "It would be interesting to know," he wrote a few weeks later, "whether, under this new doctrine of international law, if we had been defeated, the victors could plausibly assert that our supplying Britain with fifty destroyers was an act of aggression, and whether Russia was not an aggressor when it marched into Finland or in entering the war against Japan despite its treaty of peace and neutrality with Japan."[54] Charles C. Burlingham's comment that "one of the most aggressive aggressors is Russia" drew from the Chief Justice sentiments as to the entire Nuremberg venture so churlish that he advised his correspondent to tear it up.[55]

Yet irritation growing out of the accumulated inconvenience he attributed to Justice Jackson's absence provoked even more intemperate comments. "Jackson is away conducting his high-grade lynching party in Nuremberg," he remarked. "I don't mind what he does to the Nazis, but I hate to see the pretense that he is running a court and proceeding according to common law.† This is a little too sanctimonious a fraud to meet my old-fashioned ideas."[56] Jackson's absence

* In an address on April 13, 1945, Justice Jackson himself had decried "farcical judicial trials" of war criminals. But by June 1945, when he was appointed Nuremberg trials prosecutor, he had become convinced that the trials need not be "farcical." He realized, moreover, that if the trial was to accomplish anything, it could not be done by second-string men. One of the results of his appointment was that it forced other countries to send their top men to Nuremberg. (See Justice Jackson's statement at the Nuremberg Trials, *New York Times*, Nov. 22, 1945.)

As to the unwisdom or impropriety of off-Court duties for Supreme Court Justices, Jackson was in full agreement with the Chief Justice. "I feel that he was right about it," Jackson commented in an interview with the author, April 8, 1953. "I was entirely willing to quit the Court if this was the price. In those days this wasn't a pleasant place to be."

† In his letter to Charles Fairman, March 13, 1945, the Justice was much more restrained: "That just retribution ought to reach most of the accused is plain enough, but I find great difficulty in finding a firm basis in law for punishing the heads of a state or high government officials for making aggressive war, and I wonder how some of those who preside at the trials would justify some of the acts of their own government if they were placed in the status of the accused."

forced the appointment of another Justice as Circuit Justice for the Second Circuit. In his absence a number of cases, stymied by 4 to 4 votes, piled up, awaiting his return; and, of course, he was not present to do his share of opinion writing.* All this added to the tremendous burdens of the Chief Justice.

Jackson's report that his colleagues on the International Tribunal, enjoying the luxury of "free time," had voted themselves a vacation in mid-stream, heightened Stone's impatience. "We here," he wrote, January 2, 1946, "have not been troubled by too much recess over the holidays, and I found myself doing some work on both Christmas and New Year's Day in order to keep up. At the moment all of my opinions are written, but I think there is no one else on the Court in that fortunate situation, although Douglas, as usual, is not very much behind and he has had on the whole rather heavier assignments than I have given myself." The Chief Justice's reply was otherwise so friendly and considerate as to give Jackson the impression that the Court was not suffering from his absence. "I greatly appreciate your suggestion of a willingness to come over at some time for a short period," Stone told Jackson. "That, I think, ought to be avoided on your account, if not ours, and will not be necessary so long as we have enough cases to keep us busy without those which have to be reargued. I will keep you informed."

When Justice Jackson repeated his offer to return briefly, Stone again vetoed the suggestion, apparently feeling that it might be charged that Jackson had returned for certain politically delicate cases, and for these only. "It would be preferable," Stone wrote, "not to return to the work of the Court until you are ready to take it up in the regular way without further interruptions, even at the cost of putting over cases which might otherwise be disposed of in this term." "Having put your hand to the plow you should turn the furrow by completing the trial. I shall welcome the day when you are back and we have settled down to our usual course of procedure."[57]

For Stone, Justice Jackson's participation in the Nuremberg trials

---

* Jackson went to Europe at the close of Court, June 1945. In the fall Justice Reed was designated Circuit Justice for the Second Circuit. So it seems unlikely that Stone was particularly imposed upon by this aspect of Jackson's absence. Stone indicated the inconvenience he felt by sending his brethren, Sept. 29, 1945, a list of cases "of such importance as to raise the question whether they should be heard with an eight-judge Court." Among others, the list included *Duncan* v. *Kahanamoku*, 327 U.S. 304 (1946), and *United Public Workers* v. *Mitchell*, 330, U.S. 75 (1947). *Atkins* v. *Atkins*, 326 U.S. 683 (1945), another on the same list, presented a question that was decided in *Williams* v. *North Carolina*, 325 U.S. 226 (1945), by a 6 to 3 vote. "Mr. Justice Roberts and Mr. Justice Jackson were with the majority," Stone pointed out, "leaving the matter now standing as a 4 to 3. Should Mr. Justice Burton dissent, it would result in an affirmative by an equally divided Court, thus overruling the Williams case. It is highly probable that this case must be held pending Mr. Justice Jackson's return."

combined three major sources of irritation: disapproval in principle of non-judicial work, strong objection to the trials on legal and political grounds, the inconvenience and increased burden of work entailed. Even if the Chief Justice had wholly approved the trials themselves, he would have disapproved Jackson's role in them. If he had felt differently about the task in which Jackson was engaged, he might have been somewhat less annoyed by his colleague's absence. The uncertain point is whether the intemperate criticism the Chief Justice expressed in personal letters, while the case was pending and before the proceedings at Nuremberg affirmed the intention of the victors to afford a fair trial to the vanquished,* can be accepted as the expression of a considered judgment. Certainly his informal opinions ought to be placed alongside his holding in the Yamashita case—that the Japanese general might be tried by a military commission for the war crime of merely failing to prevent atrocities in the command area, without a showing that he personally ordered or knew of them.† If Stone's views had been followed, not all the Nazi leaders would have been brought before military tribunals, because their acts were not of the kind covered by the laws of war. But many of them could have been held, charged, and convicted, as was done in the case of General Yamashita.

One authoritative writer found in Stone's opinion in *Ex parte Quirin* ample support for the international trial of war criminals. In January 1946 the English jurist Lord Wright stated: "What is relevant now is that the Supreme Court, while distinguishing military courts from courts martial, affirms the jurisdiction of military courts to try offenses that by the law of war are triable by military tribunals." "From the very beginning of its history," the Chief Justice had said, "this Court has recognized and applied the law of war as including that part of the law of nations which prescribes, for the conduct of war, the status, rights, and duties of enemy nations as well as of enemy individuals."[58] Passages from Stone's opinion, Lord Wright said, "will, I am confident, be regarded as classical and authoritative statements that there is a law of nations which includes the laws of war and which defines the functions of military tribunals, and also the punishments assigned by

---

* The International Tribunal charged each of the German defendants with personal responsibility for specific offenses. After hearing, three of the defendants were acquitted and others were cleared of some charges.

† The vehement language Stone used in condemning Nuremberg is matched by what Justice Murphy said in dissenting from the Chief Justice's ruling in Yamashita. "An uncurbed spirit of revenge and retribution, masked in formal legal procedure for purposes of dealing with a fallen enemy commander," Justice Murphy said, "can do more lasting harm than all the atrocities giving rise to that spirit." (Yamashita case, p. 41.)

that law and those courts to violators of the law of war.* . . . I do not find," this writer concluded, "anything contrary to natural justice in thus giving effect to what the Chief Justice calls the common law of war."[59]

Nuremberg was not the last incident to rile Stone's sense of propriety. When President Truman added to the Chief Justice's rapidly accumulating woes by inviting him to head a committee on traffic safety, Stone took the occasion to tell the Chief Executive rather pointedly of the hardships worked by Jackson's prolonged tour of duty: "Few are aware that neither my predecessor, nor I in more than twenty years since I have been a Justice of the Supreme Court, have been able to meet the daily demands upon us without working night and holidays and Sunday. The administrative duties of the Chief Justice have increased,† and many other duties have been imposed on him by acts of Congress which my predecessors were not called on to perform. Added to this is the extra work imposed on all the Justices, and especially the Chief Justice, because of Justice Jackson's absence. Unlike the functions of an executive officer, practically none of these can be delegated."[60]

It has been suggested that Stone's letter declining this picayune assignment may have unwittingly nipped another projected raid—the plan to draft Justice William O. Douglas as Secretary of the Interior. In any event, when it became known that Douglas had refused to leave the bench, many credited Stone.‡ "Figuring in that decision,"

* "I am not at all sure that Father's views" as to the Nuremberg trials and "his opinions in the Saboteur and Yamashita cases are inconsistent. It was Father's thought from the beginning that the Nazi defendants could be dealt with through a military rather than a judicial trial—the very thing that eventually occurred in the Yamashita case. He felt that the law of nations, including the law of war, was sufficiently well established to permit a trial by a military tribunal, while there seemed to be no basis for using a judicial trial to carry out a matter of military or national policy. Another thing that bothered him was the fact that the principles of the Nuremberg trials could well be applied to certain of the activities of our Russian ally." (Lauson H. Stone to A.T.M., Feb. 24, 1954.)

† Stone no doubt had especially in mind the Administrative Office of the United States Courts, which functions under the Chief Justice. The office expanded greatly during 1941-46, and added to his burden. The Judicial Conference came into being under Hughes, but the scope and importance of its work increased under Stone. Stone told President Truman that practically none of the Chief Justice's functions could be delegated. But when Vinson came in, he named an administrative assistant, salary to commence at $10,000. A sort of executive officer, the appointee was to stand between the Chief Justice and the Clerk, the Marshal, the Librarian, the Reporter, and the Administrative Office of the Courts. Stone had but one messenger; Vinson increased it to two. Stone had only two law clerks; Vinson added a third.

‡ "The newspaper reports about my relation to the Douglas appointment are greatly exaggerated," Stone wrote Luther Ely Smith, March 6, 1946. "I should hardly interfere with an appointment of a Justice of the Court to a Cabinet position if the President saw fit to make the appointment. As a matter of fact, I think

one radio commentator observed, "was some plain talking on the part of Chief Justice Stone, who is reported to have let it be known, in no uncertain terms, that the integrity of the Supreme Court is in serious danger when it is turned into a 'fishing pond' for political appointments."[61]

In his twenty-one years on the bench Stone met many situations requiring delicate judgments as to proper judicial conduct and, by and large, he kept the veil and warded off all encroachment with remarkable constancy. Against persistent pressures, particularly during his last years, his conception of the true nature of judicial office, subtly refined by experience, sustained him. As Chief Justice, he was in the unique position of having declined requests from both Congress and the President and of having written letters of real significance on the appropriate bounds of judicial activity. Stone's capital pronouncements, especially his letters to President Roosevelt and Senator Vandenberg on the transcending importance of the judicial function in the United States, may, in time, become classic injunctions against extra-judicial service for members of the Supreme Court.

---

Douglas was reluctant to leave the Court, at least for a Cabinet position, and that that was what finally solved the problem in his case. . . . Taking Justices off the Court for temporary services is quite another matter, whether it be Justices of the Supreme Court, or the judges of the lower federal courts."

## PART SEVEN

# Savoring Life

## CHAPTER FORTY-THREE

# *Grand Gourmet*

Justice Stone relished hard work, and the record he built was a source of much pride. In 1925 a commentator listed the number of his opinions as five without noticing that Stone had not joined the Court until a few months before the end of the term. "This," the Justice objected, "makes it look very much as though I were the Court loafer." Beginning with his first full term, he pointed out that the "statistics tell a different story."[1] Even as Chief Justice he continued to do "a stout year's work," always carrying his share or more of the Court's heavy schedule. In 1942 he wrote forty-six opinions, or half the number of majority rulings, and three times the peak load of certain Supreme Court Justices since 1946.[2] This impressive record was achieved by restricting non-essential activities to the barest minimum, saving himself for the really important things. Unless the occasion might give a chance to visit his sons Marshall and Lauson, he shunned extra-judicial chores. "Life is an elective system," he said in stock replies to tempting outside invitations, "and I seem to have made my choice."

Stone's rule was to guard his time jealously. The few occasions when he found himself abreast of his schedule he preferred to take a trip with family, dine with friends, or spend a few hours in an art gallery or museum. "Stone," Judge Julian Mack commented emphatically, "certainly knows about life as well as about law."[3]

"You should adopt my practice of working just hard enough, but not too hard," he advised Harold R. Medina in 1931. "I get up every morning at six-thirty, then have the liveliest kind of game of volley-ball played with a medicine ball, work from nine until six, or a little later, walk three miles, then go out to dinner. The general result is that I feel much younger than I did when I lived in New York."[4] But he sorely missed the Long Island Country Club, the scene of many pleasant days' fishing and congenial companionship. In acknowledging a brace of pheasant from a friend, he wrote: "I take it that this means you have had an outing down at the Club, which stirs my envy. I think I shall never quite get anything to replace the fun that I got out of the Club during the years just before I left New York."[5] In Washington he took up golf and joined the Chevy Chase Club. But when the cases began coming down "like a deluge," golf, along with other time-consuming pleasures, became a thing of the past.

Meanwhile dinner invitations from Washington socialites began pouring in. Even before confirmation, Stone had exulted in the social opportunities his new station would afford. "As a Justice of the Supreme Court," he pointed out, "my social rank is higher than that of a member of the Cabinet." After four full years in Washington the social life seemed more active than ever. "I really thought that after the new wore off we would not be pursued so vigorously," Stone commented, "but there seems to be an unending number of dinners, luncheons, musical affairs and what-not, many of them very interesting." Social activities kept up with unabated vigor. "I never saw such a place as this Washington," he wrote in 1932. "It looks as though the public had taken us to feed for the rest of the winter, but I am hoping for a let-up and a little quiet life soon."[6]

The "let-up" he sought came the next year when the New Deal President took up his residence in the White House. The members of the new administration seemed "not to be very socially inclined, and everybody is more or less hard up financially." The Justice was consoled, however, by the thought that the depression might produce "sane living." The New Deal itself soon made its own special contribution to sanity when, along with much that Stone considered bad, it ended the Volstead Act. The Justice was almost gleeful in writing of the "nice little party we had here last night." For the first time since the great drought he had wine at the table. "What a strange experience our prohibition adventure has been," he observed dolefully.[7]

A strict policy of three "nights out" a week was often declared and usually carried through "by resort to conventional excuses." But frequently the policy was honored in the breach as the popular Stones "felt under obligation to accept more invitations than we really should." A typical week might include one of Mrs. Lea's famous terrapin dinners. "Old Philadelphia," Stone reported fulsomely, "she does the dinner in the grand style of former days." Or there might be a "stunning" dinner party with "old Maryland people," "a gorgeous feast of Maryland terrapin, Maryland turkey, Maryland plum pudding; and all the other Maryland good things to eat one can think of." A fondue party at the Peters' sometimes followed the Swiss country custom of "making the fondue of Swiss cheese, flavored with kirsh." When the consistency was right, everybody took a piece of bread on his fork and dipped into the common pot. "It is great fun," Stone commented, "and we usually have a very merry time over it."[8]

The Justice especially enjoyed the "very swank" embassy dinners. Before the end of his first Japanese meal he became "quite expert" with chopsticks, picking up and eating peas without difficulty. "I did so well that I even ate too much," he said. A "grand dinner" at the Russian Embassy provided more than gastronomical interest. "Quite contrary to their national policy," the Justice reported, May 23, 1935, "they seem to ape the ways of a degenerate capitalism, . . . serving oceans of caviar, vodka, red and white wine and champagne, and generally disported themselves as millionaires are supposed to do."[9]

Belittling such pastimes, he often grumbled while preparing for a social evening. If the occasion was one of duty or obligation, the Justice always "cussed" about dress shirts and the elusive collar button or stud that could not be found without Mrs. Stone's help. For all his complaining, dining out was a constant pleasure to him; and if he could look forward "to meeting Mr. Churchill or some other celebrated person" who had made his mark, all incidental annoyances were almost forgotten.[10]

The Justice played host or guest with equal relish. Parties at the Stones' were small and informal—even when they included noted dignitaries—because the Justice thought these "more fun than the larger and more formal ones." It was "good," as he said, "to cultivate the social side and to have friends whom you meet, not for show or parade, but for the mutual satisfactions that come of human contacts."[11]

The Justice made it a point to attend Mrs. Stone's Monday "At Homes." Emerging from his study late in the afternoon, he would take his seat on a large sofa, near the fireplace, facing the wide entrance to the living room. In this position guests arriving and leaving had opportunity for more than a casual salutation, and a place to sit should a conversational gambit prove rewarding. The idol worshipers found little to encourage them, though Stone was "perfectly delighted when someone would congratulate him on an opinion or indicate that he was 'a leader of the law'—unless the adulation became too sugary."[12] Shop talk was not barred, but conversation was more likely to center on Mrs. Stone's painting, the Justice's collections of *objets d'art*, or gardening. The mother of one of his law clerks, on her return to Louisville after a visit with him, was asked by friends and neighbors what in the world she could talk about with a Supreme Court Justice. "I talked about cow manure, among other things," she told them. "He argued for the merits of sheep manure on his flowers, and I liked cow manure. Mr. Stone did not tell me anything about law and the Supreme Court. He talked to me about something I could understand."[13]

Washington society satisfied the Justice's gregarious propensities, but only his consuming interest in wine matched the fun he got in earlier days from the Long Island Club.

A taste for wine is not unprecedented among Supreme Court Justices; it harks back to the great Chief Justice, John Marshall. "We are great ascetics, and even deny ourselves wine except in wet weather," Marshall's associate, Justice Story, wrote his wife in 1823. "What I say about the wine gives you our rule; but it does sometimes happen that the Chief Justice will say to me, when the cloth is removed, 'Brother Story, step to the window and see if it does not look like rain.' And if I tell him that the sun is shining brightly, Judge Marshall will sometimes reply, 'All the better, for our jurisdiction extends over so large a territory that the doctrine of chances makes it certain that it must be raining somewhere.' "[14]

Few judges in Stone's generation shared this pleasure. A friend once asked him whether any of his colleagues knew or were fond of wines. Only Frankfurter, he replied, and went on to say that Chief Justice Hughes liked champagne "but only because it fizzes."[15] Though Stone was moderate in the use of both wine and food, it might almost be said that he had taken for his own Samuel Johnson's maxim: "He who does not mind his belly will hardly mind anything else." Certainly, he did not acquire his taste for wine as Henry IV of France was said to have gotten his—by having a few drops of a rare vintage rubbed across his lips at birth. Nor is it likely that "peeled grapes, flavored with kirsch," were ever served at the Amherst homestead, though to Stone's forebears it seemed "a great trial and even a very dangerous experiment to drink water in the New World."[16] Old Simon Stone, dying on the field of battle, gasped when his rescuers administered "fair water" but was revived perceptibly by a dose of "strong waters." More likely, time, experience, and money had wrought the change. "The rich," someone has observed, "are different from you and me." "Yes," a critic replied, "they have more money." Stone seems almost to personify the ironic colloquy, as one contrasts the simple farm boy, fond of horseplay, expelled from Massachusetts Agricultural College, with the urbane, cosmopolitan lawyer, completely at ease with the most polished of his Wall Street brethren.

By the time prohibition became effective, Stone had a small wine cellar. Though he could buy no more fine wines, he determined to keep what he had. On the move from Englewood, New Jersey, to Riverside Drive in New York, the wine cellar went along too. After appointment to the Court made it very unlikely that he would return to New York, the former Attorney General was dismayed to find that no liquor could be brought into the District of Columbia. Only the taste for fine vintages went with him from Wall Street to Washington. During the Volstead drought he refused to drink even at embassy parties. "You are on foreign soil where it is not illegal to take alcoholic beverages," his more technically minded friends protested. Stone had made his decision and nothing could change it so long as prohibition lasted.

Wines are living things. Widely varying soil, climate, and method of manufacture give each a distinctive bouquet. After a good deal of thoughtful sampling and a regime of taste-training, beginning with small wines and gradually building up to great examples of the same type, Stone acquired an educated palate.* No "wine snob," he followed the basic tenet of the amateur: "Wine is good when it tastes good." In buying supplies for his cellar, a great part of the fun was to come upon a real taste sensation, a fine wine neglected, yet equal to the best. With the uncanny instinct of a New England trader, he often took a chance on a vintage or a wine judged by the experts to be somewhat below par—occasionally with pleasing results. "I have found that despite the fact that 1925 is not considered such a good year," he told a winebibber friend, "some of the clarets of that year are turning out very well."[17]

The great wines, it has been said, reserve their "splendid impressions for the tasters who know how to wait." In managing his cellar,† as on the bench, Stone displayed that prime requisite of a true son of the vine—patience. "I have some Château Pape Clément 1924 in the cellar which I have not tried," he told a friend who boasted of this rare vintage. "My curiosity being stirred, I shall be digging it up soon. I am also interested to see that you had some Château Latour 1890," he went on admiringly. "That must have been an interesting item."[18]

Stone understood the major distinctions between the principal European wines, had some knowledge of the lesser European growths, and was familiar with the principal California varieties.[19] Those qualified to judge had no doubt of his pre-eminence. He was considered to have "a palate above and beyond most of the members of wine and food societies."[20] "How much he really knew about wine," his secretary has observed, "I cannot say, but he certainly played a wonderful game of being a wine connoisseur."[21]

As his reputation grew he astonished hosts and dinner guests by identifying the wines served, down to the vintage and year. A hostess

* Palate is a curious thing. Some seem to have it naturally, while others come by it through practice. Maurice Healy tells in his book, *Claret and White Wines of Bordeaux* (London: Constable & Co., 1934) how he discovered his palate. "In truth, mine is a rather comical qualification for the authorship of a work upon wine. I was a teetotaller until I was nearly thirty. Only the accident of the war persuaded me to tolerate the taste of wine. But once I had grown to like it I found that, probably because I am a non-smoker, I had a discriminating palate." Stone was also a non-smoker. It dulls the taste, he said.

† In 1937 Stone built a wine cellar in the northwest corner of his basement. The outside walls were beneath the ground level and without sun exposure. Lined throughout with two courses of hollow tile, and well insulated at the top, the cellar was designed so as to make certain that the good vintages it contained could ripen undisturbed by high or too violent ranges of temperature.

once told him in advance that she would serve a particular vintage. At table Stone tasted the wine, and the lady asked how he liked it. "Excellent," he replied, but he also insisted it was not the wine she had said she would serve. Investigation proved that the butler had poured from the wrong bottle.* His sons once carefully wrapped a bottle of Erbacher he had received as a birthday gift and challenged their father to say from which of his shelves it came. "I was prompt to tell them," he reported to the donor, "that it didn't come from any shelf of mine, but that it did come from the Rheingau, which was as close as I could come since I do not know the Erbacher wines very well."[22] As a feat of discernment this is perhaps on a par with ability to forecast weather—it comes with experience and is fallible.

European visits added greatly to his knowledge. On trips to France he sometimes made pilgrimages to the Loire and Rhône Valleys, sampling the delicate *vins du pays*. His cellar included the fine Bordelaisan reds and the famous white Château Haut-Brion, great Burgundies from the Côte d'Or, the slope of gold; and white wines from the German Rhine and Moselle.

California wines, in Stone's judgment, were "quite good, though lacking the distinctive flavors of some of the French and the German." French wines were esteemed above all others. Of 1904 Musigny, from the heart of Burgundy, he said: "I never tasted anything quite in the same class. It is like a flower garden." The Bordeaux, Château Mouton Rothschild 1929, was rated "fairest of the fair." Developing slowly, the 1929 wine from this vineyard finally became an all-time classic. Château Ausone, from Saint-Emilion, grown on soil once cultivated by the Roman poet Ausonius, was a close rival. The poet himself however, disappointed the twentieth-century jurist. "I think I once told you that I envied the man who owned his own vineyard," Stone wrote Chaffee Hall, who had sent the "first fruits" of his own vines. "For that reason I have often been a bit envious of the poet Ausonius.

---

* Stone's skill, though striking, is by no means unprecedented. Morris Hadley tells how his father, Arthur Twining Hadley, president of Yale, while serving as Theodore Roosevelt Professor in Berlin, astounded a group of wine-loving German professors. They served a wine "blind" and asked the educator to identify it. The expert recognized at once the general district and year, but after several sips he could only say that the wine was markedly reminiscent of three well-known vineyards, which he named. The guests listened with growing excitement and at the end the host, drinking to Hadley's health, said: "Do you realize what you have done? You could never have tasted this wine. It is from a small private vineyard that has been in my family for some centuries and the wine never comes on the market. The three vineyards which you named, however, are the three by which my family's vineyard is bounded." (Morris Hadley, *Arthur Twining Hadley* (New Haven, Yale University Press [1948]), p. 185 ff.)

"The story is a good one and not at all impossible for a man who knew his Rhine wine," Stone wrote Carl P. Rollins, March, 1944.

I am also a bit annoyed at him," Stone went on. "So far as I can learn, he never wrote any poetry about his vineyard or his wine, which indicates to me very plainly that he couldn't have been much of a poet—or his wine in his day didn't have the superb quality which it has in ours."[23]

A point in favor of Stone's absorbing interest in wine was that it took little time from the important things—one must eat, and wine is the natural companion of good food. Stone often staged "wine dinners" for a few friends, planning the food to dramatize the wine. Numerous courses permitted the sampling of several wines, served in ascending order of excellence. Mrs. Stone, a superb cook, personally supervised preparation of the feasts. The cooking and serving of good food rated high among the artistic achievements the Justice appreciated. When the meal was in process his wife would often take a small quantity of soup to the library for sampling. Sometimes the Justice would go to the kitchen and taste whatever was ready.

An adept wine host, Stone developed his own vinous rituals. Taking exception to the advice of Peter Greig's Wine and Food letter that a burgundy "should breathe fifteen minutes before serving," he said: "I have always thought an hour was better, especially if the wine is old."[24] Stone much preferred to bring fine wine from the cellar and open it with his own hands. This was not possible on his seventieth birthday, when his wife gave him a surprise party.[25] The rare champagne she chose from the 1921 vintage of the century-old house of Lanson, *père et fils*, must have been at its peak, as the neatly mounted label is among an incomplete collection the Justice once started in memory of famous occasions.

Spurred by her husband's interest and enthusiasm, Mrs. Stone did her best for the little group of gourmets. "I had a small dinner party of friends here recently," Stone said of one such affair, "for whom I was able to dig up some Mouton Rothschild 1926 and some Berncasteler Badstube 1931. Both proved to be excellent although I was a bit dubious about so early a date for a Moselle. The *pièce de résistance* was pheasant, flavored with brandy introduced at some stage of the cooking procedure which Mrs. Stone has found to be the appropriate one."[26] The mere mention of this delicacy brought several requests for Mrs. Stone's secret.

Among Stone's special delights was a cheese course before dessert, not only because cheese brings out the flavor of fine wine better than almost anything else, but because he liked cheese. As with wines, he enthusiastically sampled various cheeses as he traveled. "If you have never sat under an arbor in sunny Italy," he reminisced in 1937, "with a bottle of ripe Chianti or Frascati, and a generous slab of Pavlona, you have yet to live." "Good cheese," he declared solemnly, "is one of the gifts of the Gods, a fact that is not appreciated in this country as it ought to be."[27]

Various friends generously indulged his taste. Swiss and Canadian cheese came from Carl Ganter, Monterey Jack from Dr. George Selleck, an indigenous Oregon product from Sterling Carr, a Vermont cheddar made and aged in the Crowley plant from Felix Frankfurter or Frank Buxton. This was a special favorite. Crowley, "my cheese maker extraordinary," Stone called him. The Justice sent gourmet friends many samples of this masterpiece. Three generations of Yankee know-how went into this old-fashioned New England product. The Vermont cheddar, Stone boasted, "will improve the taste of any wine." It was his custom to try out red wines for his cellar with a bit of this cheese, but he discovered that it made the wine taste too good. "Now I find that a crust of French bread does much better."[28] To ensure the makings of a delectable bedtime snack, he often poured port wine over a Crowley cheese and set it in the refrigerator for a few months to ripen.

What may have begun quite casually took on through the years seemingly pervasive importance. Good wine, "the true elixir of life,"[29] Stone said, demanded the "serious attention" of men "qualified" to appreciate it. To drink disrespectfully and without appreciation a wine that had been a decade or two in the making seemed to him a form of sacrilege. "And the Brandy!!!!" he wrote ecstatically, "it makes my eyes roll just to think of it. It is altogether the best I have tasted. I shall keep it for very special occasions. Meanwhile, from time to time, I shall uncork the bottle to get the aroma, and caress it like a sweetheart."[30]

The winebibber's ritual, to the outsider so much vinous voodoo, is devoted to getting as much out of the final moment of a wine's life as soil and sunshine, press, cask, and cellar have put into it. Sight, smell, and taste, each plays a role. He twirls the glass between his hands, warming the wine, swirling it, observing color and the slow falling back of the tears. Better to watch this phenomenon, he demands a large clear goblet. "A soap bubble cut in half," someone has rhapsodized, "would make the ideal wine glass." But the winetaster's nose, rather than his eye, is the "last court of appeal." Faint body heat imparted by the palms of the hands forces off an exquisite bouquet. Pushing his nose into the glass, the wine lover captures perfumes and experiences ecstasy's essence, bringing to mind the "twinkling feet of dancing nymphs, an army with banners, a peacock's tail."[31] Intense search with tongue and nose for "balance, bouquet, and finesse," the game of serving wine "blind," to test skill, provide pleasant and untaxing diversion. "Not only does one drink wine," a famous oenophilist has commented, "one inhales it, one looks at it, one tastes it, one swallows it . . . and one talks about it."[32]

Wine drew the Justice into a circle of like-minded friends in New York and San Francisco—Carl Ganter, Farnham Griffiths, Dr. Maynard A. Amerine, Dr. Raoul Blanquie, Henry Allen Moe, Dr. George Selleck, Robert G. Sproul, Paul Kieffer, Chaffee Hall, Sterling Carr. It gave renewed zest to friendships based on other interests. These comrades in wine demanded little and gave much—companionship, relaxation, admiration. "Perhaps," one of them commented discerningly, "our discussions of wines and our friends may be some relief from judicial cares." It may well be that winebibbing friends made more of a contribution than even they realized.

For them a luncheon or wine dinner was something of a game, relaxation into which one could pretend to put all one's energies and take a certain pride that few shared similar tastes and knowledge. "Give my regards," Stone wrote Farnham Griffiths in mock seriousness, "to all my California friends who seem determined to continue to pay proper tribute to good wine as long as it lasts, and keep some for yourself."[33] Wine lent conviviality, made the talk lighter. One anecdote told and retold the good luck of a hospitalized oenophilist whose nurses, "a Mrs. Sherry and a Miss Portwine," served as constant reminders of past pleasures. At the little stag dinners, the group regaled each other with a favorite doggerel Stone would recite almost without provocation:

> The horse and mule live thirty years
> And nothing know of wines and beers;
> The goat and sheep at twenty die,
> And never taste of Scotch or Rye;
> The cow drinks water by the ton
> And at eighteen is mostly done;
> Without the aid of rum and gin
> The dog at fifteen cashes in;
> The cat in milk and water soaks,
> And then at twelve years old she croaks;
> The modest, sober bone-dry hen
> Lays eggs for nogs and dies at ten;
> All animals are strictly dry;
> They sinless live and swiftly die,
> While sinful, gleeful rum-soaked men
> Survive for three score years and ten.
> And some of us—a mighty few—
> Stay pickled 'til we're ninety-two.

Late in 1940 these "gentlemen of large girth who are willing to have it made larger," as Stone styled the gourmets, himself included, formed an organization to pay homage to fine wine and good food. Carl Ganter, dubbed by them "Le Grand Gourmet," was generally recognized as the real connoisseur, but Justice Stone was their nominal chief. "I am highly honored—not to say a good bit puffed up—by the announcement of the Stone Society of the Sons of the Vine," the Justice wrote. "My only sorrow at the moment is that I cannot be present at the baptism of this lusty, though infant, organization. If I were anything better than a galley-slave chained to his oar, I would hotfoot it out to San Francisco forthwith, just to show you youngsters with what relish and philosophy an old-timer sips his glass of wine."[34] The Stone Society formed a sort of protective association around him, saving him from bar association dinners, public speeches, and the like for little dinners in intimate groups whose members were devoted to him. On his last trip to the West Coast in July 1941, the Stone Society tendered the new Chief Justice a luncheon, beginning with caviar and including a Madeira 1862 and a great white Burgundy, "Grand Montrachet 1929."

These pleasurable occasions were far less frequent than the Justice desired. After he became Chief Justice, San Francisco and New York, sites of most gatherings of the clan, seemed at the ends of the earth. "The work of the Court is so heavy and continuous," he wrote declining an alluring invitation from Carl Ganter, "that I find it extremely difficult to absent myself from Washington in term time."[35] Each fall and spring Ganter lay in wait, hoping the Stones would pause in New York on their annual migration long enough to allow the Chief Justice to sup with him. Others plied him with invitations equally seductive. Infrequently someone would "bag" him as a dinner or luncheon guest. When this happened the news spread quickly throughout the Stone Society.

"The Chief Justice has finally arranged to dine with the wine committee at the Century," one lucky host exulted, "and we are already digging in the cellar for him."[36] "A most delightful evening with an exceptional company of good fellows," Stone reported to the West Coast. "Unfortunately, there was no written menu, but they regaled me with Corton Charlemagne '34, Cheval Blanc '26, Château Latour '20, Richebourg '34, Château d'Yquem of an old vintage, and Bellows cognac 1865. The conversation was in keeping with the place, the occasion, and the wines."[37]

To make up for his forced absence, members of the Stone Society vied with one another in organizing dinners and luncheons and sent on detailed reports of the proceedings. "Carl Ganter was greatly elated," Farnham Griffiths wrote, "because I served sherry blind and he guessed it—Duff Gordon Fino Coquinero—which the great expert,

Dr. Selleck, missed for an Isabelita." The story of one evening was told in drawings, on the menus, by George Holl, an artist member of the San Francisco followers of the Vine and Stone. "As you will see by Mr. Holl's sketches," Griffiths explained, "the evening developed quite a debate between the proponents of Bordeaux and Burgundian wines. The suggestion that you would rather have a vineyard than be Chief Justice grew out of a remark you made at one of our luncheons in San Francisco that the one man you envied at the table was Mr. Chaffee Hall who was just then starting his vineyard at Santa Cruz."[38]

"I am much interested in the contest between the Burgundians and the rooters for Bordeaux," Stone commented longingly. "I think I could reinforce either side in that battle and would be happy if I could be present at the skirmish in July."[39] Perforce, he enjoyed these celebrations of the Sons of the Vine vicariously and saved all the menus as "souvenirs of famous occasions."

The approach of World War II threatened another drought, and Stone foresaw probable disaster for good wines long before it came. His cellar still contained "some interesting items," but he worried lest it prove too small to "carry through a proper program." In 1941 he did "war work" for blockade-frustrated wine friends, sending each a list of domestic wines adjudged worthy by the judicial palate and calling attention to his own source of solace in a war-torn world—Chilean wines, "on the whole superior to the California wines."[40] Dwindling supplies of imported vintages made it clear that he would have to resort to domestic wines. It was a step he would not take so long as he had a little Château Ausone and some other vintage wines worth tasting.

As his cellar ebbed ever lower, the Justice dug deep to entertain Court brethren and came up with some bottles of Pichon-Longueville 1928, carefully laid away ten years before. "The next day," he reported with satisfaction, "I read of a sale at auction of a private cellar at Christie's in London, in which that particular wine brought $30 a bottle." "What is one to do to repair the inroads made in our cellars by the last three lean wine years?" he asked his friend Ganter. "Will you and I ever see any more great wine?"[41]

In a bitter mood he railed at inevitable destiny: "Somehow I feel that fate has been unkind to me in denying my full share of that privilege. First—by inflicting public office and prohibition on me at one and the same time and then cutting me off from the principal source of great wine by a demanding war." For consolation, Ganter conducted him on a New York shopping tour, and he was "fortunate enough to pick up some cases which promise well." Nevertheless he reported ominously: "There is almost no good wine available, and from what I hear I think it will be some years before we begin to get good wines from the other side."[42]

Members of the Stone Society and others did what they could to console their Chief. Ganter sent along a bottle of Berry Brothers brandy, forty-four years old, "capable of giving a thrill when one even looks at it." "I don't just see how you could part with it," Stone said. Another friend contributed his last bottle of Château Rauzan Gassies, an old favorite. Though the Chief Justice accepted it gratefully, his feelings were mixed. "I am not quite certain whether I shall enjoy it more or less when I realize that it was your last bottle," he wrote.[43]

War curbs put a severe crimp in luxurious entertainment, but Stone was still eager to go. Somehow he felt the war had denied him the customary pleasures of a public figure. "We had a quiet Christmas and a still quieter New Year's," he lamented in 1945. "In the old days we went early in the morning to a White House reception, which took up a good part of the morning. Then we went to a grand reception and luncheon given by the Secretary of State in the Pan American building, and from then until evening, or until we were exhausted, we visited various receptions and eggnog parties given by government officials. It was always the rule for the Chief Justice and his wife to give a reception open to everybody, while the Associate Justices chased around to the other receptions and finally returned for the Chief Justice's to aid him, his wife and theirs, in serving the hungry and thirsty. By seven o'clock in the evening everyone was ready for bed and a long sleep. This year, so far as I know, there was not a single official reception."[44]

Despite his overtly dour outlook, he fully appreciated his good fortune. "At any rate," he told one wine *ami*, "we have accumulated some pleasant recollections." "As I think we are licking the Germans and the Japs," he wrote, putting his wartime complaints in true perspective, "I possess myself in patience and look forward to better days." With the prospect of a renewed flow of good wine from France, and with the arrival of a Crowley cheese, unobtainable during hostilities, he mellowed immediately. "I now feel for the first time," he wrote the donor, "that the war is really over."[45]

## CHAPTER FORTY-FOUR

# Lobsters, Certs, and Sights

The rigors of Court work taxed even Stone's stamina. By the end of the term he was always champing at the bit, straining to get away for "a grand and glorious holiday." He usually left Washington the very day Court adjourned, often taking the train without returning to his house. "It is important," he advised successive law clerks, "to begin the work in October in good health and with that refreshment that comes from a period of leisure and change of scene."[1]

Through the years the Justice's vacation pattern remained virtually unchanged. As a prelude to the summer, he sometimes gallivanted about a bit, taking honorary degrees from leading colleges and universities.* The first part of his vacation, perhaps six or eight weeks, was usually spent on the Continent, visiting and revisiting places of Western culture.

"Contact with other lands and races and cultures," the Justice commented in 1927, "is a worth-while experience. I have had much joy and profit from it in my own time, and I intend to get much more." Stone was a "great believer in travel." "Nothing freshens me up intellectually and spiritually," he said, "or gives me a better grasp on the day's job when I get back than seeing strange countries and people."[2]

The Stones' first trip abroad was in 1909. They had scarcely reached London when Harlan's law firm cabled him to go to Russia on a pending law suit. This visit left some indelible impressions—the terrible contrasts of wealth and poverty, the meticulous watch kept by the police on the foreigner, the many strange customs. He recalled with particular vividness a religious procession in Kishnev, where the richly vestmented priests, bearing priceless icons, were followed by scores of poor peasants, many barefoot. Before returning home, the Stones had a brief glimpse of the French capital—just enough to awaken a keen desire to return and visit its historic landmarks in a more leisurely fashion.

Two years later they were in Europe again, visiting Belgium, Hol-

---

* Honorary degrees came from Yale, 1924; Columbia, 1925; Williams, 1925; George Washington, 1927; Syracuse, 1928; Harvard, 1931; Dartmouth, 1934; Michigan, 1934; Pennsylvania, 1934; Chicago, 1938; Oberlin, 1939; Kenyon, 1940; Princeton, 1942; Tufts, 1942; Colgate, 1942; Yeshiva, 1944; Bowdoin, 1944.

land, and Switzerland. Not far from Ostend they found Knocke, a quiet
seaside resort. With this as a center, they took short trips to the cathedrals and art galleries of Brussels, Bruges, Antwerp, and Ghent. Via
Holland's rich farm lands and picturesque market places, they came
to St. Symphorien opposite Interlaken at the far end of Lake Thun,
only to be greeted by heavy, driving rain, the dull steel gray lake, the
towering Alpine peaks shrouded in a blanket of mist.

"Is this what we have traveled so many miles to see?" Stone said
gloomily as the hotel porter led them to the horse-drawn omnibus.
"There's not a mountain in sight."

But next morning he found bright sunshine streaming in through the
windows. In the distance rose snow-covered peaks—the Mönch, the
Eiger, and the Jungfrau. Up the mountainside they climbed in a slow-
moving funicular to visit the ice fields and the loftily situated village
of Mürren.

Later they went by train to Meiringen, which connected with a horse-
drawn coach for Gletsch and the Rhône glacier. But the train was late,
and the only coach for Gletsch had already gone. Harlan fumed and
cursed both train and coach. "Why not hire a horse and carriage,"
Mrs. Stone suggested. A driver turned up, and off they went over
twenty-five miles of precipitous mountain roads. Harlan rode in frigid
silence, indifferent to the magnificent scenery. Suddenly the horse
stopped, whinnied sadly, and lay down across the road.

"He must be sick," said Mrs. Stone.

No reply.

"Maybe he has the colic."

No reply.

The baffled driver crawled down from his high seat and stood by
the roadside, surveying his recumbent horse and the carriage's broken
shaft.

Time passed. Tinkling bells echoed across the pastures; a small boy
ambled down the road with his cows and goats. Darkness settled over
the valley, the horse recovered, the driver mended the shaft, and the
carriage inched along toward Gletsch. On their arrival, the inn had
long since finished serving dinner. Still Harlan kept silent. Mrs. Stone
knew the mood would pass and so it did—after sleep and awaking to
the incomparable blue of the ice on the glacier, naturally silent. There
were visits in other years—Lucerne, Lake Geneva, the Rigi—but to the
end of his days he wanted to go back to Mürren and "stay for a while."

On the way home the Stones stopped at Heidelberg, with its crumbling castle high on the hill above the dreaming river. One summer
evening there they listened to music and drank beer under the trees.
Next morning, after an evening of Bach and Mozart, they woke to the
blare of trumpets and the heavy tread of marching troops.

The Stones were indeed ensnared by the beauty of Europe. Only two years later, in 1913, they were in Saint-Briac, a small fishing village on the Brittany coast. They explored the inland villages and observed the life of the peasants—men tilling the soil with oxen, women in front of their thatched cottages loading carts for market day. From the ramparts of Saint Malo they saw the tides surge in and out and sampled Mme. Poulard's famous omelets at Mont-Saint-Michel. Quimper pottery, a souvenir of days at Dinan, Dinard, and other places in France, brightened the Stone breakfast table for many years.

Ten years passed before Stone was able to take his family abroad again. Sailing on the *Conte Rosso,* shortly after he joined Sullivan and Cromwell, they landed at Naples. After Sorrento and excursions to Capri and Pompeii, they headed for Paris via Rome, Florence, Venice, Milan, and Chamonix in the heart of the French Alps. Before proceeding by express train to Paris they went to Geneva. "I remember," Marshall Stone writes, "that my father checked some of our luggage in the luggage van and at the time when the customs examination at the Franco-Swiss border took place he contrived to lock the keys or luggage checks or both in one of the valises. While my recollection of the details is now quite hazy, I recall that considerable consternation and trouble ensued."

During the next seven years the Stones were unable to indulge their wanderlust. The pressures of establishing himself in Washington, assuming new duties on the Court, and building a house gave too little time. Instead they vacationed on the American continent or else at their summer home in Maine. In 1925 they saw something of eastern Canada—Toronto, Ottawa, Montreal, and the old French city of Quebec. Sailing up the Saguenay River, the boat docked for an hour at Murray Bay, the summer home of Chief Justice Taft. Imposing and urbane as ever, the former President came down to the pier to meet them, attracting the attention of curious steamer passengers and other onlookers. Taft insisted on taking them home with him for a hurried family dinner and accompanied them back to the boat just in time to resume their journey.

In 1928 Stone addressed the Seattle Bar Association, and thus had his first trip to the West Coast. En route they stopped at Yellowstone National Park to see its famous geysers, hot springs, and rock formations, and to catch trout in Yellowstone Lake. From Seattle they took short excursions on Puget Sound and made the trip to Vancouver and Victoria; they also drove up Mount Rainier. In San Francisco the Justice and Sterling Carr went on a gastronomic splurge, ordering after much deliberation and ceremony their favorite specialties in that city's famous restaurants. Carr showed them Lake Tahoe and the giant Redwoods, Oregon's Crater Lake, the ghost camps of the gold-seeking Forty-Niners, and the gambling dives at Reno.[3]

Stone enjoyed all this but preferred more radical changes of environment. Without a trip to Europe every year or so he felt cheated. A most memorable visit was the one to Italy in 1930 with the Adolph Millers. The Justice started out in high glee. On landing in Naples, however, the vacationers were distressed to learn that the next day would be a holiday and their projected tour of the shops impossible. They had wanted especially to visit a place dealing in reproductions of ancient Pompeiian bronzes. Deciding to make the most of their short stay, they determined to set out for the shop immediately. "We started on foot," Miller recalls, "expecting to find a taxi, but were disappointed. When a horse-drawn *carrozza* came into sight, I hailed the driver and, as the rather slender vehicle approached, wondered whether the four could possibly ride in it. I expressed my doubts to Harlan Stone, and he said, 'Well, the ladies can sit on the rear seat, and you can sit on this little drop seat, and I will get up with the driver.' The space for the driver was none too wide, and the driver himself was portly. Nothing daunted, Stone sat there, one of his legs dangling nonchalantly over the rail as the party drove down the Via Nazionale in search of the bronze shop."[4]

Stone took full advantage of his opportunities. He visited the galleries of Naples, searched out curio shops, wandered about the excavations at Pompeii and the temple ruins of Grecian Paestum, sailed on the bay of Naples, and explored the Blue Grotto of Capri. In Florence days were spent in the Uffizi Gallery and the Pitti Palace. In Rome the ruins vied with the art galleries for his attention. There he witnessed a solemn beatification and had a private audience with the Pope. The high point came at St. Peter's.

"We had all but completed our visit of the interior," Adolph Miller recalls, "and were approaching the great entrance door. Harlan led the way to 'La Pietà,' the famous sculpture by Michelangelo. We stood there together some time in silence. The ladies of our party moved toward the door. I waited a few moments and then followed. Harlan Stone remained behind. We were outside looking around for a full five minutes when I decided to go see where he was. I found him still standing in the same position before 'La Pietà.' He took no notice of my presence until I plucked him by the sleeve and told him that the ladies were waiting outside. 'Was there ever,' he asked quietly, 'such desolation and despair pictured in any human face?' "[5]

From Rome the party headed northward through the Dolomites, scarred and blasted by World War I. "We saw many sad evidences of the war," the Justice wrote his sons, "ruined villages scattered along the mountainsides and graveyards filled with Italian and Austrian dead." In Bavaria they attended the Passion Play at Oberammergau. Though "prepared to be disillusioned," Harlan was enthralled. "The performance was impressive, done with fine dramatic feeling and dignity. It made a more profound impression on me than any other stage performance I have seen. It hardly seems possible that the little village could have produced it. The characters all looked the part without make-up and the successive scenes were really a series of beautiful stage pictures based on the works of the Master painters. John and Peter might have stepped out of Dürer's famous painting in the Munich Museum. All the scenes and characters recalled paintings which we have been admiring since we left Naples."[6]

Two years later the Stones decided on a Scandinavian tour. Sailing from New York, June 1, 1932, on the S.S. *Deutschland,* they were honored as "distinguished travelers." In a setting of Alpine scenes, the ship's host had a wide selection of Austrian dishes for his guests of honor. "We were the high-muck-a-mucks on the *Deutschland,*" the Justice recounted. "The Captain gave a dinner in our honor and all sorts of attention was paid us."

After landing at Hamburg, they went first to Denmark and spent a few days in Copenhagen. Neatness and agrarian prosperity abounded in this smallest of the Scandinavian countries. "Denmark is the most beautiful farming country I have ever seen," he wrote Lauson and his wife, "and I never saw farming better done."[7] He was struck by the people's political sagacity and their civilization. When Francis Hackett's book on Denmark was published in 1941, Stone told the author of his own admiration for the Danes. "You know, I chose Denmark a good many years ago, as holding out the best promise of any country in the world for a really civilized and, therefore, happy life to its people. Your book strengthens and confirms that impression."[8]

From Denmark the Stones pushed on to Stockholm via the Göta Canal. After visiting the King's palace, Drottningholm, and the walled city of Visby on Gotland Island, they went to Rättvik on Lake Siljan for the famous midsummer festival there. Lavishly decorated carriages were fit background for men and women dancing about the Maypole in their richly embroidered costumes. Swedish ways in food came in for special comment. "I never saw a place for food like Sweden," the Justice wrote his sons. "No one takes less than four meals a day and each is a heavy one. Breakfast in Sweden consists of porridge, eggs, coffee, cheese, sausage, and innumerable dishes of cold meat and fish, both cooked and raw. Luncheon and sometimes dinner starts off with *smörgåsbord* (literally smeared bread). Various kinds of bread are brought in with a quarter of a pound or so of delicious butter; then great platters of hors d'oeuvres, shrimp, lobster, herring prepared in several different ways, assorted cold meats, curried eggs, liver preparations, etc. When one has eaten his fill of this accumulation with plenty of good Danish or Swedish beer and (if you are a Scandinavian) occasional glasses of *aqua vite* (liquid lightning), the real meal begins."[9]

In Norway's capital they visited the Folk Museum of Scandinavian artifacts, among them elaborate carved ships of the Viking period. Sailing from Oslo through the fiords, they enjoyed scenery reminiscent of the wilder coasts of northern Maine. Stone left Scandinavian lands full of enthusiasm. "The national monuments in this part of the world are not as interesting as those you have just visited," he wrote his son and daughter-in-law, "but they have their interest and their civilization so different from that of southern Europe; their customs and attractive scenery make the trip well worth while."[10]

Berlin contrasted sharply with the peaceful atmosphere and gracious ways of Scandinavia. The streets teemed with beggars, and the air was rent with cries of "Heil, Hitler" from militaristic paraders. Anxious to get away, the Stones hastened to join Emmy and Marshall in Paris, where "Father" and his adult son shared many interests—travel, art, and gastronomy. Together the two couples visited the forests and castles of Fontainebleau and Chantilly, the painter Millet's studio, and Avallon with its old gates, unchanged since the days of coaches when Napoleon stopped there on his return from Elba. Harlan and Marshall sampled the "spécialités de la maison" in some of the finest Parisian restaurants—Laperouse, La Cigogne, Au Cochon de Lait, Au Boeuf à la Mode, La Reine Pedauque, Au Vieux Logis in Montmartre, and La Rôtisserie Périgourdine on the quai across the river from Notre-Dame.

In 1933 the Stones went to the West Coast again, this time on a small Grace Line steamer, the *Santa Teresa*, which ran from New York, via the Canal. Taking several weeks for the trip, they stopped at six or eight Latin American ports, thus getting a real taste of the tropics and their first experience of this part of the world. Hoover met them at Pasadena and drove them to his home. Along the way they stopped frequently to buy cherries from orchards flourishing along the highway. The ex-President and the Supreme Court Justice left "a trail of cherry pits from Pasadena to Palo Alto."

On a final foreign tour in 1934 the Stones went first to the Isle of Wight "for a little period of loafing," then chartered an automobile and visited Salisbury, Winchester, and Bath. Years later Stone wanted very much to go back to old haunts in London, principally because of his honorary membership in the Athenaeum, an exclusive club known for wine and food. His invitation to join had come, he declared proudly, on nomination by the Lord Chief Justice of England, under the Club's Rule II—"persons eminent in science, literature, the arts, or public service."

Although Stone never saw Europe again, he sought Old World atmosphere on this side of the Atlantic. An important consideration in selecting any vacation spot was the sketching opportunities offered Mrs. Stone. In 1937 they went to Mexico, where subjects abounded— Taxco hilltop and the Borda Church, the mountains at Cuernavaca, the deserts of San Luis Potosí, and Iztaccihuatl Mountain at twilight. The next summer, in the Pacific Northwest, Mrs. Stone made her best-known picture, Mount Athabaska, now on permanent exhibition at the Corcoran Gallery. Lake Louise, Emerald Lake, Banff, Yoho Valley— such scenic gems as these kept her busy. At Yoho Valley deer crossed the trails frequently, and bears lurked in the edges of the wood. One morning Mrs. Stone settled herself not far from the Lodge with her sketchbook. All of a sudden Harlan shouted, "Don't move!" Just behind her stood a mother bear and two cubs. With the help of men at the Lodge and a powerful fire hose he frightened them away.

The following summer Dr. George C. Ruhle, a naturalist at Glacier National Park and an expert on Indian lore, introduced the Stones to the life and customs of the Blackfeet. At Browning they attended a medicine fiesta, the celebration with which the Blackfeet ended a long fast. When Dr. Ruhle asked about admission to the ceremony, he discovered it was closed to outsiders.

"Who is chief of the ceremony?" asked Dr. Ruhle.

"Yellow Kidney," replied the Indian brave.

"Tell Yellow Kidney, Ninah-Stahkoo [Ruhle's Indian name] wishes to see him and to greet him."

The boy went off and a moment later Yellow Kidney appeared at the entrance of the stockade, arms outstretched and a broad smile on his face.

"Ah, ah, Ninah-Stahkoo," he chanted, motioning to them all to enter. "Pucks-kah-poe!"

Yellow Kidney then presented the strangers to the assembled multitude and announced, "We are giving this dance in your honor."[11]

Shortly thereafter the Blackfeet, impressed by the eminence of a Justice of the Supreme Court, expressed their desire to give him a name in their language and make him a member of the tribe. This required a special powwow. For this the Indians gathered at Glacier Park Hotel. Last Star performed the ceremony. Placing his right hand on the left shoulder of the Justice, Last Star gave him a slight push forward to send him out into the world with the name of Pitavachtan, or Eagle Shield. Mrs. Stone was christened Pitaki, or Eagle Woman.

"Wherever the Blackfeet meet you," chanted the chief, "they will greet you as a brother."

By early August a Supreme Court Justice's summer work—what Holmes called "the bloody certs"—begins to pile up, and Stone had to settle down. After his "real vacation" in some exotic place, he and his

wife almost invariably returned to their beloved Isle au Haut, a remote island in Penobscot Bay off the coast of Maine.* The Stones first
saw this spot in the summer of 1900 when brother Winthrop invited
them to visit there. Accessible only by boat from Stonington, this little
island, seven miles long and two miles wide, seemed like one of the
final outposts of civilization. Traversing it was a thickly wooded moun-
tainous backbone with scattered patches of meadow and bold cliffs.
On the east the island was swept by the winds, waves, and tides of the
Atlantic Ocean; on the west it faced the bay with its myriads of rocky
islets jutting out of restless waters. At evening the sun set in splendor
behind the gentle contours of the Camden Hills.

Peopled with placid, solid, rustic folk, Isle au Haut kept the wild
charm of another era. Even now there are no shopping centers, gas
stations, movie houses, or parking meters. Only a few Model T Fords
bounce along the rocky dirt roads that wind through the woods. For
Stone such lacks were no deprivation. "The automobile is a nuisance,"
he wrote his brother Lauson in 1926. "While I ride around in one, I
despise it more than any other possession I have, for when I ride in it,
I am at the mercy of every bootlegger, incompetent driver, and scalla-
wag who is able to raise money enough to possess one of the things."[12]

At Isle au Haut the Justice found the peace and solitude, ease and
informality, he loved. Old clothes were the banner of this better life—
"the older the better, the more patches the better." When a patch wore
through, another was patched thereon. If his wife suggested "sprucing
up," he would file a rejoinder: "You are trying to make a dude of me."
Here he joined in the day-by-day routine of people who kept close to
the sea, close to the woods, close to the land. Stone's forebears had been
folk of the same sort, and much of their venturesome spirit was deeply
rooted in him. He found the island "about the only place left in the
world that changes little, if at all," keeping that "flavor of simplicity
which one should try to get in life somehow or other."[13]

Mrs. Stone saw their island world and loved it as a painter must:
the color contrasts and gradations from chalky white or tawny yellow

---

* The island's name stemmed from its discovery by Sieur de Champlain on one
of his voyages in 1603 or 1604. In describing the islands of the region the noted
explorer said: ". . . nearly in the middle, out to sea, there is another very high
ar.d remarkable island, which for this reason I called 'Ile Haute.' (Elizabeth B.
Eustis, 'Acadia's Isle au Haut Area,'" National Parks Magazine, Jan.-March, 1952,
p. 14.)

That Indians had used the island as summer camp ground is shown by shell
heaps and burial places. It was not permanently settled until 1772 and 1775. The
early settlers—Turners, Richs, Chapins, and Bartons—lived by fishing, sheep-raising,
and lumbering. The island population flourished and increased during the heyday
of the fishing industry in the 1880s and '90s, but declined with the advent of
power boats, which enabled fishermen and lobstermen to live on the mainland and
escape the rigors of winter on Isle au Haut.

in the rock ledges to the somber green of the pines or the flamboyant rose of the setting sun. Through the years she made many water colors of the vistas and characters about her—the village with its scattering of weather-worn houses, the harbor and the lighthouse beyond, the wharf where fishermen worked, the rocks, the cliffs, and the multi-tempered sea.

At first the Stones made brief visits as boarders at the home of Mrs. John Turner. When they began to bring the children there in 1908, they became renters of summer cottages but still boarded at the Turners, so Mrs. Stone might have leisure for painting and companionship with her family. In 1916 they built a house of their own on the brow of a hill overlooking the harbor. It was a shingled cottage, spacious and roomy, of weather-beaten gray with faded blue-green trim. The Stones planned their island home down to the last practical detail, relying on an architect only for technical assistance in laying out proper plans and drawing up detailed specifications for the contractor. Simple furniture, rag rugs, and colorful cretonne brightened the interior. The broad-beamed dining room was furnished in that heavy oak popular when the Stones set up housekeeping. Over the big round dining table hung a wrought iron candlestick chandelier designed by Mrs. Stone and made by Clyde Turner, the village blacksmith.

Housekeeping in this rustic setting presented a number of problems. The cooking was done on a wood range, later adapted for kerosene. Staple groceries were sent up from Boston, and twice a week Mrs. Stone shopped at Stonington either in person or by lists entrusted to the mailboat man. There was still time for painting in the shed studio a few steps from the cottage. From time to time the Justice, invariably an interested critic, dropped the certiorari he might be perusing on the porch and looked in to see "what she was up to."

At Isle au Haut his steady fare was "lobsters and certioraris."[14] "I am sorry to see that you have the illusion that my time in Maine was spent wholly in loafing," Stone chided his friend Sterling Carr, October 18, 1937. "I would just advise you that I received eight mail bags jammed full of certioraris, and that I examined them there preparatory to disposing of them in our conference the first week of the term." Working at odd moments and with his usual rapidity, he covered everything ready for examination up to September 15, so as to go back to Washington with all certiorari applications considered. This left plenty of time for life-giving pleasure with family and friends.

The Stones hiked through the wooded hills, over island trails, or sailed off on their beloved *Sabrina*. They often packed the boat with lunch, certs, books, and sketch bag to spend the day on some other part of the island. Sometimes they gave picnic parties for as many as thirty friends. Harlan loved the preparations. He went to the fisherman's wharf, picked his lobsters and clams, weighting the latter in a bag below the low-water mark a few days in advance so they could expel mud and sand. These affairs began with steamed clams, then live lobster steamed in seaweed, cod or haddock, potatoes, and corn on the cob, and wound up with doughnuts, cake, fruit, and coffee. No wonder the Justice reveled in picnics. "I love a picnic even in the winter," he once remarked, "and I think those who do not, or are unable to get one up on short notice, ought to have something done to them."[15]

On vacation Stone liked to help with the household chores. He kept the tank for the range and ice box supplied with kerosene, collected the mail twice a day, cut the alders, or painted the boat. In blackberry time he picked an extra quantity for making wine. After Mrs. Stone had fixed the brew in crocks and set it out to ferment, he stirred it twice each day for three weeks, sampling the product frequently in the process. Wine made one season was strained and bottled for use the following year, or later.

During the cool Maine evenings the family would often gather with friends to prepare Welsh rarebit. Joining in the jollification, the Justice enjoyed such rollicking tunes as the one concerning Brady O'Lynn, with or without the harmonica accompaniment provided by Professor William P. Turner of Purdue University, a son of Isle au Haut. There were also quieter evenings when the Stones gathered about the field-stone fireplace to hear "Father" read aloud from Joseph C. Lincoln's Cape Cod tales, Jacobs' sea stories, or Stephen Vincent Benét's "The Devil and Daniel Webster."

At Isle au Haut the Stones thus blended solitude and seclusion with an enthusiastic sociability. On Sundays the whole family went to the little white church where services were conducted for a good many years by Dr. Frank Snell, a medical missionary with degrees in both divinity and medicine, and later on by a seminary student on vacation. Never standing aloof from the life of the community as do many summer visitors, they developed a keen and abiding interest in all local problems. Throughout the year an extensive and warmly personal correspondence was carried on with Clyde and Clarissa Turner, who in the off season took care of all matters concerning the Stone cottage and boat. Each spring as adjournment of Court approached, detailed instructions were sent on ahead.* Clyde, in turn, kept the Justice informed about local affairs.

Toward summer, especially, the Justice's letters expressed his long-

---

* A typical letter covers: "*Cottage*—Fix floor under refrigerator. Stove for kitchen went off some time since, according to notice from Sears and Roebuck. The reference number to correspondence is No. 15770-22/FC. Get something to keep chimney from falling apart. Put on chimney cap."

*Windmill*—Leak in southeast corner of tank ought to be looked to before tank is

ing for Maine and his "island friends." No matter what exotic lands claimed him, he always spent at Isle au Haut "as much or as little time as we find convenient, but always some."[16] At this remote hideaway, free from the telephone and social obligations, the Justice rested, "vegetated a little," caught up on matter marked for reading during the busy term. Isle au Haut had the "best lobster and soft clams in the world," excellent boating, good fishing, beautiful walks—he loved them all. Here he drank again at the streams of his heritage, renewed his hold on basic human virtues, and stored up, against the trials and confusions of the winter, resources of principle and integrity.

The summer of 1940 marked the end of an era. World conflict ruled out European travel, and American involvement forced the Chief Justice to modify his vacation pattern still further. "My place at Isle au Haut, Maine," he wrote Carl Ganter in 1942, "is too far out at sea to be either safe or comfortable this year."[17] From Clyde Turner came disturbing descriptions of island life in wartime: "It was reported a tanker sighted a sub outside the island, and I think there must have been some truth in it, as there was a cruiser out by Foester Head going back and forth all through the storm. There have been a lot of planes, large C. G. boats, and blimps around. When we were in Rockland, one of the French battleships was there on her trial course, and she was well guarded by planes and destroyers. The sub may be waiting for her to come out to Seal Island for target practice."[18]

Reluctantly the Stones settled at a plush inn at Franconia in the heart of the beautiful White Mountains. "It is not the kind of holiday I ever took before or am anxious to take this time," he wrote. After a few days, however, he was somewhat reconciled. "Sugar Hill is attractive," he reported, "and Peckett's comes as near being a perfect place as any I ever saw."[19]

Peckett's, one of New Hampshire's showplaces, stood in bold contrast with the stark simplicity of Isle au Haut. The low rambling structure was luxuriously appointed and tastefully furnished in antiques. Mr. Peckett, wiry, shrewd, a connoisseur of all fine things from banjo clocks to lobster Newburg, was past master at creating quiet elegance and solid comfort. The perfection of the inn was, however, imperfect. "Alas," the Justice deplored, "it has no wine cellar."[20] The Stones

---

filled. Have Welch put in wrought iron tubing which is much less subject to rust than ordinary steel tubing. Put on new couplings for plunger rod or spear.

*Boat*—Some of the plugs in water jacket may have to be renewed. New plugs are in bag in righthand drawer of my desk at cottage. Have some sort of a stop to prevent advancing the spark too far. Put in bilge pump which can be either connected with fly wheel or shaft and keep it clear of water. Replace valve because salt water comes through exhaust. In ordering valve refer to number assigned to engine when it was bought. Number is tacked on underside of cover to forward cuddy on port side. New tubing for oil pumps is in forward starboard locker."

lodged in one of Peckett's attractive cottages and in the evening often sat on the porch with close friends and watched the setting sun fade while the moon rose above the white birches and dark pines. When the cool of night sent them indoors, they built a fire in the fireplace and spent the evening in leisurely talk.

Vacations during the war years, whether at Peckett's or at the Waumbeck Inn, were of the poultice sort, good for a much-needed rest. Days of walking, reading, and loafing, though pleasurable, "didn't compensate for the other places" he really wanted to see.[21]

Nineteen forty-five was his last summer. As the leaves began to turn and the air became brisk, he had a deep sense of regret. Signs of snow on Mount Washington reminded him that another summer had gone and another winter's work was about to begin.[22] He wasn't quite ready to face the regular grind.

CHAPTER FORTY-FIVE

# *Connoisseur*

Broad experience in New York, Washington, and Europe endowed Stone with a rich cultural background. His understanding was rooted not so much in expertness as in innate love of beauty. Only those who have "traveled with him in Europe," Adolph Miller observed, "or sat with him through an entire evening of symphonic music, could know how sensitive his nature was to beauty in all its forms."[1] If a connoisseur is one "competent to pass critical judgment in an art or in matters of taste," Justice Stone met the test.

While living in New York and Englewood the Stones attended the opera regularly, where they heard Tetrazzini, Calvé, Galli-Curci, Bori, Caruso, Chaliapin, and other immortals. On their tours abroad they took in such great musical centers as Munich, Vienna, Salzburg, and Milan. In Washington they heard all the great symphony orchestras, and a Paderewski concert at the White House.[2] The Justice and his wife went occasionally to Baltimore for performances of artists not booked to appear in Washington. Sometimes they traveled to New York to hear a favorite opera at the Metropolitan.

Stone was especially fond of symphonic music. For many years he regularly attended the concerts of the Philadelphia Symphony Orchestra, and never forgot Stokowski's rendition of Musorgski's *Pictures at an Exhibition.* His taste inclined toward the classical, but he also enjoyed Stravinsky. Perhaps the high point in Stone's musical experience came in 1936 when Justice Cardozo took him to hear the Philadelphia Symphony with the youthful Yehudi Menuhin as soloist. "It was one of the most marvelous musical events in my recollection," Stone reported. "He is now about seventeen years of age, looks and acts the part until he begins to play the violin, and then he is transformed into a master, playing with all the certainty, power, and restraint of a mature man. He played a Bach concerto as I never heard it before, Lalo's *Symphonie Espagnole,* and then wound up with Beethoven's *Concerto for Violin.*"[3]

A few days later Stone dropped in to see Justice Holmes—then ninety-two—and told him how this gangling youngster had spell-bound an audience of three thousand.

"Ah," Holmes sighed, "what a triumph! I sometimes think I would give ten years of my life to be able to play like that."

"Yes," replied the younger jurist, "but some of us would give ten years of our lives to be able to write opinions like yours."

Holmes perked up and said with a twinkle, "My boy"—Stone was then sixty-two—"God sees through all this modesty."[4]

Stone sought relaxation in music. After a day's work it gave him "peace and harmony in an inharmonious world."

To keep his mind alert and fit he turned to books. His reading matter covered a wide range—magazines, professional journals, technical works on the physical and social sciences, biographies of painters and sculptors. He read several newspapers, and in later years took the anti-New Deal *Baltimore Sun* just to follow his favorite columnist, Frank R. Kent. In less active years he was fascinated by Napoleon, a strange hero for a Yankee. Later on he was steeped in Lincoln and in the early history of the West. Among American historical figures his favorites were Jefferson, Lincoln, George Mason, and Franklin. Of the latter Stone wrote: "He has always seemed to me to be not only the most representative of our public men, but distinctly the modern man in his eighteenth-century setting."[5] He ranked Mason along with Jefferson as "one of the nation's great political thinkers."[6]

Novels and the drama, popular or not, got little notice. "I cannot recall at home seeing him read any of the works of Dickens, Thackeray, and Poe which were on our library shelves," his son Marshall has recalled.[7] "How delightful it would be," the Justice once remarked, "if I could have about three days each recess time when I could read books that are a little off the beaten path."[8]

His special aversion was George Bernard Shaw. After seeing *The Doctor's Dilemma* he wrote: "Bernard Shaw usually bores me to extinction and this was the worst ever. I think it will be a long time before I again pay good money and take valuable time to hear his wisecracks."[9] More to his liking were solid works such as Cardozo's *The Nature of the Judicial Process*—"one of the few important law books written in this country during the twentieth century"—or an authoritative work on Leonardo da Vinci, Michelangelo, Van Gogh, Winslow Homer. He got more enjoyment from seeing Shakespeare plays on the stage than from reading them, but considered it necessary to see one of them acted at least a dozen times before the beauty of language could be fully appreciated.

The strange thing is that so little of this vast outside reading ever found its way into his informal writing and correspondence. For all his love of Shakespeare, he rarely cited him or other literary worthies to prove or illustrate a point.

Election in December 1937 as Honorary Associate of Washington's Literary Society may have been in response to a deeply felt need. Stone joined with the understanding that no duties would be expected of him. By 1944, however, the pledge seems to have been forgotten. The Secretary then had the temerity to suggest that the Justice prepare a paper. "I really ought to have something to say to the Literary Society," he replied apologetically, "and I should like to say it. The difficulty is that I am a terrifically busy man, working long hours, often late at night on practically every day of the week from October until late June. After that I am supposed to have a holiday, but it is actually devoted mostly to the preparation of the work for the next term of Court and to attending Judicial Conferences, which is a part of the duties of Chief Justice."[10]

When Stanley King became president of Amherst in 1932, he asked Stone to accept membership on the Board of Trustees. "My deep affection for the College, my belief in its capacity for service, and faith in its future," he wrote in answer to a "feeler" from the Trustees' Secretary, "all afford the strongest motives for my wishing to accept the election and do what I can to promote its interests. But I am embarrassed by the fact . . . that my engagements on the Court are so exacting and peremptory that I may find it impossible to attend meetings, and difficult to give that service which the College is entitled to have from a trustee." Stone felt he simply couldn't spare the time. But King pressed his case so convincingly that the Justice finally consented.[11]

Earlier Stone had yielded to Calvin Coolidge's urgent request to accept the chairmanship of a Special Committee on Plan and Scope for the Folger Library. "I do this," Stone wrote the former President, December 31, 1931, "because of the desire I have long felt to be of service to Amherst College and because of the interest I have in this worthy undertaking."[12]

Over a period of forty-five years, Henry Clay Folger, Amherst 1879, and his wife had assembled a great Shakespearean collection and planned the construction of a beautiful building in Washington to house it. Folger died in 1930, before the Library was completed, but his will provided for its endowment, and this was to be administered by the Amherst Board of Trustees.[13]

The beauty of the structure had caught Stone's eye from the first. "Yesterday," he wrote his sons, November 21, 1931, "we stole a little time off and had a private view of the new Folger Shakespeare Library and Museum. It is a beautiful building, both exterior and interior, and a very remarkable accomplishment. The exterior of the building is modernistic, but with bas-relief decorations in classic style. The architect has really accomplished a very fine and unique result. It has as much beauty in its line and mass as a Greek temple, but is not Greek, and the touch of decoration gives it a flavor of antiquity which is very beautiful in result. The interior is Elizabethan, beautiful paneling with Tudor ornamentation, and the whole, of course, revolving around Shakespeare. It is a unique thing and will be one of the famous buildings of the world."

Beginning in 1938, the Amherst Trustees held their January sessions, which dealt primarily with Folger affairs, in Washington. After the meeting the Justice and his wife always gave the Board a dinner worthy of Lucullus. "As a practicing gourmet," Stanley King recalled, "the Justice did not believe in dulling the taste buds with cocktails before dinner. . . . With each course an appropriate wine was served, and the Justice's taste in wines was as unerring as in foods."[14] Stone was not satisfied to serve ordinary lobsters; he arranged to have them shipped from Isle au Haut, after being caught by a particular fisherman whom he considered to be the best judge of lobsters in Maine. If the main course was game, it might be sent by a hunter in the Northwest whom the Stones had befriended. The cheese came from Crowley's, and the wines served were of course especially selected by Stone himself.

The location of the Folger Library, diagonally across the street from the Supreme Court building, made it possible for the Justice to drop in frequently and discuss matters of importance with the director, William C. Slade, and later Joseph Q. Adams. Within a few years he had become deeply absorbed, especially in helping to round out the Library to the point where it became the finest collection of Elizabethan books in the world. "Personally, I never have desired to possess rare books," he wrote, "but it is really quite interesting to watch the assembling of such an extraordinary collection of rarities as we have at the Folger."[15] He did more than observe; he was instrumental in securing some of the Library's most valuable collections.

Soon after the death of Sir Leicester Harmsworth in 1937 one of the finest and most extensive Elizabethan libraries came on the market. Sir Leicester, though not particularly interested in the Shakespeare folios, had specialized in rare items shedding light on the Elizabethan Age. Adams, eager to get this precious hoard, urged President King to make every effort to obtain it.[16] In the ensuing negotiations with London solicitors Stone gave valuable legal advice and put to effective use his native and highly developed talent for bargaining. Thanks to him, the Harmsworth treasures went to Washington instead of Cambridge, though Harvard's bid exceeded the best price Folger could offer.[17] The effect of this acquisition was to transform Folger "from a collection centered on Shakespeare to the greatest collection of books on English civilization of the sixteenth and seventeenth centuries."[18]

In 1938 the Folger made another significant purchase in England—the Loseley manuscripts. World War II broke out before they could be sent here, so the directors put them in safekeeping at the Bodleian Library. When Göring's Luftwaffe threatened to destroy them, Stone asked Assistant Secretary of State Adolf Berle, Jr., if he could arrange to have the documents "forwarded to the United States in the diplomatic pouch."[19] As a result, the manuscripts were delivered to the American Embassy in London, sealed in the State Department pouch, and flown across the Atlantic.

Even day-to-day operations claimed the Justice's attention. "The director of the Library came to see him almost too often, it seemed to me," a former law clerk observed, "taking up with him every conceivable type of problem, large and small."[20] In the interminable wrangles over whether the replica of the Elizabethan theater should be used for public performances, the Folger staff stood firm against exposure of their treasures "to the tender mercies" of "an irresponsible public."[21] Stone was more sympathetic. Believing the primary function of the Library to be educational, he also envisioned a working relation with the English departments of various colleges and universities. "I think we might well consider the active encouragement of students for advanced degrees to spend part of their time, while working for the degree, at the Folger Library by acquainting them with our facilities and offering to guide their studies through the assistance of Dr. Adams," he wrote. "I feel very strongly that we should not be content with the function of the Library as a mere museum in which Folger's wonderful collection is exhibited, but that as rapidly as possible it may be made to render educational service both in the field of scholarship and of popular knowledge of and interest in Shakespeare."[22]

As an Amherst Trustee, from 1932 until 1946, Stone was not able to attend all the meetings. But when he did "his judgment on the problems presented was unsurpassed. He listened attentively and expressed his opinion. He understood scholars and scholarship, he could quickly master the essentials of any problem, and he would in a few words point out the essential question that required action. . . . I can recollect no occasion on which the Board did not follow his judgment."[23] The Justice's activities in behalf of Amherst and the Folger were but another facet of his personality. "No Renaissance institution could have had a Trustee chairman who more completely exemplified the spirit of that great age."[24]

As a small boy Stone had collected stamps. After he became a Supreme Court Justice, a philatelist, with the best of intentions, sent him three envelopes postmarked "Justice, West Virginia," "Harlan, Indiana," and "Stone, Idaho." The Justice was quite unimpressed. "We seem to raise a new crop of cranks every day," he commented. Convinced that this hobby was a waste of time, he gave his assortment to his sons, both avid collectors.[25]

Painting, sculpture, architecture, laces, tapestries, ivories, china, glass, leather work—all products of delicate handicraft—appealed to him irresistibly. "Sculpture," he said, "is decidedly part of the lawyer's training. When I go to see Justice Holmes I almost always take with me a bundle of interesting prints. The fact that he enjoys and appreciates them explains, in part at least, why he is a great lawyer."[26]

Stone was also interested in fine etchings, to which he was introduced as a law student. One day a classmate, Walter Carter, invited him to his home. The elder Mr. Carter owned a choice collection that included Whistler, Haden, and Buhot. "The intellectual appeal of the etcher's art," Stone commented years later, "is emphasized more than in other forms, and . . . good examples of it are within reach of most devotees."[27] Starting with Whistler's "Billingsgate," a Christmas present from his wife, he built a discriminating collection—Seymour Haden, Whistler, Pennell, Claude Lorrain, Platt, and others. To him many of Platt's etchings were superb—"Misty Morning," "Buttermilk Channel," and "East River from the Bridge" were among his favorites. The latter two were in his own collection. Even after etchings and engravings of eminent lawyers and judges covered the walls of his huge library-study, he was constantly on the alert for more.*

In adding to his collections he satisfied still another propensity. Like his horse-trading father, the Justice loved to bargain. His law clerk, Allison Dunham, tells of the Syrian linen merchant who called each morning at his Wyoming Street house for more than a week to display his wares. A fine linen table cloth caught the Justice's eye, and he could have bought it at a fairly reasonable price. To have done so, however, would have violated his Yankee instincts. Offer and counter-offer went

* The Justice's collection has been given to Columbia University Law School.

back and forth. The Justice finally purchased at a price somewhat below the first quotation but higher than his own original offer. The "haggle" had been half the value of the purchase.[28]

Despite ingrained thrift, he rarely refused to pose for an artist, however obscure, who wished to paint or sculpt him. Only kindness prompted him to take and pay for a product obviously destined for the attic—ultimately, the furnace. He spent freely for what seemed no more than vacation souvenirs. In many places—in San Francisco's Chinatown, along the quays by the Seine, through dingy London streets, on terraced Italian hillsides—the Stones wandered and collected. "We did some shopping in Rome and Florence," he wrote home in 1930. "We found some interesting pictures, some old Capo-di-monti, a pair of fifteenth-century carved marble urns for the garden, and a pair of Byzantine marble lions (very old) for the front steps. They are like those supporting the altar columns in the baptistery at Pisa."[29] In Belgium, France, and Italy he loved to watch the lacewomen at work on the gossamer tracery of Alençon or Point de Venise. He could rarely resist the temptation to buy; nor could he get past a jewelry shop without a brooch or ornament for his wife. Antique silver and English porcelain, carved ivory, Tang and Sung figurines, and a fragment of an old wall from Hunang, China, graced their home.

Stone was drawn solely by the aesthetic merits of the objects acquired. He never sought to buy anything just because it was rare, seldom paid a higher price just to "beat out" another collector, and never bought objets d'art as an investment. The Justice insisted on using for everyday occasions any of his prizes that were utilitarian. His "extravagances" were enjoyable, he said, because "he could live with them."

Though a connoisseur of painting and sculpture, the Justice didn't feel that he could afford to collect either. He owned only one good painting, the head and shoulders of a woman by Martin de Voos (1531-1603). In 1933, however, he fell under the spell of a piece of sculpture by Maurice Sterne. "Sitting Figure," a woman in an attitude of thoughtful repose, attracted a great deal of attention that winter at the Museum of Modern Art in New York, where Stone first saw it. Sculptured in antique Greek marble,* this was for Stone "the most beautiful piece

---

* Sterne had acquired the Pentelic marble in Italy and carved the statue in his studio in the Sabine Hills near Rome. This piece of marble with its unusual golden color had an interesting history. From an Italian stone-cutter the sculptor learned that a native of Rome, while diving in the Tiber, had seen a large block of what appeared to be Pentelic marble on the bed of the stream. Due to its long immersion and a rusting-out process, the marble had taken on a rich golden color. The diver mentioned his discovery to the stone-cutter, who succeeded in raising the block. Since it was not large enough for a life-size statue, the sculptor decided to make several smaller figures.

of sculpture I have seen, other than some of the celebrated ones of antiquity."[30]

In March the Justice told the sculptor of his consuming interest: "While the thought of possessing that beautiful statue of yours is a wild extravagance on my part, nevertheless, I entertain it. I have rarely seen anything which has lingered so persistently in my mind. If I am to have it, it is very important that I should be able to give it the proper setting, and, therefore, before reaching a final decision, I would like to have the exact size of the base and the over-all dimensions—height, length, and breadth."[31] When the Justice finally succumbed he consoled himself with the thought that "it would at least be a handsome asset when I go bankrupt."[32]

This interest in antiques, in *objets d'art*, in travel, in the history of ancient civilizations, developed an appreciation of architecture. He liked the Gothic cathedrals of England and France, the temples and amphitheaters of Greece and Rome, and admired native American colonial architecture. Gunston Hall, George Mason's eighteenth-century mansion, magnificently set on a bluff overlooking the Potomac River below Mount Vernon, was one of his favorite haunts. Purchased in 1929 by Louis Hertle, a retired Chicago merchant, this historic Georgian house, marked by an exquisite English boxwood garden and rare woodwork executed in classical style, is one of the finest in the country. Stone met Hertle when the merchant first moved to Washington, and they soon became close friends. Together they discussed a plan to make the mansion a public shrine. They decided that on Hertle's death it should go to the Commonwealth of Virginia to be cared for and run by the National Society of Colonial Dames. Though Stone had often joked about the Colonial Dames, he encouraged the whole transaction. Hertle had performed, he said, an important public service in restoring Gunston Hall and "donating it as a permanent memorial to the great statesman, who contributed so much to the establishment of our Government in its formative stages and to securing constitutional protection of civil rights."[33]

Of all Stone's hobbies art was basic for him. This interest he shared with his wife. They spent many hours together in the Louvre, the Pitti Palace, the Uffizi Gallery, the British Museum, the Metropolitan, and countless others. Whenever away from Washington, he used spare moments to visit museums or art exhibits and urged his sons to do so. "I hope by this time," he wrote them in 1940, "you have been able to see the art exhibitions in your respective cities. The Italian exhibits in New York I have seen three times, twice in San Francisco and once in Chicago. They are certainly worth going a long way to see. There were not only the things from the Bargello and Pitti, but they are also exhibiting several pieces of sculpture from small Italian towns which

I had not seen, which are quite lovely. I wish very much the Brooklyn Stones could see the medieval art exhibit now going on in Boston. They have some extraordinary things, among others a piece of woodcarving sent by our friends, the Blisses, from Washington. It is not their finest. Another piece they showed at San Francisco this summer in the same room with the Italian exhibit, and it really stole the show."[34]

He had an expert's familiarity with leading American art collections and kept this knowledge current even though his duties did not permit him to visit all of them regularly.

"I am so sorry that I did not know of your interest outside the law," he wrote the Australian jurist, Herbert Evatt, who collected water colors. "There are a number of things which you should have seen while in Washington." Sketching an art lover's tour of the United States for the visitor, Stone listed the principal galleries in the New York area, noting the outstanding characteristics of their permanent collections and describing current exhibits. "Then at Worcester, Massachusetts, midway between New York and Boston," he wrote, "there is a very fine small collection, with a very notable collection of Winslow Homer's water colors." On the way west he recommended the art galleries at Pittsburgh, Detroit, Cincinnati, Cleveland, St. Louis, and Kansas City. In Chicago, besides the Art Institute, he advised a Field Museum trip to see Malvina Hoffman's small bronzes of racial types "assembled primarily because of their anthropological value," he explained, "but they have turned out to be works of art of extraordinary interest." Stone urged Evatt not to miss "the Bali drawings made by my friend, Maurice Sterne, presented to San Francisco by Albert M. Bender. If you will let me know when you are to be in San Francisco and where you will stop, Bender, who has been the good angel of art in San Francisco, will be glad to see that you find the things in which you are interested and to show you some of his own treasures."[35]

Frequent visits to the art galleries, not systematic study, developed and refined his taste. By reading and observation he came "to understand and appreciate the ultimate aims of art." To a publisher requesting his opinion of a manuscript on art, he wrote: "My whole life has been that of the hardworking professional man, with no formal training in the field of art or aesthetics. My reading in this field, so far as it has embraced acquaintance with books seeking to expound the principles of art, has been very limited. The occasional books I have read have proved to be very unsatisfactory, because they have seemed to me to deal little, or at least inadequately, with principles and to lack anything like a systematic approach to the subject. They have seemed to be dominated more by a weak and mushy sentimentalism than by any philosophy of art. On the other hand, I have read extensively about the work of individual artists in many fields. Since young manhood, I have been a constant visitor at exhibitions and galleries here and abroad, have followed what is going on in the art world, and have enjoyed a steadily growing interest and appreciation of man's artistic achievements in almost every field."[36]

Though partial to the old masters—Titian, Rubens, Michelangelo, Rembrandt—Stone was not blind to the "genius of a Van Gogh."[37] Toward modern art he maintaincd an open mind, and confessed that Van Gogh has "a tremendous grip on me." In commenting on Samuel A. Lewisohn's "Is There Chaos in Art?" he wrote: "What is chaos often depends upon the state of mind of the observer, quite as much as the objective facts which he observes. The untrained mind might well regard law itself as chaos. I confess that a good deal of modern art seems to me like chaos, but I am not so naïve as to conclude that the chaos is in the art rather than my powers of observation."[38] His subjective conception of art led to active association with a number of young artists and to lively interest in their careers. The Public Works Art Project, headed by his former law student and artist friend, Edward Bruce, aroused a storm of criticism from those who devoutly believed that all relief workers should rake leaves. Stone strongly supported the project, explaining: "I have always felt that a nation is justified in subsidizing art. That is more true these days when the private support of it is falling and is very likely to be lacking for a long time."[39]

When the Government decided to permit Bruce to use a portion of the funds in decorating new federal buildings, Stone applauded warmly. Boardman Robinson, Maurice Sterne, and Leon Kroll all discussed their proposed work with him, including the murals in the Department of Justice. "Leon Kroll," Stone informed Bruce, "has the notion that he wants to use my head and shoulders in the figure typifying 'Law,' so he was here and made a sketch which seemed to me quite successful, probably more successful than I will be as a type."[40] Although Kroll was using Stone merely as a model symbolic of an abstract concept, the artist found it unnecessary to make many changes in his appearance. "In the painting of your head as the symbol of the Law," he wrote the Justice enthusiastically, "I took the liberty of darkening your hair a bit because the lower tone is better against the sky. I also had to turn the head slightly, whereas the drawing is a direct profile. Otherwise I tried to get it to look like you." The mural, "Triumph of Justice," which embellishes a lunette in the Attorney General's private office, shows a younger but recognizable Stone in his judicial robe, with a law book under one arm, the other hand extended to workers escaping their oppressors. "There are several reasons why you function better than any of your colleagues," the artist explained fulsomely. "In the first place, you have a magnificent head and the deep oval in profile composes well with the long oval of the girl's head.

Second, it has vigor, kindness, and understanding necessary to convey the emotional idea of the gesture. The position you have occupied and do occupy in the Government and your interpretations of the law make it historically correct. Furthermore, if I may say so, I have an enormous admiration for you."[41]

The admiration was quite mutual. "They are both beautiful compositions," Stone wrote Kroll after examining photographs of the murals, "and they seem to me also to show a complete appreciation of the essential qualities of good mural painting. Rhythm, simplicity, and power in design, and the direct expression of an easily understood but moving thought are too often lacking in present-day murals. They are all present in yours."[42]

Far from scoffing at new techniques, he appreciated the necessity for an experimental attitude. "It is interesting to see how, out of all the development of modern art, much of it probably worthless, new conceptions of permanent value are making their way," he commented. "It is a pity we cannot get an art commission here which sees something of that probability." At every turn he encouraged Bruce "to give the artists a free hand in their own compositions." There was "something so big, so vital, and genuine in the work of the federal artists as to leave no doubt that this movement will result in the production of great masterpieces of American art." In time Bruce came to rely on the Justice as "a kind of Rock of Gibraltar." "Without your help," the artist told Stone, "I should be tempted to tell them all to go to hell." "The fact is," Bruce explained apologetically, "I know of nobody holding any important position in Washington, outside of yourself and the Morgenthaus, who has the slightest interest in a cultural or artistic movement such as we are trying to develop."[43]

Outstanding among the artists whose careers he had encouraged was Mrs. Stone. When their sons, Marshall and Lauson, were ready for college, leisure hours were in prospect and on the insistence of an amateur artist at Isle au Haut, she turned her hand to painting. Enthusiastic from the first, her husband inquired about courses and teachers in New York. Mrs. Stone, however, had few lessons. Largely self-taught, she began strictly for amusement, and "dabbling in art" continued through the years with nothing more serious in mind. "I like doing it just for the doing's sake," she said in 1937, "and paint whenever there is leisure that does not conflict with the wishes of my family or the activities of my household." This policy confined her efforts largely to vacation time. After a summer's work she would return to Washington, sketch bag crammed with vivid impressions of their travels in Mexico, California, the Rockies, or on the Maine coast. Interested in the process as well as the final result, the Justice would hover at his wife's shoulder while she busied herself with easel and paint brushes in some scenic spot, frequently offering comments in the form of provocative questions: "Why did you make the sky like that?" or "Why don't you put that in?" Mrs. Stone appreciated criticism and admitted his points were not infrequently well taken.

Despite her modest design, Mrs. Stone's paintings soon began to attract attention beyond the circle of her acquaintances. In the late thirties invitations to exhibit came to her from art galleries in and around the nation's capital. Her first show at the Corcoran in 1937 followed on the heels of their Mexican summer and featured the brilliant color contrasts of that Latin country along with sketches of the stark Maine coast. Four years later the Corcoran renewed its invitation to exhibit there, and the Chief Justice was among the early visitors. "Her pictures, thirty in number, make a very good display," he wrote in an enthusiastic account to his family. "The show has a good deal of variety and seems to me especially attractive. The Museum people say it is the best show they have had for a long time, and the artists and newspapers speak very generously of it." Two weeks later he was glad to confirm this judgment: "Duncan Phillips bought one of her pictures, I suppose for his gallery, which is a high compliment indeed, as he is a rather severe critic." Baroness Maydell, a Finnish artist, bought one of the Maine pictures because "they reminded her of her own land."[44]

"Painting for Fun," the title of her largest and best-remembered show, was staged in 1945 at the Virginia Museum of Fine Arts. Sixty-four water colors, including a number from the previous summer's stay at Peckett's, filled two galleries. The Chief Justice accompanied his wife to Richmond, where they were officially received by Governor and Mrs. Colgate Darden. The local reaction to Mrs. Stone's work was extremely favorable.

Mrs. Stone had at least one point in common with Renoir. "You paint as if you were doing it for fun!" the horrified master, Gleyre, exclaimed on examining his new student's work. "If it did not give me pleasure, I swear I would never do it," Renoir responded. And so it was for both the Stones. In excited admiration her most understanding critic would lapse into the editorial pronoun, explaining how "we" achieved this color effect and what idea "we" were trying to get across in the picture. Finally an artist friend asked, "Who painted that picture, you or Agnes?"

Whenever Mrs. Stone had paintings on display in Washington art galleries, her husband would lead friends there to show them off. Sometimes he would return alone to look at them more searchingly. "Mother deserves a great deal of credit," the Justice wrote their sons, "for taking up this work and carrying it to such a point of success. It certainly has given her, as it has given me, a great deal of pleasure."[45]

It was not until Stone became Chief Justice that his knowledge and devotion to art could be put to broad constructive public use.

As chancellor of the Smithsonian Institution and chairman of the Board of Trustees of the National Gallery of Art, he presided at all meetings and acted in an advisory capacity to other officers.

During the Coolidge and Hoover administrations the Stones had become friends of Andrew Mellon, founder of the National Gallery, and frequently dined at his home. "A few nights ago we were at Mr. Mellon's dinner given to the President and Mrs. Hoover," the Justice wrote his sister, February 4, 1932. "After dinner we had a very good opportunity to examine his many pictures, priceless masterpieces of the most famous painters the world has produced." Mellon had already planned the establishment of a National Gallery of Art but died just as the excavation work began. Three years later, when the Gallery on Constitution Avenue was completed, but before any works of art had been installed, the director, Mr. David Finley, invited Justice and Mrs. Stone to inspect the building. Both were enthusiastic about the architectural design, the floor plan, the arrangements for showing the paintings and sculpture, and the backgrounds provided in the various exhibition galleries. Their enthusiasm mounted. Finally, as they were about to leave, the Justice turned to Finley and said with deep feeling: "I cannot tell you how delighted I am with this building. Mrs. Stone and I had been very worried about it, for we knew that Mr. Mellon had provided adequate funds to do whatever was necessary. We were so afraid that with so much money available, the building would be overdone and the background and installation would be too elaborate for the works of art. We were almost afraid to come and see it, and now we could not be happier or more filled with admiration for the building in every respect."[46] Thereafter the Justice and his wife followed the progress of the Gallery with keen interest, and were present at its opening on March 17, 1941, when it was accepted and formally dedicated by President Roosevelt.

On assuming his new position as chairman in 1941 Stone not only discharged the formal duties of the office in the most conscientious manner but looked upon it as pleasure and relaxation. "Tuesday was a holiday here," he wrote his sons, October 13, 1941, "and I celebrated by suspending work in the afternoon and having a look at the pictures in the Mellon Gallery." On this occasion he dwelt on the French collection, the works of Corot, Degas, Daubigny, Renoir, and Cézanne. The early Corots seemed to him more like Hobbema than like the lace-curtain pictures Corot painted later. "I felt that I found something in these artists that I had never seen before," he said.

As in his work on the Folger Library Committee, the Justice was eager to make new acquisitions and often asked Finley if he could be of any assistance. Outstanding among the untapped resources for the nation was the famous Widener Collection. Joseph Widener, a friend of Mellon, had long been interested in the National Gallery and wanted ultimately to see his collection there. Legal complications were among the causes of delay. One evening when Finley was dining with the Stones the Justice said, "Mrs. Stone and I have never seen the Widener Collection, and we would like very much to see it. Do you think it could be arranged?"[47]

On the day after Court adjourned for the summer recess the three journeyed to Philadelphia, where Mr. Widener's car met them and drove them out to Lynnewood Hall. At luncheon Widener served Château Margaux, the only wine he ever drank. It so happened that this was also a favorite with the Chief Justice. Stone's next "family" letter described what he had seen: "Thursday morning Mother and I went to Philadelphia on the invitation of Mr. Joseph E. Widener and spent the day there in his magnificent Georgian palace, looking at his great collection of pictures and sculpture. He has a well-selected and beautifully shown collection, including eight [actually fourteen] Rembrandts, numerous Franz Hals, Raphael, Bellini, the early Dutch painters, El Greco, the English classicists, Titian, together with a considerable collection of Renaissance sculpture, including Donatello, Verrochio, and numerous others. There were also some original pieces by Benvenuto Cellini. It was a good experience."[48]

"We simply must get those pictures for the National Gallery," the Chief Justice told Finley on their way home. "It is the most wonderful collection, and it would mean everything to the Gallery to have so many masterpieces come to Washington." Then, with the chuckle Stone's friends knew so well, he added, "I wish we could also get his collection of Château Margaux!"[49]

On returning to Washington, Stone urged President Roosevelt to take the initiative in bringing this "unique and priceless treasure" to the capital by sponsoring legislation transferring any tax liability to the Government. This hurdle cleared, he pressed for an immediate removal to the National Gallery. When state taxing officers demurred, Widener's lawyer guaranteed them an opportunity to make the appraisal in Washington, but without success. "We believe," the attorneys wrote Stone, "that a letter from you will most effectively remove any such objection." The Chief Justice promptly assured the state's Secretary of Revenue that "the National Gallery of Art will gladly make all the articles in the Collection available to inspection and examination by the tax officials or other representatives of the State of Pennsylvania." After this assurance the Widener Collection was soon on its way to Washington.[50]

The formal opening of the Widener Collection was celebrated at the National Gallery on December 20, 1942. Before the ceremony the director and his wife gave a luncheon for the Widener family at their Georgetown home. Because of the war Finley's stock of Château Margaux had been sadly depleted, but the thoughtful host saw to it that the two bottles left in his cellar found their proper destination—one to serve the Chief Justice, the other to serve Mr. Widener.

During the early months of the war Stone, along with many others, became deeply concerned about Europe's irreplaceable treasures. On December 8, 1942, he wrote President Roosevelt, asking his support for the "creation of an organization functioning under the auspices of the Government, for the protection and conservation of works of art and of artistic and historical monuments and records in Europe, and to aid in salvaging and returning to, or compensating in kind, the lawful owners of such objects which have been appropriated by the Axis powers or by individuals acting with their authority or consent." The President endorsed the proposal enthusiastically and referred it to the appropriate agencies for detailed study. The upshot was the appointment in 1943 of the American Commission for the Protection and Salvage of Artistic and Historic Monuments in Europe. To keep intact his rigid rule against off-Court activities, he regretfully declined to serve as the commission's Chairman, but consented to the appointment of Justice Roberts.

Upon the Roberts Commission fell the Gargantuan task of cataloguing, listing, and tracing the art objects purloined or destroyed by the Germans in France, Belgium, Poland, Italy, Holland, and other invaded countries. There were few cases of outright theft or destruction. The usual procedure of the occupying Nazis was to "buy" art pieces with occupation currency and remove them to Germany. Many such "purchases" found their way into the private collections built up during the war by Hitler, Göring, Goebbels, and other Nazi chieftains. Hitler established an art gallery in a small Austrian town near his birthplace with pieces "bought" in occupied countries. One of the major jobs of the commission was to determine how much of Naples' artistic storehouse had been removed by the Germans before the demolition of the city. "It is a tremendous task to discover all these losses, verify, and catalogue them," Stone said in a newspaper interview. "But we are preparing a bill for presentation along with other demands for reparations when the war is over."[51]

One day shortly after fighting ended in Germany a high official in the War Department asked Finley if the National Gallery would be willing to accept temporary custody and responsibility for the care of German paintings from the Kaiser Friedrich Museum in Berlin, which had been found in a salt mine in Germany. Finley telephoned Stone, then on vacation in New Hampshire, asking if he could see him the next day about an important and confidential matter concerning the Gallery. "If the Government asks us to take care of these paintings," the Chief Justice told Finley, "we must do it. It is a duty which we could not escape if we wanted to."[52] Without even lingering long enough for lunch, Finley returned to Washington and assured War Department officials that the trustees of the National Gallery would accept the responsibility and give the paintings the same care they gave their own, until they could be safely restored to Germany and cared for by their rightful owners.

Stone was blissfully unaware of the storm of protest this decision would arouse. Back in Washington, he authorized, on September 26, 1945, the following news release: "The United States is removing from Germany to the continental United States certain perishable German art objects not readily identifiable as looted property, with the sole intention of keeping such treasures safe and in trust for the people of Germany or the other rightful owners. The United States will retain these objects of art in its possession only as long as necessary to insure their physical safety or until such time as it may be possible to return them to their rightful owners." "The reason for bringing these perishable art objects to the United States," the Chief Justice explained, "is that expert personnel is not available within the American Zone to assure their safety." That same day President Truman issued the identical release.

To some of the Monuments, Fine Arts, and Archives Specialist Officers, who had been entrusted with the care of this precious store in Germany, transfer of the paintings to America seemed high-handed. They were apprehensive lest other nations, under the pretext of "protective custody," take similar steps. "We are unanimously agreed," they protested, "that the transportation of these works of art, undertaken by the United States Army, upon direction from the highest national authority, establishes a precedent which is neither morally tenable nor trustworthy."[53] Still others joined the chorus of complaint. The disgruntled officers could see no explanation for the decision to send the pictures to America other than the fact that the repositories laboriously and successfully fashioned at Wiesbaden contained "damned good pictures."*

---

* "In order to house the collections under ideal conditions," Charles L. Kuhn has written, "the MFA & A Section requisitioned the museum building at Wiesbaden which had suffered but slight war damage. This building was placed in

Stone was outraged. The good faith of the President and Chief Justice of the United States had been challenged. With anger in his voice he said to Finley, "Have these men taken leave of their senses?"[54]

On December 11 the paintings, two hundred in all, including masterpieces by Botticelli, Van Dyck, Memling, Dürer, Raphael, Titian, Giorgione, Rembrandt, and Rubens, arrived aboard the S.S. *James Parker*. They were delivered to the Gallery and placed in air-conditioned storage. Belying the fears of certain museum officials and Fine Arts officers, the works of art were sent back to Germany safely and on schedule. But before they could be returned the question arose as to whether the collection should be shown at the National Gallery and elsewhere in the United States. The War Department gave an affirmative answer. Chief Justice and Mrs. Stone attended the opening exhibition and went frequently thereafter to see these paintings, subsequently shown in twelve other cities.

The work of judging did not leave him enough time either for the formal requirements of the Gallery or for personal enjoyment of its treasures, and he often chafed because "I am so circumstanced that it is impossible for me to devote as much time as I would like to the interests of the National Gallery."[55] This forced neglect was the more regrettable because of the brilliant future he foresaw for the institution. "I have visions of the National Gallery being the greatest art institution of our times," he wrote Samuel H. Kress in 1943. "The way in which it is organized, the true spirit of the collection already assembled there, the exceptionally favorable conditions under which works of art are shown there, and the great number of people (well over three millions already), from every part of the country, who visit the Gallery, are making it unique."[56]

For Stone himself the fine arts afforded a welcome relief from the ever-growing demands of the Chief Justiceship. After 1942 it was not unusual for him to telephone the director wearily and say, "I have an hour at my disposal. I would like to come to the National Gallery and see a few paintings. I feel the need of them!"[57]

charge of Captain Walter Farmer, a Monuments Specialist Officer, a trained architect with museum experience and a man wise in the ways of the Army. For two months Captain Farmer worked night and day preparing the building to receive the objects. The roof was repaired, broken glass was replaced, special shelving was constructed, accession cards were printed, engineering and janitorial labor was procured, a highly trained German curatorial staff, a restorer, photographer, librarian, and secretaries were engaged. Captain Farmer even succeeded in obtaining the two most sought after items in the German theater—sufficient coal to keep the building warm and dry during the impending winter and a guard detail of U.S. troops to police the premises twenty-four hours a day." (Charles L. Kuhn, "German Paintings in the National Gallery: A Protest," *College Art Journal*, Jan. 1946, pp. 80-81.)

## PART EIGHT

# The Verdict

## CHAPTER FORTY-SIX

# Judging Self-Judged

The years wore on with no slackening of pace. "Ever since I arrived in Washington I have been about as busy as one could be, considering that there are only twenty-four hours in a day and that one must eat and sleep," the Chief Justice wrote his sons, October 10, 1945. The Judicial Conference, "full of difficult problems," took four days. A week of Court conferences disposed of the various applications filed during the summer. Two weeks later twenty-seven cases had been heard; the Chief having assigned them for opinions, the Justices were busily engaged writing. When these preliminaries were over Stone felt like "a sailor shipwrecked at sea, who has just made shore and got his head out of water."[1] But he did not mention the probable reason for this storm-tossed feeling.

## THE ROBERTS LETTER

In June 1945, after four hectic terms on the reconstituted bench, Justice Roberts decided to resign. The year just ended had been marked by bitter judicial skirmishes, of which Roberts' fifty-three scornful, often sharp opinions gave only a hint. Adhering to formula and custom, the Chief Justice drafted a farewell letter during the summer. Lest the lingering wounds still rankle, the tribute was cautious, almost ungenerous:

> The announcement of your resignation as a Justice of this Court brings to us a profound sense of regret, that our association with you in the daily work of the Court must now come to an end.
> During the more than fifteen years since you took office you have given to the work of the Court the benefit of your skill and wide knowledge of the law, gained through years of assiduous study and practice of your profession. You have faithfully discharged the heavy responsibility which rests upon a Justice of this Court with promptness and dispatch, and with untiring energy. You have made fidelity to principle your guide to decision.
> At parting we who have shared that responsibility with you, and who have

shared in the common endeavor to make the law realize its ideal of justice, give you this assurance of our continued good will and friendly regard. In the years to come we wish for you good health, abiding strength and, with them, the full enjoyment of those durable satisfactions which will come from the continued devotion of your knowledge and skill to worthy achievement.

As usual, the proposed letter went to senior Associate Justice Black with the request that he sign and forward it to the next oldest judge. Black demurred, suggesting omission of all the first paragraph after the words "sense of regret," and of the last sentence of the second paragraph—"You have made fidelity to principle your guide to decision."[2]

Black's objections posed a delicate question. What was the Chief to do? Should he put the matter to Black on a take-it-or-leave-it basis and run the risk of a divided Court; or should he conciliate? Hoping for unanimity, he told Black to redraft the letter and circulate it. Black did this, but took the Chief's instructions as authorizing him to pass on the revised version as though it had come in this form from the Chief Justice. Black's covering letter contained no hint that the text he was sending differed from the one he had received from Stone, except for an enigmatic explanation of the absence of the Chief's signature: "The Chief Justice had me sign it first in order to save time."[3]

Reed signed promptly, while Justice Frankfurter (who meanwhile had learned from Stone himself of Black's objections) expressed disappointment at Black's failure to enclose the Chief's first draft. "Had I not had your communications of your original views," Frankfurter commented heatedly, "I would of course have assumed that that which Black circulated was *your* draft and expressed your desire and that you had Black sign it first in order to save time—whatever that may mean. And that will be the understanding every member of the Court will derive from these enclosures who has not seen your original draft and learned of Black's objections."[4] Every member, Frankfurter suggested, ought to have the benefit of the Chief's first draft, especially as Black's revision omitted the fundamental tenet about Roberts the Justice.

Under Frankfurter's prodding, Stone crossed the Rubicon. Circulating a memorandum containing his original letter and indicating by brackets the matter Black wanted deleted, he explained: "As Justice Black objects to two phrases in it, I asked him to redraft the letter accordingly and send copies to each Justice with my original covering memorandum. This I understand has been done. While I prefer my own draft, I wrote Justice Black that I would sign the letter with his amendments in order to secure unanimity. If that cannot be accomplished I think the matter should be postponed until we meet in Washington."[5]

Black's reaction was immediate and sharp. Reminding Stone that he had redrafted the letter at the Chief Justice's own request, he was at a loss to understand just what good purpose would be served by following up his letter with Stone's own draft. If there was to be an argument, he told the Chief Justice somewhat pugnaciously, consideration of the whole subject should be deferred. To make certain that no tribute, whatever its content, would be unanimous he withdrew his name even from his own letter.[6]

Only Douglas found Black's revision "wholly agreeable"; Murphy and Rutledge took a middle ground, being willing to accept either version in order to secure unanimity.[7] Frankfurter and Jackson, meanwhile, joined in an uncompromising stand and struggled as fiercely for Stone's support as if a formal Court decision were at stake. "I am surprised," Jackson wrote the Chief, "that any issue could arise over the proposed letter to Roberts. It seemed a formal and not too cordial letter originally. To strike from it all that it contained of tribute seems to me to leave it reading like a left-handed condemnation." He thought the deletions left the letter so colorless as to suggest that "silence would be charitable."[8]

Jackson saw the whole matter in a larger frame: "My greatest concern is not justice to Roberts. Ultimately, a man who has left recorded works will come to be judged by them and not by any letter of associates. More important than that the letter be worthy of Roberts is that it be worthy of the better selves of those who write it. And if I may without offense say so, I think that is particularly true of you whose name will head the list and whose association with Roberts has been the longest. You are the two survivors of the past epoch of the Court. You often differed with him and time has vindicated you in most of those differences. Certainly you are in a position to be not only just but generous, and I know it is your temperament to be such. I hope you will not allow yourself to be compromised in this respect."[9]

Nor did pressure from Black let up. How, he asked defiantly, could "unanimity" be secured by sending the memorandum Stone had prepared at Frankfurter's request? Thus pulled and hauled by resolute contenders, Stone replied in detail:

> I had no thought that the circulation of my draft of the Roberts letter would win unanimity, but I hoped that my announced willingness to sign your draft might have that effect. My purpose in circulating it with the accompanying memorandum was only to comply with Justice Frankfurter's request which I feel he was entitled to make. Sometime in the summer before I had heard from you on the subject, in writing Frankfurter about another

matter, I mentioned the fact that I had sent my draft to you asking that it be signed and circulated and asked him if he had received it. Later, when he received your version signed by you and Reed, he asked me to circulate my draft—which I did with a memorandum repeating what I had said to you, that I would sign your draft in order to secure unanimity.

I thought that my willingness to sign your draft instead of my own which you were unwilling to sign, would win your approval and I hoped that it might induce FF and possibly some others to join in. This hope seems not likely to be realized, as I understand that FF is of the opinion that to sign your draft is to affirm that Roberts lacks qualities mentioned in mine of which yours makes no mention. So far as I am concerned, I shall, as you request, let matters rest where they now are until we meet in Washington.[10]

Why did honorable, busy men make such a furor over a merely formal matter? Emily Post would have disposed of the Justices' problem in a paragraph, along the lines of Justice Jackson's common-sense advice. But etiquette was not the real issue. Black and Frankfurter stubbornly refused to treat it as a ceremonial formality. For them Court ritual, no less than judicial decisions, must be grounded in reality, but as to that they were in complete disagreement. Black could not abandon exposure of formalism long enough to say a few kind words to a departing brother. Frankfurter, mistaking form for substance, got himself to believe that by approving Black's excisions "under challenge," he would deny Roberts' most distinctive quality. Stone jibbed about, tacking before this breeze and that, striving vainly for a clear course.

This trifling incident parodies the working Court. Even in this Lilliputian campaign, fought in dead earnest, the dominant characteristics of its leading figures are sharply etched. The line-up reflects the then current factional differences, as well as the distribution of power, among the Justices. Stone, deliberate in making up his mind, hating petty bickering and personal bitterness, let more dynamic colleagues grasp at leadership. Black, calculating and ambitious, could, in a crisis such as this, command the voices, votes, and pens of four others. In opposition, Jackson, himself a powerful personality, but Black's rival rather than Stone's, stood shoulder to shoulder with the sometimes patronizing, ever more conservative, former pedagogue, Frankfurter.

Picayune as this episode may appear, for Stone the stakes were high. Prestige, intrinsic authority among his fellows, perhaps the most essential asset of a Chief Justice, hung in the balance. Probably no man could have fashioned a unanimous farewell to Roberts out of the welter of jealousy and intrigue coloring the relations of these willful men. At various times six Justices approved Black's letter. Perhaps Stone could have made a stand there. Or ramrod tactics might have been tried at Black's first objection. The Chief Justice could have bluntly instructed him to pass the letter on to Justice Reed with or without his signature.

When the vengeful McReynolds refused to sign the brethren's encomium on Brandeis, Chief Justice Hughes had let conspicuous silence proclaim its spiteful message.

"Stone dreaded conflict," Justice Jackson later explained, "and his dread was so strong that it seemed to me that he feared action which would bring it about."[11] In Washington, with no more responsibility for getting out a letter than the pressures of a courteous custom, the Justices decided to send none at all. At the Court's first session Stone announced Roberts' resignation in substantially the language approved by Black. In the circumstances, one is inclined to agree with Jackson: silence would have been more charitable.

### OLD ISSUES IN A NEW SETTING

During the ensuing months Stone felt, as he himself said, "a good deal like the man who sticks his head through a sheet at a country fair and lets the boys throw baseballs at him."[12] They came from all directions. Bruised and sore, he clung nevertheless to tried methods—careful deliberation, exploration of fact, pragmatic solutions. In this term, as throughout his judicial career, he stood out against expanding intergovernmental tax immunities. On that issue he refused to sanction new dogma, preferring as in the past "to deal with the matter empirically." Justice Frankfurter, however, took it upon himself, in *New York v. United States*,* to dispense with criteria used in past decisions and to formulate a new basis for the immunity.[13] Relying on Holmes' famous contradiction of Marshall's dictum about the taxing power,† he said the problem could no longer be dealt with in absolutes. Frankfurter would reduce tax immunity by a rule forbidding merely discriminatory taxation of one government by another, except where the tax hit the "state as a state." In the Gerhardt case Stone had considered this approach and rejected it as too facile. Now he refused to go along. Holmes, he informed Frankfurter, was "plainly mistaken" when he intimated that Courts could invalidate federal taxes simply because they were destructive. Stone's own Sonzinsky decision had sustained a prohibitive federal license on dealers in "gangster" weapons.

"Are you intending to suggest," the Chief Justice asked, "that the rule is different where such a tax is imposed on a state, as well as the citizen, without discrimination?" Stone had no doubt Congress might lawfully destroy liquor traffic by exorbitant taxation, and taking this tack, he shredded Frankfurter's argument by pointed queries:

---

* Here the Court upheld a non-discriminatory federal excise tax on the sale, by the state of New York, of bottled mineral waters taken from state-owned springs.

† Marshall had said in *McCulloch v. Maryland*: "The power to tax involves the power to destroy." Of Marshall's dictum Holmes commented in the Panhandle case (p. 223): "The power to tax is not the power to destroy while this Court sits."

"Would such a tax be invalid if levied on a liquor business conducted by a state? If it would be valid, why cite Justice Holmes' statement? If it would be invalid, then what becomes of your thesis that a tax laid upon a state in the same way that it is laid on ordinary taxpayers, is not invalid?"* Frankfurter's whole performance, the somewhat distraught Chief lamented, boiled down to "another way of saying that the states may have an implied immunity from taxation which private individuals may not claim, and we are left where we began."[14]

Frankfurter's persistence was all the more regrettable because it doomed any possibility for a majority opinion. After twice hearing argument on the point, only Justice Rutledge could accept Frankfurter's formulation. There were four opinions, Jackson's sojourn in Nuremburg reducing the number by one, as he, apparently, would have dissented separately.†

For dissenters Douglas and Black "the major objection to the suggested test is that it disregards the Tenth Amendment, places sovereign states on the same plane as private citizens, and makes the sovereign

---

* "Nothing was further from my thought," Frankfurter responded, Dec. 21, 1945, "than to suggest that 'a federal tax in other respects constitutionally laid,' could be set aside because it is too large. I entirely agree with you that Congress could lay a tax on intoxicating liquors involving a state 'calculated to destroy the traffic.' The point of my reference to the two Holmes' opinions [Panhandle case and *Long* v. *Rockwood,* 277 U.S. 142 (1928), p. 148] was the support of my statement that in Marshall's time absolutes were more frequently employed in opinions than the complexities of our times have rendered permissible. . . . Inasmuch as you had agreed with both those opinions, I had assumed that the innuendo of my citations was clear.

"All I claim for my opinion," Frankfurter continued, "is that it tidies up one corner of the law by removing the messy criteria on which previous cases sustaining taxes falling directly on states have been based. It does so by giving a generalizing limitation upon such taxing power, i.e., that it must be non-discriminatory, so that every producer of mineral water is taxed and not merely the state as a producer of mineral water, and by making it clear that whatever other freedom from taxation the state may enjoy because of our federal system, is to be left for future adjudication unembarrassed by anything we now say.

"The difficulty that now confronts us is that prior decisions taxing state activities directly were not decided empirically, but were determined on faulty generalizations, to wit, 'proprietary' *vs.* 'governmental' and 'a business enterprise of a sort that is normally within the reach of a federal taxing power.' See *South Carolina* v. *United States; Ohio* v. *Helvering; Helvering* v. *Powers.* We have to clear the ground, reject these untenable generalizations, and find an empirical binder for all these cases. This is the only modest purpose and, I hope, execution of my opinion. I think I am breaking no fresh eggs and merely throwing away some putrid ones."

† On the ground that "neither state nor federal governments are given express immunity from taxation by the other in the Constitution. But this Court has not hesitated for the benefit of the Federal Government to imply such immunities as it deems essential to safeguard its functions. I think we should do likewise in the case of a state, although their necessities may not be identical. It seems to me that a sale of its natural resources such as water, timber, or lands would stand on a different basis from sales of liquor." (From an opinion circulated by Jackson at the October 1944 Term.)

states pay the Federal Government for the privilege of exercising powers of sovereignty guaranteed them by the Constitution." The dissent
also made manifest Black's objections to Stone's Gerhardt decision.
Black argued for state experimentation with public ownership free
from federal taxation. Douglas's opinion rejected the contention that
such immunity cripples tax power in view of modern reliance on the
income tax.[15]

Finally the Chief Justice, reiterating the stand he had taken in the
Metcalf case, said: "The problem is not one to be solved by a formula,
but we may look to the structure of the Constitution as our guide to
decision. 'In a broad sense, the taxing power of either government,
even when exercised in a manner admittedly necessary and proper,
unavoidably has some effect upon the other. The burden of federal taxation necessarily sets an economic limit to the practical operation of
the taxing power of the states, and vice versa. . . . But neither government may destroy the other nor curtail in any substantial manner the
exercise of its powers. Hence the limitation upon the taxing power of
each, so far as it affects the other, must receive a practical construction
which permits both to function with the minimum of interference each
with the other; and that limitation cannot be so varied or extended as
seriously to impair either the taxing power of the government imposing
the tax . . . or the appropriate exercise of the functions of the government affected by it.' "[16]

The Court's supervision of administrative processes also continued to
plague him. Some of his colleagues had carried "to absurd lengths the
deference which courts must pay to the rulings of administrative agencies." "It is just ridiculous," he exploded on one occasion, "to say that
the money collectors in the Treasury Department know better than
we or the federal courts what Congress intended to do by the legislation here involved."[17] Nor had he relaxed his scrutiny of NLRB rulings. In advising Justice Jackson to include in a decision the exact
wording of a modified Board order, he warned: "Otherwise, interpretation of what you have said will become a subject of debate and the
National Labor Relations Board, with its usual tendencies, will reframe
the order to suit its own purposes."[18]

Though he left the qualification of labor's great gains largely to
others, the record discloses diminishing sympathy with the majority
views. During the years 1941-45 the Supreme Court considered twenty-
one cases involving orders of the NLRB, and the Wagner Act administrators set a record of seventeen victories, and four defeats. Stone
voted to sustain Board authority in ten cases out of nineteen, but
whether decision went for or against the Board the Chief Justice either
felt unable to speak out or believed others could do it better. In an
evaluation, counting only non-unanimous opinions and taking NLRB

rulings as invariably pro-labor, Stone rolled up a meager 32 per cent score in eighty-eight controversial labor cases between 1941 and 1946, considerably below the Court's over-all 68 per cent average.[19] During the early years of labor's march to power he was able to move forthrightly because he felt the law clearly sustained the workingman's claim. Now, however, when the cases became more subtle, and the NLRB reached out for authority not plainly written into the statute, the Chief Justice retreated from the thesis he had advanced at Harvard in 1936 as to the judge's responsibility for rounding out statutory law. Falling back on "judicial self-restraint," he moved steadily in the direction of curbing union power. The Steele case shows that as late as 1944 he was still capable of judicial ingenuity when it was the Court's purpose to assert control over unions. Repeated conflicts with Black and Douglas, whom he felt were prone to resolve all doubts in labor's favor, alienated him, leading him to believe that he was again, as in 1928 and 1936, confronted with judges too anxious to write their predilections into law. But Justice Douglas's comment, "All the law I know, I learned from you, Chief," made a point that may have hurt.[20]

Evidence of Stone's reaction to changed conditions in Court and country was implicit in the doubts he had poured into his eulogy of Sutherland in 1944. The questions he then raised as to the wisdom of of the Court's retreat in 1937 were more than rhetorical flourishes. One detects sensitive awareness of the impact of that about-face on the work of the Justices, and the extent to which it had increased the difficulties of their task.

A case decided late in 1945 showed how completely "protective coloration" had vanished from the judicial process, and how effectively that struggle had punctured the myth that the judge wills nothing. With the assent of seven participating colleagues, Stone upheld congressional power to tax community property as the sole property of one spouse. The Court's decision, wiping out the favoritism that had permitted residents of Texas, California, and Louisiana to will half their estates to their wives tax free,[21] provoked scorn amongst these formerly favored taxpayers, leading Stone to observe somewhat facetiously: "Perhaps it would be better for me to go to London next summer rather than to California or Texas."[22] Such uninformed criticism nettled him almost to the point of driving him to take refuge in Roberts' discredited mechanistic theory of constitutional interpretation.

"Until I began to receive letters from disgruntled Californians and Texans about the opinion," he lashed out, "I never realized how many kinds of an SOB there are. Most of the writers do not seem to understand that Congress specifically imposed the tax in question and that Congress has very great powers of taxation. They seem to think that in some way the Court invented the tax and put it on them. I don't blame them for not liking the tax and I am sorry it fell to my lot to say that Congress could impose it. One must do his duty in this job as well as in any other."[23]

These disgruntled citizens failed to see that the Court's decision had the effect of throwing responsibility back on Congress. But the courts still had the "last say," and so long as they do "we have judicial government," as Thomas Reed Powell said in 1944, "whether courts approve or condemn what others have done."[24]

Stone did not yield to what may have been nostalgic longing for the absolute. Yet in the face of reckless criticism he sometimes seemed to regret that he and his fellow jurists could no longer retreat to that favorite fortress of the old Court—the obvious pretense that judges are but helpless instruments of the law.

It seems ironical that Stone, a peace-loving man, should have been in the crossfires of controversy throughout his entire judicial career. In Taft's Court, as during the first six years of Hughes' Chief Justiceship, he differed with colleagues who interpreted the Constitution so as to impede the power to govern. Much of the first half of his tenure was marked by an earnest plea for a more comprehensive, responsible view of the judicial function, for informed recognition of the social and economic roots of constitutional issues. Instead of giving sympathetic consideration to the stern realities prompting controverted legislation, a majority of the Justices, against his repeated admonitions, fashioned meaningless constitutional labels to preclude government regulation and control. Stone called in vain for explorations going "beyond the examination of precedents and legal formulas."[25] Finally, in two momentous dissents, he told all.[26] Only the Justices' "personal economic predilections," he said, thwarted realization of social democracy.

Nor did his troubles end in 1937, when the Court finally lifted the judicial blockade. The inconclusiveness of this judicial surrender is shown by the continuous debate among the Justices, especially since 1940, on the nature and scope of judicial power. For Stone it was essentially the same battle. Before 1937 he had found fault with right-wing colleagues who equated what they considered socially undesirable with unconstitutionality. After 1940 he was at loggerheads with judges on the left, who were equally intent on reading their social preferences into the Constitution. Thus Stone's insistence that judges should be controlled by an informed sense of judicial self-restraint was just as applicable in the new Court as in the old.

In his war on the recalcitrant four, Stone was frequently joined by Holmes and Brandeis. But this does not mean they were always in complete agreement. Though the divergence is less sharp than that separating Stone from his right- and left-wing colleagues, the Illustrious Three were not entirely agreed as to the nature of the judicial function or how it should be applied.

## UNITY IN DIVERGENCE—HOLMES, BRANDEIS, AND STONE

Among the great figures in American constitutional law, only Holmes, Brandeis, and Stone clearly emerge as a team and as a trio of equals. Despite the vast differences in their background, philosophy, and technique, they might well have been chosen to typify the American dream of unity in diversity. Each brought a unique contribution to the common fray, each pursued a distinct course in making it. This very distinctiveness seems to have solidified them as a unit in personal relations and in the public eye.

Chief among the points of agreement were their recognition of the need for a living law, their determination to maintain the Court as an institution of government, their awareness that the judiciary was most often wounded "in the house of its own guardians."* "Judicial objectivity" was, they agreed, a desirable, though not a realizable ideal. These bonds were strong, particularly in dissent against a truculent majority whose judgments and language became more dogmatic as their doctrinaire approach became increasingly out of tune with the times. But a "box score" of their alignments would show an agreement ratio lower than commonly supposed.

Holmes, Archibald MacLeish has observed, "was a man of the world who was also a philosopher, who was incidentally a lawyer. The result was that he was a very great judge."[27] Confirmed skeptic, he turned a mordant gaze even on his own beliefs and laughed with as much superiority at his own "can't helps" as at those of any thorough-going fundamentalist. Holmes welcomed and applauded the "aperçu," the brilliant flash that opened up new vistas for plodding system-builders.

---

* Judge Learned Hand states the essential agreement between Holmes, Brandeis, and Stone as follows: "These men believed that democracy was a political contrivance by which the group conflicts inevitable in all society should find a relatively harmless outlet in the give and take of legislative compromise after the contending groups had a chance to measure their relative strength; and through which the bitterest animosities might at least be assuaged, even though that reconciliation did not ensue which sometimes follows upon an open fight. They had no illusion that the outcome would necessarily be the best obtainable, certainly not that which they might themselves have personally chosen; but the political stability of such a system, and the possible enlightenment which the battle itself might bring, were worth the price. . . . Statutes were not to be held invalid so long as anyone could find a reasonable basis for not ascribing them purely to envy or greed; and, as it was seldom, if ever, that this could not be done with any confidence, most statutes were upheld." ("Chief Justice Stone's Conception of the Judicial Function," *Columbia Law Review*, Sept. 1946, p. 697.)

Razor-sharp opinions generously sprinkled with telling phrases were exposed to the public eye only after time and effort had mellowed and perfected their form. Virtually every sentence seemed to have been framed in the light of Emerson's admonition to him as a boy: "When you strike at a king you must kill him." Holmes took no chances, even with pygmies.

It is this aphoristic quality of his work that defies definitive interpretation. The same characteristic exposes his memory to bitter attack by those who glean philosophic snippets strewn through his writings. It facilitates the temptation to invoke his name for quite divergent theories of law and society, as the host of opposing groups that call Holmes master bear living proof.

Partly for stylistic reasons, partly because of his skepticism, but above all because of his individualistic quality, Holmes' judicial opinions reveal little of his own predilections. It is virtually impossible to detect in them the fact that as a personal tenet Holmes himself would gladly have enacted Herbert Spencer's *Social Statics*. This amazing ability to transcend self is one of the many truly remarkable facts about him. It is a vital part of the Olympian myth, a facet, indeed, suggesting that the Holmesian myth is firmly embedded in reality.

This passion to achieve objectivity was Holmes' answer to the problem of judicial restraint. He did not confuse himself with God and, on the whole, repulsed the temptation to embody his own values in judicial opinions. Through the pages of Holmes' opinions stalks the figure of the "reasonable man," who determines constitutionality on abstract, depersonalized grounds. This figure is, of course, not unique with Holmes, but his presence in his opinions is most conspicuous. Holmes' frequent resort to this alter ego, his striving to escape the narrow walls of personality, approaches judicial schizophrenia. Essentially, however, this was a personal solution. It provided no guidance for others, and few standards for himself. When he held legislation unconstitutional, the "reasonable man" tended to recede to the confines of Holmes' judicial robes and become one with him again. His reasons for such decisions were usually no clearer than those of the opponents he condemned for submerging their "inarticulate major premise." Indeed, when striking down legislation, the Holmesian argument was often identical with theirs.

Judiciousness is not the word that clings to the lips of Brandeis's warmest admirers. For those who regard the epitome of the judge's function as majestic indifference, Brandeis lacked "judicial temperament." Yet time has, on the whole, confirmed his judicial statesmanship.

The Brandeis brief, his marshaling of factual data to support an argument, once threatened to dissolve those granite concepts of "liberty" and "property" on which pioneer social legislation was wrecked. But experience indicates that even in evaluating objective fact the judge remains in the realm of subjective judgment. Brandeis's own judicial career indicates that strict adherence to the age-old rule of presumption of constitutionality, rather than judicial fact-finding, is the most effective bar against abuse of judicial power.

Stone, in forging his own theory of the judicial process, was aided by a judiciousness of mind and singular objectivity more akin to Holmes than to Brandeis. At the same time, unlike the Great Dissenter, he was not repelled by mundane facts. Both understood the value of Brandeis's methods; they accepted as valid his conviction that constitutional law is not primarily abstract or philosophical but concrete, embedded in the rock of economic and political reality. Within limits Stone readily utilized this method. From various mentors, Holmes and Brandeis in particular, he culled insights and fashioned them into an impressive catechism for judges.*

Stone's conception of judicial conduct was almost monastic. Yet he was not always able to live up to these high ideals.† He felt that in his utterances a judge should be extremely circumspect to limit himself precisely to the issue at hand. He should labor for consistency; contradictory precedents should usually be specifically overruled. Each case must be dealt with in the light of precedents, facts, legislative intent, and the judge's own reason and values. No monist, Stone's judicial technique, in essence, stressed complexity. To oversimplify was convenient for the pedagogue but disastrous for the judge.

Above all, Stone was a judge. Adolf Berle, Jr., sums up his meaning in relation to the other members of the great triumvirate in this way: Brandeis, social architect; Holmes, essayist; Stone, judge. [28] Holmes brought to the Court a *Weltanschauung* and unique learning. Brandeis brought an articulate social philosophy and a mastery of social phenomena. Stone brought with him full consciousness of the judge's role and a masterful technique for exercising it. In these differences lies the secret of the relatively greater popularity of Holmes' opinions. Torn from context and made into a book, Holmes' judicial writings emerge as philosophic essays of deep import and popular appeal. Similar ef-

---

* "The two phases of his life's work, the academic and the judicial, cannot be wholly separated. . . . The convictions which he formed in the University remained with him on the bench. His judicial opinions are amazingly consistent with a basic philosophy about law and its place in the social and political order, which began its evolution in the University and reached its maturity on the Court." (Young B. Smith, "Harlan Fiske Stone: Teacher, Scholar and Dean," *Columbia Law Review*, Sept. 1946, pp. 708-709.)

† Stone's conception sometimes led him to seemingly inconsistent results. See Chapters XXX and XXXI.

forts with Brandeis's opinions, while not so successful, are still engaging and instructive. The Brandeis opinion (especially in dissent) was a platform on which to state an economic and social program. In contrast, Stone's opinions tend to be limited to the case at hand; he consciously avoids philosophic byways. In book form they have limited appeal. Unlike the opinions of Holmes and Brandeis, they have little or no viability outside the legal framework.

Whether in dissent or in the majority, Stone subdued the political factor. He strove not to eliminate subjectivity but to tame it. Recognition of self was to him the first step toward judicial self-control. Awareness of the subjective element in judging must, paradoxically, end in curbing it.

"He was," Judge Learned Hand has written, "a thorough craftsman as a judge. He steered a course at times very difficult and he had the right—absolutely right—measure of a Court's limitation on constitutional questions, which appears to be in danger of being lost again. He could take over and apply the best thought of his time, but he was not an originator and, to be frank, had not an original mind."[29]

In a certain sense Stone was not an innovator. He was less original than either Holmes or Brandeis. Yet his skillful blending of their approaches made him one of the great creative judges of our time. Nothing delighted him more than to take some area in which there was a morass of conflicting decisions, sort them all out, and then restate the rule with reasons having solid substance. In a logical, as well as a chronological, sense Stone was the one who, in both the old and the new Court, carried the Holmes-Brandeis tradition to its fruition. Perforce "it fell to him to carry through the victory and then to consolidate the gain." [30]

## SUTHERLAND ON JUDICIAL SELF-RESTRAINT

In 1936 the Justices had faced alternative uses of their fearful power. At their peril, Stone thought, they could continue to follow the meandering course of Hughes and Roberts; they could adopt Sutherland's obstinate alternative, the "rigid and changeless Constitution, apparently to be applied in the same way, no matter how much the subject to which it is applied, may change."* They could relinquish power altogether, virtually surrender the duty, nowhere expressly conferred by the Constitution, of passing on the validity of legislative acts. Finally, they could take Stone's arduously responsible road of judicial self-restraint. This was the course he then earnestly urged upon the brethren.

* Stone's characterization of the position of the dissenting minority in the Washington Minimum Wage case, in a letter to his sons, April 1, 1937.

Justice Sutherland, champion of the old Court, sharply challenged his theory. Judges must "say the final word as to the validity* of a statute." [31] A judge cannot subordinate his conviction to that of his colleagues even when they number four. Stone's adjuration on self-restraint Sutherland flatly rejected as belonging in the domain of will and not judgment. When judges upset "desirable legislation" blame must rest on the document of 1787, "not upon the Court."† Stone's view that judges could by their own will construe the Constitution so as to uphold desirable legislation Sutherland denounced as "ill-considered and mischievous." The great vice of Stone's disclosures was that it lifted the veil from mystery, revealing behind judicial pageantry nine human beings, all participants in the governing process and no nearer the source of ultimate wisdom than are others. Stone had done the Court an incalculable disservice in letting the judicial cat out of the bag.

## THE TRIALS OF JUDICIAL SELF-RESTRAINT IN THE RECONSTITUTED COURT

The decisions of 1937, the backtrack under fire, unsettled rather than defined the scope of the Court's power. The retreat shocked the conservative minority, so recently its majority. Among other things, the erstwhile majority was afraid for the future because the new concept of national power might stimulate what Herbert Spencer called "political momentum." In practice, however, the Court did not vacate the arena; it did not leave the field wide open for legislative action. That is why, since 1937, so much judicial discussion centers on the meaning of the retreat. The Court has been re-examining its position as an instrument of government to determine where it might appropriately interpose a check and where it should stay out.[32] "Even for those who are not afraid to handle matters of degree in fact," Herman Pritchett has observed, "the task is difficult. Consensus is harder to achieve. . . . The old sense of certainty is gone, and judicial decisions take on the experiential quality of life itself."[33] Inevitably, reconsideration of the

* Justice McReynolds had said in the Nebbia case (p. 556): "But plainly, I think, this Court must have regard to the wisdom of the enactment."

† For Sutherland this was not a patent fiction; it was solid fact. At the height of the Court-packing struggle the Justice's friend, Senator Bailey, made a radio speech in which he said that the Court's function "is truth and righteousness. . . . It has no earthly power. . . . Its decrees prevail only by reason of the spiritual appeal of justice to the human heart." Sutherland gratefully replied: "I am unable to refrain from breaking the silence which is supposed to enshroud the judiciary to tell you how deeply your words have moved me. I am quite sincere in saying that in my judgment there never has been a better speech." (Quoted in J. Francis Paschal, *Mr. Justice Sutherland: A Man against the State* [Princeton; Princeton University Press, 1941], pp. 201-202.)

scope of judicial power brought out, as one commentator has observed, "greater recognition of the play of opinion and estimates of the wisdom of legislative action, of evaluation of interests and appraisal of their need for protection, than the Court is wont to admit."[34]

Stone did not shrink from this duty. Unlike the old judges, he did not spurn the task of reconciling "the conflicting demands of laissez faire with the exertion of regulatory power by government." "The dividing line," he said, "must be a shifting one as society becomes more complex."[35] For him the new Court's more cautious attitude meant the triumph of restraint. His labors, however, were not at an end. Applied to the New Deal justices, "self-restraint" became primarily a warning that statutory policy, like constitutional logic, must not be pressed too far. With the shift of emphasis, statutory interpretation became an area of equally bitter conflict. The work of judging was still an "elusive art," and no one was more keenly aware than Stone of "the difficulties into which the would-be omniscient judge may fall."[36] In statutory as in constitutional construction, there must be respect for the technique of law and for the materials with which judges work. Though it makes law, the Court is not a legislature. Therefore the Justices must not "legislate" wholesale, must not override popular judgment as to what the national interest requires. In resolving the question how far Congress intended legislation to go, the statute should be used as the starting point for legal reasoning; the end result should be determined, as in common law, by the judge's own concept of the wise limits of public policy.[37]

"Liberalism" of the right sort would not lead judges to enact their own economic preferences into law. "My more conservative brethren in the old days did that and read them into the Constitution as well," he reminded a liberal critic in 1945. "What they did placed in jeopardy a great and useful institution of government. The pendulum has now swung to the other extreme, and history is repeating itself. The Court is now in as much danger of becoming a legislative and Constitution-making body, enacting into law its own predilections, as it was then. The only difference is that now the interpretations of statutes whether over-'conservative' or over-'liberal' can be corrected by Congress." "Back of your criticism of the 5 to 4 decisions," he chided the correspondent, "is your recognition that Congress will not 'correct' them. It will not, because, as I believe, it never intended any other result than that which the Court reached. If that is so the Court has done its sworn duty. Are you seeking the appointment of judges who will do more?"[38]

On the Roosevelt Court, Stone's scheme of values, his convictions about the Constitution and judging, induced him to take a more cautious stand than his colleagues in cases involving statutory construction. He and the New Deal Justices were generally agreed that the

Court might use its power to rectify mistaken constitutional judgments. But they went further, insisting that the Court drastically revise previous interpretations of major congressional enactments, such as the Sherman Act. Stone disagreed. In cases such as Apex and Southeastern Underwriters, he demanded that they leave undisturbed the old Court's constructions. Perhaps, as Walton Hamilton has suggested, he was "content enough with advanced positions to which for years he never dreamed that he could bring his Court."[39] "Like a block of New England granite he stayed in place while the Court shifted around him." [40]

As his career neared its end, Stone despaired of winning the battle for restraint against judges aware of their unshackled power and determined to use it ruthlessly. In September 1945 he confessed he had "been depressed" by some judicial opinions, leading him to suspect that Newton's laws of motion might also apply to human affairs. "The time was when I thought you had worked yourself out of a job," he wrote Thomas Reed Powell early in November, "because the pendulum had swung from the extreme right, where it seemed to be when I came on the Court, much nearer the golden mean. Now that the pendulum seems to be swinging to the other extreme, I feel sure you will find plenty to write about."[41]

### THE DOCTRINE OF POLITICAL RESTRAINTS

By 1940 Stone's own position had become increasingly the subject of careful inquiry. A close student of the Court's work, seeking to get at the core of his theory, believed he had found the clue in what has been called the "doctrine of political restraints." The tenor of Stone's remarks in several opinions written between 1938 and 1940 seemed to imply that it was permissible to exercise judicial power to protect interests not adequately safeguarded by the political process; and that aside from direct interferences with democratic verities the primary restraint on legislative action is political. With respect to state interference with interstate commerce, for example, judicial intervention, under this doctrine, is justified only "when the regulation is of such a character that its burden falls principally upon those without the state, [and] legislative action is not likely to be subjected to those political restraints which are normally exerted on legislation where it affects adversely interests within the state." [42] The same doctrine was invoked in drawing the line between national and state power in the field of taxation.

"I got the impression [in 1941] from what he had written in the Tax Immunity cases, as well as from what he had said in talking to me about those cases," Professor Dowling has written, "that he was giving a lot of consideration to 'political restraints' as a factor in the judicial process in constitutional cases." But in the Darby case of that year Stone did not rule, as the doctrine of "political restraints" seemed to require, that the judiciary had no supervisory authority over federal commerce laws because all interests of the nation were, presumably, represented in Congress and could be adequately protected there. Instead, following Holmes' classic dissent in *Hammer* v. *Dagenhart,* he upheld congressional action on its merits. Failure to apply the doctrine of political restraints—indeed, failure even to mention it—made Dowling wonder what had happened. Before going on he wanted to be set straight. "Does the Darby case," he asked, "indicate that you are thinking less of that doctrine as you go along?" "I never even thought about it," the Justice chuckled good-naturedly.[43]

Still other influences may have led him to minimize the doctrine of political restraints. In 1940 Justice Frankfurter's Gobitis decision, relying in part on this doctrine, indicated how rigorous application of the theory could deprive individuals of basic rights. The Flag Salute case demonstrated that certain interests required continued judicial protection. Moreover, by February 3, 1941, the day the Darby decision came down, F.D.R. had just been inaugurated for a third term. With the alarming decline of two-party government, sole reliance on political restraints to keep national power within bounds might well invite destruction of the federal system itself. So far had he departed from his own "hands off" conception of the judicial function that when he came to write the Darby opinion, "political restraints" did not even occur to him. Dowling was satisfied that the doctrine did not hold quite so important a place in Stone's thinking as it had formerly done. "Consequently," the Columbia Law professor has observed, "I was not surprised, when, five years later, in *New York* v. *United States,* he declined to go along with Mr. Justice Frankfurter when that Justice sought to reactivate the doctrine of political restraints and make it, in part at least, the basis of the decision upholding the excise tax on state products."[44]

Stone had formulated this doctrine soon after President Roosevelt's all-out attack on the judiciary. He was then seriously concerned about the Court's future usefulness as an "implement of government." "My impression is," Dowling suggested, "that he kept it in his thinking for several years, but by the time *New York* v. *United States* came on in 1946 he had either dropped it or had concluded it was of less consequence and helpfulness than he originally believed it to be. At all events, in *New York* v. *United States,* he passed over what seems to me to be an open bid from Mr. Justice Frankfurter to join up anew on the theory of political restraints."[45]

Stone adhered to Holmes' view that the Union itself would be imperiled if the Supreme Court could not strike down state laws inimical to national interest. Justice Black, from the time he ascended the bench, had been inclined to narrow the scope of judicial power, arguing strenuously that except where the local statute discriminates against interstate commerce, relief from state regulation must be had from Congress, not the Court. In the Arizona Train Limit case of 1945 Black restated his views with characteristic vigor: "The determination of whether it is in the interest of society for the length of trains to be governmentally regulated is a matter of public policy. Someone must fix that policy—either the Congress, or the state, or the courts." But in the absence of congressional action, the Arizona law must be left undisturbed, because it was a "basic principle on which our democratic society rests" that legislators "rather than judges . . . can best determine the policies which govern the people." Black cast aside the view Stone embodied in the majority opinion as springing from "the belief . . . that both the legislature of Arizona and the Congress made wrong policy decisions in permitting a law to stand which limits the length of railroad trains."[46]

Stone disagreed. It had been "accepted constitutional doctrine," at least since *Cooley* v. *the Board of Wardens* of 1851, that the commerce clause standing alone gave the Court some power to invalidate local legislation obstructing commerce. If train lengths were to be regulated at all, plainly the rule adopted should have demanded "national uniformity." This Congress alone could prescribe. In such circumstances the Court had a clear duty to undertake the delicate task of accommodating conflicting interests. "Where Congress has not acted, this Court, and not the state legislature, is under the commerce clause the final arbiter of the competing demands of state and national interests."[47]

To Justice Black, Stone's opinion suggested that the Court was "the only agency of government that must be assumed to have the capacity to govern." Later on, Black voiced his attack in precisely the same language dissenters Holmes, Brandeis, and Stone had used against their recalcitrant colleagues: "I thought, . . . and still believe," Black wrote of Stone's Arizona Train Limit decision, "that . . . the Court was assuming the role of a 'super-legislature' in determining matters of governmental policy."[48]

### JUDICIAL SELF-RESTRAINT ON THE ANVIL OF SCHOLARLY ANALYSIS

Stone's theory of the judicial function was ripe for discussion when, in October 1945, the first full-length analysis of the Justice's twenty years on the bench appeared. "I am bound to say," Stone wrote Samuel J. Konefsky, "I am very happy about your book. . . . You make use of me as affording some human interest in your discussion of the function which a Justice of the Supreme Court performs." This "very opportune" treatise, he thought, might serve much the same purpose which his AAA dissent had performed, nearly ten years earlier, under quite different circumstances. "You have discerned and disclosed with accuracy," he told Konefsky, "what it is that I have been trying to do in the course of my judicial work. If your book will induce those who read it . . . to reflect upon what the judge ought to do when he decides constitutional questions, it will have served a very useful purpose, and enlighten many who need enlightenment about the performance of the judicial function."[49]

The book praised Stone for stopping "perhaps more often than any other member of the Court, to take stock of the processes by which it was adjudicating." It applauded the Justice's resistance to "legal or political abstractions," and commended his stress on "the necessity of deciding constitutional cases with the aid of the fullest available information." "By his labors on the Court," the author remarked, "he has demonstrated that the responsibility implicit in the exercise of judicial power, even as the responsibility inhering in high executive office, may serve to evoke latent qualities of statesmanship." The popular view, the tendency to identify "restraint" with complete objectivity, had been greatly mistaken. Refusing, for his part, to believe that any useful or genuinely patriotic purpose could be served by obscuring the personal equation in judicial review, the author observed: "There is in fact a curious dualism (some would say contradiction) to the liberal conception of the judicial function. This is as true of Chief Justice Stone as it was of Holmes, Brandeis, and Cardozo. As legal realists, all recognize the essentially subjective character of the judicial process," yet "all four have chided their colleagues for reading into the Constitution private notions of public policy."[50]

Far from evoking protest, such frank discussion greatly pleased the Chief Justice. It "really is a good book," he told his sons; Charles A. Beard's introduction he described as "a happy one." "I only wish that I were as well understood at points nearer home as I am by these two men."[51]

Obviously the brethren did not accept him uncritically, but how could he complain that they did not understand him? Did they not see his judicial opinions evolving from case to case in accord with consistent theory? Did they disagree with the judicial philosophy he championed? Or did they simply take an eclectic attitude, adopting his insights into the subjective qualities of judging while rejecting out of hand what Max Lerner has called his "agonizing cry de profundis" "—the only check upon our own exercise of power is our own sense of self-restraint?"[52]

Stone and his sophisticated associates alike realized that the harmonious application of eighteenth-century generalizations to twentieth-century existence, the perplexing search for "legislative will," calls for human sympathy, tact, curiosity, insight, intelligence—no automaton could do the job.* In matters so delicately intricate a "jurist without a philosophy of law—and of life—is lost."[53] Stone's taunt in the Tipaldo case that nothing stood in the way of minimum wage legislation except "our personal economic predilections" has usually been read as condemning the intrusion of private views into law. Yet for Stone the phrase was as much descriptive as condemnatory. "To a considerable extent," the Justice remarked on reading Jerome Frank's *Law and the Modern Mind,* "judicial opinions are rationalizations of a result which the judge has reached by subconsciously going through the processes which Frank elaborates, or perhaps without regard to them in many cases."[54] Though it is disguised and unconscious, judges do exercise the "sovereign prerogative of choice." No man, no judge, can be completely objective, if indeed one should wish him to be. Nevertheless Stone believed that the judge had the obligation to try. He had seen too many cases "where the decision is actually the result of study and comparison of the competing motivating influences to accept at full value the theory that judicial decisions are the expression of some kind of hunch arrived at quite independently of the rational process which is exhibited in the opinion."[55]

"We may try to see things as objectively as we please," Judge Cardozo wrote. "Nonetheless, we can never see them with any eyes except our own."[56] Stone urged restraint not because he believed a judge's preference should not enter law, but precisely because it inevitably did. The sharp barbs of his thought about "economic predilections" were intended for the flesh of judges, both right and left, who, without heed of consequences, irresponsibly enforced private conviction as law. His protest was directed against cavalier injection of individual bias, against the jurist who takes sides *prematurely.* Like Holmes, he believed that the assumption of responsibility for consciously weighing social advantage, would make judges "hesitate where

* Stone did not "subscribe to what has been called 'judicial automatism,' and had no delusions that judicial duty could be performed merely by laying 'the article of the Constitution which is invoked beside the statute which is challenged' and deciding 'whether the latter squares with the former.' Nor did he suffer from that other delusion that the Constitution must be interpreted like a contract with reference to what the framers had in mind at the time. He saw that, with the exception of a few specific provisions, the Constitution was the expression of great general principles of government to be applied to the changing conditions of society." (Remarks of Judge John J. Parker, In Memory of Harlan Fiske Stone, Nov. 12, 1947, *Proceedings of the Bar and Officers of the Supreme Court of the United States,* 1948.)

they are now confident," make them recognize that they were "taking sides upon debatable and often burning questions."[57]

Judges might bear their awesome responsibility more easily, Stone believed, if they would recognize the role of the legislature as a co-ordinate branch of government, empowered, as is the Court, to define social policy, but with broader limits. As his approach was pragmatic, he did not, as he once remarked critically of John Marshall, always see things in "blacks and whites." "Reasonableness," the "weighing of evidence," "accommodation"—the reshaping of our fundamental law in harmony with "that sober second thought of the community"—these are the keys to Stone's theory. In this process it is not enough to lay the statute beside the Constitution or assemble matched judicial precedents. Unlike Sutherland, Stone did not dismiss economic data as "interesting but only mildly persuasive," or as throwing "no legitimate light"[58] on matters which judges need consider. Stone, in fact, criticized lawyers who, like Sutherland, "seem to think it is sufficient to cite our decisions, without placing before us the economic data which would reveal the situation to which constitutional limitations are to be applied." On occasion he and Justice Brandeis accumulated such material—"as the Irishman played the fiddle, by main strength."[59] In 1937 Stone expressed the "need for securing an economic service—a small group of men, who have had some training as economists and statisticians, who would be qualified to assemble material for use of the Court." "I have felt hitherto," he wrote, "that the time was not ripe to advocate the establishment of such a service, but it seems to me the time is now not far away." It would, he said, be of "great assistance" in "relieving us and our very limited staff from the drudgery of such researches."[60]

Stone made no bones about it: the Supreme Court "must determine the boundaries and distribution of power under a federal constitutional system." [61] Nor is this all. The Court must invoke its power against government compulsion of belief or expression of it, "whatever may be the legislative view of the desirability of such compulsion." The epithet "judicial supremacy" never troubled him. "Our friends who prate about judicial supremacy fall into one of two classes. First, and most conspicuously, those who do not believe in the restraints of legislative power which are essential to the maintenance of an ordered conduct of a federal system of government; and second, those who have never had the lawyer's experience of interpreting legal instruments."[62] In a federal scheme, final authority must reside somewhere. For his own part, he preferred to think of the Court as an "instrument of government," one of several agencies dedicated to making the system work.

"As a practical matter," he commented in the fall of 1945, "perhaps we would have gotten on very well without the Fifth or Fourteenth Amendments, but how we could have settled all the questions arising out of distribution of power between the state and national governments without the arbitrament of a supreme court or some other body with corresponding functions, I do not know.[63] The only other alternative in many cases might well be resort to force. The Constitution, read as a whole and in the light of its background and purposes, plainly contemplated that the Supreme Court should do just that, not only in connection with the commerce clause but with other clauses whose meaning and application necessarily determine the rights of litigants."[64]

After 1935 Stone became increasingly concerned for the survival of free government, and for its keystone, a system of independent courts. "Just courts, wisely administered," were to him "the symbols of civilization and the ultimate expression of it. What hope would there be for such courts in an Asia dominated by Japan, or a Germany or a Europe overborne by the tyranny of Hitler?" he asked in a wartime address. "What hope, indeed, would there be for them if Hitler and all he symbolizes there were to triumph here?" Stone believed profoundly that the real measure of the triumph of our arms in the epic struggle then going on "will be the triumph and perpetuation of a civilization which finds its highest expression in courts and in justice administered by courts."[65]

At a time when certain of his colleagues entertained narrow conceptions of their function, he urged a broader outlook, greater consideration of non-juristic and non-personal factors. No judge had a right to jeopardize the institution he served merely because he did not like a statute. And when the New Deal Justices tended to exercise power inexorably in behalf of expanding government, "merely" because they liked certain statutory policies, he protested with a vehemence matching that stimulated by the Four Horsemen. By 1945 he had ample proof of what he had always known, or at least suspected, that economic predilection takes more than one form, that humbug and nonsense are not monopolies of the mossbacks. Clashes with Frankfurter on civil liberties, with Black as to state interference with commerce, illuminate Stone's conception of responsibly exercised judicial power and underscore his conviction that judicial review had survived the ordeal of 1937. Judicial self-restraint, not self-abnegation, was the principle he advocated. His difficulties with both old and new Courts had at least one feature in common: in both instances he had to combat the drive to elevate particular interests to the stature of principles.*

---

* Stone would, I think, subscribe to what Justice William O. Douglas wrote in 1949: "From age to age the problem of constitutional adjudication is the same. It is to keep the power of government unrestrained by the social or economic theories that one set of judges may entertain. It is to keep one age unfettered by the fears or limited vision of another. There is in that connection one tenet of faith which has crystallized more and more as a result of our long experience as a nation. It is

Neither had learned the wisdom of judicial self-restraint. "Power," said the poet Béranger, "is a bell which prevents those who set it pealing from hearing any other sound."

The entire last phase of Stone's life was a titanic struggle to prevent the Court from becoming "a mess of politicians." He had to cope with endless intrigues, with the ambition of men who wished, besides being Justices, to play a role either in American politics or foreign affairs.[66]

"Men whose fashion is to press their power to the utmost," Herbert Wechsler observed, "will never understand how much there was of self-subordination in his [Stone's] great work."[67] "About all I can do in my remaining years," the Chief Justice commented wearily in January 1945, "is to try to make apparent some of the things that in the days of yore made the Court great. But I confess I am very lonesome."[68]

## CHAPTER FORTY-SEVEN

# Law without Magic

The office of Chief Justice carries scant inherent powers. The Chief manages the docket, presents the cases, and conducts the conference; he assigns opinions (when he is one of the majority) and presides in open Court. Whatever influence he exerts actually rests on elusive personal characteristics. Those qualities that make for greatness in a judge are no sure index to success as Chief Justice. Nor do they necessarily put him in command.

What a Chief Justice does in office depends in part on his concept of it. Stone tended to minimize the role. He had said in 1930: "The post never enlarges the occupant's individual capacity for judicial work, and it may diminish it."[1] "I am frank to say," he wrote after his appointment, "that I have no particular interest in what is popularly regarded as 'promotion,' which in fact absorbs time and energies I should like to devote to what I consider more important things."[2] Consequently it

---

this: If the social and economic problems of state and nation can be kept under political management of the people, there is likely to be long-run stability. It is when a judiciary with life tenure seeks to write its social and economic creed into the Charter that instability is created. For then the nation lacks the adaptability to master the sudden storms of an era." (William O. Douglas, "Stare Decisis," *Columbia Law Review*, June 1949, p. 754.)

Stone was, perhaps, more alert than Douglas to danger from the other side—from the advocates of social justice whom Stone castigated as prone to identify as constitutional that which is socially desirable.

is not surprising that he tended to be "a bit neglectful"[3] of his administrative duties.

Besides his distaste for administration he suffered from a certain inability to master the routine details of life and work. He frequently misplaced or lost articles of dress or private papers. Accusing his wife or secretary of having moved them, he would institute a grand search that usually located the papers where he had put them.[4] The same trait carried over into Court affairs. Day after day his secretary persisted in tidying up his desk, but by mid-morning "it looked as if a storm had hit it."[5] "I approved the proposed change," he would say to a colleague, "and I think I returned it to you. At any rate I cannot find it among my papers."[6] It was customary in the Clerk's office to make two copies of everything—"one to keep and the other for the Chief to lose."[7] Stone himself boasted that he "could never find a document, but never lost one." Adding to his troubles was the difficulty during wartime of keeping two well-prepared law clerks. One sympathetic colleague, observing the Chief's distress, thought a variant of eminent domain might be invoked to ensure the services of some excellent youngsters.

Yet Stone refused to heed advice that he lighten his administrative load by distributing routine tasks. He even kept the initial sifting of petitions *in forma pauperis* in his own hands. Thus work that Hughes had attacked zestfully and dispatched efficiently was for Stone an onerous chore.

Some Supreme Court leaders have utilized every opportunity to reinforce the slender foundations of their authority, magnifying the office by magnifying themselves. Temperamentally Stone was ill equipped to do this. Pomp and circumstance were alien to him. He avoided display and kept his public appearances to a bare minimum. The attentions people normally pay their highest public servants offended his New England reserve. "I sometimes wish people were not quite so effusive," he complained, "but most of it I think springs from pure goodheartedness, and it is difficult, I suppose, for any man who is prominent in public life to avoid it."[8] To a former student's query whether to address him as "dean" or "judge," Stone replied with a chuckle, "Call me Dean. It's the only decent job I ever had."

Stone lived in an atmosphere of pure law. He ruled out the political motive as irrelevant in the judging process, even at its highest level. Each case had to be illuminated by discussion and deliberation; it did not require, or even permit, negotiation. In contrast, Hughes played on his Court as on a big organ: he knew what stops to pull. He used assignments to draw the Court together. To prevent the formation of a closely knit liberal minority, he resorted to "exceedingly clever" tactics. If the slightest difference of opinion disclosed itself between two liberal members of the Court, the Chief Justice would put "his big toe in and widen the cleavage."⁹

By employing the methods of a military commander Hughes made his administration a model of efficiency. At judicial conferences discussion was rationed. These "lasted six hours," Justice Brandeis once said, "and the Chief Justice did all the speaking." Hughes, after stating his own position in clear incisive language, thus "getting the jump on the brethren by his quickness in selecting the issue,"¹⁰ would call in due order for statements from his colleagues.* Rarely did anyone speak out of turn. Even when Hughes himself felt obliged to modify his opening remarks he did it in such a way as to suggest that interruption should be the exception rather than the rule. For him "the conference was not a debating society but a place where nine men do solos."¹¹ Stone sometimes bitterly criticized such expeditious procedures. With so little opportunity for an exchange of ideas, constitutional interpretation seemed more like counting noses, the judicial conference an administrative voting device.

A punctilious presiding officer, precise, and efficient, Hughes' goals were harmony, even though it represented no more than a *pro forma* agreement of the judges, and speedy dispatch of cases, though other values might be sacrificed.† When differences threatened to produce dissents or concurrences, one of Hughes' colleagues recalled in 1953, the C. J. would blow his whiskers straight out and say: "Brethren, the only way to settle this is to vote."¹² "Harmony," Hughes wrote in his book on the Supreme Court, "does not always wait on argumentation."¹³

Once, at conference, Stone asked permission to read an opinion he had not had time to print and circulate. It took the position that Brandeis's majority opinion was entirely wrong in theory and that unfortunate consequences would follow. Stone naturally expected full discussion, followed by the Chief's recommendation that the case go over a week to consider his views. Not so; when Stone finished reading, Hughes said: "Very powerful memorandum. Case goes down on Monday."‡

* Traditionally, in conference, discussion proceeds after the Chief Justice in order of seniority, the oldest Justice in point of service leading off.

† Hughes was chary of requests for more time to study a case. When in 1932 Stone was refused a postponement in the Scottsboro case he was furious and attributed the denial to the Chief's wish to put a stop to popular demonstrations around the Court.

‡ The case was *Bradford Electric Light Co.* v. *Clapper*, 286 U.S. 145 (1932), cited by Stone in a letter to John Bassett Moore, May 17, 1932, as "a rather striking example of what can happen under present methods." Stone, in his opinion, opposed Brandeis's somewhat inflexible approach to the full faith and credit clause, declining to give the provision its literal meaning automatically in all cases of conflict between state policies. The Bradford case had a brief career. Within three

Hughes' tendency to expedite the deciding function, sometimes led, in Stone's opinion, to serious mistakes. In May 1932 John Bassett Moore passed along a comment by one of the Justices that "under the present C. J. votes are taken practically without deliberation . . . and that the discrepancies sometimes exhibited are partly due to the lack of any previous general discussion which might have simplified the issue." Stone replied: "I think one who studied carefully the opinions of the Court would infer all that he said, perhaps more. When I first went on the Court in Taft's time the discussion was very free, although sometimes discursive. During the last of his service there was much more of an inclination to rush things through, especially if he thought he had the support of certain members of the Court."* "I have no hesitation in saying," his reply concluded, "that I think discussion of our cases should be much fuller and freer, and that in many instances an adjournment over for a week after preliminary discussion might produce more satisfactory results."[14]

As Chief, Stone, for better or worse, put this idea into practice. Under Hughes he had assuaged his distress by instituting informal Friday afternoon sessions at his house to provide a preliminary canvass of cases to come up in the Saturday conference. But only a few colleagues attended, and these were later discontinued.

In practice, as in contemplation, Stone's techniques stood in bold contrast with those of his predecessor.† Proceeding without ritual, he

---

years Stone's insistence on a limited exercise of judicial power in this field was accepted by the Court. See *Alaska Packers Association* v. *Industrial Accident Commission*, 294 U.S. 532 (1935).

* "That is the only way to explain," Stone's letter said, "the decision in *Long* v. *Rockwood*, 277 U.S. 142 (1928), overruled yesterday by no. 118, *Fox Film Corp.* v. *Doyal*, 286 U.S. 123 (1932); *Macallen Co.* v. *Massachusetts*, 279 U.S. 620 (1929), overruled by my opinion in *Educational Films Corp.* v. *Ward*, 282 U.S. 379 (1931), and in no. 270, *Pacific Co. Ltd.* v. *Johnson*, 285 U.S. 480 (1932), during the present term."

In 1939 the Court's decision in *O'Malley* v. *Woodrough*, 307 U.S. 277, brought to light further evidence of the unsubstantial quality of agreement in Taft's Court by overruling the Graham case, 268 U.S. 501 (1925), and holding that income tax on a judge's salary was not a diminution of compensation in the constitutional sense. "The Graham case," Stone wrote his sons, Nov. 16, 1939, "was argued shortly after I came on the Court, and you will be interested to know that I joined Justice Holmes and Brandeis in voting against the immunity of the judge's salary from income tax. The same principle as in the Graham case had been laid down in *Evans* v. *Gore*, 253 U.S. 245 (1920), decided a year or two before I came on the Court. Holmes had written a dissent but he thought the Graham case indistinguishable in principle from the Gore case and therefore he and I concluded that we would not record a dissent. I have since regretted my action because it puts me apparently on record as supporting the majority decision which I thought then and still think wrong." Such things occurred under Hughes as well.

† "The Chief Justice's influence," A. M. Schlesinger, Jr., has observed, "lies essentially in his management of the Saturday conference. Charles Evans Hughes kept things moving briskly and efficiently, confining discussion to issues, forbidding fruit-

stated his position tentatively. What he said sometimes revealed that he was still groping, and when he turned the case over to the brethren discussion did not march in rapid and regular sequence. Debate was free and easy, achieving the cross-fertilization of ideas, the full consideration, he longed for. His methods, peculiarly appropriate for a working court, are reminiscent of those he employed in the classroom twenty years before.

Justice delayed is justice denied, but for Stone justice hurried is sometimes justice miscarried. Under his regime no reasonable request for more time to study or to write was ever ignored.* "The conference never assumed more importance than it did under Chief Justice Stone," Justice Douglas has written. "Petitions for certiorari and jurisdictional statements were never more fully considered. And there was no cloture in discussing argued and submitted cases. Frequently the Saturday conference would continue over into Monday, Tuesday, or even Wednesday of the following week." Stone was for deliberate, not breakneck, speed. "Some might deduce from this that [he] was not an efficient chief. But the measure of efficiency is not necessarily the speed with which decisions are rendered. More often than not, justice is the product of deliberation and meditation rather than of haste. Stone's tolerance of full and free discussion produced a most healthy environment for judicial work."[15] His procedure, lending to the conference the informal air of the university seminar, made for uninhibited debate.

At the end of Stone's first conference a colleague mixed his feelings of relief with words of caution: "I should like to say to you how much I enjoyed the relaxed atmosphere and your evident desire to have our conferences an exchange of responsible views of nine men, led by a considerate moderator, and so I am full of happy days ahead." But this same colleague anticipated trouble: "Of course I understand that

---

less argument, and adjourning promptly at four-thirty. Harlan Stone, a veteran dissenter with a New Englander's faith in town-meeting democracy, found it hard to cut off talk until everyone had spoken his fill." ("The Supreme Court: 1947," *Fortune*, Jan. 1947, p. 211.) In the opinion of Judge Orie L. Phillips (quoted in a letter from Henry M. Bates to H.F.S., Dec. 17, 1945): "There is quite a contrast between him [Stone] and former Chief Justice Hughes. While Hughes' mind is trained to work with the precision of a fine watch, I do not think it has the depth of Stone's."

* Evidence of this is seen in the memorandum Stone circulated, Feb. 23, 1944: "Should we increase the length of the next recess in order to catch up with opinion writing? On Saturday, February 26, we will have completed 21 weeks of the 34-week term. During that period we have handed down 55 full opinions. As of this date 10 opinions have been circulated, in most of which there will probably be no concurrences or dissents or both. There are 23 cases assigned for opinion in which no opinion has been circulated. Unless we soon catch up with our opinion writing, we will be in serious difficulties as we approach the end of the term. We ought to avoid, if possible, the accumulation of unwritten opinions at the end of the term which embarrassed us so seriously last year."

you did not want to pull at the reins with our brethren their very first day in harness. But the deviations from the tradition against speaking out of turn only prove to me overwhelmingly how important that tradition is for the wise and effective conduct of the Court's business."[16]

Believing profoundly in freedom of expression for others no less than for himself, Stone did not budge. In his anxiety to have all issues fully explored he was slow to cut off debate. He never gave up his conviction that the Court's function was not simply to decide cases, but, through the clash of ideas, to find solutions that were considerate of the past, adequate for the present, and no obstacle to the future.

For a man of Stone's nature, it is difficult to imagine circumstances that would have moved him to expedite the decision-making process. That process he understood and accepted as inevitably time-consuming. With respect to pending decisions he sought light from every source, postponing final judgment until he had examined the case from every angle and re-examined his own first impression. Devoting himself intensively to study of material on which the decision must be founded, "including both the facts of record and the legal doctrine probably applicable," he constantly exchanged memoranda, expressed doubt about his own tentative views as well as doubts about the conclusions of others. As a direct consequence of these tedious procedures, judicial opinions during his regime were hammered out through genuine cooperative effort to an extent unequaled in any other period of Stone's judicial service. Once he had gone through this process, no man could be more firm in adherence to the conclusions he reached.[17] From this point on he became the zealous advocate.* Winning converts to his position took time, and his method may have suffered the defects of its qualities.

In the minds of certain observers, vigorous advocacy disqualified him as Chief. Machiavelli tells how Commodus, son of Marcus, lost his empire "by not maintaining his dignity, by often descending into the theatre to fight with gladiators." "Temperamentally," one commen-

---

* "At conference he was open-minded," Justice Reed has said. "But once he had come to a conclusion, neutrality ceased. He then became an indefatigable proponent for the position he had reached, an ardent advocate and a forceful writer for the ground that he deemed solid. The Chief Justice delighted to take on all comers around the conference table and armed with precedent and reason to battle, more often successfully than not, for his views. Yet the amenities of jurisprudential battle were never laid aside, nor did he nurse disappointment over an occasional defeat." (Remarks at unveiling of Chesterfield Memorial Tablet, Aug. 25, 1948.)

"A position once taken," Justice Douglas has recalled, "was seldom forsaken. He clung tenaciously to it." ("Chief Justice Stone," *Columbia Law Review*, Sept. 1946, p. 693.)

A law clerk notes the same trait: "It was extremely difficult, if not impossible, to get him to change his vote in a case after it had been cast at conference. While in process of making up his mind, he was more amenable to arguments with respect to the vote he should make." (Eugene Nickerson memorandum, May 27, 1952.)

tator close to Justice Black, observes, Stone was "too much of an intellectual partisan *himself* to get in occasional matters that leadership which can be a by-product of neutrality in most matters."[18] However well grounded, such criticism may not take fully into account the novel perplexities confronting Stone as Chief Justice: his colleagues' new and clashing notions of their function; the radically different questions posed by the far-flung extension of government;* the dilemma of a bench that took the risk of erasing the well-worn distinction between will and judgment in the judicial process; the incalculable impact of the abandonment of artificial techniques that had so often achieved the appearance of unity. To all these must be added the heterogeneous character of the Court over which he presided. Besides having to cope with sharp legal and political differences, Stone was confronted with unaccustomed ethics, manners, and even morals.

As Chief Justice, Stone felt an obligation to be fair but gave special weight to his duty to maintain the reputation of the Court by making the most of the talents of those composing it. After conference Stone would get together with his law clerks and assign the opinions. He did not have any grand strategy for "deploying his army." An especially tough or interesting opinion usually went to Douglas, Frankfurter, or Roberts, as the Chief rated their ability highly. Stone also esteemed Black but distrusted his unorthodox approach. Therefore the New Deal Justice did not get his share of the "good" cases. Justices Murphy and Rutledge Stone regarded as weak sisters. "The job of the Court," he said of one of the latter's opinions, "is to resolve doubts, not create them." The Chief Justice was well aware that he slighted Murphy; he often agreed to give him a "break," but in the end Murphy would be nosed out partly because Stone disliked leaving a fine case to the rumination of a law clerk. The Chief himself was very apt to take a case involving procedural or jurisdictional points, feeling that such matters ought to be written about by the one most concerned with them—the head of the Court.[19] Even on those triumphal occasions where he might have himself proclaimed for the majority vindication of a historic dissent, as in the Barnette and Opelika cases, he selected others to state the Court's position.

Disagreement among the diverse personalities making up the Court may in the end have been heightened by Stone's emphasis on deliberation, especially as the Bench was blessed or cursed with a number of incisive, perhaps even original minds, who could but be

---

* Writing Dean Young B. Smith, Feb. 29, 1944, Stone observed: "Congressional legislation of the past ten years has entered new constitutional fields and created new problems, the nature of which is not always fully understood by the bar and is altogether mysterious to the public. All this has put a great strain on the Court as an institution, and it seems to me that dispassionate analysis in the long run would tend to strengthen it as an institution."

stimulated by prolonged, probing discussion. Justices came away from the conference feeling that positions they had taken had never been so well explored. And yet the judge chosen to express their common sentiment must have found it difficult to assimilate the individual views to a generalized position, as the judgment of nine men must be. Certain judges took liberties with the newly enlarged scope of self-expression; dissents and concurrences rose to an all-time high.\* Unlike veteran dissenters Holmes, Brandeis, and Stone himself, they did not change pace nor let up after a trenchant attack. Rather they sometimes wrote opinions important to no one but themselves. The habit of passing along drafts that did not quite satisfy with the once familiar notations, "I think the other way, but shall not dissent," "I do not agree, but I shall go along," did not bind members of Stone's court. The Chief Justice himself was no more willing than the others to swallow real doubts in silence. "Who was Harlan Stone," someone has queried, "to cut off debate—even if he could?"[20]

The Justices sometimes took out their spite in judicial opinions, but more often than not their formal debates revealed genuine disagreements that probed the depths of the judicial process. Decision day in Stone's court, a thoughtful lawyer observed in 1945, had come to "resemble the debates on the floor of Congress." "These debates," he said, "provide rich material for research in the fields of law and political science. What has happened is that discussions previously cloaked in the secrecy of the conference room are being thrown open to the public. Most of the Justices are lawyers of exceptional stature, and the exposition of their differences of view is accompanied not only by penetrating and scholarly dissertations on the principles of government but by a brilliant display of the technique of the practicing advocate." [21]

Emphasis on deliberation, the disposition to encourage free-wheeling discussion, to magnify the role of the conference, are to Stone's credit. In the opinion of certain Justices the four or four and a half hours normally devoted to the Saturday conference is too short for adequate consideration of fourteen to seventeen cases, twenty to thirty certioraris, and miscellaneous business. Certain colleagues have praised him for exerting extraordinary influence on the deliberative side, for stimulating broad and meaningful inquiry. "Long before I came down here," one Justice told Stone, "I thought that Chief Justice Hughes was unduly emphasizing keeping the dockets clear as against the quality of the clearing." "Any Justice who kicks about the amount of time given to conference," Justice Jackson once commented, "ought to resign."

---

\* On January 29, 1945, Stone complained to Thomas Reed Powell that "the extraordinary productivity of my brethren absorbs so much of my time in reading their pieces that I have little opportunity to read any others."

"Whatever the ultimate verdict," Justice Douglas has observed, "those who stand at closer range know that the Court as an institution grew in stature under the influence of Harlan Fiske Stone."[22]

What distressed Stone and drew heavily on his energies was not genuine difference on fundamental issues but persistent personal animosity. The judicial air fairly crackled with biting repartee. "I think it is only fair to state in view of your general argument," one member of the Court informed Justice Murphy apropos his Schneiderman opinion, "that Uncle Joe Stalin is at least a spiritual co-author with Jefferson of the Virginia Statute for Religious Freedom." But horseplay among judges, like humor among the Greek gods, is likely to be taken in the wrong spirit, serving to foster rather than eliminate cleavages.

Nor did Stone himself escape his colleagues' bitter thrusts. A sensitive man, whose outstanding trait was wholesomeness of character, he writhed under the impact. He was totally unprepared to cope with the petty bickering and personal conflict in which his Court became engulfed. Stone, a man of abounding courtesy and understanding, was baffled by the ruthlessness of their drive toward the goal, no less than by the violence of their language. A Victorian liberal by instinct and sympathy, he felt hurt when colleagues, attacking his integrity, accused him of talking like a representative of "the interests." In the Hughes Court, legal differences were profound, but, with the possible exception of McReynolds, the Justices saw eye to eye on how a lawyer and a gentleman should behave. This kind of harmony gradually disappeared, and it is doubtful whether any administrative means at the disposal of the Chief Justice could have restored it.[23]

Having neglected opportunities to exalt his own standing, Stone was ill equipped to squelch unseemly sniping. Nor did he have the advantage of close relationship with all the New Deal Justices. To some observers he seemed too old, too stiff for his spry younger colleagues. Unlike their generation, his was a day of last-name associates. Outspoken himself, he would "fight with the gladiators," needle one phalanx or the other by snorting in conference: "Jackson, that's damned nonsense," or, "Douglas, you ought to know better." A "scene" or discussion descending to the level of personalities, however, was always studiously avoided. Nor could he resort to disciplinary measures even in appropriate situations. If a law clerk deviated from what he considered "correct conduct" he would appeal helplessly to his secretary, suggesting that she "do something about it."[24] Someone ought "to educate these young fellows in the ABC's of what I consider correct conduct," he implored Dean Young B. Smith.[25] But, alas, that "someone" could not be himself because "I am too busy and have too many demands made upon me."

Still less could he remonstrate with colleagues for breaches of etiquette, whether judicial or other. Stone was not born to command equals.* Having begun a memorandum rather peremptorily—"Please be prepared to discuss and vote on the case"—he would add lamely—"if that seems desirable."[26]

That Stone's solid convictions handicapped him there can be little doubt; and if success be measured by the Chief's ability to maintain the *appearance* of harmony, he certainly was a failure. Refusing to utilize backstairs diplomacy to smooth the way to decision, he thought the opinion writer should have "a good deal of scope in what he says" and that modifications should "depend on the will of the majority."[27] He also knew something of the high price Taft and Hughes had paid for success in "massing the Court." The latter had been forced to engage in double talk about "emergency,"[28] to invent meaningless distinctions,† suffer modification of his own opinions—all for the sake of unanimity. Stone was not one to employ "ingenious reasoning," good fellowship, the caucus, or other familiar political devices simply to keep the Court united. Nor would he use high pressure tactics.

"Chief Justice Stone," Irving Brant commented, "does not hammer a minority into line as some of his predecessors did, nor treat a dissent, when he is in the majority, as an affront to Jehovah."[29] Rather, he subscribed to the position Hughes had taken before he became Chief Justice. "Unanimity which is merely formal, which is recorded at the expense of strong, conflicting views, is not desirable in a court of last resort, whatever may be the effect upon public opinion at the time. This is so because what must ultimately sustain the Court in public confidence is the character and independence of the judges. They are not there simply to decide cases, but to decide them as they think they should be decided, and while it may be regrettable that they cannot always agree, it is better that their independence should be maintained and recognized than that unanimity should be secured through its sacrifice."[30]

Nor did his time-consuming procedures prevent Stone's Court from clearing its docket annually.[31] In his first year as Chief, the Justices disposed of more cases than at any previous term in the tribunal's history. Thereafter his Court continued to maintain the pace of his pred-

---

* "In the sense of having an influence as Chief any greater than that which he had as an associate," one critic has commented, "he really never became Chief at all." (John P. Frank to A.T.M., March 22, 1951.)

† Apropos *Faitoute Iron & Steel Co.* v. *Asbury Park,* 312 U.S. 502 (1942), a colleague wrote, May 16, 1942: "It is really pretty appalling the way in which Hughes differentiated the decision in the Ashton case [*Ashton* v. *Cameron County,* 298 U.S. 513 (1936)] in sustaining the Second Municipal Bankruptcy Act in the Bekins case, 304 U.S. (1938). The fact of the matter is that there was, if anything, more consent by the state for the municipal proceedings under Chapter IX of the first Act than under Chapter X of the second. Of course, the Ashton case should have been frankly overruled."

ecessor, and in the 1944 term exceeded its own record by eighty-one cases. By January that year, however, the Chief Justice seems to have lost his grip. Black and Douglas, particularly the former, began to dominate the conference, giving rise to published rumors that Black, not Stone, was the real leader.

Throughout our history judicial statesmanship has won notable political victories. This was strikingly so with John Marshall, hardly less true of Hughes who, having lost the battle to kill the New Deal, proved in the reorganization struggle of 1937 more than a match for one of the greatest political tacticians.* If Stone had brought to the Chief Justiceship comparable political cunning the tremendous pressure of Court work and the uncontrolled disputes of the conference might not have taken such a heavy toll of his lessened energies.

The continuance of dramatic cleavages kept the Court in the public eye and finally provoked bitter outcry from bar and public. Why could not five or six Justices, agreeing on a decision, agree also on the opinion? Professionals clung doggedly to the sentimental image of the law as inexorable, fixed, and certain. Even a sophisticated lawyer such as Charles C. Burlingham, who surely saw the difficulties, was deeply perturbed. "How amazing it is," Chief Justice Hughes had noted, "that, in the midst of controversies on every conceivable subject, one should expect unanimity of opinion upon difficult legal questions! In the highest ranges of thought, in theology, philosophy and science, we find differences of view on the part of the most distinguished experts—theologians, philosophers and scientists. And when we deal with questions relating to principles of law and their application, we do not suddenly rise into a stratosphere of icy certainty."[32]

Yet for lawyers, as for laymen, the law and the Court as its oracle, had lost prestige. Leading members of the bar nervously echoed charges that the Justices had unsettled the law, destroyed the rule of *stare decisis,* lowered the Court's standing. Multiplex opinions, they maintained, were valueless for them as practical forecasters of legal weather. If Holmes' view that the lawyer's job is prediction be sound, then the legal profession had reason to be grateful rather than critical of the prevailing candor on Stone's bench.† By refusing to obscure real disputes, Stone's Court provided materials from which astute lawyers could divine the lines of tension within the bench itself. When judges handed down four opinions in one case, it was apparent that the ar-

---

* "Well, Hughes hasn't been a jewel of consistency like you," Charles C. Burlingham wrote Stone, June 5, 1941, "but he read the Stars in '37, and that letter to the Senator, which he should have shown you as he did L.D.B., gave *le coup de grâce* to the Court-packing bill."

† In the Barnette case, for example, it was easy for Judge John J. Parker to predict that Gobitis would be overruled because of Black's, Douglas's, and Murphy's unprecedented announcement of their change of heart in the Opelika case.

gument was not at an end. Within those opinions one could find basic divisions, differing articulate major premises, forewarning counsel that in the next case the authority of this precedent alone would not be enough to validate his client's view. In Taft's day, as in Hughes', they would rarely have had that clue.

"Neither the law nor the Court is to be regimented so long as Stone sits," Walton Hamilton said in 1944. "In less than a decade the Court has been transformed. It has ceased to be a super-legislature; it stands today, more firmly than any other agency of State, in the great American tradition."[33] Observers who could sustain the shock of law without magic praised the new order. "It is good," Max Lerner commented, "to have Justices on the Supreme Court who pretend to no Olympian infallibility and who can stick their necks out of their enfolding robes."[34] "Never in the history of the Supreme Court of the United States has the Bill of Rights been more frequently or more ardently supported, and never have the privileges of the poor and the weak and of the minorities of race, color, and religion been more clearly asserted," another authority holds.[35]

Stone's own influence was highly salutary. "Not since Marshall have we had a Chief Justice who so fully understood the Constitution or who has so correctly judged its application to changing conditions."[36] Perhaps the *New York Times* and others who decried the Justices' disagreements as destructive of dignity, order, and authority had simply failed to "grasp the deeper and essential philosophy of which the First Amendment is only one manifestation."[37] One suspects also that their real complaint lay with what the Court was doing rather than how it was doing it. The revolution that led to judicial acceptance of New Deal legislation put the Court on the spot with respect to the older concepts of government to which vested interests clung so tenaciously. Naturally, startled cries of anguish resounded when the Court, ignoring the sanctity of sacred cows, took openly into account the social and political factors that had moved Hughes to rush through the Scottsboro and other decisions.*

Stone no less than the others felt these pressures. Nevertheless his judges stuck to their convictions. When they gave heed to such ex-

---

* "Much of the unsettling influence of the Court since 1937," Justice Douglas observed, "has been in removing from constitutional doctrine excrescences produced early in the century. The tendency has been to return to older views of constitutional interpretation, and to sanction governmental power over social and economic affairs which the Court, beginning in the '80s, and particularly in the preceding ten to thirty years, had denied." ("Stare Decisis," *Columbia Law Review*, June 1949, p. 750.)

"As usual," Alexander H. Pekelis wrote, "the quest for unity of approach, certainty of attitudes, for the 'law as it is,' is a disguise of the underlying design to prevent the development of an institution or of a body of law in a direction deemed undesirable by the critics." (*Law and Social Action*, p. 195.)

traneous considerations it was only to find out how they could do what they wanted to gracefully, without rousing destructive protest. They never found, nor did they seek, a formula for "beautifying" what was disagreeable to the sufferers, nor bother to cover grants of power with "apologetic phrases." By obscuring the lawmaking function of judges they might mislead the people and fail to bring out in the open the real responsibility of judges for what they do. Inevitably such stark candor, combined with unconcealed disagreements, robbed the "Higher Law" of its dogmatic quality. The Justices seemed to forget that the judiciary occupies, vis-à-vis the masses, a position not unlike that of the British Crown. The difference—and it is a big one—is that the Court still has real power.

The Justices on Stone's Court, along with the Chief Justice himself, did, in fact, neglect what Walter Bagehot has described as the "theatrical element."* They were neither mystic in their claims nor occult in action. Without camouflage they attempted to execute the political function of the Supreme Court in a straightforward way. They let it be known that power and individual conviction decide complex political questions. Law thus shorn of its magic seemed shockingly irreverent to people who preferred to maintain the image of changeless law.

CHAPTER FORTY-EIGHT

# Well-Deserving Pillar

On March 2, 1945, Stone completed two decades on the Supreme Bench. Newspapers throughout the country commemorated the event. "He has shared in, and indeed has greatly shaped, a significant expansion of the judicial view respecting the scope of federal authority in the economic sphere," the *Washington Post* commented in a lengthy and perceptive editorial. At the same time he had "cleaved always to

* "The mass of men," Bagehot wrote, "are uninterested in the plain, palpable ends of government; they do not prize them; they do not in the least comprehend how they should be attained. . . . The elements which excite the most easy reverence will be the theatrical elements. That which is mystic in its claims; that which is occult in its mode of action; that which is brilliant to the eye; that which is seen vividly for the moment, and then is seen no more; that which is hidden and unhidden; that which is specious, and yet interesting, palpable in its seeming, and yet professing to be more than palpable in its results; this, howsoever its form may change, or howsoever we may define it or describe it, is the sort of thing—the only sort—which yet comes home to the mass of men." (*The English Constitution and other Political Essays* [New York: D. Appleton & Co., 1914], p. 76.)

fundamentals in dealing with the rights of individuals. . . . He has never sought to govern his fellow justices, but he has brought to their deliberations an atmosphere of tolerance and friendliness which has served to temper the vigor of their intellectual differences." In congratulating him on the completion of his second decade of service to the Court, the paper expressed "the fervent hope that he will continue at his post so long as it does not overtax his strength."[1]

The Chief Justice, even then, was contemplating early retirement. "In the natural course of events," he wrote his son Lauson, July 15, 1945, "I should retire before very long. The work is heavy and nerve-wracking, and the country is entitled to have a Chief Justice who is in his prime instead of one who is on the wrong side of seventy three, as I should be in October. My retirement would also lighten the burdens on Mother. I am telling you this so that you may be free to say that my membership on the Court is not likely to be long a handicap to any firm which you might join."

In talks with his son Marshall later that summer, he made clear his intention to quit after a relatively short lapse of time. The unhappy events leading to the retirements of Justices Field and Holmes were often in his mind, underscoring the folly of prolonging judicial tenure unduly. He would withdraw before any marked signs of decline in his customary vigor had materialized. But he had not yet fixed a definite date. Various factors may have accounted for his indecision. "I would be surprised," Marshall Stone suggests, "if he had not thought of staying on long enough for a Republican President to be able to appoint his successor."[2] One thing seems certain—failing health was not a factor. On that score there appears to have been no reason whatever for planning anything but a very active life into the 1950's.

In early June 1945 the Chief Justice, reiterating an old refrain, described himself as "tied to my oar like a galley slave and pulling for dear life to keep from going down with the stream." A few months later he promptly squelched the rumor of impending retirement as "without foundation." "Perhaps the wish is 'father to the thought,' " he told Sterling Carr somewhat acidly. "After one gets into his seventy-fourth year, there is a natural expectation that he will not carry for long the heavy burden that I am carrying. Sometimes I think to myself when I see the performances that go on around me, 'Why subject oneself to that sort of thing?' And then I think what would happen if I weren't here, and what would I do if I didn't have this job and I conclude it is perhaps my duty to keep going. Who knows?"[3] Chief Justice Taft, and many others before him, had expressed similar sentiments and kept right on as long as possible.

After the war the Stone household rapidly got back to normal. Lawrence, the butler who had previously been with the family for ten years, came back ready for work; Powell, the chauffeur, was on hand; and a former cook "deigns to come in and cook a meal for us occasionally."[4] His sons, too, had returned to their respective professions. Lauson organized a new law firm in New York City; Marshall, back at his Harvard post, continued to garner academic honors and preferment.* Early in 1946 Lauson was awarded the Order of Merit by the War Department for his wartime services. The beaming Chief Justice and Mrs. Stone attended the ceremony conducted by a major general in the presence of the Secretary of War. The appointment of Republican Senator Harold Burton suggested that even the High Court might aspire to normality. "The new Justice is a very agreeable person," the Chief reported, "and I believe will be a good man. In that case, he will be a great comfort to me."[5]

The regular Court work continued to be heavy, and yet "in a moment of weakness" he relaxed his rigid rule against extra-judicial engagements and agreed to address the seventy-fifth anniversary celebration of the Association of the Bar of the City of New York. The meeting, held March 16, 1946, attracted over eight hundred lawyers. It was an inspiring occasion. "We are met," he began, "to celebrate the anniversary of the organization of this Association, an event of great significance in the history of our profession and of the struggle for good government in this city and state. It is also for me a personal anniversary, for it is now twenty-one years since I took my departure from this city."

The Chief Justice reminisced pleasantly and discursively about his early years at the bar, confessing that there had been times when he felt "nostalgic yearnings for those exciting days when I was either teaching law to young men, or practicing my profession here in New York." He proudly cited the Association's defense of the five Socialist legislators expelled from the New York Assembly as one among many notable examples of how the Association had directed its "powerful influence to the promotion . . . of good government and to the perpetuation of those principles of government upon which this nation was founded."

Coming down to the present, the speaker touched on less dramatic opportunities for constructive leadership. He noted the rise of administrative agencies, "with the accompanying increase of their functions and powers," and the expansion of the federal commerce authority—"the exercise by Congress of its power to regulate not only inter-

---

* In 1946 Marshall accepted a professorship at the University of Chicago. During the period when he was weighing the advantages of remaining at Harvard against those of moving to Chicago, his father gave freely of his advice. "I think," Marshall writes, "he was inclined to think that I would do well to remain at Harvard, though he was not dogmatic on the point." Stone died before Marshall decided to make the change.

state commerce itself, but those local matters which are regulable by Congress only because they affect the commerce." A realistic attitude toward these changes called for recognition of their "obvious need and utility." The legal profession must, moreover, open its eyes to the fact that the innovations it had so strenuously and so unsuccessfully resisted were not the result of "a judicial revolution." "If clear thinking is the first step toward effective action," the speaker suggested, "the efforts of some members of the legal profession to stay this expansion of power would perhaps have been more effective if the change had been recognized from the start for what it was—a legislative and not a judicial revolution." For those who wished to play "the role of counterrevolutionists," he recommended the method that had carried him through twenty-one years of constitutional evolution—employment of their talents in guiding change toward socially useful ends.[6]

Except for this break he had worked terribly hard all winter, preparing during three short weeks of recess in early April three opinions and two dissents. "I am busy as usual," the Chief Justice wrote an old friend, "but we are catching up with our docket all right and ought to have the decks cleared by adjournment time in June, except for cases which we are obliged to hold until Justice Jackson's return."[7] Nevertheless he yielded when David Finley invited him to speak on April 22 at the opening meeting of the American Association of Museums.[8]

In early April he suffered from a throat infection but catered to it only to the extent of staying abed until noon the following day. Later the Justice slipped on a paper he had placed beside his bed after working into the night. Fulfilling a tumbler's ambition, he came to earth unscathed. "You and I have gotten to the age and the point of dignity, where we should not be trying acrobatic stunts," he wrote Sterling Carr. "Why I didn't break my neck, I don't know, but as a matter of fact, nothing was damaged except my temper."[9]

In addition to his judicial labors he found time to take part in the now burgeoning Washington social life, missed so much during the war. At the spring dinner of the Gridiron Club a distinguished audience led by President Truman gave him one of the greatest ovations of his career.[10] On Saturday, April 20, he made one of his rare appearances at the Washington Literary Society, to hear Dr. Harold Moulton's humorous paper, "How to Buy a Farm." In the comment that followed, the Chief Justice expatiated on the joys of his boyhood work on his father's farm. As the discussion wore on, it appeared there were only two present who never had anything to do with a farm. "Of all the people in the world," Albert W. Atwood challenged, "you should observe the rights of minorities." "The thing for you to do," Stone retorted good-naturedly, "is join the majority." He moved amidst great laughter that the name of the Society be changed from Literary to Agricultural.[11] Outwardly the Justice appeared fit. Only the most discerning could see "how much the anguish of the times oppressed him."[12] Regretfully, he left the meeting early, explaining he had "quite a job to do."

The following day, Easter Sunday, April 21, was spent quietly with family and friends. "We were met by my parents at Union Station," Marshall recalls, "and driven out to the Schiffelers' country place 'Apple Hill' for lunch. H.F.S. seemed rather tired so far as appearance went, but he was in excellent spirits. It was definitely a family party, without any sense of formality. After lunch, all relaxed on the terrace in the bright sunlight. H.F.S. napped a little, stretched out in a comfortable chair. Later Mr. Schiffeler took the men for a little walk in the neighborhood. Seeing former Senator Wheeler, a neighbor of the Schiffelers, led H.F.S. to discourse philosophically on the decline of that once well-known figure. He also dwelt a little on the difficulties to which the Court had lately been put by Justice Rutledge's failure to read carefully what H.F.S. had written on a case up for decision. On the whole, the Chief Justice was in a very relaxed mood, despite these reminders of his daily concerns."[13]

After returning home the Stones entertained some young people for tea, and in the late afternoon called on former Chief Justice Hughes. Supper at home, a purely family affair, gave Marshall and his wife a rare treat. Against all precedent, "Father" lingered at the table even after it was cleared, holding his family for a talk fest as memorable as it was unusual. Rather late in the evening Lauson and his wife arrived from New York. His father joined him in a raid on the icebox, and they talked for a while before going to bed. There was the customary hearty breakfast the next morning. The fine weather continued, and everyone was in excellent spirits. A dinner party was in the offing for that evening, and the Chief Justice gave some attention to the wines to be served.

The Chief Justice was the first to leave the house, setting off for Court in a cheerful mood. On reaching the building he stopped whistling and took on judicial gravity. But when Justice Frankfurter came in with a distinguished English visitor, Lord Wright, the Chief Justice seemed "free of the burdens of office, relaxed, never more happy." Frankfurter evoked from his Chief a hearty laugh in calling Lord Wright's attention to the handsome Folger Library across the way. "Wright, look at that building," the Justice commented. "That is where this man had rather be than Chief Justice."[14] Stone did not dissent.

The Court's great marble-colonnaded chamber overflowed that day with hordes of Easter Monday tourists. At the stroke of noon the Justices seated themselves in their high-backed chairs behind the long mahogany bench. This was decision day. The Chief Justice, impressive as usual, announced the death on April 19 of Mrs. Rosamond L. Sutherland, widow of the late Justice. Leaning forward, he nodded to Justice Rutledge, who read a routine majority opinion. Stone, his solid face impassive, rattled off a brief dissent—a scene enacted many times before in his twenty-one years on the bench.

Now he was the Court's dean as well as its chief. He looked fit. His broad-chinned, wide-mouthed face reflected vigor, good nature, and a benign judicial air. Relaxed in his seat, he listened intently as Justice Douglas read the majority opinion in *Girouard* v. *United States*. The issue once again was whether a conscientious objector was eligible for citizenship, and this turned on whether that part of the oath of citizenship prescribed by the Naturalization Act of 1940, requiring the applicant "to support and defend the Constitution," etc., was to be interpreted as barring anyone who refused to bear arms. In the Schwimmer, Bland, and Macintosh cases fifteen years before, the Supreme Tribunal had turned down pacifists' pleas for citizenship on just this ground. In two of them Stone had dissented from this "tortured" interpretation of the naturalization laws. In the interim Congress had re-enacted the statutes without changing the form of oath required. Should the Court or Congress correct "error" in the judicial construction of the naturalization laws? The majority held that Congress had, in this instance, tossed back to the Court a hot potato of the Justices' own making.[15]

A cardinal feature of Stone's code of "self-restraint" had always been that the Court's obligation to remedy mistaken judicial interpretation was limited. The Court was free to reconsider and correct its own errors of Constitutional doctrine, otherwise remediable only by the cumbrous amending process. It was not free to ignore "mistaken" interpretations of legislation, since these could be overcome by Congress if the lawmakers saw fit. In the Bedford Cut Stone case early in his career and in the Apex decision at its peak, he had insisted, despite strong inclination to overrule faulty statutory construction, that the Justices should, in the absence of corrective legislation, adhere consistently to previous interpretations. The Girouard case, as he saw it, called for the straightforward application of this rule. To his law clerks, however, a departure seemed justifiable. They saw their Chief, on very slim grounds, slipping away from a position he had taken on civil liberties in the Macintosh case. This impasse, as always, made him unhappy.

"On at least two occasions during the two-week period while the opinion was in preparation," his law clerk has recalled, "the Chief made the long stomp from his office to our office on the other side of the conference room to talk about Girouard. Nickerson and I thought he was wrong, and I think Nickerson (who was helping on the dissent and who wrote parts of it) made an effort to get him to change his mind. I had the impression that the Chief was more irritated by this than usual. This impression was consistent with another impression I shared with others—that in the concurrence and admiration of his young law clerks the Chief found confirmation that he was still abreast of the times and still 'liberal.' Our refusal to give him that confirmation really stung in Girouard, where I think he sensed the dilemma of the old against the new 'liberalism.' "[16]

So different were his law clerks' views from his own that he did not even submit the draft to them until it had gone through several revisions. Finally Eugene Nickerson suggested the idea that it was Congress's duty "to make known its purpose in a controversial matter of interpretation of its former language," and that the Court must presume it had done so. "Stone was delighted; to this extent at least there was agreement with his law clerks."[17]

Thus Stone found himself dissenting from the triumph of his own views. In deference to his overriding principle of judicial self-restraint, he refused citizenship to conscientious objectors. Speaking with much less emphasis and in a lower tone than usual, he explained his stand.

"With three other Justices of the Court I dissented in the Macintosh and Bland cases, for reasons which the Court now adopts as ground for overruling them." A majority had then rejected his arguments. Now, he said, "the question, which for me is decisive of the present case, is whether Congress has likewise rejected that construction by its subsequent legislative action." The record clearly indicated to him a negative answer. "A study of congressional action taken with respect to proposals for amendment of the naturalization laws since the decision in the Schwimmer case leads me to conclude that Congress has adopted and confirmed this Court's earlier construction of the naturalization laws. For that reason alone, I think that the judgment should be affirmed."[18]

Going to the heart of his argument, stating the common ground between himself and his law clerks, he said:

It is the responsibility of Congress, in re-enacting a statute, to make known its purpose in a controversial matter of interpretation of its former language, at least when the matter has, for over a decade, been persistently brought to its attention. In the light of this legislative history, it is abundantly clear that Congress has performed that duty. In any case it is not lightly to be implied that Congress has failed to perform it and has delegated to this Court the responsibility of giving new content to language deliberately readopted after this Court has construed it. For us to make such an assumption is to discourage, if not to deny, legislative responsibility.[19]

The Chief Justice's voice rose strong and clear, and finally, at the very end of the opinion, he struck a note sounded consistently throughout his judicial career: "It is not the function of this Court to disregard the will of Congress in the exercise of its constitutional power."[20]

After Justice Black announced several opinions, it was the Chief's turn to deliver the three decisions he had prepared for the Court. He leaned back in his chair as if to begin. There were several moments of silence, enough to attract attention. "I looked over to the center chair," Justice Rutledge recalled the next day, "and saw the Chief sitting back, holding his opinions in reading position, his right hand fumbling through the pages. Then I heard him say in a low voice something like 'the case should be stayed; we decided to send this case back to conference for reconsideration.' Still it did not occur to me," Rutledge went on, "that he was ill. I thought he had suddenly decided that a case which had been announced previously had some hitch in it and was calling a recess to go off and straighten things out. Suddenly, the gavel banged, and Black adjourned the Court until two-thirty."[21]

The big round clock behind the center chair stood at one forty-five as Black and Reed assisted the Chief Justice from the bench. In a washroom off the conference chamber he lay unconscious on a couch, quietly mumbling legal talk. A few moments later a spokesman brought reassuring news; a physician had diagnosed his illness as a small case of indigestion. Shortly thereafter Stone's own physician took a more serious view but held out hope for recovery. At about three-thirty an ambulance took the stricken Chief Justice home. Surrounded by his wife and sons, he lingered without regaining consciousness and without pain. At six forty-five death from a massive cerebral hemorrhage came very peacefully and easily to the twelfth Chief Justice of the United States. There had been no tapering off. Stone was "interrupted in labor which engaged the whole of him and just after pronouncing the principle" which for him was "the pole star of the Supreme Court as he understood its place in our scheme."[22]

The nation learned of Stone's sudden death the evening of April 22. His grandchildren in Cambridge, New London, and New York heard the news in a special radio bulletin. "Words cannot express," one of them has recorded, "the way they felt about the death of this man who was so great and so dignified, and yet a truly fond grandfather."[23] In the Supreme Court building next day, the unoccupied chair at the center was draped. Senior Associate Justice Black announced a recess until April 29 and set the tone for national reaction. Stone's "distinguished" service, he said, "earned for him a high place in the affection and admiration of all the people."[24]

In the national legislature business halted to honor the departed Chief. The House of Representatives adopted a resolution solemnly recording its "profound sorrow" and adjourned as a "further mark of respect." The Senate also recessed the following day, after appointment of a committee of six senators to attend the funeral. In brief addresses several senators spoke of his meaning for them. Senator Raymond Willis of Indiana emphasized the fact that Stone's bench-mark had always been deference to the legislative will and eulogized him for sounding that note "in the last moments of his life." "If Chief Justice Stone had contributed nothing else to our American philosophy," the Senator declared, "those words alone would be worth the life which he nobly and inspiringly lived." "No Associate Justice or Chief Justice within my recollection," Senator Alben Barkley of Kentucky said, "held a more abiding place in the affections of the American people and in the affections of all who knew him intimately and personally."[25]

The funeral took place April 25 in the Washington Cathedral on a day of drizzling rain. At the right of the altar sat those closest to him in life. Some twenty-five hundred people filled the other pews, the President, his aides, and family among them. Behind the honorary pallbearers sat the Chief Justice's former colleagues, including Charles Evans Hughes, James C. McReynolds, and Owen J. Roberts. The Reverend Fleming James, Stone's friend and neighbor of Englewood days, read a prayer composed for the occasion. "Not as a great public official do we remember him now," he said, "but as a friend: understanding, companionable, kind, true, humble, simple of heart, courageous; one to whom we looked for clear direction in perplexity; one who never failed us when we needed him." As the strains of the majestic recessional, "The Strife Is O'er," resounded, the coffin was borne from the Cathedral for burial at the foot of a fir tree in the shadow of tiny century-old St. Paul's Episcopal Church, in Rock Creek Park.

From men and women throughout the nation whose lives Stone had touched, however long or briefly, came glowing tribute. "Of all the brothers, Harlan was closest to me," his sister wrote the Chief Justice's widow. "Although Winthrop and Lauson were always kind, to Harlan I turned for counsel."[26] Through all the passing years and in spite of all the honors that had come to him, "Doc" remained to his Amherst classmates the great, warmhearted, and friendly soul they had known in undergraduate days. "He stood for the truth," one of them wrote, "and he believed that the human mind could get the truth, as Professor Garman said, by 'weighing the evidence.' "[27] "No gathering could be counted complete without him;* no reunion a success if he was not

* In September 1945 the Sons of the Vine had learned from the Chief Justice himself that he had never tasted a truly great bottle of that renowned Bordeaux, Château Latour. They began at once to plan an elaborate dinner at the Century Club in New York for June 1946. Ransacking their cellars, by April they had gathered a remarkable array of vintages from the famed Château: 1900, 1920, 1926, and 1934. The Chief Justice's death intervened. On April 25, 1946, Geoffrey Parsons sent to Farnham Griffiths the following night letter: "Alas, the wine dinner with the Chief Justice is now impossible. Instead Henry [Moe], Paul [Kieffer], Carl [Ganter], and I, with [Frederick] Wildman, plan to devote the bottles which

there," his classmates' tribute said. "We admired him for his keenness of mind. We revered him for his straightforward honesty. And we loved him for the very simplicity that spelled his greatness."[28]

Miss Jessamine Dixon of high school days, and Professor Charles E. Garman of Amherst College could no longer testify, but John Bassett Moore, a professor at Columbia Law School during the nineties, had survived him. "He was once a student of mine," the elderly international jurist wrote. "I then predicted that he would have a great career, and this forecast was completely fulfilled. He united qualities of ability, independence, and integrity that are so important in the exalted position he attained."[29]

Hundreds of practicing lawyers looked back on Stone's classes as the high point of their student days. From them the testimony—"the only teacher I ever studied under who had the ability to make me think carefully and deeply"—came forth almost as a refrain. On the bench he continued to stimulate youth, retaining through his law clerks a vital link with teaching. "I often remember," one of them recounts, "the brightness with which he would smile at me, and say after we had sent an opinion off to the printer: 'Well, we learned something on that one, didn't we?' "[30]

His associate and former student, Justice William O. Douglas, wrote the Chief Justice's widow the most understanding tribute: "I had a rare affection for him. It started when I sat at his feet in law school. He was the greatest teacher I ever knew. And my affection and admiration for him grew as he moved into the public service and began to assert his influence on national problems. . . . I found in his friendship great strength and comfort. His insight and understanding were beyond compare."[31]

In death, as in life, the press singled out his most marked characteristics—integrity, humility, humaneness, independence, balance. The most discerning comment came from the obscure *Youngstown Vindicator* on April 24: "He was governed by principles which he upheld staunchly, whether it was the right or the left that infringed them." "Stone was in the tradition of all those great justices," the *Cleveland Plain Dealer* observed, "who after their elevation to the bench have never belonged to any special group, men whose integrity is beyond the understanding of those who would subvert government to their selfish purposes."[32]

---

we had assembled to share with our great friend to a dinner at the Century in his memory. We feel he would wish it so."

The dinner took place on May 18, 1946, in a quiet alcove off the Club library, surrounded by books, an atmosphere such as the Chief Justice loved. There were no formal speeches. Instead Griffiths read to the group the last paragraph of Professor Richard R. Powell's memorial address on the Chief Justice's "superlative humanity."

"Under him," Dean Erwin Griswold has observed, "we came very close to the precious ideal of a government of laws."[33]

The same theme predominated at the simple ceremonies, August 25, 1948, dedicating Stone's Chesterfield birthplace. For the first time since its founding in 1761, this placid little village of six hundred became the center of New England. Four thousand visitors poured in on all roads to see and hear Associate Justices and other notables. From the corner of Penning's store where he conducted a post office that normally did an annual business of less than $1500, the town's grocer-postmaster sold more than four hundred thousand Harlan Fiske Stone commemorative stamps, each bearing a vigorous, full-face portrait of the late Chief Justice. Friends, classmates, colleagues, tourists, and townsfolk alike sat on rough pine benches, facing a rude platform set against a backdrop of waving corn and mist-clad mountains. Under the broiling sun they heard addresses by Justice Stanley F. Reed, Senator Styles Bridges, and others. Through the years Stone's thought and words had gone back to this spot. It was fitting that his birthplace should be marked by natural New Hampshire granite.

Speakers who honored him were confident that no perspective of time would add to or detract from their estimate. "A fair and upright judge," the colleague who had known him longest declared, "one of the most judicious ever to sit on the bench."[34] Three of his pronouncements stand out: the timely AAA dissent, where he told the truth about judging and pointed the way to a prodigal Court's redemption; the Harvard Tercentenary address—an inspired essay revealing the genius of an enduring Constitution—continuity of tested values in a changing society; and, perhaps his finest achievement, the Gobitis dissent—a historic solo on the essentials of free government. In these utterances, surely, he touched the hem of greatness.

Little minds, trying to compress his meaning within the handy labels of "conservative" or "liberal," had been confounded. No tag seemed to fit. Harlan Fiske Stone was a judge, a dispassionate interpreter of the law of which he was "a well-deserving pillar."

*Bibliographic Notes*

*Chronology*

*Law Clerks to Chief Justice Stone*

*Opinions*

*Note on Stone's Legal Writings*

*Index*

# Bibliographic Notes

## PROFILE

1. H.F.S. to Charles A. Beard, Nov. 3, 1945.
2. H.F.S. to Ronald Thomson, Nov. 14, 1945.
3. H.F.S. to Alfred Lief, Feb. 17, 1944.
4. Charles A. Beard, prefatory note to Samuel J. Konefsky, *Chief Justice Stone and the Supreme Court* (New York: The Macmillan Co., 1945), p. xxi.
5. H.F.S. to Young B. Smith, Jan. 26, 1928.
6. From Stephen Vincent Benét's *The Devil and Daniel Webster* (New York: Rinehart, 1937).
7. H.F.S. to James Henry Breasted, April 1, 1935.
8. Benét, *op cit.*
9. H.F.S. to Lauson H. Stone, Feb. 28, 1936.
10. Robert H. Murray, *The History of Political Science from Plato to the Present* (Cambridge, Eng.: W. Heffer & Sons, Ltd., 1926), p. 21.
11. See Felix Frankfurter, "Harlan Fiske Stone," *Year Book of the American Philosophical Society,* 1946, p. 339.
12. Benét, *op cit.*
13. Memorandum from Herbert Wechsler to Gertrude Jenkins Regis, 1947.
14. H.F.S. to Duane R. Dills, Jan. 22, 1936.
15. H.F.S., "The Common Law in the United States," *Harvard Law Review,* Nov. 1936, p. 24.
16. H.F.S., *Law and Its Administration* (New York: Columbia University Press, 1915), p. 152.
17. H.F.S. to Charles E. Heydt, April 12, 1940.
18. Bennett Boskey, "Mr. Chief Justice Stone," *Harvard Law Review,* Oct. 1946, p. 1200.
19. H.F.S. to his sons, April 13, 1933.
20. H.F.S. to Judge Irving Lehman, Sept. 20, 1942.
21. H.F.S., "The Common Law in the United States," loc. cit., p. 25.

## PART ONE

### CHAPTER I

1. The genealogical material in this chapter is drawn primarily from J. Gardner Bartlett, *Simon Stone Genealogy, Ancestry and Descendants of Deacon Simon Stone of Watertown, Mass., 1320-1926.* (Published for the Stone Family Association, Boston, 1926.)
2. For detailed activities of the Colonial forces under Captains Henchman and Sill, in King Philip's War, and for the Narragansett grants, see: George Madison Bodge, *Soldiers in King Philip's War, being a Critical Account of that War with a concise history of the Indian War of New England, from 1620-1627* (Leominster, Mass.: printed for the Author, 1896).
3. Cotton Mather, *Magnalia Christi Americana: or, The Ecclesiastical History of New England, 1620-1698* (Hartford: Silvus Andrus, 1820), Vol. II, pp. 525-26. (First published English edition, 1702.)
4. *Massachusetts Colony Provincial Congress, 1774-1775,* pp. 612, 614.
5. H.F.S. to William A. Slade, Oct. 4, 1941.
6. Larken Mead, "Historical Sketch of Chesterfield," in J. Farmer and J. B. Moore, eds., *Collections, Topographical, Historical and Biographical, relating primarily to New Hampshire* (Concord, N.H.: Hill and Moore, 1822), Vol. I,

p. 280. A Chesterfield sketch appears also in John Farmer and Jacob B. Moore, *A Gazetteer of the State of New Hampshire* (Concord, N.H.: published by Jacob B. Moore, 1823), p. 100.

7. Spafford in the older printings; Spofford today.
8. Farmer and Moore, *A Gazetteer*, p. 19.
9. Farmer and Moore, *Collections . . .* , p. 279; Oran E. Randall, *History of Chesterfield* (Brattleboro, Vt.: D. Leonard, 1882), pp. 127-28.
10. Edwin D. Mead, "Fame of Chesterfield's Old Academy Retold," *Keene (N.H.) Evening Sentinel,* Oct. 9, 1926.
11. The Stone family history in the following pages has been taken from Claude F. Walker's talks with various people, from a memorandum by Helen Stone Willard (Oct. 1949), and from two newspapers: the *Springfield Sunday Republican,* which carried a story "The Stone Family of Amherst" on Jan. 9, 1910; and the *Springfield Daily Republican,* Sept. 13, 1916.
12. Harlan Stone's father had one brother and a half-brother, Chauncey E. Stone, son of Lauson Stone and Thankful Dodge.
13. H.F.S. to Mrs. Raymond D. Allen, Feb. 13, 1940.
14. Lauson H. Stone's memorandum on Frederick Lauson Stone.
15. The two preceding paragraphs are quoted with adaptations from Charles S. Walker's "Fifty Years of Friendships," a chapter from his unpublished ms. (Courtesy of the Jones Library, Amherst, Mass.)
16. Lauson H. Stone's memorandum on Frederick Lauson Stone.
17. H.F.S. to Albert W. Hawkes, April 26, 1945.
18. *Vermont* v. *New Hampshire,* 289 U.S. 593 (1932).
19. Benét, *op. cit.*
20. *Winthrop Ellsworth Stone. A Memorial* (published by the Trustees of Purdue University, 1922), p. 57. The chapter entitled "The Youth and the Man" is published under the name Edward H. Davis, but the text was largely supplied by Harlan Stone. "I am wondering," Stone wrote Professor Stanley Coulter of Purdue, Nov. 9, 1921, "whether we cannot find some friend outside the family who could do this better than I? If it were thought desirable, I could write what is in my own mind and heart and let him make such use of it as he may wish." The arrangement was this: Davis prepared a few introductory paragraphs (page 53 to the break on page 55); the remainder of the chapter is Stone's except for a few paragraphs at the end "to justify the use of my name as the author of the article." (Edward H. Davis to Stanley Coulter, Feb. 22, 1922.)

## CHAPTER II

1. *Winthrop Ellsworth Stone, A Memorial,* p. 57.
2. H.F.S. to H. D. Anderson, Dec. 12, 1933.
3. From memoranda prepared in 1950 by Helen Stone Willard. Circumstances and incidents relating to the family life of the Stones in Mill Valley detailed in this chapter, unless otherwise indicated, are based upon material supplied by Mrs. Willard.
4. Stone used these words to describe the impact of environment on his brother Winthrop, but they apply equally to himself. See *Winthrop Ellsworth Stone. A Memorial,* pp. 60-61.
5. Claude F. Walker's talk with Mrs. Rebecca Holley Paige (1950).
6. H.F.S. to Helen Stone Willard, Nov. 7, 1938.
7. Claude F. Walker's talk with Mrs. Rebecca Holley Paige (1950).
8. H.F.S. to Dwight L. Hubbard, Nov. 21, 1941.
9. Factual information regarding Amherst School District No. 7 in Mill Valley, and the grammar schools and high school in the Center, has been gathered from Carpenter and Morehouse, *The History of the Town of Amherst . . .* , (Amherst: 1896), p. 259 ff.; also from the personal reminiscence of early Amherst public school teachers and pupils.
10. The Reverend Warren H. Beaman, Amherst '37, was grandfather of the Reverend John D. Willard, Amherst '07, who married Helen L. Stone, Harlan's sister. The Willards lived in the "Beaman house" in Amherst while John was a member of the M.A.C. staff.
11. In June 1953 Miss King, aged ninety-five, mind clear and full of lively recollections, confirmed these stories.
12. H.F.S. to William S. Booth, Jan. 9, 1926.

13. Francis Richmond Fletcher, Harlan's classmate in high school and college, was the eldest son of William I. Fletcher, for many years Amherst College librarian.
14. H.F.S. to Luther Ely Smith, June 11, 1943.
15. Memorandum from Marshall Stone to A.T.M., 1952.
16. Claude F. Walker's talk with Warren R. Brown (1951).
17. H.F.S. to C. W. Beardsley, Jan. 10, 1925.
18. Marshall Stone's memorandum.
19. Mrs. Jessamine D. Walcott to H.F.S., Feb. 11, 1925.
20. From "The Training of Lawyers," address by H.F.S. at the induction of Huger W. Jervey as Dean of the Columbia University School of Law, Nov. 17, 1924, in *Modern Eloquence* (New York: P. F. Collier & Son Corp., 1936), Vol. VI, p. 372.
21. The quotation, and adaptations, are taken from Perlie P. Fallon's appreciation of Harlan Fiske Stone, *Club Dial* (Contemporary Club of White Plains, N.Y., Oct. 1946), p. 18.
22. Winthrop E. Stone to Charles S. Plumb, Aug. 26, 1886.
23. H.F.S. to Luther Ely Smith, June 11, 1943.

## CHAPTER III

1. For "The Revised Course of Study, at M.A.C.," signed "W." (Prof. Charles S. Walker, Sec'y of the Faculty), see *The Index*, '88, (Vol. XVIII, 1886), pp. 32-34.
2. Harlan Stone's mark in deportment for the second term, sophomore year, 1889-90, was 98, in spite of his involvement in events that resulted in his discipline by the faculty at the close of that term. Stone's record at M.A.C. for five terms was:

FRESHMAN YEAR (1888-89)

| First Term | Grade | Second Term | Grade | Third Term | Grade |
|---|---|---|---|---|---|
| Agriculture | 84 | Chemistry | 89 | Agriculture | 67 |
| Chemistry | 88 | Latin | 84 | Botany | 88 |
| Botany | 91 | Geometry | 99 | Geometry | 90 |
| Latin | 80 | English | 96 | Latin | 76 |
| Algebra | 95 | Tactics | 100 | Chemistry | 89 |
| Declamation | 80 | Drawing | 58 | English | 94 |
| Average | 86.3 | Average | 86.5 | Average | 81.8 |
| Deportment | 80 | Deportment | 85 | Deportment | 98.3 |
| Absences Ex. | 9 | Absences Ex. | 25 | Absences Ex. | 14 |
| Absences Unex. | 2 | Absences Unex. | 7 | Absences Unex. | 4 |

SOPHOMORE YEAR (1889-90)

| First Term | Grade | Second Term | Grade |
|---|---|---|---|
| Agriculture | 84 | Agriculture | 84 |
| Botany | 85 | Botany | 82 |
| Trigonometry | 90 | Mensuration | 90 |
| French | 77 | French | 60 |
| Tactics | 91.5 | Physiology | 92 |
| English | 71 | Drawing | 83 |
| Average | 83.7 | English | 75 |
| Deportment | 85 | Average | 80.8 |
| Absences Ex. | 32 | Deportment | 98 |
| | | Absences Ex. | 28 |
| | | Absences Unex. | 6 |

For this record and other kindnesses, the author is indebted to President (now Emeritus) Ralph A. Van Meter, University of Massachusetts.

3. Claude F. Walker's talk with Dr. Walter I. Boynton, M.A.C. '92 (1951).
4. Claude F. Walker's talk with Fred G. Averell, M.A.C. '94 (1952) and with Dwight L. Hubbard, M.A.C. '89 (1953). Averell and Hubbard, who lived in East Amherst, knew Harlan in school days.
5. Walker's talk with Dr. Boynton.
6. "Book of Services for the Chapel of the Massachusetts Agricultural College,

No. 2, Amherst, 1888-1891," for June 14, 1889; unpublished ms. of Charles S. Walker, Chaplain. (Courtesy of the Jones Library, Amherst, Mass.)

7. Secretary-Treasurer's Record Book, Class of '92, M.A.C. (Courtesy of the late Dr. Milton H. Williams, '92, Alumni Class Secretary.)
8. M.A.C. Minutes of the Faculty, Sept. 4, 17, 1889.
9. "Book of Services for the Chapel . . . ," for March 19, 1890.
10. Adapted from Alfred E. Stearns, *An Amherst Boyhood,* with a foreword by Chief Justice Harlan F. Stone (Amherst, Mass.: published by the College, 1946), pp. 84-86.
11. Claude F. Walker's talk with George E. Taylor, M.A.C. '92 (1951).
12. *The Index,* '92 (Vol. XXII, 1890), p. 47.
13. Jessamine Dixon to H.F.S., April 4, 1890.
14. Edith Field to H.F.S., July 5, 1890.
15. Helene May Butler Young to Mrs. Harlan F. Stone, Sept. 18, 1949.

## CHAPTER IV

1. Claude F. Walker's talk with Warren R. Brown (1951).
2. H.F.S. to Frederick S. Allis, Amherst '93, Oct. 18, 1934.
3. Claude M. Fuess, *Amherst, the Story of a New England College* (Boston: Little, Brown and Co., 1935), p. 43.
4. Thomas Le Duc, *Piety and Intellect at Amherst College, 1865-1912* (New York: Columbia University Press, 1946), pp. 41, 53.
5. H.F.S. to Stanley King, Feb. 12, 1946.
6. Fuess, *op. cit.,* p. 211.
7. Recollections of Helene May Butler Young from a memorandum prepared by Helen Stone Willard.
8. Jessamine Dixon to H.F.S., undated.
9. Edith S. Field to H.F.S., Oct. 18, 1890.
10. Will Chase to Luther Ely Smith, Oct. 22, 1947.
11. Records of the Class of '94. (Courtesy of Harry E. Whitcomb, Class Secretary.)
12. *The Amherst Student,* June 28, 1892, p. 267.
13. *The Olio '94* (1892), p. 29.
14: The donor was Joel Hayden, brother-in-law of Samuel Williston, benefactor of Williston Seminary and Amherst College. "Originally placed in the Hayden Garden in Haydenville, Mass., Sabrina caused such criticism because of her lack of draperies that Hayden solved the problem by presenting her to the College." (Stanley King, *A History of the Endowment of Amherst College* [1950], p. 47.)
15. The adventures of the bronze statue, detailed here and on pages following, except as otherwise noted, are culled from *Sabrina, The Class Goddess of Amherst College,* A History Compiled by Max Shoop, Guardian for the Class of 1910 (Springfield, Mass.: Press of Loring-Axtell, 1910), pp. 39-92.
16. Hyde's activities in his native city, and the success of his mission, may be read in Shoop, *op. cit.,* pp. 63-73.
17. The biographical references to Amherst College faculty and alumni in this chapter, and elsewhere in this work, are taken from *Amherst College Biographical Record of the Graduates and Non-Graduates,* Centennial Edition, 1821-1921, edited by Robert S. Fletcher, '97, and Malcolm O. Young, '16 (1927); also from the most recent edition of the *Record,* 1878-1950 (1951).
18. Nathan H. Weeks to Luther Ely Smith, Oct. 20, 1947.
19. This phrase is borrowed from the sketch "Sabrina," by Charles J. Staples, '96, and Professor John F. Genung, in *An Amherst Book,* edited by Herbert E. Riley, '96 (New York: The Republic Press, 1906), pp. 117-24. Staples was Guardian for '96, and Professor Genung was faculty poet and essayist, textbook author, and mentor to the Sabrina cult, if not a co-conspirator.

When, in 1921, Sabrina fell into the hands of the odd-numbered classes, the event was marked by a second Sabrina book, by Winthrop H. Smith, Guardian for the Class of 1916, and Halvor R. Seward and John G. Gibson 2nd., both '19, entitled *Sabrina, Being a Chronicle of the Life of the Goddess of Amherst College* (Concord, N.H.: The Rumford Press, 1921).

College authorities, in 1935, retired this dangerous source of interclass rivalry to the Edward Hitchcock Memorial Room, Morgan Hall, where, until June 10, 1951, it remained in permanent anchorage, a battered relic of a stormy career.

Certain adventurous spirits in the class of '51, armed with a blowtorch and deploring the fact that the spirit of the college was at a "very unfortunate low point," abducted Sabrina from her pedestal, in the hope that her absence and "possible reappearance" would start the college "thinking about at least one tradition and its place in college history." (See *The Amherst Student*, April 26, 1951, p. 3, and Sept. 19, 1951, pp. 1, 2, 3. Thomas H. Wyman, in the *Amherst Alumni News*, Oct. 1952, tells the story of the nocturnal abduction of the statue from Morgan Hall.)

One year later, June 7, 1952, Sabrina made a spectacular appearance in an airplane over Memorial Field, during the Commencement baseball game with Holy Cross, then flew away to oblivion. She left no promise, however, that the Sabrina tradition would ever recapture the prestige it enjoyed in Harlan Stone's day.

Without fanfare the statue was returned during Commencement week, 1955. (See "Wandering Statue of Sabrina Returned After Four-Year Absence," *New York Times*, June 12, 1955.)

20. *Amherst Alumni Council News*, July 1944, p. 203.
21. For a full description of the Amherst System, see John Bigham, "An Instructive Experiment in College Government," *Educational Review*, Feb. 1892, pp. 162-67; Mrs. Louise Seymour Houghton, "The Evolution of a College Republic," *Education*, 1886, pp. 485-89; "The New System in Amherst College" (a letter from the *Congregationalist*), *The Amherst Student*, Oct. 15, 1881, p. 28; "The Amherst System," *The Amherst Student*, Dec. 13, 1893, pp. 89-91; feature article by Herbert Ward in the *Boston Transcript*, April 14, 1894.
22. Words of Trustee Herbert B. Adams, Sept. 27, 1890, quoted in *Amherst Graduates' Quarterly*, Nov. 1922, pp. 4, 5.
23. For a description of Merrill Edward Gates and his hectic Amherst career, see Fuess, *op. cit.*, pp. 246-64.
24. Catalogue of Amherst College, 1892-93, p. 29.
25. From a memorandum among H.F.S.'s papers, Edward Hitchcock Memorial Room, Amherst College.
26. *The Amherst Student*, Feb. 3, 1894, p. 125; March 10, 1894, pp. 162-63; March 17, 1894, p. 174.
27. Amherst College Senate Minutes, p. 160. Carleton E. Clutia was a fellow townsman, and high school and college classmate of Harlan Stone. His chief attainment as an undergraduate seems to have been a high proficiency with the banjo. Dismissed from college for an indiscretion in 1894, he achieved success as an insurance executive. In 1916 Amherst College generously, if belatedly, granted him his A.B. degree.
28. H.F.S. to Claude M. Fuess, Sept. 9, 1939. "The president (Gates) refused to discuss the (Senate) matter with anybody, and deliberately turned his back on the president of the senior class (Stone) at his (Gate's) reception, after reproaching him, in the presence of a large number of guests, with having done the college a 'very serious injury.'" (Fuess, *op. cit.*, p. 255.)
29. Stearns, *op. cit.*, pp. 113-14. See also *The Amherst Student*, Feb. 24, 1894, p. 149, for an account of the procedures taken prior to the committee action.
30. For the full text of Stone's report, see *The Amherst Student*, March 24, 1894, p. 177.
31. Stearns, *op. cit.*, p. 115.
32. H.F.S. to Claude M. Fuess, Sept. 9, 1935; Sept. 9, 1939.
33. H.F.S. to Claude M. Fuess, Nov. 9, 1932.
34. For a description of the varsity players on the famous championship team of 1892, see *The Amherst Student*, Nov. 19, 1892, pp. 66-67.
35. *The Amherst Student*, Oct. 29, 1892, p. 46; Nov. 19, 1892, p. 65.
36. Lauson H. Stone to Luther Ely Smith, Oct. 27, 1947.
37. Feature article in *Boston Post*, April 6, 1924.
38. H.F.S. to H. J. Wheeler, Nov. 4, 1937.
39. H.F.S. to William Allen White, April 13, 1933.
40. In Alpha Delt were: "Old Doc" Hitchcock, '49; B. K. Emerson ("Emmie"), '65; and Richardson ("Richie"), '69. In Psi U.: former President Seelye, '49; Harris ("Derwall"), '55; "Tip" Tyler, '73; Estey, '60. In D.K.E.: Anson Morse, '71; J. B. Clark, '72. Garman, '72, did not join a fraternity, nor did "Davy" Todd, '75.

In an address before the Amherst Chapter of Alpha Delta Phi, June 28,

1887, President Seelye gave his favorable judgment concerning the fraternities at Amherst College:

"Now the aim of these societies is certainly good. They are not formed for pleasure simply, though they are one of the most fruitful sources of pleasure in a college student's life. Their first aim is . . . improvement in literary culture and manly character. They are all of them literary societies.

"One of the happiest features of society life at Amherst is connected with the society houses. There are no better residences in the village. . . . They are not extravagant. . . . The care of the home and its surroundings is itself a culture.

"There need be no objections to these societies on account of their secrecy. The secrecy is largely in name. . . . Treated as the societies are among us, and occupying the ground they do, no mischief comes from their secrecy. The rivalry between them is a healthy one, and is conducted openly and in a manly way." (In *The Handbook of Amherst, Massachusetts,* prepared and published by Frederick H. Hitchcock [1891], p. 147.)

41. H.F.S. to Alfred Stearns, Feb. 19, 1946.
42. H.F.S. to Clinton L. Rossiter, April 12, 1941.
43. On H.F.S.'s political activities, see *The Amherst Student,* Oct. 8, 15, 22, 29, 1892; *The Amherst Record,* Oct. 19, 26, 1892; *The Amherst Portfolio,* Class of 1894 (Boston: Charles W. Hearn, 1894).
44. H.F.S. to his cousin George Henry, in Amherst, Nov. 11, 1892.
45. Charles E. Garman, Amherst '72, B.D., Yale '79, a protégé of Seelye, taught philosophy at Amherst for twenty-six years (1881-1907), until his death in Amherst, aged fifty-six. In the 1880s he displaced Spencer's agnosticism and materialism with his own satisfying spiritual view of life. A landmark to this early phase of Garman's teaching is "An Examination of Herbert Spencer's View of the Evolution of Religion," a thesis presented to the Department of Philosophy, Amherst College, by the Reverend Charles S. Walker. In 1885, Amherst College, at Seelye's behest, granted Walker the Ph.D. degree.
46. H.F.S. to William Allen White, April 12, 1933. A slightly different version appears in White's *Puritan in Babylon* (New York: the Macmillan Co., 1939), p. 41.
47. *Letters, Lectures and Addresses of Charles Edward Garman.* A Memorial Volume. Eliza Minor Garman, in cooperation with the Class of 1884, Amherst College (Boston and New York: Houghton Mifflin Company, 1909), pp. 104-105. Hereafter referred to as *Garman Letters.* For an appreciative essay written by Walter A. Dyer, a student of Garman, see Houston Peterson, *Great Teachers* (New Brunswick: Rutgers University Press, 1946), pp. 105-119.
48. Le Duc, *op. cit.,* p. 116.
49. *Garman Letters,* p. 298.
50. *Ibid.,* p. 382.
51. From a letter to President G. Stanley Hall of Clark University, quoted in *Studies in Philosophy and Psychology,* by former students of Charles Edward Garman.
52. H.F.S. to William Allen White, April 12, 1933. See White's *A Puritan in Babylon,* p. 38.
53. *Ibid.*
54. *Ibid.*
55. Charles E. Garman's letter of recommendation, March 24, 1894.
56. *Springfield Republican,* April 6, 1924.
57. Fuess, *op. cit.,* p. 178.
58. Charles C. Seymour to Luther Ely Smith, Nov. 8, 1947.
59. Stone's Amherst grades:

| Freshman year | Grade | | Sophomore year | Grade |
|---------------|-------|---|----------------|-------|
| Elocution | B | | Declamation | B |
| Declamation | A | | Logic | C |
| Latin | D | | Oratory | B |
| German | C | | Latin | C |
| Mathematics | B | | German | B |
| Chemistry | B | | Mathematics | B |
| Anatomy | A | | Chemistry | A |
| | | | Botany | B |

| Junior year | Grade | Senior year | Grade |
|---|---|---|---|
| Public Speaking | A | Debate | A |
| Physics | A | Astronomy | A |
| Chemistry | C | Zoology | A |
| Biology | A | Philosophy | A |
| Mineralogy | A | Ethics | B |
| History | A | History | A |
| Philosophy | A | Political Economy | A |
| | | International Law | A |

General average 87.87; Phi Beta Kappa, first drawing, junior year.
60. Fuess, op. cit., p. 264 *n*. William S. Tyler, D.D., Amherst '30, "Old Ty," professor of Greek language and literature and the college historian, became emeritus in 1893, died 1897, aged eighty-seven. Harlan styled him as one of the "recent arrivals from Mount Olympus . . . worshiped from afar." (Stearns, op. cit., p. ix.) The son of William, John M. ("Tip") Tyler, Amherst '73, a botany professor, also made a classroom impress upon Harlan Stone. George D. Olds taught mathematics; Benjamin K. Emerson, mineralogy; Arthur L. Kimball, physics; Ephraim L. Wood, classics.
61. H.F.S. to Stanley King, Oct. 19, 1939.
62. H.F.S. to Nicholas Murray Butler, Dec. 22, 1925.
63. *The Amherst Student*, March 10, 1894, p. 161.
64. Luther Ely Smith to A.T.M., Aug. 5, 1950.
65. Rena Durkan to Malcolm Young, June 30, 1950.
66. *The Amherst Student*, Sept. 23, 1893, p. 4, and succeeding numbers.
67. Dr. Frederick Houk Law, Amherst, 95, to Claude F. Walker (1954).
68. *The Amherst Portfolio* (Boston: Charles W. Hearn, 1894), pp. 39-40.

## CHAPTER V

1. Frederick D. Hayward to A.T.M., Sept. 4, 1950.
2. H.F.S. to Frederick D. Hayward, June 22, 1941.
3. Claude F. Walker's talk with Wilbert A. Bishop, N.H.S. '98 (1954).
4. Webster Adams, *The Newburyport Daily News*, July 24, 1945. (Newburyport Public Library Scrapbook No. 7, p. 117.)
5. Harold A. Besse, "Saturday Smatterings," *Newburyport Daily News*, June 18, 1941.
6. H.F.S. to Harold A. Besse, April 10, 1924.
7. *School Record*, Dec. 1894.
8. *Newburyport Daily Herald*, Jan. 29, 1895.
9. Claude F. Walker's talk with Wilbert A. Bishop (1954).
10. *School Record*, June 1895.
11. Report of School Superintendent Lunt (Newburyport, Mass.), 1895, p. 70.
12. *Newburyport Daily News*, July 17, 18, 1945.
13. Ernest Foss to Mrs. Harlan F. Stone, April 24, 1946.
14. Recollections of Jackson E. Reynolds, July 1950.
15. Mrs. Walter Truslow to A.T.M., Jan. 25, 1952.
16. Cited by Mrs. Truslow in her letter of Jan. 25, 1925, to A.T.M.
17. Charles E. Garman to F. B. Dow, in *Garman Letters*, p. 549.
18. H.F.S. to John Bassett Moore, Oct. 26, 1932.
19. Nicholas Murray Butler, "The University in Action," *The Rise of a University* (New York: Columbia University Press, 1937), Vol. II, p. 292.
20. H.F.S., "After a Quarter Century at the Columbia Law School," *Columbia Alumni News*, Jan. 11, 1924, p. 219.
21. William S. Keener, 6 *Columbia Law Times* 164 (1893), reprinted (1893-94) in *Columbia Law School Announcement* 1.
    For a good description of the methods of law teaching prevailing at Columbia after 1892, see Thomas Reed Powell, "Law as a University Study," *Columbia University Quarterly*, March 1917, pp. 106-111. This discussion is to some extent based on ideas supplied by Stone. See letter, H.F.S. to Thomas Reed Powell, Jan. 26, 1917.
22. John W. Burgess, *Reminiscences of an American Scholar* (New York: Columbia University Press, 1934), p. 244.
23. George W. Kirchwey, "Columbia Law School Today," *Green Bag*, May 1898,

illustrated with photographs of the various rooms. See also *Columbia University Quarterly*, March 1899.

24. H.F.S., *op. cit.*, p. 219.
25. Horace Coon, *Columbia: Colossus on the Hudson* (New York: E. P. Dutton & Co., 1947), p. 228.
26. Recollections of Jackson E. Reynolds.
27. H.F.S., *op. cit.*
28. H. L. Satterlee, "Memorial of George Folger Canfield," *Association of the Bar of the City of New York Year Book* (1934), pp. 299-302.
29. H.F.S., *op. cit.*, p. 220.
30. Recollections of Sterling Carr, undated memorandum.
31. Edward R. Finch, Alumni Day Address upon the Presentation of the Portraits of John Bassett Moore and Harlan F. Stone, *Columbia Alumni News*, March 5, 1926, p. 455.
32. Recollections of Sterling Carr.
33. Recollections of Jackson E. Reynolds.
34. From Sterling Carr to Mrs. Harlan F. Stone, undated memorandum.
35. Finch, Alumni Day Address; Edward R. Finch to A.T.M., Oct. 26, 1950.
36. "Commencement Week, 1898," *Columbia University Quarterly*, Dec. 1898, p. 12.
37. *Ibid.*
38. H.F.S. to Ernest Cardozo, May 20, 1937.

PART TWO

## CHAPTER VI

1. H.F.S. to President Seth Low, Dec. 18, 1900.
2. H.F.S. to President Seth Low, Dec. 24, 1900.
3. H.F.S. to William S. Keener, Dec. 21, 1900.
4. H.F.S. to President Seth Low, Feb. 21, 1901.
5. H.F.S. to George W. Kirchwey, Feb. 11, 1905. Kirchwey was Dean of the Law School 1901-1910.
6. Nicholas Murray Butler to H.F.S., Dec. 20, 1906; George W. Kirchwey to H.F.S., Dec. 20, 1906.
7. *New York Times*, Nov. 20, 1909.
8. *Ibid.*
9. Charles K. Burdick to H.F.S., Dec. 19, 1909.
10. F. P. Keppel to H.F.S., Feb. 5, 1910.
11. H.F.S. to Nicholas Murray Butler, Jan. 25, 1910.
12. Anson D. Morse to H.F.S., Jan. 4, 1910.
13. H.F.S. to Nicholas Murray Butler, Jan. 15, 1910.
14. H.F.S. to Nicholas Murray Butler, Jan. 17, 1910.
15. Stone's views are set forth at some length in "The Function of the University Law School," address delivered before the American Bar Association, Boston, Aug. 28, 1911 (pamphlet).
16. *Annual Reports of Columbia University, Report of the Dean of the Faculty of Law*, 1912, pp. 67. Hereafter cited as *Annual Reports*.
17. *Annual Reports*, 1915, p. 81.
18. H.F.S. to Nicholas Murray Butler, Dec. 1, 1916.
19. *Annual Reports*, 1916, pp. 60-61.
20. H.F.S. "Fifty Years' Work of the Supreme Court," address delivered at the Semi-Centennial Meeting of the American Bar Association, Seattle, Washington, *American Bar Association Journal*, Aug.-Sept., 1928, p. 428-36.
21. Law review articles with citations are:
    "Resulting Trusts and the Statute of Frauds," *Columbia Law Review*, May 1906:
    *Steinberger v. Steinberger*, 60 Cal. App. (2d) 116, 120; 140 Pac. (2d) 31, 33 (Cal., 1943)
    "Equitable Conversion by Contract," *Columbia Law Review*, May 1913.
    "The Mutuality Rule in New York," *Columbia Law Review*, June 1916:
    *Arrow Holding Corp.* v. *McLaughlin's Sons*, 116 Misc. 555, 559, 190 N.Y. Supp. 720, 723 (N.Y., 1921)
    *Vanzandt* v. *Heilman*, 54 N.Mex. 97; 214 Pac. (2d)

864, 867 (N.Mex., 1950)
*Elder* v. *New York & Penn. Motor Express*, 284 N.Y.
350, 358; 31 N.E. (2d) 188, 192 (N.Y., 1940)
*Cavanna* v. *Brooks*, 97 N.J. Eq. 329, 332;
127 Atl. 247, 248 (N.J., 1925)
*Rizzo* v. *Stamp Realty Corp.*, 196 Misc. 615, 617;
92 N.Y. Supp. (2d) 598, 600 (N.Y., 1949)
*Epstein* v. *Gluckin*, 233 N.Y. 490; 135 N.E. 861 (1922)
"Nature of the Rights of the Cestui Que Trust," *Columbia Law Review*,
June 1917:
    *Sweeney* v. *Tabor*, 118 W.Va. 591, 595; 191 S.E.
295, 297 (W.Va., 1937)
    *Commonwealth* v. *Stewart*, 338 Pa. 9, 14; 12 A. (2d)
444, 447 (Pa., 1940)
    *Senior* v. *Braden*, 295 U.S. 422, 431; 79 L.Ed. 1520, 1524 (1935)
"Equitable Rights and Liabilities of Strangers to a Contract (I)," *Columbia
Law Review*, April 1918:
    *Bristol* v. *Woodward*, 251 N.Y. 275, 287, 288 (1929)
    *Safran* v. *Westrich*, 136 Misc. 81, 83; 240 N.Y.
Supp. 238, 241 (N.Y., 1930)
    *Neponsit P.O. Ass'n* v. *Emigrant Ind. Sav. Bank*
278 N.Y. 248, 261; 15 N.E. (2d) 793, 798 (N.Y., 1938)
"Equitable Rights and Liabilities of Strangers to a Contract (II)," *Columbia
Law Review*, May 1919:
    *Menstell* v. *Johnson*, 125 Ore. 150, 166; 262 Pac. 853, 858 (Ore., 1927)
    *Snow* v. *Van Dam*, 291 Mass. 477, 485; 197
N.E. 224, 228 (Mass., 1935)
    *Bristol* v. *Woodward*, 251 N.Y. 275, 287, 288 (1929)
"The Equitable Mortgage in New York," *Columbia Law Review*, May 1920.
"Some Legal Problems Involved in the Transmission of Funds," *Columbia
Law Review*, June 1921:
    *Equitable Trust Co.* v. *Keene*, 232 N.Y. 290, 295 (N.Y., 1922)
    *Safian* v. *Irving National Bank*, 202 A.D. 459, 463; 196 N.Y. Supp. 141,
145 (N.Y., 1922)
    *Richard* v. *American Union Bank*, 210 A.D. 22, 27; 205 N.Y. Supp. 622,
625 (N.Y., 1924)
    *Webber* v. *American Union Bank*, 128 Misc. 123, 127; 217 N.Y. Supp.
833, 836 (N.Y., 1926)
    *Euclid Holding Co.* v. *Kermacoe Realty Co., Inc.*
131 Misc. 466, 470; 227 N.Y. Supp. 103, 107 (N.Y., 1928)
    *Samuels* v. *E. F. Drew & Co.*, 296 Fed. 882, 886
(C.C.A. 2, 1924)
    *Richards* v. *Fulton*, 75 Fed. (2d) 853, 854
(C.C.A. 6, 1935)
    *Great Atlantic & Pacific Tea Co.* v. *Citizens' Nat. Bank*, 2 Fed. Supp. 29,
31 (D.C. Pa., 1932)
"A Theory of Liability of Trust Estates for the Contracts and Torts of the
Trustees," *Columbia Law Review*, June 1922:
    *In re Lathers' Will*, 137 Misc. 226, 232; 243 N.Y. Supp. 366, 374 (N.Y.,
1930)

22. H.F.S. to Nicholas Murray Butler, Dec. 1, 1916.
23. H.F.S., "University Influence," *Columbia University Quarterly*, Oct. 1918, pp.
336-37.
24. H.F.S., "The Importance of Actual Experience at the Bar as a Preparation for
Law Teaching," address delivered before the Section of Legal Education of
the American Bar Association at Milwaukee, Aug. 1912, p. 5.
25. H.F.S. to Erwin N. Griswold, April 8, 1936.
26. H.F.S., "The Function of the American University Law School."
27. *Ibid.*
28. H.F.S. to Jane Hunter Stone, May 19, 1939.
29. *Charavay & Bodvin* v. *York Silk Manufacturing Co.* (C.C. 1909), 170 Fed.
819.
30. See *In re A. E. Fountain, Inc.*, 282 Fed. 816, and Karl T. Frederick, "The
Trust Receipt as Security," *Columbia Law Review*, May and June 1922.

31. Memorandum from Karl T. Frederick to A.T.M., 1952. Frederick began work with Wilmer, Canfield and Stone on Oct. 10, 1908.
32. 233 N.Y. 300.
33. H.F.S. to George F. Kenngott, Dec. 28, 1931.
34. H.F.S., "After a Quarter Century at the Columbia Law School," *Columbia Alumni News,* Jan. 11, 1924.
35. H.F.S. to Edwin W. Patterson, Sept. 29, 1930.
36. H.F.S. in *Columbia Alumni News,* April 11, 1924, p. 374.
37. Basil N. Bass to H.F.S., July 7, 1941.
38. H.F.S., "Dr. Redlich on the Case Method," *Columbia University Quarterly,* June 1915, p. 266.
39. H.F.S., "Some Phases of American Legal Education," *Canadian Bar Review,* 1922, p. 652. (Paper read before the Ontario Bar Association.)
40. William O. Douglas, "Harlan Fiske Stone—Teacher," *California Law Review,* March 1947, pp. 4-6.
41. Quoted in Ralph W. Gifford to H.F.S., March 5, 1925.
42. Douglas, *op. cit.*
43. Herbert Haldenstein to H.F.S., Oct. 16, 1944.
44. Tom C. Johnson, Jr., to H.F.S., March 5, 1937.
45. Benjamin Berinstein to H.F.S., March 6, 1925.
46. Frank W. De Friece to H.F.S., July 12, 1941.
47. Henry Clay Greenberg to A.T.M., Jan. 17, 1951.
48. De Witt C. Jones, Jr., to A.T.M., Jan. 13, 1954.
49. H.F.S. to Nicholas Murray Butler, Dec. 12, 1927.
50. H.F.S. to Judge Elmer B. Adams, Dec. 22, 1911.
51. H.F.S., "Legal Education and Democratic Principle," *American Bar Association Journal,* Dec. 1921. See also address of the President of the American Law Schools, Dec. 30, 1919. (Reprint from *Proceedings of Association of American Law Schools,* 1919.)
52. H.F.S., "After a Quarter Century at the Columbia Law School," *loc. cit.,* p. 219.
53. H.F.S., "Some Phases of American Legal Education," *loc. cit.,* p. 668.
54. *Annual Reports,* 1922, p. 69.
55. H.F.S., "Legal Education and Democratic Principle," *loc. cit.,* p. 642.
56. H.F.S., address before the Association of the Bar of the City of New York, Oct. 7, 1920.
57. H.F.S. to Louis W. Southgate, Dec. 26, 1911.
58. H.F.S., "The Function of the American University Law School."
59. John Bassett Moore to H.F.S., Nov. 13, 1930.
60. H.F.S. to John Bassett Moore, Nov. 16, 1930.
61. *Annual Reports,* 1921, pp. 79-80.
62. H.F.S., "Some Phases of Legal Education in America," *American Law Review,* Sept. 1924, pp. 753-54.
63. H.F.S., "The Lawyer and His Neighbors," *Cornell Law Quarterly,* June 1919, pp. 185-86, 188.
64. H.F.S., "Some Phases of Legal Education in America," loc. cit., p. 755.
65. For Kent's contribution to Columbia, see *A History of the School of Law* (New York: Columbia University Press, 1955), Part I.
66. Charles Evans Hughes, "James Kent: A Master Builder of Legal Institutions," *American Bar Association Journal,* June 1923.
67. H.F.S., unpublished speech at the Kent anniversary celebration. Stone touched on the same theme in his thirteenth and final *Annual Report* submitted as Dean of the Law School.
68. H.F.S., "Obedience to Law and Social Change," New Hampshire Bar Association Proceedings (New Series), Vol. V, No. 3 (1925).

## CHAPTER VII

1. *Annual Reports,* 1917.
2. H.F.S. to William S. Booth, March 20, 1917.
3. H.F.S. to William S. Booth, Jan. 27, 1915.
4. H.F.S. to H. A. Laurie, Sept. 20, 1917.
5. H.F.S. to Winthrop Stone, Sept. 19, 1918.
6. H.F.S. to Huger W. Jervey, April 6, 1918.

7. *Annual Reports,* 1917.
8. H.F.S. to Winthrop Stone, Sept. 19, 1918.
9. H.F.S. to Colonel Raynal C. Bolling, April 6, 1918.
10. H.F.S. to Winthrop Stone, Sept. 19, 1918.
11. 40 Stat. 78 (1917).
12. Order of Dec. 19, 1917. James S. Easby-Smith, *Statement Concerning the Treatment of Conscientious Objectors in the Army* (Washington, D.C.: Government Printing Office, 1919), p. 39.
13. "Topics of the Times," *New York Times,* Jan. 24, 1919.
14. See H.F.S., "The Conscientious Objector," *Columbia University Quarterly,* Oct. 1919. Unless otherwise indicated, all quoted material is from Stone's article.
15. *New York Times,* Jan. 24, 1919. See also Major Kellogg's comment on the delicacy of the Board's work: Walter Kellogg, *The Conscientious Objector* (New York: Boni-Liveright, 1919), p. 27.
16. H.F.S. to H. M. Kallen, Feb. 25, 1944.
17. For reinforcement of Stone's views as to the numerous Hutterites, see Nanna Goodhope, "Must the Hutterites Flee Again?" *Christian Century,* Nov 13, 1940, pp. 1415-17.
18. Ernest L. Meyer, *"Hey! Yellowbacks!" The War Diary of a Conscientious Objector* (New York: John Day, 1930).
19. *Hearings before Special Committee to Investigate the Munitions Industry,* 73rd-74th Cong. (1934-37).
20. H.F.S. to Arthur Basse, March 20, 1940.
21. *Annual Reports,* 1917, p. 23.
22. Quoted in Kellogg, *op. cit.,* p. 112.
23. *New York Times,* Oct. 2, 1917.
24. H.F.S., "University Influence," *loc. cit.,* pp. 336-38 *passim.*
25. H.F.S. to J. M. Cattell, Oct. 10, 1917.
26. Remarks of Chief Justice Harlan F. Stone on the occasion of the celebration of the seventy-fifth anniversary of the Association of the Bar of the City of New York, March 16, 1946, *Record of the Association of the Bar,* Vol. I, No. 4, pp. 147-48.
27. "Charges of Illegal Practices of the Department of Justice," *Hearings before a Subcommittee of the Senate Judiciary Committee,* 66th Cong., 3rd Sess. (1921), pp. 279-80.

## CHAPTER VIII

1. Louis D. Brandeis, "The Living Law," *Illinois Law Review,* Feb. 1916, pp. 461, 464.
2. H.F.S., *Law and Its Administration* (New York: Columbia University Press, 1915), p. 152.
3. *Ibid.,* p. 2.
4. *Ives. v. South Buffalo Railway,* 201 N.Y. 271 (1911), p. 296.
5. H.F.S., *Law and Its Administration,* p. 71.
6. *Ibid.,* p. 151, quoting from the Ives decision, p. 294.
7. *Ibid.,* p. 152.
8. *Grimmer v. The Tenement House Department of the City of New York,* 204 N.Y. 370 (1912).
9. *The Survey,* March 1912.
10. H.F.S., "The Tenement House Decision," Letter to the Editor, *The Survey,* March 1912.
11. H.F.S., *Law and Its Administration,* pp. 34-44 *passim.*
12. *Ibid.,* p. 177.
13. Brandeis, *op. cit.,* p. 470.
14. *The Nation,* March 16, 1916.
15. *New Republic,* June 23, 1917. Unsigned review generally credited to Morris R. Cohen.
16. Louis N. Robinson, Book Review, *University of Pennsylvania Law Review,* May 1917.
17. H.F.S., "Changing Order and the Responsibility of the Bar," address at annual meeting of the New Jersey State Bar Association, Feb. 26, 1921, *New Jersey Bar Association Year Book,* 1921-22, pp. 55, 65.

18. H.F.S., "Some Aspects of the Problem of Law Simplification," *Columbia Law Review*, April 1923, pp. 319, 321. The substance of this paper was delivered before the Association of the Bar of the City of New York, Feb. 8, 1923. Hereafter cited as "Law Simplification." For a popular version of the same subject, see H.F.S., "The Philosophy of Law," the Literary Review of the *New York Evening Post*, Jan. 13, 1923.
19. *Ibid.*
20. *Ibid.*
21. Warren A. Seavey, "The Association of American Law Schools in Retrospect," *Journal of Legal Education*, Winter 1950, pp. 163-65.
22. Unpublished statement submitted by the Council of the American Law Institute to the Carnegie Corporation (1923). This statement contains a detailed account of the work of the Committee on the Establishment of a Permanent Organization for the Improvement of the Law, including a prospectus of the project to be carried out by the American Law Institute.
23. Minutes of the Meeting of the Committee on Juristic Center of the Association of American Law Schools, New York City, May 10, 1922.
24. American Law Institute: Report of the Committee on the Establishment of a Permanent Organization for the Improvement of the Law (1923). Quoted in unpublished statement of Herbert S. Hadley, "The Advisability of the Council of the American Institute of Law Undertaking as Its First Work a Restatement of the Law of Crimes and Criminal Procedure," March 10, 1923.
25. Seavey, *op. cit.*, p. 164.
26. H.F.S., "Law Simplification," p. 334.
27. "The Restatement of the Law," *American Bar Association Journal* (editorial), March 1924, p. 176.
28. Thurman Arnold, *Symbols of Government* (New Haven: Yale University Press, 1935), p. 51.
29. Willard Hurst, *The Growth of American Law* (Boston: Little, Brown & Co., 1950), p. 276. See also "The Significance of a Restatement of the Law," *Proceedings of the Academy of Political Science*, Vol. 10, 1922-24, pp. 309, 312.
30. H.F.S., "Law Simplification," p. 337.
31. H.F.S., "Tenement House Decision," *loc. cit.*, p. 1983.
32. H.F.S., *Law and Its Administration*, p. 42.
33. H.F.S., "Law Simplification," p. 328.
34. *Ibid.*, pp. 336, 337.
35. Thomas Reed Powell to Alfred McCormack, quoted in Alfred McCormack to A.T.M., Nov. 15, 1950.
36. H.F.S., to B. H. Levy, Oct. 1, 1938.
37. H.F.S., address at the induction of Huger Jervey as Dean of the Columbia Law School, Nov. 17, 1924. For an elaboration of this theme, see "Progress in Law Improvement in the United States, *American Bar Association Journal*, Sept. 1924; "Citizenship and the Law," address delivered at Syracuse University, June 11, 1928.

## CHAPTER IX

1. President Butler to H.F.S., Feb. 11, 1918.
2. H.F.S. to President Butler, Feb. 16, 1918.
3. *Ibid.*
4. President Butler to H.F.S., Feb. 19, 1918.
5. H.F.S. to President Butler, Feb. 25, 1918.
6. H.F.S. to President Butler, March 24, 1919.
7. H.F.S. to President Butler, April 16, 1919.
8. *Annual Reports*, 1922, p. 73.
9. H.F.S. to President Butler, May 26, 1922.
10. President Butler to H.F.S., May 29, 1922.
11. H.F.S. to President Butler, June 1, 1922.
12. *Annual Report of the President of Columbia University*, 1923, p. 6.
13. Young B. Smith to H.F.S., May 3, 1921.
14. H.F.S. to Young B. Smith, May 5, 1921.
15. H.F.S. to Charles P. Howland, Dec. 9, 1927.
16. Marion T. Byrnes, "Attorney General Stone as Former Associates and Students

of Columbia Know Him," *Sunday Brooklyn Eagle* (Magazine), April 27, 1924.
17. H.F.S., "University Influence," *loc. cit.*, p. 332.
18. *Ibid.*, pp. 330, 332.
19. H.F.S., rough draft of letter to the University of Wisconsin, 1919.
20. *Annual Report of the President of Columbia University*, 1922, pp. 27-28.
21. H.F.S. to F. C. Bangs, Oct. 31, 1925.
22. H.F.S. to President Butler, Dec. 18, 1922.
23. President Butler to H.F.S., Dec. 21, 1922.
24. President Butler to Benjamin N. Cardozo, Jan. 4, 1923.
25. H.F.S., "Some Phases of American Legal Education," *loc. cit.*, p. 653.
26. H.F.S. to President Butler, Jan. 8, 1923
27. H.F.S. to John Bassett Moore, Dec. 18, 1922.
28. H.F.S. to President Butler, Jan. 8, 1923.
29. *Annual Report of the President of Columbia University*, 1923, p. 10.
30. *Annual Reports*, 1923, pp. 44-45, 47.
31. H.F.S. to Underhill Moore, June 27, 1922.
32. President Butler to H.F.S., June 20, 28, 29, 1922.
33. H.F.S. to President Butler, July 5, 1922.
34. H.F.S. to Walter Wheeler Cook, April 5, 1928.
35. H.F.S. to John Bassett Moore, April 24, 1923.
36. H.F.S. to Garrard Glenn, Jan. 11, 1934.
37. Marshall Stone to A.T.M., 1950.
38. H.F.S. to John Bassett Moore, Nov. 20, 1913.
39. Herbert Wechsler to H.F.S., Feb. 18, 1937.
40. H.F.S. to Herbert Wechsler, Feb. 25, 1937.
41. Percival Schmuck, "Views on Laws and Politics," *Springfield Sunday Republican*, April 6, 1924.
42. John Bassett Moore to Edward R. Finch, president of the Alumni Association of the Law School of Columbia University, Dec. 12, 1923.
43. Possibly Gray, Thayer, Ames, Langdell.
44. Quoted in letter of H.F.S. to Garrard Glenn, April 22, 1931.
45. H.F.S. to Young B. Smith, Nov. 2, 1925.

## CHAPTER X

1. Quoted in *Literary Digest*, April 12, 1924, p. 6.
2. *New York Times*, Feb. 22, 1921 (editorial).
3. M. R. Werner, *Privileged Characters* (New York: McBride, 1935), p. 238. In a letter to William Allen White, Feb. 23, 1939, Stone noted Coolidge's softness toward wrongdoing: "He [the President] was irritated when I revealed to him the fact that I had personally gathered the evidence on which Daugherty was indicted and tried, and on which he should have been convicted. . . . He did not like the idea of indicting the man with whom he had sat in the Cabinet."
4. See "Select Committee on Investigation of the Attorney General," *Hearings,* 68th Cong., 1st Sess. (1924). Hereafter referred to as Brookhart Hearings.
5. Harry M. Daugherty to Smith W. Brookhart, March 27, 1924.
6. *New York World*, quoted in *Literary Digest*, April 12, 1924, p. 8.
7. Bertrand H. Snell to Luther Ely Smith, Oct. 27, 1947.
8. O. M. H. McCastline to H.F.S., Jan. 30, 1941, recalling what Stone had told him of Coolidge's remark.
9. H.F.S. to John Bassett Moore, April 3, 1924.
10. Based on material Stone sent Arthur McKeogh of *Good Housekeeping* magazine, Nov. 24, 1934, on Mrs. Stone's recollections, and on the memorandum Bertrand H. Snell sent Luther Ely Smith, Oct. 27, 1947.
11. "Stone's Name Goes to Senate as 'Unknown,'" *Vicksburg* (Miss.) *Evening Post*, April 2, 1924.
12. "Standards of Public Service," *Elkhart* (Ind.) *Truth*, April 4, 1924 (editorial).
13. "The New Attorney General," *Christian Work* (N.Y.), April 12, 1924 (editorial).
14. "The New Attorney General," *Washington* (D.C.) *Star*, April 4, 1924 (editorial).
15. Gustave Hartman to Calvin Coolidge, March 30, 1924.

16. Park T. Winslow to H.F.S., April 3, 1924.
17. "The New Attorney General," *New York Times*, April 3, 1924 (editorial).
18. "Attorney General Stone," *Dallas* (Tex.) *Morning News*, April 5, 1924 (editorial).
19. "Says Stone Reactionary," *Boston Evening Globe*, April 4, 1924.
20. "Where Mr. Vanderlip Is Right," *New York World*, April 4, 1924 (editorial).
21. *New York American*, April 8, 1924.
22. H.F.S. to Mrs. Underhill Moore, June 23, 1924.
23. H.F.S. to Solon Fieldman, Oct. 15, 1924.
24. H.F.S., address before the Women's National Committee for Law Enforcement, April 10, 1924, Washington, D.C.
25. "Stone Will Help Daugherty Inquiry," *New York Times*, April 15, 1924.
26. Mabel Walker Willebrandt to A.T.M., Jan. 31, 1951.
27. Brookhart Hearings, p. 2445.
28. *Ibid.*
29. H.F.S. to James M. Beck, June 23, 1924.
30. Felix Frankfurter to H.F.S., April 10, 1924.
31. H.F.S. to Felix Frankfurter, April 13, 1924.
32. H.F.S., "Progress in Law Improvement in the United States," address delivered at the annual meeting of the American Bar Association, Philadelphia, July 8, 1924 (mimeograph copy).
33. H.F.S. to Jack Alexander, Sept. 21, 1937.
34. H.F.S. to Jack Alexander, May 1, 1937.
35. H.F.S. to Felix Frankfurter, Feb. 9, 1925.
36. Julian Street, "Wm. J. Burns . . . Does Not Intend to Resign," *Springfield News*, April 5, 1924.
37. *Washington Evening Star*, May 9, 1924; *New York World*, May 10, 1924.
38. *Washington Herald*, May 16, 1924.
39. H.F.S. to Jack Alexander, Sept. 21, 1937.
40. A.T.M.'s interview with John Lord O'Brian, May 9, 1954.
41. Mabel Walker Willebrandt to A.T.M., Jan. 31, 1951.
42. H.F.S. to Jack Alexander, Sept. 21, 1937.
43. Memorandum from J. Edgar Hoover to A.T.M., Aug. 8, 1950.
44. Memorandum from the Attorney General for J. Edgar Hoover, Acting Director of the Bureau of Investigation, May 13, 1924. See Robert T. Small, "Days of 'Old Sleuth' Are Ended," *Washington Star*, Dec. 22, 1924.
45. H.F.S. to Felix Frankfurter, Feb. 9, 1925.
46. Memorandum of J. Edgar Hoover to Attorney General, Jan. 7, 1925.
47. Louis B. Nichols to A.T.M., Sept. 9, 1950.
48. H.F.S. to Jack Alexander, Sept. 21, 1937.
49. J. Edgar Hoover to Mrs. Harlan F. Stone, April 23, 1946.
50. H.F.S. to Felix Frankfurter, April 14, 1933.
51. H.F.S. to Jack Alexander, Sept. 21, 1937.
52. *New York Times*, May 10, 1924.
53. Mabel Walker Willebrandt to A.T.M., Jan. 31, 1951.
54. Jerome Michael to H.F.S., April 24, 1924.
55. Paul Shipman Andrews to A.T.M., Oct. 25, 1950.
56. *Ibid.*
57. *Ibid.*
58. H.F.S. to Charles D. Hilles, chairman of the Republican National Committee, Dec. 10, 1924.
59. Mabel Walker Willebrandt to A.T.M., Jan. 31, 1951.
60. James M. Hyde to Frank W. Stearns, April 4, 1924. See *San Francisco Journal*, June 9, 1924.
61. Mabel Walker Willebrandt to A.T.M., Jan. 31, 1951.
62. Sterling Carr to H.F.S., Aug. 2, 1924.
63. H.F.S. to Sterling Carr, Aug. 6, 1924.
64. H.F.S. to Sterling Carr, Sept. 17, 1924.
65. H.F.S. to Sterling Carr, Sept. 23, 1924.
66. *Ibid.*
67. Sterling Carr to H.F.S., Sept. 29, 1924.
68. Quoted in John P. Frank, *Mr. Justice Black, The Man and His Opinions* (New York: Alfred A. Knopf, 1949), p. 37.
69. *New York Times*, Dec. 16, 1924.

70. *New York Times*, Jan. 3, 1925; *New York World*, Jan. 3, 1925. For Edge's defense of Van Riper, see *The American Issue* (Waterville, Ohio), Jan. 10, 1925.
71. Mabel Walker Willebrandt to A.T.M., Jan. 31, 1951. See "Stone Ignores Edge in Jersey," New York *Evening Sun*, Dec. 17, 1924.
72. Memorandum from Rush L. Holland to H.F.S., Oct. 21, 1924.
73. *Boston Post*, Nov. 29, 1924.
74. H.F.S. to William V. Kellen, Dec. 1, 1924.
75. H.F.S. to Benjamin D. Hyde, Nov. 21, 1924.
76. H.F.S. to Benjamin D. Hyde, Nov. 26, 1924.
77. Memorandum from Mabel Walker Willebrandt to H.F.S., Dec. 21, 1924.
78. H.F.S. to Charles D. Hilles, Dec. 10, 1924.
79. *Ibid.*
80. For the full story, see *New York Times*, Oct. 3, 1924.
81. *Literary Digest*, Nov. 15, 1924, pp. 14-15. See "Untermyer Won't Tell How He Got Willebrandt Note," *Philadelphia Evening Bulletin*, Oct. 23, 1924.
82. *Washington* (D.C.) *Times*, Oct. 27, 1924; *Washington* (D.C.) *Post*, Oct. 28, 1924.
83. Mabel Walker Willebrandt to A.T.M., Jan. 31, 1951.
84. Robert H. Jackson, address at twentieth-anniversary dinner of the Federal Bar Association, Jan. 20, 1940, Washington, D.C., at which Stone was guest of honor. (*Congressional Record*, Jan. 23, 1940, p. 310, Appendix.)
85. *Boston Transcript*, Nov. 22, 1924.
86. *Annual Report of the Department of Justice*, 1924, p. 79. Stone's recommendation was embodied in the Stalker bill, introduced in the House shortly before he went to the bench. See *New York Times*, Aug. 14, 1924; *Forum*, Dec. 6, 1924.
87. H.F.S. to Sterling Carr, July 22, 1924.
88. *Annual Report of the Department of Justice*, 1924, pp. 79-80; "Department of Justice Work Four Times 10 Years Ago," *Boston Transcript*, Nov. 22, 1924; *New York Times*, Dec. 5, 1924.
89. Mabel Walker Willebrandt to A.T.M., Jan. 31, 1951.
90. H.F.S., "Federal Anti-Trust Law Enforcement, Past and Present," address before the American Whig Society, Princeton University, Jan. 19, 1925 (typescript copy), p. 16.
91. Gompers' address before National Civic Federation, *New York Times*, April 25, 1924. See also Matthew Woll, "Government Interference Menacing Industry," *Labor News* (Worcester, Mass.), July 11, 1924.
92. *Journal of Commerce* (New York), Dec. 11, 1925.
93. *Annual Report*, 1924, p. 16.
94. *Journal of Commerce* (New York), Dec. 6, 1924.
95. Mabel Walker Willebrandt to A.T.M., Jan. 31, 1951.
96. *Ibid.*
97. Paul Shipman Andrews to A.T.M., Oct. 25, 1950.

## CHAPTER XI

1. Augustus T. Seymour to Calvin Coolidge, Dec. 22, 1923.
2. *Washington Post*, May 16, 1924.
3. Memorandum from H.F.S. to Special Assistant Alfred A. Wheat, June 7, 1924.
4. *Ex parte Grossman*, 267 U.S. 87 (1925), pp. 105-106.
5. *Ibid.*, p. 106.
6. Brookhart Hearings, p. 1427.
7. Quoted in memorandum from Alfred A. Wheat to H.F.S., June 26, 1924.
8. *McGrain* v. *Daugherty*, 273 U.S. 135 (1927), pp. 146, 147-48.
9. *Ibid.*, pp. 145-46.
10. *Ibid.*, pp. 135, 138, 140.
11. *Ibid.*, p. 142.
12. *Ibid.*, pp. 143-44.
13. Memorandum from Alfred A. Wheat to H.F.S., June 26, 1924.
14. *Omaha Bee*, Sept. 15, 1924.
15. 294 Fed. 300 (1924).
16. *Philadelphia Record*, Nov. 13, 1924; *Philadelphia Evening Bulletin*, Nov. 10, 1924.

17. *New York Daily News Record,* Nov. 13, 1924.
18. Argument on behalf of Appellant by Attorney General Harlan F. Stone in *United States* v. *Chemical Foundation, Inc.* (U.S. Circuit of Appeals, 3rd District), pp. 60-61.
19. *New York Daily News Record,* Nov. 13, 1924.
20. H.F.S. to John Bassett Moore, Nov. 14, 1924.
21. 5 Fed. (2d) 191 (1926).
22. *United States* v. *Chemical Foundation, Inc.,* 272 U.S. 1 (1926). See, in this connection, A. W. Lafferty, "Should America Return German Private Property?" *Illinois Law Review,* June 1920, and *Virginia Law Review,* Dec. 1926, pp. 127-29.
23. H.F.S. to John Bassett Moore, Jan. 25, 1937.
24. H.F.S. to Nathan Abbott, June 20, 1924.
25. H.F.S. to Marshall Stone, Sept. 18, 1924.
26. H.F.S. to his sons, Oct. 1, 1924.
27. J. Q. Tilson to H.F.S., Sept. 11, 1924; H.F.S. to John Q. Tilson, Sept. 13, 1924.
28. D. M. Edwards, "Get Out Vote Campaign a Success," *American Industries,* Nov. 1924, p. 5.
29. Franklin D. Roosevelt, *His Personal Letters, 1905-1928,* edited by Elliott Roosevelt (New York: Duell, Sloane and Pearce, 1948), Vol. II, p. 566.
30. Irving Stone, *They Also Ran* (New York: Doubleday, Doran & Co., 1943), p. 335.
31. H.F.S. to his sons, Nov. 5, 1924.
32. *Ibid.*
33. "Stone Addresses Colored Voters," *Boston Sunday Herald,* Nov. 2, 1924.
34. "A Good Impression," *Des Moines Tribune,* Oct. 25, 1924.
35. H.F.S. to his sons, Dec. 17, 1924.
36. *Ibid.*
37. "Stone Pledges U.S. Investigation into Aluminum Firm," *New York Evening World,* Oct. 8, 1924; see also *Journal of Commerce* (New York), Oct. 8, 1924; *Brooklyn Daily Eagle,* Oct. 8, 1924.
38. *Journal of Commerce* (New York), Oct. 20, 1924.
39. *New York World,* Feb. 7, 1925. For Stone's final statement, indicating his belief that the company had engaged in practices violating the anti-trust laws, see *New York Times,* Feb. 7, 1925.

## CHAPTER XII

1. Learned Hand to H.F.S., Jan. 7, 1925.
2. Benjamin N. Cardozo to H.F.S., Jan. 6, 1925.
3. William Nelson Cromwell to H.F.S., Jan. 7, 1925 (telegram).
4. H.F.S. to William S. Booth, Jan. 16, 1925.
5. H.F.S. to Alfred Jaretzki, Jr., Jan. 7, 1925; to William Nelson Cromwell, Jan. 9, 1925.
6. George Sutherland to H.F.S., Jan. 8, 1925.
7. "Cabinet Changes Shake Washington," *Locomotive Engineers Journal,* Feb. 1925 (editorial).
8. "McKenna and Stone," *Nashville Tennessean,* Jan. 7, 1925 (editorial).
9. "Stone for Supreme Bench Makes Country Wonder," *Newark* (N.J.) *News,* Jan. 7, 1925 (editorial).
10. "Mr. Stone's Elevation," *Chattanooga Times,* Jan. 7, 1925 (editorial).
11. "Stone's War on Trusts Believed Reason for Nomination as Justice of Supreme Court," *New York Commercial,* Jan. 6, 1925.
12. "His Spear May Know No Brother," *Johnstown* (Pa.) *Democrat,* Feb. 14, 1925 (editorial).
13. Mabel Walker Willebrandt to A.T.M., Jan. 31, 1951.
14. *Ibid.*
15. Sterling Carr to H.F.S., March 22, 1939.
16. W. H. Taft to Robert A. Taft, July 2, 1925. Quoted in Henry Pringle, *Life and Times of William Howard Taft* (New York: Farrar and Rinehart, 1939), Vol. II, p. 1043.
17. The Papers of Calvin Coolidge, Box 41-A, Manuscripts Division of the Library of Congress. President Butler's autobiography, *Across the Busy Years* (New

York: Charles Scribner's Sons, 1939), Vol. 1, pp. 357-58, contains his letter to Coolidge.

18. H.F.S. to John Bassett Moore, Nov. 16, 1939.
19. H.F.S. to Thomas Reed Powell, Jan. 30, 1940.
20. "Stone Attacked by Old Scout as Morgan Lawyer," *New York Evening World*, Jan. 10, 1925.
21. "Warren Is to Be Attorney General; Stone Is Attacked," *New York Times*, Jan. 10, 1925.
22. Quoted in Harlan F. Stone and Willard Saulsbury, *Brief and Argument for Defendants-in-Error* (James A. Ownbey, Plaintiff-in-Error, against John Pierpont Morgan, William P. Hamilton, Herbert L. Satterlee, and Lewis C. Ledyard, as Executors of the Estate of John Pierpont Morgan, Deceased, Defendants-in-Error; in the Supreme Court of the United States, October Term, 1920), p. 3.
23. Louis Marshall, Brief and Argument for *Plaintiffs-in-Error* (James A. Ownbey, Plaintiff-in-Error, etc.)
24. Stone and Saulsbury, op. cit., p. 57.
25. *Ownbey* v. *Morgan*, 256 U.S. 94 (1921), pp. 103-104, 110-11.
26. Willard Saulsbury to H.F.S. (undated telegram).
27. J. W. Bailey to Senator Overman, Jan. 28, 1925.
28. Noel T. Dowling's memorandum prepared for A.T.M., based on conversation with Stone about *Ownbey* v. *Morgan*.
29. H.F.S. to William S. Booth, Jan. 20, 1925.
30. "Washington Topics," *San Francisco Bulletin*, Feb. 2, 1925.
31. *Congressional Record*, Jan. 27, 1925, p. 2511; Feb. 5, 1925, p. 3046.
32. *Congressional Record*, Feb. 5, 1925, p. 3047.
33. Burton K. Wheeler to A.T.M., Dec. 5, 1950.
34. Mabel Walker Willebrandt to A.T.M., Jan. 31, 1951.
35. Besides Basil Manly, vice-chairman, members of the committee included William Allen White, Josephus Daniels, H. L. Mencken, Harold Ickes, Sidney Hillman, Felix Frankfurter, Morris Ernst, Herbert Croly, and Norman Thomas. For a sample of the "literature" broadcast in Wheeler's behalf, see "The Leading Facts in the Wheeler Case," published by the Wheeler Defense Committee. Manly was director of the People's Legislative Lobby.
36. Felix Frankfurter to H.F.S., May 15, 1924.
37. H.F.S. to Felix Frankfurter, May 19, 1924.
38. Felix Frankfurter to H.F.S., May 21, 1924.
39. H.F.S. to Felix Frankfurter, May 22, 1924.
40. H.F.S. to Clinton L. Rossiter, April 12, 1941.
41. Felix Frankfurter to H.F.S., May 26, 1924.
42. H.F.S. to Felix Frankfurter, May 29, 1924.
43. Felix Frankfurter to H.F.S., June 4, 1924; H.F.S. to Felix Frankfurter, June 6, 1924.
44. H.F.S. to Nathan Abbott, June 3, 1924.
45. Memorandum, apparently prepared in the Department of Justice and approved by Stone. Hereafter cited as Department Memorandum.
46. "Testimony of Harlan F. Stone before the Senate Judiciary Committee in the Matter of His Nomination as Associate Justice of the Supreme Court of the United States," January 28, 1925, p. 3 (mimeographed copy). Hereafter referred to as Testimony.
47. Burton K. Wheeler to A.T.M., Dec. 5, 1950.
48. *New Republic*, May 13, 1925, p. 318. Senator Walsh, counsel for Wheeler, followed this group's "propaganda" line in his battle against Stone's confirmation for the Supreme Court. Compare the *New Republic* article with Walsh's speech on the floor of the Senate, *Congressional Record*, Feb. 5, 1925, p. 3039.
49. Felix Frankfurter to H.F.S., May 26, 1924.
50. H.F.S. to Senator Walsh, Jan. 24, 1925.
51. *New York Times*, Jan. 26, 29, 1925.
52. Department Memorandum, p. 5.
53. Testimony, p. 19.
54. *Ibid.*, p. 77.
55. *Ibid.*, p. 54.
56. *Ibid.*, p. 61.

57. Department Memorandum, p. 6. For a good newspaper account of the Hearings, see the *Washington* (D.C.) *Post*, Jan. 29, 1925.
58. W. H. Taft to Robert A. Taft, Feb. 1, 1925.
59. H.F.S. to Nathan Abbott, Feb. 3, 1925.
60. H.F.S. to George F. Canfield, Jan. 31, 1925.
61. H.F.S. to William Nelson Cromwell, Feb. 6, 1925.
62. H.F.S. to William H. Taft, Jan. 27, 1925.
63. *Congressional Record*, Feb. 5, 1925, pp. 3036, 3039.
64. *Ibid.*, p. 3053.
65. *Ibid.*, pp. 3053-54.
66. H.F.S. to W. S. Johnston, Feb. 2, 1943.
67. James C. McReynolds to H.F.S., Feb. 7, 1925.
68. Roger S. Lamont to H.F.S., March 4, 1925.
69. Morris R. Cohen to H.F.S., March 4, 1925.
70. H.F.S. to his sons, Feb. 26, 1925.

PART THREE

## CHAPTER XIII

1. Noel T. Dowling, Elliott E. Cheatham, Robert L. Hale, "Mr. Justice Stone and the Constitution," *Columbia Law Review*, March 1936, p. 351.
2. Edward R. Finch, Alumni Day Address upon the Presentation of the Portraits of John Bassett Moore and Harlan F. Stone, *Columbia Alumni News*, March 5, 1926, p. 457.
3. Frederick Lewis Allen, *The Big Change* (New York: Harper & Bros., 1952), p. 139.
4. *Annual Reports of Columbia University*, 1923, *University Bulletin of Information*, 24th Series, No. 43, July 26, 1924, p. 44.
5. H.F.S., address at the Ninety-sixth Convention of the Alpha Delta Phi Fraternity, Dec. 29, 1927 (pamphlet).
6. *Ibid.*, p. 2.
7. *Literary Digest*, cover design, Nov. 12, 1921.
8. S. E. Morrison and H. S. Commager, *The Growth of the American Republic* (New York: Oxford University Press, 1950), Vol. II, p. 556.
9. *Nation's Business*, June 1925, p. 40; March 1927, p. 16.
10. Charles N. Fay, *Business in Politics* (Cambridge, Mass.: The Cosmos Press, 1926), pp. 111-12.
11. *Nation's Business*, Nov. 1925, p. 26.
12. Quoted in Allen, *op. cit.*, p. 144.
13. "An Antidote to Bolshevism," *American Industries*, Jan. 1920, p. 8 (editorial).
14. Charles N. Fay, *op. cit.*, p. 164.
15. J. E. Edgerton, "Industry Has Advanced Further than Religion," *Pocket Bulletin*, April 1927, p. 4.
16. J. E. Edgerton, annual address of the President, *Proceedings of the 34th Annual Convention of the National Association of Manufacturers* (1929), p. 23.
17. *Nation's Business*, March 1926, pp. 99-100.
18. "The Businessman's Primer," *Nation's Business*, January 1926, p. 38.
19. Russell H. Conwell, *Acres of Diamonds* (New York: Harper & Bros., 1915), p. 50.
20. George Sutherland, address before the New York Bar Association, January 21, 1921, *Proceedings of the New York State Bar Association*, Vol. 44, p. 265.
21. *Literary Digest*, April 2, 1921, p. 7.
22. Quoted in *Nation's Business*, March 1926, p. 98.
23. *New York Times*, August 12, 1928.
24. Quoted from *The Engineering and Mining Journal* in *Literary Digest*, October 15, 1921, p. 5.
25. J. E. Edgerton, annual address of the President, *Proceedings of the 29th Annual Convention of the National Association of Manufacturers* (1924), p. 118.
26. William Allen White, *Masks in a Pageant* (New York: The Macmillan Co., 1928), p. 410. See Irving Stone's chapter, "Calvin Coolidge: A Study in

Inertia," included in Isabel Leighton, ed., *The Aspirin Age* (New York: Simon & Schuster, 1949).

27. H.F.S., Alpha Delta Phi address, pp. 3-4.
28. Words of Herbert Hoover accepting the Republican nomination for the Presidency, *New York Times*, August 12, 1928.
29. H.F.S., Alpha Delta Phi address, p. 4.
30. *Ibid.*, p. 5. The same ideas were expressed in his address "Obedience to Law and Social Change," *New Hampshire Bar Association Proceedings* (New Series), Vol. V, No. 3 (1925).
31. Edmund Wilson, *I Thought of Daisy* (New York: Charles Scribner's Sons, 1929), p. 61.
32. *Annual Reports of Columbia University, loc. cit.*, pp. 51, 52.
33. H.F.S. to Nicholas Murray Butler, Dec. 3, 1926.
34. W. H. Taft, "Mr. Wilson and the Campaign," *Yale Review*, Oct. 1920, pp. 19-20.
35. Henry F. Pringle, *The Life and Times of William Howard Taft* (New York: Farrar & Rinehart, 1939), Vol. II, p. 967.
36. Quoted by Judge George M. Bourguin, dissenting in *Investors' Syndicate* v. *Porter*, 52 F. (2d) 189 (1931), p. 196.
37. Edward S. Corwin, *The Constitution and What It Means Today* (Princeton: Princeton University Press, 1930), p. 125.
38. Thomas Reed Powell to H.F.S., Feb. 6, 1925.
39. H.F.S., "The Constitution of the United States," address before the League of Republican Women, Washington, D.C., May 5, 1924. (Compiled and circulated by the League.)
40. Thomas Reed Powell to H.F.S., Feb. 6, 1925.
41. Quoted in "Views of the Press," *Fort Worth Telegram*, Feb. 1, 1925.

## CHAPTER XIV

1. W. H. Taft, "The Jurisdiction of the Supreme Court under the Act of February 13, 1925," *Yale Law Journal*, Nov. 1925.
2. Public Law 415, Chap. 229, Laws of 1925, 68th Cong., 2nd Sess.
3. H.F.S. to W. H. Taft, April 8, 1925.
4. *May* v. *Henderson*, 268 U.S. 111 (1925).
5. H.F.S. to his sons, May 25, 1925.
6. H.F.S. to W. H. Taft, May 25, 1925.
7. W. H. Taft to Senator Curtis, Sept. 4, 1925.
8. W. H. Taft to H.F.S., Oct. 22, 1925.
9. H.F.S. to his sons, Nov. 19, April 2, 1925.
10. H.F.S. to John Bassett Moore, June 1, 1927.
11. *Ibid.*
12. W. H. Taft to Robert A. Taft, May 29, 1927.
13. Nathan Abbott to the Stones, Jan. 31, 1928.
14. Memorandum from Warner Gardner to A.T.M., Nov. 21, 1950.
15. H.F.S. to his sons, Feb. 9, 1928.
16. S. J. Woolf in the *Springfield Union*, June 17, 1941.
17. Gardner memorandum.
18. Memorandum from Howard Westwood to Gertrude Jenkins Regis, Oct. 30, 1947.
19. H.F.S. to his sons, April 2, 1925.
20. H.F.S. to Luther Ely Smith, Dec. 21, 1925.
21. *American Column and Lumber Co.* v. *United States*, 257 U.S. 377 (1921).
22. *Maple Flooring Mfrs. Assn.* v. *United States*, 268 U.S. 563 (1925), p. 584.
23. *Ibid.*, pp. 572, 583, 584.
24. H.F.S. to Herman Oliphant, Feb. 3, 1926. Stone also approved the substantially similar methods of the Cement Manufacturers Protective Association in an opinion handed down with the Maple Flooring decision. See *Cement Manufacturers Protective Assn.* v. *United States*, 268 U.S. 588 (1925).
25. Herbert Hoover to H.F.S., April 3, 1925.
26. Herbert Hoover to H.F.S., June 3, 1925.
27. Maple Flooring case, p. 587.
28. Alfred McCormack, "A Law Clerk's Recollections," *Columbia Law Review*,

Sept. 1946, p. 715. The case was *Louisville & Nashville Railroad* v. *Sloss-Sheffield Steel & Iron Co.*, 269 U.S. 217 (1925).
29. *Ibid.*, p. 715.
30. H.F.S. to Charles C. Burlingham, Jan. 6, 1938.
31. W. H. Taft to Robert A. Taft, Feb. 1, 1925.
32. The case was *North Laramie Land Co.* v. *Hoffman*, 268 U.S. 276 (1925).
33. These cases were *United States* v. *Katz* and *United States* v. *Feuerstein*, 271 U.S. 354 (1926); *Stebbins* v. *Riley*, 268 U.S. 137 (1925); *Provost* v. *United States*, 269 U.S. 443 (1926); *Metcalf & Eddy* v. *Mitchell*, 269 U.S. 514 (1926).
34. The case was *United States* v. *Dunn*, 268 U.S. 121 (1925).
35. W. H. Taft to H.F.S., Sept. 4, 1925.
36. *St. Louis-San Francisco Railway Co.* v. *Mills*, 271 U.S. 344 (1926), p. 346.
37. McCormack, *op. cit.*, p. 712.
38. *Ibid.*
39. *Independent Wireless Telegraph Co.* v. *Radio Corporation of America*, 269 U.S. 459 (1926), rehearing denied, 270 U.S. 84 (1926).
40. Pringle, *op. cit.*, p. 1025.
41. *Myers* v. *United States*, 272 U.S. 52 (1926). Hereafter cited as Myers case.
42. Memorandum with respect to the Effort to Secure the Removal of William S. Culbertson from the Tariff Commission, May 23, 1934.
43. *Ibid.*
44. Myers case, pp. 115, 134-35, 161, 164.
45. *Ibid.*, pp. 122, 135.
46. W. H. Taft to H.F.S., Nov. 6, 1925.
47. H.F.S. to W. H. Taft, Nov. 13, 1925.
48. Quoted in Myers case, p. 141.
49. H.F.S. to W. H. Taft, Nov. 13, 1925.
50. Alfred McCormack to A.T.M., Nov. 15, 1950.
51. H.F.S. to W. H. Taft, Nov. 13, 1925.
52. H.F.S. to W. H. Taft, Nov. 24, 1925.
53. 116 U.S. 483 (1886).
54. H.F.S. to W. H. Taft, Nov. 13, 1925.
55. H.F.S. undated memorandum to W. H. Taft, mentioned in a letter, H.F.S. to W. H. Taft, Nov. 13, 1925.
56. H.F.S. to W. H. Taft, Nov. 30, 1925.
57. Myers case, p. 161.
58. W. H. Taft to H.F.S., Dec. 8, 1925.
59. H.F.S. to W. H. Taft, March 29, 1926.
60. H.F.S. undated memorandum on Brandeis's opinion accompanying the letter of March 29, 1926.
61. H.F.S. to W. H. Taft, March 29, 1926.
62. *Ibid.*
63. The undated memorandum to Taft.
64. *Ibid.*
65. W. H. Taft to Henry Taft, Oct. 25, 1926
66. H.F.S. to W. H. Taft, Nov. 30, 1926.
67. H.F.S. undated memorandum to W. H. Taft, October Term, 1926.
68. *Humphrey's Executor* v. *United States*, 295 U.S. 602 (1935).
69. See Robert H. Jackson, *The Struggle for Judicial Supremacy* (New York: Alfred A. Knopf, 1941), pp. 107-109.
70. Humphrey case, pp. 626, 627.
71. H.F.S. to W. H. Taft, Nov. 13, 1925. (Italics the author's.)
72. Marquis Childs, "A Minority of One," *Saturday Evening Post*, Sept. 20, 1941, p. 15.

## CHAPTER XV

1. Arthur Twining Hadley, "The Constitutional Position of Property in America," *The Independent*, April 16, 1908, pp. 834, 837-38.
2. Max Lerner, "The Supreme Court and American Capitalism," *Yale Law Journal*, March 1933, p. 671.

3. *Wolff Packing Co.* v. *Court of Industrial Relations,* 262 U.S. 522 (1923), pp. 535, 536.
4. *Adkins* v. *Children's Hospital,* 261 U.S. 525 (1923), p. 554. (The Minimum Wage Case.)
5. *Block* v. *Hirsh,* 256 U.S. 135 (1921), p. 157.
6. *Tyson & Bro.* v. *Banton,* 273 U.S. 418 (1927), p. 445. Hereafter cited as Tyson case.
7. *Ibid.,* p. 451.
8. *Ibid.,* pp. 450, 451, 452.
9. *Ibid.,* pp. 450, 454.
10. H.F.S. to George Sutherland, Feb. 7, 1927.
11. H.F.S. to O. W. Holmes, Feb. 5, 1927.
12. H.F.S. to John Bassett Moore, May 4, 1927.
13. Tyson case, pp. 445-46.
14. H.F.S. to Herman Oliphant, March 3, 1917.
15. Tyson case, pp. 431, 434, 439.
16. *Ribnik* v. *McBride,* 277 U.S. 350 (1928), p. 357.
17. *Ibid.*
18. *Ibid.,* pp. 359-60, 361, 362, 373.
19. *Ibid.,* pp. 360, 374-75, 372-73.
20. *Ibid.,* pp. 358, 373-74.
21. *Ibid.,* p. 360.
22. *Ibid.,* p. 375.
23. Felix Frankfurter to H.F.S., June 6, 1928.
24. Edwin W. Patterson to H.F.S., June 15, 1928.
25. H.F.S. to Edwin W. Patterson, June 18, 1928.
26. Herman Oliphant to H.F.S., June 16, 1928.
27. H.F.S. to Herman Oliphant, June 18, 1929.
28. H.F.S. to Milton Handler, Dec. 4, 1929.
29. H.F.S. to John Bassett Moore, June 5, 1928.
30. H.F.S. to Nicholas Murray Butler, April 4, 1927.
31. *Di Santo* v. *Pennsylvania,* 273 U.S. 34 (1927), p. 44.
32. Note, *Columbia Law Review,* May 1927, pp. 574-75.
33. See *McCulloch* v. *Maryland,* 4 Wheat. 316 (1819); *Dobbins* v. *Commissioners of Erie County,* 16 Pet. 435 (1842); *Collector* v. *Day,* 11 Wal. 113 (1871); *Pollock* v. *Farmers' Loan and Trust Co.,* 157 U.S. 429 (1895).
34. *Metcalf & Eddy* v. *Mitchell,* 269 U.S. 514 (1926), pp. 521, 522, 523.
35. *Ibid.,* pp. 523-25. (Italics the author's.)
36. *Panhandle Oil Co.* v. *Mississippi,* 277 U.S. 218 (1928), p. 221.
37. *Indian Motorcycle Co.* v. *United States,* 283 U.S. 570 (1931), pp. 575, 580.
38. Dowling, Cheatham, Hale, op. cit.
39. *Liberty Warehouse Co.* v. *Grannis,* 273 U.S. 70 (1927), p. 76.
40. *Fidelity National Bank & Trust Co.* v. *Swope,* 274 U.S. 123 (1927).
41. H.F.S. to W. H. Taft, April 18, 1927; W. H. Taft to H.F.S., April 24, 1927; H.F.S. to W. H. Taft, April 25, 1927.
42. *Willing* v. *Chicago Auditorium Association,* 277 U.S. 274 (1928), pp. 289, 290, 291.
43. H.F.S. to Luther Ely Smith, March 30, 1933.
44. *Miller* v. *Schoene,* 276 U.S. 272 (1928), p. 279.
45. See *Jenkins* v. *National Surety Co.,* 277 U.S. 258 (1928).
46. H.F.S. to Milton Handler, May 28, 1928.
47. These cases were *DeForest Radio* v. *General Electric,* 283 U.S. 664 (1931), and *Saranac Automatic Machine Corp.* v. *Wirebound Patents Co.,* 282 U.S. 704 (1931).
48. *Holland Furniture Co.* v. *Perkins Glue Co.,* 277 U.S. 245 (1928), pp. 256, 257.
49. Milton Handler to H.F.S., May 26, 1928.
50. H.F.S. to Milton Handler, June 18, 1928.
51. H.F.S., "Fifty Years' Work of the United States Supreme Court," *American Bar Association Journal,* Aug.-Sept., 1928, pp. 429, 430, 431, 432, 433.
52. Felix Frankfurter to H.F.S., June 11, 1928.
53. H.F.S., "Fifty Years' Work . . . ," p. 435.
54. Henry T. Noyes to H.F.S., Feb. 8, 1929, quoting Mark Sullivan's column of Feb. 8, 1929.

## CHAPTER XVI

1. Quoted in Felix Frankfurter, "Chief Justices I Have Known," *Virginia Law Review*, Nov. 1953, pp. 899-900.
2. W. H. Taft to Robert A. Taft, May 3, 1925.
3. W. H. Taft to Charles D. Hilles, June 9, 1925.
4. H.F.S. to Louis D. Brandeis, Feb. 16, 1929.
5. McCormack, *op. cit.*, p. 712. The case was *Village of Euclid* v. *Ambler Realty Co.*, 272 U.S. 365 (1926).
6. *Murphy* v. *Sardell*, 267 U.S. 530 (1925).
7. *New Republic*, Nov. 4, 1925, pp. 270-71.
8. Harold Laski to O. W. Holmes, Nov. 10, 1925, *Holmes-Laski Letters*, ed. Mark DeWolfe Howe (Cambridge, Mass.: Harvard University Press, 1953), Vol. 1, p. 798.
9. O. W. Holmes to Harold J. Laski, loc. cit., p. 800.
10. McCormack, *op. cit.*, The case was *Schlesinger* v. *Wisconsin*, 270 U.S. 230 (1926).
11. Schlesinger case, p. 241.
12. *Weaver* v. *Palmer Bros. Co.*, 270 U.S. 402 (1926), p. 415.
13. Thomas Reed Powell to A.T.M., May 17, 1953.
14. H.F.S. to Felix Frankfurter, June 8, 1928.
15. H.F.S. to Milton Handler, May 28, 1926.
16. H.F.S. to O. W. Holmes, June 7, 1928.
17. H.F.S. to Irving Dillard, October 13, 1941.
18. W. H. Taft to Elihu Root, August 14, 1926.
19. W. H. Taft to Edward Sanford, Jan. 25, 1927.
20. W.H. Taft to George Sutherland, Jan. 25, 1927.
21. W. H. Taft to H.F.S., Jan. 26, 1927.
22. *Duplex Printing Co.* v. *Deering*, 254 U.S. 443 (1921), pp. 479, 481.
23. *Bedford Cut Stone Co.* v. *Journeymen Stone Cutters' Association*, 274 U.S. 37 (1927), p. 60. Hereafter cited as Bedford case.
24. W. H. Taft to H.F.S., Jan. 26, 1927.
25. H.F.S. to W. H. Taft, Jan. 26, 1927. The San Francisco case was *Industrial Association* v. *United States*, 268 U.S. 64 (1925).
26. W. H. Taft to H.F.S., Jan. 27, 1927.
27. W. H. Taft to George Sutherland, March 11, 1927.
28. James C. McReynolds to H.F.S., undated, hand-written note.
29. H.F.S. to James C. McReynolds, April 3, 1930.
30. W. H. Taft to Robert A. Taft, April 10, 1927.
31. Bedford case, pp. 49, 55, 65.
32. *Ibid.*, p. 56.
33. W. H. Taft to Robert A. Taft, April 10, 1927.
34. Opinions by Mr. Justice Stone, 1925 to 1930:

| | 1925 | 1926 | 1927 | 1928 | 1929 | 1930 |
|---|---|---|---|---|---|---|
| Court | 21 | 30 | 24 | 19 | 17 | 22 |
| Concur | 0 | 2 | 1 | 2 | 3 | 0 |
| Dissent | 1 | 3 | 5 | 3 | 6 | 2 |
| Ratio of separate opinions | 1-21 | 1-6 | 1-4 | 1-4 (app.) | 1-2 (app.) | 1-11 |

(See Felix Frankfurter and James M. Landis, "The Business of the Supreme Court," *Harvard Law Review*, Nov. 1930, pp. 20-21, and Dec. 1931, pp. 290-91.)

From the October Term, 1925, until the end of the 1935 term, Stone wrote forty-two dissenting opinions and recorded ninety-eight dissenting votes. In the second half of the decade, under the Chief Justiceship of Hughes, he dissented more frequently than any of his brethren. (See Dowling, Cheatham, and Hale, *op. cit.*, p. 352, note 4.)

35. H.F.S. to Felix Frankfurter, Jan. 16, 1930.
36. H.F.S. to Sterling Carr, Dec. 23, 1927.
37. H.F.S. to Felix Frankfurter, June 28, 1928.

38. Milton Handler to H.F.S., May 24, 1929.
39. Pringle, *op. cit.*, Vol. II, p. 1044.
40. W. H. Taft to Charles P. Taft, May 12, 1929. Quoted in Pringle, *op. cit.*, p. 967.
41. *Time*, May 6, 1929.
42. *The Nation*, May 7, 1930.

## CHAPTER XVII

1. Alfred McCormack to A.T.M., Nov. 15, 1950.
2. Stone included this account of his interview with the President among some "Coolidge Stories" sent Arthur McKeogh of *Good Housekeeping* magazine, Nov. 24, 1934.
3. H.F.S. to his sons, Dec. 3, 1925.
4. H.F.S. to his sons, June 13, 1928.
5. H.F.S. to Helen Stone Willard, June 16, 1928.
6. H.F.S. to his sons, Oct. 5, 1928.
7. H.F.S. to George Canfield, Oct. 13, 1928.
8. *Ibid.*
9. H.F.S. to his sons, Nov. 9, 1928.
10. William Nelson Cromwell to H.F.S., Jan. 7, 1929.
11. H.F.S. to his sons, Nov. 16, 1928.
12. H.F.S. to Herbert Hoover, Nov. 9, 1928.
13. *Ibid.*
14. H.F.S. to his sons, Feb. 21, 1929.
15. H.F.S. to Earl Davis, March 28, 1929.
16. H.F.S. to William Nelson Cromwell, Nov. 14, 1928.
17. H.F.S. to John Vance Hewitt, Feb. 7, 1929.
18. H.F.S., first draft of a memorandum, "Suggested Studies for the President's Commission on Law Enforcement," 1929.
19. T.R.B., "Washington Notes," *New Republic*, April 24, 1929, p. 279.
20. H.F.S. to Sterling Carr, Jan. 17, 1929.
21. H.F.S. to William Nelson Cromwell, Nov. 14, 1928.
22. H.F.S. to Milton Handler, Feb. 19, 1929.
23. H.F.S. to his sons, March 7, 1929.
24. H.F.S. to Herbert Hoover, May 20, 1931. For Mr. Hoover's address, see *The State Papers and Other Public Writings of Herbert Hoover* (Garden City: Doubleday, 1934), Vol. I, pp. 584-87.
25. H.F.S. to his sons, March 21, 1929.
26. Charles Evans Hughes, Jr., "Mr. Chief Justice Stone," *Harvard Law Review*, Oct. 1946, p. 1195.
27. *Ibid.*, p. 1193.
28. *Springfield Union*, May 1, 1929.
29. Hughes, *op. cit.*, p. 1195.
30. W. H. Taft to Samuel H. Fischer, May 2, 1929.
31. H.F.S. to his sons, Nov. 3, 1939.
32. W. H. Taft to Robert A. Taft, March 17, May 17, 1929.
33. W. H. Taft to Robert A. Taft, April 7, 1929.
34. Robert Barry, "Washington Day by Day," *New York Evening World*, Nov. 1, 1929.
35. George Canfield to H.F.S., Nov. 12, 1929.
36. W. H. Taft to Charles P. Taft, May 12, 1929.
37. *Ibid.*
38. Pringle, *op. cit.*, Vol. II, p. 1079.
39. 281 U.S., page v.
40. Merlo J. Pusey, *Charles Evans Hughes* (New York: The Macmillan Co., 1951), Vol. II, p. 651.
41. Herbert Hoover to Charles Evans Hughes, Feb. 25, 1937.
42. Drew Pearson and Robert S. Allen, *Washington Merry-Go-Round* (New York: Liveright, 1931), p. 316.
43. Gertrude Jenkins Regis to A.T.M., June 7, 1950.
44. *New York Times*, Feb. 4, 1930.
45. Memorandum from (brother) Lauson Stone to Gertrude Jenkins Regis, 1947.
46. Howard C. Westwood to A.T.M., Nov. 16, 1950; Richard A. Stone to Mrs.

Harlan F. Stone, June 19, 1950. See also H. F. Pringle, "Profile: Chief Justice III," *The New Yorker,* July 13, 1935.
47. See Pusey, *op. cit.,* Vol. II, pp. 650-51.
48. H.F.S. to F. C. Hicks, Feb. 5, 1930.
49. H.F.S. to his sons, Feb. 5, 1930.
50. H.F.S. to Milton Handler, Feb. 5, 1930.
51. Felix Frankfurter to H.F.S., Feb. 21, 1930.
52. H.F.S. to Felix Frankfurter, Feb. 25, 1930.
53. Herbert Hoover to A.T.M., Feb. 28, 1951.
54. Pusey, *op. cit.,* Vol. II, p. 652.
55. H.F.S. to his sons, July 8, 1930.
56. H.F.S. to John Bassett Moore, Aug. 3, 1930.
57. H.F.S. to Grosvenor H. Backus, Dec. 29, 1930.
58. Quoted in Edmund Wilson, *The American Jitters* (New York: Charles Scribner's Sons, 1932), p. 148.
59. Herbert Hoover, address to Indiana Republican Editorial Association, Indianapolis, June 15, 1931, quoted in Edward Angly, *Oh Yeah?* (New York: The Viking Press, 1931), p. 19.
60. H.F.S. to his sons, Nov. 7, 1930.
61. H.F.S. to John H. Bartlett, Jan. 6, 1938. For a brief account of the "Shame of Anacostia Flats," see Broadus Mitchell, *Depression Decade* (New York: Rinehart & Co., 1947), pp. 108-110.
62. Charles C. Burlingham passed this along to H.F.S., Dec. 16, 1930.
63. H.F.S. to his sons, April 21, 1932.
64. H.F.S. to Sterling Carr, Dec. 28, 1931.
65. Grosvenor H. Backus to H.F.S., Jan. 14, 1932.
66. Sterling Carr to H.F.S., April 5, 1932.
67. H.F.S. to Sterling Carr, April 9, 1932.
68. H.F.S. to Sterling Carr, May 15, May 25, 1932.
69. Walter Newton to H.F.S., undated, 1932. For the full text of Hoover's address, see *Campaign Speeches of 1932,* by President Hoover and Ex-President Coolidge (New York: Doubleday, Doran & Co., 1933), pp. 284-94.
70. H.F.S. to Walter Newton, Oct. 11, 1932.
71. H.F.S. to Grosvenor H. Backus, Oct. 15, 1932.
72. H.F.S. to Sterling Carr, Dec. 6, 1932.
73. H.F.S. to John Vance Hewitt, Dec. 20, 1932.
74. H.F.S. to Lawrence Richey, secretary to President Hoover, Dec. 2, 1932.
75. H.F.S. to Sterling Carr, Jan. 4, 1933.
76. H.F.S. to his sons, Feb. 10, 1933; *Washington Post,* Feb. 9, 1933.
77. H.F.S. to Helen Stone Willard, Feb. 17, 1933.
78. Memorandum from Herbert Wechsler to Gertrude Jenkins Regis, 1947.
79. Mrs. Harlan F. Stone to A.T.M., Aug. 1, 1951.

PART FOUR

## CHAPTER XVIII

1. W. H. Taft to Robert A. Taft, Oct. 21, 1928, quoted in Henry F. Pringle, *Life and Times of William Howard Taft,* Vol. II, p. 1066.
2. *Southwestern Bell Telephone Co.* v. *Public Service Commission of Missouri,* 262 U.S. 276 (1923), p. 292.
3. *St. Louis and O'Fallon Railway Co.* v. *United States,* 279 U.S. 461 (1929). Hereafter cited as O'Fallon case.
4. Congressman Sam Rayburn, then ranking Democrat on the House Commerce Committee, quoted in the *New York Times,* May 22, 1929.
5. Quoted by Justice Brandeis in the O'Fallon case, p. 541.
6. O'Fallon case, p. 550.
7. *Ibid.,* pp. 551-52.
8. *United Railways* v. *West,* 280 U.S. 234 (1930), p. 289.
9. H.F.S. to Robert Hale, Dec. 31, 1929.
10. H.F.S. to John Bassett Moore, Jan. 7, 1930.
11. Quoted in Merlo J. Pusey, *Charles Evans Hughes,* Vol. II, p. 652.
12. *New York Times,* Feb. 5, 1930.

13. This and the following paragraphs are from the *Congressional Record,* Vol. 72 (1930), p. 3373.
14. *New York Times,* Feb. 14, 1930.
15. *Congressional Record,* Vol. 72 (1930), p. 3514.
16. Words of Senator Carter Glass, *Congressional Record,* Vol. 72 (1930), p. 3553.
17. *New York Times,* Feb. 14, 1930.
18. *Congressional Record,* Vol. 72 (1930), pp. 3449, 3516, 3566.
19. *Ibid.,* p. 3642.
20. See especially *International Organization United Mine Workers* v. *Red Jacket Consolidated Coal & Coke Co.,* 18 Fed. (2d) 839 (1927).
21. H.F.S. to John J. Parker, June 4, 1930.
22. H.F.S. to his sons, April 18, April 30, 1930.
23. *Congressional Record,* Vol. 72 (1930), p. 3501.
24. *Ibid.,* p. 3573.
25. Frank R. Kent, quoted in Lief, *Democracy's Norris* (New York: Stackpole, 1939), p. 344.
26. *Washington Star,* Feb. 13, 1930.
27. *Congressional Record,* Vol. 72 (1930), p. 7949.
28. H.F.S. to his sons, April 30, 1930.
29. Felix Frankfurter, "The United States Supreme Court Molding the Constitution," *Current History,* May 1930, p. 240, and "The Supreme Court and the Public," *The Forum,* June 1930, p. 334.
30. Felix Frankfurter to H.F.S., Feb. 21, 1930.
31. H.F.S. to Milton Handler, April 9, 1930.
32. H.F.S. to John Bassett Moore, April 26, 1930.
33. H.F.S. to Felix Frankfurter, April 4, 1930. (Italics the author's.)
34. Frankfurter, "The Supreme Court and the Public," *loc. cit.,* pp. 329-30, 334, *passim.*
35. H.F.S. to Sterling Carr, Dec. 6, 1932.

## CHAPTER XIX

1. Gregory and Charlotte Hankins, *Progress of the Law in the U.S. Supreme Court, 1929-1930* (Washington, D.C.: Legal Research Service, 1930), p. 9.
2. H.F.S. to Thomas Reed Powell, Jan. 26, 1931.
3. Felix Frankfurter to H.F.S., March 18, 1931.
4. H.F.S. to Felix Frankfurter, April 4, 1931.
5. H.F.S. to Felix Frankfurter, Jan. 12, 1931.
6. Report of the Fifty-third Annual Meeting, American Bar Association, Chicago, Aug. 20-23, 1930, pp. 107-116.
7. H.F.S. to John Bassett Moore, Sept. 14, 1930.
8. *Ibid.* See, in this connection, George D. Braden, "The Search for Objectivity in Constitutional Law," *Yale Law Journal,* Feb. 1948, p. 577.
9. H.F.S. to George P. Hahn, June 2, 1931.
10. H.F.S. to Felix Frankfurter, Jan. 8, 1929.
11. 4 Wheat. 316 (1819) and 1 Wall. 113 (1871).
12. H.F.S. to Thomas Reed Powell, Jan. 30, 1931.
13. *Metcalf & Eddy* v. *Mitchell,* 269 U.S. 514 (1926).
14. *Macallen Co.* v. *Massachusetts,* 279 U.S. 620 (1929).
15. *Educational Films Corp.* v. *Ward,* 282 U.S. 379 (1931).
16. H.F.S. to his sons, Jan. 15, 1931; H.F.S. to Felix Frankfurter, Jan. 16, 1931.
17. This is one of the passages Powell sent to Stone in January 1931. The article in somewhat revised form appears in the *Harvard Law Review,* April 1931. See also Thomas Reed Powell, "The Macallen Case—and Before," *The National Income Tax Magazine,* Feb. 1930.
18. H.F.S. to Thomas Reed Powell, Jan. 26, 1931.
19. *Pacific Co.* v. *Johnson,* 285 U.S. 480 (1932).
20. H.F.S. to Charles Evans Hughes. Feb. 11, 1932.
21. H.F.S. to Felix Frankfurter, April 16, 1932.
22. H.F.S. to Thomas Reed Powell. Jan. 30, 1931.
23. H.F.S. to Thomas Reed Powell, April 16, 1932, apropos of the Pacific Company case.
24. H.F.S. to John Bassett Moore, April 2, 1932.

25. H.F.S. to Felix Frankfurter, March 30, 1932.
26. Felix Frankfurter to H.F.S., March 28, 1932.
27. H.F.S. to James C. McReynolds, March 23, 1928, re: *Untermyer* v. *Anderson*, 276 U.S. 440 (1928); *Blodgett* v. *Holden*, 275 U.S. 142 (1927); *Billings* v. *United States*, 232 U.S. 261 (1914).
28. H.F.S. to John Bassett Moore, Dec. 4, 1931.
29. Max Lowenthal, *The Investor Pays* (New York: Alfred A. Knopf, 1933), preface.
30. Commissioner Eastman, quoted in Lowenthal, *op. cit.*, p. 375.
31. Lowenthal, *op. cit.*, p. 382.
32. *United States* v. *Chicago, Milwaukee & St. Paul Railway Co.*, 282 U.S. 311 (1931), p. 325. Hereafter cited as St. Paul Railway case.
33. *Ibid.*, p. 326.
34. H.F.S., dissenting in St. Paul Railway case, p. 333.
35. Lowenthal, *op. cit.*, p. 263.
36. Jerome Frank, "Some Realistic Reflections on Some Aspects of Corporate Reorganizations," *Virginia Law Review*, April 1933, p. 568.
37. St. Paul Railway case, pp. 333, 335.
38. *Ibid.*, p. 337.
39. *Ibid.*, pp. 341, 342.
40. George W. Anderson to H.F.S., Jan. 27, 1931.
41. H.F.S. to George W. Anderson, Jan. 28, 1931.
42. Felix Frankfurter to H.F.S., Jan. 9, 1931.
43. Felix Frankfurter to H.F.S., March 7, 1932. See Robert T. Swaine, Book Review, *Columbia Law Review*, Feb. 1932, p. 403.
44. H.F.S. to Felix Frankfurter, March 11, 1932.
45. See editorials in the *Cincinnati Post*, May 21, 1931; *Topeka Daily Capital*, May 26, 1931; *Baltimore Sun*, May 28, 1931; *The Pathfinder*, June 27, 1931; also Joseph P. Pollard, "Four New Dissenters," *New Republic*, Sept. 2, 1931.
46. *State Board of Tax Commissioners* v. *Jackson*, 283 U.S. 527 (1931), p. 535.
47. H.F.S. to Milton Handler, May 26, 1931.
48. *Near* v. *Minnesota*, 283 U.S. 697 (1931).
49. *United States* v. *Macintosh*, 283 U.S. 605 (1931) and *United States* v. *Bland*, 283 U.S. 636 (1931).
50. *Baltimore Sun*, May 28, 1931.
51. *O'Gorman and Young* v. *Hartford Fire Insurance Co.*, 282 U.S. 251 (1931).
52. "The Supreme Court's Attitude toward Liberty of Contract and Freedom of Speech," *Yale Law Journal*, Dec. 1931, p. 267.
53. H.F.S. to William Nelson Cromwell, April 9, 1931.
54. H.F.S. to Garrard Glenn, May 28, 1931.

## CHAPTER XX

1. H.F.S. to his sons, Nov. 24, 1939.
2. H.F.S. to Felix Frankfurter, April 2, 1935.
3. Irving Brant, "How Liberal Is Justice Hughes?" *New Republic*, July 21, 1937. The second installment appeared on July 28.
4. H.F.S. to John Bassett Moore, May 27, 1931.
5. Charles Evans Hughes to H.F.S., Nov. 9, 1931.
6. Walter Gellhorn to Gertrude Jenkins Regis, Jan. 21, 1947.
7. *Ibid.*
8. Marquis Childs, "A Minority of One," *Saturday Evening Post*, Sept. 20, 1941, p. 15.
9. H.F.S. to Young B. Smith, March 3, 1932.
10. *Brimstone Railroad Co.* v. *United States*, 276 U.S. 104 (1928).
11. *United States* v. *Baltimore & Ohio Railroad Co.*, 284 U.S. 195 (1931), p. 205.
12. *Chicago, Rock Island & Pacific Railway Co.* v. *United States*, 284 U.S. 80 (1931).
13. *Ibid.*, pp. 116, 121, *passim.*
14. H.F.S. to Felix Frankfurter, Jan. 5, 1932.
15. *First National Bank* v. *Maine*, 284 U.S. 312 (1932) pp. 331, 333.
16. *New State Ice Co.* v. *Liebman*, 285 U.S. 262 (1932), pp. 277, 279.
17. *Ibid.*, pp. 282, 302-303.
18. *Ibid.*, pp. 306, 307, 308.

19. *Ibid.*, p. 311.
20. *Frost* v. *Corporation Commission,* 278 U.S. 515 (1929).
21. H.F.S. to Felix Frankfurter, Nov. 4, 1930.
22. *American Hide & Leather Co.* v. *United States,* 284 U.S. 343 (1932), p. 347.
23. Memorandum from Walter Gellhorn to Gertrude Jenkins Regis, Jan. 21, 1947.

## CHAPTER XXI

1. H.F.S. to Francis X. Downey, Nov. 27, 1941.
2. Max Lerner, *The Mind and Faith of Justice Holmes* (Boston: Little, Brown & Co., 1946), p. xlvi.
3. H.F.S. to Learned Hand, Jan. 14, 1932.
4. H.F.S. to the Reverend Jay T. Stocking, Feb. 7, 1932.
5. Stanley King to Luther Ely Smith, Oct. 6, 1947.
6. O. W. Holmes to H.F.S., March 1, 1928.
7. H.F.S. to O. W. Holmes, March 7, 1930.
8. H.F.S. to the Reverend Jay T. Stocking, Feb. 7, 1932.
9. H.F.S. to Harold J. Laski, June 3, 1937.
10. *Holmes-Pollock Letters,* ed. Mark DeWolfe Howe (Cambridge, Mass.: Harvard University Press, 1941), Vol. II, p. 13.
11. Alfred McCormack, "A Law Clerk's Recollections," *Columbia Law Review,* Sept. 1946, pp. 713-14.
12. *Ibid.*, p. 714.
13. H.F.S. to O.W. Holmes, May 14, 1926.
14. O. W. Holmes to H.F.S., Dec. 20, 1928; H.F.S. to O. W. Holmes, Dec. 21, 1928. The case was *Williams* v. *Standard Oil Co. of Louisiana,* 278 U.S. 235 (1929). Holmes dissented without opinion; Stone and Brandeis noted concurrence in the result.
15. H.F.S. to O.W. Holmes, May 24, 1928.
16. *Baldwin* v. *Missouri,* 281 U.S. 586 (1930), p. 595.
17. H.F.S. to Felix Frankfurter, May 31, 1930.
18. H.F.S. to the Reverend Jay T. Stocking, Feb. 7, 1932.
19. See H.F.S., "The Common Law in the United States," *Harvard Law Review,* Nov. 1936.
20. *Holmes-Laski Letters,* ed. Mark DeWolfe Howe (Cambridge, Mass.: Harvard University Press, 1953), Vol. I, p. 385.
21. *Ibid.*, Vol. II, p. 1282.
22. O. W. Holmes, "The Profession of the Law," *Collected Legal Papers* (New York: Harcourt, Brace & Co., 1920), pp. 30, 32.
23. O. W. Holmes, "The Use of Law Schools," *loc. cit.*, p. 38.
24. H.F.S. to Felix Frankfurter, March 15, 1937.
25. H.F.S. to the Reverend Jay T. Stocking, Feb. 7, 1932.
26. H.F.S. to Felix Frankfurter, March 18, 1933.
27. The case was *Silver* v. *Silver,* 280 U.S. 117 (1929).
28. H.F.S. to Clinton L. Rossiter, April 12, 1941.
29. H.F.S. to Max Lerner, May 6, 1943.
30. From the unpublished address on Justice Holmes.
31. The case was *Merchants Warehouse Co.* v. *United States,* 283 U.S. 501 (1931).
32. H.F.S. to Helen Stone Willard, Jan. 19, 1932.
33. H.F.S. to Sterling Carr, March 6, 1935.
34. H.F.S. to Sterling Carr, Jan. 22, 1932.
35. H.F.S. to Robert L. Hale, Feb. 15, 1932.
36. H.F.S. to Felix Frankfurter, Jan. 28, 1932.
37. Memorandum from Walter Gellhorn to Gertrude Jenkins Regis, Jan. 21, 1947.
38. H.F.S. to Felix Frankfurter, Feb. 9, 1932.
39. H.F.S. to Robert L. Hale, Feb. 15, 1932.
40. H.F.S. to Felix Frankfurter, Feb. 16, 1932.
41. H.F.S. to Milton Handler, Feb. 17, 1932.
42. *Crowell* v. *Benson,* 285 U.S. 22 (1932).
43. H.F.S. to Louis D. Brandeis, Feb. 19, 1932.
44. *Ibid.*
45. *Crowell* v. *Benson,* p. 94.
46. H.F.S. to Felix Frankfurter, March 2, 1932.

47. Quoted in Pearson and Allen, *The Nine Old Men*, p. 111. Stone made the same characterization of Chief Justice Hughes' opinions in a talk with Edward S. Corwin.
48. H.F.S. to Felix Frankfurter, April 16, 1932. The case was *Coombes* v. *Getz*, 285 U.S. 434 (1932).
49. H.F.S. to Milton Handler, April 20, 1932. The case was *Burnet* v. *Coronado Gas & Oil Co.*, 285 U.S. 393 (1932).
50. H.F.S. to Felix Frankfurter, April 16, 1932.
51. *Ibid.*
52. H.F.S. to Milton Handler, May 28, 1928.
53. Rev. Stat. 3224 U.S.C., Title 26, Section 154. Quoted in *Miller* v. *Standard Nut Margarine Co.*, 284 U.S. 489 (1932), p. 503.
54. Miller case, p. 511.
55. H.F.S. to Felix Frankfurter, March 2, 1932.
56. *Matthews* v. *Rodgers*, 284 U.S. 521 (1932), p. 525; see also *Stratton* v. *St. Louis Southwestern Railway Co.*, 284 U.S. 530, decided the same day.
57. Sterling Carr to H.F.S., Jan. 14, 1932.
58. H.F.S. to Felix Frankfurter, March 30, 1932.
59. Letter to H.F.S., April 2, 1932
60. *Heiner* v. *Donnan*, 285 U.S. 312 (1932), p. 327.
61. Felix Frankfurter, "Social Issues before the Supreme Court," *Yale Review*, Spring 1933, p. 490.
62. *Heiner* v. *Donnan*, pp. 343, 351. Cf. Stone's opinion in *Milliken* v. *United States*, 283 U.S. 15 (1931), upholding constitutionality of tax on "gifts in contemplation of death."
63. Gellhorn memorandum.
64. Felix Frankfurter to H.F.S., March 24, 1932.
65. H.F.S. to Felix Frankfurter, March 25, 1932.
66. Gellhorn memorandum.
67. H.F.S. to Felix Frankfurter, May 25, 1932.

## CHAPTER XXII

1. H.F.S. to Herbert Hoover, May 2, 1933.
2. H.F.S. to Goldthwaite Dorr, Feb. 5, 1933.
3. Ferdinand Pecora, *Wall Street under Oath* (New York: Simon & Schuster, 1939), p. 256.
4. H.F.S. to Herbert Hoover, Dec. 4, 1933.
5. *Ibid.*
6. H.F.S. to his sons, March 16, 1933.
7. H.F.S. to his sons, March 24, 1933.
8. *Ibid.*
9. H.F.S. to Herbert Hoover, May 2, 1933.
10. Sterling Carr to H.F.S., Dec. 30, 1932.
11. 288 U.S. 476 (1933).
12. Memorandum from Herbert Wechsler to Gertrude Jenkins Regis, 1947.
13. H.F.S. to Sterling Carr, Jan. 4, 1933.
14. H.F.S. to his sons, March 24, 1933.
15. Learned Hand to H.F.S., April 12, 1933.
16. H.F.S. to Learned Hand, April 17, 1933.
17. Franklin D. Roosevelt, "Inaugural Address," March 4, 1933, *Looking Forward* (New York: John Day, 1933), p. 267.
18. Felix Frankfurter to H.F.S., Feb. 29, 1932.
19. *Holmes-Laski Letters*, Vol. II, p. 1474. (Laski to Holmes.)
20. *Ibid.*, Vol. I, pp. 556, 675.
21. McCormack, *op. cit.*
22. *Liggett* v. *Lee*, 288 U.S. 517 (1933).
23. H.F.S. to Luther Ely Smith, March 30, 1933.
24. Learned Hand to A.T.M., Aug. 22, 1951.
25. H.F.S. to Felix Frankfurter, March 16, 1936.
26. Milton Handler, Book Review of Reavis Cox's *Competition in the American Tobacco Industry* (1934), *Harvard Law Review*, Nov. 1934, p. 160.
27. *Rogers* v. *Guaranty Trust Co.*, 288 U.S. 123 (1933). Quoted material and figures through p. 352, unless otherwise noted, are from this case.

28. H.F.S. to Felix Frankfurter, Jan. 23, 1933.
29. H.F.S. to Felix Frankfurter, Feb. 17, 1933.
30. Milton Handler to H.F.S., Jan. 25, 1933.
31. *New Republic*, July 19, 1933, p. 248.
32. H.F.S. to Sterling Carr, Feb. 17, 1933.
33. *New Republic*, March 29, 1933, p. 174.
34. Felix Frankfurter to H.F.S., April 5, 1933.
35. H.F.S. to Felix Frankfurter, April 11, 1933.
36. H.F.S. to Felix Frankfurter, March 25, 1933.
37. *Rogers* v. *Hill*, 289 U.S. 582 (1933), p. 591.
38. H.F.S. to Robert C. Rathbone, March 3, 1933.
39. Wechsler memorandum.
40. Felix Frankfurter to H.F.S., May 10, 1932.
41. Felix Frankfurter to H.F.S., March 23, 1933.
42. Sterling Carr to H.F.S., March 14, 1934; H.F.S. to Sterling Carr, March 19, 1934.
43. Felix Frankfurter to H.F.S., undated, handwritten note in the spring of 1932.

## CHAPTER XXIII

1. H.F.S. to Sterling Carr, Nov. 3, 1933.
2. H.F.S. to Sterling Carr, Jan. 3, 1934.
3. H.F.S. to Herbert Hoover, Dec. 4, 1933.
4. H.F.S. to Sterling Carr, Dec. 20, 1933.
5. H.F.S. to Sterling Carr, Dec. 20, 1933, Jan. 3, 22, Feb. 13, March 19, 1934.
6. *Adkins* v. *Children's Hospital*, 261 U.S. 523 (1923), p. 546. Hereafter cited as Adkins case.
7. Adkins, Ribnik, Tyson, New State Ice Co. cases.
8. *Lochner* v. *New York*, 198 U.S. 45 (1905), p. 75.
9. Adkins case, p. 561.
10. Franklin D. Roosevelt, address to the Commonwealth Club, Sept. 23, 1932, *The Public Papers and Addresses of Franklin D. Roosevelt* (New York: Random House, 1938), Vol. I, p. 753.
11. H.F.S. to Sterling Carr, Jan. 3, 1934.
12. William D. Prosser, "The Minnesota Mortgage Moratorium," *Selected Essays on Constitutional Law*, Vol. II, p. 361. (Published by Association of American Law Schools, 1934.)
13. *Ibid.*, pp. 362, 367.
14. Quoted in *Home Building & Loan Association* v. *Blaisdell*, 290 U.S. 398 (1934), p. 422. Hereafter cited as Blaisdell case.
15. Blaisdell case, pp. 434, 435, 444, *passim*.
16. *Ibid.*, pp. 425, 426.
17. *Ibid.*, pp. 465, 472.
18. Quoting Justice McKenna, in *Block* v. *Hirsh*, 256 U.S. 135 (1921), p. 160.
19. Blaisdell case, p. 471.
20. *Ibid.*, pp. 471-72, 483.
21. Thomas Jefferson to J. B. Colvin, Sept. 20, 1810, in *Writings of Thomas Jefferson* (1903 ed.), Vol. XII, p. 418.
22. *McCulloch* v. *Maryland*, 4 Wheat. 316 (1816), pp. 407, 415. See Hughes' opinion in Blaisdell case, p. 433.
23. *Missouri* v. *Holland*, 252 U.S. 416 (1920), p. 433.
24. Blaisdell case, especially at pp. 442, 445-47.
25. H.F.S. to Sterling Carr, Feb. 13, 1934; *Ibid.*, Jan. 22, 1934.
26. *Block* v. *Hirsh*, and *Marcus Brown Holding Co.* v. *Feldman*, 256 U.S. 170 (1921).
27. *Business Week*, March 1, 1933, p. 7.
28. Robert L. Hale, "The Constitution and the Price System: Some Reflections on *Nebbia* v. *New York*," *Columbia Law Review*, March 1943, p. 422.
29. Walton Hamilton, Book Review of Alfred Lief's *Public Control of Business*, *Columbia Law Review*, May 1941, p. 961.
30. *Nebbia* v. *New York*, 291 U.S. 502 (1934), pp. 516-17, 531-32.
31. *Ibid.*, pp. 532, 533, 536, 538-39.
32. *Ibid.*, pp. 546, 552-53.
33. *Ibid.*, pp. 551, 558.

34. *Ibid.*, p. 524.
35. T.R.B., "Washington Notes," *New Republic*, Jan. 24, 1934, p. 307.
36. Edward S. Corwin, *Twilight of the Supreme Court* (New Haven: Yale University Press, 1934), pp. 44-45. For another view see A. T. Mason, "Has the Supreme Court Abdicated?" *North American Review*, Oct. 1934, p. 353.
37. Morris Duane, "Nebbia v. People: A Milestone," *University of Pennsylvania Law Review*, April 1934, p. 622.
38. Blaisdell case, p. 448.
39. Duane, *op. cit.*, p. 619.
40. H.F.S. to Robert L. Hale, June 5, 1934; see Hale's "The Constitution and the Price System," loc. cit.
41. H.F.S. to Sterling Carr, Jan. 22, 1934.
42. H.F.S. to his sons, Nov. 9, 1933, Jan. 11, 1934.
43. Nebbia case, p. 536.

## CHAPTER XXIV

1. H.F.S. to Herbert Hoover, April 12, 1934.
2. H.F.S. to Howard Osterhout, Nov. 14, 1934.
3. H.F.S. to Garrard Glenn, Jan. 3, 1934.
4. H.F.S. to Felix Frankfurter, Nov. 8, 1933.
5. H.F.S. to Herbert Hoover, March 27, 1934. Quoted material through p. 375 is from this letter.
6. H.F.S. to Sterling Carr, Nov. 7, 1934.
7. H.F.S. to Frederick L. Allen, Oct. 5, 21, 1926.
8. Henry M. Bates to H.F.S., March 12, 1934; H.F.S. to Henry M. Bates, April 9, 1934.
9. H.F.S. to Henry M. Bates, June 7, 1934.
10. H.F.S., "The Public Influence of the Bar," reprinted in *Harvard Law Review*, Nov. 1934. Quoted material through p. 382, unless otherwise noted, is from this speech.
11. A. A. Berle, "Modern Legal Profession," *Encyclopedia of the Social Sciences* (1933), Vol. IX, p. 341.
12. *New Republic*, Dec. 26, 1934, p. 179.
13. H.F.S. to William D. Mitchell, Nov. 21, 1934.
14. Harold J. Laski, "The Decline of the Professions," *Harper's*, Nov. 1935, p. 679.
15. H.F.S. to Harold J. Laski, Nov. 19, 1935.
16. H.F.S. to Walter Gellhorn, Nov. 24, 1934.
17. William D. Guthrie, "Law School Reviews and Lawyers," *Fordham Law Review*, Jan. 1935, pp. 3, 5, 6.
18. *Ibid.*, p. 4.
19. Earle W. Evans, "Responsibility and Leadership," address of the President, Milwaukee, Aug. 28, 1934, *Reports of the American Bar Association*, Oct. 1934, Vol. 59, pp. 286-87.
20. "Proceedings of the Fifty-seventh Annual Meeting, *American Bar Association Journal*, Oct. 1934, pp. 604, 605.
21. H.F.S. to Felix Frankfurter, Oct. 9, 1934.

## CHAPTER XXV

1. Learned Hand to H.F.S., Feb. 8, 1934.
2. Robert H. Jackson, *The Struggle for Judicial Supremacy*, pp. x-xi.
3. Thurman Arnold, "The New Deal Is Constitutional," *New Republic*, Nov. 15, 1933.
4. Cf. *Swift & Co. v. United States*, 196 U.S. 375 (1905); *Second Employers' Liability Cases*, 233 U.S. 1 (1912); *Stafford v. Wallace*, 258 U.S. 495 (1922); *Board of Trade v. Olsen*, 262 U.S. 1 (1923); *McCray v. United States*, 195 U.S. 27 (1904); *Bailey v. Drexel Furniture Co.*, 259 U.S. 20 (1922).
5. Franklin D. Roosevelt, *The Public Papers and Addresses*, Vol. IV, p. 6.
6. Harold Ickes, *The Secret Diary of Harold L. Ickes: The First Thousand Days, 1933-36* (New York: Simon & Schuster, 1953), p. 101.
7. H.F.S. to his sons, May 3, 1934.
8. H.F.S. to the Marshall Stones, Dec. 13, 1934.
9. Arnold, *op. cit.*, p. 9.

10. H.F.S. to Edwin M. Borchard, Nov. 20, 1935.
11. *Borden's Farm Products Co.* v. *Baldwin,* 293 U.S. 194 (1934). Justice Stone voiced his dissatisfaction in a memorandum dated Nov. 26, 1934.
12. Russell Owen, "Nine Calm Men in the Midst of Storm," *New York Times Magazine,* Jan. 20, 1935, p. 6.
13. H.F.S. to Felix Frankfurter, April 2, 1935. The case was *Stewart Dry Goods Co.* v. *Lewis,* 294 U.S. 550 (1935).
14. See Erwin N. Griswold, "Government in Ignorance of the Law," *Harvard Law Review,* Dec. 1934.
15. *Panama Refining Co.* v. *Ryan,* 293 U.S. 388 (1935).
16. H.F.S. to his sons, Jan. 8, 1935. See Griswold, *op. cit.*
17. H.F.S. to Karl N. Llewellyn, Feb. 4, 1935.
18. H.F.S. to Felix Frankfurter, Feb. 21, 1935.
19. *Norman* v. *Baltimore & Ohio Railroad Co.,* 294 U.S. 240 (1935).
20. *Perry* v. *United States,* 294 U.S. 330 (1935), pp. 351, 354.
21. *Ibid.,* p. 358.
22. Warner Gardner to A.T.M., Nov. 16, 1950. See his "Mr. Chief Justice Stone," *Harvard Law Review,* Oct. 1946.
23. Perry case, p. 359.
24. *Ibid.,* pp. 359, 360.
25. H.F.S. to John Bassett Moore, Feb. 20, 1935.
26. H.F.S. to his sons, March 1, 1935.
27. Learned Hand to H.F.S., Oct. 5, 1935.
28. Roosevelt, *op. cit.,* Vol. IV, p. 8.
29. H.F.S. to his sons, Feb. 7, 1935.
30. *Railroad Retirement Board* v. *Alton Railroad Co.,* 295 U.S. 330 (1935), p. 368.
31. See "A Dred Scott Decision," *New Republic,* May 22, 1935.
32. H.F.S. to Felix Frankfurter, May 9, 1935.
33. Benjamin N. Cardozo to Charles Evans Hughes, April 19, 1935. Cardozo told Hughes that he and Stone had discussed the analogy but "as he is going out of town, it was agreed that I should write to you on the subject."
34. Railroad Retirement case, p. 384.
35. *Louisville Joint Stock Land Bank* v. *Radford,* 295 U.S. 555 (1935).
36. *Humphrey's Executor* v. *United States,* 295 U.S. 602 (1935).
37. Charles P. Curtis, Jr., *Lions under the Throne* (Boston: Houghton Mifflin Co., 1947), pp. 116-17.
38. NRA Release No. 11, June 25, 1933, quoted in *The ABC of the NRA* (Washington, D.C.: Brookings Institution, 1934), p. 32, note 2.
39. Jackson, *op. cit.,* p. 113.
40. *Schechter Poultry Corp.* v. *United States,* 295 U.S. 495 (1935), pp. 546, 548.
41. *Ibid.,* pp. 553, 554.
42. H.F.S .to John Bassett Moore, May 30, 1935.
43. H.F.S. to Felix Frankfurter, May 27, 1935.
44. H.F.S. to John Bassett Moore, Jan. 20, 1935.
45. Notably *Southern Railway Co.* v. *United States,* 222 U.S. 20 (1911); *Second Employers' Liability Cases,* 223 U.S. 1 (1912); *Stafford* v. *Wallace,* 258 U.S. 495 (1922); *Brooks* v. *United States,* 267 U.S. 432 (1925). See Edward S. Corwin, *The Commerce Power versus States Rights* (Princeton: Princeton University Press, 1936).
46. Mr. Justice Washington in *Ogden* v. *Saunders,* 12 Wheat. 213 (1827), p. 270.
47. Roosevelt, *op. cit.,* Vol. IV, p. 5.
48. *New York Times,* June 1, 1935.
49. President Roosevelt's characterization of the Schechter decision. *Washington Post,* June 1, 1935.
50. H.F.S. to Thomas Reed Powell, May 31, 1935.
51. Thomas Reed Powell, "Commerce, Pensions and Codes, II," *Harvard Law Review,* Dec. 1935, pp. 218, 237, 238.
52. H.F.S. to Felix Frankfurter, Feb. 17, 1936.
53. Felix Frankfurter to H.F.S., May 10, 1932.
54. H.F.S. to Thomas Reed Powell, Nov. 15, 1935.
55. Edward S. Corwin, "The Schechter Case—Landmark or What?" *New York Quarterly Review,* Jan. 1936, p. 10.
56. Felix Frankfurter and Henry Hart, "The Business of the Supreme Court at

October Term, 1934," *Harvard Law Review,* Nov. 1935, pp. 102-103, *passim.*
57. H.F.S. to Felix Frankfurter, Nov. 4, 1935.
58. H.F.S. to Thomas Reed Powell, Nov. 15, 1935.
59. H.F.S. to his sons, Dec. 20, 1935.
60. H.F.S. to his sons, Dec. 6, 1935.
61. *James C. Colgate* v. *Harvey,* Tax Commissioner of State of Vermont, 296 U.S. 404 (1935), p. 450.
62. H.F.S. to Felix Frankfurter, Dec. 20, 1935.
63. H.F.S. to Felix Frankfurter, Dec. 23, 1935.
64. H.F.S. to Owen J. Roberts, Jan. 3, 1940.
65. *Madden* v. *Kentucky,* 309 U.S. 83 (1940), p. 93.
66. H.F.S. to Felix Frankfurter, Feb. 17, 1936.
67. H.F.S. to Helen Stone Willard, Nov. 1, 1928.
68. V. R. Foley to H.F.S., May 15, 1934; H.S.F. to V. R. Foley, May 17, 1934.
69. Nathan Abbott to H.F.S., Feb. 9, 1934.
70. Unidentified newspaper clipping sent to Stone by John P. Shea in May 1935. See *Holyoke* (Mass.) *Transcript* (editorial), May 20, 1935, and Walter Lippmann, *New York Herald Tribune,* April 4, 1935.
71. H.F.S. to Edward Bruce, March 24, 1935.
72. H.F.S. to Richard B. Scandrett, Jr., Nov. 1, 1935.
73. H.F.S. to his sons, March 7, 1935.
74. H.F.S. to Helen Stone Willard, May 17, 1935.
75. H.F.S. to Edward Bruce, Dec. 18, 1935.

## CHAPTER XXVI

1. H.F.S. to his sons, Dec. 13, 1935.
2. Quoted in Curtis, *op. cit.,* p. 125.
3. *United States* v. *Butler,* 297 U.S. 1 (1936). Quoted material through p. 411, unless otherwise noted, is from this case. See particularly pp. 61, 63, 68, 72-78 *passim,* 85, 87-88.
4. *Hammer* v. *Dagenhart,* 247 U.S. 251 (1918).
5. Frances Perkins, *The Roosevelt I Knew* (New York: The Viking Press, 1946), p. 268.
6. See Raymond Moley, "So May Judicial Power Be Abused," *Today,* Jan. 18, 1936 (editorial).
7. H.F.S. to Charles A. Beard, April 15, 1936.
8. H.F.S. to Charles A. Beard, April 21, 1936.
9. *McCulloch* v. *Maryland,* 4 Wheat. 316 (1819), p. 406.
10. A. H. Feller, "The Tenth Amendment Retires," *American Bar Association Journal,* April 1941, p. 224. Feller's article was written apropos of Justice Stone's famous comment in *United States* v. *Darby* that the words of the Tenth Amendment merely stated a "truism."
11. Lloyd K. Garrison, "The Constitution and the Future," *New Republic,* Jan. 29, 1936, p. 328.
12. Howard Lee McBain, "The Issue: Court or Congress?" *New York Times Magazine,* Jan. 19, 1936, p. 2.
13. H.F.S. to DeWitt Clark, Feb. 21, 1938.
14. H.F.S. to Howard Lee McBain, Jan. 20, 1936.
15. Ickes, op. cit., p. 524.
16. Franklin D. Roosevelt, *The Public Papers and Addresses,* Vol. IV, p. 13 *passim.*
17. Edward Bauer to H.F.S., Jan. 13, 1936.
18. Robert D. Kellogg to Louis D. Brandeis, Jan. 7, 1936, who passed the letter along to Stone.
19. Senator Costigan, *Congressional Record,* Feb. 13, 1936, p. 1973.
20. "The Honorable Supreme Court," *Fortune,* May 1936, pp. 79, 80.
21. *New Republic,* Jan. 22, 1936, p. 303.
22. Louis D. Brandeis to H.F.S., Aug. 5, 1936.
23. Raoul E. Desvernine, *Democratic Despotism* (New York: Dodd, Mead & Co., 1936), pp. 175, 182.
24. National Lawyers Committee, American Liberty League, "The Welfare Clause in the Light of the AAA Decision" (1936), p. 21.
25. Desvernine, op. cit., pp. 51-52.
26. H.F.S. to Felix Frankfurter, April 7, 1936.

27. Ickes, op. cit., pp. 535, 536.
28. Arthur Twining Hadley, "The Constitutional Position of Property in America," *The Independent*, Jan.-June 1909, p. 837.
29. Moley, op. cit., p. 13.
30. Raymond Moley, *New York Times*, Jan. 12, 1936.
31. H.F.S. to Felix Frankfurter, Feb. 17, 1936.
32. H.F.S. to Howard Lee McBain, Jan. 30, 1936.
33. H.F.S. to Charles C. Burlingham, Jan. 9, 1936.
34. H.F.S. to Irving Brant, June 10, 1936.
35. H.F.S. to the Reverend Fleming James, Jan. 30, 1936.
36. H.F.S. to G. R. Farnum, Oct. 31, 1941.
37. H.F.S. to Homer F. Carey, Jan. 10, 1936.
38. A.T.M.'s interview with Adolph Miller, May 22, 1950.
39. H.F.S. to John Bassett Moore, Jan. 23, 1932.
40. Butler case, pp. 78-79.
41. *Ashwander* v. *Tennessee Valley Authority*, 297 U.S. 288 (1936).
42. Irving Brant to George Norris, Aug. 25, 1936.
43. *Great Northern Railways Co.* v. *Weeks*, 297 U.S. 135 (1936), p. 154.
44. *Carter* v. *Carter Coal Co.*, 298 U.S. 238 (1936), pp. 318, 328-29.
45. "Compare, for example," Stone suggested, "the statement in *Tax Commissioners* v. *Jackson*, 283 U.S. 527, 537, with *Mayflower Farms* v. *Ten Eyck* (decided February 10th), p. 4; *Zahn* v. *Board of Public Works*, 274 U.S. 325, with *Colgate* v. *Harvey*, p. 8; *Los Angeles Gas Co.* v. *Railroad Commission*, 289 U.S. 287, 304, 305, with the decision in *West* v. *Chesapeake & Potomac Telephone Co.*, 295 U.S. 662."
46. H.F.S. to Felix Frankfurter, Feb. 17, 1936.
47. Karl N. Llewellyn to H.F.S., May 27, 1936.
48. H.F.S. to Karl N. Llewellyn, May 28, 1936.
49. Cf. *Crowell* v. *Benson*, *Ashwander* v. *TVA*, *Schechter* v. *United States; St. Joseph Stock Yards Co.* v. *United States*, 298 U.S. 38 (1936); *Anniston Manufacturing Co.* v. *Davis*, 301 U.S. 337; see also *Carter* v. *Carter Coal Co.* (dissent); *Morehead* v. *Tipaldo* (dissent).
50. H.F.S. to Felix Frankfurter, Feb. 25, 1936.
51. H.F.S. to Felix Frankfurter, April 7, 1936.
52. *Jones* v. *Securities and Exchange Commission*, 298 U.S. 1 (1936), pp. 23, 33.
53. H.F.S. to Charles A. Beard, April 16, 1936.
54. *St. Louis Star-Times*, May 26, 1936, apropos *Ashton* v. *Cameron County Water District*, 298 U.S. 513 (1936).
55. *Morehead* v. *Tipaldo*, 298 U.S. 587, pp. 632, 633, 635, 636.
56. Charles Evans Hughes to H.F.S., May 26, 1936.
57. H.F.S. to Felix Frankfurter, June 3, 1936.
58. H.F.S. to Irving Brant, June 4, 1936.
59. See Edward S. Corwin, *Twilight of the Supreme Court*.
60. H.F.S. to Irving Brant, June 13, 1936. Brant's editorial appeared in the *St. Louis Star-Times*, June 10, 1936. For an explanation of certain misunderstandings as to Roberts' famous switch, see Felix Frankfurter, "Mr. Justice Roberts," *University of Pennsylvania Law Review*, Dec. 1955, pp. 314-16, and Erwin N. Griswold, "Owen J. Roberts as a Judge," *ibid.*, pp. 342-44.
61. *St. Louis Star-Times*, June 2, 1936.
62. *New York Times, Washington Post, Washington Daily News*, June 2, 1936.
63. "The Minimum Wage Decision," *America*, June 13, 1936, p. 217.
64. Quoted in *Congressional Record*, June 5, 1936, p. 9040.
65. *Ibid.*
66. *New York Times*, June 5, 1936.
67. H.F.S. to Sterling Carr, June 26, 1936.
68. H.F.S. to Edward Bruce, June 6, 1936.
69. H.F.S. to Louis D. Brandeis, June 20, 1936; Louis D. Brandeis to H.F.S., June 22, 1936.
70. Max Lerner, "The Fate of the Supreme Court," *The Nation*, March 25, 1936, p. 379.
71. H.F.S. to Felix Frankfurter, May 30, 1936, comment on *Ashton* v. *Cameron County Water District*.
72. H.F.S. to Felix Frankfurter, June 3, 1936.

## CHAPTER XXVII

1. H.F.S. to his sons, March 12, 1936.
2. H.F.S. to his sons, Jan. 24, 1936; to Felix Frankfurter, Jan. 17, 1936.
3. Felix Frankfurter to H.F.S., Jan. 20, 1936.
4. H.F.S. to Roscoe Pound, April 23, 1936.
5. H.F.S. to Roscoe Pound, June 1, 1936.
6. "Notes on the Common Law in American Public Law," prepared by Roscoe Pound for H.F.S. A more fertilizing influence on Stone's thinking was James M. Landis's article, "Statutes and the Sources of Law," in *Harvard Legal Essays* (Cambridge: Harvard University Press, 1934).
7. *United States* v. *Elgin, Joliet & Eastern Railway Co.*, 298 U.S. 492 (1936), pp. 504, 512.
8. H.F.S., "The Common Law in the United States," an address delivered at the Harvard Tercentenary celebration. Published under the title "The Common Law in the United States," *Harvard Law Review*, Nov. 1936. Unless otherwise noted, all quoted material in this chapter is from this article.
   Stone received an honorarium of $1000, but within a year made Harvard a gift of $750 in recognition of the three-hundredth anniversary of Harvard College.
9. *Arrow-Hart & Hegeman Electric Co.* v. *Federal Trade Commission*, 291 U.S. 587 (1934), pp. 600, 607.
10. Cf. *Prussian* v. *United States*, 282 U.S. 675 (1931) and *Leonard* v. *United States*, 279 U.S. 40 (1929).
11. O. W. Holmes, "The Path of the Law," *Collected Legal Papers*, p. 184.
12. Justice Roberts in Butler case, p. 62.
13. H.F.S. to Felix Frankfurter, May 18, 1936.
14. George Sutherland, "Principle or Expedient?" address before the annual meeting of the New York State Bar Association, Jan. 21, 1921, *Proceedings of the New York Bar Association*, Vol. 44, p. 271.
15. H.F.S. to Joseph Kise, April 4, 1938.
16. H.F.S. to Felix Frankfurter, Oct. 5, 1936.
17. "Justice Stone Warns the Courts," *St. Louis Star-Times*, Aug. 24, 1936.
18. H.F.S. to Cornelia Bryce Pinchot, Oct. 5, 1936.
19. "The Honorable Supreme Court," *Fortune*, May 1936, p. 83.

## CHAPTER XXVIII

1. "No Man's Land," *St. Louis Star-Times*, June 4, 1936.
2. Ickes, *op. cit.*, p. 274. See also Franklin D. Roosevelt, "The Three Hundred and Forty-fourth Press Conference, *The Public Papers and Addresses*, Vol. VI, p. 75.
3. *St. Louis Star-Times*, June 4, 1936.
4. *Congressional Record*, Vol. 80 (1936), p. 1616. See also Edward S. Corwin, "How Far Should the Power of the Supreme Court Extend?" *Philadelphia Record*, Jan. 12, 1936.
5. Marquis Childs, "The Supreme Court Today," *Harper's*, May 1938, p. 581.
6. *Congressional Record*, Vol. 80 (1936), p. 8636 (quoted from "Prometheus Bound," *Philadelphia Record* editorial, June 2, 1936) and pp. 9262-63, 9494, *passim*.
7. "The King Can Do No Wrong," *Philadelphia Record*, June 4, 1936; "Chiseling Is Constitutional," *Philadelphia Record*, June 3, 1936.
8. Quoted in Arthur E. Sutherland, "The Supreme Court and the General Will," *Proceedings of the American Academy of Arts and Sciences*, April 1953, p. 181.
9. Merrill E. Otis, "It Can Be Done," American Liberty League Document No. 115, Sept. 1936.
10. Senator Elmer A. Benson in *Congressional Record*, Vol. 80 (1936), p. 9041.
11. *New York Times*, June 26, 1936.
12. Ickes, *op. cit.*, p. 602.
13. *Ibid.*, p. 705. See in this connection Thomas Reed Powell, "The Next Four Years: the Constitution," *New Republic*, Jan. 13, 1937.

14. See *New York Times*, Nov. 30, 1936, p. 4, and George Creel, "Roosevelt's Plans and Purposes," *Collier's*, Dec. 26, 1936.
15. H.F.S. to Dr. Joel T. Boone, Jan. 1, 1937; H.F.S. to Edmund A. Burnham, Feb. 1, 1937.
16. H.F.S. to John Bassett Moore, Jan. 3, 1937.
17. H.F.S. to Henry W. Anderson, Feb. 1, 1937.
18. H.F.S. to Felix Frankfurter, Feb. 17, Feb. 25, 1937.
19. Irving Brant to H.F.S., Feb. 2, 1937.
20. House Documents, 75th Cong., 1st Sess., Jan. 5-Aug. 21, 1937, pp. 3, 4, 5.
21. Franklin D. Roosevelt, "Message to Congress," Feb. 5, 1937, *The Public Papers and Addresses*, Vol. VI, p. 55.
22. *Ibid.*, p. 53.
23. H.F.S. to Edward L. Tinker, Oct. 31, 1934.
24. Howard Westwood to H.F.S., April 13, 1937.
25. Rexford G. Tugwell, *Battle for Democracy* (New York: Columbia University Press, 1935), p. 12.
26. "Arouse and Beware," *American Agriculturist*, Feb. 27, 1937, p. 1.
27. "Adroit," *Emporia* (Kans.) *Gazette*, Feb. 6, 1937; "The Lines of Defense," *New York Herald Tribune* editorial, Feb. 9, 1937, quoting the New York *World-Telegram*.
28. Quoted in "What Professor Fuchs Finds Wrong with Lawyer's Report," *St. Louis Star-Times*, Feb. 19, 1937. For the arguments of other educators, showing why amendment might not meet the crisis, see "Reorganization of the Federal Judiciary," *Hearings before the Senate Judiciary*, 75th Cong., 1st Sess., Part II, pp. 168-69, 231-32, 311.
29. Franklin D. Roosevelt, address at Democratic Dinner, March 4, 1937, *loc. cit.*, p. 116. See also pp. 123-24.
30. Franklin D. Roosevelt, Fireside Chat, March 9, 1937, *loc. cit.*, pp. 125-26.
31. H.F.S. to Irving Brant, Feb. 6, 1937.
32. H.F.S. to Irving Brant, July 19, 1936.
33. H.F.S. to Irving Brant, Feb. 26, 1937.
34. H.F.S. to Grosvenor H. Backus, March 3, 1937.
35. H.F.S. to Charles C. Burlingham, March 10, 1937.
36. From notes of Alfred Lief's interview with Justice Stone, March 21, 1937.
37. H.F.S. to Irving Brant, Feb. 18, 1937.
38. H.F.S. to Charles C. Burlingham, March 14, 1937.
39. H.F.S. to Grosvenor H. Backus, March 20, 1937.
40. H.F.S. to his sons, March 30, 1937.
41. H.F.S. to Young B. Smith, April 12, 1937.
42. H.F.S. to Charles C. Burlingham, March 10, 1937.
43. H.F.S. to Irving Brant, April 20, 1937.
44. H.F.S. to his sons, March 12, 1937.
45. *United States News*, Feb. 15, 1937; the H.F.S. address was "Fifty Years' Work of the United States Supreme Court."
46. H.F.S. to Helen Stone Willard, April 7, 1937.
47. Pearson and Allen, *Washington Post*, Feb. 17, 1937.
48. Erwin N. Griswold to H.F.S., March 11, 1937.
49. H.F.S. to Felix Frankfurter, March 10, 1937.
50. H.F.S. to Charles C. Burlingham, March 10, 1931.
51. Douglas W. Johnson to H.F.S., Feb. 28, 1937.
52. H.F.S. to Douglas W. Johnson, March 3, 1937.
53. Douglas W. Johnson to H.F.S., March 12, 1937.
54. H.F.S. to Douglas W. Johnson, March 15, 1937.
55. Douglas W. Johnson to H.F.S., March 12, 1937.
56. H.F.S. to Douglas W. Johnson, March 15, 1937.
57. Douglas W. Johnson to H.F.S., March 18, 31, 1937.
58. H.F.S. to Douglas W. Johnson, March 20, 1937.
59. Draft of letter from Douglas W. Johnson to Senator Burton K. Wheeler, March 31, 1937.
60. H.F.S. to Douglas W. Johnson, April 2, 1937.
61. H.F.S. to George Biddle, April 8, 1937.
62. A.T.M.'s interview with Senator Burton K. Wheeler, Feb. 25, 1944.
63. Ickes, *op. cit.*, Vol. II, pp. 66-67.
64. Pusey, *op. cit.*, Vol. II, p. 755.

65. For the full text of Hughes' letter, see "Reorganization of the Federal Judiciary," *loc. cit.*, Part III, pp. 488-92.
66. Pusey, *op. cit.*, Vol. II, p. 756.
67. Irving Brant to A.T.M., July 22, 1951.
68. Irving Brant to H.F.S., April 15, 1937; H.F.S. to Irving Brant, April 20, 1937. For Alfred Lief's account of his interview with Justice Stone, see his *Democracy's Norris*, pp. 499-500.
69. Irving Brant to H.F.S., Oct. 23, 1937; H.F.S. to Irving Brant, Oct. 29, 1937.
70. Memorandum from H.F.S. to Irving Brant on the Court's disposition of certioraris, March 4, 1937; Irving Brant to F.D.R., April 7, 1937; H.F.S. to Irving Brant, April 20, 1937; Irving Brant to Thomas G. Corcoran, April 22, 1937, relaying Stone's sentiments.
71. Turner Catledge, "The Honorable, The Chief Justice," *New York Times Magazine*, June 22, 1941, p. 20.
72. *Congressional Record*, Vol. 81 (1937), p. 1122. In a letter to A.T.M., Aug. 6, 1951, Celler acknowledged that Stone was the jurist to whom he referred.
73. H.F.S. to Sterling Carr, April 1, 1937.
74. Jackson, *op. cit.*, p. 208.
75. *West Coast Hotel* v. *Parrish*, 300 U.S. 391 (1937), pp. 397, 399-400 *passim*.
76. Howard Brubaker, "Of All Things," *The New Yorker*, April 10, 1937, p. 34.
77. *Wright* v. *Vinton Branch*, etc., 300 U.S. 440 (1937).
78. *Sonzinsky* v. *United States*, 300 U.S. 506 (1937), pp. 513-14.
79. *Virginian Railway Co.* v. *System Federation No. 40*, 300 U.S. 515 (1937), pp. 556, 558. For Stone's pungent statement of the industrial conflict involved, see footnote 7.
80. H.F.S. to his sons, April 1, 1937.
81. Schechter case, p. 548.
82. *NLRB* v. *Jones & Laughlin Steel Corp.*, 301 U.S. 1 (1937), pp. 41-42 *passim*.
83. *NLRB* v. *Freuhauf Trailer Co.*, 301 U.S. 49 (1937); *NLRB* v. *Friedman-Harry Marks Clothing Co.*, 301 U.S. 58 (1937).
84. See *United States* v. *United States Steel Corp.*, 251 U.S. 417 (1920), *United States* v. *Trenton Potteries*, 273 U.S. 392 (1927), *Loewe* v. *Lawlor*, 208 U.S. 274 (1908), *Coronado Coal Co.* v. *United Mine Workers*, 268 U.S. 295 (1925); *Industrial Association of San Francisco* v. *United States*, 268 U.S. 64 (1925), *Bedford Cut Stone Co.* v. *Journeymen Stone Cutters' Association*, 274 U.S. 37 (1926); *Board of Trade* v. *Olsen*, 262 U.S. 1 (1923); the Shreveport case, 234 U.S. 342 (1914).
85. "Liberalized by 27,000,000 Voters," *St. Louis Star-Times*, April 13, 1937.
86. *Carmichael* v. *Southern Coal & Coke Co.*, 301 U.S. 495 (1937), pp. 522, 525, 526.
87. *Steward Machine Co.* v. *Davis*, 301 U.S. 548 (1937), *Helvering* v. *Davis*, 301 U.S. 619 (1937).
88. Jackson, *op. cit.*, pp. 192-93.
89. Pusey, *op. cit.*, Vol. II, p. 761.
90. Ickes, *op. cit.*, Vol. II, p. 153.
91. H.F.S. to Felix Frankfurter, May 20, 1937.
92. H.F.S. to his sons, Feb. 13, 1941.
93. Irving Brant to Thomas G. Corcoran, June 12, 1937.
94. Franklin D. Roosevelt, *The Public Papers and Addresses*, Vol. VI, pp. lxvi, lxix.
95. Quoted in *Law and Politics*, Occasional Papers of Felix Frankfurter, edited by Archibald MacLeish and E. F. Prichard, Jr. (New York: Harcourt, Brace & Co., 1939), p. 15.
96. H.F.S. to Felix Frankfurter, June 5, 1937.

PART FIVE

## CHAPTER XXIX

1. *Ex parte Albert LéVitt*, 302 U.S. 633 (1937).
2. H.F.S. to Hugo L. Black, Aug. 18, 1937; Hugo L. Black to H.F.S., Aug. 27, 1937.
3. *McCart* v. *Indianapolis Water Co.*, 302 U.S. 419 (1938). For this dissent Walton Hamilton awarded Black the 1938 "grand prize for the jurist's art." See his "Mr. Justice Black's First Year," *New Republic*, June 8, 1938.

4. H.F.S. to Charles Evans Hughes, Dec. 24, 1937.
5. H.F.S. to Charles Evans Hughes, Dec. 30, 1937.
6. *Connecticut General Life Insurance Co.* v. *Johnson*, 303 U.S. 77 (1938).
7. Cf. Marquis Childs, "The Supreme Court Today," *Harper's*, May 1938.
8. *Helvering* v. *Gerhardt*, 304 U.S. 405 (1938).
9. Max Lerner, "Minority Rule and the Constitutional Tradition," *University of Pennsylvania Law Review*, March 1938.
10. H.F.S. to Max Lerner, April 4, 1938.
11. Max Lerner to H.F.S., April 14, 1938.
12. H.F.S. to John Bassett Moore, Sept. 8, 1937.
13. Childs, *op. cit.*, p. 585.
14. Memorandum from Lauson H. Stone to A.T.M., 1950.
15. H.F.S. to Felix Frankfurter, Jan. 20, 1938.
16. *Ibid.*
17. A.T.M.'s interview with Marquis Childs, April 22, 1952.
18. Marquis Childs, "Minority of One," *Saturday Evening Post*, Sept. 20, 1941, p. 45.
19. See Paul Y. Anderson, "Marquis Childs and Justice Black," *The Nation*, May 21, 1938, p. 579.
20. John O'Donnell and Doris Fleeson, "Stone Denies Hand in Black Attack," *New York Daily News*, May 12, 1938.
21. *Newsweek*, May 23, 1938, p. 26.
22. Anderson, *op. cit.*, p. 579.
23. John P. Frank, *Mr. Justice Black: The Man and His Opinions* (New York: Alfred A. Knopf, 1949), p. 138; and Charlotte Williams, *Hugo L. Black, a Study in the Judicial Process* (Baltimore: Johns Hopkins University Press, 1950), p. 82.
24. "Honor among Judges," *The Nation*, May 21, 1938.
25. Walton Hamilton, "Mr. Justice Black's First Year," *New Republic*, June 8, 1938, p. 121.
26. Quoted in *Newsweek*, May 23, 1938, p. 26.
27. H.F.S., "The Common Law in the United States," *Harvard Law Review*, Nov. 1936, p. 23.
28. Childs, "Minority of One," *loc. cit.*
29. "Honor among Judges," *loc. cit.*
30. Anderson, *op. cit.*, p. 579.
31. H.F.S. to Arthur Krock, May 2, 1938. Krock responded with daily columns on the case in the *New York Times*, May 3, May 4, 1938.
32. *Swift* v. *Tyson*, 16 Peters 1 (1842), pp. 18-19.
33. Hamilton, *op. cit.*, p. 119.
34. Merlo J. Pusey, *Charles Evans Hughes*, Vol. II, p. 710.
35. H.F.S. to Louis D. Brandeis, March 23, 1938.
36. *Erie Railroad Co.* v. *Tompkins*, 304 U.S. 64 (1938), p. 91. Hereafter cited as Tompkins case.
37. Italics the author's. This statement has been severely criticized in law reviews as dictum without basis in history or precedent. See, among others: W. W. Cook, *Logical and Legal Bases of the Conflict of Laws* (1942), pp. 138-43; Lehan K. Tunks, "Categorization and Federalism: 'Substance' and 'Procedure' after *Erie Railroad* v. *Tompkins*," *Illinois Law Review*, Nov. 1939, pp. 293-95; Charles T. McCormick and Elvin Hale Hewins, "The Collapse of 'General' Law in the Federal Courts," *Illinois Law Review*, June 1938, pp. 134-36; Harry Shulman, "The Demise of *Swift* v. *Tyson*," *Yale Law Journal*, June 1938, p. 1336; Albert J. Schweppe, "What Has Happened to Federal Jurisprudence?" *American Bar Association Journal*, June 1938, p. 421.
38. H.F.S. to Louis D. Brandeis, March 25, 1938. The Holmes passage may be found in *Black & White Taxicab and Transfer Co.* v. *Brown & Yellow Taxicab and Transfer Co.*, 276 U.S. 518 (1928), p. 535.
39. Tompkins case, p. 78.
40. *Ibid.*, p. 91.
41. H.F.S. to Felix Frankfurter, April 29, 1938.
42. *NLRB* v. *Pennsylvania Greyhound Lines*, 303 U.S. 261 (1938); *NLRB* v. *Pacific Greyhound Lines*, 303 U.S. 272 (1938). Cardozo and Reed did not participate.
43. Irving Brant to Franklin D. Roosevelt, Dec. 28, 1938.

44. Harold L. Ickes, *The Secret Diary* . . . , Vol. II, pp. 551-52.
45. H.F.S. to Sterling Carr, Jan. 14, 1939.
46. H.F.S. to Felix Frankfurter, April 13, 1939.
47. Felix Frankfurter to H.F.S., April 14, 1939.
48. *NLRB* v. *Fainblatt*, 306 U.S. 601 (1939), p. 610.
49. *NLRB* v. *Fansteel Metallurgical Co.*, 306 U.S. 240 (1939), p. 265.
50. Henry M. Hart, Jr., and Edward F. Prichard, Jr., "The Fansteel Case: Employee Misconduct and the Remedial Powers of the National Labor Relations Board," *Harvard Law Review*, June 1939, p. 1317.
51. Quoted in Walter Gellhorn and Seymour L. Linfield, "Politics and Labor Relations, An Appraisal of Criticisms of NLRB Procedure," *Columbia Law Review*, March 1939, p. 340.
52. *NLRB* v. *Columbian Enameling & Stamping Co.*, 306 U.S. 292 (1939), p. 297.
53. H.F.S. to Felix Frankfurter, Feb. 16, 1939.
54. H.F.S. to Charles C. Burlingham, March 10, 1939.
55. *National Licorice Co.* v. *NLRB*, 309 U.S. 350 (1940), p. 364.
56. William O. Douglas to H.F.S., Feb. 20, 1940.
57. H.F.S. to William O. Douglas, Feb. 21, 1940.
58. *H. J. Heinz Co.* v. *NLRB*, 311 U.S. 514 (1941), pp. 520-21; cf. Justice Douglas in *International Association, etc.* v. *NLRB*, 311 U.S. 72 (1940), pp. 80-81.
59. *NLRB* v. *Express Publishing Co.*, 312 U.S. 426 (1941).
60. *Pittsburgh Plate Glass Co.* v. *NLRB*, 313 U.S. 146 (1941), p. 166.
61. *Phelps Dodge Corp.* v. *NLRB*, 313 U.S. 177 (1941), pp. 188, 210-11, 212.
62. Gellhorn and Linfield, *op. cit.*, pp. 340-41.
63. Pittsburgh Plate Glass case, pp. 176, 177.
64. H.F.S. to his sons, April 17, 1941.
65. Memorandum from Allison Dunham to A.T.M., Oct. 2, 1956.
66. H.F.S. to his sons, Feb. 13, 1941.
67. Luther Ely Smith, "Judicial Number," *Amherst News*, Dec. 26, 1942.

## CHAPTER XXX

1. H.F.S. to his sons, Feb. 25, 1933, March 21, 1929, Dec. 20, 1934.
2. H.F.S. to Felix Frankfurter, Feb. 4, 1935.
3. H.F.S. to his sons, Oct. 28, Nov. 4, 1937.
4. H.F.S. to his sons, Feb. 10, 1938. As examples of the Chief's new-found generosity Stone cited *Connecticut Life Insurance Co.* v. *Johnson; South Carolina State Highway Department* v. *Barnwell Bros.;* and *Adam* v. *Saenger.*
5. Louis Lusky to H.F.S., Nov. 11, 1938.
6. H.F.S. to Charles C. Burlingham, June 6, 1939.
7. H.F.S., "Fifty Years' Work of the Supreme Court," *American Bar Association Journal*, Aug.-Sept. 1928, p. 430.
8. *Di Santo* v. *Pennsylvania*, 273 U.S. 34 (1927), p. 44.
9. *South Carolina State Highway Department* v. *Barnwell Bros.*, 303 U.S. 177 (1938), pp. 187, 190-92. Hereafter cited as Barnwell case.
10. *Ibid.*, pp. 185-86, 189.
11. *Ibid.*, p. 185 note.
12. Noel T. Dowling, "Interstate Commerce and State Power," *Virginia Law Review*, Nov. 1940, p. 15.
13. *Western Live Stock* v. *Bureau of Revenue*, 303 U.S. 250 (1938), pp. 255-56, 258, 259.
14. Dissenting in *Adams Manufacturing Co.* v. *Storen*, 304 U.S. 307 (1938), p. 328.
15. *Gwin, White & Prince* v. *Henneford*, 305 U.S. 434 (1939), p. 441.
16. *McGoldrick* v. *Berwin-White Coal Mining Co.*, 309 U.S. 33 (1940), pp. 45, note 2, 48.
17. H.F.S. to Noel T. Dowling, Nov. 26, 1940, written apropos of Dowling's article in the *Virginia Law Review*, Nov. 1940.
18. An earlier case seeking an injunction in the Apex Hosiery strike had been dismissed in the Supreme Court as "moot"—*Leader* v. *Apex Hosiery Co.*, 302 U.S. 656 (1937).
19. *Apex Hosiery Co.* v. *Leader*, 310 U.S. 469 (1940), pp. 482, 484, 489. See A. T. Mason, Review of Edward Berman's *Labor and the Sherman Act*, *American Political Science Review*, May 1931, p. 461.

20. Apex case, pp. 488, 493, 495, 502.
21. *Ibid.*, p. 503 and note 24.
22. *Ibid.*, pp. 501, 507, note 25, 512.
23. William O. Douglas to H.F.S., May 9, 1940.
24. Apex case, pp. 507-508.
25. H.F.S. to Hugo L. Black, May 14, 1940.
26. William O. Douglas to H.F.S., May 9, 1940, and note on back of draft sent Douglas.
27. Hugo L. Black to H.F.S., May 13, 1940.
28. David Lawrence, "Chat Leaves Aftertaste of Politics," *Washington Star,* May 28, 1940.
29. "A Strange Doctrine," *Washington Star,* May 28, 1940.
30. H.F.S. to Milton Handler, June 3, 1940.
31. I. F. Stone, "The Apex Indecision," *The Nation,* June 8, 1940, p. 705; Louis Lusky, "Labor under the Apex Decision," *International Juridical Association Monthly Bulletin,* June 1940, p. 133.
32. *New York Times,* May 28, May 29, 1940.
33. Lehan Tunks, "A New Federal Charter for Trade Unionism," *Columbia Law Review,* June 1941, pp. 1013-14.
34. Charles O. Gregory, *Labor and the Law* (New York: Norton, 1946), p. 265. In his book Gregory includes a long critical account of the Apex opinion "to acquaint readers with the sort of thing our Supreme Court does when it tries to keep its output politically and socially up to date and at the same time consistent."
35. Lusky, *op. cit.,* p. 134.
36. Louis Lusky to A.T.M., May 25, 1955.
37. H.F.S. to James M. Landis, April 11, 1941.
38. Felix Frankfurter to H.F.S., Jan. 23, 1941.
39. *United States* v. *Hutcheson,* 312 U.S. 219 (1941), pp. 234-35. Hereafter cited as Hutcheson case.
40. H.F.S. to Felix Frankfurter, Jan. 21, 1941.
41. *New Republic,* April 15, 1940, pp. 494, 496.
42. Felix Frankfurter to H.F.S., Jan. 21, 1941.
43. H.F.S. to Felix Frankfurter, Jan. 21, 1941.
44. H.F.S. to Felix Frankfurter, Jan. 22, 1941.
45. Hutcheson case, pp. 241, 242, 243.
46. See, for example, Charles O. Gregory, "The New Sherman-Clayton-Norris-La Guardia Act," *University of Chicago Law Review,* April 1941; Roscoe Steffen, "Labor Activities in Restraint of Trade: The Hutcheson Case," *Illinois Law Review,* May 1941; "Pleasing to Racketeers," *Washington Post,* Feb. 6, 1941; "It's Plainly up to Congress," *Philadelphia Inquirer,* Feb. 5, 1941; but cf. I. F. Stone, "Belated Magna Carta," *The Nation,* Feb. 15, 1941.
47. H.F.S. to James M. Landis, April 11, 1941.
48. Hutcheson case, p. 246.
49. In 1934 the Court, following the 1905 decision in *South Carolina* v. *United States,* 199 U.S. 437, had upheld federal taxes on state-conducted liquor business: *Ohio* v. *Helvering,* 292 U.S. 360; *Helvering* v. *Powers,* 293 U.S. 214.
50. H.F.S. to Irving Brant, May 1, 1937.
51. See *United States* v. *California,* 297 U.S. 175 (1936).
52. H.F.S. to Irving Brant, May 1, 1937.
53. Irving Brant to A.T.M., July 22, 1951.
54. *James* v. *Dravo Contracting Co.,* 302 U.S. 134 (1937), p. 156.
55. See *Helvering* v. *Mountain Producers Corp.,* 303 U.S. 376 (1938), p. 387.
56. H.F.S. to Felix Frankfurter, Dec. 8, 1937.
57. *Ibid.* The case was *Brush* v. *Commissioner of Internal Revenue,* 300 U.S. 352 (1937). Stone refused to dissent with Roberts and Brandeis because he felt that the Government could not, in good faith, assert the right to tax a state employee's salary in the face of a Treasury regulation to the contrary.
58. Louis Lusky to A.T.M., Sept. 12, 1952.
59. H.F.S. to Felix Frankfurter, June 7, 1938.
60. *Helvering* v. *Gerhardt,* 304 U.S. 405 (1938), p. 411. Hereafter cited as Gerhardt case.
61. *Ibid.*, p. 412.
62. *Ibid.*, pp. 420, 421.

63. H.F.S. to Hugo L. Black, May 20, 1938.
64. H.F.S. to Hugo L. Black, May 18, 1938.
65. Hugo L. Black to H.F.S., May 18, 1938.
66. H.F.S. to Felix Frankfurter, June 7, 1938.
67. H.F.S. to Dudley O. McGovney, March 13, 1939.
68. *Allen* v. *Regents*, 304 U.S. 439 (1938).
69. Quoted in Felix Frankfurter to H.F.S., March 17, 1939.
70. See Robert H. Jackson, *The Struggle for Judicial Supremacy*, p. 243.
71. *Graves* v. *New York ex rel. O'Keefe*, 306 U.S. 466 (1939), pp. 480-81.
72. *Ibid.*, pp. 480, 484 note 4, 486, 487.
73. H.F.S. to Felix Frankfurter, March 23, 1939.
74. Walter Gellhorn to H.F.S., April 2, 1939.
75. H.F.S. to Walter Gellhorn, April 6, 1939.

## CHAPTER XXXI

1. Louis Lusky, "Minority Rights and the Public Interest," *Yale Law Journal,* Dec. 1942, p. 11. See also Walton Hamilton and George D. Braden, "The Special Competence of the Supreme Court," *Yale Law Journal,* June 1941, pp. 1349-57.
2. Paul A. Freund, *On Understanding the Constitution* (Boston: Little, Brown & Co., 1949).
3. Learned Hand, "Chief Justice Stone's Conception of the Judicial Function," *Columbia Law Review,* Sept. 1946, p. 698.
4. *Ibid.*
5. *Palko* v. *Connecticut,* 302 U.S. 319 (1937), p. 325. Hereafter cited as Palko case.
6. Herbert Wechsler, "Stone and the Constitution," *Columbia Law Review,* Sept. 1946, p. 793.
7. *Dennis* v. *United States,* 341 U.S. 494 (1951), p. 526.
8. *United States* v. *Carolene Products Co.,* 304 U.S. 144 (1938), pp. 152-54, note 4.
9. Louis Lusky to A.T.M., July 28, 1952.
10. Charles Evans Hughes to H.F.S., April 19, 1938.
11. H.F.S. to Charles Evans Hughes, April 19, 1938.
12. H.F.S. to Irving Lehman, April 26, 1938.
13. See Stone's significant footnote in the Barnwell case, pp. 184-85, note 2, and the Gerhardt case, p. 416. For an exposition of the underlying theory of the footnote, see the articles by Lusky and Braden cited in notes 1 and 14.
14. George D. Braden, "The Search for Objectivity in Constitutional Law," *Yale Law Journal,* Feb. 1948, pp. 580-81.
15. For Brandeis, see especially his concurrence in *Whitney* v. *California,* 274 U.S. 357 (1927), pp. 375-77; hereafter cited as the Whitney case. For Hughes, see *Stromberg* v. *California,* 283 U.S. 359 (1931), and *Near* v. *Minnesota,* 283 U.S. 697 (1931).
16. H.F.S. to Clinton L. Rossiter, April 12, 1941.
17. Palko case, pp. 325-27 *passim.*
18. H.F.S. to Raymond L. Wise, June 1, 1939.
19. *Hague* v. *CIO,* 307 U.S. 496 (1939), pp. 502, 519.
20. Slaughter-House cases, 83 U.S. (16 Wall.) 36 (1873). Writing an Amherst classmate, Wallace Keep, Oct. 7, 1939, Stone said: "I regard Samuel Miller as one of the great judges who ever sat on our Court. His influence on the decisions of the Court is still powerful."
21. H.F.S. to Irving Brant, Aug. 11, 1939.
22. Walter Gellhorn to Gertrude Jenkins Regis, Jan. 21, 1947.
23. H.F.S. to his sons, Dec. 24, 1935.
24. H.F.S. to Young B. Smith, Oct. 5, 1940.
25. *Gitlow* v. *New York,* 268 U.S. 652 (1925).
26. H.F.S. to Clinton L. Rossiter, April 12, 1941. That it was an "oversight" appears fully from an examination of the reports of the 1924 Term. The Reporter failed consistently to note cases in which Stone did not participate.
27. Whitney case, pp. 372, 375-78.
28. H.F.S. to Clinton L. Rossiter, April 12, 1941.

29. *United States* v. *Schwimmer*, 279 U.S. 644 (1929), p. 652 and *passim*.
30. H.F.S. to Pierce Butler, May 23, 1929.
31. Robert L. Hale to H.F.S., June 1, 1929; H.F.S. to Robert L. Hale, June 3, 1929.
32. Henry B. Hazard, "Supreme Court Holds Madame Schwimmer, Pacifist, Ineligible to Naturalization," *American Journal of International Law*, July 1929, p. 629; *New York Times* quoted in "Madame Schwimmer—'Without a Country,'" *Literary Digest*, June 8, 1929, p. 9; "Treason to Conscience," *The Nation*, June 12, 1929, p. 689.
33. H.F.S. to John Bassett Moore, Oct. 9, 1930.
34. John Bassett Moore to H.F.S., Oct. 18, 1930.
35. Unpublished slip opinion prepared by H.F.S. as a dissent in *United States* v. *Macintosh*, 283 U.S. 605 (1931).
36. H.F.S. to John Bassett Moore, May 27, 1931.
37. H.F.S., "The Conscientious Objector," *Columbia University Quarterly*, Oct. 1919, p. 269.
38. William O. Douglas, *An Almanac of Liberty* (New York: Doubleday & Co., 1954), p. 352.
39. *United States* v. *Bland*, 283 U.S. 636 (1931), p. 637.
40. *Hamilton* v. *Regents of the University of California*, 293 U.S. 245 (1934).
41. Pierce Butler to H.F.S., Nov. 30, 1934.
42. Benjamin N. Cardozo to H.F.S., Nov. 30, 1934.
43. See *Girouard* v. *United States*, 328 U.S. 61 (1946), p. 72, note 1.
44. Louis Lusky to A.T.M., May 25, 1955.
45. H.F.S. to Clinton L. Rossiter, April 12, 1941.
46. *Minersville School District* v. *Gobitis*, 310 U.S. 586 (1940), p. 595. Hereafter cited as Gobitis case.
47. H.F.S., "The Conscientious Objector," loc. cit., p. 270.
48. The case was *Cantwell* v. *Connecticut*, 310 U.S. 296 (1940).
49. H.F.S. to John Bassett Moore, May 22, 1940.
50. The earlier cases suffering a similar fate were *Hering* v. (N.J.) *State Board of Education*, 303 U.S. 624 (1938), and *Leoles* v. *Landers*, 302 U.S. 656 (1937).
51. Felix Frankfurter to H.F.S., May 27, 1940, reprinted in full in A. T. Mason, *Security through Freedom* (Ithaca: Cornell University Press, 1955), pp. 217-20.
52. For this pencil-written undated note I am indebted to Justice Frankfurter.
53. Gobitis case, pp. 597-98, 599, 600.
54. Allison Dunham to A.T.M., Oct. 2, 1950, June 26, 1952.
55. All quoted material through p. 531 is from the Gobitis case unless otherwise noted. See pp. 600-607 *passim*.
56. Allan Barth, *The Loyalty of Free Men* (New York: The Viking Press, 1951), p. 238.
57. Louis Lusky to H.F.S., Aug. 16, 1940.
58. Frank Grinnell to the Editor, *Boston Herald*, June 5, 1940.
59. John Haynes Holmes to H.F.S., June 14, 1940.
60. *St. Louis Post-Dispatch*, June 4, 1940; *Miami Herald*, June 5, 1940. For other editorials unfavorable to the majority opinion, see *Baltimore Sun*, *Norfolk Virginian-Pilot*, *San Francisco Chronicle*, June 4, 1940; *Christian Science Monitor*, *Columbia* (S.C.) *Record*, June 5, 1940; *New York Evening Post*, June 6, 1940. For comments in legal periodicals, see list in Note, *Yale Law Journal*, Dec. 1942, p. 175.
61. H.F.S. to Norman Meyer, Oct. 13, 1940.
62. *Boston Herald*, June 5, 1940.
63. Paul L. Blakely, "Omnipotent Schoolboards," *America*, June 22, 1940, p. 286.
64. Harold J. Laski to H.F.S., July 10, 1940.
65. "Frankfurter *v.* Stone," *New Republic*, June 24, 1940.
66. John Bassett Moore to H.F.S., July 19, 1940.
67. Leon Green to H.F.S., July 2, 1940.
68. Henry Edgerton to H.F.S., June 4, 1940; H.F.S. to Henry Edgerton, June 5, 1940.
69. H.F.S. to Francis X. Downey, June 5, 1940.
70. Italian American War Veterans of the United States, East Boston Post No. 6, to H.F.S., June 7, 1940.

71. The Reverend R. E. McDonald to H.F.S., Feb. 26, 1943.
72. Victor Rotnem and Fred G. Folsom, Jr., "Recent Restrictions upon Religious Liberty," *American Political Science Review*, Dec. 1942.
73. Robert K. Carr, *Federal Protection of Civil Rights* (Ithaca: Cornell University Press, 1947), p. 16.
74. See Justice Jackson's remarks, *West Virginia State Board of Education* v. *Barnette*, 319 U.S. 624 (1943), especially p. 626.
75. *State* v. *Lefebvre*, 91 N.H. 382, 20 A. 2d 185 (1941).
76. Samuel Hendel, "Chief Justice Stone and Judicial Review," *Lawyers Guild Review*, Oct. 1946, p. 530.
77. Hand, *op. cit.*, p. 698.
78. H.F.S. to Clinton L. Rossiter, April 12, 1941.
79. From Stone's draft of an undelivered opinion dissenting in *Martin* v. *City of Struthers*, 319 U.S. 141 (1943). This opinion later became, in substance, Justice Black's opinion for the majority.
80. H.F.S. to Wiley B. Rutledge, Jan. 23, 1944, apropos *Prince* v. *Massachusetts*, 321 U.S. 158 (1944). For recent developments on "preferred freedoms," see my article, *Yale Law Journal*, April 1956, pp. 627-28.

## CHAPTER XXXII

1. H.F.S. to R. C. Rathbone, Oct. 27, 1929.
2. H.F.S. to his sons, March 2, 1929.
3. H.F.S. to Marshall Stone, Nov. 2, 1934. Professor Edwin W. Kemmerer, a Princeton economist, flourished in the 1920s as the "money doctor."
4. H.F.S. to his sons, Oct. 26, 1925.
5. Scott Hart, "Harlan Fiske Stone: Symbol of Justice," *Coronet*, June 1946, pp. 120-26.
6. H.F.S. to F. P. Keppel, May 11, 1938.
7. H.F.S. to G. H. Dorr, Oct. 13, 1937.
8. H.F.S. to Helen Stone Willard, April 7, 1937.
9. H.F.S. to his sons, Dec. 16, 1932.
10. Memoranda, Lauson H. Stone to A.T.M., Mrs. Harlan F. Stone to A.T.M., 1950.
11. H.F.S. to his sons, Feb. 26, 1926.
12. H.F.S. to his sons, Oct. 21, 1937.
13. H.F.S. to his sons, Dec. 2, 1932.
14. H.F.S. to his sons, May 26, 1930.
15. Opinion of Dean Haskins of the Harvard Graduate School, passed on to Stone by Julien J. Champenois, May 12, 1924.
16. H.F.S. to Marshall Stone, Jan. 2, 1925.
17. H.F.S. to Helen Stone Willard, Nov. 26, 1932.
18. H.F.S. to Marshall Stone, Nov. 7, 1932.
19. H.F.S. to his sons, Feb. 25, 1933.
20. H.F.S. to F. C. Hicks, March 31, 1936.
21. H.F.S. to Marshall Stone, Nov. 2, 1934.
22. H.F.S. to his sons, Dec. 21, 1932.
23. H.F.S. to his sons, Feb. 8, 1928, Nov. 8, 1927.
24. H.F.S. to Wilbur Cummings, Nov. 8, 1927.
25. H.F.S. to his sons, Nov. 8, 1927.
26. H.F.S. to Lauson H. Stone, June 5, 1927.
27. H.F.S. to Harold R. Medina, Jan. 14, 1936.
28. H.F.S. to his sons, March 21, 1940.
29. H.F.S. to his sons, April 25, 1940; to Lauson H. Stone, April 1, 1940; to Eugene Meyer, May 2, 1940; to Horace M. Kallen, June 4, 1941. See John Dewey and H. M. Kallen, *The Bertrand Russell Case* (New York: The Viking Press, 1941.)
30. H.F.S. to Marshall Stone, May 3, 1940.
31. H.F.S. to Irving Brant, Oct. 29, 1937.
32. H.F.S. to his sons, Nov. 18, 1937.
33. H.F.S. to R. B. Scandrett, Jr., June 4, 1940.
34. See James Reston, "The Education of a Statesman," *New York Times* Book Section, April 20, 1952.
35. H.F.S. to John Bassett Moore, Oct. 17, 1938.

36. H.F.S. to Felix Frankfurter, Oct. 10, 1938. Apparently the Vienna reference is to the violent demonstrations of Nazi mobs around the home of the Archbishop, Cardinal Innitzer (*New York Times,* Oct. 9, 1938). Hitler's speech at Saarbrucken proclaimed Germany's continuing need for vigilance against the "Jewish-Bolshevist enemy" and the international press, and announced extension of the fortifications of the West (*New York Times,* Oct. 10, 1938).
37. H.F.S. to John Bassett Moore, Dec. 23, 1938.
38. John Bassett Moore to H.F.S., March 27, 1939.
39. H.F.S. to John Bassett Moore, April 18, Aug. 27, 1939.
40. H.F.S. to John Bassett Moore, Oct. 24, 26, 1939; to Felix Frankfurter, Nov. 7, 1938.
41. H.F.S. to Felix Frankfurter, Nov. 27, 1940.
42. H.F.S. to John Bassett Moore, Oct. 24, 1939.

## CHAPTER XXXIII

1. H.F.S. to John Bassett Moore, Sept. 12, 1940.
2. H.F.S. to Lauson H. Stone, Feb. 29, 1940.
3. H.F.S. to his sons, Oct. 24, 1940.
4. H.F.S. to Sterling Carr, Nov. 11, 1940.
5. H.F.S. to his sons, Jan. 23, 1941; to Sterling Carr, Feb. 5, 1941.
6. H.F.S. to his sons, Nov. 7, 1940.
7. H.F.S. to Richard B. Scandrett, Jr., Feb. 28, 1941.
8. H.F.S. to John Bassett Moore, Aug. 28, 1938.
9. H.F.S. to his sons, Jan. 7, 1938.
10. Remarks to law students at Georgetown University, quoted in *Washington Post,* May 2, 1939.
11. H.F.S. to Charles C. Burlingham, May 27, 1941.
12. H.F.S. to W. C. Johnson, March 17, 1941.
13. H.F.S. to Howard Westwood, March 3, 1939.
14. Warner W. Gardner, "Mr. Chief Justice Stone," *Harvard Law Review,* Oct. 1946, p. 1208. See also C. Herman Pritchett, *The Roosevelt Court* (New York: The Macmillan Co., 1948), p. 69.
15. H.F.S. to Alfred Lief, June 6, 1939. A partial list includes:
    *Tyson & Bro.* v. *Banton,* 273 U.S. 418 (1927), and *Ribnik* v. *McBride,* 277 U.S. 350 (1928), supplanted by *Nebbia* v. *New York,* 291 U.S. 502 (1934), and *Olsen* v. *Nebraska,* 313 U.S. 236 (1941); *Morehead* v. *New York, ex rel. Tipaldo,* 298 U.S. 587 (1936), by *West Coast Hotel* v. *Parrish,* 300 U.S. 379 (1937); *Colgate* v. *Harvey,* 296 U.S. 404 (1935), by *Madden* v. *Kentucky,* 309 U.S. 83 (1940); *Burnet* v. *Coronado Gas & Oil Co.,* 285 U.S. 393 (1932), by *Helvering* v. *Mountain Producers Corp.,* 303 U.S. 376 (1938); *Macallen Co.* v. *Massachusetts,* 279 U.S. 620 (1929), by *Educational Films Corp.* v. *Ward,* 282 U.S. 379 (1931), and *Pacific Co. Ltd.* v. *Johnson,* 285 U.S. 480 (1932); *Indian Motorcycle Co.* v. *United States,* 283 U.S. 570 (1931), by *James* v. *Dravo Contracting* Co., 302 U.S. 134 (1937); *Di Santo* v. *Pennsylvania,* 273 U.S. 34 (1927), by *California* v. *Thompson,* 313 U.S. 109 (1941); *United States* v. *Butler,* 297 U.S. 1 (1936), by *Mulford* v. *Smith,* 307 U.S. 38 (1939), and *United States* v. *Darby,* 312 U.S. 100 (1941); *United States* v. *Chicago, Milwaukee & St. Paul Railway* Co., 282 U.S. 311 (1931), by *United States* v. *Lowden,* 308 U.S. 225 (1939); *West* v. *Chesapeake & Potomac Telephone Co.,* 295 U.S. 662 (1935), by *Railroad Commission* v. *Pacific Gas Co.,* 302 U.S. 388 (1938); *United States* v. *Belmont* (concurring), 301 U.S. 324 (1937), by *Guaranty Trust Co.* v. *United States,* 304 U.S. 126 (1938). The record is even more impressive if cases in the period after 1941 are cited: *Minersville School District* v. *Gobitis,* 310 U.S. 586 (1940), by *West Virginia State Board of Education* v. *Barnette,* 319 U.S. 624 (1943); *Jones* v. *City of Opelika,* 316 U.S. 584 (1942), by *Murdock* v. *Pennsylvania,* 319 U.S. 105 (1943). He also joined dissents that later became law in *Railroad Retirement Board* v. *Alton Railroad Co.,* 295 U.S. 330 (1935), overruled by *United States* v. *Lowden,* 308 U.S. 225 (1939); *Carter* v. *Carter Coal Co.,* 298 U.S. 238 (1936), by *NLRB.* v. *Jones & Laughlin Steel Corp.,* 301 U.S. 1 (1937); *Panhandle Oil Co.* v. *Knox,* 277 U.S. 218 (1928), by *Alabama* v. *King & Boozer,* 314 U.S. 1 (1941); and *United States* v. *Macintosh,* 283 U.S. 605 (1931), by *Girouard* v. *United States,* 328 U.S. 61 (1946). See in this con-

nection Frank J. Hogan's doleful article, "Important Shifts in Constitutional Doctrine," annual address by the President of the American Bar Association, *Annual Report of the American Bar Association*, July 10-14, 1939, pp. 478-500.

16. H.F.S. to John Bassett Moore, Feb. 22, 1941.

17. Felix Frankfurter, "The 'Administrative Side' of Chief Justice Hughes," *Harvard Law Review*, Nov. 1949, p. 4. The Butler case may be the exception that proves the rule.

18. Charles Evans Hughes to H.F.S., Jan. 27, 1941.

19. *NLRB* v. *Jones & Laughlin Steel Corp.*, 301 U.S. 1, pp. 30, 37 (1937). *Kentucky Whip & Collar Co.* v. *Illinois Central Railroad Co.*, 299 U.S. 334 (1937), hardly seems an exception, since Hughes attempted to fit the proscription of convict-made goods into the rationale of *Hammer* v. *Dagenhart*, which had approved the prohibition of interstate traffic in articles deemed to be harmful in themselves or in some sense morally stigmatized. See Kentucky Whip & Collar case, pp. 347, 350-51, *passim*.

20. *Gibbons* v. *Ogden*, 9 Wheat 1 (1824), pp. 196-97.

21. Memorandum from Noel T. Dowling to A.T.M., 1951.

22. *United States* v. *Darby*, 312 U.S. 100 (1941), p. 114. Hereafter cited as Darby case.

23. *Ibid.*, pp. 113-15.

24. Dowling memorandum.

25. See *Reid* v. *Colorado*, 187 U.S. 137 (1902); *Champion* v. *Ames*, 188 U.S. 321, (1903); *Hipolite Egg Co.* v. *United States*, 220 U.S. 45 (1911), *Seven Cases* v. *United States*, 239 U.S. 510 (1916); *Caminetti* v. *United States*, 242 U.S. 470 (1917); *Clark Distilling Co.* v. *Western Maryland Railway Co.*, 242 U.S. 311 (1917); *Brooks* v. *United States*, 267 U.S. 432 (1925); *Gooch* v. *United States*, 297 U.S. 124 (1936); *Kentucky Whip & Collar Co.* v. *Illinois Central Railroad Co.*, 299 U.S. 334 (1937).

26. Darby case, pp. 115-17 *passim*.

27. H.F.S. to Charles A. Beard, April 23, 1936.

28. Darby case, pp. 123-24.

29. *Ibid.*, pp. 125-26.

30. Hugo L. Black to H.F.S., Jan. 25, 1941.

31. "Child Labor Triumph," *New York Evening Post*, Feb. 4, 1941; "Wage-Hour Decisions," *St. Louis Star-Times*, Feb. 4, 1941; "An Historic Decision," *New York Times* (editorial), Feb. 5, 1941.

32. H.F.S. to his sons, Feb. 6, 1941.

33. "Federal Powers," *Washington Post*, Feb. 5, 1941; "Labor Gains in the Courts," *Wall Street Journal*, Feb. 5, 1941; "Constitutional Change," *Asheville* (N.C.) *Citizen*, Feb. 4, 1941.

34. H.F.S. to Milton Handler, Feb. 21, 1941.

35. H.F.S. to Sterling Carr, Feb. 26, 1940.

36. H.F.S. to Sterling Carr, March 26, 1941.

37. Walton Hamilton, "Mr. Justice Black's First Year," *New Republic*, June 8, 1938, p. 118.

38. H.F.S. to Robert H. Jackson, Jan. 25, 1941; the account was in Jackson's *The Struggle for Judicial Supremacy*. The earlier case was *Railroad Retirement Board* v. *Alton Railroad Co.*

39. H.F.S. to William O. Douglas, April 24, 1941.

40. H.F.S. to Robert H. Jackson, Jan. 25, 1941.

41. See Noel T. Dowling, "The Methods of Mr. Justice Stone in Constitutional Cases," *Columbia Law Review*, Nov. 1941; see also Kenneth Sears in *American Bar Association Journal*, Feb. 1942, p. 37.

42. H.F.S. to Noel T. Dowling, Nov. 25, 1941.

43. Felix Frankfurter to Mrs. Harlan F. Stone, March 2, 1940.

44. Raymond P. Brandt, *St. Louis Post-Dispatch*, May 11, 1941.

45. H.F.S. to Alfred Lief, June 6, 1939, Feb. 13, March 7, May 1, 1940; Alfred Lief to H.F.S., Jan. 23, March 11, April 29, 1940. The book was published by Howell Soskin & Co., New York, 1940.

46. Walton Hamilton, Book Review, *Columbia Law Review*, Nov. 1941, pp. 955, 960-61 *passim*, 965.

47. H.F.S. to Walter Gellhorn, May 27, 1941.

48. *United States* v. *Morgan*, 307 U.S. 183 (1939), pp. 190-91.

49. Robert H. Jackson, address before the Public Utilities Section of the American

Bar Association, San Francisco, July 10, 1939, published in *The Legal Intelligencer*, July 25, 1939, p. 6.
50. Maury Maverick, *In Blood and Ink* (New York: Modern Age, 1939), p. 141.
51. "Possible Cabinet Changes," *Watertown* (N.Y.) *Times*, Nov. 7, 1940.
52. H.F.S. to John Bassett Moore, Feb. 22, 1941.

### PART SIX

## CHAPTER XXXIV

1. H.F.S. to his sons, June 4, 1941.
2. Irving Brant to A.T.M., July 22, 1951.
3. *Washington Post*, March 20, 1937. See also Morris L. Ernst, *The Ultimate Power* (New York: Doubleday, Doran & Co., 1937), p. 304.
4. Ernest K. Lindley, *Washington Post*, June 8, 1941.
5. Louis Lusky to H.F.S., June 13, 1941.
6. H.F.S. to John Bassett Moore, June 2, 1941.
7. Marquis W. Childs, "A Minority of One," *Saturday Evening Post*, Sept. 20, 1941, p. 45.
8. Frank R. Kent, "The Great Game of Politics," *Baltimore Sun*, June 6, 1941.
9. *St. Louis Post-Dispatch*, June 6, 1941.
10. H.F.S. to Luther Ely Smith, May 24, 1941.
11. Merlo J. Pusey, *Charles Evans Hughes*, Vol. II, pp. 787, 788.
12. Felix Frankfurter, memorandum on H.F.S. and the Chief Justiceship, written from notes made immediately after seeing the President.
13. A.T.M.'s interview with Robert H. Jackson, May 15, 1950.
14. H.F.S. to Sterling Carr, June 5, 1941.
15. Irving Brant to H.F.S., Dec. 11, 1941.
16. H.F.S. to Herbert Satterlee, June 5, 1941; to Sterling Carr, June 5, 1941.
17. Kent, *loc. cit.*
18. H.F.S. to his sons, Oct. 12, 1941.
19. *Ibid.*
20. S. J. Woolf, *Minneapolis Tribune*, June 17, 1941.
21. Archibald MacLeish to H.F.S., July 7, 1941; Morris R. Cohen to H.F.S., Oct. 5, 1941.
22. "High Court Nominations," *Springfield Republican*, June 13, 1941; *St. Louis Post-Dispatch*, June 13, 1941; "Harlan Fiske Stone," *Rocky Mountain News* (Denver), June 14, 1941.
23. *Time*, June 23, 1941, p. 15.
24. D. Stuart August to H.F.S., June 16, 1941.
25. Louis Lusky to H.F.S., June 13, 1941.
26. *American Bar Association Journal*, Aug. 1941, editorial, p. 494; "Chief Justice Harlan F. Stone," p. 469.
27. Louis D. Brandeis to H.F.S., June 13, 1941.
28. Alpheus Thomas Mason, *Brandeis: A Free Man's Life* (New York: The Viking Press, 1946), p. 635.
29. George Sutherland to H.F.S., June 20, 1941.
30. Frank Murphy to H.F.S., June 15, 1941.
31. Learned Hand to H.F.S., June 19, 1941; "Harlan F. Stone, Chief Justice of the United States," *Federal Probation*, July-Sept. 1941, pp. 31, 33.
32. To H.F.S. from E. C. Folkes, June 13, 1941; from Ella Braubart, June 18, 1941; from Margaret L. Lewisohn, June 13, 1941; from Beatrice Berle, undated; from Nicholas Murray Butler, June 14, 1941.
33. H.F.S. to Charles Evans Hughes, June 13, 1941.
34. H.F.S. to Alvin Ziegler, Oct. 22, 1941.
35. Radiogram from Herbert Cunliffe, June 12, 1941; H.F.S. to Luther Ely Smith.
36. Jessamine Dixon Walcott to H.F.S., June 20, 1941.
37. Erwin N. Griswold to H.F.S., June 14, 1941.
38. Robert H. Jackson, "The Judicial Career of Chief Justice Hughes," *American Bar Association Journal*, July 1941, pp. 408-409.
39. Augustus N. Hand to H.F.S., July 2, 1941.
40. *Congressional Record*, June 27, 1941, pp. 5618, 5619.
41. H.F.S. to Sterling Carr, April 4, 1943.

## CHAPTER XXXV

1. H.F.S., "The Chief Justice," *American Bar Association Journal*, July 1941, pp. 407-408. This article, though prepared before Stone's appointment, was published thereafter.
2. Marquis Childs, "A Minority of One," *loc. cit.*, pp. 14, 15.
3. "The New Supreme Court," *New York Herald Tribune* (editorial), June 13, 1941.
4. H.F.S. to his sons, Oct. 12, 1941; to Felix Frankfurter, Oct. 12, 1941.
5. H.F.S. to Robert H. Jackson and James F. Byrnes, Nov. 1, 1941.
6. Memorandum of Justice Byrnes, Nov. 17, 1941.
7. *Edwards* v. *California*, 314 U.S. 160 (1941), p. 181. Hereafter cited as Edwards case.
8. *Ibid.*, p. 182.
9. Byrnes memorandum.
10. Edwards case, p. 174.
11. H.F.S. to Sterling Carr, Nov. 25, 1941.
12. *Newsweek*, Dec. 8, 1941, p. 23. See also C. Herman Pritchett, *The Roosevelt Court*, Table VIII, p. 39.
13. *Wall Street Journal*, Nov. 25, 1941.
14. H.F.S. to John Vance Hewitt, Nov. 25, 1941.
15. H.F.S. to Herbert Hoover, April 15, 1942.
16. H.F.S. to his sons, Jan. 23, 1942.
17. H.F.S. to Owen J. Roberts, Jan. 27, 1942.
18. *Alabama* v. *King & Boozer*, 314 U.S. 1 (1941), p. 9, overruling the Panhandle case (1928), and *Graves* v. *Texas Co.*, 298 U.S. 393 (1936). See also *Curry* v. *United States*, 314 U.S. 14 (1941), upholding Alabama's use tax applied under similar circumstances.
19. *Arkansas* v. *Duckworth*, 314 U.S. 390 (1941), pp. 394, 396, 402.
20. *St. Louis Post-Dispatch*, Feb. 25, 1942.
21. *Bridges* v. *California*, 314 U.S. 252 (1941), p. 279.
22. See Pritchett, *op. cit.*, p. 25.
23. *Cloverleaf Butter Co.* v. *Patterson*, 315 U.S. 148 (1941), p. 170; *United States* v. *Pink*, 315 U.S. 203 (1941), p. 242.
24. *Olmstead* v. *United States*, 277 U.S. 438 (1928); *Goldstein* v. *United States*, 316 U.S. 129 (1941).
25. Jackson: *New York, Chicago & St. Louis Railway Co.* v. *Frank*, 314 U.S. 360 (1941). Reed: Cloverleaf case. Roberts: Goldman case. Douglas: Pink case. Byrnes: *Puerto Rico* v. *Hermanos*, 315 U.S. 637 (1941). Black: *Helvering* v. *Safe Deposit & Trust Co.*, 316 U.S. 56 (1942). Frankfurter: *Brillhart* v. *Excess Insurance Co.*, 316 U.S. 491.
26. *United States* v. *Local 807, I.B.T.*, 315 U.S. 521 (1942), p. 539.
27. *Ibid.*, pp. 531, 535, 536.
28. *Ibid.*, pp. 540-41.
29. H.F.S. to his sons, March 5, 1942.
30. *Thornhill* v. *Alabama*, 310 U.S. 88 (1940); *AFL* v. *Swing*, 312 U.S. 321 (1941).
31. *Milk Wagon Drivers Union* v. *Meadowmoor Dairies*, 312 U.S. 287 (1941).
32. *Bakery & Pastry Drivers* v. *Wohl*, 315 U.S. 769 (1942); *Carpenters & Joiners Union* v. *Ritters Cafe*, 315 U.S. 722 (1942).
33. *Grand Rapids* (Mich.) *Herald*, March 12, 1942.
34. May Craig, "On the Inside in Washington," *Portland* (Me.) *Press-Herald*, March 14, 1942; *Washington Post*, March 7, 1942.
35. Merlo J. Pusey, "The Roosevelt Supreme Court," *The American Mercury*, May 1944, p. 603.
36. "The Sacred Unions," *Salem* (Ore.) *Journal*, March 3, 1942; "Amend the Law," *Chicago Journal of Commerce*, March 5, 1942.
37. "A Job for a Police Court," *Wall Street Journal*, March 3, 1942.
38. George R. Farnum, *Boston Traveller*, March 29, 1942.
39. *Newberry* v. *United States*, 256 U.S. 232 (1921).
40. *United States* v. *Classic*, 313 U.S. 299 (1941), pp. 315, 316, 317. Hereafter cited as Classic case.
41. *Ibid.*, pp. 319-20.

42. *Ibid.*, pp. 332, 336.
43. *Ibid.*, p. 324.
44. William H. Hastie, "Appraisal of *Smith* v. *Allwright*," *Lawyers Guild Review*, March-April 1945, p. 68.
45. Justice Jackson in *Pollock v. Williams*, 332 U.S. 4 (1944), p. 8.
46. Alexander H. Pekelis, *Law and Social Action* (Ithaca: Cornell University Press, 1950), pp. 113-14.
47. Letter to the Editor, *New York Times*, May 28, 1944.
48. *Hearing before a Subcommittee of the Senate Judiciary Committee*, 77th Cong., 2nd Sess., 1942, pp. 367-69; cf. Classic case, p. 315.
49. Irving Brant memorandum of talk with Justice Stone on Classic case, March 1944; Irving Brant to A.T.M., July 25, 1952.
50. H.F.S. to Irving Dillard of the *St. Louis Post-Dispatch*, in a letter from H.F.S. to Irving Brant, July 31, 1941.
51. Learned Hand, quoted in Felix Frankfurter to H.F.S., March 12, 1942.
52. E. M. Morgan to Felix Frankfurter, Feb. 10, 1942.
53. "In Memoriam, Mr. Justice Van Devanter, Remarks of Chief Justice Stone," March 16, 1942, *U.S. Supreme Court Reports*, Law. Ed., Vol. 86, App. XII, pp. 1786, 1791.
54. H.F.S. to his sons, May 8, 1942.
55. *Annual Report of the Administrative Office of the United States Courts*, 1945, Table A-1, p. 69.
56. Quoted material to end of chapter is from H.F.S. address to the Twelfth Annual Judicial Conference of the Fourth Circuit, June 19, 1942, Asheville, N.C., reprinted in *American Bar Association Journal*, August 1942.

## CHAPTER XXXVI

1. See *Ex parte Quirin*, 317 U.S. 1; *Viereck* v. *United States*, 318 U.S. 236; *Hirabayashi* v. *United States*, 320 U.S. 81; *Bowles* v. *United States*, 319 U.S. 33; all decided in 1942.
2. See *Adams* v. *United States ex rel. McCann*, 317 U.S. 270, and *Galloway* v. *United States*, 319 U.S. 372; *Schneiderman* v. *United States*, 320 U.S. 118; *American Medical Association* v. *United States*, 317 U.S. 519; all decided in 1942.
3. Brethren to James F. Byrnes, James F. Byrnes to Brethren, Oct. 5, 1942, in *U.S. Supreme Court Reports*, Law. Ed., Vol. 86, App. IV, pp. 1854-55.
4. Charles C. Burlingham to H.F.S., Dec. 23, 1942; H.F.S. to Charles C. Burlingham, Jan. 4, 1943.
5. H.F.S. to Sterling Carr, Feb. 2, 1943.
6. H.F.S. to Sterling Carr, April 4, 1943.
7. *Wickard* v. *Filburn*, 317 U.S. 111 (1942); *Parker* v. *Brown*, 317 U.S. 341 (1942). Hereafter cited as Filburn case and Parker case.
8. Charles P. Curtis, Jr., *Lions under the Throne*, p. 175.
9. Robert H. Jackson to H.F.S., May 25, 1942.
10. *Ibid.*
11. *Ibid.*
12. Filburn case, p. 128.
13. The Shreveport case, 234 U.S. 342 (1914).
14. *Chicago Board of Trade* v. *Olsen*, 262 U.S. 1 (1923).
15. H.F.S. to Sterling Carr, Jan. 11, 1943.
16. All quoted material through p. 598 is from the Parker case. See pp. 351-59, 362-63.
17. H.F.S. to Charles Evans Hughes, March 24, 1941. See *Cox* v. *New Hampshire*, 312 U.S. 569 (1941); *Chaplinsky* v. *New Hampshire*, 315 U.S. 568 (1942).
18. H.F.S. to Young B. Smith, June 12, 1942.
19. *Jones* v. *City of Opelika*, 316 U.S. 584 (1941), p. 623. Hereafter cited as Opelika case.
20. *Ibid.*, pp. 597, 598, 608, 610.
21. *Ibid.*, pp. 623-24.
22. See *West Virginia State Board of Education* v. *Barnette*, 319 U.S. 624 (1943), pp. 626, 629. Hereafter cited as Barnette case.
23. *Barnette* v. *West Virginia State Board of Education*, 47 F. Supp. 251 (S.D.W. Va., 1942), pp. 252-53.

24. *Murdock* v. *Pennsylvania,* 319 U.S. 105 (1943); *Jones v. City of Opelika,* 319 U.S. 103 (1943); *Martin* v. *Struthers,* 319 U.S. 141 (1943); *Douglas* v. *City of Jeannette,* 319 U.S. 157 (1943).
25. Barnette case, p. 639.
26. *Ibid.,* pp. 638, 642.
27. *Ibid.,* p. 641.
28. H.F.S. to Robert H. Jackson, March 31, 1943.
29. H.F.S. to Robert H. Jackson, May 24, 1943.
30. Barnette case, p. 644.
31. H.F.S. to Charles C. Burlingham, June 22, 1943.
32. H.F.S. to Charles C. Burlingham, Sept. 16, 1943.
33. H.F.S. to Marshall Stone, July 15, 1943.
34. *Hendry* v. *Moore,* 318 U.S. 133 (1943).
35. Justice Stanley F. Reed, address on the occasion of the dedication of the birthplace of Chief Justice Stone, Chesterfield, N.H., Aug. 25, 1948.
36. H.F.S. to Sterling Carr, March 22, 1943.
37. *Newark* (N.J.) *Evening News,* June 26, 1943; *Macon* (Ga.) *Telegraph,* June 23, 1943.
38. *Marconi* v. *United States,* 320 U.S. 1 (1943), p. 63.
39. H.F.S. to Felix Frankfurter, June 12, 1943.
40. Wiley B. Rutledge to H.F.S., June 12, 1943.
41. *The Nation,* Aug. 12, 1944, p. 179.
42. H.F.S. to Sterling Carr, June 13, 1943.
43. H.F.S. to Wiley B. Rutledge, June 24, 1943.
44. H.F.S. to Walter Wheeler Cook, June 28, 1943.

## CHAPTER XXXVII

1. *Baltimore Sun,* Oct. 13, 1943.
2. H.F.S. to Adolf A. Berle, Jr., Oct. 18, 1943.
3. H.F.S. to Hugh Gibson, March 15, 1944.
4. H.F.S. to Farnham Griffiths, Oct. 18, 1943, Jan. 26, 1944.
5. *Mercoid Corp.* v. *Mid-Continent Investment Co.,* 320 U.S. 661 (1944), pp. 672, 673.
6. *Federal Power Commission* v. *Hope Natural Gas Co.,* 320 U.S. 591 (1944), p. 619.
7. *New York Herald Tribune,* Jan. 10, 1944, p. 16.
8. H.F.S. to Charles C. Burlingham, Jan. 20, 1944.
9. H.F.S. memorandum for the Court, Jan. 13, 1944.
10. See Merlo J. Pusey, "The Roosevelt Supreme Court," *loc. cit.*
11. Owen J. Roberts to H.F.S., Nov. 2, 1932.
12. Curtis, *op. cit.,* p. 76 *passim.*
13. Felix Frankfurter to H.F.S., Dec. 28, 1943.
14. Wesley McCune, *The Nine Young Men* (New York: Harper & Bros., 1947), p. 250.
15. *Mahnich* v. *Southern Steamship Co.,* 321 U.S. 96 (1944), pp. 112-13.
16. *Ibid.,* p. 113, citing the Gobitis, Opelika, and Barnette cases in note 9.
17. "Supreme Court Precedent," reprinted in the *Springfield Republican,* Feb. 7, 1944.
18. Lewis Wood, "Supreme Court Split Is Aired in Dissents," *New York Times,* Feb. 13, 1944.
19. *Anderson* v. *Abbott,* 321 U.S. 349 (1944), pp. 375, 380. Justice Douglas spoke for the Court.
20. Wood, *op. cit.*
21. H.F.S. to the Marshall Stones, Feb. 10, 1944; to Sterling Carr, Feb. 17, 1944.
22. Lucretius, *On the Nature of Things,* quoted in Irwin Edman, *Philosopher's Holiday* (New York: The Viking Press, 1938), p. 28.
23. H.F.S. to John Vance Hewitt, March 15, 1944; to Sterling Carr, Feb. 17, 1944.
24. H.F.S. to Felix Frankfurter, March 27, April 6, 1944. These cases were 322 U.S. 202 (1944) and 217 U.S. 91 (1910).
25. Fred G. Folsom, Jr., "Federal Elections and the 'White Primary,'" *Columbia Law Review,* Nov.-Dec. 1943, pp. 1027-28.
26. *Smith* v. *Allwright,* 321 U.S. 649 (1944), p. 660. Hereafter cited as Allwright case. *Grovey* v. *Townsend,* 295 U.S. 45 (1935).

27. H.F.S. to Stanley F. Reed, March 15, 1944.
28. Allwright case, pp. 669, 670.
29. *Paul* v. *Virginia*, 8 Wall. 168 (1869).
30. Hugo L. Black to H.F.S., May 16, 1944.
31. Owen J. Roberts to H.F.S., May 22, 1944.
32. *United States* v. *Southeastern Underwriters Association*, 322 U.S. 533 (1944), pp. 551, 553, 558, 562. All quoted material through p. 622, unless otherwise cited, is from this case. See pp. 563, 568, 579, 583.
33. Hugo L. Black to H.F.S., May 10, 1944.
34. H.F.S. to John Bassett Moore, June 5, 1935.
35. See *NLRB* v. *Fainblatt*, 306 U.S. 601 (1939).
36. Hugo L. Black to H.F.S., March 16, 1939; H.F.S. to Felix Frankfurter, March 15, 1939.
37. Owen J. Roberts memorandum. See *Yakus* v. *United States*, 321 U.S. 414 (1943), p. 452.
38. H.F.S. memorandum to the conference. See Yakus case, p. 424. Italics the author's.
39. H.F.S. to Edwin W. Patterson, June 16, 1941.
40. *The Mayor, Aldermen and Commonalty of the City of New York* v. *George Miln*, 8 Peters 12 (1834), p. 122.
41. *American Bar Association Journal*, Vol. 30, 1944: Sept., p. 485, and Frank W. Grinnell, p. 507; Nov.: J. W. Henderson, p. 597; Aug.: C. Perry Patterson, "Jefferson and Judicial Review," p. 443.
42. Thomas Reed Powell, "Our High Court Analyses," *New York Times Magazine*, June 18, 1944.
43. Quoted in Pekelis, *op. cit.*, p. 195.
44. Walton Hamilton, "The Supreme Court Today"—Part I, "Nine Independent Men"; Part II, "Nine Men, One Law"—*The Nation*, Aug. 12, 19, 1944.
45. Allwright case, p. 670.
46. Robert H. Jackson, "Decisional Law and *Stare Decisis*," address at Annual Meeting of American Law Institute, May 9, 1944, published in *American Bar Association Journal*, June 1944.
47. H.F.S. to Sterling Carr, June 16, 1944.
48. H.F.S. to Ernest Kirschten, April 17, 1944.
49. Remarks of H.F.S. at the Judicial Conference of the Fourth Circuit, June 21, 1944.
50. H.F.S. to Alfred J. Snyder, Dec. 16, 1937.

## CHAPTER XXXVIII

1. H.F.S. to Sterling Carr, Nov. 22, 1944.
2. H.F.S. to Marshall Stone, Dec. 23, 1944.
3. H.F.S. to Edward S. Corwin, Nov. 5, 1942.
4. "In Memoriam, Mr. Justice Sutherland, Remarks of Chief Justice Stone," Dec. 18, 1944, *U.S. Supreme Court Reports*, Law. Ed., Vol. 89, App. II, p. 2147. Quoted material through p. 630 is from this eulogy.
5. Learned Hand to H.F.S., Jan. 18, 1945.
6. H.F.S. to Marshall Stone, Jan. 29, 1945; to Learned Hand, Jan. 29, 1945.
7. H.F.S. to Marshall Stone, April 17, 1945.
8. H.F.S. to Sterling Carr, April 17, 1945; to John Vance Hewitt, April 20, 1945.
9. Sterling Carr to H.F.S., Feb. 20, 1945; H.F.S. to Sterling Carr, Feb. 26, 1945, apropos *Otis & Co.* v. *SEC*, 323 U.S. 624 (1945).
10. H.F.S. memorandum for the Court, Oct. 1944.
11. *Georgia* v. *Pennsylvania Railroad Co.*, 324 U.S. 439 (1945), pp. 460, 474, 489, 490.
12. *Steele* v. *Louisville & Nashville Railroad Co.*, 323 U.S. 192 (1944), p. 198.
13. Alexander H. Pekelis to H.F.S., April 4, 1944.
14. Steele case, pp. 202, 207. For an important decision in the field of "private government," showing how the seed of the Steele case may bear fruit, see *Railroad Brotherhood* v. *Howard*, 343 U.S. 768 (1952).
15. H.F.S. to Robert H. Jackson, Dec. 1, 1944.
16. *Wallace Corp.* v. *NLRB*, 323 U.S. 248 (1944), pp. 268, 271.
17. H.F.S. to Robert H. Jackson, Dec. 1, 1944.

18. Wallace case, p. 272.
19. H.F.S. to Robert H. Jackson, Dec. 1, 1944.
20. *Allen Bradley Co.* v. *Local Union No. 3, International Brotherhood of Electrical Workers*, 325 U.S. 797 (1945), p. 810.
21. Hugo L. Black to members of the conference, June 16, 1945, apropos *Hunt* v. *Crumboch*, 325 U.S. 821 (1945).
22. H.F.S. to Robert H. Jackson, June 8, 1945.
23. Edward S. Corwin, *The Constitution and What It Means Today* (Princeton: Princeton University Press, 1948 ed.), p. 198, note 51.
24. Charles O. Gregory, *Labor and the Law*, p. 288.
25. *Screws* v. *United States*, 325 U.S. 91 (1945), pp. 111, 112, 141-42, 147. See Julius Cohen, "The Screws Case: Federal Protection of Negro Rights," *Columbia Law Review*, June 1946.
26. H.F.S. to William O. Douglas, Nov. 25, 1944.
27. *Ibid.*
28. Screws case, p. 153.
29. *Western Union Telegraph Co.* v. *Lenroot*, 323 U.S. 490; *Thomas* v. *Collins*, 323 U.S. 516 (1945); *Re Summers*, 325 U.S. 561 (1945); *International Union of Mine, Mill & Smelter Workers* v. *Eagle-Picher Mining & Smelting Co.*, 325 U.S. 335 (1945); *Special Equipment Co.* v. *Coe*, 324 U.S. 370 (1945).
30. H.F.S. to Marshall Stone, Jan. 29, 1945; to Thomas A. Larremore, Jan. 9, 1945; to Luther Ely Smith, Jan. 12, 1944.
31. "To Change the Quorum of the Supreme Court of the United States," *Hearings before the House Judiciary Committee on H.R. 2808*, 78th Cong., 1st Sess., June 24, 1943, p. 25. *North American Co.* v. *SEC*, 318 U.S. 750 (1943).
32. *SEC* v. *Engineers Public Service Co.* and *Engineers Public Service Co.* v. *SEC*, petitions filed Jan. 8, Jan. 27, 1944, respectively.
33. Eugene Nickerson to A.T.M., June 18, 1952.
34. Wiley B. Rutledge to H.F.S., March 27, 1944.
35. H.F.S. to Wiley B. Rutledge, March 27, 1944.
36. *Jewell Ridge Coal Corp.* v. *Local 6167, United Mine Workers of America*, 325 U.S. 161 (1945).
37. Stanley F. Reed to H.F.S., March 12, 1945.
38. H.F.S. to Robert H. Jackson, May 3, 1945.
39. Hugo L. Black to members of the conference, May 5, 1945.
40. McCune, *op. cit.*, p. 179.
41. Text of Justice Jackson's statement, *New York Times*, June 11, 1946.
42. H.F.S. memorandum for the Court, June 11, 1945.
43. Hugo L. Black to H.F.S., June 11, 1945.
44. H.F.S. to Owen J. Roberts, Felix Frankfurter, Robert H. Jackson, June 15, 1945; Felix Frankfurter, Robert H. Jackson, Albert J. Schneider (secretary to Justice Roberts), to H.F.S., June 16, 1945. Roberts left Washington before the final decision was reached.
45. *New York Times*, June 11, 1946.
46. *Jewell Ridge Coal Corp.* v. *Local 6167, United Mine Workers of America*, 325 U.S. 897 (1945).
47. *New York Times*, June 11, 1946.
48. H.F.S. to Irving Brant, Aug. 25, 1945.
49. H.F.S. to Alexander H. Pekelis, March 27, 1945.
50. Max Lerner, "Justice Roberts: End of an Era," *PM*, July 10, 1945.
51. Kenneth Sears, "The Supreme Court and the New Deal—An Answer to Texas," *University of Chicago Law Review*, Feb. 1945, p. 176.
52. H.F.S. to DeWitt Clark, Oct. 25, 1944.
53. H.F.S. to Marshall Stone, Oct. 24, 1939.
54. The exceptions were Warner Gardner and James Morrisson, who were on duty with the Armed Forces.
55. H.F.S. to Noel T. Dowling, Dec. 14, 1926, Dec. 7, 1933; to Karl N. Llewellyn, Dec. 6, 1933; to his sons, Dec. 14, 1925.
56. H.F.S. to Noel T. Dowling, March 26, 1945.
57. Allison Dunham to H.F.S., Oct. 10, 1945.
58. H.F.S. to Warner Gardner, March 27, 1945.
59. Learned Hand to H.F.S., Jan. 18, 1945.
60. H.F.S. to Stanley King, May 24, 1945.

## CHAPTER XXXIX

1. *New York Times*, June 22, 1920.
2. H.F.S. to Sterling Carr, Dec. 9, 1941.
3. H.F.S. to Paul Shipman Andrews, Jan. 28, 1942; to Bertrand Snell, March 31, 1942.
4. H.F.S. to Sterling Carr, April 17, 1942.
5. H.F.S. to Sterling Carr, Nov. 17, 1942.
6. H.F.S. to John Foster Dulles, Oct. 13, 1945.
7. H.F.S. to John Bassett Moore, Feb. 11, 1942.
8. *United States* v. *Pink,* 315 U.S. 203 (1942), pp. 249-50.
9. John Bassett Moore to H.F.S., Feb. 13, 1942.
10. Edwin M. Borchard to H.F.S., Feb. 9, 1942; H.F.S. to Edwin M. Borchard, Feb. 11, 1942.
11. H.F.S. to Edwin M. Borchard, June 14, 1942.
12. H.F.S. to Herbert Hoover, June 4, 1942. The speech, "The Limitations on Freedom in War," is printed in full in Hoover's *Addresses upon the American Road, 1941-1945* (New York: Charles Scribner's Sons, 1946).
13. H.F.S. to Herbert Hoover, April 15, 1942. Quoted material through p. 652 is from this letter.
14. Noel T. Dowling, "The Methods of Mr. Justice Stone in Constitutional Cases," *Columbia Law Review,* Nov. 1941, p. 1181.
15. H.F.S. to Stanley F. Reed, June 24, 1942.
16. Executive Order No. 9185, *Federal Register,* Vol. 7 (1942), p. 5103.
17. Presidential Proclamation No. 2561, *Federal Register,* Vol. 7 (1942), p. 5101.
18. *Ex parte Milligan,* 71 U.S. 2 (1866).
19. Lauson H. Stone to A.T.M., June 27, 1952.
20. *New York Times,* July 29, 1942.
21. Lauson H. Stone to H.F.S., July 22, 1942.
22. Transcript of Proceedings, Vol. I, p. 4, *United States ex rel. Burger* v. *Cox,* 317 U.S. 1 (1942). Hereafter cited as Transcript.
23. *Ibid.,* p. 8.
24. *Ibid.,* pp. 8-9.
25. *Ibid.,* pp. 9-10.
26. Lauson H. Stone to A.T.M., June 27, 1952.
27. *Ex parte Quirin,* 317 U.S. 1 (1942). Hereafter cited as Quirin case.
28. See Robert E. Cushman, *"Ex parte Quirin et al.—The Nazi Saboteur Case,"* *Cornell Law Quarterly,* Nov. 1942, pp. 56-58.
29. H.F.S. to Felix Frankfurter, Sept. 28, 1941.
30. Cushman, *op. cit.,* p. 58.
31. Lauson H. Stone to A.T.M., June 27, 1952.
32. H.F.S. to Bennett Boskey, July 23, Aug. 4, 20, 21, 1942.
33. Transcript, p. 66.
34. H.F.S. to Bennett Boskey, Aug. 9, 14, 1942.
35. H.F.S. to Bennett Boskey, Aug. 21, 1942.
36. H.F.S. to Roger Nelson, Sept. 20, 1942.
37. Phrase quoted from L. P. Jacks in Randolph Bourne, *Untimely Papers* (New York: B. W. Huebsch, 1919), p. 142.
38. H.F.S. to Bennett Boskey, undated (probably after Aug. 26, 1942).
39. Act of June 1920, c. 227, arts. 46, 50½, 41 Stat. 796-97.
40. Quoted by Felix Frankfurter in following letter to H.F.S., Sept. 14, 1942.
41. H.F.S. to Felix Frankfurter, Sept. 16, 1942.
42. H.F.S. to Bennett Boskey, Sept. 5, 1942.
43. H.F.S. to Owen J. Roberts, Sept. 25, 1942.
44. H.F.S. memorandum to the Court re Saboteurs cases.
45. H.F.S. to Bennett Boskey, Sept. 5, 1942.
46. Quirin case, pp. 47-48.
47. *Ibid.,* p. 25.
48. H.F.S. to Roger Nelson, Nov. 30, 1942.
49. H.F.S. memorandum for the conference, Oct. 17, 1942.
50. H.F.S. to Sterling Carr, Nov. 17, 1942.
51. H.F.S. to John Bassett Moore, Dec. 31, 1942; John Bassett Moore to H.F.S., Jan. 4, 1943.

52. Charles C. Burlingham to H.F.S., Aug. 28, 1942.
53. Comment, "Constitutional Law—Saboteurs and the Jurisdiction of Military Commissions," *Michigan Law Review*, Dec. 1942, p. 495.
54. E. g., Note, "Federal Military Commissions," *Harvard Law Review*, Jan. 1943, p. 642.
55. Cushman, *op. cit.*, p. 65.
56. The Saboteurs opinion is so described by Edward S. Corwin in *Total War and the Constitution* (New York: Alfred A. Knopf, 1947), p. 118.
57. H.F.S. to Bennett Boskey, Aug. 19, 1942; to Felix Frankfurter, Aug. 3, 1942.
58. *In re Yamashita*, 326 U.S. 693 (1945).
59. Stanley F. Reed to H.F.S., Jan. 22, 1946.
60. *In re Yamashita*, 327 U.S. 1 (1946), pp. 45-46, 79.
61. H.F.S. memorandum for the Court, on or about Jan. 30, 1946.
62. Hugo L. Black to H.F.S., Jan. 28, 1946.
63. H.F.S. to Hugo L. Black, Jan. 29, 1946.
64. H.F.S. memorandum for the Court, Jan. 31, 1946. See Yamashita case, p. 23.
65. Yamashita case, p. 8.
66. *Ibid.*, pp. 46, 81.
67. *Ibid.*, pp. 8, 9, 30.
68. Adolf Frank Reel, *The Case of General Yamashita* (Chicago: University of Chicago Press, 1949), p. 216.
69. *Ibid.*
70. *United States v. Butler*, 297 U.S. 1 (1936), p. 87.

## CHAPTER XL

1. Justice Cardozo, *Palko v. Connecticut*, 302 U.S. 319 (1937), p. 325.
2. Public Proclamation No. 3, *Federal Register*, Vol. 7, (1943), p. 2543.
3. *Hirabayashi v. United States*, 320 U.S. 81 (1943), p. 95. Hereafter cited as Hirabayashi case.
4. *Ibid.*, p. 99.
5. *Ibid.*, pp. 99, 100, 101, 102.
6. William O. Douglas to H.F.S., May 31, 1943.
7. H.F.S. memorandum for the Court, June 4, 1943.
8. H.F.S. to William O. Douglas, June 4, 1943.
9. William O. Douglas to H.F.S., June 7, 1943.
10. H.F.S. memorandum for the conference. See Hirabayashi case, p. 93.
11. Hirabayashi case, pp. 93, 102.
12. *Ibid.*, p. 113.
13. Wiley B. Rutledge to H.F.S., June 12, 1943.
14. Hirabayashi case, p. 114.
15. Stanley F. Reed to H.F.S., June 3, 1943.
16. Morton Grodzins, *Americans Betrayed, Politics and the Japanese Evacuation* (Chicago: University of Chicago Press, 1949), p. 353.
17. *Korematsu v. United States*, 323 U.S. 214 (1944), pp. 217-18, 220.
18. *Ibid.*, pp. 232, 242, 246-47.
19. H.F.S. to Hugo L. Black, Nov. 9, 1944.
20. *Ibid.*
21. *Ex parte Endo*, 323 U.S. 283 (1944).
22. Hirabayashi case, p. 101.
23. *Ibid.*, p. 99.
24. Korematsu case, p. 246.
25. Corwin, *Total War . . .*, pp. 99-100.
26. Eugene Rostow, "The Japanese American Cases—A Disaster," *Yale Law Journal*, June 1945, pp. 520, 531.
27. Quoted in Grodzins, *op. cit.*, p. 374.
28. Harrop A. Freeman, "Genesis, Exodus, Leviticus—Genealogy, Evacuation, and Law," *Cornell Law Quarterly*, June 1943, p. 425.
29. Grodzins, *op. cit.*, p. 358.
30. Rostow, *op. cit.*, p. 533.
31. Grodzins, *op. cit.*, p. 374.
32. Barnette case, p. 636.
33. *Duncan v. Kahanamoku*, 327 U.S. 304 (1946), pp. 322, 324.
34. H.F.S. to Hugo L. Black, Jan. 17, 1946.

## CHAPTER XLI

1. Robert E. Cushman, quoted in Corwin, *Total War* . . . , p. 106.
2. H.F.S. in *Viereck* v. *United States,* 318 U.S. 236 (1943), p. 245.
3. *Ibid.,* p. 247, note 3.
4. *Ibid.,* pp. 247-48.
5. H.F.S. to Felix Frankfurter, Feb. 19, 1943.
6. H.F.S. quoted in "The Courts in Wartime," *New York Times,* March 5, 1943 (editorial).
7. "Americanism *v.* Nazism," *Youngstown* (Ohio) *Vindicator,* March 3, 1943; "Viereck Case Exemplifies Democracy at Work," *Tampa* (Fla.) *Times,* March 9, 1943; "Democracy's Concept of Justice," *St. Louis Globe-Democrat,* March 2, 1943.
8. "The Viereck Decision," *Chicago Times,* March 8, 1943; Raymond Moley, " 'Dignity and Good Order,' " *Wall Street Journal,* March 5, 1943.
9. Mrs. P. Somers Smith to H.F.S., March 1, 1943; Jane F. O'Connor to H.F.S., March 3, 1943; anonymous, March 2, 1943.
10. Alfred A. Knopf to H.F.S., March 3, 1943; H.F.S. to Alfred A. Knopf, March 16, 1943.
11. *Schneiderman* v. *United States,* 320 U.S. 115 (1943), pp. 135-36.
12. *Ibid.,* p. 181. Cf. H.F.S. to Max Lerner, April 4, 1938, Chap. XXIX, pp. 470-71.
13. *Ibid.,* pp. 171, 182, 187-88, 191, 192, 194.
14. *Ibid.,* pp. 165-67 *passim.*
15. *Ibid.,* pp. 195-97 *passim.*
16. H.F.S. to Sterling Carr, June 23, 1943.
17. Frank Murphy memorandum re Schneiderman case, June 18, 1943; cf. Schneiderman case, p. 119.
18. "Communist Victory," *Washington Star,* June 25, 1943; "High Court Adjourns," *Macon* (Ga.) *Telegraph,* June 23, 1943; "The Schneiderman Decision," *Norfolk Virginian-Pilot,* June 24, 1943; *Chicago Sun,* June 23, 1943.
19. "Belief Is Personal," *Birmingham* (Ala.) *Age-Herald,* June 24, 1943.
20. Mrs. C. H. Bromfield to H.F.S., June 30, 1943.
21. T. Ernest Switzer to H.F.S., June 25, 1943.
22. William B. Taylor to H.F.S., June 26, 1943; H.F.S. to William B. Taylor, June 26, 1943.
23. H.F.S. to Felix Frankfurter, May 16, 1944.
24. *Baumgartner* v. *United States,* 322 U.S. 665 (1944), pp. 670-71, 678-79. Frank Murphy memorandum to the Court, May 17, 1944.
25. *Hartzel* v. *United States,* 322 U.S. 680 (1944), p. 689.
26. *Keegan and Kunze* v. *United States,* 325 U.S. 478 (1945), pp. 500, 505.
27. William O. Douglas to H.F.S., March 15, 1944.
28. H.F.S. memorandum to the Court, March 22, 1944.
29. *Ibid.*
30. H.F.S. to William O. Douglas, March 15, 1944. See Corwin, *Total War* . . . , p. 125.
31. *Ibid.*
32. Hugo L. Black to H.F.S., March 25, 1944.
33. *Cramer* v. *United States,* 322 U.S. 773 (1944).
34. *Cramer* v. *United States,* 325 U.S. 1 (1945), p. 24.
35. Corwin, *Total War* . . . , p. 126.
36. *United States* v. *Macintosh,* 283 U.S. 605 (1931), p. 622.
37. *Yakus* v. *United States,* 321 U.S. 414 (1944), pp. 419, 422, 429, 431.
38. *Ibid.,* p. 432.
39. *Ibid.,* p. 435.
40. *Ibid.,* pp. 468, 483-84.
41. *Ibid.,* p. 460.
42. See Corwin, *Total War* . . ., pp. 178-79; William G. McLaren, "Can a Trial Court of the United States Be Completely Deprived of the Power to Determine Constitutional Questions?" *American Bar Association Journal,* Jan. 1944, p. 17.
43. H.F.S. in Hirabayashi case, p. 99.
44. H.F.S. in Gobitis case, p. 602.

45. Yakus case, p. 447.
46. Justice Frankfurter in Korematsu case, p. 224.
47. "In Memoriam, Harlan Fiske Stone," Remarks of Judge John J. Parker, Washington, D.C., Nov. 12, 1947, *Proceedings of the Bar and Officers of the Supreme Court of the United States.*
48. Benjamin N. Cardozo, *The Nature of the Judicial Process* (New Haven: Yale University Press, 1921), p. 66.

## CHAPTER XLII

1. Bennett Boskey to A.T.M., Dec. 18, 1953.
2. H.F.S. to his sons, May 5, 1928.
3. H.F.S. to Herbert F. Goodrich, March 21, 1934.
4. Memorandum from Mrs. Harlan F. Stone to A.T.M., 1950.
5. H.F.S. to Edward Bruce, Nov. 30, 1939.
6. H.F.S. to Young B. Smith, Jan. 30, 1937.
7. H.F.S. to Frederick William Wile, Jan. 31, 1939.
8. *Washington Post,* May 3, 1939.
9. Wendell Berge to A.T.M., Sept. 27, 1951.
10. Lauson H. Stone to A.T.M., June 25, 1952.
11. See John P. Frank, "Disqualification of Judges," *Yale Law Journal,* April 1947, p. 605.
12. He participated in three decisions where Sullivan and Cromwell represented former clients: *New York Life Insurance Co.* v. *Sliosberg,* 275 U.S. 526 (1927); *Endicott Johnson Corp.* v. *Perkins,* 317 U.S. 501 (1943); *North American Co.* v. *SEC,* 327 U.S. 686 (1946). Under similar circumstances he did not participate in two cases: *United States* v. *Goldman,* 277 U.S. 229 (1929); *Sugar Institute Inc.* v. *United States,* 297 U.S. 553 (1936). He participated in three cases argued by Sullivan and Cromwell when the party was not a former client: *Helvering* v. *Watts,* 296 U.S. 387 (1935); *Ripperger* v. *Allyn,* 311 U.S. 695 (1940); *Vinson* v. *Washington Gas Co.,* 321 U.S. 489 (1944). In similar circumstances he did not participate in: *Banque de France* v. *Supreme Court of New York,* 316 U.S. 646 (1942); *Federal Trade Commission* v. *A.P.W. Paper Co.,* 326 U.S. 704 (1945).
13. "To Change the Quorum of the Supreme Court of the United States," *Hearings before the House Judiciary Committee on H.R. 2808,* 78th Cong., 1st Sess., June 24, 1943, p. 24. Hereafter cited as Hearings.
14. *Ibid.,* p. 24.
15. H.F.S. to Frank Murphy, March 14, 1946.
16. Hearings, p. 29.
17. *Ibid.,* p. 34.
18. H.F.S. to Hugo L. Black, March 29, 1946, apropos *Gallois* v. *Commissioner,* 327 U.S. 798 (1945).
19. H.F.S. to Hugo L. Black, Nov. 2, 1945.
20. H.F.S. to Irving Brant, Aug. 25, 1945.
21. *Quarterly Publication of Historical and Philosophical Society of Ohio,* April-June 1917, p. 131.
22. H.F.S. to Henry Albert, May 9, 1940, in answer to Albert's letter of May 2.
23. W.H. Taft to Charles P. Taft, March 17, 1929.
24. H.F.S. to J. Edgar Hoover, Oct. 7, 1939.
25. H.F.S. to John Taber, Jan. 12, 1940.
26. Mrs. Stone's memorandum.
27. Allison Dunham to A.T.M., June 26, 1952.
28. H.F.S. to Sterling Carr, Dec. 30, 1941.
29. H.F.S. to his sons, Dec. 18, 1941.
30. H.F.S. to Styles Bridges, Aug. 1, 1941.
31. H.F.S. to Joseph P. Chamberlain, Sept. 2, 1944.
32. H.F.S. to Arthur H. Vandenberg, Sept. 24, 1945.
33. Emmanuel Celler to H.F.S., Aug. 13, 1942.
34. H.F.S. to Emmanuel Celler, Aug. 15, 1942.
35. H.F.S. to members of the Court, Aug. 25, 1942.
36. H.F.S. to Grosvenor H. Backus, Sept. 19, 1942, recounting an earlier conversation with an unnamed friend.

37. H.F.S. memorandum, July 24, 1942, 8:45 p.m.
38. Ben W. Gilbert in *Washington Post*, July 25, 1942.
39. President Roosevelt to H.F.S., July 30, 1942.
40. H.F.S. to President Roosevelt, Aug. 1, 1942.
41. *Lynchburg News, July* 28, 1942; *Washington Post*, July 26, 1942; Frank R. Kent, in his syndicated column, "The Great Game of Politics"—"Rubber and Mr. Stone," Aug. 3, 1942.
42. Noel T. Dowling's report, based on an interview, of what Stone said to Justice Byrnes when the latter talked to the Chief Justice about resigning from the Court. (Noel T. Dowling to A.T.M., Nov. 22, 1950.)
43. H.F.S., Remarks at the Third Judicial Conference of the District of Columbia Circuit, Feb. 25, 1943.
44. H.F.S. to Joseph Chamberlain, Sept. 2, 1944.
45. Arthur H. Vandenberg to H.F.S., Nov. 20, 1943.
46. H.F.S. to Arthur H. Vandenberg, Nov. 22, 1943.
47. H.F.S. to Arthur H. Vandenberg, Sept. 24, 1945.
48. H.F.S. to Marshall Stone, Oct. 10, 1945.
49. H.F.S. to his sons, Oct. 23, 1945.
50. H.F.S. to John Bassett Moore, Nov. 29, 1945.
51. H.F.S. to Luther Ely Smith, Jan. 2, 1946.
52. *Ibid.*
53. H.F.S. to Louis Lusky, Nov. 13, 1945.
54. H.F.S. to Luther Ely Smith, Dec. 23, 1945.
55. H.F.S. to Charles C. Burlingham, Nov. 30, 1945.
56. H.F.S. to Sterling Carr, Dec. 4, 1945.
57. H.F.S. to Robert H. Jackson, March 1, 21, 1946.
58. Quirin case, pp. 27-28.
59. Lord Wright, "War Crimes under International Law," *Law Quarterly Review*, Jan. 1946, pp. 43-44.
60. H.F.S. to President Truman, Feb. 13, 1946.
61. Ray Henle's broadcast over stations of the American Broadcasting Company, March 3, 1946 (typescript copy). Under the dateline of March 5, a New York *Sun* staff correspondent told the same story.

PART SEVEN

## CHAPTER XLIII

1. H.F.S. to Felix Frankfurter, Nov. 21, 1928.
2. See John P. Frank, "The United States Supreme Court, 1949-50," *University of Chicago Law Review*, Autumn 1950, p. 41. The Court reached a low point in 1953-54 when it handed down only seventy-one opinions. (*United States Law Week*, June 22, 1954, p. 3333.) The record for 1954-55 was seventy-nine. (*Ibid.*, June 21, 1955, p. 8315.)
3. Quoted in Felix Frankfurter to H.F.S., April 28, 1937.
4. H.F.S. to Harold R. Medina, Dec. 4, 1931.
5. H.F.S. to John Vance Hewitt, Jan. 3, 1931.
6. H.F.S. to Marshall Stone, Jan. 9, 1925; to his sons, Feb. 9, 1928, March 10, 1932.
7. H.F.S. to his sons, Oct. 21, 1933, March 9, 1934.
8. H.F.S. to his sons, March 14, 1940, Jan. 10, Feb. 13, 1941, Feb. 9, 1934, Jan. 11, 1934.
9. H.F.S. to his sons, March 29, 1928, May 23, 1935.
10. Memorandum from Mrs. Harlan F. Stone to A.T.M., 1950.
11. H.F.S. to his sons, April 15, 1937, May 8, 1930.
12. Howard Westwood to A.T.M., Nov. 16, 1950.
13. Ann K. Lusky to Mrs. Harlan F. Stone, April 25, 1946.
14. Albert J. Beveridge, *The Life of John Marshall* (Boston: Houghton Mifflin Co., 1929), Vol. IV, p. 68.
15. Farnham Griffiths to A.T.M., Dec. 17, 1951.
16. Alice Earle Hyde, *Olden Time Beverages* (undated pamphlet).
17. H.F.S. to Farnham Griffiths, April 21, 1943.
18. H.F.S. to Farnham Griffiths, March 7, 1944.

19. Dr. Maynard A. Amerine to A.T.M., August 16, 1951.
20. Farnham Griffiths to A.T.M., Dec. 17, 1951.
21. Gertrude Jenkins Regis to A.T.M., June 3, 1950.
22. Memorandum from Lauson H. Stone to A.T.M., 1950; H.F.S. to C. C. Schiffeler, Oct. 15, 1942.
23. H.F.S. to Carl Ganter, Dec. 15, 1943; to Edward L. Tinker, Jan. 6, 1938; to Chaffee Hall, March 29, 1945.
24. H.F.S. to C.C. Schiffeler, Jan. 15, 1940.
25. Mrs. Stone's memorandum.
26. H.F.S. to Farnham Griffiths, Feb. 17, 1944.
27. H.F.S. to Luther Ely Smith, April 14, 1937; to Thomas McInnerney, Oct. 13, 1937.
28. H.F.S. to Farnham Griffiths, Feb. 22, 1936; to Dr. George Selleck, Dec. 7, 1944.
29. H.F.S. to Carl Ganter, Dec. 7, 1944.
30. H.F.S. to Sterling Carr, Dec. 28, 1938.
31. Frank Schoonmaker and Tom Marvel, *The Complete Wine Book* (New York: Simon & Schuster, 1935), pp. 248, 249.
32. Edward VII quoted in Alexis Lichine, *The Wines of France* (New York: Alfred A. Knopf, 1951), p. 11.
33. H.F.S. to Farnham Griffiths, March 7, 1944.
34. H.F.S. to Carl Ganter, Dec. 31, 1940.
35. H.F.S. to Carl Ganter, Oct. 1, 1941.
36. Paul Kieffer to Farnham Griffiths, quoted by Griffiths to H.F.S., April 10, 1944.
37. H.F.S. to Farnham Griffiths, April 17, 1944.
38. Farnham Griffiths to H.F.S., August 13, 1945, March 4, 1942.
39. H.F.S. to Farnham Griffiths, March 20, 1942.
40. Mimeographed memorandum by H.F.S., Feb. 1, 1941.
41. H.F.S. to Dr. Raoul H. Blanquie, April 4, 1943; to Carl Ganter, July 30, 1943.
42. H.F.S. to Farnham Griffiths, March 20, 1942, Oct. 18, 1943.
43. H.F.S. to Carl Ganter, Dec. 19, 1944; to David E. Finley, Dec. 2, 1942.
44. H.F.S. to Edward M. Graham, Jan. 2, 1945. The same description of better days, almost verbatim, had been sent to his son Marshall twenty years before, Jan. 2, 1925, in a wide-eyed report on his first Washington New Year's.
45. H.F.S. to Farnham Griffiths, Feb. 17, 1943; to Grosvenor H. Backus, Nov. 29, 1943; to Frank Buxton, Oct. 9, 1945.

## CHAPTER XLIV

1. H.F.S. to Allison Dunham, May 11, 1939.
2. H.F.S. to Herman Oliphant, June 8, 1927; to Helen Stone Willard, Oct. 3, 1929.
3. Sterling Carr to H.F.S., April 26, 1933.
4. Memorandum from Adolph Miller to A.T.M., Oct. 23, 1950.
5. *Ibid.*
6. H.F.S. to his sons, July 8, 20, 1930.
7. H.F.S. to the Lauson H. Stones, June 18, 1932.
8. H.F.S. to Francis Hackett, June 13, 1941.
9. H.F.S. to the Lauson H. Stones, June 18, 1932.
10. *Ibid.*
11. George C. Ruhle to Mrs. Harlan F. Stone, Oct. 25, 1951.
12. H.F.S. to his brother Lauson, Dec. 4, 1928.
13. H.F.S. to Mr. and Mrs. Augustus Eustis, Jan. 8, 1935.
14. H.F.S. to Stanley King, Jan. 14, 1935.
15. H.F.S. to Edward Bruce, Nov. 28, 1941.
16. H.F.S. to F. C. Hicks, March 31, 1936.
17. H.F.S. to Carl Ganter, Sept. 20, 1942.
18. Clyde Turner to H.F.S., Sept. 20, 1942.
19. H.F.S. to Louis Hertle, June 30, 1942; to Grosvenor H. Backus, Jan. 1, 1943.
20. H.F.S. to Farnham Griffiths, Sept. 10, 1942.
21. H.F.S. to Carl Ganter, Sept. 20, 1942.
22. H.F.S. to the Marshall Stones, Sept. 16, 1945.

## CHAPTER XLV

1. Adolph Miller memorandum.
2. H.F.S. to Helen Stone Willard, Feb. 4, 1932.
3. H.F.S. to his sons, Feb. 4, 1936.
4. As told in Pearson and Allen, *The Nine Old Men*, p. 107.
5. H.F.S. to Max Farnum, May 22, 1941.
6. H.F.S. to T. Filipowicz, the Polish Ambassador, March 2, 1942.
7. Memorandum from Marshall Stone to A.T.M., 1950.
8. H.F.S. to his sons, Feb. 24, 1934.
9. H.F.S. to his sons, March 14, 1939.
10. H.F.S. to the Secretary of the Literary Society, Feb. 17, 1944.
11. H.F.S. to F. S. Allis, Oct. 17, 1932; Stanley King to Luther Ely Smith, Oct. 6, 1947.
12. H.F.S. to Calvin Coolidge, Dec. 31, 1931.
13. H.F.S. to Sir Roland Lindsay, April 10, 1935.
14. Stanley King, *Recollections of the Folger Shakespeare Library* (Published for the Trustees of Amherst College by the Cornell University Press, 1950).
15. H.F.S. to his sons, Feb. 24, 1938.
16. Joseph Q. Adams to Stanley King, Sept. 20, 1937.
17. Lauson H. Stone memorandum.
18. Dr. Louis B. Wright quoted in King, op. cit., p. 33.
19. H.F.S. to Adolf A. Berle, Jr., May 28, 1941.
20. Memorandum from Howard Westwood to Gertrude Jenkins Regis, Oct. 30, 1947.
21. Joseph Q. Adams to H.F.S., May 27, 1936.
22. H.F.S. to George A. Plimpton, Oct. 12, 1934.
23. Stanley King to Luther Ely Smith, Oct. 6, 1947.
24. "Great Patron of the Folger Library," *Report from the Folger Library*, Jan 4, 1950.
25. Marshall Stone memorandum.
26. H.F.S. to Karl N. Llewellyn, Oct. 30, 1932.
27. H.F.S. to H. S. Latham, May 30, 1931.
28. Memorandum from Allison Dunham to A T.M., Oct. 1950.
29. H.F.S. to his sons, July 8, 1930.
30. H.F.S. to his sons, April 6, 1933.
31. H.F.S. to Maurice Sterne, March 25, 1933.
32. H.F.S. to Edward Bruce, March 25, 1933.
33. H.F.S. to Colonel Richard E. Evans, Oct. 6, 1941.
34. H.F.S. to his sons, March 7, 1940.
35. H.F.S. to Herbert V. Evatt, Oct. 27, 1938.
36. H.F.S. to H. S. Latham, May 30, 1941.
37. H.F.S. to Richard Stone, April 21, 1938.
38. H.F.S. to Samuel A. Lewisohn, April 30, 1945.
39. H.F.S. to Edward Bruce, May 6, 1935.
40. H.F.S. to Edward Bruce, Jan. 30, 1936.
41. Leon Kroll to H.F.S., Feb. 8, 1937.
42. H.F.S. to Leon Kroll, April 7, 1937. Much the same appraisal went to Edward Bruce, Jan. 30, 1936.
43. H.F.S. to Edward Bruce, Jan. 8, 1936, June 7, 1938, Nov. 6, 1939; Edward Bruce to H.F.S., Dec. 7, 1935.
44. H.F.S. to his sons, Oct. 31, Nov. 13, 1941.
45. H.F.S. to his sons, Nov. 13, 1941.
46. Memorandum from David E. Finley to A.T.M., Jan. 7, 1952.
47. *Ibid.*
48. H.F.S. to Marshall Stone, June 13, 1942.
49. Finley memorandum.
50. H.F.S. to President Roosevelt, Aug. 1, 1942; Schofield Andrews to H.F.S., Sept. 17, 1942; H.F.S. to Dr. Edward B. Logan, Sept. 12, 1942.
51. *Richmond Times-Dispatch*, Nov. 6, 1943.
52. Finley memorandum.
53. Dated Nov. 7, 1945; the full text of the resolution is reprinted in *Magazine of Art*, Feb. 1946, p. 42.

54. Finley memorandum.
55. H.F.S. to Chester Dale, Nov. 29, 1943.
56. H.F.S. to Samuel Kress, April 4, 1943.
57. Finley memorandum.

PART EIGHT

CHAPTER XLVI

1. H.F.S. to Allison Dunham, Oct. 25, 1945.
2. Hugo L. Black to H.F.S., Aug. 14, 1925.
3. Hugo L. Black to Stanley F. Reed, Aug. 20, 1945.
4. Felix Frankfurter to H.F.S., Aug. 25, 1945.
5. H.F.S. memorandum for the Court, undated, about Aug. 30, 1945.
6. Hugo L. Black to H.F.S., Aug. 31, 1945.
7. William O. Douglas to H.F.S., notation scribbled on Stone's memorandum, Sept. 5, 1945; Frank Murphy to H.F.S., notation, undated, on Stone's memorandum; Wiley B. Rutledge to H.F.S., Sept. 24, 1945.
8. Robert H. Jackson to H.F.S., Sept. 8, 1945.
9. *Ibid.*
10. H.F.S. to Hugo L. Black, Sept. 10, 1945, in answer to Black's letter of Sept. 7.
11. Robert H. Jackson to A.T.M., April 15, 1953.
12. H.F.S. to L. C. Turner, Dec. 11, 1945.
13. Felix Frankfurter to the Brethren, Dec. 29, 1945.
14. H.F.S. to Felix Frankfurter, Dec. 21, 1945.
15. *New York* v. *United States*, 326 U.S. 572 (1946), pp. 591, 593-96, 598.
16. *Ibid.*, pp. 589-90. Cf. *Metcalf & Eddy* v. *Mitchell*, 269 U.S. 514 (1926), pp. 523-24.
17. H.F.S. to Felix Frankfurter, Nov. 26, 1945, regarding Justice Reed's memorandum in *Railroad Retirement Board* v. *Duquesne Warehouse Co.*, 326 U.S. 446 (1945).
18. H.F.S. to Robert H. Jackson, Feb. 24, 1944.
19. C. Herman Pritchett, *The Roosevelt Court*, p. 208.
20. A.T.M.'s interview with Justice William O. Douglas, May 8, 1951.
21. *Fernandez* v. *Wiener*, 326 U.S. 340 (1945); *United States of America* v. *Rompel*, 326 U.S. 367 (1945).
22. H.F.S. to Sterling Carr, Jan. 3, 1946.
23. *Ibid.*
24. Thomas Reed Powell, "Our High Court Analyzed," *New York Times Magazine*, June 18, 1944, p. 45.
25. H.F.S., "Fifty Years' Work of the United States Supreme Court," *American Bar Association Journal*, Aug.-Sept. 1928, p. 435.
26. The Butler and Morehead cases in 1936.
27. Archibald MacLeish's introduction to *Law and Politics, Occasional Papers of Felix Frankfurter, 1913-1918*, p. xvii.
28. A.T.M.'s interview with Adolf A. Berle, Jr., April 15, 1953. See *New York Times*, July 8, 1955, p. 24.
29. Learned Hand to A.T.M., Aug. 22, 1951.
30. Herbert Wechsler, "Stone and the Constitution," *Columbia Law Review*, Sept. 1946, p. 771.
31. *West Coast Hotel* v. *Parrish*, 300 U.S. 379 (1937), pp. 401, 402-404 *passim*.
32. Noel T. Dowling, "The Methods of Mr. Justice Stone in Constitutional Cases," *Columbia Law Review*, Nov. 1941.
33. Pritchett, *op. cit.*, p. 269.
34. Dowling, *op. cit.*, p. 1164.
35. H.F.S. to John J. Parker, Nov. 20, 1940.
36. Walton Hamilton, "Trial by Ordeal, New Style," *Yale Law Journal*, March 1941, p. 778.
37. H.F.S. to Joseph Kiser, April 28, 1938.
38. H.F.S. to Irving Brant, Aug. 25, 1945.
39. Walton Hamilton and George D. Braden, "The Special Competence of the Supreme Court," *Yale Law Journal*, June 1941, p. 1374.
40. Wesley McCune, *The Nine Young Men*, p. 249.

41. H.F.S. to Thomas Reed Powell, Nov. 8, 1945.
42. Barnwell case, p. 184, note 2.
43. Memorandum from Noel T. Dowling to A.T.M., Oct. 11, 1950.
44. *Ibid.*
45. *Ibid.*
46. *Southern Pacific Co. v. Arizona*, 325 U.S. 761 (1945), pp. 789, 792, 794-95.
47. *Ibid.*, p. 769.
48. *Morgan v. Virginia*, 328 U.S. 373 (1946), p. 387.
49. H.F.S. to Samuel J. Konefsky, Nov. 12, 1945.
50. Samuel J. Konefsky, *Chief Justice Stone and the Supreme Court* (New York: The Macmillan Co., 1945), pp. 207, 258, 260-61, 265.
51. H.F.S. to his sons, Oct. 23, 1945.
52. Max Lerner, *Ideas Are Weapons* (New York: The Viking Press, 1939), p. 464; Butler case, p. 79.
53. Hamilton and Braden, *op. cit.*, p. 1394.
54. H.F.S. to Walter Wheeler Cook, Nov. 20, 1930.
55. *Ibid.*
56. Benjamin N. Cardozo, *The Nature of the Judicial Process*, p. 13.
57. O. W. Holmes, *Collected Legal Papers*, pp. 184, 295, *passim*.
58. Adkins case, pp. 559-60.
59. H.F.S. to W. Z. Ripley, April 6, 1937. In illustration Stone cited the following cases: *Hudson v. United States*, 272 U.S. 451 (1926), translation of the Year Books; *Nielsen v. Johnson*, 277 U.S. 583 (1928), researches in medieval French law, early law of Denmark and Danish West Indies, treaty prohibitions on the discriminatory use of the *droit de détraction; Ribnik v. McBride*, 277 U.S. 350, 359 (1928), economic problems and effects growing out of employment agencies; *Chicago, Rock Island and Pacific Railway Co. v. United States*, 284 U.S. 80, 100 (1931), methods adopted for the distribution of costs of car-hire for cars passing over the rails of others than their owners; *Virginia Railway Co. v. System Federation, no. 40*, etc., 299 U.S. 529 (1937), experience in collective bargaining for settlement of labor disputes; *Indian Motorcycle Co. v. United States*, 283 U.S. 570, 580 (1931), considerations effecting the economic "passing on" to others the burden of a tax.
60. H.F.S. to W. Z. Ripley, April 6, 15, 1937.
61. "In Memoriam, Mr. Justice Sutherland, Remarks of Chief Justice Stone," Dec. 18, 1944, *U.S. Supreme Court Reports, Law. Ed.*, Vol. 89, App. II, p. 2148.
62. H.F.S. to Noel T. Dowling, Oct. 19, 1945.
63. Compare the language of Justice Holmes, *op. cit.*, pp. 295-96.
64. H.F.S. to Noel T. Dowling, Oct. 19, 1945.
65. Remarks of Chief Justice Stone at the Judicial Conference for the Fourth Circuit, June 21, 1944.
66. Adolf A. Berle, Jr., to A.T.M., July 19, 1951.
67. "In Memoriam, Harlan Fiske Stone," Remarks of Mr. Herbert Wechsler, Nov. 12, 1947, *Proceedings of the Bar and Officers of the Supreme Court of the United States*, p. 46.
68. H.F.S. to Learned Hand, Jan. 29, 1945.

## CHAPTER XLVII

1. H.F.S. to his sons, Feb. 5, 1930.
2. H.F.S. to Irving Dillard, June 7, 1941.
3. A.T.M.'s interview with Justice Jackson, April 8, 1953.
4. Memorandum from Mrs. Harlan F. Stone to A.T.M., 1950.
5. Memorandum from Eugene Nickerson to A.T.M., May 27, 1952.
6. H.F.S. to Owen J. Roberts, June 1, 1945.
7. A.T.M.'s interview with Charles Elmore Cropley, May 15, 1950.
8. H.F.S. to his sons, Oct. 12, 1942.
9. President Roosevelt made this observation to Harold Ickes in 1939, after a conference with Justice Stone. See Ickes' *The Secret Diary . . .* , Vol. II, p. 552.
10. Paul A. Freund, in *Harvard Law Review*, Dec. 1951, p. 370; Walton Hamilton, "The Supreme Court Today," Part I, *The Nation*, Aug. 12, 1944, p. 180.
11. A.T.M.'s interview with Justice Frankfurter, April 14, 1952.
12. Merlo J. Pusey, *Charles Evans Hughes*, Vol. II, p. 676.

13. Charles Evans Hughes, *The Supreme Court of the United States*, p. 72.
14. John Bassett Moore to H.F.S., May 16, 1932; H.F.S. to John Bassett Moore, May 17, 1932.
15. William O. Douglas, "Chief Justice Stone," *Columbia Law Review*, Oct. 1946, p. 695.
16. Felix Frankfurter to H.F.S., undated, apparently after first conference in 1941.
17. H.F.S. to Benjamin Shein, June 4, 1942. In this letter Stone attributed qualities to Cardozo that apply equally well to himself. See Warner Gardner's statement in "Mr. Chief Justice Stone," *Harvard Law Review*, Oct. 1946, pp. 1203-1204.
18. John P. Frank to A.T.M., March 22, 1950.
19. A.T.M.'s interview with Eugene Nickerson, Feb. 10, 1952.
20. McCune, *op. cit.*, p. 249.
21. Arthur A. Ballantine, "The Supreme Court: Principles and Personalities," *American Bar Association Journal*, March 1945, p. 113. For a brilliant development of Ballantine's thesis, see Alexander H. Pekelis, *Law and Social Action*.
22. William O. Douglas, *op. cit.*, p. 695.
23. A.T.M.'s interview with John Lord O'Brian, June 29, 1954.
24. A.T.M.'s interview with Gertrude Jenkins Regis, May 15, 1950.
25. H.F.S. to Young B. Smith, Jan. 30, 1937.
26. H.F.S. memorandum re Opelika case, May 8, 1942.
27. H.F.S. to Stanley F. Reed, March 8, 1940; to Felix Frankfurter, Dec. 14, 1942; to Owen J. Roberts, March 7, 1945.
28. Cf. the Blaisdell case, pp. 425-26, with the Schechter case, pp. 528-29.
29. Irving Brant, "Due Process and the Supreme Court," *PM*, July 31, 1945.
30. Charles Evans Hughes, *op. cit.*, pp. 67-68. Stone cited this in defense of his own Court.
31. For comparison, see Report of the Judicial Conference of Senior Circuit Judges. *Annual Report of the Director of the Administrative Office of the United States*, 1945, p. 69.

CASES FILED, DISPOSED OF, AND REMAINING ON THE DOCKET
IN THE SUPREME COURT OF THE UNITED STATES DURING THE OCTOBER TERMS 1935-44.

| | 1934 | *Hughes* | | | | | | *Stone* | | | |
|---|---|---|---|---|---|---|---|---|---|---|---|
| | 1934 | 1935 | 1936 | 1937 | 1938 | 1939 | 1940 | 1941 | 1942 | 1943 | 1944 |
| **Total cases:** | | | | | | | | | | | |
| Filed | | 983 | 950 | 981 | 942 | 981 | 977 | 1,178 | 984 | 997 | 1,237 |
| Disposed of | | 990 | 942 | 1,013 | 923 | 946 | 985 | 1,168 | 997 | 962 | 1,249 |
| Remaining on docket | 109 | 102 | 110 | 78 | 97 | 132 | 124 | 134 | 121 | 156 | 144 |

*Method of Disposition*

| | 1934 | 1935 | 1936 | 1937 | 1938 | 1939 | 1940 | 1941 | 1942 | 1943 | 1944 |
|---|---|---|---|---|---|---|---|---|---|---|---|
| **Cases disposed of:** | | | | | | | | | | | |
| By written opinions | | 187 | 180 | 180 | 174 | 151 | 195 | 175 | 196 | 154 | 199 |
| By per curiam opinions | | 72 | 80 | 102 | 65 | 97 | 86 | 201 | 63 | 56 | 75 |
| By denial or dismissal of petitions for certiorari | | 717 | 671 | 718 | 676 | 690 | 693 | 785 | 731 | 749 | 971 |
| By motion to dismiss or per stipulation | | 14 | 10 | 13 | 8 | 8 | 10 | 7 | 7 | 2 | 4 |
| By final decree— original cases | | | 1 | | | 1 | | | | 1 | |
| Number of written opinions of the court | | 145 | 149 | 152 | 139 | 137 | 165 | 151 | 147 | 130 | 156 |

32. Quoted by Felix Frankfurter in "The Job of a Supreme Court Justice," *New York Times Magazine*, Nov. 28, 1954, p. 14.
33. Walton Hamilton, "The Supreme Court Today," Part II, *The Nation*, Aug. 19, 1944, p. 209.
34. Quoted in Pekelis, *op. cit.*, p. 200.
35. Kenneth C. Sears, "The Supreme Court and the New Deal—An Answer to Texas," *University of Chicago Law Review*, Feb. 1945, p. 159.

36. William Draper Lewis to Mrs. Harlan F. Stone, April 27, 1946.
37. Pekelis, *op. cit.*, p. 196.

## CHAPTER XLVIII

1. *Washington Post*, March 2, 1945.
2. Memorandum from Marshall Stone to A.T.M., Dec. 1954.
3. H.F.S. to Luther Ely Smith, June 6, 1945; to Sterling Carr, Jan. 26, 1946.
4. H.F.S. to Sterling Carr, Oct. 6, Dec. 4, 1945.
5. H.F.S. to Helen Stone Willard, Nov. 13, 1945.
6. Remarks of Chief Justice Harlan F. Stone on the occasion of the celebration of the seventy-fifth anniversary of the Association of the Bar of the City of New York, March 16, 1946, *Record of the Association of the Bar*, Vol. I, No. 4, pp. 144-49 *passim*.
7. H.F.S. to Luther Ely Smith, April 2, 1946.
8. Memorandum from David E. Finley to A.T.M., Jan. 7, 1952.
9. H.F.S. to Sterling Carr, April 13, 1946.
10. Arthur Krock, "Stone, a Gifted Judge," *New York Times*, April 24, 1946.
11. Albert W. Atwood to A.T.M., March 13, 1951.
12. Felix Morley to Mrs. Harlan F. Stone, April 25, 1946.
13. Marshall Stone memorandum.
14. A.T.M.'s interview with Justice Frankfurter, April 7, 1953; Felix Frankfurter to Thomas Reed Powell, April 24, 1946.
15. Ralph T. Bischoff in Edmond Cahn, *Supreme Court and Supreme Law* (Bloomington, Ind.: Indiana University Press, 1954), pp. 80-81.
16. Herbert Prashker to A.T.M., Sept. 22, 1952.
17. Eugene Nickerson to A.T.M., May 27, 1952.
18. *Girouard* v. *United States*, 328 U.S. 61 (1946), p. 72, 73.
19. *Ibid.*, p. 76.
20. *Ibid.*, p. 79.
21. Wiley B. Rutledge to Luther Ely Smith, April 23, 1946.
22. Felix Frankfurter, "Harlan Fiske Stone," *Year Book of the American Philosophical Society*, 1946, pp. 334-35.
23. Phoebe Stone, "The Judge," typewritten manuscript, 1951.
24. *Washington Times-Herald*, April 24, 1946.
25. H. Res. 607, 79th Cong., 2nd Sess., April 30, 1946; *Congressional Record*, April 23, 1946, pp. 4096, 4097-98.
26. Helen Stone Willard to Mrs. Harlan F. Stone, May 1, 1946.
27. Eugene Lyman to Luther Ely Smith, June 7, 1946.
28. A tribute by his classmates, Amherst '94, signed by Alfred E. Stearns, Edward Warren Capen, Harry Estabrook Whitcomb.
29. John Bassett Moore to Mrs. Harlan F. Stone, May 5, 1946.
30. James L. Morrisson to Mrs. Harlan F. Stone, April 23, 1946.
31. William O. Douglas to Mrs. Harlan F. Stone, April 23, 1946.
32. "Harlan F. Stone," *Cleveland Plain-Dealer*, April 24, 1946.
33. Erwin N. Griswold to Mrs. Harlan F. Stone, April 23, 1946.
34. William O. Douglas, "Chief Justice Stone," *loc. cit.*, p. 694.

# Chronology

| | |
|---|---|
| 1872 | Born, Chesterfield, New Hampshire, October 11. |
| 1888-1890 | Massachusetts Agricultural College. |
| 1890-1894 | Amherst College. |
| 1894-1895 | Teacher, Newburyport High School. |
| 1895-1898 | Columbia Law School. |
| 1898-1899 | Law Clerk, Sullivan and Cromwell. |
| 1899 | Admitted to the New York Bar. |
| 1899 | Married Agnes Harvey, September 7. |
| 1899-1903 | Lecturer, Columbia Law School, and lawyer with Wilmer and Canfield. |
| 1903-1905 | Adjunct Professor of Law, Columbia Law School. |
| 1905-1910 | Lawyer, Wilmer and Canfield. |
| 1910-1915 | Professor of Law, Columbia University. |
| 1910-1923 | Dean, Columbia Law School. |
| 1915-1923 | Kent Professor of Law, Columbia University. |
| 1923-1924 | Head of litigation department, Sullivan and Cromwell. |
| 1924-1925 | Attorney General of the United States. |
| 1925-1941 | Associate Justice of the Supreme Court. |
| 1941-1946 | Chief Justice of the United States. |
| 1946 | Died, Washington, D.C., April 22. |

# Law Clerks to Chief Justice Stone

| | | PRESENT POSITION |
|---|---|---|
| Robert F. Cogswell | 1924-1925 | Lawyer, Washington, D.C. |
| Alfred McCormack | 1925-1926 | Lawyer, New York City |
| Milton Handler | 1926-1927 | Professor, Columbia Law School |
| Francis X. Downey | 1927-1928 | Lawyer, New York City |
| Oliver B. Merrill | 1928-1929 | Lawyer, New York City |
| Adrian C. Leiby | 1929-1930 | Lawyer, New York City |
| Wilbur M. Friedman | 1930-1931 | Lawyer, New York City |
| Walter F. Gellhorn | 1931-1932 | Professor, Columbia Law School |
| Herbert Wechsler | 1932-1933 | Professor, Columbia Law School |
| Howard C. Westwood | 1933-1934 | Lawyer, Washington, D.C. |
| Warner W. Gardiner | 1934-1935 | Lawyer, Washington, D.C. |
| Thomas E. Harris | 1935-1936 | Lawyer, Washington, D.C. |
| Harold Leventhal | 1936-1937 | Lawyer, Washington, D.C. |
| Louis Lusky | 1937-1938 | Lawyer, Louisville, Ky. |
| Alexis Coudert | 1938-1939 | Lawyer, New York City |
| Allison Dunham | 1939-1941 | Professor, University of Chicago Law School |
| C. Roger Nelson | 1941-1942 | Lawyer, Washington, D.C. |
| Bennett Boskey | 1941-1943 | Lawyer, Washington, D.C. |
| James L. Morrison | 1942-1944 | Lawyer, Washington, D.C. |
| Edward B. Friedman | 1943-1945 | Lawyer, New York City |
| Eugene H. Nickerson | 1944-1946 | Lawyer, New York City |
| Herbert Prashker | 1945-1946 | Lawyer, New York City |

# Opinions

## By Associate Justice Stone

### 1925-1941

*Adam* v. *Saenger*, 303 U.S. 59 (1938).
*Aetna Casualty & Surety Co.* v. *Phoenix National Bank & Trust Co.*, 285 U.S. 209 (1932).
*Aetna Insurance Co.* v. *United Fruit Co.*, 304 U.S. 430 (1938).
*Aetna Life Insurance Co.* v. *Moses*, 287 U.S. 530 (1933).
*Alaska Packers Association* v. *Industrial Accident Commission*, 294 U.S. 532 (1935).
*Alaska Steamship Co.* v. *United States*, 290 U.S. 256 (1933).
*Alford* v. *United States*, 282 U.S. 687 (1931).
*Allen* v. *Regents of the University System of Georgia*, 304 U.S. 439 (1938); concurring, p. 453.
*Altoona Publix Theatres* v. *American Tri-Ergon Corp.*, 294 U.S. 477 (1935).
*Aluminum Castings Co.* v. *Routzahn*, 282 U.S. 92 (1930).
*AFL* v. *NLRB*, 308 U.S. 401 (1940).
*American Hide & Leather Co.* v. *United States*, 284 U.S. 343 (1932).
*Apex Hosiery Co.* v. *Leader*, 310 U.S. 469 (1940).
*Arizona* v. *California*, 298 U.S. 558 (1936).
*Arkansas* v. *St. Louis-San Francisco Railway*, 269 U.S. 172 (1925).
*Arrow-Hart & Hegeman Electric Co.* v. *Federal Trade Commission*, 291 U.S. 587 (1934); dissenting, p. 599.
*Aschenbrenner* v. *United States Fidelity & Guaranty Co.*, 292 U.S. 80 (1934).
*Atchison, Topeka & Sante Fe Railway Co.* v. *Toops*, 281 U.S. 351 (1930).
*Atchison, Topeka & Sante Fe Railway Co.* v. *United States*, 295 U.S. 193 (1935); dissenting, p. 202.
*Atlas Life Insurance Co.* v. *Southern*, 306 U.S. 563 (1939).
*Awotin* v. *Atlas Exchange National Bank*, 295 U.S. 209 (1935).
*Baizley Iron Works* v. *Span*, 281 U.S. 222 (1930); dissenting, p. 237.
*Baldwin* v. *Missouri*, 281 U.S. 586 (1930); dissenting, p. 596.
*Baltimore & Ohio Railroad* v. *Berry*, 286 U.S. 272 (1932).
*Bankers' Pocahontas Coal Co.* v. *Burnet*, 287 U.S. 308 (1932).
*Barnette* v. *Wells Fargo Nevada National Bank of San Francisco*, 270 U.S. 438 (1926).
*Beadle* v. *Spencer*, 298 U.S. 124 (1936).
*Beal* v. *Missouri Pacific Railroad*, 312 U.S. 45 (1941).
*Beazell* v. *Ohio*, 269 U.S. 167 (1925).
*Becker Steel Co.* v. *Cummings*, 296 U.S. 74 (1935).
*Bedford Cut Stone Co.* v. *Journeymen Stone Cutters' Association*, 274 U.S. 37 (1927); concurring, p. 55.
*Biddle* v. *Commissioner of Internal Revenue*, 302 U.S. 573 (1938).
*Blair* v. *Birkenstock*, 271 U.S. 348 (1926).
*Blair* v. *Oesterlein Machine Co.*, 275 U.S. 220 (1927).
*Blakey* v. *Brinson*, 286 U.S. 254 (1932).
*Blatt Co.* v. *United States*, 305 U.S. 267 (1938); concurring, p. 280.
*Borden's Products Co.* v. *Baldwin*, 293 U.S. 194 (1934); concurring, p. 213.

*Boston & Maine Railroad* v. *Armburg*, 285 U.S. 234 (1932).
*Bradford Electric Light Co.* v. *Clapper*, 286 U.S. 145 (1932); concurring, p. 163.
*Brasfield* v. *United States*, 272 U.S. 448 (1926).
*Broad River Power Co.* v. *South Carolina*, 281 U.S. 537 (1930).
*Bromley* v. *McCaughn*, 280 U.S. 124 (1929).
*Brush* v. *Commissioner of Internal Revenue*, 300 U.S. 352 (1937); concurring, p. 374.
*Burnet* v. *Aluminum Goods Manufacturing Co.*, 287 U.S. 544 (1933).
*Burnet* v. *Coronado Oil & Gas Co.*, 285 U.S. 393 (1932); dissenting, p. 401.
*Burnet* v. *Harmel*, 287 U.S. 103 (1932).
*Burnet* v. *Sanford & Brooks Co.* 282 U.S. 359 (1931).
*California* v. *Thompson*, 313 U.S. 109 (1941).
*Callaghan* v. *Reconstruction Finance Corporation*, 297 U.S. 464 (1936).
*Calmar. S. S. Corp.* v. *Taylor*, 303 U.S. 525 (1938).
*Carley & Hamilton* v. *Snook*, 281 U.S. 66 (1930).
*Carmichael* v. *Southern Coal & Coke Co.*, 301 U.S. 495 (1937).
*Carpenter* v. *Shaw*, 280 U.S. 363 (1930).
*Cement Manufacturers' Protective Association* v. *United States*, 268 U.S. 588 (1925).
*Central Kentucky Gas Co.* v. *Railroad Commission of Kentucky*, 290 U.S. 264 (1933).
*Central New England Railway* v. *Boston & Albany Railroad*, 279 U.S. 415 (1929).
*Central Transfer Co.* v. *Terminal Railroad Association*, 288 U.S. 469 (1933).
*Central Vermont Transportation Co.* v. *Durning*, 294 U.S. 33 (1935).
*Chapman* v. *Hoage*, 296 U.S. 526 (1936).
*Charter Shipping Co.* v. *Bowring*, 281 U.S. 515 (1930).
*Chase National Bank* v. *United States*, 278 U.S. 327 (1929).
*Chesapeake & Ohio Railway* v. *Thompson Manufacturing Co.*, 270 U.S. 416 (1926).
*Chicago, Milwaukee, St. Paul Railway* v. *Risty*, 276 U.S. 567 (1928).
*Chicago, Rock Island & Pacific Railway* v. *United States*, 284 U.S. 80 (1931); dissenting, p. 100.
*Chicago, St. Paul, Minneapolis & Omaha Railway* v. *Holmberg*, 282 U.S. 162 (1930).
*Christopher* v. *Brusselback*, 302 U.S. 500 (1938).
*City of New York* v. *Feiring*, 313 U.S. 283 (1941).
*Clark* v. *Paul Gray*, 306 U.S. 583 (1939).
*Clyde Mallory Lines* v. *Alabama*, 296 U.S. 261 (1935).
*Colgate* v. *Harvey*, 296 U.S. 404 (1935); dissenting, p. 436.
*Collie* v. *Fergusson*, 281 U.S. 52 (1930).
*Compañía Espanola* v. *The "Navemar,"* 303 U.S. 68 (1938).
*Compañía General de Tabacos* v. *Collector*, 279 U.S. 306 (1929).
*Concrete Appliances Co.* v. *Gomery*, 269 U.S. 177 (1925).
*Connecticut General Life Insurance Co.* v. *Johnson*, 303 U.S. 77 (1938),
*Connell* v. *Walker*, 291 U.S. 1 (1934).
*Curry* v. *McCanless*, 307 U.S. 357 (1939).
*Dakin* v. *Bayly*, 290 U.S. 143 (1933); dissenting, p. 152.
*DeForest Radio Co.* v. *General Electric Co.*, 283 U.S. 664 (1931).
*Deitrick* v. *Greaney*, 309 U.S. 190 (1940).
*Delaware River Bridge Commission* v. *Colburn*, 310 U.S. 419 (1940).
*Di Giovanni* v. *Camden Fire Insurance Association*, 296 U.S. 64 (1935).
*Dimick* v. *Schiedt*, 293 U.S. 474 (1935); dissenting, p. 488.
*Di Santo* v. *Pennsylvania*, 273 U.S. 34 (1927); dissenting, p. 43.
*Dismuke* v. *United States*, 297 U.S. 167 (1936).
*District of Columbia* v. *Clawans*, 300 U.S. 617 (1937).
*District of Columbia* v. *Fred*, 281 U.S. 49 (1930).
*Dohany* v. *Rogers*, 281 U.S. 362 (1930).
*Doleman* v. *Levine*, 295 U.S. 221 (1935).
*Douglas, City of,* v. *Federal Reserve Bank*, 271 U.S. 489 (1926).
*Duignan* v. *United States*, 274 U.S. 195 (1927).
*Dumbra* v. *United States*, 268 U.S. 435 (1925).
*Edelman* v. *Boeing Air Transport*, 289 U.S. 249 (1933).
*Educational Films Corp.* v. *Ward*, 282 U.S. 379 (1931).
*Electric Cable Joint Co.* v. *Brooklyn Edison Co.*, 292 U.S. 69 (1934).

*Oxford Paper Co.* v. *The "Nidarholm,"* 282 U.S. 681 (1931).
*Pacific Co.* v. *Johnson,* 285 U.S. 480 (1932).
*Pacific Employers' Insurance Co.* v. *Industrial Accident Commission of California,* 306 U.S. 493 (1939).
*Pacific Telephone & Telegraph Co.* v. *Seattle,* 291 U.S. 300 (1934).
*Page* v. *Arkansas Natural Gas Corp.,* 286 U.S. 269 (1932).
*Pagel* v. *MacLean,* 283 U.S. 266 (1931).
*Palmer* v. *Bender,* 287 U.S. 551 (1933).
*Palmer* v. *Commissioner of Internal Revenue,* 302 U.S. 63 (1937).
*Paramount Publix Corp.* v. *American Tri-Ergon Corp.,* 294 U.S. 464 (1935).
*Pearson* v. *McGraw,* 308 U.S. 313 (1939); concurring, p. 319.
*Penn General Casualty Co.* v. *Pennsylvania,* 294 U.S. 189 (1935).
*Pennsylvania* v. *Williams,* 294 U.S. 176 (1935).
*Perry* v. *United States,* 294 U.S. 330 (1935); concurring, p. 358.
*Petroleum Exploration* v. *Burnet,* 288 U.S. 467 (1933).
*Petroleum Exploration* v. *Public Service Commission,* 304 U.S. 209 (1938); concurring, p. 223.
*Phelps Dodge Corp.* v. *NLRB,* 313 U.S. 177 (1941); dissenting, p. 208.
*Phillips* v. *Dime Trust & Safe Deposit Co.,* 284 U.S. 160 (1931).
*Pittsburgh Plate Glass Co.* v. *NLRB,* 313 U.S. 146 (1941); dissenting, p. 166.
*Pizitz Dry Goods Co.* v. *Yeldell,* 274 U.S. 112 (1927).
*Portneuf-Marsh Co.* v. *Brown,* 274 U.S. 630 (1927).
*Provost* v. *United States,* 269 U.S. 443 (1926).
*Prussian* v. *United States,* 282 U.S. 675 (1931).
*Puerto Rico* v. *Russell & Co.,* 288 U.S. 476 (1933).
*Puget Sound Co.* v. *Seattle,* 291 U.S. 619 (1934).
*Quaker City Cab Co.* v. *Pennsylvania,* 277 U.S. 389 (1928); dissenting, p. 412.
*Raffel* v. *United States,* 271 U.S. 494 (1926).
*Railroad Commission of California* v. *Los Angeles Railway,* 280 U.S. 145 (1929); dissenting, p. 166.
*Rasquin* v. *Humphreys,* 308 U.S. 54 (1939).
*Raybestos-Manhattan Co.* v. *United States,* 296 U.S. 60 (1935).
*Reading Co.* v. *Koons,* 271 U.S. 58 (1926).
*Reichelderfer* v. *Quinn,* 287 U.S. 315 (1932).
*Reinecke* v. *Gardner,* 277 U.S. 239 (1928).
*Reinecke* v. *Northern Trust Co.,* 278 U.S. 339 (1929).
*Ribnik* v. *McBride,* 277 U.S. 350 (1928); dissenting, p. 359.
*Richbourg Motor Co.* v. *United States,* 281 U.S. 528 (1930).
*Risty* v. *Chicago, Rock Island & Pacific Railway,* 270 U.S. 378 (1926).
*Roberts & Shaefer Co.* v. *Emmerson,* 271 U.S. 50 (1926).
*Rogers* v. *Guaranty Trust Co. of New York,* 288 U.S. 123 (1933); dissenting, p. 133.
*Royal Indemnity Co.* v. *United States,* 313 U.S. 289 (1941).
*Russell* v. *Todd,* 309 U.S. 280 (1940).
*Ryerson* v. *United States,* 312 U.S. 405 (1941).
*Safe Deposit & Trust Co.* v. *Virginia,* 280 U.S. 83 (1929); concurring, p. 95.
*St. Joseph Stock Yards Co.* v. *United States,* 298 U.S. 38 (1936); concurring, p. 93.
*St. Louis & O'Fallon Railroad Co.* v. *United States,* 279 U.S. 461 (1929); dissenting, p. 548.
*St. Louis-San Francisco Railway* v. *Mills,* 271 U.S. 344 (1926).
*Saltonstall* v. *Saltonstall,* 276 U.S. 260 (1928).
*Sanford's Estate* v. *Commissioner of Internal Revenue,* 308 U.S. 39 (1939).
*Saranac Machine Corp.* v. *Wirebounds Patents Co.,* 282 U.S. 704 (1931).
*Schnell* v. *The "Vallescura,"* 293 U.S. 296 (1934).
*Schriber-Schroth Co.* v. *Cleveland Trust Co.,* 305 U.S. 47 (1938).
*Schriber-Schroth Co.* v. *Cleveland Trust Co.,* 311 U.S. 211 (1940).
*Seattle Gas Co.* v. *Seattle,* 291 U.S. 638 (1934).
*Second Russian Insurance Co.* v. *Miller,* 268 U.S. 552 (1925).
*SEC* v. *United States Realty Co.,* 310 U.S. 434 (1940).
*Seeman* v. *Philadelphia Warehouse Co.,* 274 U.S. 403 (1927).
*Senior* v. *Braden,* 295 U.S. 422 (1935); dissenting, p. 433.
*Shamrock Oil & Gas Corp.* v. *Sheets,* 313 U.S. 100 (1941).
*Shaw* v. *Gibson-Zahniser Oil Corp.,* 276 U.S. 575 (1928).
*Shearer* v. *Burnet,* 285 U.S. 228 (1932).
*Shriver* v. *Woodbine Savings Bank,* 285 U.S. 467 (1932).

*United States* v. *Darby,* 312 U.S. 100, 657 (1941).
*United States* v. *Dern,* 289 U.S. 352 (1933).
*United States* v. *Dubilier Condenser Corp.,* 289 U.S. 178, 706 (1933); dissenting, p. 209.
*United States* v. *Dunn,* 268 U.S. 121 (1925).
*United States* v. *Elgin, Joliet & Eastern Railway,* 298 U.S. 492 (1936); dissenting, p. 504.
*United States* v. *Falcone,* 311 U.S. 205 (1940).
*United States* v. *Felt & Tarrant Manufacturing Co.,* 283 U.S. 269 (1931).
*United States* v. *Helvering,* 301 U.S. 540 (1937).
*United States* v. *Hutcheson,* 312 U.S. 219 (1941); concurring, p. 237.
*United States* v. *Illinois Central Railroad,* 291 U.S. 457 (1934); concurring, p. 464.
*United States* v. *Katz,* 271 U.S. 354 (1926).
*United States* v. *Klein,* 303 U.S. 276 (1938).
*United States* v. *Louisiana,* 290 U.S. 70 (1933).
*United States* v. *Lowden,* 308 U.S. 225 (1939).
*United States* v. *Madigan,* 300 U.S. 500 (1937).
*United States* v. *Morgan,* 307 U.S. 183 (1939).
*United States* v. *New York Central Railroad,* 272 U.S. 457 (1926).
*United States* v. *O'Donnell,* 303 U.S. 501 (1938).
*United States* v. *One Ford Coupe,* 272 U.S. 321 (1926); concurring, p. 335.
*United States* v. *Oregon,* 295 U.S. 1 (1935).
*United States* v. *Pelzer,* 312 U.S. 399 (1941).
*United States* v. *Ryan,* 284 U.S. 167 (1931).
*United States* v. *Santos Flores,* 289 U.S. 137 (1933).
*United States* v. *Sherwood,* 312 U.S. 584 (1941).
*United States* v. *Trenton Potteries,* 273 U.S. 392 (1927).
*United States* v. *West Virginia,* 295 U.S. 463 (1935).
*United States* v. *White Dental Manufacturing Co.,* 274 U.S. 398 (1927).
*United States Shipping Board Merchant Fleet Corp.* v. *Harwood,* 281 U.S. 519 (1930).
*Utah* v. *United States,* 284 U.S. 534 (1932).
*Vajtauer* v. *Commissioner of Immigration of New York,* 273 U.S. 103 (1927).
*Van Oster* v. *Kansas,* 272 U.S. 465 (1926).
*Vermont* v. *New Hampshire,* 289 U.S. 593 (1933).
*Vermont* v. *New Hampshire,* 300 U.S. 636 (1937).
*Virginian Railway* v. *System Federation No. 40,* 300 U.S. 515 (1937).
*Waggoner Estate* v. *Wichita County,* 273 U.S. 113 (1927).
*Washington Fidelity National Insurance Co.* v. *Burton,* 287 U.S. 97 (1932); dissenting, p. 100.
*Waxham* v. *Smith,* 294 U.S. 20 (1935).
*Welch* v. *Henry,* 305 U.S. 134 (1938).
*West* v. *American Telephone & Telegraph Co.,* 311 U.S. 223 (1940).
*West* v. *Chesapeake & Potomac Telephone Co.,* 295 U.S. 662 (1935); dissenting, p. 680.
*West India Oil Co.* v. *Domenech,* 311 U.S. 20, 729 (1940).
*West Ohio Gas Co.* v. *Public Utilities Commission* (No. 1), 294 U.S. 63 (1935); concurring, p. 86.
*Western Live Stock* v. *Bureau of Revenue,* 303 U.S. 250 (1938).
*Western Union Telegraph Co.* v. *Priester,* 276 U.S. 252 (1928).
*White* v. *United States,* 305 U.S. 281 (1938).
*Wichita Royalty Co.* v. *City National Bank of Wichita Falls,* 306 U.S. 103 (1939).
*Wilentz* v. *Sovereign Camp, Woodmen of the World,* 306 U.S. 573 (1939).
*Willing* v. *Chicago Auditorium Association,* 277 U.S. 274 (1928); concurring, p. 290.
*Wolfle* v. *United States,* 291 U.S. 7 (1934).
*Worcester County Trust Co.* v. *Riley,* 302 U.S. 292 (1937).
*Work* v. *Braffet,* 276 U.S. 560 (1928).
*Wright* v. *United States,* 302 U.S. 583 (1938); concurring, p. 598.
*Wuchter* v. *Pizzutti,* 276 U.S. 13 (1928); dissenting, p. 28.
*Yarborough* v. *Yarborough,* 290 U.S. 202 (1933); dissenting, p. 213.

# By Chief Justice Stone
## 1941-1946

# Note on Stone's Legal Writings

Scattered through fifteen volumes of the *Columbia Law Review*, Stone's technical writings are connected by a unifying thread of content and purpose. His first article, "Resulting Trusts and the Statute of Frauds" (6 *Columbia Law Review* 326), appearing in 1906, inveighed against the acquiescence of courts in certain low standards of business practice. A ninth and final essay was published in 1922 under the title, "A Theory of Liability of Trust Estates for the Contracts and Torts of the Trustee" (22 *Columbia Law Review* 527). From first to last, he urged equity to adapt its remedies so as to protect persons ignorant of the law from unconscionable impositions of "sharpers" well versed in legal technicalities. Judges were slow to follow his reasoning. As late as 1943 a California court, though citing Stone's arguments as "unanswerable," felt compelled by earlier decisions to arrive at its "more just result" by extending a well-recognized exception to the old rule, rather than by frankly adopting Stone's view. (*Steinberger* v. *Steinberger*, 1943, 60 Cal. App. [2d] 116, 120; 140 Pac. [2d] 31, 33.)

In another essay he disputed Professor Austin W. Scott's contention that the property interest of the beneficiary of a trust had been converted by modern judicial decisions into a species of legal right in the particular property held in trust. Holding to the orthodox view, Stone urged that the beneficiary was entitled to faithful performance of the duties of the trustee and nothing more. ("The Nature of the Rights of the Cestui Que Trust," *Columbia Law Review*, June 1917.) Stone's defense embodied a review of existing precedents, all but ignoring the ferment at work in this area of law. He thus fell headlong into the trap of paying too much attention to what judges said and too little to what they were doing to alter the content of traditional concepts. By 1935 he brushed aside his own fine-spun reasoning as "subtle refinements of legal doctrine" affording no guide whatever outside a very narrow field. (*Senior* v. *Braden*, 1935, 295 U.S. 422, 439.) For some time before the appearance of Stone's article, the beneficiary's interest in a trust had troubled such legal scholars as Maitland, Holdsworth, Ames, Langdell, and Pound. It continued to plague the courts. Although as late as 1937 the West Virginia Supreme Court followed Stone's thought (*Sweeney* v. *Tabor*, 118 West Va. 591, 595; 191 S.E. 295, 297, 1937), by the time of *Senior* v. *Braden* the tide of decision had definitely turned against it. "This view," the Pennsylvania Supreme Court said in 1940, "undoubtedly represents the early judicial conception of the cestui que trust. But the modern trend of equity jurisprudence has inclined toward the doctrine that, in addition to rights against the trustee, the beneficiary also has rights *in rem*, an actual property interest in the subject-matter of the trust, an equitable ownership in the trust res." (*Commonwealth* v. *Stewart*, 338 Pa. 9, 14; 12 A (2d) 444, 446-447, 1940.)

In two articles concerning the equitable rights and liabilities of strangers to a contract ("Equitable Rights and Liabilities of Strangers to a Contract," Part I, *op. cit.*, pp. 43-76, 18 *Columbia Law Review* 201. 1918; Part II, pp. 165-179, 19 *Columbia Law Review* 177, 1919), Stone argued that the same doctrine advanced to refute Scott—equity's protection of certain interests from outside "interference" —also protected the operations of businessmen in situations ranging from the enforcement of covenants restricting use of land to the exclusive personal service contract—the heart of the "star" system in movies and baseball. The Oregon Supreme Court, "much impressed" with Dean Stone's conclusions, announced that its practice was "in harmony with this rule." (*Menstell* v. *Johnson*, 125 Ore.

150, 166; 202 Pac. 853, 857-858, 1927.) (*Snow* v. *Van Dam*, 291 Mass. 477, 485; 197 N.E. 224, 228, 1935.) But judges on the Massachusetts and New York benches, including Stone's friend, Judge Benjamin N. Cardozo, did not accept his analysis. Stone, Cardozo admitted, had come up with "ingenious answers" to objections raised to his position, but the judge did not find it necessary to settle the point for New York. (*Bristol* v. *Woodward*, 1929, 251 N.Y. 275, 288.) A decade later Judge Irving Lehmann also avoided deciding "when, or even whether, covenants in a deed will be enforced, upon equitable principles, against subsequent purchasers with notice, at the suit of a party without privity of contract or estate." Nevertheless, he indicated approval of Stone's view by citing his article on the point. (*Neoponsit P.O. Ass'n* v. *Emigrant Ind. Sav. Bank*, 1938, 278 N.Y. 248, 261.)

A passion for order and symmetry in law dominated Stone's scholarly writing. It led him to distrust legal fictions, those "white lies" in the law contrived to explain decisions obviously just and in harmony with contemporary social conditions, but inconsistent with the progressive development of the law. With the patience and persistence of a harrier, he traced to its source in old English reports the fiction of "Equitable Conversion by Contract." (13 *Columbia Law Review* 369, 1913.) Cutting away the case-hardened superstructure erected on the fiction, he exposed the ordinary principles of equity operating normally in a false disguise. Again in 1920, he examined minutely the credit laws of New York in "The Equitable Mortgage in New York" (20 *Columbia Law Review* 519, 1920), showing how some of the notions of the agricultural society of medieval England still influenced twentieth-century law in the Empire State. To rid Wall Street and Main Street of "curious inconsistencies and complications" caused by the hangover of feudal rules in a society typified by skyscrapers, he urged comprehensive reform and unification of the credit laws. In his last legal essay ("A Theory of the Liability of Trust Estates for the Contracts and Torts of the Trustee," 22 *Columbia Law Review* 527, 1922) he attempted to put businesses managed by trustees on an equal footing with other forms of competitive enterprise. Trustees operated coal mines, managed farms, ran grocery stores and filling stations—inevitably they incurred legal obligations common to such commerce—yet trust property sometimes escaped paying for goods and services it obtained or for injuries committed in its administration. From the standpoint of the trust beneficiary who drew the profits but frequently took no part in the conduct of the business, it was, as Stone commented, "the one authentic instance in law where one may pay his debts with his losses." He therefore advocated substitution of the policy that "an economic enterprise should bear its own economic burdens."

For Stone legal writing was not a sterile academic exercise. Feeling that university scholars could devote to their studies the time and thought necessary to see problems whole and devise rational solutions, he wrote for lawyers and judges too much a part of the process to think objectively about it. In 1921 he ventured into unknown waters to discuss problems of foreign exchange and was delighted when, the following year, his work received the approbation of Chief Judge Hiscock of the New York Court of Appeals. "While not having the authority of a judicial decision," the doughty Chief Judge said, "we nevertheless cite in support of what has been said a very thorough and well-considered discussion of the general subject of foreign exchange by Dean Harlan F. Stone of Columbia Law School." (*Equitable Trust Co.* v. *Keene*, 232 N.Y. 290, 295, 1922.) Writing a former student who proposed to use his arguments in a brief for the New York Court, Stone commented: "They have already cited my article so they evidently think my views on the matter have some merit." (HFS to Charles C. Pearce, March 28, 1923.) Lower New York Courts, taking their cue from the Chief Judge, followed Stone consistently. (See, *Safian* v. *Irving Nat. Bank*, 1922, 202 A.D. 459, 463; 196 N.Y. Supp. 141, 145; *Richard* v. *American Union Bank*, 1924, 210 A.D. 22, 27; 205 N.Y. supp. 622, 625; *Webber* v. *American Union Bank*, 1926, 128 Misc. 123, 127; 217 N.Y. Supp. 833, 836; *Euclid Holding Co.* v. *Kermacoe Realty Co.. Inc.*, 1928, 131 Misc. 466, 470; 227 N.Y. Supp. 103, 107.) In 1924 the Federal Circuit Court of Appeals for the Second Circuit, the nation's foremost business court, endorsed his approach as to the duties of bankers procuring foreign exchange for their customers. (*Samuels* v. *E. F. Drew & Co.*, 296 Fed. 882, 886, C.C.A. 2d, 1924. *See also Great Atlantic and Pacific Tea Co.* v. *Citizens Nat. Bank*, 1932, 2 Fed. Supp. 29, 31 [D.C. WD Pa.]; *Richards* v. *Fulton*, 75 Fed. [2d] 853, 854, C.C.A. 6th, 1935.)

In at least one area, Stone's work influenced change in the law of New York state. Back in 1896, the court of that state had given an anomalous twist to the rules determining the right of an individual to have his contract enforced specifically, that is, his right to have a court of equity compel the other party to live up to his literal contractual promise. The New York bench had held that both parties must be eligible for the remedy or neither could have it. (*Stokes v. Stokes*, 148 N.Y. 708.) In 1916, Stone directed one of his most penetrating law essays, "The Mutuality Rule in New York," 16 *Columbia Law Review* 443, 1916) to a critical study of this rule. The doctrine that the remedies must be mutual had been invented to prevent the miscarriage of justice occurring if a court should order enforcement of the contract against one party, without being able to ensure that the other person would also make good on his promise. In its origin, the rule was sound, but later decisions had perverted its essential purpose, creating the injustice it had been devised to prevent. It was ludicrous, Stone thought, to deny a person who had fulfilled his contract obligations, his right to performance by the other party on the ground that his own fidelity had deprived his defaulting opponent of the right to have the contract specifically performed. Yet this was one consequence of the New York rule. "Contrasting the cases, it seems apparent," the Dean commented dryly, "that in applying the rule, the courts of this state have misinterpreted it, or at least lost sight of the reason upon which [it was] founded."

"The Dean's chapter needs revision," Garrard Glenn wrote in a review of this article when it appeared in Stone's selected essays (*Columbia Law Review*, April, 1922), "because the arguments it contains have received due acknowledgment from the courts which they have influenced." Glenn's comment was well taken. Stone had scanned New York's legal newspapers, looking for a case in which to try his theory. When he found one he suggested to the attorney in the case, trial lawyer Max Steuer, that he might find his article of "some service." (HFS to Steuer, March 23, 1917.) Steuer's appeal, however, was unsuccessful, as the court unanimously refused to budge from the "well-settled law in this jurisdiction." (*Dittenfass* v. *Horsley*, 1918, 224 N.Y. 560, 561.) Other lawyers persisted in addressing Stone's arguments to lower courts. These tribunals appreciated the force of his contentions but felt "constrained to follow," as one judge remarked, "what we understand to be a final determination of the question by the Court of Appeals." (*Schuyler* v. *Kirk Brown Co.*, 1920, 184 N.Y. Supp. 95, 98.) Lower court judges, apparently tired of hearing the thesis reiterated, gave up and began merely citing the cases decided against Stone's position. "Dean Stone, in a very able article," one judge observed, "questions the decisions, . . . but concedes that they hold as above stated." (*Ibid.*) By 1921 the jurists were driven to recognize "the unique position of the courts of this state, in adhering to the doctrine to its full and precise extent." (*Arrow Holding Co.* v. *McLaughlin's Sons*, 1921, 116 Misc. 555, 559; 190 N.Y. Supp. 720, 723.)

Finally, in 1922, a similar case was taken to the Court of Appeals. This time Stone's point of view found complete acceptance. "If there ever was a rule that mutuality of remedy existing . . . at the time of the formation of the contract is a condition of equitable relief," Judge Cardozo wrote in the celebrated case of *Epstein* v. *Gluckin*, 233 N.Y. 490 (1922), "it has been so qualified by exceptions . . . that it has ceased to be a rule of today." Cardozo's explanation of his decision pursued the track cut by Stone's essay. "What equity exacts as a condition of relief," the scholarly jurist commented, citing Stone, "is the assurance that the decree, if rendered, will operate without injustice or oppression either to plaintiff or to defendant. . . . The formula had its origin in an attempt to fit the equitable remedy to the needs of justice. We may not suffer it to petrify at the cost of its animating principle." The Epstein case was heralded in the law journals of Columbia, Harvard, Yale, and Cornell. By this decision, the *Harvard Law Review* commented, "the New York court adds its weight to that of a growing line of authorities which are making the doctrine of mutuality achieve justice." (Note, 36 *Harvard Law Review* 229, 230, 1922.)

Of course, Stone's article alone did not change the pernicious rule. "Obviously, a doctrine so out of harmony with modern business practice could not," as Stone himself later observed, "maintain itself in its unrestricted form." ("Some Aspects of the Problem of Law Simplification," 1923, 23 *Columbia Law Review* 319, 323.) But Chief Judge Cardozo recognized Stone as one of several university law professors without whose intervention "the heresy, instead of dying out, would probably have persisted and even spread. . . . What saved the day was criticism from without." (B. N. Cardozo, *The Growth of the Law*, Yale, New Haven, 1931, pp. 15-16.) Both Stone and Cardozo saw that the article had a significance for law that did not terminate with the decision in the Epstein case. Stone's reasoning in "The Mutuality Rule in New York" later became a convenient prop for decisions limiting the "mutuality" requirement in other jurisdictions. (See *Elder* v. *N. Y. & Penn. Motor Express*, 1940, 284 N.Y. 350, 358, mutuality of estoppel by judgment.)

Dean Stone's critical analysis of judicial opinions in law journals did more than provide instructive material for law students. The frequency with which his essays were referred to by courts demonstrates that he dealt primarily with living problems of genuine interest to practitioners and administrators. Because he wanted to influence law he wanted to be understood. He therefore sought clarity of expression. "I always suspect the so-called scholarly articles which cannot be understood," he wrote his son Lauson, October 25, 1927, when the latter was article revision editor for the *Columbia Law Review*. "There are a great many people in the world who are posing as scholars and succeed in doing it because they conceal their thoughts." As teacher and dean, he also insisted that criticism be constructive. He set up certain canons as properly delimiting the scope of criticism of courts and urged that comment be directed to "principles" rather than to personalities. His own technical studies were molded, perhaps cramped, by these standards. What bulks out of them is a form of legal conservatism, respect for the past and for the system, appreciative handling of the lawyer's legacy. He was primarily concerned with just results, and with the formation of a consistent body of legal rules to produce them.

In his later essays one notes a marked upturn in the impact of facts on his thinking. Foreign exchange law should, for example, be based on the realities of the banking trade, and the responsibilities of trustees should be revised to square with actualities. It may be that he now believed his work could have been more effective had his approach been less reverent, more skeptical. "What you say," he wrote Walter Wheeler Cook, zealous crusader for legal realism, "about our habit of regarding research as a mere process for putting together a patchwork of legal doctrine in such a way that it will follow some more or less harmonious design is especially true. That was Ames' contribution and a valuable one in its day, but we have been ready for the next step for a long time." (HFS to W. W. Cook, April 13, 1927.)

Common law moves glacierlike—slowly, unevenly. Ideas imported a century, to say nothing of a generation, ago are still being worked out in hesitant, *ad hoc* fashion. The influences of Stone's scholarship on this development is not yet spent. Yet the main lines of impact are clear. His theory as to the nature of the right of the trust beneficiary, his views of "mutuality" and of the duties of bankers, are now well established in most jurisdictions. Wherever courts are concerned with the responsibilities of trust property to third persons or with oral agreements to hold land in trust, his essays are relevant guides to sound social policy as well as the harmonious application of legal doctrine.

# Index

United Railways v. West, 295-96, 298
United States Law Week, 639 n.
U.S. v. American Tobacco Co., 259
U.S. v. B. and O. R. Co., 318
U.S. v. Bekins, 796 n.
U.S. v. Belmont, 650 n.
U.S. v. Bland, 315, 523, 805
U.S. v. Butler, 279, 336 n., 405-418 pas-
   sim, 422, 426, 434, 437, 444, 459 n.,
   461, 473, 553, 600 n., 671, 783, 809
U.S. v. Calif., 244, 503
U.S. v. Carolene Products Co., 470, 491,
   512-17 passim, 526, 527, 531, 534-
   35, 600 n.
U.S. v. Chemical Foundation, Inc., 171-
   74, 650 n.
U.S. v. Chicago, Milwaukee & St. Paul
   R. Co., 311-14, 383, 384 n., 556
U.S. v. Classic, 586-89, 614-17 passim,
   637-39
U.S. v. Curtiss-Wright Export Corp.,
   650 n.
U.S. v. Darby, 550-55, 622, 781
U.S. v. Elgin, Joliet & Eastern R. Co.,
   429
U.S. v. Gold, 498 n.
U.S. v. Hutcheson, 499-503, 636-37
U.S. v. E. C. Knight, 396, 555 n.
U.S. v. La Franca, 556
U.S. v. Local 807, I.R.T., 583-86
U.S. v. Lowden, 556
U.S. v. Macintosh, 315, 317, 519-24 pas-
   sim, 804, 805
U.S. v. Morgan, 559
U.S. v. Perkins, 227-31 passim
U.S. v. Pink, 582, 649-50
U.S. v. Rompel, 772
U.S. v. Schwimmer, 519-25 passim, 686
U.S. v. Southeastern Underwriters As-
   soc., 617-24 passim, 625 n., 626 n.,
   780
U.S. ex rel Burger v. Cox, see Quirin,
   Ex parte
Untermyer, Samuel, 162

Vandenberg, Arthur H., 545, 713-14,
   720
Van Devanter, Willis, as member of the
   Court, 210, 219, 220, 225, 227, 229,
   241 n., 244-45, 255, 261, 272, 276,
   307, 338, 339, 348, 352, 359, 421,
   438, 451, 454 n., 601, 705 n.; and
   H.F.S., 220; retirement of, 461-63;
   eulogized, 589-90
Van Dyke, Henry, 73
Van Meter, Ralph A., 40 n.
Van Riper, Walter D., 158-60

Vauclain, Samuel, 206
Vermont v. N.H., 19-20
Victor, Royall, 139
Viereck v. U.S., 592, 683-85
Village of Euclid v. Ambler, 252
Vinson, Fred M., 644 n., 719 n.
Virginian Ry. Co. v. System Federation,
   457
Volstead Act, see Prohibition
Votau, Herbert, 154

Wages and hours legislation, see Labor
Wagner Act (1935), 440, 494; Court
   cases involving, 457-61, 481-86 pas-
   sim, 516-17, 634-36, 771-72. See also
   Labor; National Labor Relations
   Board
Waite, Morrison R., 234, 238, 269 n.,
   366, 389, 417, 418 n.
Walker, Charles S., 37-38
Walker, James J., 699
Wallace, Henry A., 417
Wallace Corp. v. NLRB, 634-36
Wall Street Journal, 555, 581, 585
Walsh, Thomas J., 192-99 passim
Ward, Hayden and Satterlee (law
   firm), 88
War power, 674-75, 681. See also Presi-
   dent, U.S.
War Relocation Authority (World War
   II), 674, 677 n., 678
Warren, Charles, 477 n.
Warren, Charles B., 199, 203
War Trade Board, 101
Washington, Bushrod, 396
Washington, George, 576, 747
Washington Herald, 536
Washington Minimum Wage case, see
   West Coast Hotel v. Parrish
Washington News, 181, 424
Washington Post, 375 n., 391, 424, 543,
   555, 585, 617, 646, 702, 712, 799
Washington Star, 144, 271, 301, 497,
   689
Washington University Law School,
   444
Watson, James E., 194
Watson, Tom (U.S. Senator), 144
Weaver v. Palmer Bros. Co., 253-54
Wechsler, Herbert, 296 n., 512, 787
Weeks, Nathan, 47
Wellington, Prof. (at M.A.C.), 36
West Coast Hotel v. Parrish, 455-56,
   487, 776 n.
Western Livestock v. Bureau of Rev-
   enue, 492-93
Western Union v. Lenroot, 639

W. Va. School Board v. Barnette, 599-601, 793
Westwood, Howard C., 365
Wheat, Alfred A., 171
Wheeler, Burton K., 144, 147-48, 169, 199, 299, 803; controversy over conspiracy indictment of, 188-96 passim, 198 n., 297; role of in "Court-packing," 449-55 passim, 461
Wheeler Defense Committee, 189-90, 192, 196
Whitcomb, Harry, 47
White, Edward Douglass, 186, 251, 426, 566, 570
White, William Allen, 284, 403, 425, 443-44
Whiteman, Alonzo J., 61
White primary, 614-17
Whitman, Charles S., 68
Whitney v. Calif., 518-19
Wickard v. Filburn, 593-96, 620 n.
Wickersham, George W., 149, 172, 272-74 passim
Wickersham Commission on Law Observance and Enforcement, 272-74 passim
Widener, Joseph, 759-60
Wildman, Frederick, 807 n.
Wile, Frederick W., 701
Willard, Helen Stone (sister of H.F.S.), 22, 27-28, 53, 425, 537, 807
Willebrandt, Mabel Walker, 150, 154-56 passim, 159-65 passim, 183, 188 n.
Williams, Charlotte: Hugo L. Black, 468 n.
Williams, John T., 156-57
Williams, Wayne C., 375 n.
Williams College, 43, 52-53, 735 n.

Williams v. North Carolina, 717 n.
Willing v. Chicago Auditorium, 246
Willis, Raymond, 807
Willkie, Wendell, 548, 558, 686
Wilmer, William N., 87
Wilmer and Canfield (law firm), 77; becomes Wilmer, Canfield and Stone, 87; becomes Satterlee, Canfield and Stone, 88, 186
Wilson, Woodrow, 100, 102, 103, 171 n., 204, 205, 210, 220, 222, 267, 650 n., 704 n.
Wilson v. New, 386 n.
Winne, Walter G., 159
Wisconsin, University of, 131
Walcott, Jessamine Dixon, 33, 40-41, 44, 571-72, 808
Wolff Packing Co. v. Court of Industrial Rel., 234
Women's National Committee on Law Enforcement, 147
Wood, Ephriah, 60
Wood, Willis D., 45, 47
Workmen's compensation, 115-16, 221, 337-39, 392-93
Worthen Co. v. Thomas, 364 n.
Wright, Lord, 427, 718, 803
Wright v. Vinton Branch, 456
Wyeth and Sullivan (architects), 214

Yakus v. U.S., 559 n., 623, 694-97
Yale University, 129, 174, 247, 541, 735 n.; Law Journal, 481 n., 498 n., 499
Yamashita, In re, 666-70, 718 n., 719 n.
Yeshiva University, 735 n.
Youngstown Vindicator, 808